MACROECONOMICS

THIRD CANADIAN EDITION

ANDREW B. ABEL
UNIVERSITY OF PENNSYLVANIA

BEN S. BERNANKE
PRINCETON UNIVERSITY

GREGOR W. SMITH
QUEEN'S UNIVERSITY

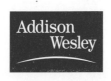
Addison
Wesley

Toronto

National Library of Canada Cataloguing in Publication Data

Abel, Andrew B., 1952-
    Macroeconomics

3rd Canadian ed.
Includes indexes.
ISBN 0-321-11522-8

1. Macroeconomics.   2. Canada—Economic conditions.   I. Bernanke, Ben.
II. Smith, Gregor W.   III. Title

HB172.5.A24 2003   339   C2002-900382-2

0-321-11522-8

Vice President, Editorial Director: Michael J. Young
Executive Editor: Dave Ward
Marketing Manager: Deborah Meredith
Developmental Editor: Paul Donnelly
Production Editor: Marisa D'Andrea
Copy Editor: Rohini Herbert
Production Coordinator: Janette Lush
Page Layout: Debbie Kumpf
Permissions Research: Amanda McCormick
Art Director: Julia Hall
Interior and Cover Design: Amy Harnden
Cover Image: Roman Konopka/Firstlight.ca

Statistics Canada information is used with the permission of the Minister of Industry, as Minister responsible for Statistics Canada. Information on the availability of the wide range of data from Statistics Canada can be obtained from Statistics Canada's Regional Offices, its World Wide Web site at http://www.statcan.ca, and its toll-free access number 1-800-263-1136.

1 2 3 4 5   07 06 05 04 03

Printed and bound in Canada.

ABOUT THE AUTHORS

ANDREW B. ABEL

The Wharton School of the University of Pennsylvania

Robert Morris Professor of Finance at The Wharton School and professor of economics at the University of Pennsylvania, Andrew Abel received his A.B. *summa cum laude* from Princeton University and his Ph.D. from the Massachusetts Institute of Technology.

Since his appointment to The Wharton School in 1986, Abel has held the Ronald O. Perelman and the Amoco Foundation Professorships. He began his teaching career at the University of Chicago and Harvard University and has held visiting appointments at both Tel Aviv University and The Hebrew University of Jerusalem.

A prolific researcher, Abel has published extensively on fiscal policy, capital formation, monetary policy, asset pricing, and social security—as well as serving on the editorial boards of numerous journals. He has been honoured as an Alfred P. Sloan Fellow, a National Science Foundation Graduate Fellow, a Fellow of the Econometric Society, and a recipient of the John Kenneth Galbraith Award for teaching excellence. Abel has served as a visiting scholar at the Federal Reserve Bank of Philadelphia, as a member of the Economics Advisory Panel of the National Science Foundation, and as a member of the Technical Advisory Panel on Assumptions and Methods for the U.S. Social Security Advisory Board. He is also a Research Associate of the National Bureau of Economic Research and a member of the Advisory Board of the Carnegie-Rochester Conference Series.

BEN S. BERNANKE

Woodrow Wilson School of Public and International Affairs, Princeton University

Howard Harrison and Gabrielle Snyder Beck Professor of Economics and Public Affairs at Princeton University, Ben Bernanke received his B.A. in economics from Harvard University, *summa cum laude*—capturing both the Allyn Young Prize for best Harvard undergraduate economics thesis and the John H. Williams Prize for outstanding senior in the economics department. Like co-author Abel, he holds a Ph.D. from the Massachusetts Institute of Technology.

Bernanke began his career at the Stanford Graduate School of Business in 1979. In 1985, he moved to Princeton University, where he is currently chair of the economics department. He has twice been visiting professor at M.I.T. and once at New York University and has taught in undergraduate, M.B.A., M.P.A., and Ph.D. programs. He has authored more than 50 publications in macroeconomics, macroeconomic history, and finance. He is the editor of *The American Economic Review*.

Bernanke has served as a visiting scholar and advisor to the Federal Reserve System. He is a Guggenhem Fellow and a Fellow of the Econometric Society. He has also been variously honoured as an Alfred P. Sloan Research Fellow, a Hoover Institution National Fellow, a National Science Foundation Graduate Fellow, and a Research Associate of the National Bureau of Economic Research.

GREGOR W. SMITH

Department of Economics, Queen's University

Douglas D. Purvis Professor of Economics at Queen's University, Gregor Smith, who is a native of Winnipeg, received his B.A. in history from Queen's University and his M.A. (first class honours) in economics from the University of St. Andrews, where he was awarded the Adam Smith medallion in economics and the Miller Prize as the outstanding arts faculty graduate. He received his D.Phil. from Oxford University, which he attended as a Rhodes Scholar.

Smith has been a visiting researcher at the Bank of Canada, a lecturer at St. Catherine's College, Oxford, a postdoctoral fellow at the University of British Columbia, a visiting professor at the University of Toronto, and a Fulbright Fellow at Princeton University. He has taught at Queen's since 1986 and in 1988 received the Polanyi Prize in economics awarded by the Government of Ontario.

Smith has published on open-economy macroeconomics, econometrics, international finance, and economic history. He is a former co-editor of the *Canadian Journal of Economics* and of the *Journal of International Economics*.

Brief Contents

DETAILED CONTENTS

Summary Tables

Key Diagrams

APPLYING MACROECONOMICS TO THE REAL WORLD

SYMBOLS USED IN THIS BOOK

A	productivity		W	nominal wage
B	government debt		Y	total income or output
$BASE$	monetary base		$\overline{Y}$	full-employment output
C	consumption			
CA	current account balance		a	individual wealth or assets
CU	currency in circulation		c	individual consumption; consumption per worker
DEP	bank deposits			
E	worker effort		cu	currency–deposit ratio
G	government purchases		d	depreciation rate
I	investment		e	real exchange rate
INT	net interest payments		e_{nom}	nominal exchange rate
K	capital stock		$\overline{e}_{nom}$	official value of nominal exchange rate
KA	capital account balance		i	nominal interest rate
M	money supply		i^m	nominal interest rate on money
MC	marginal cost		k	capital–labour ratio
MPK	marginal product of capital		n	growth rate of labour force
MPN	marginal product of labour		p_K	price of capital goods
$MRPN$	marginal revenue product of labour		r	expected real interest rate
N	employment, labour		r^w	world real interest rate
$\overline{N}$	full-employment level of employment		$r_{a\text{-}t}$	expected after-tax real interest rate
NFP	net factor payments		res	reserve–deposit ratio
NM	non-monetary assets		s	individual saving; saving rate
NX	net exports		t	income tax rate
P	price level		u	unemployment rate
P^e	expected price level		$\overline{u}$	natural unemployment rate
$PVLC$	present value of lifetime consumption		uc	user cost of capital
			w	real wage
$PVLR$	present value of lifetime resources		y	individual labour income; output per worker
R	real seignorage revenue			
RES	bank reserves		π	inflation rate
S	national saving		π^e	expected inflation rate
S_{pvt}	private saving		η_Y	income elasticity of money demand
S_{govt}	government saving		τ	effective tax rate
T	taxes			
TR	transfers			
V	velocity			

PREFACE

The first two Canadian editions of *Macroeconomics*, along with four US editions by Abel and Bernanke, have been very well received by instructors and students. In the third Canadian edition, we have added new material to keep the text modern and up to date, while building on the strengths that underlie the book's lasting appeal, including:

- ***Real-world applications.*** A perennial challenge for instructors is to help students make active use of the economic ideas developed in the text. The rich variety of applications in this book shows by example how economic concepts can be put to work in explaining real-world issues, such as increasing wage inequality, the productivity slowdown, sources of international financial crises, and alternative approaches to making monetary policy. The third Canadian edition offers new applications, as well as updates of the best applications of the previous editions.

- ***Broad modern coverage.*** From its conception, *Macroeconomics* has responded to students' desires to investigate and understand a wider range of macroeconomic issues than permitted by the course's traditional emphasis on short-run fluctuations and stabilization policy. This book provides a modern treatment of these traditional topics but also gives in-depth coverage of other important macro issues, such as the determinants of long-run economic growth, international trade and capital flows, labour markets, and the political and institutional framework of policymaking. This comprehensive coverage also makes the book a useful tool for instructors with differing views about course coverage and topic sequence.

- ***Reliance on a set of core economic ideas.*** Although we cover a wide range of topics, we avoid developing a new model or theory for each issue. Instead, we emphasize the broad applicability of a set of core economic ideas (such as the production function, the trade-off between consuming today and saving for tomorrow, and supply-demand analysis). Using these core ideas, we build a theoretical framework that encompasses all the macroeconomic analyses presented in the book: long-run and short-run, open-economy and closed-economy, and classical and Keynesian.

- ***A balanced presentation.*** Macroeconomics is full of controversies, many of which arise from the split between classicals and Keynesians (of the old, new, and neo- varieties). Sometimes, the controversies overshadow the broad common ground shared by the two schools. We emphasize that common ground. First, we pay greater attention to long-run issues (on which classicals and Keynesians have less disagreement). Second, we develop the classical and Keynesian analyses of short-run fluctuations within a single overall framework, in which we show that the two approaches differ principally in their assumptions about how quickly wages and prices adjust. Where differences in viewpoint remain—for example in the search versus efficiency wage interpretations of unemployment—we present and critique both perspectives. This balanced approach exposes students to all the best ideas in modern macro-economics. At the same time, an instructor of either classical or Keynesian inclinations can easily base a course on this book.

- **Innovative pedagogy.** The third Canadian edition, like its predecessors, provides useful tools to help students study, understand, and retain the material. Described in more detail later in the Preface, these tools include Summary tables, Key Diagrams, Key Terms, and Key Equations to aid students in organizing their study, and three types of problems for practice and developing understanding.

NEW AND UPDATED COVERAGE

What is taught in intermediate economics courses—and how it is taught—has changed substantially in recent years. Previous editions of *Macroeconomics* played a major role in these developments. The third Canadian edition provides lively and up-to-date coverage of a broad spectrum of macroeconomic issues and ideas, including a variety of new and updated topics:

- **Long-term economic growth.** Because the rate of economic growth plays a central role in determining living standards, we devote much of Part II to growth and related issues. We first discuss factors contributing to growth, such as productivity (Chapter 3) and rates of saving and investment (Chapter 4), and then, in Chapter 6, turn to a full-fledged analysis of the growth process. In Chapter 6, we use tools such as growth accounting and the Solow–Swan model to discuss various growth-related topics, including the post–1973 productivity slowdown, the factors that determine long-run living standards, the prospect for the convergence of living standards around the world, and government policies to stimulate growth. *New to this edition:* The text now includes falling computer prices and the measurement of economic growth (Chapter 2), a more extensive treatment of endogenous growth theory (Chapter 6), the information technology revolution and the behaviour of productivity (Chapter 6), and economic growth and the environment (Chapter 6).

- **International macroeconomic issues.** We address the increasing integration of the world economy in two ways. First, throughout the text, we make frequent use of cross-country comparisons and applications that draw on the experiences of countries other than Canada; for example, in Chapter 3, we compare hours of work in nations around the world; in Chapter 6, we examine the growth experiences of the East Asian tigers; in Chapter 7, we compare inflation experiences among European countries in transition; in Chapter 13, we compare sacrifice ratios among various countries; and in Chapter 14, we discuss strategies used for making monetary policy around the world. Second, we devote two chapters, Chapters 5 and 10, specifically to international issues. In Chapter 5, we show how the trade balance is related to a country's rates of saving and investment and then apply this framework to discuss such issues as the crises in Mexico, East Asia, and Russia, and the link between the trade deficit and the government budget deficit. In Chapter 10, we use a simple supply-demand framework to examine the determination of exchange rates. This chapter features innovative material on fixed exchange rates and currency unions, including an explanation of why a currency may face a speculative run.

New or substantially revised coverage: The text now covers Japanese monetary policy in the 1990s (Chapter 12), lessons for North America of European Monetary Union (Chapter 10), and the recent behaviour of the Canadian trade balance (Chapter 10).

- ***Business cycles.*** Our analysis of business cycles begins with facts, rather than theories: A unique chapter, Chapter 8, gives a history of Canadian business cycles and then describes the observed cyclical behaviour of a variety of important macroeconomic variables (the "business cycle facts"). Alternative classical and Keynesian theories of the business cycle, presented in Chapters 9 to 12, are then evaluated by how well they explain the facts.

- ***Monetary and fiscal policy.*** We discuss the effects and potential role of macroeconomic policies in nearly every chapter of the book, both in terms of theory and applications. We present classical (Chapter 11), Keynesian (Chapter 12), and monetarist (Chapter 14) views on the appropriate use of policy. Among the policy-related topics that we cover are rational expectations and monetary policy (Chapter 11), the importance of central bank credibility (Chapters 13 and 14), and inflation targeting (Chapter 14). We also provide useful background on the institutional framework of policy making; for example, Chapter 14 explains the operations of the Bank of Canada. Chapter 15 includes detailed information on provincial government spending and revenue, and discusses fiscal federalism. *New or substantially revised coverage:* The text now includes the Taylor rule (Chapter 14), the use of the target overnight interest rate in Canadian monetary policy (Chapter 14), updated generational accounts for Canada (Chapter 15), and an update on the federal budget surplus and the Canada Pension Plan (Chapter 15).

- ***Labour market issues.*** We pay close attention to issues related to employment, unemployment, and real wages. We introduce the basic supply-demand model of the labour market and discuss unemployment briefly in Chapter 3. Chapter 13 covers unemployment more extensively, including the inflation-unemployment trade-off, the costs of unemployment, and government policies for reducing unemployment. Other labour market topics include the trend to wage inequality (Chapter 3), the dynamics of job creation and job destruction in manufacturing (Chapter 11), efficiency wages (Chapter 12), hysteresis in unemployment (Chapter 13), and the effects of marginal and average tax rate changes on labour supply (Chapter 15). *New or substantially revised coverage:* The text provides updated comparisons of unemployment rates across countries and provinces (Chapter 13) and new evidence on the poverty trap (Chapter 15).

ALSO NEW TO THE THIRD CANADIAN EDITION

In preparing the third Canadian edition, we viewed our main objective to be keeping the book fresh and up to date. We have added new applications, boxes, and problems throughout and made many revisions to the text to reflect recent events and developments in the field. For example, Chapter 3 now includes updated evidence for Canada on the link between the stock market and consumption. Chapter 2 has been revised to explain the adoption of chain-weighting in measuring real GDP and its components.

A major structural change is the use of *better-integrated microfoundations*. Previous editions contained material on the microfoundations of labour supply, consumption, saving, and other aspects of household and firm behaviour. However, much of the discussion of the microfoundations of household behaviour was contained in a separate, optional chapter. The third Canadian edition integrates this material into the text, with enhanced discussions of the labour supply decision in Chapter 3 and of consumption and saving behaviour in Chapter 4. The optional chapter has been eliminated, with its more technical material now appearing in the appendix to Chapter 4. This rearrangement gives students more exposure to the basic microeconomics of household decisions, without an increase in technical difficulty and without the need to cover an optional chapter.

A FLEXIBLE ORGANIZATION

Other than the incorporation of the microfoundations material in Chapters 3 and 4, and the resulting elimination of the optional chapter on microfoundations, the basic structure of the text is unchanged from previous editions. In Part I (Chapters 1 and 2), we introduce the field of macroeconomics and discuss issues of measurement. In Part II (Chapters 3 to 7), we focus on long-run issues, including productivity, saving, investment, growth, and inflation. We devote Part III (Chapters 8 to 12) to the study of short-run economic fluctuations and stabilization policy. Finally, although we discuss macroeconomic policy throughout the book, in Part IV (Chapters 13 to 15), we look at issues and institutions of policy making in greater detail. In the Appendix at the end of the book, we review useful algebraic and graphical tools.

We recognize that instructors have different preferences about what to include in their courses and that their choices may be constrained by their students' backgrounds and the length of the term. The text is designed to be flexible in accommodating these different needs. In planning how to use *Macroeconomics* in your course, you might find the following suggestions useful:

- *Core chapters.* We recommend that every course include these six chapters:

  Chapter 1   Introduction to Macroeconomics
  Chapter 2   The Measurement and Structure of the Canadian Economy
  Chapter 3   Productivity, Output, and Employment
  Chapter 4   Consumption, Saving, and Investment
  Chapter 7   The Asset Market, Money, and Prices
  Chapter 9   The *IS–LM/AD–AS* Model: A General Framework for
               Macroeconomic Analysis

  Chapters 1 and 2 provide an introduction to macroeconomics, including national income accounting. The next four chapters on the list make up the analytical core of the book: Chapter 3 introduces the labour market, Chapters 3 and 4 together develop the goods market, and Chapter 7 discusses the asset market. Chapter 9 combines the three markets into a general equilibrium model usable for short-run analysis (in either classical or Keynesian mode).

  To a syllabus containing the above six chapters, the instructor can add various combinations of other chapters according to the course focus.

The following are some possible choices:

- **International macroeconomic issues.** Most instructors will want to add two open-economy chapters to the six chapters listed. Chapter 5 discusses saving, investment, and the trade balance in both small and large open economies with full employment. Chapter 10 discusses exchange-rate determination and macroeconomic policy in an open-economy model in which short-run deviations from full employment are possible. Each of these chapters directly follows its closed-economy partner.

- **Short-run focus.** Instructors who prefer to emphasize short-run issues (business cycle fluctuations and stabilization policy) may omit Chapter 6 without loss of continuity. They could also go directly from Chapters 1 and 2 to Chapters 8 and 9, which introduce business cycles and the *IS-LM/AD-AS* framework. Although the presentation in Chapters 8 and 9 is self-contained, it will be helpful for instructors who skip Chapters 3 to 7 to provide some background and motivation for the various behavioural relationships and equilibrium conditions.

- **Classical emphasis.** For instructors who want to teach the course with a modern classical emphasis, all the chapters in Part II are recommended. Chapters 8, 9 and 11 provide a self-contained presentation of classical business cycle theory. Other material of interest includes the Friedman–Phelps interpretation of the Phillips curve (Chapter 13), the role of credibility in monetary policy (Chapter 14), and Ricardian equivalence with multiple generations (Chapter 15).

- **Keynesian emphasis.** Instructors who prefer a Keynesian emphasis may omit Chapter 11 (classical business cycle analysis). As noted, if a short-run focus is preferred, Chapter 5 (full-employment analysis of the open economy) and Chapter 6 (long-term economic growth) may also be omitted without loss of continuity.

APPLYING MACROECONOMICS TO THE REAL WORLD

Economists sometimes get caught up in the elegance of formal models and forget that the ultimate test of a model or theory is its practical relevance. We dedicate a significant portion of each chapter to showing how the theory can be applied to real events and issues.

- **Applications.** Applications in each chapter show students how they can use theory to understand an important episode or issue. Examples of topics covered in Applications include the possible link between technical change and wage inequality (Chapter 3), calibrating the business cycle (Chapter 11), the financial crisis in East Asia (Chapter 5), and money-growth targeting versus inflation targeting (Chapter 14).

- **Boxes.** Boxes provide interesting additional information or sidelights, often drawn from current research. Representative topics covered in boxes include discussions of biases in inflation measurement (Chapter 2), flows of US currency abroad (Chapter 7), the Lucas critique (Chapter 13), and temporary and permanent components of Canadian recessions (Chapter 8).

- ***In Touch with the Macroeconomy.*** One important component of thinking like an economist is being familiar with macroeconomic data—what data are available and their strengths and shortcomings. To put students in touch with the macroeconomy, we provide a series of boxes that show where to find important macroeconomic data—such as the index of leading indicators, balance of payments data, and labour market data—and how to interpret them. Throughout the book, we give information from the *Canadian Economic Observer* or other readily available printed or online sources.

- ***The Political Environment.*** In talking about economic policy, students frequently note the discrepancy between the recommendations of economists (assuming they even agree!) and the decisions that politicians or government institutions make. We address this discrepancy in a special series of boxes that highlight the political environment of economic issues and policies. These special boxes examine such topics as the link between the state of the economy and opinion polls (Chapter 13), the relationship between democracy and economic growth (Chapter 6), and the independence of the Bank of Canada (Chapter 14).

LEARNING AIDS

The text contains many features aimed at helping students understand, apply, and retain important concepts.

- ***Detailed, colour graphs.*** The book is liberally illustrated with *data graphs*, which emphasize the empirical relevance of theory, and *analytical graphs*, which guide students through the development of model and theory in a well-paced, step-by-step manner. Both types of graphs include descriptive captions that summarize the details of events shown in the graph.

  Our use of colour in analytical graphs is demonstrated in Figure 9.14, which shows the effects of a shifting curve on a set of endogenous variables. Note that the original curve is in black, and its new position is in blue, with arrows indicating the direction of the shift. A coloured "shock box" indicates the reason for the shift, and a grey "result box" lists the main effects of the shock on endogenous variables. We consistently use these and similar conventions to make it easier for students to gain a clear understanding of the analysis.

- ***Key Diagrams.*** Key diagrams, a unique study feature found at the end of selected chapters, are self-contained descriptions of the most important analytical graphs in the book (see the list on p. xiii for their locations). For each key diagram we present the graph (the production function, p. 94, or the classical *AD–AS* diagram, p. 330, for example) and define and describe its elements in words and equations. We then present an analysis of what the graph reveals and discuss the factors that shift the curves in the graph.

- ***Summary tables.*** Throughout the book summary tables compile the main results of analyses. These summary tables reduce the amount of time the student must spend learning and writing results, allowing a greater concentration on understanding and applying these results.

- ***End-of-chapter review materials.*** To facilitate review, at the end of each chapter, the student will find a chapter summary, covering the chapter's main points; a list of key terms, with page references; an annotated list of key equations; and review questions for self-testing.

FIGURE 9.14

MONETARY NEUTRALITY IN THE *AD–AS* FRAMEWORK

If we start from general equilibrium at point *E*, a 10% increase in the nominal money supply shifts the *AD* curve up by 10% at each level of output, from *AD*¹ to *AD*². The *AD* curve shifts up by 10% because at any given level of output, a 10% increase in the price level is needed to keep the real money supply, and thus the aggregate quantity of output demanded, unchanged. In the new short-run equilibrium at point *F*, the price level is unchanged, and output is higher than its full-employment level. In the new long-run equilibrium at point *H*, output is unchanged at $\bar{Y}$, and the price level P_2 is 10% higher than the initial price level P_1. Thus, money is neutral in the long run.

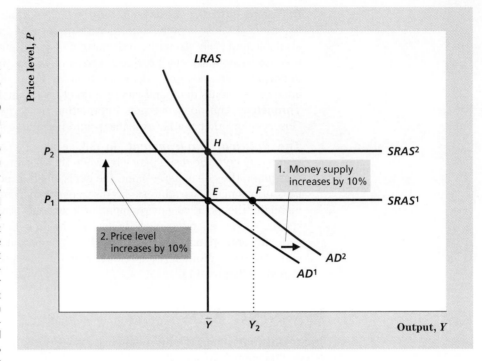

- **End-of-chapter problems.** An extensive set of problems for practice and review (more than 160 in all) includes *numerical problems*, which have explicit numerical solutions and are especially useful for checking students' understanding of basic relationships and concepts, and *analytical problems*, which ask the student to use or extend theories qualitatively. Answers and additional problems are provided in the Instructor's Manual.

- **Review of useful analytical tools.** Although we use no mathematics beyond high-school algebra, some students will find helpful a review of the main analytical tools used in the book. The Appendix (at the end of the text) succinctly discusses functions of one and several variables, graphs, slopes, exponents, and formulas for finding the growth rates of products and ratios.

- **Glossary.** The Glossary at the end of the text includes definitions of all key terms (set in boldface in the chapters and listed at the end of each chapter) and refers the student to the page on which the term is fully defined and discussed.

SUPPLEMENTS

The following supplementary materials for further learning are available:

- **Instructor's Manual.** The Instructor's Manual provides guidance for instructors on using the text in their courses, solutions to all end-of-chapter problems in the text, an extensive set of additional questions for testing and practice, and suggested topics for additional class discussion.

- **Electronic PowerPoint Slides.** The PowerPoint slides for text figures facilitate classroom presentations. You may also print transparency masters from the program, or integrate your own lecture notes with the figures. A PowerPoint viewer is provided for those who do not have the full software program.

- **Test Item File.** The Test Item File provides a generous number of multiple-choice questions and numerical problems that test the students' recall and application of key concepts and formulas.

- **Pearson Education Canada TestGen.** The TestGen is an electronic version of the Test Item File that enables instructors to edit existing questions, add new questions, and generate tests.

- **Companion Website.** New to this edition, the Companion Website (www.pearsoned.ca/abel) offers a number of review and self-test exercises for students. Instructors have access to downloadable versions of the Instructor's Manual and PowerPoint presentations.

ACKNOWLEDGMENTS

These days a textbook is not the lonely venture of its author or co-authors but is the joint project of dozens of skilled and dedicated people. We extend special thanks to Dave Ward, Executive Editor; Paul Donnelly, Developmental Editor; Marisa D'Andrea, Production Editor; Rohini Herbert, Copy Editor; Janette Lush, Production Coordinator; Debbie Kumpf, Formatter; and Amy Harnden, Designer; each of whom contributed greatly to the project. We also thank many others at Pearson Education Canada and the United States for their effort and craft.

We benefited from the advice of numerous colleagues at universities across Canada, the Bank of Canada, and Statistics Canada who patiently directed us to data sources and research studies. We appreciate the contributions of reviewers and colleagues who offered valuable comments on succeeding drafts of the book in all three editions thus far:

Robert Amano, Bank of Canada
Charles Beach, Queen's University
Russell Boyer, University of Western Ontario
Saud A. Choudhry, Trent University
Douglas Curtis, Trent University
Michael Devereux, University of British Columbia
Urvashi Dhawan, Memorial University
Christopher Ferrall, Queen's University
Stephen Ferris, Carleton University
Jim Frazer, Huron College
Ian Irvine, Concordia University
Talan Iscan, Dalhousie University
David Johnson, Wilfrid Laurier University
Stephen Jones, McMaster University
Stan Kardasz, University of Waterloo
Ronald Kneebone, University of Calgary
Leigh MacDonald, University of Western Ontario
Keith MacKinnon, York University

Lawrence McDonough, Royal Military College
Kenneth McKenzie, University of Calgary
Frank Muller, Concordia University
James Nason, University of British Columbia
Erik Poole, Simon Fraser University
Baldev Raj, Wilfrid Laurier University
Brad Reid, University of Alberta
Alistair Robertson, Wilfrid Laurier University
Liu Zeng Rung, Concordia University
Glen Stirling, University of Western Ontario
Javed Taheri, St. Mary's University
Angela Trimarchi, University of Waterloo

We are grateful to Mark Gertler, Rick Mishkin, and Steve Zeldes for valuable assistance with the first US edition, and to reviewers of the US editions. We are also grateful to several cohorts of students at the University of Pennsylvania, Princeton University, and Queen's University who—not entirely of their own free will but nonetheless very graciously—assisted us in the development of this textbook.

Last and most important, we thank our families for their patience and support. We dedicate this book to them.

Philadelphia   A.B.A.
Princeton   B.S.B.
Kingston   G.W.S.

A Great Way to Learn and Instruct Online

The Pearson Education Canada Companion Website is easy to navigate and is organized to correspond to the chapters in this textbook. Whether you are a student in the classroom or a distance learner you will discover helpful resources for in-depth study and research that empower you in your quest for greater knowledge and maximize your potential for success in the course.

[www.pearsoned.ca/abel]

Addison Wesley

Jump to...   http://www.pearsoned.ca/abel   Home   Search   Help   Profile   Companion Website

Home >

Companion Website

Macroeconomics, Third Canadian Edition, by Abel, Bernanke, and Smith

Student Resources

The modules in this section provide students with tools for learning course material. These modules may include:
- Chapter Objectives
- Destinations
- Quizzes
- Internet Exercises
- Net Search
- Glossary

In the quiz modules students can send answers to the grader and receive instant feedback on their progress through the Results Reporter. Coaching comments and references to the textbook may be available to ensure that students take advantage of all available resources to enhance their learning experience.

Instructor Resources

This module links directly to additional teaching tools. Downloadable PowerPoint Presentations, Electronic Transparencies, and an Instructor's Manual are just some of the materials that may be available in this section.

Part I INTRODUCTION

Chapter 1
INTRODUCTION TO MACROECONOMICS

1.1 WHAT MACROECONOMICS IS ABOUT

Macroeconomics is the study of the structure and performance of national economies and of the policies that governments use to try to affect economic performance. The issues that macroeconomists address include the following:

- *What determines a nation's long-run economic growth?* In 1870, income per capita in Norway was smaller than in Argentina. But today, income per capita is more than twice as high in Norway as in Argentina. Why do some nations' economies grow quickly, providing their citizens with rapidly improving living standards, while other nations' economies are relatively stagnant?

- *What causes a nation's economic activity to fluctuate?* After nearly a decade of prosperity during the 1980s, the Canadian economy began to falter in 1990. In 1991, output in Canada had fallen by more than 1.7% from its 1990 level. Even if they grow on average, why do economies sometimes experience sharp short-run fluctuations, lurching between periods of prosperity and periods of hard times?

- *What causes unemployment?* During the 1930s, one-quarter of the workforce in Canada was unemployed. A decade later, during World War II, less than 2% of the workforce was unemployed. Why does unemployment sometimes reach very high levels? Why, even during times of relative prosperity, is a significant fraction of the workforce unemployed?

- *What causes prices to rise?* The rate of inflation in Canada crept steadily upward during the 1970s, and reached 12% per year in the early 1980s before dropping to less than 4% per year in the mid-1980s, and to less than 2% per year in the early 1990s. Germany's inflation experience has been much more extreme: Although Germany has earned a reputation for low inflation in recent decades, following its defeat in World War I, Germany experienced an 18-month period (July 1922–December 1923) during which prices rose by a factor of several billion! What causes inflation, and what can be done about it?

- *How does being part of a global economic system affect nations' economies?* According to many observers, economic growth in Canada in the 1990s was boosted by rapid growth abroad, which added to the demand for Canadian products. During this period, Canadians actively debated the effect of freer trade with the United States and Mexico and the effects of the East Asian crisis. How do economic links between nations, such as international trade and borrowing, affect the performance of individual economies and the world economy as a whole?

- *Can government policies be used to improve a nation's economic performance?* A central goal of the federal government from 1993 to 1998 was to reduce its budget deficit. Provincial governments have shared this goal. If a government begins to run surpluses, should it increase spending, cut taxes, or pay down its debts? How do economic policies, such as government taxation and spending policies, affect the behaviour of the overall economy? How should economic policy be conducted in order to keep the economy as prosperous and stable as possible?

Macroeconomics seeks to offer answers to such questions, which are of great practical importance and are constantly debated by politicians, the press, and the public. In the rest of this section, we consider these key macroeconomic issues in more detail.

LONG-RUN ECONOMIC GROWTH

If you have ever travelled in a developing country, you could not help but observe the difference in living standards relative to those of such countries as Canada. The problems of inadequate food, shelter, and health care experienced by the poorest citizens of rich nations often represent the average situation for the people of a developing country. From a macroeconomic perspective, the difference between rich nations and developing nations may be summarized by saying that rich nations have, at some point in their history, experienced extended periods of rapid economic growth but that the poorer nations either have never experienced sustained growth or have had periods of growth offset by periods of economic decline.

Figure 1.1 summarizes the growth in output of the Canadian economy since 1870.[1] The record is an impressive one: Over the past century and a quarter, the annual output of Canadian goods and services has increased dramatically. The performance of the Canadian economy is not unique, however; other industrial nations have had similar, and in some cases higher, rates of growth over this period of time. This massive increase in the output of industrial economies is one of the central facts of modern history and has had enormous political, environmental, social, and even cultural implications.

In part, the long-term growth of the Canadian economy is the result of a rising population, which has meant a steady increase in the number of available workers. But another significant factor is the increase in the amount of output that can be produced with a given amount of labour. The amount of output produced per unit of labour input—for example, per worker or per hour of work—is called **average labour productivity**. Figure 1.2 shows how average labour productivity, defined in

---

1. Output is measured in Figure 1.1 by real gross domestic product (real GDP), which attempts to measure the physical volume of production in each year. We discuss the measurement of output in detail in Chapter 2.

FIGURE 1.1

OUTPUT OF THE
CANADIAN ECONOMY,
1870–2000

In this graph, the output of the
Canadian economy is mea-
sured by real gross domestic
product (real GDP) with goods
and services valued at their
1997 prices (see Chapter 2).
Note the strong upward trend
in output over time, as well as
sharp fluctuations during the
Great Depression (1930–
1938), World War II (1939–
1945), and the recessions of
1981–1982 and 1990–1992.

Sources: 1870–1926: Adapted from
M.C. Urquhart, *Gross National
Product, Canada, 1870–1926*,
McGill-Queen's University Press,
1993, Tables 1.1 and 1.6. Data
from Urquhart were rescaled.
1926–2000: Statistics Canada,
CANSIM Series D100126.

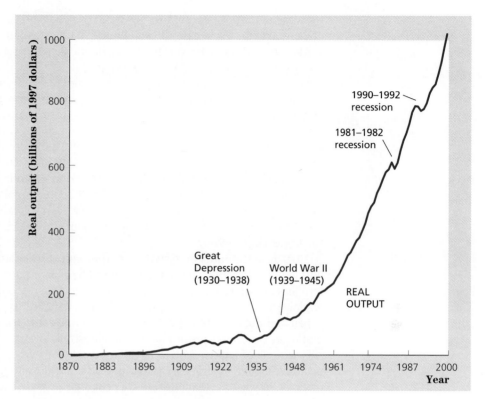

FIGURE 1.2

AVERAGE LABOUR PRO-
DUCTIVITY IN CANADA,
1921–2000

Average labour productivity
(output per employed worker)
has risen over time, with a
peak during World War II, reflecting increased wartime production and troughs during
recessions. Productivity growth
was particularly strong during
the 1950s and 1960s but has
slowed since then.

Sources: Employment: 1921–1945:
Historical Statistics of Canada,
Series D129, Civilian Over–14
Employment; 1946–1965: *Histori-
cal Statistics of Canada*, Series
D139; 1966–2000: Statistics
Canada, CANSIM Series D980595.
Average labour productivity is out-
put divided by employment.

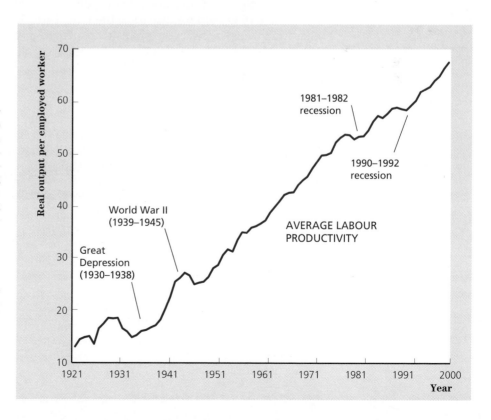

this case as output per employed worker, has changed since 1921. In 2000, the average Canadian worker produced about five times as much output as the average worker in 1921, despite working fewer hours over the course of the year. Because today's typical worker is so much more productive, Canadians enjoy a significantly higher standard of living than would have been possible earlier in the century.

Although the long-term record of productivity growth in the Canadian economy is excellent, in recent years average labour productivity in Canada has grown slowly. In the 27-year period between 1973 and 2000, output per Canadian worker grew about 36%, which compares poorly with the more than 50% total improvement that occurred in the 20-year period from 1953 to 1973. As a result, living standards rose relatively slowly in the recent period. Labour productivity growth did rise to some extent in the mid-1980s and mid-1990s, as you can see from Figure 1.2. Still, the possibility that the productivity slowdown will continue underlies many of the concerns that have been expressed about the health and long-term future of the Canadian economy.

Because the rates of growth of output and, particularly, of output per worker ultimately determine whether a nation will be rich or poor, understanding what determines growth is one of the most important goals of macroeconomics. Unfortunately, explaining why economies grow is not easy. Why, for example, did resource-poor Japan and South Korea experience growth rates that transformed them in a generation or two from war-torn nations to industrial powers, whereas several resource-rich nations of Latin America have had erratic or even negative growth in recent years? Although macroeconomists have nothing close to a complete answer to the question of what determines rates of economic growth, they do have some ideas to offer. For example, as we discuss in some detail in this book, most macroeconomists believe that rates of saving and investment are important for growth. Another key determinant of growth we discuss is the rate at which technological change and other factors help increase the productivity of machines and workers.

BUSINESS CYCLES

If you look at the history of Canadian output in Figure 1.1, you will notice that the growth of output is not always smooth but has hills and valleys. Most striking is the period between 1929 and 1945, which contains the Great Depression and World War II. During the 1929–1933 economic collapse that marked the first major phase of the Great Depression, the output of the Canadian economy fell by nearly 30%. Other countries experienced similar collapses in economic activity. Over the period 1939–1944, as Canada entered World War II and expanded production of armaments, output rose by more than 60%. No fluctuations in Canadian output since 1945 have been as severe as those of the 1929–1945 period. However, during the postwar era, there have been periods of unusually rapid economic growth, such as during the 1960s, and times during which output actually declined from one year to the next, as in 1953–1954, 1981–1982, and 1990–1992.

Macroeconomists use the term *business cycle* to describe short-run, but sometimes sharp, contractions and expansions in economic activity.[2] The downward phase of a business cycle, during which national output may be falling or perhaps growing only very slowly, is called a recession. Even when they are relatively mild, recessions

---

2. A more exact definition is given in Chapter 9. Business cycles do not include fluctuations lasting only a few months, such as the increase in activity that occurs around Christmas.

mean hard economic times for many people. Recessions are also a major political concern because almost every politician wants to be re-elected and the chances of re-election are better if the country's economy is expanding rather than declining. Macroeconomists put a lot of effort into trying to figure out what causes business cycles and into deciding what can or should be done about them. For example, business cycles are to some extent worldwide and are roughly synchronized across countries, which raises the question of whether Canada can avoid them. In this book, we describe a variety of features of business cycles, compare alternative explanations for cyclical fluctuations, and evaluate the policy options that are available for affecting the course of the cycle.

UNEMPLOYMENT

One important aspect of recessions is that they usually are accompanied by an increase in **unemployment**, the number of people who are available for work and are actively seeking work but cannot find jobs. Along with growth and business cycles, the problem of unemployment is a third major issue in macroeconomics.

The best-known measure of unemployment is the unemployment rate, which is the number of unemployed divided by the total labour force (the number of people either working or seeking work). Figure 1.3 shows the unemployment rate in Canada since 1921. The highest and most prolonged period of unemployment occurred during the Great Depression of the 1930s. In 1933, the unemployment rate was 25%, indicating that about one of every four potential workers was unable to find a job. In contrast, the tremendous increase in economic activity that occurred during

FIGURE 1.3

THE CANADIAN
UNEMPLOYMENT RATE,
1921–2000

The figure shows the percentage of the labour force that was unemployed in each year since 1921. Unemployment peaked during the Great Depression of the 1930s and reached its low point during World War II. Since World War II the highest unemployment rates have occurred during the recessions of 1981–1982 and 1990–1992.

Sources: 1921–1945: *Historical Statistics of Canada*, Series D132 and D129; 1946–1965: *Historical Statistics of Canada*, Series D233; 1966–2000: Statistics Canada, CANSIM Series D980745.

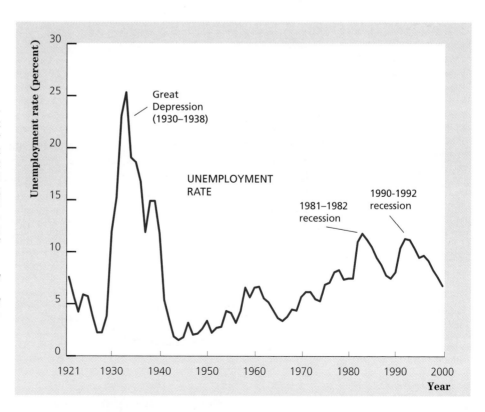

World War II significantly reduced unemployment. In 1944, at the peak of the wartime boom, the unemployment rate was 1.5%.

Recessions have led to significant increases in unemployment in recent years. For example, during the recessions of the 1981–1982 and 1990–1992, the Canadian unemployment rate exceeded 11%. Even during periods of economic expansion, however, the unemployment rate remains well above zero, as you can see from Figure 1.3. In 2000, after eight years of economic growth with no recession, the unemployment rate remained near 7%. Why the unemployment rate can remain fairly high even when the economy as a whole is doing well is doing well is another important question in macroeconomics. Canadian macroeconomists also try to explain differences among provincial unemployment rates.

INFLATION

When the prices of most goods and services are rising over time, the economy is said to be experiencing **inflation**. Figure 1.4 shows a measure of the average level of prices faced by consumers in Canada since 1913.[3] Prior to World War II, inflation usually occurred only during wartime. These wartime periods of inflation were followed by periods of **deflation**, during which the prices of most goods and services fell. The result of these offsetting periods of inflation and deflation was that over the long run, the level of prices was fairly constant.

---

3. This measure is called the consumer price index, or CPI, which is discussed in Chapter 2. Conceptually, the CPI is intended to measure the cost of buying a certain fixed set, or "basket," of consumer goods. However, the construction of a consumer price index over a period as long as 90 years involves many compromises. One is that the basket of goods priced by the CPI is not literally the same over the entire period shown in Figure 1.4 but is periodically changed to reflect the different mix of consumer goods available at different times.

FIGURE 1.4

CONSUMER PRICES IN CANADA, 1913–2000

Prior to World War II, the average level of prices faced by consumers remained relatively constant, with periods of inflation (rising prices) offset by periods of deflation (falling prices). Since World War II, however, prices have risen more than tenfold. In the figure, the average level of prices is measured by the consumer price index, or CPI (see Chapter 2). The CPI measures the cost of a fixed set, or basket, of consumer goods relative to the cost of the same basket of goods in a base period, in this case 1992. Thus, a CPI of 138 in 1997 means that a basket of consumer goods that cost $100 in 1992 would cost $138 in 1997.

Sources: 1913–1975 (1971=100): *Historical Statistics of Canada,* Series K8; 1975–2000 (1992=100): Statistics Canada, CANSIM Series P100000. Data prior to 1975 were adjusted to a base with 1992 = 100.

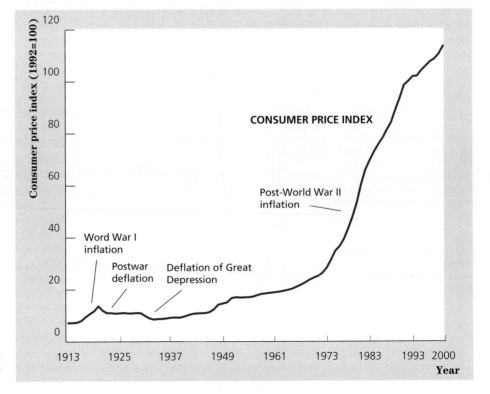

The last significant deflation in Canada occurred during 1930–1933, the initial phase of the Great Depression. Since then, inflation, without offsetting deflation, has become the normal state of affairs. Figure 1.4 shows that consumer prices have risen significantly since World War II, with the measure of prices shown increasing more than ninefold.

The percentage increase in the average level of prices over a year is called the inflation rate. If the inflation rate in consumer prices is 10%, for example, then, on average, the prices of items that consumers buy are rising by 10% per year. Rates of inflation may vary dramatically both over time and across countries, from a few percent per year in low-inflation countries (such as Canada or Switzerland) to 1,000% per year or more in countries (such as Bolivia or Argentina in recent years) that experience hyperinflations, or extreme inflations. When the inflation rate reaches an extremely high level, with prices changing daily or hourly, the economy tends to function poorly. High inflation also means that the purchasing power of money erodes quickly, which forces people to scramble to spend their money almost as soon as they receive it.

THE INTERNATIONAL ECONOMY

Today, every major economy is an **open economy**, or one that has extensive trading and financial relationships with other national economies. (A **closed economy** does not interact economically with the rest of the world.) Macroeconomists study patterns of international trade and borrowing to understand better the links between national economies. For example, an important topic in macroeconomics is how international trade and borrowing relationships can help transmit business cycles from country to country.

Another issue for which international considerations are central is trade imbalances. Figure 1.5 shows the historical behaviour of the imports and exports of goods and services by Canada. Canadian imports are goods and services produced abroad and purchased by Canadians; Canadian exports are goods and services produced in Canada and sold to foreigners. To give you a sense of the relative importance of international trade, Figure 1.5 expresses exports and imports as percentages of total Canadian output. Note that exports and imports grew rapidly during the 1990s. Both are larger fractions of Canadian output than they were during the 1950s and 1960s, reflecting both the recovery of trade from the disruptions of the Great Depression (when trade fell even faster than output) and World War II and the trend toward greater economic interdependence among nations. Note, though, that 70 years ago, exports and imports already were important in relation to the size of the overall economy. Currently, exports and imports are nearly three times as large, in proportion to output, in Canada as in the United States.

You can see from Figure 1.5 that exports and imports need not be equal each year. For example, following World War II, Canadian exports outstripped Canadian imports because the country was sending large quantities of supplies to countries whose economies had been damaged by war. When exports exceed imports, a **trade surplus** exists. In the early 1990s, however, Canadian exports declined relative to imports, as you can see from Figure 1.5. This excess of imports over exports, or **trade deficit**, received considerable attention from policymakers and the press. Surpluses emerged again after 1994 as exports grew faster than imports. What causes these trade imbalances? Are they bad for the Canadian economy or for the economies of this country's trading partners? These are among the questions that macroeconomists try to answer.

FIGURE 1.5

CANADIAN EXPORTS AND
IMPORTS, 1926–2000

The figure shows Canadian exports (blue curve) and imports (black curve), each expressed as a percentage of total output. Exports and imports need not be equal in each year: During the late 1950s and early 1990s, Canadian exports were smaller than Canadian imports (shaded blue area). Since 1994, exports have exceeded imports (shaded grey area).

Sources: Exports and imports of goods and services, in current dollars, GDP at market prices: Statistics Canada, CANSIM Series D14833, D14836, D14816.

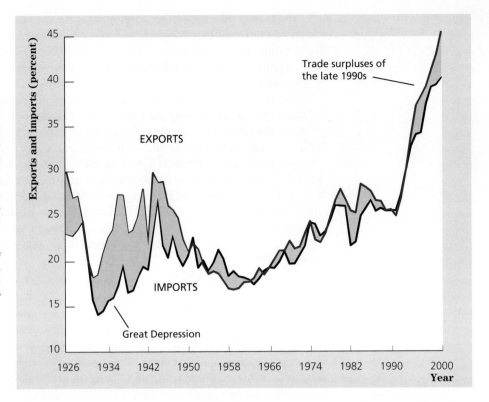

One important influence on the trade balance is the **exchange rate**. The exchange rate is the amount of Canadian dollars that can be purchased with a unit of foreign currency. Although exchange rates are quoted between many currencies, the Canada–US exchange rate is the most important one to Canada because of the very large volume of trade between the two countries.

Figure 1.6 shows the Canada–US exchange rate since 1950. During the 1960s, the exchange rate was fixed within a narrow band. Since then, the exchange rate has floated and has been subject to large swings. These movements directly affect the cost of imported goods and the price of exported goods. For example, a decrease in the exchange rate tends to raise the prices of imports but lower the prices paid by foreigners for Canadian exports. Later chapters will discuss what determines the value of the exchange rate and, in turn, how its value affects the trade balance, employment, and output.

MACROECONOMIC POLICY

A nation's economic performance depends on many factors, including its natural and human resources, its capital stock (buildings and machines), its technology, and the economic choices made by its citizens, both individually and collectively. Another extremely important factor affecting economic performance is the set of macroeconomic policies pursued by the government.

Macroeconomic policies attempt to affect the performance of the economy as a whole. The two major types of macroeconomic policies are fiscal policy and monetary policy. **Fiscal policy**, which is determined at the federal, provincial, and municipal

FIGURE 1.6

CANADA–US EXCHANGE
RATE, 1950–2001

The figure shows the exchange
rate between Canada and the
United States, quarterly since
1950. The exchange rate is the
value of the Canadian dollar
expressed in US dollars.
During the 1960s, the ex-
change rate was fixed within a
narrow band, but since then,
it has floated and has been
subject to large fluctuations,
falling below 65 US cents in
recent years.

Source: *Bank of Canada Review*,
Table A2. Reprinted with the permission of the Bank of Canada.

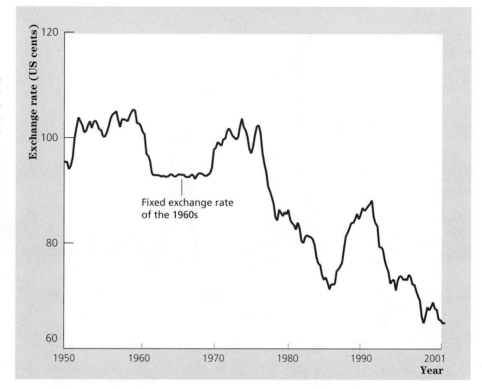

levels, concerns government spending and taxation. **Monetary policy** affects short-
term interest rates and the rate of growth of the nation's money supply and is under
the control of a government institution known as the central bank. In Canada, the
central bank is the Bank of Canada.

One of the main macroeconomic policy issues of recent years in Canada has
been in the realm of fiscal policy. This issue concerns the potential effects on the
economy of large federal and provincial government budget deficits, the annual excess of government spending over tax collections. The recent history is put into a
long-term perspective in Figure 1.7, which presents data on federal government
spending and tax revenues since 1926. Again, so that their importance in relation to
the economy as a whole is indicated, spending, tax collections, and government
budget deficits and surpluses are expressed as percentages of total output.

One obvious feature of Figure 1.7 is the peak in government spending and
deficits that resulted from World War II. At its high point during World War II,
federal government spending exceeded 40% of total output. Significant deficits
also occurred during the Great Depression of the 1930s because of a decline in
tax revenue and because the government eventually increased its spending on unemployment relief. Also shown clearly is the increase in the size of the government sector since the Great Depression, an increase reflected in both the major
upward shift in government spending and in tax collections relative to national
output that occurred in about 1940 and the mild upward trend in both variables that
occurred until about 1990.

The federal budget deficits of the 1980s and early 1990s appear in the right-hand
portion of Figure 1.7. These large and persistent deficits are historically unusual
in that they occurred during a period of peace and relative prosperity. Critics of

FIGURE 1.7

CANADIAN FEDERAL
GOVERNMENT SPENDING
AND REVENUE,
1926–2000

Canadian federal government
spending (blue curve) and revenue (black curve) are shown
as percentages of total output.
Deficits, or excesses of spending over tax collections, are
shaded in blue, and surpluses
(excesses of revenue over
spending) are shaded in grey.
The federal government's share
of the economy has grown
since the Great Depression.
Large deficits occurred during
World War II and in recent
years.

Source: Federal government spending and revenue in millions of dollars, GDP at market prices:
Statistics Canada, CANSIM Series
D15088, D15103.

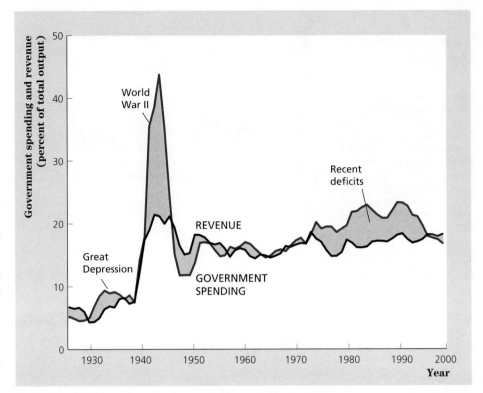

the government's fiscal policies argued that the deficits, which were financed by
borrowing from the public, diverted funds that might otherwise have gone to more
productive uses, such as investment in modern equipment. Some critics, therefore,
claim a close link between the federal budget deficits since the mid-1970s and the decline in productivity growth that occurred during the same period (see Figure 1.2).
Is this claim true? If so, will balancing the federal budget improve prospects for
growth? These questions, too, fall under the study of macroeconomics.

The possible link between the government's budget deficit and productivity
growth illustrates an important aspect of macroeconomics: Macroeconomic issues and
problems are frequently interconnected. For this reason, studying one macroeconomic
question in isolation, such as the effects of the government budget deficit, generally
is not sufficient. Instead, macroeconomists usually study the economy as a complete
system, recognizing that changes in one sector or market may affect the behaviour
of the entire economy.

AGGREGATION

Macroeconomics is one of two broad areas within the field of economics, the other
being microeconomics. Macroeconomics and microeconomics have many basic
economic ideas and methods in common; the difference between them is the level
at which the economy is studied. Microeconomists focus on individual consumers,
workers, and firms, each of whom is too small to have an impact on the national
economy. Macroeconomists ignore the fine distinctions among the many different
kinds of goods, firms, and markets that exist in the economy and, instead, focus on

national totals. For example, in their analyses, macroeconomists do not care whether consumers are buying VCRs or compact disc players, beef or chicken, Pepsi or Coke. Instead, they add consumer expenditures on all goods and services to get an overall total called aggregate consumption. The process of summing individual economic variables to obtain economywide totals is called **aggregation**. The use of aggregation and the emphasis on aggregate quantities, such as aggregate consumption, aggregate investment, and aggregate output, are the primary factors that distinguish macroeconomics from microeconomics.

1.2 WHAT MACROECONOMISTS DO

How do macroeconomists use their skills, and what do they do with all the data they gather and the theories they develop? Besides teaching economics, macroeconomists engage in a wide variety of activities, including forecasting, macroeconomic analysis, basic research, and data development.

MACROECONOMIC FORECASTING

Many people believe that economists spend most of their time trying to forecast the performance of the economy. In fact, except for a relatively small number of forecasting specialists, forecasting is a minor part of what macroeconomists do. One reason macroeconomists do not emphasize forecasting is that on the whole, they are not terribly good at it! Although short-range forecasters have some success, long-range forecasting is difficult, not only because our understanding of how the economy works is imperfect but also because of the impossibility of taking into account *all* the factors—many of them not strictly economic—that might affect future economic trends. Here are some questions that a forecaster, in trying to project the course of the economy, might have to try to answer: How will constitutional uncertainty affect Canadian interest rates? What oil price will the Organization of Petroleum Exporting Countries (OPEC) decide on at its next meeting? Will there be a severe drought in agricultural regions, with adverse effects on food quantities and prices? Will new technologies that are being developed ever come to market? Because answers to such questions are highly uncertain, macroeconomic forecasters rarely offer a single prediction. Instead, they usually combine a "most likely" forecast with "optimistic" and "pessimistic" alternative scenarios.

Does the fact that macroeconomics cannot be used to make highly accurate forecasts of economic activity mean that it is a pointless field of study? Some people may think so, but that is really an unreasonable standard. Meteorology is an example of a field in which forecasting is difficult (will it *definitely* be nice this weekend?) but in which there is also a lot of useful knowledge (meteorologists helped discover the depletion of the Earth's ozone layer and pointed out its dangers). Similarly, cardiologists cannot usually predict if or when a patient will have a heart attack—they can only talk about probabilities. Like meteorologists and doctors, economists deal with a system whose complexity makes gaining a thorough understanding difficult and forecasting the system's behaviour even more difficult. Rather than predicting what will happen, most macroeconomists are engaged in analyzing and interpreting events as they happen (macroeconomic analysis) or in trying to understand the structure of the economy in general (macroeconomic research).

MACROECONOMIC ANALYSIS

Macroeconomic analysts monitor the economy and think about the implications of current economic events. Many analysts are employed in the private sector, such as in banks or large corporations. Private sector analysts try to determine how general economic trends will affect their employers' financial investments, their opportunities for expansion, the demand for their products, and so on. Some private firms specialize in macroeconomic analysis and assist clients on a fee-for-service basis.

The public sector, which includes federal and provincial governments and international agencies, such as the World Bank and the International Monetary Fund, also employs many macroeconomic analysts. The main function of public sector analysts is to assist in policymaking—for example, by writing reports that assess various macroeconomic problems and by identifying and evaluating possible policy options. Among Canadian policymakers, the officials who set monetary policy may call on the aid of Ph.D. economists employed by the Bank of Canada, and federal and provincial cabinets have the advice of the professional staffs of numerous departments and agencies. Economic policymakers also often go outside the government to seek the advice of macroeconomists from business or academia.

If a country has many well-trained macroeconomic analysts, as is true in Canada, does that mean that its macroeconomic policies will always be intelligent and far-sighted? The answer, unfortunately, is "no." Because of the complexity of the economy, macroeconomic policy analysis, like macroeconomic forecasting, often is difficult and uncertain. Perhaps even more important, though, *politicians, not economists, usually make economic policy*. Politicians are typically less concerned with the abstract desirability of a policy than with the policy's immediate effects on their constituents. Thus, in late 1990, international talks intended to reduce trade barriers failed because European governments found it politically inadvisable to reduce high subsidy payments to their farmers—despite the nearly universal opposition of economists to both trade barriers and farm price support payments. To reflect the importance of politics in economic policymaking, at various points in this book, we include a feature called "The Political Environment," in which we discuss political aspects of macroeconomics.

Although the technical advice provided by macroeconomic analysts is not the sole basis on which macroeconomic policy is made, such advice is probably necessary for making good policy decisions, especially if dramatic changes are being considered. In recent years, for example, a number of countries in Eastern Europe, Latin America, and elsewhere have undertaken radical reforms of their economies. In most of these cases, the countries' leaders have sought the technical advice of domestic and foreign economists, and this advice has been influential in policymaking. In the former Soviet Union, economists have played an important role in the debate over restructuring and reform, both as technical specialists and as political advocates.

MACROECONOMIC RESEARCH

Macroeconomic research takes an amazing variety of forms, from abstract mathematical analysis to psychological experimentation to massive number-crunching projects in which supercomputers are used to process large amounts of economic data. Nevertheless, the goal of all macroeconomic research is to make general statements about how the economy works. The general insights about the economy gained from successful research form the basis for the analyses of specific economic problems, policies, or situations.

To see why research is important, imagine that you are an economist with the International Monetary Fund whose task is to help a small African country control its high rate of inflation. On what basis can you offer advice? Basically, you should know what inflation-fighting policies other countries had used in the past, what the results had been, how the results had depended on the characteristics of the country employing the policy, and so on. Particularly, if the situation you are analyzing is not identical to any of the previous cases, having some theoretical principles would also help you identify and understand the main factors contributing to that country's inflation. Analyzing the historical cases and working out the theoretical principles by yourself from scratch might involve many years' effort. The value of ongoing research activities is that many of the results and ideas that you need would already be available in books or professional journals or circulated in unpublished form. Because it forms the basis for activities such as economic analysis and forecasting, in a very real sense, macroeconomic research is the engine that pulls the whole enterprise of macroeconomics behind it.

Macroeconomic research takes place primarily in colleges and universities, in non-profit institutions, and in the public sector (the government and international agencies). Particularly in the public sector, the line between economic analysis and macroeconomic research is much fuzzier than we have drawn it here. The reason is that many economists move back and forth between analysis of specific problems (such as an African country's inflation problem) and more basic macroeconomic research (such as an analysis of inflation in general).

Economic Theory

How is macroeconomic research carried out? As in many other fields, macroeconomic research proceeds primarily through the formulation and testing of theories. An **economic theory** is a set of ideas about the economy that have been organized in a logical framework. Most economic theories are developed in terms of an **economic model**, which is a simplified description of some aspect of the economy, usually expressed in mathematical form. Economists evaluate an economic model or theory by applying four criteria:

1. Are its assumptions reasonable and realistic?

2. Is it understandable and manageable enough to be used in studying real problems?

3. Does it have implications that can be tested by **empirical analysis**? That is, can its implications be evaluated by comparing them with data obtained in the real world?

4. When the implications and the data are compared, are the implications of the theory consistent with the data?

For a theory or model—of any type, not just economic—to be useful, the answer to each of these questions must be "yes." Unfortunately, though, economists may not always agree in their evaluation of a particular model, which means that controversies about the best way to model a given economic situation sometimes persist.

We present a summary of the main steps in developing and testing an economic theory or model in Box 1.1.

BOX 1.1 DEVELOPING AND TESTING AN ECONOMIC THEORY

To illustrate the process of developing and testing an economic theory, suppose that we want to develop a theory that explains the routes that people take when they commute from home to work and back. Such a theory would be useful, for example, to a traffic planner who is concerned about how a proposed housing development will affect traffic patterns. Here are the steps we would take:

STEP 1. State the research question.
EXAMPLE: What determines traffic flows in the city during rush hours?

STEP 2. Make provisional assumptions that describe the economic setting and the behaviour of the economic factors. These assumptions should be simple yet capture the most important aspects of the problem.
EXAMPLE: The setting is described by the map of the city. The assumption about behaviour is that commuters choose routes that minimize driving time.

STEP 3. Work out the implications of the theory.
EXAMPLE: Use the map of the city to plot a route that minimizes driving time between home and place of work.

STEP 4. Conduct an empirical analysis to compare the implications of the theory with the data.
EXAMPLE: Conduct a survey of commuters to identify (1) home locations; (2) work locations; and (3) routes taken to work. Then, see whether the routes predicted by the model are generally the same as those reported in the commuter survey.

STEP 5. Evaluate the results of your comparisons.

If the theory fits the data well: Use the theory to predict what would happen if the economic setting or economic policies change.
EXAMPLE: Use the minimum-driving-time assumption to evaluate the traffic effects of a new housing development by figuring out which routes the residents of the development are likely to take.

If the theory fits the data poorly: Start from scratch with a new model. Repeat steps 2 through 5.
EXAMPLE: Change the provisional behavioural assumption to the following: Commuters choose the route that minimizes the distance they must drive (not the time they spend driving).

If the theory fits the data moderately well: Either make do with a partially successful theory or modify the model with additional assumptions and then repeat steps 3 through 5.
EXAMPLE: A possible modification of the minimum-driving-time assumption is that commuters will choose more scenic over less scenic routes, if driving time is not increased by more than a certain number of minutes. To test the model with this modified assumption, you must determine which routes are more scenic (those that pass a lake) and which are less scenic (those that pass a garbage dump).

DATA DEVELOPMENT

The collection of economic data is a vital part of macroeconomics, and many economists are involved in the data development process. In Canada as well as many other countries, data on thousands of economic variables are collected and analyzed. We have already presented some important macroeconomic data series, such as measures of output and the price level, and will look at these and others in more detail in Chapter 2. Macroeconomists use economic data to assess the current state of the economy, make forecasts, analyze policy alternatives, and test macroeconomic theories.

Most economic data are collected and published by the government—for example, by such agencies as Statistics Canada and the federal Department of Finance in Canada, and by central banks, such as the Bank of Canada. International data are collected and published by such organizations as the International Monetary Fund (IMF) and the Organization for Economic Cooperation and Development (OECD). To an increasing degree, however, these activities also take place in the private sector. For example, marketing firms and private economic forecasting companies are important collectors, users, and sellers of economic data. In this book, boxes called "In Touch with the Macroeconomy" describe major macroeconomic data series and tell you how they are collected and where to find them.

Much of the data collection and preparation process is routine. However, because providers of data want their numbers to be as useful as possible while keeping costs down, the organization of major data collection projects is typically the joint effort of many skilled professionals. Providers of data must decide what types of data should be collected on the basis of who is expected to use the data and how. They must take care that measures of economic activity correspond to abstract concepts (such as "capital" and "labour") that are suggested by economic theory. In addition, data providers must guarantee the confidentiality of data that may reveal information about individual firms and people in the economy. In a large data-gathering organization, such as Statistics Canada, each of these issues is exhaustively analyzed by economists and statisticians before data collection begins.[4]

1.3 WHY MACROECONOMISTS DISAGREE

Over the years, the efforts of thousands of analysts, data collectors, and researchers have greatly enhanced the understanding of macroeconomic phenomena. Yet, no matter what the macroeconomic issue, the news media seemingly can find an economist to argue either side of it. Why do macroeconomists appear to disagree so much?[5]

To a certain extent, the amount of disagreement among macroeconomists is exaggerated by the tendency of the public and the media to focus on the most difficult and controversial issues. In addition, the very fact that economic policy and performance are of such broad interest and concern contributes to the intensity of debate. More than controversies in many other fields, debates in macroeconomics tend to take place in public, rather than in the seminar room or the laboratory. Although important disagreements among macroeconomists certainly exist, there also are many areas of substantial agreement in macroeconomics.

We can provide an insight into why macroeconomists disagree by drawing the important distinction between positive and normative analyses of economic policy. A **positive analysis** of an economic policy examines the economic consequences of a policy but does not address the question of whether those consequences are desirable. A **normative analysis** of policy tries to determine whether a certain policy *should* be used. For example, if an economist is asked to evaluate the effects on the economy of a 5% rise in the income tax, the response involves a positive analysis. But if asked whether the income tax *should* be raised 5%, the economist's response requires a normative analysis. This normative analysis will involve not only the

---

4. For a readable discussion of issues that face data collectors, see Janet L. Norwood, "Distinguished Lecture on Economics in Government: Data Quality and Public Policy," *Journal of Economic Perspectives*, Spring 1990, pp. 3–12.

5. Not only do macroeconomists often seem to disagree with each other, but they also sometimes are accused of not being able to agree with themselves. American President Harry Truman expressed the frustration of many policy-makers when he said he wanted a one-handed economist—one who would not always say, "On the one hand, . . .; on the other hand. . . . "

economist's objective, scientific understanding of how the economy works but also personal value judgments—for example, about the appropriate size of the government sector or the amount of income re-distribution that is desirable.

Economists may agree on the positive analysis of a question yet disagree on the normative part because of differences in values. Value differences also are common in other fields: Physicists may be in perfect agreement on what would happen *if* a nuclear bomb were detonated (a positive analysis). But physicist "hawks" and physicist "doves" may disagree strongly about whether nuclear weapons *should* be deployed (a normative question).

Disagreement may occur on positive issues, however, and these differences are important in economics. In macroeconomics, there always have been many schools of thought, each with a somewhat different perspective on how the economy works. Examples include monetarism and supply-side economics, both of which we discuss in this book. However, the most important—and enduring—disagreements on positive issues in macroeconomics involve the two schools of thought called the classical approach and the Keynesian approach.

CLASSICALS VERSUS KEYNESIANS

The classical approach and the Keynesian approach are the two major intellectual traditions in macroeconomics. We discuss the differences between the two approaches briefly here and in much greater detail later in the book.

THE CLASSICAL APPROACH

The origins of the classical approach go back more than two centuries, at least to the famous Scottish economist Adam Smith. In 1776, Smith published his classic, *The Wealth of Nations*, in which he proposed the concept of the "invisible hand." The idea of the **invisible hand** is that if there are free markets and individuals conduct their economic affairs in their own best interests, the overall economy will work well. As Smith put it, in a market economy, individuals, while pursuing their own self-interest, seem to be led by an invisible hand to maximize the general welfare of everyone in the economy.

However, we must not overstate what Smith claimed: To say that an invisible hand is at work does *not* mean that no one in a market economy will be hungry or dissatisfied; free markets cannot insulate a nation from the effects of drought, war, or political instability. Nor does the invisible hand rule out the existence of great inequalities between the rich and the poor because in Smith's analysis, he took the initial distribution of wealth among people as given. Rather, the invisible-hand idea says that given a country's resources (natural, human, and technological) and its initial distribution of wealth, the use of free markets will make people as economically well off as possible.

The validity of the invisible-hand idea depends on a key assumption: The various markets in the economy, including financial markets, labour markets, and markets for goods and services, must function smoothly and without impediments, such as minimum wages and interest rate ceilings. In particular, wages and prices must adjust rapidly enough to maintain **equilibrium**—a situation in which the quantities demanded and supplied are equal—in all markets. In markets where quantity demanded exceeds quantity supplied, prices must rise to bring the market into equilibrium. In markets where more of a good is available than people want to buy, prices must fall to bring the market into equilibrium.

Wage and price flexibility is crucial to the invisible-hand idea because in a free-market system, changes in wages and prices are the signals that coordinate the actions of people in the economy. To illustrate, suppose that war abroad disrupts foreign oil production. This drop in supply will drive up the price of oil. A higher oil price will make it profitable for domestic oil suppliers to pump more oil and to drill more wells. The higher price will also induce domestic consumers to conserve oil and to switch to alternative sources of energy. Increased demand for alternative energy sources will raise their prices and stimulate *their* production, and so on. Thus, in the absence of impediments, such as government price controls, the adjustment of prices helps the free-market economy respond in a constructive and coordinated way to the initial disruption of supplies.

The classical approach to macroeconomics builds on Smith's basic assumptions that people pursue their own economic self-interests and that prices adjust reasonably quickly to achieve equilibrium in all markets. With these two assumptions as a basis, followers of the classical approach attempt to construct models of the macroeconomy that are consistent with the data and that can be used to answer the questions raised at the beginning of this chapter.

The use of the classical approach carries with it some strong policy implications. Because the classical assumptions imply that the invisible hand works well, classical economists often argue (as a normative proposition) that the government should have, at most, a limited role in the economy. As a positive proposition, classical economists also often argue that government policies will be ineffective or counterproductive at achieving their stated goals. Thus, for example, most classicals believe that the government should not try actively to eliminate business cycles.

THE KEYNESIAN APPROACH

Compared with the classical approach, the Keynesian approach is relatively recent. The book that introduced it, *The General Theory of Employment, Interest, and Money*, by British economist John Maynard Keynes, appeared in 1936—160 years after Adam Smith's *The Wealth of Nations*. In 1936, the world was suffering through the Great Depression. Unprecedentedly high rates of unemployment had afflicted most of the world's economies for years, and the invisible hand of free markets seemed completely ineffective. From the viewpoint of 1936, the classical theory appeared to be seriously inconsistent with the data, creating a need for a new macroeconomic theory. Keynes provided this theory.

In his book, Keynes offered an explanation for persistently high unemployment.[6] He based this explanation on an assumption about wage and price adjustment that was fundamentally different from the classical assumption. Instead of assuming that wages and prices adjust rapidly to achieve equilibrium in each market, as in the classical tradition, Keynes assumed that wages and prices adjust slowly. Slow wage and price adjustment meant that markets could be out of equilibrium—with quantities demanded not equal to quantities supplied—for long periods of time. In the Keynesian theory, unemployment can persist because wages and prices do not adjust quickly enough to equalize the number of people firms want to employ with the number of people who want to work.

Keynes's proposed solution to high unemployment was to have the government increase its purchases of goods and services, thus raising the demand for output.

---

6. Actually, Keynes presented a number of explanations of unemployment in his book, and debate continues about "what Keynes really meant." Our interpretation of what Keynes meant is the one adopted by his major followers.

Keynes argued that this policy would reduce unemployment because in order to meet the higher demands for their products, businesses would have to employ more workers. In addition, Keynes suggested, the newly hired workers would have more income to spend, creating another source of demand for output that would raise employment further. More generally, in contrast to classicals, Keynesians tend to be skeptical about the invisible hand and, thus, are more willing to advocate a role for government in improving macroeconomic performance.

THE EVOLUTION OF THE CLASSICAL–KEYNESIAN DEBATE

Because the Great Depression so strongly shook the faith of many economists in the classical approach, the Keynesian approach dominated macroeconomic theory and policy from World War II until about 1970. At the height of Keynesian influence, economists widely believed that through the skilful use of macroeconomic policies, the government could promote economic growth while avoiding inflation or recession. The main problems of macroeconomics apparently had been solved, with only some details to be filled in.

However, in the 1970s, Canada and other countries suffered from both high unemployment and high inflation—called "stagflation," or stagnation plus inflation. This experience weakened economists' and policymakers' confidence in the traditional Keynesian approach, much as the Great Depression had undermined the traditional classical approach. In addition, the Keynesian assumption that prices and wages adjust slowly, so that markets may be out of equilibrium, was criticized as being without sound theoretical foundations. While the Keynesian approach was coming under attack, developments in economic theory made classical macroeconomics look more interesting and attractive to many economists. Starting in the early 1970s, a modernized classical approach enjoyed a major resurgence among macroeconomic researchers, although classical macroeconomics did not achieve the dominance that Keynesianism enjoyed in the early postwar years.

In the past 20 years, advocates of both approaches have reworked them extensively to repair their weaknesses. Economists working in the classical tradition have improved their explanations of business cycles and unemployment. Keynesians have worked on the development of sound theoretical foundations for the slow adjustment of wages and prices, and Keynesian models can now accommodate stagflation. Currently, excellent research is being conducted with both approaches, and substantial communication and cross-fertilization are occurring between them.

A UNIFIED APPROACH TO MACROECONOMICS

In writing this book, we needed a strategy to deal with the fact that there are two major macroeconomic schools of thought. One strategy would have been to emphasize one of the two schools of thought and to treat the other only briefly. The problem with that strategy is that it would not expose you to the full range of ideas and insights that comprise modern macroeconomics. Alternatively, we might have presented the two approaches separately and then compared and contrasted their conclusions; but you would have missed the opportunity to explore the large common ground shared by the two schools of thought.

Our choice was to take an approach to macroeconomics that is as balanced and unified as possible. In keeping with this unified approach, all our analyses in this book—whether of economic growth, business cycles, inflation, or policy, and whether classical or Keynesian in spirit—are based on a single economic model, or on components or extensions of the basic model. This economic model, which draws heavily from both the classical and Keynesian traditions, has the following characteristics:

1. *Individuals, firms, and the government interact in goods markets, asset markets, and labour markets.* We have already discussed the need for aggregation in macroeconomics. In the economic model of this book, we follow standard macroeconomic practice and aggregate all the markets in the economy into three major markets: the market for goods and services, the asset market (in which assets, such as stocks, bonds, and real estate, are traded), and the labour market. We show how participants in the economy interact in each of these three markets and how these markets relate to each other and the economy as a whole.

2. *The model's macroeconomic analysis is based on the analysis of individual behaviour.* Macroeconomic behaviour reflects the behaviours of many individuals and firms interacting in markets. To understand how individuals and firms behave, we take a "bottom-up" approach and focus our analysis at the level of individual decision making (as in Box 1.1, where we discuss a model of individual choices about the route to take to work). The insights gained are then used for studying the economy as a whole.

The guiding principle in analyzing the behaviour of individuals and firms is the assumption that they *try to maximize their own economic satisfaction, given their needs, desires, and resources.* Although the founder of classical economics, Adam Smith, emphasized this assumption, it is generally accepted by Keynesians and classicals alike; and it is used in virtually all modern macroeconomic research.

3. Although Keynesians reject the classical assumption that wages and prices quickly adjust to achieve equilibrium in the short run, *Keynesians and classicals both agree that in the long run, prices and wages fully adjust to achieve equilibrium in the markets for goods, assets, and labour.* Because complete flexibility of wages and prices in the long run is not controversial, we examine the long-term behaviour of the economy (Chapters 3–7) before discussing short-run issues associated with business cycles (Chapters 8–12).

4. *The basic model that we present may be used with either the classical assumption that wages and prices are flexible or the Keynesian assumption that wages and prices are slow to adjust.* This aspect of the model allows us to compare classical and Keynesian conclusions and policy recommendations within a common theoretical framework.

CHAPTER SUMMARY

1. Macroeconomics is the study of the structure and performance of national economies and the policies that governments use to try to affect economic performance. Important topics in macroeconomics include the determinants of long-run economic growth, business cycles, unemployment, inflation, international trade and lending, and macroeconomic policy.

2. Because macroeconomics covers the economy as a whole, macroeconomists ignore the fine distinctions among different kinds of goods, firms, or markets and focus on national totals, such as aggregate consumption. The process of adding individual economic variables to obtain economy-wide totals is called aggregation.

3. The activities engaged in by macroeconomists include (in addition to teaching) forecasting, macroeconomic analysis, macroeconomic research, and data development.

4. The goal of macroeconomic research is to be able to make general statements about how the economy works. Macroeconomic research makes progress toward this goal by developing economic theories and testing them empirically—that is, by seeing whether they are consistent with data obtained from the real world. A useful economic theory is based on reasonable and realistic assumptions, is easy to use, has implications that can be tested in the real world, and is consistent with the data and the observed behaviour of the real-world economy.

5. A positive analysis of an economic policy examines the economic consequences of the policy but does not address the question of whether those consequences are desirable. A normative analysis of a policy tries to determine whether the policy should be used. Disagreements among macroeconomists may arise because of differences in normative conclusions, the result of differences in personal values and beliefs, and differences in the positive analysis of a policy proposal.

6. The classical approach to macroeconomics is based on the assumptions that individuals and firms act in their own best interests and that wages and prices adjust quickly to achieve equilibrium in all markets. Under these assumptions, the invisible hand of the free-market economy works well, with only a limited scope for government intervention in the economy.

7. The Keynesian approach to macroeconomics assumes that wages and prices do not adjust rapidly and, thus, the invisible hand may not work well. Keynesians argue that because of slow wage and price adjustment, unemployment may remain high for a long time. Keynesians are usually more inclined than classicals to believe that government intervention in the economy may help improve economic performance.

KEY TERMS

aggregation, p. 11
average labour productivity, p. 2
closed economy, p. 7
deflation, p. 6
economic model, p. 13
economic theory, p. 13
empirical analysis, p. 13
equilibrium, p. 16
exchange rate, p. 8
fiscal policy, p. 8
inflation, p. 6
invisible hand, p. 16
macroeconomics, p. 1
monetary policy, p. 9
normative analysis, p. 15
open economy, p. 7
positive analysis, p. 15
trade deficit, p. 7
trade surplus, p. 7
unemployment, p. 5

REVIEW QUESTIONS

1. How have total output and output per worker changed over time in Canada? How have these changes affected the lives of typical Canadians?

2. What is a business cycle? How does the unemployment rate behave over the course of a business cycle? Does the unemployment rate ever reach zero?

3. Define *inflation* and *deflation*. Compare the behaviour of consumer prices in Canada in the years before and after World War II.

4. Define *budget deficit*. Historically, when has the federal government been most likely to run deficits? What has been the recent experience?

5. What is meant by *aggregation*? Why is aggregation important for macroeconomic analysis?

6. List the principal professional activities of macroeconomists. What role does macroeconomic research play in each of these activities?

7. What steps are involved in developing and testing an economic theory or model? What are the criteria for a useful theory or model?

8. Might two economists agree about the effects of a particular economic policy but disagree about the desirability of implementing the policy? Explain your answer.

9. Compare the classical and Keynesian views on the speed of wage and price adjustment. What are the important consequences of the differences in their views?

NUMERICAL PROBLEMS

1. Here are some macroeconomic data for the country of Oz for the years 2001 and 2002.

	2001	**2002**
Output	12,000 tonnes of potatoes	14,300 tonnes of potatoes
Employment	1,000 workers	1,100 workers
Unemployed	100 workers	50 workers
Total labour force	1,100 workers	1,150 workers
Prices	2 shekels/tonne of potatoes	2.5 shekels/tonne of potatoes

As the data suggest, Oz produces only potatoes, and its monetary unit is the shekel. Calculate each of the following macroeconomic variables for Oz, being sure to give units.
a. Average labour productivity in 2001 and 2002.
b. The growth rate of average labour productivity between 2001 and 2002.
c. The unemployment rate in 2001 and 2002.
d. The inflation rate between 2001 and 2002.

2. In a recent issue of the *Canadian Economic Observer, Statistical Summary*, find the data section entitled "National Accounts." In Table 1, "Gross Domestic Product," find data on gross domestic product (a measure of total output), exports, and imports. In Table 3, "Government Revenue and Expenditure," find data on the federal government's total revenue (taxes) and expenditures.
a. Calculate the ratio of exports to GDP, the ratio of imports to GDP, and the ratio of the trade imbalance to GDP in the latest reported quarter. Compare the answers with the values reported for the previous two complete years.
b. Calculate the ratio of federal government revenue to GDP, the ratio of federal government expenditures to GDP, and the ratio of the budget deficit to GDP, for the most recent quarter and for the previous two complete years.

ANALYTICAL PROBLEMS

1. Can average labour productivity fall, even though total output is rising? Can the unemployment rate rise, even though total output is rising?

2. Prices were much higher in Canada in 2001 than in 1913. Does this fact mean that people were economically better off in 1913? Why, or why not?

3. State a theory for why people vote for a specific political party that potentially could satisfy the criteria for a useful theory given in the text. How would you go about testing your theory?

4. Which of the following statements are positive in nature and which are normative?
a. A tax cut will raise interest rates.
b. A reduction in the payroll tax would primarily benefit poor and middle-class workers.
c. Payroll taxes are too high.
d. A cut in the payroll tax would improve the federal government's popularity ratings.
e. Payroll taxes should not be cut unless capital gains taxes are cut also.

5. In 1993, the debate heated up in Canada about the North American Free Trade Agreement (NAFTA), which proposed to reduce barriers to trade (such as taxes on or limits to imports) among Canada, the United States, and Mexico. Some people strongly opposed the agreement, arguing that an influx of foreign goods under NAFTA would disrupt the Canadian economy, harm domestic industries, and throw Canadian workers out of work. How might a classical economist respond to these concerns? Would you expect a Keynesian economist to be more or less sympathetic to these concerns than the classical economist? Why?

Chapter 2

THE MEASUREMENT AND STRUCTURE OF THE CANADIAN ECONOMY

Measurement is a crucial part of scientific study. Accurate measurement is essential for making new discoveries, evaluating competing theories, and predicting future events or trends. During the first half of the 20th century, painstaking research on national accounting showed that careful economic measurement is not only possible but also necessary for any serious understanding of the economy. This research transformed economics from a field in which scholars relied on informal observations and broad generalizations to one in which numbers and statistical analysis play an essential role.

In this chapter, we present some of the conceptual and practical issues involved in measuring the macroeconomy. We focus on the national income accounts, a framework for measuring economic activity that is widely used by economic researchers and analysts. Learning about the national income accounts will familiarize you with some useful economic data. In addition, because the national income accounts are set up in a logical way that mirrors the structure of the economy, working through these accounts is an important first step toward understanding how the macroeconomy works. When you finish this chapter, you will have a much clearer understanding of the relationships that exist among key macroeconomic variables and among the different sectors of the economy.

2.1 NATIONAL INCOME ACCOUNTING: THE MEASUREMENT OF PRODUCTION, INCOME, AND EXPENDITURE

The **national income accounts** are an accounting framework used in measuring current economic activity. Almost all countries have some form of official national income accounts. (For background information on the Canadian national income accounts, see the box, "In Touch with the Macroeconomy: The National Income and Expenditure Accounts," p. 23.) In this section, we discuss the basic idea that underlies national income accounting. We then show how the national income accounts are used in measuring economic activity in Canada and other countries.

The national income accounts are based on the idea that the amount of economic activity that occurs during a period of time can be measured in terms of

1. the amount of output produced, excluding output used up in intermediate stages of production (the product approach);

2. the incomes received by the producers of output (the income approach); and

IN TOUCH WITH THE MACROECONOMY

THE NATIONAL INCOME AND EXPENDITURE ACCOUNTS

In Canada, the national income accounts are part of the National Economic and Financial Accounts. These accounts provide comprehensive measurements of production, income, and expenditure for the Canadian economy. Limited accounts were constructed prior to 1945 (for example, by the staff of the Rowell-Sirois Commission), but comprehensive accounts began in the Dominion Bureau of Statistics in 1945. Official accounts have been constructed as far back as 1926, and some measurements have been made for 1870–1926 by M.C. Urquhart of Queen's University.

Currently, the accounts are constructed quarterly by government economists and statisticians in Statistics Canada, as part of the System of National Accounts. Very clear guides to the system are provided by Statistics Canada, *Guide to the Income and Expenditure Accounts* (cat. no 13–603E), and by John Grant's *A Handbook of Economic Indicators.* *

In constructing the accounts, Statistics Canada relies on data provided by other departments of the federal government, by provincial governments, by the Bank of Canada, and by industry associations. For example, the data sources include the decennial census and tax returns submitted to the Canada Customs and Revenue Agency.

Initial estimates of quarterly economic activity are released about two months after the end of each quarter. Revised estimates, which may differ significantly from the initial estimates, are released another three months later. More detailed revisions are done annually. Like many series compiled by Statistics Canada, these series are available in CANSIM (a registered mark of Statistics Canada), a computer database, or at *www.statcan.ca.*

Quarterly data are quoted at annual rates, which means that the GDP flow for the quarter is multiplied by four. This gives the value that annual GDP would have if economic activity continued at the same pace for four quarters. Quarterly and monthly data are also often seasonally adjusted. That means that Statistics Canada tries to separate the part of GDP that is due to seasonal factors (such as Christmas shopping) from that due to longer-term causes.

Historical national accounts data may be obtained from the *Canadian Economic Observer, Historical Statistical Supplement*, which is updated annually, and from *Historical Statistics of Canada*. Last-quarter data appear in the business press, which gives extensive coverage to monthly releases by Statistics Canada. National income accounts for other countries are available in *National Accounts*, a publication of the Organization for Economic Cooperation and Development (OECD); in *World Economic Outlook*, published by the International Monetary Fund; and in the United Nations' *National Accounts Statistics*.

---

* John Grant, *A Handbook of Economic Indicators*, Toronto: University of Toronto Press, 1992.

3. the amount of spending by the ultimate purchasers of output (the expenditure approach).

Each approach gives a different perspective on the economy. However, the fundamental principle underlying national income accounting is that except for such problems as incomplete or misreported data, *all three approaches give identical measurements of the amount of current economic activity.*

We can illustrate why these three approaches are equivalent by an example. Imagine an economy with only two businesses, called AppleInc and JuiceInc. AppleInc owns and operates apple orchards. It sells some of its apples directly to the public. It sells the rest of its apples to JuiceInc, which produces and sells apple juice. The following table shows the transactions of each business during a year.

AppleInc Transactions

Wages paid to AppleInc employees	$15,000
Taxes paid to government	5,000
Revenue received from sale of apples	35,000
Apples sold to public	10,000
Apples sold to JuiceInc	25,000

(*Note*: After-tax profit of AppleInc = revenue – costs – taxes = $15,000)

JuiceInc Transactions

Wages paid to JuiceInc employees	$10,000
Taxes paid to government	2,000
Apples purchased from AppleInc	25,000
Revenue received from sale of apple juice	40,000

(*Note*: After-tax profit of JuiceInc = revenue – costs – taxes = $3,000)

AppleInc pays $15,000 per year in wages to workers to pick apples, and it sells these apples for $35,000 ($10,000 worth of apples to households and $25,000 worth of apples to JuiceInc). Thus, AppleInc's profit before taxes is $35,000 – $15,000 = $20,000. Because AppleInc pays taxes of $5,000, its after-tax profit is $15,000.

JuiceInc buys $25,000 of apples from AppleInc and pays wages of $10,000 to workers to process the apples into apple juice. It sells the apple juice for $40,000, so its profit before taxes is $5,000 ($40,000 – $25,000 – $10,000). After paying taxes of $2,000, its after-tax profit is $3,000. What is the total value, measured in dollars, of the economic activity generated by these two businesses? The product approach, income approach, and expenditure approach are three different ways of arriving at the answer to this question; all yield the same answer.

1.   The **product approach** measures economic activity by adding the market values of goods and services produced, excluding any goods and services used up in intermediate stages of production. This approach makes use of the value-added concept. The **value added** of any producer is the value of its output minus the value of the inputs it purchases from other producers. The product approach computes economic activity by summing the value added of all producers.

In our example, AppleInc produces output worth $35,000 and JuiceInc produces output worth $40,000. However, measuring overall economic activity by simply adding $35,000 and $40,000 would "double count" the $25,000 of apples that JuiceInc purchased from AppleInc and processed into juice. To avoid this double counting, we sum value added rather than output: Because JuiceInc processed apples worth $25,000 into a product worth $40,000, JuiceInc's value added is $15,000 ($40,000 – $25,000). AppleInc does not use any inputs purchased from other businesses so its value added equals its revenue of $35,000. Thus, total value added in the economy is $35,000 + $15,000 = $50,000.

2.   The **income approach** measures economic activity by adding all income received, including wages, taxes (the government's income), and after-tax profits (the income of the owners of AppleInc and JuiceInc). The incomes generated in the example are as follows:

Incomes Received

Wage income ($15,000 at AppleInc; $10,000 at JuiceInc)	$25,000
Taxes ($5,000 from AppleInc; $2,000 from JuiceInc)	7,000
Profits ($15,000 at AppleInc; $3,000 at JuiceInc)	18,000
Total income	$50,000

The income approach concludes that the value of economic activity is $50,000, the same amount determined by the product approach.

3. Finally, the **expenditure approach** measures activity by adding the amount spent by all ultimate users of output. In this example, households are ultimate users of apples. JuiceInc is not an ultimate user of apples because it sells the apples (in processed, liquid form) to households. Thus, ultimate users purchase $10,000 of apples from AppleInc and $40,000 of apple juice from JuiceInc for a total of $50,000, the same amount computed in both the product and the expenditure approaches.[1]

WHY THE THREE APPROACHES ARE EQUIVALENT

That the product, income, and expenditure approaches all give the same answer is no accident. The logic of these three approaches is such that they must *always* give the same answer.

To see why, first observe that the market value of goods and services produced in a given period is by *definition* equal to the amount that buyers must spend to purchase them. JuiceInc's apple juice has a market value of $40,000 only because that is what people are willing to spend to buy it. The market value of a good or service and the spending on that good or service are always the same, so the product approach (which measures market values) and the expenditure approach (which measures spending) must give the same measure of economic activity.[2]

Next, observe that what the seller receives must equal what the buyers spend. The seller's receipts in turn equal the total income generated by the economic activity, including the incomes paid to workers and suppliers, taxes paid to the government, and profits (whatever is left over). Thus, total expenditure must equal total income generated, implying that the expenditure and income approaches must also produce the same answer. Finally, as both product value and income equal expenditure, they also must be equal.

Because of the equivalence of the three approaches, over any specified time period

$$\text{total production} = \text{total income} = \text{total expenditure}, \qquad (2.1)$$

where production, income, and expenditure all are measured in the same units (for example, in dollars). Equation (2.1) is called the **fundamental identity of national income accounting** and forms the basis for national income accounting. (An identity is an equation that is true by definition.) In Section 2.2, we show how this fundamental identity is used in measuring current economic activity for the economy as a whole.

2.2 GROSS DOMESTIC PRODUCT

The broadest measure of aggregate economic activity, as well as the best-known and most often used, is the **gross domestic product**, or GDP. As in the example in Section 2.1, a country's GDP may be measured by the product approach, the expenditure approach, or the income approach. Although the three approaches

---

1. In the example, each business also purchases labour services from employees, but as these services are used in production, they are not counted as services purchased by ultimate users.

2. Our explanation implicitly assumes that everything produced is sold. What if a firm produces some goods that it cannot sell? As we demonstrate shortly, the national income accounts treat unsold goods as though they were purchased by the firm from itself, that is, accumulation of unsold goods in inventory is treated as part of expenditure. Thus, expenditure and production remain equal even if some goods remain unsold.

arrive at the same value for GDP, each views GDP differently. Using all three approaches gives a more complete picture of an economy's structure than any single approach could.

THE PRODUCT APPROACH TO MEASURING GDP

The product approach defines a nation's GDP as the market value of final goods and services newly produced within a nation during a fixed period of time. In working through the various parts of this definition, we discuss some practical issues that arise in measuring GDP.

MARKET VALUE

Goods and services are counted in GDP at their market values, that is, at the prices at which they are sold. The advantage of using market values is that it allows adding the production of different goods and services. Imagine, for example, that you want to measure the total output of an economy that produces 7 cars and 100 pairs of shoes. Adding the number of cars and the number of pairs of shoes to get a total output of 107 would not make much sense because cars and shoes are not of equal economic value. But suppose that each car sells for $10,000 and each pair of shoes sells for $60. Taking these market-determined prices as measures of relative economic values, you can calculate the value of cars produced as $70,000 (7 × $10,000) and the value of shoes produced as $6,000 (100 × $60). The total market value of production, or GDP, is $70,000 + $6,000 = $76,000. Using market values to measure production makes sense because it takes into account differences in the relative economic importance of different goods and services.

A problem with using market values to measure GDP is that some useful goods and services are not sold in formal markets. Ideally, GDP should be adjusted upward to reflect the existence of these goods and services. However, because of the difficulty of obtaining reliable measures, some nonmarket goods and services simply are ignored in the calculation of GDP. Homemaking and child-care services performed within the family without pay, for example, are not included in GDP, although homemaking and child care that are provided for pay (for example, by professional housecleaners or by private day-care centres) are included. Similarly, because the benefits of clean air and water are not bought and sold in markets, actions to reduce pollution or otherwise improve environmental quality usually are not reflected in GDP (see Box 2.1).

Some nonmarket goods and services are partially incorporated in official GDP measures. An example is activity that takes place in the so-called underground economy. The **underground economy** includes both legal activities hidden from government record keepers (to avoid payment of taxes or compliance with regulations, for example) and illegal activities, such as drug dealing, prostitution, and (in some places) gambling. Some might argue that such activities as drug dealing are "bads" rather than "goods" and should not be included in GDP anyway—although a consistent application of this argument might rule out many goods and services currently included in GDP. Clearly, though, the services of a housepainter who is paid in cash in order to avoid taxes should be included in GDP. Statistics Canada regularly adjusts GDP figures to include estimates of the underground economy's size (currently estimated at roughly 3% of GDP). Because cash is the favoured means of payment for off-the-books transactions, one clue to the size of the underground economy is the amount of cash in circulation.

Box 2.1

NATURAL RESOURCES, THE ENVIRONMENT, AND THE NATIONAL INCOME ACCOUNTS

Much of any country's economic well being flows from natural, rather than human-made, assets—land, rivers and oceans, natural resources (such as oil and timber), and, indeed, the air that everyone breathes. Ideally, for the purposes of economic and environmental planning, the use and misuse of natural resources and the environment should be appropriately measured in the national income accounts. Unfortunately, they are not. There are at least two important conceptual problems with the way the national income accounts currently handle the economic use of natural resources and the environment.

1. *Natural resource depletion.* When an oil driller pumps oil from an underground field, the value of the oil produced is counted as part of the nation's GDP; there is no offsetting deduction to account for the fact that nonrenewable resources are being depleted. In principle, the draining of the oil field can be thought of as a type of negative inventory investment because, in a sense, it reduces the inventory of oil. If it were included in the national income accounts, this negative inventory investment would reduce the computed value of GDP.

2. *The costs and benefits of pollution control.* Imagine that a company has the following choices: It can produce $100 million worth of output and, in the process, pollute the local river by dumping its wastes; alternatively, by using 10% of its workers to properly dispose of its wastes, it can avoid polluting but will get only $90 million of output. Under current national income accounting rules, if the firm chooses to pollute rather than not to pollute, its contribution to GDP will be larger ($100 million rather than $90 million) because the national income accounts attach no explicit value to a clean river. In an ideal accounting system, the economic costs of environmental degradation would be subtracted in the calculation of a firm's contribution to output, and activities that improve the environment—because they provide real economic benefits—would be added to output.

Discussing the national income accounting implications of resource depletion and pollution may seem to trivialize these important problems. Actually, because GDP and related statistics are used continually in policy analyses, abstract questions of measurement often may turn out to have significant real effects. For example, economic development experts have expressed concern that some poor countries, in attempting to raise measured GDP as quickly as possible, have done so, in part, by overexploiting their natural resources and harming the environment. Conceivably, explicitly incorporating "hidden" resource and environmental costs into official measures of economic growth might cause these policies to be modified. Similarly, in the industrialized countries, political debates about the environment at times have emphasized the impact on conventionally measured GDP of proposed pollution control measures, rather than their impact on overall economic welfare. Better accounting for environmental quality might serve to refocus these debates to the more relevant question of whether, for any particular environmental proposal, the benefits (economic and noneconomic) exceed the costs.

For these reasons, Statistics Canada developed the Canadian System of Environmental Accounts, as a complement to the existing national accounts. The additional accounts measure stocks of renewable and nonrenewable resources, waste output (including greenhouse gas emissions), and expenditures on pollution abatement and environmental protection. For example, they estimate Canadian carbon dioxide emissions in megatonnes each year, tonnes per capita, or tonnes per dollar of GDP. You can track these measures under "Environment" at *www.statcan.ca*, or in *Ecoconnections: Linking the Environment and the Economy* (Statistics Canada cat. no. 16–200-XKE).

Particularly important components of economic activity that do not pass through markets are the services provided by government, such as public education, defence, and the building and maintenance of roads and bridges. The fact that most government services are not sold in markets implies a lack of market values to use when calculating the government's contribution to GDP. In this case, the solution that has been adopted is to value government services at their cost of production.

Thus, the contribution of public education to GDP equals the government's cost of providing education: the salaries of school teachers, the costs of building and maintaining schools, and so on.

Newly Produced Goods and Services

As a measure of current economic activity, GDP includes only goods or services that are newly produced within the current period. GDP excludes purchases or sales of goods that were produced in previous periods. Thus, although the market price paid for a newly constructed house would be included in GDP, the price paid in the sale of a used house is not counted in GDP. (The value of the used house would have been included in GDP for the year it was built.) However, the value of the services of the real estate agent involved in the sale of the used house is part of GDP because those services are provided in the current period.

Final Goods and Services

Goods and services produced during a period of time may be classified as either intermediate goods and services or final goods and services. **Intermediate goods and services** are those used up in the production of other goods and services *in the same period that they themselves were produced*. For example, flour that is produced and then used to make bread in the same year is an intermediate good. The trucking company that delivers the flour to the bakery provides an intermediate service.

Final goods and services are those goods and services that are not intermediate. Final goods and services are the end products of a process. For example, bread produced by the bakery is a final good, and a shopper's bus ride home from the bakery is a final service. Because the purpose of economic activity is the production of final goods and services, with intermediate goods being but a step along the way, only final goods and services are counted in GDP.

Sometimes the distinction between intermediate goods and final goods is subtle. For example, is a new lathe sold to a furniture manufacturer an intermediate good or a final good? Although the lathe is used to produce other goods, it is not used up during the year. Therefore, it is not an intermediate good; it is a final good. In particular, the lathe is an example of a type of final good called a capital good. Other more general examples of capital goods include factory equipment, office equipment, and factories and office buildings themselves. A **capital good** is a good that is itself produced (this rules out natural resources, such as land) and is used to produce other goods; however, unlike an intermediate good, a capital good is not used up in the same period that it is produced. The preparers of the national income accounts decided to classify capital goods as final goods and, thus, to include their production in GDP. Their reasoning was that the addition to productive capacity that new capital goods represent is an important purpose of economic activity.

Another subtle distinction between intermediate and final goods arises in the treatment of inventory investment. **Inventories** are stocks of unsold finished goods, goods in process, and raw materials held by firms. Inventory investment is the amount by which inventories increase during the year.[3] For example, suppose that a baker began the year with $1,000 worth of flour in her storeroom, and at the end of the year she is holding $1,100 worth of flour. The difference between her beginning and ending stocks, or $100 worth of flour, equals the baker's inventory investment

---

3. When inventories decline during the year, inventory investment is negative.

during the year. Even though the ultimate purpose of the baker's flour is for making bread, her increase in inventory represents production of flour that is not used up during the year. As in the case of capital goods, inventory investment is treated as a final good and, thus, part of GDP because increased inventories on hand imply greater productive capacity in the future.

In the AppleInc/JuiceInc example, we showed that total economic activity could be measured by summing the value added (value of output minus value of purchased inputs) for each producer. The advantage of the value added technique is that it automatically includes final goods and excludes intermediate goods from the measure of total output. If you go back to that example, you will see that by summing the value added of the two companies, we obtained a measure of economic activity that included the value of final sales of the two businesses to the public, but that excluded the intermediate goods (unprocessed apples) sold to JuiceInc by AppleInc.

GNP VERSUS GDP

Until fairly recently, many economists focused on a measure of economic activity known as gross national product (GNP) rather than on GDP. The difference between GNP and GDP concerns the treatment of output produced by capital and labour working outside its home (domestic) country. Specifically, **gross national product** is the market value of final goods and services newly produced *by domestic factors of production* during the current period (as opposed to production taking place within a country, which is GDP).

When Canadian capital and labour—also called factors of production—are used abroad, they produce output and earn income. This output and income are included in Canadian GNP but not in Canadian GDP because they do not represent production taking place within Canada. So, for example, the value of roads built by a Canadian construction company in Saudi Arabia, as measured by the fees that the construction company receives from the Saudi government, is counted in Canadian GNP but not in Canadian GDP. Similarly, when foreign capital or labour is used in Canada, the output produced and the income earned are part of Canadian GDP (because the production occurs within Canada) but not of Canadian GNP (they are counted in the foreign country's GNP instead). For example, the portion of the value of Japanese cars built in Canada that is attributable to Japanese capital and management counts in Japanese GNP and Canadian GDP, but not in Canadian GNP.

We define **net factor payments from abroad** (*NFP*) to be income paid to domestic factors of production by the rest of the world, minus income paid to foreign factors of production by the domestic economy. Using this concept, we express the relationship between GDP and GNP as

$$GDP + NFP = GNP. \qquad (2.2)$$

For Canada, GDP and GNP give slightly different measures of economic activity. For example, in 2000, Canadian GDP was $1,056 billion and Canadian GNP was $1,031 billion, a difference of about 2%. This compares with a difference of about 0.2% between US GDP and US GNP. *NFP* is proportionally larger in Canada than in the United States (and negative) because of the scale of foreign investment in Canada. When foreign firms invest in Canada, the interest and profits they earn count in GDP but not in GNP. The distinction between GNP and GDP is even more important for such countries as Egypt and Turkey that have many citizens working abroad. The reason is that remittances sent home by workers abroad are part of a country's GNP but not its GDP.

THE EXPENDITURE APPROACH TO MEASURING GDP

A different perspective on the components of GDP is obtained by looking at the expenditure side of the national income accounts. The expenditure approach measures GDP as total spending on final goods and services produced within a nation during a specified period of time. Four major categories of spending are added to get GDP: consumption, investment, government purchases of goods and services, and net exports of goods and services. In symbols,

$$
\begin{aligned}
Y = \text{GDP} \ &= \text{total production (or output)} \\
&= \text{total income} \\
&= \text{total expenditure;} \\
C &= \text{consumption;} \\
I &= \text{investment;} \\
G &= \text{government purchases of goods and services;} \\
NX &= \text{net exports of goods and services.}
\end{aligned}
$$

With these symbols, we express the expenditure approach to measuring GDP as

$$Y = C + I + G + NX. \tag{2.3}$$

Equation (2.3), like Eq. (2.1), is one of the basic relationships in macroeconomics. Equation (2.3) is called the **income–expenditure identity** because it states that income Y equals total expenditure $C + I + G + NX$. Recent Canadian data for the four categories of spending, along with some major subcategories, are given in Table 2.1. As you read the rest of this section, you should look at Table 2.1 to get some feel for the relative sizes of different components of spending in the Canadian economy.

CONSUMPTION

Consumption is spending by domestic households on final goods and services, including those produced abroad.[4] It is the largest component of expenditure, usually accounting for about 60% of GDP in Canada. Consumption expenditures include spending in four categories:

1. *Consumer durables*, which are long-lived items, such as motor vehicles, furniture, and appliances (but not houses, which are classified under investment)

2. *Semi-durable goods*, which are shorter-lived goods, such as clothing

3. *Nondurable goods*, such as food and utilities

4. *Services*, such as health care, financial services, rent, and restaurant meals

INVESTMENT

Investment includes both spending for new capital goods, called fixed investment, and increases in firms' inventory holdings, called *inventory investment*. Fixed investment, in turn, has three components:

1. *Residential construction*, which is spending on the construction of new houses and apartment buildings. Houses and apartment buildings are treated as capital goods because they provide a service (shelter) over a long period of time

---

4. Later, we subtract imports to get total spending on the goods and services produced in the domestic economy.

TABLE 2.1

Expenditure Approach to Measuring GDP in Canada, 2000

	Billions of dollars	Percent of GDP
Personal consumption expenditures	**593.275**	**56.2**
durable goods	81.239	7.7
semi-durable goods	52.116	4.9
nondurable goods	141.112	13.4
services	318.808	30.2
Business fixed investment	**184.294**	**17.5**
residential construction	48.170	4.6
nonresidential construction	50.569	4.8
machinery and equipment	85.555	8.1
Business inventory investment	**7.144**	**0.7**
Government investment	**24.764**	**2.3**
fixed capital	24.740	2.3
inventories	0.024	0.0
Government purchases of goods and services*	**192.771**	**18.3**
Net exports	**53.227**	**5.0**
exports	479.450	45.4
imports	426.223	40.4
Statistical discrepancy	**0.535**	**0.1**
Total (equals GDP)	**1056.010**	**100.0**

Source: *Canadian Economic Observer, Statistical Summary*, Statistics Canada, cat. no. 11–010, Table 1; and *National Economic and Financial Accounts, Quarterly Estimates*, Statistics Canada, cat. no. 13–001, Table 2.

* Government *purchases of* goods and services are also referred to as government *expenditure on* goods and services.

2. *Nonresidential investment*, which is private spending on structures (factories, warehouses, and office buildings, for example)

3. *Machinery and equipment investment*, which is spending on machines, tools, and vehicles

Like consumption, investment includes spending on foreign-produced goods. Overall, fixed investment in Canada usually is about one-sixth of GDP.

As we have mentioned, increases in inventories are included in investment spending, regardless of why inventories rose. In particular, if a firm produces goods that it cannot sell, the resulting rise in inventories counts as investment by the firm. For the purposes of national income accounting, the firm has, in effect, purchased the unsold goods from itself. This accounting rule is useful because it guarantees that production and expenditure will always be equal in the national income accounts. Anything that is produced must by definition either be bought by a customer or "purchased" by the firm itself.

Government investment is also counted in GDP (as shown in Table 2.1) and is measured separately from other government spending. We include it in *I*, which, thus, measures private and public investment.

GOVERNMENT PURCHASES OF GOODS AND SERVICES

Government purchases of goods and services, which include any expenditure by the government for a currently produced good (other than capital goods) or service, foreign or domestic, is the third major component of spending. Government purchases in Canada recently have been about one-fifth of GDP. Government purchases include those made by provincial, municipal, and territorial governments.

Not all cheques written by governments are for purchases of goods and services. **Transfers**, a category that includes transfers between levels of government as well as government payments to individuals in the form of public pensions, unemployment insurance benefits, welfare payments, and so on, are payments by governments that are not made in exchange for currently produced goods or services. As a result, they are excluded from the government purchases category and are not counted in GDP as calculated by the expenditure approach. Similarly, interest payments on the national debt are not counted as part of government purchases.

NET EXPORTS

Net exports are exports minus imports. As discussed in Chapter 1, exports are the goods and services produced within a country that are purchased by foreigners; imports are the goods and services produced abroad that are purchased by a country's residents. Net exports are positive if exports are greater than imports and negative if imports exceed exports.

Exports are added to total spending because they represent spending (by foreigners) on final goods and services produced in a country. Imports are subtracted from total spending because consumption, investment, and government purchases are defined to include imported goods and services. Subtracting imports ensures that total spending, $C + I + G + NX$, reflects spending only on output produced in the country. For example, an increase in imports may mean that Canadians are buying Korean cars instead of Canadian cars. For fixed total spending by domestic residents, therefore, an increase in imports lowers spending on domestic production.

THE INCOME APPROACH TO MEASURING GDP

The third and final way to measure GDP is the income approach. It calculates GDP by adding the incomes received by producers, including profits, and taxes paid to the government. A key part of the income approach is a concept known as net national income. Net national income is the sum of four types of income (see Table 2.2 for recent Canadian data).

1. *Labour income.* This is the income of employees (excluding the self-employed) and includes wages, salaries, employee benefits (including contributions by employers to private pension plans), and employer contributions to Employment Insurance and the Canada Pension Plan. As you can see from Table 2.2, labour income is the largest component of national income, comprising 51% of GDP in 2000.[5]

2. *Corporate profits.* Corporate profits are the profits earned by corporations and represent the remainder of corporate revenue after wages, interest, rents, and other costs have been paid. Corporate profits are used to pay taxes levied on corporations and to pay dividends to shareholders. The rest of corporate profits after taxes and dividends, called retained earnings, is kept within the corporation.

---

5. Labour income overstates the take-home income of workers. As in each of the other measures of income on this list, part of the income received by employees must be paid to the government as taxes.

TABLE 2.2

Income Approach to Measuring GDP in Canada, 2000

	Billions of dollars	Percent of GDP
Labour income	536.578	50.8
Corporate profits*	139.215	13.2
Interest and investment income†	50.938	4.8
Unincorporated business income**	65.216	6.2
Total (equals Net National Income) at factor cost	791.947	75.0
Plus Indirect taxes less subsidies	130.283	12.3
Total (equals Net Domestic Product) at market prices	922.230	87.3
Plus Capital consumption allowances	134.315	12.7
Plus Statistical discrepancy††	–0.535	0.1
Equals Gross Domestic Product (GDP)	1056.010	100.0
Plus Net factor payments	–24.547	2.3
Equals Gross National Product (GNP)	1031.463	97.7

Source: *Canadian Economic Observer, Statistical Summary*, Statistics Canada, cat. no. 11-010, Table 1; and *National Economic and Financial Accounts, Quarterly Estimates*, Statistics Canada, cat. no. 13-001, Table 30.

* Includes government enterprise profits.
† Includes inventory valuation adjustment.
** Includes net farm income.
†† Statistical discrepancy reflects the difference between Statistics Canada's estimates of GDP from the expenditure approach and its estimates from the income approach. The discrepancy is an adjustment that is made so that the two estimates coincide.

Corporate profits generally are a modest fraction of GDP (13% of GDP in 2000), but the amount of profits earned by corporations may change dramatically from year to year or even from quarter to quarter.

3. *Interest and investment income.* Interest income consists of the interest earned by individuals from businesses and foreign sources minus interest paid by individuals. In 2000, interest and investment income was 5% of GDP. In Table 2.2, this category also includes any change in the value of inventories held by firms.

4. *Unincorporated business income.* Unincorporated business income is the income of the nonincorporated self-employed. As many self-employed people own some capital (examples are a farmer's tractor or a dentist's X-ray machine) unincorporated business income includes both labour and capital income. This category accounted for 6% of GDP in 2000.

In addition to the four components of net national income just described, two other items—indirect taxes (net of subsidies) and depreciation—need to be accounted for to obtain GDP.

Indirect taxes, such as provincial sales taxes and the federal goods and services tax (GST), are paid by businesses to federal, provincial, and municipal governments. Indirect taxes (net of subsidies) do not appear in any of the four categories of income discussed, but because they are income of the government, they must be added to national income in order to measure all of a country's income. National income plus indirect taxes less subsidies equals net domestic product (at market prices) as shown in Table 2.2. Net national income also is referred to as net national or domestic product at factor cost because it is constructed with before-tax prices. In contrast, net domestic product at market prices is based on after-tax prices.

Depreciation (also known as capital consumption allowances) is the value of the capital that wears out during the period over which economic activity is being measured.[6] In the calculation of the components of national income (such as corporate profits and investment income) depreciation is subtracted from total, or gross, income. Thus, to compute the total or gross amount of income we must add back in depreciation. The sum of net domestic product and depreciation is gross domestic product. Gross domestic product is called *gross* because it measures Canada's total production or output of goods and services without subtracting depreciation.

As we discussed earlier, to go from GDP to GNP, we have to add net factor payments from abroad, *NFP* (see Eq. 2.2). As we have already mentioned and as you can see from Table 2.2, for Canada *NFP* is negative and so GNP is less than GDP.

PRIVATE SECTOR AND GOVERNMENT SECTOR INCOME

In this section, we have measured economic activity as the sum of all the incomes received in an economy. Sometimes, however, economists need to know how much of total income was received by the private sector (households and businesses) and how much accrues to the government sector, which, in Canada, consists of federal, provincial, territorial, and municipal governments. For example, in trying to predict the demand for consumer goods, focusing on the income available to the private sector might be more useful than focusing on the income of the economy as a whole.

The income of the private sector, known as **private disposable income**, measures the amount of income the private sector has available to spend. In general, as for an individual family, the disposable income of the private sector as a whole equals income received from private sector activities, plus payments received by the private sector from the government, minus taxes paid to the government. The precise definition is

$$\text{private disposable income} = Y + NFP + TR + INT - T, \qquad (2.4)$$

where

$$Y = \text{gross domestic product (GDP)};$$
$$NFP = \text{net factor payments from abroad};$$
$$TR = \text{transfers received from the government};$$
$$INT = \text{interest payments on the government's debt};$$
$$T = \text{taxes}.$$

As you can see from Eq. (2.4), private disposable income equals private sector income earned at home (GDP) and abroad (net factor payments from abroad, *NFP*);[7] plus payments to the private sector from the government sector (transfers, *TR*, and interest on the government debt, *INT*); minus taxes paid to the government, *T*.

The part of GNP that is not at the disposal of the private sector is the net income of the government sector. The government's net income equals taxes paid by the private sector, *T*, minus transfer and interest payments from the government to the private sector (transfers, *TR*, and interest payments on the government debt, *INT*):

$$\text{net government income} = T - TR - INT. \qquad (2.5)$$

Adding Eqs. (2.4) and (2.5) yields the sum of private disposable income and net government income, $Y + NFP$, which is gross national product.

---

6. Depreciation (capital consumption allowances) includes both capital that physically wears out and capital that is scrapped because it is no longer economically useful. For instance, still-functioning computers that are scrapped because they have been made obsolete by later models would be included in depreciation.

7. Note that the sum of incomes earned at home and abroad, GDP + *NFP*, equals GNP.

2.3 SAVING AND WEALTH

If you wanted to assess the economic situation of a household, the current income of the household would be an important piece of information. However, someone with a high current income is not necessarily better off economically than someone with a low current income. For example, a retired tycoon who has no current earnings but owns real estate worth $10 million probably is economically better off than newly graduated doctor with a high salary but heavy debts left over from medical school. To determine how well off a household is, in addition to knowing current income, you also need to know what the household owns (its assets) and owes (its liabilities). The difference between assets and liabilities is called **wealth**.

As for a household, the economic well-being of a country depends not only on its income but also on its wealth. The wealth of an entire nation is called **national wealth**.

An important determinant of wealth is the rate of saving: A family that puts aside a quarter of its income each month will accumulate wealth much more quickly than a family that spends nearly all its income. Similarly, the rate at which national wealth increases depends on the rate at which individuals, businesses, and governments in the economy save. Thus, rates of saving and wealth accumulation are closely related.

In this section, we present some concepts of aggregate saving and wealth and examine the relationships among them. Our main interest here is measurement. Such questions as what determines the rate of saving in a country are covered in later chapters.

MEASURES OF AGGREGATE SAVING

In general, the **saving** of any economic unit is the unit's current income minus its spending on current needs. The saving rate of an economic unit is its saving divided by its income. From a macroeconomic perspective, three important measures of saving are private saving, government saving, and national saving. Summary table 1 outlines the definitions of each measure.

PRIVATE SAVING

The saving of the private sector, known as **private saving**, equals private disposable income minus consumption. Using the definition of private disposable income from Eq. (2.4), we have

$$S_{pvt} = \text{private disposable income} - \text{consumption}$$
$$= (Y + NFP - T + TR + INT) - C, \tag{2.6}$$

where S_{pvt} is private saving. Consumption is subtracted from private disposable income to obtain private saving because consumption represents the private sector's spending to meet current needs. Investment, although part of private sector spending, is not subtracted from private disposable income because capital goods are purchased to enhance future productive capacity, rather than to satisfy current needs. The private saving *rate* is private saving divided by private disposable income.[8]

---

8. A measure of aggregate saving that you may hear reported and discussed is *personal saving*, which is the saving of the household portion of the private sector. Personal saving differs from private saving by excluding saving done within businesses. However, because businesses are owned and controlled by households, it makes little economic sense to distinguish between the portion of private saving done within households and the portion done within businesses. Thus, we focus on private rather than personal saving.

GOVERNMENT SAVING

Government saving equals net government income minus government purchases of goods and services, G. With the definition of net government income from Eq. (2.5), government saving, S_{govt}, is

$$S_{govt} = \text{net government income} - \text{government purchases} \qquad (2.7)$$
$$= (T - TR - INT) - G.$$

If you think of government purchases as the government's spending to meet current needs, this definition of government saving fits the general definition of saving. In reality, though, some goods that the government purchases—roads, and government buildings, for example—are not used up during the year and, thus, are available to satisfy future needs. The national income accounts of Canada distinguish these longer-lived government purchases from spending to meet current needs. We, thus, define government saving to be net government income less current government spending, but without subtracting government investment.[9]

Another, probably more familiar, name for government saving is the government budget surplus. The government **budget surplus** equals government revenue minus government expenditure. **Government revenue** equals tax revenue, T. **Government expenditures** are the sum of government purchases of goods and services, G, transfers, TR, and interest payments on government debt, INT. Thus, the government budget surplus equals $T - (G + TR + INT)$, which, as you can see from Eq. (2.7), is the same as government saving.

When government revenue is less than government expenditure, the difference between expenditures and revenue is known as the government **budget deficit**. Thus, when the government runs a budget deficit, with its expenditure greater than its revenue, government saving is negative.

---

9. A similar argument suggests that expenditures on cars and other long-lived consumer durables should not be subtracted from disposable income in the calculation of private saving, although in practice they are subtracted.

SUMMARY 1 MEASURES OF AGGREGATE SAVING

SAVING MEASURE	DEFINITION AND FORMULA
Private saving	Private disposable income less consumption $S_{pvt} = (Y + NFP - T + TR + INT) - C$
Government saving	Government revenue less government expenditure $S_{govt} = T - (G + TR + INT)$
National saving	Private saving plus government saving; also GNP $(Y + NFP)$ less consumption and government purchases $S = S_{pvt} + S_{govt} = Y + NFP - C - G$

NATIONAL SAVING

National saving, or the saving of the economy as a whole, equals private saving plus government saving. Using the definitions of private and government saving, Eqs. (2.6) and (2.7), we obtain national saving, S:

$$S = S_{pvt} + S_{govt}$$
$$= (Y + NFP - T + TR + INT - C) + (T - TR - INT - G) \qquad (2.8)$$
$$= Y + NFP - C - G.$$

Equation (2.8) shows that national saving equals the total income of the economy, $Y + NFP$ (which equals GNP), minus spending to satisfy current needs (consumption, C, and government purchases, G).

THE USES OF PRIVATE SAVING

How is private saving in an economy put to use? Here we show that private saving is used to fund new capital investment, provide the resources the government needs to finance its budget deficits, and acquire assets from or lend to foreigners.

To derive an important identity that illustrates the uses of private saving, we first use the income–expenditure identity (Eq. 2.3) and substitute $C + I + G + NX$ for Y in the expression for national saving (Eq. 2.8):

$$S = (C + I + G + NX) + NFP - C - G.$$

Simplifying the above expression, we obtain

$$S = I + (NX + NFP). \qquad (2.9)$$

The expression for national saving in Eq. (2.9) contains the term $NX + NFP$, which is the sum of net exports and net factor payments, and is called the current account balance, CA.[10] The **current account balance** equals payments received from abroad in exchange for currently produced goods and services (including factor services), minus the analogous payments made to foreigners by the domestic economy. As we have seen, NFP principally includes interest on foreign investment in Canada, and so is negative. Substituting CA for $NX + NFP$ in Eq. (2.9), we obtain

$$S = I + CA. \qquad (2.10)$$

We now have an expression for national saving, S; our goal is an expression for private saving, S_{pvt}. Equation (2.8) shows that private saving, S_{pvt}, equals national saving, S, minus government saving, S_{govt}. Then, subtracting S_{govt} from both sides of Eq. (2.10), we get

$$S_{pvt} = I + (-S_{govt}) + CA, \qquad (2.11)$$

where $-S_{govt}$ is the government budget deficit.

Equation (2.11) is another important macroeconomic identity, called the **uses-of-saving identity**. It states that an economy's private saving is used in three ways:

1. *Investment (I).* Firms borrow from private savers to finance the construction and purchase of new capital (including residential capital) and inventory investment.

2. *The government budget deficit ($-S_{govt}$).* When the government runs a budget deficit (so that S_{govt} is negative and $-S_{govt}$ is positive), it must borrow from private savers to cover the difference between spending and revenue.

---

10. Actually, the current account balance also includes a term called transfers, which measures transfers between countries, such as private gifts or official foreign aid (see Chapter 5). In our analysis, we generally ignore this term.

3. *The current account balance (CA).* When the Canadian current account balance is positive, foreigners' receipts of payments from Canada are not sufficient to cover the payments they make to Canada. To make up the difference, foreigners must either borrow from Canadian private savers or sell to Canadian savers some of their assets, such as land, factories, stocks, and bonds. Thus, financing the current account balance is a use of a country's private saving.

In contrast, when the Canadian current account balance is negative, as it was during much of the postwar period, Canadian receipts of payments from foreigners are not sufficient to cover Canadian payments to foreigners. To offset this excess of payments over receipts, Canada must borrow from foreigners or sell to foreigners some Canadian assets. In this case, foreigners use their saving to lend to Canada or to acquire Canadian assets.[11]

RELATING SAVING AND WEALTH

Saving is a key economic variable because it is closely related to the rate of wealth accumulation. In the rest of this section, we discuss the relationship of saving and wealth. To do so, however, we must first introduce the concept of stocks versus flows.

[11] The current account and its relationship to international borrowing and lending are discussed in greater detail in Chapter 5.

APPLICATION

THE USES OF SAVING AND THE GOVERNMENT BUDGET DEFICIT IN CANADA

Understanding the uses-of-saving identity is a helpful first step for analyzing some complicated macroeconomic issues. For example, the effects of government budget deficits on the economy are argued endlessly. Equation (2.11) shows that if S_{govt} falls so that the government budget deficit increases, at least one of the following three things, or a combination of them, must happen: (1) private saving must rise, (2) investment must fall, and/or (3) the current account balance must fall.

Figure 2.1 shows the behaviour of private saving and its three uses in Canada since 1926, all measured as percentages of GDP. Note the large budget deficits during the Great Depression (1930–1938) and World War II (1939–1945) and the coinciding declines in investment. The increase in government budget deficits during the 1970s and 1980s is evident in the drops in S_{govt}, which includes the saving of all levels of government in Canada. During the early 1980s, the drop in S_{govt} was accompanied by a decline in investment relative to private saving. By 1988 and 1989, however, investment was roughly equal to private saving, so the large government budget deficit (negative S_{govt}) was matched by a large current account deficit. These "twin deficits" are discussed in more detail in Chapter 5.

Since the mid-1990s, the government budget deficit has been shrinking so that S_{govt} has been growing. By 1997, S_{govt} was positive, reflecting the emergence of surpluses for the federal government and several provincial governments. The sharp increase in S_{govt} has been accompanied by an increase in investment spending and especially by a switch of the current account balance from deficit to surplus. Thus, Canada now has "twin surpluses."

FIGURE 2.1

THE USES-OF-SAVING IDENTITY IN CANADA, 1926–2000

The figure illustrates the uses-of-saving identity— which states that private saving equals the sum of investment, the government budget deficit, and the current account balance— for Canada over the period 1926–2000. Each variable is measured as a percentage of GDP, and government saving is the combined saving of the federal, provincial, and municipal governments.

Source: *Canadian Economic Observer, Historical Statistical Supplement*, cat. no. 11-210.

STOCKS AND FLOWS

The economic variables we have discussed so far in this chapter—such as GDP and the various types of expenditure, income, and saving—are measured per unit of time (for example, per quarter or per year). For instance, annual GDP figures measure the economy's production per year. Variables that are measured per unit of time are called **flow variables**.

In contrast, some economic variables, called **stock variables**, are defined at a point in time. Examples of stock variables are the amount of money in your bank account on September 15 of this year and the total value of all houses in Canada on January 1, 2002.

In many applications, a flow variable is the rate of change in a stock variable. A classic example is a bathtub with water flowing in from a faucet. The amount of water in the tub at any moment is a stock variable. The units of a stock variable (litres, in this case) do not have a time dimension. The rate at which water enters the tub is a flow variable; its units (litres per minute) have a time dimension. In this case, the flow is equal to the rate of change of the stock.

WEALTH AND SAVING AS STOCK AND FLOW

Saving and wealth are related to each other in much the same way that the flow and stock of water in a bathtub are related. The wealth of any economic unit, also called net worth, is its assets (the things that it owns, including IOUs from other economic units) minus its liabilities (what it owes to other units). Wealth is measured in dollars at a point in time and is a stock variable. Saving is measured in dollars per unit time and is a flow variable. Because saving takes the form of an accumulation of assets or a reduction in liabilities (for example, if saving is used to pay off debts), it adds to wealth just as water flowing into a bathtub adds to the stock of water.

NATIONAL WEALTH

National wealth is the total wealth of the residents of a country. National wealth consists of two parts: (1) the country's domestic physical assets, such as its stock of capital goods and land;[12] and (2) its net foreign assets. The **net foreign assets** of a country equal the country's foreign assets (foreign stocks, bonds, and factories owned by domestic residents) minus its foreign liabilities (domestic physical and financial assets owned by foreigners). Net foreign assets are part of national wealth because they represent claims on foreigners that are not offset by foreigners' claims on the domestic economy.

Domestic financial assets held by domestic residents are not part of national wealth because the value of any domestic financial asset is offset by a domestic financial liability. For example, a chequing account held by a Canadian in a Canadian bank is an asset for the depositor but a liability for the bank; it, thus, does not represent wealth for the economy as a whole. In contrast, a Canadian's chequing account in a foreign bank has no corresponding domestic liability (it is a liability of a foreigner) and so is part of Canadian national wealth.

National wealth can change in two ways over time. First, the value of the existing assets or liabilities that make up national wealth may change. Thus, an increase in the value of Canadian farmland raises Canadian national wealth, as does an increase in the value of foreign stocks held by Canadians. The wearing out or depreciation of physical assets, which corresponds to a fall in the value of those assets, reduces national wealth.

The second way that national wealth can change is through national saving. Over any particular period of time, with the value of existing assets and liabilities held constant, each extra dollar of national saving adds a dollar to national wealth. That is,

$$S = I + CA,$$

which you will recognize as Eq. (2.10). This equation shows that national saving has two uses: (1) to increase the stock of domestic physical capital through investment, I, and (2) to increase the nation's stock of net foreign assets by lending to foreigners or acquiring foreign assets in an amount equal to the current account balance, CA. But each dollar by which domestic physical assets or net foreign assets increase is a dollar by which national wealth increases. Thus, as we claimed, increases in national saving increase national wealth dollar for dollar. As in the example of water flowing into a bathtub, the more rapid the flow of national saving, the more quickly the stock of national wealth will rise. On the other hand, an increase in the government budget deficit that is only partially offset by increased private saving would lead to a fall in $I + CA$ and, therefore, a fall in future wealth.

How do national saving and investment in Canada compare with those in other countries? Saving and investment rates in Canada are close to the averages for industrialized countries. In contrast, the United States is a low-saving country. Using the relationship $S = I + CA$, we see that if investment, I, is greater than saving, S, then

---

12. In principle, national wealth should also include the value of the skills and training of the country's residents— what economists call human capital. In practice, because of measurement problems, human capital is not usually included in measures of national wealth.

the current account balance, *CA*, must be negative. In recent years, the US has run large current account deficits. In contrast, high-saving countries, such as Japan, Singapore, and Switzerland, have typically had investment rates lower than their saving rates, resulting in consistently positive current account balances for those countries. As we saw in Figure 2.1, Canada also has run current account surpluses in recent years.

2.4 REAL GDP, PRICE INDEXES, AND INFLATION

All the key macroeconomic variables that we have discussed so far in this chapter—GDP, the components of expenditure and income, national wealth, and saving—are measured in terms of current market values. Such variables are called **nominal variables**. The advantage of using market values to measure economic activity is that it allows summing of different types of goods and services.

However, a problem with measuring economic activity in nominal terms arises if you want to compare the values of an economic variable—GDP, for example—at two different points in time. If the current market value of the goods and services included in GDP changes over time, you cannot tell whether this change reflects changes in the quantities of goods and services produced, changes in the prices of goods and services, or a combination of these factors. For example, a large increase in the current market value of GDP might mean that a country has greatly expanded its production of goods and services, or it might mean that the country has experienced inflation, which raised the prices of goods and services.

REAL GDP

Economists have devised methods for breaking down changes in nominal variables into the part owing to changes in physical quantities and the part owing to changes in prices. Consider the numerical example in Table 2.3, which gives production and price data for an economy that produces two types of goods: computers and bicycles. The data are presented for two different years. In year 1, the value of GDP is $46,000 (5 computers worth $1,200 each and 200 bicycles worth $200 each). In year 2, the value of GDP is $66,000 (10 computers worth $600 each and 250 bicycles worth $240 each), which is 43.5% higher than the value of GDP in year 1. This 43.5% increase in nominal GDP does not reflect either a 43.5% increase in physical output or a 43.5% increase in prices. Instead, it reflects changes in both output and prices.

How much of the 43.5% increase in nominal output is attributable to an increase in physical output? A simple way to remove the effects of price changes, and thus to focus on changes in quantities of output, is to measure the value of production in each year by using the prices from some base year. For this example, let us choose year 1 as the base year. Using the prices from year 1 ($1,200 per computer and $200 per bicycle) to value the production in year 2 (10 computers and 250 bicycles) yields a value of $62,000, as shown in Table 2.4. We say that $62,000 is the value of real GDP in year 2, measured using the prices of year 1.

In general, an economic variable that is measured by the prices of a base year is called a **real variable**. Real economic variables measure the physical quantity of economic activity. Specifically, **real GDP**, also called *constant-dollar GDP*, measures the physical volume of an economy's final production using tile prices of a base year. **Nominal GDP**, also called *current-dollar GDP*, is the dollar value of an economy's

TABLE 2.3

Production and Price Data

	Year 1	Year 2	Percent change from Year 1 to Year 2
Product (Quantity)			
Computers	5	10	+100%
Bicycles	200	250	+25%
Price			
Computers	$1,200/computer	$600/computer	–50%
Bicycles	$200/bicycle	$240/bicycle	+20%
Value			
Computers	$6,000	$6,000	0
Bicycles	$40,000	$60,000	+50%
Total	$46,000	$66,000	+43.5%

TABLE 2.4

Calculation of Real Output with Alternative Base Years

Calculation of real output with base year = Year 1

	Current quantities		Base-year prices		
Year 1					
Computers	5	×	$1,200	=	$6,000
Bicycles	200	×	$200	=	$40,000
				Total =	**$46,000**
Year 2					
Computers	10	×	$1,200	=	$12,000
Bicycles	250	×	$200	=	$50,000
				Total =	**$62,000**

Percentage growth of real GDP = ($62,000 – $46,000)/$46,000 = **34.8%**

Calculation of real output with base year = Year 2

	Current quantities		Base-year prices		
Year 1					
Computers	5	×	$600	=	$3,000
Bicycles	200	×	$240	=	$48,000
				Total =	**$51,000**
Year 2					
Computers	10	×	$600	=	$6,000
Bicycles	250	×	$240	=	$60,000
				Total =	**$66,000**

Percentage growth of real GDP = ($66,000 – $51,000)/$51,000 = **29.4%**

final output measured at current market prices. Thus, nominal GDP in year 2 for our example is $66,000, which we computed earlier using current (that is, year 2) prices to value output.

What is the value of real GDP in year 1? Continuing to treat year 1 as the base year, use the prices of year 1 ($1,200 per computer and $200 per bicycle) to value production. The production of 5 computers and 200 bicycles has a value of $46,000. Thus, the value of real GDP in year 1 is the same as the value of nominal GDP in year 1. This result is a general one: Because current prices and base-year prices are the same in the base year, real and nominal values are always the same in the base year. Specifically, real GDP and nominal GDP are equal in the base year.

Now we are prepared to calculate the increase in the physical production from year 1 to year 2. Real GDP is designed to measure the physical quantity of production. Because real GDP in year 2 is $62,000 and real GDP in year 1 is $46,000, output, as measured by real GDP, is 34.8% higher in year 2 than in year 1.

PRICE INDEXES

We have seen how to calculate the portion of the change in nominal GDP owing to a change in physical quantities. We now turn our attention to the change in prices by using price indexes. A **price index** is a measure of the average level of prices for some specified set of goods and services, relative to the prices in a specified base year. For example, the **GDP deflator** is a price index that measures the overall level of prices of goods and services included in GDP and is defined by the formula

$$\text{real GDP} = \text{nominal GDP/GDP deflator.}$$

The GDP deflator is the amount by which nominal GDP must be divided, or "deflated," to obtain real GDP. In our example, we have already computed nominal GDP and real GDP, so we can now calculate the GDP deflator by rewriting the preceding formula as

$$\text{GDP deflator} = \text{nominal GDP/real GDP.}$$

In year 1 (the base year in our example), nominal GDP and real GDP are equal, so the GDP deflator equals 1.[13] This result is an example of the general principle that the GDP deflator always equals 1 in the base year. In year 2, nominal GDP is $66,000 (see Table 2.3), and real GDP is $62,000 (see Table 2.4), so the GDP deflator in year 2 is $66,000/$62,000 = 1.065, which is 6.5% higher than the value of the GDP deflator in year 1. Thus, the overall level of prices, as measured by the GDP deflator, is 6.5% higher in year 2 than in year 1.

The measurement of real GDP and the GDP deflator depends on the choice of a base year. Box 2.2 demonstrates that the choice of a base year can have important effects on the calculated growth of real output, which in turn affects the calculated change in the price level.

THE CONSUMER PRICE INDEX

The GDP deflator measures the average level of prices of goods and services included in GDP. The **consumer price index**, or CPI, measures the prices of consumer goods. Unlike the GDP deflator, which is calculated quarterly, the CPI is available

---

13. The GDP deflator often is multiplied by 100, so that it equals 100 rather than 1.00 in the base year.

Box 2.2 THE COMPUTER REVOLUTION AND CHAIN-WEIGHTED GDP

The widespread use of computers has revolutionized business, education, and leisure throughout much of the developed world. The fraction of the real spending in Canada devoted to computers grew rapidly between the mid-1980s and the mid-1990s, while computer prices fell by more than 10% per year on average. The sharp increase in the real quantity of computers and the sharp decline in computer prices highlight the problem of choosing a base year in calculating the growth of real GDP.

We can use the example in Tables 2.3 and 2.4, which includes a large increase in the quantity of computers coupled with a sharp decrease in computer prices, to illustrate the problem. We have shown that when we treat year 1 as the base year, real output increases by 34.8% from year 1 to year 2. However, as we will see in this box, using Table 2.4, we get a substantially different measure of real output growth if we treat year 2 as the base year. Treating year 2 as the base year means that we use the prices of year 2 to value output. Specifically, each computer is valued at $600 and each bicycle is valued at $240. Thus, the real value of the 5 computers and 200 bicycles produced in year 1 is $51,000. If we continue to treat year 2 as the base year, the real value of output in year 2 is the same as the nominal value of output, which we have already calculated to be $66,000. Thus, by treating year 2 as the base year, we see real output grow from $51,000 in year 1 to $66,000 in year 2, an increase of 29.4%.

Let us summarize our calculations so far. Using year 1 as the base year, the calculated growth of output is 34.8%, but using year 2 as the base year, the calculated growth of output is only 29.4%. Why does this difference arise? In this example, the quantity of computers grows by 100% (from 5 to 10) and the quantity of bicycles grows by 25% (from 200 to 250) from year 1 to year 2. The computed growth of overall output—34.8% using year 1 as the base year or 29.4% using year 2 as the base year—is between the growth rates of the two individual goods. The overall growth rate is a sort of weighted average of the growth rate of the individual goods. When year 1 is the base year, we use year 1 prices to value output, and in year 1 computers are much more expensive than bicycles. Thus, the growth of overall output is closer to the very high growth rate of computers than when the growth rate is computed using year 2 as the base year.

Which base year is the "right" one to use? There is no clear reason to prefer one over the other. To deal with this problem, in May 2001, Statistics Canada introduced chain-weighted indexes to measure real GDP. These indexes, sometimes called chain Fisher volume indexes, represent a mathematical compromise between using the current period as the base period and using the previous period as the base period. In practice, Statistics Canada chain weights using quarters, not years as in our example. The growth rate of real GDP computed using chain weighting is a sort of average of the growth rate computed using the previous quarter as the base and the growth rate computed using the current quarter as the base. For a discussion of chain weighting, see *www.statcan.ca/english/concepts/chainfisher/methodology. htm*.

Before Statistics Canada adopted chain weighting, it used 1997 as the base year to compute real GDP. As time passed, it became necessary to update the base year so that the prices used to compute real GDP would reflect the true values of various goods being produced. Every time the base year was changed, Statistics Canada had to calculate new historical data for real GDP. Chain weighting effectively updates the base year automatically. The growth rate for a given quarter is computed using that quarter and the preceding quarter as base quarters. As time goes on, there is no need to recompute historical growth rates of real GDP using new base years. Nevertheless, chain-weighted real GDP has a peculiar feature. Although the income–expenditure identity, $Y = C + I + G + NX$, always holds exactly in nominal terms, for technical reasons, this relationship need not hold exactly when GDP and its components are measured in real terms when chain weighting is used. Because the discrepancy is usually small, we assume in this book that the income–expenditure identity holds in both real and nominal terms.

The United States has used chain weighting since 1995, but using a year-to-year chain instead. So, an added advantage of the switch to chain weighting in Canada is that it makes comparisons between the US and Canadian growth rates more accurate.

Chain weighting was introduced to solve the problem of choosing a given year as a base year in calculating real GDP. How large a difference does chain weighting make? Using 1997 as a base year, real GDP from 1999 to 2000 grew 4.6%. Using chain weighting, real GDP growth was measured to be 4.4%. The downward revision when more recent weights are used reflects the growth of the IT sector, and its falling prices, just as in our example in Table 2.3. The effects of the change to chain weighting are even larger for some components of GDP, such as investment or imports, where IT spending is a major component.

monthly. Statistics Canada constructs the CPI by sending people out each month to find the current prices of a fixed list, or "basket," of consumer goods and services, including many specific items of food, clothing, housing, and fuel. The CPI for that month is then calculated as the current cost of the basket of consumer items divided by the cost of the same basket of items in the base year.[14]

The calculation of the consumer price index requires the use of a base year. If a base year—say 1992—is chosen and then never changed, the basket of goods and services established for the base year would eventually become outdated compared with the goods and services that people are actually consuming today. (Not only do people change their buying patterns—switching, for example, from beef to chicken—but some goods on the market today did not even exist in 1992.) This problem suggests that the base year should be updated occasionally, so that the base-year basket of goods and services better resembles the basket of goods and services that consumers choose in the current year. Box 2.3 discusses another concern with using the CPI to measure prices.

INFLATION

An important variable that is measured with price indexes is the rate of inflation. The rate of inflation equals the percentage rate of increase in the price index per period. Thus, if the CPI rises from 100 in one year to 105 the next, the rate of inflation between the two years is $(105 - 100)/100 = 5/100 = 0.05 = 5\%$ per year. If in the third year the CPI is 112, the rate of inflation between the second and third years is $(112 - 105)/105 = 7/105 = 0.0667 = 6.67\%$ per year. More generally, if P_t is the price level in period t and P_{t+1} is the price level in period $t + 1$, the rate of inflation between t and $t + 1$, or π_{t+1}, is

$$\pi_{t+1} = \frac{(P_{t+1} - P_t)}{P_t} = \frac{\Delta P_{t+1}}{P_t},$$

where ΔP_{t+1}, or $P_{t+1} - P_t$, represents the change in P_t.

Figure 2.2 shows the Canadian inflation rate for 1951–2000, based on the GDP deflator as the measure of the price level. Inflation rose during the 1960s and 1970s, fell sharply in the early 1980s, and fell further in the 1990s.

2.5 INTEREST RATES

Interest rates are another important—and familiar—type of economic variable. An **interest rate** is a rate of return promised by a borrower to a lender. If, for example, the interest rate on a $100, one-year loan is 8%, the borrower has promised to repay the lender $108 one year from now, or $8 interest plus repayment of the $100 borrowed.

As we discuss in more detail in Chapter 4, there are many different interest rates in the economy. Interest rates vary according to who is doing the borrowing, how long the funds are borrowed for, and other factors. There are also many assets in the economy, such as shares of corporate stock, that do not pay a specified interest rate but do pay their holders a return; for shares of stock the return comes in the form of dividends and capital gains (increases in the stock's market price). The existence

---

14. As with the GDP deflator, the CPI often is multiplied by 100, so base-year prices equal 100 rather than 1.00.

Box 2.3   DOES CPI INFLATION OVERSTATE INCREASES IN THE COST OF LIVING?

In recent years, economists have debated the accuracy of official inflation measures. In Canada, inflation, as measured by the CPI, may overstate true increases in the cost of living by up to 0.5 percentage points each year.*

In other words, if the official inflation rate is 1%, the true inflation rate may well be only 0.5% per year. While this difference may seem small, its cumulative effect may be large. In the United States, a government commission concluded that this bias may be as much as 1 to 2 percentage points per year.

Why might increases in the CPI overstate the actual rate at which the cost of living rises? One reason is the difficulty that government statisticians face in trying to measure changes in the quality of goods. For example, if the design of an air-conditioner is improved so that it can put out 10% more cold air without an increased use of electricity, then a 10% increase in the price of the air-conditioner should not be considered inflation; although paying 10% more, the consumer is also receiving 10% more cooling capacity. However, if government statisticians fail to account for the improved quality of the air-conditioner and simply note its 10% increase in price, the price change will be incorrectly interpreted as inflation.

Although measuring the output of an air-conditioner is not difficult, for some products (especially services) quality change is hard to measure. For example, by what percentage does the availability of 24-hour cash machines improve the quality of banking services? To the extent that the CPI fails to account for quality improvements in the goods and services people use, inflation will be overstated. This overstatement is called the *quality adjustment bias*.

Another problem with CPI inflation as a measure of cost of living increases can be illustrated by the following example. Suppose that consumers like chicken and turkey about equally well and in the base year consume equal amounts of each. But then, for some reason, the price of chicken rises sharply, leading consumers to switch to eating turkey almost exclusively. Because consumers are about equally satisfied with chicken and turkey, this switch does not make them significantly worse off; their true cost of living has not been affected much by the rise in the price of chicken. However, the official CPI, which measures the cost of buying the base-year basket of goods and services, will register a significant increase when the price of chicken skyrockets. Thus, the rise in the CPI exaggerates the true increase in the cost of living. The problem is that the CPI is based on the assumption that consumers purchase a basket of goods and services that is fixed over time, ignoring the fact that consumers can (and do) substitute cheaper goods or services for more expensive ones. This source of overstatement of the true increase in the cost of living is called the *substitution bias*.

If official inflation measures do, in fact, overstate true inflation, there are important implications. First, if cost of living increases are overstated, then increases in important quantities, such as real family income (the purchasing power of a typical family's income), are correspondingly understated. As a result, the bias in the CPI may lead to too gloomy a view of how the Canadian economy has done over the past few decades. Second, some government payments (such as pension benefits) and taxes are indexed to the CPI. If CPI inflation overstates true inflation, then some public pension recipients have been receiving greater benefit increases than necessary to compensate them for increases in the cost of living. Third, monetary policy that targets the inflation rate (see Chapters 7 and 14) may have to adjust for the CPI's overstatement of the true inflation rate.

_____

*See Allan Crawford, "Measurement Biases in the Canadian CPI," *Bank of Canada Technical Report 64*, 1993.

of so many different assets, each with its own rate of return, has the potential to complicate greatly the study of macroeconomics. Fortunately, however, most interest rates and other rates of return tend to move up and down together. For purposes of macroeconomic analysis, we usually speak of "the" interest rate, as if there were only one. If we say that a certain policy causes "the" interest rate to rise, for example, we mean that interest rates and rates of return, in general, are likely to rise.

FIGURE 2.2

THE INFLATION RATE IN CANADA, 1951–2000
Here, inflation is measured as the annual percentage change in the GDP deflator. Inflation fell after the Korean War, then rose during the 1960s and 1970s, before falling sharply in the 1980s and again in the 1990s.

Source: Statistics Canada, CANSIM Series D100465.

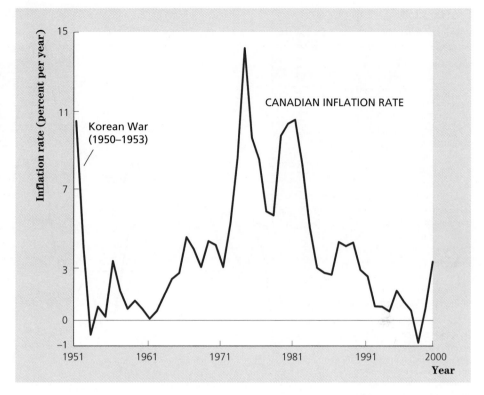

REAL VERSUS NOMINAL INTEREST RATES

Interest rates and other rates of return share a measurement problem with nominal GDP: An interest rate indicates how quickly the nominal or dollar value of an interest-bearing asset increases over time, but it does not reveal how quickly the value of the asset changes in real, or purchasing-power, terms. Consider, for example, a savings account with an interest rate of 4% per year that has $300 in it at the beginning of the year. At the end of the year, the savings account is worth $312, which is a relatively good deal for the depositor if inflation is zero; with no inflation, the price level is unchanged over the year, and $312 buys 4% more goods and services in real terms than the initial $300 did a year earlier. If inflation is 4%, however, what cost $300 a year earlier now costs $312, and in real terms the savings account is worth no more today than it was a year ago.

To distinguish changes in the real value of assets from changes in nominal value, economists frequently use the concept of the real interest rate. The **real interest rate** (or real rate of return) on an asset is the rate at which the real value or purchasing power of the asset increases over time. To distinguish them from real interest rates, we refer to conventionally measured interest rates, such as those reported in the newspaper, as nominal interest rates. The **nominal interest rate** (or nominal rate of return) tells us the rate at which the nominal value of an asset increases over time. The symbol for the nominal interest rate is i.

The real interest rate is related to the nominal interest rate and the inflation rate:

$$\text{real interest rate} = \text{nominal interest rate} - \text{inflation rate} \tag{2.12}$$
$$= i - \pi$$

FIGURE 2.3

NOMINAL AND REAL

INTEREST RATES IN

CANADA, 1951–2001
The nominal interest rate shown is the interest rate on three-to-five-year Government of Canada bonds. The real interest rate is measured as the nominal interest rate minus the average inflation rate (using the GDP deflator) over the current and subsequent two years. The real interest rate was unusually low (actually negative) in the mid–1970s. In the early 1980s, both nominal and real interest rates were very high. Nominal interest rates did not fall as much as inflation did, so real interest rates were high again in the mid–1990s.

Source: The implict price deflator for GDP is the same as that in Figure 2.2. Inflation rates for 1998–2000 are assumed to be 1%. The average interest rate on three-to-five-year federal government bonds is reprinted with permission from the Bank of Canada, *Banking and Financial Statistics,* Table F1 or Statistics Canada, CANSIM B14010.

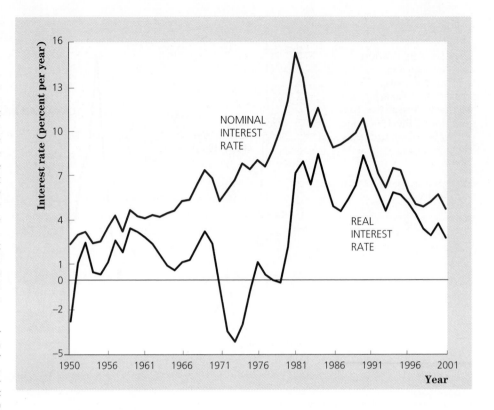

We derive and discuss Eq. (2.12) further at the end of the book in the appendix, Section A.7.[15] For now, consider again the savings account paying 4% interest. If the inflation rate is zero, the real interest rate on that savings account is the 4% nominal interest rate minus the 0% inflation rate, or 4%. A 4% real interest rate on the account means that the depositor will be able to buy 4% more goods and services at the end of the year than at the beginning. But if inflation is 4%, the real interest rate on the savings account is the 4% nominal interest rate minus the 4% inflation rate, or 0%. In this case, the purchasing power of the account is no greater at the end of the year than at the beginning.

Nominal and real interest rates for Canada for 1951–2001 are shown in Figure 2.3. The real interest rate was unusually low in the mid–1970s; indeed, it was negative, which means that the real values of interest-bearing assets actually were declining over time. Both nominal and real interest rates rose to record highs in the early 1980s before returning to a more normal level. In the 1990s, inflation fell earlier than the nominal interest rate, so real interest rates were high. The real interest rate fell after 2000 as the nominal rate declined further.

THE EXPECTED REAL INTEREST RATE

Usually, when you borrow, lend, or make a bank deposit, the nominal interest rate is specified in advance. But what about the real interest rate? For any nominal interest rate, Eq. (2.12) states that the real interest rate depends on the rate of inflation

---

15. Equation (2.12) is an approximation, rather than an exact relationship. This approximation holds most closely when interest rates and inflation rates are not too high.

over the period of the loan or deposit, say, a year. However, the rate of inflation during the year generally cannot be determined until the year is over. Thus, at the time that a loan or deposit is made, the real interest rate that will be received is uncertain.

Because borrowers, lenders, and depositors do not know what the actual real interest rate will be, they must make their decisions about how much to borrow, lend, or deposit on the basis of the real interest rate they expect to prevail. They know the nominal interest rate in advance, so the real interest rate they expect depends on what they think inflation will be. The **expected real interest rate** is the nominal interest rate minus the expected rate of inflation, or

$$r = i - \pi^e, \tag{2.13}$$

where r is the expected real interest rate and π^e is the expected rate of inflation.

Comparing Eqs. (2.13) and (2.12), you can see that if people are correct in their expectations—so that expected inflation and actual inflation turn out to be the same—the expected real interest rate and the real interest rate actually received will be the same.

The expected real interest rate is the correct interest rate to use for studying most types of economic decisions, such as people's decisions about how much to borrow or lend. However, a problem in measuring the expected real interest rate is that economists generally do not know exactly what the public's expected rate of inflation is. Economists use various means to measure expected inflation. One approach is to survey the public and simply ask what rate of inflation people expect. A second method is to assume that the public's expectations of inflation are the same as publicly announced government or private forecasts. A third possibility is to assume that people's inflation expectations are an extrapolation of recently observed rates of inflation. Unfortunately, none of these methods is perfect, so the measurement of the expected real interest rate always contains some error.

CHAPTER SUMMARY

1. The national income accounts are an accounting framework used in measuring current economic activity. The national income accounts measure activity in three ways: the product approach, the expenditure approach, and the income approach. Although each gives the same value for current economic activity, all three approaches are used because each gives a different perspective on the economy.

2. Gross domestic product (GDP) is the broadest measure of aggregate economic activity occurring during a specified period of time. The product approach measures GDP by adding the market values of final goods and services newly produced in an economy; this approach is implemented by summing the value added by all producers. The expenditure approach measures GDP by adding the four categories of spending: consumption, investment, government purchases, and net exports. The income approach measures GDP by adding all the incomes, including taxes and profits, generated by economic activity.

3. The income of the private sector (domestic households and businesses) is called private disposable income. Private disposable income equals income received from private sector activities (GDP plus net factor payments from abroad, or GNP) plus payments received from the government

(transfers and interest on government debt) minus taxes paid to the government. The net income of the government sector equals taxes collected minus transfer payments and interest paid on government debt. Private disposable income and net government income sum to GNP, which is the income of all domestic factors of production.

4. Saving is the portion of an economic unit's current income that it does not spend to meet current needs. Saving by the private sector, called private saving, equals private disposable income minus consumption. Government saving, which is the same as the government budget surplus, equals the government's net income minus its purchases of goods and services; equivalently, government saving equals government revenue minus government spending. National saving is the sum of private saving and government saving; it equals GDP plus net factor payments from abroad minus consumption and government purchases.

5. The uses-of-saving identity states that private saving equals the sum of investment, the government budget deficit, and the current account balance. Equivalently, national saving equals the sum of investment and the current account balance.

6. The national wealth of a country equals its physical assets, such as capital, plus its net foreign assets. National wealth increases in two ways: through changes in the value of existing assets and through national saving. National saving adds to national wealth because national saving is used either for investment, thus adding to physical capital, or for lending to foreigners an amount that equals the current account balance, which increases the country's net foreign assets.

7. Nominal GDP is the value of an economy's final output measured at current market prices. Real GDP is a measure of the physical volume of the economy's final output. Real GDP equals nominal GDP divided by the GDP deflator.

8. A price index is a measure of the current price level relative to a base year. The GDP deflator measures the overall price level of goods and services included in GDP. The consumer price index (CPI) measures the price level of a basket of consumer goods. The rate of inflation is the percentage rate of change of the price level, measured by percentage rate of change of a price index, such as the GDP deflator or the CPI.

9. An interest rate is a rate of return promised by a borrower to a lender. The nominal interest rate is the rate at which the nominal value of an interest-bearing asset increases over time. The real interest rate, or the nominal interest rate minus the rate of inflation, is the rate at which the value of an asset grows in real, or purchasing-power, terms. Borrowing and lending decisions are based on the expected real interest rate, which is the nominal interest rate less the expected rate of inflation.

KEY TERMS

KEY EQUATIONS

Total production = total income = total expenditure

$$(2.1)$$

The fundamental identity of national income accounting states that the same measure of total economic activity is obtained whether activity is measured by the production of final goods and services, the amount of income generated by the economic activity, or the expenditure on final goods and services.

$$Y = C + I + G + NX \qquad (2.3)$$

According to the income–expenditure identity, total income or product or output, Y, equals the sum of the four types of expenditure: consumption, C, investment, I, government purchases, G, and net exports, NX.

$$S_{pvt} = (Y + NFP - T + TR + INT) - C \qquad (2.6)$$

Private saving equals private disposable income less consumption, C. Private sector disposable income equals gross domestic product, Y, plus net factor payments from abroad, NFP, plus transfers, TR, and interest, INT, received from the government, less taxes paid, T.

$$S_{govt} = (T - TR - INT) - G \qquad (2.7)$$

Government saving equals government revenue from taxes, T, less expenditures for transfers, TR, interest on the national debt, INT, and government purchases, G. Government saving is the same as the government budget surplus and is the negative of the government budget deficit.

$$S = S_{pvt} + S_{govt} = Y + NFP - C - G \qquad (2.8)$$

National saving, S, is the sum of private saving and government saving. Equivalently, national saving equals gross domestic product, Y, plus net factor payments from abroad, NFP, less consumption, C, and government purchases, G.

$$S = I + CA \qquad (2.10)$$

National saving, S, has two uses: to finance investment, I, and to lend to foreigners (or to acquire foreign assets) an amount that equals the current account balance, CA. The current account balance equals the increase in net foreign assets.

$$S_{pvt} = I + (-S_{govt}) + CA \qquad (2.11)$$

According to the uses-of-saving identity, private saving is used to finance investment spending, I, to provide the government with the funds it needs to cover its budget deficit, $-S_{govt}$, and to lend to foreigners (or to acquire foreign assets) an amount that equals the current account balance, CA.

$$r = i - \pi^e \qquad (2.13)$$

The expected real interest rate, r, equals the nominal interest rate, i, minus expected inflation π^e.

REVIEW QUESTIONS

1. What are the three approaches to measuring economic activity? Why do they give the same answer?
2. Why are goods and services counted in GDP at market value? Are there any disadvantages or problems in using market values to measure production?
3. What is the difference between intermediate and final goods and services? In which of these categories do capital goods, such as factories and machines, fall? Why is the distinction between intermediate and final goods important for measuring GDP?
4. List the four components of total spending. Why are imports subtracted when GDP is calculated in the expenditure approach?
5. Define private saving. How is private saving used in the economy? What is the relationship between private saving and national saving?
6. What is national wealth, and why is it important? How is national wealth linked to national saving?
7. For the purposes of assessing an economy's growth performance, which is the more important statistic: real GDP or nominal GDP? Why?
8. Describe how the CPI deflator and CPI inflation are calculated. What are some reasons that CPI inflation may overstate true inflation?
9. Explain the differences among the nominal interest rate, the real interest rate, and the expected real interest rate. Which interest rate concept is the most important for the decisions made by borrowers and lenders? Why?

NUMERICAL PROBLEMS

1. After a boat rescues everyone else from Gilligan's Island, the Professor and Gilligan remain behind, afraid of getting shipwrecked again with the same bunch of people. The Professor grows coconuts and catches fish. Last year he harvested 1,000 coconuts and caught 500 fish. He values one fish as worth two coconuts. The Professor gave 200 coconuts to Gilligan in exchange for help in the harvest, and he gave Gilligan 100 fish in exchange for collecting worms for use in fishing. The Professor stored 100 of his coconuts in his hut for consumption at some future time. He also used 100 fish as fertilizer for the coconut trees, as he must every year to keep the trees producing. Gilligan consumed all his coconuts and fish.

    In terms of fish, what is the GDP of Gilligan's Island? What are consumption and investment? What are the incomes of the Professor and Gilligan?

2. National income and product data are generally revised. What effects would the following revisions have on consumption, investment, government purchases, net exports, and GDP?

    a. It is discovered that consumers bought $600 million more furniture than previously thought. This furniture was manufactured in Quebec.

    b. It is discovered that consumers bought $600 million more furniture than previously thought. This furniture was manufactured in Sweden.

    c. It is discovered that businesses bought $600 million more furniture than previously thought. This furniture was manufactured in Quebec.

    d. It is discovered that businesses bought $600 million more furniture than previously thought. This furniture was manufactured in Sweden.

3. ABC Computer Company has a $20,000,000 factory in Kanata. During the current year, ABC builds $2,000,000 worth of computer components. ABC's costs are labour, $1,000,000; interest on debt, $100,000; and taxes, $200,000.

    ABC sells all its output to XYZ Supercomputer. Using ABC's components, XYZ builds four supercomputers at a cost of $800,000 each ($500,000 worth of components, $200,000 in labour costs, and $100,000 in taxes per computer). XYZ has a $30,000,000 factory. XYZ sells three of the supercomputers for $1,000,000 each; but at year's end, it had not sold the fourth. The unsold computer is carried on XYZ's books as an $800,000 increase in inventory.

    a. Calculate the contributions to GDP of these transactions, showing that all three approaches give the same answer.

    b. Repeat part (a), but now assume that in addition to its other costs, ABC also paid $500,000 for imported computer chips.

4. For each of the following transactions, determine the contribution to the current year's GDP. Explain the effects on the product, income, and expenditure accounts.

    a. On January 1, you purchase 10 sheets of plywood at $20 per sheet. The lumber store purchased the plywood the previous week at a wholesale price (transportation included) of $15 per sheet.

    b. Colonel Hogwash purchases a West Vancouver mansion for $1,000,000. The broker's fee is 6%.

    c. A homemaker enters the workforce, taking a job that will pay $20,000 over the year. The homemaker must pay $8,000 over the year for professional child-care services.

    d. The Japanese build an auto plant in Quebec for $100,000,000, using only local labour and materials. (*Hint*: The auto plant is a capital good produced by Canadians and purchased by the Japanese.)

    e. You are informed that you have won $3,000,000 in Lotto 6/49, to be paid to you, in total, immediately.

    f. The lottery corporation pays you an additional $5,000 fee to appear in a TV commercial publicizing the provincial lottery.

    g. Discount Car Rentals replaces its rental fleet by buying $100,000,000 worth of new cars from General Motors. It sells its old fleet to a consortium of used-car dealers for $40,000,000. The consortium resells the used cars to the public for a total of $60,000,000.

5. You are given the following information about an economy:

Gross private domestic investment	40
Government purchases of goods and services	30
Gross national product (GNP)	200
Current account balance	–20
Taxes	60
Government transfer payments	25
Interest payments from the government (all to domestic households)	15
Factor income from the rest of the world	7
Factor payments to the rest of the world	9

    Find the following, assuming that government investment is zero:

    a. Consumption

    b. Net exports

    c. GDP

d. Net factor payments

e. Private saving

f. Government saving

g. National saving

6. Consider an economy that produces only three types of fruit: apples, oranges, and bananas. In the base year (a few years ago), the production and price data were as follows:

Fruit	Quantity	Price
Apples	3,000 bags	$2 per bag
Bananas	6,000 bunches	$3 per bunch
Oranges	8,000 bags	$4 per bag

In the current year, the production and price data are as follows:

Fruit	Quantity	Price
Apples	4,000 bags	$3 per bag
Bananas	14,000 bunches	$2 per bunch
Oranges	32,000 bags	$5 per bag

a. Find nominal GDP in the current year and in the base year. What is the percentage increase since the base year?

b. Find real GDP in the base year and in the current year. By what percentage does real GDP increase from the base year to the current year?

c. Find the GDP deflator for the current year and the base year. By what percentage does the price level change from the base year to the current year?

d. Would you say that the percentage increase in nominal GDP in this economy since the base year is due more to increases in prices or increases in the physical volume of output?

7. For the consumer price index values shown, calculate the rate of inflation in each year from 1930 to 1933. What is unusual about this period, relative to recent experience?

Year	1929	1930	1931	1932	1933
CPI	14.2	14.0	12.7	11.5	10.9

8. Hy Marks buys a one-year government bond on January 1, 2002, for $500. He receives principal plus interest totalling $545 on January 1, 2003. Suppose that the CPI is 200 on January 1, 2002, and 214 on January 1, 2003. This increase in prices is more than Hy had anticipated; his guess was that the CPI would be at 210 by the beginning of 2003.

Find the nominal interest rate, the inflation rate, the real interest rate, Hy's expected inflation rate, and Hy's expected real interest rate.

9. The GDP deflator in Econoland is 200 on January 1, 2002. The deflator rises to 242 by January 1, 2004, and to 266.2 by January 1, 2005.

a. What is the annual rate of inflation over the two-year period between January 1, 2002, and January 1, 2004? In other words, what constant yearly rate of inflation would lead to the price rise observed over those two years?

b. What is the annual rate of inflation over the three-year period from January 1, 2002, to January 1, 2005?

c. In general, if P_0 is the price level at the beginning of an n-year period, and P_n is the price level at the end of that period, show that the annual rate of inflation π over that period satisfies the equation $(1 + \pi)^n = (P_n /P_0)$.

ANALYTICAL PROBLEMS

1. A reputable study shows that a particular new workplace safety regulation will reduce the growth of real GDP. Is this an argument against implementing the regulation? Explain.

2. Consider a closed economy with a single telephone company, Calls-R-Us. The residents of the country make two million phone calls per year and pay $3 per phone call. One day, a new phone company, CheapCall, enters the market and charges only $2 per phone call. All the residents immediately stop using Calls-R-Us and switch to CheapCall. They still make two million phone calls per year. The executives of CheapCall are proud of their market share. They post billboards stating " Our country has increased its national saving by $2 million per year by switching to CheapCall." Comment on the accuracy of the statement on the billboards.

3. Economists have tried to measure the GDPs of virtually all the world's nations. This problem asks you to think about some practical issues that arise in that effort.

a. Before the fall of communism, the economies of the Soviet Union and Eastern Europe were centrally planned. One aspect of central planning is that most prices are set by the government. A government-set price may be too low in that people want to buy more of the good at the fixed price than there are supplies available; or the price may be too high so that large stocks of the good sit unsold on store shelves. During the past several years, central planning has been largely eliminated in Eastern Europe and the former Soviet Union, but government price-setting has not been completely abandoned. For example, Russia still keeps energy prices well below market-clearing levels.

What problem does government control of prices create for economists attempting to measure a country's GDP? Suggest a strategy for dealing with this problem.

b. In very poor, agricultural countries, many people grow their own food, make their own clothes, and provide services for each other within a family or village group. Official GDP estimates for these countries are often extremely low, perhaps just a few hundred dollars per person. Some economists have argued that the official GDP figures underestimate these nations' actual GDPs. Why might this be so? Again, can you suggest a strategy for dealing with this measurement problem?

4. In a recent issue of *Canadian Economic Observer, Statistical Summary,* find the current account balance (Table 17), government saving (Table 3), and investment (Table 1) in Canada for the past two years. Find private saving from the uses-of-saving identity. (You can check your findings using the *National Economic and Financial Accounts*, Statistics Canada, cat. no. 13–001.)

LONG-RUN ECONOMIC PERFORMANCE

Chapter 3

PRODUCTIVITY, OUTPUT, AND EMPLOYMENT

In Chapter 2, we discussed the measurement of several economic variables used to gauge the economy's health. The measurement of economic performance is a prelude to the main objective of macroeconomics: *to understand how the economy works*. Understanding how the economy works requires a shift from economic *measurement* to economic *analysis*.

In Part II of this book, which begins with this chapter, we have two main goals. The first is to analyze the factors that affect the longer-term performance of the economy, including the rate of economic growth, productivity and living standards, the long-run levels of employment and unemployment, saving and capital formation, and the rate of inflation, among others.

The second goal is to develop a theoretical model of the macroeconomy that you can use to analyze the economic issues covered in this book and others that you may encounter in the future. As outlined in Chapter 1, our model is based on the assumption that individuals, firms, and the government interact in three composite markets: the labour market (covered in this chapter), the goods market (Chapter 4), and the asset market (Chapter 7). In developing and using this model in Part II , we generally assume that the economy is at full employment, with quantities supplied and demanded equal in each of the three major markets. As we are focusing on the long-term behaviour of the economy, this assumption is a reasonable one. In Part III, in which we explore business cycles, we allow for the possibility that quantities supplied and demanded may not be equal in the short run.

This chapter begins the discussion of how the economy works with what is perhaps the most fundamental determinant of economic well-being in a society: the economy's productive capacity. Everything else being equal, the greater the quantity of goods and services an economy can produce, the more people will be able to consume in the present and the more they will be able to save and invest for the future.

The first section of the chapter shows that the amount of output an economy produces depends on two factors: (1) the quantities of inputs (such as labour, capital, and raw materials) utilized in the production process; and (2) the **productivity** of the inputs, that is, the effectiveness with which they are used. As discussed in

Chapter 1, an economy's productivity is basic to determining living standards. In this chapter, we show how productivity affects people's incomes by helping determine how many workers are employed and how much they receive in wages.

Of the various inputs to production, the most important (as measured by share of total cost) is labour. For this reason, we spend most of the chapter analyzing the labour market, using the tools of supply and demand. We first consider the factors that affect how much labour employers demand and workers supply and then look at the forces that tend to bring the labour market into equilibrium. Equilibrium in the labour market determines wages and employment; in turn, the level of employment, together with the quantities of other inputs (such as capital) and the level of productivity, determine how much output an economy produces.

Our basic model of the labour market rests on the assumption that the quantities of labour supplied and demanded are equal so that all labour resources are fully utilized. In reality, however, some fraction of workers is always unemployed. The latter part of the chapter introduces unemployment and looks at the relationship between the unemployment rate and the amount of output produced in the economy.

3.1 HOW MUCH DOES THE ECONOMY PRODUCE? THE PRODUCTION FUNCTION

Every day the business news reports many economic variables that influence the economy's performance—the rate of consumer spending, the value of the dollar, the gyrations of the stock market, the growth rate of the money supply, and so on. All of these variables are important. However, no determinant of economic performance and living standards is more basic than the economy's physical capacity to produce goods and services. If an economy's factories, farms, and other businesses all shut down for some reason, other economic factors would not mean much.

What determines the quantity of goods and services that an economy can produce? A key factor is the quantity of inputs—such as capital goods, labour, raw materials, land, and energy—that producers in the economy use. Economists refer to inputs to the production process as **factors of production**. All else being equal, the greater the quantities of factors of production used, the more goods and services are produced. Of the various factors of production, the two most important are capital (factories and machines, for example) and labour (workers). Hence we focus on these two factors in discussing an economy's capacity to produce goods and services. In modern economies, however, output often responds strongly to changes in the supply of other factors, such as energy or raw materials. Later in this chapter, the Application, "Output, Employment, and the Real Wage During Oil Price Shocks," (p. 82) discusses the effects of a disruption in oil supplies on the economy.

The quantities of capital and labour (and other inputs) used in production do not completely determine the amount of output produced. Equally important is how effectively these factors are used. For the same stocks of capital and labour, an economy with superior technologies and management practices, for example, will produce more output than an economy without those strengths.

The effectiveness with which capital and labour are used may be summarized by a relationship called the production function. The **production function** is a mathematical expression relating the amount of output produced to quantities of capital and labour utilized. A convenient way to write the production function is

$$Y = AF(K, N), \tag{3.1}$$

where

Y = real output produced in a given period of time;
A = a number measuring overall productivity;
K = the capital stock, or quantity of capital used in the period;
N = the number of workers employed in the period;
F = a function relating output Y to capital K and labour N.

The production function in Eq. (3.1) applies both to an economy as a whole (where Y, K, and N refer to the economy's output, capital stock, and number of workers) and to an individual firm, in which case Y, K, and N refer to the firm's output, capital, and number of workers.

According to Eq. (3.1), the amount of output Y that an economy (or firm) can produce during any period of time depends on the size of the capital stock K and the number of workers N. The symbol A in Eq. (3.1), which multiplies the function $F(K, N)$, is a measure of the overall effectiveness with which capital and labour are used. We refer to A as **total factor productivity**, or simply productivity. Note that for any values of capital and labour, an increase in productivity A of, say, 10% implies a 10% increase in the amount of output that can be produced. Thus, increases in productivity A correspond to improvements in production technology or to any other change in the economy that allows capital and labour to be utilized more effectively.

APPLICATION

THE PRODUCTION FUNCTION AND PRODUCTIVITY GROWTH IN CANADA

Empirical studies show that the relationship between output and inputs in the Canadian economy is described reasonably well by the following production function:[1]

$$Y = AK^{0.3} N^{0.7}. \tag{3.2}$$

The production function in Eq. (3.2) is a specific example of the general production function in Eq. (3.1), in which we set the general function $F(K, N)$ equal to $K^{0.3}N^{0.7}$. (Note that this production function contains exponents; if you need to review the properties of exponents, see the Appendix, Section A.6.)

Equation (3.2) shows how output Y relates to the use of factors of production, capital K and labour N, and to productivity A in Canada. Table 3.1 presents data on these variables for the Canadian economy for 1981 to 2000. Columns (1), (2), and (3) show output (real GDP), capital stock, and labour for each year. Real GDP and the capital stock are measured in billions of 1997 dollars, and labour is measured in millions of employed workers. Column (4) shows the Canadian economy's productivity for each year.

Output, capital, and labour in Table 3.1 are measured directly, but there is no way to measure productivity directly. Instead, the productivity index A shown in column (4) is measured indirectly by assigning to A the value necessary to satisfy Eq. (3.2). Specifically, for each year A is determined by the formula $A = Y/(K^{0.3}N^{0.7})$, which is

---

1. This type of production function is called a Cobb–Douglas production function. Cobb–Douglas production functions take the form $Y = AK^aN^{1-a}$, where $0 < a < 1$. Under certain conditions, the parameter a in the Cobb–Douglas production function corresponds to the share of income received by owners of capital, whereas labour receives a share of income equal to $1 - a$. Thus, observing the actual shares of income received by capital and labour provides a way of estimating the parameter a.

just another way of writing Eq. (3.2). In 2000, for example, Table 3.1 reports that Y = 1009, K = 808, and N = 14.9; therefore, the value of A for 2000 is $1009/[(808)^{0.3} (14.9)^{0.7}]$, or A = 20.43. Calculating productivity in this way ensures that the production function relationship, Eq. (3.2), is satisfied exactly for each year.

The levels of the productivity index A reported in Table 3.1 depend on the units in which output, capital, and labour are measured—for example, the values of A would change if we measured workers in thousands rather than millions—and, thus, are hard to interpret. In contrast, the year-to-year growth rates of the productivity measure shown in column (5) are units-free and are, therefore, easier to work with. A close look at the productivity growth rates shown in Table 3.1 emphasizes two points.

First, productivity growth can vary sharply from year to year. Most strikingly, productivity in Canada fell 1.5% in 1982, a deep recession year, then rose 1.9% in 1983 and 3.8% in 1984, a period of economic recovery. Productivity also fell during the 1990–1992 recession. Productivity normally falls in recessions and rises in recoveries, but explanations for its behaviour over the business cycle are controversial. We return to this issue in Part III of this book, which is devoted to business cycles.

TABLE 3.1

The Production Function for Canada, 1981–2000

Production function: $Y = AK^{0.3}N^{0.7}$

Year	(1) Real GDP, Y (Billions of 1997 dollars)	(2) Capital, K (Billions of 1997 dollars)	(3) Labour, N (Millions of workers)	(4) Total Factor Productivity, A*	(5) Growth in Total Factor Productivity (% Change in A)
1981	603	525	11.3	16.87	– –
1982	586	538	10.9	16.63	−1.5
1983	602	544	11.0	16.95	1.9
1984	637	548	11.3	17.58	3.8
1985	667	559	11.6	17.95	2.1
1986	683	569	12.0	17.91	−0.3
1987	712	583	12.3	18.17	1.5
1988	747	605	12.7	18.45	1.5
1989	766	629	13.0	18.42	−0.1
1990	768	650	13.1	18.18	−1.3
1991	751	670	12.8	17.86	−1.8
1992	758	682	12.7	18.01	0.8
1993	776	690	12.9	18.28	1.5
1994	813	693	13.1	18.85	3.2
1995	836	704	13.4	19.04	1.0
1996	849	705	13.5	19.22	0.9
1997	885	729	13.8	19.54	1.7
1998	920	751	14.1	19.76	1.1
1999	966	775	14.5	20.17	2.1
2000	1009	808	14.9	20.43	1.3

*Total factor productivity is calculated by the formula $A = Y/K^{0.3}N^{0.7}$.

Second, since 1981, productivity in Canada has been growing relatively slowly, averaging about 1% per year during the 1981–2000 period. This result is comparable with the performance of the 1970s, but notably less than in the 1950–1970 period, when productivity growth exceeded 2% a year.[2] This trend is bad news for the economy because the rate of productivity growth is closely related to the rate of improvement of living standards. Chapter 6 discusses the relationship between productivity and living standards in greater detail.

THE SHAPE OF THE PRODUCTION FUNCTION

The production function in Eq. (3.1) can be shown graphically. The easiest way to graph it is to hold one of the two factors of production, either capital or labour, constant and then graph the relationship between output and the other factor.[3] Suppose that we use the Canadian production function for the year 2000 and hold labour N at its actual 2000 value of 14.9 million workers (see Table 3.1). We also use the actual 2000 value of 20.43 for A. The production function (Eq. 3.2) becomes

$$Y = AK^{0.3}N^{0.7} = (20.43)(K^{0.3})(14.9^{0.7}) = 135.36K^{0.3}.$$

This relationship is graphed in Figure 3.1, on the next page, with capital stock K on the horizontal axis and output Y on the vertical axis. With labour and productivity held at their 2000 values, the graph shows the amount of output that could have been produced in that year for any value of the capital stock. Point A on the graph shows the situation that actually occurred in 2000: The value of the capital stock ($808 billion) appears on the horizontal axis, and the value of real GDP ($1,009 billion) appears on the vertical axis.

The Canadian production function graphed in Figure 3.1 shares two properties with most production functions:

1. *The production function slopes upward from left to right.* The slope of the production function tells us that as the capital stock increases, more output can be produced.

2. *The slope of the production function becomes flatter from left to right.* This property implies that although more capital always leads to more output, it does so at a decreasing rate.

Before discussing the economics behind the second property of the production function, we can illustrate it numerically using Figure 3.1. Suppose that we are initially at point B, where the capital stock is $400 billion. Adding $100 billion in capital moves us to point C, where the capital stock is $500 billion. How much extra output has this expansion in capital provided? The difference in output between points B and C is $56 billion ($873 billion output at C minus $817 billion output at B). This extra $56 billion in output is the benefit from raising the capital stock from $400 billion to $500 billion, with productivity and employment held constant.

Now, suppose that starting at C, we add another $100 billion of capital. This new addition of capital takes us to D, where the capital stock is $600 billion. The difference in output between C and D is only $49 billion ($922 billion output at D

---

2. Other countries also have experienced slower productivity growth since the mid-1970s, as discussed further in Chapter 6.

3. To show the relationship among output and both factors of production simultaneously would require a three-dimensional graph.

FIGURE 3.1

THE PRODUCTION

FUNCTION RELATING

OUTPUT AND CAPITAL

This production function shows how much output the Canadian economy could produce for each level of Canadian capital stock, holding labour and productivity at 2000 levels. Point A corresponds to the actual 2000 output and capital stock. The production function has diminishing marginal productivity of capital: Raising the capital stock by $100 billion in order to move from point B to point C raises output by $56 billion, but adding another $100 billion in capital to go from point C to point D increases output by only $49 billion.

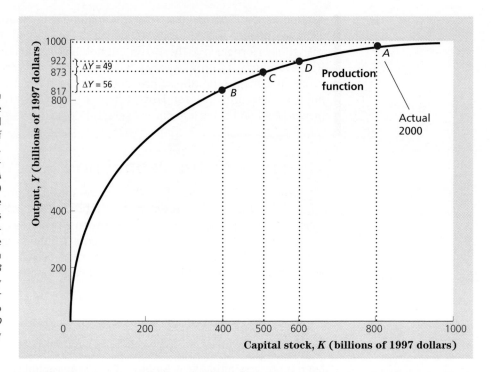

minus $873 billion output at C), which is less than the $56 billion increase in output between B and C. Thus, although the second $100 billion of extra capital raises total output, it does so by less than did the first $100 billion of extra capital. This result illustrates that the production function rises less steeply between points C and D than between points B and C.

THE MARGINAL PRODUCT OF CAPITAL

The two properties of the production function are closely related to a concept known as the marginal product of capital. To understand this concept, let us suppose that we start from some given capital stock K and increase the capital stock by some amount ΔK (other factors held constant). This increase in capital would cause output Y to increase by some amount ΔY. The **marginal product of capital**, or MPK, is the increase in output produced resulting from a one-unit increase in the capital stock. Because ΔK additional units of capital permit the production of ΔY additional units of output, the amount of additional output produced per additional unit of capital is $\Delta Y/\Delta K$. Thus, the marginal product of capital is $\Delta Y/\Delta K$.

The marginal product of capital $\Delta Y/\Delta K$ is the change in the variable on the vertical axis of the production function graph (ΔY) divided by the change in the variable on the horizontal axis (ΔK), which you might recognize as a slope.[4] For small increases in the capital stock, the MPK can be measured by the slope of a line drawn tangent to the production function. Figure 3.2 illustrates this way of measuring the MPK. When the capital stock is 400, for example, the MPK equals the slope of the line tangent to the production function at point B.[5] We can use the concept of the marginal product of capital to restate the two properties of production functions listed earlier.

---

4. For definitions and a discussion of slopes of lines and curves, see the Appendix, Section A.2.
5. We often refer to the slope of the line tangent to the production function at a given point as simply the slope of the production function at that point, for short.

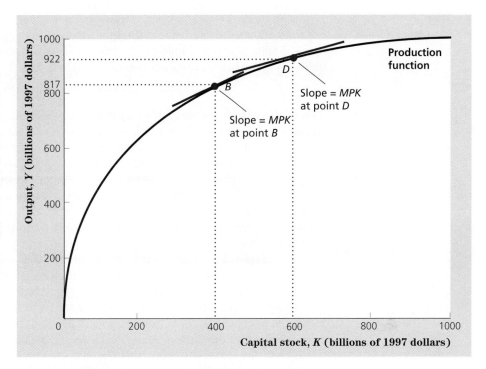

FIGURE 3.2

THE MARGINAL PRODUCT OF CAPITAL

The marginal product of capital (*MPK*) at any point can be measured as the slope of the line tangent to the production function at that point. Because the slope of the line tangent to the production function at point *B* is greater than the slope of the line tangent to the production function at point *D*, we know that the *MPK* is greater at *B* than at *D*. At higher levels of capital stock, the *MPK* is lower, reflecting diminishing marginal productivity of capital.

1. *The marginal product of capital is positive.* Whenever the capital stock is increased, more output can be produced. Because the marginal product of capital is positive, the production function slopes upward from left to right.

2. *The marginal product of capital declines as the capital stock is increased.* Because the marginal product of capital is the slope of the production function, the slope of the production function decreases as the capital stock is increased. As Figure 3.2 shows, the slope of the production function at point *D*, where the capital stock is 600, is smaller than the slope at point *B*, where the capital stock is 400. Thus, the production function becomes flatter from left to right.

The tendency for the marginal product of capital to decline as the amount of capital in use increases is called the **diminishing marginal productivity** of capital. The economic reason for diminishing marginal productivity of capital is as follows: When the capital stock is low, there are many workers for each machine, and the benefits of increasing capital further are great; but when the capital stock is high, workers already have plenty of capital to work with, and little benefit is to be gained from expanding capital further. For example, in a secretarial pool in which there are many more secretaries than computers, each computer is constantly being utilized and secretaries must waste time waiting for a free machine. In this situation, the benefits in terms of increased output of adding extra computers are high. However, if there are already as many computers as secretaries, so that computers often are idle and there is no waiting for a machine to become available, little additional output can be obtained by adding yet another computer.

THE MARGINAL PRODUCT OF LABOUR

In Figures 3.1 and 3.2, we graphed the relationship between output and capital implied by the 2000 Canadian production function, holding constant the amount of labour. Similarly, we can look at the relationship between output and labour, holding constant the quantity of capital. Suppose that we fix capital K at its actual 2000 value of \$808 billion and hold productivity A at its actual 2000 value of 20.43 (see Table 3.1). The production function (Eq. 3.2) becomes

$$Y = AK^{0.3}N^{0.7} = (20.43)(808^{0.3})(N^{0.7}) = 152.22N^{0.7}.$$

This relationship is shown graphically in Figure 3.3. Point A, where $N = 14.9$ million workers and $Y = \$1{,}009$ billion, corresponds to the actual 2000 values.

The production function relating output and labour looks generally the same as the production function relating output and capital.[6] As in the case of capital, increases in the number of workers raise output but do so at a diminishing rate. Thus, the principle of diminishing marginal productivity also applies to labour, and for similar reasons: the greater the number of workers already using a fixed amount of capital and other inputs, the smaller is the benefit (in terms of increased output) of adding even more workers.

The **marginal product of labour**, or MPN, is the additional output produced by each additional unit of labour, $\Delta Y/\Delta N$. As with the marginal product of capital, for small increases in employment, the MPN can be measured by the slope of the line tangent to a production function that relates output and labour. In Figure 3.3, when employment equals 6 million workers, the MPN equals the slope of the line tangent to the production function at point B; and when employment is 10 million workers, the MPN is the slope of the line that touches the production function at point C. Because of the diminishing marginal productivity of labour, the slope of the production function relating output to labour is greater at B than at C, and the production function flattens from left to right.

SUPPLY SHOCKS

The production function of an economy does not usually remain fixed over time. Economists use the term **supply shock**—or, sometimes, productivity shock—to refer to a change in an economy's production function.[7] A positive, or beneficial, supply shock raises the amount of output that can be produced for given quantities of capital and labour. A negative, or adverse, supply shock lowers the amount of output that can be produced for each capital–labour combination.

Real-world examples of supply shocks include changes in the weather, such as a drought or an unusually cold winter; inventions or innovations in management techniques that improve efficiency, such as minicomputers or statistical analysis in quality control; and changes in government regulations, such as anti-pollution laws, that affect the technologies or production methods used. Also included in the category of supply shocks are changes in the supplies of factors of production other than capital and labour that affect the amount that can be produced. All these shocks are reflected in changes in productivity, A, which we measured for Canada in Table 3.1.

Figure 3.4, on the next page, shows the effects of an adverse supply shock on the production function relating output and labour. The negative supply shock shifts the production function downward so that less output can be produced for specific

---

6. Because N is raised to the power of 0.7 but K is raised to the power of 0.3, the production function relating output and labour is not as sharply bowed as the production function relating output and capital.

7. The term *shock* is a slight misnomer. Not all changes in the production function are sharp or unpredictable, although many are.

FIGURE 3.3

THE PRODUCTION
FUNCTION RELATING
OUTPUT AND LABOUR

This production function
shows how much output the
Canadian economy could
produce at each level of
employment (labour input),
holding productivity and the
capital stock constant at 2000
levels. Point A corresponds to
actual 2000 output and
employment. The marginal
product of labour (MPN) at
any point is measured as the
slope of the line tangent to the
production function at that
point. The MPN is lower at
higher levels of employment,
reflecting diminishing marginal
productivity of labour.

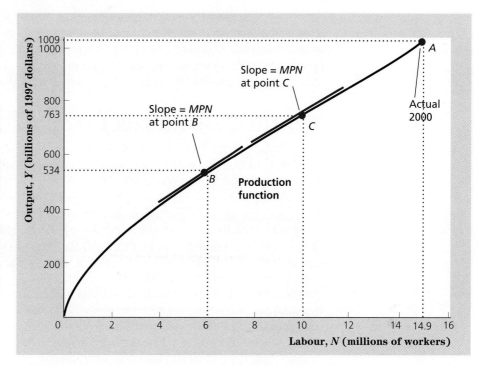

FIGURE 3.4

AN ADVERSE SUPPLY
SHOCK THAT LOWERS THE
MPN

An adverse supply shock is a
downward shift of the
production function. For any
level of labour, the amount of
output that can be produced
is now less than before. The
adverse shock reduces the
slope of the production function at every level of employment.

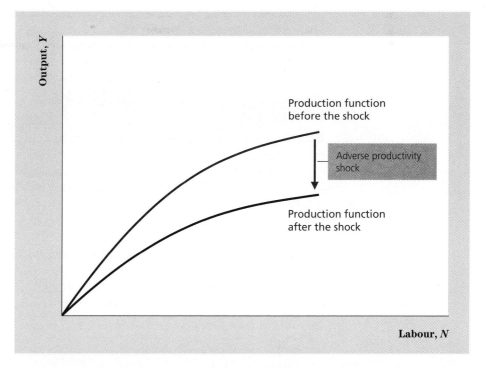

quantities of labour and capital. In addition, the supply shock shown reduces the slope of the production function so that the output gains from adding a worker (the marginal product of labour) are lower at every level of employment.[8] Similarly, a beneficial supply shock makes possible the production of more output with given quantities of capital and labour and, thus, shifts the production function upward.[9]

3.2 THE DEMAND FOR LABOUR

We have shown that the amount of output produced by a country, or by a firm, depends both on productivity and the quantities of inputs used in the production process. In Section 3.1 our focus was on productivity—its measurement and factors such as supply shocks that cause it to change. In this section, we examine what determines the quantities of inputs that producers use. Recall that the two most important inputs are capital and labour. The capital stock in an economy changes over time as a result of investment by firms and the scrapping of worn-out or obsolete capital. However, because the capital stock is long-lived and has been built up over many years, new investment and the scrapping of old capital only slowly have a significant effect on the overall quantity of capital available. Thus, for analyses spanning only a few quarters or years, economists often treat the economy's capital stock as fixed. For now, we follow this practice and assume a fixed capital stock. In taking up long-term economic growth in Chapter 6, we drop this assumption and examine how the capital stock evolves over time.

In contrast to the amount of capital, the amount of labour employed in the economy can change fairly quickly. For example, firms may lay off workers or ask them to work overtime without much notice. Workers may quit or decide to enter the workforce quickly. Thus, year-to-year changes in production often can be traced to changes in employment. To explain why employment changes, for the remainder of this chapter, we focus on how the labour market works, using a supply and demand approach. In this section we look at labour demand, and in Section 3.3 we discuss factors affecting labour supply.

As a step toward understanding the overall demand for labour in the economy, we consider how an individual firm decides how many workers to employ. To keep things simple for the time being, we make the following assumptions:

1. *Workers are all alike.* We ignore differences in workers' aptitudes, skills, ambition, and so on.

2. *Firms view the wage of the workers they hire as being determined in a competitive labour market and not set by the firms themselves.* For example, a competitive firm in Halifax that wants to hire machinists knows that it must pay the going local wage for machinists if it wants to attract qualified workers. The firm then decides how many machinists to employ.

3. *In making the decision about how many workers to employ, a firm's goal is to earn the highest possible level of profit* (the value of its output minus its costs of production, including taxes). The firm will demand the amount of labour that maximizes its profit.

---

8.   Logically, an adverse supply shock need not always reduce the marginal products of labour and capital; for example, the production function could make a parallel downward shift. However, thinking of an adverse supply shock reducing marginal products as being the normal case seems reasonable. A shift of the production function like that shown in Figure 3.4 would occur if there were a decline in total factor productivity A, for example.

9.   The effects of supply shocks on the production function relating output and capital would be similar.

To figure out the profit-maximizing amount of labour, the firm must compare the costs and benefits of hiring each additional worker. The cost of an extra worker is the worker's wage, and the benefit of an extra worker is the value of the additional goods or services the worker produces. As long as the benefits of additional labour exceed the costs, hiring more labour will increase the firm's profits. The firm will continue to hire additional labour until the benefit of an extra worker (the value of extra goods or services produced) equals the cost (the wage).

THE MARGINAL PRODUCT OF LABOUR AND LABOUR DEMAND: AN EXAMPLE

Let us make the discussion of labour demand more concrete by looking at The Clip Joint, a small business that grooms dogs. The Clip Joint uses both capital, such as clippers, tubs, and brushes, and labour to produce its output of groomed dogs.

The production function that applies to The Clip Joint appears in Table 3.2, on the next page. For given levels of productivity and the capital stock, it shows how The Clip Joint's daily output of groomed dogs, column (2), depends on the number of workers employed, column (1). The more workers The Clip Joint has, the greater its daily output is.

The *MPN* of each worker at The Clip Joint is shown in column (3). Employing the first worker raises The Clip Joint's output from 0 to 11, so the *MPN* of the first worker is 11. Employing the second worker raises The Clip Joint's output from 11 to 20, an increase of 9, so the *MPN* of the second worker is 9; and so on. Column (3) also shows that as the number of workers at The Clip Joint increases, the *MPN* falls so that labour at The Clip Joint has diminishing marginal productivity. The more workers there are on the job, the more they must share the fixed amount of capital (tubs, clippers, brushes) and the less benefit there is to adding yet another worker.

The marginal product of labour measures the benefit of employing an additional worker in terms of the extra *output* produced. A related concept, the **marginal revenue product of labour**, or *MRPN*, measures the benefit of employing an additional worker in terms of the extra *revenue* produced. To calculate the *MRPN*, we need to know the price of the firm's output. If The Clip Joint receives $10 for each dog it grooms, the *MRPN* of the first worker is $110 per day (11 additional dogs groomed per day at $10 per grooming). More generally, the marginal revenue product of an additional worker equals the price of the firm's output, P, times the extra output gained by adding the worker, *MPN*:

$$MRPN = P \times MPN. \tag{3.3}$$

At The Clip Joint the price of output P is $10 per grooming, so the MRPN of each worker, column (4), equals the MPN of the worker, column (3), multiplied by $10.

Now, suppose that the wage W that The Clip Joint must pay to attract qualified workers is $80 per day. (We refer to the wage W, when measured in the conventional way in terms of today's dollars, as the nominal wage.) How many workers should The Clip Joint employ in order to maximize its profits? To answer this question, The Clip Joint compares the benefits and costs of employing each additional worker. The benefit of employing an additional worker, in dollars per day, is the worker's marginal revenue product *MRPN*. The cost of an additional worker, in dollars per day, is the nominal daily wage W.

TABLE 3.2

The Clip Joint's Production Function

(1) Number of Workers, N	(2) Number of Dogs Groomed, Y	(3) Marginal Product of Labour, MPN	(4) Marginal Revenue Product of Labour, $MRPN =$ $MPN \times P$ (when $P = \$10$ per grooming)
0	0		
		11	$110
1	11		
		9	$90
2	20		
		7	$70
3	27		
		5	$50
4	32		
		3	$30
5	35		
		1	$10
6	36		

Table 3.2 shows that the $MRPN$ of the first worker is $110 per day, which exceeds the daily wage of $80, so employing the first worker is profitable for The Clip Joint. Adding a second worker increases The Clip Joint's profit as well because the $MRPN$ of the second worker ($90 per day) also exceeds the daily wage. However, employing a third worker reduces The Clip Joint's profit because the third worker's $MRPN$ of $70 per day is less than the $80 daily wage. Therefore, The Clip Joint's profit-maximizing level of employment at $80/day—equivalently, the quantity of labour demanded by The Clip Joint—is two workers.

In finding the quantity of labour demanded by The Clip Joint, we measured the benefits and costs of an extra worker in nominal, or dollar, terms. If we measure the benefits and costs of an extra worker in real terms, the results are the same. In real terms, the benefit to The Clip Joint of an extra worker is the number of extra groomings that the extra worker provides, which is the marginal product of labour, MPN. The real cost of adding another worker is the **real wage**, which is the wage measured in terms of units of output. Algebraically, the real wage, w, equals the nominal wage, W, divided by the price of output, P.

In this example, the nominal wage W is $80 per day and the price of output P is $10 per grooming, so the real wage w equals ($80 per day)/($10 per grooming), or 8 groomings per day. To find the profit-maximizing level of employment, The Clip Joint compares this real cost of an additional worker with the real benefit of an additional worker, the MPN. The MPN of the first worker is 11 groomings per day, which exceeds the real wage of 8 groomings per day, so employing this worker is profitable. The second worker also should be hired, as the second worker's MPN of 9 groomings per day also exceeds the real wage of 8 groomings per day. However, a third worker should not be hired, as the third worker's MPN of 7 groomings per day is less than the real wage. The quantity of labour demanded by The Clip Joint is, therefore, two workers, which is the same result we got when we compared costs and benefits in nominal terms.

This example shows that when the benefit of an additional worker exceeds the cost of an additional worker, the firm should increase employment in order to maximize profits. Similarly, if at the firm's current employment level the benefit of the last worker employed is less than the cost of the worker, the firm should reduce employment. Summary table 2 compares benefits and costs of additional labour in both real and nominal terms. In the choice of the profit-maximizing level of employment, comparison of benefits and costs in real or nominal terms is equally valid.

A CHANGE IN THE WAGE

The Clip Joint's decision to employ two workers was based on a nominal wage of $80 per day. Now suppose that for some reason the nominal wage needed to attract qualified workers drops to $60 per day. How will the reduction in the nominal wage affect the number of workers that The Clip Joint wants to employ?

To find the answer, we can compare costs and benefits in either nominal or real terms. Let us make the comparison in real terms. If the nominal wage drops to $60 per day while the price of groomings remains at $10, the real wage falls to ($60 per day)/($10 per grooming), or 6 groomings per day. Column (3) of Table 3.2 shows that the MPN of the third worker is 7 groomings per day, which is now greater than the real wage. Thus, at the lower wage, expanding the quantity of labour demanded from two to three workers is profitable for The Clip Joint. However, the firm will not hire a fourth worker because the MPN of the fourth worker (5 groomings per day) is less than the new real wage (6 groomings per day).

This example illustrates a general point about the effect of the real wage on labour demand: All else being equal, *a decrease in the real wage raises the amount of labour demanded. Similarly, an increase in the real wage decreases the amount of labour demanded.*

SUMMARY 2 COMPARING THE BENEFITS AND COSTS OF CHANGING THE AMOUNT OF LABOUR

TO MAXIMIZE PROFITS, THE FIRM SHOULD	INCREASE EMPLOYMENT IF	DECREASE EMPLOYMENT IF
Real terms	$MPN > w$ ($MPN > W/P$)	$MPN < w$ ($MPN < W/P$)
Nominal terms	$P \times MPN > W$ ($MRPN > W$)	$P \times MPN < W$ ($MRPN < W$)

MPN = marginal product of labour
P = price of output
$MRPN$ = marginal revenue product of labour = $P \times MPN$
W = nominal wage
w = real wage = W/P

THE MARGINAL PRODUCT OF LABOUR AND THE LABOUR DEMAND CURVE

Using The Clip Joint as an example, we showed the negative relationship between the real wage and the quantity of labour that a firm demands. Figure 3.5 shows in more general terms how the link between the real wage and the quantity of labour demanded is determined. The amount of labour N is on the horizontal axis. The MPN and the real wage, both of which are measured in goods per unit of labour, are on the vertical axis. The downward-sloping curve is the MPN curve; it relates the marginal product of labour, MPN, to the amount of labour employed by the firm, N. The MPN curve slopes downward because of the diminishing marginal productivity of labour. The horizontal line represents the real wage faced by firms in the labour market, which the firms take as given. Here, the real wage is w^*.

For any real wage w^*, the amount of labour that yields the highest profit (and therefore the amount of labour demanded) is determined at point A, the intersection of the real-wage line and the MPN curve. At A, the quantity of labour demanded is N^*. Why is N^* a firm's profit-maximizing level of labour input? At employment levels of less than N^*, the marginal product of labour exceeds the real wage (the MPN curve lies above the real-wage line); thus, if the firm's employment is initially less than N^*, it can increase its profit by expanding the amount of labour it uses. Similarly, if the firm's employment is initially greater than N^*, the marginal product of labour is less than the real wage *(MPN < w*)* and the firm can raise profits by reducing employment. Only when employment equals N^* will the firm be satisfied with the number of workers it has. More generally, for any real wage, the profit-maximizing amount of labour input—labour demanded—corresponds to the point at which the MPN curve and the real-wage line intersect.

FIGURE 3.5

THE DETERMINATION OF LABOUR DEMAND

The amount of labour demanded is determined by locating the point on the *MPN* curve at which the *MPN* equals the real wage rate; the amount of labour corresponding to that point is the amount of labour demanded. For example, when the real wage is w^*, the *MPN* equals the real wage at point A and the quantity of labour demanded is N^*. The labour demand curve, *ND*, shows the amount of labour demanded at each level of the real wage. The labour demand curve is identical to the *MPN* curve.

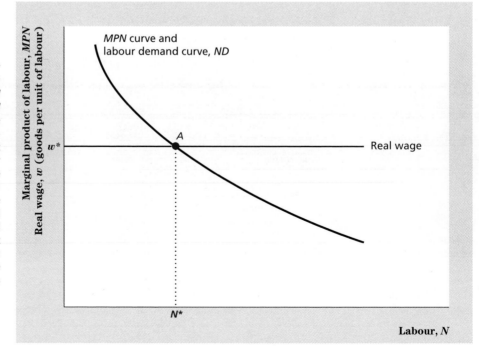

The graph of the relationship between the amount of labour demanded by a firm and the real wage that the firm faces is called the *labour demand curve*. Because the *MPN* curve also shows the amount of labour demanded at any real wage, *the labour demand curve is the same as the MPN curve*, except that the vertical axis measures the real wage for the labour demand curve and measures the marginal product of labour for the *MPN* curve.[10] Like the *MPN* curve, the labour demand curve slopes downward, indicating that the quantity of labour demanded falls as the real wage rises.

This labour demand curve is more general than that in the example of The Clip Joint in a couple of ways that are worth mentioning. First, we referred to the demand for labour and not specifically to the demand for workers, as in The Clip Joint example. In general, labour N can be measured in various ways—for example, as total hours worked, total weeks worked, or the number of employees—depending on the application. Second, although we assumed in the example that The Clip Joint had to hire a whole number of workers, the labour demand curve shown in Figure 3.5 allows labour N to have any positive value, whole or fractional. Allowing N to take any value is sensible because people may work fractions of an hour.

FACTORS THAT SHIFT THE LABOUR DEMAND CURVE

Because the labour demand curve shows the relation between the real wage and the amount of labour that firms want to employ, changes in the real wage are represented as movements *along* the labour demand curve. Changes in the real wage do not cause the labour demand curve to shift. The labour demand curve shifts in response to factors that change the amount of labour that firms want to employ *at any given level of the real wage.* For example, we showed earlier in this chapter that beneficial or positive supply shocks are likely to increase the *MPN* at all levels of labour input, and adverse or negative supply shocks are likely to reduce the *MPN* at all levels of labour input. Thus, a beneficial supply shock shifts the *MPN* curve upward and to the right and raises the quantity of labour demanded at any given real wage; an adverse supply shock does the reverse.

The effect of a supply shock on The Clip Joint's demand for labour can be illustrated by imagining that the proprietor of The Clip Joint discovers that playing New Age music soothes the dogs. It makes them more cooperative and doubles the number of groomings per day that the same number of workers can produce. This technological improvement gives The Clip Joint a new production function, as described in Table 3.3. Note that doubling total output doubles the *MPN* at each employment level.

The Clip Joint demanded two workers when faced with the original production function (Table 3.2) and a real wage of 8 groomings per day. Table 3.3 shows that the productivity improvement increases The Clip Joint's labour demand at the given real wage to four workers because the *MPN* of the fourth worker (10 groomings per day) now exceeds the real wage. The Clip Joint will not hire a fifth worker, however, because this worker's *MPN* (6 groomings per day) is less than the real wage.

The effect of a beneficial supply shock on a labour demand curve is shown in Figure 3.6. The shock causes the *MPN* to increase at any level of labour input, so the

---

10. Recall that the real wage and the *MPN* are measured in the same units, goods per unit of labour.

TABLE 3.3

The Clip Joint's Production Function after a Beneficial Productivity Shock

(1) Number of Workers, N	(2) Number of Dogs Groomed, Y	(3) Marginal Product of Labour, MPN	(4) Marginal Revenue Product of Labour, $MRPN = MPN \times P$ (when $P = \$10$ per grooming)
0	0		
		22	$220
1	22		
		18	$180
2	40		
		14	$140
3	54		
		10	$100
4	64		
		6	$60
5	70		
		2	$20
6	72		

MPN curve shifts upward and to the right. Because the *MPN* and labour demand curves are identical, the labour demand curve also shifts upward and to the right, from ND^1 to ND^2 in Figure 3.6. When the labour demand curve is ND^2, the firm hires more workers at any real wage level than when the labour demand curve is ND^1. Thus, worker productivity and the amount of labour demanded are closely linked. A reduction in payroll taxes (such as employer contributions to unemployment

FIGURE 3.6

THE EFFECT OF A BENEFICIAL SUPPLY SHOCK ON LABOUR DEMAND

A beneficial supply shock that raises the *MPN* at every level of labour shifts the *MPN* curve upward and to the right. Because the labour demand curve is identical to the *MPN* curve, the labour demand curve shifts upward and to the right from ND^1 to ND^2. For any real wage, firms demand more labour after a beneficial supply shock.

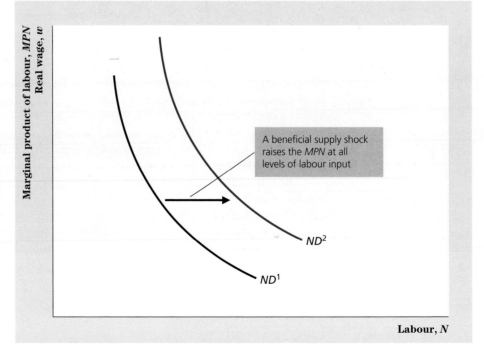

insurance) would have the same effect as a beneficial supply shock. This tax change would raise the after-tax marginal product of labour and, so, shift the labour demand curve to the right.

Another factor that may affect labour demand is the size of the capital stock. Generally, an increase in the capital stock K—by giving each worker more machines or equipment to work with—raises workers' productivity and increases the MPN at any level of labour. Hence an increase in the capital stock will cause the labour demand curve to shift upward and to the right, raising the amount of labour that a firm demands at any particular real wage.[11]

AGGREGATE LABOUR DEMAND

So far, we have focused on the demand for labour by an individual firm, such as The Clip Joint. For macroeconomic analysis, however, we usually work with the concept of the **aggregate demand for labour**, or the sum of the labour demands of all the firms in an economy.

Because the aggregate demand for labour is the sum of firms' labour demands, the factors that determine the aggregate demand for labour are the same as for an individual firm. Thus, the aggregate labour demand curve looks the same as the labour demand curve for an individual firm (see Figure 3.5). Like the firm's labour demand curve, the aggregate labour demand curve slopes downward, showing that an increase in the economywide real wage reduces the total amount of labour that firms want to use. Similarly, a beneficial supply shock or an increase in the aggregate capital stock shifts the aggregate labour demand curve upward and to the right; an adverse supply shock or a drop in the aggregate capital stock shifts it downward and to the left. The factors affecting aggregate labour demand are listed for convenience in Summary table 3.

---

11. An increase in the capital stock may reduce the demand for labour if the new capital substitutes for the use of labour. For example, the installation of automatic elevators reduced the marginal product of elevator operators and, thus, the demand for these workers.

SUMMARY 3 FACTORS THAT SHIFT THE AGGREGATE LABOUR DEMAND CURVE

AN INCREASE IN	CAUSES THE LABOUR DEMAND CURVE TO SHIFT	REASON
Productivity	Right	Beneficial supply shock increases MPN and shifts MPN curve up and to the right.
Capital stock	Right	Higher capital stock increases MPN and shifts MPN curve up and to the right.

3.3 THE SUPPLY OF LABOUR

The demand for labour is determined by firms, but the supply of labour is determined by individuals or members of a family making a joint decision. Each person of working age must decide how much (if at all) to work in the wage-paying sector of the economy versus non–wage-paying alternatives, such as taking care of the home and children, going to school, or being retired. The **aggregate supply of labour** is the sum of the labour supplied by everyone in the economy.

Recall that in determining how much labour to demand, firms compare the costs and benefits of hiring additional workers. Similarly, in deciding how much to work, an individual weighs the benefits against the costs of working. Beyond any psychological satisfaction gained from having a job, the principal benefit of working is the income earned, which can be used to buy necessities and luxuries. The principal cost of working is that it involves time and effort that are no longer available for other activities. Economists use the term **leisure**[12] for all off-the-job activities, including eating, working around the house, spending time with family and friends, and so on. To make themselves as well off as possible, individuals choose to supply labour up to the point at which the income obtained from working an extra hour just makes up for the extra hour of leisure they have to forgo.

THE INCOME–LEISURE TRADE-OFF

To illustrate how the trade-off between income and leisure affects the labour supply decision, let us look at an example. Consider a tennis instructor named Ace who offers tennis lessons. After paying taxes and job-related expenses, Ace can earn $35 per hour, which we will call his (after-tax) nominal wage rate. Ace enjoys a reputation as an outstanding tennis instructor and could work as many hours per year as he chooses. He is reluctant to work too much, however, because every day he spends teaching tennis means one less day available to devote to his real passion, skydiving. The decision Ace faces is how many hours to work this year—or, in other words, how much labour to supply.

Ace approaches this question by asking himself: Economically speaking, what really makes me happy? After a little reflection, Ace concludes that his level of happiness, or *utility*, depends on the amount of goods and services he consumes and on the amount of leisure time he has available to jump out of airplanes. His question can, therefore, be recast as follows: How much should I work this year so as to obtain the highest possible level of utility?

To find the level of labour supply that maximizes his utility, Ace must compare the costs and benefits of working an extra hour. The cost of an extra hour of work is the loss of an hour of leisure; this cost can be measured as the loss in utility that Ace experiences when he must work for an hour instead of skydive. The benefit of working an extra hour is an increase of $35 in income, which allows Ace to enjoy more consumption.

If the benefit of working an extra hour (the utility gained from extra income) exceeds the cost (the utility lost by reducing leisure), Ace should work the extra hour. In fact, he should continue to increase his time at work until the utility he receives from the additional income of $35 just equals the loss of utility associated with missing an hour of leisure. Ace's labour supply at that point is the one that maximizes

---

12. The term *leisure* does not imply that all off-the-job activities (housework or schoolwork, for example) are "leisurely"!

his utility.[13] Using the idea that the labour supply decision results from a trade-off of leisure against income, we can discuss factors that influence the amount of labour supplied by Ace.

REAL WAGES AND LABOUR SUPPLY

The real wage is the amount of real income that a worker receives in exchange for giving up a unit of leisure (an hour, a day, or a week, for example) for work. It is an important determinant of the quantity of labour that is supplied.

Generally, an increase in the real wage affects the labour supply decision in two ways. First, an increase in the real wage raises the benefit (in terms of additional real income) of working an additional hour and, thus, tends to make the worker want to supply more labour. The tendency of workers to supply more labour in response to a higher reward for working is called the **substitution effect of a higher real wage** on the quantity of labour supplied.

Second, an increase in the real wage makes workers effectively wealthier because for the same amount of work, they now earn a higher real income. Someone who is wealthier will be better able to afford additional leisure and, as a result, will supply less labour. The tendency of workers to supply less labour in response to becoming wealthier is called the **income effect of a higher real wage** on the quantity of labour supplied. Note that the substitution and income effects of a higher real wage operate in opposite directions, with the substitution effect tending to raise the quantity of labour supplied and the income effect tending to reduce it.

A PURE SUBSTITUTION EFFECT: A ONE-DAY RISE IN THE REAL WAGE

We can illustrate the substitution effect by supposing that after some consideration, Ace decides to work 48 hours per week, by working eight hours per day for six days each week. He leaves every Wednesday free to go skydiving. Although Ace could work and earn $35 per hour each Wednesday, his highest utility is obtained by taking leisure on that day instead.

Now imagine that one Tuesday, an eccentric tennis player calls Ace and requests a lesson on Wednesday to help him prepare for a weekend amateur tournament. He offers Ace his regular wage of $35 per hour, but Ace declines, explaining that he plans to go skydiving on Wednesday. Not willing to take "no" for an answer, the tennis player then offers to pay Ace $350 per hour for an all-day lesson on Wednesday. When Ace hears this offer to work for 10 times his usual wage rate, he thinks: "I don't get offers like this one every day. I'll go skydiving some other day, but this Wednesday I'm going to work."

Ace's decision to work rather than skydive (that is, to substitute labour for leisure) on this particular Wednesday represents a response to a very high reward, in terms of additional income, that each additional hour of work on that day will bring. His decision to work the extra day results from the substitution effect. Because receiving a very high wage for only one day does not make Ace substantially wealthier, the income effect of the one-day wage increase is negligible. Thus, the effect of a one-day increase in the real wage on the quantity of labour supplied by Ace is an almost pure example of the substitution effect.

---

13. Not everyone can choose his or her labour supply as flexibly as Ace; for example, some jobs are available for 40 hours a week or not at all. Nevertheless, by choosing to work overtime, part-time, or at a second job, or by varying the number of family members who are working, households do have a significant amount of latitude over how much labour to supply.

A Pure Income Effect: Winning the Lottery

In addition to skydiving, Ace enjoys playing the provincial lottery. As luck would have it, a week after spending the Wednesday teaching the eccentric tennis player, Ace wins $300,000 in the lottery. Ace's response is to reduce his workweek from six to five days, because the additional $300,000 of wealth enables him to afford to take more time off from work—and so he does. Because the lottery prize has made him wealthier, he reduces his labour supply. As the lottery prize does not affect the current reward for giving up an hour of leisure to work—Ace's real wage is still $35 per hour—there is no substitution effect. Thus, winning the lottery is an example of a pure income effect.

Another example of a pure income effect is an increase in the expected future real wage. Suppose that the aging tennis pro at the posh country club in Ace's community announces that he will retire the following year, and the country club agrees to hire Ace beginning one year from now. Ace will earn $50 per hour (after taxes) for as many hours as he wants to teach tennis.[14] Ace recognizes that this increase in his future wage has effectively made him wealthier by increasing the future income he will receive for any given amount of labour supplied in the future. Looking at his lifetime income, Ace realizes that he is better able to afford leisure today. That is, the increase in the future real wage has an income effect that leads Ace to reduce his current labour supply. Because this increase in the future wage does not change Ace's current wage and, thus, does not affect the current reward for giving up an hour of leisure to work an additional hour, there is no substitution effect on Ace's current labour supply. Thus, the increase in the future real wage has a pure income effect on Ace's labour supply.

The Substitution Effect and the Income Effect Together: A Long-Term Increase in the Real Wage

The aging tennis pro at the country club quits suddenly, and the country club asks Ace to start work immediately. Ace accepts the offer and earns $50 per hour (after taxes) for as many hours as he wants to teach tennis.

On his new job, will Ace work more hours or fewer hours than he did before? In this case, the two effects work in opposite directions. On the one hand, because the reward for working is greater, Ace will be tempted to work more than he did previously. This tendency to increase labour supply in response to a higher real wage is the substitution effect. On the other hand, at his new, higher wage, Ace can pay for food, rent, and skydiving expenses by working only three or four days each week, so he is tempted to work less and spend more time skydiving. This tendency to reduce labour supply because he is wealthier is the income effect.

Which effect wins? One factor that will influence Ace's decision is the length of time he expects his new, higher wage to last. The longer the higher wage is expected to last, the larger its impact on Ace's lifetime resources is, and the stronger the income effect is. Thus, if Ace expects to hold the new job until he retires, the income effect is strong (he is much wealthier) and he is more likely to reduce the amount of time that he works. In contrast, if Ace believes that the job may not last very long, the income effect is weak (the increase in his lifetime resources is small) and he may choose to work more so as to take advantage of the higher wage while he can. In general, the longer an increase in the real wage is expected to last, the

---

14. We assume that zero inflation is expected over the next year, so the $50 per hour wage rate in the following year is an increase in Ace's real wage rate as well as an increase in his nominal wage rate.

larger the income effect is and the more likely it is that the quantity of labour supplied will be reduced.

EMPIRICAL EVIDENCE ON REAL WAGES AND LABOUR SUPPLY

Because of conflicting income and substitution effects, there is some ambiguity about how a real-wage change will affect labour supply. What is the empirical evidence?

Derek Hum and Wayne Simpson of the University of Manitoba have reviewed evidence from Canada and the United States.[15] The evidence comes from surveys, like those conducted by Statistics Canada, and also from some large-scale experiments. For example, during the Manitoba Basic Annual Income Experiment of 1975 to 1979, participants received a guaranteed annual income (sometimes called a negative income tax). Hum and Simpson compared the labour supply of participants in the income experiment with the labour supply of a control group. They also measured the effects of marriage and children on the labour supply of both men and women. Overall, they found that the income and substitution effects of most real-wage changes were almost offsetting. Thus, increases in real wages may not lead to large increases in labour supply. This finding has important implications for how macroeconomists model business cycles and for the design of tax and unemployment insurance systems, as we will see in later chapters.

In his book on labour supply, Mark Killingsworth,[16] of Rutgers University, surveyed the results of more than 60 studies of the labour supply decision in the United States, the United Kingdom, Canada, West Germany, Japan, and Taiwan. Although the studies differed in many respects and did not all yield precisely the same results, generally they showed that the aggregate amount of labour supplied rises in response to a temporary increase in the real wage but falls in response to a permanent increase in the real wage. The finding that a temporary increase in the real wage raises the amount of labour supplied confirms the substitution effect: If the reward for working rises for a short period, people will take advantage of the opportunity to work more. The result that a permanent increase in the real wage lowers the aggregate amount of labour supplied indicates that for long-lived increases in the real wage the income effect outweighs the substitution effect: If permanently higher wages make workers much better off, they will choose to work less. The effect of permanent increases in real wages is further illustrated in the Application "Weekly Hours of Work and the Wealth of Nations" on page 77.

THE LABOUR SUPPLY CURVE

We have discussed how the amount of labour supplied by an individul depends on the current and expected future real wage rates. The *labour supply curve* of an individual worker relates the amount of labour supplied to the current real wage, with other factors (including the expected future real wage) held constant. Figure 3.7 (on the next page) is a graph of a typical labour supply curve. The current real wage is measured on the vertical axis, and the amount of labour supplied is measured on the horizontal axis. The labour supply curve slopes upward because an increase in the current real wage leads to an increase in the amount of labour supplied.

15. *Income Maintenance, Work Effort, and the Canadian Mincome Experiment*, Ottawa: Economic Council of Canada, 1991.
16. *Labour Supply*, Cambridge, England: Cambridge University Press, 1983. See especially Tables 3.1–3.5 and 4.2–4.4.

FIGURE 3.7

FIGURE 3.7

THE LABOUR SUPPLY CURVE OF AN INDIVIDUAL WORKER

The horizontal axis shows the amount of labour that a worker will supply for any given current real wage on the vertical axis. The labour supply curve slopes upward, indicating that—with other factors including the expected future real wage held constant—an increase in the current real wage raises the amount of labour supplied.

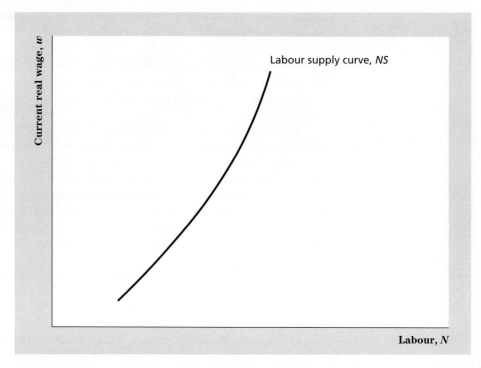

FACTORS THAT SHIFT THE LABOUR SUPPLY CURVE

Any factor that changes the amount of labour supplied at a given level of the current real wage shifts the labour supply curve. Specifically, any factor that increases the

FIGURE 3.8

THE EFFECT ON LABOUR SUPPLY OF AN INCREASE IN WEALTH

An increase in wealth reduces the amount of labour supplied at any real wage. Therefore, an increase in wealth causes the labour supply curve to shift to the left. Similarly, an increase in the expected future real wage, which has the effect of making the worker wealthier, reduces the amount of labour supplied at any given current real wage and shifts the labour supply curve to the left.

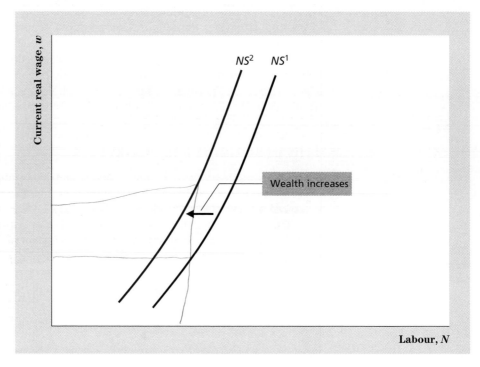

amount of labour supplied at a given level of the real wage shifts the labour supply curve to the right, and any factor that decreases the amount of labour supplied at a given level of the real wage shifts the labour supply curve to the left. We have already discussed how an increase in wealth (say, from winning the lottery) has a pure income effect that reduces the amount of labour supplied at a given real wage. Thus, as shown in Figure 3.8, an increase in wealth shifts the labour supply curve to the left. We also have discussed how an increase in the expected future real wage has a pure income effect that reduces the amount of labour supplied at a given real wage. Figure 3.8 also depicts the response of the labour supply curve to an increase in the expected future real wage.

APPLICATION

WEEKLY HOURS OF WORK AND THE WEALTH OF NATIONS

In 1900, the typical worker in the Canadian manufacturing sector worked about 55 hours per week. However, as shown in Figure 3.9, on page 78, the average workweek in Canadian manufacturing declined steadily into the 1970s. Although various forces contributed to the shortening of the workweek before 1970, the major reason was sharply rising real wages. Increases in real wages during the early 20th century in Canada were driven by technological innovation and increased productivity and thus were largely permanent. In response to permanent increases in the real wage, workers reduced the amount of labour they supplied.

The response of labour supply to increases in real wages does not explain all the changes in weekly hours worked. For example, the relatively low number of hours worked per week during the 1930s reflects primarily the general economic collapse that occurred during the Great Depression; and the sharp increase in weekly hours of work during the 1940s resulted, in part, from the threat posed by World War II, which induced workers to work more hours per week. Since World War II, the average workweek in Canadian manufacturing has declined slowly from about 42 hours to about 38 hours even though the real wage rose substantially in the 1950s and 1960s. However, since World War II workers have reduced the quantities of labour supplied in other ways, notably by retiring earlier and taking more vacation time.

The historical data in Figure 3.9 provide some evidence that in response to a permanent increase in the real wage, workers choose to have more leisure and to work fewer hours per week. Figure 3.10, on page 79, presents additional evidence, drawn from 35 nations. Each point in the diagram represents a different country. The horizontal axis measures real gross domestic product (GDP) per person, and the vertical axis measures the average number of hours worked per week by production workers in manufacturing. Workers in richer countries with higher wage rates (United States, Canada) tend to work fewer hours per week than workers in poorer countries with lower wage rates (South Korea, Philippines). Because the differences in wages among countries reflect long-term differences in productivity, the fact that high-wage countries have shorter workweeks provides further support for the finding that permanent increases in the real wage cause workers to supply less labour.

FIGURE 3.9

AVERAGE WEEKLY HOURS,
CANADIAN
MANUFACTURING

Reflecting the income effect of
wages on labour supply, the
steady increase in the real
wage in Canada during the
20th century tended to reduce
the average weekly hours of
manufacturing workers. Weekly hours fluctuated sharply
during the Great Depression
and World War II, then declined further in the postwar
period.

Source: For 1901–1927, average
weekly hours of machinists in
Halifax, Montreal, Toronto, Winnipeg, and Vancouver: Adapted from
*Wages and Hours of Labour in
Canada, 1901–1920,* Report No.
1, Department of Labour, Canada,
Table II(d) and *Wages and Hours
of Labour in Canada, 1920–1927,*
Report No. 11, Department of
Labour, Canada, Table I(b). For
1926–1955, average weekly hours
of non-agricultural workers:
Historical Statistics of Canada, (1st
ed., 1965), Series D408. For
1945–2000, average weekly hours
in manufacturing: *Historical
Statistics of Canada,* Series E131,
and *Employment, Earnings, and
Wages,* Statistics Canada, cat. no.
72-002.

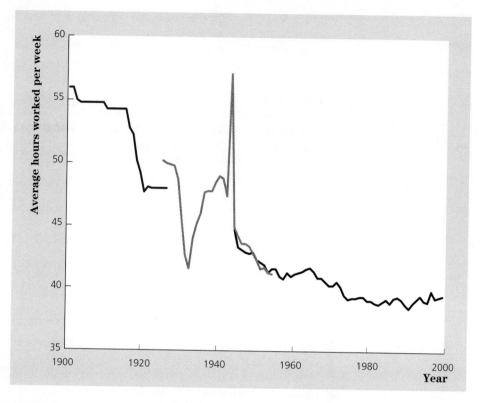

AGGREGATE LABOUR SUPPLY

As we mentioned earlier, the aggregate supply of labour is the total amount of labour
supplied by everyone in the economy. Just as the quantity of labour supplied by an
individual rises when the person's current real wage rises, the aggregate quantity of
labour supplied increases when the economywide real wage rises. An increase in
the current economywide real wage raises the aggregate quantity of labour supplied for two reasons. First, when the real wage rises, people who are already working may supply even more hours—by offering to work overtime, by changing from
part-time to full-time work, or by taking a second job. Second, a higher real wage may
entice some people who are not currently in the labour force to decide to look for
work. Because higher current real wages induce people to want to work more, the
aggregate labour supply curve—which shows the relation between the aggregate
amount of labour supplied and the current real wage—slopes upward.

Factors other than the current real wage that change the amount of labour that
people want to supply cause the aggregate labour supply curve to shift. Summary
table 4 on p. 79, lists the factors that shift aggregate labour supply. We discussed the
first two factors in the table, wealth and the expected future real wage, when we
considered the individual's labour supply decision. Aggregate labour supply will also
increase if the country's working-age population increases (for example, because of an
increased birth rate or immigration), or if changes in the social or legal environment
cause a greater proportion of the working-age population to enter the labour force
(increased labour force participation). For example, evolving attitudes about the role
of women in society contributed to a large increase in the number of women in the
Canadian labour market during the 1970s and 1980s; and the elimination of mandatory
retirement in many fields might increase the participation rates of older workers.

FIGURE 3.10

THE WORKWEEK AND REAL GDP PER PERSON IN 35 COUNTRIES

The point corresponding to each country shows the country's real GDP per person in 1988 on the horizontal axis and the average number of hours worked per week in manufacturing on the vertical axis. Because of the income effect on labour supply, richer countries tend to have short workweeks.

Source: Average hours per week: Based on *United Nations Statistical Yearbook, 1988–1989*, Table 41, p. 316; real GDP per capita in 1985 dollars: Based on Robert Summers and Alan Heston, "The Penn World Table (Mark 5): An Expanded Set of International Comparisons, 1950–1988," *Quarterly Journal of Economics*, May 1991, pp. 327–368, Table II.

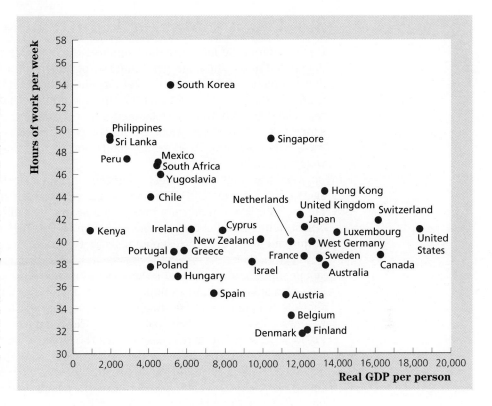

SUMMARY 4 FACTORS THAT SHIFT THE AGGREGATE LABOUR SUPPLY CURVE

AN INCREASE IN	CAUSES THE LABOUR SUPPLY CURVE TO SHIFT	REASON
Wealth	Left	Increase in wealth increases amount of leisure workers can afford.
Expected future real wage	Left	Increase in expected future real wage increases amount of leisure workers can afford.
Working-age population	Right	Increased number of potential workers increases amount of labour supplied.
Participation rate	Right	Increased number of people wanting to work increases amount of labour supplied.

3.4 LABOUR MARKET EQUILIBRIUM

Equilibrium in the labour market requires that the aggregate quantity of labour demanded equal the aggregate quantity of labour supplied. The basic supply–demand model of the labour market introduced here (called the *classical model of the labour market*) is based on the assumption that the real wage adjusts reasonably quickly to equate labour supply and labour demand. Thus, if labour supply is less than labour demand, firms competing for scarce workers bid up the real wage, whereas if many workers are competing for relatively few jobs, the real wage will tend to fall.

Labour market equilibrium is represented graphically by the intersection of the aggregate labour demand curve and the aggregate labour supply curve at point E in Figure 3.11. The equilibrium level of employment, achieved after the complete adjustment of wages and prices, is known as the **full-employment level of employment**, $\bar{N}$. The corresponding market-clearing real wage is $\bar{w}$.

Factors that shift either the aggregate labour demand curve or the aggregate labour supply curve affect both the equilibrium real wage and the full-employment level of employment. An example of such a factor is a temporary adverse supply shock. A temporary adverse supply shock—because of, say, a spell of unusually bad weather—decreases the marginal product of labour at every level of employment. As Figure 3.12 shows, this decrease causes the labour demand curve to shift to the left, from ND^1 to ND^2. Because the supply shock is temporary, however, it is not expected to affect future marginal products or the future real wage, so the labour supply curve does not shift. Equilibrium in the labour market moves from point A to point B. Thus, the model predicts that a temporary supply shock will lower both the current real wage (from w_1 to w_2) and the full-employment level of employment (from $\bar{N}_1$ to $\bar{N}_2$).

The classical supply–demand model of the labour market has the virtue of simplicity and is quite useful for studying how economic disturbances or changes in economic policy affect employment and the real wage. However, a significant drawback of this basic model is that it cannot be used to study unemployment. Because it assumes that any worker who wants to work at the equilibrium real wage can find a job, the model implies zero unemployment, which never occurs.

One way to get unemployment into the model is to drop the assumption that the real wage adjusts rapidly to equate supply and demand. The assumption that the real wage is slow to adjust underlies the Keynesian approach to business cycle analysis (Chapter 12). Another way to extend the model of the labour market to allow for unemployment is to recognize that the process of matching people who would like to work with the appropriate available jobs is not immediate but takes time. Because matching workers with jobs is a time-consuming process, at any particular time, some workers will be without jobs. We discuss the matching process and its relationship to unemployment later in this chapter.

FULL-EMPLOYMENT OUTPUT

By combining labour market equilibrium and the production function, we can determine how much output firms want to supply. **Full-employment output**, $\bar{Y}$, sometimes called *potential output*, is the level of output that firms in the economy supply when wages and prices have fully adjusted. Equivalently, full-employment output is the level of output supplied when aggregate employment equals its full-

FIGURE 3.11

LABOUR MARKET
EQUILIBRIUM

The quantity of labour demanded equals the quantity of labour supplied at point *E*. The equilibrium real wage is $\overline{w}$, and the corresponding equilibrium level of employment is $\overline{N}$, the full-employment level of employment.

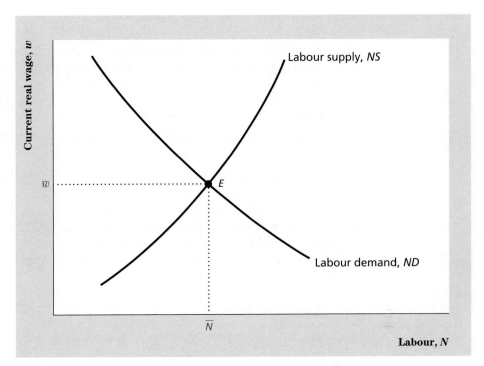

FIGURE 3.12

EFFECTS OF A TEMPORARY
ADVERSE SUPPLY SHOCK
ON THE LABOUR MARKET

An adverse supply shock that lowers the marginal product of labour (see Figure 3.4) reduces the quantity of labour demanded at any real wage level. Thus, the labour demand curve shifts left, from ND^1 to ND^2, and the labour market equilibrium moves from point *A* to point *B*. The adverse supply shock causes the real wage to fall from $\overline{w}_1$ to $\overline{w}_2$ and reduces the full-employment level of employment from $\overline{N}_1$ to $\overline{N}_2$.

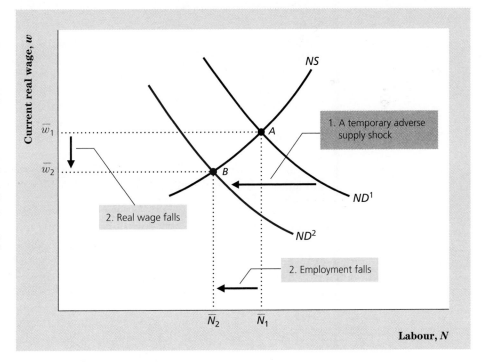

employment level $\overline{N}$. Algebraically, we can define full-employment output $\overline{Y}$ by using the production function (Eq. 3.1):

$$\overline{Y} = AF(K, \overline{N}).$$

(3.4)

Equation (3.4) shows that for constant capital stock K, full-employment output is determined by two general factors: the full-employment level of employment $\overline{N}$ and the production function relating output to employment.

Anything that changes either the full-employment level of employment $\overline{N}$ or the production function will change full-employment output $\overline{Y}$. For example, an adverse supply shock that reduces the MPN (see Figure 3.12) works in two distinct ways to lower full-employment output:

1. The adverse supply shock lowers output directly, by reducing the quantity of output that can be produced with any fixed amounts of capital and labour. This direct effect can be thought of as a reduction in the productivity measure A in Eq. (3.4).

2. The adverse supply shock reduces the demand for labour and, thus, lowers the full-employment level of employment $\overline{N}$, as Figure 3.12 shows. A reduction in $\overline{N}$ also reduces full-employment output $\overline{Y}$, as Eq. (3.4) confirms.

APPLICATION

OUTPUT, EMPLOYMENT, AND THE REAL WAGE DURING OIL PRICE SHOCKS

Among the most severe supply shocks hitting the Canadian and world economies since World War II were sharp increases in the prices of oil and other energy products. Figure 3.13 shows how the industrial price of petroleum, measured relative to the GDP deflator (the general price level of all output), varied during the period 1956–2001. Five adverse oil price shocks stand out. In 1956, the Suez crisis disrupted supplies and caused prices to rise. In the period 1973–1974, the Organization of Petroleum Exporting Countries (OPEC) imposed an oil embargo and then greatly increased crude oil prices. In the period 1979–1980, the Iranian revolution disrupted oil supplies. This shock turned out to be temporary, as energy prices subsequently fell. A fourth increase in oil prices followed Iraq's invasion of Kuwait in August 1990. However, the 1990 shock had a lesser impact on overall energy prices than the previous two oil price shocks and, thus, does not appear as much more than a blip in Figure 3.13. Most recently, OPEC production cuts in 1999 led to higher energy prices in 2000.

In Canada, oil price increases benefit oil producing firms and their employees, as well as governments (like Alberta's) that earn revenue from oil royalties. But when energy prices rise, most firms cut back on energy use, implying that less output is produced at any particular levels of capital and labour. Thus, an increase in energy prices is an adverse supply shock. How important were these supply shocks? In an empirical study of Canada from 1974 through 1982, John Helliwell[17] of the University of British Columbia estimated a production function for Canada, in which he allowed for effects of oil price changes. He attributed most of the changes in output during this period to oil price changes and to the parallel output changes in other industrial economies. His results suggest a large impact on the supply of output from oil price shocks, at least for the shocks of the 1970s.

---

17. "Stagflation and Productivity Decline in Canada, 1974–1982," *Canadian Journal of Economics*, May 1984, pp. 191–216.

Our analysis predicts that an adverse supply shock will lower labour demand, reducing employment and the real wage, as well as reducing the supply of output. John Burbidge and Alan Harrison of McMaster University studied the effects of oil price shocks in Canada, the United States, Germany, Japan, and the United Kingdom during the 1960s and 1970s. They found that changes in oil prices led to declines in industrial production and in real wages in each country.[18] In Canada, the economy went into a recession following both the 1979–1980 and 1990 oil shocks, with negative GDP growth each time.[19] In both cases, the fraction of the adult population employed and the real wage fell. The real wage (average weekly industrial earnings divided by the CPI) declined by about 1% between 1981 and 1982 and between 1990 and 1991. Care must be taken in interpreting these results because macroeconomic policies and other factors were changing at the same time, but Helliwell found that domestic policies (such as anti-inflation policy and the National Energy Program) did not account for much of the changes in output in the 1970s. Our model, thus, appears to account for the response of the economy to historical oil price shocks.

Does this analysis mean that the recent spike in energy prices will again cause output, employment, and real wages to fall in Canada? This scenario now seems unlikely, for three reasons. First, as Figure 3.13 shows, the most recent increase in energy prices was relatively short-lived and was largely reversed during 2001. Second, total energy use as a percentage of real GDP in Canada has declined by about 25 percent since 1978. Since GDP is less energy intensive, oil price shocks should now have smaller effects. Third, Canada is a large exporter of energy, especially natural gas, which is a substitute for oil. As a result, the positive macroeconomic effects of oil price shocks may almost outweigh the negative effects for Canada.[20]

APPLICATION

TECHNICAL CHANGE AND WAGE INEQUALITY

Because many families have little income other than wage income, trends in real wages have important implications for the standard of living of a large segment of the society. During the 25 years after World War II, real wages in Canada grew strongly. Since about 1970, however, there have been two trends: (1) overall real wage growth has slowed considerably; and (2) real wages have become more unequal, with wages of the best-paid workers continuing to rise but wages of the worst-paid workers actually falling in real terms.

These two trends are illustrated by Table 3.4, which is drawn from a study by Charles Beach, of Queen's University, and George Slotsve, of Vanderbilt University. The table shows the percentages of employed women and men (including part-time workers) earning either less than $20,000 or more than $40,000, in constant (1990) dollars for 1967, 1975, 1985, and 1997.

---

18. "Testing for the Effects of Oil-Price Rises using Vector Autoregressions," *International Economic Review*, June 1984, pp. 459–484.

19. Canada also experienced a recession in 1974-1975 after the 1973 OPEC price increase. That recession was relatively mild, though, partly because the government limited the adjustment of the domestic oil price to the world price.

20. For an analysis of the recent oil price increase, see Gerald Stuber, "The Changing Effects of Energy Price Shocks on Economic Activity and Inflation," *Bank of Canada Review*, Summer 2001, pp. 3-14.

FIGURE 3.13

RELATIVE PRICE OF OIL, 1956–2001

The figure shows the industrial product price index of refined petroleum relative to the GDP deflator. Note the impact of the 1973-1974 and 1979-1980 oil shocks, the decline in petroleum prices during the second half of the 1980s, and the temporary jump in the price of oil in 2000 following output reductions by OPEC.

Source: GDP deflator: Statistics Canada, CANSIM Series D100465. Data prior to 1981 are not chain-weighted and so have been spliced. Oil price: industrial product price index, refined petroleum, Statistics Canada, CANSIM P3275.

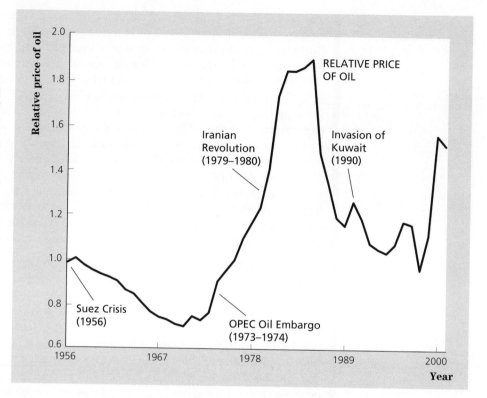

If real wages were growing for all groups, then the entries in the first two rows would decline steadily and the entries in the last two rows would rise steadily. In fact, the largest shifts occurred before 1975, particularly for men, so real wage growth clearly has slowed. Moreover, the proportion of men earning less than $20,000 has risen since 1975, so some real wages have declined.

The other trend in Canada—toward wage inequality by skill level—is most marked for men. Roughly speaking, over the past 30 years, the percentage of workers earning more than $40,000 has grown faster than the percentage earning less than $20,000 has declined.[21]

The trends to slower and more unequal wage growth also are evident for other countries. For example, in the United States, from 1963 through 1993, real wages of the top decile rose 40%, while those of the bottom decile fell 5%.[22] Although the increase in wage inequality has been greatest in the United States, it seems evident in many industrial countries.[23]

The explanations offered by most economists for both these trends focus on the pattern of technological change. The overall slowdown in real wage growth is generally

---

21. A third trend also is suggested by the table. The ratio of women's wages to men's wages—sometimes called the earnings ratio—has risen steadily. In this sense, wage inequality has declined. Most explanations of this trend focus on changes in labour supply, particularly the increased participation of women in the full-time labour force. While an increase in labour supply tends to lower the real wage, increased full-time job experience tends to raise the real wage by raising productivity.

22. Chinhui Juhn, Kevin M. Murphy, and Brooks Pierce, "Wage Inequality and the Rise in Returns to Skill," *Journal of Political Economy*, June 1993, pp. 410–442.

23. Francine D. Blau and Lawrence M. Kahn, "International Differences in Male Wage Inequality: Institutions versus Market Forces," *Journal of Political Economy*, August 1996, pp. 791–836.

TABLE 3.4

Wage Inequality since 1967

Constant (1990) dollar earnings of all workers

	1967	1975	1985	1997
Percentage of women less than $20,000	86.6	73.1	67.9	58.5
Percentage of men less than $20,000	44.7	35.1	42.3	40.0
Percentage of women more than $40,000	0.6	2.6	5.3	8.3
Percentage of men more than $40,000	9.9	23.3	24.5	25.9

Source: Adapted from Charles M. Beach and George A. Slotsve, "Polarization of Earnings in the Canadian Labour Market," in *Stabilization, Growth, and Distribution*, Thomas J. Courchene, ed., *Bell Canada Papers on Economic and Public Policy*, John Deutsch Institute for the Study of Economic Policy: Kingston, 1994, Tables 2 and 3. Data for 1997 are estimates from *Earnings of Men and Women*, Statistics Canada, cat. no. 13–217.

attributed to the slowdown in productivity growth in the world economy over the past two decades (discussed in the Application, "The Production Function and Productivity Growth in Canada," earlier in the chapter). Because of slow productivity growth, the marginal product of labour, *MPN*, and, thus, labour demand have grown slowly. Coupled with relatively rapid increases in labour supply (the fraction of the adult population in the workforce has risen from about 57% to roughly 66% during this period), slow growth in labour demand has held down the growth of real wages. Chapter 6 discusses further the general slowdown in productivity growth and its implications.

Some economists link the rising inequality in real wages to the character, not the pace, of technical change.[24] In particular, they argue that technical change during the past two decades has been *skill-biased*, meaning that it has raised the productivity of highly trained or educated workers more than that of the less skilled. For example, some new manufacturing techniques rely considerably more on worker initiative and problem solving than did the traditional assembly-line approach and, thus, require better-skilled workers. Computerization is another development that has, in many cases, increased the productivity of more skilled workers while squeezing out those without the education or training to use this new tool effectively. For example, a study by Alan Krueger of Princeton University found that US workers who are able to use computers in their jobs enjoy a 10% to 15% wage premium over similar workers who are not trained to use computers.[25]

Figure 3.14 illustrates the labour market effects of a skill-biased technical change. Here, we drop the simplifying assumption made earlier that all workers are identical and instead allow for two types of workers, skilled and unskilled.[26] Supply and demand for each type of worker are shown separately, with the market for skilled

24. For a discussion of this and alternative explanations—such as international trade or changes in labour supply—see Peter Kuhn, "Labour Market Polarization: Canada in International Perspective," *Bell Canada Papers on Economic and Social Policy*, 1995, pp. 283–322.

25. "How Computers Have Changed the Wage Structure: Evidence from Microdata, 1984–1989," *Quarterly Journal of Economics*, February 1993, pp. 33–60.

26. With two types of workers, there are three factors of production: capital, skilled labour, and unskilled labour. The production function thus becomes $Y = AF(K, N_{sk}, N_{unsk})$, where N_{sk} is the number of skilled and N_{unsk} the number of unskilled workers employed. A skill-biased technical change changes the function F so that the marginal product of skilled workers rises relative to the marginal product of unskilled workers.

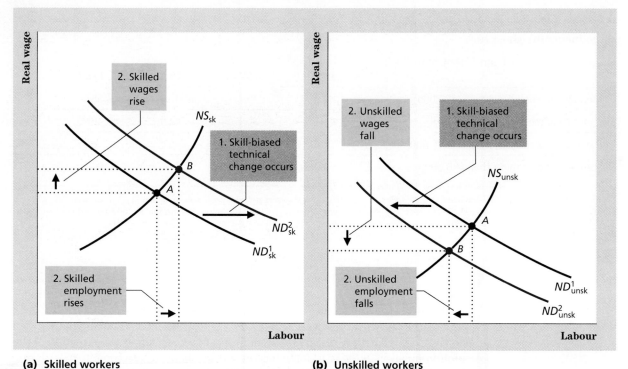

(a) Skilled workers   **(b) Unskilled workers**

FIGURE 3.14

THE EFFECTS OF SKILL-BIASED TECHNICAL CHANGE ON WAGE
INEQUALITY
The supply and demand for skilled labour is shown in (a), and the
supply and demand for unskilled labour is shown in (b). The initial
equilibrium is shown as point *A* in both parts. Because skilled
workers have a higher *MPN* than unskilled workers, their real wage
is higher.

A skill-biased technical change increases the *MPN* of skilled workers
relative to the *MPN* of unskilled workers. A rise in the *MPN* of
skilled workers raises the demand, from ND^1_{sk} to ND^2_{sk} in (a). If
the *MPN* of unskilled workers actually falls, demand for unskilled
labour falls, from ND^1_{unsk} to ND^2_{unsk} in (b). At the new equilibrium,
point *B* in both parts, the wages of skilled workers have risen relative
to those of unskilled workers.

workers shown in Figure 3.14(a) and the market for unskilled workers shown in
Figure 3.14(b). The supply of each type of worker reflects the number of people in
the labour force with each level of skills. For simplicity, and to focus on the effects
of a skill-biased technical change, we ignore population growth and changing
participation rates and assume that the labour supply curves are fixed. The demand
for each type of worker depends on the *MPN* of that type of worker, for constant
capital stock and number of employed workers of the other type.

The initial labour demand curves are ND^1_{sk} in Figure 3.14(a) and ND^1_{unsk} in
Figure 3.14(b), and the initial labour market equilibrium is at point *A* in both parts.
The real wages of skilled workers are higher than those of unskilled workers (i.e., the
equilibrium real wage at point *A* in Figure 3.14(a) is higher than the equilibrium
real wage at point *A* in Figure 3.14(b). This difference reflects the higher *MPN* and
lower supply of skilled workers, relative to unskilled workers.

A skill-biased technical change, such as the introduction of computers, raises the *MPN*
of skilled workers (who can accomplish more with the aid of a computer than they
could without one) but reduces the *MPN* of unskilled workers (who do not have
the training to be productive in a computerized workplace). Because the *MPN* curve

and the demand curve for labour are the same, this technical change raises the demand for skilled workers (from ND^1_{sk} to ND^2_{sk} in Figure 3.14(a)), but reduces the demand for unskilled workers (from ND^1_{unsk} to ND^2_{unsk} in Figure 3.14(b)). At the new equilibrium, at point B in both parts, skilled workers' real wages and employment have risen, and the wages and employment of the unskilled have fallen. The increased wage inequality predicted by this analysis is consistent with the facts. It also appears to be true that the fraction of employment composed of skilled workers has increased, while the fraction composed of unskilled workers has decreased.[27]

3.5 UNEMPLOYMENT

Our classical model of the labour market, which relies on supply–demand analysis, is useful for studying the wage rate and the level of employment in an economy and for showing how these variables are linked to output and productivity. However, this model of the labour market is based on the strong assumption that when the labour market is in equilibrium, all workers who are willing to work at the prevailing wage are able to find jobs. In reality, of course, not everyone who would like to work has a job; there is always some unemployment. The existence of unemployment implies that at any time, not all of society's labour resources are actively involved in producing goods and services.

We discuss the problem of unemployment several times in this book, notably in Chapter 13. Here, we introduce the topic by presenting some basic facts about unemployment and then turning to a preliminary economic analysis of it.

MEASURING UNEMPLOYMENT

In order to estimate the unemployment rate in Canada, each month, Statistics Canada surveys about 52,000 households. Each person over 15 years old in the surveyed households is assigned to one of three categories:

1. *Employed*, if the person worked full-time or part-time during the past week (or was on sick leave, on vacation, or on strike)

2. *Unemployed*, if the person was without work during the past week, had actively sought work in the past four weeks, and was available for work

3. *Not in the labour force*, if the person did not work during the past week and did not look for work during the past four weeks (examples are full-time students, retirees, and homemakers)

Table 3.5 shows the number of people in each category in August 2001. (A good source for these and other data about the labour market is described in the box, "In Touch with the Macroeconomy: Labour Market Data," p. 88.) In that month, there were 15.1 million employed and 1.1 million unemployed workers. The **labour force**

---

27. A complication not shown in Figure 3.14 arises if workers expect the skill bias of technical change to be permanent. In that case, skilled workers expect both their current and future wages to rise, which shifts their labour supply curve left; expected declines in the future wage of the unskilled shifts their labour supply curve to the right. This complication may reverse the predictions of the analysis about employment but only reinforces the main conclusion drawn here, that skilled workers' wages rise relative to those of unskilled workers. A second complication is that unskilled workers may respond to lower relative wages by acquiring skills through training. This response would reduce the supply of unskilled labour and increase the supply of skilled labour, reducing wage inequality. This adjustment seems to be very slow, however.

TABLE 3.5

Employment Status of the Canadian Adult Population, August 2001

Category	Number (Millions)	Share of Labour Force (Percent)	Share of Adult Population (Percent)
Employed workers	15.1	93.2	61.4 (employment ratio)
Unemployed workers	1.1	6.8 (unemployment rate)	4.5
Labour force (employed + unemployed workers)	16.2	100.0	65.9 (participation rate)
Not in labour force	8.4		34.1
Adult population (labour force + not in labour force)	24.6		100.0

Source: *Labour Force Information*, Statistics Canada, cat. no. 71-001.
Data are seasonally adjusted.

IN TOUCH WITH THE MACROECONOMY

LABOUR MARKET DATA

Statistics Canada collects and distributes a remarkable variety of data pertaining to the labour market. Information on employment and unemployment is available from *Labour Force Information* (cat. no. 71-001), which is issued monthly. This publication presents data for the aggregate Canadian economy and for various categories of workers based on age, gender, family status, education status, province, and industry. Historical data are published annually in *Historical Labour Force Statistics* (cat. no. 71-201).

The data in *Labour Force Information* are obtained from the monthly labour force survey of approximately 52,000 households (as described earlier in this chapter) involving approximately 97,000 respondents, carried out by personal interview or by telephone. One-sixth of the sample is replaced each month. Changes in labour market status, such as the transitions between employment and unemployment (and the other transitions shown in Figure 3.15), thus can be studied because five-sixths of those surveyed in any month also were surveyed in the previous month.

While information from the labour force survey is widely publicized in the press, further information on unemployment is available from censuses (every five years) and from the number of unemployment insurance (officially called employment insurance in Canada) claimants.

Information on wages and hours worked is available in *Employment, Earnings, and Hours* (cat. no. 72-002). This publication provides monthly data on average hourly earnings, which is a key measure of wage costs. Again, the data are disaggregated by industry and province. An increase in the labour input in the production function may occur because more people are working (total employment rises) or because average hours per worker rise (due to overtime, for example, or part-time jobs becoming full-time). This publication allows one to disentangle these changes.

consists of all employed and unemployed workers, so in August 2001, it totalled 16.2 million workers (15.1 million employed plus 1.1 million unemployed). The working-age population in August 2001 was 24.6 million, which leaves 8.4 million adults not in the labour force (total population of 24.6 million less 16.2 million in the labour force).

Some useful measures of the labour market are the unemployment rate, the participation rate, and the employment ratio. The **unemployment rate** is the fraction of the labour force that is unemployed. In August 2001, the unemployment rate was 6.8% (1.1 million unemployed divided by 16.2 million in the labour force). Figure 1.3 on page 5 shows the Canadian unemployment rate for the period since 1921.

The fraction of the working-age population in the labour force is the **participation rate**. Of the 24.6 million working-age people in Canada in August 2001, 16.2 million were in the labour force, so the participation rate was 65.9%. In contrast, the participation rate 35 years ago was 57%. The increase is due to a rise in the participation rate of women, from 35% to 60%. During the same period, the participation rate of men fell from 80% to 72%.

The **employment ratio** is the employed fraction of the working-age population. In August 2001, the employment rate was 61.4% (15.1 million employed divided by the working-age population of 24.6 million). With an employment ratio of 61.4%, 38.6% of the adult population was not employed in August 2001. Of this 38.6%, 4.5% reflected unemployment and the remaining 34.1% reflected people not in the labour force. Thus, a large majority of working-age people who are not employed at any given time are not in the labour force rather than unemployed.

CHANGES IN EMPLOYMENT STATUS

The labour market is in a constant state of flux. Even when the unemployment rate remains unchanged from one month to the next, during the month hundreds of thousands of Canadian workers become unemployed and hundreds of thousands become employed.

Figure 3.15, based on research by Stephen Jones of McMaster University and Craig Riddell of the University of British Columbia, shows how workers change their employment status (that is, whether they are employed, unemployed, or not in the labour force) in a typical month. The arrow between each pair of boxes represents a change from one employment status to another, and the number on the arrow shows the number of people in one status who switch to the other status in a typical month. Thus, for example, the arrow from the employed box to the unemployed box has the label 195,690, indicating that 195,690 of employed workers in a typical month will become unemployed by the following month. Typically less than half of all those becoming unemployed have lost their jobs, while the remainder are job leavers or are entering or re-entering the labour force.

What are the employment prospects of an unemployed worker? Figure 3.15 shows that 21.8% of the unemployed people in a typical month will be employed the following month and that 17.2% of the unemployed people will be out of the labour force the next month. The remaining 61% of the unemployed people will still be unemployed the following month. Of the 17.2% of the unemployed who leave the labour force each month, some are **discouraged workers**, or people who have become so discouraged by lack of success at finding a job that they stop searching. Other unemployed workers leave the labour force to engage in some activity outside the labour market, such as homemaking or going to school.

FIGURE 3.15

CHANGES IN EMPLOYMENT
STATUS IN A TYPICAL
MONTH

The arrow between two boxes represents a change from one employment status to another; the label on the arrow shows the number of people in one status who switched to the other status in a typical month, during the period 1990–1994. For example, the arrow from the unemployed box to the employed box shows that 326,346 unemployed workers (21.8% of the unemployed) became employed the following month. The arrow from the employed box to the unemployed box shows that 195,690 employed workers (1.5% of the employed) became unemployed during the following month.

Source: Adapted from Stephen R. G. Jones and W. Craig Riddell, "Gross Flows of Labour in Canada and the United States," *Canadian Public Policy*, February 1998, pp. 103–120.

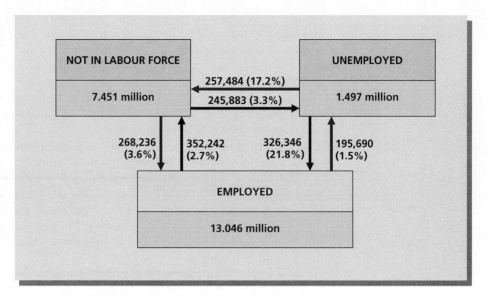

HOW LONG ARE PEOPLE UNEMPLOYED?

Of the 61% of those unemployed in a typical month who remain unemployed the following month, some may remain unemployed for a considerable period of time. The length of time that an individual is continuously unemployed is called an **unemployment spell**. The length of time that an unemployment spell lasts is called its **duration**. The duration of an unemployment spell determines, in large part, the degree of hardship suffered by an unemployed worker. At one extreme, a one-week unemployment spell will cost a worker a week's pay but probably will not seriously affect the worker's standard of living. At the other extreme, an unemployment spell that lasts for several months may force an unemployed worker to exhaust his or her life savings or to sell the car or house.

The duration of unemployment spells in Canada is characterized by two seemingly contradictory statements:

1. Most unemployment spells are of short duration, about two months or less.

2. Most people who are unemployed on a given date are experiencing unemployment spells with long duration.

To understand how both these statements can be true, consider an economy with 100 people in the labour force. Suppose that at the beginning of every month, two workers become unemployed and remain unemployed for one month before finding a new job. In addition, at the beginning of every year, four workers become unemployed and remain unemployed for the entire year.

In this example, there are 28 spells of unemployment during a year: 24 spells that last one month, and four spells that last one year. Thus, 24 of 28, or 86%, of the spells last only one month, which is consistent with the first statement: Most spells are short.

How many people are unemployed on a given day, say, on May 15? There are six unemployed workers on May 15: two unemployed workers who began one-month spells of unemployment on May 1, and four unemployed workers who began one-year spells of unemployment on January 1. Thus, four of six, or 67%, of the workers unemployed on May 15 are experiencing one-year spells of unemployment, which is consistent with the second statement: Most people who are unemployed on a given date are experiencing long spells of unemployment.

WHY THERE ALWAYS ARE UNEMPLOYED PEOPLE

Even when the economy is growing vigorously and many new jobs are being created, some people remain unemployed. Why is unemployment apparently a permanent feature of the economy? Here, we discuss frictional unemployment and structural unemployment, two types of unemployment that always exist in the labour market and, thus, prevent the unemployment rate from ever reaching zero.

FRICTIONAL UNEMPLOYMENT

The labour market is characterized by a great deal of searching by both workers and firms. Unemployed workers search for suitable jobs, and firms with vacancies search for suitable workers. If all workers were identical and all jobs were identical, these searches would be short and easy: Unemployed workers would simply have to find firms that had vacancies, and they would immediately be hired. The problem, of course, is that neither jobs nor workers are identical. Workers vary in their talents, skills, experience, goals, geographic location (and willingness to move), and in the amount of time and energy they are willing to commit to their job. Similarly, jobs vary in the skills and experience required, working conditions, location, hours, and pay. Because of these differences, an unemployed worker may search for several weeks or more before finding a suitable job; similarly, a firm may search for a considerable time before it is able to hire a suitable worker.

   The unemployment that arises as workers search for suitable jobs and firms search for suitable workers is called **frictional unemployment**. Because the economy is dynamic, with jobs continually being created and destroyed and workers continually entering and exiting the labour force, there is always some frictional unemployment as workers are matched with appropriate jobs.

STRUCTURAL UNEMPLOYMENT

In addition to those suffering long spells of unemployment, many people are chronically unemployed. Although their unemployment spells may be broken by brief periods of employment or being out of the labour force, workers who are **chronically unemployed** are unemployed a large part of the time. Long spells of unemployment and chronic unemployment cannot be attributed primarily to the matching process. People in these situations do not seem to search for work very intensively and do not generally find stable employment. The long-term and chronic unemployment that exists even when the economy is not in a recession is called **structural unemployment**.

   Structural unemployment occurs for two primary reasons. First, unskilled or low-skilled workers often are unable to obtain desirable, long-term jobs. The jobs available to them typically offer relatively low wages and little chance for training or advancement. Most directly related to the issue of structural unemployment is the fact that jobs held by low-skilled workers often do not last long. After a few months, the job may end or the worker may quit or be fired, thus entering another spell of unemployment. Some workers with low skill levels eventually get enough training or experience to obtain more secure, long-term jobs. Because of such factors as inadequate education, discrimination, and language barriers, however, some unskilled workers never make the transition to long-term employment and remain chronically unemployed.

The second source of structural unemployment is the reallocation of labour from industries that are shrinking, or regions that are depressed, to areas that are growing. When industries find that their product is no longer in demand (for example, buggy whip manufacturers) or that they are no longer competitive (for example, Canadian garment producers who lost much of the market to overseas manufacturers), workers in these industries lose their jobs. At the same time, some industries will be growing (for example, health-care providers and computer software developers). To prevent unemployment from rising requires that workers who lose jobs in declining industries be matched somehow with jobs in growing industries. This matching may involve a long period of unemployment, especially if workers need to relocate to another city or province or be trained for a new job.

THE NATURAL RATE OF UNEMPLOYMENT

Because of the combination of frictional and structural unemployment, an economy's unemployment rate is never zero, even when the economy is at its full-employment level. The rate of unemployment that prevails when output and employment are at the full-employment level is called the **natural rate of unemployment**, $\bar{u}$. The natural rate of unemployment reflects unemployment owing to frictional and structural causes. Although there is no single official measure of the natural rate of unemployment, many economists believe that the natural rate was roughly 5% during the 1960s, increased gradually to about 8% in the 1980s, then fell to about 7% in the 1990s. Chapter 13 discusses the reasons for the increase in the natural rate.

As output fluctuates around its full-employment level, the unemployment rate fluctuates around the natural rate. The difference between actual unemployment rate and the natural rate of unemployment is called **cyclical unemployment**. Specifically, cyclical unemployment = $u - \bar{u}$, where u is the actual unemployment rate and $\bar{u}$ is the natural rate. Cyclical unemployment is positive whenever the economy's output and employment are below full-employment levels; it is negative when output and employment exceed full-employment levels.

CHAPTER SUMMARY

1. The production function tells us the amount of output that can be produced with any given quantities of capital and labour. The production function can be graphed as a relationship between output and capital, holding labour fixed, or as a relationship between output and labour, holding capital fixed. In either case, the production function slopes upward, implying that greater use of capital or labour leads to more output. A shift in the production function, which indicates a change in the amount of output that can be produced with given amounts of capital and labour, is called a supply shock.

2. The extra output that can be produced when the capital stock is increased by one unit, with labour held constant, is called the marginal product of capital (*MPK*). In a graph of the production function relating output to capital, the *MPK* can be measured as the slope of the production function. The *MPK* falls as the capital stock increases, reflecting the diminishing marginal productivity of capital. Similarly, the marginal product of labour (*MPN*) is the extra output that can be produced when labour increases by one unit, with capital held constant. The *MPN*—which can be measured as the slope of the production function relating

output to labour—falls as employment rises, indicating that labour also has diminishing marginal productivity.

3. To maximize profits, firms demand labour to the point that the marginal revenue product of labour (*MRPN*) equals the nominal wage, *W*; or, equivalently, to the point that the *MPN* equals the real wage, *w*.

4. The labour demand curve is identical to the *MPN* curve. Because an increase in the real wage causes firms to demand less labour, the labour demand curve slopes downward. Factors that increase the amount of labour demanded at any real wage, such as a beneficial supply shock or an increase in the capital stock, shift the labour demand curve to the right. Aggregate labour demand is the sum of the labour demands of firms in the economy.

5. An individual's decision about how much labour to supply reflects a comparison of the benefit and cost of working and additional hour. The benefit of working an additional hour is the additional real income earned, which can be used to increase consumption. The cost of working an extra hour is the loss of an hour's leisure. An individual's happiness, or utility, is maximized by supplying labour to the point where the cost of working an extra hour (the utility lost because of reduced leisure) equals the benefit (the utility gained because of increased income).

6. An increase in the real wage has competing substitution and income effects on the amount of labour supplied. The substitution effect of a higher real wage increases the amount of labour supplied, as the worker responds to the increased reward for working. The income effect reduces the amount of labour supplied, as the higher real wage makes the worker wealthier and, thus, able to afford more leisure. The longer an increase in the real wage is expected to last, the stronger the income effect is. Thus, a temporary increase in the real wage will increase the amount of labour supplied. A permanent increase in the real wage will increase the amount of labour supplied by a smaller amount than a temporary increase in the real wage of the same size, however, and may even lead to a decrease in the amount of labour supplied.

7. The labour supply curve relates the amount of labour supplied to the current real wage. The labour supply curve slopes upward, indicating that an increase in the current real wage—with other factors, including the expected future real wage, held fixed—raises the amount of labour supplied. Factors that decrease the quantity of labour supplied at the current real wage and, thus, shift the labour supply curve to the left include an increase in wealth and an increase in the expected future real wage. Aggregate labour supply, which is the sum of labour supplies of the individuals in the economy, is also influenced by changes in the working-age population and social or legal factors that affect the number of people participating in the labour market.

8. The classical supply–demand model of the labour market is based on the assumption that the real wage adjusts relatively quickly to equalize the quantities of labour demanded and supplied. The equilibrium level of employment, which arises when wages and prices in the economy have fully adjusted, is called the full-employment level of employment. Fluctuations in employment and the real wage are the result of factors that shift the labour supply curve and/or the labour demand curve.

9. Full-employment output, or potential output, is the amount of output produced when employment is at its full-employment level. Increases in the full-employment level of employment or beneficial supply shocks increase the full-employment level of output.

10. Working-age people without jobs are classified as unemployed if they looked for work during the preceding four weeks; they are classified as not in the labour force if they have not been looking for work. The labour force consists of all employed workers plus all unemployed workers. The unemployment rate is the fraction of the labour force that is unemployed.

11. Frictional unemployment reflects the time required for potential workers to find suitable jobs and for firms with vacancies to find suitable workers. Structural unemployment—long-term and chronic unemployment that exists even when the economy is not in recession—occurs because some workers do not have the skills needed to obtain long-term employment or because of delays in reallocating workers from economically depressed areas to those that are growing. Frictional and structural unemployment together account for the natural rate of unemployment, which is the unemployment rate that exists when employment is at its full-employment level. Cyclical unemployment is the excess of the actual unemployment rate over the natural rate of unemployment.

KEY DIAGRAM 1

THE PRODUCTION FUNCTION

The production function indicates how much output an economy or a firm can produce with any given quantities of capital and labour.

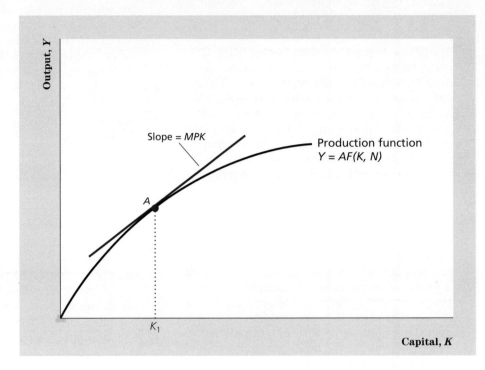

DIAGRAM ELEMENTS

- The production function graphed here has the amount of output produced, Y, on the vertical axis and the quantity of capital used, K, on the horizontal axis, with labour, N, held constant. It can also be drawn as a relationship between output and labour, with capital held constant. The production function relating output to labour looks like the graph shown here.

- The equation for the production function is $Y = AF(K, N)$, where A (total factor productivity, or simply productivity) measures how effectively the economy uses capital and labour.

ANALYSIS

- The production function slopes upward, reflecting the fact that an increase in the quantity of capital will allow more output to be produced.

- The production function becomes flatter from left to right, implying that the larger the capital stock already is, the less extra output is gained by adding another unit of capital. The fact that extra capital becomes less productive as the capital stock grows is called diminishing marginal productivity of capital.

- With labour held constant, if an increase in capital of ΔK leads to an increase in output of ΔY, then $\Delta Y / \Delta K$ is called the marginal product of capital, or MPK. The MPK is measured graphically by the slope of the line tangent to the production function. For example, in the diagram, the MPK when the capital stock is K_1 equals the slope of the line tangent to the production function at point A.

FACTORS THAT SHIFT THE CURVE

- Any change that allows more output to be produced for given quantities of capital and labour—a beneficial supply shock—shifts the production function upward. Examples of beneficial supply shocks include new inventions and improved management techniques.

- Any change that reduces the amount of output that can be produced for given quantities of capital and labour—an adverse supply shock—shifts the production function downward. Examples of adverse supply shocks include bad weather and the depletion of natural resources.

KEY DIAGRAM 2

THE LABOUR MARKET

An economy's level of employment and the real wage are determined in the labour market.

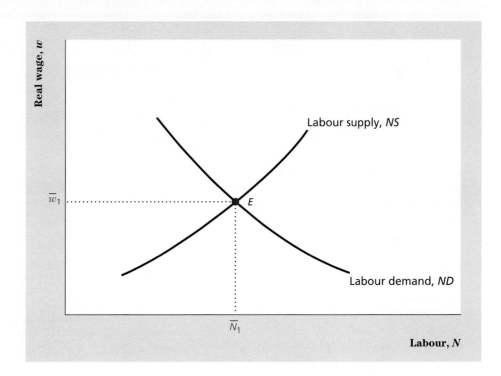

DIAGRAM ELEMENTS

- The current real wage, w, is on the vertical axis, and the level of employment, N, is on the horizontal axis. The variable N may also represent alternative measures of labour, such as total hours worked.

- The labour demand curve, ND, shows the amount of labour that firms want to employ at each current real wage. The labour demand curve slopes downward because firms find hiring more labour profitable when the real wage falls. The labour demand curve for an individual firm is the same as the MPN curve, which shows the marginal product of labour at each level of employment.

- The labour supply curve, NS, shows the amount of labour offered by workers at each current real wage. The labour supply curve slopes upward because an increase in the current real wage, with other factors held constant, increases the amount of labour supplied.

ANALYSIS

- Equilibrium in the labour market occurs when the quantity of labour demanded equals the quantity of labour supplied. In the figure, equilibrium employment is $\overline{N}_1$, and the equilibrium real wage is $\overline{w}_1$. The equilibrium level of employment, which occurs after wages and prices have fully adjusted, is called the full-employment level of employment.

FACTORS THAT SHIFT THE CURVES

- Any factor that increases the amount of labour demanded at a given current real wage shifts the labour demand curve to the right. Such factors include an increase in the marginal product of labour at any given level of employment and an increase in the capital stock. See Summary table 3.

- Any factor that increases the amount of labour supplied at a given current real wage shifts the labour supply curve to the right. Such factors include a decline in wealth, a drop in the expected future real wage, a rise in the working-age population, and an increase in labour force participation. See Summary table 4.

KEY TERMS

KEY EQUATIONS

$$Y = AF\,(K,\,N) \qquad (3.1)$$

The production function indicates how much output Y can be produced for given quantities of capital K and labour N and for a given level of total factor productivity A.

$$\overline{Y} = AF\,(K,\,\overline{N}) \qquad (3.4)$$

Full-employment output $\overline{Y}$ is the quantity of output supplied by firms when wages and prices have fully adjusted, and employment equals its equilibrium value $\overline{N}$.

REVIEW QUESTIONS

1. What is a production function? What are some factors that can cause a nation's production function to shift over time? What do you have to know besides an economy's production function to know how much output the economy can produce?

2. The production function slopes upward, but its slope declines from left to right. Give an economic interpretation of each of these properties of the production function.

3. Define marginal product of capital, or *MPK*. How can the *MPK* be shown graphically?

4. Explain why the profit-maximizing level of employment for a firm occurs when the marginal revenue product of labour equals the nominal wage. How can this profit-maximizing condition be expressed in real terms?

5. What is the *MPN* curve? How is the *MPN* curve related to the production function? How is it related to labour demand?

6. Use the concepts of income effect and substitution effect to explain why a temporary increase in the real wage increases the amount of labour supplied, but a permanent increase in the real wage may decrease the quantity of labour supplied.

7. What two variables are related by the aggregate labour supply curve? What are some factors that cause the aggregate labour supply curve to shift?

8. Define full-employment output. How is full-employment output affected by an increase in labour supply? by a beneficial supply shock?

9. Why is the classical model of the labour market discussed in this chapter not very useful for studying unemployment?

10. Define the following: *labour force*, *unemployment rate*, *participation rate*, and *employment ratio*.

11. Define unemployment spell and duration. What are the two seemingly contradictory facts about unemployment spells? Why are the two facts not actually contradictory?

12. What is frictional unemployment? Why is a certain amount of frictional unemployment probably necessary in a well-functioning economy?

13. What is structural unemployment? What are the two principal sources of structural unemployment?

14. Define the natural rate of unemployment and cyclical unemployment. What does negative cyclical unemployment mean?

NUMERICAL PROBLEMS

1. The following data give real GDP, Y, capital, K, and labour, N, for the Canadian economy in various years.

Year	Y	K	N
1960	223	225	5.9
1970	368	352	7.9
1980	577	498	11.1
1990	768	650	13.1

Units and sources are the same as in Table 3.1. Assume that the production function is $Y = AK^{0.3}N^{0.7}$.

a. How much did Canadian total factor productivity grow between 1960 and 1970? between 1970 and 1980? between 1980 and 1990?

b. What happened to the marginal product of labour between 1960 and 1990? Calculate the marginal product numerically as the extra output gained by adding one million workers in each of the two years. (The data for employment, N, is measured in millions of workers, so an increase of one million workers is an increase of 1.0.)

2. An economy has the production function

$$Y = 0.2(K + \sqrt{N}).$$

In the current period $K = 100$ and $N = 100$.

a. Graph the relationship between output and capital, holding labour constant at its current value. What is the *MPK*? Does the marginal productivity of capital diminish?

b. Graph the relationship between output and labour, holding capital constant at its current value. Find the *MPN* for an increase of labour from 100 to 110. Compare this result with the *MPN* for an increase in labour from 110 to 120. Does the marginal productivity of labour diminish?

3. Acme Widget, Inc. has the following production function

Number of Workers	Number of Widgets Produced
0	0
1	8
2	15
3	21
4	26
5	30
6	33

a. Find the *MPN* for each level of employment.

b. Acme can get $5 for each widget it produces. How many workers will it hire if the nominal wage is $38? if it is $27? if it is $22?

c. Graph the relationship between Acme's labour demand and the nominal wage. How does this graph differ from a labour demand curve? Graph Acme's labour demand curve.

d. With the nominal wage fixed at $38, the price of widgets doubles from $5 each to $10 each. What happens to Acme's labour demand and production?

e. With the nominal wage fixed at $38 and the price of widgets fixed at $5, the introduction of a new automatic widget maker doubles the number of widgets that the same number of workers can produce. What happens to labour demand and production?

f. What is the relationship between your answers to part (d) and part (e)? Explain.

4. The marginal product of labour (measured in units of output) for a certain firm is

$$MPN = A(100 - N),$$

where A measures productivity and N is the number of labour hours used in production. The price of output is $2 per unit.

a. If $A = 1.0$, what will be the demand for labour if the nominal wage is \$10? if it is \$20? Graph the demand curve for labour. What is the equilibrium real wage if the supply of labour is fixed at 95?

b. Repeat part (a) for $A = 2.0$.

5. Consider an economy in which the marginal product of labour MPN is $MPN = 309 - 2N$, where N is the amount of labour used. The amount of labour supplied, NS, is given by $NS = 22 + 12w + 2T$, where w is the real wage and T is a lump-sum tax levied on individuals.

a. Use the concepts of income effect and substitution effect to explain why an increase in lump-sum taxes will increase the amount of labour supplied.

b. Suppose that $T = 35$. What are the equilibrium values of employment and the real wage?

c. With T remaining equal to 35, the government passes minimum-wage legislation that requires firms to pay a real wage greater than or equal to 7. What are the resulting values of employment and the real wage?

6. Suppose that the production function is

$$Y = 9K^{0.5}N^{0.5}.$$

With this production function, the marginal product of labour is

$$MPN = 4.5K^{0.5}N^{-0.5}.$$

The capital stock is

$$K = 25.$$

The labour supply curve is

$$NS = 100[(1 - t)w]^2,$$

where w is the real wage rate, t is the tax rate on labour income, and hence

$$(1 - t)w$$

is the after-tax real wage rate.

a. Assume that the tax rate on labour income, t, equals zero. Find the equation of the labour demand curve. Calculate the equilibrium levels of the real wage and employment, the level of full-employment output, and the total after-tax wage income of workers.

b. Repeat part (a) under the assumption that the tax rate on labour income, t, equals 0.6.

c. Suppose that a minimum wage of $w = 2$ is imposed. If the tax rate on labour income, t, equals zero, what are the resulting values of employment and the real wage? Does the introduction of the minimum wage increase the total income of workers, taken as a group?

7. Consider an economy with 500 people in the labour force. At the beginning of every month, five people lose their jobs and remain unemployed for exactly one month; one month later, they find new jobs and become employed. In addition, on January 1 of each year, 20 people lose their jobs and remain unemployed for six months before finding new jobs. Finally, on July 1 of each year, 20 people lose their jobs and remain unemployed for six months before finding new jobs.

a. What is the unemployment rate in this economy in a typical month?

b. What fraction of unemployment spells lasts for one month? What fraction lasts for six months?

c. What is the average duration of an unemployment spell?

d. On any particular date, what fraction of the unemployed are suffering a long spell (six months) of unemployment?

8. Use the data in Figure 3.15 to calculate how many people become unemployed during a typical month. How many become employed? How many leave the labour force?

9. If you have studied multivariate calculus, you can use that tool to find marginal products and the firm's demand for labour. Suppose that the production function is:

$$Y = AK^a N^{1-a},$$

and that a is a positive fraction.

a. By differentiating the production function with respect to capital, find the marginal product of capital. Similarly, find the marginal product of labour.

b. How are the marginal products affected by an adverse supply shock?

c. Suppose that a competitive firm tries to maximize profits, given by:

$$P \cdot AK^a N^{1-a} - WN,$$

with its capital stock fixed in the short run. By differentiating profits with respect to N, find the firm's labour demand curve and graph it.

ANALYTICAL PROBLEMS

1. **a.** A technological breakthrough raises a country's total factor productivity A by 10%. Show how this change affects the graphs of both the production function relating output to capital and the production function relating output to labour.

b. Show that a 10% increase in A also increases the MPK and the MPN by 10% at any level of capital and labour. (*Hint*: What happens to ΔY for any increase in capital ΔK or for any increase in labour ΔN?)

c. Can a beneficial supply shock leave the *MPK* and *MPN* unaffected? Show graphically.

2. How would each of the following affect the current level of full-employment output? Explain.

a. A large number of immigrants enter the country.

b. Energy supplies become depleted.

c. New teaching techniques improve the educational performance of high school students.

d. A new law mandates the shutdown of some unsafe forms of capital.

3. During the 1980s and 1990s, the average rate of unemployment in Europe was high. Some economists claimed that this rate was in part the result of "real-wage rigidity," a situation in which unions kept real wages above their market-clearing levels.

a. Accepting for the sake of argument that real wages were too high in Europe in the 1980s and 1990s, show how this would lead to unemployment (a situation where people who would like to work at the going wage cannot find jobs).

b. What is the effect of real-wage rigidity on the output actually supplied by firms, relative to the output they would supply if there were no real-wage rigidity?

4. How would each of the following affect Helena Handbasket's supply of labour?

a. The value of Helena's home triples in an unexpectedly hot real estate market.

b. Originally an unskilled worker, Helena acquires skills that give her access to a higher-paying job. Assume that her preferences about leisure are not affected by the change in jobs.

c. A temporary income tax surcharge raises the percentage of her income that she must pay in taxes, for the current year only. (Taxes are proportional to income in Helena's country.)

5. Suppose that under a new law all businesses must pay a tax equal to 6% of their sales revenue. Assume that this tax is not passed on to consumers. Instead, consumers pay the same prices after the tax is imposed as they did before. What is the effect of this tax on labour demand? If the labour supply curve is unchanged, what will be the effect of the tax on employment and the real wage?

6. Can the unemployment rate and the employment ratio rise during the same month? Can the participation rate fall at the same time that the employment ratio rises? Explain.

Chapter 4
CONSUMPTION, SAVING, AND INVESTMENT

Chapter 3 focused on some of the factors determining the amount of output produced, or *supplied*, in the economy. This chapter considers the factors that underlie the economywide *demand* for goods and services. In other words, we move from examining how much is produced to examining how that production is used.

Recall from Chapter 2 that aggregate demand (spending) in the economy has four components: the demand for consumer goods and services by households (consumption), the demand for new capital goods by firms and governments (investment), government purchases of goods and services, and the net demand for domestic goods by foreigners (net exports). Because the levels of government purchases and investment are determined primarily by the political process, macroeconomic analysis usually treats these components of spending as given. For this chapter, we also assume that the economy is closed so that net exports are zero (we drop the closed-economy assumption in Chapter 5). That leaves two major components of spending—consumption and private investment—to be discussed in this chapter. Section 4.1 presents the factors that determine how much households choose to consume, and Section 4.2 looks at the decision by firms about how much to invest.

We have said that this chapter is about the aggregate demand for goods and services. However, we could just as easily say that it is about a seemingly very different (but equally important) topic: the determination of saving and capital formation. Studying the aggregate demand for goods and services is the same as studying the factors that determine saving and capital formation for the following reasons: First, saving is simply what is left after an economic unit (say, a household) decides how much of its income to consume. Thus, the decision about how much to consume is the same as the decision about how much to save. Second, investment spending is part of the aggregate demand for goods and services, but it also represents the acquisition of new capital goods by firms; and so, in studying investment spending, we are also looking at the factors that lead an economy to acquire new factories, machines, and housing. In effect, we do two things at once in this chapter:

- We explore the determinants of the aggregate demand for goods, which prepares you for future discussions of topics such as the role of spending fluctuations in business cycles.

- While exploring aggregate demand we also examine the factors affecting saving and capital formation, which prepares you for future discussions of the sources of economic growth and other issues.

In making many economic decisions, including those we consider in this chapter, people must trade off the present against the future. In deciding how much to consume and save, for example, a household must weigh the benefits of enjoying more consumption today against the benefits of putting aside some of its income as saving for consumption in the future. Similarly, in deciding how much to invest, a firm's manager must determine how much to spend today in order to increase the firm's productive capacity one, five, or even 20 years from now. In making these trade-offs, households and firms must take into account their expectations about the future of the economy, including expectations about government policy.

In Chapter 3 , we asked, "What forces act to bring the labour market into equilibrium?" We close this chapter by asking the same question for the goods market. The goods market is in equilibrium when the quantity of goods and services that producers want to supply (discussed in Chapter 3) equals the quantity of goods and services demanded by households, firms, and the government (discussed in this chapter). Equivalently, the goods market is in equilibrium when desired saving in the economy equals desired investment. We show that the real interest rate plays a key role in bringing the goods market into equilibrium.

4.1 CONSUMPTION AND SAVING

We begin consideration of the demand for goods and services by discussing the factors that affect consumer spending. Because consumption spending by households is, by far, the largest component of the demand for goods and services—accounting for about 60% of total spending—changes in consumers' willingness to spend have major implications for the behaviour of the economy.

Besides the sheer size of consumption spending, another reason to study consumption is that the individual's or household's decision about how much to consume is closely linked to another important economic decision, the decision about how much to save. Indeed, for given levels of disposable income, the decision about how much to consume and the decision about how much to save are really the same decision. For example, a college student with a part-time job that pays $4,000 per year after taxes might decide to spend $3,700 per year on clothes, food, entertainment, and other consumption. If she does consume this amount, her saving will automatically be $300 ($4,000 minus $3,700) per year. Equivalently, she might decide to save $300 per year. If she succeeds in saving $300, her consumption automatically is $3,700 ($4,000 minus $300) per year. Because the decision about how much to consume and the decision about how much to save actually are two sides of the same coin, we analyze them together.

From a macroeconomic perspective, we are interested in the aggregate, or national, levels of consumption and saving. We define the national level of *desired consumption*, C^d, as the aggregate quantity of goods and services that households want to consume, given income and other factors that determine households' economic opportunities. We will analyze desired consumption and its response to various factors, such as income and interest rates, by examining the consumption decisions of individual households. The aggregate level of desired consumption, C^d, is obtained by adding up the desired consumption of all households. Thus, any factor that increases the desired consumption of individual households will increase C^d, and any factor that decreases the desired consumption of individual households will decrease C^d.

Just as a household's consumption decision and saving decision are closely linked, a country's desired consumption is closed linked to its desired national saving. Specifically, *desired national saving*, S^d, is the level of national saving that occurs when aggregate consumption is at its desired level. Recall from Chapter 2

(Eq. 2.8) that if net factor payments from abroad (*NFP*) equal zero (as must be true in a closed economy), national saving, *S*, equals $Y - C - G$, where *Y* is output, *C* is consumption, and *G* is government purchases. Because desired national saving, S^d, is the level of national saving that occurs when consumption equals its desired level, we obtain an expression for desired national saving by substituting desired consumption, C^d, for consumption, *C*, in the definition of national saving. This substitution yields

$$S^d = Y - C^d - G. \tag{4.1}$$

We can gain insight into the factors that affect consumption and saving at the national level by considering how consumption and saving decisions are made at the individual level. Appendix 4.A provides a more formal analysis of this decision-making process.

THE CONSUMPTION AND SAVING DECISION OF AN INDIVIDUAL

Let us consider the case of Prudence, a bookkeeper for the Spectacular Eyeglasses Company. Prudence earns $20,000 per year after taxes. Hence she could, if she chose, consume $20,000 worth of goods and services every year. Prudence, however, has two other options.

First, she can save by consuming less than $20,000 per year. Why should Prudence consume less than her income allows? The reason is that she is thinking about the future. By consuming less than her current income, she will accumulate savings that will allow her, at some time in the future, to consume more than her income. For example, Prudence may expect her income to be very low when she retires; by saving during her working life, she will be able to consume more than her income during retirement. Indeed, the desire to provide for retirement is an important motivation for saving in the real world.

Alternatively, Prudence could consume more than her current income by borrowing or by drawing down previously accumulated savings. If she borrows $5,000 from a bank, for example, she could consume as much as $25,000 worth of goods and services this year, even though her income is only $20,000. Consuming more than her income is enjoyable for Prudence, but the cost to her is that at some future time, when she must repay the loan, she will have to consume less than her income.

If Prudence consumes less today, she will be able to consume more in the future, and vice versa. In other words, she faces a trade-off between current consumption and future consumption. The rate at which Prudence trades off current and future consumption depends on the real interest rate prevailing in the economy. Suppose that Prudence can earn a real interest rate of *r* per year on her saving and, for simplicity, suppose that if she borrows, she must pay the same real interest rate *r* on the loan. These assumptions imply that Prudence can trade one unit of current (this year's) consumption for $1 + r$ units of future (next year's) consumption. For example, suppose Prudence reduces her consumption today by one dollar, thereby increasing her saving by one dollar. Because she earns a real interest rate of *r* on her saving, the dollar she saves today will be worth $1 + r$ dollars one year from now.[1]

---

1. We are assuming that there is zero inflation over the coming year so that $1 purchases the same amount of real goods in each period. Alternatively, we could say that since the real interest rate is *r*, each *real* dollar Prudence saves today will be worth $1 + r$ *real* dollars one year from now.

Under the assumption that Prudence uses the extra $1 + r$ dollars to increase her next year's consumption, she has effectively traded one dollar's worth of consumption today for $1 + r$ dollars of consumption a year from now.

Similarly, Prudence can trade $1 + r$ real dollars of future consumption for one extra dollar of consumption today. She does so by borrowing and spending an extra dollar today. In a year, she will have to repay the loan with interest, a total of $1 + r$ dollars. Because she has to repay $1 + r$ dollars next year, her consumption next year will be $1 + r$ dollars less than it would be otherwise. So, the "price" to Prudence of one dollar's worth of extra consumption today is $1 + r$ dollars' worth of consumption in the future.

The real interest rate, r, determines the relative price of current consumption and future consumption. Given this relative price, how should Prudence choose between consuming today and consuming in the future? One extreme possibility would be for her to borrow heavily and consume much more than her income today. The problem with this strategy is that after repaying her loan, Prudence would be able to consume almost nothing in the future. The opposite, but equally extreme, approach would be for Prudence to save nearly all of her current income. This strategy would allow her to consume a great deal in the future, but at the cost of near-starvation today.

Realistically, most people would choose neither of those extreme strategies but would instead try to avoid sharp fluctuations in consumption. The desire to have a relatively even pattern of consumption over time—avoiding periods of very high or very low consumption—is known as the **consumption-smoothing motive**. Because of her consumption-smoothing motive, Prudence will try to spread her consumption spending more or less evenly over time, rather than bingeing in one period and starving in another.

Next, we will see how the consumption-smoothing motive guides Prudence's behaviour when changes occur in some important determinants of her economic well being, including her current income, her expected future income, and her wealth. As we consider each of these changes, we will hold constant the real interest rate r and, hence, the relative price of current consumption and future consumption. Later, we will discuss what happens if the real interest rate changes.

EFFECT OF CHANGES IN CURRENT INCOME

Current income is an important factor affecting consumption and saving decisions. To illustrate, suppose that Prudence receives a one-time bonus of $3,000 at work, which increases her current year's income by $3,000. (We ignore income taxes; equivalently, we can assume that the bonus is actually larger than $3,000 but that after paying her taxes, Prudence finds that her current income has increased by $3,000.) What will she do with this extra income? Prudence could splurge and spend the entire bonus on a trip to Hawaii. If she spends the entire bonus, her current consumption will increase by $3,000 but because she has not increased her saving, her future consumption will be unchanged. Alternatively, she could save the entire bonus, leaving her current consumption unchanged but using the bonus plus the interest it earns to increase her consumption in the future. Because of the consumption-smoothing motive, however, Prudence is unlikely to follow either of these extreme strategies. Instead, she will spend part of the bonus (increasing current consumption) and save the rest (enabling her to increase future consumption as well).

The portion of her bonus that Prudence spends will depend on such factors as her willingness to defer gratification and her assessment of her current and future needs. We define Prudence's **marginal propensity to consume**, or MPC, as the fraction of additional current income that she consumes in the current period. Because Prudence consumes some but not all of her extra income, her MPC will be between zero and one. Suppose, for example that Prudence has an MPC equal to 0.4, so that she consumes 0.4, or 40%, of an increase in current income. Then, when she receives a $3,000 bonus, Prudence will increase her current consumption by $(0.4)(\$3,000) = \$1,200$. Because the part of income that is not consumed is saved, her saving also increases by the amount of $\$3,000 - \$1,200 = \$1,800$.

The marginal propensity to consume also applies to declines in current income. For example, if Prudence were temporarily laid off from her bookkeeping job so that her current year's income decreased by $4,000, she would reduce both her consumption and her saving. If we assume that her marginal propensity to consume remains 0.4, she would reduce her consumption by $(0.4)(\$4,000) = \$1,600$, and her saving would, therefore, have to diminish by $\$4,000 - \$1,600 = \$2,400$.

Aggregate income and consumption reflect the decisions of millions of individuals and households so that the lessons we learned from thinking about the case of Prudence also apply at the macroeconomic level. Just as an increase in Prudence's income caused her to consume more, we would expect an increase in aggregate output (income) Y to lead to an increase in aggregate desired consumption, C^d, as well. Because marginal propensities to consume are less than 1, however, the increase in C^d will be less than the increase in Y. As not all of the increase in Y is spent, desired national saving S^d will also rise when Y rises.

EFFECT OF CHANGES IN EXPECTED FUTURE INCOME

Today's consumption decisions may depend not only on current income but also on the income that one expects to earn in the future. For example, an individual who is currently not employed but who has a contract to begin a high-paying job in three months will probably consume more today than another unemployed individual with no job prospects.

To illustrate the effect of changes in expected future income, suppose that instead of receiving the $3,000 bonus during the current year, Prudence learns that she will receive a $3,000 bonus (after taxes) next year. The promise of the bonus is legally binding, and Prudence has no doubt that she will receive the extra income next year. How will this information affect Prudence's consumption and saving in the current year?

Because her current income is unaffected, Prudence could leave her current consumption and saving unchanged, waiting until she actually receives the bonus to increase her consumption. If her decisions are guided by a consumption-smoothing motive, however, she will prefer to use the bonus to increase her current consumption as well as her future consumption. She can increase her current consumption, despite the fact that her current income remains unchanged, by reducing her current saving (she could even "dissave," or have negative current saving, with current consumption exceeding current income, by using her accumulated assets or by borrowing). Suppose, for example, that Prudence decides to consume $1,000 more this year. Because her current income is unchanged, Prudence's $1,000 increase in current consumption is equivalent to a $1,000 reduction in current saving.

The $1,000 reduction in current saving will reduce Prudence's available resources in the next year, relative to the situation in which her saving is unchanged, by $1,000 $(1 + r)$. For example, if the real interest rate is 0.05, cutting current saving by $1,000 reduces Prudence's available resources next year by $1,000(1.05) = $1,050. Overall, her available resources next year will increase by $3,000 because of the bonus but will decrease by $1,050 because of reduced current saving, giving a net increase in resources of $3,000 – $1,050 = $1,950, which can be used to increase consumption next year or in the following years. Effectively, Prudence can use the increase in her expected future income to increase consumption both in the present and in the future.

To summarize, an increase in an individual's expected future income is likely to lead that person to increase current consumption and decrease current saving. The same result applies at the macroeconomic level: If people expect that aggregate output and income, Y, will be higher in the future, current desired consumption, C^d, should increase and current desired national saving, S^d, should decrease.

Economists cannot measure expected future income directly, so how do they take this variable into account when predicting consumption and saving behaviour? One approach is to survey consumers and ask them about their expectations. Their answers can be useful for assessing developments in the macroeconomy, as the Application "Consumer Attitudes and Recessions" shows.

APPLICATION

CONSUMER ATTITUDES AND RECESSIONS

The theory of consumer behaviour tells us that consumers' decisions on how much to consume and how much to save depend on their expectations about the economy's future. When consumers are generally optimistic about the future, they consume more and save less than when they are pessimistic about it. Thus, economic forecasters and other analysts may find it useful to know what consumers are thinking about the future at any particular time.

In this application, we focus on the "index of consumer attitudes" constructed by the Conference Board of Canada from its consumer attitudes survey. The survey has been conducted quarterly since 1960 and involves 1,500 telephone interviews with randomly selected households. Respondents are asked to give their views about their household's current and expected financial positions and the short-term employment outlook. They are also asked whether now is a good time to make a major purchase. The index is seasonally adjusted, and measured relative to a value of 100 for 1991, with higher values corresponding to greater consumer optimism.

Historically, the index has been a sensitive indicator of recessions and other macroeconomic shocks. Figure 4.1(a) shows quarterly data for the index of consumer attitudes for the period from 1981 to 2001. Figure 4.1(b) shows quarterly data for real total consumption and real consumption expenditure on durable goods during the same period. Expenditures on durable goods, which are measured on the scale on the right side of the figure, are only about one-seventh of total consumption expenditures, which are measured on the scale on the left side of the figure. We show expenditures on durable goods in addition to total consumption because expenditures on durable goods (such as automobiles, appliances, and furniture) tend to display sharper fluctuations than expenditures on other components of consumption (such as food and heating oil). When consumers become pessimistic about the future, they may

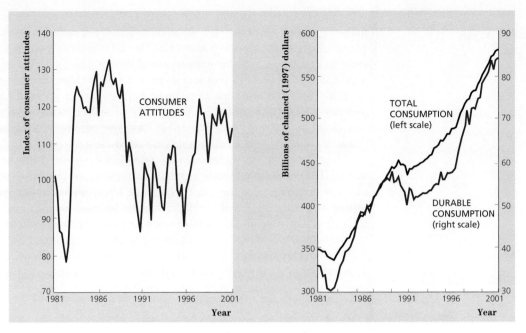

FIGURE 4.1(a)

THE INDEX OF CONSUMER ATTITUDES, 1981–2001

The quarterly index of consumer attitudes is based on what consumers tell interviewers about their expectations for the future of the economy. The index of consumer attitudes dipped deeply but briefly during the early 1980s. In the early 1990s it fell for a longer period, then rose to a higher level during the late 1990s.

Source: CBISA—Index of Consumer Attitudes, All Respondents, Canada & Regions, Seasonally Adjusted. The Conference Board of Canada, 2001. The Conference Board of Canada is a membership-based, not-for-profit, independent applied-research organization.

FIGURE 4.1(b)

TOTAL CONSUMPTION EXPENDITURES AND CONSUMPTION EXPENDITURES ON DURABLE GOODS, 1981–2001

Total consumption expenditures are measured on the left vertical axis, and consumption expenditures on durable goods are measured on the right vertical axis. Total consumption expenditures fell but then recovered quickly in the early 1980s. In the early 1990s, they fell again but recovered more slowly. Consumption expenditures on durable goods reacted more strongly, but with a similar pattern over the past twenty years.

Source: Personal consumption expenditures and durable goods consumption expenditures in billions of chained 1997 dollars: Statistics Canada, CANSIM Series D100199 and D100200.

delay the purchase of a new car more easily than they would delay the purchase of food or heating oil, so the effects of consumer sentiment may be more readily evident in durable goods expenditures than in overall consumption.

The index of consumer attitudes dropped sharply during the 1981–1982 recession but also recovered rapidly. In contrast, the decline in the index was more gradual during the early 1990s, while its recovery was more erratic. Reflecting this consumer pessimism and uncertainty, growth in real consumption expenditures was slow and erratic during the uneven recovery that began in 1992. Not until 1996–1997 did the index of consumer attitudes grow strongly, while consumption expenditures grew at the same time. In 2000 and 2001, the index was volatile, perhaps reflecting a new period of uncertainty for consumers.

EFFECT OF CHANGES IN WEALTH

Another factor that affects consumption and saving is wealth. Recall from Chapter 2 that the wealth of any entity, such as a household or an entire nation, equals its assets minus its liabilities.

To see how consumption and saving respond to an increase in wealth, suppose that while cleaning out her attic, Prudence finds a stock certificate for 50 shares of stock in a pharmaceutical company. Prudence's grandmother bought this stock for Prudence when she was born, and Prudence did not know about it. She immediately calls her broker and learns that the stock is now worth $3,000. This unexpected $3,000 increase in Prudence's wealth has the same effect on her available resources as the $3,000 increase in current income that we examined earlier. As in the case involving an increase in her current income, Prudence will use her increase in wealth to increase her current consumption by an amount smaller than $3,000 so that she can use some of the additional $3,000 to increase her future consumption. Because Prudence's current income is not affected by finding the stock certificate, the increase in her current consumption is matched by a decrease in current saving of the same size. In this way, an increase in wealth increases current consumption and reduces current saving. The same line of reasoning leads to the conclusion that a decrease in wealth reduces current consumption and increases saving.

The ups and downs in the stock market are an important source of changes in wealth, and the effects on consumption of changes in the stock market are explored in the following Application.

APPLICATION

The 1987 Stock Market Crash and Consumer Spending

On October 19, 1987, stock prices took their biggest ever one-day plunge. That week, the Toronto Stock Exchange's composite index of 300 stock prices (TSE 300) lost 520 points or about 15% of its value, as part of a worldwide decline in stock prices. Although estimates differ, apparently about $100 billion in financial wealth (equal in value to more than two months of GDP) was eliminated through declining stock values from August to December 1987.

According to economic theory, how should a stock market crash affect consumers' spending? There are two possible channels.

First, the crash reduced households' wealth, which should have reduced consumption. According to the theory, however, the effect on current consumption should have been much smaller than the $100 billion reduction in wealth; the reason is that consumers would be expected to spread the effects of their losses in wealth over a long period of time, reducing the consumption they had planned for future years as well as current consumption. We can get a quick estimate of the effect of a $100 billion drop in stock values on current consumption by supposing that consumers spread their reduction in consumption over 25 years. Also, for simplicity, let us assume that the real interest rate is zero.[2] Hence, in response to a $100 billion loss in wealth, consumers would plan to reduce their consumption in each of the next 25 years by 1/25 of $100 billion or $4 billion per year (about 1.3% of personal disposable income). To the extent that current income was unaffected by the crash, saving would have to rise by the same amount that consumption falls.

---

2. If the real interest rate were positive, in calculating the effect on consumption we would have to take into account the interest that the lost $100 billion would have earned in future years.

The second way a crash could affect consumption is that it might lead consumers to expect bad economic times ahead and falling future incomes. As discussed previously, a reduction in expected future income tends to reduce current consumption and raise current saving. The index of consumer attitudes did decline in the fourth quarter of 1987 (see the preceding Application, "Consumer Attitudes and Recessions"), but the decline was small and was associated with consumers' plans for major purchases; the proportion of respondents who thought economic conditions would improve within six months actually rose.

What, then, was the actual effect of the October crash on consumption? Consumption behaviour is affected by many factors, and isolating the influence of any single factor is not easy. However, the Conference Board of Canada estimated that the crash reduced consumer spending (in all categories) by about $1.1 billion over 1988.[3]

The theory was correct, then, in predicting that the loss of financial wealth should reduce consumption and increase saving, but the effects on consumption and saving appeared to be even smaller than the small effect predicted by the theory. In fact, researchers at the Bank of Canada in early 1988 found "no visible evidence that the stock market decline has had an effect on the pace of economic activity in Canada."[4]

Why? One possible explanation is connected with the unusually erratic behaviour of stock prices during 1987. The tremendous decline in stock prices after August mirrored equally impressive gains earlier in the year—33% from January to August 1987. Because the earlier increase in stock prices was so rapid, it is possible that by August 1987 stockholders had not yet fully adjusted their consumption and saving behaviour to their higher level of wealth. Thus, when the market fell, consumption did not have to decline by very much in order to fall back into line with wealth.

Other explanations for the small effect of the crash on consumption focus on the subsequent recovery in stock prices, the fact that many consumers hold stocks through pension plans and may not have perceived the changes in wealth, and the possibility that stock-owning consumers have relatively low marginal propensities to consume. Moreover, the crash was followed by a sharp decline in interest rates, which may have had an offsetting effect on consumption.

We have seen that a precipitous decline in the stock market can cause consumption to fall below the level it would have attained otherwise. But does the relationship between the stock market and consumption hold when stock market rises sharply?

Figure 4.2 shows the value of the TSE 300 price index, adjusted for inflation by dividing by the consumer price index. This measure of the real value of the stock market is shown on the left scale. The figure also shows consumption expenditure as a percentage of national income, on the right scale. You can see that consumption and the stock market both boomed during the late 1990s, but the timing does not suggest that the stock market was the main cause of the consumption boom. From 1995 to 1998, the consumption share of GDP rose by about 2 percentage points. Although the real value of the TSE 300 index rose at the same time, the consumption share continued to rise in 1998, after stock prices fell. When the rise in the value of the stock market continued in 1999 and 2000, the consumption share of GDP fell. Thus, the timing of the two booms, with the consumption share of GDP peaking

3. Conference Board of Canada, *Canadian Outlook*, Winter 1988, vol. 3, no. 2.
4. "Economic Developments in Canada in the Second Half of 1987," *Bank of Canada Review*, March 1988, p. 18.

two years before the stock market peaked, suggests that factors other than wealth—such as the real interest rate or expected future income—may have been more important in explaining fluctuations in consumption spending.

For example, interest rates were rising during 1998 and 1999, encouraging saving, then falling during 2001, encouraging consumption. These changes may have offset the effects of stock market wealth on consumption. Research on the US stock market and consumption booms of the 1990s reaches the same conclusion.[5]

EFFECT OF CHANGES IN THE REAL INTEREST RATE

We have seen that the real interest rate is the price of current consumption in terms of future consumption. We held the real interest rate fixed when we examined the effects of changes in current income, expected future income, and wealth. Now, we let the real interest rate vary, examining the effect on current consumption and saving of changes in the real interest rate.

How would Prudence's consumption and saving change in response to an increase in the real interest rate? Her response to such an increase reflects two opposing tendencies. On the one hand, because each real dollar of saving in the current year grows to $1 + r$ real dollars next year, an increase in the real interest rate means that each dollar of current saving will have a higher payoff in terms of increased future consumption. This increased reward for current saving tends to increase saving.

---

5. See Jonathan Parker, "Spendthrift in America? On Two Decades of Decline in the U.S. Saving Rate," in *NBER Macroeconomics Annual* 1999, pp. 317–370.

FIGURE 4.2

STOCK MARKET VALUE AND CONSUMPTION AS A SHARE OF GDP, 1995–2001

The real value of the TSE 300 price index (found by dividing by the CPI) is measured on the left vertical axis. Personal consumption expenditures, measured as a percentage of GDP, are measured on the right vertical axis. Note that the measure of stock market wealth and the consumption share rose together during the mid–1990s. But the consumption share of GDP peaked near 59% in the middle of 1998, even though stock prices fell early in 1998. The peak in the consumption share long preceded the peak in the real value of the stock market, which suggests that factors other than stock market wealth were the main causes of changes in consumption during this period.

Source: Quarterly average value of the TSE 300: Statistics Canada, CANSIM Series B4237; quarterly average CPI: CANSIM Series P100000; personal consumption expenditures and GDP in current dollars: CANSIM Series D14817 and D14840. Dividends have not been included in valuing the stock market.

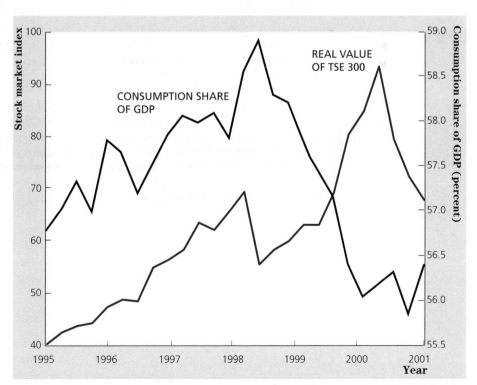

On the other hand, a higher real interest rate means that Prudence can achieve any future savings target with a smaller amount of current saving. For example, suppose that she is trying to accumulate $1,400 to buy a new laptop computer next year. An increase in the real interest rate means that any current saving will grow to a larger amount by next year, so the amount that she needs to save this year to reach her goal of $1,400 is lower. Because she needs to save less to reach her goal, she can increase her current consumption and, thus, reduce her saving.

The two opposing effects described above are known as the substitution effect and the income effect of an increase in the real interest rate. The **substitution effect of the real interest rate on saving** reflects the tendency to reduce current consumption and increase future consumption as the price of current consumption, $1 + r$, increases. In response to an increase in the price of current consumption, consumers *substitute* away from current consumption, which has become relatively more expensive, toward future consumption, which has become relatively less expensive. The reduction in current consumption implies that current saving increases. Thus, the substitution effect implies that current saving increases in response to an increase in the real interest rate.

The **income effect of the real interest rate on saving** reflects the change in current consumption that results when a higher real interest rate makes a consumer richer or poorer. For example, if Prudence has a savings account and has not borrowed any funds, she is a recipient of interest payments. She, therefore, benefits from an increase in the real interest rate because her interest income increases. With a higher interest rate, she can afford to have the same levels of current and future consumption as before the interest rate change, and she would have some additional resources to spend. These extra resources are effectively the same as an increase in her wealth, so she will increase both her current and her future consumption. Thus, for a saver, who is a recipient of interest payments, the income effect of an increase in the real interest rate is to increase current consumption and reduce current saving. Therefore, for a saver, the income and substitution effects of an increase in the real interest rate work in opposite directions, with the income effect reducing saving and the substitution effect increasing saving.

The income effect of an increase in the real interest rate is different for a payer of interest, such as a borrower. An increase in the real interest rate increases the amount of interest payments that a borrower must make, thereby making the borrower unable to afford the same levels of current and future consumption as before the increase in the real interest rate. The borrower has effectively suffered a loss of wealth as a result of the increase in the real interest rate, and responds to this decline in wealth by reducing both current consumption and future consumption. The reduction in current consumption means that current saving increases (that is, borrowing decreases). Hence, for a borrower, the income effect of an increase in the real interest rate is to increase saving. Thus, both the substitution effect and the income effect of an increase in the real interest rate increase the saving of a borrower.

Let us summarize the effect of an increase in the real interest rate. For a saver, who is a recipient of interest, an increase in the real interest rate tends to increase saving through the substitution effect but to reduce saving through the income effect. Without additional information, we cannot say which of these two opposing effects is larger. For a borrower, who is a payer of interest, both the substitution effect and the income effect operate to increase saving. Consequently, the saving of a borrower unambiguously increases.

What is the effect of an increase in the real interest rate on national saving? Because the national economy is composed of both borrowers and savers, and because, in principle, savers could either increase or decrease their saving in response to an increase in the real interest rate, economic theory cannot answer this question. As economic theory does not indicate whether national saving increases or decreases in response to an increase in the real interest rate, we must rely on empirical studies that examine this relationship using actual data. Unfortunately, interpretation of the empirical evidence from the many studies done continues to inspire debate. The most widely accepted conclusion seems to be that an increase in the real interest rate reduces current consumption and increases saving, but this effect is not very strong.

Taxes and the Real Return to Saving

In discussing the real return that savers earn, we have not yet mentioned an important practical consideration: Interest earnings (and other returns on savings) are taxed. Because part of interest earnings must be paid as taxes, the real return earned by savers is actually less than the difference between the nominal interest rate and expected inflation.

A useful measure of the returns received by savers that recognizes the effects of taxes is the *expected after-tax real interest rate*. To define this concept, we let i represent the nominal interest rate and t the rate at which interest income is taxed. In Canada, for example, most interest earnings are taxed as ordinary income, so t is the income tax rate. Savers retain a fraction $(1 - t)$ of total interest earned so that the after-tax nominal interest rate, received by savers after payment of taxes, is $(1 - t)i$. The **expected after-tax real interest rate**, $r_{a\text{-}t}$, is the after-tax nominal interest rate minus the expected inflation rate π^e, or

$$r_{a\text{-}t} = (1 - t)i - \pi^e. \tag{4.2}$$

The expected after-tax real interest rate is the appropriate interest rate for consumers to use in making consumption and saving decisions because it measures the increase in the purchasing power of their saving after payment of taxes.

Table 4.1 shows how to calculate the after-tax nominal interest rate and the expected after-tax real interest rate. Note that given the nominal interest rate and expected inflation, a reduction in the tax rate on interest income increases the nominal and real after-tax rates of return that a saver receives. Thus, by reducing the rate at which it taxes interest, the government can increase the real rate of return earned by savers and (possibly) increase the rate of saving in the economy. The

Table 4.1

Calculating After-Tax Interest Rates

i = nominal interest rate = 5% per year
π^e = expected inflation rate = 2% per year

Example 1
t = tax rate on interest income = 30%
After-tax nominal interest rate = $(1 - t)i = (1 - 0.30)5\% = 3.5\%$
Expected after-tax real interest rate = $(1 - t)i - \pi^e = (1 - 0.30)5\% - 2\% = 1.5\%$

Example 2
t = tax rate on interest income = 20%
After-tax nominal interest rate = $(1 - t)i = (1 - 0.20)5\% = 4\%$
Expected after-tax real interest rate = $(1 - t)i - \pi^e = (1 - 0.20)5\% - 2\% = 2\%$

IN TOUCH WITH THE MACROECONOMY

INTEREST RATES

Although in our theoretical discussions, we refer to "the" interest rate, as if there were only one, actually there are many different interest rates, each of which depends on the identity of the borrower and the terms of the loan. Here are some interest rates that appeared on the Bank of Canada's web site under "Financial Rates and Statistics" (*www.bank-banque-canada-ca/en/rates.htm*) on September 19, 2001*:

	19 Sept. 2001	19 Sept. 2000
Target overnight rate	3.50%	5.75%
Prime rate	5.25	7.50
3-month Treasury bills	3.10	5.57
1-year Treasury bills	3.01	5.81
10-year Canadian bonds	5.25	5.79
3-month commercial paper	3.31	5.84
3-month U.S. commercial paper	3.28	6.56

A complete list of interest rates (including previous months' values) for Canada and the United States is also available in print in the monthly *Bank of Canada Banking and Financial Statistics*, Table F1. Some of these rates are available for many other countries in the weekly issues of *The Economist*.

The target overnight rate is the centre of the central bank's target range for the overnight rate, which, in turn, is the interest rate at which chartered banks make short-term loans to one another. The target overnight rate is the key indicator of monetary policy, which Chapter 14 describes in more detail. The prime rate is the basic rate that chartered banks and trust companies charge on loans to their best customers. These first two rates are called administered rates, while the other rates vary continuously as financial market conditions change. Treasury bills and Government of Canada bonds are debt of the federal government, and commercial paper is a debt of a private issuer.

The interest rates charged on these different types of loans need not be the same. One reason for this variation is differences in the risk of non-repayment, or default. Federal government debt is believed to be free from default risk, but there is always a chance that a business, bank, or province may not be able to repay what it borrowed. Lenders charge risky borrowers extra interest to compensate themselves for the risk of default. Thus, the prime rate and the commercial paper rate are higher than they would be if there were no default risk. Note that the three-month commercial paper rate was greater than the three-month treasury bill rate by 0.21% (21 basis points).

A second factor affecting interest rates is the length of time for which the funds are borrowed. The relationship between the life of a bond (its *maturity*) and the interest rate it pays is called the *yield curve*. Because longer maturity bonds typically pay higher interest rates than shorter maturity bonds (as you can see for 2000 and 2001), the yield curve generally slopes up. But note that the yield curve was much steeper in September 2001 than in September 2000, that is, the difference between long-term and short-term interest rates was larger in September 2001 than in September 2000. Interestingly, historical experience suggests that when the yield curve is relatively steep, the economy is likely to have relatively strong growth in subsequent months.

A third factor influencing interest rates is the country of issue. This discrepancy in nominal interest rates could reflect different rates of expected inflation acorss countries. It also may compensate international lenders for the risk of changes in the value of the Canadian dollar in terms of the US dollar (see Appendix 10B).

Although the levels of various interest rates are quite different, interest rates go up and down together most of the time. All of the interest rates discussed here fell between September 2000 and September 2001. As a general rule, interest rates tend to move together, so in our economic analysis, we usually refer to "the" interest rate, as if there were only one.

---

*Reprinted with permission of the Bank of Canada.

stimulation of saving is one of the motivations for tax provisions, such as Registered Retirement Savings Plans (RRSPs), which allow savers to shelter part of their interest earnings from taxes and, thus, earn higher after-tax rates of return. Unfortunately, because economists disagree about the effect of higher real interest rates on saving, the effectiveness of RRSPs and similar tax breaks for saving also is in dispute.

Fiscal Policy

We have just demonstrated how government tax policies can affect the real return earned by savers and thus, perhaps, the saving rate. However, even when government fiscal policies—its decisions about spending and taxes—are not intentionally directed at affecting the saving rate, these policies have important implications for the amount of consumption and saving that takes place in the economy. Although understanding the links between fiscal policy and consumer behaviour requires some difficult economic reasoning, these links are so important that we introduce them here. We discuss several of these issues further in this book, particularly in Chapter 15.

To make the discussion of fiscal policy effects as straightforward as possible, we take the economy's aggregate output Y as a given. That is, we ignore the possibility that the changes in fiscal policy that we consider affect the aggregate supply of goods and services. This assumption is valid if the economy is at full employment (as we are assuming throughout Part II of this book) and if the fiscal policy changes do not significantly affect the capital stock or labour supply. Later, we review the fixed-output assumption and discuss both the classical and Keynesian views about how fiscal policy changes can affect output.

In general, fiscal policy affects *desired consumption, C^d*, primarily by affecting households' current and expected future incomes. More specifically, fiscal changes that increase the tax burden on the private sector, either by raising current taxes or by leading people to expect that taxes will be higher in the future, will cause people to consume less.

For a given level of output Y, government fiscal policies affect desired national saving S^d, or $Y - C^d - G$, in two basic ways. First, as we just noted, fiscal policy can influence desired consumption: For any levels of output Y and government purchases G, a fiscal policy change that reduces desired consumption C^d by one dollar will at the same time raise desired national saving S^d by one dollar. Second, for any levels of output and desired consumption, increases in government purchases directly lower desired national saving, as is apparent from the definition of desired national saving, $S^d = Y - C^d - G$.

To illustrate these general points, we consider how desired consumption and desired national saving would be affected by two specific fiscal policy changes: an increase in government purchases and a tax cut.

Government Purchases

Suppose that current government purchases G increase by $1 billion, say, because the government increases defence spending. Assume that this increase in G is temporary so that plans for future government purchases are unchanged. (Analytical Problem 5 at the end of this chapter looks at the case of a permanent increase in government purchases.) For any level of output Y, how will this change in fiscal policy affect desired consumption and desired national saving in the economy?

Let us start by finding the effect of the increased government purchases on consumption. As already mentioned, changes in government purchases affect consumption because they affect private sector tax burdens. Suppose for example that the government pays for the extra $1 billion in defence spending by raising current taxes by $1 billion. For given total (before-tax) output Y, this tax increase implies a $1 billion decline in consumers' current (after-tax) incomes. We know that consumers respond to a decline in their current incomes by reducing consumption, although by less than the decline in current income.[6] So, in response to the $1 billion tax increase, consumers might reduce their current consumption by $600 million.

What happens to consumption if the government does not raise current taxes when it increases its purchases? The analysis in this case is more subtle. If the government does not raise current taxes, it will have to borrow the $1 billion to pay for the extra spending. The government will have to repay the $1 billion it borrows, plus interest, sometime in the future, implying that future taxes will have to rise.[7] If taxpayers are clever enough to understand that increased government purchases today mean higher taxes in the future, households' expected future (after-tax) incomes will fall, and again they will reduce desired consumption. For the sake of illustration, we can imagine that they again reduce their current consumption by $600 million, although the reduction in consumption might be less if some consumers do not understand that their future taxes are likely to rise. What about the effects on desired national saving? The increase in government purchases affects desired national saving, or $Y - C^d - G$, directly by increasing G and indirectly by reducing desired consumption C^d. In our example, the increase in government purchases reduces desired consumption by $600 million, which by itself would raise national saving by $600 million. However, this effect is outweighed by the increase in G of $1 billion so that overall desired national saving $Y - C^d - G$ falls by $400 million, with output Y held constant.[8] More generally, because the decline in desired consumption can be expected to be less than the initial increase in government purchases, a temporary increase in government purchases will lower desired national saving.

To summarize, for the current level of output Y, we conclude that a temporary increase in government purchases reduces both desired consumption and desired national saving.

Taxes

Now, suppose that government purchases G remain constant but that the government reduces current taxes T by $1 billion. To keep things as simple as possible, we suppose that the tax cut is a *lump sum*, giving each taxpayer the same amount (think of the country's 10 million taxpayers receiving $100 each). With government purchases G and output Y held constant, desired national saving $Y - C^d - G$ will change only if desired consumption C^d changes. So, the question is, how will desired consumption respond to the cut in current taxes?

Again the key issue is, how does the tax cut affect people's current and expected future incomes? The $1 billion current tax cut directly increases current (after-tax) incomes by $1 billion, so the tax cut should increase desired consumption (by somewhat less than $1 billion). However, the $1 billion current tax cut also should lead people to expect *lower* after-tax incomes in the future. The reason is that because the government has not changed its spending, to cut taxes by $1 billion today the government must also increase its current borrowing by $1 billion. Because the extra $1 billion of government debt will have to be repaid with interest in the

---

6. Recall that the marginal propensity to consume out of current income is positive but less than 1.
7. For example, federal and provincial governments may increase taxes to help control budget deficits, much of which reflect interest on earlier government borrowing.
8. Note that national saving would fall by even more than $400 million if consumers ignored the prospect of future tax increases and thus did not reduce their current consumption.

future, future taxes will have to be higher, which, in turn, implies lower future disposable incomes for households. All else being equal, the decline in expected future incomes will cause people to consume less today, offsetting the positive effect of increased current income on desired consumption. Thus, in principle, a current tax cut—which raises current incomes but lowers expected future incomes—could either raise or lower current desired consumption.

Interestingly, some economists argue that the positive effect of increased current income and the negative effect of decreased future income on desired consumption should exactly cancel so that the overall effect of a current tax cut on consumption is zero! The idea that tax cuts do not affect desired consumption and (therefore) also do not affect desired national saving,[9] is called the **Ricardian equivalence proposition**.[10]

The Ricardian equivalence idea can be briefly explained as follows (see Chapter 15 for a more detailed discussion). In the long run, all government purchases must be paid for by taxes. Thus, if the government's current and planned purchases do not change, a cut in current taxes can affect the *timing* of tax collections but (advocates of Ricardian equivalence emphasize) not the ultimate tax burden borne by consumers. A current tax cut with no change in government purchases does not really make consumers any better off (any reduction in taxes today is balanced by tax increases in the future), so they have no reason to respond to the tax cut by changing their desired consumption.

Although the logic of the Ricardian equivalence proposition is sound, many economists question whether it makes sense in practice. Most of these sceptics argue that even though the proposition predicts that consumers will not increase consumption when taxes are cut, in reality, lower current taxes likely will lead to increased desired consumption and, thus, reduced desired national saving. One reason that consumption may rise after a tax cut is that many, perhaps most, consumers do not understand that increased government borrowing today is likely to lead to higher taxes in the future. Thus, consumers may simply respond to the current tax cut, as they would to any other increase in current income, by increasing their desired consumption.

The effects of a tax cut on consumption and saving may be summarized as follows: According to the Ricardian equivalence proposition, with no change in current or planned government purchases, a tax cut does not change desired consumption and desired national saving. However, the Ricardian equivalence proposition may not apply if consumers fail to take account of possible future tax increases in their planning; in that case, a tax cut will increase desired consumption and reduce desired national saving.

The factors that affect consumption and saving are listed in Summary table 5 on the next page.

4.2 INVESTMENT

Let us now turn to a second major component of spending: investment spending by firms. Like consumption and saving decisions, the decision about how much to invest depends largely on expectations about the economy's future. Investment also

---

9. In this example, private disposable income rises by $1 billion, so if desired consumption does not change, desired private saving rises by $1 billion. However, the government deficit also rises by $1 billion because of the tax cut, so government saving falls by $1 billion. Therefore, desired national saving—private saving plus government saving—does not change.

10. The argument was first advanced by the 19th century economist David Ricardo, although he expressed some reservations about its applicability to real-world situations. The word "equivalence" refers to the idea that if Ricardian equivalence is true, taxes and government borrowing have equivalent effects on the economy.

SUMMARY 5   DETERMINANTS OF DESIRED NATIONAL SAVING

An increase in	Causes desired national saving to	Reason
Current output, Y	Rise	Part of the extra income is saved to provide for future consumption.
Expected future output	Fall	Anticipation of future income raises current desired consumption, lowering current desired saving.
Wealth	Fall	Some of the extra wealth is consumed, which reduces saving for given income.
Expected real interest rate, r	Probably rise	An increased return makes saving more attractive, probably outweighing the fact that less must be saved to reach a specific savings target.
Government purchases, G	Fall	Higher government purchases directly lower desired national saving.
Taxes, T	Remain unchanged or rise	Saving does not change if consumers take into account an offsetting future tax cut; saving rises if consumers do not take into account a future tax cut and thus reduce current consumption.

shares in common with saving and consumption the idea of a trade-off between the present and the future. In making a capital investment, a firm commits its current resources (which could otherwise be used, say, to pay increased dividends to shareholders) to increasing its capacity to produce and earn profits in the future.

Recall from Chapter 2 that investment refers to the purchase or construction of capital goods, including residential and nonresidential buildings, machines and equipment used in production, and additions to inventory stocks. From a macroeconomic perspective, there are two main reasons to study investment behaviour. First, more so than the other components of aggregate spending, investment spending fluctuates sharply over the business cycle, falling in recessions and rising in booms. Even though investment is only about one-sixth of GDP, in the typical recession, half or more of the total decline in spending is reduced investment spending. Hence explaining the behaviour of investment is important for understanding the business cycle, which we explore further in Part III.

The second reason for studying investment behaviour is that investment plays a crucial role in determining the long-run productive capacity of the economy. Because investment creates new capital goods, a high rate of investment means that the capital stock is growing quickly. As discussed in Chapter 3, capital is one of the two most important factors of production (the other is labour). All else being equal, output will be higher in an economy that has invested rapidly and, thus, built up a large capital stock than in an economy that has not acquired much capital.

THE DESIRED CAPITAL STOCK

To understand what determines the amount of investment, we must consider how firms decide how much capital they want. If firms attempt to maximize profit, as we assume, a firm's **desired capital stock** is the amount of capital that allows the firm to earn the largest expected profit. Managers can determine the profit-maximizing level of the capital stock by comparing the costs and benefits of using additional capital—a new machine, for example. If the benefits outweigh the costs, expanding the capital stock will raise profits. But if the costs outweigh the benefits, the firm should not increase its planned capital stock and may even want to reduce it. As you might infer from this brief description, the economic logic underlying a firm's decision about how much capital to use is similar to the logic of its decision about how many workers to employ, discussed in Chapter 3.

In real terms, the benefit to a firm of having an additional unit of capital is the marginal product of capital, MPK. Recall from Chapter 3 that the MPK is the increase in output that a firm can obtain by adding a unit of capital, holding constant the firm's workforce and other factors of production. Because lags occur in obtaining and installing new capital, the expected *future* marginal product of capital, MPK^f, is the benefit from increasing investment today by one unit of capital. This expected future benefit must be compared with the expected cost of using that extra unit of capital, or the user cost of capital.

THE USER COST OF CAPITAL

To make the discussion of the user cost of capital more concrete, let us consider the case of Tony's Bakery, Inc., a company that produces specialty cookies. Tony, the bakery's owner-manager, is considering investing in a new solar-powered oven that will allow him to produce more cookies in the future. If he decides to buy such an oven, he must also determine its size. In making this decision, Tony has the following three items of information:

1. A new oven can be purchased in any size at a price of $1,000 per cubic metre, measured in real (base-year) dollars.

2. Because the oven is solar powered, using it does not involve energy costs. The oven also does not require maintenance expenditures.[11] However, the oven becomes less efficient as it ages: With each year that passes, the oven produces 10% fewer cookies. Because of this depreciation, the real value of an oven falls 10% per year. For example, after one year of use, the real value of the oven is $900 per cubic metre.

3. Tony can borrow (from a bank) or lend (to the government, by buying a one-year government bond) at the prevailing expected real interest rate of 8% per year.

---

11. These assumptions simplify the example. If there were operating costs, such as fuel and maintenance costs, we would subtract them from the expected future marginal product of capital when calculating the benefit of using the machine.

In calculating the user cost of capital, we use the following symbols (the numerical values are from the example of Tony's Bakery):

p_K = real price of capital goods ($1,000 per cubic metre)
d = rate at which capital depreciates (10% per year)
r = expected real interest rate (8% per year)

The **user cost of capital** is the expected real cost of using a unit of capital for a specified period of time. For Tony's Bakery, we consider the expected costs of purchasing a new oven, using it for a year, then selling it. The cost of using the oven has two components: a depreciation cost and an interest cost.

In general, the depreciation cost of using capital is the value lost as the capital wears out. Because of depreciation, after one year, the oven that Tony pays $1,000 per cubic metre for when new will be worth only $900 per cubic metre. The $100-per-cubic-metre loss that Tony suffers over the year is the depreciation cost of using the oven. Even if Tony does not sell the oven at the end of a year, he suffers this loss because at the end of the year, the asset's (the oven's) economic value will be 10% less.

The interest cost of using capital equals the expected real interest rate times the price of the capital. As the expected real interest rate is 8%, Tony's interest cost of using the oven for a year is 8% of $1,000 per cubic metre, or $80 per cubic metre. To see why the interest cost is a cost of using capital, imagine first that Tony must borrow the funds necessary to buy the oven; in this case, the interest cost of $80 per cubic metre is the interest he pays on the loan, which is obviously part of the total cost of using the oven. Alternatively, if Tony uses profits from the business to buy the oven, he gives up the opportunity to use those funds to buy an interest-bearing asset, such as a government bond. For every $1,000 that Tony puts into the oven, he is sacrificing $80 in interest that he would have earned by purchasing a $1,000 government bond. This forgone interest is a cost to Tony of using the oven. Thus, the interest cost is part of the true economic cost of using capital, whether the capital's purchase is financed with borrowed funds or with the firm's own retained profits.

The user cost of capital is the sum of the depreciation cost and the interest cost. The interest cost is rp_K, the depreciation cost is dp_K, and the user cost of capital, uc, is

$$uc = rp_K + dp_K = (r + d)p_K. \tag{4.3}$$

In the case of Tony's Bakery,

$$uc = 0.08(\$1,000 \text{ per cubic metre}) + 0.10(\$1,000 \text{ per cubic metre})$$
$$= \$180 \text{ per cubic metre.}$$

Thus, Tony's user cost of capital is $180 per cubic metre per year.

Determining the Desired Capital Stock

Now we can find a firm's profit-maximizing capital stock, or desired capital stock. A firm's desired capital stock is the capital stock at which the expected future marginal product of capital equals the user cost of capital.

Figure 4.3 shows the determination of the desired capital stock for Tony's Bakery. The capital stock K, expressed as cubic metres of oven capacity, is measured along the horizontal axis. Both the MPK^f and the user cost of capital are measured along the vertical axis.

FIGURE 4.3

DETERMINATION OF THE
DESIRED CAPITAL STOCK

The desired capital stock (50 cubic metres of oven capacity in this example) is the capital stock that maximizes profits. When the capital stock is 50 cubic metres, the expected future marginal product of capital MPK^f is equal to the user cost of capital uc. If the MPK^f is larger than uc, as it is when the capital stock is 40 cubic metres, the benefit of extra capital exceeds the cost, and the firm should increase its capital stock. If the MPK^f is smaller than uc, as it is at 60 cubic metres, the cost of extra capital exceeds the benefit, and the firm should reduce its capital stock.

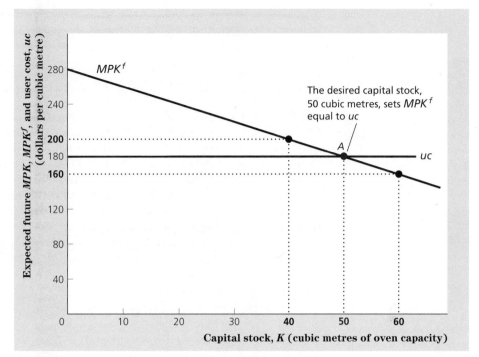

The downward-sloping curve shows the value of the MPK^f for different sizes of the capital stock K; at each level of K, the MPK^f equals the expected real value of the extra cookies that could be produced if oven capacity were expanded an additional cubic metre. The MPK^f curve slopes downward because the marginal product of capital falls as the capital stock is increased (we discussed reasons for the diminishing marginal productivity of capital in Chapter 3). The user cost (equal to $180 per cubic metre in the example) does not depend on the amount of capital and is represented by a horizontal line.

The amount of capital that maximizes the expected profit of Tony's Bakery is 50 cubic metres, represented by point A in Figure 4.3. At A, the expected benefit of an additional unit of capital, MPK^f, equals the user cost, uc. For any amount of oven capacity of less than 50 cubic metres, Tony's Bakery could increase its expected profit by increasing oven capacity. For example, Figure 4.3 shows that at a planned capacity of 40 cubic metres, the MPK^f of an additional cubic metre is $200 worth of cookies per year, which exceeds the $180 expected cost of using the additional cubic metre of capacity. Starting from a planned capacity of 40 cubic metres, if Tony adds an extra cubic metre of capacity, he will gain an additional $200 worth of future output while incurring only $180 in expected future costs. Thus, expanding beyond 40 cubic metres is profitable for Tony. Similarly, Figure 4.3 shows that at an oven capacity of more than 50 cubic metres, the expected future marginal product of capital, MPK^f, is less than the user cost, uc; in this case, Tony's Bakery could increase expected profit by reducing its capital stock. Only when $MPK^f = uc$ will the capital stock be at the level that maximizes expected profit.

As mentioned earlier, the determination of the desired capital stock is similar to the determination of the firm's labour demand, described in Chapter 3. Recall that the firm's profit-maximizing level of employment is the level at which the marginal product of labour equals the wage. Analogously, the firm's profit-maximizing level of capital is the level at which the expected future marginal product of capital equals the user cost, which can be thought of as the "wage" of capital (the cost of using capital for one period).

CHANGES IN THE DESIRED CAPITAL STOCK

Any factor that shifts the MPK^f curve or changes the user cost of capital changes the firm's desired capital stock. For Tony's Bakery, suppose that the real interest rate falls from 8% to 6%. If the real interest rate r is 0.06 and the depreciation rate d and the price of capital p_K remain at 0.10 and $1,000 per cubic metre, respectively, the decline in the real interest rate reduces the user cost of capital $(r + d)p_K$ from $180 per cubic metre to $(0.06 + 0.10)$ $1,000 per cubic metre, or $160 per cubic metre.

This decline in the user cost is shown as a downward shift of the user cost line, from uc^1 to uc^2 in Figure 4.4. After that shift, the MPK^f at the original desired capital stock of 50 cubic metres (point A), or $180 per cubic metre, exceeds the user cost of capital, now $160 per cubic metre (point B). Tony's Bakery can increase its profit by raising planned oven capacity to 60 cubic metres, where the MPK^f equals the user cost of $160 per cubic metre (point C). This example illustrates that a decrease in the expected real interest rate—or any other change that lowers the user cost of capital—increases the desired capital stock.

Technological changes that affect the MPK^f curve also affect the desired stock of capital. Suppose that Tony invents a new type of cookie dough that requires less baking time, allowing 12.5% more cookies to be baked daily. Such a technological advance would cause the MPK^f curve for ovens to shift upward by 12.5% at each value of the capital stock. Figure 4.5 shows this effect as a shift of the MPK^f curve from MPK^{f1} to MPK^{f2}. If the user cost remains at $180 per cubic metre, the technological advance causes Tony's desired capital stock to rise from 50 to 60 cubic metres. At

FIGURE 4.4

A DECLINE IN THE REAL INTEREST RATE RAISES THE DESIRED CAPITAL STOCK

For the Tony's Bakery example, a decline in the real interest rate from 8% to 6% reduces the user cost, uc, of a cubic metre of oven capacity from $180 to $160 per cubic metre and shifts the user cost line down from uc^1 to uc^2. The desired capital stock rises from 50 (point A) to 60 (point C) cubic metres of oven capacity. At 60 cubic metres, the MPK^f and the user cost of capital again are equal, at $160 per cubic metre.

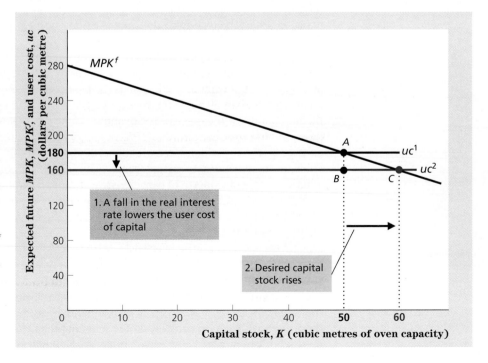

1. A fall in the real interest rate lowers the user cost of capital

2. Desired capital stock rises

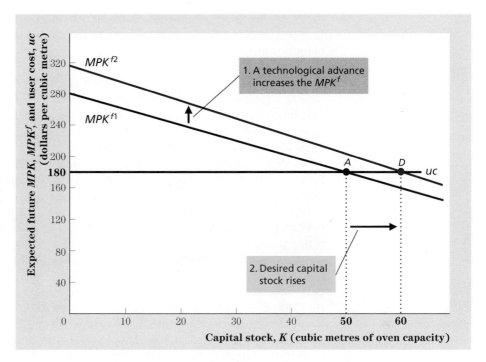

60 cubic metres (point *D*), the *MPK^f* again equals the user cost of capital. In general, with the user cost of capital held constant, an increase in the expected future marginal product of capital at any level of capital raises the desired capital stock.

TAXES AND THE DESIRED CAPITAL STOCK

So far, we have ignored the role of taxes in the investment decision. But Tony is interested in maximizing the profit his firm gets to keep after paying taxes. Thus, he must take into account taxes in evaluating the desirability of an additional unit of capital.

Suppose that Tony's Bakery pays 20% of its revenues in taxes. In this case, extra oven capacity that increases the firm's future revenues by, say, $200 will raise Tony's after-tax revenue by only $160, with $40 going to the government. To decide whether to add this extra capacity, Tony should compare the after-tax *MPK^f* of $160—not the before-tax *MPK^f* of $200—with the user cost. In general, if τ is the tax rate on firm revenues, the after-tax future marginal product of capital is $(1-\tau)MPK^f$. The desired capital stock is the one for which the after-tax future marginal product equals the user cost, or

$$(1-\tau)MPK^f = uc.$$

Dividing both sides of this equation by $1 - \tau$, we obtain

$$MPK^f = \frac{uc}{1-\tau} = \frac{(r+d)p_K}{1-\tau}. \qquad (4.4)$$

In Eq. (4.4), the term $uc/(1-\tau)$ is called the **tax-adjusted user cost of capital**. The tax-adjusted user cost of capital shows how large the before-tax future marginal product of capital must be for a firm to willingly add another unit of capital. An increase in the tax rate τ raises the tax-adjusted user cost and, thus, reduces the desired stock of capital.

To derive the tax-adjusted user cost, we assumed that taxes are levied as a proportion of firms' revenues. However, actual corporate taxes in Canada and other countries are much more complicated. Firms generally pay taxes on their profits rather than on their revenues, and the part of profit that is considered taxable may depend on how much the firm invests. For example, when a firm purchases some capital, it is allowed to deduct part of the purchase price of the capital from its taxable profit in both the year of purchase and in subsequent years. By reducing the amount of profit to be taxed, these deductions, known as *depreciation allowances*, allow the firm to reduce its total tax payment.

Another important tax provision, which was used from 1975 to 1987 in Canada, is the investment tax credit. *An investment tax credit* permits the firm to subtract a percentage of the purchase price of new capital directly from its tax bill. So, for example, if the investment tax credit is 10%, a firm that purchases a $15,000 piece of equipment can reduce its taxes by $1,500 (10% of $15,000) in the year the equipment is purchased.

Economists summarize the many provisions of the tax code affecting investment by a single measure of the tax burden on capital called the **effective tax rate**. Essentially, the idea is to ask what tax rate, τ, on a firm's revenue would have the same effect on the desired capital stock as would the actual provisions of the tax code. The hypothetical tax rate that answers this question is the effective tax rate. Changes in the tax law that, for example, raise the effective tax rate are equivalent to an increased tax on firm revenue and a rise in the tax-adjusted user cost of capital. Thus, all else being equal, an increase in the effective tax rate lowers the desired capital stock.

Table 4.2 shows effective tax rates on capital for the G7 countries and Mexico in 1998, based on work by Kenneth McKenzie, Mario Mansour, and Ariane Brûlé of the technical committee on business taxation, which reported to the federal finance minister in 1998. You can see that the effective tax rate on capital in Canada was lower than those in Japan, Germany, or Italy, but higher than those in France, the United Kingdom, the United States, and Mexico.

Effective tax rates also vary for different types of investment. Table 4.3 shows the effective tax rates on investment in machinery and equipment, buildings and

TABLE 4.2

Effective Tax Rates on Capital, 1998, G7 Countries plus Mexico

Country	Effective Tax Rate on Capital (Percent)
Canada	26.2
United States	20.8
United Kingdom	19.4
Germany	31.2
France	24.3
Italy	30.1
Japan	33.3
Mexico	17.3

Source: Effective tax rates on investment, by country for 1998, from Kenneth J. McKenzie, Mario Mansour, and Ariane Brûlé, "The Calculation of Marginal Effective Tax Rates," Working Paper 97–15, Technical Committee on Business Taxation, May 1998, Table 4.3.

TABLE 4.3

Canadian Effective Tax Rates 1980–2000

Category	1980	1990	2000
Buildings and structures	5.4	21.1	22.1
Equipment and machinery	14.2	25.6	19.1
Inventories	59.0	43.2	35.0
Land	−36.0	20.2	24.5

Source: 1980, 1990: Adapted from Kenneth J. McKenzie and Jack M. Mintz, "Tax Effects on the Cost of Capital," in John B. Shoven and John Whalley, eds., *Canada–U.S. Tax Comparisons*, Chicago:University of Chicago Press, 1992, Table 5.1; 2000: Duanjie Chen, *The Marginal Effective Tax Rate*, C.D. Howe Institute Backgrounder, August 2000, Figure 1.

structures, inventories, and land as calculated in studies by Kenneth McKenzie, of the University of Calgary, and Jack Mintz and Duanjie Chen of the University of Toronto. In 1980, investments in buildings and structures faced very low tax rates, and investment in land was even subsidized. By 2000, effective tax rates on the four categories of capital were more equal, with investment in machinery and equipment having the lowest tax rate.

APPLICATION

MEASURING THE EFFECTS OF TAXES ON INVESTMENT

Does the effective tax rate significantly affect investment patterns? Determining the empirical relationship between tax rates and investment is not easy. One problem is that the factors other than taxes that affect the desired capital stock—such as the expected future marginal product of capital and real interest rates—are always changing, so that isolating the "pure" effects of tax changes is difficult. Another problem is that changes in the tax code do not happen randomly but reflect the government's assessment of economic conditions. For example, in order to boost economic activity, the federal government is likely to reduce taxes on investment when investment spending is expected to be unusually low. But if the government does so, then low taxes on capital will tend to be associated with periods of low investment, and the econometrician might mistakenly conclude that tax cuts reduce rather than increase investment spending.

To solve the first problem, Kenneth McKenzie of the University of Calgary and Aileen Thompson of Carleton University compared investment spending in Canada and the United States since 1970.[12] They reasoned that changes in the expected future marginal product of capital and in real interest rates are quite similar across the two countries in similar industries. Thus, changes in investment in Canada relative to investment in the United States might be explained by changes in relative taxes. They found a small but noticeable effect of taxes on investment in machinery and equipment, but not on investment in structures.

---

12. "Taxes, the Cost of Capital, and Investment: A Comparison of Canada and the United States," Working Paper 97–3, Technical Committee on Business Taxation, Department of Finance, 1997.

An interesting study that attempted to solve both problems in detecting the effects of taxes was carried out by Jason Cummins of New York University, Kevin Hassett of the Board of Governors of the Federal Reserve System, and R. Glenn Hubbard of Columbia University.[13] To get around the problem that factors other than taxes are always changing, Cummins, Hassett, and Hubbard focused on periods around major tax reforms in 14 different countries. For example, they examined investment before and after the cut in corporate income taxes in Canada in 1988. Their idea was that by looking at occasions when the tax code changed significantly in a short period of time, they could reasonably assume that most of the ensuing change in investment was the result of the tax change rather than other factors. To get around the second problem, that tax cuts tend to take place when aggregate investment is low, Cummins, Hassett, and Hubbard did not look at the behaviour of aggregate investment; instead, they compared the investment responses of a large number of individual corporations with each tax reform. Because the tax laws treat different types of capital differently (as you can see in Table 4.3) and because companies use capital in different combinations, the authors believed that observing how different companies changed their investment after each tax reform would provide information on the effects of tax changes. For example, if a tax reform cuts taxes on machines relative to taxes on structures and if taxes are an important determinant of investment, then companies whose investment is concentrated in machinery should respond relatively more strongly to the tax change than companies who invest primarily in buildings.

Cummins, Hassett, and Hubbard found stronger effects of tax changes on investment than reported in previous studies, possibly because the earlier studies did not deal effectively with the two problems that we identified. These authors found a significant response of investment to tax changes in 12 of the 14 countries they studied, including Canada.

FROM THE DESIRED CAPITAL STOCK TO INVESTMENT

Now let us look at the link between a firm's desired capital stock and the amount it invests. In general, the capital stock (of a firm or of a country) changes over time through two opposing channels. First, the purchase or construction of new capital goods increases the capital stock. We have been calling the total purchase or construction of new capital goods that takes place each year "investment," but its precise name is **gross investment**. Second, the capital stock depreciates or wears out, which reduces the capital stock.

Whether the capital stock increases or decreases over the course of a year depends on whether gross investment is greater or less than depreciation during the year; when gross investment exceeds depreciation, the capital stock grows. The change in the capital stock over the year—or, equivalently, the difference between gross investment and depreciation—is **net investment**.

We express these concepts algebraically with the symbols:

I_t = gross investment during year t,

K_t = capital stock at the beginning of year t, and

K_{t+1} = capital stock at the beginning of year $t + 1$ (equivalently, at the end of year t).

---

13. "Tax Reforms and Investment: A Cross-Country Comparison," *Journal of Public Economics*, October 1996, pp. 237–273.

Net investment, the change in the capital stock during period t, equals $K_{t+1} - K_t$. The amount of depreciation during year t is dK_t, where d is the fraction of capital that depreciates each year. The relationship between net and gross investments is

$$net\ investment = gross\ investment - depreciation;$$
$$K_{t+1} - K_t = I_t - dK_t. \tag{4.5}$$

In most but not all years, gross investment is larger than depreciation so that net investment is positive and the capital stock increases. Figure 4.6 shows the behaviour since 1926 of gross and net investments in Canada, expressed as percentages of GDP; the difference between gross and net investments is depreciation. Note the occasional large swings in both gross and net investments and the negative rates of net investment that occurred in several years during the Great Depression of the 1930s and World War II.

We can use Eq. (4.5) to illustrate the relationship between the desired capital stock and investment. First, rewriting Eq. (4.5) gives

$$I_t = K_{t+1} - K_t + dK_t,$$

which states that gross investment equals net investment plus depreciation.

Now, suppose that firms use information available at the beginning of year t about the expected future marginal product of capital and the user cost of capital and determine the desired capital stock K^* they want by the end of year t (beginning of year $t + 1$). For the moment, suppose also that capital is easily obtainable so that firms can match the actual capital stock at the end of year t, K_{t+1}, with the desired capital stock K^*. Substituting K^* for K_{t+1} in the preceding equation yields

$$I_t = K^* - K_t + dK_t. \tag{4.6}$$

FIGURE 4.6

GROSS AND NET INVESTMENTS, 1926–2000

The figure shows private gross and net investments in Canada since 1926 as percentages of GDP. During some years of the Great Depression and World War II, net investment was negative, implying that the private capital stock was shrinking.

Source: *Canadian Economic Observer, Historical Statistical Supplement*, cat. no. 11-210, Table 1. Gross investment is investment in business fixed capital, and depreciation is capital consumption allowances.

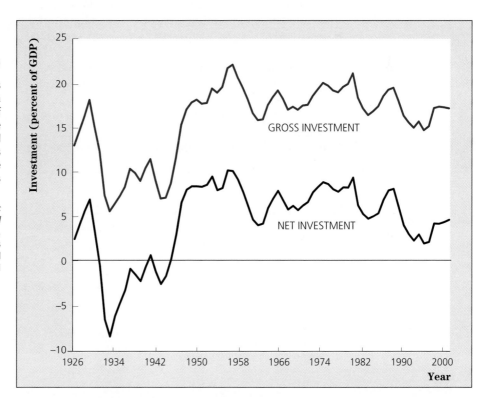

Equation (4.6) shows that firms' gross investment, I_t, during a year has two parts: (1) the desired net increase in the capital stock over the year, $K^* - K_t$; and (2) the investment needed to replace worn-out or depreciated capital, dK_t. The amount of depreciation that occurs during a year is determined by the depreciation rate and the initial capital stock. However, the desired net increase in the capital stock over the year depends on the factors—such as taxes, interest rates, and the expected future marginal product of capital—that affect the desired capital stock. Indeed, Eq. (4.6) shows that any factor that leads to a change in the desired capital stock K^* results in an equal change in gross investment I_t.

LAGS AND INVESTMENT

The assumption just made, that firms can obtain capital quickly enough to match actual capital stocks with desired levels each year, is not realistic in all cases. Although most types of equipment are readily available, a skyscraper or a nuclear power plant may take years to construct. Thus, in practice, a $1 million increase in a firm's desired capital stock may not translate into a $1 million increase in gross investment within the year; instead, the extra investment may be spread over several years as planning and construction proceed. Despite this qualification, factors that increase firms' desired capital stocks also tend to increase the current rate of investment. Summary table 6 brings together the factors that affect investment.

INVESTMENT IN INVENTORIES AND HOUSING

Our discussion so far has emphasized what is called business fixed investment, or investment by firms in structures (such as factories and office buildings) and equipment (such as drill presses and jetliners). However, there are two other components of investment spending: inventory investment and residential investment. As discussed in Chapter 2, inventory investment equals the increase in firms' inventories of unsold goods, unfinished goods, or raw materials. During business cycles, inventory investment is the most volatile component of investment spending. Residential investment is the construction of housing, such as single-family homes, condominiums, or apartment buildings.

Fortunately, the concepts of future marginal product and the user cost of capital, which we used to examine business fixed investment, apply equally well to inventory investment and residential investment. Consider, for example, a new-car dealer

SUMMARY 6   DETERMINANTS OF DESIRED INVESTMENT

AN INCREASE IN	CAUSES DESIRED INVESTMENT TO	REASON
Real interest rate, r	Fall	The user cost increases, which reduces desired capital stock.
Effective tax rate	Fall	The tax-adjusted user cost increases, which reduces desired capital stock.
Expected future, MPK	Rise	The desired capital stock increases.

trying to decide whether to increase the number of cars she normally keeps on her lot from 100 to 150, that is, to make an inventory investment of 50 cars. The benefit of having more cars to show is that potential car buyers will have a greater variety of models to select from and may not have to wait for delivery, enabling the car dealer to sell more cars. The increase in sales commissions the car dealer expects to make, measured in real terms and with the same sales force, is the expected future marginal product of the increased inventory. The cost of holding more cars reflects (1) depreciation of the cars sitting on the lot, and (2) the interest the car dealer must pay on the loan obtained to finance the higher inventory. The car dealer will make the inventory investment if the expected benefits of increasing her inventory, in terms of increased sales, are at least as great as the interest and depreciation costs of adding 50 cars. This principle is the same one that applies to business fixed investment.

We can also use this same approach to analyze residential investment. The expected future marginal product of an apartment building, for example, is the real value of rents that can be collected from the tenants, minus taxes and operating costs. The user cost of capital for an apartment building during a year is its depreciation, or loss of value from wear and tear, plus the interest cost (reflected in mortgage payments, for example). As for other types of capital, constructing an apartment building is profitable only if its expected future marginal product is at least as great as its user cost.

4.3 GOODS MARKET EQUILIBRIUM

In Chapter 3, we showed that the quantity of goods and services supplied in an economy depends on the level of productivity—as determined, for example, by the technology used—and on the quantity of inputs, such as the capital and labour used. In this chapter, we have discussed the factors that affect the demand for goods and services, particularly the demand for consumption goods by households and the demand for investment goods by firms. But how do we know that the amount of goods and services that consumers and investors want to buy will be the same as the amount that producers are willing to provide? Putting the question another way, what economic forces bring the goods market into equilibrium, with quantities demanded equal to quantities supplied? In this section, we show that the real interest rate is the key economic variable whose adjustments help bring the quantities of goods supplied and demanded into balance; thus, a benefit of our analysis is an explanation of what determines interest rates. Another benefit is that by adding the analysis of goods market equilibrium to the analysis of labour market equilibrium in Chapter 3, we take another large step toward constructing a complete model of the macroeconomy.

The goods market is in equilibrium when the aggregate quantity of goods supplied equals the aggregate quantity of goods demanded. (For brevity, we refer only to "goods" rather than to "goods and services," but services always are included.) Algebraically, this condition is

$$Y = C^d + I^d + G. \tag{4.7}$$

The left-hand side of Eq. (4.7) is the quantity of goods Y supplied by firms, which is determined by the factors discussed in Chapter 3. The right-hand side of Eq. (4.7) is the aggregate demand for goods. If we continue to assume no foreign sector, so that net exports are zero, the quantity of goods demanded is the sum of desired consumption by households, C^d, desired investment by firms, I^d, and government purchases G.[14] Equation (4.7) is called the goods market equilibrium condition.

The goods market equilibrium condition is different in an important way from the income–expenditure identity for a closed economy, $Y = C + I + G$ (this identity is Eq. 2.3, with $NX = 0$). The income–expenditure identity is a relationship between actual income (output) and actual spending, which, by definition, is always satisfied. In contrast, the goods market equilibrium condition does not always have to be satisfied. For example, firms may produce output faster than consumers want to buy it so that undesired inventories pile up in firms' warehouses. In this situation, the income–expenditure identity is still satisfied (because the undesired additions to firms' inventories are counted as part of total spending—see Chapter 2); but the goods market would not be in equilibrium because production exceeds *desired* spending (which does *not* include the undesired increases in inventories). Although in principle the goods market equilibrium condition need not always hold, strong forces act to bring the goods market into equilibrium fairly quickly.

A different, but equivalent, way to write the goods market equilibrium condition emphasizes the relationship between desired saving and desired investment. To obtain this alternative form of the goods market equilibrium condition, we first subtract $C^d + G$ from both sides of Eq. (4.7):

$$Y - C^d - G = I^d.$$

The left-hand side of this equation, $Y - C^d - G$, is desired national saving, S^d (see Eq. 4.1). Thus, the goods market equilibrium condition becomes

$$S^d = I^d. \tag{4.8}$$

This alternative way of writing the goods market equilibrium condition says that the goods market is in equilibrium when desired national saving equals desired investment.

Because saving and investment are central to many issues we present in this book, and because the desired-saving-equals-desired-investment form of the goods market equilibrium condition often is easier to work with, we utilize Eq. (4.8) in most of our analyses. However, we emphasize once again that Eq. (4.8) is equivalent to the condition that the supply of goods equals the demand for goods, Eq. (4.7).

THE SAVING–INVESTMENT DIAGRAM

For the goods market to be in equilibrium, then, the aggregate supply of goods must equal the aggregate demand for goods, or equivalently, desired national saving must equal desired investment. We demonstrate in this section that adjustments of the real interest rate allow the goods market to attain equilibrium.[15]

The determination of goods market equilibrium can be shown graphically with a saving–investment diagram (Figure 4.7). The real interest rate is measured along the vertical axis, and national saving and investment are measured along the horizontal axis. The saving curve, S, shows the relationship between desired national saving and the real interest rate. The upward slope of the saving curve reflects the empirical finding (see Section 4.1) that a higher real interest rate raises desired

---

14. We assume that G always equals the level desired by the government and so do not distinguish between desired and actual G.

15. Strictly speaking, we should refer to the expected real interest rate rather than simply the real interest rate. The two are the same if expected inflation and actual inflation are equal.

national saving. The investment curve, I, shows the relationship between desired investment and the real interest rate. The investment curve slopes downward because a higher real interest rate increases the user cost of capital and, thus, reduces desired investment.

Goods market equilibrium is represented by point E, at which desired national saving equals investment, as required by Eq. (4.8). The real interest rate corresponding to E (6% in this example) is the only real interest rate that clears the goods market. When the real interest rate is 6%, both desired national saving and desired investment equal 100.

How does the goods market come to equilibrium at E, where the real interest rate is 6%? Suppose instead that the real interest rate is 3%. As Figure 4.7 shows, when the real interest rate is 3%, the amount of investment that firms want to do (150) exceeds desired national saving (85). With investors wanting to borrow more than savers want to lend, the "price" of saving—the real interest rate that lenders receive—will be bid up. The return to savers will rise until it reaches 6%, and desired national saving and desired investment are equal. Similarly, if the real interest rate exceeds 6%, the amount that savers want to lend will exceed what investors want to borrow, and the real return paid to savers will be bid down. Thus, adjustments of the real interest rate, in response to an excess supply or excess demand for saving, bring the goods market into equilibrium.

Although Figure 4.7 shows goods market equilibrium in terms of equal saving and investment, keep in mind that an equivalent way to express goods market equilibrium is that the supply of goods, Y, equals the demand for goods, $C^d + I^d + G$ (Eq. 4.7). Table 4.4 illustrates this point with a numerical example consistent with the values shown in Figure 4.7. Here the assumption is that output Y and government purchases G are fixed at values of 450 and 150, respectively. Desired consumption C^d and desired investment I^d depend on the real interest rate. Desired consumption depends

FIGURE 4.7

GOODS MARKET EQUILIBRIUM

Goods market equilibrium occurs when desired national saving equals desired investment. In the figure, equilibrium occurs when the real interest rate is 6% and both desired national saving and desired investment equal 100. If the real interest rate were, say, 3%, desired investment (150) would not equal desired national saving (85), and the goods market would not be in equilibrium. Competition among borrowers for funds would then cause the real interest rate to rise until it reaches 6%.

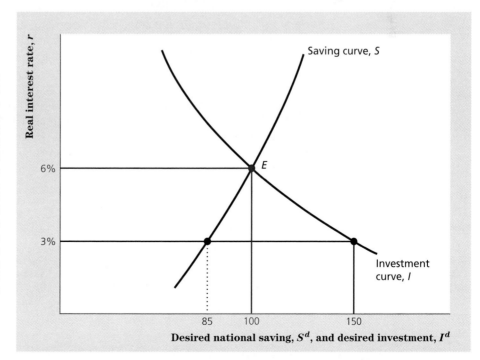

on the real interest rate because a higher real interest rate raises desired saving, which necessarily reduces desired consumption. Desired investment depends on the real interest rate because an increase in the real interest rate raises the user cost of capital, which lowers desired investment.

In the example in Table 4.4, when the real interest is 6%, desired consumption $C^d = 200$. Therefore, desired national saving $S^d = Y - C^d - G = 450 - 200 - 150 = 100$. Also, when the real interest rate is 6%, desired investment $I^d = 100$. As desired national saving equals desired investment when $r = 6\%$, the equilibrium real interest rate is 6%, as in Figure 4.7.

Note, moreover, that when the real interest rate is at the equilibrium value of 6%, the aggregate supply of goods, Y, which is 450, equals the aggregate demand for goods, $C^d + I^d + G = 200 + 100 + 150 = 450$. Thus, both forms of the goods market equilibrium condition, Eqs. (4.7) and (4.8), are satisfied when the real interest rate equals 6%.

Table 4.4 also illustrates how adjustments of the real interest rate bring about equilibrium in the goods market. Suppose that the real interest rate initially is 3%. Both components of private sector demand for goods (C^d and I^d) are higher when the real interest rate is 3% than when it is 6%. The reason is that consumers save less and firms invest more when real interest rates are relatively low. Thus, at a real interest of 3%, the demand for goods ($C^d + I^d + G = 215 + 150 + 150 = 515$) is greater than the supply of goods ($Y = 450$). Equivalently, at a real interest rate of 3%, Table 4.4 shows that desired investment ($I^d = 150$) exceeds desired saving ($S^d = 85$). As Figure 4.7 shows, an increase in the real interest rate to 6% eliminates the disequilibrium in the goods market by reducing desired investment and increasing desired national saving. An alternative explanation is that the increase in the real interest rate eliminates the excess of the demand for goods over the supply of goods by reducing both consumption demand and investment demand.

SHIFTS OF THE SAVING CURVE

For any real interest rate, a change in the economy that raises desired national saving shifts the saving curve to the right, and a change that reduces desired national saving shifts the saving curve to the left. (Summary table 5 on page 116, lists the factors affecting desired national saving.)

A shift of the saving curve leads to a new goods market equilibrium with a different real interest rate and different amounts of saving and investment. Figure 4.8 illustrates the effects of a decrease in desired national saving—resulting, for example, from a temporary increase in current government purchases. The initial equilibrium point is at E, where (as in Figure 4.7) the real interest rate is 6% and desired national saving and desired investment both equal 100. When current government purchases

TABLE 4.4

Components of Aggregate Demand for Goods (An example)

Real Interest Rate, r	Output, Y	Desired Consumption, C^d	Desired Aggregate Investment, I^d	Government Purchases, G	National Saving, $S^d = Y - C^d - G$	Demand for Goods, $C^d + I^d + G$
3%	450	215	150	150	85	515
6%	450	200	100	150	100	450

FIGURE 4.8

A DECLINE IN DESIRED SAVING

A change that reduces desired national saving, such as a temporary increase in current government purchases, shifts the saving curve to the left, from S^1 to S^2. The goods market equilibrium point moves from E to F. The decline in desired saving raises the real interest rate, from 6% to 7%, and lowers saving and investment, from 100 to 85.

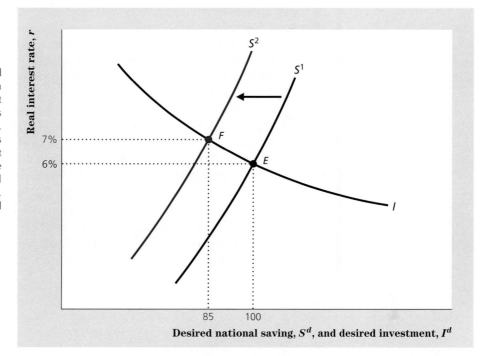

increase, the resulting decrease in desired national saving causes the saving curve to shift to the left, from S^1 to S^2. At the new goods market equilibrium point, F, the real interest rate is 7%, reflecting the fact that at the initial real interest rate of 6% the demand for funds by investors now exceeds the supply of saving.

Figure 4.8 also shows that in response to the increase in government purchases, national saving and investment both fall, from 100 to 85. Saving falls because of the initial decrease in desired saving, which is only partially offset by the increase in the real interest rate. Investment falls because the higher real interest rate raises the user cost of capital that firms face. When increased government purchases cause investment to decline, economists say that investment has been *crowded out*. The crowding out of investment by increased government purchases occurs, in effect, because the government is using more real resources, some of which would otherwise have gone into private investment.

APPLICATION

THE EFFECT OF WARS ON INVESTMENT AND THE REAL INTEREST RATE

Economically, an important aspect of war is that government purchases rise sharply as expenditures for military pay and equipment increase. Also, to a greater degree than other types of increases in government purchases, increases owing to war are temporary because military expenditures tend to return to lower peacetime levels after a war. Thus, thinking of a war as a largely temporary increase in current government purchases is reasonable. Our model predicts that a temporary increase in government purchases associated with a war will increase the real interest rate and reduce investment.

How well do these predictions hold up? Historically, wars (especially large ones) often have had negative effects on investment. Figure 4.9 shows Canadian real investment spending and real government purchases, measured relative to real GDP, for the period 1926–2000. During World War II a large decline in private investment spending mirrored the sharp increase in government purchases.

Besides predicting that wars will crowd out investment, our analysis also implies that real interest rates will be higher during wars.[16] Robert Barro of Harvard University has studied the behaviour of US real interest rates during wars.[17] He found that this prediction of the model does not fit the data well for the United States: Although real interest rates were slightly above normal during the Korean and Vietnam wars, they were below normal during the Civil War, World War I, and World War II.

For the US case, especially during the two world wars, government price controls, rationing, and control of production decisions may have prevented the private economy from functioning normally. As an alternative test of the theory, Barro used British data for the period 1730–1913. The British fought many wars, both large and small, during that period, and they rarely invoked price or production controls. Thus, the British data should provide a good test of the theory.

FIGURE 4.9

SHARES OF GOVERNMENT PURCHASES AND INVESTMENT IN CANADIAN GDP, 1926–2000

The graph shows the percentages of Canadian GDP devoted to government purchases and to private investment since 1926. Note the sharp increase in government purchases during World War II and the tendency for investment's share to mirror that of government spending.

Source: *Canadian Economic Observer, Historical Statistical Supplement*, cat. no. 11-210, Table 7.

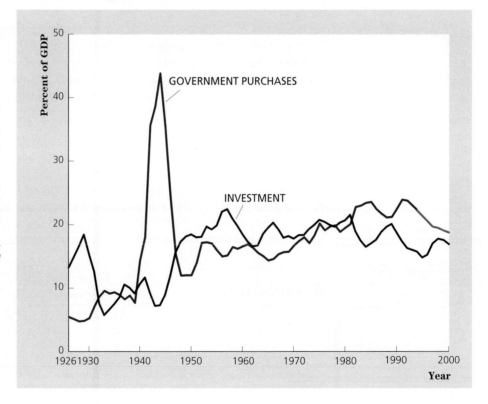

---

16. In Chapter 5, we will see that for small countries, we might expect an effect on the current account, but not on the interest rate.

17. "The Neoclassical Approach to Fiscal Policy," in Robert Barro, ed., *Modern Business Cycle Theory*, Cambridge, Mass.: Harvard University Press, 1989.

Barro found evidence in the British data that real interest rates do rise during wars. Long-term nominal interest rates (which, because inflation was essentially zero over this period, were about the same as real rates) were normally about 3.5% in Britain for this time span. During the American War of Independence, however, British rates rose to about 5.5%, and they reached 6% during the Napoleonic Wars. This effect is not huge, but it is statistically significant. For the British case, at least, Barro's evidence is consistent with the prediction that wars raise real interest rates.

SHIFTS OF THE INVESTMENT CURVE

Like the saving curve, the investment curve can shift. For any real interest rate, a change in the economy that raises desired investment shifts the investment curve to the right, and a change that lowers desired investment shifts the investment curve to the left.(See Summary table 6 for the factors affecting desired investment.)

The effects on goods market equilibrium of an increase in desired investment are shown in Figure 4.10. Suppose that a new invention or, at the aggregate level, an economic reform in an emerging market economy raises the expected future marginal product of capital. The increase in desired investment shifts the investment curve to the right, from I^1 to I^2, changing the goods market equilibrium point from E to G. The real interest rate rises from 6% to 8% because the increased demand for investment funds causes the real interest rate to be bid up. Saving and investment also increase, from 100 to 110, with the higher saving reflecting the willingness of savers to save more when the real interest rate rises.

In these last two chapters, we have presented supply–demand analyses of the labour and goods markets and developed tools needed to understand the behaviour of various macroeconomic variables, including employment, the real wage, output,

FIGURE 4.10

AN INCREASE IN DESIRED INVESTMENT

A change in the economy that increases desired investment, such as an invention that raises the expected future *MPK*, shifts the investment curve to the right, from I^1 to I^2. The goods market equilibrium point moves from E to G. The real interest rate rises from 6% to 8%, and saving and investment also rise, from 100 to 110.

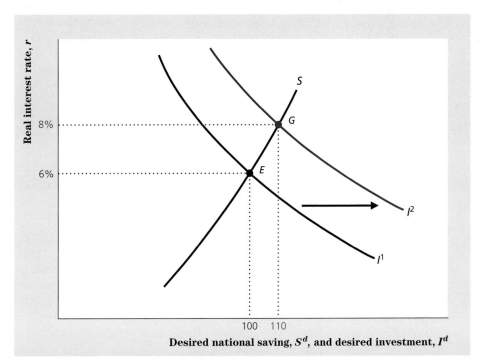

Desired national saving, S^d, and desired investment, I^d

saving, investment, and the real interest rate. These concepts—and a few more developed in the study of asset markets in Chapter 7—form the basis for the economic analysis presented in the rest of this book. In Chapter 5, we use the concepts developed so far to examine the determinants of trade flows and international borrowing and lending. In Chapter 6, we use them to tackle the fundamental question of why some countries' economies grow more quickly than others'.

CHAPTER SUMMARY

1. Because saving equals income minus consumption, a household's decisions about how much to consume and how much to save are really the same decision. Individuals and households save because they value both future consumption and current consumption; for the same amount of income, an increase in current saving reduces current consumption but increases the amount that the individual or household will be able to consume in the future.

2. For an individual or household, an increase in current income raises both desired consumption and desired saving. Analogously, at the national level, an increase in current output raises both desired consumption and desired national saving. At both the household and national levels, an increase in expected future income or in wealth raises desired consumption; however, because these changes raise desired consumption without affecting current income or output, they cause desired saving to fall.

3. An increase in the real interest rate has two potentially offsetting effects on saving. First, a higher real interest rate increases the price of current consumption relative to future consumption (each unit of current consumption costs $1+r$ units of forgone future consumption). In response to the increased relative price of current consumption, people substitute future consumption for current consumption by saving more today. This tendency to increase saving in response to an increase in the relative price of current consumption is called the substitution effect of the real interest rate on saving. Second, a higher real interest rate increases the wealth of savers by increasing the interest payments they receive, while reducing

the wealth of borrowers by increasing the amount of interest they must pay. By making savers wealthier, an increase in the real interest rate leads savers to consumer more and reduce their saving; however, because it makes borrowers poorer, an increase in the real interest rate causes borrowers to reduce their consumption and increase their saving. The change in current consumption that results because a consumer is made richer or poorer by an increase in the real interest rate is called the income effect of the real interest rate on saving.

For a saver, the substitution effect of an increase in the real interest rate (which tends to boost saving) and the income effect (which tends to reduce saving) work in opposite directions, so that the overall effect is ambiguous. For a borrower, both the substitution effect and the income effect of a higher real interest rate act to increase saving. Overall, empirical studies suggest that an increase in the real interest rate increases desired national saving and reduces desired consumption, but not by very much.

The real interest rate that is relevant to saving decisions is the expected after-tax real interest rate, which is the real return that savers expect to earn after paying a portion of the interest they receive in taxes.

4. With total output held constant, a temporary increase in government purchases reduces desired consumption. The reason is that higher government purchases imply increases in present or future taxes, which makes consumers feel poorer. However, the decrease in desired consumption is smaller than the increase in government purchases, so that desired national saving,

$Y - C^d - G$, falls as a result of a temporary increase in government purchases.

5. According to the Ricardian equivalence proposition, a current lump-sum tax cut should have no effect on desired consumption or desired national saving. The reason is that if there is no change in current or planned government purchases, a tax cut that increases current income must be offset by future tax increases that lower expected future income. If consumers do not take account of expected future tax changes, however, the Ricardian equivalence proposition will not hold, and a tax cut is likely to raise desired consumption and lower desired national saving.

6. The desired capital stock is the level of capital that maximizes expected profits. At the desired capital stock the expected future marginal product of capital equals the user cost of capital. The user cost of capital is the expected real cost of using a unit of capital for a period of time; it is the sum of the depreciation cost (the loss in value because the capital wears out) and the interest cost (the interest rate times the price of the capital good).

7. Any change that reduces the user cost of capital or increases the expected future marginal product of capital increases the desired capital stock. A reduction in the taxation of capital, as measured by the effective tax rate, also increases the desired capital stock.

8. Gross investment is spending on new capital goods. Gross investment minus depreciation (worn-out or scrapped capital) equals net investment, or the change in the capital stock. Firms invest in order to achieve their desired level of capital stock; when the desired capital stock increases, firms invest more.

9. The goods market is in equilibrium when the aggregate quantity of goods supplied equals the aggregate quantity of goods demanded, which (in a closed economy) is the sum of desired consumption, desired investment, and government purchases of goods and services. Equivalently, the goods market is in equilibrium when desired national saving equals desired investment. For any given level of output, the goods market is brought into equilibrium by changes in the real interest rate.

10. The determination of goods market equilibrium, for any supply of output Y, is represented graphically by the saving–investment diagram. The saving curve slopes upward because empirical evidence suggests that a higher real interest rate raises desired saving. The investment curve slopes downward because a higher real interest rate raises the user cost of capital, which lowers firms' desired capital stocks and, thus, the amount of investment they do. At constant output, changes in variables that affect desired saving or investment shift the saving or investment curves and change the real interest rate that clears the goods market.

KEY DIAGRAM 3

THE SAVING–INVESTMENT DIAGRAM

DIAGRAM ELEMENTS

- The real interest rate r is on the vertical axis; desired national saving S^d and desired investment I^d are on the horizontal axis.

- The saving curve, S, shows the level of desired national saving at each real interest rate. The saving curve slopes upward because a higher real interest rate increases the reward for saving and causes households to save more. (Empirically, this effect outweighs the tendency of a higher

real interest rate to lower saving by reducing the amount of saving necessary to reach any specified target.) Desired national saving is defined as $S^d = Y - C^d - G$, where Y is output, C^d is desired consumption, and G is government purchases.

- The investment curve, I, shows the amount that firms want to invest in new capital goods at each real interest rate. The investment curve slopes downward because a higher real interest rate raises the user cost of capital and thus lowers the amount of capital that firms want to use.

In an economy with no foreign trade, the goods market is in equilibrium when desired national saving equals desired investment. Equivalently, the goods market is in equilibrium when the aggregate quantity of goods supplied equals the aggregate quantity of goods demanded.

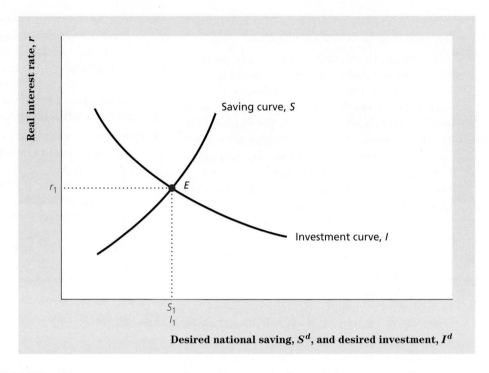

Desired national saving, S^d, and desired investment, I^d

ANALYSIS

- Goods market equilibrium requires that desired national saving equal desired investment, or $S^d = I^d$.

- Goods market equilibrium occurs in the diagram at point E, where the saving curve and investment curve intersect. At E desired national saving equals S_1, desired investment equals I_1, and $S_1 = I_1$. The real interest rate at E, r_1, is the real interest rate that clears the goods market.

- An alternative way to express the goods market equilibrium condition is as follows: The quantity of goods supplied, Y, equals the quantity of goods demanded by households, C^d, firms, I^d, and the government, G, or $Y = C^d + I^d + G$. As $S^d = Y - C^d - G$, this condition is equivalent to $S^d = I^d$.

FACTORS THAT SHIFT THE CURVES

- Any factor that raises desired national saving at a given real interest rate shifts the saving curve to the right; similarly, any factor that lowers desired national saving shifts the saving curve to the left. Factors that affect desired national saving are listed in Summary table 5. Similarly, factors that change desired investment for a given interest rate shift the investment curve; see Summary table 6 for factors that affect desired investment. Shifts of either curve change the goods market equilibrium point and thus change national saving, investment, and the real interest rate.

KEY TERMS

KEY EQUATIONS

$$S^d = Y - C^d - G \qquad (4.1)$$

Desired national saving, S^d, is the level of national saving that occurs when consumption is at its desired level. Equation (4.1) is obtained by substituting desired consumption C^d for actual consumption C in the definition of national saving.

$$r_{\text{a-t}} = (1 - t)i - \pi^e \qquad (4.2)$$

The expected after-tax real interest rate, $r_{\text{a-t}}$, is the after-tax nominal interest rate, $(1 - t)i$, minus the expected rate of inflation π^e. The expected after-tax real interest rate is the real return earned by a saver when a portion t of interest income must be paid as taxes.

$$uc = rp_K + dp_K = (r + d)p_K \qquad (4.3)$$

The user cost of capital, uc, is the sum of the interest cost, rp_K, and the depreciation cost, dp_K, where d is the depreciation rate and p_K is the price of a new capital good.

$$MPK^f = \frac{uc}{1 - \tau} = \frac{(r + d)p_K}{1 - \tau} \qquad (4.4)$$

The desired capital stock, or the capital stock that maximizes the firm's expected profits, is the capital stock for which the expected future marginal product of capital, MPK^f, equals the tax-adjusted user cost of capital, $uc/(1 - \tau)$, where τ is the tax rate on firm revenues (equivalently, the effective tax rate).

$$Y = C^d + I^d + G \qquad (4.7)$$

The goods market equilibrium condition says that the goods market is in equilibrium when the aggregate quantity of goods supplied, Y, equals the aggregate quantity of goods demanded, $C^d + I^d + G$.

$$S^d = I^d \qquad (4.8)$$

Another way of stating the goods market equilibrium condition is that desired national saving, S^d, must equal desired investment, I^d. This equation is equivalent to Eq. (4.7).

REVIEW QUESTIONS

1. Given income, how are consumption and saving linked? What is the basic motivation for saving?
2. How are desired consumption and desired saving affected by increases in current income, expected future income, and wealth?
3. Use the concepts of income effect and substitution effect to explain why the effect on desired saving of an increase in the expected real interest rate is potentially ambiguous.

4. What effect does a temporary increase in government purchases—for example, to fight a war—have on desired consumption and desired national saving, for a constant level of output? What is the effect on desired national saving of a lump-sum tax increase? Why is the effect of a lump-sum tax increase controversial?
5. What are the two components of the user cost of capital? Explain why each is a cost of using a capital good.
6. What is the desired capital stock? How does it depend on the expected future marginal product of capital, the user cost of capital, and the effective tax rate?
7. What is the difference between gross investment and net investment? Can gross investment be positive when net investment is negative?
8. Give two equivalent ways of describing equilibrium in the goods market. Use a diagram to show how goods market equilibrium is attained.
9. Explain why the saving curve slopes upward and the investment curve slopes downward in the saving–investment diagram. Give two examples of changes that would shift the saving curve to the right, and two examples of changes that would shift the investment curve to the right.

NUMERICAL PROBLEMS

1. A consumer is making saving plans for this year and next. She knows that her real income after taxes will be $25,000 in both years. Any part of her income saved this year will earn a real interest rate of 10% between this year and next year. Currently, the consumer has no wealth (no money in the bank or other financial assets, and no debts). There is no uncertainty about the future.

   The consumer wants to save an amount this year that will allow her to (1) make university tuition payments next year equal to $6,300 in real terms; (2) enjoy exactly the same amount of consumption this year and next year, not counting tuition payments as part of next year's consumption; and (3) have neither assets nor debts at the end of next year.
   a. How much should the consumer save this year? How much should she consume?

   How are the amounts that the consumer should save and consume affected by each of the following changes (taken one at a time, with other variables held at their original values)?
   b. Her current income rises from $25,000 to $27,100.
   c. The income she expects to receive next year rises from $25,000 to $27,100.

d. During the current year she receives an inheritance of $525 (an increase in wealth, not income).

e. The expected tuition payment for next year rises from $6,300 to $7,350.

f. The real interest rate rises from 10% to 25%.

2. Hula hoop fabricators cost $100 each. The Hi-Ho Hula Hoop Company is trying to decide how many of these machines to buy. HHHHC expects to produce the following number of hoops each year for each level of capital stock shown:

Number of Fabricators	Number of Hoops Produced per Year
0	0
1	100
2	150
3	180
4	195
5	205
6	210

Hula hoops have a real value of $1 each. HHHHC has no other costs besides the cost of fabricators.

a. Find the expected future marginal product of capital (in terms of dollars) for each level of capital. The MPK^f for the third fabricator, for example, is the real value of the extra output obtained when the third fabricator is added.

b. If the real interest rate is 12% per year and the depreciation rate of capital is 20% per year, find the user cost of capital (in dollars per fabricator per year). How many fabricators should HHHHC buy?

c. Repeat part (b) for a real interest rate of 8% per year.

d. Repeat part (b) for a 40% tax on HHHHC's sales revenues.

e. A technical innovation doubles the number of hoops a fabricator can produce. How many fabricators should HHHHC buy when the real interest rate is 12% per year? 8% per year? Assume that there are no taxes and that the depreciation rate is still 20% per year.

3. You have just taken a job that requires you to move to a new city. In relocating, you face the decision of whether to buy or rent a house. A suitable house costs $200,000 and you have saved enough for the down payment. The (nominal) mortgage interest rate is 10% per year, and you can also earn 10% per year on savings. Interest earnings on savings are taxable, and you are in a 30% tax bracket. Interest is paid or received, and taxes are paid, on the last day of the year. The expected inflation rate is 5% per year.

The cost of maintaining the house (replacing worn-out roofing, painting, and so on) is 6% of the value of the house. Assume that these expenses also are paid entirely on the last day of the year. If the maintenance is done, the house retains its full real value. There are no other relevant costs or expenses.

a. What is the expected after-tax real interest rate on the home mortgage?

b. What is the user cost of the house?

c. If all you care about is minimizing your living expenses, at what (annual) rent level would you be just indifferent between buying a house and renting a house of comparable quality? Rent is also paid on the last day of the year.

4. Consider a firm that faces the following expected future marginal product of capital:

$$MPK^f = 1,000 - 2K,$$

where MPK^f is the expected future marginal product of capital and K is the capital stock. The price of capital, p_K, is 1,000, the real interest rate, r, is 10%, and the depreciation rate, d, is 15%.

a. What is the user cost of capital?

b. What is the value of the firm's desired capital stock?

c. Now suppose that the firm must pay a 50% tax on its revenue. What is the value of the desired capital stock?

d. Now suppose that in addition to the 50% tax rate on revenue, the firm can take advantage of a 20% investment tax credit, which allows it to reduce its taxes paid by 20% of the value of new capital purchased. What is the firm's desired capital stock now? (*Hint*: An investment tax credit effectively reduces the price of capital to the firm.)

5. An economy has full-employment output of 900, and government purchases are 200. Desired consumption and desired investment are as follows:

Real Interest Rate (%)	Desired Consumption	Desired Investment
2	610	150
3	600	140
4	590	130
5	580	120
6	570	110

a. Why do desired consumption and desired investment fall as the real interest rate rises?

b. Find desired national saving for each value of the real interest rate.

c. If the goods market is in equilibrium, what are the values of the real interest rate, desired national saving, and desired investment? Show that both forms of the goods market equilibrium condition, Eqs. (4.7) and (4.8), are satisfied at the equilibrium. Assume that output is fixed at its full-employment level.

d. Repeat part (c) for the case in which government purchases fall to 160. Assume that the amount people desire to consume at each real interest rate is unchanged.

6. An economy has full-employment output of 600. Government purchases, G, are 120. Desired consumption and desired investment are

$$C^d = 360 - 200r + 0.10Y, \text{ and}$$
$$I^d = 120 - 400r,$$

where Y is output and r is the real interest rate.

a. Find an equation relating desired national saving S^d to r and Y.

b. Using both versions of the goods market equilibrium condition, Eqs. (4.7) and (4.8), find the real interest rate that clears the goods market. Assume that output equals full-employment output.

c. Government purchases rise to 144. How does this increase change the equation describing desired national saving? Show the change graphically. What happens to the market-clearing real interest rate?

7. Suppose that the economywide expected future marginal product of capital is $MPK^f = 20 - 0.02K$, where K is the future capital stock. The depreciation rate of capital, d, is 20% per period. The current capital stock is 900 units of capital. The price of a unit of capital is 1 unit of output. Firms pay taxes equal to 50% of their output. The consumption function in the economy is $C = 100 + 0.5Y - 200r$, where C is consumption, Y is output, and r is the real interest rate. Government purchases equal 200, and full-employment output is 1,000.

a. Suppose that the real interest rate is 10% per period. What are the values of the tax-adjusted user cost of capital, the desired future capital stock, and the desired level of investment?

b. Now consider the real interest rate determined by goods market equilibrium. This part of the problem will guide you to this interest rate.

    i. Write the tax-adjusted user cost of capital as a function of the real interest rate r. Also write the desired future capital stock and desired investment as functions of r.

    ii. Use the investment function derived in part (i) along with the consumption function and government purchases, to calculate the real interest rate that clears the goods market. What are the goods market-clearing values of consumption, saving, and investment? What are the tax-adjusted user cost of capital and the desired capital stock in this equilibrium?

8. (Appendix 4.A) A consumer has initial real wealth of 20, current real income of 90, and future real income of 110. The real interest rate is 10% per period.

a. Find the consumer's *PVLR*.

b. Write the equation for the consumer's budget constraint (using the given numerical values) and graph the budget line.

    Suppose that the consumer's goal is to smooth consumption completely. That is, he wants to have the same level of consumption in both the current and the future periods.

c. How much will he save and consume in the current period?

d. How will his current saving and consumption be affected by an increase of 11 in current income?

e. How will his current saving and consumption be affected by an increase of 11 in future income?

f. How will his current saving and consumption be affected by an increase of 11 in his initial wealth?

9. (Appendix 4.A) A consumer lives three periods, called the learning period, the working period, and the retirement period. Her income is 200 during the learning period, 800 during the working period, and 200 again during the retirement period. The consumer's initial assets are 300. The real interest rate is zero. The consumer desires perfectly smooth consumption over her lifetime.

a. What are consumption and saving in each period, assuming no borrowing constraints? What happens if the consumer faces a borrowing constraint that prevents her from borrowing?

b. Assume that the consumer's initial wealth is zero instead of 300. Repeat part (a). Does being borrowing-constrained mean that consumption is lower in all three periods of the consumer's life than it would be if no borrowing constraints applied?

ANALYTICAL PROBLEMS

1. Use the saving–investment diagram to analyze the effects of the following on national saving, investment, and the real interest rate. Explain your reasoning.

a. Consumers become more future-oriented and, thus, decide to save more.

b. The government announces a large, one-time bonus payment to farmers because of a drought. The bonus will be financed by additional taxes levied on the general population over the next five years.

c. The government introduces an investment tax credit (offset by other types of taxes, so total tax collections remain unchanged).

d. A large number of accessible oil deposits are discovered, which increases the expected future marginal product of oil rigs and pipelines. It also causes an increase in expected future income.

2. A country loses much of its capital stock to a war.

a. What effects should this event have on the country's current employment, output, and real wage?

b. What effect will the loss of capital have on desired investment?

c. The effects on desired national saving of the wartime losses are ambiguous. Give one reason for desired saving to rise and one reason for it to fall.

d. Assume that desired saving does not change. What effect does the loss of capital have on the country's real interest rate and the quantity of investment?

3. Analyze the following:

a. The effects of a temporary increase in the price of oil (a temporary adverse supply shock) on current output, employment, the real wage, national saving, investment, and the real interest rate. Because the supply shock is temporary, you should assume that the expected future *MPK* and households' expected future incomes are unchanged. Assume throughout that output and employment remain at full-employment levels (which may change).

b. The effects of a permanent increase in the price of oil (a permanent adverse supply shock) on current output, employment, the real wage, national saving, investment, and the real interest rate. Show that in this case, unlike the case of a temporary supply shock, the real interest rate need not change. (*Hint*: A permanent adverse supply shock lowers the current productivity of capital and labour, just as a temporary supply shock does. In addition, a permanent supply shock lowers both the expected future *MPK* and households' expected future incomes.)

4. Economists often argue that a temporary increase in government purchases, say, for military purposes, will crowd out private investment. Use the saving–investment diagram to illustrate this point, explaining why the curve(s) shift. Does it matter whether the temporary increase in military spending is funded by taxes or by borrowing?

Alternatively, suppose that the temporary increase in government purchases is for infrastructure (roads, sewers, bridges) rather than for military purposes. The gov-

ernment spending on infrastructure makes private investment more productive, increasing the expected future *MPK* at each level of the capital stock. Use the saving–investment diagram to analyze the effects of government infrastructure spending on current consumption, national saving, investment, and the real interest rate. Does investment by private firms get crowded out by this kind of government investment? If not, what kind of spending, if any, does get crowded out? Assume that there is no change in current productivity or current output and assume also (for simplicity) that households do not expect a change in their future incomes.

5. "A permanent increase in government purchases has a larger effect than a temporary increase of the same amount." Use the saving–investment diagram to evaluate this statement, focusing on effects on consumption, investment, and the real interest rate for a fixed level of output. (*Hint*: The permanent increase in government purchases implies larger increases in current and future taxes.)

6. (Appendix 4.A) Draw a budget line and indifference curves for a consumer who initially is a borrower. Be sure to indicate the no-borrowing, no-lending point and the optimal consumption point. Then show the effect on the budget line and the consumer's optimal consumption of an increase in the real interest rate. Using an intermediate budget line, show the income effect and the substitution effect. Do they work in the same direction or in opposite directions? Explain your answer.

7. (Appendix 4.A) Consumers typically pay a higher real interest rate to borrow than they receive when they lend (by making bank deposits, for example). Draw a consumer's budget line under the assumption that the real interest rate earned on funds lent, r_l, is lower than the real interest rate paid to borrow, r_b. Show how the budget line is affected by an increase in r_l, an increase in r_b, or an increase in the consumer's initial wealth.

Show that changes in r_l and r_b may leave current and future consumption unchanged. (*Hint*: Draw the consumer's indifference curves so that the consumer initially chooses the no-borrowing, no-lending point.)

APPENDIX 4.A

A FORMAL MODEL OF CONSUMPTION AND SAVING

This appendix analyzes more formally the decision about how much to consume and how much to save. We focus on the decisions of a consumer named Prudence. To help keep the analysis manageable, we make three simplifying assumptions:

1. The time horizon over which Prudence makes plans consists of only two periods: the present, or current, period and the future period. The current period might represent Prudence's working years and the future period might represent her retirement years, for example.

2. Prudence takes her current income, future income, and wealth as given.

3. Prudence faces a given real interest rate and can choose how much to borrow or save at that rate.

HOW MUCH CAN THE CONSUMER AFFORD? THE BUDGET CONSTRAINT

To analyze Prudence's decision about how much to consume and save, we first examine the choices available to her. To have some specific numbers to analyze, let us suppose that Prudence receives a fixed after-tax income, measured in real terms,[1] of 14,000 in the current period and expects to receive a real income of 11,000 in the future period. In addition, she begins the current period with real wealth of $6,000 in a savings account, and she can borrow or lend at a real interest rate of 10% per period.

Next, we list the symbols used to represent Prudence's situation:

y = Prudence's current real income (14,000);
y^f = Prudence's future real income (11,000);[2]
a = Prudence's real wealth (assets) at the beginning of the current period (6000);
r = real interest rate (10%);
c = Prudence's current real consumption (not yet determined);
c^f = Prudence's future real consumption (not yet determined).

In general, any amount of current consumption, c, that Prudence chooses will determine the amount of future consumption, c^f, that she will be able to afford. To work out this relationship, note that the funds that Prudence has on hand in the current period are her current income, y, and her initial wealth, a. If her current consumption is c, then at the end of the current period she has $y + a - c$ left.

Prudence can put these leftover current resources, $y + a - c$, in the bank to earn interest. If the real interest rate that she can earn on her deposit is r, the real

---

1. The units in which Prudence's income is measured are base-year dollars.
2. We do not include in future income y^f, the interest that Prudence earns on her saving. Future income, y^f, includes only labour income or transfers received, such as Canada Pension Plan payments.

value of her bank account (principal plus interest) in the future period will be $(y + a - c)(1 + r)$. In addition to the real value of her bank account in the future period, Prudence receives income of y^f, so her total resources in the future period equal $(y + a - c)(1 + r) + y^f$. Because the future period is the last period of Prudence's life, she spends all of her remaining resources on consumption.[3] Thus, Prudence's future consumption, c^f, is

$$c^f = (y + a - c)(1 + r) + y^f. \tag{4.A.1}$$

Equation (4.A.1) is called the *budget constraint.* It shows for any level of current consumption, c, how much future consumption, c^f, Prudence can afford, based on her current and future income and initial wealth.[4] The budget constraint in Eq. (4.A.1) is represented graphically by the *budget line,* which shows the combinations of current and future consumption that Prudence can afford, based on her current and future income, her initial level of wealth, and the real interest rate. Figure 4.A.1 depicts Prudence's budget line, with current consumption, c, on the horizontal axis and future consumption, c^f, on the vertical axis.

The budget line slopes downward, reflecting the trade-off between current and future consumption. If Prudence increases her current consumption by one unit, her saving falls by one unit. Because saving earns interest at rate r, a one-unit decline in saving today implies that Prudence's future resources—and thus her

FIGURE 4.A.1

THE BUDGET LINE

The budget line shows the combinations of current and future consumption, c and c^f, available to Prudence. The slope of the budget line is $-(1 + r) = -1.10$. The horizontal intercept is at $c = PVLR = 30,000$. You can verify that the combinations of current and future consumption at each of the lettered points (as well as any point on the budget line) satisfy $c + c^f / (1 + r) = PVLR = 30,000$.

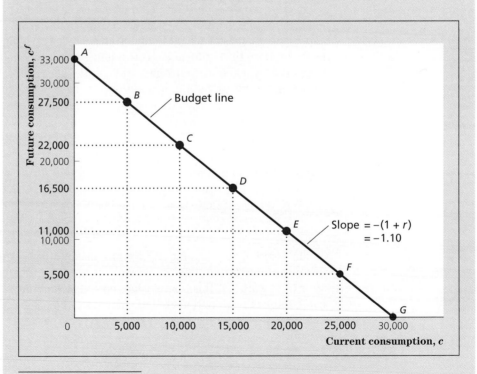

3. Here we assume that Prudence does not wish to leave a bequest to anyone. Later, we will briefly examine the effect of bequests on saving decisions.
4. In our derivation of Eq. (4.A.1), we assumed that Prudence's current consumption was less than her total current resources so that she had some resources left to deposit in the bank. However, the budget constraint, Eq. (4.A.1), still works if Prudence's current consumption exceeds her total current resources so that she must borrow from the bank.

future consumption—will be lower by $1 + r$ units. Because a one-unit increase in current consumption lowers future consumption by $1 + r$ units, the slope of the budget line is $-(1 + r)$. In our numerical example, the real interest rate is 10%, so the slope of the budget line in Figure 4.A.1 is -1.10.

PRESENT VALUES

We can conveniently represent Prudence's budget constraint by using the concept of *present value*. The present value measures the value of payments to be made in the future in terms of today's dollars or goods. To illustrate this concept, suppose that you must make a payment of $13,200 one year from now. How much money would you have to put aside today so that you could make that future payment? The answer to this question is the present value of $13,200.

The present value of a future payment depends on the interest rate. If the current nominal interest rate, i, is 10% per year, the present value of $13,200 to be paid one year from now is $12,000. The reason is that $12,000 deposited in the bank today at a 10% interest rate will earn $1,200 (10% of $12,000) of interest in one year, which, when added to the initial $12,000, gives the $13,200. Therefore, at an interest rate of 10%, having $13,200 one year from now is economically equivalent to having $12,000 today.

More generally, if the nominal interest rate is i per year, each dollar in the bank today is worth $1 + i$ dollars one year from now. To have $13,200 one year from now requires $13,200/(1 + i)$ in the bank today; thus, the present value of $13,200 to be paid one year from now is $13,200/(1 + i)$. As we have already shown, if $i = 10\%$ per year, the present value of $13,200 one year from now is $13,200/1.10 = $12,000$. If $i = 20\%$ per year, the present value of $13,200 one year in the future is $13,200/1.20 = $11,000$. Hence an increase in the interest rate reduces the present value of a future payment.

If future payments are measured in nominal terms, as in the preceding example, the appropriate interest rate for calculating present values is the nominal interest rate, i. If future payments are measured in real terms, present values are calculated in exactly the same way, except that we use the real interest rate, r, rather than the nominal interest rate, i. In analyzing Prudence's consumption–saving decision, we are measuring everything in real terms, so we use the real interest rate, r, to calculate the present values of Prudence's future income and consumption.

PRESENT VALUE AND THE BUDGET CONSTRAINT

We define the *present value of lifetime resources (PVLR)* as the present value of the income that a consumer expects to receive in current and future periods plus initial wealth. In the two-period case, the present value of lifetime resources is

$$PVLR = y + y^f/(1+r) + a \qquad (4.A.2)$$

which is the sum of current income, y,[5] the present value of future income, $y^f/(1 + r)$, and current wealth, a. In our example, Prudence has $PVLR = 14{,}000 + 11{,}000/1.10 + 6{,}000 = 30{,}000$.

---

5. Note that the present value of current income is just current income.

Next, we divide both sides of Eq. (4.A.1) by $(1 + r)$ and then add c to both sides to get

$$c + c^f/(1 + r) = y + y^f/(1 + r) + a$$
$$PVLC = PVLR \qquad\qquad (4.A.3)$$

The left side of Eq. (4.A.3) is the present value of lifetime consumption, $c + c^f/(1 + r)$, which we denote $PVLC$. The budget constraint in Eq. (4.A.3) states that the *present value of lifetime consumption (PVLC)*, equals the present value of lifetime resources $PVLR$.

In terms of Figure 4.A.1, and indeed for any graph of the budget line, $PVLR$ equals the value of current consumption, c, at the horizontal intercept of the budget line because the horizontal intercept is the point on the budget line at which future consumption, c^f, equals zero. Setting future consumption, c^f, to zero in Eq. (4.A.3) yields current consumption, c, on the left side of the equation, which must equal $PVLR$ on the right side. Thus, $c = PVLR$ at the horizontal intercept of the budget line.

What Does the Consumer Want? Consumer Preferences

The budget constraint, represented graphically as the budget line, shows the combinations of current and future consumption *available* to Prudence. To determine which of the many possible consumption combinations Prudence will choose, we need to know something about Prudence's preferences for current versus future consumption.

Economists use the term *utility* to describe the satisfaction or well being of an individual. Preferences about current versus future consumption are summarized by how much utility a consumer obtains from each combination of current and future consumption. We can graphically represent Prudence's preferences for current versus future consumption through *indifference curves*, which represent all combinations of current and future consumption that yield the same level of utility. Because Prudence is equally happy with all consumption combinations on an indifference curve, she does not care (that is, she is indifferent to) which combination she actually gets. Figure 4.A.1 shows two of Prudence's indifference curves. Because the consumption combinations corresponding to points X, Y, and Z all are on the same indifference curve, IC^1, Prudence would obtain the same level of utility at X, Y, and Z.

Indifference curves have three important properties, each of which has an economic interpretation and each of which appears in Figure 4.A.2:

1. *Indifference curves slope downward from left to right.* To understand why, let us suppose that Prudence has selected the consumption combination at point Y, where $c = 15{,}000$ and $c^f = 15{,}000$.[6] Now, suppose that Prudence must reduce her current consumption to $c = 13{,}000$. Clearly, if she reduces current consumption while maintaining future consumption at 15,000, she will suffer a

---

6. Point Y lies below Prudence's budget line, shown in Figure 4.A.1, which means that not only could Prudence afford this consumption combination but she would also have resources left over at the end of the future period. Unless she wants to leave a bequest, she would not actually choose such a combination for the resources shown in Figure 4.A.1.

FIGURE 4.A.2

INDIFFERENCE CURVES

All points on an indifference curve represent consumption combinations that yield the same level of utility. Indifference curves slope downward because a consumer can be compensated for a reduction in current consumption by an appropriate increase in future consumption. All points on IC^2 represent consumption combinations that are preferred to all consumption combinations represented by points on IC^1. Indifference curves are bowed toward the origin to reflect the consumption-smoothing motive. Prudence prefers the consumption combination at point W, which is an average of the combinations at point X and Z because W represents a smoother pattern of consumption. Thus the indifference curve containing $W(IC^2)$ lies above and to the right of the indifference curve containing X, Y, and Z (IC^1).

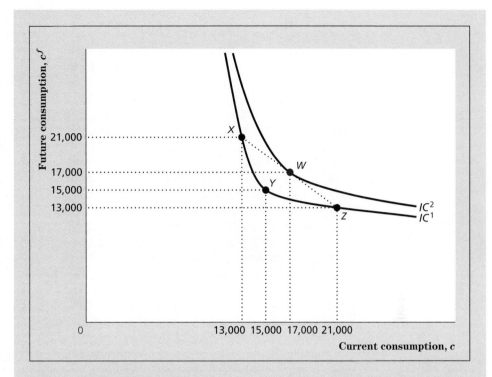

reduction in utility. However, Prudence can be compensated for this reduction in current consumption by additional future consumption. Suppose that if she increases her future consumption to $c^f = 21,000$ when her current consumption falls to $c = 13,000$, so that she moves to point X, her level of utility remains unchanged. In such a case, she is indifferent to the consumption combinations at X and Y, and points X and Y must lie on the same indifference curve. In general, any change in the level of current consumption must be accompanied by a change in the *opposite* direction in the level of future consumption so as to keep Prudence's level of utility unchanged. Thus, indifference curves, which represent consumption combinations with equal levels of utility, must slope downward from left to right.

2. *Indifference curves that are farther up and to the right represent higher levels of utility.* Consider for example point W, which lies above and to the right of point Y in Figure 4.A.2. Both current consumption and future consumption are higher at W than at Y. Because Prudence obtains utility from both current and future consumption, W offers a higher level of utility than does Y; that is, Prudence prefers W to Y. In fact, as all points on the indifference curve IC^1 yield the same level of utility as Y, Prudence prefers W to all points on the indifference curve IC^1. Furthermore, as all points on indifference curve IC^2 yield the same level of utility as W, Prudence prefers all points on IC^2 to all points on IC^1. In general, for any two indifference curves, consumers prefer consumption combinations on an indifference curve that is above and to the right of the other indifference curve.

3. *Indifference curves are bowed toward the origin.* This characteristic shape of indifference curves captures the consumption-smoothing motive, discussed in Chapter 4. Under the consumption-smoothing motive, consumers prefer a relatively smooth pattern of consumption over time to having large amounts of consumption in one period and small amounts in another period. We can illustrate the link between the shape of indifference curves and the consumption-smoothing motive by considering the following three consumption combinations in Figure 4.A.2: point X ($c = 13,000$; $c^f = 21,000$), point W ($c = 17,000$; $c^f = 17,000$), and point Z ($c = 21,000$; $c^f = 13,000$). Note that W corresponds to complete consumption smoothing, with equal consumption occurring in both periods. In contrast, X and Z represent consumption combinations with large changes in consumption between the first period and the second period. In addition, note that W represents a consumption combination that is the average of the consumption combinations at X and Z: Current consumption at W, 17,000, is the average of current consumption at X and Z, 13,000 and 21,000, respectively; similarly, future consumption at W, also 17,000, is the average of future consumption at X and Z, 21,000 and 13,000, respectively.

Even though point W essentially is an average of points X and Z, and Prudence is indifferent between X and Z, she prefers W to X and Z because W represents much "smoother" (more even) consumption. Graphically, her preference for W over X and Z is indicated by W's position above and to the right of indifference curve IC^1 (which runs through X and Z). Note that W lies on a straight line drawn between X and Z. The only way that W can lie above and to the right of IC^1 is if IC^1 bows toward the origin, as depicted in Figure 4.A.2. Thus, the bowed shape of the indifference curve reflects the consumption-smoothing motive.

THE OPTIMAL LEVEL OF CONSUMPTION

Combining Prudence's budget line (which describes her available consumption combinations) and her indifference curves (which describe her preferences for current versus future consumption), we can find the levels of current consumption and saving that make her happiest. This best available, or *optimal*, level of current consumption and saving is represented graphically by the point at which Prudence's budget line is tangent to an indifference curve, shown as point D in Figure 4.A.3.

To see why Prudence achieves her highest possible level of satisfaction, or utility, at point D, first note that D lies on indifference curve IC^*, which means that all consumption combinations on IC^* yield the same level of utility as D. All points on Prudence's budget line other than point D—points such as B and E, for example—lie on indifference curves that are below and to the left of IC^*. Thus, the consumption combinations represented by all of these other points yield a lower level of utility than the consumption combination at D. Prudence would prefer the consumption combination represented by a point such as T in Figure 4.A.3 to the consumption combination represented by D, because T lies on an indifference curve above and to the right of IC^*; because T also lies above the budget line, however, Prudence cannot afford the consumption combination represented by that point. With her budget constraint, Prudence cannot do any better than D.

We conclude that Prudence's utility-maximizing consumption and saving choice is represented by point D, where her budget line is tangent to an indifference curve. Here, her optimal level of current consumption is 15,000, and her optimal level of future consumption is 16,500. Prudence's choice of current

FIGURE 4.A.3

THE OPTIMAL
CONSUMPTION
COMBINATION

The optimal (highest utility) combination of current and future consumption is represented by the point of tangency between the budget line and an indifference curve (point *D*). All other points on the budget line, such as *B* and *E*, lie on indifference curves below and to the left of indifference curve *IC** and thus yield lower utility than the consumption combination at *D*, which lies on *IC**. Prudence would prefer the consumption combination at point *T* to the one at *D*, but as *T* lies above the budget line she cannot afford the consumption combination that *T* represents.

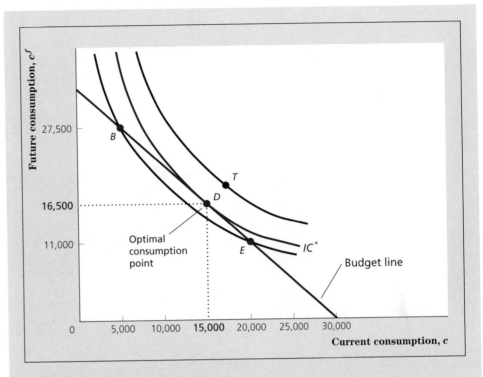

consumption automatically determines her current saving, *s*, which equals her current income, minus her optimal current consumption:

$$s = y - c = 14{,}000 - 15{,}000 = -1{,}000.$$

Thus, Prudence chooses to dissave (decrease her initial assets) by 1,000.

THE EFFECTS OF CHANGES IN INCOME AND WEALTH ON CONSUMPTION AND SAVING

The formal model developed in this appendix provides a helpful insight: *The effect on consumption of a change in current income, expected future income, or wealth depends only on how that change affects the consumer's present value of lifetime resources, or PVLR.*

AN INCREASE IN CURRENT INCOME

Suppose that Prudence receives a bonus at work of 4,000, which raises her current real income from 14,000 to 18,000. Her initial assets (6,000), future income (11,000), and the real interest rate (10%) remain unchanged; hence the increase of 4,000 in current income implies an equal increase in Prudence's present value of lifetime resources, or *PVLR*. If she has not yet committed herself to her original consumption–saving plan, how might Prudence revise that plan in light of her increased current income?

We use the graph in Figure 4.A.4 to answer this question. In Figure 4.A.4, BL^1 is Prudence's original budget line, and point *D*, where *c* = 15,000 and c^f = 16,500, represents Prudence's original, pre-bonus consumption plan. Prudence's

An increase in current
income, future income,
and/or initial wealth that
raises Prudence's *PVLR* by
4,000 causes the budget
line to make a parallel shift
to the right by 4000, from
BL^1 to BL^2. If Prudence's
original consumption plan
was to consume at point *D*,
she could move to point *H*
by spending all the in-
crease on future consump-
tion and none on current
consumption; or she could
move to point *K* by spending all the increase on
current consumption and
none on future consump-
tion. However, if Prudence
has a consumption-
smoothing motive she will
move to point *J*, which has
both higher current con-
sumption and higher future
consumption than *D*. Point
J is optimal because it lies
where the new budget line
BL^2 is tangent to an indifference curve, IC^{**}.

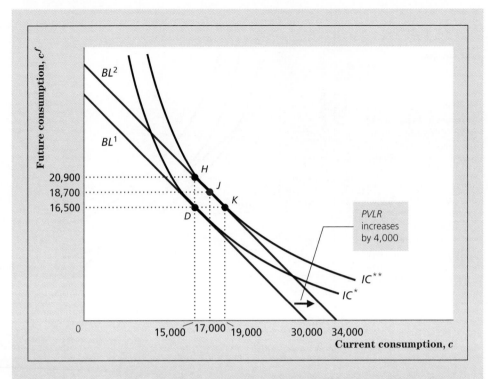

bonus will allow her to consume more, both now and in the future, so the increase
in her income causes her budget line to shift. To see exactly how it shifts, note that
the increase of 4,000 in Prudence's current income implies that her *PVLR* also
increases by 4,000. Because the horizontal intercept of the budget line occurs at
$c = PVLR$, the bonus shifts the horizontal intercept to the right by 4,000. The
slope of the budget line, $-(1 + r) = -1.10$, remains unchanged because the real interest rate r is unchanged. Thus, the increase in current income of 4,000 causes
a parallel shift of the budget line to the right by 4,000, from BL^1 to BL^2.

That shift demonstrates graphically that after receiving her bonus, Prudence
can enjoy greater current and future consumption. One strategy for Prudence,
represented by point *K* on the new budget line BL^2, is to use the entire bonus to
increase her current consumption by 4,000 while leaving her future consumption
unchanged. Another strategy, represented by point *H* on BL^2, is to save all of
her bonus while keeping her current consumption unchanged, and then use both
the bonus and the interest of 400 earned on the bonus to increase her future
consumption by 4,400.

If Prudence operates under a consumption-smoothing motive, she will use
her bonus to increase *both* her current consumption and (by saving part of her
bonus) her future consumption, thereby choosing a point on BL^2 between point
K (consume the entire bonus) and point *H* (save the entire bonus). If her indifference curves are as shown in Figure 4.A.4, she will move to *J*, where her new budget line, BL^2, is tangent to the indifference curve IC^{**}. At *J*, current consumption,
c, is 17,000, future consumption, c^f, is 18,700, and saving, *s*, is 18,000 − 17,000
= 1,000. Both current and future consumption are higher at *J* than at *D* (where *c*
= 15,000 and c^f = 16,500). Prudence's current saving of 1,000 at *J* is higher than her
saving was at *D* (where she dissaved by 1,000) because the increase in her current

consumption of 2,000 is less than the increase in her current income of 4,000. This example illustrates that an increase in current income raises both current consumption and current saving.

AN INCREASE IN FUTURE INCOME

Suppose that Prudence does not receive her bonus of 4,000 in the current period, so that her current income, y, remains at its initial level of 14,000. Instead, because of an improved company pension plan, she learns that her future income will increase by 4,400, so y^f rises from 11,000 to 15,400. How will this good news affect Prudence's current consumption and saving?

At a real interest rate of 10%, the improvement in the pension plan increases the present value of Prudence's future income by 4,400/1.10, or 4,000. So, as in the case of the current-period bonus just discussed, the improved pension plan raises Prudence's *PVLR* by 4,000 and causes a parallel shift of the budget line to the right by that amount. The effects on current and future consumption are therefore exactly the same as they were for the increase of 4,000 in current income (and Figure 4.A.4 applies equally well here).

Although increases in current income and expected future income that are equal in present value will have the same effects on current and planned future consumption, the effects of these changes on current saving are different. Previously, we showed that an increase in current income raises current saving. In contrast, because the increase in future income raises current consumption (by 2,000 in this example) but does not affect current income, it causes saving to fall (by 2,000, from –1,000 to –3,000). Prudence knows that she will be receiving more income in the future, so she has less need to save today.

AN INCREASE IN WEALTH

Changes in wealth also affect consumption and saving. As in the cases of current and future income, the effect of a change in wealth on consumption depends only on how much the *PVLR* changes. For example, if Prudence finds a passbook savings account in her attic worth 4,000, her *PVLR* increases by 4,000. To illustrate this situation, we use Figure 4.A.4 again. Prudence's increase in wealth raises her *PVLR* by 4,000 and, thus, shifts the budget line to the right by 4,000, from BL^1 to BL^2. As before, her optimal consumption choice goes from point D (before she finds the passbook) to point J (after her increase in wealth). Because the increase in wealth raises current consumption (from 15,000 at D to 17,000 at J) but leaves current income (14,000) unchanged, it results in a decline in current saving (from –1,000 at D to –3,000 at J). Being wealthier, Prudence does not have to save as much of her current income (actually, she is increasing her dissaving) to provide for the future.

The preceding analyses show that changes in current income, future income, and initial wealth all lead to parallel shifts of the budget line by the amount that they change the *PVLR*. Economists use the term *income effect* to describe the impact of any change that causes a parallel shift of the budget line.

THE PERMANENT INCOME THEORY

In terms of our model, a temporary increase in income represents a rise in current income, y, with future income, y^f, held constant. A permanent increase in income raises *both* current income, y, *and* future income, y^f. Therefore, a permanent one-unit increase in income leads to a larger increase in *PVLR* than does a temporary one-unit increase in income. Because income changes affect consumption only to the extent that they lead to changes in *PVLR*, our theory predicts that a permanent one-unit increase in income will raise current and future consumption more than a temporary one-unit increase in income will.

This distinction between the effects of permanent and temporary income changes is emphasized in the *permanent income theory* of consumption and saving, developed in the 1950s by Nobel laureate Milton Friedman. He pointed out that income should affect consumption only through the *PVLR* in a many-period version of the model we present here. Thus, permanent changes in income, because they last for many periods, may have much larger effects on consumption than temporary changes in income. As a result, temporary income increases would be mostly saved, and permanent income increases would be mostly consumed.[7]

CONSUMPTION AND SAVING OVER MANY PERIODS: THE LIFE-CYCLE MODEL

The two-period model suggests that a significant part of saving is intended to pay for retirement. However, it does not reflect other important aspects of a consumer's lifetime income and consumption patterns. For example, income typically rises over most of a person's working life, and people save for reasons other than retirement. The *life-cycle model* of consumption and saving, originated in the 1950s by Nobel laureate Franco Modigliani and his associates, extends the model from two periods to many periods and focuses on the patterns of income, consumption, and saving throughout an individual's life.

The essence of the life-cycle model is shown in Figure 4.A.5. In Figure 4.A.5(a), the typical consumer's patterns of income and consumption are plotted against the consumer's age, from age 20 years (the approximate age of economic independence) to age 80 years (the approximate age of death). Two aspects of Figure 4.A.5(a) are significant.

First, the average worker experiences steadily rising real income, with peak earnings typically occurring between the ages of 50 and 60 years. After retirement, income (excluding interest earned from previous saving) drops sharply.

Second, the lifetime pattern of consumption is much smoother than the pattern of income over time, which is consistent with the consumption-smoothing motive discussed earlier. Although shown as perfectly flat in Figure 4.A.5(a), consumption, in reality, varies somewhat by age; for example, it will be higher during years of high child-rearing expenses. An advantage of using the life-cycle model to study consumption and saving is that it may be easily modified to allow for various patterns of lifetime income and consumption.

---

7. Friedman also provided some of the first empirical evidence for this theory. For example, he found that the consumption of farm families, on average, responded less to changes in income than did the consumption of nonfarm families. Friedman's explanation was that because farm incomes depend heavily on weather and crop prices, both of which are volatile, changes in farm incomes are much more likely to be temporary than are changes in nonfarm incomes. Current changes in farm incomes have a smaller effect on the *PVLR* and therefore have a smaller effect on current consumption.

FIGURE 4.A.5

LIFE-CYCLE
CONSUMPTION,
INCOME, AND SAVING

(a) Income and consumption are plotted against age. Income typically rises gradually throughout most of a person's working life and peaks shortly before retirement. The desire for a smooth pattern of consumption means that consumption varies less than income over the life cycle. Consumption here is constant.

(b) Saving is the difference between income and consumption; the saving pattern is hump-shaped. Early in a person's working life consumption is larger than income, so saving is negative. In the middle years saving is positive; the excess of income over consumption is used to repay debts incurred earlier in life and to provide for retirement. During retirement people dissave.

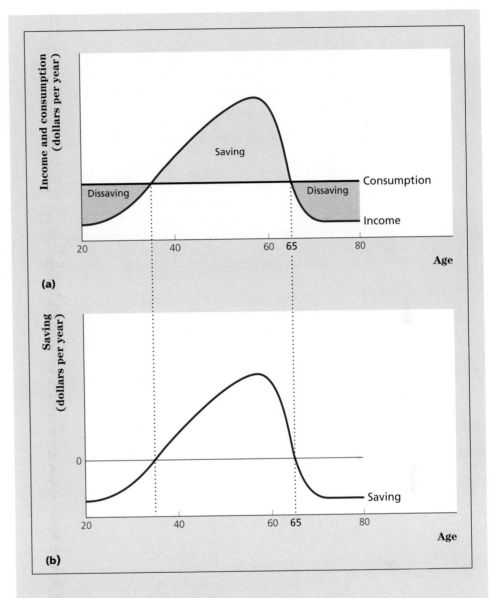

The lifetime pattern of saving, shown in Figure 4.A.5(b), is the difference between the income and consumption curves in Figure 4.A.5(a). This overall hump-shaped pattern has been confirmed empirically. Saving is minimal or even negative during the early working years, when income is low. Maximum saving occurs when the worker is between ages 50 and 60 years, when income is highest. Finally, dissaving occurs during retirement as the consumer draws down accumulated wealth to meet living expenses.

An important implication of the hump-shaped pattern of saving is that national saving rates depend on the age distribution of a country's population. Countries with unusually young or unusually old populations have low saving rates, and countries with relatively more people in their middle years have higher saving rates.

Bequests and Saving

We have assumed that the consumer plans to spend all of his or her wealth and income during his or her lifetime, leaving nothing to heirs. In reality, many people leave bequests, or inheritances, to children, charities, and others. To the extent that consumers desire to leave bequests, they will consume less and save more than when they simply consume all their resources during their lifetimes.

Ricardian Equivalence

One of the most significant results of analyzing our model is that changes in income or wealth affect desired consumption only to the extent that they affect the consumer's *PVLR*. The point made by advocates of Ricardian equivalence, discussed in Chapter 4, is that, holding current and future government purchases constant, *a change in current taxes does not affect the consumer's PVLR and thus should not affect desired consumption, C^d, or desired national saving, $Y - C^d - G$.*

To illustrate this idea, suppose that the government cuts Prudence's current taxes by 100. This tax reduction increases Prudence's current income by 100, which (all else being equal) would cause her to consume more. Because the government's revenue has been reduced by 100 and its expenditures have not changed, however, the government must increase its current borrowing from the public by 100 (per taxpayer). Furthermore, the government must pay interest on its borrowings. For example, if the real interest rate that the government must pay on its debt is 10%, in the future period the government's outstanding debt will be 110 greater than it would have been without the tax cut.

As a taxpayer, Prudence is ultimately responsible for the government's debts. Suppose that the government decides to repay its borrowings and accumulated interest in the future period (Chapter 15 discusses what happens if the government's debt is left for Prudence's descendants to repay). To repay its debt plus interest, the government must raise taxes in the future period by 110, so Prudence's expected future income falls by 110. Overall, then, the government's tax program has raised Prudence's current income by 100 but reduced her future income by 110. At a real interest rate of 10%, the present value of the future income change is –100, which cancels out the increase in current income of 100. Thus, Prudence's *PVLR* is unchanged by the tax cut, and (as the Ricardian equivalence proposition implies) she should not change her current consumption.

Excess Sensitivity and Borrowing Constraints

A variety of studies have confirmed that consumption is affected by current income, expected future income, and wealth, and that permanent income changes have larger effects on consumption than do temporary income changes—all of which are outcomes implied by the model. Nevertheless, some studies show that the response of consumption to a change in current income is greater than would be expected on the basis of the effect of the current income change on *PVLR*. This tendency of consumption to respond to current income more strongly than the model predicts is called the *excess sensitivity* of consumption to current income.

One explanation for excess sensitivity is that people are more short-sighted than assumed in our model and, thus, consume a larger portion of an increase in current income than predicted by it. Another explanation, which is more in the spirit of the model, is that the amount that people can borrow is limited. A restriction imposed by lenders on the amount that someone can borrow against future income is called a *borrowing constraint.*

The effect of a borrowing constraint on the consumption–saving decision depends on whether the consumer would want to borrow in the absence of a borrowing constraint. If the consumer would not want to borrow even if borrowing were possible, the borrowing constraint is said to be *nonbinding.* When a consumer wants to borrow but is prevented from doing so, the borrowing constraint is said to be *binding.* A consumer who faces a binding borrowing constraint will spend all available current income and wealth on current consumption so as to come as close as possible to the consumption combination desired in the absence of borrowing constraints. Such a consumer would consume the entire amount of an increase in current income. Thus, the effect of an increase in current income on current consumption is greater for a consumer who faces a binding borrowing constraint than is predicted by our simple model without borrowing constraints. In macroeconomic terms, this result implies that—if a significant number of consumers face binding borrowing constraints—the response of aggregate consumption to an increase in aggregate income will be greater than implied by the basic theory in the absence of borrowing constraints. In other words, if borrowing constraints exist, consumption may be excessively sensitive to current income.[8]

THE REAL INTEREST RATE AND THE CONSUMPTION–SAVING DECISION

To explore the effects of a change in the real interest rate on consumption and saving, let us return to the two-period model and Prudence's situation. Recall that Prudence initially has current real income, y, of 14,000, future income, y^f, of 11,000, initial wealth, a, of 6,000, and that she faces a real interest rate, r, of 10%. Her budget line, which is the same as in Figure 4.A.1, is shown in Figure 4.A.6 as BL^1. Now let us see what happens when for some reason the real interest rate jumps from 10% to 76%.[9]

THE REAL INTEREST RATE AND THE BUDGET LINE

To see how Prudence's budget line is affected when the real interest rate rises, let us first consider point E on the budget line BL^1. Point E is special in that it is the only point on the budget line at which current consumption equals current income plus initial wealth ($c = y + a = 20,000$) and future consumption equals

---

8. Although we have no direct way of counting how many consumers are constrained from borrowing, estimates suggest that to account for the observed relationship between consumption and current income, during any year some 13% to 25% of Canadian consumers face binding borrowing constraints. See Tony S. Wirjanto, "Testing the Permanent Income Hypothesis: The Evidence from Canadian Data," *Canadian Journal of Economics*, August 1991, pp. 563–577.

9. A 76% real interest rate is not realistic, but assuming this large a change makes its effects more obvious.

FIGURE 4.A.6

THE EFFECT OF AN
INCREASE IN THE REAL
INTEREST RATE ON THE
BUDGET LINE

The figure shows the effect
on Prudence's budget line
of an increase in the real
interest rate, r, from 10% to
76%. Because the slope of
a budget line is $-(1 + r)$ and
the initial real interest rate
is 10%, the slope of
Prudence's initial budget
line, BL^1, is -1.10. The
initial budget line, BL^1, also
passes through the no-
borrowing, no-lending
point, E, which represents
the consumption combina-
tion that Prudence obtains
by spending all her current
income and wealth on
current consumption.
Because E can still be
obtained when the real
interest rate rises, it also lies
on the new budget line,
BL^2. However, the slope of
BL^2 is -1.76, reflecting the
rise in the real interest rate
to 76%. Thus, the higher
real interest rate causes the
budget line to pivot clockwise around the no-borrowing, no-lending point.

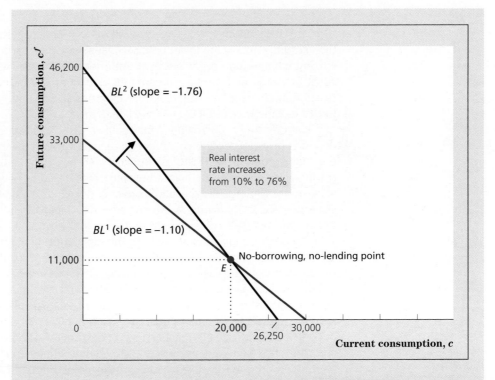

future income ($c^f = y^f = 11,000$). If Prudence chooses this consumption combination, she does not need to borrow (her current income and initial wealth are just
sufficient to pay for her current consumption), nor does she have any current
resources left to deposit in (lend to) the bank. Thus, E is the *no-borrowing, no-
lending point.* Because E involves neither borrowing nor lending, the consumption combination it represents is available to Prudence regardless of the
real interest rate. Thus, the no-borrowing, no-lending point remains on the budget line when the real interest rate changes.

Next, recall that the budget line's slope is $-(1 + r)$. When the real interest
rate, r, jumps from 10% to 76%, the slope of the budget line changes from -1.10
to -1.76; that is, the new budget line becomes steeper. Because the budget line becomes steeper but still passes through the no-borrowing, no-lending point, E, it
pivots clockwise around point E.

THE SUBSTITUTION EFFECT

As we discussed in Chapter 4, the price of current consumption in terms of future
consumption is $1 + r$, because if Prudence increases her consumption by one
unit today, thereby reducing her saving by one unit, she will have to reduce her
future consumption by $1 + r$ units. When the real interest rate increases, current consumption becomes more expensive relative to future consumption. In
response to this increase in the relative price of current consumption, Prudence
substitutes away from current consumption toward future consumption by increasing her saving. This increase in saving reflects *the substitution effect of the
real interest rate on saving,* introduced in Chapter 4.

The substitution effect is illustrated graphically in Figure 4.A.7. Initially, the real interest rate is 10% and the budget line is BL^1. Suppose for now that Prudence's preferences are such that BL^1 is tangent to an indifference curve, IC^1, at the no-borrowing, no-lending point, E.[10] At a real interest rate of 10%, Prudence chooses the consumption combination at E.

When the real interest rate rises from 10% to 76%, the budget line pivots clockwise to BL^2. Because Prudence's original consumption point—the no-borrowing, no-lending point, E—also lies on the new budget line, BL^2, she has the option of remaining at E and enjoying the same combination of current and future consumption after the real interest rate rises. Points along BL^2 immediately above and to the left of E lie above and to the right of IC^1, however. These points represent consumption combinations that are available to Prudence and yield a higher level of utility than the consumption combination at E. Prudence can attain the highest level of utility along BL^2 at point V, where indifference curve IC^2 is tangent to BL^2. In response to the increase in the relative price of current consumption, Prudence reduces her current consumption, from 20,000 to 17,000, and moves from E to V on BL^2. Her reduction of 3,000 in current consumption between E and V is equivalent to an increase of 3,000 in saving. The increase in saving between E and V reflects the substitution effect on saving of a higher real interest rate.

THE INCOME EFFECT

If Prudence's current consumption initially equals her current resources (current income plus initial wealth) so that she is neither a lender nor a borrower, a change

FIGURE 4.A.7

THE SUBSTITUTION EFFECT OF AN INCREASE IN THE REAL INTEREST RATE

We assume that Prudence's preferences are such that when the real interest rate is 10% she chooses the consumption combination at the no-borrowing, no-lending point E, on the initial budget line BL^1. Point E lies on the indifference curve IC^1. An increase in the real interest rate to 76% causes the budget line to pivot clockwise from BL^1 to BL^2, as in Fig. 4.A.6. By substituting future consumption for current consumption along the new budget line, BL^2, Prudence can reach points that lie above and to the right of IC^1; these points represent consumption combinations that yield higher utility than the consumption combination at E. Her highest utility is achieved by moving to point V, where the new budget line, BL^2, is tangent to indifference curve IC^2. The drop in current consumption (by 3,000) and the resulting equal rise in saving that occur in moving from E to V reflect the substitution effect of the increase in the real interest rate.

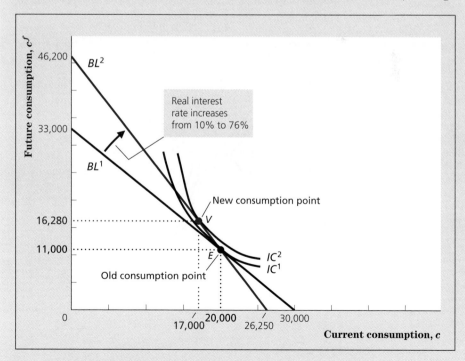

10. Note that Prudence's indifference curves in Figure 4.A.7 are different from those in Figure 4.A.4.

in the real interest rate has only a substitution effect on her saving, as shown in Figure 4.A.7. If her current consumption initially is not equal to her current resources, however, then an increase in the real interest rate also has an income effect. As we discussed in Chapter 4 if Prudence is initially a saver (equivalently, a lender), with current consumption less than her current resources (current income plus initial wealth), an increase in the real interest rate makes her financially better off by increasing the future interest payments that she will receive. In response to this increase in future interest income, she increases her current consumption and reduces her current saving. On the other hand, if Prudence is initially a borrower, with current consumption exceeding her current resources, an increase in the real interest rate increases the interest she will have to pay in the future. Having to make higher interest payments in the future makes Prudence financially worse off overall, leading her to reduce her current consumption. Thus, for a borrower, the income effect of an increase in the real interest rate leads to reduced current consumption and increased saving.

THE SUBSTITUTION EFFECT AND THE INCOME EFFECT TOGETHER

Figure 4.A.8 illustrates the full impact of an increase in the real interest rate on Prudence's saving, including the substitution and income effects—assuming that Prudence initially is a lender. As before, Prudence's original budget line is BL^1 when the real interest rate is 10%. We now assume that Prudence's preferences are such that BL^1 is tangent to an indifference curve, IC^1, at point D. Thus, at a 10% real interest rate, Prudence plans current consumption of 15,000 and future consumption of 16,500. Her current resources equal 20,000 (current income of

FIGURE 4.A.8

AN INCREASE IN THE REAL INTEREST RATE WITH BOTH AN INCOME EFFECT AND A SUBSTITUTION EFFECT

We assume that Prudence initially consumes at point D on the original budget line, BL^1. An increase in the real interest rate from 10% to 76% causes the budget line to pivot clockwise, from BL^1 to the new budget line, BL^2. We break the overall shift of the budget line into two parts: (1) a pivot around the original consumption point, D, to yield an intermediate budget line, BL^{int}, and (2) a parallel shift from BL^{int} to the final budget line, BL^2. The substitution effect is measured by the movement from the original consumption point, D, to point P on BL^{int}, and the income effect is measured by the movement from P to Q on BL^2. As drawn, the substitution effect is larger than the income effect so that the overall effect is for current consumption to fall and saving to rise.

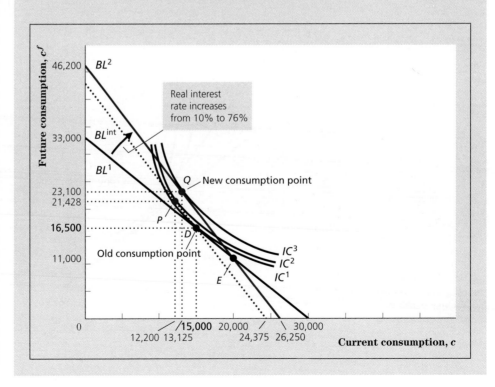

14,000 plus initial assets of 6,000), so if she enjoys current consumption of 15,000 she will have resources of 5,000 to lend. Her chosen point, D, is located to the left of the no-borrowing, no-lending point, E (current consumption is lower at D than at E) showing that Prudence is a lender.

The increase in the real interest rate from 10% to 76% causes Prudence's budget line to pivot clockwise through the no-borrowing, no-lending point, E, ending at BL^2 as before. To separate the substitution and income effects of the increase in the real interest rate, think of the movement of the budget line from BL^1 to BL^2 as taking place in two steps.

First, imagine that the original budget line, BL^1, pivots clockwise around Prudence's original consumption combination, point D, until it is parallel with the new budget line, BL^2 (that is, its slope is –1.76). The resulting intermediate budget line is the dotted line, BL^{int}. Second, imagine that BL^{int} makes a parallel shift to the right to BL^2.

The response of Prudence's saving and current consumption to the increase in the real interest rate can also be broken into two steps. First, consider her response to the pivot of the budget line through point D, from BL^1 to BL^{int}. If this change were the only one in Prudence's budget line, she would move from D to P ($c = 12,200$ and $c^f = 21,428$) on BL^{int}. At P, she would save more and enjoy less current consumption than at D. The increase in saving between D and P, similar to Prudence's shift from E to V in Figure 4.A.7, measures the substitution effect on Prudence's saving of the increase in the real interest rate.

Second, consider the effect of the parallel shift from BL^{int} to BL^2. The new budget line, BL^2, is tangent to an indifference curve, IC^3, at point Q, so Prudence will choose the consumption combination at Q. Current and future consumption are higher, and saving is lower, at Q than at P. The increase in current consumption and the decrease in saving between P and Q reflect the income effect of the increase in the real interest rate. Thus, as discussed earlier, income effects occur when a change in some variable causes a parallel shift of the budget line.

The total change in Prudence's consumption and saving resulting from the rise in the real interest rate is depicted in Figure 4.A.8 as the change in saving between point D and point Q. This change is the sum of the substitution effect, measured by the increase in saving in moving from D to P, and the income effect, measured by the decline in saving in moving from P to Q. In Figure 4.A.8, current consumption is lower and saving is higher at the final point, Q, than at the original point, D. However, we could just as easily draw the curves so that saving is less at the final point, Q, than at the initial point, D. Thus, the theory fails to predict whether Prudence's saving will rise or fall in response to an increase in the real interest rate because the income and substitution effects work in opposite directions for a lender.

As we discussed in Chapter 4, for a borrower the income and substitution effects work in the same direction (Analytical Problem 6 at the end of Chapter 4 asks you to explain this result). A higher real interest rate increases a borrower's reward for saving (equivalently, it increases the relative price of current consumption), so he or she tends to save more (the substitution effect); because a borrower pays rather than receives interest, a higher real interest rate also makes him or her poorer, leading to less consumption and more saving.

To summarize, the two-period model implies that an increase in the real interest rate increases saving by borrowers. Nevertheless, because of conflicting income and substitution effects, economic theory is not decisive about the effect of the real interest rate on the saving of lenders. As we discussed in Chapter 4, empirical studies have shown that an increase in the real interest rate tends to increase desired national saving, though this effect is not very strong.

Chapter 5

SAVING AND INVESTMENT IN THE OPEN ECONOMY

With virtually no exceptions, modern economies are open economies, which means that they engage in international trade of goods and services and in international borrowing and lending. Economic openness is of tremendous benefit to the average person. Because Canada is an open economy, Canadian consumers can enjoy products from around the world (Japanese video cassette recorders, Italian shoes, Irish woollens) and Canadian businesses can find new markets abroad for their products (paper, wheat, engineering services). Similarly, the internationalization of financial markets means that Canadian savers have the opportunity to purchase German government bonds or shares in Taiwanese companies as well as domestic assets, and Canadian firms who want to finance investment projects can borrow in London or New York as well as in Toronto or Montreal.

Beyond the economic diversity and opportunity it creates, economic openness carries another important implication: In an open economy, *a country's spending need not equal its production in every period*, as would be required in a closed economy with no foreign trade and no international borrowing and lending. In particular, by importing more than they export and borrowing from abroad to pay for the difference, the residents of an open economy can temporarily spend more than they produce.

The ability of an open economy to spend more than it produces is both an opportunity and a potential problem. For example, by borrowing abroad, Canada was able to finance an excess of imports over exports during the early 1990s. As a result, Canadians enjoyed higher levels of consumption, investment, and government purchases than they could have otherwise. At the same time, however, they incurred foreign debts that may be a future burden to the Canadian economy. Similarly, by borrowing heavily from abroad during the 1970s, some less developed countries (LDCs) were able to avoid large reductions in domestic spending, even though the two oil price shocks of that decade caused sharp declines in their output. During the 1980s, however, many LDC borrowers were unable to cope with the burden of their foreign debts—a situation that became known as the LDC debt crisis—and perhaps as a result suffered severely reduced economic growth.

Why do countries sometimes borrow abroad to pay for an excess of imports over exports but at other times export more than they import and lend the difference to other countries? Why doesn't each country just balance its books and import as much as it exports each year? As this chapter explains, the fundamental determinants of a country's trade position are the country's saving and investment decisions. Thus, although the issues of trade balances and international lending introduced here may seem at first to be unrelated to the topics covered in Chapter 4, the two sets of questions actually are closely related.

To explore how desired national saving and desired investment help determine patterns of international trade and lending, we extend the idea of goods market equilibrium, described by the saving–investment diagram, to include a foreign sector. We show that unlike the situation in a closed economy, in an open economy, desired national saving and desired investment do not have to be equal. Instead, we show that when a country's desired national saving exceeds its desired investment, the country will be a lender in the international capital market and will have a current account surplus. Similarly, when a country's desired national saving is less than its desired investment, the country will be an international borrower and will have a current account deficit.

By emphasizing saving and investment, this chapter develops an important theme of this part of the book. However, in order to focus on the role of saving and investment, we ignore some other factors that also influence international trade and lending. The most important of these factors is the exchange rate, or the rate at which domestic currency can be exchanged for foreign currency. We discuss exchange rates and their role in the open economy fully in Chapter 10.

5.1 BALANCE OF PAYMENTS ACCOUNTING

Examining the factors that affect international trade and lending first requires an understanding of the basics of balance of payments accounting. The **balance of payments accounts**, which are part of the national income accounts discussed in Chapter 2, are the record of a country's international transactions. (The box, "In Touch with the Macroeconomy: The Balance of Payments Accounts," p. 162, contains information about how the balance of payments accounts are constructed and where to find these data.) As you read this section, you should refer to Table 5.1, which presents Canadian balance of payments data for 2000; note that some of the numbers are positive and that others are negative. To sort out which international transactions are entered with a plus sign and which are entered with a minus sign, keep the following principle in mind: Any transaction that involves a flow of funds *into* Canada is a *credit* item and is entered with a plus sign; any transaction that involves a flow of funds *out of* Canada is a *debit* item and is entered with a minus sign. We illustrate this principle as we discuss the various components of the balance of payments accounts.

THE CURRENT ACCOUNT

The **current account** measures a country's trade in currently produced goods and services, along with net transfers between countries. For convenience, we divide the current account into three separate components: (1) net exports of goods and services, (2) investment income from assets abroad, and (3) current transfers.

NET EXPORTS OF GOODS AND SERVICES

We discussed the concept of net exports, *NX*, or exports minus imports, as part of the expenditure approach to measuring GDP in Chapter 2. Here, we point out that net exports often are broken into two categories: merchandise (goods) and services.

Merchandise consists of currently produced goods, such as American soybeans, French perfume, Brazilian coffee, and Japanese cars. When a Canadian buys a Japanese car, for example, the transaction is recorded as a merchandise import for

TABLE 5.1

Canada's Balance of International Payments, 2000 (Billions of Dollars)

CURRENT ACCOUNT

Net exports			**52.6**
Exports		477.9	
Goods	422.6		
Services	55.3		
Imports		−425.3	
Goods	−363.3		
Services	−62.0		
Net income from assets			−27.2
Income receipts on investments		42.3	
Income payments on investments		−69.5	
Current transfers			1.4
Current Account Balance (*CA*)				26.8

CAPITAL AND FINANCIAL ACCOUNT

Increase in Canadian-owned assets abroad			−134.9
(capital outflow)			
Canadian official reserve assets		−5.5	
Other Canadian assets		−129.4	
Increase in foreign-owned assets in Canada			114.5
(capital inflow)			
Financial account			−20.4
Capital account			5.3
Capital and Financial Account Balance (*KA*)				−15.1
Statistical discrepancy				−11.7

Source: Bank of Canada, *Banking and Financial Statistics*, Tables J1 and J2. Reprinted with the permission of the Bank of Canada.

Canada (a debit item for Canada, because funds flow out of Canada to pay for the car) and a merchandise export for Japan (a credit item for Japan because funds flow into Japan to pay for the car). The difference between a country's merchandise exports and its merchandise imports is called the **merchandise trade balance**, or simply the trade balance. The merchandise trade balance receives a lot of attention from the public and the press.[1] This attention does not seem entirely warranted, however, because merchandise trade is only one component of the current account.

Internationally traded services include transportation, tourism, insurance, education, and financial services, among others. When a Canadian family spends a week's vacation in Mexico, for example, the family's expenditures for accommodations, food, sightseeing tours, and so on, are counted in the Canadian current account as an import of tourism services (a debit item for Canada because funds are flowing out of the country). The family's expenditures count as an export of tourism services for Mexico (a credit item in the Mexican current account). Similarly, when a foreign student attends a university in Canada, her tuition payments are included as an export of services for Canada and an import of services for her home country.

---

1. This attention may in part reflect the availability of merchandise trade data monthly, whereas most balance of payments data are available only quarterly. See the box, "In Touch with the Macroeconomy: The Balance of Payments Accounts."

IN TOUCH WITH THE MACROECONOMY

THE BALANCE OF PAYMENTS ACCOUNTS

The data on Canadian international transactions that make up the balance of payments accounts are produced quarterly by Statistics Canada, and published in Canada's *Balance of International Payments* (cat. no. 67–001), part of the system of national accounts. Like the National Income and Expenditure Accounts, the data are released about two months after the end of the quarter to which they apply, and are subject to periodic revisions. Summary data, much like those in Table 5.1, appear in the *Canadian Economic Observer, Statistical Summary*, the Bank of Canada Review, and at *www.statcan.ca*.

In 1997, Statistics Canada revised its accounting to conform to international reporting standards agreed to by member countries of the International Monetary Fund. The revised format mainly involves separating the financial and capital accounts and is described in *Canada's Balance of International Payments* for the first quarter of 1997. The revised data also are available for previous years since 1926.

Canada's Balance of International Payments also provides details on the bilateral accounts between Canada and the United States,

the European Union, Japan, and other OECD countries, and on investment transactions by type (direct or portfolio), industry, and geographic area. Statistics Canada also publishes annual data in Canada's *International Investment Position* (cat. no. 67–202), which provides detail on Canadian investment abroad and foreign investment in Canada.

Although full information about the balance of payments accounts is available only quarterly, some components of the accounts are released monthly. The best-known example is the merchandise trade balance, which equals exports of goods minus imports of goods. The import data are initially collected by the Canada Customs and Revenue Agency at border crossings. As a rule, import data are more reliable than export data. Since 1990, estimates of Canada's exports to the United States have been based on import data collected by US Customs. The benefit of exchanging trade information is that it allows Statistics Canada to find out, for example, whether Canadian estimates of exports shipped to the United States are similar to US estimates of imports received from Canada. In principle, of course, the two numbers should be the same.

INVESTMENT INCOME FROM ASSETS ABROAD

Investment income received from assets abroad includes interest payments, dividends, royalties, and other returns that residents of a country receive from assets (such as bonds, stocks, or patents) that they own outside their own country. For example, the interest that a Canadian saver receives from a French government bond he owns, or the profits a Canadian company receives from a foreign subsidiary, are income receipts from assets abroad. These are credit items in the current account because the receipts are payments from foreigners to domestic residents.

Payment of investment income to foreign owners of assets in a country are debit items because they represent funds that flow out of the country. *Net* investment income from assets abroad equals investment income received from assets abroad minus investment income paid to foreign owners of domestic assets.

For Canada, net investment income from assets abroad is quantitatively almost the same as net factor payments from abroad, *NFP*, discussed in Chapter 2. The difference between the two concepts is that net factor payments from abroad also include wages and salaries of Canadians working outside the country, less the wages and salaries of foreigners working in Canada. In practice, the wage and salary component of *NFP* is very small, so we ignore it and treat *NFP* and net investment income from abroad as equivalent concepts.

CURRENT TRANSFERS

Current transfers are payments from one country to another that do not correspond to the purchase of any good, service, or asset. Examples are official foreign aid (a payment from one government to another), pension payments, or a gift of money from a resident of one country to family members living in another country. When Canada makes a transfer to another country, the amount of the transfer is a debit item because funds flow out of Canada. A country's current transfers equal transfers received by the country minus transfers flowing out of the country. The positive value of current transfers in Table 5.1 shows that Canada was a net recipient of transfers from other countries.

CURRENT ACCOUNT BALANCE

Adding all the credit items and subtracting all the debit items in the current account yields a number called the **current account balance**. If the current account balance is positive—with the value of credit items exceeding the value of debit items—the country has a current account surplus. If the current account balance is negative—with the value of debit items exceeding the value of credit items—the country has a current account deficit. As Table 5.1 shows, in 2000, Canada had a $26.8 billion current account surplus, equal to the sum of net exports (NX = $52.6 billion), net investment income from abroad (NFP = –$27.2 billion), and current transfers ($1.4 billion).

THE CAPITAL ACCOUNT

Not all transactions with foreign countries are tallied in the current account. If a Japanese investor purchases a 10-year-old vacation house in Canmore, Alberta, for example, the purchase is *not* included in the current account of either Canada or Japan. The reason is that the current account includes only the trade of currently produced goods and services. A 10-year-old house is an existing asset, rather than a currently produced good or service, so its sale is not part of the current account.

Trade between countries in existing assets, either real (direct investment) or financial (portfolio investment), is recorded in the **capital and financial account**. When the home country sells an asset to another country, the transaction is recorded as a **financial inflow** for the home country and as a credit item in the capital account. So, for example, if a Canadian bond is sold to Italian investors, the transaction is counted as a capital inflow to Canada and as a credit item in the Canadian capital account. (Why is a capital inflow a credit item? Because when a Canadian sells an asset to a foreigner, funds flow into Canada.) Similarly, when the home country buys an asset from abroad—say, a Canadian obtains a Swiss bank account—the transaction is a **financial outflow** from the home country (Canada in this example) and a debit item in the home country's capital account (funds are flowing out of Canada).

Since 1997, the capital and financial account has been divided into two parts called the financial account and the capital account. The financial account records direct and portfolio investment, while the capital account records migrants' funds, inheritances, and transactions in intellectual property, such as patents. Economists usually refer to the capital and financial account simply as the **capital account** (even though most of the transactions involved are in the financial account), and we will follow this usage here.

The **capital account balance** equals the value of capital inflows (credit items) minus the value of capital outflows (debit items). When residents of a country sell more assets to foreigners than they buy from foreigners, the capital account balance is positive, creating a capital account surplus. When residents of the home country purchase more assets from foreigners than they sell, the capital account balance is negative, creating a capital account deficit. Table 5.1 shows that in 2000, Canadians increased their holdings of foreign assets by $134.9 billion, while foreigners increased their holdings of Canadian assets by $114.5 billion. Thus, the financial account balance was -$20.4 billion. There was an added capital inflow in the form of migrants' funds and purchases of Canadian intellectual property of $5.3 billion, so the capital and financial account balance was -$15.1 billion ($5.3 billion plus $114.5 billion minus $134.9 billion). Thus, in 2000, Canada experienced a net capital outflow or capital account deficit.

The Official Settlements Balance

In Table 5.1, one set of capital account transactions, transactions in official reserve assets, has been listed separately. These transactions differ from other capital account transactions in that they are conducted by central banks (such as the Bank of Canada), which are the official institutions that determine national money supplies. Held by central banks, **official reserve assets** are assets, other than domestic money or securities, that can be used in making international payments. Historically, gold was the primary official reserve asset, but now the official reserves of central banks also include government securities of major industrialized economies, foreign bank deposits, and special assets created by the International Monetary Fund (an international agency that facilitates trade and financial relationships among countries).

Central banks can change the quantity of official reserve assets they hold by buying or selling reserve assets on open markets. For example, the Bank of Canada could increase its reserve assets by using dollars to buy gold. According to Table 5.1 (see the line "Canadian official reserve assets"), in 2000, the Canadian central bank bought $5.5 billion of official reserve assets.[2] The **official settlements balance**—also called the **balance of payments**—is the net increase (domestic less foreign) in a country's official reserve assets. A country that increases its net holdings of reserve assets during a year has a balance of payments surplus, and a country that reduces its net holdings of reserve assets has a balance of payments deficit.

For the issues we discuss in this chapter, the balances on current account and capital account play a much larger role than the balance of payments. The macroeconomic significance of the balance of payments is explained in Chapter 10, when we discuss the determination of exchange rates.

The Relationship between the Current Account and the Capital Account

The logic of balance of payments accounting implies a close relationship between the current account and the capital account. Except for errors arising from problems of measurement, *in each period, the current account balance and the capital account balance must sum to zero*. That is, if

$$CA = \text{current account balance},$$
$$KA = \text{capital account balance},$$

---

2. Remember that a negative number in the capital account indicates a capital outflow, or a purchase of assets.

then

$$CA + KA = 0. \qquad (5.1)$$

The reason that Eq. (5.1) holds is that every international transaction involves a swap of goods, services, or assets between countries. The two sides of the swap always have offsetting effects on the sum of the current and capital account balances, $CA + KA$. Thus, the sum of the current and capital account balances must equal zero.

Table 5.2 helps clarify this point. Suppose that a Canadian buys an imported British sweater, paying $75 for it. This transaction is an import of goods to Canada and, thus, reduces the Canadian current account balance by $75. However, the British exporter who sold the sweater now holds $75. What will he do with it? There are several possibilities, any of which will offset the effect of the purchase of the sweater on the sum of the current and capital account balances.

TABLE 5.2

Why the Current Account Balance and the Capital Account Balance Sum to Zero: An Example (Balance of Payments Data Refer to Canada)

Case I: **Canada Imports $75 Sweater from Britain; Britain Imports $75 Telephone from Canada**

Current Account	
Exports	+$75
Imports	−$75
Current account balance, CA	0
Capital Account	
No transaction	
Capital account balance, KA	0
Sum of current and capital account balances, $CA + KA$	0

Case II: **Canada Imports $75 Sweater from Britain; Britain Buys $75 Bond from Canada**

Current Account	
Imports	−$75
Current account balance, CA	−$75
Capital Account	
Capital inflow	+$75
Capital account balance, KA	+$75
Sum of current and capital account balances, $CA + KA$	0

Case III: **Canada Imports $75 Sweater from Britain; Bank of Canada Sells $75 of British Pounds to British Bank**

Current Account	
Imports	−$75
Current account balance, CA	−$75
Capital Account	
Capital inflow (reduction in Canadian official reserve assets)	+$75
Capital account balance, KA	+$75
Sum of current and capital account balances, $CA + KA$	0

The Briton may use the $75 to buy a Canadian product, say, a telephone. This purchase is a $75 export for Canada. This Canadian export together with the original import of the sweater into Canada results in no net change in the Canadian current account balance *CA*. The Canadian capital account balance *KA* has not changed, as no assets have been traded. Thus, the sum of *CA* and *KA* remains the same.

A second possibility is that the Briton will use the $75 to buy a Canadian asset, say, a bond issued by a Canadian corporation. The purchase of this bond is a capital inflow to Canada. This $75 increase in the Canadian capital account offsets the $75 reduction in the Canadian current account caused by the original import of the sweater. Again, the sum of the current and capital account balances, *CA* + *KA*, is unaffected by the combination of transactions.

Finally, the Briton may decide to go to his bank and trade his dollars for British pounds. If the bank sells these dollars to another Briton for the purpose of buying Canadian exports or assets, or if it buys Canadian assets itself, one of the previous two cases is repeated. Alternatively, the bank may sell the dollars to the Bank of Canada in exchange for pounds. But in giving up $75 worth of British pounds, the Bank of Canada reduces its holdings of official reserve assets by $75, which counts as a capital inflow. As in the previous case, the capital account balance rises by $75, offsetting the decline in the current account balance caused by the import of the sweater.[3]

This example shows why, conceptually, the current account balance and capital account balance must always sum to zero. In practice, problems in measuring international transactions prevent this relationship from holding exactly. The amount that would have to be added to the sum of the current and capital account balances for this sum to reach its theoretical value of zero is called the **statistical discrepancy**. As Table 5.1 shows, in 2000 the statistical discrepancy was -$11.7 billion. Box 5.1 discusses a puzzle that arises because of statistical discrepancies in the balance of payments accounts.

NET FOREIGN ASSETS AND THE BALANCE OF PAYMENTS ACCOUNTS

In Chapter 2, we defined the net foreign assets of a country as the foreign assets held by the country's residents (including, for example, foreign stocks, bonds, or real estate) minus the country's foreign liabilities (domestic physical and financial assets owned by foreigners). Net foreign assets are part of a country's national wealth, along with the country's domestic physical assets, such as land and the capital stock. The total value of a country's net foreign assets can change in two ways: (1) the value of existing foreign assets and foreign liabilities can change, as when stock held by a Canadian in a foreign corporation increases in value or the value of Canadian farmland owned by a foreigner declines; and (2) the country can acquire new foreign assets or incur new foreign liabilities.

What determines the quantity of new foreign assets that a country can acquire? In any period, *the net amount of new foreign assets that a country acquires equals its current account surplus*. For example, suppose a country exports

---

3. In this case, the balance of payments falls by $75, reflecting the Bank's loss of official reserves. We did not consider the possibility that the Briton would just hold $75 in Canadian currency. As dollars are an obligation of Canada, the Briton's acquisition of dollars would be a credit item in the Canadian capital account, which would offset the effect of the sweater import on the Canadian current account.

BOX 5.1 DOES MARS HAVE A CURRENT ACCOUNT SURPLUS?

The exports and imports of any individual country need not be equal in value. However, as every export is somebody else's import, for the world as a whole exports must equal imports and the current account surplus must be zero.

Or must it? When official current account figures for all nations are added up, the result usually is a current account deficit for the world. For example, International Monetary Fund (IMF) projections for 2001 (in US dollars) were that advanced economies would have a collective $223.1 billion current account deficit, developing countries would have a $22.4 billion surplus, and countries in transition would have a $13.9 billion surplus, all of which adds up to a current account deficit of $186.9 billion (about 0.6% of world GDP). During the 1990s, the world current account balance ranged from a surplus of $8.6 billion to a deficit of $161 billion, and the average deficit was about $70 billion. Is planet Earth a net importer, and does Mars have a current account surplus?

Since extraterrestrial trade seems unlikely, the explanation of the Earth's current account deficit must lie in statistical and measurement problems. Most research concludes that the main problem is the misreporting of income from assets held abroad. For example, interest earned by a Canadian on a foreign bank account should, in principle, be counted as a credit item in the Canadian current account and a debit item in the current account of the foreign country. However, if the Canadian fails to report this interest income to the Canadian government, it may show up only as a debit to the foreign current account, leading to a measured Earth-wide current account deficit. The fact that the world's current account deficit is generally larger during periods of high interest rates provides some support for this explanation.

Sources: Based on IMF, *World Economic Outlook*, October 2000, Appendix II: The Global Current Account Discrepancy; and IMF, *World Economic Outlook*, October 2001, Table A27.

$10 billion more in goods and services than it imports and, thus, runs a $10 billion current account surplus (assuming that net investment income from abroad and current transfers both are zero). The country must then use this $10 billion to acquire foreign assets or reduce foreign liabilities. In this case, we say that the country has undertaken net foreign lending of $10 billion.

Similarly, if a country has a $10 billion current account deficit, it must cover this deficit either by selling assets to foreigners or borrowing from foreigners. Either action reduces the country's net foreign assets by $10 billion. We describe this situation by saying that the country has engaged in net foreign borrowing of $10 billion.

Equation (5.1) emphasizes the link between the current account and the acquisition of foreign assets. Because $CA + KA = 0$, if a country has a current account surplus, it must have an equal capital account deficit. In turn, a capital account deficit implies that the country is experiencing capital outflows, or a net increase in holdings of foreign assets. Similarly, a current account deficit implies a capital account surplus and a decline in the country's net holdings of foreign assets. Summary table 7 presents some equivalent ways of describing a country's current account position and its acquisition of foreign assets.

In evaluating the significance of a country's foreign assets or debt, you must remember that net foreign assets are only one component of national wealth, the other being domestic physical assets. If national wealth is growing at a healthy rate overall, there is not much reason to be concerned if one of its components is falling. For example, if a country were to incur large foreign debts in order to build up its capital stock, and if the new capital were highly productive, the foreign debt would not be an economic burden. Canada's current account deficit of the mid-1950s can

SUMMARY 7   EQUIVALENT MEASURES OF A COUNTRY'S INTERNATIONAL TRADE AND LENDING

EACH ITEM DESCRIBES THE SAME SITUATION

A current account surplus of $10 billion
A capital account deficit of $10 billion
Net acquisition of foreign assets of $10 billion
Net foreign lending of $10 billion
Net exports of $10 billion (if net factor payments, *NFP*,
  and current transfers equal zero)

be viewed in this light. In the mid-1950s, investment accounted for a large share of output, and Canadian output and wealth grew rapidly.

After growing slowly during most of the 1990s, Canadian wealth grew by 4.5% during 2000. As we saw in Table 5.1, Canada has been running current account surpluses in recent years. That means that part of the growth in national wealth has taken the form of increased net foreign assets or, in Canada's case, decreased foreign debt. During 2000, the combined foreign debts of Canadians fell to less than 25% of GDP, the lowest value of this share of GDP in the past 40 years, and much lower than the peak value of 45% in 1993.

5.2 GOODS MARKET EQUILIBRIUM IN AN OPEN ECONOMY

We are now ready to investigate the economic forces that determine international trade and borrowing. In the remainder of this chapter, we demonstrate that a country's current account balance and foreign lending are closely linked to its domestic spending and production decisions. Understanding these links first requires developing the open-economy version of the goods market equilibrium condition.

In Chapter 4, we derived the goods market equilibrium condition for a closed economy. We showed that this condition can be expressed either as desired national saving equals desired investment or, equivalently, as the aggregate supply of goods equals the aggregate demand for goods. With some modification, we can use these same two conditions to describe goods market equilibrium in an open economy.

Let us begin with the open-economy version of the condition that desired national saving equals desired investment. In Chapter 2, we derived the national income accounting identity (Eq. 2.9):

$$S = I + CA = I + (NX + NFP). \tag{5.2}$$

Equation (5.2) is a version of the uses-of-saving identity. It states that national saving S has two uses: (1) to increase the nation's stock of capital by funding investment I, and (2) to increase the nation's stock of net foreign assets by lending to foreigners (recall that the current account balance CA equals the amount of funds that the country has available for net foreign lending). Equation (5.2) also reminds us that (assuming no current transfers) the current account CA is the sum of net exports NX and net factor payments from abroad NFP.

Because Eq. (5.2) is an identity, it must always hold (by definition). For the economy to be in goods market equilibrium, actual national saving and investment must also equal their desired levels. If actual and desired levels are equal, Eq. (5.2) becomes

$$S^d = I^d + CA = I^d + (NX + NFP),$$ (5.3)

where S^d and I^d represent desired national saving and desired investment, respectively. Equation (5.3) is the goods market equilibrium condition for an open economy, in which the current account balance CA equals net lending to foreigners, or capital outflows. Hence Eq. (5.3) states that *in goods market equilibrium in an open economy, the desired amount of national saving S^d must equal the desired amount of domestic investment I^d plus the amount lent abroad CA*. Note that the closed-economy equilibrium condition is a special case of Eq. (5.3), with $CA = 0$.

In general, net factor payments NFP are determined by past investments and are not much affected by current macroeconomic developments. If, for simplicity, we assume that net factor payments NFP are zero, the current account equals net exports and the goods market equilibrium condition, Eq. (5.3), becomes

$$S^d = I^d + NX.$$ (5.4)

Equation (5.4) is the form of the goods market equilibrium condition that we will work with. Under the assumption that net factor payments are zero, we can refer to the term NX interchangeably as net exports or as the current account balance.

As for the closed economy, we can also write the goods market equilibrium condition for the open economy in terms of the aggregate supply and aggregate demand for goods. In an open economy, where net exports NX are part of the aggregate demand for goods, this alternative condition for goods market equilibrium is

$$Y = C^d + I^d + G + NX,$$ (5.5)

where Y is output, C^d is desired consumption spending, and G is government purchases. This way of writing the goods market equilibrium condition is equivalent to the condition in Eq. (5.4).[4]

We can rewrite Eq. (5.5) as

$$NX = Y - (C^d + I^d + G).$$ (5.6)

Equation (5.6) states that in goods market equilibrium, the amount of net exports a country sends abroad equals the country's total output (gross domestic product) Y less total desired spending by domestic residents, $C^d + I^d + G$. Total spending by domestic residents is called **absorption**. Thus, Eq. (5.6) states that an economy in which output exceeds absorption will send goods abroad ($NX > 0$) and have a current account surplus and that an economy that absorbs more than it produces will be a net importer ($NX < 0$), with a current account deficit.

5.3 SAVING AND INVESTMENT IN A SMALL OPEN ECONOMY

To show how saving and investment are related to international trade and lending, we first present the case of a small open economy, such as Canada. A **small open**

---

4. To see that Eq. (5.5) is equivalent to Eq. (5.4), subtract $C^d + G$ from both sides of Eq. (5.5) to obtain $Y - C^d - G = I^d + NX$. The left-hand side of this equation equals desired national saving S^d, so it is the same as Eq. (5.4).

economy is an economy that is too small to affect the world real interest rate. The **world real interest rate** is the real interest rate that prevails in the international capital market, the market in which individuals, businesses, and governments borrow and lend across national borders. Because changes in saving and investment in the small open economy are not large enough to affect the world real interest rate, this interest rate is fixed in our analysis, which is a convenient simplification. Later in this chapter, we consider the case of an open economy, such as the US economy, that is large enough to affect the world real interest rate.

As with the closed economy, we can describe the goods market equilibrium in a small open economy by using the saving–investment diagram. The important new assumption that we make is that residents of the economy can borrow or lend in the international capital market at the (expected) world real interest rate r^w, which for now we assume is fixed. If the world real interest rate is r^w, the domestic real interest rate must be r^w as well, as no domestic borrower with access to the international capital market would pay more than r^w to borrow, and no domestic saver with access to the international capital market would accept less than r^w to lend.[5]

Figure 5.1 shows the saving and investment curves for a small open economy. In a closed economy, goods market equilibrium would be represented by point E, the intersection of the curves. The equilibrium real interest rate in the closed economy would be 4% (per year), and national saving and investment would be $3 billion (per year). In an open economy, however, desired national saving need not equal desired investment. If the small open economy faces a fixed world real interest rate r^w higher than 4%, desired national saving will be greater than desired investment. For example, if r^w is 6%, desired national saving is $5 billion and desired investment is $1 billion, so desired national saving exceeds desired investment by $4 billion.

FIGURE 5.1

A SMALL OPEN ECONOMY
THAT LENDS ABROAD

The graph shows the saving–investment diagram for a small open economy. The country faces a fixed world real interest rate of 6%. At this real interest rate national saving is $5 billion (point B) and investment is $1 billion (point A). The part of national saving not used for investment is lent abroad, so foreign lending is $4 billion (distance AB).

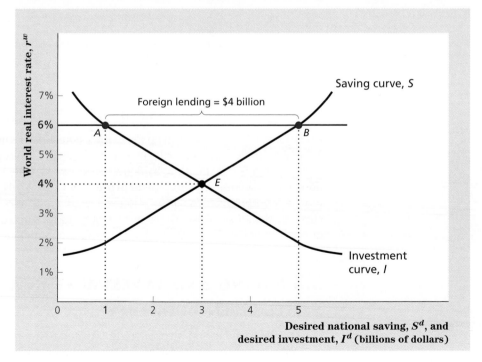

5. In Chapter 10, we will see that when countries produce different goods, real interest rates need not be equal across countries. For simplicity, we ignore such factors as differences in risk or taxes that might cause the domestic real interest rate to differ from the world rate. We also assume that there are no legal barriers to international borrowing and lending (when they exist, such barriers are referred to as capital controls).

FIGURE 5.2

A SMALL OPEN ECONOMY
THAT BORROWS ABROAD

The same small open economy
shown in Figure 5.1 now faces
a fixed world real interest rate
of 2%. At this real interest rate
national saving is $1 billion
(point C) and investment is $5
billion (point D). Foreign borrowing of $4 billion (distance
CD) makes up the difference
between what investors want
to borrow and what domestic
savers want to lend.

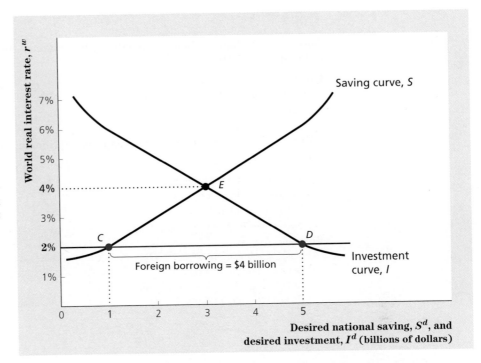

Can the economy be in equilibrium when desired national saving exceeds desired
investment by $4 billion? In a closed economy, it could not. The excess saving would
have no place to go, and the real interest rate would have to fall to bring desired
saving and desired investment into balance. However, in the open economy, the excess $4 billion of saving can be used to buy foreign assets. This capital outflow uses
up the excess national saving so that there is no disequilibrium. Instead, the goods
market is in equilibrium with desired national saving of $5 billion, desired invest-
ment of $1 billion, and net foreign lending of $4 billion (see Eq. 5.4 and recall that
net exports NX and net foreign lending are the same).

Alternatively, suppose that the world real interest rate r^w is 2% instead of 6%.
As Figure 5.2 shows, in this case desired national saving is $1 billion and desired
investment is $5 billion so that desired investment exceeds desired saving by $4
billion. Now, firms desiring to invest will have to borrow $4 billion in the interna-
tional capital market. Is this also a goods market equilibrium? Yes it is, because desired national saving ($1 billion) again equals desired investment ($5 billion) plus net
foreign lending (minus $4 billion). Indeed, a small open economy can achieve goods
market equilibrium for any value of the world real interest rate. All that is required
is that net foreign lending equal the difference between the country's desired national
saving and its desired investment.

A more detailed version of the example illustrated in Figures 5.1 and 5.2 is
presented in Table 5.3 on the next page. As shown in the top panel, we assume that
in this small country gross domestic product Y is fixed at its full-employment value
of $20 billion and government purchases G are fixed at $4 billion. The middle panel
shows three possible values for the world real interest rate r^w and the assumed
levels of desired consumption and desired investment at each of these values of the
real interest rate. Note that higher values of the world real interest rate imply lower
levels of desired consumption (because people choose to save more) and lower
desired investment. The bottom panel shows the values of various economic quantities
implied by the assumed values in the top two panels.

Table 5.3

**Goods Market Equilibrium in a Small Open Economy: An Example
(Billions of Dollars)**

Given

Gross domestic product, Y	20
Government purchases, G	4

Effect of real interest rate on desired consumption and investment

	(1)	(2)	(3)
(1) World real interest rate, r^w (%)	2	4	6
(2) Desired consumption, C^d	15	13	11
(3) Desired investment, I^d	5	3	1

Results

	(1)	(2)	(3)
(4) Desired absorption, $C^d + I^d + G$	24	20	16
(5) Desired national saving, $S^d = Y - C^d - G$	1	3	5
(6) Net exports, $NX = Y -$ desired absorption	−4	0	4
(7) Desired foreign lending, $S^d - I^d$	−4	0	4

Note: We assume that net factor payments, NFP, equal zero.

The equilibrium in this example depends on the value of the world real interest rate r^w. Suppose that $r^w = 6\%$, as shown in Figure 5.1. Column (3) of Table 5.3 shows that, if $r^w = 6\%$, desired consumption C^d is \$11 billion (row 2) and that desired investment I^d is \$1 billion (row 3). With C^d at \$11 billion, desired national saving, $Y - C^d - G$, is \$5 billion (row 5). Desired net foreign lending, $S^d - I^d$, is \$4 billion (row 7)—the same result illustrated in Figure 5.1. If $r^w = 2\%$, as in Figure 5.2, column (1) of Table 5.3 shows that desired national saving is \$1 billion (row 5) and that desired investment is \$5 billion (row 3). Thus, desired foreign lending, $S^d - I^d$, equals −\$4 billion (row 7)—that is, foreign borrowing totals \$4 billion. Again, the result is the same as illustrated in Figure 5.2.

An advantage of working through the numerical example in Table 5.3 is that we can also use it to demonstrate how the goods market equilibrium, which we have been interpreting in terms of desired saving and investment, can be interpreted in terms of output and absorption. Suppose again that $r^w = 6\%$, giving a desired consumption C^d of \$11 billion and a desired investment I^d of \$1 billion. Government purchases G are fixed at \$4 billion. Thus, when r^w is 6%, desired absorption (the desired spending by domestic residents), $C^d + I^d + G$, totals \$16 billion (row 4, column 3).

In goods market equilibrium a country's net exports—the net quantity of goods and services that it sends abroad—equal gross domestic product Y minus desired absorption (Eq. 5.6). When r^w is 6%, Y is \$20 billion and desired absorption is \$16 billion so that net exports NX are \$4 billion. Net exports of \$4 billion imply that the country is lending \$4 billion abroad, as in Figure 5.1. If the world real interest rate drops to 2%, desired absorption rises (because people want to consume more and invest more) from \$16 billion to \$24 billion (row 4, column 1). Because in this case absorption (\$24 billion) exceeds domestic production (\$20 billion), the country has to import goods and services from abroad ($NX = -\$4$ billion). Note that desired net imports of \$4 billion imply net foreign borrowing of \$4 billion, as shown in Figure 5.2.

THE EFFECTS OF ECONOMIC SHOCKS IN A SMALL OPEN ECONOMY

The saving–investment diagram can be used to determine the effects of various types of economic disturbances in a small open economy. Briefly, any change that increases desired national saving relative to desired investment at a given world real interest rate will increase net foreign lending, the current account balance, and net exports (which are all equivalent[6]). A decline in desired national saving relative to desired investment reduces those quantities. Let us look at two examples, both of which are useful in the Application that follows.

EXAMPLE 1: A TEMPORARY ADVERSE SUPPLY SHOCK

Suppose that a small open economy is hit with a severe drought—an adverse supply shock—that temporarily lowers output. The effects of the drought on the nation's saving, investment, and current account are shown in Figure 5.3 below. The initial saving and investment curves are S^1 and I^1. For the world real interest rate r^w, initial net foreign lending (equivalently, net exports or the current account balance) is length AB.

The drought brings with it a temporary decline in income. A drop in current income causes people to reduce their saving at any prevailing real interest rate, so the saving curve shifts left, from S^1 to S^2. If the supply shock is temporary, as we have assumed, the expected future marginal product of capital is unchanged. As a result, desired investment at any real interest rate is unchanged, and the investment curve does not shift. The world real interest rate is given and does not change.

In the new equilibrium, net foreign lending and the current account have shrunk to length AD. The current account shrinks because the country saves less and thus is not able to lend abroad as much as before.

FIGURE 5.3

A TEMPORARY ADVERSE SUPPLY SHOCK IN A SMALL OPEN ECONOMY

Curve S^1 is the initial saving curve, and curve I^1 is the initial investment curve of a small open economy. With a fixed world real interest rate of r^w, national saving equals the distance OB and investment equals distance OA. The current account surplus (equivalently, net foreign lending) is the difference between national saving and investment, shown as distance AB. A temporary adverse supply shock lowers current output and causes consumers to save less at any real interest rate, which shifts the saving curve left, from S^1 to S^2. National saving decreases to distance OD, and the current account surplus decreases to distance AD.

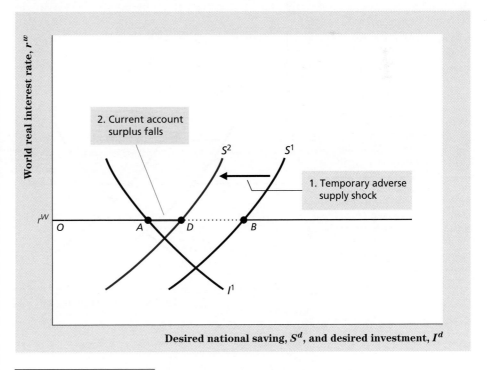

Desired national saving, S^d, and desired investment, I^d

---

6. Remember that we are assuming that net factor payments from abroad and net transfers are zero so that net exports equal the current account balance.

In this example we assumed that the country started with a current account surplus, which is reduced by the drought. If, instead, the country had begun with a current account deficit, the drought would have made the deficit larger. In either case, the drought reduces (in the algebraic sense) net foreign lending and the current account balance.

EXAMPLE 2: AN INCREASE IN THE EXPECTED FUTURE MARGINAL PRODUCT OF CAPITAL

Suppose that technological innovations increase the expected future marginal product MPK^f of current capital investments. The effects on a small open economy are shown in Figure 5.4. Again, the initial national saving and investment curves are S^1 and I^1 so that the initial current account surplus equals length AB.

An increase in the MPK^f raises the capital stock that domestic firms desire to hold so that desired investment rises at every real interest rate. Thus, the investment curve shifts right, from I^1 to I^2. The current account and net foreign lending shrink to length FB. Why does the current account fall? Because building capital has become more profitable in the home country, more of the country's output is absorbed by domestic investment, leaving less to send abroad.[7]

FIGURE 5.4

AN INCREASE IN THE EXPECTED FUTURE MPK IN A SMALL OPEN ECONOMY

As in Figure 5.3, the small open economy's initial national saving and investment curves are S^1 and I^1. At the fixed world real interest rate of r^w, there is an initial current account surplus equal to the distance AB. An increase in the expected future marginal product of capital (MPK^f) shifts the investment curve right, from I^1 to I^2, causing investment to increase from OA to distance OF. The current account surplus, which is national saving minus investment, decreases from distance AB to distance FB.

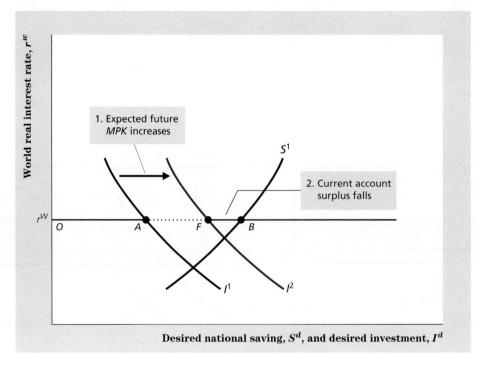

Desired national saving, S^d, and desired investment, I^d

---

7. A possibility that we have neglected so far is that technological innovations also cause savers to expect a higher future income, which would reduce current saving at every level of the world real interest rate. A leftward shift of the saving curve would further reduce the current account balance. This effect would only reinforce the effect on the country's current account of the rightward shift of the investment curve, so for simplicity we continue to ignore this potential change in desired saving.

APPLICATION

THE LDC DEBT CRISIS

During the 1970s, many less developed countries (LDCs) greatly increased their international borrowing, which allowed them to run large current account deficits. Over the 1972–1981 period, a group of 15 developing countries that were later to be designated as "heavily indebted" by the International Monetary Fund (IMF) ran current account deficits averaging more than 18% of their exports of goods and services.[8] These current account deficits were financed by borrowing abroad, primarily from private commercial banks in the United States, Japan, Canada, and Europe. For example, by 1986, Canadian banks held more than $25 billion in loans to those countries, mainly Mexico, Chile, Brazil, Venezuela, and Argentina.[9] By that year, the outstanding debt of these countries exceeded 60% of their combined annual GDPs.

During 1982, for reasons that we discuss shortly, banks began to lose confidence that their LDC loans would be repaid as promised and refused to make new loans. Unable to obtain new credit to replace maturing loans or to make planned investments, dozens of countries came under intense financial pressure. Negotiations with the banks and international agencies, such as the International Monetary Fund and the World Bank, resulted in some modest reductions in outstanding LDC debt, as did some unilateral decisions by debtor countries to reduce or delay payments to the banks. Mainly, though, the debtors did not default on (refuse to repay) their debts and attempted to keep making the interest and principal payments as promised.

In the years following 1982, interest payments on international debt were a heavy burden on LDC economies. For the 15 heavily indebted countries tracked by the IMF, interest payments to foreigners during the 1982–1989 period were between a quarter and a third of the value of those countries' exports. In the balance of payments accounts, payments of interest on international debt are part of investment income paid to foreigners and, thus, are debit items in the current account. Because the LDCs could not get new loans (capital inflows) for use in making interest payments, the only way they could keep up their payments was to expand exports and cut imports of goods and services. This surplus in trade in goods and services allowed the LDCs to make interest payments while bringing their current accounts toward balance. Unfortunately, lower imports, especially reductions in imports of capital goods and intermediate goods, contributed to slow, often negative, growth during the 1980s, and, as a result, living standards in some debtor countries fell sharply.

In March 1989, US Treasury Secretary Nicholas Brady announced what has become known as the Brady plan. The plan amounted to a three-way deal among the commercial banks holding LDC debt, the international agencies, such as the World Bank, that make loans to poor countries, and the debtor nations themselves. The Brady plan called on the commercial banks to accept significant reductions in the interest and principal owed to them by the developing countries, in exchange for guarantees that the reduced LDC debt would be repaid. The role of the international agencies

---

8. The 15 countries, 10 of which are in Latin America, were Argentina, Bolivia, Brazil, Chile, Colombia, Côte d'Ivoire, Ecuador, Mexico, Morocco, Nigeria, Peru, the Philippines, Uruguay, Venezuela, and Yugoslavia. Data on this group of countries can be found in issues of the IMF's *World Economic Outlook* through 1994, after which the IMF no longer felt the need to track these countries as a group.

9. For the history of Canadian bank lending during the crisis, see James Powell, "The Evolution of Canadian Bank Claims on Heavily Indebted Developing Countries," *Bank of Canada Review*, November 1991, pp. 3–20.

was to help the debtor nations meet their reduced debt payments by providing loans and other assistance. For their part, besides making continued debt payments, the LDC debtors were required to undertake reforms to improve the performance of their economies. These reforms included reducing government spending and increasing reliance on markets.

The Brady plan, together with falling world interest rates, contributed to a reduced burden of LDC debt after 1989. Private lenders, encouraged by these developments, began to make new loans to developing countries. However, the economic troubles of the LDC debtors were not over: The worldwide recession of the early 1990s reduced demand for LDC exports, and LDC trade balances and GDP growth rates deteriorated. Then, new crises in Mexico in 1994, Asia in 1997, Russia in 1998 (see the Application, "The Crises in Mexico, East Asia, and Russia" on p. 179), and Argentina in 2001 once again raised doubts about loans to developing countries.

However, despite these crises and worries about loans to developing countries, no country defaulted on Brady bonds until September 1999, when Ecuador failed to make a $98 million payment on its Brady bonds.

The LDC debt crisis raises several important questions:

1. *Why Did the LDCs Borrow So Much in the First Place, and Why Were Lenders Willing to Lend?* There were two main causes of the increase in LDC debt, both of which can be analyzed with our model of the small open economy. The first cause is that heavy foreign borrowing is a normal part of the process of economic development. Canada and the United States, for example, both piled up large international debts during their early growth. Figure 5.5 illustrates the reasons. In a developing economy, the capital stock is low, whereas other types of resources (labour, land, minerals) may be relatively abundant. As a result, the expected future marginal product of capital investments is potentially high. This high expected future *MPK* is reflected by a desired investment curve that is quite far to the right.

At the same time, at early stages of development, a country's income is low, so desired national saving is low. Reflecting this low desired saving, the saving curve is far to the left. The combination of high desired investment and low desired national saving at the given world real interest rate results in large capital inflows, or foreign borrowing, represented by length *AB*. Corresponding to the capital inflows are current account deficits, which arise because the developing country is importing large quantities of capital goods and other supplies without yet producing much for export. In a growing LDC, attractive investment opportunities exceed the domestic population's capacity to save, so borrowing abroad is profitable for domestic investors, and lending is profitable for foreign lenders. For these reasons, capital flows to some LDCs once again boomed in the mid-1990s, though typically not in the form of bank lending to governments.

The second cause of the increase in LDC debt was specific to the 1970s. The oil shocks of 1973–1974 and 1979–1980 represented severe adverse supply shocks, which sharply depressed income in non-oil-exporting LDCs. Presumably because they thought that these shocks would be temporary, consumers in non-oil-exporting LDCs responded by reducing saving, so they would not have to reduce current consumption by as much as the current drop in output. Lower desired saving at given values of the world real interest rate led to increased current account deficits and foreign borrowing. Our analysis of a temporary adverse supply shock in Figure 5.3 predicts such a result.

FIGURE 5.5

INTERNATIONAL
BORROWING IN A
DEVELOPING COUNTRY

In a small developing economy, income and national
saving are low, so the saving
curve *S* is far to the left.
Investment opportunities are
good (the expected future *MPK*
is high), so the investment
curve *I* is far to the right. At the
world real interest rate of r^w,
investment (distance *OB*)
greatly exceeds national saving
(distance *OA*). To fund its
desired investment, the country must borrow abroad.
Distance *AB* is the developing
country's foreign borrowing or,
equivalently, its current account deficit.

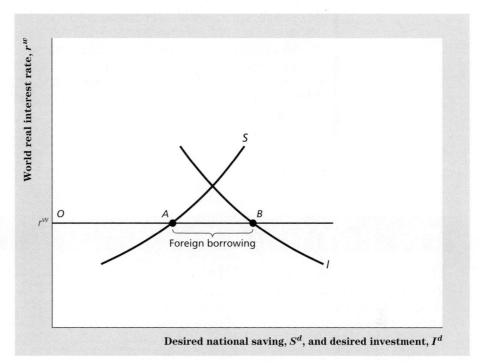

Ironically, the ultimate source of a significant portion of the funds borrowed by
LDCs was the oil-exporting countries themselves, which needed somewhere to
invest the huge increase in their oil revenues created by the higher prices. In practice,
the oil exporters lent to banks in industrialized countries, who then re-lent the funds
to LDCs in a process known as "recycling petro-dollars."

2. *If the LDC Lending Was Justified, Why Did the Loans Go Bad?* Various
adverse macroeconomic developments, not foreseen when most of the LDC loans
were made, caused problems for the LDC debtors. Among these developments was
a worldwide recession from 1979 through 1982 that lowered the demand for LDC
exports. Reduced export sales kept LDC borrowers from achieving the large surpluses
on the merchandise and services portion of the current account that they needed to
pay interest on their debts. Another adverse macroeconomic development of the
early 1980s was a sharp increase in interest rates. Because most LDC debt was in the
form of floating-rate loans, whose required interest payments rise automatically
when current interest rates rise, the interest obligations of the LDC debtors increased
greatly.

Although the macroeconomic problems that arose generally were unexpected,
many of the loans made to the LDCs in the 1970s probably were not adequately
researched by lenders, and some borrowing firms and governments wasted or mis-
managed the funds they received. The rapidity with which lending was expanded in
the 1970s may have been one reason that careless lending and investment decisions
were made.

3. *Why Did the LDC Debt Crisis Take So Long to Be Resolved?* Because the
true economic values of LDC loans fell dramatically below their "paper" values,
someone had to bear large losses; the long delay in resolving the crisis was a result
of continuing disagreement over how the losses should be shared. The borrowers, of
course, could have escaped their debts by defaulting. However, default itself may

impose sufficient economic and political costs on the borrowers to make it unattractive (see the box, "The Political Environment: Default and Sovereign Debt," below). The banks that made the LDC loans had little incentive to make concessions, particularly when their own financial health was at serious risk early in the decade. Only over a long period of time, as the costs of an ongoing debt crisis became clear, did political leaders begin to take some steps toward finding a resolution of the debt problem.

THE POLITICAL ENVIRONMENT

DEFAULT AND SOVEREIGN DEBT

If an individual consumer defaults on a loan, the creditors have well-established legal means to try to force repayment. For example, they may be able to seize the consumer's assets, or a court may rule that part of the consumer's future wages may be attached in repayment. In contrast, default on sovereign debt, or debt owed by an independent nation, leaves creditors with limited options. There is no international authority to enforce repayment of sovereign debts, and creditors can neither seize the debtors' domestic assets nor "attach" its income.

With this lack of legal enforceability, why do sovereign debtors usually try to repay what they owe, even when doing so imposes economic hardship on their people? Some researchers emphasize that defaulting countries may face significant economic costs. Such costs may include seizure of the country's assets held abroad, disruption of international trade (as creditors interfere with shipments or payments), and denial of future international loans.

Although the economic costs of default are part of the reason that international debtors usually repay, key political considerations are equally important:

1. *Creditors' political power within their own country.* When there were widespread defaults on foreign bonds during the Great Depression, the American holders of the foreign bonds were politically unorganized and received little help from the US government (well-organized British bondholders got much more help from their government in the 1930s).* In the 1980s, in contrast, concern about the health of the domestic banking system (which stood to suffer from LDC defaults) prompted the United States to put diplomatic and political pressures on the debtor countries to repay.

2. *Relations between creditor and debtor countries.* History has shown that debtors are more likely to repay when they value the political, economic, and military relations they have with creditors. A debt-laden Australia did not default during the Great Depression because it wanted good relations with its main creditor, Great Britain. At the opposite extreme, in 1990, Iraq tried to "solve" its foreign debt problems by invading a principal creditor, Kuwait. Similarly, creditors are less likely to be tough when they value their relationships with the debtors. After World War II, Canada forgave some of the war debts owed by its military allies, for example.

3. *Relations among the debtor countries.* If many LDC debtors defaulted simultaneously, the creditor countries would have much greater difficulty punishing them. Enforcing trade sanctions against one country is easier than enforcing them against 30 countries, for example. For this reason, some LDC leaders have called for the formation of a "debtors' cartel," an organization of debtor countries that would negotiate with the creditors as a bloc. The feasibility of such debtor cooperation depends on the ability of the debtors to get along and cooperate politically. So far, differing goals among debtors and political pressures from the creditor nations have prevented the emergence of a debtors' cartel.

*For an interesting discussion of the debt crisis in historical perspective, see Barry Eichengreen, "Historical Research on International Lending and Debt," *Journal of Economic Perspectives*, Spring 1991, pp. 149–169.

APPLICATION

THE CRISES IN MEXICO, EAST ASIA, AND RUSSIA

In the 1990s, economic crises in Mexico, East Asia, and Russia again focused attention on international borrowing and lending. Were these regions the victims of speculators? Or do international capital markets serve the useful purpose of disciplining imprudent government policy? Exploring these questions begins with the origins of the crises. All three episodes originated in current account deficits, although the deficits themselves had different sources.

In Mexico, the signing of the North American Free Trade Agreement (NAFTA) in 1993 promised to lower trade barriers among Mexico, the United States, and Canada. Foreign private investors, who had been wary of making financial investments in Mexcio during the debt crisis period, came flocking back. During 1992 and 1993, net capital inflows to Mexico amounted to about 8% of Mexican GDP, an extraordinarily high rate. Of course, as we have emphasized in this chapter, the mirror image of a surplus in the capital account is a deficit in the current account. Hence Mexico also ran a current account deficit of about 8% of GDP in 1992 and 1993. Essentially, Mexico was importing large quantities of goods and services and paying for these imports by borrowing abroad. One of the underlying causes of these current account deficits was a low private saving rate.

The crisis in East Asia in 1997 also was preceded by large current account deficits, but in this case, the deficits cannot be attributed to low private saving. Private and government savings rates in East Asia were high, but investment rates were even higher. As Figure 5.5 shows, a developing economy with a high expected future marginal product of capital has high desired investment. These high investment rates in such countries as Thailand, Malaysia, and Indonesia led to very high current account deficits. For example, in 1996 Thailand ran a current account deficit of 8% of GDP.

Russia, which experienced a financial crisis a year after East Asia, ran current account deficits for a different reason. There, low government saving was the source. The Russian government had great difficulty collecting revenue, which led to a government budget deficit of 6.9% of GDP in 1997.

In all three places, the capital inflow largely took the form of portfolio investment (purchases of stocks and bonds) rather than foreign direct investment (purchases of physical assets). Much of the portfolio investment was at short maturities and, therefore, quite liquid, and except in Russia, the borrowers generally were private, rather than sovereign. Thus, these assets could be quickly sold if investor sentiment changed.

What triggered such asset sales is not completely clear. In Mexico, the uprising in Chiapas and several political assassinations—notably that of the ruling party's presidential candidate, Luis Donaldo Colosio—raised doubts about the country's political stability. In December 1994, investors began to sell Mexican assets and a financial crisis followed.[10] In East Asia, concerns about the stability of banking systems played a role in the loss of confidence, which began in Thailand in May 1997 and soon

---

10. For an introductory account of the December 1994 crisis in Mexico, see Joseph A. Whitt, Jr. "The Mexican Peso Crisis," *Economic Review*, Federal Reserve Bank of Atlanta, January/February 1996, pp. 1–20, or "Factors Behind the Financial Crisis in Mexico," *World Economic Outlook*, May 1995, pp. 90–97.

spread to the Philippines, Malaysia, and Indonesia and later affected Korea, Taiwan, Singapore, and Hong Kong.[11] In Russia, the Duma did not agree to the Kiriyenko government's revenue plan in July 1998, and so the government declared a moratorium on foreign debt repayments.

Whatever the cause, the reversal of capital flows was dramatic. For example, by February 1998, equity markets in Indonesia, Malaysia, the Philippines, South Korea, and Thailand had fallen by more than 50% from their 1996–1997 peaks, and their growth forecasts were revised down from a range of 6–8% to a range of 0–4%. In several countries, notably Indonesia, GDP fell sharply in 1998 as a severe and protracted recession began. As the analysis of this chapter shows, the curtailment of foreign borrowing in a small open economy leads to a higher real interest rate and lower investment in physical capital. In the economy illustrated in Figure 5.2, for example, the removal of foreign capital moves the economy from point D to point E.

Another prominent feature of these crises was a contagion—called the "tequila effect" in 1994 and the "Asian flu" in 1997—that seemed to spread them to other countries. For example, in 1994, Argentina also suffered a sharp withdrawal of foreign lending and experienced a deep recession. In 1997, the Asian crisis spread to Singapore and Hong Kong, while in 1998, the Russian default led to speculation that Brazil would follow. One source of this contagion is that investors who have made losses in one emerging market may need to sell assets in other countries to cover those losses. Also, foreign investors may exhibit herd behaviour and simply follow the example of other investors.

Some countries began to recover quite rapidly from these financial crises. For example, most East Asian countries ran current account surpluses in 1998, though their recovery was slowed by the ongoing recession in Japan, a major market for their exports. In others, such as Indonesia and Russia, continued political crisis prolonged the economic crisis.

What lessons for economic policy can be drawn from these financial crises? First, the Mexican and East Asian crises were largely unforeseen, so they have led to macroeconomic research focusing on early warnings of crises.[12] So far, this research suggests that large current account deficits alone do not seem to lead to crises, but reliable indicators seem difficult to find.

Second, the crises have focused debate on the possibility of *moral hazard* in the international financial system. Moral hazard occurs when insuring against a risk makes risk-taking behaviour more likely. In international borrowing and lending, it may have occurred if the the bail-out of Mexico in early 1995 encouraged investors to buy assets in East Asia that they otherwise would not have bought. However, moral hazard probably cannot explain the scale of these crises. While some investors, such as banks which held Korean debt, were bailed out, many others suffered enormous losses in East Asia and Russia.

Third, the crises have led to some criticism of the policy recommendations made by the IMF to countries that borrow from it. Influential critics include Paul Krugman of the Massachusetts Institute of Technology and Jeffrey Sachs of Harvard University.

---

11. For a chronology of the Asian crisis, see the IMF's booklet *World Economic Outlook: Interim Assessment — Crisis in Asia: regional and global implications*, December 1997.
12. See the review in "Financial Crises: Characteristics and Indicators of Vulnerability," *World Economic Outlook*, May 1998, pp. 74–97.

In Indonesia, Thailand, and Korea, the IMF required a tighter fiscal policy to raise the current account balance, though this advice was revised as the depth of the crisis became clear. But the IMF's critics have argued that government saving should be reduced to fight a recession after a crisis. We discuss this stabilizing role for fiscal policy in Chapters 9 to 12.

Fourth, the crises also have led to exploration of the policy choices made by small open economies. Some countries have considered controls on capital inflows and outflows, as used in Chile. Malaysia adopted such controls in 1998. Other policies reconsidered by domestic governments include greater supervision of banking systems and more frequent reporting of economic statistics. Since the crises led to collapses in currency values (such as the Mexican peso and Russian ruble) governments also have re-examined their exchange rate arrangements, a decision we study in Chapter 10.

These three crises show that large capital inflows to a developing country (and hence large current account deficits) are a two-edged sword.[13] On the one hand, a continued inflow of foreign capital can help the country develop much more quickly; several developing countries have used foreign investment successfully in just this way. On the other hand, if the foreign investors lose confidence in the economic or political stability of the country, the sudden withdrawal of foreign funds can lead to a wrenching period of adjustment.

5.4 SAVING AND INVESTMENT IN LARGE OPEN ECONOMIES

Although the model of a small open economy facing a fixed real interest rate is appropriate for studying many of the countries in the world, it is not the right model to use for analyzing the world's largest developed economies. The problem is that significant changes in the saving and investment patterns of a major economy can and do affect the world real interest rate, which violates the assumption made for the small open economy that the world real interest rate is fixed. Fortunately, we can readily adapt the analysis of the small open economy to the case of a **large open economy**, that is, an economy large enough to affect the world real interest rate.

To begin, let us think of the world as comprising only two large economies: (1) the home or domestic economy, and (2) the foreign economy (representing the economies of the rest of the world combined). Figure 5.6 shows the saving–investment diagram that applies to this case. Figure 5.6(a) shows the saving curve S and the investment curve I of the home economy. Figure 5.6(b) displays the saving curve S_{For} and the investment curve I_{For} of the foreign economy. These saving and investment curves are just like those for the small open economy.

Instead of taking the world real interest rate as given, as we did in the model of a small open economy, we determine the world real interest rate within the model for a large open economy. What determines the value of the world real interest rate? Remember that for the closed economy, the real interest rate was set by the condition that the amount that savers want to lend must equal the amount that investors

---

13. For a history of policy toward international lending, see Maurice Obstfeld, "The Global Capital Market: Benefactor or Menace?" *Journal of Economic Perspectives*, Fall 1998, pp. 9–30.

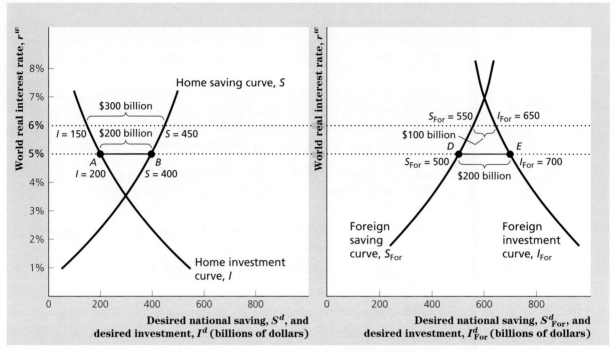

(a) Home country

(b) Foreign country

FIGURE 5.6

THE DETERMINATION OF THE WORLD REAL INTEREST RATE
WITH TWO LARGE OPEN ECONOMIES

The equilibrium world real interest rate is the real interest rate at
which desired international lending by one country equals desired
international borrowing by the other country. In the figure, when the
world real interest rate is 5%, desired international lending by the
home country is $200 billion ($400 billion desired national saving
less $200 billion desired investment, or distance *AB*), which equals
the foreign country's desired international borrowing of $200 billion
($700 billion desired investment less $500 billion desired national
saving, or distance *DE*). Thus, 5% is the equilibrium world real
interest rate. Equivalently, when the interest rate is 5%, the current
account surplus of the home country equals the current account
deficit of the foreign country (both are $200 billion).

want to borrow. Analogously, in the case of two large open economies, *the world
real interest rate will be such that desired international lending by one country equals desired international borrowing by the other country.* At this real
interest rate, desired world saving equals desired world investment.

To illustrate the determination of the equilibrium world real interest rate, we
return to Figure 5.6. Suppose, arbitrarily, that the world real interest rate r^w is 6%.
Does this rate result in a goods market equilibrium? Figure 5.6(a) shows that at a 6%
real interest rate, in the home country, desired national saving is $450 billion and
desired investment is $150 billion. Because desired national saving exceeds desired
investment by $300 billion, the amount that the home country would like to lend
abroad is $300 billion.

To find how much the foreign country wants to borrow, we turn to Figure 5.6(b).
When the real interest rate is 6%, desired national saving is $550 billion and desired
investment is $650 billion in the foreign country. Thus, at a 6% real interest rate,
the foreign country wants to borrow $100 billion ($650 billion less $550 billion) in the
international capital market. Because this amount is less than the $300 billion, the
home country wants to lend, 6% is not the real interest rate that is consistent with
equilibrium in the international capital market.

At a real interest rate of 6%, desired international lending exceeds desired international borrowing, so the equilibrium world real interest rate must be less than 6%. Let us try a real interest rate of 5%. Figure 5.6(a) shows that at that interest rate desired national saving is $400 billion and desired investment is $200 billion in the home country, so the home country wants to lend $200 billion abroad. In Figure 5.6(b), when the real interest rate is 5%, desired national saving in the foreign country is $500 billion and desired investment is $700 billion, so the foreign country's desired international borrowing is $200 billion. At a 5% real interest rate, desired international borrowing and desired international lending are equal (both are $200 billion), so the equilibrium world real interest rate is 5% in this example.

Graphically, the home country's desired lending when r^w equals 5% is length AB in Figure 5.6(a), and the foreign country's desired borrowing is length DE in Figure 5.6(b). Because length AB equals length DE, desired international lending and borrowing are equal when the world real interest rate is 5%.

We defined international equilibrium in terms of desired international lending and borrowing. Equivalently, we can define equilibrium in terms of international flows of goods and services. The amount the lending country desires to lend (distance AB in Figure 5.6(a)) is the same as its current account surplus. The amount the borrowing country wants to borrow (distance DE in Figure 5.6(b)) equals its current account deficit. Thus, saying that desired international lending must equal desired international borrowing is the same as saying that the desired net outflow of goods and services from the lending country (its current account surplus) must equal the desired net inflow of goods and services to the borrowing country (its current account deficit).

In summary, for a large open economy the equilibrium world real interest rate is the rate at which the desired international lending by one country equals the desired international borrowing of the other country. Equivalently, it is the real interest rate at which the lending country's current account surplus equals the borrowing country's current account deficit.

Unlike the situation in a small open economy, for large open economies, the world real interest rate is not fixed but will change when desired national saving or desired investment changes in either country. Generally, any factor that increases desired international lending relative to desired international borrowing at the initial world real interest rate causes the world real interest rate to fall. Similarly, a change that reduces desired international lending relative to desired international borrowing at the initial world real interest rate will cause the world real interest rate to rise. We illustrate this principle further in an Application .

APPLICATION

GERMAN REUNIFICATION, CURRENT ACCOUNT BALANCES, AND THE WORLD REAL INTEREST RATE

In 1990, West Germany and East Germany, which had been divided since the end of World War II, reunited into a single country. The two parts of the new united Germany, however, were not on equal footing economically. West Germany had developed into a modern industrial nation, but the legacy of communism in East Germany included outmoded factories and equipment, inadequate infrastructure, and major environmental problems. In an attempt to help the economy of eastern Germany catch up, the new united nation undertook a program of increased government spending (to rebuild eastern Germany's infrastructure and provide income support for its citizens) and encouragement of private investment there. Indeed, private investment surged during the reunification period.

How did the reunification program affect the current account balances of both the united Germany and its trading partners? Also, how did it affect the world real interest rate? Figure 5.7 provides an analysis to help you answer these questions. The home economy, shown in Figure 5.7(a), is a united Germany. We label the foreign economy in Figure 5.7(b) as the United States, although the foreign economy might more accurately be taken to represent all of Germany's trading partners as a group.

In Figure 5.7 the initial (before reunification) equilibrium world real interest rate is r_1^w. At that interest rate, Germany has a current account surplus, represented by the distance AB, and the United States has a current account deficit, represented by distance DE. As required for equilibrium, before reunification the US current account deficit equals the German current account surplus. That is, distances AB and DE are equal.

Two key results of reunification are (1) temporarily increased German government purchases as the infrastructure in eastern Germany is rebuilt; and (2) an increase in the expected future marginal product, MPK^f, for German investment, resulting from eastern Germany's switch to a capitalist system and the opening up of the economy. To determine the impact of reunification, we consider how these two factors should affect desired national saving and desired investment in a united Germany.

Recall that a temporary increase in government purchases lowers desired national saving at any real interest rate. Thus, the German saving curve shifts leftward, from S^1 to S^2 in Figure 5.7(a). The effect of the increase in the MPK^f in eastern Germany is to raise desired investment at any real interest rate, leading the German investment curve to shift rightward, from I^1 to I^2. There is no reason to expect any change in desired national saving or desired investment in the United Sates at any given world real interest rate.

Because of the reduction in desired national saving and the increase in desired investment in Germany, the international capital market is no longer in equilibrium at the original world real interest rate, r_1^w. At that real interest rate the amount the Germans want to lend abroad has fallen, so desired international borrowing exceeds desired international lending. Thus, the world real interest rate must rise. Figure 5.7 shows that the new equilibrium interest rate is r_2^w. When the real interest rate is r_2^w, desired international lending by Germany, distance JK, equals desired international borrowing by the United States, distance LM. Because r_2^w is greater than r_1^w, we conclude that German reunification will tend to raise the world real interest rate. In addition, Figure 5.7 shows that German reunification should both lower the German account surplus and reduce the current account deficits of its trading partners.

The predictions obtained from this analysis hold up reasonably well for the period immediately following reunification.[14] The German current account surplus, which was 4.1% of German GDP in 1988 and 4.8% of GDP in 1989, became a current account deficit of 1% of GDP in 1991 and remained at about that level for several years. The US current account deficit, which was 2.5% of US GDP in 1988, fell to only 0.2% of GDP in 1991. Real interest rates, although certainly also affected by factors other

---

14. Data in the last two paragraphs of Section 5.4 are from the International Monetary Fund, *World Economic Outlook*, October 1996, Tables A9, A18, and A28.

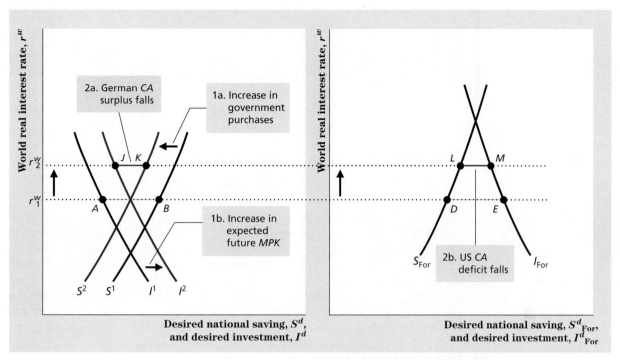

(a) Home country (Germany)   **(b) Foreign country (United States)**

FIGURE 5.7

GERMAN REUNIFICATION AND THE
WORLD REAL INTEREST RATE

The figure represents two large open economies, Germany (the home economy) and the United States (the foreign economy). Before reunification, the German saving and investment curves are S^1 and I^1. The equilibrium world real interest rate, r_1^w, is the real interest rate at which the German current account surplus AB just equals the

US current account deficit DE. Reunification raises government purchases in Germany, which shifts the German saving curve left from S^1 to S^2, and also improves investment opportunities in Germany, which shifts the German investment curve right from I^1 to I^2. The US saving and investment curves do not shift. The new world real interest rate is r_2^w, where the German current account surplus JK again equals the US current account deficit LM. Reunification raises the world real interest rate, lowers the German current account surplus, and lowers the US current account deficit.

than the ones discussed here,[15] also were unusually high in 1990 and 1991. In Germany, the short-term real interest rate rose from 2.8% in 1988 to 5.2% in 1990 and 5.3% in 1991; in the United States, the short-term real interest rate increased by less, from 3% in 1988 to 3.9% in 1989, but then fell to 3.2% in 1990. Real interest rates also rose in Japan, Canada, and other industrialized countries. All these results are consistent with the analysis shown in Figure 5.7.

Since 1991, however, although the German current account has remained in deficit, world real interest rates generally have come down, suggesting that other factors have outweighed the effects of German reunification on interest rates. One factor that probably has contributed to the fall in world real interest rates is a general decline in fiscal deficits in the industrialized countries. (Falling fiscal deficits can shift the saving curve to the right; see Section 5.5.) For example, the federal government budget deficits in the United States and Canada have declined and moved into

---

15. The effects of monetary policy on the real interest rate, which were probably important during this period, are discussed in the second half of this book.

surplus. Another factor leading to reduced government budget deficits is the Maastricht treaty, agreed to by most of the countries of Western Europe. This treaty specified the conditions under which countries could adopt the single European currency (see Chapter 10). One of its requirements was that member countries must keep their government budget deficits below 3% of GDP.

5.5 FISCAL POLICY AND THE CURRENT ACCOUNT

The late 1980s and early 1990s in Canada were characterized by large government budget deficits and large current account deficits. Were these two phenomena related? Many economists and other commentators argue that they were, suggesting that, in fact, the budget deficit was the primary cause of the current account deficit. Those supporting this view often use the phrase "twin deficits" to convey the idea that the government budget deficit and the current account deficit were closely linked. Not all economists agree with this interpretation, however; some argue that the two deficits were largely unrelated. In this section, we briefly discuss what the theory has to say about this issue and then turn to the evidence.

THE CRITICAL FACTOR:
THE RESPONSE OF NATIONAL SAVING

In theory, the issue of whether there is a link between the government budget deficit and the current account deficit revolves around the following proposition: An increase in the government budget deficit will raise the current account deficit only if the increase in the budget deficit reduces desired national saving.

Let us first look at why the link to national saving is crucial. Figure 5.8 shows the case of the small open economy. The world real interest rate is fixed at r^w. We draw the initial saving and investment curves S^1 and I so that, at the world real interest rate r^w, the country is running a current account surplus, represented by length AB. Now, suppose that the government budget deficit rises. For simplicity, we assume throughout this section that the change in fiscal policy does not affect the tax treatment of investment so that the investment curve does not shift. Hence, as Figure 5.8 shows, the government deficit increase will change the current account balance only if it affects desired national saving.

The usual claim made by supporters of the twin-deficits idea is that an increase in the government budget deficit reduces desired national saving. If it does, the increase in the government deficit shifts the desired national saving curve left, from S^1 to S^2. The country still has a current account surplus, now equal to distance AC, but it is less than the original surplus AB.

We conclude that in a small open economy an increase in the government budget deficit reduces the current account balance by the same amount that it reduces desired national saving. By reducing saving, the increased budget deficit reduces the amount that domestic residents want to lend abroad at the world real interest rate, thus lowering capital outflows. Equivalently, reduced national saving means that a greater part of domestic output is absorbed at home; with less output to send abroad, the country's current account falls. Similar results hold for the large open economy (you are asked to work out this case in Analytical Problem 4 at the end of the chapter).

FIGURE 5.8

THE GOVERNMENT BUDGET
DEFICIT AND THE CURRENT
ACCOUNT IN A SMALL
OPEN ECONOMY

An increase in the government
budget deficit affects the
current account only if the
increased budget deficit
reduces national saving.
Initially, the saving curve is S^1
and the current account
surplus is distance AB. If an
increase in the government
deficit reduces national saving,
the saving curve shifts left,
from S^1 to S^2. With no change
in the effective tax rate on
capital, the investment curve I
does not move. Thus, the
increase in the budget deficit
causes the current account
surplus to decrease from
distance AB to distance AC. In
contrast, if the increase in the
budget deficit has no effect on
national saving, the current
account is also unaffected and
remains equal to distance AB.

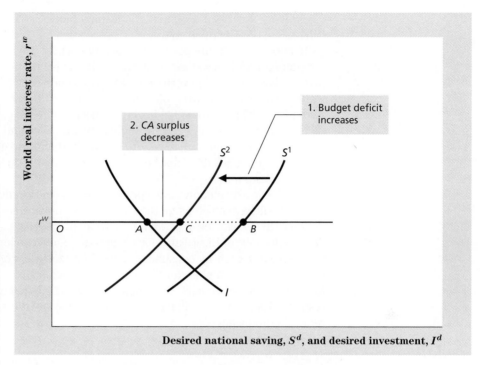

THE GOVERNMENT BUDGET DEFICIT AND NATIONAL SAVING

Let us now turn to the link between the budget deficit and saving and consider two cases: a budget deficit arising from an increase in government purchases and a deficit arising from a cut in taxes.

A DEFICIT CAUSED BY INCREASED GOVERNMENT PURCHASES

Suppose that the source of the government budget deficit is a temporary increase in government purchases, perhaps owing to a war. In this case, there is no controversy: Recall (Chapter 4) that with output Y held constant at its full-employment level, an increase in government purchases G directly reduces desired national saving, $S^d = Y - C^d - G$.[16, 17] Because economists agree that a deficit owing to increased government purchases reduces desired national saving, they also agree that a deficit resulting from increased government purchases reduces the nation's current account balance.

A DEFICIT RESULTING FROM A TAX CUT

Suppose instead that the government budget deficit is the result of a cut in current taxes, with current and planned future government purchases unchanged. With government purchases G unchanged and with output Y held constant at its full-employment level, the tax cut will cause desired national saving, $S^d = Y - C^d - G$, to fall only if it causes desired consumption C^d to rise.

---

16. Because the increase in government purchases also means that taxes may be raised in the future, lowering consumers' expected future income, desired consumption C^d may fall. However, because the increase in G is temporary so that the future tax increase need not be too large, this drop in C^d should not offset the effect of increased G on desired national saving.

17. In general, in an open economy, $S^d = Y + NFP - C^d - G$, but we are assuming that $NFP = 0$ so that $S^d = Y - C^d - G$.

Will a tax cut cause people to consume more? As we discussed in Chapter 4, believers in the Ricardian equivalence proposition argue that a lump-sum tax change (with current and future government purchases held constant) will not affect desired consumption or desired national saving. These economists point out that a cut in taxes today forces the government to borrow more to pay for its current purchases; when this extra borrowing plus interest is repaid in the future, future taxes will have to rise. Thus, although a tax cut raises consumers' current after-tax incomes, the tax cut creates the need for higher future taxes and lowers the after-tax incomes that consumers can expect to receive in the future. Overall, according to this argument, a tax cut does not benefit consumers and, thus, will not increase their desired consumption.

If the Ricardian equivalence proposition is true, a budget deficit resulting from a tax cut will have no effect on the current account because it does not affect desired national saving. However, as we noted in Chapter 4, many economists argue that—despite the logic of Ricardian equivalence—in practice, many consumers do respond to a current tax cut by consuming more. For example, consumers simply may not understand that a higher deficit today makes higher taxes tomorrow more likely. If for any reason consumers do respond to a tax cut by consuming more, the deficit resulting from a tax cut will reduce national saving and, thus, also will reduce the current account balance.

APPLICATION

THE TWIN DEFICITS

The relationship between the Canadian government budget deficit and the Canadian current account deficit—the twin deficits—is shown in Figure 5.9 (on the next page) for the period 1961–2001. Here fiscal policy is measured by government purchases and net government income (taxes less transfers and interest paid), in both cases relative to GDP and for combined federal, provincial, territorial, and municipal governments. The difference between government purchases and net receipts is the government budget deficit, shown by the shaded area. Figure 5.9 also shows the current account balance. Negative values of the current account balance indicate a current account deficit.

Notice that the current account balance tends to move in the opposite direction to government purchases, which is consistent with the theory in this chapter, for a small open economy. In addition, the government budget balance and the current account balance have moved in tandem in recent years. Both were in deficit in the early and mid-1990s. Both moved into surplus later in that decade. In 2000, the government budget surplus was about 3.5% of GDP, while the current account surplus was 2.5% of GDP.

This apparently close relationship between the Canadian government budget balance and the current account balance is evidence in favour of the twin deficits idea. David Johnson, of Wilfrid Laurier University, has reviewed the statistical evidence and concluded that Canadian budget deficits do reduce national saving.[18] The growth of

---

18. "Ricardian Equivalence: Assessing the Evidence for Canada," pp. 81–118 in W. Robson and W. Scarth, eds., *Deficit Reduction: What Pain, What Gain?* Toronto: C. D. Howe Institute, 1994.

FIGURE 5.9

THE GOVERNMENT BUDGET
BALANCE AND THE
CURRENT ACCOUNT
BALANCE IN CANADA,
1961–2001

The figure shows government
purchases, net government
income (taxes less transfers
and interest), and the current
account balance for Canada
for the period 1961–2001.
Government data are for
federal, provincial, territorial,
and municipal governments,
and each series is measured as
a percentage of GDP. The
government deficit (shaded
area) is the difference between
government purchases and net
receipts. The expansion of both
the government deficit and
the current account deficit in the
late 1980s and early 1990s is
the twin-deficits phenomenon.
Canada currently has twin
surpluses.

Source: *Canadian Economic
Observer, Historical Statistical
Supplement,* Tables 1, 3, and 19,
or Statistics Canada, CANSIM
Series D15665, D58032, D15886,
and D15892.

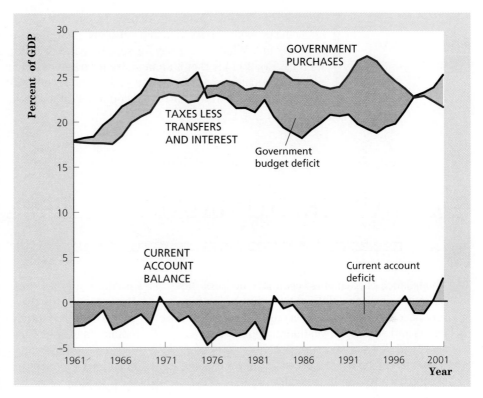

the government budget deficit in the mid-1980s, for example, primarily reflected declines in tax revenue (or increases in transfers and interest, which reduced net government receipts) rather than increased government purchases. Figure 5.9 shows that the current account went into deficit at the same time. Thus, the behaviour of the two deficits seems also to contradict the Ricardian equivalence proposition, which says that tax cuts should have no effect on national saving or the current account.

However, even though these experiences seem to confirm the link between the government budget and the current account, the evidence from other episodes is less supportive of the hypothesis. For example, Canada simultaneously ran large government budget deficits and large current account surpluses during World War II (see Figure 2.1). Other periods in which the twin-deficits idea failed to hold include 1997 and 1998, when the current account went into deficit, while the government budget went into surplus.

The evidence from other countries on the relationship between the government budget and the current account balances also is mixed. In the 1980s, the US had twin deficits, apparently due to tax cuts. But during the late 1990s, the US government budget balance was in surplus, yet the US current account balance remained deeply in deficit because private saving fell and investment rose as a share of GDP at the same time. This situation was reversed in Japan, where the current account continued to be in surplus even as the government budget deficit approached 9% of GDP.

> Because of the lack of clear evidence, a good deal of disagreement remains among economists about the relationship between government budget deficits and the current account. What we can say for sure (because it is implied by the uses-of-saving identity, Eq. 2.11) is that if an increase in the government budget deficit is not offset by an equal increase in private saving, the result must be a decline in domestic investment, a rise in the current account deficit, or both.

CHAPTER SUMMARY

1. The balance of payments accounts consist of the current account and the capital account. The current account records trade in currently produced goods and services, investment income from assets held abroad, and transfers between countries. The capital account records trade in existing assets, both real and financial.

2. In the current account, exports of goods and services, receipts of investment income from assets held abroad, and transfers received from abroad count as credit (plus) items. Imports of goods and services, payments of investment income to foreigners holding assets in the home country, and transfers sent abroad are debit (minus) items in the current account. The current account balance, CA, equals the value of credit items less debit items in the current account. Setting net factor payments and net transfers to zero makes the current account balance the same as net exports, NX. The capital account balance, KA, is the value of assets sold to foreigners (capital inflows) minus the value of assets purchased from foreigners (capital outflows).

3. In each period, except for measurement errors, the current account balance and the capital account balance must sum to zero. The reason is that any international transaction amounts to a swap of goods, services, or assets between countries; the two sides of the swap always have offsetting effects on the sum of the current account and capital account balances.

4. In an open economy, goods market equilibrium requires that the desired amount of national saving equal the desired amount of domestic investment plus the amount the country lends abroad. Equivalently, net exports must equal the country's output (gross domestic product) less desired total spending by domestic residents (absorption).

5. A small open economy faces a fixed real interest rate in the international capital market. In goods market equilibrium in a small open economy, national saving and investment equal their desired levels at the prevailing world real interest rate; foreign lending, net exports, and the current account all equal the excess of national saving over investment. Any factor that increases desired national saving or reduces desired investment at the world real interest rate will increase the small open economy's foreign lending (equivalently, its current account balance).

6. The levels of saving and investment of a large open economy affect the world real interest rate. In a model of two large open economies, the equilibrium real interest rate in the international capital market is the rate at which desired international lending by one country equals desired international borrowing by the other country. Equivalently, it is the rate at which the lending country's current account surplus equals the borrowing country's current account deficit. Any factor that increases desired national saving or reduces desired investment at the initial interest rate for either large country will increase the supply of international loans relative to the demand and cause the world real interest rate to fall.

7. According to the "twin-deficits" hypothesis, the large Canadian and US government budget deficits of the 1980s and early 1990s helped cause the sharply increased current account deficits of that period in these countries. Whether budget deficits cause current account deficits is the subject of disagreement. In theory, and if we assume no change in the tax treatment of invest-ment, an increase in the government budget deficit will raise the current account deficit only if it reduces national saving. Economists gener-ally agree that an increase in the budget deficit caused by a temporary increase in government purchases will reduce national saving, but whether an increase in the budget deficit caused by a tax cut reduces national saving is controversial.

KEY DIAGRAM 4

NATIONAL SAVING AND INVESTMENT IN A SMALL OPEN ECONOMY

This open-economy version of the saving–investment diagram shows the determination of national saving, investment, and the current account balance in a small open economy that takes the world real interest rate as given.

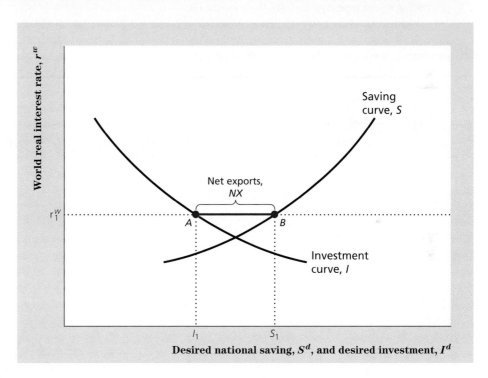

DIAGRAM ELEMENTS

- The world real interest rate is measured on the vertical axis, and the small economy's desired national saving S^d and desired investment I^d are measured on the horizontal axis.

- The world real interest rate r^w is fixed, as indi-cated by the horizontal line.

- The saving curve S and the investment curve I are the same as in the closed-economy saving–investment diagram, Key Diagram 3 (p. 135).

ANALYSIS

- Goods market equilibrium in a small open econ-omy requires that desired national saving equal desired investment plus net exports (Eq. 5.4). In the diagram when the world real interest rate is r_1^w desired national saving is S_1 and desired invest-ment is I_1. The country's net exports NX and current account balance CA, or $S_1 - I_1$, is distance AB. Equivalently, distance AB, the excess of desired national saving over desired investment, is the amount that the small open economy is lending abroad, or its capital account deficit.

FACTORS THAT SHIFT THE CURVES

- Anything that increases desired national saving in the small open economy, for a fixed value of the world real interest rate, shifts the saving curve right. Factors that shift the saving curve right (see Summary table 5, p. 116) include
  - an increase in current output, Y,
  - a decrease in expected future output,
  - a decrease in wealth,
  - a decrease in current government purchases, G, and
  - an increase in current taxes, T, if Ricardian equivalence doesn't hold and taxes affect saving.

- Anything that increases desired investment at the prevailing real interest rate shifts the investment curve right. Factors that shift the investment curve right (see Summary table 6, p. 126) include an increase in the expected future marginal product of capital, MPK^f, and a decrease in the effective tax rate on capital.

- An increase in desired national saving shifts the saving curve right and raises net exports and the current account balance. Equivalently, an increase in desired national saving raises the country's net foreign lending, which equals its capital account deficit. Similarly, an increase in desired investment shifts the investment curve right and lowers net exports, the current account balance, net foreign lending, and the capital account deficit.

- An increase in the world real interest rate r^w raises the horizontal line in the diagram. Because an increase in the world real interest rate increases national saving and reduces investment, it raises net foreign lending, net exports, the current account surplus, and the capital account deficit.

KEY DIAGRAM 5

NATIONAL SAVING AND INVESTMENT IN LARGE OPEN ECONOMIES

This diagram shows the determination of national saving, investment, and the current account balance in large open economies, economies large enough to affect the world real interest rate.

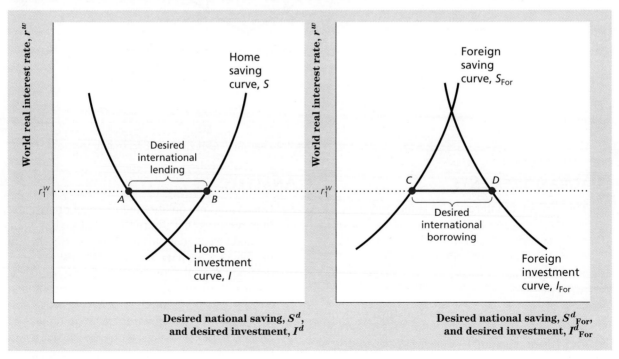

(a) Home country

(b) Foreign country

DIAGRAM ELEMENTS

- The figure consists of two saving–investment diagrams, one for the home country and one for the foreign country (representing the rest of the world).
- The world real interest rate r^w, measured on the vertical axis, is the real interest rate faced by both countries in the international capital market.
- The saving and investment curves in the home country (S and I) and in the foreign country (S_{For} and I_{For}) are the same as the saving and investment curves presented before (Key Diagram 3, p. 135, and Key Diagram 4, p. 191).

ANALYSIS

- This case differs from the case of the small open economy (Key Diagram 4) in that the world real interest rate r^w is determined within the model, not given.
- Goods market equilibrium for large open economies requires that the desired international lending of one country equal the desired international borrowing of the other. Equivalently, because a country's international lending equals its current account balance, goods market equilibrium requires that one country's current account surplus equal the other country's current account deficit.

- The world real interest rate adjusts to achieve goods market equilibrium. In the diagram r_1^w is the equilibrium world real interest rate, because at that interest rate the home country's desired international lending (its desired national saving less desired investment, or distance AB) equals the foreign country's desired international borrowing (its desired investment less desired national saving, or distance CD).

FACTORS THAT SHIFT THE CURVES

- The saving and investment curves in the two countries are shifted by the same factors as in Key Diagram 3, p. 135 , and Key Diagram 4, p. 191.
- The world real interest rate changes when desired national saving or desired investment changes in either country. Any change that increases desired international lending relative to desired international borrowing at the initial world real interest rate will cause the world real interest rate to fall to restore equilibrium in the international capital market. Changes that increase desired international lending relative to desired international borrowing include an increase in desired national saving or a decrease in desired investment in either country. Similarly, a decrease in desired national saving or an increase in desired investment in either country reduces desired international lending relative to desired international borrowing and raises the world real interest rate.

KEY TERMS

KEY EQUATIONS

$$CA + KA = 0 \qquad (5.1)$$

Except for problems of measurement, the current account balance, CA, and the capital account balance, KA, always sum to zero. The reason is that every international transaction involves a swap of goods, services, or assets; and the two sides of the swap always have offsetting effects on $CA + KA$.

$$S^d = I^d + NX \qquad (5.4)$$

The goods market equilibrium condition in an open economy holds that desired national saving, S^d, must equal desired investment, I^d, plus the amount lent abroad. The amount lent abroad equals the current account balance, which (if we assume that net factor payments and transfers are zero) also equals net exports, NX.

$$NX = Y - (C^d + I^d + G) \qquad (5.6)$$

An alternative way of writing the goods market equilibrium condition, this equation states that net exports must equal the country's output, Y, less its desired absorption, $C^d + I^d + G$.

REVIEW QUESTIONS

1. List the categories of credit items and debit items that appear in a country's current account. What is the current account balance? What is the relationship between the current account balance and net exports?
2. What is the key difference that determines whether an international transaction appears in the current account or the capital account?
3. A Canadian publisher sells $200 worth of books to a resident of Brazil. By itself, this item is a credit item in the Canadian current account. Describe some offsetting transactions that could ensure that the Canadian current and capital account balances would continue to sum to zero.
4. How do a country's current and capital account balances affect its net foreign assets? If country A has greater net foreign assets per citizen than does country B, is country A necessarily better off than country B?
5. Explain why, in a small open economy, (a) national saving does not have to equal investment, and (b) output does not have to equal absorption.
6. Generally, what types of factors will cause a small open economy to run a large current account deficit and thus borrow abroad? More specifically, what two major factors contributed to heavy LDC borrowing in the 1970s?
7. In a world with two large open economies, what determines the world real interest rate? What relationship between the current accounts of the two countries is satisfied when the world real interest rate is at its equilibrium value?
8. How does an increase in desired national saving in a large open economy affect the world real interest rate? How does an increase in desired investment affect it? Why do changes in desired saving or investment in large open economies affect the world real interest rate, while changes in desired saving or investment in small open economies do not?
9. Under what circumstances will an increase in the government budget deficit affect the current account balance in a small open economy? In the cases in which the current account balance changes, by how much does it change?
10. What are the twin deficits? What is the connection between them?

NUMERICAL PROBLEMS

1. Here are some balance of payments data (without pluses and minuses):

    Merchandise exports, 100
    Merchandise imports, 125
    Service exports, 90
    Service imports, 80
    Investment income receipts from assets, 110
    Investment income payments on assets, 140
    Transfers from home country to other countries, 10
    Increase in home country's ownership of assets abroad, 160
    Increase in foreign ownership of assets in home country, 200
    Increase in home reserve assets, 30
    Increase in foreign reserve assets, 35

    Find the merchandise trade balance, net exports, the current account balance, the capital account balance, the official settlements balance, and the statistical discrepancy.

2. In a small open economy, output (gross domestic product) is $25 billion, government purchases are $6 billion, and net factor payments from abroad are zero. Desired consumption and desired investment are related to the world real interest rate in the following manner:

World Real Interest Rate	Desired Consumption	Desired Investment
5%	$12 billion	$3 billion
4%	$13 billion	$4 billion
3%	$14 billion	$5 billion
2%	$15 billion	$6 billion

    For each value of the world real interest rate, find national saving, foreign lending, and absorption. Calculate net exports as the difference between output and absorption. What is the relationship between net exports and foreign lending?

3. In a small open economy,

    desired national saving, $S^d = \$10 \text{ billion} + (\$100 \text{ billion})r^w$;

    desired investment, $I^d = \$15 \text{ billion} - (\$100 \text{ billion})r^w$;

    output, $Y = \$50$ billion;

    government purchases, $G = \$10$ billion;

    world real interest rate, $r^w = 0.03$.

    a. Find the economy's national saving, investment, current account surplus, net exports, desired consumption, and absorption.

b. Owing to a technological innovation, the country's desired investment rises by $2 billion at each level of the world real interest rate. Repeat part (a).

4. Consider two large open economies, the home economy and the foreign economy. In the home country the following relationships hold:

$$\text{desired consumption, } C^d = 320 + 0.4(Y - T) - 200r^w;$$

$$\text{desired investment, } I^d = 150 - 200r^w;$$

$$\text{output, } Y = 1,000;$$

$$\text{taxes, } T = 200;$$

$$\text{government purchases, } G = 275.$$

In the foreign country the following relationships hold:

$$\text{desired consumption, } C^d_{For} = 480 + 0.4(Y_{For} - T_{For}) - 300r^w;$$

$$\text{desired investment, } I^d_{For} = 225 - 300r^w;$$

$$\text{output, } Y_{For} = 1,500;$$

$$\text{taxes, } T_{For} = 300;$$

$$\text{government purchases, } G_{For} = 300.$$

a. What is the equilibrium interest rate in the international capital market? What are the equilibrium values of consumption, national saving, investment, and the current account balance in each country?

b. Suppose that in the home country government purchases increase by 50 to 325. Taxes also increase by 50 to keep the deficit from growing. What is the new equilibrium interest rate in the international capital market? What are the new equilibrium values of consumption, national saving, investment, and the current account balance in each country?

5. Consider a world with only two countries, which are designated the home country (H) and the foreign country (F). Output equals its full-employment level in each country. You are given the following information about each country:

Home Country

Consumption:	$C_H = 100 + 0.5Y_H - 500r$
Investment:	$I_H = 300 - 500r$
Government Purchases:	$G_H = 155$
Full-employment Output:	$\overline{Y}_H = 1,000$

Foreign Country

Consumption:	$C_F = 225 + 0.7Y_F - 600r$
Investment:	$I_F = 250 - 200r$
Government Purchases:	$G_F = 190$
Full-employment Output:	$\overline{Y}_F = 1,200$

a. Write national saving in the home country and in the foreign country as functions of the world real interest rate r.

b. What is the equilibrium value of the world real interest rate?

c. What are the equilibrium values of consumption, national saving, investment, the current account balance, and absorption in each country?

6. A small island nation is endowed with indestructible coconut trees. These trees live forever and no new trees can be planted. Every year $1 million worth of coconuts fall off the trees and can be eaten locally or exported to other countries. In past years, the island nation ran current account surpluses and capital account deficits, acquiring foreign bonds. It now owns $500,000 of foreign bonds. The interest rate on these bonds is 5% per year. The residents of the island nation consume $1,025,000 per year. What are the values of investment, national saving, the current account balance, the capital account balance, net exports, GDP, and GNP in this country?

ANALYTICAL PROBLEMS

1. Explain how each of the following transactions would enter the Canadian balance of payments accounts. Discuss only the transactions described. Do not be concerned with possible offsetting transactions.

a. The Canadian government sells military equipment to a foreign government.

b. A London bank sells yen to, and buys Canadian dollars from, a Swiss bank.

c. The Bank of Canada sells yen to, and buys dollars from, a Swiss bank.

d. A Canadian bank receives the interest on its loans to Brazil.

e. A Canadian collector buys some ancient artifacts from a collection in Egypt.

f. A Canadian oil company buys insurance from Lloyds of London to insure its oil rigs in the Beaufort Sea.

g. A Canadian company borrows from a U.S. bank.

2. For each transaction described in Analytical Problem 1 that by itself changes the sum of the Canadian current account balance, CA, and the Canadian capital account balance, KA, give an example of an offsetting transaction that would leave $CA + KA$ unchanged.

3. A large country imposes capital controls that prohibit foreign borrowing and lending by domestic residents. Analyze the effects on the country's current account balance, national saving, and investment, and on domestic and world real interest rates. Assume that before the capital controls were imposed, the large country was running a capital account surplus.

4. The text showed that for a small open economy, an increase in the government budget deficit raises the current account deficit only if it affects desired national saving in the home country. Show that this result is true also for a large open economy. Then assume that an increase in the government budget deficit does affect desired national saving in the home country. What effects will the increased budget deficit have on the foreign country's current account, investment in both countries, and the world real interest rate?

5. How would each of the following affect national saving, investment, the current account balance, and the real interest rate in a large open economy?

   a. An increase in the domestic willingness to save (which raises desired national saving at any given real interest rate).

   b. An increase in the willingness of foreigners to save.

   c. An increase in foreign government purchases.

   d. An increase in foreign taxes (consider both the case in which Ricardian equivalence holds and the case in which it does not hold).

6. Analyze the effects on a large open economy of a temporary adverse supply shock that hits only the foreign economy. Discuss the impact on the home country's national saving, investment, and current account balance—and on the world real interest rate. How does your answer differ if the adverse supply shock is worldwide?

7. The chief economic advisor of a small open economy makes the following announcement: "We have good news and bad news: The good news is that we have just had a temporary beneficial productivity shock that will increase output; the bad news is that the increase in output and income will lead domestic consumers to buy more imported goods, and our current account balance will fall." Analyze this statement, taking as given that a beneficial productivity shock has indeed occurred.

8. The world is made up of only two large countries: Eastland and Westland. Westland is running a large current account deficit and often appeals to Eastland for help in reducing this current account deficit. Currently, the government of Eastland purchases $10 billion of goods and services, and all these goods and services are produced in Eastland. The finance minister of Eastland proposes that the government purchase half of its goods from Westland. Specifically, the government of Eastland will continue to purchase $10 billion of goods, but $5 billion will be from Eastland and $5 billion will be from Westland. The finance minister gives the following rationale: "Both countries produce identical goods, so it does not really matter to us which country produced the goods we purchase. Moreover, this change in purchasing policy will help reduce Westland's large current account deficit." What are the effects of this change in purchasing policy on the current account balance in each country and on the world real interest rate? (*Hint:* What happens to net exports by the private sector in each country after the government of Eastland changes its purchasing policy?)

Chapter 6

LONG-RUN ECONOMIC GROWTH

A country's ability to provide improving standards of living for its people depends crucially on its long-run rate of economic growth. Over a long period of time, even an apparently small difference in the rate of economic growth can translate into a large difference in the income of the average person.

Compare, for example, the historical experiences of Australia and Japan. In 1870, real GDP per person was about five times greater in Australia than in Japan, as the data on national growth performances in Table 6.1 show. Indeed, of 16 major economies considered by British economist Angus Maddison in his important research on long-run growth (and from whose work some of the data in Table 6.1 are taken), Australia was the richest and Japan the poorest in 1870. Australia's economy did not stand still after 1870. Over the next 126 years, according to Maddison's data, Australian real GDP per person grew by 1.3% per year so that by 1996 the real income of the average Australian was almost five times higher than it had been in 1870. However, during the same period, Japanese real GDP per person grew at a rate of 2.7% per year, reaching a level in 1996 that was more than 28 times larger than it had been in 1870.

The Japanese growth rate of 2.7% per year may not seem dramatically greater than the Australian growth rate of 1.3% per year. Yet, by 1996, Japan, which had been far poorer than Australia a century earlier, had surpassed its Pacific neighbour in per capita GDP by a margin of 15%. Other, similar comparisons can be drawn from Table 6.1; compare, for example, the long-term growth performance of the United Kingdom against that of Canada or Sweden. Note, however, that even those countries that grew relatively slowly have dramatically increased their output per person during the past century.

Although the comparisons highlighted by Table 6.1 span a long period of time, a change in the rate of economic growth can have important effects over even a decade or two. For example, since about 1973, Canada and other industrialized countries have experienced a sustained slowdown in their rates of growth. Between 1947 and 1973, total (not per capita) real GDP in Canada grew by about 5% per year, but between 1973 and 2000, Canada's real GDP grew by only 3% per year. To appreciate the significance of this slowdown, imagine that the 1947–1973 growth trend had continued—that is, suppose that real GDP in Canada had continued to grow at 5% per year instead of at the 3% per year rate actually achieved. Then, in 2000, the Canadian real GDP would have been about 70% higher than its actual value—a bonus of about $690 billion, or $22,000 per person (in 1997 dollars).

No one understands completely why economies grow, and no one has a magic formula for inducing rapid growth. Indeed, if such a formula existed, there would be no poor countries. Nevertheless, economists have gained useful insights about the

TABLE 6.1

Economic Growth in Eight Major Countries, 1870–1996

| Country | Levels of Real GDP per Capita | | | | Annual growth rate (%) |
	1870	1913	1950	1996	1870–1996
Australia	3,123	4,523	5,931	15,076	1.3
Canada	1,347	3,560	6,113	17,453	2.1
France	1,571	2,734	4,149	14,631	1.8
Germany	1,300	2,606	3,339	15,313	2.0
Japan	618	1,114	1,563	17,346	2.7
Sweden	1,316	2,450	5,331	14,912	1.9
United Kingdom	2,610	4,024	5,651	14,440	1.4
United States	2,247	4,854	8,611	19,638	1.7

Note: Figures are in US dollars at 1985 prices, adjusted for differences in the purchasing power of the various national currencies.

Sources: Data from 1870, 1913, and 1950 adapted from Angus Maddison, *Dynamic Forces in Capitalist Development: A Long-Run Comparative View*, New York: Oxford University Press, 1991, Table 1.1. Data for 1996 computed by the authors using growth rates of real GDP from 1989 to 1996 reported in *OECD National Accounts, Main Aggregates, 1960-1996*, Volume 1 Part Four, Growth Triangles, and 1989 levels of GDP per capita from Maddison. (The 1996 data for Germany apply the growth rate for unified Germany to the 1989 GDP per capita for West Germany and thus overstate GDP per capita for unified Germany in 1996 because income per capita was higher in West Germany than in East Germany in 1989.)

growth process. In this chapter, we identify the forces that determine the growth rate of an economy over long periods of time and examine various policies that governments may use to try to influence the rate of growth. Once again, saving and investment decisions play a central role in the analysis. Along with changes in productivity, the rates at which a country saves and invests—and, thus, the rate at which it accumulates capital goods—are important factors in determining the standard of living that the country's people can attain.

6.1 THE SOURCES OF ECONOMIC GROWTH

An economy's output of goods and services depends on the quantities of available inputs, such as capital and labour, and on the productivity of those inputs. The relationship between output and inputs is described by the production function, introduced in Chapter 3:

$$Y = AF(K, N). \tag{6.1}$$

Equation (6.1) relates total output Y to the economy's use of capital K and labour N and to productivity A.

If inputs and productivity are constant, the production function states that output also will be constant—there will be no economic growth. For the quantity of output to grow, either the quantity of inputs must grow or productivity must improve, or both. The relationship between the rate of output growth and the rates of input growth and productivity growth is

$$\frac{\Delta Y}{Y} = \frac{\Delta A}{A} + a_K \frac{\Delta K}{K} + a_N \frac{\Delta N}{N},$$ (6.2)

where

$\dfrac{\Delta Y}{Y}$ = rate of output growth;

$\dfrac{\Delta K}{K}$ = rate of capital growth;

$\dfrac{\Delta N}{N}$ = rate of labour growth;

$\dfrac{\Delta A}{A}$ = rate of productivity growth;

a_K = elasticity of output with respect to capital;

a_N = elasticity of output with respect to labour.

In Eq. (6.2) the elasticity of output with respect to capital, a_K, is the percentage increase in output resulting from a 1% increase in the capital stock, and the elasticity of output with respect to labour, a_N, is the percentage increase in output resulting from a 1% increase in the amount of labour used. The elasticities a_K and a_N both are numbers between 0 and 1 that must be estimated from historical data.[1]

Equation (6.2), called the **growth accounting equation**, is the production function (Eq. 6.1) written in growth rate form. Some examples will be helpful for understanding the growth accounting equation.

Suppose that a new invention allows firms to produce 10% more output for the same amount of capital and labour. In terms of the production function, Eq. (6.1), for constant capital and labour inputs, a 10% increase in productivity A raises output Y by 10%. Similarly, from the growth accounting equation, Eq. (6.2), if productivity growth $\Delta A/A$ equals 10% and capital and labour growth are zero, output growth $\Delta Y/Y$ will be 10%. Thus, the production function and the growth accounting equation give the same result, as they should.

Now, suppose that firms' investments cause the economy's capital stock to rise by 10% ($\Delta K/K = 10\%$) while labour input and productivity remain unchanged. What will happen to output? The production function shows that if the capital stock grows, output will increase. However, because of the diminishing marginal productivity of capital (see Chapter 3), the extra capital will be less productive than that used previously, so the increase in output will be less than 10%. Diminishing marginal productivity of capital is the reason that the growth rate of capital, $\Delta K/K$, is multiplied by a factor less than 1 in the growth accounting equation. For Canada this factor, a_K, the elasticity of output with respect to capital, is about 0.3. Thus, the growth accounting equation, Eq. (6.2), indicates that a 10% increase in the capital stock, with labour and productivity held constant, will increase Canadian output by about 3%, or (0.3)(10%).

---

1. Elasticities and growth rate formulas such as Eq. (6.2) are discussed further in the Appendix, Sections A.3 and A.7.

Similarly, the elasticity of output with respect to labour a_N is about 0.7 in Canada. Thus, according to Eq. (6.2), a 10% increase in the amount of labour used $(\Delta N/N = 10\%)$, with no change in capital or productivity, will raise Canadian output by about 7%, or $(0.7)(10\%)$.[2]

GROWTH ACCOUNTING

According to Eq. (6.2), output growth $\Delta Y/Y$ can be divided into three parts:

1. that resulting from productivity growth, $\Delta A/A$,
2. that resulting from increased capital inputs, $a_K \, \Delta K/K$, and
3. that resulting from increased labour inputs, $a_N \, \Delta N/N$.

Growth accounting measures empirically the relative importance of these three sources of output growth. A typical growth accounting analysis involves the following four steps (see Table 6.2, on the next page, for a summary and numerical example).

- *Step 1.* Obtain measures of the growth rates of output, $\Delta Y/Y$, capital, $\Delta K/K$, and labour, $\Delta N/N$, for the economy over any period of time. In the calculation of growth rates for capital and labour, more sophisticated analyses make adjustments for changing quality as well as quantity of inputs. For example, to obtain a quality-adjusted measure of N, an hour of work by a skilled worker is counted as more labour than an hour of work by an unskilled worker. Similarly, to obtain a quality-adjusted measure of K, a machine that can turn 50 bolts a minute is treated as being more capital than a machine that can turn only 30 bolts a minute.

- *Step 2.* Estimate values for the elasticities a_K and a_N from historical data. Keep in mind the estimates for Canada of 0.3 for a_K and 0.7 for a_N.

- *Step 3.* Calculate the contribution of capital to economic growth as $a_K \, \Delta K/K$ and the contribution of labour to economic growth as $a_N \, \Delta N/N$.

- *Step 4.* The part of economic growth assignable to neither capital growth nor labour growth is attributed to improvements in total factor productivity. The rate of productivity change $\Delta A/A$ is calculated from the formula

$$\frac{\Delta A}{A} = \frac{\Delta Y}{Y} - a_K \frac{\Delta K}{K} - a_N \frac{\Delta N}{N},$$

which is the growth accounting equation, Eq. (6.2), rewritten with $\Delta A/A$ on the left-hand side. Thus, the growth accounting technique treats productivity change as a residual, that is, the portion of growth not otherwise explained.[3]

---

2. Chapter 3 examined the production function for the Canadian economy, $Y = AK^{0.3} N^{0.7}$. In that production function, called a Cobb–Douglas production function, the exponent on the capital stock K, 0.3, equals the elasticity of output with respect to capital, and the exponent on the quantity of labour input N, 0.7, equals the elasticity of output with respect to labour. See the Appendix, Section A.7.

3. The growth accounting method for calculating productivity growth is similar to the method we used to find productivity growth in Section 3.2, where we also determined productivity growth as the part of output growth not explained by increases in capital and labour. The differences are that growth accounting uses the growth accounting equation, which is the production function in growth rate form, instead of using the production function directly, as we did in Chapter 3; and growth accounting analyses usually adjust measures of capital and labour for changes in quality, which we did not do in Chapter 3.

TABLE 6.2

The Steps of Growth Accounting: A Numerical Example

Step 1. Obtain measures of output growth, capital growth, and labour growth over the period to be studied.

Example:

$$\text{Output growth} = \frac{\Delta Y}{Y} = 40\%;$$

$$\text{Capital growth} = \frac{\Delta K}{K} = 20\%;$$

$$\text{Labour growth} = \frac{\Delta N}{N} = 30\%.$$

Step 2. Using historical data, obtain estimates of the elasticities of output with respect to capital and labour, a_K and a_N.

Example:

$$a_K = 0.3 \quad \text{and} \quad a_N = 0.7.$$

Step 3. Find the contributions to growth of capital and labour.

Example:

$$\begin{array}{c}\text{Contribution to output growth} \\ \text{of growth in capital}\end{array} = a_K \frac{\Delta K}{K} = (0.3)(20\%) = 6\%;$$

$$\begin{array}{c}\text{Contribution to output growth} \\ \text{of growth in labour}\end{array} = a_N \frac{\Delta N}{N} = (0.7)(30\%) = 21\%.$$

Step 4. Find productivity growth as the residual (the part of output growth not explained by capital or labour).

Example:

$$\text{Productivity growth} = \frac{\Delta A}{A} = \frac{\Delta Y}{Y} - a_K \frac{\Delta K}{K} - a_N \frac{\Delta N}{N}$$

$$= 40\% - 6\% - 21\% = 13\%.$$

APPLICATION

GROWTH ACCOUNTING AND THE EAST ASIAN "MIRACLE"

Several East Asian countries—sometimes called the East Asian tigers—exhibited remarkable rates of economic growth during the final third of the 20th century. Between 1966 and 1991, Hong Kong averaged real GDP growth of more than 7% per year, and between 1966 and 1990, Singapore, South Korea, and Taiwan averaged real GDP growth of more than 8% per year. An 8% annual growth rate sustained over 25 years translates into a level of real output nearly seven times as high at the end of the period as at the beginning. These countries were hit by a severe financial crisis in the late 1990s, which slowed their GDP growth—and even caused negative GDP growth in some cases (see the Application "The Crises in Mexico, East Asia, and Russia," p. 179). Nevertheless, the East Asian miracle remains an interesting example to economists, political leaders, and businesspeople who would like to find a way to create similar miracles in their own countries.

What caused the East Asian miracle? And will it continue? To address these questions, Alwyn Young of the University of Chicago applied growth accounting in a particularly careful study of East Asian growth.[4] Young used a variety of data sources to develop comprehensive measures of the growth of output, capital, and labour for Hong Kong, Singapore, South Korea, and Taiwan. He found that to a surprising degree, the rapid economic growth of these East Asian economies has resulted from rapid growth in capital and labour inputs, rather than improvements in total factor productivity (TFP). For example, all four countries experienced remarkable increases in labour force participation rates, as well as general population growth. Similarly, extremely high rates of national saving (in some cases, enforced by government regulations) led to rapid growth in capital stocks.

After accounting for increases in inputs, Young found that rates of growth in TFP in the four East Asian countries were not so high as many people had thought: 2.3% for Hong Kong, 1.7% for South Korea, 2.6% for Taiwan, and only 0.2% for Singapore! These are good rates of TFP growth (except for Singapore's) but not "miraculous" rates; for example, over approximately the same period, Italy enjoyed TFP growth of about 2% per year.

As we discuss in detail in this chapter, the declining marginal productivity of capital makes it very difficult to sustain growth over the very long term by increasing inputs alone. At some point, only advances in TFP can keep an economy on a path of rapid growth. Thus, an implication of Young's research is that (even without the Asian financial crisis) the rapid growth in East Asia may have run out of steam on its own. Furthermore, the rapid growth of the East Asian tigers is unlikely to resume, unless those countries can find ways to stimulate growth in TFP.

Growth Accounting and the Productivity Slowdown

What does growth accounting say about the sources of Canadian economic growth? Table 6.3 summarizes some of the research, much of it originated by Harvey Lithwick, of Carleton University.

The last entry in Column (3) shows, for example, that over the 1926–1956 period, output grew at an average rate of 3.9% per year. According to these measurements, the growth of labour accounted for output growth of 0.6% per year. The growth of labour, in turn, resulted primarily from an increase in population, an increase in the percentage of the population in the labour force, and higher educational levels, which raised workers' skills. (Offsetting these trends to a degree was a decline in the number of hours worked per person.) The growth of the capital stock also accounted for output growth of 0.6% per year. So, together, labour and capital growth contributed 1.2% to the annual growth rate of output.

The difference between total growth (3.9%) and the amount of growth attributed to capital and labour growth (1.2%) from 1926 through 1956 is 2.7%. By the growth accounting method, this remaining 2.7% per year of growth is attributed to increases in productivity. Thus, increased quantities of factors of production and improvements in the effectiveness with which those factors were used both played important roles in Canadian growth after 1926.

---

4. Alwyn Young, "The Tyranny of Numbers: Confronting the Statistical Realities of the East Asian Growth Experience," *Quarterly Journal of Economics*, August 1995, pp. 641–680.

TABLE 6.3

Sources of Economic Growth in Canada (Percent per Year)

	(1) 1891–1910	(2) 1910–1926	(3) 1926–1956
Source of Growth			
Labour growth	1.8	1.0	0.6
Capital growth	0.8	0.3	0.6
Total input growth	2.6	1.3	1.2
Productivity growth	0.8	1.2	2.7
Total output growth	**3.4**	**2.5**	**3.9**
	(4) 1962–1973	(5) 1974–1986	(6) 1984–1998
Source of Growth			
Labour growth	2.8	2.0	1.1
Capital growth	0.6	0.7	0.5
Total input growth	3.4	2.7	1.6
Productivity growth	2.0	0.7	0.9
Total output growth	**5.4**	**3.4**	**2.5**

Source: 1891–1956: N. Harvey Lithwick, *Economic Growth in Canada: A Quantitative Analysis*, 2nd ed., Toronto: University of Toronto Press, 1970; 1962–1986: P. Someshwar Rao and Tony Lemprière, *Canada's Productivity Performance*, *Economic Council of Canada*, 1992. 1984-1998: Centre for the Study of Living Standards Productivity Tables, (*www.csls.ca/ptables.html*). The Lithwick findings do not incorporate the recent Urquhart revisions to pre-1926 GDP.

Data for periods after 1956 are given in Columns (4) to (6) of Table 6.3 and are based on research at the Economic Council of Canada by P. Someshwar Rao and Tony Lemprière and, more recently, by the Centre for the Study of Living Standards. They show rapid output growth during 1962–1973, which has slowed since. Comparing column (4) with column (5), for 1974–1986, or with column (6), for 1984–1998, shows that much of the decline in output growth can be accounted for by a decline in productivity growth.

The finding of a significant slowdown in productivity growth beginning in the early 1970s has been confirmed by many studies, both for Canada and for other industrialized countries. Michael Denny and other economists at the University of Toronto and Carleton University have carefully studied productivity growth in manufacturing in Canada, the United States, and Japan for 1953–1986.[5] They found the slowdown after 1973 to be most evident for Japan (partly because Japanese productivity growth was so high during the 1960s) and least evident for Canada. In manufacturing, there was some tendency for productivity growth to increase in the 1980s, but it did not return to pre-1973 levels. Both the slowdown and any increases in the 1980s in productivity growth were highly correlated across industries in the three countries. For example, in all three countries, productivity grew rapidly in the electrical equipment industry and very slowly in primary metals industries.[6]

5. M. Denny, J. Bernstein, M. Fuss, S. Nakamura, and L. Waverman, "Productivity in Manufacturing Industries, Canada, Japan, and the United States, 1953–1986: Was the 'Productivity Slowdown' Reversed?" *Canadian Journal of Economics*, August 1992, pp. 584–603.

6. There is also evidence of country-specific factors (across industries) in productivity growth, though. See Donna M. Costello, "A Cross-Country, Cross-Industry Comparison of Productivity Growth," *Journal of Political Economy*, April 1993, pp. 207–222.

The widespread slowdown in productivity growth of the past two decades is a major economic concern and has a direct impact on living standards, real wages, and other basic economic issues. Unfortunately, the source of the slowdown remains something of a puzzle, as the following Application, "The Post-1973 Slowdown in Productivity Growth," discusses.

APPLICATION

THE POST-1973 SLOWDOWN IN PRODUCTIVITY GROWTH

The rate of economic growth, both in Canada and in other industrialized countries, has declined significantly since about 1973. This slowdown has had serious consequences for real wages and living standards in Canada. At the same time, the complete explanation cannot lie in Canada because of the worldwide nature of the slowdown.

Growth accounting was useful in showing that the slowdown in output growth largely reflected reduced growth of productivity, rather than slower growth in the amount of capital and labour available. But this finding only deepens the puzzle. The next obvious question is, What caused productivity performance to deteriorate so sharply? In this Application, we discuss some alternative explanations, including possible measurement problems, reduced rates of technological innovation, the effects of high oil prices, and the information technology revolution.

Measurement. Interestingly, several economists have suggested that the productivity slowdown really is not a genuine economic problem. Instead, they argue, the slowdown is an illusion, the result of measurement problems that have overstated the extent of the decline.

The key issue in productivity measurement is whether the official output statistics adequately capture changes in quality. Consider the case of a firm producing air-conditioners that, using unchanged quantities of capital and labour, makes the same number of air-conditioners this year as last year. However, this year's air-conditioners are of much higher quality than last year's because they are more reliable and energy efficient. The firm's output this year has a greater real economic value than last year's output, so the true productivity of the firm's capital and labour has risen over the year, even though the firm produces the same number of air-conditioners as before. However, if statisticians measuring the firm's output counted only the number of air-conditioners produced and failed to adjust for quality change, they would miss this improvement in productivity. Similar issues arise in the construction of price indexes; see Box 2.2, "Does CPI Inflation Overstate Increases in the Cost of Living?" (p. 46).

In fact, official output measures do try to account for quality improvements—for example, by counting a more energy-efficient air-conditioner as contributing more to output than a less efficient model. Also, mismeasuring quality of intermediate goods may affect the separate measurement of productivity in the firms that produce them and use them, without affecting the measurement of aggregate productivity. However, measuring quality change is difficult, and to the extent that improvements in final goods are not fully accounted for in the data, productivity growth will be underestimated.

Productivity growth can appear to slow if improvements in the quality of outputs are not taken into account, as the case of the air-conditioner firm illustrates. But a slow-down also may appear to occur if the quality of inputs declines. For example, if the firm employs the same number of workers this year as last year, but the workers are less skilled, then output per worker (productivity) will decline. Some economists have suggested that part of the slowdown is due to a decline in labour skills, measured by real wages or by educational attainment. Again, however, careful measurements of the labour input do account for the quality of inputs, so this problem is unlikely to account for much of the slowdown. Whether the quality of labour input in fact declined is also controversial.

Aggregate productivity also will slow down if there is a shift in production from sectors with rapid productivity growth to those with slow productivity growth. For this reason, a shift of inputs from manufacturing to services may reduce productivity growth. However, this is not the complete explanation for the productivity slow-down. There is widespread evidence of slower productivity growth even within manufacturing industries since 1973, as we have already noted for Canada, the United States, and Japan.

Finally, measurement problems are not new but also existed before 1973. For in-adequate measurement to explain the post-1973 productivity decline, we must show not only that current measurement procedures understate productivity growth but also that recent productivity growth is understated by much more than it was before 1973 and for many countries.[7] Thus, the productivity slowdown is not, for the most part, simply a measurement problem.

Technological Depletion and Slow Commercial Adaptation. Improvements in technology are a fundamental source of productivity growth and economic growth. The production processes used and the products and services available today are vastly different from those of 50 years ago. One explanation for the productivity slowdown is that the major technological advances of the past have now been largely exploited, but commercially significant new technologies have not arrived fast enough to maintain earlier rates of productivity growth. The idea that technological innovation has at least temporarily dried up is part of the "depletion hypothesis."[8]

Why should the pace of technological innovation have slowed down since 1973? One answer is that the high rate of innovation in the decades following World War II was abnormal, reflecting a backlog of technological opportunities that were not ex-ploited earlier because of the Great Depression and World War II. A related argument is that it is the rapid productivity growth from 1945 to 1973 that is the anomaly.[9] Table 6.3 shows that productivity growth also was slower (less than 2% per year) earlier in Canada's history. Perhaps rapid productivity growth in the early postwar period resulted from reconstruction in Europe and Japan, reallocation of resources after the Great Depression and World War II, trade liberalization, and the export of US technology.

7.   See Robert J. Gordon and Martin N. Baily, "Measurement Issues and the Productivity Slowdown in Five Major Industrial Countries," pp. 187–206 in *Technology and Productivity: The Challenge for Economic Policy*, Paris: OECD, 1991.
8.   William D. Nordhaus, "Economic Policy in the Face of Declining Productivity Growth," *European Economic Review*, May/June 1982, pp. 131–147.
9.   Moses Abramowitz, "The Postwar Productivity Spurt and Slowdown," pp. 19–33 in *Technology and Productivity: The Challenge for Economic Policy*, Paris: OECD, 1991.

According to this view, in recent years we have simply returned to a more normal rate of innovation. Some economists also point out that nothing requires economically valuable inventions to arrive at a steady rate. Perhaps we have simply been unlucky in that recent scientific and engineering breakthroughs in computerization and genetic engineering, for example, have not yet produced all the expected economic payoffs.

Some indicators of technological change—such as patents and R&D spending—do not seem to have declined in ways that would explain the productivity slowdown.[10] Thus, a variation of the technological depletion hypothesis holds that there is no shortage of breakthroughs in basic science. Instead, the problem is that firms have been slow or unable to adapt the most recent breakthroughs to commercial uses. For example, some studies have found that Japanese firms are better than North American firms at bringing new scientific results into the marketplace—even when the original scientific breakthroughs occurred in other countries.[11] Recall, however, that productivity growth slowed in Japan, too, after 1973.

The Oil Price Explanation. A popular explanation for the productivity slowdown is the large increase in energy prices that followed the OPEC oil embargo in 1973. (Figure 3.13 showed the relative price of oil in Canada.) The idea is that as companies responded to high energy prices by using less energy, the amount of output they could produce with the same amount of capital and labour declined, reducing productivity. What makes this explanation plausible is not only that the timing is right—the decline in productivity growth appears to have begun in earnest in about 1973[12]—but also that the oil price story explains why all major industrial countries experienced a slowdown.

Pinning the blame for the productivity slowdown on oil price increases is not easy, though. For many industries energy costs are a relatively small part of total costs. Why, then, should energy price increases have had such dramatic effects? One answer is that the rise in oil prices may have made many older, more energy-intensive machines and factories unprofitable to operate, thus effectively reducing the capital stock. Such a decline in the "true" capital stock below the measured capital stock would show up in the data as a drop in productivity. If this explanation were correct, however, the prices of capital goods should have dropped sharply when oil prices rose, reflecting their diminished economic value. Generally though, the predicted decline in the prices of used capital goods did not happen.

Several detailed studies of multiple industries and countries support the oil price explanation.[13] Moreover, low energy prices during the 1962–1973 period might then account for rapid productivity growth during that period. Despite these possibilities, however, proponents of the oil price explanation face the problem of explaining why productivity growth did not resurge when oil prices fell in real terms in the 1980s.

---

10. See Zvi Griliches, "Productivity Puzzles and R&D: Another Nonexplanation," *Journal of Economic Perspectives*, Fall 1988, pp. 9–21.

11. The argument that the US problem is slow commercial adaptation of new scientific findings is made by an influential MIT study; *see MIT Commission on Industrial Productivity, Made in America: Regaining the Productive Edge*, Cambridge, Mass.: MIT Press, 1989.

12. For an argument that the timing is not exactly right, see Michael Denny, "The Prospects for Productivity," Chapter 1 in John Sargent, ed., *Economic Growth: Prospects and Determinants, Royal Commission on the Economic Union and Development Prospects for Canada*, volume 22, Toronto: University of Toronto Press, 1986.

13. See Dale Jorgenson, "Productivity and Postwar U.S. Economic Growth," *Journal of Economic Perspectives*, Fall 1988, pp. 23–41, and John F. Helliwell, Peter H. Sturm, and Gérard Salou, "International Comparison of the Sources of Productivity Slowdown 1973–1982," *European Economic Review*, June/July 1985, pp. 157–191.

The Beginning of a New Industrial Revolution? In an article titled simply "1974," Jeremy Greenwood of the University of Rochester and Mehmet Yorukoglu of the University of Chicago[14] argue that the slowdown in productivity after 1973 may have resulted from the onset of the information technology (IT) revolution. The development and commercial implementation of new information technologies required a substantial period of learning by both the developers of the new technology and the skilled workers who would work with the technology. During the learning process, productivity was temporarily depressed as developers and workers groped toward developing more powerful technologies and operating those technologies more efficiently. To support their view that productivity was depressed following the introduction of a new range of technologies, Greenwood and Yorukoglu present data showing that productivity in Great Britain fell in the late 18th century during the early part of the Industrial Revolution in that country. In the United States, productivity fell in the 1830s as the young country was beginning its industrialization.

This view of the post-1973 productivity slowdown offers an optimistic prospect for the future. In the previous industrial revolutions examined by Greenwood and Yorukoglu, the revolutionary ideas eventually paid off in terms of very large increases in productivity after a few decades of learning. If the productivity slowdown of the 1970s did, in fact, result from the IT revolution, then we should see increases in productivity growth in the not-too-distant future. In fact, proponents of this view suggest that some improved productivity growth in the 1990s (relative to the 1980s) reflects the IT revolution.

Conclusion. The problem involved in explaining the post-1973 slowdown in productivity growth may not be a lack of reasonable explanations but too many. We should not dismiss the possibility that there was no single cause of the slowdown but that many factors contributed to it. Unfortunately, if there are multiple explanations for the slowdown, no single policy action by itself is likely to rev up the productivity engine. Instead, policies to improve productivity growth will have to address many problems at the same time.

6.2 Growth Dynamics: The Neoclassical Growth Model

Although growth accounting provides useful information about the sources of economic growth, it does not completely explain a country's growth performance. Because growth accounting takes the economy's rates of input growth as given, it cannot explain why capital and labour grow at the rates that they do. The growth of the capital stock, in particular, is the result of the myriad saving and investment decisions of households and firms. By taking the growth of the capital stock as given, the growth accounting method leaves out an important part of the story.

In this section, we take a closer look at the dynamics of economic growth, or how the growth process evolves over time. In doing so, we drop the assumption made in Chapter 3 that the capital stock is fixed and study the factors that cause the economy's stock of capital to grow. Our analysis is based on a famous model of economic growth developed in the late 1950s by Nobel laureate Robert Solow of

---

14. Jeremy Greenwood and Mehmet Yorukoglu, "1974," *Carnegie-Rochester Conference Series on Public Policy*, June 1997, pp. 49-95.

MIT, and Trevor Swan of the Australian National University, called the **neoclassical growth model**.[15] This model has become the basic framework for most subsequent research on growth. Besides clarifying how capital accumulation and economic growth are interrelated, the Solow–Swan model is useful for examining three basic questions about growth:

1. What is the relationship between a nation's long-run standard of living and such fundamental factors as its saving rate, its population growth rate, and its rate of technical progress?

2. How does a nation's rate of economic growth evolve over time? Will economic growth stabilize, accelerate, or stop?

3. Do economic forces exist that will ultimately allow poorer countries to catch up with the richest countries in terms of living standards?

SETUP OF THE MODEL

The growth model examines an economy as it evolves over time. In order to analyze the effects of labour force growth as well as changes in capital, we assume that the population is growing and that at any particular time a fixed share of the population is of working age. For any year t,

$$N_t = \text{the number of workers available.}$$

We assume that the population and workforce both grow at fixed rate n. So, if $n = 0.05$, the number of workers in any year is 5% greater than in the previous year.

At the beginning of each year, t, the economy has available a capital stock K_t. (We demonstrate shortly how this capital stock is determined.) During each year t capital, K_t, and labour, N_t, are used to produce the economy's total output, Y_t. Part of the output produced each year is invested in new capital or in replacing worn-out capital. We further assume that the economy is closed and that there are no government purchases,[16] so the uninvested part of output is consumed by the population. If

$$Y_t = \text{output produced in year } t,$$
$$I_t = \text{gross (total) investment in year } t, \text{ and}$$
$$C_t = \text{consumption in year } t,$$

the relationship among consumption, output, and investment in each year is

$$C_t = Y_t - I_t. \tag{6.3}$$

Equation (6.3) states that the uninvested part of the economy's output is consumed.

Because the population and the labour force are growing in this economy, focusing on output, consumption, and the capital stock per worker is convenient. Hence we use the following notation:

$$y_t = \frac{Y_t}{N_t} = \text{output per worker in year } t;$$

$$c_t = \frac{C_t}{N_t} = \text{consumption per worker in year } t;$$

15. For simplicity, we shall often refer to the neoclassical growth model simply as the growth model. The original articles are by Robert M. Solow, "A Contribution to the Theory of Economic Growth," *Quarterly Journal of Economics*, February 1956, pp. 65–94, and Trevor W. Swan, "Economic Growth and Capital Accumulation," *Economic Record*, November 1956, pp. 334–361.
16. Analytical Problem 3 at the end of this chapter adds government purchases to the model.

$$k_t = \frac{K_t}{N_t} = \text{capital stock per worker in year } t.$$

The capital stock per worker, k_t, is also called the **capital–labour ratio**. An important goal of the model is to understand how output per worker, consumption per worker, and the capital–labour ratio change over time.[17]

The per-Worker Production Function

In general, the amount of output that can be produced by specific quantities of inputs is determined by the production function. Until now, we have written the production function as a relationship between total output Y and the total quantities of capital and labour inputs K and N. However, we can also write the production function in per worker terms as

$$y_t = f(k_t). \tag{6.4}$$

Equation (6.4) indicates that, in each year t, output per worker y_t depends on the amount of available capital per worker k_t.[18] Here, we use a small f instead of a capital F for the production function to emphasize that the measurement of output and capital is in per-worker terms. For the time being, we focus on the role of the capital stock in the growth process by assuming no productivity growth and, thus, leave the productivity term out of the production function, Eq. (6.4).[19] We bring productivity growth back into the model later.

The per-worker production function is graphed in Figure 6.1. The capital–labour ratio (the amount of capital per worker) k_t is measured on the horizontal axis, and output per worker y_t is measured on the vertical axis. The production function slopes upward from left to right because an increase in the amount of capital per worker allows each worker to produce more output. As with the standard production function, the bowed shape of the per-worker production function reflects the diminishing marginal productivity of capital. Thus, when the capital–labour ratio is already high, an increase in the capital–labour ratio has a relatively small effect on output per worker.

Steady States

One of the most striking conclusions obtained from the neoclassical growth model is that in the absence of productivity growth the economy reaches a steady state in the long run. A **steady state** is a situation in which the economy's output per worker, consumption per worker, and capital stock per worker are constant—that is, in the steady state, y_t, c_t, and k_t do not change over time.[20] To explain how the growth model works, we first examine the characteristics of a steady state and then discuss how the economy might attain it.

---

17. For purposes of analysis, discussing output and consumption per worker is more convenient than discussing output and consumption per member of the population as a whole. Under the assumption that the workforce is a fixed fraction of the population, anything we say about the growth rate of output or consumption per worker also will be true of the growth rate of output or consumption per member of the population.

18. To write the production function in the form of Eq. (6.4) requires the assumption of constant returns to scale, which means that an equal percentage increase in both capital and labour inputs results in the same percentage increase in total output. So, for example, with constant returns to scale, a 10% increase in both capital and labour raises output by 10%. In terms of the growth accounting equation, Eq. (6.2), constant returns to scale requires that $a_K + a_N = 1$. See Analytical Problem 6 at the end of this chapter.

19. More precisely, we set the total factor productivity term A at 1.

20. Note that if output, consumption, and capital per worker are constant, then total output, consumption, and capital all are growing at rate n, the rate of growth of the workforce.

FIGURE 6.1

THE PER-WORKER
PRODUCTION FUNCTION

The per-worker production
function, $y_t = f(k_t)$, relates the
amount of output produced
per worker, y_t, to the capital–
labour ratio, k_t. For example,
when the capital–labour ratio
is k_1, output per worker is y_1.
The per-worker production
function slopes upward from
left to right because an
increase in the capital–labour
ratio raises the amount of
output produced per worker.
The bowed shape of the
production function reflects
the diminishing marginal
productivity of capital.

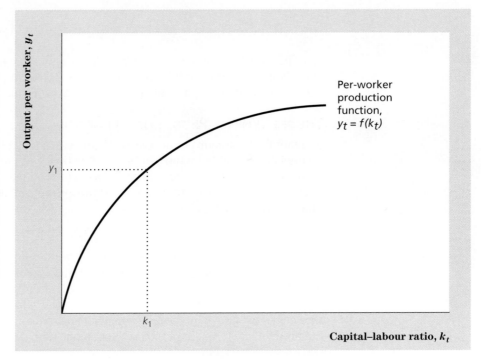

Let us begin by looking at investment in a steady state. In general, gross (total) investment in year t, I_t, is devoted to two purposes: (1) replacing worn-out or depreciated capital, and (2) expanding the size of the capital stock. If d is the capital depreciation rate, or the fraction of capital that wears out each year, the total amount of depreciation in year t is dK_t. The amount by which the capital stock is increased is net investment. What is net investment in a steady state? Because capital per worker, K_t/N_t, is constant in a steady state, the total capital stock grows at the same rate as the labour force, that is, at rate n. Net investment is therefore nK_t in a steady state.[21] To obtain steady-state investment, we add net investment nK_t and depreciation dK_t:

$$I_t = (n + d)K_t \text{ (in a steady state).} \tag{6.5}$$

To obtain steady-state consumption (output less investment), we substitute Eq. (6.5) into Eq. (6.3):

$$C_t = Y_t - (n + d)K_t \text{ (in a steady state).} \tag{6.6}$$

Equation (6.6) measures consumption, output, and capital as economywide totals, rather than in per-worker terms. To put them in per-worker terms, we divide both sides of Eq. (6.6) by the number of workers N_t, recalling that $c_t = C_t/N_t$, $y_t = Y_t/N_t$, and $k_t = K_t/N_t$. Then we use the per-worker production function, Eq. (6.4), to replace y_t with $f(k_t)$ and obtain

$$c = f(k) - (n + d)k \text{ (in a steady state).} \tag{6.7}$$

---

21. Algebraically, net investment in year t is $K_{t+1} - K_t$. If total capital grows at rate n, then $K_{t+1} = (1 + n)K_t$. Substituting for K_{t+1} in the definition of net investment, we find that net investment $= (1 + n)K_t - K_t = nK_t$ in a steady state.

Equation (6.7) shows the relationship between consumption per worker c and the capital–labour ratio k in the steady state. Because consumption per worker and the capital–labour ratio are constant in the steady state, we dropped the time subscripts, t.

Equation (6.7) shows that an increase in the steady-state capital–labour ratio k has two opposing effects on steady-state consumption per worker c. First, an increase in the steady-state capital–labour ratio raises the amount of output each worker can produce, $f(k)$. Second, an increase in the steady-state capital–labour ratio also increases the amount of output per worker that must be devoted to investment, $(n + d)k$. More goods devoted to investment leaves fewer goods to consume.

Figure 6.2, on the next page, shows the trade-off between these two effects. In Figure 6.2(a) different possible values of the steady-state capital–labour ratio k are measured on the horizontal axis. The curve is the per-worker production function, $y = f(k)$, as in Figure 6.1. The straight line shows steady-state investment per worker, $(n + d)k$. Equation (6.7) indicates that steady-state consumption per worker c equals the height of the curve $f(k)$ minus the height of the straight line $(n + d)k$. Thus, consumption per worker is the height of the shaded area.

The relationship between consumption per worker and the capital–labour ratio in the steady state is shown more explicitly in Figure 6.2(b). For each value of the steady-state capital–labour ratio k, steady-state consumption c is the difference between the production function and investment in Figure 6.2(a). Note that starting from low and medium values of k (values less than k_1 in Figure 6.2(b)), increases in the steady-state capital–labour ratio lead to greater steady-state consumption per worker. However, for high values of k (values greater than k_1), increases in the steady-state capital–labour ratio may actually result in lower steady-state consumption per worker because so much investment is needed to maintain the high level of capital per worker. In the extreme case, where $k = k_{max}$ in Figure 6.2, all output has to be devoted to replacing and expanding the capital stock, with nothing left to consume!

Policymakers often try to improve long-run living standards with policies aimed at stimulating saving and investment—and thus increasing the rate of capital formation. Figure 6.2 shows the limits to this strategy. A country with a low amount of capital per worker may hope to improve long-run (steady-state) living standards substantially by increasing rates of saving and investment. However, a country that already has a high level of capital per worker may find that further increases in saving and investment fail to raise steady-state consumption much. The fundamental reason for this outcome is the diminishing marginal productivity of capital—that is, the larger the capital stock already is, the smaller is the benefit from expanding the capital stock still further. Indeed, Figure 6.2 shows that theoretically, capital per worker can be so high that further increases will actually lower steady-state consumption per worker. The level of the capital stock that maximizes consumption per worker in the steady state, shown as k_1 in Figure 6.2, is known as the **Golden Rule** level of the capital stock, so-called because it maximizes the economic welfare of future generations.[22]

In any economy in the world today, could a higher capital stock lead to less consumption in the long run? A recent study of seven advanced industrial countries concluded that the answer is "no." Even for high-saving Japan, further increases in

---

22. Readers familiar with calculus might try to use Eq. (6.7) to show that at the Golden Rule level of the capital stock the marginal product of capital equals $n + d$.

FIGURE 6.2

THE RELATIONSHIP OF
CONSUMPTION PER
WORKER TO THE
CAPITAL–LABOUR RATIO IN
THE STEADY STATE

(a) For each value of the capital–labour ratio, k, steady-state output per worker, y, is given by the per-worker production function, $f(k)$. Steady-state investment per worker, $(n + d)k$, is a straight line with slope $n + d$. Steady-state consumption per worker, c, is the difference between output per worker and investment per worker (the shaded area). For example, if the capital–labour ratio is k_1, steady-state consumption per worker is c_1.
(b) For each value of the steady-state capital–labour ratio, k, steady-state consumption per worker, c, is derived in (a) as the difference between output per worker and investment per worker. Thus, the shaded area in (b) corresponds to the shaded area in (a). Note that starting from a low value of the capital–labour ratio, an increase in the capital–labour ratio raises steady-state consumption per worker. However, starting from a capital–labour ratio greater than k_1, an increase in the capital–labour ratio actually lowers consumption per worker. When the capital–labour ratio equals k_{max}, all output is devoted to investment, and steady-state consumption per worker is zero.

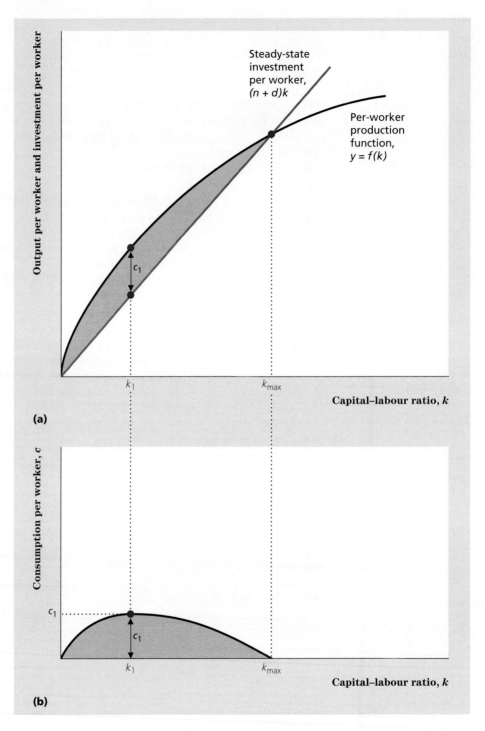

capital per worker would lead to higher steady-state consumption per worker.[23] Thus, in our analysis, we will always assume that an increase in the steady-state capital–labour ratio raises steady-state consumption per worker.

23. See Andrew B. Abel, N. Gregory Mankiw, Lawrence H. Summers, and Richard J. Zeckhauser, "Assessing Dynamic Efficiency: Theory and Evidence," *Review of Economic Studies*, January 1989, pp. 1–20.

REACHING THE STEADY STATE

Our discussion of steady states leaves two loose ends. First, we need to say something about why an economy like the one we describe here eventually will reach a steady state, as we claimed earlier. Second, we have not yet shown which steady state the economy will reach; that is, we would like to know the steady-state level of consumption per worker and the steady-state capital–labour ratio that the economy will eventually attain.

To tie up these loose ends, we need one more piece of information: the rate at which people save. To keep things as simple as possible, suppose that saving in this economy is proportional to current income:

$$S_t = sY_t, \tag{6.8}$$

where S_t is national saving[24] in year t, and s is the saving rate, which we assume to be constant. Because a \$1 increase in current income raises saving, but by less than \$1 (see Chapter 4), we take s to be a number between 0 and 1. Equation (6.8) ignores some other determinants of saving discussed in earlier chapters, such as the real interest rate. However, including these other factors would not change our basic conclusions, so for simplicity we omit them.

In every year, national saving S_t equals investment I_t. Therefore,

$$sY_t = (n + d)K_t \text{ (in a steady state)}, \tag{6.9}$$

where the left-hand side of Eq. (6.9) is saving (see Eq. 6.8) and the right-hand side of Eq. (6.9) is steady-state investment (see Eq. 6.5). As in Chapter 4, saving equals investment (which implies a real interest rate), but we now study the dynamic evolution of the economy as the capital stock changes.

Equation (6.9) shows the relation between total output Y_t and the total capital stock K_t that holds in the steady state. To determine steady-state capital per worker, we divide both sides of Eq. (6.9) by N_t. We then use the production function, Eq. (6.4), to replace y_t with $f(k_t)$:

$$sf(k) = (n + d)k \text{ (in the steady state)}. \tag{6.10}$$

Equation (6.10) indicates that saving per worker $sf(k)$ equals steady-state investment per worker $(n + d)k$. Because the capital–labour ratio k is constant in the steady state, we again drop the subscripts t from the equation.

With Eq. (6.10), we can now determine the steady-state capital–labour ratio that the economy will attain, as shown in Figure 6.3. The capital–labour ratio is measured along the horizontal axis. Saving per worker and investment per worker are measured on the vertical axis.

The bowed curve shows how the amount of saving per worker $sf(k)$ is related to the capital–labour ratio. This curve slopes upward because an increase in the capital–labour ratio implies higher output per worker and, thus, more saving per worker. The saving-per-worker curve has the same general shape as the per-worker production function because saving per worker equals the per-worker production function $f(k)$ multiplied by the fixed saving rate s.

The line in Figure 6.3 represents steady-state investment per worker $(n + d)k$. The steady-state investment line slopes upward because as the capital–labour ratio rises, more investment per worker is required to replace depreciating capital and equip new workers with the same high level of capital.

---

24. With no government in this model, national saving and private saving are the same.

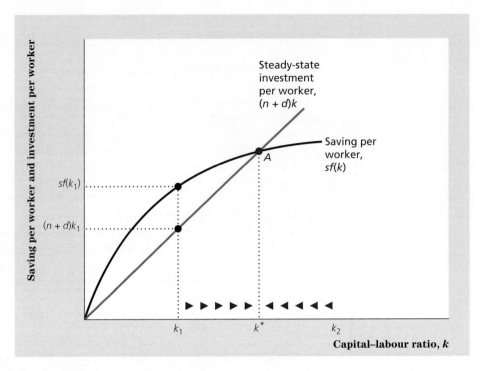

According to Eq. (6.10), the steady-state capital–labour ratio must ensure that saving per worker and steady-state investment per worker are equal. The one level of the capital–labour ratio for which this condition is satisfied is shown in Figure 6.3 as k^*, the value of k at which the saving curve and the steady-state investment line cross. For any other value of k, saving and investment will not be equal in the steady state. Thus, k^* is the only possible steady-state capital–labour ratio for this economy.[25]

With the unique steady-state capital–labour ratio k^*, we can also find steady-state output and consumption per worker. From the per-worker production function, Eq. (6.4), if the steady-state capital–labour ratio is k^*, steady-state output per worker y^* is

$$y^* = f(k^*).$$

From Eq. (6.7), steady-state consumption per worker, c^*, equals steady-state output per worker, $f(k^*)$, minus steady-state investment per worker, $(n + d)k^*$:

$$c^* = f(k^*) - (n + d)k^*.$$

Recall that in the empirically realistic case, a higher value of the steady-state capital–labour ratio k^* implies greater steady-state consumption per worker c^*.

Using the condition that in a steady state, national saving equals steady-state investment, we found the steady-state capital–labour ratio k^*. When capital per worker is k^*, the amount that people choose to save will just equal the amount of investment necessary to keep capital per worker at k^*. Thus, when the economy's capital–labour ratio reaches k^*, it will remain there forever.

---

25. Actually, there is also a steady state at the point $k = 0$, at which the capital stock, output, and consumption are zero forever. However, as long as the economy starts out with a positive amount of capital, it will never reach the zero-capital steady state.

But is there any reason to believe that the capital–labour ratio will ever reach k^* if it starts at some other value? Yes, there is. Suppose that the capital–labour ratio happens to be less than k^*; for example, it equals k_1 in Figure 6.3. When capital per worker is k_1, the amount of saving per worker, $sf(k_1)$, is greater than the amount of investment needed to keep the capital–labour ratio constant, $(n + d)k_1$. When this extra saving is converted into capital, the capital–labour ratio will rise. As indicated by the arrows on the horizontal axis, the capital–labour ratio will increase from k_1 toward k^*.

If capital per worker is initially greater than k^*—for example, if k equals k_2 in Figure 6.3—the explanation of why the economy converges to a steady state is similar. If the capital–labour ratio exceeds k^*, the amount of saving that is done will be less than the amount of investment that is necessary to keep the capital–labour ratio constant. (In Figure 6.3 when k equals k_2, the saving curve lies below the steady-state investment line.) Thus, the capital–labour ratio over time will fall from k_2 toward k^*, as indicated by the arrows. Output per worker will also fall until it reaches its steady-state value.

To summarize, if we assume no productivity growth, the economy must eventually reach a steady state. In this steady state, the capital–labour ratio, output per worker, and consumption per worker remain constant over time. (However, total capital, output, and consumption grow at rate n, the rate of growth of the labour force.) This conclusion might seem gloomy, since it implies that living standards must eventually stop improving. However, we shall see that this conclusion can be avoided if, in fact, productivity continually increases.

THE FUNDAMENTAL DETERMINANTS OF LONG-RUN LIVING STANDARDS

What determines how well off the average person in an economy will be in the long run? If we measure long-run well being by the steady-state level of consumption per worker, we can use the growth model to answer this question. Here, we discuss three factors that affect long-run living standards: the saving rate, population growth, and productivity growth (see Summary table 8).

THE SAVING RATE

According to the neoclassical growth model, a higher saving rate implies higher living standards in the long run, as illustrated in Figure 6.4. Suppose that the economy's initial saving rate is s_1 so that saving per worker is $s_1 f(k)$. The saving curve when the saving rate is s_1 is labelled "Initial saving per worker." The initial steady-state capital–labour ratio k_1^* is the capital–labour ratio at which the initial saving curve and the investment line cross (point A).

Suppose now that, say, because the government introduces policies that strengthen the incentives for saving, the country's saving rate rises from s_1 to s_2. The increased saving rate raises saving at every level of the capital–labour ratio. Graphically, the saving curve shifts upward from $s_1 f(k)$ to $s_2 f(k)$. The new steady-state capital–labour ratio k_2^* corresponds to the intersection of the new saving curve and the investment line (point B). Because k_2^* is larger than k_1^*, the higher saving rate has increased the steady-state capital–labour ratio. Gradually, this economy will move to the higher steady-state capital–labour ratio, as indicated by the arrows on the horizontal axis. In the new steady state, output per worker and consumption per worker will be higher than in the original steady state.

SUMMARY 8 THE FUNDAMENTAL DETERMINANTS OF LONG-RUN LIVING STANDARDS

AN INCREASE IN	CAUSES LONG-RUN OUTPUT, CONSUMPTION, AND CAPITAL PER WORKER TO	REASON
The saving rate, s	Rise	Higher saving allows for more investment and a larger capital stock.
The rate of population growth, n	Fall	With higher population growth more output must be used to equip new workers with capital, leaving less output available to increase consumption or capital per worker.
Productivity	Rise	Higher productivity directly increases output; by raising incomes, it also raises saving and the capital stock.

FIGURE 6.4

THE EFFECT OF AN INCREASED SAVING RATE ON THE STEADY-STATE CAPITAL–LABOUR RATIO

An increase in the saving rate from s_1 to s_2 raises the saving curve from $s_1 f(k)$ to $s_2 f(k)$. The point where saving per worker equals steady-state investment per worker moves from point A to point B, and the corresponding capital–labour ratio rises from k_1^* to k_2^*. Thus, a higher saving rate raises the steady-state capital–labour ratio.

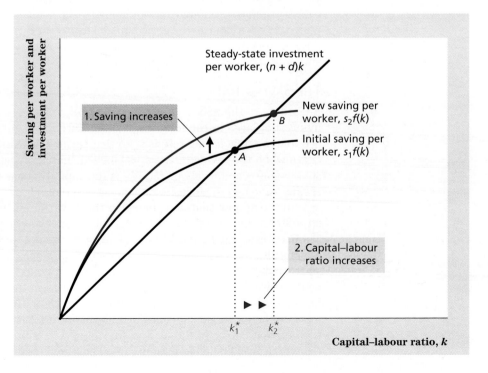

An increased saving rate leads to higher output, consumption, and capital per worker in the long run, so it seems that a policy goal should be to make the country's saving rate as high as possible. However, this conclusion is not necessarily correct: Although a higher saving rate raises consumption per worker in the long run, an increase in the saving rate initially causes consumption to fall. This decline occurs because at the initial level of output, increases in saving and investment leave less available for current consumption. Thus, higher future consumption has a cost in terms of lower present consumption. Society's choice of a saving rate should take into account this trade-off between current and future consumption. Beyond a certain point, the cost of reduced consumption today will outweigh the long-run benefits of a higher saving rate.

POPULATION GROWTH

In many developing countries, a high rate of population growth is considered to be a major problem, and reducing it is a primary policy goal. What is the relationship between population growth and a country's level of development, as measured by output, consumption, and capital per worker?

The growth model's answer to this question is shown in Figure 6.5. An initial steady-state capital–labour ratio k_1^* corresponds to the intersection of the steady-state investment line and the saving curve at point A. Now, suppose that the rate of population growth, which is the same as the rate of labour force growth, rises from an initial level of n_1 to n_2. What happens?

An increase in the population growth rate means that workers are entering the labour force more rapidly than before. These new workers must be equipped with capital. Thus, to maintain the same steady-state capital–labour ratio, the amount of investment per current member of the workforce must rise. Algebraically, the rise in n increases steady-state investment per worker from $(n_1 + d)k$ to $(n_2 + d)k$.

FIGURE 6.5

THE EFFECT OF A HIGHER POPULATION GROWTH RATE ON THE STEADY-STATE CAPITAL–LABOUR RATIO

An increase in the population growth rate from n_1 to n_2 increases steady-state investment per worker from $(n_1 + d)k$ to $(n_2 + d)k$. The steady-state investment line pivots up and to the left as its slope rises from $n_1 + d$ to $n_2 + d$. The point where saving per worker equals steady-state investment per worker shifts from point A to point B, and the corresponding capital–labour ratio falls from k_1^* to k_2^*. A higher population growth rate therefore causes the steady-state capital–labour ratio to fall.

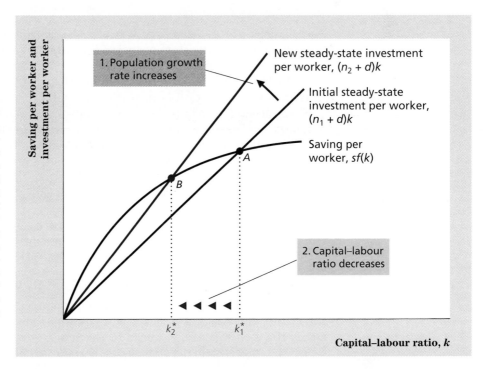

This increase in the population growth rate causes the steady-state investment line to pivot up and to the left, as its slope rises from $(n_1 + d)$ to $(n_2 + d)$.

After the pivot of the steady-state investment line, the new steady state is at point B. The new steady-state capital–labour ratio is k_2^*, which is lower than the original capital–labour ratio k_1^*. Because the new steady-state capital–labour ratio is lower, the new steady-state output per worker and consumption per worker will be lower as well.

Thus, the growth model implies that increased population growth will lower living standards. The basic problem is that when the workforce is growing rapidly, a large part of current output must be devoted just to providing capital for the new workers to use. This result suggests that policies to control population growth will indeed improve living standards.

There are some counterarguments to the conclusion that policy should aim to reduce population growth. First, although a reduction in the rate of population growth n raises consumption *per worker*, it also reduces the growth rate of *total* output and consumption, which grow at rate n in the steady state. Having fewer people means more for each person but also less total productive capacity. For some purposes (military, political), a country may care about its total output as well as output per person. Thus, for example, some countries of Western Europe are concerned about projections that their populations will actually shrink in the next century, possibly reducing their ability to influence world events.

Second, an assumption in the growth model is that the proportion of the total population that is of working age is fixed. When the population growth rate changes dramatically, this assumption may not hold. For example, declining birth rates in Canada imply that the ratio of working-age people to retirees will become unusually low later in the 21st century, a development that may cause problems in funding pension plans and health care.

PRODUCTIVITY GROWTH

A significant aspect of the basic growth model is that ultimately, the economy reaches a steady state in which output per capita is constant. But in the introduction to this chapter, we described how Japanese output per person has grown by a factor of 28 since 1870! How can the model account for that sustained growth? The key is a factor that we have not yet made part of the analysis: productivity growth.

The effects of a productivity improvement—the result of, say, a new technology—are shown in Figures 6.6 and 6.7. An improvement in productivity corresponds to an upward shift in the per-worker production function because at any prevailing capital–labour ratio, each worker can produce more output. Figure 6.6 shows a shift from the original production function $y = f_1(k)$ to a "new, improved" production function $y = f_2(k)$. The productivity improvement corresponds to a beneficial supply shock, as explained in Chapter 3.

Figure 6.7 shows the effects of this productivity improvement in the growth model. As before, the initial steady state is determined by the intersection of the saving curve and the steady-state investment line at point A; the corresponding steady-state capital–labour ratio is k_1^*. The productivity improvement raises output per worker for any level of the capital–labour ratio. As saving per worker is a constant fraction s of output per worker, saving per worker also rises at any capital–labour ratio. Graphically, the saving curve shifts upward from $sf_1(k)$ to $sf_2(k)$, now intersecting the steady-state investment line at point B. The new steady-state capital–labour ratio is k_2^*, which is higher than the original steady-state capital–labour ratio k_1^*.

FIGURE 6.6

AN IMPROVEMENT IN
PRODUCTIVITY

An improvement in productivity shifts the per-worker production function upward from the initial production function $y = f_1(k)$ to the new production function $y = f_2(k)$. After the productivity improvement, more output per worker y can be produced at any capital–labour ratio k.

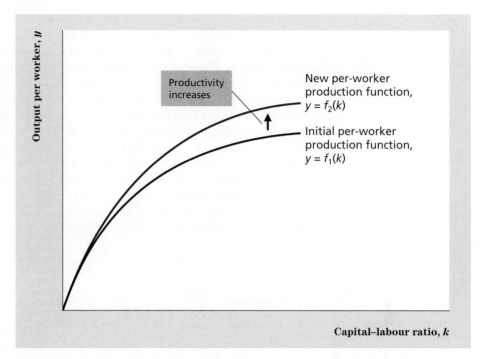

FIGURE 6.7

THE EFFECT OF A
PRODUCTIVITY
IMPROVEMENT ON THE
STEADY-STATE
CAPITAL–LABOUR RATIO

A productivity improvement shifts the production function upward from $f_1(k)$ to $f_2(k)$, raising output per worker for any capital–labour ratio. Because saving is proportional to output, saving per worker also rises, from $sf_1(k)$ to $sf_2(k)$. The point where saving per worker equals steady-state investment per worker shifts from point A to point B, and the corresponding steady-state capital–labour ratio rises from k_1^* to k_2^*. Thus, a productivity improvement raises the steady-state capital–labour ratio.

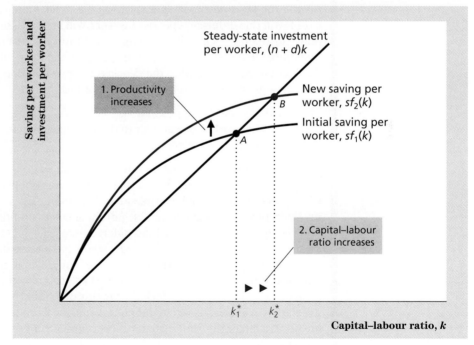

Overall, a productivity improvement raises steady-state output and consumption per worker in two ways. First, it directly increases the amount that can be produced at any capital–labour ratio. Second, as Figure 6.7 shows, by raising the supply of saving, a productivity improvement also causes the long-run capital–labour ratio to rise. Thus, a productivity improvement has a doubly beneficial impact on the standard of living.

Like a one-time increase in the saving rate or decrease in the population growth rate, a one-time productivity improvement shifts the economy only from one steady state to a higher one. When the economy reaches the new steady state, consumption per worker once again becomes constant. Is there some way to keep consumption per worker growing indefinitely?

In reality, there are limits to how high the saving rate can rise (it certainly cannot exceed 100%!) or how low the population growth rate can fall. Thus, higher saving rates or slower population growth are not likely sources of continually higher living standards. However, since the Industrial Revolution, if not before, people have shown remarkable ingenuity in becoming more and more productive. In the very long run, according to the neoclassical growth model, only these continuing increases in productivity hold the promise of perpetually better living standards. Thus, we conclude that in the long run, *the rate of productivity improvement is the dominant factor determining how quickly living standards rise.*

APPLICATION

DO ECONOMIES CONVERGE?

A wide gulf separates living standards in the richest and the poorest nations of the world. Will this difference persist forever? Will, indeed, the "rich get richer and the poor get poorer"? Or will national living standards ultimately converge? These questions obviously are of immense importance for humanity's future. In this Application, we discuss what the neoclassical growth model says about the prospects for convergence and then turn to the empirical evidence.[26]

There are at least three possible scenarios for the evolution of living standards throughout the world: We will refer to them as unconditional convergence, conditional convergence, and no convergence.

By **unconditional convergence** we mean that the poor countries eventually will catch up to the rich countries so that in the long run, living standards around the world become more or less the same. The neoclassical growth model predicts unconditional convergence under certain special conditions. For example, let us suppose that the world's economies differed principally in terms of their capital–labour ratios, with rich countries having high capital–labour ratios and high levels of output per worker, and poor countries having low capital–labour ratios and low levels of output per worker. Suppose, however, that on other dimensions—specifically in terms of saving rates, population growth rates, and the production functions to which they had access—rich and poor countries were the same. If each of a group of countries has the same saving rate, population growth rate, and production function, the Solow–Swan model predicts that—despite any differences in initial capital–labour ratios—these countries all will eventually reach the same steady state. In other words, according to the model, if countries have the same fundamental characteristics, capital–labour ratios and living standards will unconditionally converge, even though some countries may start from way behind.

---

26. For an excellent discussion of international disparities in growth rates see James A. Brander, "Comparative Economic Growth: Evidence and Interpretation," *Canadian Journal of Economics*, November 1992, pp. 792–818.

But if countries differ in such characteristics as their saving rates, population growth rates, and access to technology, according to the model they will converge to different steady states, with different capital–labour ratios and different living standards in the long run. If countries differ in fundamental characteristics, the growth model predicts **conditional convergence**, by which we mean that living standards will converge only within groups of countries having similar characteristics. For example, if there is conditional convergence, a poor country with a low saving rate may catch up someday to a richer country that also has a low saving rate, but it will never catch up to a rich country that has a high saving rate.

For a variety of reasons (such as different cultures, political systems, and economic policies), countries do differ in such characteristics as saving rates, so conditional convergence seems to be the most likely outcome. However, our discussion, so far, assumes that these economies are all closed economies. According to the model, if economies are open and international borrowing and lending flow freely, some additional economic forces support unconditional convergence. In particular, as poor countries have less capital per worker and, thus, higher marginal products of capital than do rich countries, savers in all countries will be able to earn the highest return by investing in poor countries. Thus, foreign investment should cause capital stocks in poor countries to grow rapidly, even if domestic saving rates are low. Eventually, borrowing abroad should allow initially poor countries' capital–labour ratios and output per worker to be the same as in initially rich countries.[27]

The third possibility is *no convergence*, by which we mean that poor countries do not catch up over time. Living standards may even diverge (the poor get poorer and the rich get richer). Although reconciling no convergence with the neoclassical growth model is not impossible (for example, permanent differences in productivity growth rates across countries could lead to divergence), this outcome would be inconsistent with the spirit of that model, which tends to favour the general idea of convergence.

What is the evidence? Unfortunately (from the perspective of the world's poor countries), there is little empirical support for unconditional convergence: Most studies have uncovered little tendency for poor countries to catch up with rich ones. For example, in a study of 72 countries over the period from 1950 through 1985, William Baumol[28] of Princeton University and New York University found no overall tendency toward convergence. Using data beginning in 1870, Baumol did find some evidence for convergence among a group of 16 major free-market economies, with the countries in the sample that were relatively poorest in 1870 growing somewhat faster over the period. However, J. Bradford DeLong[29] of the University of California at Berkeley pointed out that the countries Baumol studied were the richest countries as of 1980. In choosing this set of countries, DeLong argued, Baumol created a bias in favour of finding convergence because countries that failed to converge to high levels of output per hour would not be included among the sample of currently rich countries. DeLong showed that if Baumol's sample were expanded to include countries that were relatively rich in 1870 but are not among the richest countries

27. Although output per worker in poor countries converges to that of rich countries, consumption per worker will remain at a lower level in poor countries because part of output must be used to repay foreign investors.
28. "Productivity Growth, Convergence, and Welfare: What the Long-Run Data Show," *American Economic Review*, December 1986, pp. 1072–1085.
29. "Productivity Growth, Convergence and Welfare: Comment," *American Economic Review*, December 1988, pp. 1138–1154.

today—such countries as Argentina, Chile, the former East Germany, Ireland, New Zealand, Portugal, and Spain—Baumol's evidence for convergence disappears.

The evidence for conditional convergence, however, seems much better. For example, an article by N. Gregory Mankiw of Harvard University, David Romer of the University of California at Berkeley, and David Weil[30] of Brown University examined a sample of 98 countries for the period from 1960 through 1985. While finding no evidence for unconditional convergence in their data, Mankiw, Romer, and Weil showed that the failure of poor countries to catch up reflected high rates of population growth and low rates of saving (defined broadly to include resources devoted to education along with those devoted to accumulation of physical capital). After correcting for differences in national saving rates and population growth rates, Mankiw, Romer, and Weil found strong tendencies for countries with similar characteristics to converge. Similar results were obtained by Serge Coulombe of the University of Ottawa and Frank Lee[31] of Industry Canada, who also demonstrated a convergence of living standards among the provinces of Canada. Because the provinces are similar in fundamental economic characteristics, such as saving rates and access to technology, this result also is consistent with conditional convergence.

The findings in support of conditional convergence are encouraging for the growth model, and they provide some empirical confirmation that such factors as the saving rate (including the provision of resources for education) are important for growth. These results also suggest that international capital markets linking rich and poor countries are not as efficient as we might hope, since, evidently, foreign investment in poor countries has been insufficient to overcome the problem of low domestic saving rates. Possibly, political barriers, such as legal limits or high taxes on foreign investment, prevent enough foreign lending from flowing into poor countries. Alternatively, potential lenders in rich nations may not be able to obtain adequate information about investment opportunities in countries that are both physically distant and also have different languages, cultures, and legal systems. Chapter 5 discussed some of the problems associated with sovereign lending.

ENDOGENOUS GROWTH THEORY

The traditional model of economic growth has proved quite useful, but it nevertheless has at least one serious shortcoming as a model of economic growth. According to the neoclassical growth model, productivity growth is the only source of long-run growth of output per capita, so a full explanation of long-run economic growth requires an explanation of productivity growth. The model, however, simply takes the rate of productivity growth as given, rather than trying to explain how it is determined. That is, the neoclassical growth model *assumes*, rather than *explains*, the behaviour of the crucial determinant of the long-run growth rate of output per capita.

In response to this shortcoming of the neoclassical growth model, a new branch of growth theory, **endogenous growth theory**, has been developed to try to explain

---

30. "A Contribution to the Empirics of Economic Growth," *Quarterly Journal of Economics*, May 1992, pp. 407–438.

31. "Convergence Across Canadian Provinces, 1961 to 1991," *Canadian Journal of Economics*, November 1995, pp. 886–898.

productivity growth—and hence the growth rate of output—*endogenously*, or *within the model*.[32] As we will see, an important implication of endogenous growth theory is that a country's long-run growth rate depends on its rate of saving and investment, not only on exogenous productivity growth (as implied by the neoclassical growth model).

Here we present a simple endogenous growth model in which the number of workers remains constant, a condition implying that the growth rate of output per worker is simply equal to the growth rate of output. Our simple endogenous growth model is based on the aggregate production function

$$Y = AK \tag{6.11}$$

where Y is aggregate output and K is the aggregate capital stock. The parameter A in Eq. (6.11) is a positive constant. According to the production function in Eq. (6.11), each additional unit of capital increases output by A units, regardless of how many units of capital are used in production. Because the marginal product of capital, equal to A, does not depend on the size of the capital stock K, the production function in Eq. (6.11) does not imply diminishing marginal productivity of capital. The assumption that the marginal productivity is constant, rather than diminishing, is a key departure from the neoclassical growth model.

Endogenous growth theorists have provided a number of reasons to explain why, for the economy as a whole, the marginal productivity of capital may not be diminishing. One explanation emphasizes the role of **human capital**, the economist's term for the knowledge, skills, and training of individuals. As economies accumulate capital and become richer, they devote more resources to "investing in people," through improved nutrition, schooling, health care, and on-the-job training. This investment in people increases the country's human capital, which, in turn, raises productivity. If the physical capital stock increases while the stock of human capital is remains fixed, there will be diminishing marginal productivity of physical capital, as each unit of physical capital effectively works with a smaller amount of human capital. Endogenous growth theory argues that as an economy's physical capital stock increases, its human capital stock tends to increase in the same proportion. Thus, when the physical capital stock increases, each unit of physical capital effectively works with the same amount of human capital, so the marginal productivity of capital need not decrease.

A second rationalization of a constant marginal productivity of capital is based on the observation that in a growing economy, firms have incentives to undertake research and development (R&D) activities. These activities increase the stock of commercially valuable knowledge, including new products and production techniques. According to this R&D-focused explanation, increases in capital and output tend to generate increases in technical know-how, and the resulting productivity gains offset any tendency for the marginal productivity of capital to decline.

Having examined why a production function like Eq. (6.11) might be a reasonable description of the economy as a whole, once such factors as increased human capital and research and development are taken into account, let us work out the implications of this equation. As in the neoclassical growth model, let us assume that national

---

32. Two important early articles in endogenous growth theory are Paul Romer, "Increasing Returns and Long-Run Growth," *Journal of Political Economy*, October 1986, pp. 1002–1037, and Robert E. Lucas, Jr., "On the Mechanics of Economic Development," *Journal of Monetary Economics*, July 1988, pp. 3–42. A more accessible description of endogenous growth theory is in Paul Romer, "The Origins of Endogenous Growth," *Journal of Economic Perspectives*, Winter 1994, pp. 3–22.

saving, S, is a constant fraction s of aggregate output, AK, so that $S = sAK$. In a closed economy, investment must equal saving. Recall that total investment equals net investment (the net increase in the capital stock) plus depreciation, or $I = \Delta K + dK$. Therefore, setting investment equal to saving, we have

$$\Delta K + dK = sAK. \tag{6.12}$$

Next, we divide both sides of Eq. (6.12) by K and then subtract d from both sides of the resulting equation to obtain the growth rate of the capital stock.

$$\frac{\Delta K}{K} = sA - d. \tag{6.13}$$

Because output is proportional to the capital stock, the growth rate of output equals the growth rate of the capital stock. Therefore Eq. (6.13) implies

$$\frac{\Delta Y}{Y} = sA - d. \tag{6.14}$$

Equation (6.14) shows that in the endogenous growth model, the growth rate of output depends on the saving rate s. As we are assuming that the number of workers remains constant over time, the growth rate of output per worker equals the growth rate of output given in Eq. (6.14) and, thus, depends on the saving rate s. The result that the saving rate affects the long-run growth rate of output stands in sharp contrast to the results of the neoclassical growth model, in which the saving rate does not affect the long-run growth rate. Saving affects long-run growth in the endogenous growth framework because in that framework, higher rates of saving and capital formation stimulate greater investment in human capital and R&D. The resulting increases in productivity help spur long-run growth. In summary, in comparison to the neoclassical growth model, the endogenous growth model places greater emphasis on saving, human capital formation, and R&D as sources of long-run growth.

Although endogenous growth theory remains in a developmental stage, the approach appears promising in at least two dimensions. First, this theory attempts to explain, rather than assumes, the economy's rate of productivity growth. Second, it shows how the long-run growth rate of output may depend on such factors as the country's saving rate, which can be affected by government policies. Many economists working in this area are optimistic that endogenous growth theory will yield further insights into the creative processes underlying productivity growth, while providing lessons that might be applied to help the poorest nations of the world achieve substantially higher standards of living.

ECONOMIC GROWTH AND THE ENVIRONMENT

The growth models studied so far—both the neoclassical growth model and the endogenous growth model—do not allow for the possibility that economic growth may be limited by available stocks of natural resources or by the environment more generally. Brian Copeland, of the University of British Columbia, has recently surveyed the environmental costs of economic growth in Canada.[33] If the environmental costs rise as growth proceeds, then eventually growth should come to an end as these costs come to exceed the benefits of greater consumption.

---

[33]. *Economics and the Environment: The Recent Canadian Experience and Prospects for the Future.* Industry Canada Report, Canada in the 21st Century Series, No. 8.

Macroeconomists are hard at work on growth models that incorporate effects of economic growth on the environment and, in turn, effects of environmental change (such as rising sea levels) on economic choices. For example, William Nordhaus and Joseph Boyer, of Yale University, have developed a model which can be used to assess the impact on growth of following the Kyoto Protocol on greenhouse gases.[34] Their model consists of many equations in a spreadsheet program and is too complicated to summarize here, but it involves many of the same interactions seen in the growth models we have introduced so far.

Nancy Stokey, of the University of Chicago, has introduced this feedback from growth to the environment in the theoretical growth models studied in this chapter.[35] She showed that steady growth is possible with emissions standards gradually becoming stricter but that growth will be at a lower rate than in the original growth models that do not have negative effects of growth on the environment. Earlier, we found that productivity improvements are the key source of long-run growth. Stokey noted that new technologies can continue to lead to growth only if they allow more consumption *and* environmental improvements.

Does economic growth generally lead to deterioration in the environment? In poor countries, increases in GDP often are associated with declines in environmental quality. But Gene Grossman and Alan Krueger, of Princeton University, have showed that most economics reach a turning point in this relationship.[36] Once GDP per capita reaches a certain threshold, environmental quality begins to improve again. They found this pattern for several different indicators of pollution, including urban air pollution and heavy metal contamination of rivers. Thus, graphing environmental quality against GDP per capita gives a graph with a U-shape; quality first falls but later rises as economic growth proceeds. The optimistic conclusion one can draw from this evidence is that cities with poor air quality today, such as Mexico City, may have better air quality in the future as GDP rises. After all, the air quality in London, England, has improved dramatically since the 19th century. Grossman and Krueger emphasize that improvements like these are not automatic, though, but instead result from policy decisions.

Finding that some countries have passed the turning point and begun to experience improved air quality might not be as encouraging as it seems, for two reasons. First, it could be that industrialized countries improved their air quality by transferring polluting industries to poorer regions or countries. In that case, the poorest regions may may inherit the pollution and not grow out of it because they have no one else to pass it on to. Grossman and Krueger find little evidence of this environmental "dumping," however, for the pollutants they studied. Second, no country seems to have yet reached a point at which carbon dioxide emissions decline as GDP per capita rises. It remains to be seen whether the U-shape found for some more obvious forms of pollution—such as lead, mercury, or sulphur dioxide emissions—carries over to carbon dioxide or to threats to biodiversity.

---

34. *Warming the World.* Cambridge MA: MIT Press, 2000.

35. "Are There Limits to Growth?" *International Economic Review,* February 1998, pp. 1-31. For a clear discussion of the environment and growth models, see Chapter 9, "Natural Resources and Economic Growth" in Charles I. Jones, *Introduction to Economic Growth,* second edition, New York: W.W. Norton, 2002.

36. Gene M. Grossman and Alan B. Krueger, "Economic Growth and the Environment," *Quarterly Journal of Economics,* April 1995, 353-377.

6.3 GOVERNMENT POLICIES TO RAISE LONG-RUN LIVING STANDARDS

Increased growth and a higher standard of living in the long run often are cited by political leaders as primary policy goals. Let us take a closer look at government policies that may be useful in raising a country's long-run standard of living. ("The Political Environment: Economic Growth and Democracy," p. 227, discusses whether the form of government—democratic or nondemocratic—affects the long-run growth rate of an economy.)

POLICIES TO AFFECT THE SAVING RATE

The neoclassical growth model suggests that the rate of national saving is a principal determinant of long-run living standards. However, this conclusion does not necessarily mean that policymakers should try to force the saving rate upward because more saving means less consumption in the short run. Indeed, if markets are working well, the saving rate freely chosen by individuals should be the one that optimally balances the benefit of saving more (higher future living standards) against the cost of saving more (less present consumption).

Even though the private saving rate is higher in Canada than in the United States, it is significantly lower than that in, say, Japan. Despite the argument that saving decisions are best left to individuals and the free market, some people, thus, claim that Canadians save too little and that policy should aim at raising the saving rate. One possible justification for this claim is that existing tax laws discriminate against saving by taxing away part of the returns to saving; a "pro-saving" policy, thus, is necessary to offset this bias. Another, stronger view is that Canadians are simply too shortsighted in their saving decisions and must be encouraged to save more.

What policies can be used to increase saving? If saving were highly responsive to the real interest rate, tax changes that increased the real return that savers receive would be effective. For example, some economists advocate taxing households on how much they consume rather than on how much they earn, thereby exempting from taxation the income that is saved. But as Chapter 4 noted, although saving appears to increase when the expected real return available to savers rises, most studies find this response to be small. For example, during the 1980s, the tax rate on investment earnings fell for upper-income Canadians, with little effect on the saving rate. Thus, there may not be much scope for policies to influence the level of private saving.[37]

An alternative and perhaps more direct way to increase the national saving rate is to increase the amount that governments save; in other words, governments should try to reduce their deficits. Our analysis of the "twin deficits" debate (Chapter 5) showed that reducing deficits by reducing government purchases will lead to more national saving. Many economists also argue that raising taxes to reduce deficits will also increase national saving by leading people to consume less. However, believers in Ricardian equivalence contend that tax increases without changes in current or planned government purchases will not affect consumption or national saving.

---

37. For example, the private rate of saving may be lower in Canada now than it was in the 1920s, say, because of health insurance and public pensions, yet few observers would suggest limiting social insurance to create risk and boost saving.

THE POLITICAL ENVIRONMENT

ECONOMIC GROWTH AND DEMOCRACY

Economic growth is an important social goal, but it is certainly not the only one. Most people also highly value political freedom and a democratic political process. Are these two goals conflicting or mutually supporting? If the citizens of poor countries succeed in achieving democracy, as many did during the 1980s and early 1990s, can they expect to enjoy faster economic growth as well? Or does increased political freedom involve economic sacrifice?

There are several reasons to believe that democracy may promote growth. Relative to dictatorships, democratic governments that command popular support might be expected to be more stable, to be less likely to start wars, and to have better relations with the advanced industrial nations, most of which are democracies. Constitutional protections of both human and property rights should increase the willingness of both foreigners and residents to invest in the country, and freedoms of speech and expression probably are essential for the full development of a nation's educational and scientific potential. However, the ability of a democratic government to undertake unpopular but necessary economic reforms or make other tough choices may be hampered by pressures of interest groups or fluctuations of public opinion. Similarly, a dictatorial government may be better able than a democratic one to enforce a high national saving rate and keep government spending under control.

What does empirical evidence show about the relationship between democracy and economic growth? A simple fact is that for the most part, the richest countries of the world are democratic, and the poorest nations are nondemocratic. (There are exceptions: India is poor but is more democratic than wealthy Saudi Arabia or Singapore.) Not too much should be read into this fact, however, because many wealthy nations that are currently democratic initially achieved economic leadership under monarchies.

A more direct empirical test is to examine the growth performance of countries that experienced sharp changes in their level of democracy. Jenny Minier of the University of Miami identified 13 countries that experienced sharp increases in democracy and 22 countries that experienced sharp decreases in democracy during the period 1965-1987*. To get a clear measure of the impact of changes in the level of democracy on the subsequent rate of economic growth, for each change in the level of democracy, Minier formed a control group of countries. She chose the control groups so that prior to the change in democracy, the levels of income per capita and of democracy were the same in the control group as in the country undergoing the change. She found that over the five-year period following an increase in democracy, countries experienced economic growth that averaged almost 2%, compared with growth of -1% in the control groups. Countries that experienced a decrease in democracy had economic growth of almost 8% in the five-year period following the change, compared with almost 15% growth in the control groups. Thus, relative to the control groups, increases in democracy tended to increase economic growth, and decreases in democracy tended to decrease economic growth. These findings were strengthened by Minier's examination of growth in the 15-year period following a change in the level of democracy. Countries that increased democracy experienced economic growth of 32% in the 15 years after a change (compared with 6% growth for the control groups), and countries that decreased democracy saw their economies grow by less than 8% in the 15 years after the change (compared with 35% for the control groups).

---

*Jenny A. Minier, "Democracy and Growth: Alternative Approaches," *Journal of Economic Growth*, September 1998, pp. 241-266.

POLICIES TO RAISE THE RATE OF PRODUCTIVITY GROWTH

Of the factors affecting long-run living standards, the rate of productivity growth may well be the most important in that—according to the neoclassical growth model—only ongoing productivity growth can lead to continuing improvement in output and consumption per worker. Government policy can attempt to increase productivity in several ways.

IMPROVING INFRASTRUCTURE

Some research findings suggest a significant link between productivity and the quality of a nation's infrastructure—its highways, bridges, utilities, dams, airports, and other publicly owned capital.[38] The construction of the Trans-Canada highway system, for example, significantly reduced the cost of transporting goods and stimulated tourism and other industries. In the past two decades, the rate of government investment in infrastructure has fallen, leading some economists to argue that reversing this trend might help achieve higher productivity. Increased federal investment in infrastructure was called for by some Canadian provincial and municipal governments during the recession of the early 1990s.

However, not everyone agrees that more infrastructure investment is needed.[39] For example, some critics have argued that the links between productivity growth and infrastructure are not clear. Cross-country differences in growth rates cannot be readily explained by differences in public investment.[40] Moreover, if rich countries are more likely to build roads and hospitals, perhaps higher productivity growth leads to more infrastructure, rather than vice versa. Others worry that infrastructure investments by governments may involve political considerations (for example, favouring the ridings of powerful members of Parliament) more than promoting economic efficiency.

BUILDING HUMAN CAPITAL

Recent research findings point to a strong connection between productivity growth and human capital. Governments affect human capital through educational policies, worker training or relocation programs, health programs, and in other ways. Specific programs should be examined carefully to see whether benefits exceed costs, but a case may be made for greater commitment to human capital formation as a way to fight productivity slowdown.

One crucial form of human capital, which we have not yet mentioned, is entrepreneurial skill. People with the ability to build successful new businesses or to bring a new product to market play key roles in economic growth. Productivity growth may increase if the government were to remove unnecessary barriers to entrepreneurial activity (such as excessive red tape) and give people with entrepreneurial skills greater incentives to use those skills productively.[41]

---

38. David A. Aschauer, "Is Public Expenditure Productive?" *Journal of Monetary Economics*, March 1989, pp. 177–200; Alicia H. Munnell, "Infrastructure and Economic Growth," *Journal of Economic Perspectives*, Fall 1992, pp. 189–198.
39. For a variety of viewpoints, see Jack M. Mintz and Ross S. Preston, eds., *Infrastructure and Competitiveness, Tenth Roundtable*, John Deutsch Institute for the Study of Economic Policy, Queen's University, 1994.
40. Ross Levine and D. Renelt, "A Sensitivity Analysis of Cross-Country Growth Regressions," *American Economic Review*, September 1992, pp. 942–963.
41. For a discussion of the importance of entrepreneurial activity and how it is affected by government policy and the social environment, see William J. Baumol, "Entrepreneurship: Productive, Unproductive, and Destructive," *Journal of Political Economy*, October 1990 (part 1), pp. 893–921.

ENCOURAGING RESEARCH AND DEVELOPMENT

Governments also may be able to stimulate productivity growth by affecting rates of scientific and technical progress. The Canadian government directly supports much basic scientific research (through its research councils, for example). Most economists agree with this type of policy because the benefits of scientific progress, like those of human capital development, spread throughout the economy. Basic scientific research, thus, may be a good investment from society's point of view, even if no individual firm finds such research profitable. Some economists would go further and say that even more applied, commercially oriented research deserves government aid.

Is there scope for policies to promote R&D in Canada? Several types of evidence suggest that there is. The federal government's expenditures on R&D have declined, as a percentage of GDP, over the last 20 years. Moreover, Canada spends a significantly smaller proportion of output on R&D than any other G-7 country, except Italy.[42] Some commentators, thus, argue that R&D expenditures, both public and private, should be more strongly encouraged.

International comparisons of R&D spending can be misleading, because R&D spending in such countries as the United States and the United Kingdom includes substantial spending in the defence sector, which may have few benefits for economic productivity. Also, Canada already provides very generous tax credits for private R&D. So, is there still a case for promoting growth this way? Dan Trefler, of the University of Toronto, has argued that Canada needs more spending on basic research and that obstacles to sharing that research can be lowered by changes to patent policy.[43] By studying productivity growth in a range of Canadian manufacturing firms, he also shows that relying on the benefits of R&D spending to spread from US companies to their Canadian subsidiaries is unlikely to lead to enhanced productivity growth in Canada.

INDUSTRIAL POLICY

Beyond support for basic science and technology, an aggressive approach that has been proposed for encouraging technological development is industrial policy. Generally, **industrial policy** is a growth strategy in which the government—using taxes, subsidies, or regulation—attempts to influence the country's pattern of industrial development. More specifically, some advocates of industrial policy argue that the government should subsidize and promote "high-tech" industries, in order to try to achieve or maintain national leadership in technologically dynamic areas.

The idea that the government should try to determine the country's mix of industries is controversial. Economic theory and practice suggest that under normal circumstances the free market can allocate resources well without government assistance. Thus, advocates of industrial policy must explain why the free market fails in the case of high technology. Two possible sources of market failure that have been suggested are borrowing constraints and spillovers.

Borrowing constraints are limits imposed by lenders on the amounts that individuals or small firms can borrow.[44] Because of borrowing constraints, private companies, especially start-up firms, may have difficulty obtaining enough financing for

---

42. The G-7 countries are Canada, France, Germany, Italy, Japan, the United Kingdom, and the United States.

43. "Does Canada Need a Productivity Budget?" *Policy Options*, July-August 1999, pp. 66-71.

44. Appendix 4A presents a discussion of borrowing constraints.

some projects. Development of a new supercomputer, for example, is likely to require heavy investment in research and development and involve a long period during which expenses are high and no revenues are coming in.

Spillovers occur when a given company's innovation—say, the development of an improved computer memory chip or CT scanner—stimulates a flood of related innovations and technical improvements by other companies and industries. The innovative company, thus, may enjoy only some of the total benefits of its breakthrough while bearing the full development cost. Without a government subsidy (argue advocates of industrial policy), such companies may not have a sufficiently strong incentive to innovate.

A third argument for industrial policy has less to do with market failure and more with nationalism. In some industries (such as aerospace), the efficient scale of operation is so large that the world market has room for only a few firms. For the world, the most desirable outcome is that those few firms be the most efficient, lowest-cost producers. However, in terms of a single country, say, Canada, at least some of the firms in the market should be Canadian so that profits from the industry will accrue to Canada. This perceived benefit might lead Canada to subsidize its firms in that industry, helping them to compete with the firms of other nations in the race to capture the world market. Of course, other nations may well retaliate by introducing or increasing existing subsidies to their own firms.

These theoretical arguments for government intervention assume that the government is skilled at picking "winning" technologies and that its decisions about which industries to subsidize would be free from purely political considerations. However, both assumptions are questionable. A danger of industrial policy is that the favoured industries would be those with the most powerful political supporters, rather than those with the most economic promise. Alternative polices—such as R&D tax credits—promote technological change without requiring the government to target specific industries.[45]

---

45. For a review of the evidence, see Gene Grossman, "Promoting New Industrial Activities: A Survey of Recent Arguments and Evidence," *OECD Economic Studies*, Spring 1990, pp. 87–125.

CHAPTER SUMMARY

1. Economic growth is the principal source of improving standards of living over time. Over long periods, even small differences in growth rates can have a large effect on nations' standards of living.

2. Growth accounting is a method for breaking total output growth into the portions resulting from growth in capital inputs, growth in labour inputs, and growth in productivity. All three factors have contributed to long-run economic growth in Canada. However, the slowdown in output growth after 1973 in Canada (and in other countries)

primarily reflects a sharp decline in productivity growth. This decline in productivity growth, in turn, is the result of various factors, including slower technical progress and increased oil prices.

3. The neoclassical growth model examines the interaction of growth, saving, and capital accumulation over time. It predicts that in the absence of productivity growth the economy will reach a steady state in which output, consumption, and capital per worker are constant.

4. According to the growth model, each of the following leads to higher output, consumption,

and capital per worker in the long run: an increase in the saving rate, a decline in the population growth rate, and an increase in productivity.

5. The growth model implies that living standards of countries with similar saving rates, population growth rates, and production functions will tend to converge over time (conditional convergence). Empirical evidence tends to support conditional convergence. Unconditional convergence—the idea that living standards in most poor countries will eventually catch up to those of rich countries—is not supported by the data.

6. Endogenous growth theory attempts to explain, rather than assume, the economywide rate of productivity growth. One strand of this approach emphasizes the formation of human capital, including the acquisition of skills and training by workers. A second strand focuses on research and development activity by firms. Endogenous growth theorists argue that because growth in capital and output engenders increased human capital and innovation, the marginal productivity of capital may not be diminishing for the economy as a whole. An implication of this theory is that the saving rate can affect the long-run rate of economic growth.

7. Government policies to raise long-run living standards include raising the rate of saving and increasing productivity. Possible ways of increasing productivity involve investing in public capital (infrastructure), encouraging the formation of human capital, and increasing research and development. A more aggressive strategy is industrial policy, in which the government uses subsidies and other tools to influence the pattern of industrial development and, in particular, to stimulate high-tech industries. Theoretical arguments for the use of industrial policy include the possible existence of borrowing constraints and spillovers. Critics of this approach contend that in practice, the government cannot successfully pick and subsidize only "winning" technologies.

KEY TERMS

capital–labour ratio, p. 209
conditional convergence, p. 221
endogenous growth theory, p. 222
Golden Rule, p. 211

growth accounting, p. 200
growth accounting equation, p. 199
human capital, p. 223
industrial policy, p. 229
neoclassical growth model, p. 208
steady state, p. 209
unconditional convergence, p. 220

KEY EQUATIONS

$$\frac{\Delta Y}{Y} = \frac{\Delta A}{A} + a_K \frac{\Delta K}{K} + a_N \frac{\Delta N}{N} \qquad (6.2)$$

The growth accounting equation states that output growth, $\Delta Y/Y$, depends on the growth rate of productivity, $\Delta A/A$, the growth rate of capital, $\Delta K/K$, and the growth rate of labour, $\Delta N/N$. The elasticity of output with respect to capital, a_K, gives the percentage increase in output that results when capital increases by 1%. The elasticity of output with respect to labour, a_N, gives the percentage increase in output that results when labour increases by 1%.

$$y_t = f(k_t) \qquad (6.4)$$

For any year t, the per-worker production function relates output per worker, y_t, to capital per worker (also called the capital–labour ratio), k_t

$$c = f(k) - (n + d)k \qquad (6.7)$$

Steady-state consumption per worker c equals steady-state output per worker $f(k)$ minus steady-state investment per worker $(n + d)k$. Steady-state output per worker is determined by per-worker production $f(k)$, where k is the steady-state capital–labour ratio. Steady-state investment per worker has two parts: equipping new workers with the per-worker capital stock, nk, and replacing worn-out or depreciated capital, dk.

$$sf(k) = (n + d)k \qquad (6.10)$$

The steady state is determined by the condition that saving per worker $sf(k)$ equals steady-state investment per worker $(n + d)k$. Saving per worker equals the saving rate s times output per worker $f(k)$.

$$Y = AK \qquad (6.11)$$

Endogenous growth theory replaces the assumption of diminishing marginal productivity of capital with the assumption that the marginal productivity of capital is independent of the level of the capital stock. In the production function relating aggregate output Y to the aggregate capital stock K in Eq. (6.11), the marginal product of capital is constant and equal to the parameter A.

$$\Delta Y/Y = sA - d \qquad (6.14)$$

In an endogenous growth model, the growth rate of output is determined endogenously by the saving rate, s. An increase in the saving rate increases the growth rate of output.

REVIEW QUESTIONS

1. According to the growth accounting approach, what are the three sources of economic growth? From what basic economic relationship is the growth accounting approach derived?

2. Of the three sources of growth identified by growth accounting, which one is primarily responsible for the slowdown in Canadian economic growth after 1973? What explanations have been given for the decline in this source of growth?

3. According to the neoclassical growth model, if there is no productivity growth, what will happen to output per worker, consumption per worker, and capital per worker in the long run?

4. True or false? The higher the steady-state capital–labour ratio is, the more consumption each worker can enjoy in the long run. Explain your answer.

5. What effect should each of the following have on long-run living standards, according to the neoclassical growth model?
   a. An increase in the saving rate.
   b. An increase in the population growth rate.
   c. A one-time improvement in productivity.

6. What is convergence? Explain the difference between unconditional convergence and conditional convergence. What prediction does the neoclassical growth model make about convergence? What does the evidence say?

7. What two explanations of productivity growth does endogenous growth theory offer? How does the production function in an endogenous growth model differ from the production function in the neoclassical growth model?

8. What types of policies are available to a government that wants to promote economic growth? For each type of policy you identify, explain briefly how the policy is supposed to work, and list its costs or disadvantages. How does endogenous growth theory possibly change our thinking about the effectiveness of various pro-growth policies, such as increasing the saving rate?

NUMERICAL PROBLEMS

1. Two economies, Hare and Tortoise, each start with a real GDP per person of $5,000 in 1950. Real GDP per person grows 3% a year in Hare and 1% a year in Tortoise. In the year 2000, what will be real GDP per person in each economy? Make a guess first; then use a calculator to get the answer.

2. Over the past 20 years, an economy's total output has grown from 1,000 to 1,300, its capital stock has risen from 2,500 to 3,250, and its labour force has increased from 500 to 575. All measurements are in real terms. Calculate the contributions to economic growth of growth in capital, labour, and productivity
   a. assuming that $a_K = 0.3$ and $a_N = 0.7$.
   b. assuming that $a_K = 0.5$ and $a_N = 0.5$.

3. For a particular economy, the following capital input K and labour input N were reported in four different years.

Year	K	N
1	200	1,000
2	250	1,000
3	250	1,250
4	300	1,200

The production function in this economy is

$$Y = K^{0.3}N^{0.7},$$

where Y is total output.
   a. Find total output, the capital–labour ratio, and output per worker in each year. Compare year 1 with year 3 and year 2 with year 4. Can this production function be written in per-worker form? If so, write algebraically the per-worker form of the production function.
   b. Repeat part (a) but assume now that the production function is $Y = K^{0.3}N^{0.8}$.

4. Use the data from Table 6.1 to calculate annual growth rates of GDP per capita for each country listed over the period 1950–1996. (*Note*: The annual growth rate z will satisfy the equation $(1 + z)^{46} = \text{GDP}_{1996}/\text{GDP}_{1950}$. To solve this equation for z using a calculator, take logs of both sides of the equation.) You will find that Germany and Japan, two countries that suffered extensive damage in World War II, had the two highest growth rates after 1950. Give a reason, based on the analysis of the growth model, for these countries' particularly fast growth during this period.

5. An economy has the per-worker production function

$$y_t = 3k_t^{0.5},$$

where y_t is output per worker and k_t is the capital–labour ratio. The depreciation rate is 0.1, and the population growth rate is 0.05. Saving is

$$S_t = 0.3Y_t,$$

where S_t is total national saving, and Y_t is total output.
a. What are the steady-state values of the capital–labour ratio, output per worker, and consumption per worker?
The rest of the problem shows the effects of changes in the three fundamental determinants of long-run living standards.
b. Repeat part (a) for a saving rate of 0.4 instead of 0.3.
c. Repeat part (a) for a population growth rate of 0.08 (with a saving rate of 0.3).
d. Repeat part (a) for a production function of

$$y_t = 4k_t^{0.5}.$$

Assume that the saving rate and population growth rate are at their original values.

6. Consider a closed economy in which the population grows at the rate of 1% per year. The per-worker production function is $y = 6\sqrt{k}$, where y is output per worker and k is capital per worker. The depreciation rate of capital is 14% per year.
a. Households consume 90% of income and save the remaining 10% of income. There is no government. What are the steady-state values of capital per worker, output per worker, consumption per worker, and investment per worker?
b. Suppose that the country wants to increase its steady-state value of output per worker. What steady-state value of the capital–labour ratio is needed to double the steady-state value of output per capita? What fraction of income would households have to save to achieve a steady-state level of output per worker that is twice as high as in part (a)?

7. Both population and the work force grow at the rate of $n = 1\%$ per year in a closed economy. Consumption is $C = 0.5(1 - t)Y$, where t is the tax rate on income and Y is total output. The per-worker production function is $y = 8\sqrt{k}$, where y is output per worker and k is the capital–labour ratio. The depreciation rate of capital is $d = 9\%$ per year. Suppose for now that there are no government purchases and the tax rate on income is $t = 0$.
a. Find expressions for national saving per worker and the steady-state level of investment per worker as

functions of the capital–labor ratio, k. In the steady state, what are the values of the capital–labour ratio, output per worker, consumption per worker, and investment per worker?
b. Suppose that the government purchases goods each year and pays for these purchases using taxes on income. The government runs a balanced budget in each period and the tax rate on income is $t = 0.5$. Repeat part (a) and compare your results.

ANALYTICAL PROBLEMS

1. According to the neoclassical growth model, how would each of the following affect consumption per worker in the long run (that is, in the steady state)? Explain.
a. The destruction of a portion of the country's capital stock in a war.
b. A permanent increase in the rate of immigration (which raises the overall population growth rate).
c. A permanent increase in energy prices.
d. A temporary rise in the saving rate.
e. A permanent increase in the fraction of the population in the labour force (the population growth rate is unchanged).

2. An economy is in a steady state with no productivity change. Because of an increase in acid rain, the rate of capital depreciation rises permanently.
a. According to the neoclassical growth model, what are the effects on steady-state capital per worker, output per worker, consumption per worker, and the long-run growth rate of the total capital stock?
b. In an endogenous growth model, what are the effects on the growth rates of output, capital, and consumption of an increase in the depreciation rate of capital?

3. This problem adds the government to the growth model. Suppose that a government purchases goods in the amount of g per worker every year; with N_t workers in year t, total government purchases are gN_t. The government has a balanced budget so that its tax revenue in year t, T_t, equals total government purchases. Total national saving S_t is

$$S_t = s(Y_t - T_t),$$

where Y_t is total output and s is the saving rate.
a. Graphically show the steady state for the initial level of government purchases per worker.
b. Suppose that the government permanently increases its purchases per worker. What are the effects on the steady-state levels of capital per

worker, output per worker, and consumption per worker? Does your result imply that the optimal level of government purchases is zero?

4. In a Solow–Swan-type economy, total national saving S_t is

$$S_t = sY_t - hK_t.$$

The extra term, $-hK_t$, reflects the idea that when wealth (as measured by the capital stock) is higher, saving is lower. (Wealthier people have less need to save for the future.)

Find the steady-state values of per-worker capital, output, and consumption. What is the effect on the steady state of an increase in h?

5. Two countries are identical in every way except that one has a much higher capital–labour ratio than the other. According to the neoclassical growth model, which country's total output will grow more quickly? Does your answer depend on whether one country or the other is in a steady state? In general terms, how will your answer be affected if the two countries are allowed to trade with each other?

6. Suppose that total capital and labour both increase by the same percentage amount so that the amount of capital per worker k does not change. Writing the production function in per-worker terms, $y = f(k)$, requires that this increase in capital and labour must not change the amount of output produced per worker y. Use the growth accounting equation to show that equal percentage increases in capital and labour will leave output per worker unaffected only if $a_K + a_N = 1$.

7. An economy has a per-capita production function $y = Ak^a h^{1-a}$, where A and a are fixed parameters, y is per-worker output, k is the capital–labour ratio, and h is human capital per worker, a measure of the skills and training of the average worker. The production function implies that for a given capital–labour ratio, increases in average human capital raise output per worker.

The economy's saving rate is s, and all saving is used to create physical capital, which depreciates at rate d. Workers acquire skills on the job by working with capital; the more capital with which they have to work, the more skills they acquire. We capture this idea by assuming that human capital per worker is always proportional to the amount of capital per worker, or $h = Bk$, where B is a fixed parameter.

Find the long-run growth rates of physical capital, human capital, and output in this economy.

Chapter 7

The Asset Market, Money, and Prices

Chapters 3 and 4 discussed the labour market and the goods market, two of the three markets in our model of the macroeconomy. In this chapter, we consider the third market, the asset market. By asset market we mean the entire set of markets in which people buy and sell real and financial assets, including, for example, gold, houses, stocks, and bonds.

A type of asset that has long been believed to have special macroeconomic significance is money. Money is the economist's term for assets that can be used in making payments, such as cash and chequing accounts. One reason that money is important is that most prices are expressed in units of money, such as dollars, yen, or francs. Because prices are measured in money terms, understanding the role of money in the economy is basic to studying issues related to the price level, such as inflation and its causes. In addition, many economists believe that the amount of money in the economy affects real economic variables, such as output and employment. If it does, then it may be possible to use monetary policy to promote stable output growth and fight unemployment, as we discuss in Part III.

Because money is such an important asset, it is the focus of our discussion of the asset market. The first part of the chapter explains what money is and why people choose to hold it. We show that a person's decision about how much money to hold (his or her money demand) is part of a broader decision about how to allocate wealth among the various assets that are available. We then bring together the demand for money and the supply of money (which is determined by the central bank) to analyze equilibrium in the asset market. This analysis demonstrates that the price level in an economy is closely related to the amount of money in the economy. Thus, high rates of inflation—that is, rapid increases in prices—are likely when the money supply is growing rapidly.

7.1 What Is Money?

In economics, the meaning of the term *money* is different from its everyday meaning. People often say *money* when they mean *income* or *wealth*, as in: That job pays good money, or Her family has a lot of money. In economics, however, **money** refers specifically to assets that are widely used and accepted as payment. Historically, the forms of money have ranged from beads and shells to gold and silver—and even to cigarettes (see Box 7.1). In modern economies, the most familiar forms of money are coins and paper money, or currency. Another common form of money is chequable deposits, or bank accounts on which cheques can be written for making payments.

THE FUNCTIONS OF MONEY

Since the earliest times, almost all societies—from the most primitive to the most sophisticated and with many types of political and economic systems—have used money. Money has three useful functions in an economy: It is a medium of exchange, a unit of account, and a store of value.

MEDIUM OF EXCHANGE

In an economy with no money, trading takes the form of barter, or the direct exchange of certain goods for other goods. Even today some people belong to barter clubs, in which members swap goods and services among themselves. Generally, though, barter is an inefficient way to trade, because finding someone who has the item you want and is willing to exchange that item for something you have is both difficult and time-consuming. In a barter system, if one of the authors of this book wanted a restaurant meal, he would first have to find a restauranteur willing to trade his blue-plate special for an economics lecture—which might not be easy to do.

Money makes searching for the perfect trading partner unnecessary. In an economy that utilizes money, the economics professor does not have to find a restaurant owner who is hungry for knowledge. Instead, he can first exchange his economics lecture to students (and taxpayers) for money and then use the money to buy a meal. In functioning as a **medium of exchange**, or a device for making transactions, money permits people to trade at less cost in time and effort. Having a medium of exchange also raises productivity by allowing people to specialize in economic activities at which they are most skilled. In an economy with money, specialized producers have no problem trading their goods or services for the things they need. In a barter economy, though, the difficulty of trading would leave people no choice but to produce most of their own food, clothing, and shelter. Thus, in a barter economy, the opportunity to specialize is greatly reduced.

UNIT OF ACCOUNT

As a **unit of account**, money is the basic unit for measuring economic value. In Canada, for example, virtually all prices, wages, asset values, and debts are expressed in dollars. Having a single, uniform measure of value is convenient. For example, pricing all goods in Canada in dollars—instead of some goods being priced in yen, some in gold, and some in Canadian Pacific shares—simplifies comparison among different goods.

The medium-of-exchange and unit-of-account functions of money are closely linked. Because goods and services are most often exchanged for money (the medium-of-exchange function), expressing economic values in money terms (the unit-of-account function) is natural. Otherwise, we could just as well express economic values in terms of, say, bushels of wheat. However, the medium of exchange and the unit of account are not always the same. In countries with high and erratic inflation, for example, fluctuating currency value makes money a poor unit of account because prices must be changed frequently. In such cases, economic values are commonly stated in terms of a more stable unit of account, such as US dollars or ounces of gold, even though transactions may continue to be carried out in the local currency.

BOX 7.1 MONEY IN A PRISONER-OF-WAR CAMP

Among the Allied soldiers liberated from German prisoner-of-war (POW) camps at the end of World War II was a young man named R. A. Radford. Radford had been trained in economics, and shortly after his return home, he published an article entitled "The Economic Organisation of a POW Camp*." This article, a minor classic in the economics literature, is a fascinating account of the daily lives of soldiers in several POW camps. It focuses particularly on the primitive "economies" that grew up spontaneously in the camps.

The scope for economic behaviour in a POW camp might seem severely limited, and to a degree that is so. There was little production of goods within the camps, although there was some trade in services, such as laundry or tailoring services and even portraiture. However, prisoners were allowed to move around freely within the compound, and they actively traded goods obtained from the Red Cross, the Germans, and other sources. Among the commodities exchanged were tinned milk, jam, butter, biscuits, chocolate, sugar, clothing, and toilet articles. In one particular camp, which at various times had up to 50,000 prisoners of many nationalities, active trading centres were run entirely by the prisoners.

A key practical issue was how to organize the trading. At first, the camp economies used barter, but it proved to be slow and inefficient. Then the prisoners hit on the idea of using cigarettes as money. Soon prices of all goods were quoted in terms of cigarettes, and cigarettes were accepted as payment for any good or service. Even nonsmoking prisoners would happily accept cigarettes as payment because they knew that they could easily trade the cigarettes for other things they wanted. The use of cigarette money greatly simplified the problem of making trades and helped the camp economy function much more smoothly.

Why were cigarettes, rather than some other commodity, used as money by the POWs? Cigarettes satisfied a number of criteria for a good money: A cigarette is a fairly standardized commodity whose value was easy for both buyers and sellers to ascertain. An individual cigarette is low enough in value that making "change" was not a problem. Cigarettes are portable, are easily passed from hand to hand, and do not spoil quickly.

A drawback was that as a commodity money (a form of money with an alternative use), cigarette money had a resource cost: Cigarettes that were being used as money could not simultaneously be smoked. In the same way, the traditional use of gold and silver as money was costly, in that it diverted these metals—and the labour and capital used to locate and mine them—from alternative uses.

The use of cigarettes as money is not restricted to POW camps. Just before the collapse of communism in Eastern Europe, cigarette money reportedly was used in Romania and other countries instead of the nearly worthless official money.

---

*Economica, November 1945, pp. 189–201.

STORE OF VALUE

As a **store of value**, money is a way of holding wealth. An extreme example is a miser who keeps his life's savings in cash under the mattress. But even someone who spends his cash wages 15 minutes after receiving them is using money as a store of value for that short period.

In most cases, only money functions as a medium of exchange or a unit of account, but any asset—for example, stocks, bonds, or real estate—can be a store of value. As these other types of assets normally pay the holder a higher return than money does, why do people use money as a store of value? The answer is that money's usefulness as a medium of exchange makes it worthwhile to hold, even though its return is relatively low.

MEASURING MONEY: THE MONETARY AGGREGATES

Money is defined as those assets that are widely used and accepted in payment. This definition suggests a hard-and-fast line between assets that should be counted as money and those that should not. Actually, the distinction between monetary assets and non-monetary assets is not so clear.

Consider, for example, money market mutual funds (MMMFs), which became popular in the late 1980s. MMMFs are organizations that sell shares to the public and invest the proceeds in short-term government and corporate debt. MMMFs strive to earn a high return for their shareholders. At the same time, MMMFs typically allow their shareholders to write a small number of cheques each month against their accounts, perhaps for a fee. Thus, although MMMF shares can be used to make payments, they are not as convenient as cash or regular chequing accounts for this purpose. Should MMMF shares be counted as money or not? There is no definitive answer.

Because assets differ in their "moneyness," no single measure of the amount of money in the economy—or the money stock, as it is often called—is likely to be completely satisfactory. For this reason, in most countries, economists and policymakers use several different measures of the money stock. These official measures are known as **monetary aggregates**. The various monetary aggregates differ in how narrowly they define the concept of money. In Canada, the two most widely used monetary aggregates are called M1 and M2. Summary definitions and data for these two aggregates are given in Table 7.1. Information about where to find data on the monetary aggregates is presented in the box, "In Touch with the Macroeconomy: The Monetary Aggregates."

THE M1 MONETARY AGGREGATE

The most narrowly defined official money measure, **M1**, consists primarily of currency and balances held in chequing accounts. More precisely, M1 is made up of currency held by the public, demand deposits (personal chequing accounts), and other chequable deposits (current accounts). The category "personal chequing accounts" includes interest-bearing chequable deposits, such as daily interest chequing accounts, while current accounts are held by firms. M1 is perhaps the closest counterpart to the theoretical definition of money because all its components are actively used and widely accepted for making payments.[1]

As usual, one way to bring the astronomical numbers in Table 7.1 down to earth is to divide by the population. In June 2001, the Canadian population was 31 million, so the stock of currency per person was $1,142 ($35.4 billion divided by 31 million). This strikes most students as a surprisingly large number. For a discussion of the even larger value for the US, see Box 7.2, "Where Have All the US Dollars Gone?" on page 240.

---

1. The Bank of Canada distinguishes between gross M1, which includes payments in transit, and net M1, which excludes them.

TABLE 7.1

The Canadian Monetary Aggregates (June 2001)

M1	**$115.5 billion**
Currency	$35.4 billion
Personal chequing accounts	$23.7 billion
Current accounts	$56.4 billion
M2	**$509.3 billion**
Components of M1	$115.5 billion
Personal savings deposits	$345.4 billion
Nonpersonal notice deposits	$48.4 billion
M2+	**$731.0 billion**
Components of M2	$509.3 billion
Deposits at trust and mortgage loan companies	$7.7 billion
Deposits at caisses populaires and credit unions	$111.4 billion
Annuities and deposits at government savings institutions	$45.4 billion
Money market mutual funds	$56.5 billion
M3	**$698.1 billion**
Components of M2	$509.3 billion
Nonpersonal fixed-term deposits	$122.2 billion
Foreign currency deposits held by residents	$66.6 billion

Source: *Bank of Canada Banking and Financial Statistics*, September 2001, Tables E1 and C2. Components do not sum exactly to the aggregates because of adjustments listed in the source. Reprinted with permission from the Bank of Canada.

IN TOUCH WITH THE MACROECONOMY

THE MONETARY AGGREGATES

The official monetary aggregates—currently net M1, gross M1, M2, M2+, and M3—are compiled and reported by the Bank of Canada in Ottawa. The definitions of the monetary aggregates have changed several times, reflecting the evolution of the financial system.

The Bank reports estimates of the aggregates both weekly and monthly, using data supplied by banks and other deposit-taking institutions. Each Friday, the Bank releases estimates for the previous week's aggregates (Wednesday to Wednesday) in its *Weekly Financial Statistics*, available at *www.bank-banque-canada.ca*. The same publication gives the aggregates for the previous month (average of Wednesdays), with and without seasonal adjustments. These announcements are regularly reported by the business media. Caisses populaires and credit unions do not report to the central bank as frequently as chartered banks do, and so aggregates (notably M2+) that include their deposits are not available with the immediacy of the narrower measures. Monthly historical data on the aggregates and their components are available in the *Bank of Canada Review* and in the CANSIM database. Monetary data are revised frequently, reflecting the receipt of new data by the Bank of Canada or changes in the definitions of the monetary aggregates.

Monetary policy can influence the monetary aggregates, although the Bank of Canada does not directly control them, and so changes in M1, for example, are sometimes viewed as reflecting policy. An important practical use for the aggregates, because of their timeliness and comprehensiveness, is as leading indicators of future changes in real GDP and in the price level.

BOX 7.2 WHERE HAVE ALL THE US DOLLARS GONE?

In 1999, the stock of US currency was $488 billion, or about $1,800 for every man, woman, and child in the United States. This figure is surprisingly high. After all, how many people actually have $1,800 cash on hand at any given time, and how many families of four hold $7,200 in cash? In fact, studies have found that the average person in the United States holds not much more than $100 in currency. So, where is the remaining $1,700 per person?

Businesses, especially retailers, hold currency for making transactions, but the amount of currency held by US businesses appears to account for less than $100 of the "missing" $1,700 per person. Currency is also extensively used in the underground economy, either to conduct illegal transactions (such as trade in illegal drugs) or to hide legal transactions from tax collectors. However, the US Federal Reserve estimates that the amount of currency in the domestic underground economy amounts to less than $125 per person. Studies have found that most of the "missing" US currency—amounting to 55% to 70% of currency outstanding—is held abroad. Indeed, about 75% of the increase in US currency in the first half of the 1990s flowed abroad.

Why would people in other countries want to hold US dollars? Even though the dollar may not serve as medium of exchange or as a unit of account in a country, it can be a relatively attractive store of value, especially in countries that are economically or politically unstable. For example, in countries with high rates of inflation, the local currency is a particularly poor store of value because the real value (purchasing power) of the local currency decreases at the rate of inflation. In high-inflation countries the dollar, which has had a relatively stable purchasing power, may be much more attractive than local currency as a means of holding wealth. Political instability in a country might also induce residents to demand US dollars because if political upheaval forces people to flee the country, carrying dollars out may be the easiest way for them to take some of their wealth with them. About half the US currency sent overseas between 1988 and 1995 went to Europe, much of it to Russia and other nations of Eastern Europe, which, in recent years, have experienced substantial economic and political instability (see the Application "Money Growth and Inflation in European Countries in Transition," p. 257)

Because currency is more than one-third of M1 in the United States and more than half of all US currency is held abroad, more than one-sixth of US M1 is, in fact, held by foreign interests. Therefore, events abroad that change the foreign demand for US dollars can cause substantial changes in measured US monetary aggregates. Since 1960, the month with the highest (seasonally adjusted) growth rate of US currency outstanding was January 1991, when the United States began bombing Iraq after Iraq's invasion of Kuwait in August 1990. In fact, four of the seven highest monthly growth rates of currency since 1960 occurred between August 1990 and February 1991. These large increases in US currency outstanding were driven by foreign concerns about political and military instability, rather than by domestic factors determining money demand in the US economy.

Although foreign holdings of US dollars reduce the reliability of measured monetary aggregates as indicators of conditions in the US economy, the United States gets an important benefit from the foreign holdings of its currency. US currency is a liability of the Federal Reserve System and, thus, represents a loan to the Federal Reserve System (and ultimately to the US government, to which most Federal Reserve profits go). However, currency pays no interest, so this loan being provided by foreign holders of US currency to the United States is interest-free! The interest savings associated with this interest-free loan to the US government amount to several billion dollars each year.

Most of the data in this box (except the months of most rapid currency growth) are reported in Richard D. Porter and Ruth A. Judson, "The Location of U.S. Currency: How Much Is Abroad?" *Federal Reserve Bulletin*, October 1996, pp. 883–903.

THE M2 MONETARY AGGREGATE

Everything in M1 plus other assets that are somewhat less "moneylike" comprises **M2**. The main additional assets in M2 include personal savings deposits and nonpersonal notice deposits. Personal savings deposits include those with a fixed term, where early withdrawal usually involves a penalty.

THE M2+ MONETARY AGGREGATE

M2 includes most bank accounts, but it does not include accounts at other financial institutions, even though those accounts may be very similar to bank accounts. **M2+**, thus, adds these accounts to M2. As Table 7.1 shows, the largest additional components of M2+ are deposits at caisses populaires and credit unions.

THE M3 MONETARY AGGREGATE

A different way of broadening M2 is to add to it other types of deposits at banks. This leads to **M3**, which augments M2 with term deposits held by businesses and with the foreign currency holdings of Canadian residents but does not include deposits at caisses populaires. Many of the assets included in M2, M2+, and M3 are not money in the strict sense of being directly acceptable in payment. For example, assets such as US-dollar accounts, which are part of M3, cannot be used directly for making purchases. However, because these assets can be quickly and cheaply converted into currency or chequable deposits, economists include them in the broader measures of money.

WEIGHTED MONETARY AGGREGATES

The monetary aggregates are constructed by simply adding the outstanding amounts of various types of assets. Thus, a dollar of currency contributes no more to the measured money stock than does a dollar of savings deposits. This standard way of measuring the money stock ignores the fact that some assets, such as currency, are more moneylike than others. Recently, some economists have experimented with weighted monetary aggregates. In this approach, a dollar of a very moneylike asset, such as currency, is given a greater weight in the total than is a dollar of a less moneylike asset, such as a savings deposit. Several studies conclude that weighted monetary aggregates are more useful measures of money than are the standard aggregates.[2] Disagreements about the best way to weight the various monetary assets remain, however, and so far this approach has not been officially adopted.

THE MONEY SUPPLY

The **money supply** is the amount of money available in an economy.[3] In modern economies, the money supply is partly determined by the central bank—in Canada, the Bank of Canada.

For simplicity, we can assume that the Bank of Canada sets the money supply. In fact, the Bank influences the money supply indirectly by influencing short-term interest rates. A detailed explanation of how central banks control the money supply

---

2. For a recent technical discussion of weighted aggregates, see William A. Barnett, Douglas Fisher, and Apostolos Serletis, "Consumer Theory and the Demand for Money," *Journal of Economic Literature*, December 1992, pp. 2086–2119.
3. The terms money supply and money stock are used interchangeably.

raises issues that would take us too far afield at this point, so we defer that discussion to Chapter 14. To grasp the basic idea, however, let us consider the simple hypothetical situation in which the only form of money is currency. In this case, to increase the money supply, the central bank only needs to increase the amount of currency in circulation. How can it do so?

One way—which is close to what happens in practice—is for the central bank to use newly minted currency to buy financial assets, such as government bonds, from the public. In making this swap, the public increases its holdings of money, and the amount of money in circulation rises. When the central bank uses money to purchase government bonds from the public, thus raising the money supply, it is said to have conducted an *open-market purchase*.

To reduce the money supply, the central bank can make this trade in reverse, selling government bonds that it holds to the public in exchange for currency. After the central bank removes this currency from circulation, the money supply is lower. When the central bank sells government bonds to the public to reduce the money supply, the transaction is an *open-market sale*. Open-market purchases and sales together are called **open-market operations**.

In addition to buying government bonds from the public, the central bank can also increase the money supply by buying newly issued government bonds directly from the government itself. For example, if a country's treasury needs $1 billion to pay for some new highways, it might give an IOU for $1 billion (government bonds) to the central bank in exchange for $1 billion in newly minted currency. The treasury then gives the $1 billion of currency to the road builders. After the treasury has distributed this currency, the amount of money in circulation—the money supply—will be higher by $1 billion. Effectively, this second way of increasing the money supply amounts to the government financing its expenditures by printing money.[4] This practice is most common in developing countries with limited sources of tax revenue or in countries wracked by war or natural disaster, in which government spending often greatly exceeds the amount that can be raised through taxes.[5]

For the rest of this chapter, we assume that the economy has a money supply of M dollars, which is determined by the central bank. The term M may represent M1, M2, or some other measure of money. For the purpose of developing the theoretical model, which measure of money M refers to does not matter.

7.2 PORTFOLIO ALLOCATION AND THE DEMAND FOR ASSETS

Our next goal is to understand how people determine the amount of money they choose to hold. We begin by considering the broader question of how people allocate their wealth among the many different assets that are available, of which money is only one example.

A consumer, a business, a pension fund, a university, or any other holder of wealth must decide how to distribute that wealth among many types of assets. The

---

4. In Chapter 2, we said that the portion of government spending not covered by taxes had to be borrowed from the private sector. Is this still true when the government has the option of paying for its spending by printing money? Yes; for national income accounting purposes, the Bank of Canada is treated as part of the private sector. So, when the government sells government bonds to the Bank in exchange for currency, it is still technically borrowing from the private sector.

5. The financing of government spending through money creation is discussed further in Chapter 15.

set of assets that a holder of wealth chooses to own is called a *portfolio*. The decision about which assets and how much of each asset to hold is called the **portfolio allocation decision**.

The portfolio allocation decision can be complex. Many people make their living by giving financial advice to holders of wealth, and a major branch of economics, called financial economics, is devoted largely to the study of the portfolio allocation decision. But, fundamentally, only three characteristics of assets matter for the portfolio allocation decision: expected return, risk, and liquidity.

EXPECTED RETURN

The rate of return to an asset is the rate of increase in its value per unit of time. For example, the return on a bank account is the interest rate on the account. The return on a share of stock is the dividend paid by the stock plus any increase in the stock's price. Clearly, a high return is a desirable feature for an asset to have: All else being equal, the higher the return a wealth holder's portfolio provides, the more consumption she can enjoy in the future for any given amount of saving done today.

Of course, the return on an asset is not always known in advance. Stock prices may go up or down, for example. Thus, holders of wealth must base their portfolio allocation decisions on **expected returns**, or their best guesses about returns on assets. Everything else being equal, the higher an asset's expected return (after subtracting taxes and fees such as brokers' commissions), the more desirable the asset is and the more of it holders of wealth will want to own.[6]

RISK

The uncertainty about the return an asset will earn relates to the second important characteristic of assets—riskiness. An asset or a portfolio of assets has high **risk** if there is a significant chance that the actual return received will be very different from the expected return. An example of a risky asset is a share in a start-up gene-splicing company that will be worthless if the company fails but will triple in value if the company succeeds. Because most people do not like risk, they hold risky assets only if the expected return is higher than that on relatively safe assets, such as government bonds.

LIQUIDITY

Besides risk and return a third characteristic, liquidity, affects the desirability of assets. The **liquidity** of an asset is the ease and quickness with which it can be exchanged for goods, services, or other assets. Because it is accepted directly in payment, money is a highly liquid asset. An example of an illiquid asset is your automobile: Time and effort are required to exchange a used car for other goods and services; you must find someone interested in buying the car and arrange legal transfer of ownership. Between liquid money and illiquid autos are many assets, such as stocks and bonds, of intermediate liquidity. A share of stock, for example,

---

6. For the purpose of comparing expected returns among assets, returns may be expressed in either real or nominal terms. For any expected rate of inflation, if asset A's nominal return is 1% higher than asset B's nominal return, asset A's expected real return (its nominal return minus expected inflation) will also be 1% higher than asset B's expected real return.

cannot be used directly to pay for groceries as cash can, but stock can be transformed into cash with a short delay and at the cost of a broker's fee.

In addition to making transactions easier and cheaper, liquidity provides flexibility to the holder of wealth. A liquid asset can easily be disposed of if there is an emergency need for funds or if an unexpectedly good financial investment opportunity arises. Thus, everything else being equal, the more liquid an asset is, the more attractive it will be to holders of wealth.

ASSET DEMANDS

Typically, there is a trade-off among the three characteristics that make an asset desirable: a high expected return, safety (low risk), and liquidity. For example, a safe and liquid asset, such as a chequing account, is likely to have a low expected return. The essence of the portfolio allocation decision is determining which assets, taken together, achieve the wealth holder's preferred combination of expected return, safety, and liquidity.

The amount of each particular asset that a holder of wealth desires to include in her portfolio is called her demand for that asset. Because all wealth must be held as some type of asset, the sum of a wealth holder's asset demands must equal her total wealth. For example, suppose that you have wealth of $10,000 and decide to hold $5,000 in stock, $4,000 in bonds, and $1,000 in cash. The sum of your three asset demands must equal your total wealth of $10,000.

7.3 THE DEMAND FOR MONEY

The **demand for money** is the quantity of monetary assets, such as cash and chequing accounts, that people choose to hold in their portfolios. Choosing how much money to demand is, thus, a part of the broader portfolio allocation decision. In general, the demand for money—like the demand for any other asset—will depend on the expected return, risk, and liquidity of money and of other assets.

In practice, two features of money are particularly important. First, money is the most liquid asset. This liquidity is the primary benefit of holding money.[7] Second, money pays a low return (indeed, currency pays a zero nominal return). The low return earned by money, relative to other assets, is the major cost of holding money. People's demand for money is determined by how they trade off their need for liquidity against the cost of a lower return.

In this section, we look at how some key macroeconomic variables affect the demand for money. Although we primarily consider the aggregate, or total, demand for money, the same economic arguments apply to individual money demands. This relation is to be expected, as the aggregate demand for money is the sum of all individual money demands.

The macroeconomic variables that have the greatest effects on money demand are the price level, real income, and interest rates. Higher prices or incomes increase people's need for liquidity and, thus, raise the demand for money. Interest rates affect money demand through the expected return channel: The higher the interest rate on money, the more money people will demand; however, the higher the interest rate paid on alternative assets to money, the more people will want to switch from money to those alternative assets.

---

7. Money also has low risk, but many alternative assets (such as short-term government bonds) are no riskier than money and pay a higher return.

THE PRICE LEVEL

The higher the general level of prices, the more dollars people need to conduct transactions and, thus, the more dollars people will want to hold. For example, 55 years ago, the price level in Canada was about one-tenth of its level today; as your grandfather will tell you, in 1945, a good restaurant meal cost a dollar. Because less money was needed for transactions, the number of dollars your grandfather held in the form of currency or chequing accounts—his nominal demand for money— was probably much smaller than the amount of money you hold today. The general conclusion is that a higher price level, by raising the need for liquidity, increases the nominal demand for money. In fact, because prices are 10 times higher today than they were in 1945, an identical transaction takes 10 times as many dollars today as it did back then. Thus, everything else being equal, the nominal demand for money is *proportional* to the price level.

REAL INCOME

The more transactions that individuals or businesses conduct, the more liquidity they need and the greater is their demand for money. An important factor determining the number of transactions is real income. For example, a large, high-volume supermarket has to deal with a larger number of customers and suppliers and pay more employees than does a corner grocery. Similarly, a high-income individual makes more and larger purchases than a low-income individual. Because higher real income means more transactions and a greater need for liquidity, the amount of money demanded should increase when real income increases.

Unlike the response of money demand to changes in the price level, the increase in money demand need not be proportional to an increase in real income. Actually, a 1% increase in real income usually leads to less than a 1% increase in money demand. One reason that money demand grows more slowly than income is that higher-income individuals and firms typically use their money more efficiently. For example, a high-income individual may open a special cash management account in which money not needed for current transactions is automatically invested in non-monetary assets paying a higher return. Because of minimum-balance requirements and fees, such an account might not be worthwhile for a lower-income individual.

Another reason that money demand grows more slowly than income is that nations' financial sophistication tends to increase as national income grows. In poor countries, people may hold much of their savings in the form of money, for lack of anything better; in richer countries, people have many attractive alternatives to money. Money substitutes, such as credit cards, also become more common as a country becomes richer, again leading to aggregate money demand's growing more slowly than income.

INTEREST RATES

The theory of portfolio allocation implies that with risk and liquidity held constant, the demand for money depends on the expected returns of both money and alternative, non-monetary assets. An increase in the expected return on money increases the demand for money, and an increase in the expected return on alternative assets causes holders of wealth to switch from money to higher-return alternatives, thus lowering the demand for money.

For example, suppose that of your total wealth of $10,000, you have $8,000 in government bonds earning 8% interest and $2,000 in an interest-bearing chequing account earning 3%. You are willing to hold the bank account at a lower return because of the liquidity it provides. But if the interest rate on bonds rises to 10%, and the bank account interest rate remains unchanged, you may decide to switch $1,000 from the bank account into bonds. In making this switch, you reduce your holding of money (your money demand) from $2,000 to $1,000. Effectively, you have chosen to trade some liquidity for the higher return offered by bonds.

Similarly, if the interest rate paid on money rises, holders of wealth will choose to hold more money. In the example, if the bank account begins paying 5% instead of 3%, with bonds still at 8%, you may sell $1,000 of your bonds, lowering your holdings of bonds to $7,000 and increasing your bank balance to $3,000. The sacrifice in return associated with holding money is less than before, so you increase your bank account balance and enjoy the flexibility and other benefits of extra liquidity. Thus, a higher interest rate on money makes the demand for money rise.

In principle, the interest rate on each of the many alternatives to money should affect money demand. However, as previously noted, the many interest rates in the economy generally tend to move up and down together. For the purposes of macroeconomic analysis, therefore, assuming that there is just one nominal interest rate, i, which measures the nominal return on non-monetary assets, is simpler and not too misleading. The nominal interest rate i minus the expected inflation rate π^e gives the expected real interest rate r that is relevant to saving and investment decisions, as discussed in Chapter 4.

Also, in reality, various interest rates are paid on money. For example, currency pays zero interest, but different types of chequable accounts pay varying rates. Again for simplicity, let us assume that there is just one nominal interest rate for money, i^m. The key conclusions are that an increase in the interest rate on nonmonetary assets, i, reduces the amount of money demanded, and an increase in the interest rate on money, i^m, raises the amount of money demanded.

THE MONEY DEMAND FUNCTION

We express the effects of the price level, real income, and interest rates on money as

$$M^d = P \times L\ (Y,\ i), \tag{7.1}$$

where

M^d = the aggregate demand for money, in nominal terms;
P = the price level;
Y = real income or output;
i = the nominal interest rate earned by alternative, non-monetary assets;
L = a function relating money demand to real income and the nominal interest rate.

Equation (7.1) holds that nominal money demand M^d is proportional to the price level P. Hence, if the price level P doubles (and real income and interest rates do not change), nominal money demand M^d also will double, reflecting the fact that twice as much money is needed to conduct the same real transactions. Equation (7.1) also indicates that for any price level P, money demand depends (through the function L) on real income Y and the nominal interest rate on non-monetary assets i. An increase in real income Y raises the demand for liquidity and, thus, increases money demand. An increase in the nominal interest rate i makes nonmonetary assets more attractive, which reduces money demand.

We could have included the nominal interest rate on money, i^m, in Eq. (7.1) because an increase in the interest rate on money makes people more willing to hold money and, thus, increases money demand. Historically, however, the nominal interest rate on money has varied much less than the nominal interest rate on nonmonetary assets (for example, currency and a portion of chequing accounts always have paid zero interest) and, thus, has been ignored by many statistical studies of Eq. (7.1). Thus, for simplicity, we do not explicitly include i^m in the equation.

An equivalent way of writing the demand for money expresses the nominal interest rate i in terms of the expected real interest rate and the expected rate of inflation. Recall from Eq. (2.13) that the expected real interest rate r equals the nominal interest rate i minus the expected rate of inflation π^e. Therefore, the nominal interest rate i equals $r + \pi^e$. Substituting $r + \pi^e$ for i in Eq. (7.1) yields

$$M^d = PL(Y, r + \pi^e). \qquad (7.2)$$

Equation (7.2) shows that for any expected rate of inflation π^e, an increase in the real interest rate increases the nominal interest rate and reduces the demand for money. Similarly, for any real interest rate, an increase in the expected rate of inflation increases the nominal interest rate and reduces the demand for money.

Nominal money demand M^d measures the demand for money in terms of dollars (or yen, or euros). But, sometimes, measuring money demand in real terms is more convenient. If we divide both sides of Eq. (7.2) by the price level P, we get

$$\frac{M^d}{P} = L(Y, \ r + \pi^e). \qquad (7.3)$$

The expression on the left-hand side of Eq. (7.3), M^d/P, is called real money demand or, sometimes, the demand for real balances. Real money demand is the amount of money demanded in terms of the goods it can buy. Equation (7.3) states that real money demand M^d/P depends on real income (or output) Y and on the nominal interest rate, which is the sum of the real interest rate r and expected inflation π^e. The function L that relates real money demand to output and interest rates in Eq. (7.3) is called the **money demand function**.

Other Factors Affecting Money Demand

The money demand function in Eq. (7.3) captures the main macroeconomic determinants of money demand, but some other factors should be mentioned. Besides the nominal interest rate on money, which we have already discussed, additional factors influencing money demand include wealth, risk, liquidity of alternative assets, and payment technologies. Summary table 9 contains a comprehensive list of variables that affect the demand for money.

Wealth

When wealth increases, part of the extra wealth may be held as money, increasing total money demand. However, with income and the level of transactions held constant, a holder of wealth has little incentive to keep extra wealth in money, rather than in higher-return alternative assets. Thus, the effect of an increase in wealth on money demand is likely to be small.

SUMMARY 9   MACROECONOMIC DETERMINANTS OF THE DEMAND FOR MONEY

AN INCREASE IN	CAUSES MONEY DEMAND TO	REASON
Price level, P	Rise proportionally	A doubling of the price level doubles the number of dollars needed for transactions.
Real income, Y	Rise less than proportionally	Higher real income implies more transactions and thus a greater demand for liquidity.
Real interest rate, r	Fall	Higher real interest rate means a higher return on alternative assets and thus a switch away from money.
Expected inflation, π^e	Fall	Higher expected inflation means a higher return on alternative assets and thus a switch away from money.
Nominal interest rate on money, i^m	Rise	A higher return on money makes people more willing to hold money.
Wealth	Rise	Part of an increase in wealth may be held in the form of money.
Risk	Rise, if risk of alternative asset increases	Higher risk of alternative asset makes money more attractive.
	Fall, if risk of money increases	Higher risk of money makes it less attractive.
Liquidity of alternative assets	Fall	Higher liquidity of alternative assets makes these assets more attractive.
Efficiency of payments technologies	Fall	People can operate with less money.

RISK

Money usually pays a fixed nominal interest rate (zero in the case of cash), so holding money itself usually is not risky. However, if the risk of alternative assets, such as stocks and real estate, increases greatly, people may demand safer assets, including money. Thus, increased riskiness in the economy may increase money demand.

However, money does not always carry a low risk. In a period of erratic inflation, even if the nominal return on money is fixed, the real return on money (the nominal return minus inflation) may become quite uncertain, making money risky. Money demand then will fall as people switch to inflation hedges (assets whose real returns are less likely to be affected by erratic inflation), such as gold, consumer durable goods, and real estate.

LIQUIDITY OF ALTERNATIVE ASSETS

The more quickly and easily alternative assets can be converted into cash, the less need there is to hold money. In recent years, the joint impact of deregulation, competition, and innovation in financial markets has made alternatives to money more liquid. We have mentioned individual cash management accounts whose introduction allowed individuals to switch wealth easily between high-return assets, such as stocks, and more liquid forms. As alternative assets become more liquid, the demand for money declines.

PAYMENT TECHNOLOGIES

A last factor affecting money demand is the technology available for making and receiving payments. For example, the introduction of credit cards allowed people to make transactions without money—at least until the end of the month, when a cheque must be written to pay the credit card bill. Automatic teller machines (ATMs) probably have reduced the demand for cash because people know that they can obtain cash quickly whenever they need it. Other innovations like direct payment systems (debit cards) undoubtedly also are reducing the demand for cash. Ultimately, we may live in a "cashless society," in which almost all payments will be made through immediately accessible computerized accounting systems and the demand for traditional forms of money will be close to zero.

ELASTICITIES OF MONEY DEMAND

The theory of portfolio allocation helps economists identify factors that should affect the aggregate demand for money. However, for many purposes—such as forecasting and quantitative analyses of the economy—economists need to know not just which factors affect money demand but also how strong the various effects are. This information can be obtained only through statistical analysis of the data.

Over the past three decades, economists have performed hundreds of statistical studies of the money demand function. The results of these studies often are expressed in terms of elasticities, which measure the change in money demand resulting from changes in factors affecting the demand for money. Specifically, the **income elasticity of money demand** is the percentage change in money demand resulting from a 1% increase in real income. Thus, for example, if the income elasticity of money demand is 2/3, a 3% increase in real income will increase money demand by 2% ($2/3 \times 3\% = 2\%$). Similarly, the **interest elasticity of money demand** is the percentage change in money demand resulting from a 1% increase in the interest rate.

When we work with the interest elasticity of money demand, some care is needed to avoid a potential pitfall. To illustrate, suppose that the interest rate increases from 5% per year to 6% per year. To describe this increase in the interest rate as a 1% increase in the interest rate is tempting (but incorrect). In fact, it is a 20% increase in the interest rate, because 6 is 20% larger than 5.[8] If the interest elasticity of money demand is –0.1, for example, an increase in the interest rate from 5% to 6% reduces money demand by 2% ($-0.1 \times 20\% = -2\%$). Note that if the interest elasticity of money demand is negative, as in this example, an increase in the interest rate reduces money demand.

---

8. The change from 5% to 6% can be described as "a 1 *percentage point* increase", or as "a 20 *percent* increase," or as a "100 *basis point* increase."

What are the actual values of the income elasticity and interest elasticity of money demand? Although the many statistical studies of money demand provide a range of answers, some common results emerge. First, there is widespread evidence that the income elasticity of money demand is positive. For example, in his classic 1973 study of US M1 demand, which established the framework for many later studies, Stephen Goldfeld of Princeton University found this elasticity to be about 0.67.[9] Studies by economists at the Bank of Canada in the 1970s found income elasticities in Canadian M1 demand of about 0.8.[10] A positive income elasticity of money demand implies that money demand rises when income rises, as predicted by our theory. These findings that the income elasticity of money demand is less than 1 are similar to those of many other empirical analyses, although some studies have found values for this elasticity (for example for Canadian M2) as large as 1. An income elasticity of money demand smaller than 1 implies that money demand rises less than proportionally with income. Earlier in the chapter, we discussed some reasons why the demand for money might be expected to grow more slowly than income as an individual or nation becomes richer.

Second, for the interest elasticity of money demand, most studies find a small negative value. For example, the interest elasticity of Canadian M1 demand in the 1970s was estimated to be about –0.3. A negative value for the interest elasticity of money demand implies that when interest rates on non-monetary assets rise, people reduce their holdings of money, again as predicted by the theory.

Finally, many studies have confirmed empirically that the nominal demand for money is proportional to the price level.[11] Again, this result is consistent with the theory, as reflected in the money demand equation, Eq. (7.3).

Application

Financial Innovation and "A Place to Stand"

In the 1970s, a money demand function for M1 in a form similar to Eq. (7.3) fit the Canadian data well. From 1975 to 1982, the Bank of Canada relied on this relationship as part of its strategy of gradualism. During this period, the Bank announced target ranges for the growth rate of M1 with a view to gradually reducing the inflation rate. Section 7.5 explains the economic theory behind this idea. Meanwhile, we shall see that problems arose with relying on the money demand equation in this way.

Almost as soon as the Bank began to announce target growth rates for M1, the demand for M1 turned out to be lower than that predicted from its principal macroeconomic determinants—the price level, income, and interest rates. Numerous explanations have been offered for the instability of money demand. One factor emphasized by many economists was an increased pace of innovation in the financial system during the 1970s and 1980s. Spurred by computerization and in response

9. "The Demand for Money Revisited," *Brookings Papers on Economic Activity*, 1973:4, pp. 577–638. Goldfeld reported elasticities of money demand that applied to the short run and the long run. The figures we present here are long-run elasticities.
10. See, for example, William R. White, "The Demand for Money in Canada and the Control of Monetary Aggregates: Evidence from the Monthly Data," *Bank of Canada Staff Research Study 12*, Ottawa: Bank of Canada, 1976; and Kevin Clinton and Kevin Lynch, "Monetary Base and Money Stock in Canada," *Bank of Canada Technical Report no. 16*, Ottawa: Bank of Canada, 1979.
11. The evidence on this and other aspects of money demand is summarized in David E. W. Laidler, *The Demand for Money*, 4th ed., New York: HarperCollins, 1993.

to high nominal interest rates during the late 1970s, banks and other financial institutions provided the public with many new financial assets to choose from, as well as a variety of new portfolio management techniques. Most of these innovations reduced the demand for narrowly defined money (M1).

For example, in 1976, most banks began to offer improved cash management techniques to large firms. These methods allowed businesses to consolidate their current accounts so that M1 was less than would have been predicted.[12] Financial innovation also reduced households' demand for deposits included in M1. For example, banks introduced daily interest savings accounts (DISAs) in 1979, and daily interest chequing accounts (DICAs) in 1981. DISAs encouraged a shift from M1 to M2 because amounts in savings deposits now earned some interest, even if they were deposited for short periods of time. DICAs were not included in the definition of M1 then, but since they were a close substitute for traditional chequing accounts, their introduction reduced M1 demand.

The Bank of Canada tried to adjust its M1 targets for these shifts in the narrow aggregate, and also redefined M1 to include DICAs. But the Bank eventually concluded that controlling M1 would not lead to reliable control of inflation because of the instability in the demand function.[13] In November 1982, it announced that it had abandoned its M1 targets.

Since 1982, the Bank has not targeted the growth rate of any monetary aggregate, although it has published explicit targets for the rate of inflation since February 1991. However, the Bank argues that real M1 holdings can help predict real output, while M2+ helps predict inflation, and it provides interpretations of changes in the aggregates.[14] Although financial innovation is good for the economy in general, changes in the financial system may continue to make money demand hard to predict.

VELOCITY AND THE QUANTITY THEORY OF MONEY

A concept related to money demand, which at times is used in discussions of monetary policy, is velocity. It measures how often the money stock "turns over" each period. Specifically, **velocity** is nominal GDP (the price level P times real output Y) divided by the nominal money stock M. If we let V represent velocity,

$$V = \frac{\text{nominal GDP}}{\text{nominal money stock}} = \frac{PY}{M}. \tag{7.4}$$

If velocity rises, each dollar of the money stock is being used in a greater dollar volume of transactions in each period, if we assume that the volume of transactions is proportional to GDP. Figure 7.1 shows the M1 and M2 velocities for Canada during the period 1968–2001. The concept of velocity comes from one of the earliest theories

12. See Charles Freedman, "Financial Innovation in Canada: Causes and Consequences," *American Economic Review*, Papers and Proceedings, May 1983, pp. 101–106.

13. See Gerald K. Bouey, "Monetary Policy—Finding a Place to Stand," *Bank of Canada Review*, September 1992, pp. 3–17; and Thomas J. Courchene, *No Place to Stand? Abandoning Monetary Targets: An Evaluation*, Toronto: C. D. Howe Institute, 1983.

14. See, for example, Joseph Atta-Mensah, "Recent Developments in the monetary aggregates, and their implications," *Bank of Canada Review*, Spring 2000, pp. 3–10, or the semi-annual *Monetary Policy Report*.

of money demand, the **quantity theory of money**.[15] The quantity theory of money asserts that real money demand is proportional to real income, or

$$\frac{M^d}{P} = kY, \tag{7.5}$$

where M^d/P is real money demand, Y is real income, and k is a constant. In Eq. (7.5), the real money demand function $L(Y, r + \pi^e)$ takes the simple form kY. This way of writing money demand is based on the strong assumption that velocity is a constant, $1/k$, and does not depend on income or interest rates.[16]

Is velocity actually a constant? As Figure 7.1 shows, M1 velocity clearly is not a constant: M1 velocity rose steadily during the 1970s, then became more volatile in the 1980s, before declining in the 1990s. Financial innovations played a role in slowing the growth of M1 velocity in the 1980s. As discussed, the popularity of new interest-bearing chequing accounts during this period raised the demand for M1 at any level of GDP and thereby lowered its velocity. But, in addition, the quantity theory's assumption that interest rates do not affect money demand—an assumption contradicted by most empirical studies—probably contributed to that theory's misprediction of M1 demand in the 1990s. Lower interest rates on non-monetary assets in the early 1990s increased people's willingness to hold low-interest or zero-

---

15. The quantity theory of money was developed by several classical economists, notably Irving Fisher, in the late 19th and early 20th centuries. A famous statement of the theory is contained in Fisher's book *The Purchasing Power of Money*, New York: Macmillan, 1911.

16. To derive velocity under the quantity theory, we must assume that nominal money demand M^d equals the actual money stock M, an assumption that we justify later in the chapter. Under this assumption, you should verify that $V = 1/k$.

Figure 7.1

Velocity of M1 and M2, 1968–2001

M1 velocity is nominal GDP divided by M1, and M2 velocity is nominal GDP divided by M2. M1 velocity rose through the 1970s, then became more erratic in the 1980s, before falling in the 1990s. M2 velocity, while declining steadily, has been more stable than M1 velocity, but it has been unpredictable over some short time periods.

Source: Statistics Canada, CANSIM Series B1627 (M1), B1630 (M2), D14816 (GDP). Series are in millions of dollars, quarterly, and seasonally adjusted.

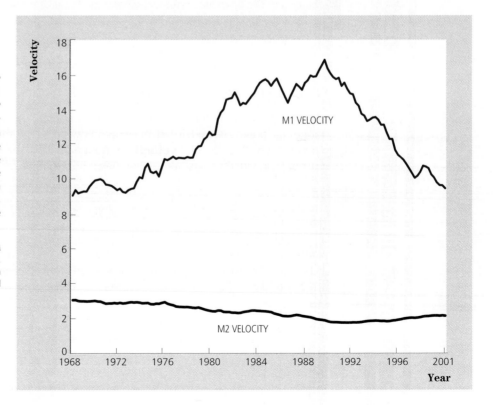

interest money, which raised the demand for M1 at any level of GDP and thus reduced M1 velocity.

M2 velocity, also shown in Figure 7.1, is more stable. It shows a gradual downward trend over the period 1968–2001. However, even M2 velocity has been somewhat unpredictable over short periods. During the late 1990s, for example, M2 velocity rose significantly more than economists predicted, as savings shifted into mutual funds, which are not included in M2. Thus, although M2 velocity is more stable than M1 velocity, most economists would be reluctant to treat M2 velocity as a constant.

7.4 ASSET MARKET EQUILIBRIUM

Recall that the asset market actually is a set of markets, in which real and financial assets are traded. The demand for any asset (say, government bonds) is the quantity of the asset that holders of wealth want in their portfolios. The demand for each asset depends on its expected return, risk, and liquidity relative to other assets. The supply of each asset is the quantity of that asset that is available. At any particular time, the supplies of individual assets are typically fixed, although over time asset supplies change (the government may issue more bonds, firms may issue new shares, more gold may be mined, and so on).

The asset market is in equilibrium when the quantity of each asset that holders of wealth demand equals the (fixed) available supply of that asset. In this section, we examine asset market equilibrium, focusing on the role of money. We then show how asset market equilibrium is linked to the price level.

ASSET MARKET EQUILIBRIUM: AN AGGREGATION ASSUMPTION

In analyzing the labour market in Chapter 3 and the goods market in Chapter 4, we relied on aggregation to keep things manageable. That is, instead of looking at the supply of and demand for each of the many different types of labour and goods in the economy, we studied the supply of and demand for both labour and goods in general. Aggregating in this way allowed us to analyze the behaviour of the economy as a whole without getting lost in the details.

Because there are many different types of assets, aggregation is equally necessary for studying the asset market. Thus, we adopt an aggregation assumption for the asset market that economists often make for macroeconomic analysis: We assume that all assets may be grouped into two categories, money and non-monetary assets. Money includes assets that can be used in payment, such as currency and chequing accounts. All money is assumed to have the same risk and liquidity and to pay the same nominal interest rate, i^m. The fixed nominal supply of money is M. Non-monetary assets include all assets other than money, such as stocks, bonds, land, and so on. All non-monetary assets are assumed to have the same risk and liquidity and to pay a nominal interest rate of $i = r + \pi^e$, where r is the expected real interest rate and π^e is the expected rate of inflation. The fixed nominal supply of non-monetary assets is NM.

Although the assumption that assets can be aggregated into two types ignores many interesting differences among assets, it greatly simplifies our analysis and has proved to be very useful. One immediate benefit of making this assumption is that if we allow for only two types of assets, *asset market equilibrium reduces to the condition that the quantity of money supplied equals the quantity of money demanded.*

To demonstrate this point, let us look at the portfolio allocation decision of an individual named Ed. Ed has a fixed amount of wealth that he allocates between money and non-monetary assets. If m^d is the nominal amount of money and nm^d is the nominal amount of non-monetary assets that Ed wants to hold, the sum of Ed's desired money holdings and his desired holdings of non-monetary assets must be his total wealth, or

$$m^d + nm^d = \text{Ed's total nominal wealth.}$$

This equation has to be true for every holder of wealth in the economy.

Suppose that we sum this equation across all holders of wealth in the economy. Then, the sum of all individual money demands m^d equals the aggregate demand for money M^d. The sum of all individual demands for non-monetary assets is the aggregate demand for non-monetary assets, NM^d. Finally, adding nominal wealth for all holders of wealth gives the aggregate nominal wealth of the economy, or

$$M^d + NM^d = \text{aggregate nominal wealth.} \tag{7.6}$$

Equation (7.6) states that the total demand for money in the economy plus the total demand for non-monetary assets must equal the economy's total nominal wealth.

Next, we relate the total supplies of money and non-monetary assets to aggregate wealth. Because money and non-monetary assets are the only assets in the economy, aggregate nominal wealth equals the supply of money M plus the supply of non-monetary assets NM, or

$$M + NM = \text{aggregate nominal wealth.} \tag{7.7}$$

Finally, we subtract Eq. (7.7) from Eq. (7.6) to obtain

$$(M^d - M) + (NM^d - NM) = 0. \tag{7.8}$$

The term $M^d - M$ in Eq. (7.8) is the *excess demand for money*, or the amount by which the total amount of money demanded exceeds the money supply. Similarly, the term $NM^d - NM$ in Eq. (7.8) is the *excess demand for non-monetary assets*.

Now, suppose that the demand for money M^d equals the money supply M so that the excess demand for money $M^d - M$ is zero. Equation (7.8) shows that if $M^d - M$ is zero, $NM^d - NM$ must also be zero; that is, if the amounts of money supplied and demanded are equal, the amounts of non-monetary assets supplied and demanded also must be equal. By definition, if quantities supplied and demanded are equal for each type of asset, the asset market is in equilibrium.

If we make the simplifying assumption that assets can be lumped into monetary and non-monetary categories, the asset market is in equilibrium only if the quantity of money supplied equals the quantity of money demanded. This result is convenient because it means that in studying asset market equilibrium, we only have to look at the supply of and demand for money and can ignore non-monetary assets. As long as the amounts of money supplied and demanded are equal, the entire asset market will be in equilibrium.

THE ASSET MARKET EQUILIBRIUM CONDITION

Equilibrium in the asset market occurs when the quantity of money supplied equals the quantity of money demanded. This condition is valid whether money supply and demand are expressed in nominal terms or real terms. We work with this condition in real terms, or

$$\frac{M}{P} = L(Y, \ r + \pi^e). \tag{7.9}$$

The left-hand side of Eq. (7.9) is the nominal supply of money M divided by the price level P, which is the supply of money measured in real terms. The right-hand side of the equation is the same as the real demand for money M^d/P, as in Eq. (7.3). Equation (7.9), which states that the real quantity of money supplied equals the real quantity of money demanded, is called the asset market equilibrium condition.

The asset market equilibrium condition involves five variables: the nominal money supply M, the price level P, real income Y, the real interest rate r, and the expected rate of inflation π^e. The nominal money supply M is determined by the central bank through its open-market operations. For now, we treat the expected rate of inflation π^e as fixed (we return to the determination of expected inflation later in the chapter). That leaves three variables in the asset market equilibrium condition whose values we have not yet specified: output Y, the real interest rate r, and the price level P.

In this part of the book, we have made the assumption that the economy is at full employment or, equivalently, that all markets are in equilibrium. Both classical and Keynesian economists agree that the full-employment assumption is reasonable for analyzing the long-term behaviour of the economy. If we continue to assume full employment,[17] we can use the analysis from previous chapters to describe how output and the real interest rate are determined. Recall from Chapter 3 that if the labour market is in equilibrium—with employment at its full-employment level— output equals full-employment output $\bar{Y}$. Chapter 4 showed that, for any level of output, the real interest rate must take the value that makes desired national saving and desired investment equal (the goods market equilibrium condition).

With the values of output and the real interest rate established by equilibrium in the labour and goods markets, the only variable left to be determined by the asset market equilibrium condition is the price level P. To emphasize that the price level is the variable determined by asset market equilibrium, we multiply both sides of Eq. (7.9) by P and divide both sides by real money demand, $L(Y, r + \pi^e)$, to obtain

$$P = \frac{M}{L(Y, \ r + \pi^e)}. \tag{7.10}$$

According to Eq. (7.10), the economy's price level P equals the ratio of the nominal money supply M to the real demand for money $L(Y, r + \pi^e)$. For given values of real output Y, the real interest rate r, and the expected rate of inflation π^e, the real demand for money $L(Y, r + \pi^e)$ is fixed. Thus, Eq. (7.10) states that the price level is proportional to the nominal money supply. A doubling of the nominal money supply M, for instance, would double the price level P, with other factors held constant. The existence of a close link between the price level and the money supply in an economy is one of the oldest and most reliable conclusions about macroeconomic behaviour, having been recognized in some form for hundreds if not thousands of years. We discuss the empirical support for this link in Section 7.5.

What forces lead the price level to its equilibrium value, Eq. (7.10)? A complete description of how the price level adjusts to its equilibrium value involves an analysis of the goods market as well as the asset market; we leave this task until Chapter 9, where we discuss the links among the three main markets of the economy in more

---

17. We relax this assumption in Part III when we discuss short-run economic fluctuations.

detail. Briefly, in Chapter 9, we show that an increase in the money supply leads people to increase their nominal spending on goods and services; this increased nominal demand for output leads prices to rise. Prices continue to rise until people are content to hold the increased nominal quantity of money in their portfolios, satisfying the asset market equilibrium condition (rewritten as Eq. 7.10).

7.5 MONEY GROWTH AND INFLATION

In Section 7.4, we established that when the markets for labour, goods, and assets are all in equilibrium, the price level P is proportional to the nominal money supply M. However, the price level itself generally is of less concern to policymakers and the public than is the rate of inflation, or the percentage rate of increase of the price level. In this section, we extend our analysis of the price level to show how inflation is determined. We conclude that the inflation rate, which is the growth rate of the price level, is closely related to the growth rate of the nominal money supply.

To obtain an equation for the rate of inflation in a full-employment economy, we set the growth rate of the left-hand side of Eq. (7.10) equal to the growth rate of its right-hand side to obtain

$$\frac{\Delta P}{P} = \frac{\Delta M}{M} - \frac{\Delta L(Y, \; r + \pi^e)}{L(Y, \; r + \pi^e)}, \qquad (7.11)$$

where the symbol Δ indicates the change in a variable from one year to the next. The left-hand side of Eq. (7.11) is the growth rate of the price level, $\Delta P/P$, which is the same as the inflation rate π. The right-hand side of Eq. (7.11) expresses the growth rate of the ratio on the right-hand side of Eq. (7.10) as the growth rate of the numerator, M, minus the growth rate of the denominator, $L(Y, r + \pi^e)$. (Appendix Section A.7 provides some useful formulas for calculating growth rates.) Equation (7.11) shows that if the asset market is in equilibrium, *the rate of inflation equals the growth rate of the nominal money supply minus the growth rate of real money demand.*

Equation (7.11) highlights the point that the rate of inflation is closely related to the rate of growth of the nominal money supply. However, to use Eq. (7.11) to predict the behaviour of inflation, we must also know how quickly real money demand is growing. The money demand function, Eq. (7.3), focused on two macroeconomic variables with significant effects on real money demand: income (or output) Y and the nominal interest rate $r + \pi^e$. We show later in this section that in a long-run equilibrium with a constant growth rate of money, the nominal interest rate will be constant. Therefore, here we look only at growth in income as a source of growth in real money demand.

Earlier, we defined the income elasticity of money demand to be the percentage change in money demand resulting from a 1% increase in real income. If $\Delta Y/Y$ is the percentage change in real income from one year to the next and η_Y is the income elasticity of money demand, $\eta_Y \Delta Y/Y$ is the resulting increase in the real demand for money, with other factors affecting money demand held constant. Substituting π for $\Delta P/P$ and $\eta_Y \Delta Y/Y$ for the growth rate of real money demand in Eq. (7.11) yields

$$\pi = \frac{\Delta M}{M} - \eta_Y \frac{\Delta Y}{Y}. \qquad (7.12)$$

Equation (7.12) is a useful simple expression for the rate of inflation. According to Eq. (7.12), the rate of inflation equals the growth rate of the nominal money supply minus an adjustment for the growth rate of real money demand arising from growth in real output. For example, suppose that nominal money supply growth is 10% per year, real income is growing by 3% per year, and the income elasticity of money demand is 2/3. Then, Eq. (7.12) predicts that the inflation rate will be 10% − (2/3)(3%), or 8% per year.

APPLICATION

MONEY GROWTH AND INFLATION IN EUROPEAN COUNTRIES IN TRANSITION

The fall of communism in Eastern Europe and the breakup of the Soviet Union led to economic, political, and social upheaval. All these countries, to varying degrees, have introduced reforms intended to make their economies more market oriented, and many (particularly the new countries formed from the breakup of the Soviet Union) have introduced new currencies. However, Russia and many of the Eastern European economies have continued to face serious problems, including very high rates of inflation. The main reason for the high inflation rates is the rapid rates of money growth in these countries.

In general, both the growth of the nominal money supply and the growth of real money demand (resulting from real income growth, for example) affect the rate of inflation (see Eq. 7.12). In countries with high inflation, however, the growth of the nominal money supply usually is the much more important of these two factors. To illustrate, if the income elasticity of money demand in a country is 2/3, and real output were to grow at the stunning rate of 15% per year, then, according to Eq. (7.12), real money demand would grow at 10% per year (2/3 × 15%) in that country. If a second country also has an income elasticity of 2/3, but its income is falling at the painful rate of 15% per year, the rate of growth of real money demand is −10% per year. Thus, even with these radically different income growth rates, the difference in the growth rates of real money demand is only 20% per year.

In contrast to the relatively modest differences among countries in the growth rates of real money demand, rates of growth of nominal money supplies may vary among countries by hundreds of percentage points per year. Thus, large differences in inflation rates among countries almost always are the result of large differences in rates of money growth.

The link between money growth and inflation is illustrated in Figure 7.2, which shows the average annual values of these rates during 1998–2000 for the European countries designated by the International Monetary Fund as "countries in transition." Most of these countries (with the exception of Turkey) are in the process of moving away from communism toward market-based systems. Belarus experienced the highest rates of money growth and inflation during this three-year period. Its average annual money growth rate was 148 percent, and its average annual inflation rate was 178 percent. Those high rates are not shown on Figure 7.2 so that the scale of the figure allows you to see differences among the other countries. The two countries that had the highest inflation rates—Belarus and Turkey—also had the highest money growth rates.

Whether we compare inflation rates between these two countries or compare their high inflation rates with the lower inflation rates of the remaining twelve countries shown, large differences in inflation rates clearly are associated with large differences in rates of money growth.

FIGURE 7.2

THE RELATIONSHIP
BETWEEN MONEY GROWTH
AND INFLATION

Nominal money growth and
inflation during the period
1998–2000 are plotted for the
European countries in transition. There is a strong relationship between money
growth rates and inflation
rates, with countries having
double-digit inflation rates also
having double-digit money
growth rates.

Source: Money growth rates and
consumer price inflation from
International Financial Statistics,
August 2001, pp. 60–61.

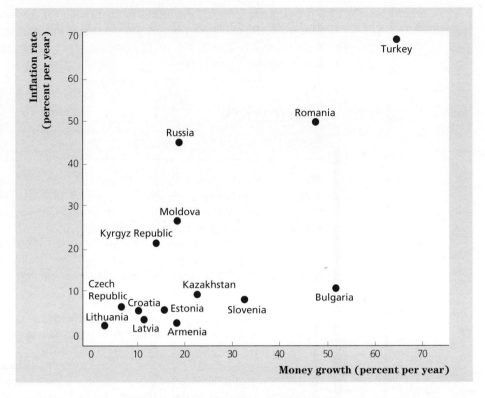

If rapid money growth causes inflation, why do countries allow their money supplies
to grow so quickly? As we discussed earlier, governments sometimes find that
printing money (borrowing from the central bank) is the only way that they can
finance their expenditures. This situation is most likely to occur in poor countries or
countries that undergo economic upheaval associated with war, natural disaster, or
(as in the case of the Eastern European countries) major political and economic
change. Unfortunately, the almost inevitable result of financing government
expenditures in this way is increased inflation.

THE EXPECTED INFLATION RATE AND THE NOMINAL INTEREST RATE

In our earlier discussion of asset market equilibrium, we made the assumption that
the expected inflation rate is fixed. For a given real interest rate r (which is
determined by the goods market equilibrium condition), if the expected inflation
rate π^e is fixed, so is the nominal interest rate, at $r + \pi^e$. We close the chapter with
a brief look at the factors that determine the expected inflation rate and the nominal
interest rate.

What should holders of wealth and others expect the inflation rate to be in the
future? As we demonstrated, Eq. (7.12), which relates inflation to the growth rates
of the nominal money supply and real income, is useful for predicting inflation. For
expected values of money growth (based, for example, on plans announced by the
central bank) and real income growth, as well as an estimate of the income elasticity

of money demand, Eq. (7.12) can be used to calculate the expected inflation rate. Suppose that people in a particular country expect their nation's money supply to grow much more rapidly over the next two years because the government is committed to large military expenditures and can pay for these expenditures only by printing money. In this case, Eq. (7.12) shows that people should expect much higher inflation rates in the future.

The inflation prediction equation, Eq. (7.12), is particularly easy to apply when the growth rates of the nominal money supply and real income are constant over time. In this case, the expected growth rates of the nominal money supply and real income equal their current growth rates, and (from Eq. 7.12) the expected inflation rate equals the current inflation rate (assuming no change in the income elasticity of money demand). In practice, the current inflation rate often approximates the expected inflation rate, as long as people do not expect money or income growth to change too much in the near future.

The public's expected inflation rate is not directly observable, except perhaps through surveys and similar methods. However, an observable economic variable that is strongly affected by expected inflation is the nominal interest rate. At any real interest rate r, which is determined by the goods market equilibrium condition that desired national saving equals desired investment, the nominal interest rate $r + \pi^e$ changes one-for-one with changes in the expected inflation rate π^e. Thus, policy actions (such as rapid expansion of the money supply) that cause people to fear future increases in inflation should cause nominal interest rates to rise, all else being equal.

But, as already noted, if people do not expect large changes in the growth rates of the money supply or real income, expected inflation will not be much different from current inflation. In this case, nominal interest rates and current inflation rates

FIGURE 7.3

INFLATION AND THE NOMINAL INTEREST RATE IN CANADA, 1949–2001

The figure shows the nominal interest rate on one- to three-year government bonds and the annual rate of inflation as measured by the CPI. The nominal interest rate tends to move together with inflation, although there are periods, such as the early 1980s and mid-1990s, when the two variables diverge.

Source: Nominal interest rate is the annual average yield on one- to three-year Government of Canada bonds from the *Bank of Canada Review,* Table F1 (reprinted with permission of the Bank of Canada) or Statistics Canada, CANSIM Series B14009. Inflation is the rate of change of the consumer price index from *Canadian Economic Observer, Historical Statistical Summary,* Table 12 or CANSIM P100000.

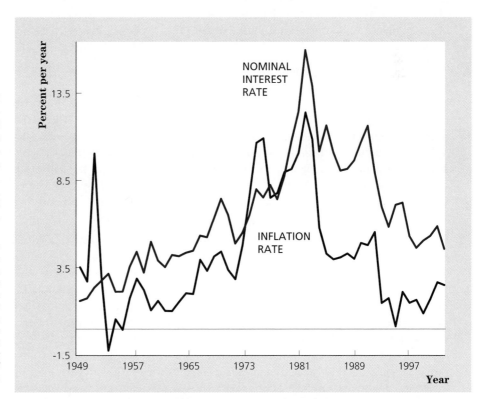

should move together. If current inflation is high, for example, expected inflation also is likely to be high; but high expected inflation also causes nominal interest rates to be high, all else being equal.

The historical relationship between nominal interest rates and inflation is illustrated by Figure 7.3, which shows the nominal interest rate on one- to three-year Government of Canada bonds and the annual inflation rate measured by the CPI in Canada from 1949 to 2001. The nominal interest rate and the inflation rate have tended to move together, rising during the 1960s and 1970s and then falling sharply after reaching a peak in 1981. However, movements in the inflation rate are not perfectly matched by movements in the nominal interest rate because the real interest rate has not been constant over this period. In particular, during the late 1970s and early 1980s, the rise in the nominal interest rate was much greater than the rise in the inflation rate, reflecting an increase in the real interest rate from a negative value in the mid-1970s to much higher, positive values in the 1980s. The real interest rate declined in the 1990s, but remained above the levels observed in the 1960s and 1970s. (See Figure 2.3, p. 48, for a graph of the real interest rate.)

CHAPTER SUMMARY

1. Money is the set of assets that are widely used and accepted as payment, such as currency and chequing accounts. Money functions as a medium of exchange, a unit of account, and a store of value.

2. The supply of money is influenced by the central bank—the Bank of Canada in Canada. The central bank's official measures of money are called the monetary aggregates. M1, which is made up primarily of currency and chequing accounts, and M2, which includes a broader set of monetary assets, are the monetary aggregates that are most widely watched.

3. A portfolio allocation decision is made by a holder of wealth when determining which assets and how much of each asset to hold. The three characteristics of assets that most affect their desirability are expected return, risk, and liquidity.

4. Money demand is the total amount of money that people choose to hold in their portfolios. The principal macroeconomic variables that affect money demand are the price level, real income, and interest rates. Nominal money demand is proportional to the price level. Higher real income increases the number of transactions and, thus,

raises real money demand. A higher interest rate on alternative, non-monetary assets lowers real money demand by making the alternative assets more attractive than money. The money demand function measures the relationship between real money demand and these macroeconomic variables.

5. Velocity is the ratio of nominal GDP to the nominal money stock. The quantity theory of money is an early theory of money demand that assumes that velocity is constant so that money demand is proportional to income. Historically, M2 velocity has been more stable than M1 velocity, although even M2 velocity is not constant.

6. Under the simplifying assumption that assets can be grouped into two categories—money and non-monetary assets—the asset market is in equilibrium if the quantity of money supplied equals the quantity of money demanded. When all markets are in equilibrium (the economy is at full employment), the level of output is determined by equilibrium in the labour market, the real interest rate is determined by equilibrium in the goods market, and the price level is determined by

equilibrium in the asset market. The equilibrium price level is proportional to the nominal money supply.

7. When all markets are in equilibrium, the inflation rate equals the growth rate of the nominal money supply minus the growth rate of real money demand. The growth rate of real money demand, in turn, depends primarily on the real income growth rate. Expected inflation depends on expected growth rates of the nominal money supply and real income. For a given real interest rate, the nominal interest rate responds one-for-one to changes in expected inflation.

KEY TERMS

demand for money, p. 244
expected returns, p. 243
income elasticity of money demand, p. 249
interest elasticity of money demand, p. 249
liquidity, p. 243
M1, p. 238
M2, p. 241
M2+, p. 241
M3, p. 241
medium of exchange, p. 236
monetary aggregates, p. 238
money, p. 235
money demand function, p. 247
money supply, p. 241
open-market operations, p. 242
portfolio allocation decision, p. 243
quantity theory of money, p. 252
risk, p. 243
store of value, p. 237
unit of account, p. 236
velocity, p. 251

KEY EQUATIONS

$$\frac{M^d}{P} = L(Y,\ r + \pi^e) \qquad (7.3)$$

According to the money demand function, the real quantity of money demanded, M^d/P, depends on output and the nominal interest rate on alternative, non-monetary assets. An increase in output, Y, raises the number of transactions people make and, thus, raises the demand for money. An increase in the nominal interest rate on non-monetary assets, i (which equals the real interest rate, r, plus the expected

rate of inflation, π^e) raises the attractiveness of alternative assets and, thus, reduces the demand for money.

$$V = \frac{\text{nominal GDP}}{\text{nominal money stock}} = \frac{PY}{M} \qquad (7.4)$$

Velocity V is nominal GDP, or P times Y, divided by the nominal money stock, M. Velocity is assumed to be constant by the quantity theory of money.

$$\frac{M}{P} = L(Y,\ r + \pi^e) \qquad (7.9)$$

The asset market equilibrium condition states that the real supply of money, M/P, and the real demand for money, $L(Y, r + \pi^e)$, are equal.

$$\pi = \frac{\Delta M}{M} - \eta_Y \frac{\Delta Y}{Y} \qquad (7.12)$$

The inflation rate, π, equals the growth rate of the nominal money supply, $\Delta M/M$, minus the growth rate of real money demand. The growth rate of real money demand equals the income elasticity of money demand, η_Y, times the growth rate of real income or output, $\Delta Y/Y$.

REVIEW QUESTIONS

1. Define *money*. How does the economist's use of this term differ from its everyday meaning?
2. What are the three functions of money? How does each function contribute to a more smoothly operating economy?
3. Who determines the country's money supply? Explain how the money supply could be expanded or reduced in an economy in which all money is in the form of currency.
4. What are the three characteristics of assets that are most important to holders of wealth? How does money compare with other assets for each characteristic?
5. List and discuss the macroeconomic variables that affect the aggregate demand for money.
6. Define velocity. Discuss the role of velocity in the quantity theory of money.
7. Why is equilibrium in the asset market described by the condition that real money supply equal real money demand? What is the aggregation assumption that is needed to allow ignoring the markets for other assets?
8. What is the relationship between the price level and the nominal money supply when all markets are in equilibrium? What is the relationship between inflation and the nominal money supply?

9. Give an example of a factor that would increase the public's expected rate of inflation. All else being equal, how would this increase in the expected inflation rate affect interest rates?

NUMERICAL PROBLEMS

1. Money demand in an economy in which no interest is paid on money is

$$\frac{M^d}{P} = 500 + 0.2Y - 1{,}000i$$

a. You know that $P = 100$, $Y = 1{,}000$, and $i = 0.10$. Find real money demand, nominal money demand, and velocity.

b. The price level doubles from $P = 100$ to $P = 200$. Find real money demand, nominal money demand, and velocity.

c. Starting from the values of the variables given in part (a) and assuming that the money demand function as written holds, determine how velocity is affected by an increase in real income, by an increase in the nominal interest rate, and by an increase in the price level.

2. Mr. Midas has wealth of $100,000 that he invests entirely in money (a chequing account) and government bonds. Mr. Midas instructs his broker to invest $50,000 in bonds, plus $5,000 more in bonds for every percentage point that the interest rate on bonds exceeds the interest rate on his chequing account.

a. Write an algebraic formula that gives Mr. Midas's demand for money as a function of bond and chequing account interest rates.

b. Write an algebraic formula that gives Mr. Midas's demand for bonds. What is the sum of his demand for money and his demand for bonds?

c. Suppose that all holders of wealth in the economy are identical to Mr. Midas. Fixed asset supplies per person are $80,000 of bonds and $20,000 of chequing accounts. Chequing accounts pay no interest. What is the interest rate on bonds in asset market equilibrium?

3. Assume that the quantity theory of money holds and that velocity is constant at 5.0. Output is fixed at its full-employment value of 10,000, and the price level is 2.0.

a. Determine the real demand for money and the nominal demand for money.

b. In this same economy, the government fixes the nominal money supply at 5,000. With output fixed at its full-employment level and with the assumption that prices are flexible, what will be the new price level? What happens to the price level if the nominal money supply rises to 6,000?

4. Consider an economy with a constant nominal money supply, a constant level of real output $Y = 100$, and a constant real interest rate $r = 0.10$. Suppose that the income elasticity of money demand is 0.5 and the interest elasticity of money demand is -0.1.

a. By what percentage does the equilibrium price level differ from its initial value if output increases to $Y = 106$ (and r remains at 0.10)? (*Hint*: Use Eq. 7.11.)

b. By what percentage does the equilibrium price level differ from its initial value if the real interest increases to $r = 0.11$ (and Y remains at 100)?

c. Suppose that the real interest rate increases to $r = 0.11$. What would real output have to be in order for the equilibrium price level to remain at its initial value?

5. Suppose that the real money demand function is

$$L(Y, \ r + \pi^e) = \frac{0.01Y}{(r + \pi^e)},$$

where Y is real output, r is the real interest rate, and π^e is the expected rate of inflation. Real output is constant over time at $Y = 150$. The real interest is fixed in the goods market at $r = 0.05$ per year.

a. Suppose that the nominal money supply is growing at the rate of 10% per year and that this growth rate is expected to persist forever. Currently, the nominal money supply is $M = 300$. What are the values of the real money supply and the current price level? (*Hint*: What is the value of the expected inflation rate that enters the money demand function?)

b. Suppose that the nominal money supply is $M = 300$. The central bank announces that from now on, the nominal money supply is going to grow at the rate of 5% per year. If everyone believes this announcement, and if all markets are in equilibrium, what are the values of the real money supply and the current price level? Explain the effects on the real money supply and the current price level of a slowdown in the rate of money growth.

6. The income elasticity of money demand is 2/3 and the interest elasticity of money demand is -0.1. Real income is expected to grow by 4.5% over the next year, and the real interest rate is expected to remain constant over the next year. The rate of inflation has been zero for several years.

a. If the central bank wants zero inflation over the next year, then what growth rate of the nominal money supply should it choose?

b. By how much will velocity change over the next year if the central bank follows the policy that achieves zero inflation?

ANALYTICAL PROBLEMS

1. All else being equal, how would each of the following affect the demand for M1? The demand for M2? Explain.

   a. The maximum number of cheques per month that can be written on money market mutual funds is raised from 3 to 30.

   b. Banks begin to pay interest on current accounts held by firms.

   c. The stock market crashes, and further sharp declines in the market are widely feared.

   d. Banks introduce overdraft protection, under which funds are automatically transferred from savings to chequing as needed to cover cheques.

   e. A crackdown reduces the illegal drug trade (which is carried out largely in currency).

2. Figure 7.1 shows that before the 1990s, M1 velocity generally rose over time. Suggest some explanations for this upward trend.

3. The prisoner-of-war camp described by Radford (Box 7.1) periodically received large shipments of cigarettes from the Red Cross or other sources.

   a. How did cigarette shipments affect the price level (the prices of goods in terms of cigarettes) in the POW camp?

   b. (More difficult) On some occasions the prisoners knew in advance when the cigarette shipments were to arrive. What happened to the demand for cigarette money and the price level in the camp in the days just before an anticipated shipment?

4. Assume that prices and wages adjust rapidly so that the markets for labour, goods, and assets are always in equilibrium. What are the effects of each of the following on output, the real interest rate, and the current price level?

   a. A temporary increase in government purchases.

   b. A reduction in expected inflation.

   c. A temporary increase in labour supply.

   d. An increase in the interest rate paid on money.

Part III
BUSINESS CYCLES AND MACROECONOMIC POLICY

Chapter 8
BUSINESS CYCLES

Since the Industrial Revolution, the economies of Canada and many other countries have grown tremendously. That growth has transformed economies and greatly improved living standards. Yet, even in prosperous countries, economic expansion has been periodically interrupted by episodes of declining production, income, and spending and rising unemployment. Sometimes—fortunately, not very often—these episodes have been severe and prolonged. But whether brief or more extended, declines in economic activity have been followed almost invariably by a resumption of economic growth.

This repeated sequence of economic expansion giving way to temporary decline followed by recovery, is known as the *business cycle*. The business cycle is a central concern in macroeconomics because business cycle fluctuations—the ups and downs in overall economic activity—are felt throughout the economy. When the economy is growing strongly, prosperity is shared by most of the country's industries and their workers and owners of capital. When the economy weakens, many sectors of the economy experience declining sales and production, and the number of unemployed workers increases. Because the effects of business cycles are so widespread, and because economic downturns can cause great hardship, economists have tried to find the causes of these episodes and to determine what, if anything, can be done to counteract them. The two basic questions (1) what causes business cycles, and (2) how policymakers should respond to cyclical fluctuations are the main concern of Part III of this book.

The answers to these two questions remain highly controversial. Much of this controversy involves the proponents of the classical and Keynesian approaches to macroeconomics, introduced in Chapter 1. In brief, classical economists view business cycles as generally representing the economy's best response to disturbances in production or spending. Thus, classical economists do not see much, if any, need for government action to counteract these fluctuations. In contrast, Keynesian economists argue that because wages and prices adjust slowly, disturbances in production or spending may drive the economy away from its most desirable level of output and employment for long periods of time. According to the Keynesian view, there may be a role for government to smooth business cycle fluctuations.

We explore the debate between classicals and Keynesians, and the implications of that debate for economic analysis and macroeconomic policy, in Chapters 9 to 12. This chapter provides essential background for that discussion by presenting the basic features of the business cycle. We begin with a definition and a brief history of the business cycle in Canada. We then turn to a more detailed discussion of business cycle characteristics, or "business cycle facts." We conclude the chapter with a brief preview of the alternative approaches to the analysis of business cycles.

8.1 WHAT IS A BUSINESS CYCLE?

Countries have experienced ups and downs in overall economic activity since they began to industrialize. Economists have measured and studied these fluctuations for more than a century. Marx and Engels referred to "commercial crises," an early term for business cycles, in their *Communist Manifesto* in 1848. In the United States, the National Bureau of Economic Research (NBER), a private nonprofit organization of economists founded in 1920, pioneered business cycle research. The NBER developed and continues to update the **business cycle chronology**, a detailed history of business cycles in the United States and other countries. The NBER has also sponsored many studies of the business cycle: One landmark study was the 1946 book *Measuring Business Cycles*, by Arthur Burns and Wesley Mitchell. This work was among the first to document and analyse the empirical facts about business cycles. It begins with the following definition:

> Business cycles are a type of fluctuation found in the aggregate economic activity of nations that organize their work mainly in business enterprises. A cycle consists of expansions occurring at about the same time in many economic activities, followed by similarly general recessions, contractions, and revivals which merge into the expansion phase of the next cycle; this sequence of changes is recurrent but not periodic; in duration business cycles vary from more than one year to ten or twelve years.[1]

Five points in this definition should be clarified and emphasized.

1. *Aggregate economic activity.* Business cycles are defined broadly as fluctuations of "aggregate economic activity," rather than as fluctuations in a single, specific economic variable, such as real GDP. Although real GDP may be the single variable that most closely measures aggregate economic activity, Burns and Mitchell also thought it important to look at other indicators of activity, such as employment and financial market variables.

2. *Expansions and contractions.* Figure 8.1—a diagram of a typical business cycle—helps explain what Burns and Mitchell meant by expansions and contractions. The dashed line shows the average, or normal, growth path of aggregate economic activity, and the solid curve shows the rises and falls of actual business activity. The period of time during which aggregate economic activity is falling is a **contraction** or **recession**. If the recession is particularly severe, it becomes a **depression**. After reaching the low point of the contraction, the **trough** (T), economic activity begins to increase. The period of time during which aggregate economic activity grows is an **expansion** or a **boom**. After reaching the high point of the expansion, the **peak** (P), aggregate economic activity begins to decline again. The entire sequence of

---

1. Burns and Mitchell, *Measuring Business Cycles*, New York: National Bureau of Economic Research, 1946, p. 1.

decline followed by recovery, measured from peak to peak or trough to trough, is a **business cycle**.

Figure 8.1 suggests that business cycles are purely temporary deviations from the economy's long-run growth path. However, part of the output losses and gains that occur during a business cycle may become permanent (see Box 8.1, on the next page).

Peaks and troughs in the business cycle are known collectively as **turning points**. One goal of business cycle research is to identify when turning points occur. Aggregate economic activity is not measured directly by any single variable, so there is no simple formula that tells economists when a peak or trough has been reached.[2] In practice, economists at Statistics Canada examine a variety of economic data using methods similar to those of the NBER. They evaluate whether a peak or trough has been reached and, if so, the month it happened. However, the precise dating of turning points usually comes well after a peak or trough occurs, so these judgements are more useful for historical analysis of business cycles than as a guide to current policymaking.

3. *Co-movement.* Business cycles do not occur in just a few sectors or in just a few economic variables. Instead, expansions or contractions "occur at about the same time in many economic activities." Thus, although some industries are more sensitive to the business cycle than others, output and employment in most industries tend to fall in recessions and rise in expansions. Many other economic variables, such as prices, productivity, investment, and unemployment, also have regular and predictable patterns of behaviour over the course of the business cycle. This tendency is called **co-movement**.

---

2. A conventional definition used by the media—that a recession has occurred when there are two consecutive quarters of negative real GDP growth—is not widely accepted by economists. The reason that economists tend not to like this definition is that real GDP is only one of many possible indicators of economic activity.

FIGURE 8.1

A BUSINESS CYCLE

The solid curve graphs the behaviour of aggregate economic activity over a typical business cycle. The dashed line shows the economy's normal growth path. During a contraction, aggregate economic activity falls until it reaches a trough, *T*. The trough is followed by an expansion during which economic activity increases until it reaches a peak, *P*. A complete cycle is measured from peak to peak or trough to trough.

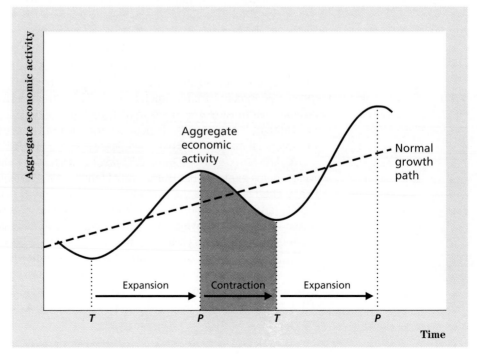

Box 8.1   TEMPORARY AND PERMANENT COMPONENTS OF RECESSIONS

Until the 1980s, economists generally believed that business cycles were temporary events. According to this view, after the economy recovers from a recession, it returns to the level it would have reached had the recession not occurred. Thus, although a recession creates short-run problems, it has no important long-run effects on a country's standard of living.

However, in a 1982 article,* Charles Nelson, of the University of Washington, and Charles Plosser, of the University of Rochester, showed that business cycles are not entirely temporary events. Instead, some permanent reduction in output is associated with the typical recession. Nelson and Plosser examined many macroeconomic variables, including measures of output and employment. Using statistical techniques, they found that for every variable except the unemployment rate, part of a typical cyclical fluctuation represents a permanent change. Only in the unemployment rate did they find fluctuations to be completely transitory.

The severe 1981–1982 recession illustrates the potential permanence of cyclical changes in output. The solid curve in Figure 8.2 shows actual real GDP in Canada from 1947 to the second quarter of 2001. The dashed curve in the figure shows the trend in real output, based on the period 1947–1981 and extended through 2001.[†] In the 1980s and 1990s GDP remained well below the levels it would have reached on the basis of the earlier trend, suggesting that the 1981–1982 recession was associated with a permanent reduction in real GDP. Of course, we cannot conclude that the 1981–1982 recession directly caused the subsequent slowdown. External factors may have caused both the recession and the subsequent slowdown. Alternatively, the slowdown of growth after 1982 may have been purely coincidental and unrelated to the recession. Whatever the reason, much of the 1981–1982 drop in output became permanent.

(continued)

FIGURE 8.2

PERMANENT COMPONENTS OF THE BUSINESS CYCLE

The figure shows actual Canadian GDP (measured quarterly) and a trend line based on real GDP growth from 1947 to 1981. The economy did not return to the earlier trend line after the 1981–1982 recession. Hence much of the output loss of the 1981–1982 recession was permanent.

Source: Real GDP quarterly, seasonally adjusted: *Canadian Economic Observer, Statistical Summary* or CANSIM D100-126; data prior to 1981 have been rescaled.

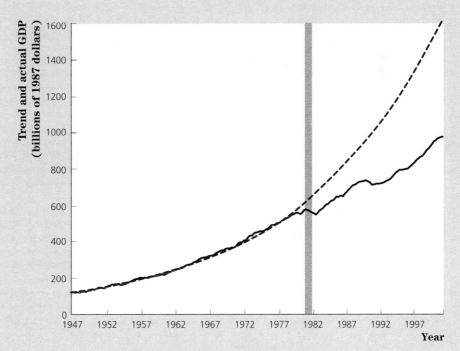

In a typical recession, what fraction of the decline in output is permanent? Although some studies have estimated that as much as 70% of business cycle changes in Canadian output are permanent,[‡] this question is not easily answered. One problem is that the nature of a decline in output—temporary or permanent—cannot be determined until several years afterward. Another problem is that all cyclical output changes may not be alike in their degree of permanence. For example, it is perhaps not so surprising that a portion of the output decline during the 1974–1975 recession turned out to be permanent because that recession was associated with a large and long-lasting change in the economy: a doubling of the relative price of oil. Output declines in recessions not associated with long-lasting supply shocks, in contrast, may well be less permanent.

Indeed, one recent statistical analysis—by Pierre Perron of the Boston University—concluded that of post–World War II US recessions, only the 1973–1974 downturn had a significant permanent effect on the level of output.[§]

---

[*] "Trends and Random Walks in Macroeconomic Time Series: Some Evidence and Implications," *Journal of Monetary Economics*, September 1982, pp. 139–162.
[†] The trend line in the figure curves upward slightly because it is based on the assumption of a constant growth rate. The graph of a variable that grows by the same percentage every year will curve upward over time, rather than being a straight line.
[‡] See Timothy Cogley, "International Evidence on the Size of the Random Walk in Output," *Journal of Political Economy*, June 1990, pp. 501–518.
[§] "The Great Crash, the Oil Price Shock, and the Unit Root Hypothesis," *Econometrica*, November 1989, pp.1361–1401.

4. *Recurrent but not periodic.* The business cycle is not periodic in that it does not occur at regular, predictable intervals and does not last for a fixed or predetermined length of time. (Box 8.2, p. 285, discusses the seasonal cycle—or economic fluctuations over the seasons of the year—which, unlike the business cycle, is periodic.) Although the business cycle is not periodic, it is recurrent; that is, the standard pattern of contraction–trough–expansion–peak recurs again and again in industrial economies.

5. *Persistence.* The duration of a complete business cycle can vary greatly, from about a year to more than a decade, and predicting it is extremely difficult. However, once a recession begins, the economy tends to keep contracting for a period of time, perhaps for a year or more. Similarly, an expansion once begun usually lasts awhile. This tendency for declines in economic activity to be followed by further declines, and for growth in economic activity to be followed by more growth, is called **persistence**. Because movements in economic activity have some persistence, economic forecasters are always on the lookout for turning points, which are likely to indicate a change in the direction of economic activity.

8.2 THE CANADIAN BUSINESS CYCLE: THE HISTORICAL RECORD

An overview of Canadian business cycle history is provided by the monthly business cycle chronology, as summarized in Table 8.1. The chronology gives the dates of the troughs and peaks of the 25 complete business cycles that the Canadian economy has experienced since 1873. Table 8.1 also shows the number of months that each contraction and expansion lasted. The dates were established by Edward Chambers, of the University of Washington, Keith Hay, of Carleton University, and more recently by the Current Analysis Section at Statistics Canada. The selection of peaks and troughs is based on the NBER's methods, which involve study of a large number of economic variables and require an element of judgment.

TABLE 8.1

Canadian Business Cycle Turning Points and Durations

Trough	Expansion (Months from Trough to Peak)	Peak	Contraction (Months from Peak to Next Trough)
		Nov. 1873	66
May 1879	38	July 1882	32
Mar. 1885	23	Feb. 1887	12
Feb. 1888	29	July 1890	9
Mar. 1891	23	Feb. 1893	13
Mar. 1894	17	Aug. 1895	12
Aug. 1896	44	Apr. 1900	10
Feb. 1901	22	Dec. 1902	18
June 1904	30	Dec. 1906	19
July 1908	20	Mar. 1910	16
July 1911	16	Nov. 1912	26
Jan. 1915	36 (WWI)	Jan. 1918	15
Apr. 1919	14	June 1920	15
Sep. 1921	21	June 1923	14
Aug. 1924	56	Apr. 1929	47 (Depression)
Mar. 1933	52	July 1937	15 (Depression)
Oct. 1938	80 (WWII)	June 1945	8
Feb. 1946	33	Oct. 1948	11
Sep. 1949	44 (Korean War)	May 1953	14
July 1954	31	Feb. 1957	12
Feb. 1958	26	Apr. 1960	10
Feb. 1961	160	June 1974	10
Apr. 1975	58	Feb. 1980	6
July 1980	12	July 1981	16
Nov. 1982	89	Apr. 1990	24
Apr. 1992			

Sources: 1873–1897:Edward J. Chambers, "Late Nineteenth Century Business Cycles in Canada," *Canadian Journal of Economics and Political Science*, August 1964, pp. 391–412; 1900–1919; Keith A. J. Hay, "Early Twentieth Century Business Cycles in Canada," *Canadian Journal of Economics and Political Science*, August 1966, pp. 354–365; 1919–1954: Edward J. Chambers, "Canadian Business Cycles since 1919: A Progress Report," *Canadian Journal of Economics and Political Science*, May 1958, pp. 166–189; 1952–1982: Philip Cross and Francine Roy-Mayrand, "Statistics Canada's New System of Leading Indicators," *Canadian Economic Observer*, February 1989, pp. 3.1–3.37; 1982–1992: Philip Cross, "Alternative Measures of Business Cycles in Canada: 1947–1992," *Canadian Economic Observer*, February 1996, pp. 3.1–3.40. Contractions in 1967 and 1970 were too mild to count as recessions. Alternative postwar dates are given by Geoffrey H. Moore and Victor Zarnowitz, "The Development and Role of the National Bureau of Economic Research's Business Cycle Chronologies," Appendix A in Robert J. Gordon, ed., *The American Business Cycle: Continuity and Change*, Chicago: University of Chicago Press and National Bureau of Economic Research, 1986, Table A8. For an evaluation of Canadian business cycle turning points, and a method to find recent points, see Philip M. Bodman and Mark Crosby, "Phases of the Canadian Business Cycle," *Canadian Journal of Economics*, August 2000, pp. 618–633.

THE PRE–WORLD WAR I PERIOD

The period between Confederation (1867) and World War I (1914–1918) was one of rapid economic growth in Canada. Nevertheless, as Table 8.1 shows, recessions were a serious problem during that time. Indeed, the longest contraction on record is the 66-month-long decline between November 1873 and May 1879, a contraction that was worldwide in scope and is referred to by economic historians as the Depression of the 1870s. Overall, during the 1873–1914 period, the economy suffered 233 months of contraction, or nearly as many as the 262 months of expansion. In contrast, from the end of World War II in 1945 through December 2001, the number of months of expansion (572) outnumbered the months of contraction (109) by more than five to one.

For many years the standard interpretation of Canadian economic growth before World War I described the years 1873 to 1896 as a period of stagnation, and 1896 to 1914 as a period of growth brought about by a "wheat boom."[3] This interpretation was an extension of the "staples theory" developed by Harold A. Innis, of the University of Toronto, which attributed pre-Confederation Canadian economic growth and cycles to the exploitation of a series of natural resources—fur, fish, timber, and so on. Some economic historians have challenged this interpretation, arguing that growth was neither as slow before 1896 nor as fast after 1896, as this view suggested, and that the growth of the Prairie wheat economy was not the central cause of growth before World War I. However, extensive recent research on Canadian GDP by Malcolm C. Urquhart, of Queen's University, and his collaborators tends to support the original interpretation.[4] Nevertheless, future research may well lead to revisions in the business cycle chronology for this period.

THE GREAT DEPRESSION AND WORLD WAR II

Canada experienced a sharp but brief contraction after World War I, in 1920–1921. However, the worst economic contraction in the history of Canada was the Great Depression of the 1930s. After a prosperous decade in the 1920s, aggregate economic activity reached a peak in April 1929, six months before the stock market crash in October 1929. Between the 1929 peak and the 1933 trough, real GDP fell by more than 30%. During the same period, the unemployment rate rose from about 3% to 25%, with many of those lucky enough to have jobs able to work only part time. To appreciate how severe the Great Depression was, compare it with the two worst post–World War II recessions, those of 1981–1982 and 1990–1992. In contrast to the 30% real GDP decline and 25% unemployment rate of the Depression, in the 1981–1982 recession, real GDP fell by 3.5%, and the unemployment rate rose from about 7% to about 12%; in the 1990–1992 recession, real GDP fell by 3.3%, and the unemployment rate rose from about 7% to about 11%.

Although no sector escaped the Great Depression, some were particularly hard hit. In agriculture, farmers were bankrupted by low crop prices, and a prolonged drought on the Prairies turned thousands of farm families into homeless migrants. Investment, both business and residential, fell to extremely low levels and a "trade

---

3. See Oscar D. Skelton, *General Economic History of the Dominion, 1867–1912*, Toronto: Publishers Associations of Canada, 1913; and William A. Mackintosh, *The Economic Background of Dominion-Provincial Relations*, Appendix III to the Rowell-Sirois Report, Ottawa: King's Printer, 1939.
4. Malcolm C. Urquhart, *Gross National Product, Canada, 1870–1926: The Derivation of the Estimates*, Kingston: McGill-Queen's University Press, 1993.

war"—in which countries competed in erecting barriers to imports—virtually halted international trade.

Although most people think of the Great Depression as a single episode, technically, it consisted of two business cycles, as Table 8.1 shows. The contraction phase of the first cycle lasted 47 months, from April 1929 until March 1933, and was the most precipitous economic decline in Canadian history. Largely because of expansion in the United States under the New Deal (and not because of Canadian policy) an expansion began in March 1933 and continued for 52 months, until July 1937. By 1937, real GDP was almost back to its 1929 level, although at 12% the unemployment rate remained high. Unemployment remained high in 1937 despite the recovery of real GDP because the number of people of working age had grown since 1929 and because increases in productivity allowed employment to grow more slowly than output.

The second cycle of the Great Depression began in July 1937 with a contraction phase that lasted more than a year. Despite a new recovery that began in October 1938, the unemployment rate was still more than 14% in 1939.

The Great Depression ended dramatically with the advent of World War II. With the demand for armaments and other supplies for the war effort, real output by 1944 exceeded its 1938 level by 80%. Unemployment dropped sharply, averaging less than 2% of the labour force from 1943 through 1945.

POST–WORLD WAR II CANADIAN BUSINESS CYCLES

As World War II was ending in 1945, economists and policymakers were concerned that the economy would relapse into depression. As an expression of this concern, governments in several countries committed themselves to fighting recessions with macroeconomic policy and to avoiding the tariff wars of the 1930s. But instead of falling into a new depression as feared, the Canadian economy began to grow strongly.

Only a few relatively brief and mild recessions interrupted the expansion of the early postwar period. Only one of the six contractions that occurred between 1945 and 1974 lasted more than a year, whereas 14 of the previous 16 cyclical contractions had lasted a year or more. The largest drop in real GDP between 1945 and 1974 was 4.3% during the 1953–1954 recession, and throughout this period, the unemployment rate never exceeded 7% of the workforce. Again, there was a correlation between expansion and war: The 1949–1953 expansion corresponded closely to the Korean War, and the strong expansion of the 1960s occurred while the United States was fighting the Vietnam War.

Because no serious recession occurred between 1945 and 1970, some economists suggested that the business cycle had been "tamed," or even that it was "dead." This view was especially popular during the record 160-month-long expansion of the period 1961–1974, which was widely attributed not only to US wartime spending but also to macroeconomic policies. Some economists argued that policymakers should stop worrying about recessions and focus their attention on inflation, which had been gradually increasing during the 1960s.

Unfortunately, reports of the business cycle's death proved premature. Shortly after the Organization of Petroleum Exporting Countries (OPEC) succeeded in quadrupling oil prices in the autumn of 1973, the Canadian economy fell into recession, partly because of the recession experienced by many other economies. The 1974–1975 recession was much less severe in Canada than in the United States, but the unemployment rate rose to more than 7%. Also disturbing was the fact that inflation, which had fallen during most previous recessions, shot up to double-digit levels. Inflation continued to be a problem for the rest of the 1970s, even as the economy recovered from the 1974–1975 recession.

More evidence that the business cycle was not dead came with the sharp 1981–1982 recession. That contraction lasted 16 months, and the unemployment rate reached 12.8%, a postwar high. Many economists claim that central banks knowingly created this recession to reduce inflation. Inflation did drop dramatically, from about 13% to less than 5% per year. The recovery from this recession was strong, however, and the ensuing expansion continued until the spring of 1990.

In April 1990, the expansion of more than seven years ended, and the economy entered a recession. This recession was longer and shallower than the 1981–1982 recession. In particular, recovery from the 1990–1992 recession was slow and erratic, prompting public concern about the state of the economy two years or more after the trough had passed. Although the Canadian economy has expanded since 1992, growth slowed in 2000 and 2001. Many commentators attributed the slowdown to increases in energy prices and also to the loss of wealth associated with the steep fall in stock market prices in 2000 (especially in the information technology sector). During 2001, a recession began to seem even more likely, especially because of the uncertainty following the terrorist attacks in the United States on September 11, 2001, which led to lower consumption and investment spending in the United States and hence lower demand for Canadian exports. The behaviour of Canada's index of leading indicators (discussed in the box "In Touch with the Macroeconomy: The Index of Leading Indicators") suggested that a period of slow growth was imminent. Thus, the business cycle is with us still.

HAVE BUSINESS CYCLES BECOME LESS SEVERE?

Until recently, macroeconomists believed that business cycles generally have become less severe. Obviously, no recession in Canada since World War II can begin to rival the severity of the Great Depression. Even putting aside the Depression, economists generally believed that business downturns before 1929 were longer and deeper than those since 1945. According to the business cycle chronology (see Table 8.1), for example, the average contraction before 1929 lasted nearly 20 months, and the average expansion lasted slightly more than 27 months. Since 1945, contractions have shortened to an average of 12 months, and expansions have lengthened to an average of 64 months. Standard measures of economic fluctuations, such as real GDP growth and the unemployment rate, also show considerably less volatility since 1945, relative to data available for the pre-1929 era.

Since World War II, a major goal of economic policy has been to reduce the size and frequency of recessions. If researchers found—contrary to the generally accepted view—that business cycles had not moderated in the postwar period, serious doubt would be cast on the ability of economic policymakers to achieve this goal. For this reason, although the question of whether the business cycle has moderated over time may seem to be a matter of interest only to economic historians, this issue is of great practical importance.

Thus, Christina Romer, of the University of California at Berkeley, sparked a heated controversy in the United States by writing a series of articles denying the claim that the business cycle had moderated over time.[5] Romer's main point

---

5. The articles included "Is the Stabilization of the Postwar Economy a Figment of the Data?" *American Economic Review*, June 1986, pp. 314–334.

concerned the dubious quality of the pre-1929 data. Unlike today, in earlier periods, governments did not collect comprehensive data on economic variables, such as GDP. Instead, economic historians, using whatever fragmentary information they could find, have had to estimate historical measures of these variables. Romer argued that methods for estimating historical data typically overstated the size of earlier cyclical fluctuations, largely because the early measurements were based on volatile sectors of the economy and underrepresented less volatile sectors, such as services.

Since Romer raised the issue, much new research has been done, both for the United States and for other countries.[6] For example, David Backus, of New York University, and Patrick Kehoe, of the University of Pennsylvania, have studied fluctuations for 10 developed countries before World War I, in the interwar period, and since World War II.[7] They found that output growth in Canada since World War II has been only about half as volatile as it was before World War I. While some part of this discrepancy may be due to measurement error, a similar pattern is found for the United Kingdom and the United States (though not for Japan or Germany). Further research for Canada may clarify this issue, but it seems that cycles have been significantly moderated in the postwar period.

ARE BUSINESS CYCLES MADE IN CANADA?

Another key question about business cycle history in Canada concerns the extent to which business cycles have originated in Canada or been caused by cycles in the world or US economy. The answer to this question also has important implications for macroeconomic policy. If recessions largely originate in Canada then domestic policy may be able to moderate or prevent them. But if recessions are an unavoidable side effect of participating in the world economy then international macroeconomic policies (in the United States, Europe, and Japan, for example) may be more important influences on Canadian cycles.

The historical data show a strong coincidence between cycle turning points in Canada (see Table 8.1) and in the United States, even in the 19th century. However, there also are notable differences between the two countries' business cycle histories. For example, the United States suffered a sharp recession in the period 1973–1975, whereas Canada experienced a much milder recession in the period 1974–1975. The 1990–1992 recession in Canada was longer and deeper than the 1990–1991 recession in the United States. Most recently, the US recession of 2001 was not shared by Canada.

Recent research by Allan Gregory and Allen Head, of Queen's University, and Jacques Raynauld, of l'École des Hautes Études Commerciales, has measured the part of fluctuations in GDP growth in the G–7 countries since 1970 that can be explained by the world business cycle.[8] Figure 8.3 illustrates this common cycle by showing real GDP since 1970 in each of these seven major industrial countries. Note in particular the effects of worldwide recessions in about 1975, 1982, and 1991. Figure 8.3 also shows that each economy experiences many small fluctuations not shared by the others. Gregory, Head, and Raynauld found that in Japan, Germany, Italy, and France

---

6. See for example, Steven Sheffrin, "Have Economic Fluctuations Been Dampened? A Look at Evidence Outside the United States," *Journal of Monetary Economics*, January 1988, pp. 73–83; and Nathan Balke and Robert Gordon, "The Estimation of Prewar Gross National Product: Methodology and New Evidence," *Journal of Political Economy*, February 1989, pp. 38–92.

7. "International Evidence on the Historical Properties of Business Cycles," *American Economic Review*, September 1992, pp. 864–888.

8. "Measuring World Business Cycles," *International Economic Review*, August 1997, pp. 677–701.

Figure 8.3

Real GDP in G–7 Countries

The worldwide effect of business cycles is reflected in the similar behaviour of real GDP in each of the seven countries shown. But individual countries also have fluctuations not shared with other countries.

Note: The scales for output differ by country; for example, the figure does not imply that Canada's output is the highest of the seven countries.

Source: Real GDP, quarterly, seasonally adjusted: International Monetary Fund, *International Financial Statistics*.

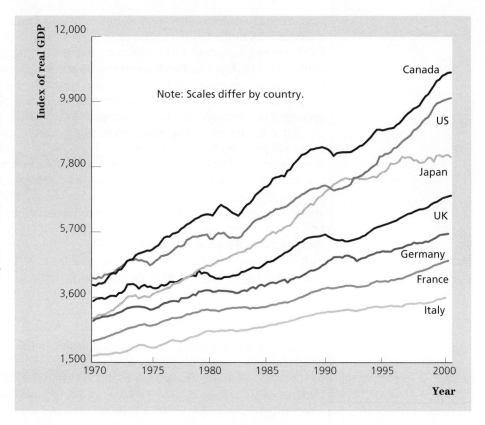

more than half the fluctuation in GDP could be accounted for by the world business cycle. For Canada, the United Kingdom, and the United States, the role of the world business cycle appears to be smaller. Thus, a significant component of the business cycle does seem to be made in Canada.

8.3 Business Cycle Facts

The business cycle also is an international phenomenon in another sense. Within many countries, the behaviour of a range of economic variables tends to repeat itself from cycle to cycle. Although no two business cycles are identical, all (or most) cycles have features in common. This point has been made strongly by a leading business cycle theorist, Robert E. Lucas, Jr., of the University of Chicago:

> Though there is absolutely no theoretical reason to anticipate it, one is led by the facts to conclude that, with respect to the qualitative behavior of co-movements among series [that is, economic variables], *business cycles* are all alike. To theoretically inclined economists, this conclusion should be attractive and challenging, for it suggests the possibility of a unified explanation of business cycles, grounded in the *general* laws governing market economies, rather than in political or institutional characteristics specific to particular countries or periods.[9]

9. Robert E. Lucas, Jr., "Understanding Business Cycles," in K. Brunner and A. H. Meltzer, eds., *Carnegie-Rochester Conference Series on Public Policy*, vol. 5, Autumn, 1977, p. 10.

Lucas's statement that business cycles are all alike (or more accurately, that they have many features in common) is based on examinations of co-movements among economic variables over the business cycle. In this section, we study these co-movements, which we call business cycle facts, for the post–World War II period in Canada. Knowing these business cycle facts is useful for interpreting economic data and evaluating the state of the economy. In addition, they provide guidance and discipline for developing economic theories of the business cycle. When we discuss alternative theories of the business cycle in Chapters 11 and 12, we evaluate the theories principally by determining how well they account for business cycle facts. To be successful, a theory of the business cycle must explain the cyclical behaviour of not just a few variables, such as output and employment, but of a wide range of key economic variables.

THE CYCLICAL BEHAVIOUR OF ECONOMIC VARIABLES: DIRECTION AND TIMING

Two characteristics of the cyclical behaviour of macroeconomic variables are important to our discussion of the business cycle facts. The first is the direction in which a macroeconomic variable moves, relative to the direction of aggregate economic activity. An economic variable that moves in the same direction as aggregate economic activity (up in expansions, down in contractions) is **procyclical**. A variable that moves oppositely to aggregate economic activity (up in contractions, down in expansions) is **countercyclical**. Variables that do not display a clear pattern over the business cycle are **acyclical**.

The second characteristic is the timing of the variable's turning points (peaks and troughs) relative to the turning points of the business cycle. An economic variable is a **leading variable** if it tends to move in advance of aggregate economic activity. In other words, the peaks and troughs in a leading variable occur before the corresponding peaks and troughs in the business cycle. A **coincident variable** is one whose peaks and troughs occur at about the same time as the corresponding business cycle peaks and troughs. Finally, a **lagging variable** is one whose peaks and troughs tend to occur later than the corresponding peaks and troughs in the business cycle.

In some cases, the cyclical timing of a variable is obvious from a graph of its behaviour over the course of several business cycles; in other cases, elaborate statistical techniques are needed to determine timing. The fact that some economic variables consistently lead the business cycle suggests that they might be used to forecast the future course of the economy. This idea is behind the index of leading indicators, discussed in the box, "In Touch with the Macroeconomy: The Index of Leading Indicators," pp. 276–77.

Let us now examine the cyclical behaviour of some key macroeconomic variables. We showed the historical behaviour of several of these variables in Figures 1.1 to 1.5. Those figures covered a long time period and were based on annual data. To provide a better view of short-run cyclical behaviour, we now look at quarterly or monthly data. The direction and timing of the variables considered are presented in Summary table 10 on p. 278.

PRODUCTION

Because the level of production is a basic indicator of aggregate economic activity, peaks and troughs in production tend to occur at about the same time as peaks and

IN TOUCH WITH THE MACROECONOMY

THE INDEX OF LEADING INDICATORS

The **index of leading indicators** is a weighted average of 10 economic variables that lead the business cycle. Statistics Canada releases the index in the first week of each month and publishes it in the *Canadian Economic Observer*. The index was modelled on the US index begun by the NBER and currently issued by the Commerce Department.

The 10 variables that make up the index of leading indicators are listed in the accompanying table. They were chosen because each has a tendency to predict (lead) economic activity (whatever the cause of the cycle) and because data on them are frequently and promptly reported. This second characteristic is essential because a variable cannot be of much help in forecasting if accurate data on the variable arrive only after a long delay.

Although the components of the index are varied, there are good economic reasons why each component helps predict economic activity. For example, new orders for durable goods and the length of the workweek in manufacturing both are direct measures of the amount of future production being planned in the economy. The index of stock prices reflects the optimism or pessimism of stock market participants about the economy's future. An indicator from the service sector also is included because services account for 70% of employment. The US leading index is a component of the Canadian index because exports account for more than 30% of Canadian GDP, and about three-quarters of exports go to the United States. Thus, expansions or contractions in the US economy have large and immediate effects on the Canadian economy.

The percentage change in the index of leading indicators is reported monthly, with two or three consecutive monthly declines being regarded as the warning sign that a recession is on the way. The behaviour of the index of leading indicators since 1952 is shown in Figure 8.4. Note how the index tends to turn down in advance of cyclical peaks. On the whole, the index is a valuable and closely watched forecasting device, correctly predicting a large majority of economic turning points during the post–World War II period. However, the index is not without problems, including the following:

1. Despite the emphasis on the use of data that are promptly available, the data on the 10 components of the index and, thus, the index of leading indicators itself are usually revised during the first four or five months after their initial release. A typical revision is about 0.2%. As a result, an early signal of recession or recovery may be reversed when the revised data become available.

2. Precisely because its components are cyclically sensitive, the index has given false warnings on several occasions, predicting a recession when, in fact, no recession occurred in the several months following the drop in the index.

3. Although it may forecast that a recession is coming, the index does not provide much information about how far in the future the recession is or how severe it will be when it arrives.

4. Changes in the structure of the economy over time may cause some variables to become better predictors of the economy and others to become worse. For this reason, the index of leading indicators must be revised periodically, either to change the list of component indicators or to change the weights of the components.

COMPONENTS OF THE INDEX OF LEADING INDICATORS
1. Retail sales of furniture and appliances
2. Retail sales of other durable goods
3. Housing outlays index
4. Shipment to inventory ratio for finished manufactured goods
5. New orders for durable goods
6. Average workweek in manufacturing
7. Employment in business and personal services
8. Toronto Stock Exchange 300 composite stock price index
9. Money supply (M1)
10. U.S. composite leading index

FIGURE 8.4

THE INDEX OF LEADING INDICATORS

Used for forecasting, the index of leading indicators is a weighted average of 10 economic variables that typically lead the business cycle. The index turns down in advance of business cycle peaks, signalling the onset of recession. Shaded areas represent recessions.

Source: *Canadian Economic Observer, Statistical Summary*, Table 5 (unsmoothed) or CANSIM D100052.

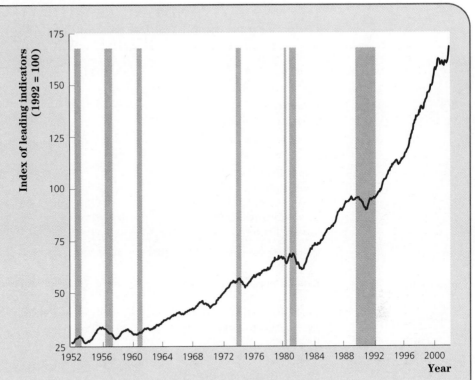

In 1989, Statistics Canada revised the index, partly because of these problems.* The revisions included the addition of employment in business and personal services, which includes employment in legal, architectural, computing, and job placement services as measured by the Labour Force Survey. The components also were selected to ensure that the index clearly leads turning points and can be published rapidly. In 1993, the index was revised to include the most recent data on variables like M1 and the TSE 300 index, before data on some other components are available.†

The index leads peaks (when recessions begin) by 6.3 months and troughs by 3.8 months on average.

---

*See Philip Cross and Francine Roy-Mayrand, "Statistics Canada's New System of Leading Indicators," *Canadian Economic Observer*, February 1989, pp. 3.1–3.37.

†Francine Roy, "A New Composite Index," *Canadian Economic Observer*, February 1993, pp. 3.1–3.5.

troughs in aggregate economic activity. Thus, production is a coincident and procyclical variable. Figure 8.5 shows the behaviour of industrial production in Canada since 1961. The vertical lines *P* and *T* in Figures 8.5 to 8.14 indicate the dates of business cycle peaks and troughs, as listed in Table 8.1. The turning points in industrial production correspond closely to the turning points of the cycle.

Although almost all types of production rise in expansions and fall in recessions, the cyclical sensitivity of production in some sectors of the economy is greater than in others. Industries that produce relatively durable, or long-lasting, goods—houses, consumer durables (refrigerators, cars, washing machines), or capital goods (drill presses, computers, factories)—respond strongly to the business cycle, producing at high rates during expansions and at much lower rates during recessions. In contrast, industries that produce relatively nondurable or short-lived goods (foods, paper products) or services (education, insurance) are less sensitive to the business cycle.

SUMMARY 10

THE CYCLICAL BEHAVIOUR OF KEY MACROECONOMIC VARIABLES (THE BUSINESS CYCLE FACTS)

VARIABLE	DIRECTION	TIMING
Production		
Industrial production	Procyclical	Coincident
Durable goods industries are more volatile than nondurable goods and services.		
Expenditure		
Consumption	Procyclical	Coincident
Business fixed investment	Procyclical	Coincident
Inventory investment	Procyclical	Leading
Trade balance	Procyclical	Leading
Investment is more volatile than consumption.		
Labour Market Variables		
Employment	Procyclical	Coincident
Unemployment	Countercyclical	Coincident
Average labour productivity	Procyclical	Leading
Real wage	Acyclical	—
Money Growth and Inflation		
Money growth	Procyclical	Leading
Inflation	Procyclical	Lagging
Financial Variables		
Stock prices	Procyclical	Leading
Nominal interest rates	Procyclical	Lagging
Real interest rates	Acyclical	—

EXPENDITURE

For components of expenditure, as for types of production, durability is the key to determining sensitivity to the business cycle. Figure 8.6 shows the cyclical behaviour of consumption spending and fixed investment (both measured in real terms). Fixed investment, which consists of business fixed investment (structures, equipment) and residential investment, is made up primarily of spending on durable goods and is strongly procyclical. However, consumption expenditures, which include expenditures on nondurable goods and services, in addition to consumer durables, are relatively smoother. A breakdown of consumption into its components would show that spending on consumer durables is strongly procyclical (sales of cars, furniture, and washing machines go up sharply during an economic expansion) but that consumption of nondurable goods and services is much less affected by the business cycle. With respect to timing, consumption and investment are generally coincident with the business cycle, although individual components of fixed investment vary in their cyclical timing.

FIGURE 8.5

CYCLICAL BEHAVIOUR OF INDUSTRIAL PRODUCTION

Industrial production, an aggregate of production in all industries, is procyclical and coincident with the business cycle. The peaks and troughs of the business cycle are shown by the vertical lines *P* and *T*. The shaded areas represent recessions.

Source: Monthly industrial production, seasonally adjusted: *Canadian Economic Observer, Statistical Summary* or CANSIM I56010.

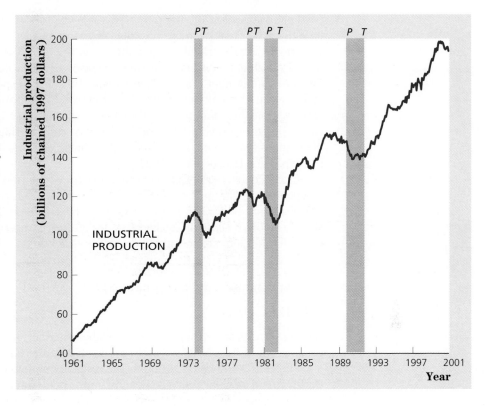

FIGURE 8.6

CYCLICAL BEHAVIOUR OF CONSUMPTION AND INVESTMENT

Both consumption and investment are procyclical. However, investment is more sensitive than consumption to the business cycle, reflecting the fact that durable goods are a larger part of investment spending than they are of consumption spending.

Source: Consumption and business fixed investment, real, quarterly, and seasonally adjusted: 1946–1980 Statistics Canada, CANSIM D15372 and D14851; 1981–2001 CANSIM D100103 and D100111. Data prior to 1981 are not chain-weighted and have been rescaled.

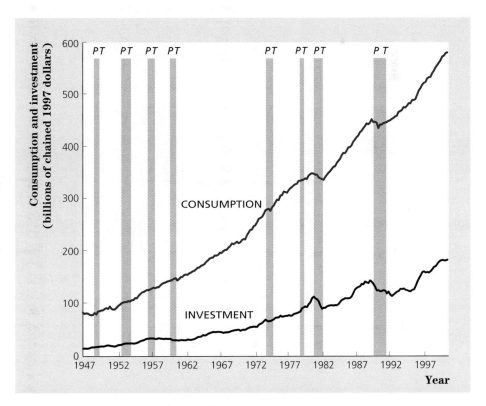

One component of spending that seems to follow its own rules is inventory investment, or changes in business inventories, shown in Figure 8.7, below. Inventory investment is procyclical and leading. Even though goods kept in inventory need not be durable, inventory investment is also very volatile. Although, on average, inventory investment is a small part (about 1%) of total spending, sharp declines in inventory investment represented a large part of the total decline in spending in some recessions, most notably those of 1981–1982 and 1990–1992. The sense in which inventory investment follows its own rules is that it often displays large fluctuations that are not associated with business cycle peaks and troughs, as during the expansion that began in 1992.

In an economy oriented to international trade, the trade balance is an important component of aggregate expenditure. Figure 8.8, p. 281, shows the Canadian trade balance since 1947. The trade balance is procyclical and leading, usually falling sharply before recessions. Business cycles often are transmitted between countries through the trade balance, as we discuss in Chapter 10.

EMPLOYMENT, UNEMPLOYMENT, AND LABOUR PRODUCTIVITY

Business cycles are strongly felt in the labour market. In a recession, employment grows slowly or falls, many workers are laid off, and jobs become more difficult to find.

Figure 8.9 shows the number of workers employed in Canada since 1966. Employment is clearly procyclical, as more people have jobs in booms than in recessions, and also is coincident with the cycle. Figure 8.10 shows the unemployment

FIGURE 8.7

CYCLICAL BEHAVIOUR OF CHANGES IN BUSINESS INVENTORIES

Inventory investment, or changes in business inventories, is procyclical and leading but also extremely volatile. For example, between 1992 and 2000, inventory investment fluctuated sharply despite the fact that the economy was continually in expansion.

Source: Real, quarterly inventory investment, seasonally adjusted: 1947–1980 Statistics Canada, CANSIM D14858; 1981–2001 CANSIM D100116. Data prior to 1981 are not chain-weighted and have been rescaled.

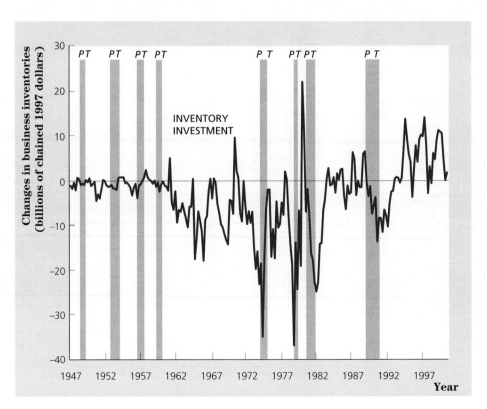

rate, which is the fraction of the labour force (the number of people who are available for work and want to work) that is unemployed. The unemployment rate is strongly countercyclical, rising sharply in contractions but falling more slowly in expansions. Figure 8.10 illustrates a somewhat unusual aspect of the 1990–1992 recession: The unemployment rate continued to climb for several months after the recession's trough was reached.

Another significant labour market variable is average labour productivity. As discussed in Chapter 1, average labour productivity is output per unit of labour input. Figure 8.11, p. 283, shows average labour productivity measured as total real output in the Canadian economy divided by the total number of employed people who produced that output. Average labour productivity tends to be procyclical: In booms workers produce more output during each hour of work than they do in recessions.[10] Also, average labour productivity tends to lead the business cycle.

One labour market variable we have not shown is the real wage. Recall from Chapter 3 that the real wage is the compensation received by workers per unit of time (such as an hour or a week) measured in real, or purchasing-power, terms. The real wage is an especially important variable in the study of business cycles because it is one of the main determinants of the amount of labour supplied by workers and demanded by firms.

Generally speaking, two types of studies attempt to characterize the cyclical behaviour of real wages. One examines the average real wage for the economy as a whole. In these studies, the wage usually is measured as the total real compensation

---

10. The Application in Chapter 3, "The Production Function and Productivity Growth in Canada," p. 57, made the point that total factor productivity *A* also tends to be procyclical.

FIGURE 8.8

CYCLICAL BEHAVIOUR OF THE TRADE BALANCE

The trade balance (the difference between exports and imports) tends to be procyclical and leading, falling prior to recessions.

Source: Real, quarterly exports and imports, seasonally adjusted: 1947–1980 Statistics Canada, CANSIM D14862-D14866; 1981–2001 CANSIM D100119-D1001422. Data prior to 1981 are not chain-weighted and have been rescaled.

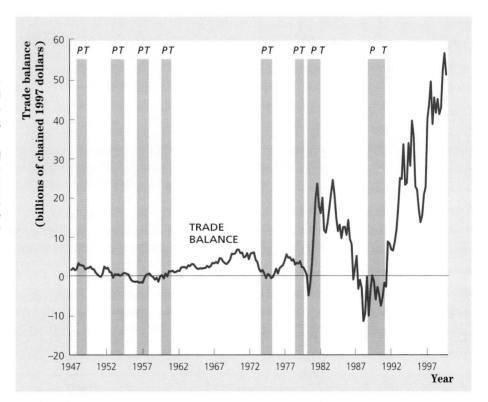

FIGURE 8.9

CYCLICAL BEHAVIOUR OF
EMPLOYMENT

Employment is procyclical and
coincident with the business
cycle.

Source: Total employment, month-
ly, seasonally adjusted: *Canadian
Economic Observer, Statistical
Summary* or CANSIM D980595.

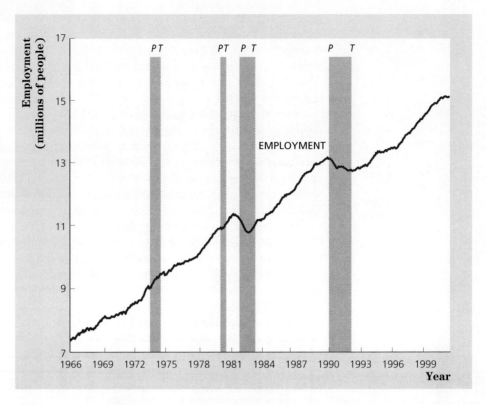

paid to all workers in the economy divided by the total number of hours worked.
In Canada, the real wage measured in this way is acyclical or perhaps mildly
procyclical.

However, some economists point out that the economywide average real wage
may not be a good indicator of the real wage received by the typical worker. An
example illustrates the potential problem. Imagine that an economy consisted of
two employed workers, each earning $9 per hour, and one unemployed worker.
Clearly, the average wage paid to workers in this economy is $9 per hour. Now,
suppose that this economy expands, with the result that the two employed workers
get raises to $10 per hour and that the previously unemployed worker finds a job that
pays $7 per hour. If all three workers work the same number of hours, the
economywide average wage is the same as before: ($10 + $10 + $7)/3, or $9 per
hour. Thus, although all three workers are earning more in the expansion than they
did before, the economywide average wage has not changed. The reason is that the
increase in the employed individuals' wages has been offset by a change in the
composition of the workforce, which now includes a relatively low-wage worker who
was not working before the expansion.

To eliminate effects of changing labour force composition on the measured real
wage, the second type of study attempts to measure the cyclical behaviour of the real
wages of specific individual workers. Unfortunately, this type of study suffers from
a lack of good data on individual wages and from a number of technical statistical
problems. Because of these problems, results range from the finding that real wages
are acyclical to the finding that they are highly procyclical.

FIGURE 8.10

CYCLICAL BEHAVIOUR OF
THE UNEMPLOYMENT RATE

The unemployment rate is
countercyclical and very
sensitive to the business cycle.
It rises rapidly in contractions
but falls more slowly in
expansions.

Source: Monthly unemployment
rate, seasonally adjusted: *Canadian
Economic Observer, Statistical
Summary* or CANSIM D980745.

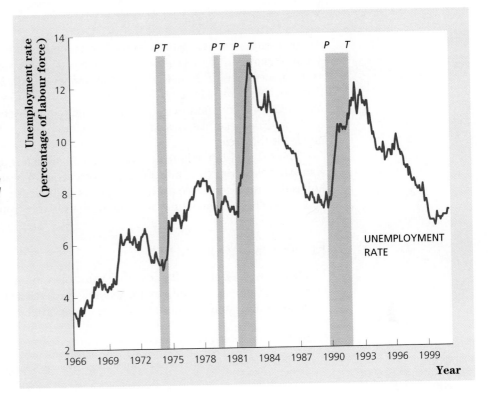

FIGURE 8.11

CYCLICAL BEHAVIOUR OF
AVERAGE LABOUR
PRODUCTIVITY

Average labour productivity,
measured as real output per
person employed, is pro-
cyclical and leading.

Source: Monthly GDP at factor cost
and monthly employment, both
seasonally adjusted: *Canadian
Economic Observer, Statistical
Summary* or CANSIM I56001 and
D980595.

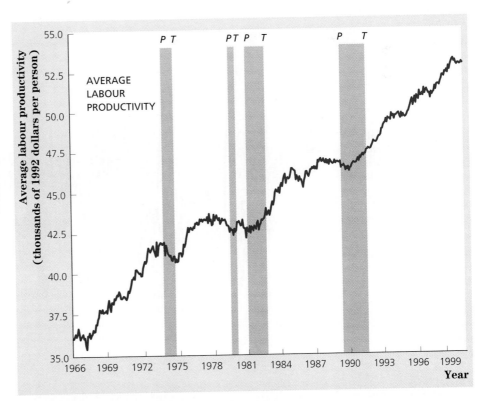

MONEY GROWTH AND INFLATION

Another variable whose cyclical behaviour is somewhat controversial is the money supply. Figure 8.12 shows the behaviour since 1953 of the growth in the M1 measure of the money supply.[11] Note that (nominal) money growth fluctuates a great deal and does not always display an obvious cyclical pattern. However, as Figure 8.12 shows, money growth often falls sharply at or just before the onset of a recession. Moreover, many statistical and historical studies demonstrate that money growth is procyclical and leads the cycle.

The cyclical behaviour of inflation, also shown in Figure 8.12, presents a somewhat clearer picture. Inflation is procyclical but with some lag. Inflation typically builds during an economic expansion, peaks slightly after the business cycle peak, and then falls until some time after the business cycle trough is reached.

FINANCIAL VARIABLES

Financial variables are another class of economic variables that are sensitive to the cycle. For example, stock prices are generally procyclical (stock prices rise in good economic times) and leading (stock prices usually fall in advance of a recession).

---

11. See Table 7.1 for a definition of M1. To reduce the effect of high month-to-month volatility in money growth, Figure 8.12 presents a six-month moving average of money growth rates; that is, the reported growth rate in each month is actually the average of the growth rate in the current month and in the previous five months.

FIGURE 8.12

CYCLICAL BEHAVIOUR OF NOMINAL MONEY GROWTH AND INFLATION

Nominal money growth, here measured as the six-month moving average of monthly growth rates in M1 (expressed in annual rates) is volatile. However, the figure shows that money growth often falls at or just before a cyclical peak. Generally, money growth is procyclical and leading.

Inflation, here measured as the six-month moving average of monthly growth rates of the CPI (expressed in annual rates), is procyclical and lags the business cycle. A typical pattern is for inflation to build up during the expansion and then to fall after the cyclical peak.

Source: M1 monthly, seasonally adjusted: *Bank of Canada Review*, Table E1, reprinted with permission of the Bank of Canada, or CANSIM B1627; monthly CPI, all items: *Canadian Economic Observer, Statistical Summary* or CANSIM P100000.

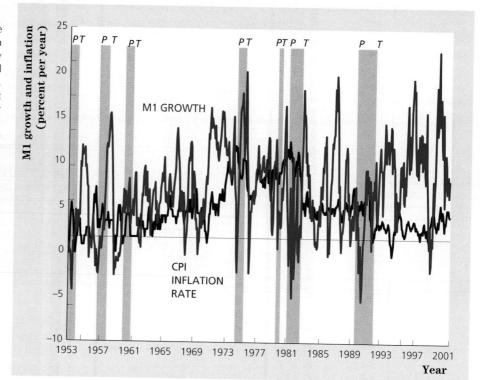

BOX 8.2 THE SEASONAL CYCLE AND THE BUSINESS CYCLE

Did you know that Canada has a large economic boom, followed by a deep recession, every year? The boom always occurs in the third quarter of the year (July through September). During this quarter, output is 7% higher than in the second quarter (April–June) and 3% higher than in the following fourth quarter (October–December). The winter recession then continues, as output falls by about 5% in the following first quarter (January – March). Fortunately, the recession is always a brief one, as output rises by 4% on average in the second quarter. This regular seasonal pattern, known as the seasonal cycle, actually accounts for more than 70% of the total fluctuation in the growth rate of real output!

Why don't large seasonal fluctuations appear in Figures 8.3–8.13? Normally, macroeconomic data are seasonally adjusted, meaning that regularly recurring seasonal fluctuations are removed from the data. Seasonal adjustment allows users of economic data to ignore seasonal changes and focus on business cycle fluctuations and longer-term movements in the data. However, researchers still study unadjusted data in case seasonal adjustment conceals information that could help economists better understand the business cycle.

The seasonal cycle illustrates a potential source of aggregate economic fluctuations: changes in productivity, as when construction workers and farmers become less productive because of winter weather in the first and fourth quarters. Other seasonal shocks include changes in consumer demand, as at Christmas, and changes in labour supply, as when people take summer vacations and students enter the full-time labour force in the third quarter. The seasonal pattern in output—with a boom in the second and third quarters—suggests that in Canada seasonal productivity shocks are most important, though.

As we discuss in Chapter 11, classical economists believe that business cycles generally represent the economy's best response to changes in the economic environment, a response that macroeconomic policy need not try to eliminate. Although it does not necessarily confirm this view, the seasonal cycle shows that large economic fluctuations may be desirable responses to various factors (such as the weather) and do not need to be offset by government policy.

Nominal interest rates are procyclical and lagging. The nominal interest rate shown in Figure 8.13, on the next page, is the rate on three-month corporate paper. However, other interest rates, such as the prime rate (charged by banks to their best customers) and the rates on Treasury bills, also are procyclical and lagging. Note that nominal interest rates have the same general cyclical pattern as inflation; Chapter 7 discussed why nominal interest rates tend to move up and down with the inflation rate.

The real interest rate does not have an obvious cyclical pattern. For instance, the real interest rate actually was negative during the 1974–1975 recession but was very high during the 1981–1982 recession. (Annual values of the real interest rate are shown in Figure 2.3.) The acyclicality of the real interest rate does not necessarily mean its movements are unimportant over the business cycle. Instead, the lack of a stable cyclical pattern may reflect the facts that individual business cycles have different causes and that these different sources of cycles have different effects on the real interest rate.

8.4 BUSINESS CYCLE ANALYSIS: A PREVIEW

The business cycle facts presented in this chapter would be useful even if we took them no further. For example, being familiar with the typical cyclical patterns of

FIGURE 8.13

CYCLICAL BEHAVIOUR OF
THE NOMINAL INTEREST
RATE

The nominal interest rate,
measured here as the interest
rate on 90-day corporate
paper, is procyclical and recently has lagged the business
cycle.

Source: Monthly average, 90-day
corporate paper rate: *Bank of
Canada Review,* Table F1 reprinted
with permission of the Bank of
Canada, or CANSIM B14017.

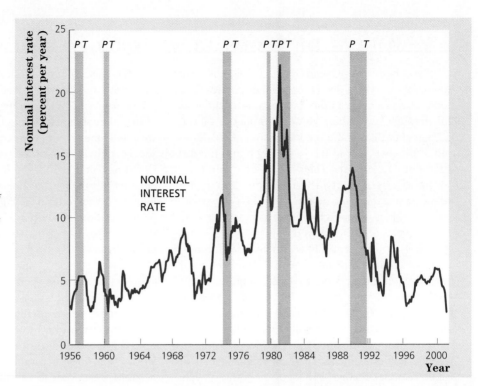

key macroeconomic variables helps forecasters project the course of the economy,
as we showed when discussing the index of leading indicators. Knowing the facts
about cycles also is important for businesspeople making investment and hiring
decisions and for financial investors trying to choose portfolios that provide the
desired combinations of risk and return. However, macroeconomists are interested
not only in *what* happens during business cycles but also in *why* it happens. This
desire to understand cycles is not just idle intellectual curiosity. For example, as
we demonstrate in Chapters 9 to 12, the advice that macroeconomists give to
policymakers about how to respond to a recession depends on what they think is
causing the recession. Thus, with the business cycle facts as background, in the
rest of Part III we describe the primary alternative explanations of business cycle
fluctuations, as well as policy recommendations based on these explanations.

In general, theories of the business cycle have two main components. The first is
a description of the types of factors that have major impacts on the economy—wars,
new inventions, harvest failures, and changes in government policy are examples.
Economists often refer to these (typically unpredictable) forces hitting the economy
as *shocks*. The other component of a business cycle theory is a *model* of how the
economy responds to the various shocks. Think of the economy as a car moving down
a poorly maintained highway: The shocks can be thought of as the potholes and bumps
in the road; the model describes how the components of the car (its tires and shock
absorbers) act to smooth out or amplify the effects of the shocks on the passengers.

The two principal business cycle theories that we discuss in this book are the
classical and the *Keynesian* theories. Fortunately, to present and discuss these
two theories we do not have to develop two completely different models. Instead, both
can be considered within a general framework called the *aggregate demand–
aggregate supply*, or *AD–AS, model*. To introduce some of the key differences

between the classical and Keynesian approaches to business cycle analysis, in the rest of this chapter, we preview the *AD–AS* model and how it is used to analyze business cycles.

AGGREGATE DEMAND AND AGGREGATE SUPPLY: A BRIEF INTRODUCTION

We develop and apply the *AD–AS* model, and a key building block of the *AD–AS* model, the *IS–LM* model, in Chapters 9 to 12. Here, we simply introduce and briefly explain the basic components of the *AD–AS* model. The *AD–AS* model has three components, as illustrated in Figure 8.14: (1) the aggregate demand curve, (2) the short-run aggregate supply curve, and (3) the long-run aggregate supply curve. Each curve represents a relationship between the aggregate price level, *P*, measured on the vertical axis in Figure 8.14, and output, *Y*, measured along the horizontal axis.

The aggregate demand (AD) curve shows for any price level, *P*, the total quantity of goods and services, *Y*, demanded by household, firms, and governments. The *AD* curve slopes downward in Figure 8.14, implying that when the general price level is higher, people demand fewer goods and services. We give the precise explanation for this downward slope in Chapter 9 . The intuitive explanation for the downward slope of the *AD* curve—that when prices are higher people can afford to buy fewer goods—is *not* correct. The problem with the intuitive explanation is that although an increase in the general price level does reflect an increase in the prices of most goods, it also implies an increase in the incomes of the people who produce and sell those goods. Thus, to say that a higher price level reduces the quantities of goods and services that people can afford to buy is not correct because their incomes, as well as prices, have gone up.

FIGURE 8.14

THE AGGREGATE DEMAND–AGGREGATE SUPPLY MODEL

The aggregate demand (*AD*) curve slopes downward, reflecting the fact that the aggregate quantity of goods and services demanded, *Y*, falls when the price level, *P*, rises. The short-run aggregate supply (*SRAS*) curve is horizontal, reflecting the assumption that in the short run, prices are fixed and firms simply produce whatever quantity is de-manded. In the long run, firms produce their normal levels of output, so the long-run aggregate supply (*LRAS*) curve is vertical at the full-employment level of output, $\bar{Y}$. The economy's short-run equilibrium is at the point where the *AD* and *SRAS* curves intersect, and its long-run equilibrium is where the *AD* and *LRAS* curves intersect. In this example, the economy is in both short-run and long-run equilibrium at point *E*.

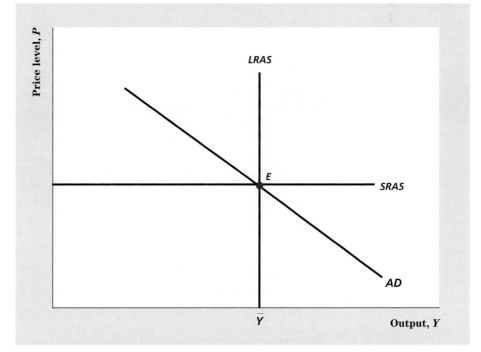

The *AD* curve relates the amount of output demanded to the price level, if we hold other economic factors constant. However, for a specific price level, any change in the economy that increases the aggregate quantity of goods and services demanded will shift the *AD* curve to the right (and any change that decreases the quantity of goods and services demanded will shift the *AD* curve to the left.) For example, a sharp rise in the stock market, by making consumers wealthier, would likely increase households' demand for goods and services, shifting the *AD* curve to the right. Similarly, the development of more efficient capital goods would increase firms' demand for new capital goods, again shifting the *AD* curve to the right. Government policies also can affect the *AD* curve. For example, a decline in government spending on military hardware reduces the aggregate quantity of goods and services demanded and shifts the *AD* curve to the left.

An aggregate supply curve indicates the amount of output producers are willing to supply at any particular price level. Two aggregate supply curves are shown in Figure 8.14—one that holds in the short run and one that holds in the long run. The short-run aggregate supply (*SRAS*) curve, shown in Figure 8.14, is a horizontal line. The horizontal *SRAS* curve captures the ideas that in the short run, the price level is fixed and that firms are willing to supply any amount of output at that price. If the short run is a very short period of time, such as a day, this assumption is realistic. For instance, an ice cream store posts the price of ice cream in the morning and sells as much ice cream as is demanded at that price (up to its capacity to produce ice cream). During a single day, the owner typically will not raise the price of ice cream if the quantity demanded is unusually high; nor does the owner lower the price of ice cream if the quantity demanded is unusually low. The tendency of a producer to set a price for some time and then supply whatever is demanded at that price is represented by a horizontal *SRAS* curve.

However, suppose that the quantity of ice cream demanded remains high day after day, to the point that the owner is straining to produce enough ice cream to meet demand. In this case, the owner may raise her price in order to reduce the quantity of ice cream demanded to a more manageable level. The owner will keep raising the price of ice cream as long as the quantity demanded exceeds normal production capacity. In the long run, the price of ice cream will be whatever it has to be to equate the quantity demanded to the owner's normal level of output. Similarly, in the long run, all other firms in the economy will adjust their prices as necessary so as to be able to produce their normal level of output. As discussed in Chapter 3, the normal level of production for the economy as a whole is called the full-employment level of output, denoted $\bar{Y}$. Thus, the long-run aggregate supply (*LRAS*) curve is vertical, as shown in Figure 8.14, at the point that output supplied, Y, equals $\bar{Y}$.

Figure 8.14 represents an economy that is simultaneously in short-run and long-run equilibrium. The short-run equilibrium is represented by the intersection of the *AD* and *SRAS* curves, shown as point *E*. The long-run equilibrium is represented by the intersection of the *AD* and *LRAS* curves, also shown as point *E*. However, when some change occurs in the economy, the short-run equilibrium can differ from the long-run equilibrium.

AGGREGATE DEMAND SHOCKS

Recall that a theory of business cycles has to include a description of the shocks hitting the economy. The *AD–AS* framework identifies shocks by their initial effects—on aggregate demand or aggregate supply. An aggregate demand shock is a change in the economy that shifts the *AD* curve. For example, a negative aggregate demand shock would occur if consumers became more pessimistic about the future and, thus, reduced their current consumption spending, shifting the AD curve to the left.

To analyze the effect of an aggregate demand shock, let us suppose that the economy initially is in both short-run and long-run equilibrium at point E in Figure 8.15. We assume that because consumers become more pessimistic, the aggregate demand curve shifts down and to the left from AD^1 to AD^2. In this case, the new short-run equilibrium (the intersection of AD^2 and $SRAS$) is at point F, where output has fallen to Y_2 and the price level remains unchanged at P_1. Thus, the decline in household consumption demand causes a recession, with output falling below its normal level. However, the economy will not stay at point F forever because firms will not be content to keep producing below their normal capacity. Eventually, firms will respond to lower demand by adjusting their prices—in this case downward—until the economy reaches its new long-run equilibrium at point H, the intersection of AD^2 and $LRAS$. At point H, output is at its original level, $\overline{Y}$, but the price level has fallen to P_2.

Our analysis shows that an adverse aggregate demand shock, which shifts the AD curve down, will cause output to fall in the short run but not in the long run. How long does it take for the economy to reach the long run? This question is crucial to economic analysis and is one to which classical economists and Keynesian economists have very different answers. Their answers help explain why classicals and Keynesians have different views about the appropriate role of government policy in fighting recessions.

The classical answer is that prices adjust quite rapidly to imbalances in quantities supplied and demanded so that the economy gets to its long-run equilibrium quickly—in a few months or less. Thus, a recession caused by a downward shift of the AD curve is likely to end rather quickly, as the price level falls and the economy reaches the original level of output, $\overline{Y}$. In the strictest versions of the classical model, the

FIGURE 8.15

AN ADVERSE AGGREGATE DEMAND SHOCK

An adverse aggregate demand shock reduces the aggregate quantity of goods and services demanded at a given price level; an example is that consumers become more pessimistic and, thus, reduce their spending. This shock is represented by a shift to the left of the aggregate demand curve from AD^1 to AD^2. In the short run, the economy moves to point F. At this short-run equilibrium, output has fallen to Y_2 and the price level is unchanged. Eventually, price adjustment causes the economy to move to the new long-run equilibrium at point H, where output returns to its full-employment level, $\overline{Y}$, and the price level falls to P_2. In the strict classical view, the economy moves almost immediately to point H, so the adverse aggregate demand shock essentially has no effect on output in both the short run and the long run. Keynesians argue that the adjustment process takes longer so that the adverse aggregate demand shock may lead to a sustained decline in output.

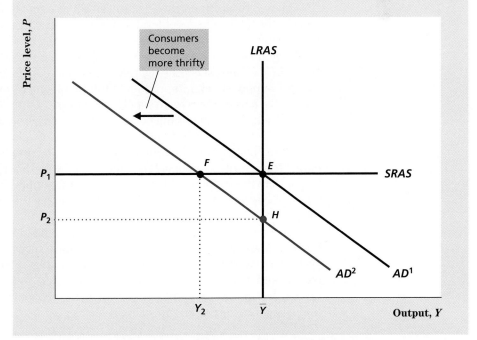

economy is assumed to reach its long-run equilibrium essentially immediately, implying that the short-run aggregate supply curve is irrelevant and that the economy always operates on the long-run aggregate supply (*LRAS*) curve. Because the adjustment takes place quickly, classical economists argue that little is gained by the government actively trying to fight recessions. Note that this conclusion is consistent with the "invisible hand" argument described in Chapter 1, according to which the free market and unconstrained price adjustments are sufficient to achieve good economic results.

In contrast to the classical view, Keynesian economists argue that prices (and wages, which are the price of labour) do not necessarily adjust quickly in response to shocks. Hence the return of the economy to its long-run equilibrium may be slow, taking, perhaps, years rather than months. In other words, although Keynesians agree with classicals that the economy's level of output will eventually return from its recessionary level (represented by Y_2 in Figure 8.15) to its full-employment level, $\overline{Y}$, they believe that this process may be slow. Because they lack confidence in the self-correcting powers of the economy, Keynesians tend to see an important role for the government in fighting recessions. For example, Keynes himself originally argued that government could fight recessions by increasing spending. In terms of Figure 8.15, an increase in government spending could in principle shift the *AD* curve to the right, from AD^2 back to AD^1, restoring the economy to full employment.

AGGREGATE SUPPLY SHOCKS

Because classical economists believe that aggregate demand shocks do not cause sustained fluctuations in output, they generally view aggregate supply shocks as the major force behind changes in output and employment. An aggregate supply shock is a change in the economy that causes the long-run aggregate supply (*LRAS*) curve to shift. The position of the *LRAS* curve depends only on the full-employment level of output, $\overline{Y}$, so aggregate supply shocks can also be thought of as factors—such as changes in productivity or labour supply, for example—that lead to changes in $\overline{Y}$.

Figure 8.16 illustrates the effects of an adverse supply shock, that is, a shock that reduces the full-employment level of output (an example would be a severe drought that greatly reduces crop yields). Suppose that the economy is initially in long-run equilibrium at point E in Figure 8.16, where the initial long-run aggregate supply curve, $LRAS^1$, intersects the aggregate demand curve, *AD*. Now imagine that the adverse supply shock hits, reducing full-employment output from $\overline{Y}_1$ to $\overline{Y}_2$ and causing the long-run aggregate supply curve to shift to the left from $LRAS^1$ to $LRAS^2$. The new long-run equilibrium occurs at point F, where the level of output is lower than at point E. According to the classical view, the economy moves quickly from point E to point F and then remains at point F. The drop in output as the economy moves from point E to point F is a recession. Note that the new price level, P_2, is higher than the initial price level, P_1, so adverse supply shocks cause prices to rise during recessions. We return to this implication for the price level and discuss its relation to the business cycle facts in Chapter 11.

Although classical economists first emphasized supply shocks, Keynesian economists also recognize the importance of supply shocks in accounting for business cycle fluctuations in output. Keynesians agree that an adverse supply shock will reduce output and increase the price level in the long run. In Chapter 12, we discuss the Keynesian view of the process by which the economy moves from the short run to the long run in response to a supply shock.

FIGURE 8.16

AN ADVERSE AGGREGATE
SUPPLY SHOCK

An adverse aggregate supply shock, such as a drought, reduces the full-employment level of output from $\bar{Y}_1$ to $\bar{Y}_2$. Equivalently, the shock shifts the long-run aggregate supply curve from the left, from $LRAS^1$ to $LRAS^2$. As a result of the adverse supply shock, the long-run equilibrium moves from point E to point F. In the new long-run equilibrium, output has fallen from $\bar{Y}_1$ to $\bar{Y}_2$ and the price level has increased from P_1 to P_2.

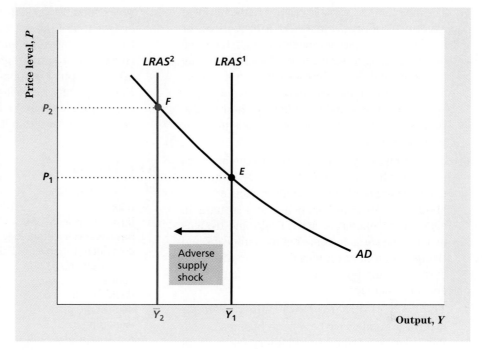

CHAPTER SUMMARY

1. A business cycle consists of a period of declining aggregate economic activity (a contraction or recession) followed by a period of rising economic activity (an expansion or a boom). The low point of the contraction is called the trough, and the high point of the expansion is called the peak. Business cycles have been observed in market economies since the beginning of industrialization.

2. Many economic variables have regular and predictable patterns of behaviour over the course of the cycle. That tendency is called co-movement. We refer to the typical cyclical patterns of key macroeconomic variables as the "business cycle facts."

3. The fluctuations in aggregate economic activity that constitute business cycles are recurrent, having been observed again and again in industrialized market economies. However, they

are not periodic, in that they do not occur at regular or predictable intervals. Business cycle fluctuations also are persistent, which means that once a recession or expansion begins, it usually lasts for awhile.

4. Economists believe that the Canadian economy before 1929 had longer recessions and more cyclical volatility than the post–World War II economy. However, data problems prevent precise measurements of how much more cyclical the pre–World War I economy was. The Great Depression that began in 1929 and did not end until the onset of World War II was the most severe cyclical decline in Canadian history. Moderation of the business cycle after World War II led to premature pronouncements that the cycle was "dead." However, the Canadian economy suffered severe recessions in 1981–1982 and 1990–1992.

5. The direction of a variable relative to the business cycle can be procyclical, countercyclical, or acyclical. A procyclical variable moves in the same direction as aggregate economic activity, rising in booms and falling in recessions. A counter-cyclical variable moves oppositely to aggregate economic activity, falling in booms and rising in recessions. An acyclical variable has no clear cyclical pattern.

6. The timing of a variable relative to the business cycle may be coincident, leading, or lagging. A coincident variable's peaks and troughs occur at about the same time as peaks and troughs in aggregate economic activity. Peaks and troughs in a leading variable come before and peaks and troughs in a lagging variable come after the corresponding peaks and troughs in aggregate economic activity.

7. The cyclical direction and timing of major macroeconomic variables—the business cycle facts—are described in Summary table 10. In brief, production, consumption, and investment are procyclical and coincident. Investment is much more volatile over the business cycle than consumption is. Employment and average labour productivity are procyclical, but the unemploy-ment rate is countercyclical. Money and stock prices are procyclical and lead the cycle. Inflation and nominal interest rates are procyclical and lagging. The real interest rate is acyclical.

8. A theory of business cycles consists of (1) a description of shocks that affect the economy and (2) a model, such as the aggregate demand–aggregate supply (AD–AS) model, that describes how the economy responds to these shocks. In the AD–AS model, shocks to the aggregate demand (AD) curve cause output to change in the short run, but output returns to its full-employment level, $\overline{Y}$, in the long run. Shocks to the aggregate supply (AS) curve can affect output both in the long run and the short run.

9. Classical economists argue that the economy reaches its long-run equilibrium quickly because prices adjust rapidly. This view implies that aggregate demand shocks have only short-lived effects on real variables, such as output; instead, classical economists emphasize aggregate supply shocks as the source of business cycles. Classicals also see little role for government policies to fight

recessions. Keynesian economists, in contrast, believe that it takes a long time for the economy to reach long-run equilibrium. They conclude, therefore, that aggregate demand shocks can affect output for substantial periods of time. Further, many Keynesians believe that govern-ment policies may be useful in speeding the economy's return to full employment.

KEY TERMS

acyclical, p. 275
boom, p. 265
business cycle, p. 266
business cycle chronology, p. 265
coincident variable, p. 275
co-movement, p. 266
contraction, p. 265
countercyclical, p. 275
depression, p. 265
expansion, p. 265
index of leading indicators, p. 276
lagging variable, p. 275
leading variable, p. 275
peak, p. 265
persistence, p. 268
procyclical, p. 275
recession, p. 265
trough, p. 265
turning points, p. 266

REVIEW QUESTIONS

1. Draw a diagram showing the phases and turning points of a business cycle. Using the diagram, illustrate the concepts of recurrence and persistence.

2. What is co-movement? How is co-movement related to the business cycle facts presented in this chapter?

3. What is the evidence for the view that the Canadian business cycle has become less severe over time? Why is the question of whether the cycle has moderated over time an important one?

4. What terms are used to describe the way a variable moves when economic activity is rising or falling? What terms are used to describe the timing of cyclical changes in economic variables?

5. If you knew that the economy was falling into a recession, what would you expect to happen to production during the next few quarters? to investment? to average labour productivity? to the unemployment rate?

6. How is the fact that some economic variables are known to lead the cycle used in macroeconomic forecasting?

7. What are the two components of a theory of business cycles?

8. How do Keynesian and classical economists differ in their beliefs about how long it takes the economy to reach long-run equilibrium? What implications do these differences in beliefs have for Keynesian and classical views about the usefulness of anti-recessionary policies? About the types of shocks that cause most recessions?

ANALYTICAL PROBLEMS

1. Consumer expenditures on durable goods, such as cars and furniture, as well as purchases of new houses, fall much more than expenditures on nondurable goods and services during recessions. Why do you think that is?

2. Output, total hours worked, and average labour productivity all are procyclical. Which variable, output or total hours worked, increases by a larger percentage in expansions and falls by a larger percentage in recessions? (*Hint*: Average labour productivity = output ÷ total hours worked so that the percentage change in average labour productivity equals the percentage change in output minus the percentage change in total hours worked.)

3. During the period 1973–1975, many industrialized countries experienced a deep recession with a simultaneous sharp rise in the price level. Would you conclude that the recession was the result of a supply shock or a demand shock? Illustrate, using *AD–AS* analysis.

4. It is sometimes argued that economic growth that is "too rapid" will be associated with inflation. Use *AD-AS* analysis to show how this statement might be true. When this claim is made, what type of shock is implicitly assumed to be hitting the economy?

Chapter 9

THE *IS–LM/AD–AS* MODEL: A GENERAL
FRAMEWORK FOR MACROECONOMIC ANALYSIS

The main goal of Chapter 8 was to describe business cycles by presenting the business cycle facts. This and the following three chapters explain business cycles and how policymakers should respond to them. First, we must develop a macroeconomic model that we can use to analyze cyclical fluctuations and the effects of policy changes on the economy. By examining the labour market in Chapter 3, the goods market in Chapters 4 and 5, and the asset market in Chapter 7, we already have identified the three components of a complete macroeconomic model. Now we put these three components together into a single framework that allows us to analyze them simultaneously. This chapter, and its open-economy partner Chapter 10, consolidate our previous analyses to provide the theoretical structure for the rest of the book.

The macroeconomic model developed in this chapter is the *IS–LM* model. (As we discuss later, this name originates in two of its basic equilibrium conditions: that investment, *I*, must equal saving, *S*, and that money demanded, *L*, must equal money supplied, *M*.) The *IS–LM* model was developed in 1937 by Nobel laureate Sir John Hicks,[1] who intended it as a graphical representation of the ideas presented by Keynes in his famous 1936 book, *The General Theory of Employment, Interest, and Money*. Reflecting Keynes's belief that wages and prices do not adjust quickly to clear markets (see Section 1.3), in his original *IS–LM* model, Hicks assumed that the price level was fixed, at least temporarily. Since Hicks, several generations of economists have worked to refine the *IS–LM* model, and it has been widely applied in analyses of cyclical fluctuations and macroeconomic policy, and in forecasting.

Because of its origins, the *IS–LM* model is commonly identified with the Keynesian approach to business cycle analysis. Classical economists—who believe that wages and prices move rapidly to clear markets—would reject Hicks's *IS–LM* model because of his assumption that the price level is fixed. However, the conventional *IS–LM* model may be easily adapted to allow for rapidly adjusting wages and prices. Thus, the *IS–LM* framework, although originally developed by Keynesians, also may be used to present and discuss the classical approach to business cycle analysis. In addition, the *IS–LM* model is equivalent to the *AD–AS* model that we previewed in Section 8.4. We show how the *AD–AS* model is derived from the *IS–LM* model and illustrate how the *AD–AS* model can be used with either a classical or a Keynesian perspective.

Using the *IS–LM* model (and the equivalent *AD–AS* model) as a framework for both classical and Keynesian analyses has several practical benefits: First, using a single model for both classical and Keynesian analyses avoids the need to learn two

---

1. Hicks outlined the IS–LM framework in an article entitled "Mr. Keynes and the Classics: A Suggested Interpretation," *Econometrica*, April 1937, pp. 137–159.

different models. Second, utilizing a single framework emphasizes the large areas of agreement between the Keynesian and classical approaches while showing clearly how the two approaches differ. Moreover, because versions of the *IS–LM* model (and its concepts and terminology) are so often applied in analyses of the economy and macroeconomic policy, studying this framework will help you understand and participate more fully in current economic debates.

We use a graphical approach to develop the *IS–LM* model. Appendix 9.A presents the identical analysis in algebraic form. If you have difficulty understanding why the curves used in the graphical analysis have the slopes they do or why they shift, you may find the algebra in the Appendix helpful.

To keep things as simple as possible, in this chapter, we assume that the economy is closed. In Chapter 10, we show how to extend the *IS–LM* model to allow for a foreign sector.

9.1 THE *FE* LINE:
EQUILIBRIUM IN THE LABOUR MARKET

In previous chapters, we discussed the three main markets of the economy: the labour market, the goods market, and the asset market. We also identified some of the links among these markets, but now we want to be more precise about how they fit into a complete macroeconomic system.

Let us turn first to the labour market and recall from Chapter 3 the concepts of the full-employment level of employment and full-employment output. The *full-employment level of employment* $\overline{N}$ is the equilibrium level of employment reached after wages and prices have fully adjusted so that the quantity of labour supplied equals the quantity of labour demanded. *Full-employment output* $\overline{Y}$ is the amount of output produced when employment is at its full-employment level, given the current level of the capital stock and the production function. Algebraically, full-employment output $\overline{Y}$ equals $AF(K, \overline{N})$, where K is the capital stock, A is productivity, and F is the production function (see Eq. 3.4).

Our ultimate goal is a diagram that has the real interest rate on the vertical axis and output on the horizontal axis. In such a diagram, equilibrium in the labour market is represented by the **full-employment line**, or *FE*, in Figure 9.1, on the next page. The *FE* line is vertical at $Y = \overline{Y}$ because when the labour market is in equilibrium, output equals its full-employment level, regardless of the interest rate.[2]

FACTORS THAT SHIFT THE *FE* LINE

The full-employment level of output is determined by the current levels of labour, capital, and productivity. Any change that affects the full-employment level of output $\overline{Y}$ will cause the *FE* line to shift. Recall that full-employment output $\overline{Y}$ increases—and, thus, the *FE* line shifts to the right—when the labour supply increases (which raises equilibrium employment $\overline{N}$) or when there is a beneficial supply shock. Similarly, a drop in the labour supply or an adverse supply shock lowers full-employment output $\overline{Y}$ and shifts the *FE* line to the left. Summary table 11 lists the factors that shift the *FE* line.

---

2. The real interest rate affects investment and thus the amount of capital that firms will have in the future, but it does not affect the current capital stock, and hence does not affect current output.

FIGURE 9.1

THE *FE* LINE

The full-employment (*FE*) line represents labour market equilibrium. When the labour market is in equilibrium, employment equals its full-employment level $\bar{N}$ and output equals its full-employment level $\bar{Y}$, regardless of the value of the real interest rate. Thus, the *FE* line is vertical at $Y = \bar{Y}$.

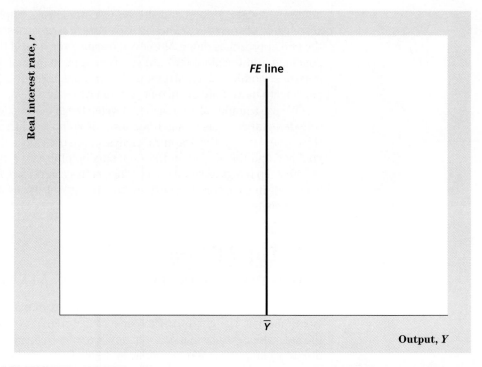

SUMMARY 11 FACTORS THAT SHIFT THE FULL-EMPLOYMENT (*FE*) LINE

A(N)	SHIFTS THE *FE* LINE	REASON
Beneficial supply shock	Right	**1.** More output can be produced for the same amount of capital and labour. **2.** If the *MPN* rises, labour demand increases and raises employment. Full-employment output increases for both reasons.
Increase in labour supply	Right	Equilibrium employment rises, raising full-employment output.
Increase in the capital stock	Right	More output can be produced with the same amount of labour. In addition, increased capital may increase the *MPN*, which increases labour demand and equilibrium employment.

Some classical economists argue that increases in government purchases lead to increases in the labour supply as follows: the government pays for its increased spending by raising taxes, which reduces workers' wealth. Recall from Summary table 4 in Chapter 3 that a fall in wealth leads to an increase in labour supply. Thus, these classical economists suggest that increases in government spending shift the *FE* line to right. We review this argument in Chapter 11, when we study the classical model in detail.

9.2 THE *IS* CURVE:
EQUILIBRIUM IN THE GOODS MARKET

The second of the three markets in our model is the goods market. Recall from Chapter 4 that the goods market is in equilibrium when desired investment and desired national saving are equal or, equivalently, when the aggregate quantity of goods supplied equals the aggregate quantity of goods demanded. In Chapter 4, we demonstrated that adjustments in the real interest rate help bring about equilibrium in the goods market.

In a diagram with the real interest rate on the vertical axis and real output on the horizontal axis, equilibrium in the goods market is described by a curve called the **IS curve**. Specifically, for any level of output (or income) Y, the *IS* curve shows the real interest rate r for which the goods market is in equilibrium. The *IS* curve is so named because at all points on the curve desired investment, I, equals desired national saving, S.

Figure 9.2, on the next page, shows the derivation of the *IS* curve from the saving–investment diagram introduced in Chapter 4 and used extensively in Chapters 4 and 5 (see Chapter 4 Key Diagram 3, p. 135). Figure 9.2(a) shows the saving–investment diagram drawn for two randomly chosen levels of output, 400 and 500. Corresponding to each level is a saving curve, with the value of output indicated in parentheses next to it. Each saving curve slopes upward because an increase in the real interest rate causes households to increase their desired level of saving. An increase in current output (income) leads to more desired saving at any real interest rate, so the saving curve S for $Y = 500$ lies to the right of the saving curve S for $Y = 400$.

Figure 9.2(a) also shows an investment curve. Recall from Chapter 4 that the investment curve slopes downward because an increase in the real interest rate increases the user cost of capital, which reduces the desired capital stock and hence desired investment. Desired investment is not affected by current output, so the investment curve is the same whether $Y = 400$ or $Y = 500$.

Each level of output implies a different market-clearing real interest rate. When output is 400, goods market equilibrium is at point D and the market-clearing real interest rate is 7%. When output is 500, goods market equilibrium occurs at point F and the market-clearing real interest rate is 5%.

Figure 9.2(b) shows the *IS* curve for this economy, with output on the horizontal axis and the real interest rate on the vertical axis. For any level of output, the *IS* curve shows the real interest rate that clears the goods market. Thus, $Y = 400$ and $r = 7\%$ at point D on the *IS* curve. (Note that point D in Figure 9.2(b) corresponds to point D in Figure 9.2(a).) Similarly, when output is 500, the real interest rate that clears the goods market is 5%. This combination of output and the real interest rate occurs at point F on the *IS* curve in Figure 9.2(b); it corresponds to point F in Figure 9.2(a). In general, because a rise in output increases national desired saving,

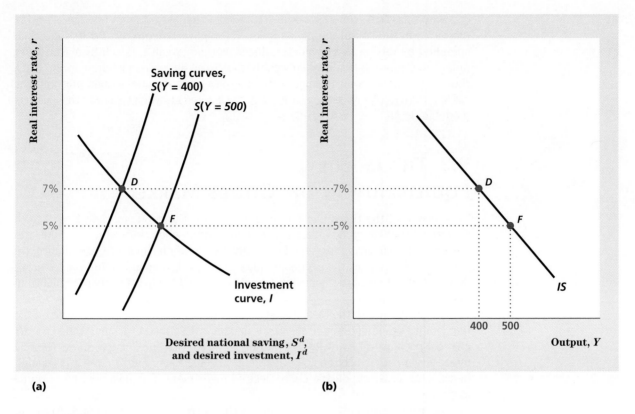

(a)   **(b)**

FIGURE 9.2

DERIVING THE *IS* CURVE

(a) The graph shows the goods market equilibrium for two different levels of output: 400 and 500 (the output corresponding to each saving curve is indicated in parentheses next to the curve). Higher levels of output (income) increase desired national saving and shift the saving curve to the right. When output is 400, the real interest rate that clears the goods market is 7% (point *D*). When output is 500, the market-clearing interest rate is 5% (point *F*).

(b) For each level of output the *IS* curve shows the corresponding real interest rate that clears the goods market. Thus, each point on the *IS* curve corresponds to an equilibrium point in the goods market. As in (a), when output is 400, the real interest rate that clears the goods market is 7% (point *D*); when output is 500, the market-clearing interest rate is 5% (point *F*). Because higher output raises saving and leads to a lower market-clearing interest rate, the *IS* curve slopes downward.

thereby reducing the real interest rate that clears the goods market, the *IS* curve slopes downward.

The slope of the *IS* curve may also be interpreted in terms of the alternative (but equivalent) version of the goods market equilibrium condition, which states that in equilibrium the aggregate quantity of goods demanded must equal the aggregate quantity of goods supplied. To illustrate, suppose that the economy is initially at point *F* in Figure 9.2(b). The aggregate quantities of goods supplied and demanded are equal at point *F*, because *F* lies on the *IS* curve, which means that the goods market is in equilibrium at that point.[3] Now, suppose that for some reason the real interest rate *r* rises from 5% to 7%. Recall from Chapter 4 that an increase in the real interest rate reduces both desired consumption C^d (because people

---

3.   We have just showed that desired national saving equals desired investment at point *F*, or $S^d = I^d$. Substituting the definition of desired national saving, $Y - C^d - G$, for S^d in the condition that desired national saving equals desired investment shows also that $Y = C^d + I^d + G$ at *F*.

desire to save more when the real interest rate rises) and desired investment I^d, thereby reducing the aggregate quantity of goods demanded. If output Y remained at its initial level of 500, the increase in the real interest rate would imply that more goods were being supplied than demanded. For the goods market to reach equilibrium at the higher real interest rate, the quantity of goods supplied has to fall. At point D in Figure 9.2(b), output has fallen enough (from 500 to 400) that the quantities of goods supplied and demanded are equal, and the goods market has returned to equilibrium.[4] Again, higher real interest rates are associated with less output in goods market equilibrium, so the *IS* curve slopes downward.

FACTORS THAT SHIFT THE *IS* CURVE

For any level of output, the *IS* curve shows the real interest rate needed to clear the goods market. With output held constant, any economic disturbance or policy change that changes the value of the goods-market-clearing real interest rate will cause the *IS* curve to shift. More specifically, *for constant output, any change in the economy that reduces desired national saving relative to desired investment will increase the real interest rate that clears the goods market and, thus, shift the IS curve up.* Similarly, for constant output, changes that increase desired saving relative to desired investment, thereby reducing the market-clearing real interest rate, shift the *IS* curve down. Factors that shift the *IS* curve are described in Summary table 12, on the next page.

We can use a change in current government purchases to illustrate *IS* curve shifts in general. The effects of a temporary increase in government purchases on the *IS* curve are shown in Figure 9.3, on page 301. Figure 9.3(a) shows the saving–investment diagram, with an initial saving curve S^1 and an initial investment curve I. The S^1 curve represents saving when output (income) is fixed at $Y = 450$. Figure 9.3(b) shows the initial *IS* curve, IS^1. The initial goods market equilibrium when output Y equals 450 is represented by point E in both (a) and (b). At E, the initial market-clearing real interest rate is 6%.

Now, suppose that the government increases its current purchases of goods, G. Desired investment at any level of the real interest rate is not affected by the increase in government purchases, so the investment curve does not shift. However, as discussed in Chapter 4, a temporary increase in government purchases reduces desired national saving (see Summary table 5, p. 116), so the saving curve shifts to the left from S^1 to S^2 in Figure 9.3(a). As a result of the reduction in desired national saving, the real interest rate that clears the goods market when output equals 450 increases from 6% to 7% (point F in Figure 9.3(a)).

The effect on the *IS* curve is shown in Figure 9.3(b). With output constant at 450, the real interest rate that clears the goods market increases from 6% to 7%, as shown by the shift from point E to point F. The new *IS* curve, IS^2, passes through F and lies above and to the right of the initial *IS* curve, IS^1. Thus, a temporary increase in government purchases shifts the *IS* curve up.

---

4. Although a drop in output Y obviously reduces the quantity of goods supplied, it also reduces the quantity of goods demanded. The reason is that a drop in output is also a drop in income, which reduces desired consumption. However, although a drop in output of one dollar reduces the supply of output by one dollar, a drop in income of one dollar reduces desired consumption C^d by less than one dollar (that is, the marginal propensity to consume, defined in Chapter 4, is less than 1). Thus, a drop in output Y reduces goods supplied more than goods demanded and therefore reduces the excess supply of goods.

SUMMARY 12 FACTORS THAT SHIFT THE *IS* CURVE

AN INCREASE IN	SHIFTS THE *IS* CURVE	REASON
Expected future output	Up	Desired saving falls (desired consumption rises), raising the real interest rate that clears the goods market.
Wealth	Up	Desired saving falls (desired consumption rises), raising the real interest rate that clears the goods market.
Government purchases, G	Up	Desired saving falls (demand for goods rises), raising the real interest rate that clears the goods market.
Taxes, T	No change or Down	No change, if consumers take into account an offsetting future tax cut and do not change consumption (Ricardian equivalence); down, if consumers do not take into account a future tax cut and reduce desired consumption, increasing desired national saving and lowering the real interest rate that clears the goods market.
Expected future marginal product of capital, MPK^f	Up	Desired investment increases, raising the real interest rate that clears the goods market.
Effective tax rate on capital	Down	Desired investment falls, lowering the real interest rate that clears the goods market.

So far, our discussion of *IS* curve shifts has focused on the goods market equilibrium condition that desired national saving must equal desired investment. However, factors that shift the *IS* curve may also be described in terms of the alternative (but equivalent) goods market equilibrium condition—that the aggregate quantities of goods demanded and supplied are equal. In particular, for a given level of output, *any change that increases the aggregate demand for goods shifts the IS curve up*. This rule works because for the initial level of output, an increase in the aggregate demand for goods causes the quantity of goods demanded to exceed the quantity supplied. Goods market equilibrium can be restored at the same level of output by an increase in the real interest rate, which reduces desired

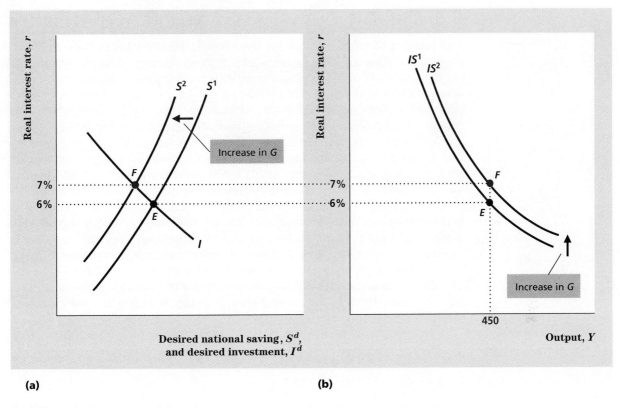

(a)

(b)

FIGURE 9.3

EFFECT ON THE *IS* CURVE OF A TEMPORARY INCREASE IN
GOVERNMENT PURCHASES

(a) The saving–investment diagram shows the effects of a temporary increase in government purchases, *G*, with output *Y* constant at 450. The increase in *G* reduces desired national saving and shifts the saving curve to the left, from S^1 to S^2. The goods market equilibrium point moves from point *E* to point *F*, and the real interest rate rises from 6% to 7%.

(b) The increase in *G* raises the real interest rate that clears the goods market for any level of output. Thus, the *IS* curve shifts upward from IS^1 to IS^2. In this example, with output held constant at 450, an increase in government purchases raises the real interest rate that clears the goods market from 6% (point *E*) to 7% (point *F*).

consumption C^d and desired investment I^d. For any level of output, an increase in aggregate demand for goods raises the real interest rate that clears the goods market, so we conclude that an increase in the aggregate demand for goods shifts the *IS* curve up.

To illustrate this alternative way of thinking about *IS* curve shifts, we again use the example of a temporary increase in government purchases. Note that an increase in government purchases, *G*, directly raises the demand for goods, $C^d + I^d + G$, leading to an excess demand for goods at the initial level of output. The excess demand for goods can be eliminated and goods market equilibrium at the initial level of output restored by an increase in the real interest rate, which reduces C^d and I^d. Because a higher real interest rate is required for goods market equilibrium when government purchases increase, an increase in *G* causes the *IS* curve to shift up.

9.3 THE *LM* CURVE: ASSET MARKET EQUILIBRIUM

The third and final market in our macroeconomic model is the asset market, presented in Chapter 7. The asset market is in equilibrium when the quantities of assets demanded by holders of wealth for their portfolios equal the supplies of those assets in the economy. In reality, there are many different assets, both real (houses, consumer durables, office buildings) and financial (chequing accounts, government bonds). Recall, however, that we aggregated all assets into two categories—money and non-monetary assets. We assumed that the nominal supply of money is M and that money pays a fixed nominal interest rate i^m. Similarly, we assumed that the nominal supply of non-monetary assets is NM and that these assets pay a nominal interest rate i and (given expected inflation π^e) an expected real interest rate r.

With this aggregation assumption, we showed that the asset market equilibrium condition reduces to the requirement that the quantities of money supplied and demanded be equal. In this section, we show that asset market equilibrium can be represented by the *LM* curve. However, in order to discuss how the asset market comes into equilibrium—a task that we did not complete in Chapter 7—we first introduce an important relationship used every day by traders in financial markets: the relationship between the *price* of a non-monetary asset and the *interest rate* on that asset.

THE INTEREST RATE AND THE PRICE OF A NON-MONETARY ASSET

The price of a non-monetary asset, such as a government bond, is what a buyer has to pay for it. Its price is closely related to the interest rate that it pays (sometimes called its *yield*). To illustrate this relationship with an example, let us consider a bond that matures in one year. At maturity, we assume, the bondholder will redeem it and receive $10,000; the bond does not pay any interest before it matures.[5] Suppose that this bond can now be purchased for $9,615. At this price, over the coming year the bond will increase in value by $385 ($10,000 – $9,615), or approximately 4% of its current price of $9,615. Therefore, the nominal interest rate on the bond, or its yield, is 4% per year.

Now, suppose that for some reason the current price of a $10,000 bond that matures in one year drops to $9,524. The increase in the bond's value over the next year will be $476 ($10,000 – $9,524), or approximately 5% of the purchase price of $9,524. Therefore, when the current price of the bond falls to $9,524, the nominal interest rate on the bond increases to 5% per year. More generally, given the promised schedule of repayments of a bond or other non-monetary asset, the higher the price of the asset, the lower is the nominal interest rate that the asset pays. Thus, a media report that in yesterday's trading, the bond market "strengthened" (bond prices rose), is equivalent to saying that nominal interest rates fell.

We have just indicated why the price of a non-monetary asset and its nominal interest rate are negatively related to each other. For a given expected rate of inflation π^e, movements in the nominal interest rate are matched by equal movements in the real interest rate, so the price of a non-monetary asset and its real interest rate are also inversely related. This relationship is a key to deriving the *LM* curve and explaining how the asset market comes into equilibrium.

---

5. A bond that does not pay any interest before maturity is called a discount bond.

THE EQUALITY OF MONEY DEMANDED AND MONEY SUPPLIED

To derive the *LM* curve, which represents asset market equilibrium, recall again that the asset market is in equilibrium only if the quantity of money demanded equals the currently available money supply. We depict the equality of money supplied and demanded using the money supply–money demand diagram, shown in Figure 9.4(a). The real interest rate is on the vertical axis and money, measured in real terms, is on the horizontal axis.[6] The *MS* line shows the economy's real money supply, *M/P*. For simplicity, we may suppose that the central bank sets the nominal money supply *M*.[7] Thus, for a given price level *P*, the real money supply *M/P* is a fixed number and the *MS* line is vertical. For example, if *M* = 200 and *P* = 2, the *MS* line is vertical at *M/P* = 100.

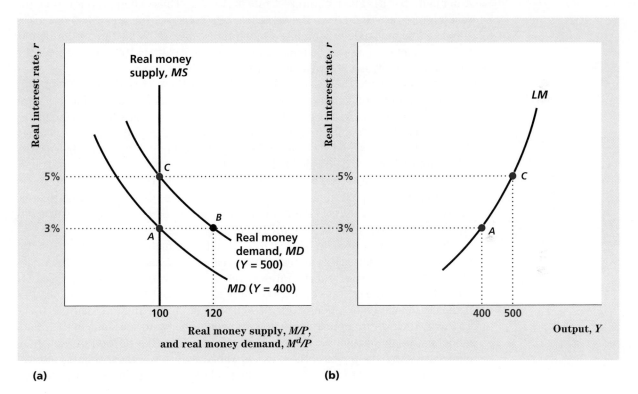

(a)   **(b)**

FIGURE 9.4

DERIVING THE *LM* CURVE

(a) The curves show real money demand and real money supply. Real money supply is fixed at 100. When output is 400, the real money demand curve is *MD* (*Y* = 400); the real interest rate that clears the asset market is 3% (point *A*). When output is 500, more money is demanded at the same real interest rate, so the real money demand curve shifts to the right to *MD* (*Y* = 500). In this case, the real interest rate that clears the asset market is 5% (point *C*).

(b) The graph shows the corresponding *LM* curve. For each level of output, the *LM* curve shows the real interest rate that clears the asset market. Thus, when output is 400, the *LM* curve shows that the real interest rate that clears the goods market is 3% (point *A*). When output is 500, the *LM* curve shows a market-clearing real interest rate of 5% (point *C*). Because higher output raises money demand, and thus raises the real interest rate that clears the asset market, the *LM* curve slopes upward.

---

6. Asset market equilibrium may be expressed as either nominal money supplied equals nominal money demanded, or as real money supplied equals real money demanded. As in Chapter 7, we work with the condition expressed in real terms.

7. Chapter 14 describes the tools of Canadian monetary policy.

Real money demand at two different levels of income Y is shown by the two *MD* curves in Figure 9.4(a). Recall from Chapter 7 that a higher real interest rate r increases the relative attractiveness of non-monetary assets and causes holders of wealth to demand less money. Thus, the money demand curves slope downward. The money demand curve *MD* for $Y = 400$ shows the real demand for money when output is 400; similarly, the *MD* curve for $Y = 500$ shows the real demand for money when output is 500. Because an increase in income increases the amount of money demanded at any real interest rate, the money demand curve for $Y = 500$ is farther to the right than the money demand curve for $Y = 400$.

Graphically, asset market equilibrium occurs at the intersection of the money supply and money demand curves, where the real quantities of money supplied and demanded are equal. For example, when output is 400 so that the money demand curve is *MD* $(Y = 400)$, the money demand and money supply curves intersect at point A in Figure 9.4(a). The real interest rate at A is 3%. Thus, when output is 400, the real interest rate that clears the asset market (equalizes the quantities of money supplied and demanded) is 3%. At a real interest rate of 3% and an output of 400, the real quantity of money demanded by holders of wealth is 100, which equals the real money supply made available by the central bank.

What happens to the asset market equilibrium if output rises from 400 to 500? People need to conduct more transactions, so their real money demand increases at any real interest rate. As a result, the money demand curve shifts to the right, to *MD* for $Y = 500$. If the real interest rate remained at 3%, the real quantity of money demanded would exceed the real money supply. At point B in Figure 9.4(a), the real quantity of money demanded is 120, which is greater than the real money supply of 100. To restore equality of money demanded and supplied and, thus, bring the asset market back into equilibrium, the real interest rate must rise to 5%. When the real interest rate is 5%, the real quantity of money demanded declines to 100, which is equal to the fixed real money supply (point C in Figure 9.4(a)).

How does an increase in the real interest rate eliminate the excess demand for money, and what causes this increase in the real interest rate? Recall that the prices of non-monetary assets and the interest rates they pay are negatively related. At the initial real interest rate of 3%, the increase in output from 400 to 500 causes people to demand more money (the *MD* curve shifts to the right in Figure 9.4(a)). To satisfy their desire to hold more money, people will try to sell some of their non-monetary assets for money. But when people rush to sell a portion of their non-monetary assets, the prices of these assets will fall, which will cause the real interest rates on these assets to rise. Thus, it is the public's attempt to increase its holdings of money by selling non-monetary assets that causes the real interest rate to rise.

Because the real supply of money in the economy is fixed, the public, as a whole, cannot increase the amount of money it holds. As long as people attempt to do so by selling non-monetary assets, the real interest rate will continue to rise. But the increase in the real interest rate paid by non-monetary assets makes those assets more attractive relative to money, reducing the real quantity of money demanded (here the movement is *along* the *MD* curve for $Y = 500$, from point B to point C in Figure 9.4(a)). The real interest rate will rise until the real quantity of money demanded again equals the fixed supply of money and restores asset market equilibrium. The new asset market equilibrium is at C, where the real interest rate has risen from 3% to 5%.

The preceding example shows that when output rises, increasing real money demand, a higher real interest rate is needed to maintain equilibrium in the asset

market. In general, the relationship between output and the real interest rate that
clears the asset market is expressed graphically by the **LM curve**. For any level of
output, the *LM* curve shows the real interest rate for which the asset market is in
equilibrium, with equal quantities of money supplied and demanded. The term *LM*
comes from the asset market equilibrium condition that the real quantity of money
demanded, as determined by the real money demand function *L*, must equal the
real money supply *M/P*.

The *LM* curve corresponding to our numerical example is shown in Figure 9.4(b),
with the real interest rate *r* on the vertical axis and output *Y* on the horizontal axis.
Points *A* and *C* lie on the *LM* curve. At *A*, which corresponds to point *A* in the
money supply–money demand diagram of Figure 9.4(a), output *Y* is 400, and the
real interest rate *r* is 3%. Because *A* lies on the *LM* curve, when output is 400, the
real interest rate that clears the asset market is 3%. Similarly, because *C* lies on the
LM curve, when output is 500, the real interest rate that equalizes money supplied
and demanded is 5%; this output–real interest rate combination corresponds to the
asset market equilibrium at point *C* in Figure 9.4(a).

Figure 9.4(b) illustrates the general point that the *LM* curve always slopes
upward from left to right. It does so because increases in output, by raising money
demand, also raise the real interest rate on non-monetary assets needed to clear
the asset market.

Factors That Shift the *LM* Curve

In deriving the *LM* curve, we varied output but held constant other factors, such as
the price level, that affect the real interest rate that clears the asset market. Changes
in any of these other factors will cause the *LM* curve to shift. In particular, for constant
output, *any change that reduces real money supply relative to real money
demand will increase the real interest rate that clears the asset market and
cause the LM curve to shift up*. Similarly, for constant output, anything that raises
real money supply relative to real money demand will reduce the real interest rate that
clears the asset market and shift the *LM* curve down. Here, we discuss in general
terms how changes in real money supply or demand affect the *LM* curve. Summary
table 13, shown on the next page, describes the factors that shift the LM curve.

Changes in the Real Money Supply

An increase in the real money supply *M/P* will reduce the real interest rate that
clears the asset market and shift the *LM* curve down. Figure 9.5, on page 307,
illustrates this point and extends our previous numerical example.

Figure 9.5(a) contains the money supply–money demand diagram. Initially,
suppose that the real money supply *M/P* is 100 and output is 400, so the money
demand curve is *MD* (*Y* = 400). Then, equilibrium in the asset market occurs at
point *A* with a market-clearing real interest rate of 3%. The *LM* curve corresponding
to the real money supply of 100 is shown as *LM* (*M/P* = 100) in Figure 9.5(b). At point
A on this *LM* curve, as at point *A* in the money supply–money demand diagram in
Figure 9.5(a), output is 400 and the real interest rate is 3%. Because *A* lies on the
initial *LM* curve, when output is 400 and the money supply is 100, the real interest
rate that clears the asset market is 3%.

Now, suppose that with output constant at 400, the real money supply rises
from 100 to 120. This increase in the real money supply causes the vertical money
supply curve to shift to the right, from MS^1 to MS^2 in Figure 9.5(a). The asset market

SUMMARY 13   FACTORS THAT SHIFT THE *LM* CURVE

AN INCREASE IN	SHIFTS THE *LM* CURVE	REASON
Nominal money supply, M	Down	Real money supply increases, lowering the real interest rate that clears the asset market (equates money supplied and money demanded).
Price level, P	Up	Real money supply falls, raising the real interest rate that clears the asset market.
Expected inflation, π^e	Down	Demand for money falls, lowering the real interest rate that clears the asset market.
Nominal interest rate on money, i^m	Up	Demand for money increases, raising the real interest rate that clears the asset market.

In addition, for constant output, any factor that increases real money demand raises the real interest rate that clears the asset market and shifts the *LM* curve up. Other factors that increase real money demand (see Summary table 9, p. 248) include

■ an increase in wealth;

■ an increase in the risk of alternative assets relative to the risk of holding money;

■ a decline in the liquidity of alternative assets; and

■ a decline in the efficiency of payment technologies.

equilibrium point is now point D, where, with output remaining at 400, the market-clearing real interest rate has fallen to 2%.

Why has the real interest rate that clears the asset market fallen? At the initial real interest rate of 3%, there is an excess supply of money—that is, holders of wealth have more money in their portfolios than they want to hold, and consequently, they have a smaller share of their wealth than they would like in non-monetary assets. To eliminate this imbalance in their portfolios, holders of wealth will want to use some of their money to buy non-monetary assets. However, when holders of wealth as a group try to purchase non-monetary assets, the price of non-monetary assets is bid up and hence the real interest rate paid on these assets declines. As the real interest rate falls, non-monetary assets become less attractive relative to money. The real interest rate continues to fall until it reaches 2% at point D in Figure 9.5(a), where the excess supply of money and the excess demand for non-monetary assets are eliminated and the asset market is back in equilibrium.

The effect of the increase in real money supply on the *LM* curve is illustrated in Figure 9.5(b). With output constant at 400, the increase in the real money supply lowers the real interest rate that clears the asset market, from 3% to 2%. Thus, point D, where $Y = 400$ and $r = 2\%$, is now a point of asset market equilibrium, and point

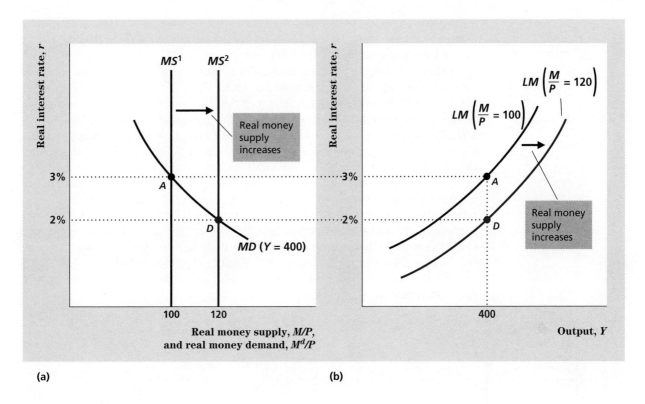

(a)   **(b)**

FIGURE 9.5

AN INCREASE IN THE REAL MONEY SUPPLY SHIFTS THE *LM*
CURVE DOWN

(a) An increase in the real supply of money shifts the money supply
curve to the right, from MS^1 to MS^2. For a constant level of output,
the real interest rate that clears the asset market falls. If output is
fixed at 400, for example, the money demand curve is *MD* ($Y =$
400) and the real interest rate that clears the asset market falls from
3% (point *A*) to 2% (point *D*).

(b) The graph shows the effect of the increase in real money supply
on the *LM* curve. For any level of output, the increase in the real
money supply causes the real interest rate that clears the asset market to fall. So, for example, when output is 400, the increase in the
real money supply causes the real interest rate that clears the asset
market to fall from 3% (point *A*) to 2% (point *D*). Thus, the *LM*
curve shifts down, from *LM* for *M/P* = 100 to *LM* for *M/P* = 120.

A no longer is. More generally, for any given level of output, an increase in the real
money supply lowers the real interest rate that clears the asset market. Therefore, the
entire *LM* curve shifts down. The new *LM* curve, *LM* for *M/P* = 120, passes through
the new equilibrium point *D* and lies below the old *LM* curve, *LM* for *M/P* = 100.

　　Thus, with fixed output, an increase in the real money supply lowers the real
interest rate that clears the asset market and causes the *LM* curve to shift down. A
similar analysis would show that a drop in the real money supply causes the *LM*
curve to shift up.

　　What might cause the real money supply to increase? In general, because the real
money supply equals *M/P*, the real money supply will increase whenever the nominal
money supply *M*, which is controlled by the central bank, grows more quickly than
the price level *P*.

CHANGES IN REAL MONEY DEMAND

A change in any variable that affects real money demand, other than output or the
real interest rate, will also shift the *LM* curve. More specifically, with output constant,

an increase in real money demand raises the real interest rate that clears the asset market and, thus, shifts the LM curve up. Analogously, with output constant, a drop in real money demand shifts the LM curve down.

Figure 9.6 shows a graphical analysis of an increase in money demand similar to that for a change in money supply shown in Figure 9.5. As before, the money supply–money demand diagram is shown on the left, Figure 9.6(a). Output is constant at 400, and the real money supply again is 100. The initial money demand curve is MD^1. The initial asset market equilibrium point is at A, where the money demand curve MD^1 and the money supply curve MS intersect. At initial equilibrium, point A, the real interest rate that clears the asset market is 3%.

Now, suppose that for a fixed level of output, a change occurs in the economy that increases real money demand. For example, if banks decided to increase the interest rate paid on money, i^m, the public would want to hold more money at the same levels of output and the real interest rate. Graphically, the increase in money demand shifts the money demand curve to the right, from MD^1 to MD^2 in Figure 9.6(a). At the initial real interest rate of 3% the real quantity of money demanded is 130, which exceeds the available supply of 100; so, 3% is no longer the value of the real interest rate that clears the asset market.

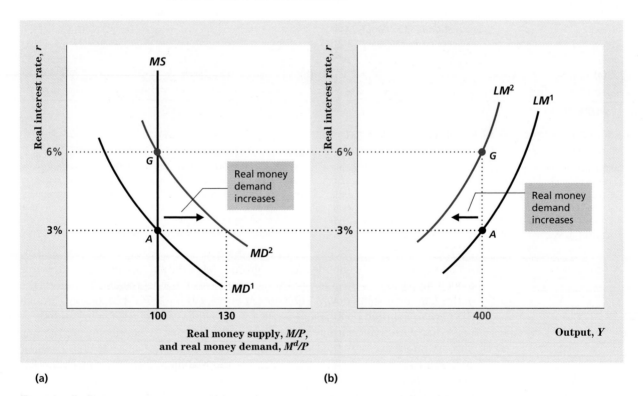

(a)   (b)

FIGURE 9.6

AN INCREASE IN REAL MONEY DEMAND SHIFTS THE LM CURVE UP

(a) With output constant at 400 and the real money supply at 100, an increase in the interest rate paid on money raises real money demand. The money demand curve shifts to the right, from MD^1 to MD^2, and the real interest rate that clears the asset market rises from 3% (point A) to 6% (point G).

(b) The graph shows the effect of the increase in real money demand on the LM curve. When output is 400, the increase in real money demand raises the real interest rate that clears the asset market from 3% (point A) to 6% (point G). More generally, for any level of output, the increase in real money demand raises the real interest rate that clears the asset market. Thus, the LM curve shifts up, from LM^1 to LM^2.

How will the real interest rate that clears the asset market change after the increase in money demand? If holders of wealth want to hold more money, they will exchange non-monetary assets for money. Increased sales of non-monetary assets will drive down their price and, thus, raise the real interest rate that they pay. The real interest rate will rise, reducing the attractiveness of holding money, until the public is satisfied to hold the available real money supply (100). The real interest rate rises from its initial value of 3% at A to 6% at G.

Figure 9.6(b) shows the effect of the increase in money demand on the *LM* curve. The initial *LM* curve, LM^1, passes through point A, showing that when output is 400 the real interest rate that clears the asset market is 3%. (Point A in Figure 9.6(b) corresponds to point A in Figure 9.6(a)). Following the increase in money demand, with output fixed at 400, the market-clearing real interest rate rises to 6%. Thus, the new *LM* curve must pass through point G (corresponding to point G in Figure 9.6(a)), where $Y = 400$ and $r = 6\%$. The new *LM* curve, LM^2, is higher than LM^1 because the real interest rate that clears the asset market is now higher for any level of output.

9.4 GENERAL EQUILIBRIUM IN THE COMPLETE *IS–LM* MODEL

The next step is to put the labour market, the goods market, and the asset market together and examine the equilibrium of the economy as a whole. A situation in which all markets in an economy are simultaneously in equilibrium is called a **general equilibrium**. Figure 9.7 shows the complete *IS–LM* model, illustrating how the general equilibrium of the economy is determined. The figure shows

- the full-employment, or *FE*, line, along which the labour market is in equilibrium;

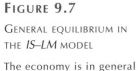

FIGURE 9.7

GENERAL EQUILIBRIUM IN THE *IS–LM* MODEL

The economy is in general equilibrium when quantities supplied equal quantities demanded in every market. The general equilibrium point, *E*, lies on the *IS* curve, the *LM* curve, and the *FE* line. Thus, at *E*, and only at *E*, the goods market, the asset market, and the labour market are simultaneously in equilibrium.

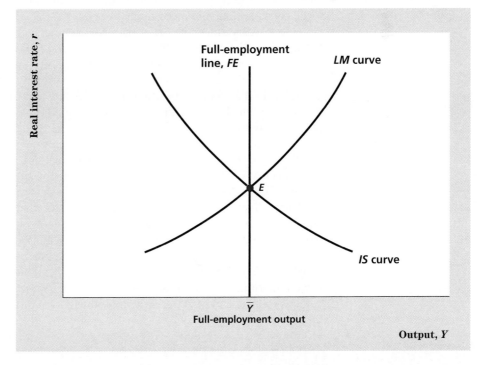

- the *IS* curve, along which the goods market is in equilibrium; and

- the *LM* curve, along which the asset market is in equilibrium.

The three curves intersect at point E, indicating that all three markets are in equilibrium at that point. Therefore, E represents a general equilibrium, and because it is the only point that lies on all three curves, it represents the only general equilibrium for this economy.

Although point E obviously is a general equilibrium point, it is not so clear what forces, if any, act to bring the economy to that point. To put it another way, although the *IS* curve and *FE* line must intersect somewhere, we have not explained why the *LM* curve must pass through that same point. In Section 9.5, we discuss the economic forces that lead the economy to general equilibrium. There we show that (1) the general equilibrium of the economy always occurs at the intersection of the *IS* curve and the *FE* line; and (2) adjustments of the price level cause the *LM* curve to shift until it passes through the general equilibrium point defined by the intersection of the *IS* curve and the *FE* line. Before discussing the details of this adjustment process, however, let us consider an example that illustrates the use of the complete *IS–LM* model.

APPLYING THE *IS–LM* FRAMEWORK: A TEMPORARY ADVERSE SUPPLY SHOCK

An economic shock relevant to business cycle analysis is an adverse supply shock. Specifically, suppose that (because of bad weather or a temporary increase in oil prices) the productivity parameter A in the production function drops temporarily.[8] We can use the *IS–LM* model to analyze the effects of this shock on the general equilibrium of the economy and the general equilibrium values of such economic variables as the real wage, employment, output, the real interest rate, the price level, consumption, and investment.

Suppose that the economy is initially in general equilibrium at point E in Figure 9.8(a), where the initial *FE* line, FE^1, *IS* curve, and *LM* curve, LM^1, for this economy intersect. To determine the effects of a temporary supply shock on the general equilibrium of this economy, we must consider how the temporary drop in productivity A affects the positions of the *FE* line and the *IS* and *LM* curves.

The *FE* line describes equilibrium in the labour market. Hence to find the effect of the supply shock on the *FE* line, we must start by looking at how the shock affects labour supply and labour demand. In Chapter 3, we demonstrated that an adverse supply shock reduces the marginal product of labour and, thus, shifts the labour demand curve down (see Figure 3.12). Because the supply shock is temporary, we assume that it does not affect workers' wealth or expected future wages and so does not affect labour supply. As a result of the decline in labour demand, the equilibrium values of the real wage and employment, $\overline{N}$, fall. The *FE* line shifts only to the degree that full-employment output $\overline{Y}$ changes. Does $\overline{Y}$ change? Yes. Recall from Chapter 3 that an adverse supply shock reduces full-employment output $\overline{Y}$, which equals $AF(K, \overline{N})$, for two reasons: (1) as we just mentioned, the supply shock reduces the equilibrium level of employment $\overline{N}$, which lowers the amount of output that can be produced; and (2) the drop in productivity A directly reduces the amount of

---

8. Recall that the production function, Eq. (3.1), is $Y = AF(K, N)$, so a drop in A reduces the amount of output that can be produced for any quantities of capital K and labour N.

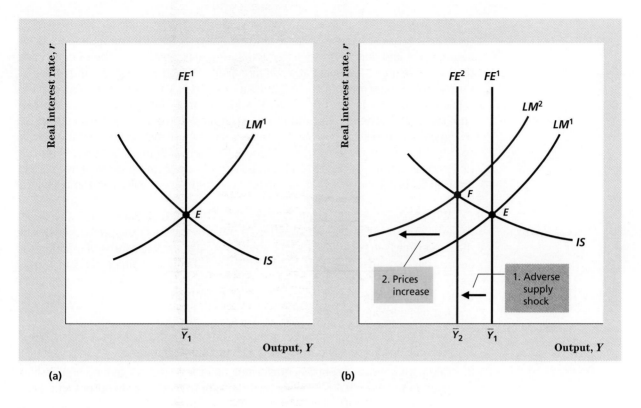

(a)   (b)

Figure 9.8

Effects of a temporary adverse supply shock

(a) Initially, the economy is in general equilibrium at point *E*, with output at its full-employment level $\bar{Y}_1$.
(b) A temporary adverse supply shock reduces full-employment output from $\bar{Y}_1$ to $\bar{Y}_2$ and shifts the *FE* line to the left from FE^1 to FE^2. The new general equilibrium is represented by point *F*, where FE^2

intersects the unchanged *IS* curve. The price level increases and shifts the *LM* curve up and to the left, from LM^1 to LM^2, until it passes through *F*. At the new general equilibrium point, *F*, output is lower, the real interest rate is higher, and the price level is higher than at the original general equilibrium point, *E*.

output produced by any combination of capital and labour. The reduction in $\bar{Y}$ is represented by a shift to the left of the *FE* line, from FE^1 to FE^2 in Figure 9.8(b).

Now, consider the effects of the temporary adverse supply shock on the *IS* curve. Recall that we derived the *IS* curve by changing the level of current output in the saving–investment diagram (see Figure 9.2) and finding for each level of current output the real interest rate for which desired saving equals desired investment. A *temporary* adverse supply shock reduces current output but does not change any other factor affecting desired saving or investment (such as wealth, expected future income, or the future marginal product of capital). Therefore, a temporary supply shock is just the sort of change in current output that we used to trace out the *IS* curve. We conclude that a temporary adverse supply shock is a movement *along* the *IS* curve, *not a shift* of the *IS* curve, leaving it unchanged.[9]

Finally, we consider the *LM* curve. A temporary supply shock has no direct effect on the demand for or supply of money and thus does not shift the *LM* curve.

9. Analytical Problem 2 at the end of the chapter examines the effect of a permanent adverse supply shock and identifies factors that shift the *IS* curve in that case.

We now look for the new general equilibrium of the economy. In Figure 9.8(b), there is no point at which FE^2 (the new FE line), IS, and LM^1 all intersect. As we mentioned—and demonstrate in Section 9.5—when the FE line, the IS curve, and the LM curve do not intersect at a common point, the LM curve shifts until it passes through the intersection of the FE line and IS curve. This shift in the LM curve is caused by changes in the price level P, which change the real money supply M/P and, thus, affect the equilibrium of the asset market. As Figure 9.8(b) shows, to restore general equilibrium at point F, the LM curve must shift up and to the left, from LM^1 to LM^2. For it to do so, the real money supply M/P must fall (see Summary table 13) and, thus, the price level P must rise. We infer (although we have not yet given an economic explanation) that an adverse supply shock will cause the price level to rise.

What is the effect of a temporary supply shock on the inflation rate, as distinct from the price level? As the inflation rate is the growth rate of the price level, during the period in which prices are rising to their new, higher level, a burst of inflation will occur. However, after the price level stabilizes at its higher value (and is no longer rising), inflation subsides. Thus, a temporary supply shock should cause a temporary rather than a permanent increase in the rate of inflation.

Let us pause and review our results.

1. As we had already shown in Chapter 3, a temporary adverse supply shock lowers the equilibrium values of the real wage and employment.

2. Comparing the new general equilibrium, point F, to the old general equilibrium, point E, in Figure 9.8(b), we see that the supply shock lowers output and raises the real interest rate.

3. The supply shock raises the price level and causes a temporary burst in inflation.

4. Because in the new general equilibrium the real interest rate is higher and output is lower, consumption must be lower than before the supply shock. The higher real interest rate also implies that investment must be lower after the shock.

In the Application, "Oil Price Shocks Revisited," we see how well our model explains the historical behaviour of the economy. However, note that economic models, such as the IS–LM model, also are used extensively in forecasting economic conditions (see Box 9.1 on page 314).

APPLICATION

OIL PRICE SHOCKS REVISITED

In Chapter 3, we pointed out that an increase in the price of oil is an example of an adverse supply shock, and we looked at the effects of the 1973–1974 and 1979–1980 oil price shocks on the Canadian economy (see the Application, "Output, Employment, and the Real Wage during Oil Price Shocks," p. 82). The theory's predictions—that adverse supply shocks reduce output, employment, and the real wage—were confirmed for those two episodes. Our analysis using the complete IS–LM model is consistent with that earlier discussion. However, it adds the predictions that following an oil price shock, consumption and investment decline, inflation increases, and the real interest rate rises.

Figure 8.4 shows that consumption fell slightly and that investment fell sharply immediately after these oil price shocks. During 1974, real consumption fell by 0.5%, and real investment fell by 5.0%. Following the onset of the recession in the first quarter of 1980, real consumption fell by 0.2%, and real investment fell by 2.6% in just one quarter. Inflation also behaved as predicted by our analysis, surging temporarily in 1973–1974 and again in 1979–1980 (see Figure 7.3 or Figure 8.10).

Our analysis also predicted that an oil price shock will cause the real interest rate to rise. However, this result depends somewhat on the assumption we made that people expected the oil price shock to be temporary. In Analytical Problem 2 at the end of the chapter, you will find that if the adverse supply shock is expected to be permanent, the rise in the real interest rate will be less than when the adverse supply shock is expected to be temporary (and the real interest rate may not rise). However, we do not really know what people's expectations were about the duration of the two major oil price shocks. Therefore, we cannot state with confidence what the effect of such a shock on the real interest rate should have been. Actually, the real interest rate rose during the 1979–1980 shock but not during the 1973–1974 shock (see Figure 2.3). On the basis of these data only, our model suggests that people expected the 1973–1974 oil shock to be permanent and the 1979–1980 shock to be temporary. Interestingly, those expectations were essentially correct: Figure 3.13 shows that the oil price increase of 1979–1980 was reversed rather quickly but that the price increase of 1973–1974 was not.

9.5 PRICE ADJUSTMENT AND THE ATTAINMENT OF GENERAL EQUILIBRIUM

We now explain the economic forces that lead prices to change and shift the *LM* curve until it passes through the intersection of the *IS* curve and the *FE* line. In discussing the role of price adjustments in bringing the economy back to general equilibrium, we also show the basic difference between the two main approaches to business cycle analysis: classical and Keynesian.

To illustrate the adjustment process, let us use the complete *IS–LM* model to consider what happens to the economy if the nominal money supply increases. This analysis allows us to discuss monetary policy (the control of the money supply) and to introduce some ongoing controversies about the effects of monetary policy on the economy.

THE EFFECTS OF A MONETARY EXPANSION

Suppose that the central bank decides to raise the nominal money supply M by 10%. For now, we hold the price level P constant so that the real money supply M/P also increases by 10%. What effects will this monetary expansion have on the economy? Figure 9.9, on the next page, helps us answer this question with the complete *IS–LM* model.

The three parts of Figure 9.9 show the sequence of events involved in the analysis. For simplicity, suppose that the economy initially is in general equilibrium so that in Figure 9.9(a), the *IS* curve, the *FE* line, and the initial *LM* curve, LM^1, all pass through the general equilibrium point, E. At E, output equals its full-employment

Box 9.1 ECONOMETRIC MODELS AND MACROECONOMIC FORECASTS

The *IS–LM* model developed in this chapter is a relatively simple example of a macroeconomic model. Much more complicated models of the economy, many, though not all, of them based on the *IS–LM* framework, are used in applied macroeconomic research and analysis. These models are used by public institutions (such as the Department of Finance and the Bank of Canada), by research groups at universities, and by private sector firms, including banks, investment dealers, and specialized forecasting firms.

A common use of macroeconomic models is to help economists forecast the course of the economy. In general, using a macroeconomic model to obtain quantitative economic forecasts involves three steps. First, numerical values for the parameters of the model (such as the income elasticity of money demand) must be obtained. In econometric models, these values are estimated through statistical analyses of the data. Second, projections must be made of the likely behaviour of relevant *exogenous* variables, or variables whose values are not determined within the model. Examples of exogenous variables include policy variables (such as government spending), foreign variables, oil prices, and changes in productivity. Third, on the basis of the expected path of the exogenous variables and the model parameters, the model can be solved (usually on a computer) to give forecasts of variables determined within the model (such as output, employment, and interest rates). Variables determined within the model are *endogenous* variables.

Although a relatively simple model, such as the *IS–LM* model developed in this chapter, could be used to create real forecasts, the results probably would not be very good. Because real-world economies are complex, macroeconomic models actually used in forecasting tend to be much more detailed than the *IS–LM* model presented here. For example, instead of a single aggregate production function, an econometric model used for forecasting might include production functions estimated separately for many individual industries. The complexity of models used in forecasting is illustrated by the accompanying table, which shows that models include hundreds or even thousands of equations.

Despite the amount of detail in some econometric models, they typically do not capture all information relevant to forecasting the economy. Most forecasters combine the results from their econometric models with other forecasting techniques, including personal judgment, time-series methods (statistical methods that attempt to extrapolate economic trends without the explicit use of an economic model), and detailed analysis of current data (including partial and preliminary data). Studies have shown that combining several different forecasting methods usually provides more accurate forecasts than relying on a single approach.

Forecaster	Model Name	Frequency	Number of Equations
DRI McGraw-Hill	DRI	Quarterly	674
University of Toronto	FOCUS	Quarterly	344
University of British Columbia	MACE	Annual	613
Conference Board of Canada	MTFM	Quarterly	893
Department of Finance	QFS	Quarterly	668
Bank of Canada	QPM	Quarterly	310
Informetrica Ltd.	TIM	Annual	3914

Sources: Grady Economics and Associates Ltd., *The State of the Art in Canadian Macroeconomic Modelling,* Ottawa: Department of Finance, 1985; "The Bank of Canada's New Quarterly Projection Model (QPM): An Introduction," *Bank of Canada Review,* Autumn 1994, pp. 23–38.

value of 1,000, and the real interest rate is 5%. Both the *IS* and *LM* curves pass through *E*, so we know that 5% is the market-clearing real interest rate in both the goods and asset markets. For the moment, the price level, *P*, is fixed at its initial level of 100.

FIGURE 9.9

EFFECTS OF A MONETARY EXPANSION

(a) The economy is in general equilibrium at point *E*. Output equals the full-employment level of 1,000, the real interest rate is 5%, and the price level is 100.

(b) With the price level fixed, a 10% increase in the nominal money supply *M* raises the real money supply *M/P* and shifts the *LM* curve down from LM^1 to LM^2. At point *F*, the intersection of the *IS* curve and the new *LM* curve, LM^2, the real interest rate has fallen to 3%, which raises the aggregate demand for goods. If firms produce extra output to meet the increase in aggregate demand, output rises to 1,200 (higher than full-employment output of 1,000).

(c) Because aggregate demand exceeds full-employment output at point *F*, firms raise prices. A 10% rise in *P*, from 100 to 110, restores the real money supply to its original level and shifts the *LM* curve back to its original position at LM^1. This returns the economy to point *E*, where output again is at its full-employment level of 1,000, but the price level has risen 10% from 100 to 110.

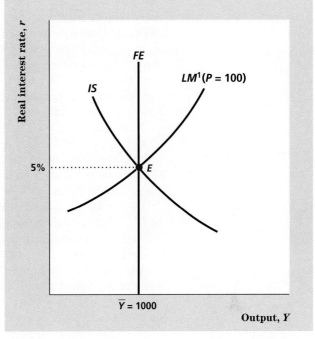

(a)

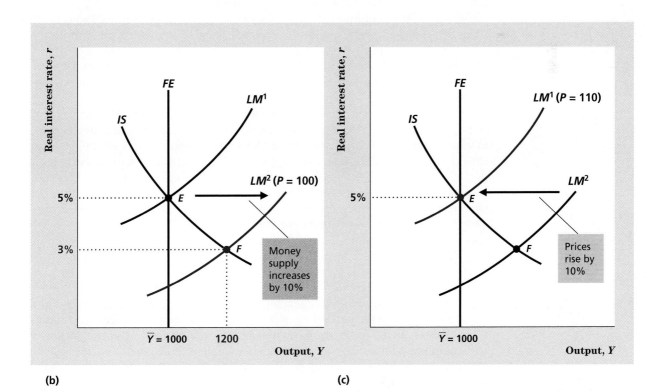

(b)   **(c)**

The 10% increase in the real supply of money M/P does not shift the IS curve or the FE line because with output and the real interest rate held constant, a change in M/P does not affect desired national saving, desired investment, labour demand, labour supply, or productivity. However, Figure 9.5 showed that an increase in the real money supply does shift the LM curve down, which we show here as a shift of the LM curve from LM^1 to LM^2, in Figure 9.9(b). The LM curve shifts down because at any level of output, an increase in the money supply lowers the real interest rate needed to clear the asset market.

Note that after the LM curve has shifted down to LM^2, there is no point in Figure 9.9(b) at which all three curves intersect. In other words, the goods market, the labour market, and the asset market no longer are simultaneously in equilibrium. We now must make some assumptions about how the economy behaves when it is not in general equilibrium.

Of the three markets in the IS–LM model, the asset market (represented by the LM curve) undoubtedly adjusts the most quickly because financial markets can respond within minutes to changes in economic conditions. The labour market (the FE line) is probably the slowest to adjust because the process of matching workers and jobs takes time and wages may be renegotiated only periodically. The adjustment speed of the goods market (IS curve) probably is somewhere in the middle. We assume that when the economy is not in general equilibrium, the asset market and the goods market are in equilibrium *so that output and the real interest rate are given by the intersection of the IS and LM curves.* Note that when the economy is not in general equilibrium, the IS–LM intersection does not lie on the FE line, so the labour market is not in equilibrium.

Immediately after the increase in the nominal money supply, therefore, the economy is out of general equilibrium with the level of output and the real interest rate represented by point F in Figure 9.9(b), where the new LM curve, LM^2, intersects the IS curve. At F, output (1,200) is higher and the real interest rate (3%) is lower than at the original general equilibrium, point E. We refer to F, the point at which the economy comes to rest before any adjustment occurs in the price level, as the *short-run equilibrium* point. (Although we refer to F as a short-run equilibrium point, keep in mind that only the asset and goods markets are in equilibrium there—the labour market is not.)

In economic terms, why does the increase in the money supply shift the economy to point F? The sequence of events can be described as follows: After the increase in the money supply, holders of wealth are holding more money in their portfolios than they desire at the initial values of output and the real interest rate. To bring their portfolios back into balance, they will try to use their excess money to buy non-monetary assets. However, as holders of wealth bid for non-monetary assets, they put upward pressure on the price of those assets, which reduces their interest rate. Thus, after an increase in the money supply, wealth-holders' attempts to achieve their desired mix of money and non-monetary assets cause the interest rate to fall.

The drop in the real interest rate is not the end of the story, however. Because the lower real interest rate increases the demand by households for consumption, C^d, and the demand by firms for investment, I^d, the aggregate demand for goods rises. Here, we make a fundamental assumption, to which we return shortly: When demanders increase their spending on goods, firms are willing (at least temporarily) to produce enough to meet the extra demand for their output. After the decline in the real interest rate raises the aggregate demand for goods, therefore, we assume that firms respond by increasing production, leading to higher output at the short-run equilibrium point, F.

To summarize, with the price level constant, an increase in the nominal money supply takes the economy to the short-run equilibrium point, F, in Figure 9.9(b), at which the real interest rate is lower and output is higher than at the initial general equilibrium point, E. We made two assumptions: (1) when the economy is not in general equilibrium, the economy's short-run equilibrium occurs at the intersection of the *IS* and *LM* curves; and (2) when the aggregate demand for goods rises, firms are willing (at least temporarily) to produce enough extra output to meet the expanded demand.

THE ADJUSTMENT OF THE PRICE LEVEL

So far, we have simply taken the price level P as fixed. In reality, prices respond to conditions of supply and demand in the economy. The price level P refers to the price of output (goods), so to think about how prices are likely to adjust in this example, let us reconsider the effects of the increase in the money supply on the goods market.

In Figure 9.9(b), the short-run equilibrium point, F, lies on the *IS* curve, implying that the goods market is in equilibrium at that point with equal aggregate quantities of goods supplied and demanded. Recall our assumption that firms are willing to meet any increases in aggregate demand by producing more. In that sense, then, the aggregate quantity of goods supplied equals the aggregate quantity of goods demanded. However, in another sense, the goods market is *not* in equilibrium at point F. The problem is that in order to meet the aggregate demand for goods at F, firms have to produce more output than their full-employment level of output $\overline{Y}$. Full-employment output $\overline{Y}$ is the level of output that maximizes firms' profits because that level of output corresponds to the profit-maximizing level of employment (Chapter 3). Therefore, in meeting the higher level of aggregate demand, firms are producing more output than they want to. In the sense that, at point F, the production of goods by firms is *not* the level of output that maximizes their profits, the goods market is not truly in equilibrium.

At point F the aggregate demand for goods exceeds firms' desired supply of output $\overline{Y}$, so we can expect firms to begin raising their prices, causing the price level P to rise. With the nominal money supply M set by the central bank, an increase in the price level P lowers the real money supply M/P, which, in turn, causes the *LM* curve to shift up. Indeed, as long as the aggregate quantity of goods demanded exceeds what firms want to supply, prices will keep rising. Thus, the *LM* curve will keep shifting up and to the left until the aggregate quantity of goods demanded equals full-employment output. Aggregate demand equals full-employment output only when the *LM* curve has returned to its initial position, LM^1 in Figure 9.9(c), where it passes through the original general equilibrium point, E. At E, all three markets of the economy again are in equilibrium, with output at its full-employment level.

Compare Figure 9.9(c) with the initial situation in Figure 9.9(a) and note that after the adjustment of the price level, the 10% increase in the nominal money supply has had no effect on output or the real interest rate. Employment also is unchanged from its initial value, as the economy has returned to its original level of output. However, as a result of the 10% increase in the nominal money supply, the price level is 10% higher (so that $P = 110$). How do we know that the price level changes by exactly 10%? To return the *LM* curve to its original position, the increase in the price level had to return the real money supply M/P to its original value. Because the nominal money supply M was raised by 10%, to return M/P to its original value, the price level P had to rise by 10% as well. Thus, the change in the nominal money supply causes the price level to change proportionally. This result is the same result obtained in Chapter 7 (see Eq. 7.10), where we assumed that all markets are in equilibrium.

Note that because in general equilibrium the price level has risen by 10% but real economic variables are unaffected, all nominal economic variables must also rise by 10%. In particular, for the real wage to have the same value after prices have risen by 10% as it did before, the nominal wage must rise by 10%. Thus, the return of the economy to general equilibrium requires adjustment of the nominal wage (the price of labour) as well as the price of goods.

TREND MONEY GROWTH AND INFLATION

In Figure 9.9, we analyzed the effects of a one-time 10% increase in the nominal money supply, followed by a one-time 10% adjustment in the price level. In reality, in most countries, the money supply and the price level grow continuously. Our framework easily handles this situation. Suppose that in some country, both the nominal money supply M and the price level P are growing steadily at 7% per year, which implies that the real money supply M/P is constant. The LM curve depends on the real money supply M/P, so in this situation the LM curve will not shift, even though the nominal money supply and prices are rising.

Now, suppose that for one year, the money supply of this country is increased an additional 3%—for a total of 10%—while prices rise 7%. Then the real money supply M/P grows by 3% (10% minus 7%), and the LM curve shifts down and to the right. Similarly, if for one year, the nominal money supply increased by only 4%, with inflation still at 7% per year, the LM curve would shift up, reflecting the 3% drop (–3% = 4% – 7%) in the real money supply.

This example illustrates that changes in M or P *relative to the expected or trend rate of growth of money and inflation* (7% in this example) shift the LM curve. Thus, when we analyze the effects of "an increase in the money supply," we have in mind an increase in the money supply relative to the expected, or trend, rate of money growth (for example, a rise from 7% to 10% growth for one year); by a "decrease in the money supply," we mean a drop relative to a trend rate (such as a decline from 7% to 4% growth in money). Similarly, if we say something like "the price level falls to restore general equilibrium," we do not necessarily mean that the price level literally falls but only that it rises by less than its trend or expected rate of growth would suggest.

CLASSICAL VERSUS KEYNESIAN VERSIONS OF THE *IS–LM* MODEL

Our diagrammatic analysis of the effects of a change in the money supply highlights two questions that are central to the debate between the classical and Keynesian approaches to macroeconomics: (1) How rapidly does the economy reach general equilibrium? (2) What are the effects of monetary policy on the economy? We previewed the first of these questions in Section 8.4, using the *AD–AS* model. Now we examine both questions, using the *IS–LM* model.

PRICE ADJUSTMENT AND THE SELF-CORRECTING ECONOMY

In our analysis of the effects of a monetary expansion, we showed that the economy is brought into general equilibrium by adjustment of the price level. In graphical terms, if the intersection of the *IS* and *LM* curves lies to the right of the *FE* line—so that the aggregate quantity of goods demanded exceeds full-employment output, as in Figure 9.9(b)—the price level will rise. The increase in P shifts the LM curve up, reducing the quantity of goods demanded, until all three curves intersect at the general equilibrium point, as in Figure 9.9(c). Similarly, if the $IS–LM$ intersection lies to the left of the full-employment line—so that desired spending on goods is below firms' profit-maximizing level of output—firms will cut prices. A decrease in the price level raises the real money supply and shifts the LM curve down, until all three curves again intersect, returning the economy to general equilibrium.

There is little controversy about the idea that after some sort of economic disturbance, price level adjustments will eventually restore the economy to general equilibrium. However, the speed at which this process takes place is a much-debated issue in macroeconomics. Under the classical assumptions that we used in Chapters 3, 4, and 7, prices are flexible and the adjustment process is rapid. When prices are flexible, the economy is effectively self-correcting, automatically returning to full employment after a shock moves it away from general equilibrium. Indeed, if firms respond to increased demand by raising prices, rather than by temporarily producing more (as we earlier assumed), the adjustment process would be almost immediate.

According to the opposing Keynesian view, however, sluggish adjustment of prices (and of wages, the price of labour) might prevent general equilibrium from being attained for a much longer period, perhaps even several years. While the economy is not in general equilibrium, Keynesians argue, output is determined by the level of aggregate demand, represented by the intersection of the IS and LM curves; the economy is not on the FE line, and the labour market is not in equilibrium. This assumption of sluggish price adjustment, and the consequent disequilibrium in the labour market, distinguishes the Keynesian version of the $IS–LM$ model from the classical version.

MONETARY NEUTRALITY

Closely related to the issue of how fast the economy reaches general equilibrium is the question of how a change in the nominal money supply affects the economy. We showed that after the economy reaches its general equilibrium, an increase in the nominal money supply has no effect on real variables, such as output, employment, or the real interest rate, but raises the price level. Economists say that there is **monetary neutrality**, or simply that money is neutral, if a change in the nominal money supply changes the price level proportionally but has no effect on real variables. Our analysis shows that after the complete adjustment of prices, money is neutral in the $IS–LM$ model.

The practical relevance of monetary neutrality is much debated by classicals and Keynesians.[10] The basic issue again is the speed of price adjustment. In the classical view, a monetary expansion is rapidly transmitted into prices and has, at most, a transitory effect on real variables; that is, the economy moves quickly from the situation shown in Figure 9.9(a) to the situation shown in Figure 9.9(c), spending little time in the position shown in Figure 9.9(b). Keynesians agree that money is neutral after prices fully adjust but believe that because of slow price adjustment, the economy may spend a long time in disequilibrium. During this period, the increased money supply causes output and employment to rise and the real interest rate to fall (compare Figure 9.9(b) with Figure 9.9(a)).

---

10. For a history of the idea of monetary neutrality and a review of some international and historical evidence, see Parts I and II of Robert E. Lucas, Jr., "Nobel Lecture: Monetary Neutrality," *Journal of Political Economy*, August 1996, pp. 661–682.

In brief, Keynesians believe in monetary neutrality in the long run (after prices adjust) but not in the short run. Classicals are more accepting of the view that money is neutral even in the relatively short run. We return to the issue of monetary neutrality when we develop the classical and Keynesian models of the business cycle in more detail in Chapters 11 and 12.

9.6 THE AGGREGATE DEMAND–AGGREGATE SUPPLY MODEL

The *IS–LM* model introduced in this chapter is a complete model representing the general equilibrium of the economy. In this section, we use the *IS–LM* model to develop the aggregate demand–aggregate supply (*AD–AS*) model, which we previewed in Chapter 8. The *AD–AS* model appears to be different from the *IS–LM* model, but in fact, the two models are equivalent. They are based on the same assumptions about economic behaviour and price adjustment, and they give the same answers when used to analyze the effects of various shocks on the economy. Why then do we bother to present both models? The reason is that depending on the issue being addressed, one way of representing the economy may be more convenient than the other. The *IS–LM* model relates the real interest rate to output, and the *AD–AS* model relates the price level to output. Thus, the *IS–LM* model is more useful for examining the effect of various shocks on the real interest rate and on variables, such as saving and investment, that depend on the real interest rate. In Chapter 10, for example, when we discuss international borrowing and lending in open economies, the behaviour of the real interest rate is crucial; and so, in that chapter, we emphasize the *IS–LM* approach. However, for issues related to the price level, or inflation, use of the *AD–AS* model is more convenient. For example, we rely on the *AD–AS* framework in Chapter 13 when we describe the relationship between inflation and unemployment. Keep in mind, though, that the choice of the *IS–LM* framework or the *AD–AS* framework is a matter of convenience; the two models express the same basic macroeconomic theory.

THE AGGREGATE DEMAND CURVE

The **aggregate demand curve** shows the relation between the aggregate quantity of goods demanded, $C^d + I^d + G$, and the price level, P. The aggregate demand curve slopes downward, as does the demand curve for a single product (apples, for example). Despite the superficial similarity between the *AD* curve and the demand curve for a specific good, however, there is an important difference between these two types of curves. The demand curve for apples relates the demand for apples to the price of apples *relative to the prices of other goods*. In contrast, the *AD* curve relates the aggregate quantity of output demanded to the *general price level*. If the prices of all goods increase by 10%, the price level, P, also increases by 10%, even though all relative prices of goods remain unchanged. Nevertheless, the increase in the price level reduces the aggregate quantity of goods demanded.

The reason that an increase in the price level, P, reduces the aggregate quantity of output demanded is illustrated in Figure 9.10. Recall that for a *given price level*, the aggregate quantity of output that households, firms, and the government choose to demand is where the *IS* curve and the *LM* curve intersect. Suppose that the nominal money supply is M and that the initial price level is P_1. Then the real money

FIGURE 9.10

DERIVATION OF THE
AGGREGATE DEMAND
CURVE

For a given price level, the aggregate quantity of output demanded is determined where the *IS* and *LM* curves intersect. If the price level, *P*, is P_1 and the initial *LM* curve is LM^1, the initial aggregate quantity of output demanded is Y_1, corresponding to point *E* in both (a) and (b). To derive the aggregate demand curve, we examine what happens to the quantity of output demanded when the price level changes. **(a)** An increase in the price level from P_1 to P_2 reduces the real money supply and shifts the *LM* curve up and to the left, from LM^1 to LM^2. Therefore, the aggregate quantity of output demanded, represented by the intersection of the *IS* and *LM* curves, falls from Y_1 to Y_2. **(b)** The increase in the price level from P_1 to P_2 reduces the aggregate quantity of output demanded from Y_1 to Y_2, so the aggregate demand curve slopes downward.

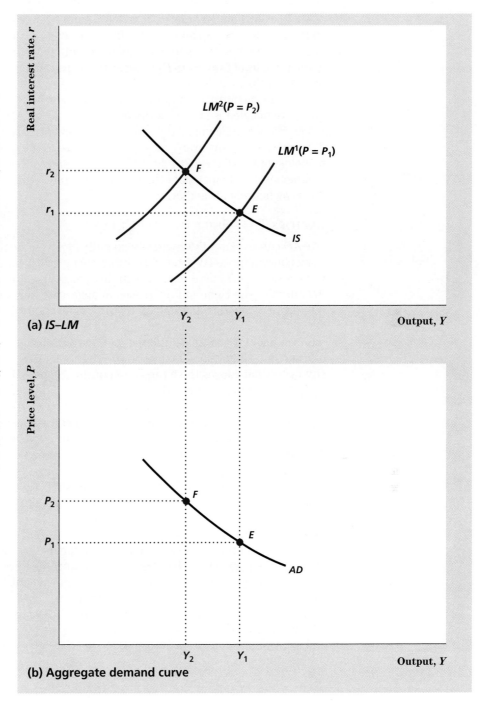

(a) *IS–LM*

(b) **Aggregate demand curve**

supply is M/P_1, and the initial *LM* curve is LM^1 in Figure 9.10(a). The *IS* and LM^1 curves intersect at point *E*, where the amount of output that households, firms, and the government want to buy is Y_1. Thus, we conclude that when the price level is P_1, the aggregate amount of output demanded is Y_1.

Now, suppose that the price level increases to P_2. With a nominal money supply of *M*, this increase in the price level reduces the real money supply from M/P_1 to

M/P_2. Recall (Summary table 13, p. 306) that a decrease in the real money supply shifts the LM curve up and to the left, to LM^2. The IS and LM^2 curves intersect at point F, where the aggregate quantity of output demanded is Y_2. Thus, the increase in the price level from P_1 to P_2 reduces the aggregate quantity of output demanded from Y_1 to Y_2.

This negative relation between the price level and the aggregate quantity of output demanded is shown as the downward-sloping AD curve in Figure 9.10(b). Points E and F in Figure 9.10(b) correspond to points E and F in Figure 9.10(a). The AD curve slopes downward because an increase in the price level reduces the real money supply, which shifts the LM curve up and to the left; the reduction in the real money supply increases the real interest rate, which reduces the demand for goods by households and firms.

FACTORS THAT SHIFT THE *AD* CURVE

The AD curve relates the aggregate quantity of output demanded to the price level. For a constant price level, any factor that changes the aggregate demand for output will cause the AD curve to shift, with increases in aggregate demand shifting the AD curve to the right and decreases in aggregate demand shifting it to the left. Aggregate demand is determined by the intersection of the IS and LM curves, so we can also say that holding the price level constant, any factor that causes the intersection of the IS curve and the LM curve to shift to the right raises aggregate demand and shifts the AD curve to the right. Similarly, for a constant price level, any factor that causes the intersection of the IS and LM curves to shift to the left shifts the AD curve to the left.

An example of a factor that shifts the AD curve to the right, which we have considered before, is a temporary increase in government purchases. The effect of the increase in government purchases on the AD curve is illustrated in Figure 9.11. The initial IS curve, IS^1, intersects the LM curve at point E in Figure 9.11(a) so that the initial aggregate quantity of output demanded is Y^1. As we have shown, a temporary increase in government purchases shifts the IS curve to the right to IS^2. With the price level held constant at its initial value of P_1, the intersection of the IS and LM curves moves to point F so that the aggregate quantity of output demanded increases from Y_1 to Y_2.

The shift of the AD curve resulting from the increase in government purchases is shown in Figure 9.11(b). The increase in the aggregate quantity of output demanded at price level P_1 is shown by the movement from point E to point F. Because the increase in government purchases raises the aggregate quantity of output demanded at any price level, the entire AD curve shifts to the right, from AD^1 to AD^2. Other factors that shift the AD curve are listed in Summary table 14 and an algebraic derivation of the AD curve is presented in Appendix 9.A.

THE AGGREGATE SUPPLY CURVE

The **aggregate supply curve** shows the relation between the price level and the aggregate amount of output that firms supply. Recall from the preview in Chapter 8 and our discussion of the IS–LM model that firms are assumed to behave differently in the short run and in the long run. That is, the assumption is that prices remain fixed in the short run and that firms supply the quantity of output demanded at this fixed price level. Thus, the **short-run aggregate supply curve**, or $SRAS$, is a horizontal line, as shown in Figure 9.12.

FIGURE 9.11

THE EFFECT OF AN
INCREASE IN GOVERNMENT
PURCHASES ON THE
AGGREGATE DEMAND
CURVE

(a) An increase in government
purchases shifts the *IS* curve
up and to the right, from IS^1 to
IS^2. At price level P_1, the aggregate quantity of output demanded increases from Y_1 to
Y_2, as shown by the shift of the
IS–LM intersection from point
E to point *F*.
(b) Because the aggregate
quantity of output demanded
rises at any price level, the *AD*
curve shifts to the right. Points
E and *F* in part (b) correspond
to points *E* and *F* in part (a).

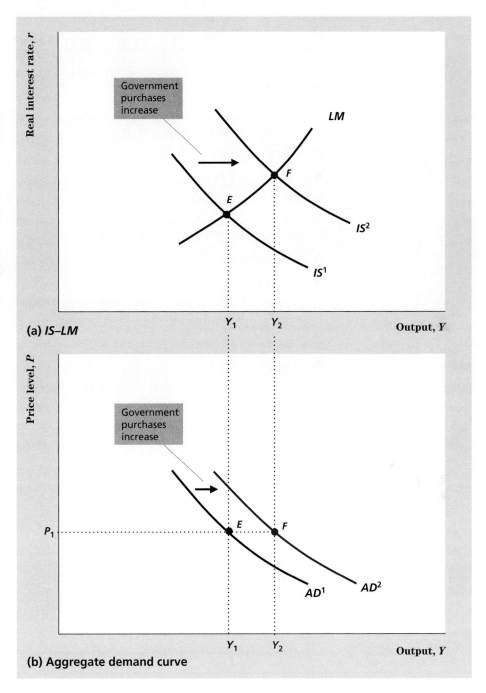

(a) *IS–LM*

(b) Aggregate demand curve

In the long run, prices and wages adjust to clear all markets in the economy. In
particular, the labour market clears so that employment equals $\overline{N}$, which is the level
of employment that maximizes firms' profits. When employment equals $\overline{N}$, the
aggregate amount of output supplied is the full-employment level, $\overline{Y}$, which equals
$AF(K,\overline{N})$, regardless of the price level. In the long run firms supply $\overline{Y}$ at any price level,
so the **long-run aggregate supply curve**, or *LRAS*, is a vertical line at $Y = \overline{Y}$, as
shown in Figure 9.12.

SUMMARY 14   FACTORS THAT SHIFT THE *AD* CURVE

For a constant price level, any factor that shifts the intersection of the *IS* and *LM* curves to the right increases aggregate output demanded and shifts the *AD* curve to the right.

Factors that shift the *IS* curve up and to the right, and thus shift the *AD* curve to the right (see Summary table 12, p. 300) include

■ an increase in expected future output;

■ an increase in wealth;

■ an increase in government purchases, *G*;

■ a reduction in taxes, *T* (assuming no Ricardian equivalence so that consumers respond by raising desired consumption);

■ an increase in the expected future *MPK*; and

■ a reduction in the effective tax rate on capital.

Factors that shift the *LM* curve down and to the right, and thus shift the *AD* curve to the right (see Summary table 13, p. 306) include

■ an increase in the nominal money supply, *M*;

■ a rise in expected inflation, π^e;

■ a decrease in the nominal interest rate on money, i^m; and

■ any other change that reduces the real demand for money.

FIGURE 9.12

THE SHORT-RUN AND LONG-RUN AGGREGATE SUPPLY CURVES

In the short run, firms supply the amount of output demanded at the fixed price, so the short-run aggregate supply (*SRAS*) curve is a horizontal line. In the long run, when the labour market clears, firms supply the full-employment level of output, $\bar{Y}$, regardless of the price level. Thus, the long-run aggregate supply (*LRAS*) curve is a vertical line at $Y = \bar{Y}$.

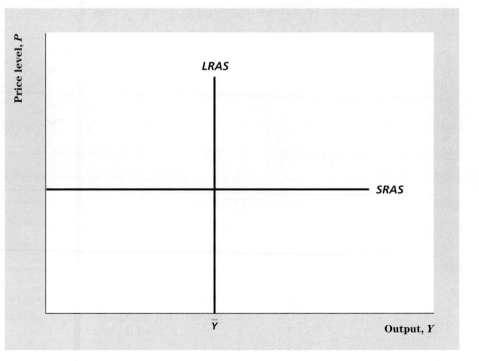

FACTORS THAT SHIFT THE AGGREGATE SUPPLY CURVES

Any factor that increases the full-employment level of output, $\overline{Y}$, shifts the long-run aggregate supply (*LRAS*) curve to the right, and any factor that reduces $\overline{Y}$ shifts the *LRAS* curve to the left. Thus, any change that shifts the *FE* line to the right in the *IS–LM* diagram also shifts the *LRAS* curve to the right. For instance, an increase in the labour force raises the full-employment level of employment and output, shifting the *LRAS* curve to the right.

The short-run aggregate supply curve shifts whenever firms change their prices in the short run. Any factor, such as an increase in costs, that leads firms to increase prices in the short run will shift the *SRAS* curve up, and any factor that leads firms to decrease prices in the short run will shift the *SRAS* curve down.

EQUILIBRIUM IN THE *AD–AS* MODEL

When we previewed the *AD–AS* model in Section 8.4, we introduced the distinction between short-run equilibrium (equilibrium when prices are fixed) and long-run equilibrium (equilibrium when prices have fully adjusted). Short-run equilibrium is represented by the intersection of the *AD* and *SRAS* curves, as at point *E* in Figure 9.13. Long-run equilibrium is represented by the intersection of the *AD* and *LRAS* curves, which is also at point *E* in Figure 9.13. Thus, point *E* represents both the short-run and long-run equilibrium of the economy. When the economy is in long-run equilibrium, output equals its full-employment level, $\overline{Y}$. Long-run equilibrium is the same as general equilibrium because in long-run equilibrium, all markets clear.

When the economy reaches general, or long-run equilibrium, all three curves—*AD*, *SRAS*, and *LRAS*—intersect at a common point, as in Figure 9.13. This condition is not a coincidence. As with the *IS* curve, the *LM* curve, and the *FE* line, strong

FIGURE 9.13

EQUILIBRIUM IN THE
AD–AS MODEL

Short-run equilibrium is represented by the intersection of the *AD* and *SRAS* curves at point *E*. At short-run equilibrium, prices are fixed and firms meet demand at those prices. Long-run equilibrium, which occurs after prices have fully adjusted, is represented by the intersection of the *AD* and *LRAS* curves, also at point *E*. Long-run equilibrium is the same as general equilibrium because in long-run equilibrium all markets clear.

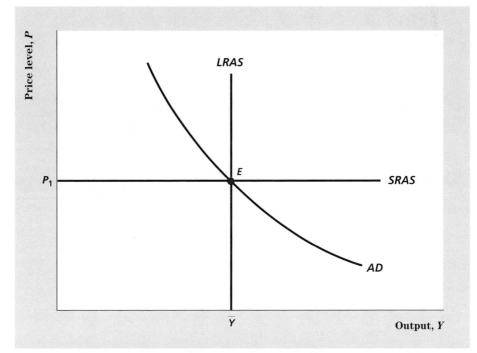

economic forces lead the economy to arrive eventually at a common point of intersection of the three curves. Indeed, the forces leading the AD, $SRAS$, and $LRAS$ curves to intersect at a common point are the same as the forces leading the IS curve, the LM curve, and FE line to intersect at a common point. To illustrate, we use the AD–AS framework to examine the effects on the economy of an increase in the money supply, which we previously analyzed with the IS–LM model.

MONETARY NEUTRALITY IN THE AD–AS MODEL

Suppose that the economy is initially in equilibrium at point E in Figure 9.14, where the level of output is $\overline{Y}$ and the price level is P_1, and that the money supply then increases by 10%. In the IS–LM model an increase in the money supply shifts the LM curve down and to the right, raising the aggregate quantity of output demanded at any particular price level. Thus, an increase in the money supply also shifts the AD curve up and to the right, from AD^1 to AD^2.

Moreover, *when the money supply rises by 10%, the AD curve shifts vertically upward by 10% at each level of output demanded*. To see why, compare points E and H. Because H lies on AD^2 and E lies on AD^1, the nominal money supply, M, is 10% higher at H than at E. However, the aggregate quantity of output demanded is the same ($\overline{Y}$) at H and E. The aggregate quantity of output demanded can be the same at H and E only if the real money supply, M/P, which determines the position of the LM curve and hence the aggregate quantity of output demanded, is the same at H and E. With the nominal money supply 10% higher at H, for the real money supply to be the same at the two points the price level at H must be 10% higher than at E. Therefore, P_2 is 10% higher than P_1. Indeed, for every level of output the price level is 10% higher on AD^2 than on AD^1.

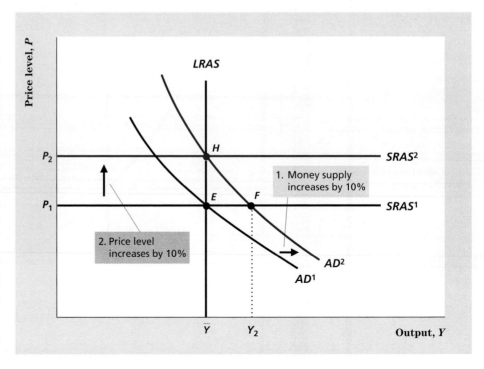

In the short run, the price level remains fixed, and the increase in the nominal money supply shifts the aggregate demand curve from AD^1 to AD^2. Thus, the short-run equilibrium moves from point E to point F (which corresponds to movement from point E to point F in the *IS–LM* diagram in Figure 9.9(b)). Thus, in the short run, the nominal money supply increases output from $\overline{Y}$ to Y_2, causing an economic boom.

However, the economy will not remain at point F indefinitely. Because the amount of output, Y_2, is higher than the profit-maximizing level of output, $\overline{Y}$, firms will eventually increase their prices. Rising prices cause the short-run aggregate supply curve to shift up from $SRAS^1$. Firms will increase their prices until the quantity of output demanded falls to the profit-maximizing level of output, $\overline{Y}$. The new long-run equilibrium is represented by point H, where the AD curve, the $LRAS$ curve, and the new short-run aggregate supply curve, or $SRAS^2$, all intersect. In the new long-run equilibrium, the price level has increased by 10%, which is the same amount that the nominal money supply has increased. Output is the same in the new long-run equilibrium at point H as at point E. Thus, we conclude that money is neutral in the long run, as we did when using the *IS–LM* model.

Our analysis highlights the distinction between the short-run and long-run effects of an increase in the money supply, but it leaves open the crucial question of how long it takes the economy to reach long-run equilibrium. As we have emphasized in both Chapter 8 and this chapter, classical and Keynesian economists have very different answers to this question. Classical economists argue that the economy reaches its long-run equilibrium quickly. Indeed, in its strictest form, the classical view is that the economy reaches long-run equilibrium almost immediately so that the long-run aggregate supply ($LRAS$) curve is the only aggregate supply curve that matters (the short-run aggregate supply ($SRAS$) curve is irrelevant). However, Keynesians argue that the economy may take years to reach long-run equilibrium and that in the meantime, output will differ from its full-employment level. We elaborate on these points of view in Chapter 11, which is devoted to the classical model, and in Chapter 12, which is devoted to the Keynesian model.

CHAPTER SUMMARY

1. The *IS–LM* model represents the three main markets of the economy—the labour market, the goods market, and the asset market—simultaneously, in a diagram that has the real interest rate on the vertical axis and output on the horizontal axis. Although the *IS–LM* model was originally developed by Keynesians, it may be used to illustrate both classical and Keynesian analyses of the economy.

2. In the *IS–LM* model, equilibrium in the labour market is represented graphically by the full-employment, or *FE*, line, which is vertical at full-employment output. Factors that raise full-employment output shift the *FE* line to the right, and factors that reduce full-employment output shift the *FE* line to the left.

3. For any level of output, the *IS* curve shows the value of the real interest rate that clears the goods market. The *IS* curve slopes downward because higher output leads to more desired saving and, thus, a lower goods-market-clearing real interest rate. For constant output, any change that reduces desired national saving relative to desired investment increases the real interest rate that clears the goods market and shifts the *IS* curve up. Equivalently, for constant output, any change

that increases the aggregate demand for goods increases the real interest rate that clears the goods market and shifts the *IS* curve up.

4. For any level of output, the *LM* curve identifies the real interest rate that equates the quantities of money supplied and demanded and, thus, clears the asset market. The *LM* curve slopes upward because an increase in output raises money demand, implying that a higher real interest rate is needed to clear the asset market. With output fixed, any change that reduces the money supply relative to money demand increases the real interest rate that clears the asset market and causes the *LM* curve to shift up.

5. General equilibrium in the macroeconomy occurs when all markets are in equilibrium. Graphically, the general equilibrium point is where the *IS* curve, the *FE* line, and the *LM* curve intersect. Price level adjustments push the economy toward general equilibrium. Specifically, changes in the price level, P, change the real money supply, M/P, which causes the *LM* curve to shift until it passes through the point at which the *FE* line and the *IS* curve intersect.

6. A temporary adverse supply shock causes the general equilibrium levels of the real wage, employment, output, consumption, and investment to fall, and the general equilibrium levels of the real interest rate and price level to increase.

7. A change in the money supply is neutral if it leads to a proportional change in the price level but does not affect real variables. In the *IS–LM* model, money is neutral after prices have adjusted and the economy has returned to general equilibrium.

8. The aggregate demand–aggregate supply (*AD–AS*) model is based on the *IS–LM* model and, in fact, is equivalent to it. However, the two models allow us to focus on the behaviour of different macroeconomic variables: The *IS–LM* model is most useful for studying the relationship between the real interest rate and the level of output, whereas the *AD–AS* model focuses on the relation between the price level and the level of output.

9. The aggregate demand (*AD*) curve relates the aggregate quantity of output demanded—the level of output at the intersection of the *IS* and *LM* curves—to the price level. An increase in the price

level reduces the real money supply and shifts the *LM* curve up and to the left, thereby reducing the aggregate quantity of output demanded. Because an increase in the price level reduces the aggregate quantity of goods demanded, the aggregate demand curve slopes downward. Factors that increase the aggregate quantity of output demanded at a given price level, such as increases in government purchases or the money supply, shift the *AD* curve to the right.

10. The aggregate supply curve relates the quantity of output supplied to the price level. In the short run, the price level is fixed and firms supply whatever level of output is demanded, so the short-run aggregate supply (*SRAS*) curve is horizontal. In the long run, after prices and wages have fully adjusted and all markets are in equilibrium, firms produce the profit-maximizing level of output. Hence in the long run aggregate output, Y, equals its full-employment level, $\overline{Y}$. In the long run firms supply $\overline{Y}$ regardless of the price level, so the long-run aggregate supply (*LRAS*) curve is a vertical line at $Y = \overline{Y}$.

11. Classical macroeconomists argue that prices and wages adjust rapidly in response to changes in supply or demand. This argument implies that following shocks or changes in policy, the economy quickly reaches its general equilibrium, represented by the *IS–LM–FE* intersection or, equivalently, by the intersection of the *AD* and *LRAS* curves. In contrast, Keynesian macroeconomists argue that prices and wages adjust slowly enough that the economy can remain away from its general equilibrium (long-run equilibrium) for a prolonged period of time. Keynesians agree with classicals, however, that eventually prices and wages fully adjust so that the economy reaches its general equilibrium.

12. Classicals and Keynesians agree that money is neutral in the long run, after the economy has reached its general equilibrium. Because classicals believe that long-run equilibrium is reached quickly, they dismiss the short-run equilibrium in which money is not neutral as essentially irrelevant. Keynesians, who believe that it may take several years for the economy to reach general equilibrium, ascribe much more importance to the short-run period in which money is not neutral.

KEY DIAGRAM 6

THE *IS–LM* MODEL

The *IS–LM* model shows general equilibrium in the goods, asset, and labour markets. It can be used to analyze the effects of economic shocks on output, the real interest rate, the price level, and other macroeconomic variables.

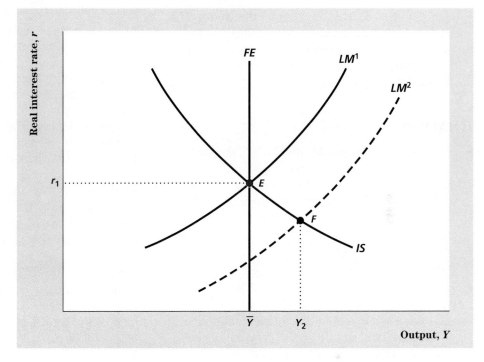

DIAGRAM ELEMENTS

- The real interest rate, r, is on the vertical axis, and output, Y, is on the horizontal axis.

- The full-employment line, FE, is vertical at full-employment output. Full-employment output, $\overline{Y}$, is the level of output that firms supply when wages and prices have fully adjusted, so employment is at its full-employment level, $\overline{N}$. Full-employment output is determined by the equation $Y = AF(K, \overline{N})$.

- For any level of output Y, the *IS* curve gives the real interest rate r that clears the goods market—or, in other words, the rate that equalizes desired national saving, S^d, and desired investment, I^d. Because higher output raises desired saving and lowers the real interest rate that clears the goods market, the *IS* curve slopes downward. Equivalently, the *IS* curve gives combinations of output Y and the real interest rate r that equalize the

aggregate quantities of goods supplied and demanded, $Y = C^d + I^d + G$.

- For given values of the price level and output, the *LM* curve gives the real interest rate that clears the asset market, making the real money supply, M/P, and the real quantity of money demanded, $L(Y, r + \pi^e)$, equal. Because an increase in income raises real money demand, which raises the real interest rate that clears the asset market, the *LM* curve slopes upward.

FACTORS THAT SHIFT THE CURVES

- Any factor that raises full-employment output shifts the *FE* line to the right. See Summary table 11.

- For constant output, any change that reduces desired national saving relative to desired investment increases the real interest rate that clears the goods market and shifts the *IS* curve up. Equivalently, any change that increases the aggregate demand for goods at a specific level of income raises the real interest rate that clears the goods market and shifts the *IS* curve up. See Summary table 12.

- For constant output, any change that reduces real money supply relative to real money demand increases the real interest rate that clears the asset market and shifts the *LM* curve up. See Summary table 13.

ANALYSIS

- If we assume that the *LM* curve is LM^1, the economy is in general equilibrium at point E, which lies on all three curves. At E, the labour market (*FE* line), the goods market (*IS* curve), and the asset market (*LM* curve) are all in equilibrium. At E, output equals full-employment output $\bar{Y}$; and the real interest rate, r_1, clears both the goods and asset markets.

- If we assume that the *LM* curve is LM^2, the *FE* line and *IS* and *LM* curves do not all intersect, and the economy is out of general equilibrium. We assume that when the economy is out of general equilibrium, the short-run equilibrium of the

economy occurs at the intersection of the *IS* and *LM* curves (point F), where the goods and asset markets are in equilibrium but the labour market is not. If we further assume that (at least temporarily) firms produce enough output to meet the increased aggregate demand at F, in short-run equilibrium the economy's output is Y_2.

- At the short-run equilibrium point, F, output Y_2 is greater than firms' profit-maximizing level of output $\bar{Y}$. Because aggregate demand at F exceeds what firms want to produce, they raise prices. An increase in the price level P lowers the real money supply M/P and shifts the *LM* curve up to LM^1, and general equilibrium is reached at E. At E, output again equals full-employment output $\bar{Y}$. Similarly, if the short-run equilibrium had been to the left of the *FE* line, declines in the price level P would have shifted the *LM* curve to the right and restored general equilibrium at E.

- According to classical economists, the price adjustment process quickly restores the economy to general equilibrium at point E, so the economy spends little or no time away from full employment at point F. Keynesians argue that prices and wages are slow to adjust, so the economy may remain at the short-run equilibrium point, F, with output different from $\bar{Y}$, for an extended period of time.

KEY DIAGRAM 7
THE AGGREGATE DEMAND–AGGREGATE SUPPLY MODEL

DIAGRAM ELEMENTS

- The price level, P, is on the vertical axis, and the level of output, Y, is on the horizontal axis.

- The aggregate demand (*AD*) curve shows the aggregate quantity of output demanded at each price level. The aggregate amount of output demanded is determined by the intersection of the *IS* and *LM* curves (see Figure 9.10). An increase in the price level, P, reduces the real money supply, shifting the *LM* curve up and to the left, and reduces the aggregate quantity of output demanded. Thus, the *AD* curve slopes downward.

- The aggregate supply curves show the relationship between the price level and the aggregate quantity of output supplied in the short run and in the long run. In the short run, the price level is fixed at $\bar{P}$, and firms supply whatever level of output is demanded. Thus, the short-run aggregate supply (*SRAS*) curve is horizontal at $P = \bar{P}$. In the long run firms produce the amount of output that maximizes their profits, which is the full-employment level of output, $\bar{Y}$. Because aggregate output in the long run equals $\bar{Y}$, regardless of the price level, P, the long-run aggregate supply (*LRAS*) curve is a vertical line at $Y = \bar{Y}$.

The *AD–AS* model shows the determination of the price level and output. In the short run, before prices adjust, equilibrium occurs at the intersection of the *AD* and *SRAS* curves. In the long run, equilibrium occurs at the intersection of the *AD* and *LRAS* curves.

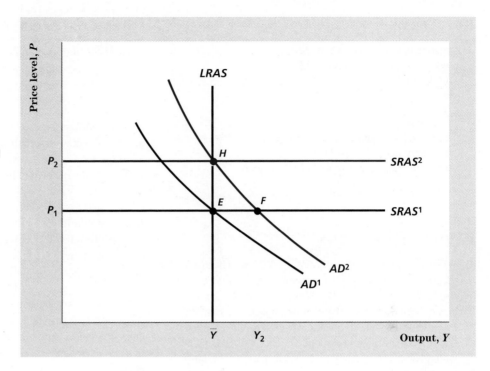

FACTORS THAT SHIFT THE CURVES

- The aggregate quantity of output demanded is determined by the intersection of the *IS* and the *LM* curves. At a constant price level, any factor that shifts the *IS–LM* intersection to the right increases the aggregate quantity of goods demanded and, thus, also shifts the *AD* curve to the right. Factors that shift the *AD* curve are listed in Summary table 14.

- Any factor, such as an increase in the costs of production, that leads firms to increase prices in the short run will shift the short-run aggregate supply (*SRAS*) curve up. Any factor that increases the full-employment level of output, $\bar{Y}$, shifts the long-run aggregate supply (*LRAS*) curve to the right. Factors that increase $\bar{Y}$ include beneficial supply shocks and an increase in labour supply.

ANALYSIS

- The economy's short-run equilibrium is represented by the intersection of the *AD* and *SRAS* curves, as at point *E*. The long-run equilibrium of the economy is represented by the intersection of the *AD* and the *LRAS* curves, also at point *E*. In the long run, output equals its full-employment level, $\bar{Y}$.

- The short-run equilibrium can temporarily differ from the long-run equilibrium as a result of shocks or policy changes that affect the economy. For instance, an increase in the nominal money supply shifts the aggregate demand curve up from AD^1 to AD^2. The new short-run equilibrium is represented by point *F*, where output is higher than its full-employment level, $\bar{Y}$. At point *F*, firms produce an amount of output that is greater than the profit-maximizing level, and they begin to increase prices. In the new long-run equilibrium at point *H*, output is at its full-employment level and the price level is higher than its initial value, $\bar{P}$. Because the new price level is P_2, the short-run aggregate supply curve shifts up to $SRAS^2$, which is a horizontal line at $P = P_2$.

KEY TERMS

aggregate demand curve, p. 320
aggregate supply curve, p. 322
full-employment line, p. 295
general equilibrium, p. 309
IS curve, p. 297
LM curve, p. 305
long-run aggregate supply (*LRAS*) curve, p. 323
monetary neutrality, p. 319
short-run aggregate supply (*SRAS*) curve, p. 322

REVIEW QUESTIONS

1. What determines the position of the *FE* line? Give two examples of changes in the economy that would shift the *FE* line to the right.
2. What relationship does the *IS* curve capture? Derive the *IS* curve graphically and show why it slopes as it does. Give two examples of changes in the economy that would cause the *IS* curve to shift down and to the left.
3. What relationship does the *LM* curve capture? Derive the *LM* curve graphically and show why it slopes as it does. Give two examples of changes in the economy that would cause the *LM* curve to shift down and to the right.
4. For constant output, if real money supply exceeds the real quantity of money demanded, what will happen to the real interest rate that clears the asset market? In describing the adjustment of the real interest rate, use the relationship that exists between the price of a non-monetary asset and the interest rate that it pays.
5. Define general equilibrium and show the general equilibrium point in the *IS–LM* diagram. If the economy is not in general equilibrium, what determines output and the real interest rate? What economic forces act to bring the economy back to general equilibrium?
6. Define monetary neutrality. Show that after prices adjust completely, money is neutral in the *IS–LM* model. What are the classical and Keynesian views about whether money is neutral in the short run? in the long run?
7. What two variables are related by the aggregate demand (*AD*) curve? Why does the *AD* curve slope downward? Give two examples of changes in the economy that shift the *AD* curve to the right and explain why the shifts occur.
8. Describe the short-run aggregate supply (*SRAS*) curve and the long-run aggregate supply (*LRAS*) curve. Why is one of these curves horizontal and the other vertical?
9. Use the *AD–AS* framework to analyze whether money is neutral in the short run and whether it is neutral in the long run.

NUMERICAL PROBLEMS

1. Desired consumption and investment are

$$C^d = 360 - 200r + 0.10Y;$$
$$I^d = 120 - 400r.$$

As usual, Y is output and r is the real interest rate. Government purchases G are 120.

a. Find an equation relating desired national saving S^d to r and Y.

b. What value of the real interest rate clears the goods market when $Y = 600$? Use both forms of the goods market equilibrium condition. What value of the real interest rate clears the goods market when $Y = 640$? Graph the *IS* curve.

c. Government purchases rise to 132. How does this increase change the equation for national saving in part (a)? What value of the real interest rate clears the goods market when $Y = 600$? Use both forms of the goods market equilibrium condition. How is the *IS* curve affected by the increase in G?

2. In a particular economy the real money demand function is

$$\frac{M^d}{P} = 200 + 0.2Y - 2000i.$$

Assume that $M = 300$, $P = 2.0$, and $\pi^e = 0.05$.

a. What is the real interest rate r that clears the asset market when $Y = 500$? when $Y = 600$? Graph the *LM* curve.

b. Repeat part (a) for $M = 360$. How does the *LM* curve in this case compare with the *LM* curve in part (a)?

c. Use $M = 300$ again and repeat part (a) for $\pi^e = 0.04$. Compare the *LM* curve in this case with the one in part (a).

3. An economy has full-employment output of 1,000. Desired consumption and desired investment are

$$C^d = 200 + 0.8(Y - T) - 500r;$$
$$I^d = 200 - 500r.$$

Government purchases are 196 and taxes are

$$T = 20 + 0.25Y.$$

Money demand is

$$\frac{M^d}{P} = 0.5Y - 250(r + \pi^e),$$

where the expected rate of inflation $\pi^e = 0.10$. The nominal supply of money $M = 9890$.

a. What are the general equilibrium values of the real interest rate, price level, consumption, and investment?

b. Suppose that government purchases are increased to $G = 216$. What are the new general equilibrium values of the real interest rate, the price level, consumption, and investment?

4. The production function in an economy is

$$Y = A(5N - 0.0025N^2),$$

where A is productivity. With this production function, the marginal product of labour is

$$MPN = 5A - 0.005AN.$$

Suppose that $A = 2$. The labour supply curve is

$$NS = 55 + 10(1 - t)w,$$

where NS is the amount of labour supplied, w is the real wage, and t is the tax rate, which is 0.5.

Desired consumption and investment are

$$C^d = 300 + 0.8(Y - T) - 200r;$$
$$I^d = 258.5 - 250r.$$

Taxes and government purchases are

$$T = 20 + 0.5Y;$$
$$G = 50.$$

Money demand is

$$\frac{M^d}{P} = 0.5Y - 250(r + \pi^e).$$

The expected rate of inflation π^e is 0.02, and the nominal money supply M is 9150.

a. What are the general equilibrium levels of the real wage, employment, and output?

b. For any level of output Y, find an equation that gives the real interest rate r that clears the goods market; this equation describes the *IS* curve. (*Hint:* Write the goods market equilibrium condition and solve for r in terms of Y and other variables.) What are the general equilibrium values of the real interest rate, consumption, and investment?

c. For any level of output Y, find an equation that gives the real interest rate that clears the asset market; this equation describes the *LM* curve. (*Hint:* As in part (b), write the appropriate equilibrium condition and solve for r in terms of Y and other variables.) What is the general equilibrium value of the price level?

d. Suppose that government purchases increase to $G = 72.5$. Now what are the general equilibrium values of the real wage, employment, output, the real interest rate, consumption, investment, and the price level?

5. (Appendix) This question asks you to use the formulas in Appendix 9.A to find the general equilibrium values of variables for the economy described in Numerical Problem 4. Assume that $G = 50$.

a. Use the data from Numerical Problem 4 to find the numerical values of the parameters $A, f_1, f_2, n_0, n_w, c_0, c_Y, c_r, t_0, t, i_0, i_r, \ell_0, \ell_Y,$ and, ℓ_r defined in Appendix 9.A.

b. Substitute the values of these behavioural parameters into the relevant equations in Appendix 9.A to compute the general equilibrium values of the real wage, employment, output, the real interest rate, and the price level.

c. Assume that government purchases G increase to 72.5, and repeat part (b).

6. Consider the following economy:

Desired consumption	$C^d = 1275 + 0.5(Y - T) - 200r.$
Desired investment	$I^d = 900 - 200r.$
Real money demand	$L = 0.5Y - 200i.$
Full-employment output	$\bar{Y} = 4600.$
Expected inflation	$\pi^e = 0.$

a. Suppose that $T = G = 450$ and that $M = 9000$. Find an equation describing the *IS* curve. (*Hint:* Set desired national saving and desired investment equal, and solve for the relationship between r and Y, given P.) Finally, find an equation for the aggregate demand curve. (*Hint:* Use the *IS* and *LM* equations to find a relationship between Y and P.) What are the equilibrium values of output, consumption, investment, the real interest rate, and the price level?

b. Suppose that $T = G = 450$ and that $M = 4500$. What is the equation for the aggregate demand curve now? What are the equilibrium values of output, consumption, investment, the real interest rate, and the price level? Assume that full-employment output $\bar{Y}$ is fixed.

c. Repeat part (b) for $T = G = 330$ and $M = 9000$.

ANALYTICAL PROBLEMS

1. Use the *IS–LM* model to determine the effects of each of the following on the general equilibrium values of the real wage, employment, output, the real interest rate, consumption, investment, and the price level.

a. A reduction in the effective tax rate on capital that increases desired investment.

b. The expected rate of inflation rises.

c. An influx of working-age immigrants increases labour supply (ignore any other possible effects of increased population).

d. The introduction of automatic teller machines reduces the demand for money.

2. Use the *IS–LM* model to analyze the general equilibrium effects of a permanent increase in the price of oil (a permanent adverse supply shock) on current output, employment, the real wage, national saving, consumption, investment, the real interest rate, and the price level. Assume that besides reducing the current productivity of capital and labour, the permanent supply shock lowers both the expected future *MPK* and households' expected future incomes. Show that if the real interest rate rises at all, it will rise less than in the case of a temporary supply shock that has an equal effect on current output.

3. Suppose that the price level is fixed in the short run so that the economy does not reach general equilibrium immediately after a change in the economy. For each of the following changes, what are the short-run effects on the real interest rate and output? Assume that when the economy is in disequilibrium, only the labour market is out of equilibrium; assume also that for a short period firms are willing to produce enough output to meet the aggregate demand for output.

    a. A decrease in the expected rate of inflation.

    b. An increase in consumer optimism that increases desired consumption at each level of income and the real interest rate.

    c. An increase in government purchases.

    d. An increase in lump-sum taxes, with no change in government purchases (consider both the case in which Ricardian equivalence holds and the case in which it does not).

    e. A scientific breakthrough increases the expected future *MPK*.

4. (Appendix) In some macroeconomic models, desired investment depends on the current level of output as well as on the real interest rate. One possible reason that desired investment may depend on output is that when current production and sales are high, firms may expect continued strong demand for their products in the future, which leads them to want to expand capacity.

    Algebraically, we can allow for a link between desired investment and current output by replacing Eq. (9.A.10) with

    $$I^d = i_0 - i_r\, r + i_Y\, Y,$$

    where i_Y is a positive number. Use this alternative equation for desired investment to derive the algebraic expressions for the general equilibrium values of employment, the real wage, output, the real interest rate, and the price level.

5. (Appendix) Recall from Chapter 7 that an increase in i^m, the nominal interest rate on money, increases the demand for money. To capture that effect, let us replace Eq. (9.A.17) with

    $$\frac{M^d}{P} = \ell_0 + \ell_Y\, Y - \ell_r\, (r + \pi^e - i^m).$$

    How does this modification change the solutions for the general equilibrium values of the variables discussed in Appendix 9.A, including employment, the real wage, output, the real interest rate, and the price level?

APPENDIX 9.A

ALGEBRAIC VERSIONS OF THE *IS–LM* AND *AD–AS* MODELS

In this appendix, we present algebraic versions of the *IS–LM* and *AD–AS* models. For each of the three markets—labour, goods, and assets—we first present equations that describe demand and supply in that market, then find the market equilibrium. After considering each market separately, we solve for the general equilibrium of the complete *IS–LM* model. We use the *IS–LM* model to derive the aggregate demand (*AD*) curve and then introduce the short-run and long-run aggregate supply curves to derive the short-run and long-run equilibria.

THE LABOUR MARKET

The demand for labour is based on the marginal product of labour, as determined by the production function. Recall from Chapter 3 (Eq. 3.1) that the production function can be written as $Y = AF(K, N)$, where Y is output, K is the capital stock, N is labour input, and A is productivity. Holding the capital stock K fixed, we can write the production function with output Y as a function only of labour input N and productivity A. A useful specific production function is

$$Y = A\left(f_1 N - \frac{1}{2} f_2 N^2\right), \tag{9.A.1}$$

where f_1 and f_2 are positive numbers.

The marginal product of labour, *MPN*, is the slope of the production function. The slope of the production function in Eq. (9.A.1) at any level of employment N equals[11] $A(f_1 - f_2 N)$, so the marginal product of labour is

$$MPN = A(f_1 - f_2 N) \tag{9.A.2}$$

Firms hire labour to the point at which the marginal product of labour equals the real wage. Thus, the relation between the real wage w and the amount of labour demanded *ND* is

$$w = A(f_1 - f_2 ND) \tag{9.A.3}$$

The supply of labour is an increasing function of the current, after-tax real wage. If t is the tax rate on wage income (we assume that $0 < t < 1$) so that $(1 - t)w$ is the after-tax real wage, a simple form of the labour supply curve is

$$NS = n_0 + n_w (1 - t)w, \tag{9.A.4}$$

where *NS* is the amount of labour supplied, and n_0 and n_w are positive numbers. Factors other than the after-tax real wage that affect labour supply, such as wealth or the working-age population, are captured by the constant term n_0 in Eq. (9.A.4).

---

11. Students who know calculus can derive the slope of the production function by taking the derivative of Eq. (9.A.1) with respect to N.

EQUILIBRIUM IN THE LABOUR MARKET

In equilibrium, the amounts of labour demanded ND and supplied NS are equal; their common value is the full-employment level of employment $\overline{N}$. If we substitute $\overline{N}$ for NS and ND in Eqs.(9.A.3) and (9.A.4), we have two linear equations in the two variables $\overline{N}$ and w. Solving these equations for w and $\overline{N}$ yields[12]

$$w = A\left[\frac{f_1 - f_2 n_0}{1 + (1-t)Af_2 n_w}\right] \tag{9.A.5}$$

and

$$\overline{N} = \frac{n_0 + (1-t)Af_1 n_w}{1 + (1-t)Af_2 n_w}. \tag{9.A.6}$$

Using the full-employment level of employment $\overline{N}$ in Eq. (9.A.6), we obtain the full-employment level of output $\overline{Y}$ by substituting $\overline{N}$ into the production function (9.A.1):

$$\overline{Y} = A\left[f_1\overline{N} - \frac{1}{2}f_2\overline{N}^2\right], FE \text{ line.} \tag{9.A.7}$$

The value of full-employment output in Eq. (9.A.7) is the horizontal intercept of the FE line.

We can use these equations to analyze the effects on the labour market of changes in productivity and in labour supply. First, consider an increase in productivity A. Equation (9.A.5) shows that an increase in A leads to an increase in the equilibrium real wage (an increase in A raises the ratio $A/[1 + (1-t)Af_2 n_w]$). Although not directly evident from Eq. (9.A.6), an increase in A also increases $\overline{N}$.[13] To see why, note first that an increase in A does not affect the labour supply curve, Eq. (9.A.4). Second, an increase in A raises the real wage. Hence the implication is that an increase in A raises the equilibrium amount of labour supplied and, thus, also the full-employment level of employment $\overline{N}$. Because an increase in A raises $\overline{N}$, it must also raise full-employment output $\overline{Y}$ (see Eq. 9.A.7) and shift the FE line to the right.

Now, consider an increase in the amount of labour supplied at each level of the after-tax real wage, represented algebraically as an increase in n_0 in Eq. (9.A.4). Equations (9.A.5) and (9.A.6) show that an increase in n_0 reduces the equilibrium real wage and increases employment $\overline{N}$. Because an increase in labour supply raises $\overline{N}$, it also raises full-employment output $\overline{Y}$ and shifts the FE line to the right.

THE GOODS MARKET

To find equilibrium in the goods market, we start with equations describing desired consumption and desired investment. Desired consumption is

---

12. We assume that the constants f_1, f_2, and n_0 are such that $f_1 - f_2 n_0 > 0$. This assumption is needed to guarantee that the marginal product of labour and the equilibrium real wage are positive.

13. Students who know calculus can compute the derivative of $\overline{N}$ with respect to A in Eq. (9.A.6) and will find that the sign of this derivative is positive only if $f_1 - f_2 n_0 > 0$. As we have assumed that $f_1 - f_2 n_0 > 0$ (see preceding footnote), an increase in A does indeed increase $\overline{N}$.

$$C^d = c_0 + c_Y (Y - T) - c_r r; \tag{9.A.8}$$

where $Y - T$ is disposable income (income Y minus taxes T), r is the real interest rate, and c_0, c_Y, and c_r are positive numbers. The number c_Y in Eq. (9.A.8) is the marginal propensity to consume, as defined in Chapter 4; because people consume only part of an increase in disposable income, saving the rest, a reasonable assumption is that $0 < c_Y < 1$. According to Eq. (9.A.8), an increase in disposable income causes desired consumption to increase, and an increase in the real interest rate causes desired consumption to fall (and desired saving to rise). Other factors that affect desired consumption, such as wealth or expected future income, are included in the constant term c_0.[14]

Taxes in Eq. (9.A.8) are

$$T = t_0 + tY, \tag{9.A.9}$$

where t is the tax rate on income (the same tax rate that is levied on wages) and t_0 is a lump-sum tax. As mentioned earlier, $0 \leq t < 1$, so an increase in income Y increases total taxes T and also increases disposable income $Y - T$.

Desired investment is

$$I^d = i_0 - i_r r; \tag{9.A.10}$$

where i_0 and i_r are positive numbers. Equation (9.A.10) indicates that desired investment falls when the real interest rate rises. Other factors affecting desired investment, such as the expected future marginal product of capital, are included in the constant term i_0.

EQUILIBRIUM IN THE GOODS MARKET

The goods market equilibrium condition in a closed economy is given by Eq. (4.7), which we repeat here:

$$Y = C^d + I^d + G. \tag{9.A.11}$$

Equation (9.A.11) is equivalent to the goods market equilibrium condition, $S^d = I^d$, which could be used equally well here.

If we substitute the equations for desired consumption (Eq. 9.A.8, with taxes T as given by Eq. 9.A.9) and desired investment (Eq. 9.A.10) into the goods market equilibrium condition (Eq. 9.A.11), we get

$$Y = c_0 + c_Y (Y - t_0 - tY) - c_r r + i_0 - i_r r + G. \tag{9.A.12}$$

Collecting the terms that multiply Y on the left-hand side yields

$$[1 - (1 - t)c_Y]Y = c_0 + i_0 + G - c_Y t_0 - (c_r + i_r)r. \tag{9.A.13}$$

---

14. Because an increase in taxes T reduces desired consumption in Eq. (9.A.8), this formulation of desired consumption appears, at first glance, to be inconsistent with the Ricardian equivalence proposition discussed in Chapter 4. However, essential to the idea of Ricardian equivalence is that consumers expect an increase in current taxes T to be accompanied by lower taxes in the future. This decrease in expected future taxes would increase desired consumption, which would be captured in Eq. (9.A.8) as an increase in c_0. According to the Ricardian equivalence proposition, after an increase in T with no change in current or planned government purchases, an increase in c_0 would exactly offset the reduction in $c_Y (Y - T)$ so that desired consumption would be unchanged.

Equation (9.A.13) relates output Y to the real interest rate r that clears the goods market. This relationship between Y and r defines the *IS* curve. Because the *IS* curve is graphed with r on the vertical axis and Y on the horizontal axis, we rewrite Eq. (9.A.13) with r on the left-hand side and Y on the right-hand side. Solving Eq. (9.A.13) for r gives

$$r = \alpha_{IS} - \beta_{IS}Y, \; IS \text{ curve.} \tag{9.A.14}$$

In Eq. (9.A.14), α_{IS} and β_{IS} are positive numbers defined as

$$\alpha_{IS} = \frac{c_0 + i_0 + G - c_Y t_0}{c_r + i_r} \tag{9.A.15}$$

and

$$\beta_{IS} = \frac{1 - (1-t)c_Y}{c_r + i_r}. \tag{9.A.16}$$

Equation (9.A.14) yields the graph of the *IS* curve. In Eq. (9.A.14), the co-efficient of Y, or $-\beta_{IS}$, is the slope of the *IS* curve; because this slope is negative, the *IS* curve slopes downward. Changes in the constant term α_{IS} in Eq. (9.A.14), which is defined in Eq. (9.A.15), shift the *IS* curve. Anything that increases α_{IS}—such as (1) an increase in consumer optimism that increases desired consumption by increasing c_0; (2) an increase in the expected future marginal product of capital MPK^f that raises desired investment by raising i_0; or (3) an increase in government purchases G—shifts the *IS* curve up. Similarly, anything that decreases α_{IS} shifts the *IS* curve down.

THE ASSET MARKET

In general, the real demand for money depends on real income Y and on the nominal interest rate on non-monetary assets i, which in turn equals the expected real interest rate r plus the expected rate of inflation π^e. We assume that the money demand function takes the form

$$\frac{M^d}{P} = \ell_0 + \ell_Y Y - \ell_r (r + \pi^e), \tag{9.A.17}$$

where M^d is the nominal demand for money, P is the price level, and ℓ_0, ℓ_Y, and ℓ_r are positive numbers. The constant term ℓ_0 includes factors other than output and the interest rate that affect money demand, such as the liquidity of alternative assets. The real supply of money equals the nominal supply of money M, which is determined by the central bank, divided by the price level P.

EQUILIBRIUM IN THE ASSET MARKET

As we showed in Chapter 7, if we assume that there are only two types of assets (money and non-monetary assets), the asset market is in equilibrium when the real quantity of money demanded equals the real money supply M/P. Using the money demand function in Eq. (9.A.17), we write the asset market equilibrium condition as

$$\frac{M}{P} = \ell_0 + \ell_Y Y - \ell_r (r + \pi^e). \tag{9.A.18}$$

For fixed levels of the nominal money supply M, price level P, and expected rate of inflation π^e, Eq. (9.A.18) relates output Y and the real interest rate r that clears the asset market. Thus, Eq. (9.A.18) defines the *LM* curve. To get Eq. (9.A.18) into a form that is easier to interpret graphically, we rewrite the equation with r alone on the left-hand side:

$$r = \alpha_{LM} - \left(\frac{1}{\ell_r}\right)\left(\frac{M}{P}\right) + \beta_{LM}Y, \quad \textit{LM curve}, \tag{9.A.19}$$

where

$$\alpha_{LM} = \left(\frac{\ell_0}{\ell_r}\right) - \pi^e \tag{9.A.20}$$

and

$$\beta_{LM} = \left(\frac{\ell_Y}{\ell_r}\right). \tag{9.A.21}$$

The graph of Eq. (9.A.19) is the *LM* curve. In Eq. (9.A.19), the coefficient of Y, or β_{LM}, is the slope of the *LM* curve; because this coefficient is positive, the *LM* curve slopes upward. Variables that change the intercept of the equation in Eq. (9.A.19), $\alpha_{LM} - (1/\ell_r)(M/P)$, shift the *LM* curve. An increase in the real money supply M/P reduces this intercept and, thus, shifts the *LM* curve down and to the right. An increase in the expected rate of inflation π^e reduces α_{LM} and shifts the *LM* curve down. An increase in real money demand arising from (for example) reduced liquidity of alternative assets raises, ℓ_0, which raises α_{LM} and shifts the *LM* curve up.

GENERAL EQUILIBRIUM IN THE *IS–LM* MODEL

From the supply and demand relationships and equilibrium conditions in each market, we can calculate the general equilibrium values for the most important macroeconomic variables. We have already solved for the general equilibrium levels of the real wage, employment, and output in the labour market: The real wage is given by Eq. (9.A.5); employment equals its full-employment level $\bar{N}$, given by Eq. (9.A.6); and, in general equilibrium, output equals its full-employment level $\bar{Y}$, as given by Eq. (9.A.7).

Turning to the goods market, we obtain the general equilibrium real interest rate by substituting $\bar{Y}$ for Y in Eq. (9.A.14):

$$r = \alpha_{IS} - \beta_{IS}\bar{Y}. \tag{9.A.22}$$

Having output $\bar{Y}$ and the real interest rate r (determined by Eq. 9.A.22), we use Eqs. (9.A.9), (10.A.8), and (9.A.10) to find the general equilibrium values of taxes T, consumption C, and investment I, respectively.

The final important macroeconomic variable whose equilibrium value needs to be determined is the price level P. To find the equilibrium price level, we work with the asset market equilibrium condition, Eq. (9.A.18). In Eq. (9.A.18), we substitute full-employment output $\bar{Y}$ for Y and use Eq. (9.A.22) to substitute the equilibrium value of the real interest rate for r. Solving Eq. (9.A.18) for the price level gives

$$P = \frac{M}{\ell_0 + \ell_Y \bar{Y} - \ell_r(\alpha_{IS} - \beta_{IS}\bar{Y} + \pi^e)}. \tag{9.A.23}$$

Equation (9.A.23) confirms that the equilibrium price level P is proportional to the nominal money supply M.

We can use these equations to analyze the effects of an adverse productivity shock on the general equilibrium, as in the text. We have already shown that an increase in the productivity parameter A increases the equilibrium real wage, the full-employment level of employment, and the full-employment level of output. Thus, an adverse productivity shock (a reduction in A) reduces the general equilibrium levels of the real wage, employment, and output. Equation (9.A.22) indicates that an adverse productivity shock, because it reduces $\bar{Y}$, must increase the equilibrium real interest rate. Lower output and a higher real interest rate imply that both consumption and investment must decline (Eqs. 9.A.8 and 9.A.10). Finally, the decrease in $\bar{Y}$ resulting from an adverse productivity shock reduces the denominator of the right-hand side of Eq. (9.A.23), so the price level P must rise. All these results are the same as those found by graphical analysis.

THE *AD–AS* MODEL

Building on the algebraic version of the *IS–LM* model just derived, we now derive an algebraic version of the *AD–AS* model presented in this chapter. We present algebraic versions of the aggregate demand (*AD*) curve, the short-run aggregate supply (*SRAS*) curve, and the long-run aggregate supply (*LRAS*) curve and then solve for short-run and long-run equilibrium.

THE AGGREGATE DEMAND CURVE

Aggregate output demanded at any price level, P, is the amount of output corresponding to the intersection of the *IS* and *LM* curves. We find the value of Y at the intersection of the *IS* and *LM* curves by setting the right-hand sides of Eqs. (9.A.14) and (9.A.19) equal and solving for Y:

$$Y = \frac{\alpha_{IS} - \alpha_{LM} + (1/\ell_r)(M/P)}{\beta_{IS} + \beta_{LM}}. \tag{9.A.24}$$

Equation (9.A.24) is the aggregate demand curve. For constant nominal money supply, M, Eq. (9.A.24) shows that the aggregate quantity of goods demanded, Y, is a decreasing function of the price level, P, so that the *AD* curve slopes downward. Note that the numerator of the right-hand side of Eq. (9.A.24) is the intercept of the *IS* curve minus the intercept of the *LM* curve. Thus, for a constant price level, any change that shifts the *IS* curve up (such as an increase in government purchases) or shifts the *LM* curve down (such as an increase in the nominal money supply) increases aggregate output demanded and shifts the *AD* curve to the right.

THE AGGREGATE SUPPLY CURVE

In the short run, firms supply the output demanded at the fixed price level, which we denote $\bar{P}$. Thus, the short-run aggregate supply (*SRAS*) curve is a horizontal line:

$$P = \bar{P}, \qquad SRAS. \qquad (9.A.25)$$

The long-run aggregate supply curve is a vertical line at the full-employment level of output, $\bar{Y}$, or

$$Y = \bar{Y}, \qquad LRAS. \qquad (9.A.26)$$

SHORT-RUN AND LONG-RUN EQUILIBRIUM

The short-run equilibrium of the economy is represented by the intersection of the aggregate demand (*AD*) curve and the short-run aggregate supply (*SRAS*) curve. We find the quantity of output in short-run equilibrium simply by substituting the equation of the *SRAS* curve (Eq. 9.A.25) into the equation of the *AD* curve (Eq. 9.A.24) to obtain

$$Y = \frac{\alpha_{IS} - \alpha_{LM} + (1/\ell_r)(M/\bar{P})}{\beta_{IS} + \beta_{LM}}. \qquad (9.A.27)$$

The long-run equilibrium of the economy, which is reached when the labour, goods, and asset markets are all in equilibrium, is represented by the intersection of the aggregate demand curve and the long-run aggregate supply curve. Thus, $Y = \bar{Y}$ in the long-run equilibrium, from the *LRAS* curve in Eq. (9.A.26). We find the price level in long-run equilibrium by setting the left-hand sides of the equation of the *AD* curve (Eq. 9.A.24) and the equation of the *LRAS* curve (Eq. 9.A. 26) equal and solving for P to obtain

$$P = \frac{M}{\ell_r[\alpha_{LM} - \alpha_{IS} + (\beta_{IS} + \beta_{LM})\bar{Y}]} \qquad (9.A.28)$$

The long-run equilibrium price level in Eq. (9.A.28) is the same as that at the *IS–LM–FE* intersection in Eq. (9.A.23). You can verify that the price level is the same in both equations by substituting the definitions of α_{LM} and β_{LM} from Eqs. (9.A.20) and (9.A.21), respectively, into Eq. (9.A.28).

Chapter 10

EXCHANGE RATES, BUSINESS CYCLES, AND MACROECONOMIC POLICY IN THE OPEN ECONOMY

In Chapter 9, we focused on a closed economy, or one that does not interact with other economies. For some purposes, ignoring the foreign sector simplifies the analysis. But the reality is that today, more than ever, we live in a highly interdependent world economic system.

There are two primary aspects of the interdependence of the world's economies. The first is international trade in goods and services, which has increased steadily in volume since World War II. Today, firms produce goods and services with an eye on foreign *and* domestic markets, and they obtain many raw materials from distant sources. Expanded international trade has increased productivity by allowing economies to specialize in producing the goods and services best suited to their natural and human resources. However, expanded trade also implies that national economies are more dependent on what happens in other countries. For example, because Canada sells so much of its output to the United States, a US recession or macroeconomic policy change may affect the Canadian economy as well.

The second is the worldwide integration of financial markets, which allows borrowers to obtain funds and savers to look for their best lending opportunities almost anywhere in the world, not just in their own countries. By allowing savings to flow to the highest-return uses, regardless of where savers and investors happen to live, the integration of world financial markets increases worldwide productivity, as does the development of an integrated world trading system. But financial market linkages, such as trade linkages, increase the sensitivity of individual economies to developments abroad. For example, because of closely connected financial markets, macroeconomic policies that change the real interest rate in one country may affect real interest rates and economic activity in other countries.

In this chapter, we build on earlier analyses of the open economy (Chapter 5) and cyclical fluctuations (Chapters 8 and 9) to examine the macroeconomic implications of trading and financial links among countries. We are particularly concerned in this chapter with how economic openness affects fiscal and monetary policies and how macroeconomic policy changes affect the economies of a country's trading partners. We begin our discussion by introducing two new variables that play central roles in the international economy: the nominal exchange rate and the real exchange rate.

10.1 EXCHANGE RATES

In discussing exchange rates, we must distinguish between nominal and real exchange rates. Briefly stated, the nominal exchange rate is the answer to the question: How many units of a foreign *currency* can I get in exchange for one unit of my domestic *currency*? The real exchange rate is the answer to the question: How many units of the foreign *good* can I get in exchange for one unit of my domestic *good*?

NOMINAL EXCHANGE RATES

Most countries have their own national currencies: The Canadian and US dollars, the Japanese yen, and the British pound are but a few well-known currencies. The exceptions include countries that belong to the European Monetary Union, which have a common currency, the euro, as well as some Latin American countries, such as Ecuador and Panama, that use the US dollar. If someone in one country (or area with a common currency) wants to buy goods, services, or assets from someone in another country, normally she will first have to exchange her country's currency for that of her trading partner's country.

The rate at which two currencies can be traded is the nominal exchange rate between the two currencies. For example, if the nominal exchange rate between the Canadian dollar and the Japanese yen is 78 yen per dollar, a dollar can buy 78 yen (ignoring transaction fees) in the **foreign exchange market**, which is the market for international currencies. Equivalently,78 yen can buy one dollar in the foreign exchange market. More precisely, the **nominal exchange rate** between two currencies, e_{nom}, is the number of units of foreign currency that can be purchased with one unit of the domestic currency. For residents of Canada, the domestic currency is the Canadian dollar, and the nominal exchange rate between the Canadian dollar and the Japanese yen is expressed as e_{nom} =78 yen per dollar. The nominal exchange rate often is simply called the **exchange rate**, so whenever someone mentions the exchange rate without specifying real or nominal, the reference is taken to mean the *nominal* exchange rate.

The dollar–yen exchange rate is not constant. The Canadian dollar might trade for 78 yen one day, but the next day it might rise in value to 80 yen or fall in value to 76 yen. Such changes in the exchange rate are normal under a flexible-exchange-rate system, the type of system in which many of the world's major currencies (including the Canadian dollar and the yen) are currently traded. In a **flexible-exchange-rate system**, or **floating-exchange-rate system**, exchange rates are not officially fixed but are determined by conditions of supply and demand in the foreign exchange market. Under a flexible-exchange-rate system, exchange rates move continuously and respond quickly to any economic or political news that might influence the supplies and demands for various currencies. The box, "In Touch with the Macroeconomy: Exchange Rates," p. 352, discusses exchange rate data. Figure 1.6, in Chapter 1, shows the nominal exchange rate between the Canadian and US dollars since 1950.

The values of currencies have not always been determined by a flexible-exchange-rate system. In the past, some type of **fixed-exchange-rate system**, under which exchange rates were set at officially determined levels, often operated. Usually, these official rates were maintained by the commitment of nations' central banks to buy and sell their own currencies at the fixed exchange rate. For example, under the international gold standard system that operated in the late 1800s and early 1900s, the central bank of each country maintained the value of its currency in terms of gold by agreeing to buy or sell gold in exchange for currency at a fixed rate of exchange. The gold standard was suspended during World War I, was temporarily restored in the late 1920s, and then collapsed during the economic and financial crises of the 1930s.

A more recent example of a fixed-exchange-rate system was the Bretton Woods system, named after the town in New Hampshire where the 1944 conference establishing the system was held. Under the Bretton Woods system, the values of various currencies were fixed in terms of the US dollar, and the value of the dollar was set at $35 per ounce of gold. The Bretton Woods system functioned until the early 1970s, when inflation in the United States made keeping the price of gold from rising above $35 per ounce virtually impossible (see the Application, "Policy Coordination / Failure...," p. 380, for a further discussion of the collapse of the Bretton Woods system). Since the breakdown of the Bretton Woods system, no fixed-exchange-rate system has encompassed all the world's major currencies.

Although no worldwide system of fixed exchange rates currently exists, fixed exchange rates have not disappeared entirely. Many individual countries, especially smaller ones, attempt to fix their exchange rates against a major currency. For example, several African countries tie their currencies to the euro, and Argentina until recently adopted a system under which its currency, the peso, traded one-for-one with the US dollar. By doing so, these countries hope to stabilize their own currencies and reduce the sharp swings in import and export prices that may result from exchange rate fluctuations. We discuss fixed exchange rates in Section 10.6.

REAL EXCHANGE RATES

The nominal exchange rate does not tell you all you need to know about the purchasing power of a currency. If you were told, for example, that the nominal exchange rate between the Canadian dollar and the Japanese yen is 78 yen per dollar, but you did not know anything else about the Canadian or Japanese economies, you might be tempted to conclude that someone from Vancouver could visit Tokyo very cheaply—after all, 78 yen for just one dollar seems like a good deal. But even at 78 yen per dollar, Japan is an expensive place to visit. The reason is that although one dollar can buy a lot of yen, it also takes a lot of yen (thousands or hundreds of thousands) to buy everyday goods in Japan.

Suppose, for example, that you want to compare the price of hamburgers in Tokyo and Vancouver. Knowing that the exchange rate is 78 yen per dollar does not help much. But if you also know that a hamburger costs three dollars in Vancouver and 312 yen in Tokyo, you can compare the price of a hamburger in the two cities by asking how many dollars are needed to buy a hamburger in Japan. Because a hamburger costs 312 yen in Tokyo, and 78 yen cost one dollar, the price of a hamburger in Tokyo is four dollars (calculated by dividing the price of a Japanese hamburger, ¥312, by ¥78/$1, to obtain $4 per hamburger). The price of a Canadian hamburger relative to a Japanese hamburger is, therefore, ($3 per Canadian hamburger)/($4 per Japanese hamburger) = 0.75 Japanese hamburgers per Canadian hamburger. The Japanese hamburger is expensive in the sense that (in this example) one Canadian hamburger equals only three-quarters of a Japanese hamburger.

The price of domestic goods relative to foreign goods—equivalently, the number of foreign goods someone gets in exchange for one domestic good—is called the **real exchange rate**. In the hamburger example, the real exchange rate between Canada and Japan is 0.75 Japanese hamburgers per Canadian hamburger.

In general, the real exchange rate is related to the nominal exchange rate and to prices in both countries. To write this relation, we use the following symbols:

e_{nom} = the nominal exchange rate
(78 yen per dollar);
P_{For} = the price of foreign goods, measured in the foreign currency
(312 yen per Japanese hamburger);
P = the price of domestic goods, measured in the domestic currency
(3 dollars per Canadian hamburger).

The real exchange rate e is the number of foreign goods (Japanese hamburgers) that can be obtained in exchange for one unit of the domestic good (Canadian hamburgers). The general formula for the real exchange rate is

$$e = \frac{e_{\text{nom}} P}{P_{\text{For}}}$$

$$= \frac{(\yen 78 / \$1)(\$3 / \text{Canadian hamburger})}{\yen 312 / \text{Japanese hamburger}}$$

$$= 0.75 \text{ Japanese hamburgers per Canadian hamburger.} \quad (10.1)$$

In defining the real exchange rate as the number of foreign goods that can be obtained for each domestic good, we assume that each country produces a single, unique good. (Think of France producing only bottles of wine and Saudi Arabia producing only barrels of oil; then the French real exchange rate with respect to Saudi Arabia is the number of barrels of oil that can be purchased for one bottle of wine.) The assumption that each country produces a single good (which is different from the good produced by any other country) simplifies the theoretical analysis in this chapter.[1]

Of course, in reality, countries produce thousands of different goods, so real exchange rates must be based on price indexes (such as the GDP deflator or the CPI) to measure P and P_{For}. Thus, the real exchange rate is not actually the rate of exchange between two specific goods but, instead, is the rate of exchange between a typical basket of goods in one country and a typical basket of goods in the other country. Each of these baskets contains some goods that are not traded internationally. Changes in the real exchange rate over time indicate that on average, the goods of the country whose real exchange rate is rising are becoming more expensive relative to the goods of the other country.

APPRECIATION AND DEPRECIATION

When the nominal exchange rate e_{nom} falls so that, say, a dollar buys fewer units of foreign currency, we say that the dollar has undergone a **nominal depreciation**. This is the same as saying that the dollar has become "weaker." If the dollar's nominal exchange rate e_{nom} rises, then the dollar has had a **nominal appreciation**. When the dollar appreciates, it can buy more units of foreign currency and, thus, has become "stronger."[2] The terms "appreciation" and "depreciation" are associated with flexible exchange rates. Under a fixed-exchange-rate system, in which exchange rates are changed only by official government action, different terms are used. Instead of a depreciation, a weakening of the currency is called a **devaluation**. A strengthening of the currency under fixed exchange rates is called a **revaluation**, rather than an appreciation. These terms are listed for convenience in Summary table 15.

---

1. The assumption that different countries produce different goods is a change from Chapter 5, where we implicitly assumed that all countries produce an identical good that can be used for all purposes (consumption, investment, etc.). The assumption that all countries produce the same good implied that, in the analysis of that chapter, the real exchange rate was always equal to 1.

2. You will sometimes see the exchange rate defined as the number of units of domestic currency per unit of foreign currency, which is the reciprocal of how we have defined it. For example, the exchange rate between the British pound and the Canadian dollar is typically quoted in this form (for example, $2.50 per pound). Under this alternative definition, an appreciation of the dollar corresponds to a fall in the nominal exchange rate. The two ways of defining the exchange rate are equally valid, as long as consistency is maintained. We have chosen to define the exchange rate as the number of units of foreign currency per unit of home currency because it is easier to remember that an appreciation (when the value of the dollar goes up) is associated with a rise in the exchange rate.

Summary 15

Terminology for Changes in Exchange Rates

Type of Exchange Rate System	Exchange Rate Increases (Currency Strengthens)	Exchange Rate Decreases (Currency Weakens)
Flexible exchange rates	Appreciation	Depreciation
Fixed exchange rates	Revaluation	Devaluation

An increase in the real exchange rate e is called a **real appreciation**. With a real appreciation, the same quantity of domestic goods can be traded for more of the foreign good than before because e, the price of domestic goods relative to the price of foreign goods, has risen. A drop in the real exchange rate, which decreases the quantity of foreign goods that can be purchased with the same quantity of domestic goods, is called a **real depreciation**.

Purchasing Power Parity

How are nominal exchange rates and real exchange rates related? A simple hypothetical case that allows us to think about this question occurs when all countries produce the same good (or same set of goods) and goods are freely traded among countries. In this case, no one would trade domestic goods for foreign goods except on a one-for-one basis, so (ignoring transportation costs) the real exchange rate, e, would always equal 1. If $e = 1$, we can use Eq. (10.1) to write

$$P = \frac{P_{\text{For}}}{e_{\text{nom}}}. \tag{10.2}$$

Equation (10.2) says that the price of the domestic good must equal the price of the foreign good when the price of the foreign good is expressed in terms of the domestic currency. (To express the foreign price in terms of the domestic currency, divide by the exchange rate.) The idea that similar foreign and domestic goods, or baskets of goods, should have the same price in terms of the same currency is called **purchasing power parity** (PPP). Equivalently, as implied by Eq. (10.2), purchasing power parity says that the nominal exchange rate should equal the foreign price level divided by the domestic price level, so that

$$e_{\text{nom}} = \frac{P_{\text{For}}}{P}.$$

There is some empirical evidence that PPP holds in the very long run, but (as Box 10.1 suggests) over shorter periods, PPP does not describe exchange rate behaviour very well. The failure of PPP in the short to medium run occurs for various reasons. For example, countries produce very different baskets of goods and services, not the same goods as assumed for PPP; some types of goods, and most services, are not internationally traded; and transportation costs and legal barriers to trade may prevent the prices of traded goods and services from being equalized in different countries.

To find a relationship between real and nominal exchange rates that holds more generally, we can use the definition of the real exchange rate in Eq. (10.1), $e = e_{nom} P/P_{For}$, to calculate $\Delta e/e$, the percentage change in the real exchange rate. Because the real exchange rate is expressed as a ratio, its percentage change equals the percentage change in the numerator minus the percentage change in the denominator.[3] The percentage change in the numerator of the expression for the real exchange rate[4] is $\Delta e_{nom}/e_{nom} + \Delta P/P$, and the percentage change in the denominator is $\Delta P_{For}/P_{For}$. Thus, the percentage change in the real exchange rate is

$$\frac{\Delta e}{e} = \frac{\Delta e_{nom}}{e_{nom}} + \frac{\Delta P}{P} - \frac{\Delta P_{For}}{P_{For}}$$

In the preceding equation, the term $\Delta P/P$, the percentage change in the domestic price level, is the same as the domestic rate of inflation π, and the term $\Delta P_{For}/P_{For}$, the percentage change in the foreign price level, is the same as the foreign rate of inflation π_{For}. Making these substitutions and re-arranging the equation, we rewrite this equation as

$$\frac{\Delta e_{nom}}{e_{nom}} = \frac{\Delta e}{e} + \pi_{For} - \pi. \tag{10.3}$$

Equation (10.3) is purely definitional and, thus, must always be satisfied. It states that the rate of the nominal exchange rate appreciation $\Delta e_{nom}/e_{nom}$ equals the rate of real exchange rate appreciation $\Delta e/e$ plus the excess of foreign inflation over domestic inflation, $\pi_{For} - \pi$. Hence two factors contribute to strengthening a currency (a nominal appreciation): (1) an increase in the relative price of a country's exports (a real appreciation), which might occur if, for example, foreign demand for those exports rises; and (2) a rate of domestic inflation, π, lower than that of the country's trading partners, π_{For}.

A special case of Eq. (10.3) occurs when the real exchange rate is constant, so that

$$\frac{\Delta e_{nom}}{e_{nom}} = \pi_{For} - \pi.$$

In this case, the equation above expresses a relationship called relative purchasing power parity. According to **relative purchasing power parity**, the rate of appreciation of the nominal exchange rate equals the foreign inflation rate minus the domestic inflation rate. Relative purchasing power parity usually works well for high-inflation countries because in those countries, changes in relative inflation rates are usually much larger than changes in the real exchange rate.

For low-inflation countries, such as Canada, relative purchasing power parity is not a good guide. Changes in the nominal exchange rate in Canada usually are not matched by changes in Canadian inflation, at least in the short run. Eq. (10.3) shows that if a nominal depreciation, say, is not accompanied by much domestic inflation (relative to foreign inflation), then there also will be a real depreciation. In that case, the nominal and real exchange rates will tend to move together.

---

3. Appendix, Section A.7, describes how to calculate growth rates of products and ratios.
4. This result is obtained by using the rule that the percentage change in a product XY is the percentage change in X plus the percentage change in Y. See Appendix, Section A.7.

Box 10.1 McParity

If PPP holds, similar goods produced in different countries should cost about the same when their prices are expressed in a common currency, say, US dollars. As a test of this hypothesis, *The Economist* magazine has long recorded the price of Big Mac hamburgers in different countries. The following are the dollar prices of Big Macs in selected countries, as reported in *The Economist* on April 19, 2001.

Country	US Dollar Price of a Big Mac
Canada	$2.14
United States	2.54
Britain	2.85
Japan	2.38
China	1.20
Russia	1.21
Switzerland	3.65
Denmark	2.93
Brazil	1.64
Thailand	1.21
Euro area	2.27

Big Macs are not exactly the same product the world over. For example, in Italy and Holland, ketchup is about 50 cents extra, instead of being included in the price as in the United States and Canada. Nevertheless, the prices shown reveal that PPP definitely does not hold for Big Macs.

Even though PPP fails to hold at any particular time, Big Mac prices in different countries still might gradually come closer together. One way in which such a convergence could occur would be for the currencies in countries in which Big Macs are relatively expensive to depreciate relative to the currencies of countries in which Big Macs are cheap. Such a calculation would suggest that the British pound, Swiss franc, and Danish kroner are likely to depreciate in value relative to the US dollar (because Bic Macs are most expensive in those countries). In contrast, the Big Mac index suggests that the Chinese yuan, Thai baht, and Russian ruble may appreciate. It also forecasts an appreciation of the Canadian dollar against the US dollar.

Source: © 2001 The Economist Newspaper Group, Inc. Reprinted with permission. Further reproduction prohibited. *www.economist.com*.

THE REAL EXCHANGE RATE AND NET EXPORTS

We have defined the real exchange rate, but so far we have not indicated why it is important in macroeconomic analysis. One reason that policymakers and the public should care about the real exchange rate is that it represents the rate at which domestic goods and services can be traded for those produced abroad. An increase in the real exchange rate is good for a country in the sense that its citizens are able to obtain more foreign goods and services in exchange for a given amount of domestic production.

A second reason is that the real exchange rate affects a country's net exports, or exports less imports. Changes in net exports, in turn, have a direct impact on the domestic industries that produce for export or that compete with imported goods in the domestic market. In addition, as we discuss later in the chapter, changes in net exports affect a country's overall level of economic activity and are a primary channel through which business cycle disturbances and macroeconomic policy changes are transmitted internationally.

What is the link between the real exchange rate and net exports? A basic determinant of the demand for any good or service—say, coffee or taxi rides—is the price of that good or service relative to alternatives. If the price of coffee is too high, some people will switch to tea; if taxi fares rise, more people will take the bus. Similarly, the real exchange rate—the price of domestic goods relative to foreign goods—helps determine the demand for domestic goods both in home and foreign markets.

Suppose that the real exchange rate is high so that a unit of the domestic good can buy relatively many units of the foreign good. For example, let us say that a domestically produced car costs twice as much as a comparable foreign car (both prices are measured in terms of the same currency). Domestic residents will then find that foreign cars are less expensive than domestic cars, so (all else being equal) their demand for imported autos will be high. Foreign residents, in contrast, will find that the domestic country's cars are more expensive than their own, so they will want to purchase relatively few of the domestic country's exports. With few cars being sold abroad and many cars being imported, the country's net exports of cars will be low, probably even negative.

Conversely, suppose that the real exchange rate is low; for example, imagine that a domestically produced automobile costs only half what a comparable foreign car costs. Then, all else being equal, the domestic country will be able to export relatively large quantities of cars and will import relatively few so that its net exports of cars will be high.

The general conclusion, then, is that *the higher the real exchange rate is, the lower a country's net exports will be*, holding constant other factors affecting export and import demand. The reason for this result is the same reason that higher prices reduce the amount of coffee people drink or the number of taxi rides they take. Because the real exchange rate is the relative price of a country's goods and services, an increase in the real exchange rate induces both foreigners and domestic residents to consume less domestic production and more goods and services produced abroad, which lowers net exports.

APPLICATION

THE VALUE OF THE DOLLAR AND CANADIAN NET EXPORTS

In the early 1970s, the major industrialized countries of the world switched from fixed to flexible exchange rates. Figure 10.1 shows the Canadian nominal exchange rate, measured as a trade-weighted index of the exchange rates with 19 currencies. It also shows the corresponding real exchange rate (the "real value of the dollar"), illustrating that movements in nominal and real exchange rates are very similar. Figure 10.1 also graphs real Canadian net exports since the exchange rate began to float. Because the Canadian real exchange rate is the relative price of Canadian goods, the real value of the dollar and Canadian net exports should move in opposite directions (assuming that changes in the real exchange rate are the primary source of changes in net exports).

An apparent confirmation that the real exchange rate and net exports move in opposite directions occurred during the late 1980s. From 1986 to 1989, the real value of the dollar increased by about 20%. This sharp increase was followed, with a brief delay, by a large decline in Canadian net exports. At the time, many Canadian firms complained that the strong dollar was pricing their products out of foreign markets and, by making imported goods cheap for Canadian consumers, also reducing their sales at home.

After peaking in early 1989, the real value of the dollar fell for the next five years. Despite this precipitous decline, Canadian net exports continued to fall until late in 1991, when they finally began to increase. During the two and a half years in which Canadian net exports continued to decline despite the rapid depreciation of the

Figure 10.1

Canadian real and nominal exchange rates and net exports, 1970–2001

Canadian real net exports are measured along the left vertical axis and the Canadian nominal exchange rate and real exchange rate are measured along the right vertical axis, as trade-weighted indexes relative to other countries. Note that the nominal and real exchange rates tend to move together. Note also that net exports generally rise when the real exchange rate falls.

Source: Net exports in billions of chained 1997 dollars, seasonally adjusted, quarterly: 1947-1980 CANSIM D14862-D14866; 1981-2001 D100119-D100122. Data prior to 1981 are not chain-weighted and have been rescaled. Real and nominal effective exchange rates, 1990=100: J.P. Morgan.

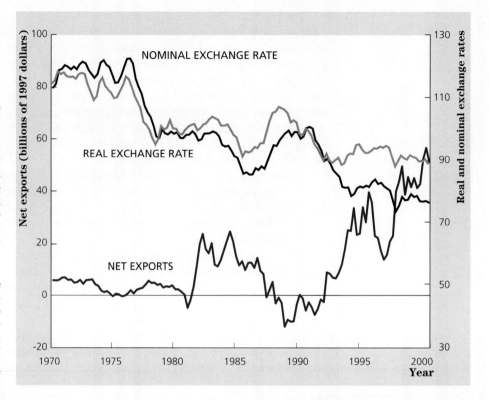

dollar, the public and policymakers expressed increasing scepticism about economists' predictions that the depreciation would lead to more net exports. Finally, Canadian real net exports did recover substantially, although they remained negative.

What took so long? One explanation suggests that because the dollar was so strong in the late 1980s (which made Canadian goods very expensive relative to foreign goods), Canadian firms lost many of their foreign customers. Once these foreign customers were lost, regaining them or adding new foreign customers was difficult, especially as many Canadian exporters reduced production capacity and cut back foreign sales operations when the value of the dollar was high. Similarly, the strong dollar gave foreign producers, including some who had not previously sold their output to Canada, a chance to make inroads into the Canadian domestic market. Having established sales networks and customer relationships in Canada, these foreign companies were better able than before to compete with Canadian firms when the dollar began its decline in 1989.

The idea that the strong dollar permanently increased the penetration of the Canadian market by foreign producers, while similarly reducing the capability of Canadian firms to sell in foreign markets, has been called the "beachhead effect."[5] According to this view, sometimes also called "hysteresis," for the effects of the strong-dollar period on Canadian net exports to be undone, the real value of the dollar had to fall back not just to its 1986 level, before the appreciation, but to a still lower level. Only with a very weak dollar could Canadian firms regain the markets they lost when the dollar was unusually strong.

---

5.   Empirical support for the beachhead effect is presented in Richard E. Baldwin, "Hysteresis in Import Prices: The Beachhead Effect," *American Economic Review*, September 1988, pp. 773–785.

Testing for the beachhead effect in the early 1990s is difficult, partly because the Canada–US Free Trade Agreement, which also affected trade between the two countries, began in 1989. However, statistical research by Robert Amano and Lawrence Schembri, of the Bank of Canada, and Eugene Beaulieu, of the University of Calgary, suggests that there is little evidence of hysteresis in Canadian net exports.[6] By 1994, the real value of the dollar fell to roughly 3.5% below its 1986 level, and net exports reached and then exceeded the levels of the mid-1980s.

Does that mean that the real exchange rate is the only macroeconomic variable that affects net exports? Confirmation of the link between the two came during 1996 and 1997, when a real appreciation of the Canadian dollar again was accompanied by a temporary fall in net exports. But Figure 10.1 shows that Canadian net exports trended strongly upwards during the rest of the 1990s, even though the real exchange rate was no lower than it had been during 1993 and 1994. What explained this trend?

Economists point to two other influences which probably explain the boom in Canadian net exports. First, free trade agreements with the United States and Mexico may have enhanced the response of net exports to the real exchange rate, by reducing the costs of trading between the three countries. Second, the US economy grew quickly during the late 1990s and 2000. As US incomes rose, the demand for Canadian exports rose, too. In fact, the business cycle in US incomes may also explain the puzzling, slow growth in Canadian net exports at the beginning of the 1990s, because the US was in recession then. We discuss the effects of national income on imports and exports in the next section.

10.2 HOW EXCHANGE RATES ARE DETERMINED: A SUPPLY-AND-DEMAND ANALYSIS

In flexible-exchange-rate systems, exchange rates change constantly. In fixed-exchange-rate systems, by definition, exchange rates are stable most of the time; but even under a fixed-rate system, large devaluations or revaluations are not uncommon. Exchange-rate changes are notoriously difficult to explain. What economic forces cause a nation's exchange rate to rise or fall? In this section, we address this question by using supply and demand to analyze the determination of exchange rates in a flexible-exchange-rate system (we return to fixed exchange rates in Section 10.6).

For clarity, our supply-and-demand analysis focuses on the nominal exchange rate, rather than on the real exchange rate. However, recall from Eq. (10.1) that for given levels of domestic and foreign prices, the real exchange rate and the nominal exchange rate are proportional. Because we hold price levels constant in this section, *all our conclusions about the nominal exchange rate apply equally to the real exchange rate*.

The nominal exchange rate e_{nom} is the value of a currency, say, the dollar. The value of the dollar, like that of any asset, is determined by supply and demand in the relevant market. For dollars, the relevant market is the foreign exchange market, where banks and currency traders continuously trade dollars for other currencies.

Figure 10.2 shows the supply and demand for dollars. The horizontal axis of the diagram measures the quantity of dollars supplied or demanded, and the vertical

---

6. "Trade Hysteresis: Theory and Evidence for Canada," in *The Exchange Rate and the Economy*, Ottawa: Bank of Canada, 1993, pp. 403–468.

IN TOUCH WITH THE MACROECONOMY

EXCHANGE RATES

Exchange rates are determined in foreign exchange markets, in which the currencies of different countries are traded. Principal foreign exchange markets are located in London, New York, Tokyo, Toronto, and other financial centres. Because foreign exchange markets are in widely separated time zones, at least one of the markets is open at almost any time of the day, so trading in foreign currencies essentially takes place around the clock. In 2001, Canadian financial institutions traded more than $42 billion (US) of foreign exchange each day, while worldwide foreign exchange transactions exceeded $1.5 trillion (US) daily. These enormous numbers are actually smaller than the corresponding values for 1998 because the introduction of the euro (the common currency of the European Monetary Union) has eliminated foreign exchange trades between the German mark and French franc, for example.

Exchange rates among major currencies often are reported daily on radio and television, and daily quotations of exchange rates are printed in major newspapers. Exchange rates are also available on the Internet, for example at Werner Antweiler's Pacific Exchange Rate Service site at the University of British Columbia: *http://pacific.commerce.ubc. ca/xr/*. The exchange rates in the accompanying table were reported in the "Foreign Exchange" section of *The Globe and Mail* on November 30, 2001, and apply to transactions of November 29, 2001.

Four exchange rates relative to the Canadian dollar are reported in the table for each country: a spot rate and three forward rates. All are expressed as units of foreign currency per Canadian dollar. The spot rate is the rate at which foreign currency can be traded immediately for Canadian dollars. For instance, the spot exchange rate for

Japan, 78.25, means that on November 29, 2001, once Canadian dollar could buy 78.25 yen for immediate delivery.

Forward exchange rates are prices at which you can agree now to buy foreign currency at a specified date in the future. For example, on November 29, 2001, you could have arranged to buy or sell Japanese yen one month later at an exchange rate of 78.08 yen per dollar. Note that for the yen and the US dollar, the one-month forward exchange rate is lower than the spot exchange rate and that forward exchange rates decrease for dates farther into the future (six months and 12 months).

This pattern of falling forward rates shows that as of November 29, 2001, participants in the foreign exchange market expected the value of the Canadian dollar relative to the yen and US dollar to decrease over the next year. In contrast, for the pound and the euro, the forward rates rise with maturity, which suggests that traders expected the value of the Canadian dollar to rise against these two currencies.

Exchange Rate Against Canadian Dollar

Country	Spot	1-Month Forward	6-Month Forward	12-Month Forward
United States (U.S. dollars per Canadian dollar)	0.6319	0.6317	0.6316	0.6315
United Kingdom (pounds per Canadian dollar)	0.4439	0.4445	0.4479	0.4513
European Union (euros per Canadian dollar)	0.7117	0.7123	0.7157	0.7170
Japan (yen per Canadian dollar)	78.25	78.08	77.43	76.38

axis measures the value of the dollar in terms of other currencies, or the nominal exchange rate e_{nom}. The supply curve for dollars, S, shows the number of dollars that people want to supply to the foreign exchange market at each "price" (nominal exchange rate). To supply dollars to the foreign exchange market means to offer to exchange dollars for some other currency. When the dollar's value in terms of other currencies is high, people are more willing to supply dollars to the market; thus, the supply curve slopes upward. Similarly, the demand curve for dollars, D,

FIGURE 10.2

THE SUPPLY OF AND
DEMAND FOR THE DOLLAR

The figure shows the determination of the value of the dollar in the foreign exchange market. The supply curve for dollars, S, indicates the number of dollars that people are willing to sell in the foreign exchange market at each value of the Canadian nominal exchange rate e_{nom}. The demand curve for dollars, D, shows the number of dollars that people want to buy at each nominal exchange rate. At equilibrium, point E, the value of the dollar, e^1_{nom}, is the nominal exchange rate at which the quantity of dollars supplied equals the quantity of dollars demanded.

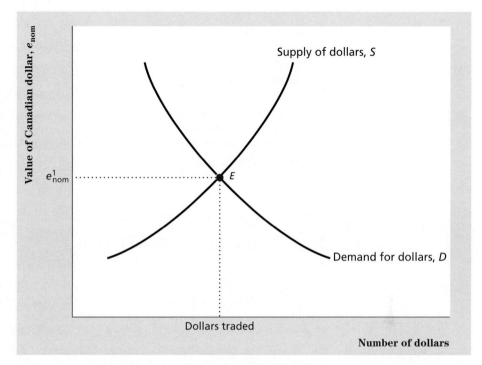

shows the quantity of dollars that people want to buy in the foreign exchange market at each exchange rate. When the dollar is more expensive in terms of other currencies, people demand fewer dollars, so the demand curve slopes downward. The equilibrium value of the dollar at point E is e^1_{nom}, the exchange rate at which the quantity of dollars supplied and the quantity of dollars demanded are equal.

Figure 10.2 aids in understanding the forces that determine the value of the dollar, or any other currency. To go any further, though, we must ask why people decide to demand or supply dollars. Unlike apples or haircuts, dollars are not demanded because people value them in themselves; rather, people value dollars because of what they can buy.[7] Specifically, foreign individuals or firms demand dollars in the foreign exchange market for two reasons:

1. to be able to buy Canadian goods and services (Canadian exports), and
2. to be able to buy Canadian real and financial assets (Canadian capital inflows).

Note that the two types of transactions for which foreigners need dollars (to purchase Canadian exports and Canadian assets) correspond to the two components of the balance of payments accounts: the current account and the capital account.[8]

Similarly, Canadians supply dollars to the foreign exchange market, thereby acquiring foreign currencies, for two reasons:

1. to be able to buy foreign goods and services (Canadian imports), and
2. to be able to buy real and financial assets in foreign countries (Canadian capital outflows).

---

7. Appendix 10.B contains a more detailed discussion of the behaviour in goods and asset markets, which underlies the supply of and demand for foreign exchange.

8. The current account and the capital account are defined and discussed in Chapter 5. The idea that foreigners must hold dollars to buy Canadian goods or assets is not completely accurate because many transactions between Canadians and foreigners are done without anyone ever literally holding a supply of dollars or the foreign currency. Nevertheless, this way of thinking about the determination of exchange rates is fairly simple and gives the same answers as would a more complex analysis.

Thus, factors that increase foreigners' demand for Canadian exports and assets will also increase the foreign-exchange-market demand for dollars, raising the dollar exchange rate. Likewise, the value of the dollar will rise if Canadians' demand for foreign goods and assets declines, so Canadians supply fewer dollars to the foreign exchange market.

As an example, suppose that Canadian goods improve in quality so that foreigners demand more of them. This increase in the demand for Canadian exports would translate into an increase in the demand for Canadian dollars. In Figure 10.3, the demand for dollars shifts to the right, from D^1 to D^2, and the equilibrium value of the dollar rises from e^1_{nom} to e^2_{nom}. All else being equal, then, improvements in the quality of Canadian goods would lead to an appreciation of the dollar.

MACROECONOMIC DETERMINANTS OF THE EXCHANGE RATE AND NET EXPORT DEMAND

In the *IS–LM* analysis of Chapter 9, we emphasized two key macroeconomic variables: real output (income) Y and the real interest rate r. In anticipation of the open-economy version of the *IS–LM* model presented in Section 10.3, we now consider how changes in real output or the real interest rate (either at home or abroad) are linked to the exchange rate and net exports. Again, because we are holding domestic and foreign price levels constant, the results we discuss here apply equally to the nominal exchange rate and the real exchange rate.

EFFECTS OF CHANGES IN OUTPUT (INCOME)

Imagine that domestic output (equivalently, domestic income) Y increases but that other factors (such as the real interest rate) remain unchanged. How would the increase in Y affect the exchange rate and net exports?

FIGURE 10.3

THE EFFECT OF INCREASED EXPORT QUALITY ON THE VALUE OF THE DOLLAR

An increase in the quality of Canadian exports raises foreigners' demands for Canadian goods and, hence, their demand for Canadian dollars, which are needed to buy Canadian goods. The demand curve for dollars shifts, from D^1 to D^2, raising the value of the dollar (the nominal exchange rate) from e^1_{nom} to e^2_{nom}.

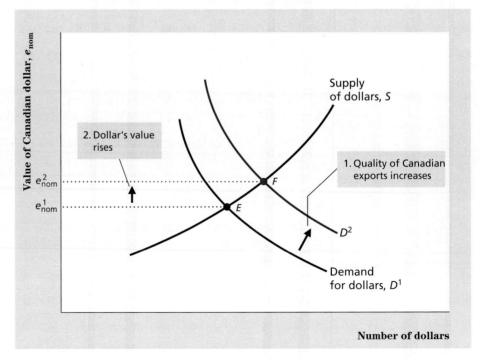

To consider the effect on net exports first is easier. We know that spending by consumers depends, in part, on their current incomes. When domestic income rises, consumers will spend more on all goods and services, *including imports*. Thus, when domestic output (income) rises, net exports (exports minus imports) must fall, other factors held constant.[9]

To determine the effect of increased domestic output on the exchange rate, recall that in order to increase their purchases of imports, domestic residents must obtain foreign currencies. Equivalently, domestic residents must supply more domestic currency to the foreign exchange market. An increased supply of domestic currency causes it to depreciate, that is, the exchange rate falls.

We can also analyze the effects of an increase in the real output of the country's trading partners, Y_{For} (foreign output or income). An increase in Y_{For} leads foreign consumers to increase their spending on all goods and services, including the exports of the domestic country. Thus, an increase in the income of Germany and Japan, for example, would increase those countries' demand for Canadian exports and raise Canadian net exports. The increase in foreign demand for Canadian goods also would increase foreigners' demand for Canadian dollars, raising the value of the dollar. Note that the effects of changes in foreign income are the opposite of the effects of changes in domestic income.

EFFECTS OF CHANGES IN REAL INTEREST RATES

A second key macroeconomic variable to be considered is the real interest rate. Imagine that the domestic country's real interest rate r rises, with other factors (including the foreign real interest rate) held constant.[10] In this case, the country's real and financial assets will become more attractive to foreign savers seeking the highest return on their funds. Because domestic currency can be used to buy domestic assets, a rise in the domestic real interest rate also increases the demand for domestic currency. An increased demand for domestic currency, in turn, leads to exchange rate appreciation.

A rise in the domestic real interest rate r has no *direct* effect on net exports, but it does have an *indirect* effect through the exchange rate. An increase in r raises the exchange rate so that domestic exports become more expensive and imports from abroad become cheaper. Thus, other factors being constant, an increase in r reduces the domestic country's net exports.

The effects of a change in the foreign real interest rate, r_{For}, are the opposite of the effects of a change in the domestic real interest rate. If the foreign real interest rate rises, for example, foreign assets will become more attractive to domestic savers. To get the foreign currency needed to buy foreign assets, domestic savers will supply domestic currency to the foreign exchange market. The increased supply of domestic currency will lead to a depreciation of the exchange rate. The depreciation of the exchange rate caused by the rise in r_{For}, in turn, raises the domestic country's net exports.

---

9. The conclusion that an increase in output reduces net exports seems to contradict a result obtained in Chapter 5—that an increase in output owing to a beneficial supply shock raises net exports. There is no contradiction because a supply shock does not hold variables other than output constant as we are assuming here. See Analytical Problem 4 at the end of the chapter.

10. Note that by holding the foreign real interest rate constant, we no longer assume (as we did in Chapter 5) that the domestic and foreign countries face the same world real interest rate. In general, real interest rates in different countries need not be the same when countries produce different goods, as we assume in this chapter. The reason is that real interest rates in different countries measure different things. For example, the Japanese real interest rate measures the growth of an asset's purchasing power in terms of Japanese goods, whereas the German real interest rate measures the growth of an asset's purchasing power in terms of German goods. If the Japanese–German real exchange rate is changing, the two need not be the same.

Summary tables 16 and 17, on the next page, list the effects of the various macroeconomic factors on the exchange rate and net exports.

10.3 THE *IS–LM* MODEL FOR AN OPEN ECONOMY

Now we are ready to explore how exchange rates and international trade interact with the behaviour of the economy as a whole. To do so, we extend the *IS–LM* model to allow for trade and lending among nations. An algebraic version of this analysis is presented in Appendix 10.A. We use the *IS-LM* diagram, rather than the *AD-AS* diagram, because we want to focus on the real interest rate, which plays a key role in determining exchange rates and the flows of goods and assets.

Recall that the components of the *IS–LM* model are the *IS* curve, which describes goods market equilibrium; the *LM* curve, which describes asset market equilibrium; and the *FE* line, which describes labour market equilibrium. Nothing discussed in this chapter affects our analysis of the supply of or demand for money; so, in developing the open-economy *IS–LM* model, we use the same *LM* curve that we used for the closed-economy model. Similarly, the labour market and the production function are not directly affected by international factors, so the *FE* line also is unchanged.[11]

However, because net exports are part of the demand for goods, we have to modify the *IS* curve in order to describe the open economy. Three main points need to be made about the *IS* curve in the open economy:

1. Although the open-economy *IS* curve is derived somewhat differently than the closed-economy *IS* curve, it is a downward-sloping relationship between output and the real interest rate, as the closed-economy *IS* curve is.

2. All factors that shift the *IS* curve in the closed economy shift the *IS* curve in the open economy in the same way.

3. In an open economy, factors that change net exports also shift the *IS* curve. Specifically, for given values of domestic output and the domestic real interest rate, factors that raise a country's net exports shift the open-economy *IS* curve up; and factors that lower a country's net exports shift the *IS* curve down.

After discussing each point, we use the open-economy *IS–LM* model to analyze the international transmission of business cycles and the operation of macroeconomic policies in an open economy.

THE OPEN-ECONOMY *IS* CURVE

For any level of output, the *IS* curve gives the real interest rate that brings the goods market into equilibrium. In a closed economy, the goods market equilibrium condition is that desired national saving S^d must equal desired investment I^d, or $S^d - I^d = 0$. In an open economy, as we showed in Chapter 5, the goods market equilibrium condition is that desired saving S^d must equal desired investment I^d plus net exports NX. Writing the goods market equilibrium condition for an open economy, we have

$$S^d - I^d = NX. \tag{10.4}$$

---

11. A case in which the *FE* line does depend on international considerations arises when some raw materials (such as oil) are imported. In this book, we have modelled oil price shocks as productivity shocks, which captures the main domestic macroeconomic effects. A full analysis that includes all the international aspects of an oil price shock is complex, so we do not present it here.

SUMMARY 16 DETERMINANTS OF THE EXCHANGE RATE (REAL OR NOMINAL)

AN INCREASE IN	CAUSES THE EXCHANGE RATE TO	REASON
Domestic output (income), Y	Fall	Higher domestic output raises demand for imports and increases supply of domestic currency.
Foreign output (income), Y_{For}	Rise	Higher foreign output raises demand for exports and increases demand for domestic currency.
Domestic real interest rate, r	Rise	Higher real interest rate makes domestic assets more attractive and increases demand for domestic currency.
Foreign real interest rate, r_{For}	Fall	Higher foreign real interest rate makes foreign assets more attractive and increases supply of domestic currency.
World demand for domestic goods	Rise	Higher demand for domestic goods increases demand for domestic currency.

SUMMARY 17 DETERMINANTS OF NET EXPORTS

AN INCREASE IN	CAUSES NET EXPORTS TO	REASON
Domestic output (income), Y	Fall	Higher domestic output raises demand for imports.
Foreign output (income), Y_{For}	Rise	Higher foreign output raises foreign demand for exports.
Domestic real interest rate, r	Fall	Higher real interest rate raises the real exchange rate and makes domestic goods more expensive relative to foreign goods.
Foreign real interest rate, r_{For}	Rise	Higher foreign real interest rate lowers the real exchange rate and makes domestic goods cheaper relative to foreign goods.
World demand for domestic goods	Rise	Higher demand for domestic goods directly increases net exports.

To interpret Eq. (10.4), recall that $S^d - I^d$, the excess of national saving over investment, is the amount that domestic residents desire to lend abroad. Recall also that net exports NX (which, if net factor payments are zero, is the same as the current account balance) equals the amount that foreigners want to borrow from domestic savers. Thus, Eq. (10.4) indicates that for the goods market to be in equilibrium, desired foreign lending must equal desired foreign borrowing. An equivalent way to write the goods market equilibrium condition is as follows:

$$Y = C^d + I^d + G + NX. \qquad (10.5)$$

We obtained Eq. (10.5) from Eq. (10.4) by replacing desired saving, S^d, with its definition, $Y - C^d - G$, and rearranging. Equation (10.5) states that the goods market is in equilibrium when the supply of goods, Y, equals the demand for goods, $C^d + I^d + G + NX$. Note that in an open economy, the total demand for goods includes spending on net exports.

Figure 10.4 illustrates goods market equilibrium in an open economy. The horizontal axis measures desired saving minus desired investment, $S^d - I^d$, and net exports, NX. Note that the horizontal axis includes both positive and negative values. The vertical axis measures the domestic real interest rate, r.

The upward-sloping curve, $S - I$, shows the difference between desired national saving and desired investment for each value of the real interest rate r. This curve slopes upward because with output held constant, an increase in the real interest rate raises desired national saving and reduces desired investment, raising the country's desired foreign lending.

The downward-sloping curve in Figure 10.4, NX, shows the relationship between the country's net exports and the domestic real interest rate, other factors held constant. As discussed in Section 10.2, a rise in the real interest rate raises the exchange rate, which, in turn, reduces net exports (see Summary table 17). Hence the NX curve slopes downward.

FIGURE 10.4

GOODS MARKET EQUILIBRIUM IN AN OPEN ECONOMY

The upward-sloping curve shows desired saving S^d less desired investment I^d. This curve slopes upward because a higher domestic real interest rate increases the excess of desired saving over desired investment. The NX curve relates net exports to the domestic real interest rate. This curve slopes downward because a higher domestic real interest rate causes the real exchange rate to rise, reducing net exports. Goods market equilibrium occurs at point E, where the excess of desired saving over desired investment equals net exports (equivalently, where desired lending abroad equals desired borrowing by foreigners). The real interest rate that clears the goods market is r_1.

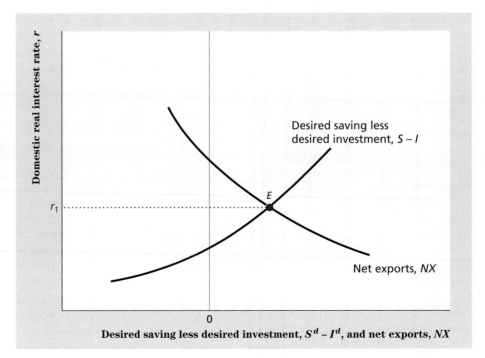

Desired saving less desired investment, $S - I$

r_1

E

Net exports, NX

0

Desired saving less desired investment, $S^d - I^d$, and net exports, NX

Domestic real interest rate, r

Goods market equilibrium requires that the excess of desired saving over desired investment equal net exports (Eq. 10.4). This condition is satisfied at the intersection of the $S - I$ and NX curves at point E. Thus, the domestic real interest rate that clears the goods market is the interest rate at E, or r_1.

To derive the open-economy IS curve, we need to know what happens to the real interest rate that clears the goods market when the current level of domestic output rises (Figure 10.5). Suppose that domestic output initially equals Y_1 and that goods market equilibrium is at point E, with a real interest rate of r_1. Now, suppose that output rises to Y_2. An increase in current output raises desired national saving but does not affect desired investment, so the excess of desired saving over desired investment rises at any real interest rate. Thus, the curve measuring the excess of desired saving over desired investment shifts to the right, from $(S - I)^1$ to $(S - I)^2$ in Figure 10.5(a).

What about the NX curve? An increase in domestic income causes domestic consumers to spend more on imported goods, which (other factors held constant) reduces net exports (see Summary table 17). Thus, when output rises from Y_1 to Y_2, net exports fall, and the NX curve shifts to the left, from NX^1 to NX^2.

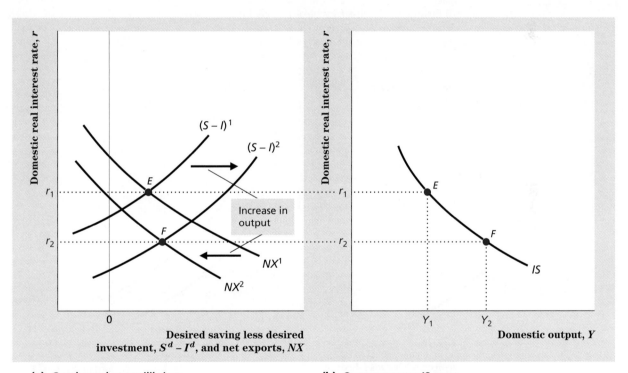

(a) Goods market equilibrium

(b) Open-economy IS curve

FIGURE 10.5

DERIVATION OF THE IS CURVE IN AN OPEN ECONOMY

The initial equilibrium in the goods market is represented by point E in both (a) and (b).

(a) At point E, domestic output is Y_1 and the domestic real interest rate is r_1. An increase in domestic output from Y_1 to Y_2 raises desired national saving at each real interest rate and does not affect desired investment. Therefore, the $S - I$ curve shifts to the right, from

$(S - I)^1$ to $(S - I)^2$. The increase in output also raises domestic spending on imports, reducing net exports and causing the NX curve to shift to the left, from NX^1 to NX^2. At the new equilibrium point, F, the real interest rate is r_2.

(b) Because an increase in output from Y_1 to Y_2 lowers the real interest rate that clears the goods market from r_1 to r_2, the IS curve slopes downward.

After the increase in output from Y_1 to Y_2, the new goods market equilibrium is at point F in Figure 10.5(a), with the real interest rate at r_2. The IS curve in Figure 10.5(b) shows that when output equals Y_1, the real interest rate that clears the goods market is r_1; and that when output equals Y_2, the real interest rate that clears the goods market is r_2. Because higher current output lowers the real interest rate that clears the goods market, the open-economy IS curve slopes downward, as for a closed economy.

FACTORS THAT SHIFT THE OPEN-ECONOMY *IS* CURVE

As in a closed economy, in an open economy any factor that raises the real interest rate that clears the goods market at a constant level of output shifts the IS curve up. This point is illustrated in Figure 10.6, which shows the effects on the open-economy IS curve of a temporary increase in government purchases. With output held constant at Y_1, the initial equilibrium is at point E, where the real interest rate is r_1. A temporary increase in government purchases lowers desired national saving at every level of output and the real interest rate. Thus, the $S - I$ curve shifts to the left, from $(S - I)^1$ to $(S - I)^2$, as shown in Figure 10.6(a). The new goods market equilibrium is at point F, where the real interest rate is r_2.

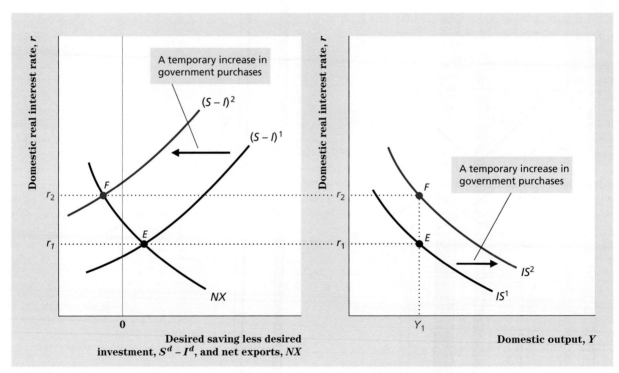

(a) Goods market equilibrium   **(b) Open-economy *IS* curve**

FIGURE **10.6**

EFFECT OF AN INCREASE IN GOVERNMENT PURCHASES ON THE OPEN-ECONOMY *IS* CURVE

Initial equilibrium is at point E, where output is Y_1 and the real interest rate is r_1, in both (a) and (b).

(a) A temporary increase in government purchases lowers desired national saving at every level of output and the real interest rate. Thus, the $S - I$ curve shifts to the left, from $(S - I)^1$ to $(S - I)^2$.
(b) For output Y_1, the real interest rate that clears the goods market is now r_2, at point F in both (a) and (b). Because the real interest rate that clears the goods market has risen, the IS curve shifts up and to the right, from IS^1 to IS^2.

Figure 10.6(b) shows the effect on the *IS* curve. For output Y_1, the increase in government purchases raises the real interest rate that clears the goods market from r_1 to r_2. Thus, the *IS* curve shifts up and to the right, from IS^1 to IS^2.

In general, any factor that shifts the closed-economy *IS* curve up does so by reducing desired national saving relative to desired investment. Because a change that reduces desired national saving relative to desired investment shifts the $S - I$ curve to the left (Figure 10.6(a)), such a change also shifts the open-economy *IS* curve up.

In addition to the standard factors that shift the *IS* curve in a closed economy, some new factors affect the position of the *IS* curve in an open economy. In particular, anything that raises a country's net exports, given domestic output and the domestic real interest rate, will shift the open-economy *IS* curve up. This point is illustrated in Figure 10.7.

At the initial equilibrium point, E, in both Figure 10.7(a) and (b), domestic output is Y_1 and the domestic real interest rate is r_1. Now, suppose that some change raises the country's net exports at any level of domestic output and the domestic real interest rate. This increase in net exports is shown as a shift to the right of the *NX* curve in Figure 10.7(a), from NX^1 to NX^2. At the new goods market equilibrium point, F, the real interest rate has risen to r_2. Because the real interest rate that clears the goods market has risen for constant output, the *IS* curve shifts up and to the right, as shown in Figure 10.7(b), from IS^1 to IS^2.

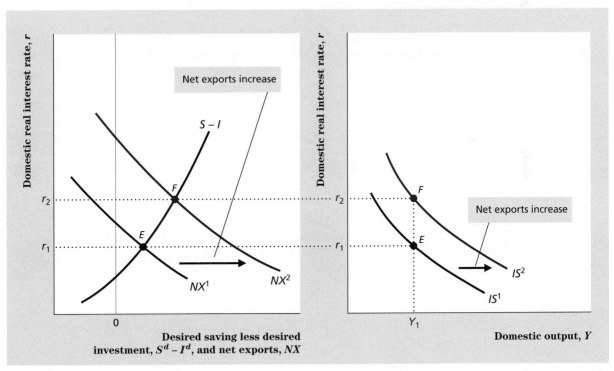

(a) Goods market equilibrium

(b) Open-economy *IS* curve

FIGURE 10.7

EFFECT OF AN INCREASE IN NET EXPORTS ON THE OPEN-
ECONOMY *IS* CURVE

In both (a) and (b), at the initial equilibrium point, E, output is Y_1 and the real interest rate that clears the goods market is r_1.

(a) If some change raises the country's net exports at any given domestic output and domestic real interest rate, the *NX* curve shifts to the right, from NX^1 to NX^2.

(b) For output Y_1, the real interest rate that clears the goods market has risen from r_1 to r_2, at point F in both (a) and (b). Thus, the *IS* curve shifts up and to the right, from IS^1 to IS^2.

What might cause a country's net exports to rise, for any given domestic output and domestic real interest rate? We have discussed three possibilities at various points in this chapter: an increase in foreign output, an increase in the foreign real interest rate, and a shift in world demand toward the domestic country's goods (see Summary table 17).

- *An increase in foreign output*, Y_{For}, increases purchases of the domestic country's goods by foreigners, directly raising the domestic country's net exports and shifting the *IS* curve up.

- *An increase in the foreign real interest rate*, r_{For}, makes foreign assets relatively more attractive to domestic savers, increasing the supply of domestic currency and causing the exchange rate to fall. A lower real exchange rate stimulates net exports, shifting the domestic country's *IS* curve up.

- *A shift in world demand toward the domestic country's goods*, as might occur if the quality of domestic goods improved, raises net exports and, thus, also shifts the *IS* curve up. A similar effect would occur if, for example, the domestic country imposed trade barriers that reduced imports (thereby increasing net exports); see Analytical Problem 1 at the end of the chapter. Summary table 18 lists factors that shift the open-economy *IS* curve.

THE INTERNATIONAL TRANSMISSION OF BUSINESS CYCLES

In the introduction to this chapter, we discussed briefly how trade and financial links among countries transmit cyclical fluctuations across borders. The analysis here shows that the impact of foreign economic conditions on the real exchange rate and net exports is one of the principal ways by which cycles are transmitted internationally.

For example, consider the impact of a recession in the United States on the economies for which the United States is a major export market, such as Canada. In the *IS–LM* model a decline in US output lowers the demand for Canadian net exports,

SUMMARY 18 INTERNATIONAL FACTORS THAT SHIFT THE *IS* CURVE

AN INCREASE IN	SHIFTS THE IS CURVE	REASON
Foreign output, Y_{For}	Up	Higher foreign output raises demand for home country exports.
Foreign real interest rate, r_{For}	Up	Higher foreign real interest rate lowers the real exchange rate and raises net exports.
Demand for domestic goods relative to foreign goods	Up	Higher demand for domestic goods raises net exports.

which shifts the Canadian *IS* curve down. In the Keynesian version of the model, this downward shift of the *IS* curve throws the Canadian economy into a recession, with output below its full-employment level, until price adjustment restores full employment. However, in the basic classical model, in which the aggregate supply curve is vertical at full-employment output, the decline in net exports would not affect Canadian output.

Similarly, a country's domestic economy can be sensitive to shifts in international tastes for various goods. For example, a shift in demand away from Canadian goods—induced perhaps by trade restrictions against Canadian products—would shift the Canadian *IS* curve down, with the same contractionary effects as the decrease in foreign (US) output had.

10.4 MACROECONOMIC POLICY IN A SMALL OPEN ECONOMY WITH FLEXIBLE EXCHANGE RATES

A primary reason for developing the *IS–LM* model for the open economy is to determine how borrowing and trading links among countries affect fiscal and monetary policies. When exchange rates are flexible, the effects of macroeconomic policy on domestic variables, such as output and the real interest rate, are largely unchanged when foreign trade is added. We first use the *IS–LM* model to find the effects of the policies on domestic output and the domestic real interest rate. This step is the same as in our analysis of the closed economy model in Chapter 9.

Next, we now can see how fiscal and monetary policy affect a country's real exchange rate and net exports. We apply the results of Section 10.2 (especially Summary tables 16 and 17) to determine how changes in output and the interest rate affect the exchange rate and net exports.

In this section, we first study an economy that is small in the sense that it cannot affect macroeconomic variables in other countries. However, it can influence its own interest rate and prices. This treatment of a small open economy is appropriate, since we have assumed in this chapter that countries produce different goods. This perspective also is realistic; the Canadian real interest rate can differ persistently from the US real interest rate. However, at the end of this section, we also consider an extreme case in which the small open economy cannot influence its interest rate even in the short run.

A FISCAL EXPANSION

To consider the effects of fiscal policy in a small open economy, let us look at a temporary increase in domestic government purchases. In analyzing this policy change, we discuss both the Keynesian and classical versions of the *IS–LM* model.

Figure 10.8 shows the *IS–LM* diagram for the small open economy. Suppose that the original equilibrium is at point *E*. The increase in government purchases shifts the *IS* curve up and to the right from IS^1 to IS^2.[12] In the Keynesian model, the short-run equilibrium is represented by point *F*, the intersection of IS^2 and LM^1. Comparing point *F* with point *E* reveals that the increase in government purchases increases both output and the real interest rate in the short run.

---

12. Some classical economists argue that the increase in government purchases also shifts the *FE* line. The mechanism is that an increase in taxes leads to an increase in labour supply. We discuss this mechanism in detail in Chapter 11.

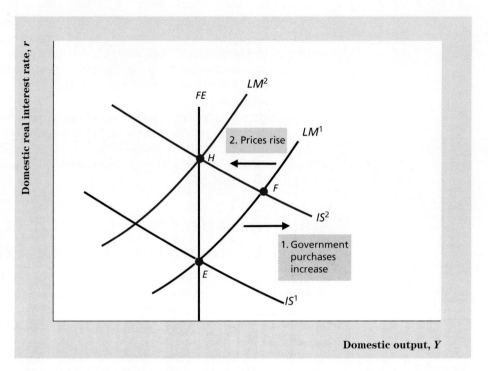

Then the domestic price level rises, shifting the *LM* curve to the left, from *LM*[1] to *LM*[2]. The long-run equilibrium is represented by point *H*. In the long-run, in both the Keynesian and classical models, the effect of the fiscal expansion is to raise the domestic real interest rate.

To examine the effects of international trade, we first consider the effects on the exchange rate of the increases in domestic output and the domestic real interest rate. Recall that an increase in output *Y* causes domestic residents to demand more imports and, thus, to supply more currency to the foreign exchange market. The increase in domestic output therefore lowers the exchange rate. However, the rise in the domestic real interest rate makes domestic assets more attractive, causing foreign savers to demand the domestic currency and raising the exchange rate. The overall effect of the increase in government purchases is theoretically ambiguous: We cannot be sure whether the increase in government purchases will raise or lower the exchange rate. However, most empirical evidence suggests that the second effect dominates. The box "In Touch with the Macroeconomy: Exchange Rates," on p. 352, describes the enormous daily volume of foreign exchange transactions. Most of these transactions are by international investors concerned with interest rate differentials, and do not directly concern trade in goods. Thus, the net effect of an increase in government purchases generally is an appreciation, as a result of the response by these investors to the higher domestic interest rate.

The effect of the fiscal expansion on the country's net export demand is not ambiguous. Recall that the increase in domestic output (which raises domestic consumers' demand for imports) and the increase in the real interest rate (which tends to raise the exchange rate) both cause net exports to fall. Thus, the overall effect of the fiscal expansion clearly is to move the country's trade balance toward deficit. This result is consistent with the analysis of the "twin deficits" (the government budget deficit and the trade deficit) of Chapter 5.

Once prices adjust, at point H, the effect of the increase in government purchases is to raise the real interest rate, but not output. Hence, the long-run effect of the fiscal expansion is to raise the exchange rate and lower net exports.

A MONETARY CONTRACTION

We can also use the open-economy IS–LM model to study the effects of monetary policy when exchange rates are flexible. For the Keynesian version of the IS–LM model, we analyze the effects of a drop in the money supply in both the short and long run. Because the effects of monetary policy are the same in the basic classical model and the long-run Keynesian model, our analysis applies to the classical model as well.

The effects of a monetary contraction are shown in Figure 10.9, which shows the IS–LM diagram for the small open economy. Suppose that the initial equilibrium is represented by point E and that a decrease in the money supply shifts the domestic LM curve up and to the left, from LM^1 to LM^2. In the Keynesian model, the price level is constant in the short run, so the short-run equilibrium is at point F, the intersection of the IS and LM^2 curves. Comparing points F and E reveals that in the short run, domestic output falls and the domestic real interest rate rises. This result is the same as for the closed economy (Chapter 9).

After the monetary contraction, the domestic currency appreciates in the short run, for two reasons. First, the drop in domestic income reduces the domestic demand for imports, leading domestic consumers to demand less foreign currency to buy imported goods. Second, the rise in the domestic real interest rate makes domestic assets relatively more attractive to foreign savers, increasing foreign savers' demand for the domestic currency.

FIGURE 10.9

A DECREASE IN THE MONEY SUPPLY IN A SMALL OPEN ECONOMY

A decrease in the money supply shifts the LM curve up and to the left, from LM^1 to LM^2. In the short-run Keynesian model, output falls and the domestic real interest rate rises. The exchange rate rises, and net exports fall (though theoretically net exports could rise if they were more responsive to output than to the interest rate). In the long-run, or in the classical model, price adjustment restores general equilibrium at point E, with real variables unchanged but a lower price level and a higher nominal exchange rate.

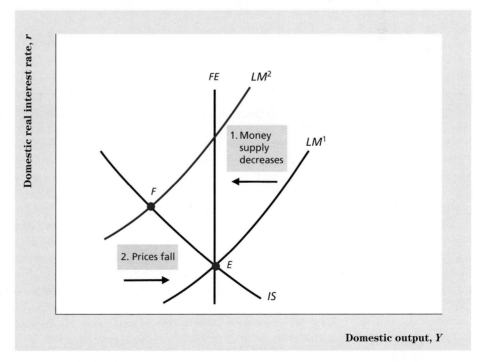

What happens to the country's net exports? Here there are two competing effects: (1) The drop in domestic income created by the monetary contraction reduces the domestic demand for foreign goods and, thus, tends to increase the country's net exports; but (2) the rise in the real interest rate, which leads to exchange rate appreciation, tends to reduce net exports. The theory does not indicate for certain which way net exports will change. Nevertheless, most empirical evidence suggests that the second effect dominates. In a small open economy, net exports are more responsive to changes in the exchange rate than to changes in domestic income. Overall, then, the country's net exports will decrease as a result of the monetary contraction.

In the long run after a monetary contraction, prices decline as output is below its full-employment level. The domestic LM curve returns to its original position, LM^1 in Figure 10.9, so that money is neutral in the long run. As all real variables return to their original levels, the real exchange rate and the domestic demand for foreign goods also return to their original levels. Hence, in the long run, the real exchange rate and net exports are not affected by the monetary contraction.

Although monetary neutrality holds in the long run in the Keynesian model, it holds immediately in the classical model. So, in the classical model, monetary policy changes have no effect on the real exchange rate or trade flows; they affect only the price level. In a monetary contraction, the domestic price level will fall.

Although money cannot affect the *real* exchange rate in the long run, it does affect the *nominal* exchange rate by changing the domestic price level. (This is one case where the responses of the real and nominal exchange rates to a change in macroeconomic conditions differ.) As we have shown, the long-run neutrality of money implies that a 10% decrease in the nominal money supply will decrease the domestic price level by 10%. Recall (Eq. 10.1) that the nominal exchange rate e_{nom} equals eP_{For}/P, where e is the real exchange rate, P_{For} is the foreign price level, and P is the domestic price level. Because the real exchange rate e and the foreign price level P_{For} are unchanged in the long run by a domestic monetary contraction, the 10% drop in the domestic price level P raises the nominal exchange rate e_{nom} by (approximately) 10%. Thus, a monetary contraction reduces the domestic price level and raises the nominal exchange rate (an appreciation) by the same percentage as the drop in the money supply.

THE MUNDELL–FLEMING MODEL

Let us also consider a more extreme definition of a small open economy in which the domestic interest rate always equals the foreign interest rate, even in the short run. Such a situation does not apply to Canada, but it is worth studying to see how the effects of monetary and fiscal policy depend on a country's integration with the rest of the world. The *IS–LM* model that results from this assumption is known as the Mundell–Fleming model.[13]

What might bring about an equality between the domestic and foreign interest rates? In this case, any tendency for the domestic interest rate r to fall below the foreign interest rate r_{For} leads to an immediate capital outflow so that the domestic interest rate rises. Similarly, any tendency for r to rise above r_{For} leads to a large capital inflow, which drives r down. This is exactly the situation we considered in Chapter 5, where the domestic and foreign economies produce the same goods.

---

13. See Robert A. Mundell, "Flexible Exchange Rates and Employment Policy," *Canadian Journal of Economics and Political Science*, November 1961, pp. 509–517; J. Marcus Fleming, "Domestic Financial Policies under Fixed and under Floating Exchange Rates," *IMF Staff Papers*, November 1962, pp. 369–379.

To see the effect of these capital flows on the open-economy *IS* curve, we again need to consider the behaviour of net exports. Suppose that there is some tendency for r to rise above r_{For}, leading to a capital inflow. Recall that a capital inflow leads to an appreciation (see Summary table 16), which, in turn, leads to a fall in net exports (Summary table 17). Only when $r = r_{For}$ will net exports cease to fall, and equilibrium in the goods market be restored. Thus, net exports are extremely elastic in response to changes in the interest rate around the foreign level. As a result, the open-economy *IS* curve is perfectly flat when r cannot deviate from r_{For}. (Numerical problem 4, at the end of this chapter, asks you to derive this result.)

Our analysis of Figure 10.8 showed that a fiscal expansion in a small open economy leads to an appreciation and reduces net exports. In the limiting case when the interest rate cannot differ from the foreign real interest rate, this appreciation and the resulting fall in net exports are so large that fiscal policy has no net effect on output, even in the short run. Thus, the Mundell–Fleming model has the surprising implication that fiscal policy is ineffective when there is a floating exchange rate and no possible international interest rate differential.

The situation is very different in the case of monetary policy, which is illustrated in Figure 10.10. In Figure 10.10, the foreign interest rate, which is also the domestic interest rate, is shown as a horizontal line. The general equilibrium is given at point *E*, where the *LM* and *FE* lines intersect at this world interest rate. Next, suppose that a decrease in the money supply shifts the *LM* curve up and to the left, from LM^1 to LM^2. In the Keynesian model the short-run equilibrium occurs at point *F*, where the new *LM* curve intersects the foreign interest rate (or equivalently, the *IS* curve).

At point *F*, the monetary contraction has tended to raise the interest rate so that e has risen and *NX* has fallen. Because the monetary contraction has caused an appreciation and hence a fall in net exports, it has a larger effect on output than it would in a closed economy. The interest rate does not rise because once again

FIGURE 10.10

A DECREASE IN THE MONEY
SUPPLY IN THE
MUNDELL–FLEMING
MODEL

The economy is in general equilibrium at point *E*. The *IS* curve is horizontal at r_{For}. A decrease in the domestic money supply shifts the *LM* curve up and to the left, from LM^1 to LM^2. The short-run equilibrium in the Keynesian model is at point *F*, with lower output and net exports, and a higher real exchange rate. In the long run, prices fall and the economy returns to equilibrium at point *E*. Thus, in the long run, money is neutral.

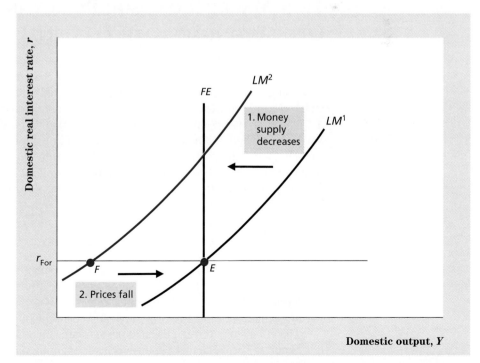

$r = r_{For}$. Thus, the full effect of the fall in the money supply is reflected in a decrease in output.

At point F, output is below its full employment level and prices begin to fall. When price adjustment is complete, the LM curve shifts back to its original position. In the long run, (or in the short run in the classical model), the change in monetary policy affects nominal variables but not real ones. So, the economy returns to point E with a lower pice level and a higher nominal exchange rate, but no long-run change in the real exchange rate, net exports, or output.

This potent effect of monetary policy on output in the short run, in a small open economy with a flexible exchange rate, plays an important role in macroeconomic history. For example, central banks that have restricted the growth of the money supply to try to reduce inflation generally have experienced exchange-rate appreciations, and declines in net exports, output, and employment. A classic example of this effect occurred in the UK from 1979 to 1981, under the first Thatcher government. A more recent example took place in Canada during the period 1989–1991, when the Bank of Canada's use of monetary policy to reduce inflation led to an appreciation of the Canadian dollar and caused a significant part of the 1990–1992 recession.

This extreme case, with $r = r_{For}$, is a useful reminder of how fiscal policy has a limited effect on output and monetary policy has a strong effect on output, in a small open economy with a flexible exchange rate. Fiscal policy has little effect because a fiscal expansion, for example, causes an appreciation, which reduces net exports, an effect that works against the original expansion. In the case of monetary policy, an expansion causes a depreciation, which adds to net exports and so enhances the effect of the policy on output. As we shall see in Section 10.6, the consequences of fiscal and monetary policy are very different under a fixed exchange rate.

10.5 MACROECONOMIC POLICY IN A LARGE OPEN ECONOMY WITH FLEXIBLE EXCHANGE RATES

In the previous section, we assumed that the economy was too small for its macroeconomic policies to affect other countries. Such an assumption is reasonable for Canada, but not for such countries as the United States, Germany, and Japan. In an interconnected world, the effects of macroeconomic policies in a large country are not limited to that country but also are felt abroad. On the basis of the analysis we have just finished, taking the extra step and finding out how a policy change affects a country's trading partners is not difficult. To study the effects of macroeconomic policy in these large economies, we simply use two IS–LM models; one for the large economy (such as the United States) and one for its trading partner, assumed to be a small economy (such as Canada).

A FOREIGN FISCAL EXPANSION

Figure 10.11 describes the effects of a fiscal expansion in the United States. The top panel, Figure 10.11(a), is the same as Figure 10.8, except that it now applies to a foreign country. The bottom panel, Figure 10.11(b), represents the small trading partner, which we refer to as the domestic economy or Canada.

The effects of a foreign fiscal expansion are transmitted through the change in net exports. The US fiscal expansion leads unambiguously to a decline in its net

FIGURE 10.11

EFFECTS OF AN INCREASE IN FOREIGN GOVERNMENT
PURCHASES

(a) An increase in foreign government purchases shifts the *IS* curve
up and to the right, from IS^1_{For} to IS^2_{For}. In the short-run Keynesian
model, foreign output and the foreign real interest rate both rise. Net
exports fall and the exchange rate rises (though theoretically the
exchange rate could fall if it were more responsive to output than to
the real interest rate). In the long-run, or classical, model, price
adjustment restores general equilibrium at point *H*, with a higher
foreign real interest rate and exchange rate, and lower foreign net
exports than at point *E*.

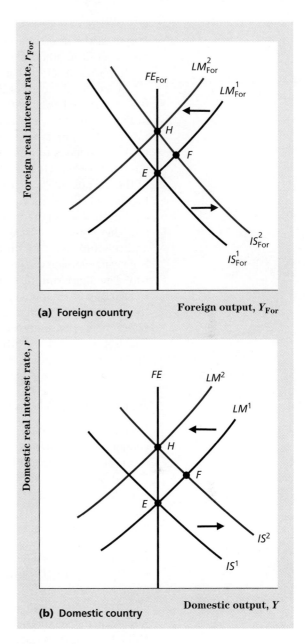

(a) Foreign country

(b) Because the foreign economy's exports are the domestic economy's
imports and vice versa, the decrease in the foreign economy's net
exports is equivalent to a rise in the domestic economy's net exports.
This increase shifts the domestic *IS* curve up, from *IS*^{1} to *IS*^{2}. In the
classical model, prices adjust rapidly, shifting the *LM* curve from *LM*^{1}
to *LM*^{2}. The new equilibrium is at point *H*, where the domestic real
interest rate and price level are higher but output is unchanged. In
the Keynesian model, price stickiness causes a temporary increase in
domestic output at point *F* before price adjustment restores equilibrium
at point *H*.

(b) Domestic country

exports. Because the foreign country's exports are the domestic country's imports
and vice versa, this is equivalent to an increase in net exports for the domestic
economy. Thus, the domestic country's *IS* curve shifts up, from *IS*^{1} to *IS*^{2}. Also recall
from Section 10.4 that the increase in government purchases probably leads to an
appreciation of the US dollar; hence the Canadian dollar depreciates.

In the classical model, the upward shift in the domestic *IS* curve does not affect
output; instead, the price level rises immediately to restore general equilibrium (the
LM curve shifts up from *LM*^{1} to *LM*^{2}). The domestic economy ends up at point *H*, with
the real interest rate and the price level higher than they were initially.

If prices are sticky, as in the Keynesian model, the effects of the shift in the *IS*
curve are slightly different. If prices do not adjust in the short run, then the shift in

the *IS* curve implies that the domestic economy would have temporarily higher output at the intersection of the *IS* and *LM* curves at point *F* in Figure 10.11(b); only after firms adjust their prices would the economy arrive at point *H*. Otherwise, the implications of the classical and Keynesian analyses are the same.

A technical aspect of the Keynesian model is worth noting. As prices adjust in the US and the US *LM* curve shifts back, US output falls and the real interest rate rises in Figure 10.11(a). In Canada, the fall in foreign (US) income and the rise in the foreign real interest rate have opposite effects on the Canadian *IS* curve. The fall in US income leads to a fall in Canadian net exports, while the rise in the US real interest rate leads to a rise in Canadian net exports, due to the further appreciation of the US dollar. The net effect of these two changes is unclear, so for simplicity, Figure 10.11(b) is drawn so that they are offsetting. Whether or not there is a further shift in the Canadian *IS* curve, the Canadian *LM* curve shifts up as shown.

Therefore, a US fiscal expansion leads to an increase in the Canadian price level and real interest rate and a decline in the value of the Canadian dollar. In the Keynesian version of the model, Canadian output also rises, but only in the short run. The short-run boom caused by the fiscal expansion in the United States is transmitted internationally by net exports because an increase in US output increases the demand for Canadian goods. The appreciation of the US dollar has the same effect. While this sounds like a favourable outcome for Canada, remember that our analysis implies that a fiscal contraction in the United States also may lead to a decline in Canadian net exports and a recession in Canada.

A FOREIGN MONETARY CONTRACTION

We can use the same two-country model to analyze the effect on the Canadian economy of a monetary contraction in the United States. Figure 10.12 illustrates this scenario. Figure 10.12(a), which is just like Figure 10.9 but now applies to the United States, shows the foreign monetary contraction. Recall from Section 10.4 that a reduction in the money supply leads to an appreciation but has an ambiguous effect on net exports. The appreciation of the US dollar lowers US net exports, while the fall in output raises US net exports. So, a monetary contraction in the US leads to a depreciation of the Canadian dollar, but we cannot be sure of the effect on Canadian net exports.

Figure 10.12(b) shows the effect on Canada. There, the *IS* curve shifts down from IS^1 to IS^2, illustrating the case in which the fall in US income outweighs the effect of the Canadian dollar depreciation so that Canadian net exports fall. In the Keynesian model, the short-run equilibrium is given by point *F*, where output and the real interest rate in Canada have both fallen.

Note that in the short-run, output is less than its full-employment level in both countries. Once again, the business cycle has been transmitted internationally, and both countries are in recession. As prices fall and the US *LM* curve shifts down, the US real interest rate and output will return to their original levels, so the Canadian *IS* curve will also return to IS^1. In the long-run, the original real exchange rate will be restored, and the Canadian economy will return to point *E*, an implication of monetary neutrality.

In this example, we cannot be sure of the net effect of the US monetary contraction on Canadian net exports. But we do know that if the Canadian dollar were not allowed to float (and depreciate), the Canadian *IS* curve would have shifted down by much more because of the fall in US output. Thus, the floating exchange rate

FIGURE 10.12

EFFECTS OF A DECREASE IN THE FOREIGN MONEY SUPPLY

(a) A foreign monetary contraction shifts the foreign *LM* curve up and to the left, from LM^1_{For} to LM^2_{For}. In the short-run Keynesian model, output falls and the foreign real interest rate rises. The exchange rate rises, but net exports can rise or fall. In this example, the effect of lower output dominates, and foreign net exports rise.

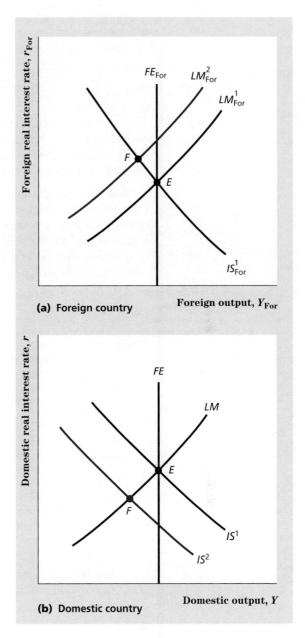

(a) Foreign country

(b) Because the foreign economy's net exports rise, the domestic economy's net exports fall, and the domestic *IS* curve shifts down, from IS^1 to IS^2. Thus, output falls in the domestic economy in the short run. In the long-run, or classical, model, foreign output and the foreign real interest rate return to their original levels, the domestic *IS* curve shifts back to IS^1, and both economies return to equilibrium at point *E*. Thus, in the long run, money is neutral.

(b) Domestic country

has partly insulated the Canadian economy from the contractionary US monetary policy. The Application "Golden Fetters" describes an important historical example of this insulating property of floating exchange rates.

The key result of this section is that macroeconomic changes in other countries are transmitted to Canada through the open-economy *IS* curve. Working out the effects of those changes on the Canadian economy simply involves seeing how this curve shifts. Note also that in both examples we have considered, a change in US macroeconomic policy that causes US output to change also leads to a change in Canadian output in the same direction. Thus, the theory is consistent with the existence of an international business cycle, even though domestic Canadian policies also affect domestic output and the real interest rate.

APPLICATION

GOLDEN FETTERS

Perhaps the most dramatic example of how the choice of exchange rate system affects an economy occurred during the Great Depression of the 1930s. In the late 1920s, most western economies participated in the gold standard, a system of fixed exchange rates, with all currency values set in terms of gold. This system broke down during the Depression as, one by one, these countries left the gold standard and allowed their exchange rates to float.

A remarkable pattern appears in the sequence in which countries recovered from the Depression: countries that left gold standard recovered from the Depression more quickly, while no country recovered while remaining on the gold standard. Typically, a country that left the gold standard increased its money supply so that its currency depreciated. This pattern of floating and macroeconomic recovery is striking evidence of the importance of monetary factors in this business cycle.

Some economic historians have argued that the Depression also was *caused* by monetary factors. For example, monetary policy in the United States became contractionary in 1928, to curb speculation on the stock market. In that year, the Federal Reserve began to raise interest rates so that speculators had to pay more to invest with borrowed money. As the analysis of this chapter shows, this contraction in the US money supply would tend to cause an appreciation of the US dollar and hence depreciations of other currencies. But under the system of fixed exchange rates, other countries then responded by contracting their own monetary policies to maintain the value of their currencies. Thus, the contractionary monetary policy was spread around the world. (Section 10.6 shows how a fixed-exchange-rate system requires coordination of monetary policies across countries.)

As the Depression began, the international monetary system also transmitted a second shock. In 1931, a series of banking panics, including the failure of Credit Anstalt (the largest bank in Austria) led to increases in money demand in several countries, as asset-holders preferred holding money to holding less liquid non-monetary assets. Like the decrease in the money supply, this increase in money demand shifted the *LM* curve back in countries with banking panics. Once again, the result was an exchange-rate appreciation, which then spread contagiously as countries tried to maintain fixed exchange rates.

How did these monetary factors propagate (and perhaps cause) the Depression? Recall that when the *LM* curve shifts up and to the left, in the short run, output falls when prices and wages are sticky (see Figure 10.9). Thus, output and employment both fell sharply. In addition, with output below its full-employment level, prices began to fall not only relative to trend but in absolute terms. Several countries experienced deflations, which caused widespread bankruptcy, as firms were not able to sell their products at prices that would cover their costs.

As we have discussed in Section 10.5, a country can partly insulate itself against a foreign monetary contraction if it has a flexible exchange rate. The Great Depression provided an unpleasant experiment that demonstrated this insulating property of flexible exchange rates. The experiment involves comparing the macroeconomic performance of countries that allowed their exchange rates to float with that of countries that imported the monetary contraction by maintaining the gold standard. Spain, for example, was not on the gold standard during the interwar period. Argentina left in 1929, the United Kingdom, Germany, and Canada in 1931, and the United States in 1933. France and Switzerland remained on the gold standard until late 1936.

Statistical evidence on the relation between allowing the exchange rate to float and recovering from the Depression has been reviewed by Ben Bernanke, of Princeton University.[14] In studying 24 countries during the period from 1932 to 1935, Bernanke found a cumulative difference in output of 31% in favour of countries that adopted flexible exchange rates. These countries also had higher employment growth, lower real exchange rates, and higher net exports.

Is it possible that this finding is a coincidence and that countries that floated earlier would have prospered anyway? This explanation for the pattern in the historical data seems implausible. Barry Eichengreen, of the University of California at Berkeley, has comprehensively examined the monetary history of the interwar period.[15] Eichengreen found that economic conditions in 1929 and 1930 were similar across countries that adopted flexible exchange rates soon after and those that did not. Thus, it seems unlikely that the floating countries were poised for growth for some reason unrelated to monetary and exchange rate policy. Eichengreen also found that in most countries, the decision to adopt a flexible exchange rate or not was largely determined by political factors and so was not generally a response to macroeconomic indicators.

The experience of countries with flexible exchange rates during the Depression does not imply that a flexible-exchange-rate regime should always be chosen, though. First, not all international shocks are monetary shocks, and a flexible exchange rate may not insulate a small open economy against foreign fiscal shocks, for example. Second, there are other arguments for adopting a fixed exchange rate, for example to constrain domestic monetary policy that is too expansionary or to promote trade, as the next section discusses.

10.6 FIXED EXCHANGE RATES

Canada has had a flexible exchange rate since 1970, and the Canadian dollar also floated in the 1950s. However, fixed-exchange-rate systems—in which exchange rates are officially set by international agreement—have been important historically and are still used by many countries. Let us now consider fixed-exchange-rate systems and address two questions: (1) How does the use of a fixed-exchange-rate system affect an economy and macroeconomic policy? (2) Ultimately, which is the better system: flexible or fixed exchange rates?

FIXING THE EXCHANGE RATE

In contrast to flexible-exchange-rate systems—where exchange rates are determined by supply and demand in foreign exchange markets—in a fixed-exchange-rate

---

14. "The Macroeconomics of the Great Depression: A Comparative Approach," *Journal of Money, Credit and Banking,* February 1995, pp. 1–28.
15. *Golden Fetters: The Gold Standard and the Great Depression, 1919–1939,* New York: Oxford University Press, 1992.

system, the value of the nominal exchange rate is officially set by the government, perhaps in consultation or agreement with other countries.[16]

A potential problem with fixed-exchange-rate systems is that the value of the exchange rate set by the government may not be the exchange rate determined by the supply of and demand for currency. Figure 10.13, on the next page, shows a situation in which the official exchange rate, e_{nom}, is higher than the **fundamental value of the exchange rate**, e_{nom}^1, or the value that would be determined by free market forces without government intervention. When an exchange rate is higher than its fundamental value, it is an **overvalued exchange rate** (often referred to as an overvalued currency).

How can a country deal with a situation in which its official exchange rate is different from the fundamental value of its exchange rate? There are several possible strategies: First, the country can simply change the official value of its exchange rate so that it equals, or is close to, its fundamental value. For example, in the case of overvaluation shown in Figure 10.13, the country could simply devalue (lower) its nominal fixed exchange rate from e_{nom} to e_{nom}^1. However, although occasional devaluations or revaluations can be expected under fixed-exchange-rate systems, if a country continuously adjusts its exchange rate it might as well switch to a flexible-rate system.

Second, the government could restrict international transactions—for example, by limiting or taxing imports or capital outflows. Such policies reduce the supply of the domestic currency to the foreign exchange market, thus raising the fundamental value of the exchange rate toward its fixed value. Some countries go even further and prohibit people from trading the domestic currency for foreign currencies without government approval; a currency that cannot be freely traded for other currencies is said to be an **inconvertible currency**. However, direct government intervention in international transactions has many economic costs, including reduced access to foreign goods and credit.

Third, the government itself may become a demander or supplier of its currency in the foreign exchange market, an approach used by most of the industrialized countries having fixed exchange rates. For example, in the case of overvaluation shown in Figure 10.13, the supply of the country's currency to the foreign exchange market (point B) exceeds private demand for the currency (point A) at the official exchange rate by the amount AB. To maintain the value of the currency at the official rate, the government could buy back its own currency in the amount AB in each period.

Usually, these currency purchases are made by the nation's central bank using official reserve assets. Recall that official reserve assets are assets other than domestic money or securities that can be used to make international payments (examples are gold, foreign bank deposits, or special assets created by international agencies, such as the International Monetary Fund). During the gold standard period, for example, gold was the basic form of official reserve asset, and central banks offered to exchange gold for their own currencies at a fixed price. If Figure 10.13 represented a gold standard country, AB would represent the amount of gold the central bank would have to use to buy back its currency in each period to equalize the quantities of its currency supplied and demanded at the official exchange rate. Recall also that the decline in a country's official reserve assets during a year equals its *balance of payments deficit*. Thus, amount AB measures the reserves the central bank must use to support the currency and corresponds to the country's balance of payments deficit.

---

16. In some fixed-exchange-rate systems, the exchange rate is allowed to fluctuate within a narrow, prespecified band. For simplicity, we shall assume in this section that the exchange rate is fixed at a single value.

FIGURE 10.13

AN OVERVALUED

EXCHANGE RATE

The figure shows a situation in which the officially fixed nominal exchange rate, $\bar{e}_{nom}$, is higher than the fundamental value of the exchange rate, e^1_{nom}, as determined by supply and demand in the foreign exchange market. In this situation, the exchange rate is said to be overvalued. The country's central bank can maintain the exchange rate at the official rate by using its reserves to purchase its own currency in the foreign exchange market, in the amount of AB in each period. This loss of reserves also is referred to as the country's balance of payments deficit.

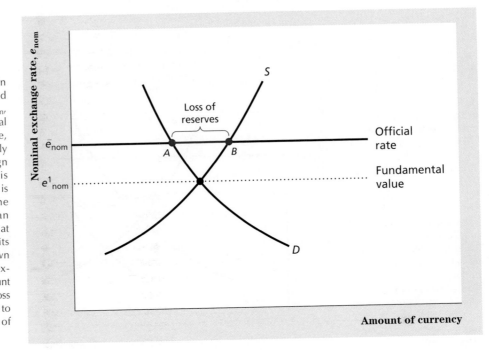

Although a central bank can maintain an overvalued exchange rate for a time by offering to buy back its own currency at a fixed price, it cannot do so forever because it has only a limited supply of official reserve assets. During the gold standard period, for example, central banks did not own unlimited amounts of gold. Attempting to support an overvalued currency for a long period of time would have exhausted a central bank's limited gold reserves, leaving the country no choice but to devalue its currency.

A central bank's attempts to support an overvalued currency can be ended quickly and dramatically by a speculative run. A **speculative run** occurs when financial investors begin to fear that an overvalued currency may soon be devalued, reducing the value of assets denominated in that currency relative to assets denominated in other currencies. To avoid losses, financial investors frantically sell assets denominated in the overvalued currency. The panicky sales of domestic assets associated with a speculative run on a currency shift the supply curve for that currency sharply to the right (Figure 10.14), increasing the gap between the quantities supplied and demanded of the currency from amount AB to amount AC. This widening gap increases the rate at which the central bank has to spend its official reserve assets to maintain the overvalued exchange rate, speeding devaluation and confirming the financial investors' expectations.

Such a speculative run occurred in December 1994 on the Mexican peso. A capital outflow necessitated a 15% devaluation of the peso against the US dollar and eventually led the Mexican authorities to allow the peso to float and depreciate further. Speculative runs or attacks also occurred during the East Asian crisis that began in 1997 and in Argentina in January 2002. We discussed some of these crises in an Application, "The Crises in Mexico, East Asia, and Russia," in Chapter 5. Figure 10.15 shows daily exchange rates from May 1997 through April 1998 for Indonesia, Singapore, the Philippines, Taiwan, Korea, and Malaysia. During the speculative runs and subsequent floats, several of these currencies depreciated by as much as 50%.

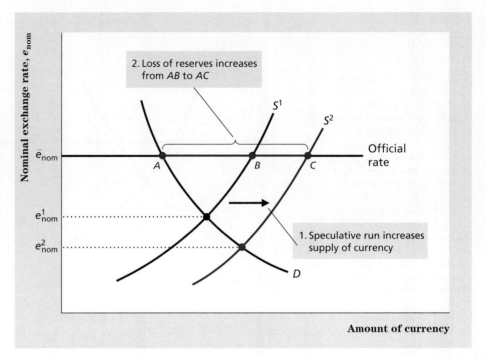

Without strong restrictions on international trade and finance (themselves
economically costly), we conclude that an overvalued exchange rate is not sustainable
for long. If the exchange rate is overvalued, the country must either devalue its
currency or make some policy change to raise the fundamental value of the exchange
rate. We show in the next section that the basic tool for changing the fundamental
value of the exchange rate is monetary policy.

We have focused on overvaluation, but an exchange rate also could be
undervalued. As illustrated in Figure 10.16 on the next page, an **undervalued
exchange rate** (or undervalued currency) exists if the officially fixed value is less
than the value determined by supply and demand in the foreign exchange market.
In this case, instead of buying its own currency, the central bank sells its currency
to the foreign exchange market and accumulates reserves in the amount AB each
period. With no limit to the quantity of reserve assets (gold, for example) a central
bank could accumulate, an undervalued exchange rate could apparently be
maintained indefinitely. However, a country with an undervalued exchange rate can
accumulate reserves only at the expense of trading partners who have overvalued
exchange rates and are, therefore, losing reserves. Because the country's trading
partners cannot continue to lose reserves indefinitely, eventually they will put
political pressure on the country to bring the fundamental value of its exchange
rate back in line with the official rate.

MONETARY POLICY AND THE FIXED EXCHANGE RATE

Suppose that a country wants to eliminate currency overvaluation by raising the
fundamental value of its nominal exchange rate until it equals the fixed value of the
exchange rate. How can it achieve this goal? Economists have long recognized that
the best way for a country to do so is through contraction of its money supply.

FIGURE 10.15

CURRENCY VALUES IN THE
EAST ASIAN CRISIS

The figure shows daily values
for six East Asian exchange
rates, from May 1, 1997, to
April 30, 1998. Rates are in US
dollars and apply to the
Indonesian rupiah, Malaysian
ringgit, Philippine peso, Singapore dollar, Taiwanese dollar,
and Korean won. The ex-
change rates are scaled so that
they are equal to 1.0 in May
1997. These sharp depreciations reflect speculative runs
or attacks.

Source: Based on statistics accessed
from Pacific Exchange Rate Service,
pacific.commerce.ubc. ca/xr/.

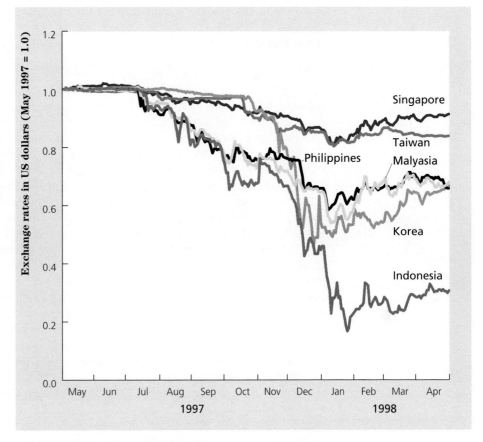

FIGURE 10.16

AN UNDERVALUED
EXCHANGE RATE

The exchange rate is undervalued when the officially
determined nominal exchange
rate, $\bar{e}_{nom}$, is less than the
fundamental value of the
exchange rate as determined
by supply and demand in the
foreign exchange market, e^1_{nom}.
To maintain the exchange rate
at its official level, the central
bank must supply its own
currency to the foreign
exchange market in the
amount AB each period,
thereby accumulating foreign
reserves.

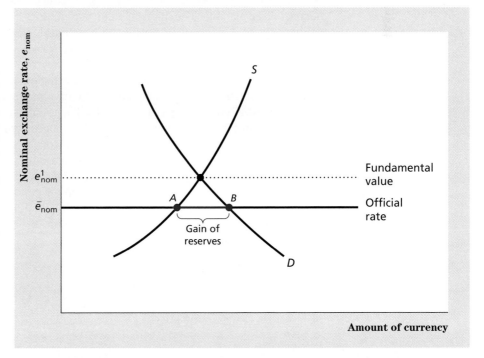

To demonstrate why a monetary contraction raises the fundamental value of the nominal exchange rate, we first rewrite Eq. (10.1), which defined the relationship of the real and nominal exchange rates:

$$e_{\text{nom}} = \frac{eP_{\text{For}}}{P}.$$

(10.6)

Equation (10.6) states that, for any foreign price level P_{For}, the nominal exchange rate e_{nom} is proportional to the real exchange rate e and inversely proportional to the domestic price level P.

In our earlier discussion of monetary policy in the Keynesian model with flexible exchange rates, we showed that a monetary contraction causes the real exchange rate to rise in the short run by reducing domestic output and increasing the real interest rate. Because short-run domestic and foreign price levels are fixed in the Keynesian model, Eq. (10.6) indicates that the short-run rise in the real exchange rate also implies a short-run rise in the nominal exchange rate. In the long run, money is neutral; hence a monetary contraction has no effect on the real exchange rate, but it does cause the domestic price level to fall. In the long run, the domestic price level P falls, but the real exchange rate e is unaffected, so Eq. (10.6) implies that the nominal exchange rate rises (appreciates) both in the long run and the short run. Thus, in both the short and long runs, a monetary contraction increases the fundamental value of the nominal exchange rate, or the value of the nominal exchange rate determined by supply and demand in the foreign exchange market.[17] Conversely, a monetary easing reduces the fundamental value of the nominal exchange rate in both the short and long runs.

Figure 10.17 illustrates the relationship between the nominal exchange rate and the money supply in a country with a fixed exchange rate.[18] The downward-sloping curve shows the relationship of the money supply to the fundamental value of the nominal exchange rate. This curve slopes downward because, other factors being equal, an increase in the money supply reduces the fundamental value of the nominal exchange rate. The horizontal line in Figure 10.17 is the officially determined exchange rate. The value of M_1 on the horizontal axis is the money supply that equalizes the fundamental value of the exchange rate and its officially fixed value. If the money supply is more than M_1, the country has an overvaluation problem (the fundamental value of the exchange rate is below the official value), and if the money supply is less than M_1 the country has an undervaluation problem.

Figure 10.17 suggests that in a fixed-exchange-rate system, individual countries typically are *not* free to expand their money supplies in order to try to raise output and employment. Instead, the money supply is governed by the condition that the official and fundamental values of the exchange rate be the same. If the country represented in Figure 10.17 wanted to expand its money supply to fight a recession, for example, it could do so only by creating an overvaluation problem (most likely leading to a future devaluation) or by devaluing its currency immediately. Under fixed exchange rates, then, a central bank cannot use monetary policy to pursue macroeconomic stabilization goals.

---

17. Because money is neutral in both the short and long runs in the basic classical model, a monetary contraction increases the fundamental value of the nominal exchange rate in both the short and long run in the basic classical model also.

18. The country's money supply is the amount of money in circulation domestically, as in previous chapters. It is not the supply of currency to foreign exchange markets, which depends only on domestic residents' demands for foreign goods and assets.

FIGURE 10.17

DETERMINATION OF THE
MONEY SUPPLY UNDER
FIXED EXCHANGE RATES

The downward-sloping fundamental value curve shows that
a higher domestic money
supply causes a lower fundamental value of the exchange
rate. The horizontal line shows
the officially fixed nominal
exchange rate. Only when the
country's money supply equals
M_1 does the fundamental
value of the exchange rate
equal the official rate. If the
central bank increased the
money supply above M_1, the
exchange rate would become
overvalued. A money supply
below M_1 would result in an
undervalued currency.

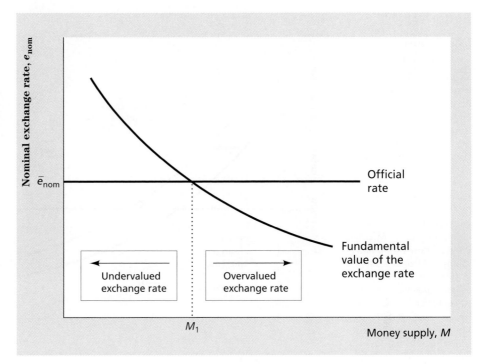

Although one member of a group of countries in a fixed-exchange-rate system
generally is not free to use monetary policy by itself, the group *as a whole* may be
able to do so, *if* they coordinate their policies. For example, suppose that Spain and
Portugal have a fixed exchange rate between their two currencies and that because
of a recession in both countries, both want to expand their money supplies. If
Portugal attempts a monetary expansion on its own, from M_1 to M_2 in Figure 10.18,
its exchange rate will become overvalued (its fundamental value, at the intersection
of M_2 and FV^1, would be lower than the official exchange rate). As a result, the Bank
of Portugal would lose reserves, ultimately forcing Portugal to undo its attempted
expansion.

Suppose, however, that Spain goes ahead with its own money supply expansion.
If Portugal's money supply remains constant, an increase in Spain's money supply
reduces Spain's (nominal) exchange rate, which is equivalent to raising Portugal's
exchange rate. In Figure 10.18, the increase in Spain's money supply increases the
fundamental value of Portugal's exchange rate at any level of its money supply. The
fundamental value curve in Figure 10.18 shifts up from FV^1 to FV^2. Now Portugal
can expand its money supply, from M_1 to M_2, without creating an overvaluation
problem (the fundamental value of the Portuguese exchange rate, at the intersection
of M_2 and FV^2, is the same as the official exchange rate). Thus, if Spain and Portugal
cooperate by changing their money supplies in the same direction, both countries can
achieve their stabilization goals without either country experiencing overvaluation.

As this example shows, fixed exchange rates are most likely to work well when
the countries in the system have similar macroeconomic goals and can cooperate on
monetary policies. As the following Application illustrates, the failure of nations to
cooperate within a fixed-exchange-rate system can lead to severe problems, including
the potential breakdown of the system.

FIGURE 10.18

COORDINATED MONETARY EXPANSION

Suppose that Spain and Portugal are members of a fixed-exchange-rate system and that both are suffering from recessions. Initially, the fundamental value of Portugal's exchange rate as a function of the country's money supply is FV^1, and its money supply level consistent with maintenance of the official exchange rate is M_1. If Portugal raises its money supply to M_2 in an attempt to stimulate its economy, the fundamental value of its exchange rate will fall below the official fixed rate, and Portugal's currency would be overvalued.

Now, suppose that Spain also expands its money supply in a coordinated effort to stimulate both economies. For any level of Portugal's money supply, the increase in Spain's money supply will lower the fundamental value of Spain's exchange rate and raise the fundamental value of Portugal's exchange rate. The fundamental value curve of Portugal's exchange rate shifts up from FV^1 to FV^2. Portugal can now increase its money supply to M_2 without creating an overvaluation problem. Thus, Spain and Portugal have achieved a coordinated monetary expansion.

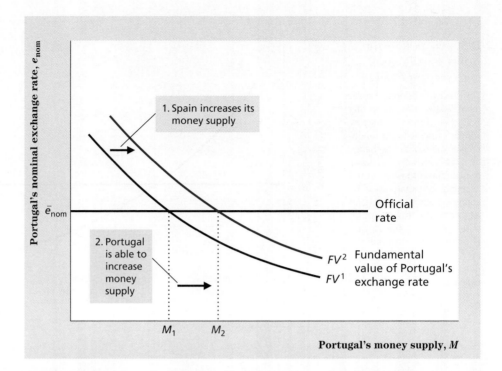

APPLICATION

POLICY COORDINATION FAILURE AND THE COLLAPSE OF FIXED EXCHANGE RATES: THE CASES OF BRETTON WOODS AND THE EMS

After World War II, the world's industrialized nations established the Bretton Woods system, under which exchange rates were fixed (with occasional adjustments).[19] The United States, by far the world's largest economy at the time, played a central role in the system and US dollars were widely used by other countries as official reserve assets. Other countries were willing to do so because the United States pledged to maintain the exchange rate between dollars and gold at $35 per ounce. Canada participated in the system from 1962 to 1970, with the exchange rate fixed at 92.5 US cents. All in all, the Bretton Woods system seemed to perform well. While the system was fully operational (1959–1971),[20] most countries recorded solid macroeconomic growth and stability. However, the inability of the principal member countries to coordinate their monetary policies created severe strains in the system and eventually led to its collapse.

Several international disputes erupted over monetary policy during the Bretton Woods era, but the one that ultimately proved fatal was triggered by American monetary policy during the 1960s. The US money supply grew more and more rapidly, reflecting the Federal Reserve's aggressive attempts to promote growth in output and employment and its desire to keep interest rates low despite expansionary fiscal policies. (US government spending increased significantly during the 1960s both because of the Vietnam War and expansion of social programs.) Increasing money growth and the inflation that followed caused the dollar to become increasingly overvalued.

19. For a detailed recent study of the Bretton Woods system, see Michael D. Bordo and Barry Eichengreen, eds., *A Retrospective on the Bretton Woods System*, Chicago: University of Chicago Press for NBER, 1993.
20. Before 1959, not all currencies in the system were convertible.

Normally, in a fixed-exchange-rate system, a country's loss of international reserves makes sustaining an overvalued currency impossible. However, the United States avoided the loss of its reserves for a time by persuading foreign central banks to buy the excess supply of dollars in the foreign exchange market. Foreign central banks at first were willing to use their own currencies to buy US dollars because they could use the dollars as international reserves. Ultimately, however, the foreign central banks grew tired of accumulating dollars and complained about what they considered to be overexpansionary US monetary policy.

To limit money supply growth and avoid importing inflation, the Canadian authorities allowed the Canadian dollar to float (and appreciate) in mid-1970. Meanwhile, the solution suggested by US policymakers was for the other Bretton Woods members to increase their money supplies, thereby eliminating the dollar overvaluation problem. However, several countries, notably Germany, refused to accept the inflationary consequences of this proposal and began to demand instead that the United States redeem its dollars with gold. Fearing a huge drain on its gold reserves, the United States was reluctant to redeem its dollars. A series of crises in the foreign exchange markets followed and, in August 1971, President Nixon announced that the United States would no longer exchange gold for dollars. This announcement effectively ended the Bretton Woods system and left the world's major currencies to float freely against each other.

Two decades later a different kind of dispute over monetary policy threatened the European Monetary System (EMS), a system of fixed exchange rates among Western European nations. Because of its large economy, Germany was the most influential country in the EMS. In 1992, concerned about increased inflation after German re-unification, the Bundesbank tightened Germany's monetary policy, raising interest rates significantly. This action undervalued the mark and overvalued other EMS currencies, putting considerable pressure on other members of the EMS to tighten monetary policies as well. However, the UK and other countries at the time were mired in serious recessions and did not want to go along with German contractionary policies.

In September 1992, participants in the foreign exchange market became convinced that the UK would not tighten monetary policy and that, as a result, the Bank of England would eventually have to devalue the pound. This fear led to a speculative run on the pound. After losing large quantities of reserves in attempts to maintain the value of the pound relative to other currencies in the EMS, the UK decided to leave the fixed-exchange-rate system and allowed the value of the pound to fall. Several other countries refused to match Germany's tight monetary policies and were forced to devalue or leave the system. The 1992 EMS crisis substantially delayed progress toward the ultimate goal of a single European currency. Indeed, new speculative crises occurred in the summer of 1993.[21]

In the Bretton Woods case, the dominant country in the system followed a monetary policy that was more expansionary than the other members wanted; in the EMS case, the dominant country followed a monetary policy that was tighter than the other members preferred. In both instances, however, international disagreements about the appropriate rate of monetary growth posed a severe threat to the existence of the fixed-exchange-rate system.

---

21. For a description of the 1992 crisis and the roles played by different market participants see Morris Goldstein et al., *International Capital Markets. Part I. Exchange Rate Management and International Capital Flows*, Washington, D.C.: International Monetary Fund, 1993.

FIXED VERSUS FLEXIBLE EXCHANGE RATES

We have discussed some of the problems that arose in the Bretton Woods and EMS fixed-exchange-rate systems. However, flexible-exchange-rate systems have problems of their own, primarily the volatility of exchange rates, which introduces uncertainty for people and businesses in their transactions with other countries. Each type of system has its problems, so which is preferable?

Proponents of fixed-exchange-rate systems stress two major benefits. First, relative to a situation in which exchange rates fluctuate continuously, stable exchange rates make trading goods and assets among countries easier and less costly. Thus, a system of fixed rates may promote economic and financial integration and improve economic efficiency. Second, fixed exchange rates may improve monetary policy "discipline," in the sense that countries with fixed exchange rates typically are less able to carry out highly expansionary monetary policies; the result may be lower inflation in the long run. For these reasons, even countries that have floating exchange rates frequently use monetary policy to influence the value of their currency. Their central banks also intervene directly in the foreign exchange market by buying and selling foreign currencies. The resulting hybrid is sometimes called a *managed float* or a *dirty float*.

The other side of the monetary discipline argument is that fixed exchange rates take away a country's ability to use monetary policy flexibly to deal with recessions.[22] This inability is particularly serious if the different countries in the fixed-exchange-rate system have different policy goals and face different types of economic shocks. As the preceding Application illustrated, disagreements among countries in a fixed-exchange-rate system about the conduct of monetary policy may even lead to the breakdown of the system.

A helpful way to think of the choice of an exchange-rate system is in terms of the **open-economy trilemma**.[23] In selecting a system, a country can choose only two of the following three features: (1) a fixed exchange rate to promote trade; (2) free international movements of capital; and (3) autonomy for domestic monetary policy. For example, a country can retain some independence for monetary policy while maintaining a fixed exchanged rate only if it uses taxes or controls to limit capital flows. Or a country can choose a fixed exchange rate and allow capital mobility if it devotes monetary policy to the goal of maintaining the exchange rate.[24]

Which system is better depends on the circumstances. Fixed exchange rates (or even a common currency) among a group of countries are useful when large benefits can be gained from increased trade and integration and when the countries in the system coordinate their monetary policies closely. Countries that value the ability to use monetary policy independently—perhaps because they face different macroeconomic shocks than other countries or hold different views about the relative costs of recessions and inflation—should retain a floating exchange rate.

---

22. Keynesians consider this a cost, but classicals do not.

23. The trilemma is used to describe the history of the international monetary system by Maurice Obstfeld and Alan Taylor, "The Great Depression as a Watershed: International Capital Mobility over the Long Run," in Michael Bordo, Claudia Goldin, and Eugene White, eds., *The Defining Moment: The Great Depression and the American Economy in the Twentieth Century*, Chicago: University of Chicago Press, 1998, pp. 353–402.

24. For a lively history of Canada's resolutions of the trilemma, see James Powell, *A History of the Canadian Dollar*, Ottawa: Bank of Canada, 1999.

CURRENCY UNIONS

An alternative to fixing exchange rates is for a group of countries to form a **currency union**, under which they agree to share a common currency. Members of a currency union also typically cooperate economically and politically.

An effective currency union usually requires more than just cooperation of national central banks. For a currency union to work, the common monetary policy must be controlled by a single institution. Because countries are typically reluctant to give up their own currency and monetary policies, currency unions have been rare. However, if politically feasible, a currency union has at least two advantages over fixed exchange rates. First, the costs of trading goods and assets among countries are even lower with a single currency than under fixed exchange rates. Second, if national curencies are eliminated in favour of the common currency, speculative attacks on the national currencies no longer can occur.[25]

However, a currency union shares the major disadvantage of a fixed-exchange-rate system. It requires all its members to share a common monetary policy. Thus, if one member of a currency union is in a recession while another is concerned about inflation, the common monetary policy cannot deal with both countries' problems simultaneously. In contrast, under flexible exchange rates, each country could set its own monetary policy independently.

APPLICATION

EUROPEAN MONETARY UNION: LESSONS FOR NORTH AMERICA?

In December 1991, at a meeting in Maastricht in the Netherlands, the member countries of the European Community adopted the Treaty on European Union, usually called the Maastricht Treaty. This treaty took effect in November 1993, after being ratified (with some opposition) by popular votes in the member countries. One of the most important provisions of the treaty was that those countries meeting certain criteria (including the achievement of low inflation rates and small government budget deficits) would adopt a common currency, to be called the euro. The common currency was introduced on January 1, 1999, and co-existed with national currencies until 2002, when it became the sole currency of members of the European Monetary Union (EMU). The United Kingdom, Sweden, and Denmark were eligible to join but decided to retain their own currencies and float against the euro.

The common monetary policy for the euro countries is determined by the Governing Council of the European Central Bank (ECB), based in Frankfurt. The council includes six members of an executive board, appointed jointly by the member countries, plus the eleven governors of the central banks of those countries. Except through their representation on the Council, the national central banks, such as Germany's Bundesbank and the Bank of France, have of necessity given up their power to make monetary policy for their countries.[26]

The monetary unification of Europe is an important development, but one whose long-term implications remain unknown as yet. Possible advantages of the currency union

---

25. Some economists argue that fixed-exchange-rate systems are not viable for this reason so that the choice is between flexible exchange rates and a currency union. See Maurice Obstfeld and Kenneth Rogoff, "The Mirage of Fixed Exchange Rates," *Journal of Economic Perspectives*, Fall 1995, pp. 73–96.
26. For a history of the EMU see Werner Antweiler's Euro pages at *http://pacific.commerce.ubc.ca/xr/euro/euro.html.*

include easier movement of goods, capital, and labour among European countries; lower costs of financial transactions; and enhanced political and economic cooperation. A risk is that member countries might disagree about whether the common monetary policy should be expansionary or contractionary at a particular time. Indeed, at the time of the introduction of the euro, a recession in Europe affected member countries to differring degrees. The ECB, thus, faced the decision of whether to ease the common monetary policy, to assist those countries worst hit by the recession (such as Italy), or to leave monetary policy unchanged, as desired by those countries (such as Ireland) doing relatively better. When the euro depreciated significantly against the US dollar, the ECB also faced criticism that its monetary stance was inappropriate.

Perhaps inspired by the European example, some Canadian economists have begun to debate the costs and benefits of a currency union with the United States, sometimes called North American Monetary Union (NAMU). As we have discussed, one of the benefits of currency union may be increased trade. Andrew Rose, of the University of California at Berkeley, has estimated that countries with the same currency trade three times as much as they would with different currencies, given other influences on trade, such as the distance between the two countries.[27]

Members of the EMU have relinquished independent monetary policies partly for political reasons. They have viewed closer economic ties as a way to ensure long-term peace in Europe and also to allow Europe to serve as a counterweight to the United States in international trade negotiations. These factors do not seem to apply to NAMU, though, where the United States seems unlikely to replace the US dollar with a North American currency or give Canada and Mexico a voice in the Federal Reserve System, its central bank.

For these reasons, countries in the western hemisphere that want to pursue currency union with the United States have done so unilaterally, through *dollarization* (adopting the US dollar as their official currency, as in Ecuador). These countries generally have a history of high money growth and high inflation and so have decided that they may have little to lose by giving up monetary independence.

---

27. "One Money, One Market," *Economic Policy* 2000, pp. 7–46. Rose's estimates are mainly from small, less-developed countries that currently belong to currency unions.

CHAPTER SUMMARY

1. The nominal exchange rate is the number of units of foreign currency that can be obtained for one unit of domestic currency. The real exchange rate is the number of units of foreign goods that can be obtained for one unit of the domestic good. The idea that similar foreign and domestic goods should have the same prices in terms of the same currency is called purchasing power parity (PPP).

2. There are two major types of exchange rate systems: flexible- or floating-exchange-rate systems, in which the value of the nominal exchange rate is determined by market forces; and fixed-exchange-rate systems, in which the value of the exchange rate is officially set by a government or group of governments. In a flexible-exchange-rate system, an exchange rate increase is called an appreciation, and an exchange rate decrease is called a depreciation.

3. The real exchange rate is important because it affects net exports, or exports minus imports. Other factors held constant, a decline in the real exchange rate makes domestic goods cheaper relative to foreign goods and, thus, tends to increase net exports.

4. In a flexible-exchange-rate system, the value of the (nominal) exchange rate is determined by supply and demand in the foreign exchange market. Foreigners demand the domestic currency to buy domestic goods and assets. Domestic residents supply the domestic currency to obtain the foreign currency needed to buy foreign goods and assets.

5. Other factors held constant, an increase in domestic output leads domestic residents to demand more imports, reducing the country's net exports and depreciating its exchange rate. An increase in the domestic real interest rate makes domestic assets more attractive, increasing the demand for the domestic currency and appreciating the exchange rate; the higher exchange rate, in turn, reduces net exports. The effects of changes in foreign output and the foreign real interest rate on the domestic country's net exports and exchange rate are the opposite of the effects of changes in domestic output and the domestic real interest rate.

6. The *IS–LM* model for an open economy is similar to that for the closed economy. The principal difference is that in the open-economy *IS–LM* model, factors (other than output or the real interest rate) that increase a country's net exports cause the *IS* curve to shift up. Among the factors that increase net exports are a rise in foreign output, an increase in the foreign real interest rate, or a shift in world demand toward the domestic country's goods. Economic shocks or policy changes are transmitted from one country to another by changes in net exports that lead to *IS* curve shifts.

7. In a small open economy with flexible exchange rates, a fiscal expansion increases domestic output, domestic prices, and the domestic real interest rate, as in a closed economy. The effect on the exchange rate is ambiguous (because an increase in the real interest rate tends to cause an appreciation, while an increase in output adds to import demand and tends to cause a depreciation), but usually, the exchange rate appreciates. Net exports fall. Thus, fiscal policy may not have a large effect on output even in the short run, because it leads to an opposite movement in net exports.

8. In a small open economy with flexible exchange rates, changes in the money supply are neutral in the basic classical model. Changes in the money supply also are neutral in the long run in the Keynesian model. In the short run in the Keynesian model, however, a decrease in the domestic money supply reduces domestic output and raises the domestic real interest rate, causing the current real exchange rate to appreciate. Lower output tends to increase net exports, while the appreciation tends to decrease net exports. The net effect usually is a decrease in net exports. Thus, monetary policy has a large effect on output in the short run because it leads to a parallel change in net exports.

9. Changes in macroeconomic policy in a large open economy are transmitted to its trading partners through shifts in their *IS* curves caused by changes in the large economy's net exports. This transmission produces an international business cycle. A fiscal expansion in a foreign, large economy leads to an increase in its trading partner's net exports so that output rises in the short run in both countries. A monetary contraction in a foreign, large economy has an ambiguous effect on its trading partner's net exports, but a flexible exchange rate can partly insulate the domestic economy from changes in foreign monetary policy.

10. In a fixed-exchange-rate system, nominal exchange rates are officially determined. If the officially determined exchange rate is greater than the fundamental value of the exchange rate as determined by supply and demand in the foreign exchange market, the exchange rate is said to be overvalued. The central bank can maintain the exchange rate at an overvalued level for a time by using official reserves (such as gold or foreign-currency bank deposits) to buy its own currency in the foreign exchange market. A country that tries to maintain an overvalued exchange rate for too long will run out of reserves and be forced to devalue its currency. If financial investors expect a devaluation, they may sell large quantities of domestic assets (a speculative run). A speculative run increases the supply of the domestic currency in the foreign exchange market and increases the rate at which the central bank must pay out its reserves.

11. To raise the fundamental value of its exchange rate, the central bank can tighten monetary policy. There is only one value of the domestic money supply at which the fundamental value of the exchange rate equals its officially fixed rate. With fixed exchange rates, individual countries are not free to use expansionary monetary policies to fight recessions because such policies result in an overvalued exchange rate. However, a group of countries in a fixed-exchange-rate system can use expansionary monetary policies effectively if they coordinate their policies.

12. The advantages of a fixed-exchange-rate system are that it may promote economic and financial integration among countries and that it imposes discipline on the monetary policies of individual countries. A fixed-exchange-rate system will not work well if member countries have different macroeconomic policy goals or face different macroeconomic disturbances and, thus, are unable or unwilling to coordinate their monetary policies.

KEY TERMS

currency union, p. 383
devaluation, p. 345
exchange rate, p. 343
fixed-exchange-rate system, p. 343
flexible-exchange-rate system, p. 343
floating-exchange-rate system, p. 343
foreign exchange market, p. 343
fundamental value of the exchange rate, p. 374
inconvertible currency, p. 374
intertemporal external balance, p. 392
nominal appreciation, p. 345
nominal depreciation, p. 345
nominal exchange rate, p. 343
nominal interest rate parity condition, p. 397
open-economy trilemma, p. 382
overvalued exchange rate, p. 374
purchasing power parity, p. 346
real appreciation, p. 346
real depreciation, p. 346
real exchange rate, p. 344
real interest rate parity condition, p. 398
relative purchasing power parity, p. 347
revaluation, p. 345
speculative run, p. 375
undervalued exchange rate, p. 376

KEY EQUATIONS

$$e = \frac{e_{\text{nom}} P}{P_{\text{For}}} \qquad (10.1)$$

The real exchange rate, e, or the number of foreign goods that can be obtained for one domestic good, is defined in terms of the nominal exchange rate e_{nom} (the amount of foreign currency that can be obtained for one unit of domestic currency), the domestic price level P, and the foreign price level P_{For}.

$$\frac{\Delta e_{\text{nom}}}{e_{\text{nom}}} = \frac{\Delta e}{e} + \pi_{\text{For}} - \pi. \qquad (10.3)$$

The percentage change in the nominal exchange rate, $\Delta e_{\text{nom}}/e_{\text{nom}}$, equals the percentage change in the real exchange rate, $\Delta e/e$, plus the excess of the foreign rate of inflation over the domestic rate of inflation, $\pi_{\text{For}} - \pi$.

$$S^d - I^d = NX \qquad (10.4)$$

In an open economy, goods market equilibrium (the *IS* curve) requires that the excess of desired national saving over desired investment equal net exports. Equation (10.4) is equivalent to the condition that output, Y, must equal the aggregate demand for goods, $C^d + I^d + G + NX$, Eq. (10.5).

REVIEW QUESTIONS

1. Define *nominal exchange rate* and *real exchange rate*. How are changes in the real exchange rate and the nominal exchange rate related?

2. What are the two main types of exchange rate systems? Currently, which type of system determines the values of the Canadian dollar and major currencies, such as the US dollar, yen, pound, and euro?

3. Define *purchasing power parity* or *PPP*. Does *PPP* work well empirically? Explain.

4. For a given real exchange rate, how are a country's net exports affected by an increase in domestic income? an increase in foreign income? How does an increase in the domestic real interest rate affect the real exchange rate and net exports? Explain.

5. Why do foreigners demand dollars in the foreign exchange market? Why do Canadians supply dollars to the foreign exchange market? Give two examples of changes that would lead to an increased demand for dollars and two examples of changes that would lead to an increased supply of dollars in the foreign exchange market.

6. How does the *IS–LM* model for an open economy differ from the *IS–LM* model for a closed economy? Illustrate

the use of the open-economy *IS–LM* model in describing
how a recession in one country may be transmitted to
other countries.

7. How are net exports affected by expansionary fiscal
policy? by expansionary monetary policy? What is the
potential ambiguity in determining these effects?

8. What effects does expansionary monetary policy have on
the nominal exchange rate in both the short and long
runs? Explain.

9. What does the Mundell–Fleming model imply about the
short-run effect on output of fiscal and monetary policies
in a Keynesian, small open economy?

10. What is the fundamental value of a currency? What does
saying that a currency is overvalued mean? Why is an
overvalued currency a problem? What can a country do
about an overvalued currency?

11. Why is a country limited in changing its money supply
under a fixed-exchange-rate system? Explain how policy
coordination among countries on a fixed-exchange-rate
system can increase the degree to which monetary policy
may be used to pursue macroeconomic goals.

12. What is the open-economy trilemma? Explain why each
element in the trilemma might be desirable and why the
three elements are incompatible.

NUMERICAL PROBLEMS

1. West Bubble makes ordinary soap bars that are sold for
5 guilders each. East Bubble makes deluxe soap bars
that are sold for 100 florins each. The real exchange
rate between West and East Bubble is two ordinary soap
bars per deluxe soap bar.

   a. What is the nominal exchange rate between the
   two countries?

   b. During the following year, West Bubble has 10%
   domestic inflation and East Bubble has 20% domestic
   inflation. Two ordinary soap bars are still traded for a
   deluxe soap bar. At the end of the year, what has
   happened to the nominal exchange rate? Which
   country has had a nominal appreciation? Which has
   had a nominal depreciation?

2. Consider the following classical economy:

Desired consumption	$C^d = 300 + 0.5Y - 200r$.
Desired investment	$I^d = 200 - 300r$.
Government purchases	$G = 100$.
Net exports	$NX = 150 - 0.1Y - 0.5e$.
Real exchange rate	$e = 20 + 600r$.
Full-employment output	$\overline{Y} = 900$.

   a. What are the equilibrium values of the real interest
   rate, the real exchange rate, consumption, investment, and net exports?

   b. Now, suppose that full-employment output
   increases to 940. What are the equilibrium values of
   the real interest rate, the real exchange rate,
   consumption, investment, and net exports?

   c. Suppose that full-employment output remains at
   940 and that government purchases increase to 132.
   What are the equilibrium values of the real interest
   rate, the real exchange rate, consumption,
   investment, and net exports?

3. Consider the following Keynesian economy:

Desired consumption	$C^d = 200 + 0.6(Y - T) - 200r$.
Desired investment	$I^d = 300 - 300r$.
Taxes	$T = 20 + 0.2Y$.
Government purchases	$G = 152$.
Net exports	$NX = 150 - 0.08Y - 500r$.
Money demand	$L = 0.5Y - 200r$.
Money supply	$M = 924$.
Full-employment output	$\overline{Y} = 1000$.

   a. What are the general equilibrium (that is, long-
   run) values of output, the real interest rate,
   consumption, investment, net exports, and the price
   level?

   b. Starting from full employment, government
   purchases are increased by 62, to 214. What are the
   effects of this change on output, the real interest rate,
   consumption, investment, net exports, and the price
   level in the short run? in the long run?

   c. With government purchases at their initial value of
   152, net exports increase by 62 at any income and
   real interest rate so that $NX = 212 - 0.08Y - 500r$.
   What are the effects of this change on output, the real
   interest rate, consumption, investment, net exports,
   and the price level in the short run? in the long run?
   Compare your answer to that for part (b).

4. Consider the following Keynesian small open economy:

Desired consumption	$C^d = 15 + 0.69Y$
Desired investment	$I^d = 83 - 20r$
Net exports	$NX = 85 - 0.1Y - e$
Real exchange rate	$e = 10 - 0.01Y + e_r(r - r_{For})$
Full-employment output	$\overline{Y} = 500$

   where we use a general coefficient e_r so that we may
   study several values.

   a. Graph NX and $S^d - I^d$ against the real interest rate,
   as in Figure 10.5.

   b. Derive the *IS* curve for arbitrary values of G, r_{For},
   and e_r.

   c. What is the slope of the *IS* curve if e_r is very large?

   d. Suppose now that e_r is very large, so that $r = r_{For}$.
   Suppose also that $r_{For} = 0.05$, $G = 28$, the *LM* curve is

$$M/P = Y - 100r,$$

and that initially $M^S = 495$. What are the values of Y, e, and P? Find the short-run and long-run effects on output Y, the price level P, and the real exchange rate e of an increase in the money supply to 544.5.

5. Consider the following classical economy:

Output $Y = \bar{Y} = 1,000$
IS $r = 800 - Y$
LM $\dfrac{M}{P} = 0.01Y - 0.01\,r$

This economy produces only wine, its output is measured in terms of wine, and its currency is francs. It trades with a country that produces only cheese, and the currency of that country is crowns. The real exchange rate e equals 5 wedges of cheese per bottle of wine. The foreign price level is 20 crowns per wedge of cheese, and the domestic money supply is 48 francs.

a. Find the aggregate demand curve for this economy.

b. What is the domestic price level? What is the fundamental value of the (nominal) exchange rate?

c. Suppose that the domestic country fixes its exchange rate at 50 crowns per franc. Is its currency overvalued, undervalued, or neither? What will happen to the domestic central bank's stock of official reserve assets if it maintains the exchange rate at 50 crowns per franc?

d. Suppose that the domestic country wants a money supply level that equalizes the fundamental value of the exchange rate and the fixed rate of 50 crowns per franc. What level of the domestic money supply achieves this goal? (*Hint*: For the given real exchange rate and foreign price level, what domestic price level is consistent with the official rate? What domestic money supply level will yield this price level?)

ANALYTICAL PROBLEMS

1. Recessions often lead to calls for protectionist measures to preserve domestic jobs. Suppose that a country that is in a recession imposes restrictions that sharply reduce the amount of goods imported by the country.

a. Using the Keynesian *IS–LM* model, analyze the effects of import restrictions on the domestic country's employment, output, real interest rate, and real exchange rate, keeping in mind that the country is initially in a recession.

b. What are the effects of the country's action on foreign employment, output, real interest rates, and

real exchange rates? What happens if the foreign country retaliates by imposing restrictions on goods exported by the domestic country?

c. Suppose that the domestic economy is at full employment when it imposes restrictions on imports. Using the classical model, find the effects on the country's employment, output, real interest rate, and real exchange rate.

2. "Japanese government budget deficits not only crowd out investment in Japan but also reduce capital formation in other countries."

Is this statement true? To analyze it, use the Keynesian model to work out the effects on investment, both at home and abroad, of a government budget deficit. Assume that the deficit was the result of a large tax cut and assume also that households respond to the tax cut by increasing desired consumption (Ricardian equivalence does not hold). Consider both the short and long runs. Does your answer change if Ricardian equivalence holds so that desired consumption is unaffected by the tax cut?

3. East Bubble's main trading partner is West Bubble. To fight inflation, West Bubble undertakes a contractionary monetary policy.

a. What is the effect of West Bubble's contractionary monetary policy on East Bubble's real exchange rate in the short run, assuming no change in East Bubble's policies? in the long run? Use the Keynesian model with flexible exchange rates.

b. What is the effect of West Bubble's monetary contraction on East Bubble's nominal exchange rate in the short run and in the long run?

c. Suppose now that East Bubble has fixed its exchange rate with West Bubble. If East Bubble wants to keep the exchange rate equal to its fundamental value, how will East Bubble have to respond to West Bubble's monetary tightening? What will happen to East Bubble's output, real exchange rate, and net exports in the short run if it maintains the fixed exchange rate at its fundamental value? Compare your answer with that for part (a).

d. Suppose that, after West Bubble's monetary tightening, East Bubble decides not to change any of its own macroeconomic policies (the exchange rate is still fixed). What will happen? Describe some alternative scenarios.

4. Use a diagram like Figure 10.5 to analyze the effect on a country's net exports of a beneficial supply shock that temporarily raises full-employment output by 100 per person. Assume that the basic classical model applies so that income is always at its full-employment level.

a. Suppose that in response to the temporary increase in income, the residents of the country do not change the amount they desire to spend at any real interest rate (on either domestic or foreign goods). What is the effect of the supply shock on the country's net exports? (*Hint*: What is the effect of the increase in income on the curve representing desired saving minus desired investment? What is the effect on the curve representing net exports?)

b. Now, suppose that in response to a temporary increase in income, the residents of the country increase their desired spending at any real interest rate by 100 per person. A portion of this increased spending is for foreign-produced goods. What is the effect on the country's net exports?

c. (More difficult) If the increase in income is temporary, would the spending behaviour assumed in part (a) or the spending behaviour assumed in part (b) be more likely to occur? On the basis of your answer, do the results of this problem confirm or contradict the prediction of the model in Chapter 5 of the response of net exports to a supply shock? Explain.

5. Suppose that the Netherlands is a small open economy in which the real interest rate does not deviate from the world real interest rate. According to the Mundell–Fleming model, what happens to Dutch macroeconomic variables when the world interest rate increases?

APPENDIX 10.A

AN ALGEBRAIC VERSION OF THE OPEN ECONOMY *IS–LM* MODEL

The *IS–LM* model for the open economy is basically the same as the closed-economy *IS–LM* model derived in Appendix 9.A, with the exception that the goods market equilibrium condition (the *IS* curve) is expanded to include net exports. The *LM* curve and the *FE* line are unchanged from previous analyses.

To derive the *IS* curve for the open economy, we begin with the equations describing desired consumption and desired investment, Eqs. (9.A.8) and (9.A.10):

$$C^d = c_0 + c_Y [Y - (t_0 + tY)] - c_r r, \tag{10.A.1}$$

$$I^d = i_0 - i_r r. \tag{10.A.2}$$

Equation (10.A.1) shows that desired consumption depends positively on disposable income, $Y - T$, and negatively on the real interest rate, r. (In Eq. 10.A.1 we used Eq. 9.A.9 to substitute for taxes, T.) Equation (10.A.2) states that desired investment depends negatively on the real interest rate r. Other factors influencing desired consumption and desired investment are included in the constant terms c_0 and i_0, respectively.

In an open economy, net exports also are a source of demand for domestic output. We assume that net exports are

$$NX = x_0 - x_Y Y + x_{YF} Y_{\text{For}} - x_r r + x_{rF} r_{\text{For}}, \tag{10.A.3}$$

where x_0, x_Y, x_{YF}, x_r, and x_{rF} are positive numbers. According to Eq. (10.A.3), a country's net exports depend negatively on domestic income Y (increased domestic income raises spending on imports) and positively on foreign income Y_{For} (increased foreign income raises spending on exports). Net exports also depend negatively on the domestic real interest rate r (a higher real interest rate raises the real exchange rate, making domestic goods relatively more expensive) and positively on the foreign real interest rate r_{For} (a higher foreign real interest rate lowers the domestic country's real exchange rate). Other factors influencing net exports, such as the qualities of domestic and foreign goods, are reflected in the constant term x_0 in Eq. (10.A.3). The goods market equilibrium condition for an open economy, Eq. (5.5), is

$$Y = C^d + I^d + G + NX. \tag{10.A.4}$$

The alternative version of the open-economy goods market equilibrium condition, $S^d = I^d + NX$, which is emphasized in the text, could be used equally well.

If we substitute the equations for desired consumption, Eq. (10.A.1), desired investment, Eq. (10.A.2), and net exports, Eq. (10.A.3), into the goods market equilibrium condition, Eq. (10.A.4), we get

$$Y = c_0 + c_Y (Y - t_0 - tY) - c_r r + i_0 - i_r r + G + x_0 - x_Y Y + x_{YF} Y_{For}$$
$$- x_r r + x_{rF} r_{For}. \tag{10.A.5}$$

Collecting the terms that multiply Y on the left-hand side yields

$$[1 - (1 - t)c_Y + x_Y]Y = c_0 + i_0 + G - c_Y t_0 + x_0 + x_{YF} Y_{For} + x_{rF} r_{For}$$
$$- (c_r + i_r + x_r)r. \tag{10.A.6}$$

Equation (10.A.6) relates output Y to the real interest rate r that clears the goods market and, thus, defines the open-economy IS curve. To put Eq. (10.A.6) in a form that is easier to interpret graphically, we rewrite it with r on the left-hand side and Y on the right side to obtain

$$r = \alpha'_{IS} - \beta'_{IS} Y, \qquad \text{open-economy } IS \text{ curve.} \tag{10.A.7}$$

Here, α'_{IS} and β'_{IS} are positive numbers defined as

$$\alpha'_{IS} = \frac{c_0 + i_0 + G - c_Y t_0 + x_0 + x_{YF} Y_{For} + x_{rF} r_{For}}{c_r + i_r + x_r}; \tag{10.A.8}$$

and

$$\beta'_{IS} = \frac{1 - (1 - t)c_Y + x_Y}{c_r + i_r + x_r}. \tag{10.A.9}$$

If there are no net exports, so that $x_0 = x_Y = x_{YF} = x_r = x_{rF} = 0$, the coefficients α'_{IS} and β'_{IS} reduce to the coefficients of the closed-economy IS curve, α_{IS} and β_{IS} (compare Eqs. 10.A.8 and 10.A.9 with Eqs. 9.A.15 and 9.A.16).

We use the open-economy IS curve equation, Eq. (10.A.7), to confirm the three points made about the curve in the text. First, it slopes downward (the slope of the IS curve is $-\beta'_{IS}$, which is negative). Second, any factor that shifts the closed-economy IS curve also shifts the open-economy IS curve (any factor that changes the intercept α_{IS} also changes the intercept α'_{IS} in the same direction). Finally, for a given output and real interest rate, any factor that increases net exports shifts the open-economy IS curve up. That is, an increase in Y_{For} or r_{For}, or some other change that increases the demand for net exports as reflected in an increase in x_0, raises the intercept term α'_{IS} and thus shifts the IS curve up.

General equilibrium in the open-economy *IS–LM* model is determined as in
the closed-economy model, except that the open-economy *IS* curve (Eq. 10.A.7)
replaces the closed-economy *IS* curve (Eq. 9.A.14).

For values of output Y, the real interest rate r, and the price level P determined by the open-economy *IS–LM* model, exchange rates can be determined
from:

$$e = e_0 - e_Y Y + e_{YF} Y_{\text{For}} + e_r r - e_{rF} r_{\text{For}}, \tag{10.A.10}$$

where e_0, e_Y, e_{YF}, e_r, and e_{rF} are positive numbers; and

$$e_{\text{nom}} = \frac{e P_{\text{For}}}{P}. \tag{10.A.11}$$

According to Eq. (10.A.10), an increase in foreign income Y_{For} or the domestic interest rate r, either of which raises the demand for the domestic currency,
raises the real exchange rate e. Also, an increase in domestic income Y or the
foreign real interest rate r_{For}, either of which increases the supply of domestic currency, lowers the real exchange rate. Eq. (10.A.11), which is the same as Eqs.
(10.1) and (10.6), states that the nominal exchange rate e_{nom} depends on the
real exchange rate e and the foreign and domestic price levels, P_{For} and P.

To illustrate the use of Eqs. (10.A.10) and (10.A.11), let us consider the effects of a monetary expansion in the Keynesian model. In the short run, an increase
in the money supply raises domestic output Y, lowers the domestic real interest
rate r, and leaves the domestic price level P unchanged. For these changes Eqs.
(10.A.10) and (10.A.11)—holding constant foreign output Y_{For} and the foreign real
interest rate r_{For} —imply a lower real exchange rate e and a lower nominal exchange rate e_{nom} (both a real and a nominal depreciation). In the long run, money
is neutral, so Y and r return to their original levels. Equation (10.A.10) indicates,
therefore, that the real exchange rate e also returns to its original value in the
long run. However, a monetary expansion leads to a long-run increase in the domestic price level P. Hence from Eq. (10.A.11) we see that the nominal exchange
rate e_{nom} also falls in the long run.

APPENDIX 10.B

INTERTEMPORAL EXTERNAL BALANCE AND INTEREST RATE PARITY

The real exchange rate, the quantity of foreign goods that can be acquired in exchange for one unit of the domestic good, is an important determinant of a country's net exports and, therefore, of domestic production and employment. But what determines a country's real exchange rate? Section 10.2 used a supply-and-demand analysis to describe how exchange rates are determined. This appendix gives a deeper analysis. We will see that the real exchange rate is determined by two equilibrium conditions, each of which is economically significant in its own right. One of these conditions applies to the international market for goods and one applies to the international market for assets. We study these conditions in turn below.

THE INTERNATIONAL FLOW OF GOODS: INTERTEMPORAL EXTERNAL BALANCE

As discussed in Chapter 5, a country with positive net exports produces more goods than are purchased by its consumers, firms, and governments. The country's excess of output over spending equals its lending to other countries. In the future, the country will be paid back what it has lent with interest, which will allow it to spend more than it produces and have negative net exports.

Similarly, a country with negative net exports produces less output than is bought by domestic consumers, firms, and governments and, therefore, must borrow from abroad an amount equal to the excess of its spending over its output. Ultimately, the country must repay with interest the funds that it borrows from other countries. In order to repay foreign loans, countries with negative net exports today must at some point in the future achieve positive net exports.

The requirement that countries that have positive net exports and lend today have negative net exports in the future—and similarly, that countries that have negative net exports and borrow today have positive net exports in the future—is known as **intertemporal external balance**. (*External* refers to the flow of goods across international borders, and *intertemporal* emphasizes that the flow of goods between countries need not balance in every period but must balance over time.) Put simply, intertemporal external balance—or external balance, for short—says that no country can borrow abroad indefinitely without repaying and that no country would want to lend abroad indefinitely without being repaid.

To illustrate the concept of external balance, consider a numerical example with only two periods, the current period and the future period. Suppose that a country's current net exports NX are negative, equal to –100 home goods. To pay for this deficit, the country borrows in the international capital market at a real interest rate r of 8% per period. In the future period, the country must repay its international borrowing with interest, for a total repayment of 108 goods. Where will the country get the 108 goods it needs to repay its foreign debt? To obtain the 108 goods it needs, in the future period the country must spend 108 goods less than it produces so that its future net exports NX^f equals 108 goods.

In general, for a country to achieve external balance, its future net exports NX^f must equal $-(1 + r)NX$, where NX is current net exports and r is the real interest rate. (For simplicity, we continue to assume two periods.) In our example, $NX = -100$ and $r = 0.08$, so $NX^f = 108$, as we found. Alternatively, suppose that the country's current net exports were positive and equal to 100 home goods. With net exports of 100 goods, the country lends 100 goods abroad today. If the real interest rate is 0.08, the country will be repaid 108 goods in the future, which means that it will be able to have future net exports of –108 goods. This result is once again as implied by the formula $NX^f = -(1 + r)NX$.

Formally, we write the intertemporal external balance (IEB) condition as

$$NX(e,...) + \frac{NX^f(e^f,...)}{(1 + r)} = 0, \qquad (10.B.1)$$

which is a rearrangement of the condition that $NX^f = -(1 + r)NX$. In Eq. (10.B.1), e is the real exchange rate in the current period and e^f is the real exchange rate in the future period. The notations $NX(e,...)$ and $NX^f (e^f,...)$ emphasize that the country's net exports in each period depend on the real exchange rate in that period, as well as on other factors. (Those readers who covered Appendix 4.A will recognize that Eq. 10.B.1 requires the present value of net exports to equal zero.)

THE INTERTEMPORAL EXTERNAL BALANCE CURVE

The intertemporal external balance curve IEB in Figure 10.B.1 shows the combinations of the current real exchange rate e and the future real exchange rate

FIGURE 10.B.1

THE INTERTEMPORAL
EXTERNAL BALANCE
CURVE

The intertemporal external balance (IEB) condition requires that future net exports equal $-(1 + r)$ times current net exports. If we start at point A, which satisfies the IEB condition, an increase in the current real exchange rate from e_A to e_B causes a fall in current net exports. To restore external balance, future net exports must increase, which is achieved by a fall in the future real exchange rate from e^f_A to e^f_B. Thus, point B also satisfies the IEB condition. Since both point A and point B lie on the IEB curve, the IEB curve slopes downward.

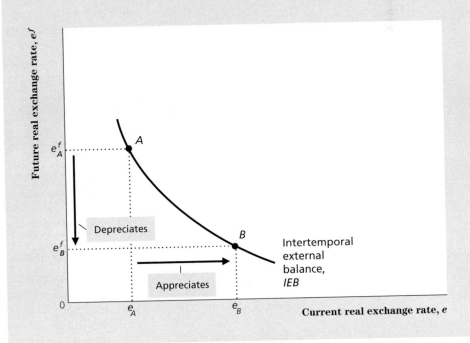

e^f that satisfy the external balance condition, Eq. (10.B.1). To understand why this relation slopes downward, suppose the economy starts with the combination of current and future real exchange rates represented by point a in Figure 10.B.1. The exchange rates at point A, e_A, and e^f_A, lie on the *IEB* curve and, thus, satisfy the external balance condition. Now, suppose that the current real exchange rate increases to e_B, a real appreciation. The real appreciation reduces the country's net exports in the current period. So that external balance is maintained and the country can repay foreign borrowings, lower net exports today must be offset by higher net exports in the future. This increase in future net exports can be achieved by real depreciation in the second period, or a decrease in the future real exchange rate to e^f_B. The new equilibrium combination of exchange rates, e_B and e^f_B, is represented by point B in Figure 10.B.1. Since points A and B both satisfy external balance, the *IEB* curve slopes downward.

In general, external balance requires that an increase in the current real exchange rate be offset by a decline in the expected future real exchange rate. Intuitively, a high real exchange rate today causes negative net exports today, so a low real exchange rate in the future is needed to allow net exports to be positive in the future. Thus, the *IEB* curve slopes downward, as shown in Figure 10.B.1.

FACTORS THAT SHIFT THE *IEB* CURVE

The *IEB* curve shows the combinations of current and future real exchange rates that lead to external balance. Factors other than real exchange rates that affect current net exports or future net exports will shift the *IEB* curve. We discuss three important *IEB* curve shifters: a change in domestic income, a change in foreign income, and shifts in demand.

1. *Domestic income.* Suppose that a country is initially in external balance. Now imagine that current income (output) increases. At the initial values of e and e^f the increase in income makes domestic consumers wealthier, leading them to spend more on all goods, including imported foreign goods, in both the current and future periods. The increase in imports reduces net exports in both periods so that the country is no longer in external balance. For external balance to be restored, either the current or future real exchange rate (or both) must fall. Thus, the increase in domestic income causes the *IEB* curve to shift downward.

2. *Foreign income.* The effect of an increase in foreign income on the *IEB* curve is just the opposite of the effect of an increase in domestic income. Because foreign consumers are made wealthier by the increase in income, they will buy more of the goods produced by the home country in the current period and in the future, which increases net exports by the home country in both periods. An appreciation of the current real exchange rate, or of the future real exchange rate, will reduce the net exports of the home country and restore external balance; so the *IEB* curve shifts upward.

3. *Shifts in demand.* A shift in demand away from foreign goods toward goods produced by the home country shifts the *IEB* curve upward, just as an increase in foreign income does. The reason is that like an increase in foreign income, a shift in demand toward domestic goods increases both current and

future net exports by the home country. For external balance to be restored, the current real exchange rate or the future real exchange rate must appreciate; so the *IEB* curve shifts upward.

The International Asset Market: Interest Rate Parity

Besides affecting the international flow of goods, the real exchange rate also plays a key role in international asset markets. We will see in this section that there is a close link between the expected behaviour of the exchange rate and the interest rates that are paid on assets in different countries.

Returns on Domestic and Foreign Assets

To illustrate the role of the real exchange rate in international asset markets, we again use a numerical example. Imagine that you want to invest $10,000 in a financial asset for one year, and suppose that you have limited your choice to either Canadian government bonds or German government bonds. Canadian government bonds are denominated in dollars and pay a nominal interest rate of 8% for one year (that is, $i = 0.08$). German government bonds, which are denominated in euros, pay a nominal interest rate of 6% for one year ($i_{For} = 0.06$). The two financial investments have comparable risk and liquidity. If you want to maximize your financial return, which bonds should you buy?

At first glance, the answer seems obvious: Buy the Canadian government bonds because they offer a higher interest rate. But this answer may not be right. The correct answer depends on what you think is going to happen to the exchange rate between the Canadian dollar and the euro over the next year.

We can compare the financial returns on the two assets by calculating the value in dollars one year from now of $10,000 invested in each asset. For the Canadian government bond the answer is easy. At a nominal interest rate of 8% per year, the bond will earn $800 in interest and will be worth $10,800 in one year. For the German bond, however, we must take into account that the $10,000 must first be converted into euros in order to buy the bond; then when the German bond matures in one year, the principal and interest (which will be in euros) must be converted back into dollars.

Table 10.B.1 illustrates the calculation of the future dollar value of the German bond, assuming that (1) the current nominal exchange rate e_{nom} is 0.7 euros per dollar, and that (2) the exchange rate is expected to depreciate by 3% over the coming year so that the expected future nominal exchange rate e^f_{nom} equals 0.679 euros per dollar (0.679 is 97% of 0.7). Converting $10,000 to euros at an exchange rate of 0.7 euros per dollar yields 7,000 euros (step 1 in Table 10.B.1), which are used to buy a German bond. At a 6% nominal interest rate the German bond earns 420 euros interest and is worth 7,420 euros at the end of one year (step 2). Finally, converting 7,420 euros to dollars at 0.679 euros per dollar yields $10,928 (step 3)—which is higher than the $10,800 that would be obtained from investing in a Canadian bond! Thus, the German bonds have a higher expected rate of return in this case, even though they pay a lower nominal interest rate.

TABLE 10.B.1

Calculating the Gross Nominal Rate of Return for a Foreign Asset

Example

Today: $e_{\text{nom}} = 0.7$ euros/dollar $i_{\text{For}} = 0.06$ *Future:* $e^f_{\text{nom}} = 0.679$ euros/dollar

Step 1	**Step 2**	**Step 3**
Convert home currency to foreign currency	Earn interest on foreign bond	Convert foreign currency to home currency
$10,000 → 7,000 euros	→ 7,420 euros	→ $10,928

General Case

Today   *Future*

Step 1	**Step 2**	**Step 3**
Convert home currency to foreign currency	Earn interest on foreign bond	Convert foreign currency to home currency
1 unit of → e_{nom} units of home currency foreign currency	$(1 + i_{\text{For}})e_{\text{nom}}$ units of foreign currency	→ $[(1 + i_{\text{For}})e_{\text{nom}}]/e^f_{\text{nom}}$ units of home currency

The German bonds have a higher rate of return in this example because, relative to the dollar asset, the German bonds have two sources of return. The first source is the nominal interest paid on the bonds ($i_{\text{For}} = 0.06$). The second source of return is the appreciation of the euro relative to the dollar. At the end of the year, when you convert your investment back into dollars, the value of a euro in terms of dollars is 3% higher than at the beginning of the year, when you converted your dollars into euros.

The gross nominal rate of return on an investment is the value at the end of the year (in terms of dollars) of one dollar invested at the beginning of the year. The gross nominal rate of return from investing in Canadian government bonds is $1 + i$, which is 1.08 in this example because each dollar invested in these bonds is worth $1.08 at the end of the year. The bottom section of Table 10.B.1 calculates the gross nominal rate of return on the German bond. One dollar will buy e_{nom} euros (step 1), which can be invested in a German bond at a nominal interest rate of i_{For} to yield $(1 + i_{\text{For}})\, e_{\text{nom}}$ euros at the end of a year (step 2). Converting the $(1 + i_{\text{For}})\, e_{\text{nom}}$ euros to dollars yields $(1 + i_{\text{For}})\, e_{\text{nom}} / e^f_{\text{nom}}$ dollars at the end of the year (step 3). Thus, the gross nominal rate of return from investing in the German government bond is

$$
\begin{aligned}
\text{gross nominal rate of} \atop \text{return on foreign bond} \quad &= (1 + i_{\text{For}})\frac{e_{\text{nom}}}{e^f_{\text{nom}}} \\
&= (1.06)\frac{(0.7 \text{ euros per dollar})}{0.679 \text{ euros per dollar}} \qquad (10.B.2)\\
&= 1.0928.
\end{aligned}
$$

With a gross nominal rate of return equal to 1.0928, a $10,000 investment grows to a value of $10,928 at the end of one year, just as we calculated previously.

Equation (10.B.2) is an exact expression for the gross nominal rate of return. A simple approximation ($\approx$) to the gross nominal rate of return is

$$\text{gross nominal rate of return on foreign bond} \approx 1 + i_{\text{For}} - \frac{\Delta e_{\text{nom}}}{e_{\text{nom}}} \quad \text{(10.B.3)}$$

In our example of the German government bond with $i_{\text{For}} = 0.06$ and $\Delta e_{\text{nom}}/e_{\text{nom}} = -0.03$, Eq. (10.B.3) indicates that the gross nominal rate of return from investing in the German government bond is approximately 1.09, which is very close of the exact value of 1.0928. The approximation in Eq. (10.B.3) permits easy calculation of the gross nominal return, generally without using pencil and paper (or a calculator). The other virtue of this approximation is that it makes clear the two sources of return from holding the German government bond: the interest on the bond i_{For}, and the nominal appreciation of the euro relative to the dollar over the course of the year, $-\Delta e_{\text{nom}}/e_{\text{nom}}$.

INTEREST RATE PARITY

In our example, the gross nominal rate of return expected on the German government bond exceeded the gross nominal rate of return on the Canadian government bond. However, if both types of government bonds have the same risk and liquidity, this difference in rates of return would not persist for long. If savers are free to choose between German bonds and Canadian bonds, they will choose the German bonds as long as they offer a higher gross nominal rate of return than Canadian bonds. But if investors choose German bonds in preference to Canadian bonds, the rate of return on German bonds will fall and the rate of return on Canadian bonds will increase until the two rates of return are equal.

In general, when the international asset market is in equilibrium, the gross nominal rates of return to domestic and foreign assets of comparable risk and liquidity must be the same. This equilibrium condition can be written as

$$\left(\frac{e_{\text{nom}}}{e^{f}_{\text{nom}}} \right) \left(1 + i_{\text{For}} \right) = 1 + i, \quad \text{(10.B.4)}$$

where the left side is the gross nominal rate of return on the foreign bond (Eq. 10.B.2) and the right side is the gross nominal rate of return on the domestic bond. The equilibrium condition in Eq. (10.B.4) is the nominal interest rate parity condition, which says that the nominal returns on foreign and domestic financial investments with equal risk and liquidity, when measured in a common currency, must be the same. (With the approximation in Eq. 10.B.3 the **nominal interest rate parity condition** can also be expressed more simply as $i_{\text{For}} - \Delta e_{\text{nom}}/e_{\text{nom}} \approx i$. According to this approximate formula for interest rate parity, the difference between nominal interest rates in two countries equals the rate at which the currency of the country with the higher nominal interest rate is expected to depreciate.)

Interest rate parity can also be expressed in terms of real interest rates and real exchange rates as the **real interest rate parity condition**:

$$\left(\frac{e}{e^f}\right)\left(1 + r_{\text{For}}\right) = 1 + r, \tag{10.B.5}$$

where r_{For} is the foreign real interest rate, r is the domestic real interest rate, and e and e^f are the current and future real exchange rates. The real interest rate parity condition, Eq. (10.B.5), is identical to the nominal interest parity condition, Eq. (10.B.4), except that the nominal interest and exchange rates in Eq. (10.B.4) are replaced by real interest and exchange rates in Eq. (10.B.5).

Note that real interest rate parity does not require that the domestic real interest rate r and the foreign real interest rate r_{For} be equal. The two real interest rates are not directly comparable, since r is measured in terms of the domestic good and r_{For} is measured in terms of the foreign good. Instead, real interest rate parity requires that the real returns on domestic and foreign assets be equal when real returns are measured in terms of the same good. (If there is only one good, as we assumed in Chapter 5, then $e = e^f = 1$, and Eq. 10.B.5 reduces to $r_{\text{For}} = r$.)

The Interest Rate Parity Line

Like the intertemporal external balance condition in the international goods market, the real interest rate parity condition in the international asset market can be shown graphically as a relationship between the current and future real exchange rates, e and e^f. To write the real interest rate parity condition in a form that is easily graphed, we multiply both sides of Eq. (10.B.5) by e^f and then divide both sides by $1 + r$, to obtain

$$e^f = \left[\frac{(1 + r_{\text{For}})}{(1 + r)}\right] e. \tag{10.B.6}$$

Figure 10.B.2

Real interest rate parity

According to the real interest rate parity (*IRP*) condition, the future real exchange rate is proportional to the current real exchange rate. Specifically, the future real exchange rate equals the current real exchange rate multiplied by $(1 + r_{\text{For}})/(1 + r)$, so that $(1 + r_{\text{For}})/(1 + r)$ is the slope of the *IRP* line.

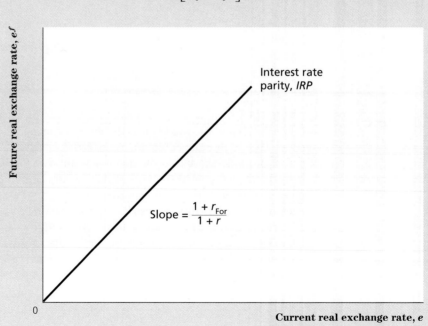

Equation (10.B.6) shows that the future real exchange rate e^f is proportional to the current real exchange rate e if the domestic and foreign real interest rates are held constant. Equation (10.B.6) also shows that if the foreign real interest rate is greater than the domestic real interest rate, then the future real exchange rate must exceed the current real exchange rate. The reason is that no financial investor will hold domestic assets paying a lower real return than is available on foreign assets unless a real appreciation of the domestic exchange rate is expected. Similarly, if the real return on foreign assets is lower than the real return on domestic assets, a real depreciation must be expected. An expected real depreciation implies that the future real exchange rate is lower than the current real exchange rate.

Figure 10.B.2 graphs the real interest rate parity (*IRP*) condition in Eq. (10.B.6). Given values of r and r_{For}, the *IRP* line relates the expected future real exchange rate e^f to the current real exchange rate e. Because the future real exchange rate e^f is proportional to the current real exchange rate e, the *IRP* line is a straight line through the origin.

FACTORS THAT SHIFT THE *IRP* LINE

The position of the *IRP* line depends on only two factors: the domestic real interest rate r and the foreign real interest rate r_{For}. As you can see in Eq. (10.B.6), the slope of the *IRP* line is $(1 + r_{For})/(1 + r)$. So, if we are given the values of r and r_{For}, the *IRP* line is completely determined.

A fall in the foreign real interest rate r_{For} or a rise in the domestic real interest rate r reduces the slope of the *IRP* line, $(1 + r_{For})/(1 + r)$, thus causing the *IRP* line to pivot clockwise (see Figure 10.B.3). A decline in the real rate of return

FIGURE 10.B.3

THE *IRP* LINE WHEN
INTEREST RATES CHANGE

Either an increase in the domestic real interest rate r or a decrease in the foreign real interest rate r_{For} makes domestic bonds more attractive than foreign bonds. To be willing to hold foreign bonds, financial investors must expect the domestic currency to depreciate. For a given value of the real exchange rate e, therefore, the future real exchange rate e^f must fall, and the *IRP* line pivots clockwise. Equivalently, an increase in the domestic real interest rate r or a decrease in the foreign real interest rate r_{For} reduces the slope of the *IRP* line, $(1 + r_{For})/(1 + r)$, resulting in the rotation of the *IRP* line from IRP^1 to IRP^2.

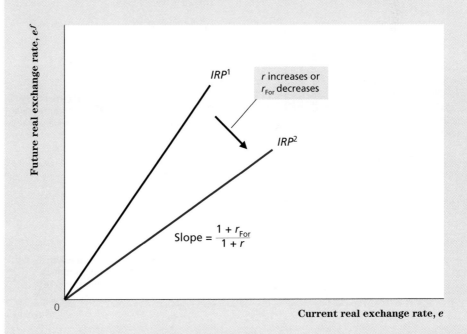

on the foreign asset relative to the domestic asset is possible only if financial investors expect the domestic real exchange rate to depreciate. Thus, for any given current real exchange rate e, the future real exchange rate e^f must fall, which causes the IRP line to pivot clockwise. Similarly, a rise in the real return on foreign assets relative to the real return on domestic assets would increase the slope of the IRP line and cause it to pivot counterclockwise.

THE DETERMINATION OF THE REAL EXCHANGE RATE

In the previous two sections, we focused on the role of real exchange rates in the international markets for goods and assets. We derived and discussed two equilibrium conditions, the intertemporal external balance (IEB) condition in the goods market and the real interest rate parity (IRP) condition in the asset market. In this section, we put these two conditions together to discuss the determinants of real exchange rates.

The determination of the current and future real exchange rates is shown in Figure 10.B.4, which graphs both the intertemporal external balance (IEB) curve and the interest rate parity (IRP) line. As you can see in the figure, the only combination of e and e^f that simultaneously satisfies both the intertemporal external balance condition and the real interest rate parity condition is represented by point E, the intersection of the IEB curve and the IRP line. The values of the current and future real exchange rates that correspond to point E are the values that will occur in equilibrium.

Using the diagram in Figure 10.B.4, we can examine the factors that influence real exchange rates. As an aid to intuition, it is helpful to keep in mind that the real

FIGURE 10.B.4

EQUILIBRIUM OF REAL
EXCHANGE RATES

Equilibrium in the international market for goods requires that the IEB condition hold, and equilibrium in the international market for assets requires that the IRP condition hold. The only combination of current and future real exchange rates that satisfies both conditions is located at point E, the intersection of the IEB curve and the IRP line.

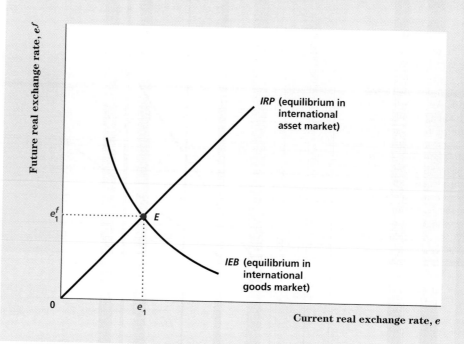

value of a currency, say the Canadian dollar, depends on supplies and demands in the foreign exchange market. When foreigners want to buy Canadian goods or assets, they must trade their own currency for dollars (they demand dollars in the foreign exchange market); and when Canadians want to buy foreign goods or assets, they must trade dollars for foreign currencies (they supply dollars to the foreign exchange market). Thus, factors that make Canadian goods or assets more attractive to foreigners raise the demand for dollars and increase the real value of the dollar (the real exchange rate). Likewise, factors that make foreign goods or assets more attractive to Canadians increase the supply of dollars and thus reduce the real value of the dollar.

FACTORS THAT CHANGE THE REAL EXCHANGE RATE

Any factor that shifts the IEB curve or the IRP line will change the equilibrium combination of current and future real exchange rates.

1. *Domestic income (output).* An increase in domestic income raises the home country's demand for foreign goods. To buy foreign goods, domestic residents supply their own currency to the foreign exchange market, which—by the intuitive argument suggested above—lowers the real exchange rate. In terms of the IEB–IRP diagram (Figure 10.B.5), if we start from an initial equilibrium at point E, an increase in domestic income raises imports by the home country and causes the IEB curve to shift downward, from IEB^1 to IEB^2. The interest rate parity line is unaffected by the change in domestic income. At the new equilibrium, point F, both the current and the future real exchange rates have fallen. The fall in the current and future real exchange rates restores external balance while maintaining interest rate parity.

FIGURE 10.B.5

REAL EXCHANGE RATES
WHEN DOMESTIC
INCOME INCREASES

At the initial exchange rates at point E, an increase in domestic income raises the domestic demand for imported goods and thus reduces current and future net exports. For external balance to be restored, real exchange rates must fall; so the IEB curve shifts downward, from IEB^1 to IEB^2. The interest rate parity (IRP) line is unaffected by the change in domestic income. Thus, the increase in domestic income shifts the equilibrium from point E to point F. The current and future exchange rates both fall (from e_1 to e_2 and e^f_1 to e^f_2, respectively).

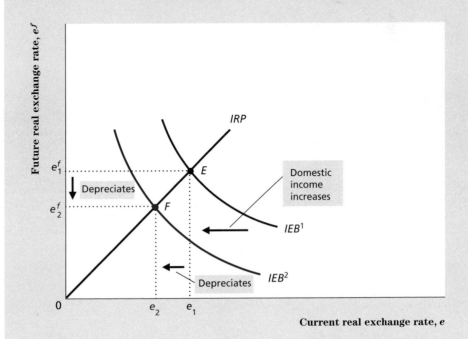

2. *Foreign income (output).* An increase in foreign income has exactly the opposite effect of an increase in domestic income. Intuitively, higher foreign income increases the demand for home country exports, raises the demand for the home country's currency, and, thus, causes the real exchange rate to rise. In terms of Figure 10.B.6, an increase in foreign income shifts the *IEB* curve upward, from IEB^1 to IEB^2. The *IRP* line is not affected by the change in foreign income. At point *F*, the new equilibrium, the values of the current and future real exchange rates both increase. The higher real exchange rates restore external balance in a way that is consistent with interest rate parity. Again, note that the effects of the increase in foreign income are just the opposite of the effects of an increase in the home country's income.

3. *Shifts in demand.* A shift in demand toward the goods produced by the home country increases the demand for the home country's currency and, thus, raises the real exchange rate. In terms of the *IEB–IRP* diagram, a shift in demand toward the home country's exports causes the *IEB* curve to move upward. The *IRP* line is not affected by the shift in the demand for goods. Figure 10.B.6, which was introduced to illustrate the effects of an increase in foreign income, applies to the shift in demand toward home goods as well. As a result of the shift in demand toward the goods produced by the home country, both the current and future equilibrium values of the real exchange rate increase.

4. *The domestic real interest rate.* An increase in the domestic real interest rate makes domestic assets more attractive, which increases the demand for the home country's currency and thus causes the current real exchange rate to

FIGURE 10.B.6

REAL EXCHANGE RATES WHEN FOREIGN INCOME INCREASES

At the initial combination of real exchange rates at point *E*, either an increase in foreign income or a shift in demand toward the domestic good increases net exports. For net exports to be reduced and for external balance to be restored, real exchange rates must rise. Therefore, the *IEB* curve shifts upward, from IEB^1 to IEB^2. The *IRP* line is unaffected by an increase in foreign income or a shift in demand toward the domestic good. Thus, the current and real exchange rates both rise (from e_1 to e_2 and e_1^f to e_2^f respectively), as shown by the shift from point *E* to point *F*, where IEB^2 intersects *IRP*.

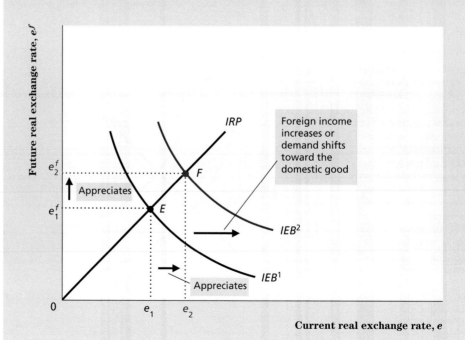

appreciate. Diagrammatically, an increase in the domestic real interest rate reduces the slope of the *IRP* line and causes it to pivot clockwise, from *IRP*^{1} to *IRP*^{2} in Figure 10.B.7. The *IEB* curve is unaffected by the change in the domestic real interest rate. (To say that the domestic real interest rate does not affect the *IEB* curve is not quite accurate, since the real interest rate r does appear in the external balance condition, Eq. (10.B.1). A change in r has no effect on the *IEB* curve at the point at which exports equal imports in both periods ($NX = NX^f = 0$), and the effect is small at points at which exports and imports in each period are close to being in balance. Since allowing for an effect of the domestic real interest rate on the *IEB* curve does not significantly affect our results, for simplicity we ignore this effect.) Therefore, the equilibrium moves from point E to point F, where *IEB* intersects *IRP*^{2}. The result of an increase in the domestic real interest rate is a rise in the current real exchange rate and a fall in the future real exchange rate, or a larger expected rate of exchange rate depreciation. Since the domestic real interest rate has increased, the larger expected depreciation is needed to make financial investors willing to hold foreign assets.

5. *The foreign real interest rate.* An increase in the foreign real interest rate has the opposite effects of an increase in the domestic real interest rate. As you can verify, an increase in the foreign real interest rate (by rotating the *IRP* line counterclockwise and leaving the *IEB* curve unaffected) lowers the current real exchange rate and raises the future real exchange rate. Intuitively, the fall in the current real exchange rate occurs because the rise in the foreign real interest rate makes foreign assets more attractive.

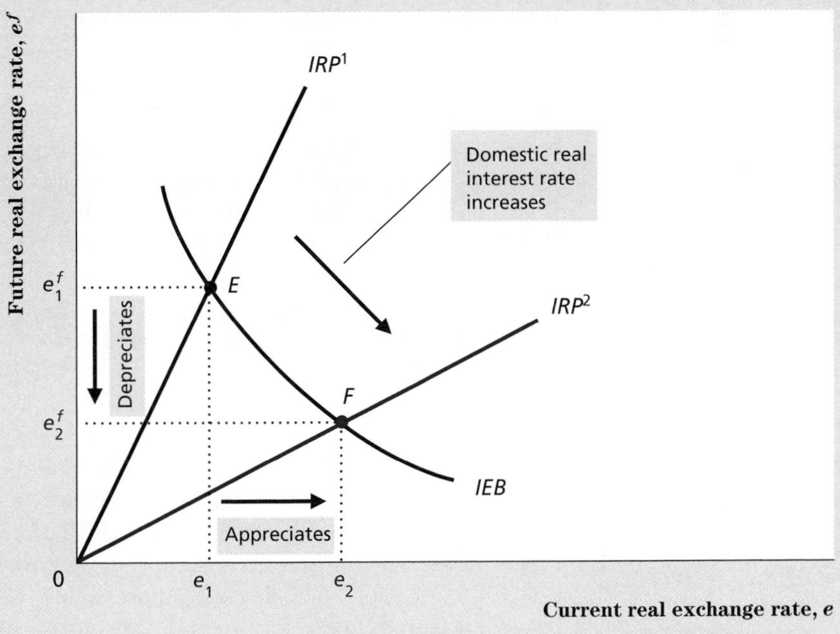

FIGURE 10.B.7

REAL EXCHANGE RATES
WHEN THE DOMESTIC
REAL INTEREST RATE
INCREASES

If we start from an initial equilibrium at point *E*, an increase in the domestic real interest rate makes domestic assets more attractive than foreign assets. As foreigners acquire domestic currency to buy domestic assets, the current real exchange rate rises. In the new international asset market equilibrium, the current real exchange rate has increased relative to the future real exchange rate, as shown by the clockwise rotation of the *IRP* line from *IRP*^{1} to *IRP*^{2}. The *IEB* curve is unaffected by the change in the real interest rate. At the new equi-librium at point *F*, the current real exchange rate has risen from e_1 to e_2 (an appreciation) and the future real exchange rate has fallen from e_1^f to e_2^f.

Chapter 11

CLASSICAL BUSINESS CYCLE ANALYSIS: MARKET-CLEARING MACROECONOMICS

Economists generally agree about the basic business cycle facts outlined in Chapter 8. They know that economic growth is not necessarily smooth and that occasionally there are periods of recession in which output declines and unemployment rises. They know that recessions typically are followed by periods of recovery, in which the economy grows more strongly than normal. And they also know a great deal about how other macroeconomic variables—such as productivity, interest rates, and inflation—behave during recessions.

Recall that recessions and booms in the economy raise two basic questions: (1) What are the underlying economic causes of these business cycles? (2) What, if anything, should government policymakers do about them? Unfortunately, economists agree less about the answers to these two questions than about the basic business cycle facts.

The main disagreements about the causes and cures of recessions are between two broad groups of macroeconomists, the classicals and the Keynesians. As discussed first in Chapter 1 and again in Chapters 8 and 9, classicals and Keynesians—although agreeing on many points—differ primarily in their views on how rapidly prices and wages adjust to restore general equilibrium after an economic shock. Classical macroeconomists assume that prices and wages adjust quickly to equate quantities supplied and demanded in each market; as a result, they argue, a market economy is largely "self-correcting," with a strong tendency to return to general equilibrium on its own when it is disturbed by an economic shock or a change in public policy. Keynesians usually agree that prices and wages *eventually* change as needed to clear markets; however, they believe that *in the short run* price and wage adjustment is likely to be incomplete. That is, in the short run, quantities supplied and demanded need not be equal and the economy may remain out of general equilibrium. Although this difference in views may seem purely theoretical, it has a practical implication: Because Keynesians are sceptical about the economy's ability to reach equilibrium rapidly on its own, they are more inclined than are classicals to recommend that the government act to raise output and employment during recessions and to moderate economic growth during booms.

In this chapter and Chapter 12, we develop and compare the classical and Keynesian theories of the business cycle and the policy recommendations of the two groups, beginning with the classical perspective in this chapter. Conveniently, both the classical and Keynesian analyses can be expressed in terms of a common analytical framework, the *IS–LM/AD–AS* model. In this chapter, we use the classical (or market-clearing) version of the *IS–LM/AD–AS* model, comprising the *IS–LM/AD–AS* model and the assumption that prices and wages adjust rapidly. The assumption that prices and wages adjust rapidly implies that the economy always is in or near general equilibrium and, therefore, that such variables as output and employment are always close to their general equilibrium levels.

In comparing the principal competing theories of the business cycle, we are particularly interested in how well the various theories explain the business cycle facts. The classical theory is consistent with many of the most important facts about the cycle. However, one business cycle fact that challenges the classical theory is the observation that changes in the money stock lead the cycle. Recall the implication of the classical assumption that wages and prices adjust quickly to clear markets: Money is neutral so that changes in the money supply do not affect output and other real variables. However, most economists interpret the fact that money leads the cycle as evidence that money is *not* neutral in all situations. If money is *not* neutral, we must either modify the basic classical model to account for monetary non-neutrality or abandon the classical model in favour of alternative theories (such as the Keynesian approach) that are consistent with non-neutrality. In Section 11.3, we extend the classical model to allow for non-neutrality of money. We then examine the implications of this extended classical approach for macroeconomic policy.

11.1 BUSINESS CYCLES IN THE CLASSICAL MODEL

We have identified two basic questions of business cycle analysis: What causes business cycles? What can (or should) be done about them? Let us examine the classical answers to these questions, beginning with what causes business cycles.

THE REAL BUSINESS CYCLE THEORY

In general, a complete theory of the business cycle must have two components. The first component is a description of the types of shocks or disturbances believed to affect the economy the most. Examples of economic disturbances emphasized by various theories of the business cycle include supply shocks, changes in monetary or fiscal policy, and changes in consumer spending. The second component is a model that describes how key macroeconomic variables, such as output, employment, and prices, respond to economic shocks. The model preferred by classical economists is the market-clearing version of the *IS–LM* model or some similar framework. However, the issue of which shocks are crucial in driving cyclical fluctuations remains.

An influential group of classical macroeconomists developed a theory that takes a strong stand on the sources of shocks that cause cyclical fluctuations. This theory, the **real business cycle theory** (or RBC theory), argues that real shocks to the economy are the primary cause of business cycles.[1] **Real shocks** are disturbances to the "real side" of the economy, such as shocks that affect the production function, the size of the labour force, the real quantity of government purchases, and the spending and saving decisions of consumers. Economists contrast real shocks with **nominal shocks**, or shocks to money supply or money demand. In terms of the *IS–LM* model, real shocks directly affect only the *IS* curve or the *FE* line, whereas nominal shocks directly affect only the LM curve.

Although many types of real shocks could contribute to the business cycle, RBC theorists give the largest role to production function shocks—what we have called

---

1.   For a more detailed introduction to real business cycles, see Charles Plosser, "Understanding Real Business Cycles," *Journal of Economic Perspectives*, Summer 1989, pp. 51–78. The original research is described by Finn E. Kydland and Edward C. Prescott, "Time to Build and Aggregate Fluctuations," *Econometrica*, November 1982, pp. 1345–1370, and John B. Long and Charles I. Plosser, "Real Business Cycles," *Journal of Political Economy*, February 1983, pp. 39–69.

supply shocks and what the RBC theorists usually refer to as **productivity shocks**. Productivity shocks include the development of new products or production methods, the introduction of new management techniques, changes in the quality of capital or labour, changes in the availability of raw materials or energy, unusually good or unusually bad weather, changes in government regulations affecting production, and any other factor affecting productivity. According to RBC theorists, most economic booms result from beneficial productivity shocks, and most recessions are caused by adverse productivity shocks.

The Recessionary Impact of an Adverse Productivity Shock

Does the RBC theorists' idea that adverse productivity shocks lead to recessions (and, similarly, that beneficial productivity shocks lead to booms) make sense? We examined the theoretical effects on the economy of a temporary adverse productivity shock in Chapters 3, 8, and 9.[2] In Chapter 3, we showed that an adverse productivity shock (or supply shock), such as an increase in the price of oil, reduces the marginal product of labour (MPN) and the demand for labour at any real wage. As a result, the equilibrium values of the real wage and employment both fall (see Figure 3.12). The equilibrium level of output (the full-employment level of output $\overline{Y}$) also falls, both because equilibrium employment declines and because the adverse productivity shock reduces the amount of output that can be produced by any amount of capital and labour.

We later used the complete *IS–LM* model (see Figure 9.8) to explore the general equilibrium effects of a temporary adverse productivity shock. We confirmed our earlier conclusion that an adverse productivity shock lowers the general equilibrium levels of the real wage, employment, and output. In addition, we showed that an adverse productivity shock raises the real interest rate, depresses consumption and investment, and raises the price level.

Broadly, then, our earlier analyses of the effects of an adverse productivity shock support the RBC theorists' claim that such shocks are recessionary in that they lead to declines in output. Similar analyses show that a beneficial productivity shock leads to a rise in output (a boom). Note that in the RBC approach, output declines in recessions and rises in booms because the general equilibrium (or full-employment) level of output has changed and because rapid price adjustment ensures that actual output always equals full-employment output. As classical economists, RBC theorists would reject the Keynesian view (discussed in Chapter 12) that recessions and booms are periods of disequilibrium, during which actual output is below or above its general equilibrium level for a protracted period of time.

Real Business Cycle Theory and the Business Cycle Facts

Although the RBC theory—which combines the classical, or market-clearing, version of the *IS–LM* model with the assumption that productivity shocks are the dominant form of economic disturbance—is relatively simple, it is consistent with many of the basic business cycle facts. First, under the assumption that the economy is being continuously buffeted by productivity shocks, the RBC approach predicts recurrent fluctuations in aggregate output, which actually occur. Second, the RBC theory correctly predicts that employment will move procyclically—that is, in the same direction as output. Third, the RBC theory predicts that real wages will be higher during booms than during recessions (procyclical real wages), as also occurs.

---

2. RBC theorists analyze permanent as well as temporary productivity shocks; we focus on temporary shocks because it is the slightly easier case.

A fourth business cycle fact explained by the RBC theory is that average labour productivity is procyclical; that is, output per worker is higher during booms than during recessions. This fact is consistent with the RBC theorists' assumption that booms are periods of beneficial productivity shocks, which tend to raise labour productivity, whereas recessions are the results of adverse productivity shocks, which tend to reduce labour productivity. The RBC theorists point out that without productivity shocks—allowing the production function to remain stable over time— average labour productivity would not be procyclical. With no productivity shocks, the expansion of employment that occurs during booms would tend to reduce average labour productivity because of the principle of diminishing marginal productivity of labour. Similarly, without productivity shocks, recessions would be periods of relatively higher labour productivity instead of lower productivity, as observed. Thus, RBC theorists regard the procyclical nature of average labour productivity as strong evidence supporting their approach.

Macroeconomists also try to explain facts about international business cycles. One such fact is that saving and investment tend to move together closely in most countries even though (as we saw in Chapter 5) they need not be equal in an open economy.[3] Real business cycle theorists have had some success in accounting for this fact by showing that productivity shocks in many countries also tend to move together. For example, if two countries both experience a favourable productivity shock then saving and investment will increase in both countries and hence will tend to move together country-by-country. Recall from Chapter 5 that the current account is equal to the difference between saving and investment, so we can think of this approach as trying to explain the behaviour of the current account over the business cycle. For example, Enrique Mendoza, of Duke University, showed that a model of a small open economy that experiences shocks to productivity, foreign prices, and foreign interest rates can produce current account behaviour similar to that of the postwar Canadian economy.[4] Researchers also use international real business cycle models to account for the similarities in movements in consumption and output across countries.[5]

A business cycle fact that does *not* seem to be consistent with the simple RBC theory is that inflation tends to slow during or immediately after a recession. The theory predicts that an adverse productivity shock will both cause a recession and increase the general price level. Thus, according to the RBC approach, periods of recession should also be periods of inflation, contrary to the business cycle fact.

Some RBC theorists have responded by taking issue with the conventional view that inflation is procyclical. The evidence has been examined by R. Todd Smith, of the University of Alberta, who studied a century of prices in 10 industrialized countries, including Canada.[6] Smith found that the price level in most countries has been countercyclical since World War II and that this conclusion holds for various ways of measuring business cycles.

The standard view that the price level and inflation are procyclical does seem to hold for the period before World War II, and especially during the Great Depression,

3. See Martin Feldstein and Charles Horioka, "Domestic Saving and International Capital Flows," *Economic Journal*, June 1980, pp. 314–329.

4. "Real Business Cycles in a Small Open Economy," *American Economic Review*, September 1991, pp. 797–818.

5. See David K. Backus, Patrick J. Kehoe, and Finn E. Kydland, "International Real Business Cycles," *Journal of Political Economy*, August 1992, pp. 745–775.

6. "The Cyclical Behavior of Prices," *Journal of Money, Credit, and Banking*, November 1992, pp. 413–430. See also John Judd and Bharat Trehan, "The Cyclical Behavior of Prices: Interpreting the Evidence," *Journal of Money, Credit, and Banking*, August 1995, pp. 789–797.

when the world economy had a different structure and was subject to different types of shocks than in more recent history. The fact that inflation surged following the oil price shocks of 1973–1974 and 1979–1980 is consistent with the prediction of the RBC theory. The issue of the cyclical behaviour of prices remains controversial, however.[7]

APPLICATION

CALIBRATING THE BUSINESS CYCLE

If we put aside the debate about price level behaviour, the RBC theory can account for some of the business cycle facts, including the procyclical behaviour of employment, productivity, and real wages. However, real business cycle theorists argue that an adequate theory of the business cycle should be *quantitative* as well as *qualitative*. In other words, in addition to predicting generally how key macroeconomic variables move throughout the business cycle, the theory should predict numerically the size of economic fluctuations and the strength of relationships among the variables.

To examine the quantitative implications of their theories, RBC theorists developed a method called *calibration*. The idea is to work out a detailed numerical example of a more general theory. The results are then compared to observations to see whether model and reality broadly agree.

The first step in calibration is to write a simple classical model of the economy—such as the classical version of the *IS–LM* model—except that specific functions replace general functions. For example, instead of representing the production function in general terms as

$$Y = AF(K, N),$$

the person doing the calibration uses a specific algebraic form for the production function, such as[8]

$$Y = AK^a N^{1-a},$$

where a is a number between 0 and 1. Similarly, specific functions are used to describe the behaviour of consumers and workers.

Next, the specific functions chosen are made even more specific by expressing them in numerical terms. For example, for $a = 0.3$, the production function becomes

$$Y = AK^{0.3} N^{0.7}.$$

In the same way, specific numbers are assigned to the functions describing the behaviour of consumers and workers. Where do these numbers come from? Generally, they are *not* estimated from macroeconomic data but are based on other sources. For example, the numbers assigned to the functions in the model may come from previous studies of the production function or of the saving behaviour of individuals and families.

---

7. Another RBC response to this criticism is to note that in reality the money supply is not literally fixed, as we assumed in our analysis of the effects of a productivity shock in Chapter 9. To the extent that the money supply declines in recessions, the tendency for prices to rise will be less.

8. This production function is the Cobb–Douglas production function (see Chapter 3). As we noted, although it is relatively simple, it fits data quite well.

The third step, which must be carried out on a computer, is to find out how the numerically specified model behaves when it is hit by random shocks, such as productivity shocks. The shocks are created on the computer with a random number generator, with the size and persistence of the shocks (unlike the numbers assigned to the specific functions) being chosen to fit the actual macroeconomic data. For these shocks, the computer tracks the behaviour of the model over many periods and reports the implied behaviour of key macroeconomic variables, such as output, employment, consumption, and investment. The results are then compared with the behaviour of the actual economy to determine how well the model fits reality.

One of the developers of RBC theory, Edward Prescott,[9] of the University of Minnesota, performed an early and influential calibration exercise. Prescott used a model similar to the RBC model we present here, the main difference being that our version of the RBC model is essentially a two-period model (the present and the future), and Prescott's model allowed for many periods. The results of Prescott's computer simulations are shown in Figures 11.1 and 11.2.

Figure 11.1 compares the actually observed volatilities of six macroeconomic variables, as calculated from post–World War II US data, with the volatilities predicted by Prescott's calibrated RBC model.[10] Prescott set the size of the random productivity

---

9. "Theory Ahead of Business Cycle Measurement," *Carnegie-Rochester Conference Series on Public Policy*, Volume 25, Autumn 1986, pp. 11–39. Reprinted in *Quarterly Review*, Federal Reserve Bank of Minneapolis, Fall 1986, pp. 9–22.
10. The measure of volatility used is called the *standard deviation*. The higher the standard deviation, the more volatile is the variable being measured.

FIGURE 11.1

ACTUAL VERSUS SIMULATED
VOLATILITIES OF KEY
MACROECONOMIC
VARIABLES

The figure compares the actual volatilities of key macroeconomic variables observed in post–World War II US data with the volatilities of the same variables predicted by computer simulations of Edward Prescott's calibrated RBC model. Prescott set the size of the random productivity shocks in his simulations so that the simulated volatility of GNP would match the actually observed volatility of GNP exactly. For these random productivity shocks, the simulated volatilities of the other five macroeconomic variables (with the possible exception of consumption) match the observed volatilities fairly well.

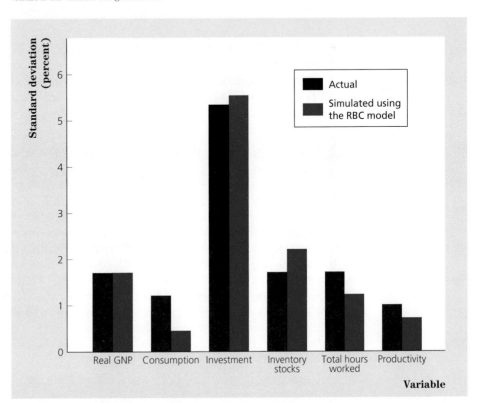

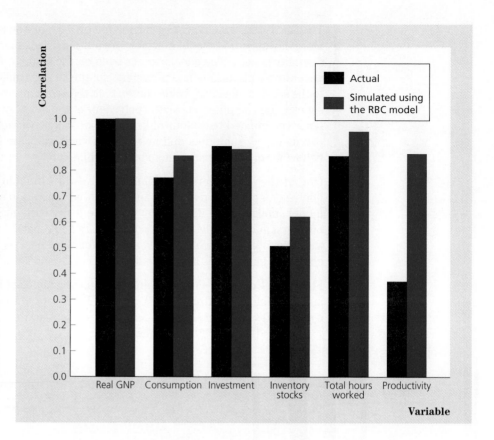

FIGURE 11.2

ACTUAL VERSUS SIMULATED
CORRELATIONS OF KEY
MACROECONOMIC
VARIABLES WITH GNP

How closely a variable moves with GNP over the business cycle is measured by its correlation with GNP, with higher correlations implying a closer relationship. The figure compares the correlations of key variables with GNP that were actually observed in the post–World War II US economy with the correlations predicted by computer simulations of Prescott's calibrated RBC model. Except for productivity, whose predicted correlation with GNP is too high, the simulations predicted correlations of macroeconomic variables with GNP that closely resemble the actual correlations of these variables with GNP.

shocks in his simulations so that the volatility of GNP in his model would match the actual volatility in US GNP.[11] That choice explains why the actual and simulated volatilities of GNP are equal in Figure 11.1. But he did nothing to guarantee that the simulation would match the actual volatilities of the other five variables. Note, however, that the simulated and actual volatilities for the other variables in most cases are quite close.

Figure 11.2 compares the actual economy with Prescott's calibrated model in another respect: how closely important macroeconomic variables move with GNP over the business cycle. The statistical measure of how closely variables move together is called *correlation*. If a variable's correlation with GNP is positive, the variable tends to move in the same direction as GNP over the business cycle (that is, the variable is procyclical). A correlation with GNP of 1.0 indicates that the variable's movements track the movements of GNP perfectly (thus, the correlation of GNP with itself is 1.0), and a correlation with GNP of 0 indicates no relationship to GNP. Correlations with GNP between 0 and 1.0 reflect relationships with GNP of intermediate strength. Figure 11.2 shows that Prescott's model generally accounts well for the strength of the relationships between some of the variables and GNP, although the correlation of productivity and GNP predicted by Prescott's model is noticeably larger than the actual correlation.

---

11. At the time of Prescott's study, the national income and product accounts of the US focused on GNP rather than GDP, so Prescott also focused on GNP.

> The degree to which relatively simple calibrated RBC models can match the actual data is impressive. In addition, the results of calibration exercises help guide further development of the model. For example, the version of the RBC model discussed here has been modified to improve the match between the actual and predicted correlations of productivity with GNP.

Are Productivity Shocks the Only Source of Recessions?

Although RBC theorists agree, in principle, that many types of real shocks buffet the economy, in practice much of their work rests on the assumption that productivity shocks are the dominant, or even the only, source of recessions. Many economists, including both classicals and Keynesians, have criticized this assumption as being unrealistic. For example, some economists challenged the RBC theorists to identify the specific productivity shocks that they believe caused each of the recessions since World War II. The critics argue that except for the oil price shocks of 1973, 1979, and 1990, historical examples of economywide productivity shocks are virtually nonexistent.

An interesting RBC response to that argument is that, in principle, economywide fluctuations could also be caused by the cumulative effects of a series of small productivity shocks. Moreover, the effects of shocks can persist as the economy adjusts to them. For example, Chapter 6 showed that a beneficial productivity shock leads to an increase in the capital–labour ratio in the neoclassical growth model. This capital accumulation propagates shocks in RBC models.

To illustrate the point that small shocks can cause large fluctuations, Figure 11.3 shows the results of a computer simulation of productivity shocks and the associated behaviour of output for a simplified RBC model. In this simple RBC model, the change in output from one month to the next has two parts: (1) a fixed part that arises from normal technical progress or from a normal increase in population and employment; and (2) an unpredictable part that reflects a random shock to productivity during the current month.[12] The random, computer-generated productivity shocks are shown at the bottom of Figure 11.3, and the implied behaviour of output is displayed above them. Although none of the individual shocks is large, the cumulative effect of the shocks causes large fluctuations in output that look something like business cycles. Hence business cycles may be the result of productivity shocks, even though identifying specific, large shocks is difficult.

Does the Solow Residual Measure Technology Shocks?

Because productivity shocks are the primary source of business cycle fluctuations in RBC models, RBC theorists have attempted to measure the size of these shocks. The most common measure of productivity shocks is known as the **Solow residual**, which is an empirical measure of total factor productivity, A. The Solow residual is named after the originator of modern growth theory Robert Solow, who used this measure in the 1950s.[13]

---

12. Specifically, the model is $Y_t = Y_{t-1} + 0.01 + e_t$, where Y_t is output in month t, Y_{t-1} is output in the previous month, and e_t is the random productivity shock in month t. The productivity shocks are randomly chosen numbers between -1.0 and 1.0. A similar example is given in Numerical Problem 6 at the end of this chapter.

13. "Technical Change and the Aggregate Production Function," *Review of Economics and Statistics*, 1957, pp. 312–320. In Chapter 6, we described Solow's contributions to growth theory.

FIGURE 11.3

SMALL SHOCKS AND LARGE
CYCLES

A computer simulation of a
simple RBC model is used to
find the relationship between
computer-generated random
productivity shocks (shown at
the bottom of the figure) and
aggregate output (shown in the
middle of the figure). Even
though all the productivity
shocks are small, the simulation produces large cyclical
fluctuations in aggregate output. Thus, large productivity
shocks are not necessary to
generate large cyclical fluctuations.

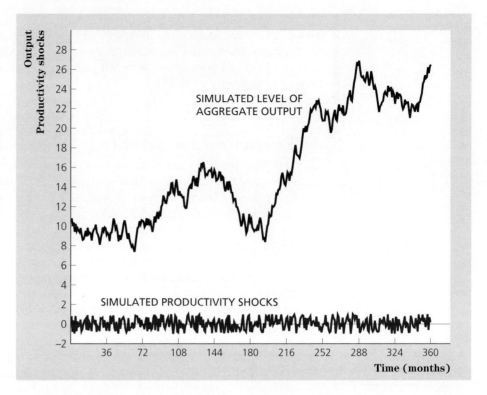

Recall from Chapter 3 that to measure total factor productivity A, we need data on output, Y, and the inputs of capital, K, and labour, N. In addition, we need to use a specific algebraic form for the production function, such as $Y = AK^a N^{1-a}$. We then compute the value of the productivity parameter, A, also known as the Solow residual, as

$$\text{Solow residual} = \frac{Y}{K^a N^{1-a}} = A. \qquad (11.1)$$

The Solow residual is called a "residual" because it is the part of output that cannot be directly explained by measured capital and labour inputs.

When the Solow residual is computed from actual data, using Eq. (11.1), it turns out to be strongly procyclical, rising in economic expansions and falling in recessions. Figure 11.4 shows Canadian and US Solow residuals from 1980 to 2000. Note that the Canadian residuals fell sharply during the recessions of 1981–1982 and 1990–1992. This procyclical behaviour is consistent with the premise of RBC theory that cyclical fluctuations in aggregate output are driven largely by productivity shocks.

Recently, however, some economists have questioned whether the Solow residual should be interpreted solely as a measure of technology, as RBC proponents tend to do. If changes in the Solow residual reflect only changes in the technologies available to an economy, it should be unrelated to such factors as government purchases or monetary policy that do not directly affect scientific and technological progress (at least in the short run). However, statistical studies reveal that the Solow residual is, in fact, correlated with such factors as government expenditures, suggesting that movements in the Solow residual may also reflect the impacts of other factors.[14]

---

14. Changes in technology might well be correlated with changes in government spending on research and development (R&D). However, the Solow residual is also highly correlated with non-R&D government spending and with lags too short to be accounted for by the effects of spending on the rate of invention.

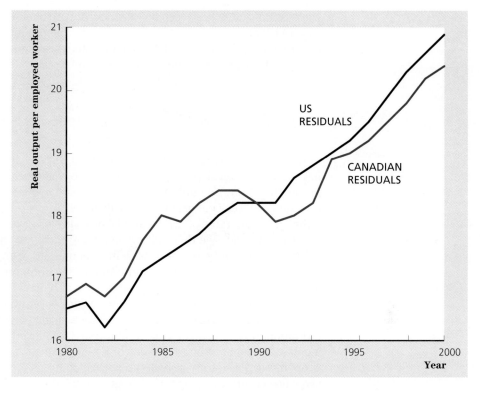

FIGURE 11.4

CANADIAN AND US
SOLOW RESIDUALS,
1980–2000

Solow residuals are constructed from annual output, employment, and capital series, with $a = 0.3$. Note that both Canadian and US Solow residuals are procyclical.

Sources: Canadian data: table 3.1; US data: output is real GDP in chained 1996 dollars, employment is civilian employment, from *Economic Report of the president* tables B2 and B36; capital is a quantity index of the non-residential fixed capital stock from the Bureau of Economic Analysis, *www.bea.gov.doc,* table 4.2. US residuals have been rescaled to have the same average as Canadian residuals.

To understand why measured productivity can vary, even if the actual technology used in production does not change, we need to recognize that capital and labour sometimes are used more intensively than at other times and that more intensive use of inputs leads to higher output. For instance, a printing press used full time contributes more to production than an otherwise identical printing press used half the time. Similarly, workers working fast (for example, restaurant workers during a busy lunch hour) will produce more output and revenue than the same number of workers working more slowly (the same restaurant workers during the afternoon lull). To capture the idea that capital and labour resources can be used more or less intensively at different times, we define the *utilization rate of capital*, u_K, and the *utilization rate of labour*, u_N. The utilization rate of a factor measures the intensity at which it is being used. For example, the utilization rate of capital for the printing press run full time would be twice as high as for the printing press used half the time; similarly, the utilization rate of labour is higher in the restaurant during lunch hour. The actual usage of the capital stock in production, which we call *capital services*, equals the utilization rate of capital times the stock of capital, or $u_K K$. Capital services are a more accurate measure of the contribution of the capital stock to output than is the level of capital itself because the definition of capital services adjusts for the intensity at which capital is used. Similarly, we define *labour services* to be the utilization rate of labour times the number of workers (or hours) employed by the firm, or $u_N N$. Thus, the labour services received by an employer are higher when the same number of workers are working hard and fast than when they are working slowly (that is, the utilization of labour is higher).

Recognizing that capital services and labour services go into the production of output, we rewrite the production function as

$$Y = AF(u_K K, u_N N) = A(u_K K)^a (u_N N)^{1-a}, \qquad (11.2)$$

where we have replaced the capital stock, K, with capital services, $u_K K$, and labour, N, with labour services, $u_N N$. Now we can use the production function in Eq. (11.2) to substitute for Y in Eq. (11.1) to obtain an expression for the Solow residual that incorporates utilization rates for capital and labour.

$$\text{Solow residual} = \frac{A(u_K K)^a (u_N N)^{1-a}}{K^a N^{1-a}} = A u_K{}^a u_N{}^{1-a}. \qquad (11.3)$$

Equation (11.3) shows that the Solow residual, as conventionally measured, includes not only parameter A (which reflects technology and perhaps other factors affecting productivity) but also utilization rates of capital and labour u_K and u_N. Thus, even if technology were unchanging, the calculated Solow residual would be procyclical if the utilization rates of capital and labour were procyclical.

There is evidence that utilization is procyclical (so that capital and labour are worked harder in boom periods than in economic slumps). For example, Craig Burnside, of the World Bank, and Martin Eichenbaum and Sergio Rebelo, of Northwestern University, studied the cyclical behaviour of capital utilization by using data on the amount of electricity used by producers.[15] Their rationale for using data on electricity is that additional electricity is needed to increase capital utilization, whether the increased utilization is achieved by operating capital for an increased number of hours per day or by increasing the speed at which the capital is operated. This study revealed that electricity used per unit of capital rises in economic upturns, leading the authors to conclude that capital utilization is strongly procyclical. In addition, this study showed that a measure of technology, analogous to the term A in Eq. (11.2), is much less procyclical than is the Solow residual.

Measuring the cyclical behaviour of labour utilization is more difficult, but various studies have found evidence that the utilization rate of labour is also procyclical. For example, Jon Fay and James Medoff,[16] of Harvard University, sent questionnaires to large manufacturing enterprises, asking about employment and production during the most recent downturn experienced at each plant. Fay and Medoff found that during a downturn, the average plant surveyed cut production by 31% and cut its total use of blue-collar hours to 23% below the normal level. Plant managers estimated that total hours could have been reduced by an additional 6% of the normal level without further reducing output. Of the 6% of normal hours, about half (3% of normal hours) were typically assigned to various types of useful work, including equipment maintenance and overhaul, painting, cleaning, reworking output, and training. The remaining 3% of normal hours were assigned to "make-work" and other unproductive activities. These numbers suggest that firms utilize labour less intensively during recessions.

Another interesting study by R. Anton Braun and Charles L. Evans,[17] of the Federal Reserve Banks of Minnesota and Chicago, respectively, examined the behaviour of the US Solow residual over the seasons of the year. Using data that had not been adjusted for normal seasonal variation, Braun and Evans found that the measured Solow residual was especially high during the period around Christmas,

---

15. "Capital Utilization and Returns to Scale," in B. Bernanke and J. Rotemberg, eds., *NBER Macroeconomics Annual*, 1995.

16. "Labor and Output Over the Business Cycle," *American Economic Review*, September 1985, pp. 638–655.

17. "Seasonal Solow Residuals and Christmas: A Case for Labor Hoarding and Increasing Returns," *Journal of Money, Credit, and Banking*, August 1998, part 1, pp. 306-330.

growing by 16% between the third and fourth quarters of the year and then dropping by 24% between the fourth and first quarters. The most reasonable explanation for this finding, as Braun and Evans pointed out, is that US manufacturers and retailers work particulalry hard during the Christmas shopping season to meet the surge in demand. In other words, the temporary rise in the Solow residual around Christmas is due, in large part, to higher labour utilization rates, rather than to changes in productive technology.

The tendency to use workers less intensively in recessions than in expansions has been referred to as labour hoarding. **Labour hoarding** occurs when due to the costs of firing and hiring workers, firms retain some workers in a recession that they would otherwise lay off. Firms keep these workers on the payroll to avoid costs of laying off workers and then rehiring them or hiring and training new workers when the economy revives. Hoarded labour either works less hard during the recession (there is less to do) or is put to work doing tasks, such as maintaining equipment, that are not measured as part of the firm's output. When the economy revives, the hoarded labour goes back to working in the normal way. In much the same way, it may not pay the restaurant owner to send her workers home between the lunch and dinner rush hours, with the result that restaurant workers are less productive during the slow afternoon period. This lower rate of productivity during recessions (or during the afternoon slow period, in the restaurant) does not reflect changes in the available technology, but only changes in the rate at which firms utilize capital and labour. Hence you should be cautious about interpreting cyclical changes in the Solow residual (equivalently, total factor productivity, A) as solely reflecting changes in technology.

Although changes in technology or the utilization rates of capital and labour can cause aggregate cyclical fluctuation, history suggests that shocks other than productivity shocks also affect the economy; wars are but one obvious example. Thus, many classical economists favour a broader definition of classical business cycle theory that allows for both productivity and other types of shocks to have an impact on the economy.

The macroeconomic effects of shocks other than productivity shocks can be analyzed with the classical *IS–LM* model. Let us use it to examine the effects of a fiscal policy shock.

FISCAL POLICY SHOCKS IN THE CLASSICAL MODEL

Another type of shock that can be a source of business cycles in the classical model is a change in fiscal policy, such as an increase or decrease in real government purchases of goods and services.[18] Examples of shocks to government purchases include wars and the initiation of large road-building or other public works programs. Because government purchases are procyclical—and, in particular, because national output tends to be above normal during wars and at other times when military spending is high—we need to explore how shocks to government purchases affect aggregate output and employment.

---

18. Another important example of a change in fiscal policy is a change in the structure of the tax code. Classical economists argue that the greatest effects of tax changes are those that affect people's incentives to work, save, and invest and, thus, affect full-employment output. Because most classical economists accept the Ricardian equivalence proposition, they would not expect lump-sum changes in taxes without accompanying changes in government purchases to have much effect on the economy, however.

Let us consider what happens when the government purchases more goods, as it would, for example, when the government begins a program of infrastructure spending or drought relief or when the country is at war. (Think of the increase in government purchases as temporary. Analytical Problem 2 at the end of the chapter asks you to work out what happens if the increase in government purchases is permanent.)

Figure 11.5, on the next page, illustrates the effects of an increase in government purchases in the classical *IS–LM* model. Before the fiscal policy change the economy's general equilibrium is represented by point *E* in both (a) and (b). To follow what happens after purchases rise, we start with the labour market in Figure 11.5(a). The change in fiscal policy does not affect the production function or the marginal product of labour (the *MPN* curve), so the labour demand curve does not shift.

However, classical economists argue that an increase in government purchases will affect labour supply by reducing workers' wealth. People are made less wealthy because if the government increases the share of the nation's output that it takes for public spending, less output will be left for private consumption and investment. This negative impact of increased government purchases on private wealth is most obvious if the government pays for its increased spending by raising current taxes.[19] However, even if the government does not raise current taxes to pay for the extra spending and borrows the funds it needs, taxes will still have to be raised in the future to pay the principal and interest on this extra government borrowing. So, whether taxes are currently raised or not, under the classical assumption that output is always at its full-employment level, an increase in government spending effectively makes people poorer.

In Chapter 3, we showed that a decrease in wealth increases labour supply because someone who is poorer can afford less leisure. Thus, according to the classical analysis, an increase in government purchases—which makes people financially worse off—should lead to an increase in aggregate labour supply.[20] The increase in government purchases causes the labour supply curve to shift to the right, from NS^1 to NS^2 in Figure 11.5(a). Following the shift of the labour supply curve, the equilibrium in the labour market shifts from point *E* to point *F*, with employment increasing and the real wage decreasing.[21]

The effects of the increase in government purchases in the classical *IS–LM* framework are shown in Figure 11.5(b). First, note that because equilibrium employment increases, full-employment output $\overline{Y}$ also increases. Thus, the *FE* line shifts to the right, from FE^1 to FE^2.

In addition to shifting the *FE* line to the right, the fiscal policy change also shifts the *IS* curve. Recall that at any level of output, a temporary increase in government purchases reduces desired national saving and raises the real interest rate that clears the goods market. Thus, the *IS* curve shifts up, from IS^1 to IS^2. (See also Summary table 12, p. 300.) The *LM* curve is not directly affected by the change in fiscal policy.

---

19. For simplicity, assume that the tax increase is lump-sum. A tax increase that is not lump-sum—for example, if it changes the effective tax rate on capital—has complicating effects.

20. In theory, the effect on labour supply of an increase in government purchases should be the strongest for spending, such as military spending, that extracts resources without providing any direct benefits to the private sector. Government purchases that effectively replace private consumption expenditures—for example, purchases of medical services, roads, or playgrounds—should, in principle, have a smaller negative impact on people's economic well being and, thus, a smaller positive effect on labour supply.

21. Note that this labour supply effect was omitted from our discussion of the impact of increased government purchases in Chapter 4, as illustrated in Figure 4.8.

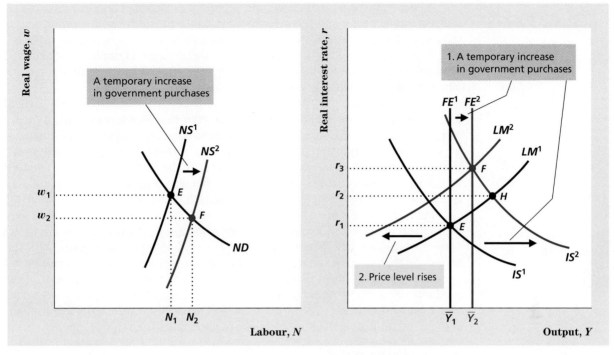

(a) Labour market

(b) General equilibrium

FIGURE 11.5

EFFECTS OF A TEMPORARY INCREASE IN GOVERNMENT
PURCHASES

Initial equilibrium is at point E in both (a) and (b).

(a) A temporary increase in government purchases raises workers'
current or future taxes. Because workers feel poorer, they supply
more labour and the labour supply curve shifts to the right, from NS^1
to NS^2. The shift in the labour supply curve reduces the real wage
and increases employment, as indicated by point F.

(b) The increase in employment raises full-employment output and
shifts the FE line to the right, from FE^1 to FE^2. The increase in
government purchases also reduces desired national saving and
shifts the IS curve up, from IS^1 to IS^2. Because the intersection of IS^2
and LM^1 is to the right of FE^2, the aggregate quantity of output
demanded is higher than the full-employment level of output $\overline{Y}_2$, so
the price level rises. The rise in the price level reduces the real
money supply and shifts the LM curve up, from LM^1 to LM^2, until
the new general equilibrium is reached at point F. The effect of the
increase in government purchases is to increase output, the real
interest rate, and the price level.

The new IS curve, IS^2, the initial LM curve, LM^1, and the new FE line, FE^2,
have no common point of intersection. For general equilibrium to be restored, prices
must adjust, shifting the LM curve until it passes through the intersection of IS^2
and FE^2 (point F). Will prices rise or fall? The answer to this question is ambiguous
because the fiscal policy change has increased both the aggregate demand for goods
(by reducing desired saving and shifting the IS curve up) and the full-employment
level of output (by increasing labour supply and shifting the FE line to the right). If
we assume that the effect on labour supply and full-employment output of the
increase in government purchases is not too large (probably a reasonable
assumption), after the fiscal policy change, the aggregate quantity of goods demanded
is likely to exceed full-employment output. In Figure 11.5(b) the aggregate quantity
of goods demanded (point H at the intersection of IS^2 and LM^1) exceeds full-
employment output $\overline{Y}_2$. Thus, the price level must rise, shifting the LM curve to the
left and causing the economy to return to general equilibrium at F. At F, both output
and the real interest rate are higher than at the initial equilibrium point, E.

Therefore, the increase in government purchases increases output, employment, the real interest rate, and the price level. Because the increase in employment is the result of an increase in labour supply, rather than an increase in labour demand, real wages fall when government purchases rise. Because of diminishing marginal productivity of labour, the increase in employment also implies a decline in average labour productivity when government purchases rise.

That fiscal shocks play some role in business cycles seems reasonable, which is itself justification for including them in the model. However, including fiscal shocks along with productivity shocks in the RBC model has the additional advantage of improving the match between model and data. We previously noted that government purchases are procyclical, which is consistent with the preceding analysis. Another advantage of adding fiscal shocks to a model that also contains productivity shocks is that it improves the model's ability to explain the behaviour of labour productivity.

Refer back to Figure 11.2 to recall a weakness of the RBC model with only productivity shocks: It predicts that average labour productivity and GNP are highly correlated. In fact, RBC theory predicts a correlation that is more than twice the actual correlation. However, as we have just shown, a classical business cycle model with shocks to government purchases predicts a negative correlation between labour productivity and GNP because a positive shock to government purchases raises output but lowers average productivity. A classical business cycle model that includes *both* shocks to productivity *and* shocks to government purchases can match the empirically observed correlation of productivity and GNP well, without reducing the fit of the model in other respects.[22] Thus, adding fiscal shocks to the real business cycle model seems to improve its ability to explain the actual behaviour of the economy.

SHOULD FISCAL POLICY BE USED TO DAMPEN THE CYCLE?

Our analysis shows that changes in government purchases can have real effects on the economy. Changes in the tax laws can also have real effects on the economy in the classical model, although these effects are more complicated and depend mainly on the nature of the tax, the type of income or revenue that is taxed, and so on. Potentially, then, changes in fiscal policy could be used to offset cyclical fluctuations and stabilize output and employment; for example, the government could increase its purchases during recessions. This observation leads to the second of the two questions posed in the introduction to the chapter: Should policymakers use fiscal policy to smooth business cycle fluctuations?

Recall that classical economists generally oppose active attempts to dampen cyclical fluctuations because of Adam Smith's invisible-hand argument that free markets produce efficient outcomes without government intervention. The classical view holds that prices and wages adjust fairly rapidly to bring the economy into general equilibrium, allowing little scope for the government to improve the macroeconomy's response to economic disturbances. Therefore, although, in principle, fiscal policy could be used to fight recessions and reduce output fluctuations, classical economists advise against using this approach. Instead, classicals argue that not interfering in the economy's adjustment to disturbances is better.

This scepticism about the value of active anti-recessionary policies does *not* mean that classical economists do not regard recessions as a serious problem. If an

---

22. See Lawrence Christiano and Martin Eichenbaum, "Current Real-Business-Cycle Theories and Aggregate Labor-Market Fluctuations," *American Economic Review*, June 1992, pp. 430–450. The analysis of this paper is technically complex, but it gives a flavour of much recent work in classical business cycle analysis.

adverse productivity shock causes a recession, for example, real wages, employment, and output all fall, which means that many people experience economic hardship. But would offsetting the recession by, for example, increasing government purchases help? In the classical analysis, a rise in government purchases increases output by raising the amount of labour supplied, and the amount of labour supplied is increased by making workers poorer (as a result of higher current or future taxes). Thus, under the classical assumption that the economy is always in general equilibrium, increasing government purchases for the sole purpose of increasing output and employment makes people worse off, rather than better off. Classical economists conclude that government purchases should be increased only if the benefits of the expanded government program—in terms of improved military security or public services, for example—exceed the costs to taxpayers. Classicals apply this criterion for useful government spending—that the benefits should exceed the costs—whether the economy is currently in recession or not.

So far, we have assumed that because fiscal policy affects the equilibrium levels of employment and output, the government is capable of using fiscal policy to achieve the levels of employment and output it chooses. In fact, the legislative process can lead to lengthy delays, or *lags*, between the time that a fiscal policy change is proposed and the time that it is enacted. Additional lags occur in implementing the new policies and in the response of the economy to the policy changes. Because of these lags, fiscal policy changes contemplated today should be based on where the economy will be several quarters in the future; but, unfortunately, forecasting the future of the economy is an inexact art at best. Beyond the problems of forecasting, policymakers also face uncertainties about how and by how much to modify their policies to get the desired output and employment effects. Classical economists cite these practical difficulties as another reason for not using fiscal policy to fight recessions.

UNEMPLOYMENT IN THE CLASSICAL MODEL

A major weakness of the classical model is that it does not explain why unemployment rises during business downturns. Indeed, in the simple classical, or supply-and-demand, model of the labour market, unemployment is literally zero: Anyone who wants to work can find a job at the market-clearing wage. Of course, in reality unemployment is never zero. Furthermore, the sharp increases in unemployment that occur during recessions are a principal reason that policymakers and the public are so concerned about economic downturns.

Classical economists are perfectly aware of this issue, and they have developed more sophisticated versions of the classical business cycle model to account for unemployment. The main modification they make to the simple supply-and-demand model of the labour market is to drop the model's implicit assumption that all workers and jobs are the same. Rather than all being the same, workers in the real world have different abilities, skills, and interests, among other things; jobs entail different skill requirements, work environments, locations, and other characteristics. Because workers and jobs both vary in so many ways, matching workers to jobs is not instantaneous and free, but time consuming and costly. The fact that someone who has lost a job or has just entered the labour force must spend time and effort to find a new job helps explain why there always are some unemployed people.

Some classical economists suggest that differences among workers and among jobs explain not only why the unemployment rate is always greater than zero but also why unemployment rises so sharply in recessions. They argue that productivity shocks and other macroeconomic disturbances that cause recessions also often increase the degree of mismatch between workers and firms.[23] Thus, a major adverse productivity shock might affect the various industries and regions within the country differently, with jobs being destroyed in some sectors but new opportunities emerging in others. An oil price shock, for example, would eliminate jobs in energy-intensive industries but create new opportunities in industries that supply energy or are light energy users.

Following such a shock, workers in industries and regions where labour demand has fallen will be induced to search elsewhere for jobs, which raises the frictional component of unemployment. Some of these workers will find that their skills do not match the requirements of industries with growing labour demand; these workers may become chronically unemployed, raising structural unemployment.[24] With many unemployed workers looking for jobs, and because creating new jobs takes a while, the time necessary to find a new job is likely to increase. For all these reasons, an adverse productivity shock may raise unemployment as well as reduce output and employment. Note that this predicted rise in frictional and structural unemployment during recessions is the same as an increase in the natural rate of unemployment (the sum of frictional and structural unemployment rates).

What is the evidence of worker–job mismatch and unemployment? Statistics Canada conducts an annual census of the Canadian manufacturing sector, which provides some answers. During the 1974–1992 period, about 11% of all manufacturing jobs disappeared, on average, each year, reflecting plant closings and cutbacks. During a typical year, though, about as many new jobs were created in the manufacturing sector. Thus, a great deal of "churning" of jobs and workers occurs in the economy. Much of this churning has reflected closing of old plants and opening of new ones within the same industries, rather than a general decline in some industries and growth in others. Thus, reallocation of workers within industries seems to be as important as movement of workers between industries as a source of unemployment.

Table 11.1, on the next page, shows the rates of job creation and destruction in manufacturing. Note that in recession years, such as 1982 and 1991, many more jobs were lost than were created; but a significant number of new jobs were created even in recession years, reflecting shifts of workers in the labour market.

It seems clear that increased mismatches between workers and jobs cannot account for all the increase in unemployment that occurs during recessions. Much of that increase is in the form of temporary layoffs; rather than search for new jobs, many workers who are temporarily laid off simply wait until they are called back by their old firm. Moreover, if recessions were times of increased mismatch in the labour market, more postings of vacancies and help-wanted ads during recessions would be expected; but, in fact, both vacancies and new job openings fall in recessions. Despite these objections, however, economists generally agree that the dynamic reallocation of workers from shrinking to growing sectors is an important source of unemployment.

Modifying the classical model to allow for unemployment does not change the classical view that fiscal policy should not be actively used to combat recessions. Classical economists point out that raising the aggregate demand for goods (by

23. This idea was proposed in David Lilien, "Sectoral Shifts and Cyclical Unemployment," *Journal of Political Economy*, August 1982, pp. 777–793.

24. See Chapter 3 for definitions and discussion of frictional and structural unemployment.

TABLE 11.1

Rates of Job Creation and Destruction in Canadian Manufacturing, 1974–1992

Year	Job Creation	Job Destruction
1974	9.7%	7.6%
1975	9.3%	11.8%
1976	9.4%	9.2%
1977	7.8%	10.0%
1978	13.1%	8.2%
1979	11.9%	8.4%
1980	9.6%	10.0%
1981	9.6%	9.4%
1982	7.4%	15.3%
1983	10.6%	12.5%
1984	12.2%	9.2%
1985	11.8%	9.2%
1986	12.7%	10.4%
1987	13.2%	10.1%
1988	15.5%	11.1%
1989	12.9%	11.7%
1990	9.8%	15.0%
1991	8.8%	15.6%
1992	11.7%	15.3%

Note: Job creation is the number of new manufacturing jobs created during the year, as a percentage of existing manufacturing jobs. Job destruction is the number of manufacturing jobs lost during the year, as a percentage of existing jobs.

Source: Table 1 in John Baldwin, Timothy Dunne, and John Haltiwanger, "A Comparison of Job Creation and Job Destruction in Canada and the United States," *Review of Economics and Statistics*, August 1998, pp. 347–356.

increasing government purchases, for example) does not directly address the problem of unemployment arising from the mismatch that exists at the microeconomic level between workers and jobs. A better approach, in the classical view, is to eliminate barriers to labour market adjustment, such as regulations that raise businesses' costs of employing additional workers.

11.2 MONEY IN THE CLASSICAL MODEL

So far, we have focused on real shocks to the economy, such as productivity shocks and changes in government purchases. However, many macroeconomists believe that nominal shocks—shocks to money supply and money demand—also affect the business cycle. In the rest of the chapter, we discuss the role of money and monetary policy in the classical approach to the business cycle.

MONETARY POLICY AND THE ECONOMY

Monetary policy refers to the central bank's decisions about how much money to supply to the economy (see Chapter 7). Recall that the central bank (the Bank of Canada in Canada) can affect the money supply through open-market operations, in which it sells government bonds to the public in exchange for money (to reduce the money supply) or uses newly created money to buy bonds from the public (to increase the money supply).

In Chapter 9, we examined the effects of changes in the money supply using the *IS–LM* model (see Figure 9.9) and the *AD–AS* model (see Figure 9.14). With both models we found that after prices fully adjust, changes in the money supply are neutral: A change in the nominal money supply M causes the price level P to change proportionally, but a change in the money supply has no effect on real variables, such as output, employment, or the real interest rate. Our analysis left open the possibility that a change in the money supply would affect real variables, such as output, in the short run before prices had a chance to adjust. However, because classical economists believe that the price adjustment process is rapid, their theory predicts that money will be neutral even in the short run.

MONETARY NON-NEUTRALITY AND REVERSE CAUSATION

The prediction that money is neutral is a striking result of the classical model, but it seems inconsistent with the business cycle fact that money is a leading, procyclical variable. If an expansion of the money supply has no effect, why are expansions of the money supply typically followed by increased rates of economic activity? And, similarly, why are reductions in the money supply often followed by recessions?

Some classical economists have responded to these questions by pointing out that although increases in the money supply tend to precede expansions in output, this fact does not necessarily prove that economic expansions are caused by those increases. After all, just because people put storm windows on their houses before winter begins does not mean that winter is caused by putting on storm windows. Rather, people put storm windows on their houses because they know that winter is coming.

Many classical economists, including RBC theorists in particular, argue that the link between money growth and economic expansion is like the link between putting on storm windows and the onset of winter, a relationship they call reverse causation. Specifically, **reverse causation** means that expected future increases in output cause increases in the current money supply and that expected future decreases in output cause decreases in the current money supply, rather than the other way around. Reverse causation explains how money could be a procyclical and leading variable, even if the classical model is correct and changes in the money supply are neutral and have no real effects.

Reverse causation might arise in one of several ways. One possibility (which you are asked to explore in more detail in Analytical Problem 4 at the end of the chapter) is based on the idea that money demand depends on expected future output as well as current output. Suppose that a firm's managers expect business to pick up considerably in the next few quarters. To prepare for this expected increase in output, the firm may need to increase its current transactions (for example, to purchase raw materials, hire workers, and so on), and thus, it will demand more money now. If many firms do so, the aggregate demand for money may rise in advance of the actual increase in output.

Now, suppose that the Bank of Canada observes this increase in the demand for money. If the Bank does nothing, leaving the money supply unchanged, the increase in money demand will cause the equilibrium value of the price level to fall. As one of the Bank's objectives is stable prices, it will not like this outcome; to keep prices stable, instead of doing nothing, the Bank should provide enough extra money to the economy to meet the higher money demand. But if the Bank does so, the money supply will rise in advance of the increase in output, consistent with the business cycle fact—even though money is neutral.

Undoubtedly, reverse causation explains at least some of the tendency of money to lead output (see Box 11.1, on p. 424, for a seasonal example). However, this explanation does not rule out the possibility that changes in the money supply also sometimes cause changes in output so that money is non-neutral. That is, a combination of reverse causation and monetary non-neutrality could account for the procyclical behaviour of money.

THE NON-NEUTRALITY OF MONEY: ADDITIONAL EVIDENCE

Because of reverse causation, the leading and procyclical behaviour of money cannot by itself establish that money is non-neutral. To settle the issue of whether money is neutral, we need additional evidence. One useful source is a historical analysis of monetary policy. For example, for the United States, the classic study is Milton Friedman and Anna J. Schwartz's, *A Monetary History of the United States, 1867–1960*.[25] Using a variety of sources, including Federal Reserve policy statements and the journals and correspondence of monetary policymakers, Friedman and Schwartz carefully described and analyzed the causes of money supply fluctuations and the interrelation of money and other economic variables. They concluded:

> Throughout the near-century examined in detail, we have found that:
>
> **1.** Changes in the behavior of the money stock have been closely associated with changes in economic activity, [nominal] income, and prices.
>
> **2.** The interrelation between monetary and economic change has been highly stable.
>
> **3.** Monetary changes have often had an independent origin; they have not been simply a reflection of changes in economic activity. (p. 676)

The first two conclusions restate the basic business cycle fact that money is procyclical. The third conclusion states that reverse causation cannot explain the entire relationship between money and real income or output. Friedman and Schwartz focused on historical episodes in which changes in the supply of money were not (they argued) responses to macroeconomic conditions but instead resulted from other factors, such as gold discoveries (which affected money supplies under the gold standard), changes in monetary institutions, or changes in the leadership of the Federal Reserve. In the majority of these cases, "independent" changes in money growth were followed by changes in the same direction in real output. This evidence suggests that money is not neutral.

These conclusions have been disputed using other historical episodes in which rapid monetary growth has not led to inflation.[26] Also, there has been no comparable historical case made that would link Canadian business cycles to changes in the money supply. Nevertheless, there seem to be some clear examples of non-neutrality in Canada. For example, during World War I, Canada and other countries left the gold standard (a system of fixed exchange rates in which exchange rates were

25. Princeton, N.J.: Princeton University Press for NBER, 1963.
26. See Bruce D. Smith, "Mischief and Monetary History: Friedman and Schwartz Thirty Years Later," *Journal of Monetary Economics*, August 1994, pp. 27–45.

Box 11.1   MONEY AND ECONOMIC ACTIVITY AT CHRISTMASTIME

According to the reverse causation argument, the association of higher-than-normal money growth with economic booms and lower-than-normal money growth with recessions occurs because money growth responds to changes in output, not because money growth causes changes in output. An example of reverse causation is provided by the behaviour of money and economic activity at Christmastime, as shown in the accompanying table.

In Canada, both the money supply and retail sales grow rapidly in December. Clearly, the sharp increase in December retail sales (measured in real terms) results from Christmas gift buying and not from the December increase in the money supply. Thus, at Christmastime, higher economic activity must cause a higher money supply, rather than vice versa. Where does the extra money come from? The Bank of Canada regularly increases the money supply in December to meet the demands of merchants and shoppers for more money.

The existence of reverse causation from output to money in December does not rule out monetary non-neutrality, but it does mean that we have to be cautious in interpreting the positive association between money and output over the course of the business cycle. This association could arise because of monetary non-neutrality, reverse causation, or both. The relationship between money and economic activity at Christmastime shows that reverse causation does in fact occur and can be important.

Month	Growth of Money Supply	Growth of Real Retail Sales
November	1.4%	1.2%
December	2.6	15.8
January	–2.2	–27.8
February	–0.5	–3.7

Note: Growth rates are measured month to month.
Sources: Real retail sales: retail trade, all stores, in constant (1992) dollars, CANSIM D658050; money supply: M1, CANSIM B2033. Both series are for 1991–2001 and are not seasonally adjusted.

quoted in terms of gold) and allowed their exchange rates to float. Wartime inflation led to a depreciation of currency values in terms of gold. At the end of the war, governments sought to return to pre-war exchange rates, which required an appreciation. Tight monetary policy was implemented in Canada, the United Kingdom, and other gold-standard countries, and a brief but severe recession followed in 1921–1922. The Application "Golden Fetters," in Chapter 10, also described evidence of non-neutrality as countries abandoned the gold standard in the 1930s.

More recently, many economists have attributed the depth of the 1990–1992 recession to restrictive monetary policy on the part of the Bank of Canada. Because of episodes like these (and similar experiences in other countries), most economists now believe that money is not neutral. If we accept that evidence, contrary to the prediction of the classical model, we are left with two choices: Either we must adopt a different framework for macroeconomic analysis or we must modify the classical model. In Section 11.3, we take the second approach and consider how monetary non-neutrality can be explained in a classical model.

11.3 THE MISPERCEPTIONS THEORY AND THE NON-NEUTRALITY OF MONEY

According to the classical model, prices do not remain fixed for any substantial period of time, so the horizontal short-run aggregate supply curve developed in

Chapter 9 is irrelevant. The only relevant aggregate supply curve is the long-run aggregate supply curve. As we showed in Figure 9.14, changes in the money supply cause the *AD* curve to shift; but because the aggregate supply curve is vertical, the effect of the *AD* shift is simply to change prices without changing the level of output. Thus, money is neutral in the classical model.

For money to be non-neutral, the relevant aggregate supply curve must not be vertical. In this section, we extend the classical model to incorporate the assumption that producers have imperfect information about the general price level and, thus, sometimes misinterpret changes in the general price level as changes in the relative prices of the goods that they produce. We demonstrate that the assumption that producers may misperceive the aggregate price level—the *misperceptions theory*—implies a short-run aggregate supply curve that is not vertical. Unlike the short-run aggregate supply curve developed in Chapter 9, however, the short-run aggregate supply curve based on the misperceptions theory does not require the assumption that prices are slow to adjust. Even though prices may adjust instantaneously, the short-run aggregate supply curve slopes upward, so money is non-neutral in the short run.

The misperceptions theory was originally proposed by Nobel laureate Milton Friedman and then was rigorously formulated by another Nobel laureate, Robert E. Lucas, Jr., of the University of Chicago.[27] According to the **misperceptions theory**, *the aggregate quantity of output supplied rises above the full-employment level, $\overline{Y}$, when the aggregate price level, P, is higher than expected.* Thus, for any expected price level, the aggregate supply curve relating the price level and the aggregate quantity of output supplied slopes upward.

If you took a course in the principles of economics, you learned that supply curves generally slope upward, with higher prices leading to increased production. However, just as the demand curves for individual goods differ from the aggregate demand curve, the supply curves for individual goods differ from the aggregate supply curve. An ordinary supply curve relates the supply of some good to the price of that good *relative to other prices*. In contrast, the aggregate supply curve relates the aggregate amount of output produced to the *general price level*. Changes in the general price level can occur while the relative prices of individual goods remain unchanged.

To understand the misperceptions theory and why it implies an upward-sloping aggregate supply curve, let us think about an individual producer of a particular good, say, bread. For simplicity, consider a bakery owned and operated by one person, a baker. The baker devotes all his labour to making bread and earns all his income from selling bread. Thus, the price of bread is effectively the baker's nominal wage, and the price of bread relative to the general price level is the baker's real wage. When the relative price of bread increases, the baker responds to this increase in his current real wage by working more and producing more bread. Similarly, when the price of bread falls relative to the other prices in the economy, the baker's current real wage falls and he decreases the amount of bread he produces.

But how does an individual baker know whether the relative price of bread has changed? To calculate the relative price of bread, the baker needs to know both the nominal price of bread and the general price level. The baker knows the nominal price of bread because he sells bread every day and observes the price directly. However, the baker probably is not as well informed about the general price level

27. See Friedman, "The Role of Monetary Policy," *American Economic Review*, March 1968, pp. 1–17. Lucas's formalization of Friedman was first presented in Lucas's article, "Expectations and the Neutrality of Money," *Journal of Economic Theory*, April 1972, pp. 103–124.

because he observes the prices of the many goods and services he might want to buy less frequently than he observes the price of bread. Thus, in calculating the relative price of bread, the baker cannot use the actual current price level. The best he can do is use his previously formed expectation of the current price level to estimate the actual price level.

Suppose that before he observes the current market price of bread, the baker expected an overall inflation rate of 5%. How will he react if he then observes that the price of bread increases by 5%? The baker reasons as follows: I expected the overall rate of inflation to be 5%, and now I know that the price of bread has increased by 5%. This 5% increase in the price of bread is consistent with what I had expected. My best estimate is that all prices increased by 5%, and thus, I think that the relative price of bread is unchanged. There is no reason to change my output.

The baker's logic applies equally to suppliers of output in the aggregate. Suppose that all suppliers expected the nominal price level to increase by 5% and that, in fact, all prices do increase by 5%. Then each supplier will estimate that her relative price has not changed and will not change her output. Hence, if expected inflation is 5%, an actual increase in prices of 5% will not affect aggregate output.

For a change in the nominal price of bread to affect the quantity of bread produced, the increase in the nominal price of bread must differ from the expected increase in the general price level. For example, suppose that the baker expected the general price level to increase by 5% but then observes that the price of bread rises by 8%. The baker then estimates that the relative price of bread has increased so that the real wage she earns from baking is higher. In response to the perceived increase in the relative price, she increases the production of bread.

Again, the same logic applies to the economy in the aggregate. Suppose that everyone expects the general price level to increase by 5% but, instead, it actually increases by 8%, with the prices of all goods increasing by 8%. Now all producers will estimate that the relative prices of the goods they make have increased, and hence the production of all goods will increase. Thus, a greater-than-expected increase of the price level will tend to raise output. Similarly, if the price level actually increases by only 2% when all producers expected a 5% increase, producers will think that the relative prices of their own goods have declined; in response, all suppliers reduce their output.

Thus, according to the misperceptions theory, the amount of output that producers choose to supply depends on the actual general price level as compared with the expected general price level. When the price level exceeds what was expected, producers are fooled into thinking that the relative prices of their own goods have risen, and they increase their output. Similarly, when the price level is lower than expected, producers believe that the relative prices of their goods have fallen, and they reduce their output. This relation between output and prices is captured by the equation:

$$Y = \overline{Y} + b(P\text{-}P^e), \tag{11.4}$$

where b is a positive number that describes how strongly output responds when the actual price level exceeds the expected price level. Equation (11.4) summarizes the misperceptions theory by showing that output Y exceeds full-employment output $\overline{Y}$ when the price level P exceeds the expected price level P^e.

To obtain an aggregate supply curve from the misperceptions theory, we graph Eq. (11.4) in Figure 11.6. For given full-employment output $\overline{Y}$ and expected price level P^e, the aggregate supply curve slopes upward, illustrating the relation between the amount of output supplied Y and the actual price level P. Because an increase in

FIGURE 11.6

THE AGGREGATE SUPPLY
CURVE IN THE
MISPERCEPTIONS THEORY

The misperceptions theory
holds that for a given value of
the expected price level P^e, an
increase in the actual price
level P fools producers into
increasing output. This relationship between output and
the price level is shown by the
short-run aggregate supply
curve SRAS. Along the SRAS
curve, output equals $\overline{Y}$ when
prices equal their expected
level ($P = P^e$, at point E), output
exceeds $\overline{Y}$ when the price
level is higher than expected
($P > P^e$), and output is less than
$\overline{Y}$ when the price level is lower
than expected ($P < P^e$). In the
long run, the expected price
level equals the actual price
level so that output equals $\overline{Y}$.
Thus, the long-run aggregate
supply curve LRAS is vertical
at $Y = \overline{Y}$.

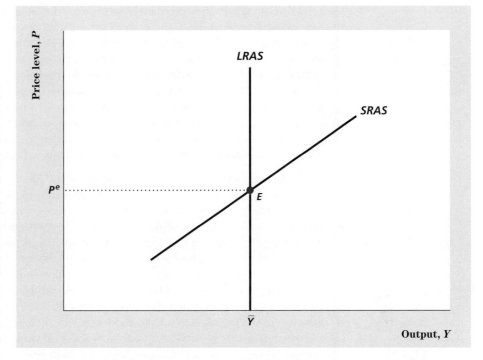

the price level of ΔP increases the amount of output supplied by $\Delta Y = b\Delta P$, the
slope of the aggregate supply curve is $\Delta P/\Delta Y = 1/b$. Thus, the aggregate supply curve
is steep if b is small and is relatively flat if b is large.

Point E helps us locate the aggregate supply curve. At E, the price level P equals
the expected price level P^e so that (from Eq. 11.4) the amount of output supplied
equals full-employment output $\overline{Y}$. When the actual price level is higher than expected
($P > P^e$), the aggregate supply curve shows that the amount of output supplied is
greater than $\overline{Y}$; when the price level is lower than expected ($P < P^e$), output is less
than $\overline{Y}$.

The aggregate supply curve in Figure 11.6 is called the short-run aggregate
supply curve (SRAS) because it applies only to the short period of time that P^e
remains unchanged. In the long run, people learn what is actually happening to
prices, and the expected price level adjusts to the actual price level ($P = P^e$). When
the actual price level equals the expected price level, no misperceptions remain
and producers supply the full-employment level of output. In terms of Eq. (11.4), in
the long run, P equals P^e, and output Y equals full-employment output $\overline{Y}$. In the
long run, then, the supply of output does not depend on the price level. Thus, as
in Chapters 9 and 10, the long-run aggregate supply (LRAS) curve is vertical at the
point where output equals $\overline{Y}$.

APPLICATION

INTERNATIONAL EVIDENCE ON THE SLOPE OF THE
SHORT-RUN AGGREGATE SUPPLY CURVE

According to the misperceptions theory, when the actual price level, P, is higher
than the expected price level, P^e, output is higher than the full-employment level, $\overline{Y}$.
Extra output is produced because all producers believe (mistakenly) that the relative

prices of the goods they produce have increased. The amount by which producers increase their output when the general price level rises depends on how much they believe that their relative prices have increased. For example, when the general price level increases, if producers believe that the increase in their individual relative prices is small, they will not increase output by much. In this case, the coefficient b in the equation for the *SRAS* curve, Eq. (11.4), which measures the response of output to changes in $P - P^e$, will be small; the slope of the *SRAS* curve, $1/b$, will be steep. Alternatively, if producers interpret a rise in the price level as meaning that their individual relative prices have increased a lot, they will increase their output substantially so that the coefficient b is large; the *SRAS* curve will be relatively flat (its slope, $1/b$, is small).

Under the misperceptions theory, the slope of the *SRAS* curve depends on the degree to which producers tend to interpret increases in the price level above its expected value as changes in their own relative prices. But what determines whether producers believe that a positive value of $P - P^e$ represents a large or small increase in relative prices? Robert E. Lucas, Jr. was the first to argue that if the aggregate price level in a country is generally stable, when producers perceive increases in the prices of their own goods, they are likely to conclude that the overall price level has changed little and, thus, that the relative prices of their individual goods must have increased. Lucas concluded that in countries with stable prices, an unanticipated increase in prices will lead output to increase by a large amount, and so the short-run aggregate supply curve will be relatively flat. However, in countries with highly variable price levels (for example, high-inflation countries), producers are more likely to attribute increases in the prices of their own goods to a rise in the general price level, implying that the relative prices of their own goods probably have not changed much. Thus, in countries with unstable price levels, output will increase only a little in response to a general increase in prices, and the aggregate supply curve will be relatively steep.

One way to test the misperceptions theory is to compare the *SRAS* curves in different countries, to determine whether the *SRAS* curves are, indeed, flatter in countries with more stable prices, as the theory predicts. Lucas performed this test after developing the misperceptions theory in the early 1970s.[28] He examined aggregate supply curves in 18 countries. Of these 18 countries, 16 had relatively stable inflation rates and, thus, relatively predictable price levels, and two—Argentina and Paraguay—had unstable inflation rates and, hence, unpredictable price levels. Lucas found that the *SRAS* curves in Argentina and Paraguay were more than 10 times as steep as the short-run aggregate supply curves in any of the other 16 countries. The finding that countries with unpredictable prices have steep *SRAS* curves is exactly what the misperceptions theory predicts.

MONETARY POLICY AND THE MISPERCEPTIONS THEORY

Let us now re-examine the neutrality of money in the extended version of the classical model. This framework highlights an important distinction between anticipated and unanticipated changes in the money supply: Unanticipated changes in the nominal money supply have real effects, but anticipated changes are neutral and have no real effects.

---

28. "Some International Evidence on Output–Inflation Tradeoffs," *American Economic Review*, June 1973, pp. 326–334.

UNANTICIPATED CHANGES IN THE MONEY SUPPLY

Suppose that the economy is initially in general equilibrium at point E in Figure 11.7, where AD^1 intersects $SRAS^1$. Here, output equals the full-employment level $\overline{Y}$, and the price level and the expected price level both equal P_1. Suppose that everyone expects the money supply and the price level to remain constant but that the Bank of Canada unexpectedly and without publicity increases the money supply by 10%. A 10% increase in the money supply shifts the AD curve up to AD^2, increasing the price level at each level of output by 10%. Given the expected price level P_1 the $SRAS$ curve remains unchanged, still passing through point E.

The increase in aggregate demand bids up the price level to the new equilibrium level P_2, where AD^2 intersects $SRAS^1$ (point F). In the new short-run equilibrium at F, the actual price level exceeds the expected price level and output exceeds $\overline{Y}$. Because the increase in the money supply leads to a rise in output, money is not neutral in this analysis.

The reason is that producers are fooled. Each producer misperceives the higher nominal price of his output as an increase in its relative price, rather than as an increase in the general price level. Although output increases in the short run, producers are not better off. They end up producing more than they would have if they had known the true relative prices.

The economy cannot stay long at the equilibrium represented by point F because at F the actual price level P_2 is higher than the expected price level P_1. Over time, people obtain information about the true level of prices and adjust their expectations accordingly. The only equilibrium that can be sustained in the long run is one in which people do not permanently underestimate or overestimate the price level so that the expected price level and the actual price level are equal. Graphically, when people learn the true price level, the relevant aggregate supply curve is the long-run aggregate supply curve $LRAS$, along which P always equals P^e. In Figure 11.7, the

FIGURE 11.7

AN UNANTICIPATED
INCREASE IN THE MONEY
SUPPLY

If we start from the initial equilibrium at point E, an unanticipated 10% increase in the money supply shifts the AD curve up by 10% at each level of output, from AD^1 to AD^2. The short-run equilibrium is located at point F, the intersection of AD^2 and the short-run aggregate supply curve $SRAS^1$, where prices and output are both higher than at point E. Thus, an unanticipated change in the money supply is not neutral in the short run. In the long run, people learn the true price level and the equilibrium shifts to point H, the intersection of AD^2 and the long-run aggregate supply curve $LRAS$. In the long-run equilibrium at H, the price level has risen by 10% but output returns to its full-employment level $\overline{Y}$ so that money is neutral in the long run. As expectations of the price level rise from P_1 to P_3, the $SRAS$ curve also shifts up until it passes through H.

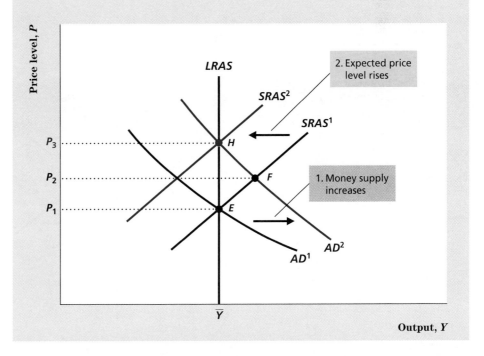

long-run equilibrium is point H, the intersection of AD^2 and $LRAS$. At H, output equals its full-employment level $\overline{Y}$, and the price level P_3 is 10% higher than the initial price level P_1. Because everyone now expects the price level to be P_3, a new $SRAS$ curve, $SRAS^2$, passes through H.

Thus, according to the misperceptions theory, an unanticipated increase in the money supply raises output and is not neutral *in the short run*. However, an unanticipated increase in the money supply is neutral in the long run, after people have learned the true price level.

ANTICIPATED CHANGES IN THE MONEY SUPPLY

In the extended classical model based on the misperceptions theory, the effects of an anticipated money supply increase are different from the effects of a surprise money supply increase. Figure 11.8 illustrates the effects of an anticipated money supply increase. Again, we suppose that the initial general equilibrium point is at E, where output equals its full-employment level and the actual and expected price levels both equal P_1. We assume that the Bank of Canada announces that it is going to increase the money supply by 10% and that the public believes this announcement.

As we have shown, a 10% increase in the money supply shifts the AD curve up by 10% at each level of output, from AD^1 to AD^2. However, in this case, the $SRAS$ curve also shifts up. The reason is that the public's expected price level rises as soon as people learn of the increase in the money supply. Suppose that people expect—correctly—that the price level will also rise by 10% so that P^e rises by 10%, from P_1 to P_2. Then the new $SRAS$ curve, $SRAS^2$, passes through point F in Figure 11.8, where Y equals $\overline{Y}$ and both the actual and expected price levels equal P_2. The new equilibrium also is at F, where AD^2 and $SRAS^2$ intersect. At the new equilibrium, output equals its full-employment level, and prices are 10% higher than they were initially. The anticipated increase in the money supply has not affected

FIGURE 11.8

AN ANTICIPATED INCREASE
IN THE MONEY SUPPLY

The economy is in initial equilibrium at point *E* when the Bank of Canada publicly announces a 10% increase in the money supply. When the money supply increases, the *AD* curve shifts upward by 10%, from AD^1 to AD^2. But in addition, because the increase in the money supply is anticipated by the public, the expected price level increases by 10%, from P_1 to P_2. Thus, the short-run aggregate supply curve shifts up from $SRAS^1$ to $SRAS^2$. The new short-run equilibrium, which is the same as the long-run equilibrium, is at point *F*. At *F*, output is unchanged at $\overline{Y}$ and the price level is 10% higher than in the initial equilibrium at *E*. Thus, an anticipated increase in the money supply is neutral in the short run as well as in the long run.

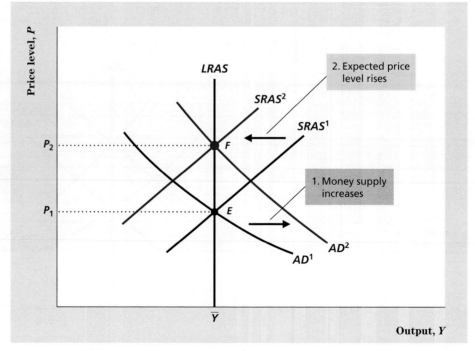

output but has raised prices proportionally. Similarly, an anticipated drop in the money supply would lower prices but not affect output or other real variables. Thus, anticipated changes in the money supply are neutral in the short run as well as in the long run. The reason is that if producers know that increases in the nominal prices of their products are the result of an increase in the money supply and do not reflect a change in relative prices, they will not be fooled into increasing production when prices rise.

RATIONAL EXPECTATIONS AND THE ROLE OF MONETARY POLICY

In the extended classical model based on the misperceptions theory, unanticipated changes in the money supply affect output, but anticipated changes in the money supply are neutral. Thus, if the Bank of Canada wanted to use monetary policy to affect output, it seemingly should use only unanticipated changes in the money supply. So, for example, when the economy is in recession, the Bank would try to use surprise increases in the money supply to raise output; when the economy is booming, the Bank would try to use surprise decreases in the money supply to slow the economy.

A serious problem for this strategy is the presence of private economic forecasters in financial markets. These people spend a good deal of time and effort trying to forecast macroeconomic variables, such as the money supply and the price level, and their forecasts are well publicized. If the Bank began a pattern of raising the money supply in recessions and reducing it in booms, forecasters would quickly understand and report this fact. As a result, the Bank's manipulations of the money supply would no longer be unanticipated, and the changes in the money supply would have no effect other than possibly causing instability in the price level. More generally, according to the misperceptions theory, to achieve any systematic change in the behaviour of output, the Bank must conduct monetary policy in a way that systematically fools the public. But there are strong incentives in the financial markets and elsewhere for people to try to figure out what the Bank is doing. Thus, most economists believe that attempts by the Bank to surprise the public in a systematic way cannot be successful.

The idea that a central bank cannot systematically surprise the public is part of a larger hypothesis that the public has rational expectations. The hypothesis of **rational expectations** states that the public's forecasts of various economic variables, including the money supply, the price level, and GDP, are based on reasoned and intelligent examination of available economic data.[29] (The evidence for rational expectations is discussed in Box 11.2, on the next page.) If the public has rational expectations, it will eventually understand the Bank of Canada's general pattern of behaviour. If expectations are rational, purely random changes in the money supply may be unanticipated and, thus, non-neutral. However, because the Bank will not be able to surprise the public systematically, it cannot use monetary policy to stabilize output. Thus, even if smoothing business cycles were desirable, according to the combination of the misperceptions theory and rational expectations, the Bank cannot systematically use monetary policy to do so.

---

29. The idea of rational expectations was first discussed by John F. Muth in his classic 1961 paper, "Rational Expectations and the Theory of Price Movements," *Econometrica*, July 1961, pp. 315–335. However, this idea was not widely used in macroeconomics until the new classical "revolution" of the early 1970s.

Box 11.2 ARE PRICE FORECASTS RATIONAL?

Most classical economists assume that people have rational expectations about future economic variables; that is, people make intelligent use of available information in forecasting variables that affect their economic decisions. The rational expectations assumption has important implications. For example, as we have demonstrated, if monetary non-neutrality is the result of temporary misperceptions of the price level and people have rational expectations about future prices, monetary policy is not able to affect the real economy systematically.

The rational expectations assumption is attractive to economists—including many Keynesian as well as classical economists—because it fits well economists' presumption that people intelligently pursue their economic self-interests. If people's expectations are not rational, the economic plans that individuals make will not generally be as good as they could be. But the theoretical attractiveness of rational expectations obviously is not enough; economists would like to know whether people really do have rational expectations about important economic variables.

The rational expectations idea can be tested with data from surveys, in which people are asked their opinions about the future of the economy. To illustrate how such a test would be conducted, suppose that we have data from a survey in which people were asked to make a prediction of the price level one year in the future. Imagine that this survey is repeated each year for several years. Now suppose that for each individual in the survey, we define

P^e_t = the individual's forecast, made in year $t - 1$, of the price level in year t.

Suppose also that we let P_t represent the price level that actually occurs in year t. Then the individual's forecast error for year t is the difference between the actual price level and the individual's forecast:

$P_t - P^e_t$ = the individual's forecast error in year t.

If people have rational expectations, these forecast errors should be unpredictable random numbers. However, if forecast errors are consistently positive or negative—meaning that people systematically tend to underpredict or overpredict the price level—expectations are not rational. If forecast errors have a systematic pattern—for example, if people tend to overpredict the price level when prices have been rising in the recent past—again, expectations are not rational.

Many statistical studies of price level forecasts made by consumers, journalists, academic economists, and others reject the rational expectations theory. A common finding is that people are too slow to incorporate new information into their forecasts. However, supporters of the rational expectations idea argue that the typical survey respondent is not likely to think very hard about the forecast she gives to the survey-taker because she has little or no economic stake in the quality of her answer. They argue that a fairer test of rational expectations is to examine the expectations of people who do have a real stake in the quality of their forecasts—namely, professional economic forecasters. Michael Keane and David Runkle,* of the Federal Reserve Bank of Minneapolis, studied the US price level forecasts of a panel of professional forecasters who have been surveyed by the American Statistical Association and the National Bureau of Economic Research since 1968. Perhaps not too surprisingly, Keane and Runkle found no evidence to refute the hypothesis that the professional forecasters had rational expectations. A plausible conclusion to draw from the research is that the greater a person's economic incentives to make good forecasts about the future, the more likely that person is to have rational expectations.

---

*"Testing the Rationality of Price Forecasts: New Evidence from Panel Data," *American Economic Review*, September 1990, pp. 714–735.

PROPAGATING THE EFFECTS OF UNANTICIPATED CHANGES IN THE MONEY SUPPLY

The misperceptions theory implies that unanticipated changes in the money supply are non-neutral because individual producers are temporarily fooled about the price level. However, money supply data are available weekly and price level data are reported monthly, suggesting that any misperceptions about monetary policy or the price level—and, thus, any real effects of money supply changes—should be quickly eliminated.

To explain how changes in the money supply can have real effects that last more than a few weeks, classical economists stress the role of propagation mechanisms. A **propagation mechanism** is an aspect of the economy that allows short-lived shocks to have relatively long-term effects on the economy.

An important example of a propagation mechanism is the behaviour of inventories. Consider a manufacturing firm that has both a normal level of monthly sales and a normal amount of finished goods in inventory that it tries to maintain. Suppose that an unanticipated rise in the money supply increases aggregate demand and raises prices above their expected level. Because increasing production sharply in a short period of time is costly, the firm will respond to the increase in demand partly by producing more goods and partly by selling some finished goods from inventory, thus depleting its inventory stocks below their normal level.

Next month, suppose that everyone learns the true price level and that the firm's rate of sales returns to its normal level. Despite the fact that the monetary shock has passed, the firm may continue to produce for a while at a higher-than-normal rate. The reason for the continued high level of production is that besides meeting its normal demand, the firm wants to replenish its inventory stock. The need to rebuild inventories illustrates a propagation mechanism that allows a short-lived shock (a monetary shock, in this case) to have a longer-term effect on the economy.

CHAPTER SUMMARY

1. Classical business cycle analysis utilizes the classical *IS–LM* model along with the assumption that wages and prices adjust quickly to bring the economy into general equilibrium.

2. The real business cycle (RBC) theory is a version of the classical theory that emphasizes productivity shocks (shocks to the production function) as the source of business cycle fluctuations. In the classical *IS–LM* model, a temporary decline in productivity reduces the real wage, employment, and output, while raising the real interest rate and the price level. The RBC theory can account for the observed procyclical behaviour of employment, real wages, and labour productivity. However, the prediction of the RBC theory that prices are countercyclical is viewed by some as a failing.

3. The Solow residual is an empirical measure of total factor productivity, A, in the production function. It increases as a result of technical progress that increases the amount of output that can be produced with the same amounts of labour and capital services (inputs). However, the Solow residual also changes as a result of changes in the utilization rates of capital and labour. The Solow residual is procyclical, at least partly because the utilization rates of capital and labour are procyclical. The procyclical behaviour of the utilization rate of labour may reflect labour hoarding, which occurs when firms continue to employ workers during recessions but use them less intensively or on tasks, such as maintenance, that do not contribute directly to measured output.

4. Classical business cycle analysis allows for other shocks to the economy besides changes in productivity, including changes in fiscal policy. According to the classical *IS–LM* model, an increase in government purchases raises employment, output, the real interest rate, and the price level. Including both fiscal and productivity shocks in the classical model improves its ability to fit the data. Although fiscal policy can affect employment and output, classical economists argue that it should not be used to smooth the business cycle because the invisible hand leads the economy to an efficient outcome without government interference. Instead, decisions about government purchases should be based on comparisons of costs and benefits.

5. In the basic classical model (which includes RBC theory), money is neutral, which means that changes in the nominal money supply change the price level proportionally but do not affect real variables, such as output, employment, and the real interest rate.

6. The basic classical model can account for the procyclical and leading behaviour of money if there is reverse causation, that is, if anticipated changes in output lead to changes in the money supply in the same direction. For example, if firms increase their money demand in anticipation of future output increases, and if the central bank (to keep the price level stable) supplies enough extra money to meet the increase in money demand, increases in the money stock precede increases in output. This result holds even though changes in the money stock do not cause subsequent changes in output.

7. Examination of historical monetary policy actions suggests that money is not neutral. More recent experiences, such as the economic slowdown that accompanied the Bank of Canada's pursuit of price stability, also provide evidence for the view that money is not neutral.

8. The misperceptions theory is based on the idea that producers have imprecise information about the current price level. According to the misperceptions theory, the amount of output supplied equals the full-employment level of output $\overline{Y}$ only if the actual price level equals the expected price level. When the price level is higher than expected, suppliers are fooled into thinking that the relative prices of the goods they supply have risen, so they supply a quantity of output that exceeds $\overline{Y}$. Similarly, when the price level is lower than expected, the quantity of output supplied is less than $\overline{Y}$.

The short-run aggregate supply curve (*SRAS*) based on the misperceptions theory slopes upward in describing the relation between output and the actual price level, with the expected price level held constant. In the long run, the price level equals the expected price level so that the supply of output equals $\overline{Y}$; thus, the long-run aggregate supply curve (*LRAS*) is a vertical line at the point where output equals $\overline{Y}$.

9. With the upward-sloping *SRAS* curve based on the misperceptions theory, an unanticipated increase in the money supply increases output (and is, thus, non-neutral) in the short run. However, because the long-run aggregate supply curve is vertical, an unanticipated increase in the money supply does not affect output (and so is neutral) in the long run. An anticipated increase in the money supply causes price expectations to adjust immediately and leads to no misperceptions about the price level; thus, an anticipated increase in the money supply is neutral in both the short and long runs.

10. According to the extended classical model based on the misperceptions theory, only surprise changes in the money supply can affect output. If the public has rational expectations about macroeconomic variables, including the money supply, the Bank of Canada cannot systematically surprise the public because the public will understand and anticipate the Bank's pattern of behaviour. Thus, classical economists argue that the Bank cannot systematically use changes in the money supply to affect output.

KEY DIAGRAM 8

THE MISPERCEPTIONS VERSION OF THE *AD–AS* MODEL

The misperceptions version of the *AD–AS* model shows how the aggregate demand for output and the aggregate supply of output interact to determine the price level and output in a classical model in which producers misperceive the aggregate price level.

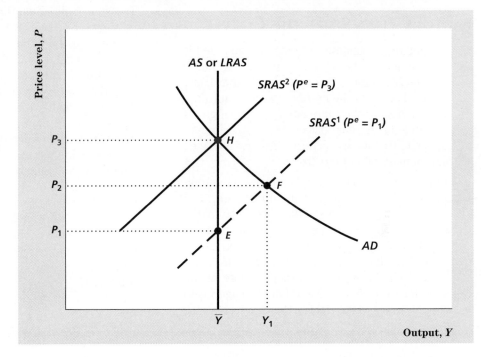

DIAGRAM ELEMENTS

- The price level, P, is on the vertical axis, and the level of output, Y, is on the horizontal axis.

- The aggregate demand (*AD*) curve shows the aggregate quantity of output demanded at each price level. It is identical to the *AD* curve in Key Diagram 7, p. 330. The aggregate amount of output demanded is determined by the intersection of the *IS* and *LM* curves (see Figure 9.10). An increase in the price level, P, reduces the real money supply, shifting the *LM* curve up and to the left and reducing the aggregate quantity of output demanded. Thus, the *AD* curve slopes downward.

- The misperceptions theory is based on the assumption that producers have imperfect information about the general price level and hence do not know precisely the relative prices of their products. When producers misperceive the price level, an increase in the general price level above the expected price level fools suppliers into thinking

that the relative prices of their goods have increased, so all suppliers increase output. The short-run aggregate supply (*SRAS*) curve shows the aggregate quantity of output supplied at each price level, with the expected price level held constant. Because an increase in the price level fools producers into supplying more output, the short-run aggregate supply curve slopes upward, as shown by $SRAS^1$.

- The short-run aggregate supply curve, $SRAS^1$, is drawn so that the expected price level, P^e, equals P_1. When the actual price level equals the expected price level, producers are not fooled and so supply the full-employment level of output, $\overline{Y}$. Therefore, at point E, where the actual price level equals the expected price level (both equal P_1), the short-run aggregate supply curve, $SRAS^1$, shows that producers supply $\overline{Y}$.

- In the long run, producers learn about the price level and adjust their expectations until the actual price level equals the expected price level. Producers then supply the full-employment level of output, $\overline{Y}$, regardless of the price level. Thus, the long-run aggregate supply (*LRAS*) curve is vertical at $Y = \overline{Y}$, just as in the basic *AD–AS* model in Key Diagram 7.

FACTORS THAT SHIFT THE CURVES

- The aggregate quantity of output demanded is determined by the intersection of the *IS* curve and the *LM* curve. At a constant price level, any factor that shifts the *IS–LM* intersection to the right increases the aggregate quantity of goods demanded and, thus, also shifts the *AD* curve to the right. Factors that shift the *AD* curve are listed in Summary table 14, p. 324.

- Any factor that increases full-employment output, $\overline{Y}$, shifts both the short-run and the long-run aggregate supply curves to the right. Factors that increase full-employment output include beneficial supply shocks or an increase in labour supply. An increase in government purchases because it induces workers to supply more labour, also shifts the short-run and long-run aggregate supply curves to the right in the classical model.

- An increase in the expected price level shifts the short-run aggregate supply curve up.

ANALYSIS

- The short-run equilibrium is at the intersection of the *AD* curve and the *SRAS* curve. For example, if the expected price level is P_1, the *SRAS* curve is $SRAS^1$, and the short-run equilibrium is at point *F*. At *F*, output, Y_1, is higher than the full-employment level, $\overline{Y}$, and the price level, P_2, is higher than the expected price level, P_1. As producers obtain information about the price level, the expected price level is revised upward, which shifts the *SRAS* curve up. The long-run equilibrium is at point *H*, where the long-run aggregate supply (*LRAS*) curve intersects the *AD* curve. In the long run, (1) output equals $\overline{Y}$, and (2) the price level equals the expected price level (both equal P_3). In the long run, when the expected price level has risen to P_3, the short-run aggregate supply curve, $SRAS^2$, passes through *H*.

KEY TERMS

labour hoarding, p. 415
misperceptions theory, p. 425
nominal shocks, p. 405
productivity shocks, p. 406
propagation mechanism, p. 433
rational expectations, p. 431
real business cycle theory, p. 405
real shocks, p. 405
reverse causation, p. 422
Solow residual, p. 411

KEY EQUATION

$$Y = \overline{Y} + b(P - P^e) \qquad (11.4)$$

The short-run aggregate supply curve, based on the misperceptions theory, indicates that the aggregate amount of output supplied, Y, equals full-employment output, $\overline{Y}$, when the price level, P, equals the expected price level, P^e. When the price level is higher than expected ($P > P^e$), output exceeds $\overline{Y}$; when the price level is lower than expected ($P < P^e$), output is less than $\overline{Y}$.

REVIEW QUESTIONS

1. What main feature of the classical *IS–LM* model distinguishes it from the Keynesian *IS–LM* model? Why is the distinction of practical importance?

2. What are the two main components of any theory of the business cycle? Describe these two components for the real business cycle theory.

3. Define *real shock* and *nominal shock*. What type of real shock do real business cycle theorists consider the most important source of cyclical fluctuations?

4. What major business cycle facts does the RBC theory explain successfully? Does it explain any business cycle facts less well?

5. What is the Solow residual and how does it behave over the business cycle? What factors cause the Solow residual to change?

6. What effects does an increase in government purchases have on the labour market, according to the classical theory? What effects does it have on output, the real interest rate, and the price level? According to classical economists, should fiscal policy be used to smooth out the business cycle? Why, or why not?

7. In the context of the relationship between the money supply and real economic activity, what is meant by reverse causation? Explain how reverse causation could occur. What business cycle fact is it intended to explain?

8. According to the misperceptions theory, what effect does an increase in the price level have on the amount of output supplied by producers? Explain. Does it matter whether the increase in the price level was expected?

9. What conclusion does the basic classical model (with no misperceptions of the price level) allow about the neutrality or non-neutrality of money? In what ways is this conclusion modified by the extended classical model based on the misperceptions theory?

10. Define *rational expectations*. According to the classical model, what implications do rational expectations have for the ability of the central bank to use monetary policy to smooth business cycles?

NUMERICAL PROBLEMS

1. In a certain economy the production function is

$$\bar{Y} = A(100N - 0.5N^2),$$

where Y is output, A is productivity, and N is total hours worked. The marginal product of labour associated with this production function is

$$MPN = A(100 - N).$$

Initially, $A = 1.0$, but a beneficial productivity shock raises A to 1.1.

a. The supply of labour is

$$NS = 45 + 0.1w,$$

where w is the real wage. Find the equilibrium levels of output, hours worked, and the real wage before and after the productivity shock. Recall (from Chapter 3) that the MPN curve is the same as the labour demand curve, with the real wage replacing the MPN.

b. Repeat part (a) if the labour supply is

$$NS = 10 + 0.8w.$$

c. Some studies show that the real wage is only slightly procyclical. Assume for the sake of argument that this finding is correct. Would a calibrated RBC model fit the facts better if the labour supply is relatively insensitive to the real wage, or if it is relatively sensitive? Justify your answer diagrammatically and relate it to your answers to parts (a) and (b).

2. A closed economy is described as follows:

Desired consumption	$C^d = 600 + 0.5(Y - T) - 50r.$
Desired investment	$I^d = 450 - 50r.$
Real money demand	$L = 0.5Y - 100i.$
Full-employment output	$\bar{Y} = 2,210.$
Expected inflation	$\pi^e = 0.05.$

In this economy, the government always has a balanced budget, so $T = G$, where T is total taxes collected.

a. Suppose that $M = 4,320$ and $G = 150$. Use the classical *IS–LM* model to find the equilibrium values of output, the real interest rate, the price level, consumption, and investment. (*Hint*: In the classical model, output always equals its full-employment level.)

b. The money supply rises to 4,752. Repeat part (a). Is money neutral?

c. With the money supply back at 4,320, government purchases and taxes rise to 190. Repeat part (a). Assume, for simplicity, that $\bar{Y}$ is fixed (unaffected by G). Is fiscal policy neutral in this case? Explain.

3. Consider the following economy:

Desired consumption	$C^d = 1,275 + 0.5(Y - T) - 200r.$
Desired investment	$I^d = 900 - 200r.$
Real money demand	$L = 0.5Y - 200i.$
Full-employment output	$\bar{Y} = 4,600.$
Expected inflation	$\pi^e = 0.$

a. Suppose that $T = G = 450$ and that $M = 9,000$. Find an equation describing the *IS* curve. (*Hint*: Set desired national saving and desired investment equal, and solve for the relationship between r and Y.) Find an equation describing the *LM* curve. (*Hint*: Set real money supply and real money demand equal, and again solve for the relationship between r and Y, given P.) Finally, find an equation for the aggregate demand curve. (*Hint*: Use the *IS* and *LM* equations to find a relationship between Y and P.) What are the equilibrium values of output, consumption, investment, the real interest rate, and the price level? Assume that there are no misperceptions about the price level.

b. Suppose that $T = G = 450$ and that $M = 4,500$. What is the equation for the aggregate demand curve now? What are the equilibrium values of output, consumption, investment, the real interest rate, and the price level? Assume that full-employment output $\bar{Y}$ is fixed.

c. Repeat part (b) for $T = G = 330$ and $M = 9,000$.

4. An economy has the following *AD* and *AS* curves:

AD curve	$Y = 300 + 30(M/P).$
AS curve	$Y = \bar{Y} + 10(P - P^e).$

Here, $\bar{Y} = 500$ and $M = 400$.

a. Suppose that $P^e = 60$. What are the equilibrium values of the price level P and output Y? (*Hint*: The solutions for P in this part and in part (b) are multiples of 10.)

b. An unanticipated increase raises the money supply to $M = 700$. Because the increase is unanticipated, P^e remains at 60. What are the equilibrium values of the price level P and output Y?

c. The Bank of Canada announces that the money supply will be increased to $M = 700$, which the public believes. Now what are the equilibrium values of the price level P, the expected price level P^e, and output Y?

5. Output in an economy is given by the production function $Y = AK^{0.3}N^{0.7}$, where Y is output, A measures productivity, the capital stock K is fixed at 30, and employment N is fixed at 100. Output equals 100 in the year 2000 and equals 105 in 2001.

a. Find the Solow residual in the years 2000 and 2001, and its growth rate between those two years.

b. What is the relationship between the growth in the Solow residual between 2000 and 2001 and the growth in productivity (as measured by the parameter A) in the same years? Assume that the rates of utilization of capital and labour remain unchanged.

c. Repeat part (b) under the assumption that utilization of labour increases by 3% between 2000 and 2001. You will have to modify the production function along the lines of Eq. (9.2).

d. Repeat part (b) under the assumption that the utilization rates of both labour and capital increase by 3% between 2000 and 2001.

6. Try the following experiment: Flip a coin 50 times, keeping track of the results. Think of each "heads" as a small positive shock that increases output by one unit; similarly, think of each "tails" as a small negative shock that reduces output by one unit. Let the initial value of output Y be 50, and graph the level of output over time as it is hit by the "positive" and "negative" shocks (coin flips). For example, if your first four flips are three heads and a tail, output takes the values 51, 52, 53, 52. After 50 flips, have your small shocks produced any large cycles in output?

7. In a particular economy, the labour force (the sum of employed and unemployed workers) is fixed at 10 million. In this economy, each month 1% of the workers who were employed at the beginning of the month lose their jobs, and 19% of the workers who were unemployed at the beginning of the month find new jobs.

a. The January unemployment rate is 8%. For the rates of job loss and job finding given, what will the unemployment rate be in February? in March?

b. In April an adverse productivity shock raises the job loss rate to 3% of those employed. The job loss rate returns to 1% in May, while the job finding rate remains unchanged at 19% throughout. Find the unemployment rate for April, May, June, and July.

8. (Appendix) Consider the following economy:

IS curve	$r = 2.47 - 0.0004Y$.
Real money demand	$L = 0.5Y - 500(r + \pi^e)$.
Short-run aggregate supply	$Y = \bar{Y} + 100(P - P^e)$.

Here, r is the real interest rate, Y is output, and P is the price level. Assume that expected inflation $\pi^e = 0$, nominal money supply $M = 88,950$, and full-employment output $\bar{Y} = 6,000$.

a. Use the notation of Appendixes 9.A and 11.A. What are the values of the parameters a_{IS}, b_{IS}, a_{LM}, β_{LM}, ℓ_r, and b? (*Hint*: Solve for asset market equilibrium to obtain the coefficients of the *LM* equation.)

b. What is the equation of the aggregate demand curve?

c. Suppose that the expected price level $P^e = 29.15$. What are the short-run equilibrium values of the price level P and output Y?

d. What are the long-run equilibrium values of the price level P and output Y?

ANALYTICAL PROBLEMS

1. The discovery of a new technology increases the expected future marginal product of capital.

a. Use the classical *IS–LM* model to determine the effect of the increase in the expected future *MPK* on current output, the real interest rate, employment, real wages, consumption, investment, and the price level. Assume that expected future real wages and future incomes are unaffected by the new technology. Assume also that current productivity is unaffected.

b. Find the effects of the increase in the expected future *MPK* on current output and prices from the *AD–AS* diagram based on the misperceptions theory. What accounts for the difference with part (a)?

2. Use the classical *IS–LM* model to analyze the effects of a permanent increase in government purchases of 100 per year (in real terms). The increase in purchases is financed by a permanent increase in lump-sum taxes of 100 per year.

a. Begin by finding the effects of the fiscal change on the labour market. How does the effect of the permanent increase in government purchases of 100 compare with the effect of a temporary increase in purchases of 100?

b. Because the tax increase is permanent, assume that at any constant levels of output and the real interest rate consumers respond by reducing their consumption each period by the full amount of the tax increase. Under this assumption, how does the permanent increase in government purchases affect desired national saving and the *IS* curve?

c. Use the classical *IS–LM* model to find the effects of the permanent increase in government purchases and taxes on output, the real interest rate, and the price level in the current period. What happens if consumers reduce their current consumption by less than 100 at any level of output and the real interest rate?

3. Consider a business cycle theory that combines the classical *IS–LM* model with the assumption that temporary changes in government purchases are the main source of cyclical fluctuations. How well would this theory explain the observed cyclical behaviour of each of the following variables? Give reasons for your answers.

a. Employment

b. The real wage

c. Average labour productivity

d. Investment

e. The price level

4. This problem asks you to work out in more detail the example of reverse causation described in the text. Suppose that firms that expect to increase production in the future have to increase their current transactions (for example, they may need to purchase more raw materials). For this reason, current real money demand rises when expected future output rises.

a. Under the assumption that real money demand depends on expected future output, use the classical *IS–LM* model to find the effects of an increase in expected future output on the current price level. For simplicity, assume that any effects of the increase in expected future output on the labour market or on desired saving and investment are small and can be ignored.

b. Suppose that the Bank of Canada wants to stabilize the current price level. How will the Bank respond to the increase in expected future output? Explain why the Bank's response is an example of reverse causation.

5. Two countries called East and West agree to unify. The real value of full-employment output in East is 1 trillion widgets, and in West it is 2 trillion widgets. The combined full-employment output of the unified country is expected to be the sum of the two full-employment outputs, or 3 trillion widgets.

Real money demand in the West is 10% of West's real output and will remain so after unification. In the East, people do not have access to financial instruments, such as stocks and bonds, and so are forced to save in the form of money. As a result, real money demand in the East is 40% of East's real output. However, after unification, Easterners will have access to a full range of financial assets, and thus, their real money demand will drop to 10% of output.

The unified country will use only the West's currency. As part of the unification plan, the West central bank has agreed to print new Western currency and trade it for Eastern currency, which will be destroyed. At the initial price levels, the total real value of the Western currency received by Easterners equals the total real value of the Eastern currency they give up.

Use the classical *IS–LM* model to find the effects on post-unification output and prices of the currency swap. Give a quantitative estimate of the effect on the price level (measured in the Western currency). Qualitatively, does your answer change if you use the *AD–AS* model based on the misperceptions theory? What can West's central bank do to offset the effects of the currency swap on the price level?

6. Starting from a situation with no government spending and no taxes, the government introduces a foreign aid program (in which domestically produced goods are shipped abroad) and pays for it with a temporary 10% tax on current wages. Future wages are untaxed.

What effects will the temporary wage tax have on labour supply? Use the classical *IS–LM* model to find the effects of the fiscal change on output, employment, the (before-tax) real wage, the real interest rate, and the price level.

APPENDIX 11.A

AN ALGEBRAIC VERSION OF THE CLASSICAL *AD–AS* MODEL WITH MISPERCEPTIONS

Building on the algebraic version of the *IS–LM* model developed in Appendix 9.A, in this appendix we derive an algebraic version of the classical *AD–AS* model presented in this chapter. We present algebraic versions of the aggregate demand (*AD*) curve and the aggregate supply (*AS*) curve and then solve for the general equilibrium.

THE AGGREGATE DEMAND CURVE

Because misperceptions by producers do not affect the demand for goods, the aggregate demand curve is the same as in Appendix 9.A. Recall from Eq. (9.A.27) that the equation of the aggregate demand (AD) curve is

$$Y = \frac{\alpha_{IS} - \alpha_{LM} + (1/\ell_r)(M/P)}{\beta_{IS} + \beta_{LM}}. \tag{11.A.1}$$

where the coefficients of the *IS* curve, α_{IS} and β_{IS}, are given by Eqs. (9.A.15) and (9.A.16), respectively, the coefficients of the *LM* curve, α_{LM} and β_{LM}, are given by Eqs. (9.A.20) and (9.A.21) respectively, and ℓ_r is the coefficient of the nominal interest rate in the money demand equation, Eq. (9.A.17).

THE AGGREGATE SUPPLY CURVE

The short-run aggregate supply curve based on the misperceptions theory is represented by Eq. (11.4), which, for convenience, we repeat here:

$$Y = \bar{Y} + b(P - P^e), \tag{11.A.2}$$

where *b* is a positive number.

GENERAL EQUILIBRIUM

For a given expected price level P^e, the short-run equilibrium value of the price level is determined by the intersection of the aggregate demand curve (Eq. 11.A.1) and the short-run aggregate supply curve (Eq. 11.A.2). Setting the right-hand sides of Eqs. (11.A.1) and (11.A.2) equal and multiplying both sides of the resulting equation by *P* yields a quadratic equation for the price level *P*:

$$a_2 P^2 + a_1 P - a_0 = 0, \tag{11.A.3}$$

where

$$a_2 = (\beta_{IS} + \beta_{LM})b;$$
$$a_1 = (\beta_{IS} + \beta_{LM})(\bar{Y} - bP^e) - \alpha_{IS} + \alpha_{LM};$$
$$a_0 = \frac{M}{\ell_r}.$$

The coefficients a_2 and a_0 are positive, and the coefficient a_1 could be positive, negative, or zero. Because both a_2 and a_0 are both positive, the solution of Eq. (11.A.3) yields one positive value of P and one negative value of P. The price level cannot be negative, so the short-run equilibrium price level is the positive solution of this equation. Using the standard quadratic formula, we find the positive solution of Eq. (11.A.3) to be

$$P = \frac{-a_1 + \sqrt{a_1^2 + 4a_2 a_0}}{2a_2}.$$
(11.A.4)

We obtain the short-run equilibrium level of output by substituting the value of the price level from Eq. (11.A.4) into either the aggregate demand curve Eq. (11.A.1) or the aggregate supply curve Eq. (11.A.2).

Note that an increase in the nominal money supply M increases the constant a_0, and thus, according to Eq. (11.A.4), it increases the equilibrium price level. Because an increase in M does not affect the aggregate supply curve but does increase the equilibrium price level, Eq. (11.A.2) shows that it increases output.

We focused on short-run equilibrium in this appendix. In the long run, the actual price level equals the expected price level so that, according to Eq. (11.A.2), output equals its full-employment level $\overline{Y}$. In the long run, the economy reaches the general equilibrium described in Appendix 9.A .

Chapter 12

KEYNESIANISM: THE MACROECONOMICS OF WAGE AND PRICE RIGIDITY

In Chapter 11, we presented the classical, or market-clearing, approach to business cycle analysis. In the classical approach, wages and prices are assumed to adjust quickly so that markets are almost always in equilibrium. Classical economists argue that business cycles represent the economy's best response to disturbances, such as productivity shocks, so there is little justification for government attempts to smooth the cycle.

In contrast to the classicals, Keynesians are less optimistic about the ability of free-market economies to respond quickly and efficiently to shocks. One of the central ideas of Keynesianism is that wages and prices are "rigid" or "sticky" and do *not* adjust quickly to market-clearing levels. Wage and price rigidity implies that the economy can be away from its general equilibrium for significant periods of time. Thus, a deep recession is not an optimal response of the free market to outside shocks; rather, it is a disequilibrium situation in which high unemployment reflects an excess of labour supplied over labour demanded. Many Keynesians believe that the government should act to eliminate—or at least minimize—these periods of low output and high unemployment. Others—sometimes called *new Keynesians*— think that rigidities or market imperfections cause cycles but do not think that macroeconomic policy should necessarily be used to try to stabilize the economy.

As wage and price rigidity is the basis for Keynesian theory and policy recommendations, understanding the potential causes of rigidity is important. A telling criticism that the classicals aimed at the Keynesians in the early 1970s was that the Keynesians simply assumed that wages and prices are rigid, without giving a good economic explanation of why these rigidities occur. After all, argued the classicals, wages and prices are not simply "given" to the economy but are the results of decisions made by millions of individuals and firms. If excessively high wages are causing unemployment, why don't unemployed workers offer to work for lower wages until firms are willing to hire them? If prices are not at the levels at which quantities supplied equal quantities demanded, why don't firms just change their prices? In effect, the classicals challenged the Keynesians to show how wage and price rigidity could be consistent with the idea—basic to almost all of economics— that individuals and firms are economically rational; that is, they do the best they can for themselves when making economic decisions.

Keynesian researchers accepted this challenge and have made progress in explaining wage and price rigidity in terms consistent with economic rationality. In the first part of this chapter, we discuss some leading Keynesian explanations for wage and price rigidity. We then show how slow adjustment of wages and prices can be incorporated into the *IS–LM* model, converting it from a classical model to a Keynesian model. Using this model, we discuss the Keynesian answers to the two central questions about business cycles, namely, what causes business cycles and what should policymakers do about them?

12.1 REAL-WAGE RIGIDITY

Because Keynesian analysis and policy prescriptions depend so greatly on the assumption that wages and prices do not move rapidly to clear markets, we begin by discussing in some detail the possible economic reasons for slow or incomplete adjustment. In this section, we focus on the rigidity of real wages, and in Section 12.2, we look at the slow adjustment of prices.

The main reason that Keynesians bring wage rigidity into their analysis is their dissatisfaction with the classical explanation of unemployment. Recall that classicals believe that most unemployment, including the increases in unemployment that occur during recessions, arises from mismatches between workers and jobs (frictional or structural unemployment). Keynesians do not dispute that mismatch is a major source of unemployment, but they are sceptical that it explains all unemployment.

Keynesians are particularly unwilling to accept the classical idea that recessions are periods of increased mismatch between workers and jobs. If higher unemployment during downturns reflected increased mismatch, Keynesians argue, recessions should be periods of particularly active search by workers for jobs and by firms for new employees. However, surveys suggest that unemployed workers spend relatively little time searching for work (many are simply waiting, hoping to be recalled to their old jobs), and help-wanted advertising and vacancy postings by firms fall, rather than rise during recessions. Rather than times of increased worker–job mismatch, Keynesians believe that recessions are periods of generally low demand for both output and workers throughout the economy.

To explain the existence of unemployment without relying solely on worker–job mismatch, Keynesians argue for rejecting the classical assumption that real wages adjust relatively quickly to equate the quantities of labour supplied and demanded. In particular, if the real wage is above the level that clears the labour market, unemployment (an excess of labour supplied over labour demanded) will result. From the Keynesian perspective, the idea that the real wage moves "too little" to keep the quantity of labour demanded equal to the quantity of labour supplied is called **real-wage rigidity**.

SOME REASONS FOR REAL-WAGE RIGIDITY

For a rigid real wage to be the source of unemployment, the real wage that firms are paying must be higher than the market-clearing real wage, at which quantities of labour supplied and demanded are equal. But if the real wage is higher than necessary to attract workers, why don't firms save labour costs by simply reducing the wage that they pay, as suggested by the classical analysis?

Various explanations have been offered for why real wages might be rigid, even in the face of an excess supply of labour. One possibility is that there are legal and institutional factors that keep wages high, such as minimum-wage laws and union contracts. However, most Canadian workers are neither union members nor minimum-wage earners (about 30% are unionized), so these barriers to wage cutting cannot be the main reason for real-wage rigidity. Furthermore, the minimum wage in Canadian provinces is specified in nominal terms so that workers who are paid the minimum wage would have rigid nominal wages rather than rigid real wages. (Union contracts may help explain real-wage rigidity in Western European and other countries in which a high proportion of workers are unionized, and in which nominal wages are typically adjusted for inflation in order to maintain the real wage at its negotiated level.)

Another explanation for why a firm might pay a higher real wage than it "has" to is that this policy might reduce the firm's **turnover costs**, or the costs associated with hiring and training new workers. By paying a high wage, the firm can keep more of its current workers, which saves the firm the cost of hiring and training replacements. Similarly, by developing a reputation for paying well, the firm can assure itself of more and better applicants for any position that it may have to fill.

A third reason that firms might pay real wages above market-clearing levels is that workers who are paid well may have greater incentives to work hard and effectively. If highly paid workers are more productive, the firm may profit from paying its employees well, even though it could attract all the workers it needs at a lower real wage. The idea that a worker's productivity depends on the real wage received and that, therefore, firms may pay wages above the market-clearing level is the essence of the **efficiency wage model**. Because this model of wage determination has played a key role in recent Keynesian analyses and because it has several interesting aspects, we focus on it for the remainder of this section.

THE EFFICIENCY WAGE MODEL

If better-paid workers are more productive, firms may gain by paying wages higher than the minimum necessary to attract workers. But why might a worker's productivity depend on the real wage received? The answer has both "carrot" and "stick" aspects.

The *carrot* or positive incentive is based on the idea that workers who feel well treated will work harder and more efficiently. Nobel Laureate George Akerlof, of the University of California at Berkeley, argued that workers who believe that their employer is treating them fairly—say, by paying higher wages than required to retain them and by not cutting wages in slack times—will, in turn, want to treat the employer fairly by doing a good job. Akerlof called this motivation the *gift exchange motive*[1] because it is similar to the one that leads people to exchange gifts.

The *stick* or threat aspect of why a firm would pay a higher wage than necessary has been analyzed in an economic model called the "shirking" model of wage determination.[2] According to the *shirking model*, if a worker is paid only the minimum amount needed to attract her to a particular job, she will not be too concerned about the possibility of being fired if she does not perform well. After all, if the job pays the minimum amount necessary to induce her to take the job, she is not much happier with the job than without the job. In this case, the worker will be more inclined to take it easy at work and shirk her duties, and the employer will have to bear the cost either of the shirking or of paying supervisors to make sure that the work gets done. In contrast, a worker receiving a higher wage will place a greater value on keeping her job (it is not that easy to find another job as good) and will work hard to avoid being fired for shirking.

The gift exchange idea and the shirking model both imply that workers' efforts on the job depend on the real wages they receive. Graphically, the relation between the real wage and the level of effort is shown by the **effort curve** in Figure 12.1, on the next page. The real wage w is measured along the horizontal axis, and the level

---

1. See George Akerlof, "Labor Contracts as Partial Gift Exchange," *Quarterly Journal of Economics*, November 1982, pp. 543–569.
2. See Carl Shapiro and Joseph E. Stiglitz, "Equilibrium Unemployment as a Worker Discipline Device," *American Economic Review*, June 1984, pp. 433–444.

FIGURE 12.1

DETERMINATION OF THE
EFFICIENCY WAGE

The effort curve shows the relation between worker effort, E, and the real wage workers receive, w. A higher real wage leads to more effort, but above a certain point, higher wages are unable to spur effort much, so the effort curve is S-shaped. For any point on the curve, the amount of effort per dollar of real wage is the slope of the line from the origin to that point. At point A, effort per dollar of real wage is E_A/w_A. The highest level of effort per dollar of real wage is at point B, where the line from the origin is tangent to the curve. The real wage rate at B is the efficiency wage w^*, and the corresponding level of effort is E^*.

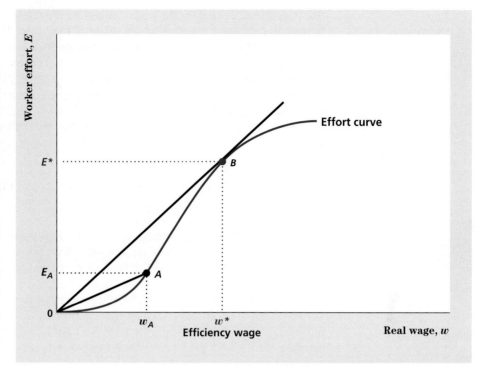

of effort E is measured along the vertical axis. The effort curve passes through points O, A, and B. When real wages are higher, workers choose to work harder, for either "carrot" or "stick" reasons; therefore, the effort curve slopes upward. We assume that the effort curve is S-shaped. At the lowest levels of the real wage, workers make hardly any effort, and effort rises only slowly as the real wage increases. At higher levels of the real wage, effort rises sharply, as shown by the steeply rising portion of the curve. The curve flattens at very high levels of the real wage because there is some maximum level of effort that workers really cannot exceed no matter how motivated they are.

WAGE DETERMINATION IN THE EFFICIENCY WAGE MODEL

The effort curve shows that effort depends on the real wage, but what determines the real wage? To make as much profit as possible, *firms will choose the level of the real wage that gets the most effort from workers for each dollar of real wages paid.* The amount of effort per dollar of real wages equals the amount of effort E divided by the real wage w. The ratio of E to w can be found graphically from Figure 12.1. Consider, for example, point A on the effort curve, at which the real wage w_A induces workers to supply effort E_A. The slope of the line from the origin to A equals the height of the curve at point A, E_A, divided by the horizontal distance, w_A. Thus, the slope of the line from the origin to A equals the amount of effort per dollar of real wages at A.

The real wage that achieves the highest effort per dollar of wages is at point B. The slope of the line from the origin to B, which is the amount of effort per dollar of real wage at B, is greater than the slope of the line from the origin to any other point on the curve. In general, to locate the real wage that maximizes effort per dollar of real wage, draw a line from the origin tangent to the effort curve; the real wage at the tangency point maximizes effort per dollar of real wage. We call the real wage that maximizes effort or efficiency per dollar of real wages the **efficiency wage**. In Figure 12.1, the efficiency wage is w^*, and the corresponding level of effort is E^*.

The efficiency wage theory helps explain real-wage rigidity. Because the employer chooses the real wage that maximizes effort received per dollar paid, as long as the effort curve does not change, the employer will not change the real wage. Therefore, the theory implies that the real wage is permanently rigid and equals the efficiency wage.

EMPLOYMENT AND UNEMPLOYMENT IN THE EFFICIENCY WAGE MODEL

According to the efficiency wage theory, the real wage is rigid at the level that maximizes effort per dollar of wages paid. We now consider how the levels of employment and unemployment in the labour market are determined.

The workings of the labour market when there is an efficiency wage are shown in Figure 12.2, on the next page. The efficiency wage w^* is indicated by a horizontal line. Because the efficiency wage is determined solely by the effort curve, for the purpose of analyzing the labour market we can take w^* to be fixed. Similarly, we can take the level of effort E^* induced by the efficiency wage w^* as fixed at this stage of the analysis.

The upward-sloping curve is the standard labour supply curve, *NS*. As in the classical model, this curve shows the number of hours of work that people would like to supply at each level of the real wage.[3]

The downward-sloping curve is the demand curve for labour in the efficiency wage model. Recall from Chapter 3 that the amount of labour demanded by a firm depends on the marginal product of labour, or *MPN*. Specifically, the labour demand curve is identical to the *MPN* curve, which, in turn, relates the marginal product of labour *MPN* to the quantity of labour input *N* being used. The *MPN* curve—and hence the labour demand curve—slopes down because of the diminishing marginal productivity of labour.

In the classical model, the marginal product of labour depends only on the production function and the capital stock. A complication of the efficiency wage model is that the amount of output produced by an extra worker (or hour of work) also depends on the worker's effort. Fortunately, as we noted, the efficiency wage w^* and the effort level induced by that wage, E^*, are fixed at this stage of the analysis. Thus, the labour demand curve in Figure 12.2, ND^*, reflects the marginal product of labour when worker effort is held fixed at E^*. As in the classical case, an increase in productivity or in the capital stock shifts the labour demand curve ND^* to the right. In addition, any change in the effort curve that led to an increase in the optimal level of effort E^* would raise the *MPN* and the labour demand curve ND^* again would shift to the right.

Now, we can put the elements of Figure 12.2 together to show how employment is determined. Point *A* on the labour demand curve ND^* indicates that when the real wage is fixed at w^*, firms want to employ $\overline{N}$ hours of labour. Point *B* on the labour supply curve indicates that when the real wage is fixed at w^*, workers want

---

3.   For simplicity, we assume that the number of hours of labour that people want to supply does not depend on the effort they must exert while on the job.

Figure 12.2

Excess supply of labour
in the efficiency wage
model

When the efficiency wage w^*
is paid, the firm's demand for
labour is $\bar{N}$, represented by
point A. However, the amount
of labour that workers want to
supply at a real wage of w^* is
NS_1. The excess supply of
labour equals distance AB. We
assume that the efficiency
wage w^* is higher than the
market-clearing wage w_E that
would prevail if the supply of
labour equalled the demand
for labour at point E.

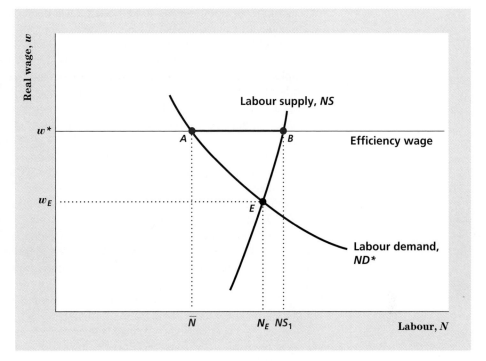

to supply NS_1 hours of labour, which is greater than the amount demanded by firms. At the efficiency wage, the quantity of labour supplied is greater than the quantity demanded,[4] so the level of employment is determined by the labour demand of firms and hence equals $\bar{N}$. The demand-determined level of employment is labelled $\bar{N}$ because it represents the full-employment level of employment for this model; that is, $\bar{N}$ is the level of employment reached after full adjustment of wages and prices. (Note that the value of $\bar{N}$ in the efficiency wage model differs from the full-employment level of employment in the classical model of the labour market, which would correspond to N_E in Figure 12.2.) Because the efficiency wage is rigid at w^*, in the absence of shocks the level of employment in this economy remains at $\bar{N}$ indefinitely.

Perhaps the most interesting aspect of Figure 12.2 is that it provides a new explanation of unemployment. It shows that even when wages have adjusted as much as they are going to and the economy is technically at "full employment," an excess supply of labour, $NS_1 - \bar{N}$ remains.[5]

Why don't the unemployed bid down the real wage and, thus, gain employment, as they would in the classical model of the labour market? Unlike the classical case, in a labour market with an efficiency wage, the real wage cannot be bid down by people offering to work at lower wages because employers will not hire them. Employers know that people working at lower wages will not put out as much effort per dollar of real wages as workers receiving the higher efficiency wage. Thus, the

4. The result that there is an excess supply of labour requires the assumption that the efficiency wage w^* is higher than the real wage that would clear the labour market, shown as w_E in Figure 12.2. We always assume that the efficiency wage is higher than the market-clearing wage; if it were not, firms would have to pay the market-clearing wage to attract workers.

5. Because the unemployment represented by the excess supply of labour persists even when the economy is at full employment, it is considered part of structural unemployment.

excess supply of labour shown in Figure 12.2 will persist indefinitely. The efficiency wage model, thus, implies that unemployment will exist even if there is no mismatch between jobs and workers.

The efficiency wage model is an interesting theory of real wages and unemployment, but does it explain actual behaviour? Box 12.1 interprets a famous episode in labour history in terms of efficiency wage theory. In addition to this anecdotal evidence, studies of wages and employment in various firms and industries provide some support for the efficiency wage model. For example, Peter Cappelli, of the University of Pennsylvania, and Keith Chauvin, of the University of Kansas,[6] found that consistent with one aspect of the theory, US plants that paid higher wages to workers experienced less shirking, measured by the number of workers fired for disciplinary reasons.

A criticism of the efficiency wage model presented here is that it predicts that the real wage is literally fixed (for no change in the effort curve). Of course, this result is too extreme because the real wage does change over time (and over the business cycle). However, the basic model can be extended to allow for changes in the effort curve that bring changes in the efficiency wage over time. For example, a reasonable assumption would be that workers are more concerned about losing their jobs during recessions, when finding a new job is more difficult, than during booms. Under this assumption, the real wage necessary to obtain any specific level of effort will be lower during recessions; hence the efficiency wage paid in recessions also may be lower. This extension may help the efficiency wage model match the business cycle fact that real wages are lower in recessions than in booms (procyclical real wages).

EFFICIENCY WAGES AND THE *FE* LINE

In the Keynesian version of the *IS–LM* model, as in the classical version, the *FE* line is vertical, showing the full-employment level of output $\overline{Y}$. If we assume that employers pay efficiency wages, full-employment output $\overline{Y}$, in turn, is the output produced when employment is at the full-employment level of employment $\overline{N}$, as shown in Figure 12.2, and the level of worker effort is E^*.

As in the classical model, anything that changes full-employment output $\overline{Y}$ shifts the *FE* line. The classical model emphasizes two factors that shift the *FE* line: changes in the supply of labour and changes in productivity. In the efficiency wage model, however, labour supply does not affect employment, *so changes in labour supply do not affect the FE line in the Keynesian model* with efficiency wages. A change in productivity, however, does affect the *FE* line in the Keynesian model, as in the classical model. A drop in productivity reduces full-employment output $\overline{Y}$ and shifts the *FE* line to the left, for two reasons. First, by reducing the marginal product of labour at any given level of employment, a drop in productivity reduces the demand for labour at any fixed real wage. With the real wage fixed at w^*, the full-employment level of employment $\overline{N}$ falls. Second, a drop in productivity reduces the amount of output that can be produced with any particular amount of capital, labour, and effort.

---

6. "An Interplant Test of the Efficiency Wage Hypothesis," *Quarterly Journal of Economics*, August 1991, pp. 769–787.

Box 12.1 HENRY FORD'S EFFICIENCY WAGE

During the period 1908–1914, Henry Ford instituted at Ford Motor Company a radically new way of producing automobiles.* Prior to Ford's innovations, automobile components were not produced to uniform specifications. Instead, cars had to be assembled one by one by skilled craftsmen, who could make the parts fit even if sizes or shapes were off by fractions of an inch. Ford introduced a system of assembly-line production, in which a standardized product, the Model T automobile, was produced from precisely made, interchangeable components. The production process also was broken into numerous small, simple steps, replacing the skilled craftsmen who had built cars from start to finish with unskilled workers who performed only a few operations over and over.

The high speed at which Ford ran the assembly line and the repetitiveness of the work were hard on the workers. As one labourer said, "If I keep putting on Nut No. 86 for about 86 more days, I will be Nut No. 86 in the Pontiac bughouse."[†] As a result, worker turnover was high, with the typical worker lasting only a few months on the job. Absenteeism also was high—about 10% on any given day—and morale was low. Worker slowdowns and even sabotage occurred.

In January 1914, Ford announced that the company would begin paying $5 a day to workers who met

certain criteria, one being that the worker had been with the company at least six months. Five dollars a day was more than double the normal wage for production workers at the time. Although the motivation for Ford's announcement has been debated, its effect was stunning: Thousands of workers lined up outside the plant, hoping for jobs. Within the plant, the number of people quitting dropped by 87%, absenteeism dropped by 75%, and productivity rose by 30% or more. The productivity increases helped increase Ford's profits, despite the higher wage bill and a cut in the price of a Model T.

Many results of Ford's $5 day can be predicted by the efficiency wage model, including improved efficiency and higher profits. As other automakers adopted Ford's technological innovations, they also adopted his wage policies. By 1928, before unions were important in the industry, auto industry wages were almost 40% higher than those in the rest of manufacturing.

---

* The source for this box is Daniel M. G. Raff and Lawrence H. Summers, "Did Henry Ford Pay Efficiency Wages?" *Journal of Labor Economics*, October 1987, pp. S57–S86.
[†] This quotation is originally from Stephen Meyer, *The Five-Dollar Day: Labor Management and Social Control in the Ford Motor Company, 1908–1921*, Albany: State University of New York Press, 1981.

12.2 PRICE STICKINESS

The rigidity created by efficiency wages is a real rigidity in that the real wage, rather than the nominal wage, remains fixed. Keynesian theories also emphasize nominal rigidities that occur when a price or wage is fixed in nominal, or dollar, terms and does not readily change in response to changes in supply or demand. Keynesians often refer to rigidity of nominal prices—a tendency of prices to adjust only slowly to changes in the economy—as **price stickiness**.

We explained in Section 12.1 that Keynesians introduced real-wage rigidity because of their dissatisfaction with the classical explanation of unemployment. Similarly, the assumption of price stickiness addresses what Keynesians believe is another significant weakness of the basic classical model: the classical prediction that monetary policy is neutral.

Recall that in the basic classical model, without misperceptions, the assumption that wages and prices adjust quickly implies that money is neutral. If money is neutral, an increase or decrease in the money supply changes the price level by the same proportion but has no effect on real variables, such as output, employment, or the real interest rate. However, recall also that empirical studies—including analyses of historical episodes—have led most economists to conclude that money probably is not neutral in the real world.

One approach to accounting for monetary non-neutrality (pursued in Chapter 11) is to extend the classical model by assuming that workers and firms have imperfect information about the current price level (the misperceptions theory). However, Keynesians favour an alternative way to explain monetary non-neutrality: Modify the classical assumption that prices adjust quickly. If prices are sticky, the price level cannot adjust immediately to offset changes in the money supply, and money is not neutral. Thus, for Keynesians, the importance of price stickiness is that it helps explain monetary non-neutrality.

Although we focus on nominal-price rigidity in this section, a long Keynesian tradition emphasizes nominal-wage rigidity instead of nominal-price rigidity. An alternative version of the Keynesian model that rests on the assumption of nominal-wage rigidity is discussed in Appendix 12.A. This alternative model has similar implications to the Keynesian model with price rigidity, in particular, that money is not neutral.

SOURCES OF PRICE STICKINESS: MONOPOLISTIC COMPETITION AND MENU COSTS

To say that price stickiness gives rise to monetary non-neutrality does not completely explain non-neutrality because it raises another question: Why are prices sticky? The Keynesian explanation for the existence of price rigidity relies on two main ideas: (1) Most firms actively set the prices of their products, rather than taking the prices of their output as given by the market; and (2) when firms change prices, they incur a cost, known as a menu cost.

MONOPOLISTIC COMPETITION

Talking about price stickiness in a highly competitive, organized market—such as the market for wheat or the stock exchange—would not make much sense. In these markets, prices adjust rapidly to reflect changes in supply or demand. Principal reasons for price flexibility in these competitive, highly organized markets include standardization of the product being traded (one tonne of wheat, or one share of Nortel Networks stock, is much like any other) and the large number of actual or potential market participants. These two factors make it worthwhile to organize a centralized market (such as the Toronto Stock Exchange) in which prices can react swiftly to changes in supply and demand. These same two factors also promote keen competition among buyers and sellers, which greatly reduces the ability of any individual to affect prices.

Most participants in the wheat market or stock market think of themselves as price takers. A *price taker* is a market participant who takes the market price as given. For example, a small farmer correctly perceives that the market price of wheat is beyond his control. In contrast, a *price setter* has some power to set prices.

Markets having fewer participants and less standardized products than the wheat or stock markets may exhibit price-setting rather than price-taking behaviour. For example, consider the market for movies in a medium-sized city. This market may be fairly competitive, with many different movie theatres, each trying to attract customers from other theatres, home video stores, and so on. Although the market for movies is competitive, it is not competitive to the same degree as the wheat market. If a farmer tried to raise the price of a kilogram of his wheat by 5¢ above the market price, he would sell no wheat; but a movie theatre that raised its ticket prices by 5¢ above its competitors' prices would not lose all its customers. Because the movie theatre's product is not completely standardized (it is showing a different movie from those in other theatres, its location is better for some people, it has different candy bars in the concession stand, a larger screen, or more comfortable seats, and so on), the theatre has some price-setting discretion. It is a price setter, not a price taker.

Generally, a situation in which all buyers and sellers are price takers (such as the market for wheat) is called **perfect competition**. In contrast, a situation in which there is some competition, but in which a smaller number of sellers and imperfect standardization of the product allow individual producers to act as price setters, is called **monopolistic competition**.

Perfect competition is the model underlying the classical view of price determination, and as we have said, price rigidity or stickiness is extremely unlikely in a perfectly competitive market. Keynesians agree that price rigidity would not occur in a perfectly competitive market but point out that a relatively small part of the economy is perfectly competitive. Keynesians argue that price rigidity is possible, even likely, in a monopolistically competitive market.

To illustrate the issues, let us return to the example of the competing movie theatres. If the market for movie tickets were perfectly competitive, how would tickets be priced? Presumably, there would be some central meeting place where buyers and sellers of tickets would congregate. Market organizers would call out "bids" (prices at which they are willing to buy) and "asks" (prices at which they are willing to sell). Prices would fluctuate continuously as new information hit the market, causing supplies and demands to change. For example, a favourable review would instantly drive up the price of tickets to that movie, but news of a prospective shortage of babysitters would cause all movie ticket prices to fall.

Obviously, though, this is not how movie tickets are priced. Actual pricing by most theatres has the following three characteristics, which are also common to most price-setting markets:

1. Rather than accept the price of movies as completely determined by the market, a movie theatre sets the price of tickets (or a schedule of prices), in nominal terms, and maintains the nominal price for some period of time.

2. At least within some range, the theatre meets the demand that is forthcoming at the fixed nominal price. By "meets the demand," we mean that the theatre will sell as many tickets as people want to buy at its fixed price, to the point that all its seats are filled.

3. The theatre readjusts its price from time to time, generally when its costs or the level of demand changes significantly.

Can this type of pricing behaviour maximize profits? Keynesian theory suggests that it can, if there are costs associated with changing nominal prices and if the market is monopolistically competitive.

MENU COSTS AND PRICE SETTING

The classic example of a cost of changing prices is the cost that a restaurant faces when it has to reprint its menu to show changes in the prices of its offerings. Hence the cost of changing prices is called a **menu cost**. More general examples of menu costs (which can apply to any kind of firm) include costs of re-marking merchandise, reprinting price lists and catalogues, and informing potential customers. Clearly, if firms incur costs when changing prices, they will change prices less often than they would otherwise, which creates a certain amount of price rigidity.

A potential problem with the menu cost explanation for price rigidity is that these costs seem to be rather small. How, then, can they be responsible for an amount of nominal rigidity that could have macroeconomic significance?

Here is the first point at which the monopolistic competition assumption is important. For a firm in a perfectly competitive market, getting the price "a little bit wrong" has serious consequences: The farmer who prices his wheat 5¢ a kilogram above the market price sells no wheat. Therefore, the existence of a menu cost would not prevent the farmer from pricing his product at precisely the correct level. However, the demand for the output of a monopolistically competitive firm responds much less sharply to changes in its price; the movie theatre does not lose many of its customers if its ticket price is 5¢ higher than its competitors'. Thus, as long as the monopolistic competitor's price is in the right general range, the loss of profits from not getting the price exactly right is not too great. If the loss in profits is less than the cost of changing prices—the menu costs—the firm will not change its price.

Over time, the production function and the demand curve the firm faces will undergo a variety of shocks so that eventually the profit-maximizing price for a firm may be significantly different from the preset price. When the profits lost by having the "wrong" price clearly exceed the cost of changing the price, the firm will change its nominal price. Thus, movie theatres periodically raise their ticket and popcorn prices to reflect general inflation and other changes in market conditions.

EMPIRICAL EVIDENCE ON PRICE STICKINESS

Several studies have examined the degree of rigidity or stickiness in actual prices. Using data first collected by Nobel laureate George Stigler and James Kindahl for the low-inflation period 1957–1966, Dennis Carlton,[7] of the University of Chicago, documented that US industrial prices can be very sticky. Table 12.1, taken from Carlton's study, shows the average number of months between price changes for various industrial product groups. Note that for three of eleven groups the average time between price changes is more than a year. Using a statistical analysis, Carlton also found that prices were less rigid in relatively more competitive industries, a finding that fits the theory.

More recent data on price stickiness were obtained by Alan Blinder,[8] of Princeton University. Assisted by a team of Princeton graduate students, during 1990–1992 Blinder interviewed the managers of 200 randomly selected firms about their pricing behaviour. Table 12.2 summarizes the evidence on price stickiness by showing the percentage of firms in the study that reported changing their prices at various frequencies. For example, the first line of Table 12.2 tells us that 10.2% of these firms reported changing their prices less than once per year.

Blinder and his team found a degree of price stickiness comparable to what Carlton had uncovered. As Table 12.2 shows, almost half (49.5%) the managers interviewed said that their firms changed prices once a year or less. Only 22% of the firms changed prices more than four times per year.

Besides probing into pricing behaviour, Blinder and his students also asked firm managers *why* they tend to change prices infrequently. Direct costs of changing

7. "The Rigidity of Prices," *American Economic Review*, September 1986, pp. 637–658.

8. "On Sticky Prices: Academic Theories Meet the Real World," in N. G. Mankiw, ed., *Monetary Policy*, University of Chicago Press, 1994.

TABLE 12.1

Average Times between Price Changes for Various Industries

Product Group (Most to Least Rigid)	Average Time between Price Changes (Months)
Cement	13.2
Steel	13.0
Chemicals	12.8
Glass	10.2
Paper	8.7
Rubber tires	8.1
Petroleum	5.9
Truck motors	5.4
Plywood	4.7
Non-ferrous metals	4.3
Household appliances	3.6

Source: Dennis W. Carlton, "The Rigidity of Prices," *American Economic Review*, September 1986, pp. 637–658, Table 1.

TABLE 12.2

Frequency of Price Adjustments among Interviewed Firms

Frequency of Price Change (Number of Times per Year)	Percentage of Firms
Less than once	10.2%
Once	39.3
1.01 to 2	15.6
2.01 to 4	12.9
4.01 to 12	7.5
12.01 to 52	4.3
More than fifty-two	10.2

Alan S. Binder, "On Sticky Prices: Academic Theories Meet the Real World," in N.G. Mankiw. ed., *Monetary Policy*, University of Chicago Press, 1994, Table 4.1.

prices (menu costs) did appear to play a role for many firms. Nevertheless, many managers stressed as a reason for price stickiness their concern that, if they changed their own prices, their competitors would not necessarily follow suit. Managers were particularly reluctant to be the first in their market to raise prices, fearing that they would lose customers to their rivals. For this reason, many firms reported delaying price changes until it was evident throughout the industry that changes in costs or demand made price adjustment necessary.

In another study of price stickiness, Anil Kashyap,[9] of the University of Chicago, examined the prices of 12 individual items listed in the catalogues of L.L. Bean, Orvis, and Recreational Equipment, Inc., over a 35-year period. Changing the prices listed in a new catalogue is virtually costless, yet Kashyap found that the nominal prices of many goods remained fixed in successive issues of the catalogue. When nominal prices were changed, Kashyap found both large and small changes. He

---

9. "Sticky Prices: New Evidence from Retail Catalogs," *Quarterly Journal of Economics*, February 1995, pp. 245–274.

interpreted the combination of small price changes and long periods of unchanged prices as evidence against menu costs. If menu costs are the reason that prices are not changed frequently, prices should be changed only when they are relatively far out of line, and the price changes should be large; small changes seem to contradict this implication of menu costs. Even if menu costs are not the underlying cause of pricing behaviour, however, Kashyap's study confirms the findings by Carlton and Blinder of substantial nominal-price rigidity in the economy.

Another way to study price stickiness is to see if prices change in response to changes in the exchange rate. For example, when the Canadian dollar depreciates, foreign goods eventually become more expensive for Canadians to buy. Thus, you might expect the retail prices of imported goods in Canada to rise promptly in response to depreciations. However, some studies find that this **pass-through** from the exchange rate to domestic prices is slow or incomplete. Prices do not all adjust fully to the changes in the exchange rate, which suggests that firms are partly absorbing exchange rate changes in changes in their profits. A situation in which firms can price discriminate across markets and in which they absorb part of exchange rate changes in profits, while keeping prices more stable in each market, is called **pricing to market**.

Export prices also might be expected to adjust when the exchange rate changes. A careful study of this adjustment was undertaken by Lawrence Schembri, of the Bank of Canada, who examined data from the Census of Manufacturers on a Canadian export industry during the period 1973–1985.[10] During this time, the Canadian dollar depreciated on average, which would have lowered the US prices of Canadian exports had prices adjusted fully. Yet firms did not pass on the depreciation to their US customers. Schembri estimated that a 1% depreciation caused US dollar prices to fall by only 0.15% and domestic Canadian prices to rise by only 0.22%. This evidence of incomplete pass-through is an important example of price stickiness.

MEETING THE DEMAND AT THE FIXED NOMINAL PRICE

When prices are sticky, firms react to changes in demand by changing the amount of production, rather than by changing prices. According to Keynesians, why are firms willing to meet demand at a fixed nominal price? To answer this question, we again rely on the assumption of monopolistic competition. We have stated that a monopolistically competitive firm can raise its price to some extent without risk of losing all its customers. The profit-maximizing strategy for a monopolistically competitive firm is to charge a price higher than its **marginal cost**, or the cost of producing an additional unit of output. The excess of the price over the marginal cost is the **markup**. For example, if a firm charges a price 15% above its marginal cost, the firm has a markup of 15%. More generally, if the firm charges a constant markup of η over marginal cost, the following markup rule describes its price:

$$P = (1 + \eta)\, MC, \tag{12.1}$$

where P is the nominal price charged by the firm and MC is the nominal marginal cost.[11]

---

10. "Export Prices and Exchange Rates: An Industry Approach," Chapter 6 in Robert C. Feenstra, ed., *Trade Policies for International Competitiveness*, Chicago: University of Chicago Press and NBER, 1989.

11. Technical note: For a monopolistically competitive firm that faces a demand curve with a constant price elasticity and a fixed wage, the constant-markup rule in Eq. (13.1) will maximize profit. Also, in this case, the labour demand curve is proportional to (rather than equal to) the marginal product of labour curve. Specifically, to maximize profits the firm equates the MPN to $(1 + \eta)w^*$, where w^* is the efficiency wage, rather than equating the MPN to w^* itself. This qualification does not affect any conclusions presented in this chapter.

When the firm sets its price according to Eq. (12.1), it has an idea of how many units will sell. Now, suppose that to the firm's surprise, customers demand several more units than the firm expected to sell at that price. Will it be profitable for the firm to meet the demand at this price?

The answer is "yes." Because the price the firm receives for each extra unit exceeds its cost of producing that extra unit (its marginal cost), the firm's profits increase when it sells additional units at the fixed price. Thus, as long as the marginal cost remains below the fixed price of its product, the firm gladly supplies more units at this fixed price. Furthermore, if the firm is paying an efficiency wage, it can easily hire more workers to produce the units needed to meet the demand because there is an excess supply of labour.

The macroeconomic importance of firms' meeting demand at the fixed nominal price is that *the economy can produce an amount of output that is not on the full-employment line*. Recall that the *FE* line shows the amount of output that firms would produce after complete adjustment of all wages and prices. However, with nominal-price stickiness, the prices of goods do not adjust rapidly to their general equilibrium values. During the period in which prices have not yet completely adjusted, the amount of output produced need not be on the *FE* line. Instead, as long as marginal cost is below the fixed price, monopolistically competitive firms will produce the level of output demanded.

EFFECTIVE LABOUR DEMAND

When a firm meets the demand for its output at a specific price, it may produce a different amount of output and employ a different amount of labour than it had planned. How much labour will a firm actually employ when it meets the demand? The answer is given by the effective labour demand curve, $ND^e(Y)$, shown in Figure 12.3. For any amount of output Y, the **effective labour demand curve** indicates how much labour is needed to produce that output, with productivity, the capital stock, and effort held constant.

We already have a concept that expresses the relationship between the amount of labour used and the amount of output produced: the production function. Indeed, the effective labour demand curve in Figure 12.3 is simply a graph of the production function relating output and labour input, except that output Y is measured on the horizontal axis and labour N is measured on the vertical axis. (Reversing the units on the axes is convenient later.) The effective labour demand curve slopes upward from left to right because a firm needs more labour in order to produce more output.

We use the effective labour demand curve to determine the level of employment in the Keynesian model in Section 12.3. When the economy is not on the *FE* line and the price level is fixed, the effective labour demand curve gives the level of employment. Then, after complete adjustment of wages and prices, the economy returns to the *FE* line and the level of employment is given by the labour demand curve ND^* (see Figure 12.2). After wages and prices have completely adjusted, with output at its full-employment level $\overline{Y}$, the effective labour demand curve indicates that employment equals $\overline{N}$, as shown in Figure 12.3.

12.3 MONETARY AND FISCAL POLICY IN THE KEYNESIAN MODEL

Let us now consider the complete Keynesian model. Like the classical model, the Keynesian model can be expressed in terms of the *IS–LM* diagram, or alternatively,

FIGURE 12.3

THE EFFECTIVE LABOUR
DEMAND CURVE

When a firm meets the
demand for its output, it
employs just the amount of
labour needed to produce the
quantity of output demanded.
Because more labour is
required to produce more
output, firms must employ
more labour when the demand
for output is high. This relation
between the amount of output
demanded and the amount of
labour employed is the
effective labour demand curve.
The effective labour demand
curve is the same as the
production function relating
output and labour, except that
labour is plotted on the vertical
axis and output is plotted on
the horizontal axis.

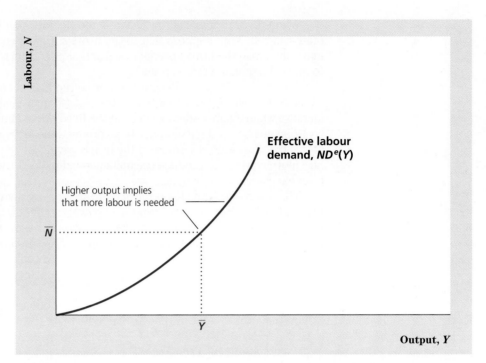

in terms of the *AD–AS* diagram. Rather than describe the Keynesian model in the
abstract, we put it to work analyzing the effects of monetary and fiscal policy.

MONETARY POLICY

The main reason for introducing nominal-price stickiness into the Keynesian model
was to explain monetary non-neutrality. We examine the link between price stickiness
and monetary non-neutrality first in the Keynesian *IS–LM* framework and then in the
AD–AS version of the Keynesian model.

MONETARY POLICY IN THE KEYNESIAN *IS–LM* MODEL

The Keynesian version of the *IS–LM* model is quite similar to the *IS–LM* model
discussed in Chapters 9 to 11. In particular, the *IS* curve and the *LM* curve are the
same as in our earlier analyses. The *FE* line in the Keynesian model also is similar to
the *FE* line used earlier. The Keynesian *FE* line is vertical at the full-employment level
of output $\overline{Y}$, which, in turn, depends on the full-employment level of employment
determined in the labour market. However, the Keynesian and classical *FE* lines
are different in two respects. First, in the Keynesian model, the full-employment
level of employment is determined at the intersection of the labour demand curve and
the efficiency wage line, not at the point where the quantities of labour demanded
and supplied are equal, as in the classical model. Second, because labour supply
does not affect employment in the efficiency wage model, changes in labour supply
do not affect the Keynesian *FE* line, although changes in labour supply do affect
the classical *FE* line.

Because of price stickiness, in the Keynesian model the economy does not have
to be in general equilibrium in the short run. However, in the long run, when prices
adjust, the economy reaches its general equilibrium at the intersection of the *IS*
curve, the *LM* curve, and the *FE* line, as in the classical model.

According to Keynesians, what happens to the economy in the short run, if sticky prices prevent it from reaching general equilibrium? Keynesians assume that the asset market clears quickly and that the level of output is determined by aggregate demand. Thus, according to Keynesians, *the economy always lies at the intersection of the IS and LM curves*. However, because monopolistically competitive firms are willing to meet the demand for goods at fixed levels of prices, output can differ from full-employment output and the economy may not be on the *FE* line in the short run. When the economy is off the *FE* line, firms use just enough labour to produce the output needed to meet demand. Under the assumption that the efficiency wage is higher than the market-clearing real wage, there are always unemployed workers who want to work, and firms are able to change employment as needed to meet the demand for output without changing the wage.

Figure 12.4 analyzes the effect of a decrease in the nominal money supply in the Keynesian *IS–LM* model. We assume that the economy starts at its general equilibrium point, E. Recall that a decrease in the money supply shifts the *LM* curve up and to the left, from LM^1 to LM^2 (see Figure 12.4(a)). Because a decrease in the money supply does not directly affect the goods or labour markets, the *IS* curve and the *FE* line are unaffected. So far, this analysis is like that of the classical model.

Unlike the classical model, however, the Keynesian model assumes temporarily fixed prices (because of menu costs) so that the general equilibrium at E is not restored immediately. Instead, the short-run equilibrium of the economy—that is, the resting point of the economy at the fixed price level—lies at the intersection of *IS* and LM^2 (point F), where output drops to Y_2 and the real interest rate rises to r_2.

Because the *IS–LM* intersection at point F is to the left of the *FE* line, aggregate output demanded Y_2 is less than the full-employment level of output $\overline{Y}$. Monopolistically competitive firms facing menu costs do not cut their prices in the short run, as competitive firms do. Instead, they cut production to Y_2 to satisfy the lower level of demand. To reduce production, firms cut employment—for example, by laying off workers or putting some employees on part-time schedules. The level of employment is given by the effective labour demand curve in Figure 12.4(b). Because the level of output falls from $\overline{Y}$ to Y_2 in the short run, the level of employment falls from $\overline{N}$ to N_2.

We refer to a monetary policy that shifts the *LM* curve up and to the left—and, thus, reduces output and employment—as a contractionary monetary policy, or "tight" money. Analogously, an expansionary monetary policy, or "easy" money, is an increase in the money supply that shifts the *LM* curve down and to the right, raising output and employment.

Why does tight money reduce output in the Keynesian model? In the Keynesian model, prices are fixed in the short run, so a reduction in the nominal money supply M also is a reduction in the real money supply M/P. Recall that for holders of wealth to be willing to hold more non-monetary assets and less real money the real interest rate must rise.[12] Finally, the higher real interest rate reduces both consumption spending (because saving rises) and investment spending. With less demand for their output, firms cut production and lay off workers, taking the economy to point F in Figure 12.4.

The rigidity of the price level is not permanent. Eventually, firms will review and readjust their prices, allowing the economy to reach its long-run equilibrium. In the case

---

12. As we discussed in Chapter 9, the real interest rate is driven up by wealth-holders' attempts to exchange non-monetary assets for money. The selling of non-monetary assets drives down their prices, which is the same as increasing the real interest rate that they pay.

FIGURE 12.4

A DECREASE IN THE MONEY SUPPLY

(a) If we start from an initial general equilibrium at point E, a decrease in the money supply shifts the LM curve up and to the left, from LM^1 to LM^2; the IS curve and the FE line remain unchanged. Because prices are fixed and firms meet the demand for output in the short run, the economy moves to point F, which is to the left of the FE line. Output falls to Y_2 and the real interest rate rises. **(b)** Because firms produce less output, employment falls to N_2, as shown by the effective labour demand curve.

In the long run, the price level falls in the same proportion as the money supply, the real money supply returns to its initial level, and the LM curve returns to its initial position, LM^1, in (a). The economy returns to E in both (a) and (b), and money is neutral in the long run.

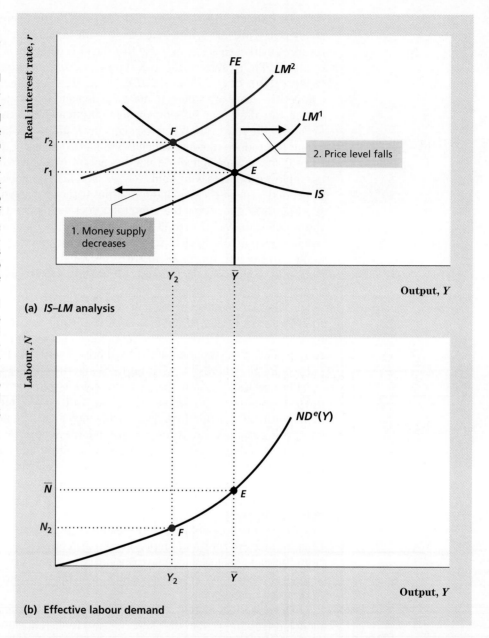

(a) *IS–LM analysis*

(b) **Effective labour demand**

of monetary contraction, firms find that demand for their products in the short run is less than they had planned (aggregate output demanded Y_2 is less than full-employment output $\overline{Y}$), so eventually, they lower their prices. The decline in the price level returns the real money supply to its initial level, which shifts the LM curve back to LM^1 and restores the general equilibrium at point E in Figure 12.4(a). This adjustment process is exactly the same as in the classical model, but it proceeds more slowly.

Thus, the Keynesian model predicts that *money is not neutral in the short run but is neutral in the long run*. In this respect, the predictions of the Keynesian model are the same as those of the extended classical model with misperceptions. In the Keynesian model, short-run price stickiness prevents the economy from reaching its general equilibrium, but in the long run, prices are flexible, ensuring general equilibrium.

MONETARY POLICY IN THE KEYNESIAN *AD–AS* MODEL

We can also analyze the effect of monetary policy on real output and the price level by using the Keynesian version of the *AD–AS* model. In fact, we have already performed this analysis in Figure 9.14, where we used the *AD–AS* model to examine the effects of a 10% increase in the nominal money supply. Although we did not identify that analysis as specifically Keynesian or classical, it can be readily given a Keynesian interpretation.

The distinguishing feature that determines whether an analysis is Keynesian or classical is the speed of price adjustment. As we emphasized in Chapter 11, classical economists argue that prices adjust quickly so that the economy reaches its long-run equilibrium quickly. In the extreme version of the classical model, the long-run equilibrium is reached virtually immediately, and the short-run aggregate supply (*SRAS*) curve is irrelevant. However, in the Keynesian model, monopolistically competitive firms that face menu costs keep their prices fixed for a while, producing the amount of output demanded at the fixed price level. This behaviour is represented by a horizontal short-run aggregate supply curve, such as $SRAS^1$ in Figure 9.14. If we assume that firms maintain fixed prices and simply meet the demand for output for a substantial period of time so that the departure from long-run equilibrium lasts for months or perhaps even years, the analysis illustrated in Figure 9.14 reflects the Keynesian approach.

Let us briefly review that analysis from an explicitly Keynesian perspective. Figure 9.14 depicts the effects of a 10% increase in the nominal money supply on an economy that is initially in both short-run and long-run equilibrium (at point *E*). The increase in the nominal money supply causes the *AD* curve to shift up from AD^1 to AD^2. In fact, as we explained in Chapter 9, the 10% increase in the nominal money supply shifts the *AD* curve up by 10% at each level of output. The initial effect of this shift in the *AD* curve is to move the economy to a short-run equilibrium at point *F*, where output is higher than its full-employment level, $\overline{Y}$. Because of menu costs, firms do not immediately react to increased demand by raising prices, but instead increase production to meet the higher demand. Thus, at point *F*, firms are producing more output than the amount that would maximize their profits in the absence of menu costs. Because output is temporarily higher than its full-employment level, we conclude that in the Keynesian model money is not neutral in the short run. Eventually, however, firms will increase their prices to bring the quantity of output demanded back to the profit-maximizing level of output. In the long-run equilibrium, represented by point *H* in Figure 9.14, output equals the full-employment level, $\overline{Y}$, and the price level, P_2, is 10% higher than the initial price level, P_1. In the long-run equilibrium the expansion of the money supply affects only nominal quantities, such as the price level, not real quantities, such as output or employment, so we conclude that in the Keynesian model (as in the classical model) money is neutral in the long run.

FISCAL POLICY

The Keynesian model was initially developed during the Great Depression as economists struggled to explain the worldwide economic collapse and find policies to help the economy return to normal. The early Keynesians stressed that fiscal policy, the government's decisions about government purchases and taxes, can significantly affect output and employment levels. Let us look at the Keynesians' conclusion that both increased government purchases and lower taxes can be used to raise output and employment.

THE EFFECT OF INCREASED GOVERNMENT PURCHASES

The Keynesian analysis of how increased government purchases affect the economy is shown in Figure 12.5, on the next page. Again, we assume that the economy starts from full employment (later we discuss what happens if the economy starts from a recession). Point E represents the initial equilibrium in both (a) and (b). As before, a temporary increase in government purchases increases the demand for goods and reduces desired national saving at any level of the real interest rate, so that the IS curve shifts up and to the right, from IS^1 to IS^2 (see Summary table 12, p. 300). In the short run, before prices can adjust, the economy moves to point F in Figure 12.5(a), where the new IS curve, IS^2, and LM^1 intersect. At F, both output and the real interest rate have increased. Because firms meet the higher demand at the fixed price level, employment also rises, as shown by the movement from point E to point F along the effective labour demand curve in Figure 12.5(b). A fiscal policy change, such as this one, that shifts the IS curve up and to the right and raises output and employment is an expansionary change. Similarly, a fiscal policy (such as a reduction in government purchases) that shifts the IS curve down and to the left and reduces output and employment is a contractionary change.

In discussing the effects of increased government purchases or other types of spending, Keynesians often use the multiplier concept. The **multiplier** associated with any particular type of spending is the short-run change in total output resulting from a one-unit change in that type of spending. So, for example, if the increase in government purchases analyzed in Figure 12.5 is ΔG and the resulting short-run increase in output between points E and F in Figure 12.5 is ΔY, the multiplier associated with government purchases is $\Delta Y / \Delta G$. Keynesians usually argue that the fiscal policy multiplier is greater than 1 so that if government purchases rise by $1 billion, output will rise by more than $1 billion. Unlike the classical analysis, which indicates that government spending diverts resources from the private sector, Keynesian analysis indicates that fiscal expansion can actually increase private sector resources in the short run, if the government purchases multiplier is greater than 1. We derive an algebraic expression for the government purchases multiplier in Appendix 12.B.

Recall that the classical version of the IS–LM model also predicts that a temporary increase in government purchases increases output, but in a different way. The classical analysis focuses on the fact that increased government purchases require higher current or future taxes to pay for the extra spending. Higher taxes make workers (who are taxpayers) effectively poorer, which induces them to supply more labour. This increase in labour supply shifts the FE line to the right and causes output to rise in the classical model. In contrast, the FE line in the Keynesian model does not depend on labour supply (because of efficiency wages) and, thus, is unaffected by the increase in government purchases. Instead, the increase in government purchases affects output by raising aggregate demand (that is, by shifting the IS–LM intersection to the right). Output increases above its full-employment level in the short run as firms satisfy extra demand at the initial price level.

The effect of increased government purchases on output in the Keynesian model lasts only as long as needed for the price level to adjust. (However, many Keynesians believe that price adjustment is sufficiently slow that this effect could be felt for several years.) In the long run, when firms adjust their prices, the LM curve moves up and to the left, from LM^1 to LM^2 in Figure 12.5(a), and the economy reaches general equilibrium at point H, with output again at $\overline{Y}$. Thus, an increase in government purchases does not raise output in the long run.

FIGURE 12.5

AN INCREASE IN
GOVERNMENT PURCHASES

(a) If we start from the general equilibrium at point E, an increase in government purchases reduces desired national saving and shifts the IS curve up and to the right, from IS^1 to IS^2. The short-run equilibrium is at point F, with output increasing to Y_2 and the real interest rate rising to r_2.
(b) As firms increase production to meet the demand, employment increases from $\bar{N}$ to N_2, as shown by the effective labour demand curve. However, the economy does not remain at point F. Because aggregate output demanded exceeds $\bar{Y}$ in the short run, the price level increases, reducing the real money supply and shifting the LM curve up and to the left, from LM^1 to LM^2. In the long run, with equilibrium at point H, output returns to $\bar{Y}$ and employment returns to $\bar{N}$, but the real interest rate rises further to r_3.

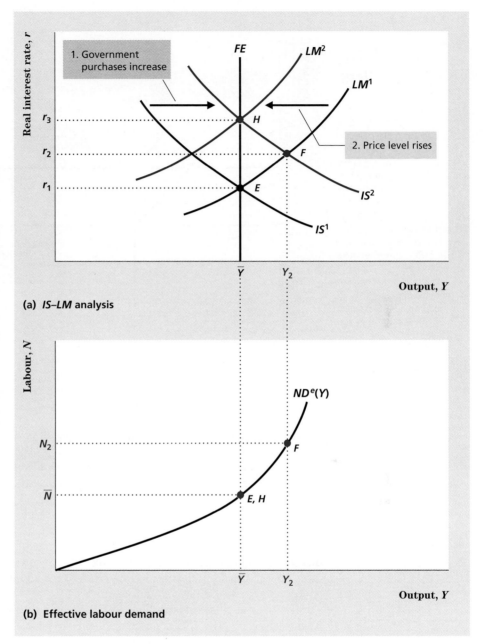

(a) *IS–LM* analysis

(b) **Effective labour demand**

The effects of more government purchases also appear in the Keynesian *AD–AS* framework (Figure 12.6). Increased government purchases shift the *IS* curve up and to the right and raise the aggregate demand for output at any given price level. Thus, as a result of expansionary fiscal policy, the aggregate demand curve shifts to the right, from AD^1 to AD^2. The increase in aggregate demand raises output above $\bar{Y}$, as shown by the shift from the initial equilibrium at point E to the short-run equilibrium at point F. At F, the aggregate demand for output is greater than full-employment output, so firms eventually raise their prices. In the long run, the economy reaches the full-employment general equilibrium at point H, with output again at $\bar{Y}$ and with a higher price level. These results are identical to those we obtained using the Keynesian *IS–LM* framework.

FIGURE 12.6

AN INCREASE IN GOVERNMENT PURCHASES IN THE KEYNESIAN *AD–AS* FRAMEWORK

An increase in government purchases raises the aggregate demand for output at any price level (see Figure 12.5). Thus, the aggregate demand curve shifts to the right, from AD^1 to AD^2. In the short run, the increase in aggregate demand increases output to Y_2 (point *F*) but does not affect the price level, because prices are sticky in the short run. Because aggregate output demanded Y_2 exceeds $\overline{Y}$ at *F*, firms eventually raise their prices. The long-run equilibrium is at *H*, where AD^2 intersects the long-run aggregate supply curve *LRAS*. At *H*, output has returned to $\overline{Y}$ and the price level has risen from P_1 to P_2. The higher price level raises the short-run aggregate supply curve, from $SRAS^1$ to $SRAS^2$.

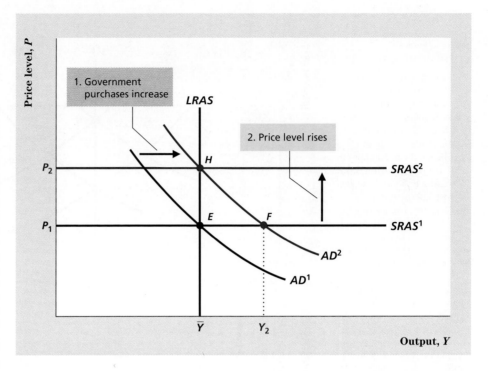

THE EFFECT OF LOWER TAXES

Keynesians generally believe that like an increase in government purchases, a lump-sum reduction in current taxes is expansionary. In other words, they expect that a tax cut will shift the *IS* curve up and to the right, raising output and employment in the short run. Similarly, they expect a tax increase to be contractionary, shifting the *IS* curve down and to the left.

Why does a tax cut affect the *IS* curve, according to Keynesians? The argument is that if consumers receive a tax cut, they will spend part of it on increased consumption. For any output *Y* and level of government purchases *G*, an increase in desired consumption arising from a tax cut will lower desired national saving, $Y - C^d - G$. A drop in desired saving raises the real interest rate that clears the goods market and shifts the *IS* curve up.[13]

If a tax cut raises desired consumption and shifts the *IS* curve upward, as Keynesians claim, the effects on the economy are similar to the effects of increased government purchases (see Figures 12.5 and 12.6). In the short run, a tax cut raises aggregate demand and, thus, output and employment at the initial price level. In the long run, after complete price adjustment, the economy returns to full employment with a higher real interest rate than in the initial general equilibrium. The only difference between the tax cut and the increase in government purchases is that instead of raising the portion of full-employment output devoted to government purchases, a tax cut raises the portion of full-employment output devoted to consumption.

---

13. In arguing that a tax cut raises desired consumption and lowers desired national saving, Keynesian economists reject the Ricardian equivalence proposition (Chapter 4), which states that a lump-sum tax cut should not affect consumption or national saving. Ricardian equivalence is discussed further in Chapter 15.

12.4 THE KEYNESIAN THEORY OF BUSINESS CYCLES AND MACROECONOMIC STABILIZATION

Recall that there are two basic questions about business cycles that a macroeconomic theory should try to answer: (1) What causes recurrent fluctuations in the economy? (2) What, if anything, should policymakers try to do about cycles? We are now ready to give the Keynesian answers to these two questions.

KEYNESIAN BUSINESS CYCLE THEORY

An explanation of the business cycle requires not only a macroeconomic model but also some assumptions about the types of shocks hitting the economy. For example, RBC theorists believe that productivity shocks, which directly shift the *FE* line, are the most important type of macroeconomic shock.

In contrast to RBC theorists, most Keynesians believe that aggregate demand shocks are the primary source of business cycle fluctuations. **Aggregate demand shocks** are shocks to the economy that shift either the *IS* curve or the *LM* curve and, thus, affect the aggregate demand for output. Examples of aggregate demand shocks affecting the *IS* curve are changes in fiscal policy, changes in desired investment arising from changes in the expected future marginal product of capital,[14] and changes in consumer confidence about the future that affect desired saving. Examples of aggregate demand shocks affecting the *LM* curve are changes in the demand for money or changes in the money supply. The Keynesian version of the *IS–LM* model, combined with the view that most shocks are aggregate demand shocks, constitutes the Keynesian theory of business cycles.

Figure 12.7 uses the Keynesian model to illustrate a recession caused by an aggregate demand shock. Suppose that consumers become pessimistic about the long-term future of the economy and, thus, reduce their current desired consumption; equivalently, they raise their current desired saving. For any level of income, an increase in desired saving lowers the real interest rate that clears the goods market and, thus, shifts the *IS* curve down, from IS^1 to IS^2. The economy goes into recession at point *F*, and, as prices do not adjust immediately to restore full employment, the economy remains in recession for some period of time with output below its full-employment level. Because firms face below-normal levels of demand, they also cut employment.

Note that a decline in investment spending (reflecting, for example, pessimism of business investors) or reduced government purchases would have similar recessionary effects as the decline in consumer spending analyzed in Figure 12.7. Alternatively, a shift to the left of the *LM* curve (because of either increased money demand or reduced money supply) also could cause a recession in the Keynesian framework; in this case, high real interest rates caused by the "shortage" of money would cause the declines in consumer spending and investment. Thus, Keynesians attribute recessions to "not enough demand" for goods, in contrast to classical economists who attribute recessions to "not enough supply."

Like the real business cycle theory, the Keynesian theory of cycles can account for several of the business cycle facts: (1) in response to occasional aggregate

---

14. A change in the expected future *MPK* might also be thought of as a technological shock because it involves a change in the future production function. However, because a change in the future *MPK* shifts the *IS* curve but does not affect the current *FE* line, Keynesians classify it as an aggregate demand shock.

FIGURE 12.7

A RECESSION ARISING
FROM AN AGGREGATE
DEMAND SHOCK

The figure illustrates how an adverse aggregate demand shock can cause a recession in the Keynesian model. The economy starts at general equilibrium at point E. A decline in consumer confidence about the future of the economy reduces desired consumption and raises desired saving so that the IS curve shifts down, from IS^1 to IS^2. The economy falls into recession at point F, with output below its full-employment level $\overline{Y}$.

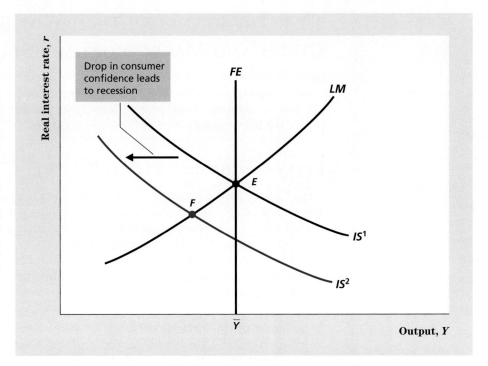

demand shocks, the theory predicts recurrent fluctuations in output; (2) the theory correctly implies that employment will fluctuate in the same direction as output; and (3) because it predicts that shocks to the money supply will be non-neutral, the theory is consistent with the business cycle fact that money is procyclical and leading.

A business cycle fact that we previously emphasized (Chapter 8) is that spending on investment goods and other durable goods is strongly procyclical and volatile. This cyclical behaviour of durable goods spending can be explained by the Keynesian theory if shocks to durable goods demand are themselves a main source of cycles. The demand for durable goods would be a source of cyclical fluctuations if, for example, investors frequently reassessed their expectations of the future MPK. Keynes himself thought that waves of investor optimism and pessimism, which he called "animal spirits," were a significant source of cyclical fluctuations. A rise in the demand for investment goods or consumer durables (at fixed levels of output and the real interest rate) is expansionary because it shifts the IS curve to the right. Investment will also be procyclical in the Keynesian model whenever cycles are caused by fluctuations in the LM curve; for example, an increase in the money supply that shifts the LM curve down and to the right both increases output and (by reducing the real interest rate) increases investment.

Another important business cycle fact that is consistent with the Keynesian theory is the observation that inflation tends to slow during or just after recessions (inflation is procyclical and lagging). In the Keynesian view, as Figure 12.7 illustrates, during a recession aggregate output demanded is less than the full-employment level of output. Thus, when firms do adjust their prices, they will be likely to cut them in order to increase their sales. According to the Keynesian model, because demand pressure is low during recessions, inflation will tend to subside when the economy is weak.

PROCYCLICAL LABOUR PRODUCTIVITY AND LABOUR HOARDING

Although the Keynesian model is consistent with many of the business cycle facts, one fact—that labour productivity is procyclical—presents problems for this approach. Recall that procyclical labour productivity is consistent with the real business cycle assumption that cycles are caused by productivity shocks—that recessions are times when productivity is unusually low and booms are times when productivity is unusually high. Unlike the RBC theorists, however, Keynesians assume that demand shocks, rather than supply (productivity) shocks, cause most cyclical fluctuations.

Because supply shocks are shifts of the production function, the Keynesian assumption that supply shocks usually are unimportant is the same as saying that the production function is fairly stable over the business cycle. But if the production function is stable, increases in employment during booms should reduce average labour productivity because of the diminishing marginal productivity of labour. Thus, the Keynesian model predicts that average labour productivity is countercyclical, contrary to the business cycle fact.

To explain the procyclical behaviour of average labour productivity, Keynesians modified their models to include labour hoarding.[15] As discussed in Section 11.1, labour hoarding occurs if firms retain, or "hoard," labour in a recession, rather than laying off or firing workers. The reason that firms might hoard labour during a recession is to avoid the costs of letting workers go and then having to rehire them or train new workers when the recession ends. Thus, hoarded labour may be used less intensively (for example, store clerks may wait on fewer customers in a day) or be assigned to such activities as training or maintenance. If labour is utilized less intensively during a recession, or workers spend time on such activities as maintenance that do not directly contribute to measured output, then labour productivity may fall during a recession even though the production function is stable. Thus, labour hoarding provides a way of explaining the procyclical behaviour of average labour productivity without assuming that recessions and expansions are caused by productivity shocks.

However, there also is evidence that in the last two recessions Canadian firms reduced their demand for workers more rapidly and on a larger scale than they did in previous downturns. In the 1950s and 1960s, employment tended to be stable (while hours decreased) during recessions, whereas now employment falls alongside output. One possible explanation for this decline in labour hoarding is based on the observation that the average unemployment rate is higher than it was in the 1960s. Therefore, firms face little risk that they will be unable to find workers when a recession ends.[16]

MACROECONOMIC STABILIZATION

From the Keynesian explanation of why business cycles occur we turn to the Keynesian view on how policymakers should respond to recessions and booms.

---

15. There also is some evidence that markups decline and labour demand rises in response to demand shocks, which may explain the fact that productivity is procyclical. See Julio J. Rotemberg and Michael Woodford, "Oligopolistic Pricing and the Effects of Aggregate Demand on Economic Activity," *Journal of Political Economy*, December 1992, pp. 1153–1207.

16. See Philip Cross, "Year-End Review of Labour Markets," *Canadian Economic Observer*, Statistics Canada, cat. no. 11-010, February 1991, pp. 3.1–3.20, and Garnett Picot, G. Lemaitre, and Peter Kuhn, "Labour Markets and Layoffs During the Last Two Recessions," *Canadian Economic Observer*, March 1994, pp. 4.1–4.13.

Briefly, Keynesians—unlike classical economists—generally favour policy actions to "stabilize" the economy by eliminating large fluctuations in output and employment. Keynesian support of more active policy measures follows from the theory's characterization of business cycle expansions and contractions as periods in which the economy is temporarily away from its general equilibrium (or not at the *IS–LM–FE* intersection). According to Keynesians, recessions are particularly undesirable because in a recession, employment may be far below the amount of labour that workers want to supply, which leads to hardships for the unemployed and to output that is "too low." Keynesians, therefore, argue that average economic well-being would be increased if governments tried to reduce cyclical fluctuations, especially recessions.

The Keynesian analysis of monetary and fiscal policies suggests that these policies could be used to smooth the business cycle. To understand how, consider Figure 12.8. Suppose that the economy, initially in general equilibrium at point *E*, has been driven into recession at point *F*. Various types of shocks could have caused this recession. In Figure 12.7, for example, we considered a drop in consumer confidence about the future of the economy. A drop in confidence would reduce current desired consumption and increase current desired saving, thereby shifting the *IS* curve down from IS^1 to IS^2. This sort of change in consumer attitudes may have contributed to the 1990–1992 recession (see the Application "Consumer Attitudes and Recessions," p. 105).

How might policymakers respond to this recession? We consider three possibilities: (1) no change in monetary or fiscal policy; (2) an increase in the money supply; and (3) an increase in government purchases.

- *Scenario 1*: No change in macroeconomic policy. One policy option is to do nothing. With no government intervention, the economy eventually will correct itself. At point *F* in Figure 12.8, aggregate output demanded is below the full-employment level of output $\overline{Y}$. Therefore, over time, prices will begin to fall, increasing the real money supply and shifting the *LM* curve down and to the right. In the long run, price declines shift the *LM* curve from LM^1 to LM^2, restoring the economy to general equilibrium at point *H*. However, a disadvantage of this strategy is that during the (possibly lengthy) price adjustment process, output and employment remain below their full-employment levels.

- *Scenario 2*: An increase in the money supply. Instead of waiting for the economy to reach general equilibrium through price adjustment, the Bank of Canada could increase the money supply, which also would shift the *LM* curve from LM^1 to LM^2 in Figure 12.8. If prices adjust slowly, this expansionary policy would move the economy to general equilibrium at point *H* more quickly than would doing nothing.

- *Scenario 3*: An increase in government purchases. An alternative policy of raising government purchases will shift the *IS* curve up and to the right, from IS^2 to IS^1. This policy also takes the economy to full employment, although at point *E* in Figure 12.8, rather than at point *H*.

In all three scenarios, the economy eventually returns to full employment. However, the use of monetary or fiscal policy to achieve full employment leads to two important differences from the scenario in which no policy action is taken. First, if the government uses monetary or fiscal expansion to end the recession, the economy returns directly to full employment; if policy is not changed, the economy remains in recession in the short run, returning to full employment only when prices have fully

FIGURE 12.8

STABILIZATION POLICY IN
THE KEYNESIAN MODEL

From point *E*, the economy is driven into a recession at point *F* by a drop in consumer confidence and spending, which shifts the *IS* curve down, from *IS¹* to *IS²*. If the government took no action, in the long run, price adjustment would shift the *LM* curve from *LM¹* to *LM²* and restore general equilibrium at point *H* (scenario 1). Alternatively, the government could try to offset the recession through stabilization policy. For example, the Bank of Canada could increase the money supply, which would shift the *LM* curve directly from *LM¹* to *LM²*, speeding the recovery in output (scenario 2). Another possibility is a fiscal expansion, such as an increase in government purchases, which would shift the *IS* curve from *IS²* back to *IS¹*, again restoring full employment at *E* (scenario 3). Compared with a strategy of doing nothing, expansionary monetary or fiscal policy helps the economy recover more quickly but leads to a higher price level in the long run.

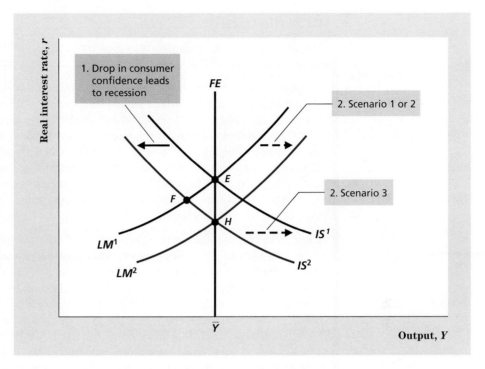

adjusted. Second, if there is no policy change (scenario 1), in the long run, the price level falls relative to the nominal money supply. Indeed, the drop in the price level relative to the money supply increases the real money supply, shifts the *LM* curve down and to the right, and restores full employment at point *H*. In contrast, when monetary or fiscal policy is used to restore full employment (scenarios 2 and 3), the downward adjustment of the price level does not occur because expansionary policy directly returns aggregate demand to the full-employment level. Thus, according to the Keynesian analysis, using expansionary monetary or fiscal policy has the advantage of bringing the economy back to full employment more quickly but the disadvantage of leading to a higher price level than if no policy action is undertaken.

Either monetary or fiscal policy can be used to bring the economy back to full employment. Does it matter which policy is used? Yes, there is at least one basic difference between the outcomes of the two policies: Monetary and fiscal policies affect the composition of spending (the amount of output that is devoted to consumption, the amount to investment, and so on) differently. In Figure 12.8, although total output is the same at the alternative general equilibrium points *E* and *H*, at *E* (reached by an increase in government purchases) government purchases are higher than at *H* (reached by an increase in the money supply). Because government purchases are higher at *E*, the remaining components of spending—consumption, investment, and net exports—must be lower at *E* than at *H*. Relative to a monetary expansion, an increase in government purchases crowds out consumption, investment, and net exports by raising the real interest rate, which is higher at *E* than at *H*. In addition, increased government purchases imply higher current or future tax burdens, which also reduces consumption relative to what it would be with monetary expansion.

APPLICATION

FISCAL AND MONETARY POLICY IN THE GREAT JAPANESE SLUMP

Between 1960 and 1990, the Japanese economy was the envy of the world. The rate of Japanese economic growth exceeded 6% per year over that period, with real GDP per capita reaching levels close to those of the United States. Japanese-manufactured goods, from automobiles to consumer electronics, became renowned for their quality and sophistication, and Japanese banks and financial investors acquired large stakes in foreign economies. Japanese stock prices and land prices skyrocketed, and Tokyo real estate prices were the world's highest. Best-selling books argued that Japan would soon be the world's preeminent economy—if it was not already—and other countries were urged to copy Japanese business practices and economic policies.

Then, to the surprise of many commentators, GDP growth during the 1990s slowed to an average rate of 1.5% per year, with negative growth rates in several years. During 2000, the unemployment rate reached 5%, an all time high. What went wrong? The recession coincided with deep declines in the prices of real estate and other assets, following a speculative rise in these prices in the late 1980s, sometimes called a "bubble." During the 1990s, the price of land in cities fell to 40% of its 1990 peak value, while the Nikkei stock price index fell by 60% in three years. Many asset purchases had been financed with bank loans, so the collapse of asset prices left borrowers unable to repay their debts and banks with many bad loans. In turn, this problem made banks less willing to finance new investment projects, choking off credit to potential borrowers. Investment in new capital goods fell particularly sharply, as many companies became convinced that the golden era of Japanese growth had ended and hence new investments would not be profitable. In addition, the decline in wealth may have reduced consumption spending. As Chapter 9 showed, both a decline in desired investment and a decline in desired consumption lead the *IS* curve to shift down and to the left, which in the Keynesian model reduces both output and the interest rate.

From a Keynesian perspective, the appropriate policy response was clear: Use expansionary fiscal and monetary policies. The Japanese authorities made repeated efforts to stabilize the economy using fiscal policy. The fiscal stimulus measures included tax cuts and increases in public investment.[17] As Chapter 9 showed, an increase in government purchases shifts the *IS* curve up and to the right. A reduction in taxes adds to this shift if households do not take into account the increase in future taxes. The effect of the fiscal stimulus packages is illustrated in Figure 12.9. The economy begins at point *F*, with output below the full-employment level. In the absence of policy measures, the *LM* curve would shift down and to the right as prices tend to fall, thus restoring full employment (not shown here). Keynesians predict that this price adjustment might be very slow. An expansionary fiscal policy may bring about a faster recovery, as the *IS* curve shifts up from IS^1 to IS^2. However, if that is the only policy change then the interest rate will increase (as at point *D*) and private investment expenditure will be discouraged. Moreover, if the interest rate rises then the yen will appreciate, which will reduce net exports. These effects of higher interest rates will limit the effect on output of the fiscal stimulus.

---

17. For a summary of these packages see "Japan's Economic Crisis and Policy Options," Part IV in *International Monetary Fund World Economic Outlook*, October 1998, pp. 45-73.

For this reason, the Japanese policy also included a monetary expansion by the Bank of Japan. The Bank lowered its official discount rate (by increasing the money supply) from 6% in 1991 to 0.5% in 1995, where it remained. In response, longer term interest rates also fell to less than 1%. This monetary policy was designed to shift the LM curve down and to the right from LM^1 to LM^2. As a result, output would rise without an increase in interest rates (at point E).

However, this policy mix did not solve Japan's macroeconomic problems, for three main reasons. First, the yen appreciated during much of the 1990s. For example, the nominal exchange rate against the US dollar was 150 yen per dollar during 1990 and 120 yen per dollar during 2001. The causes of this appreciation are not completely clear, but its negative effect on net exports partly offset the effects of the fiscal stimulus packages.

Second, in 1990, Japan had been in a position to use fiscal policy for stabilization because of its low government debt. But a series of government budget deficits (approaching 10% of GDP during 2000) led to a debt buildup and a ratio of government debt that rose well over 100% of GDP. Of course, this increase in government debt resulted from the fiscal stimulus measures, but when those measures were not successful, the debt buildup limited the scope for further government spending.

Third, note in Figure 12.9 that monetary policy accomodates an expansionary fiscal policy by lowering the interest rate. But by 1995, the official discount rate was only 0.5%. Nominal interest rates cannot go below zero because no one will lend at a negative nominal interest rate (it is always possible to hold cash, which pays a zero nominal return, instead). Because monetary policy stimulates the economy, in large

FIGURE 12.9

FISCAL EXPANSION WITH
MONETARY
ACCOMMODATION

The Japanese economy was in a recession in the early 1990s (point *F*). The Japanese government increased public spending several times (and also reduced taxes) to try to hasten the economy's recovery. The fiscal expansions shifted the *IS* curve up and to the right from *IS¹* to *IS²*. At the same time, the Bank of Japan expanded the money supply so that the *LM* curve shifted down and to the right from *LM¹* to *LM²*. This monetary accommodation prevented the interest rate from rising and reinforced the expansionary policy, leading to an increase in output (point *E*). Without the monetary expansion (at point *D*) interest rates would have risen and so private investment would have been discouraged and the yen might have appreciated even more, leading to a fall in net exports.

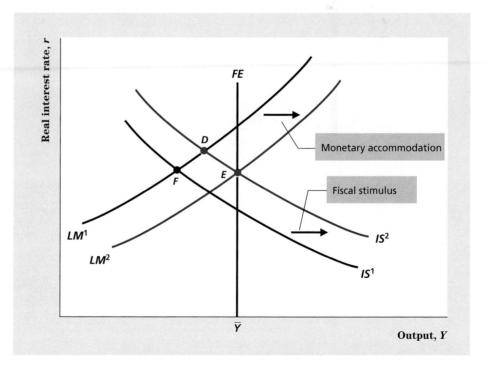

part by lowering interest rates, it becomes ineffective in these conditions. Keynes (in Chapter 15 of *The General Theory of Employment, Interest, and Money*) called this situation the **liquidity trap**. It is illustrated in Figure 12.10.

Is Japan in a liquidity trap, and if so, how can it escape? Paul Krugman, of Princeton University, has argued that the Japanese equilibrium real interest rate may be negative.[18] His argument is that an aging population trying to save for retirement leads to very high desired saving so that the desired saving and desired investment curves intersect only at a negative real interest rate. In Chatpers 9 and 10, we showed how the position of the *IS* curve can be derived from those of the desired saving and investment curves. In Figure 12.10, note that the *IS* curve intersects the *FE* line at a negative real interest rate. Meanwhile, a zero or low inflation rate makes the actual real interest rate positive and, thus, limits aggregate demand.

One way out of this trap might be to shift desired investment out, by opening international capital markets to allow more foreign investment in Japan. Another method might be to again increase government spending, to shift the desired saving curve back (or the *IS* curve out). But Krugman argued that the trap can be escaped most rapidly if the Bank of Japan creates expected inflation, by rapidly expanding the money supply. Recall that the real interest rate equals the nominal interest rate minus the expected rate of inflation. To lower the real interest rate and spur aggregate demand, the Bank of Japan could create positive inflation expectations. Lars Svensson, also of Princeton University, has suggested a "foolproof way" to create these expectations. He proposes that the Japanese authorities peg the nominal exchange rate at some depreciated level—such as 140 or 150 yen per US dollar—and keep it there until prices rise.[19]

Krugman also suggested that the Bank of Japan had not followed these policies because like many central banks, it wished to avoid inflation. The Bank also may have feared repeating the bubble of the late 1980s. Instead, recent policy has focused on addressing the problems of the banking sector, rather than on fiscal and monetary policy.

The continued slow growth in Japan does not necessarily mean that stabilization policy is ineffective. During the 1990s, Japanese consumption did not fall significantly, and the unemployment rate generally remained low. Thus, monetary and fiscal policies may have prevented a deeper recession in the early 1990s, even if they could not restore growth.

DIFFICULTIES OF MACROECONOMIC STABILIZATION

The use of monetary and fiscal policies to smooth or moderate the business cycle is called **macroeconomic stabilization**. Using macroeconomic policies to try to smooth the cycle is also sometimes called **aggregate demand management** because monetary and fiscal policies shift the aggregate demand curve. Macroeconomic stabilization was a popular concept in the heyday of Keynesian economics in the 1960s, and it still influences policy discussions. Unfortunately, even putting aside

---

18. "It's Baaack: Japan's Slump and the Return of the Liquidity Trap," *Brookings Papers on Economic Activity,* Autumn 1998. See also his essay "Japan: Still Trapped," at www.wws.princeton.edu/~pkrugman/
19. "How Japan Can Recover," *Financial Times,* 25 September 2001, also available at www.princeton.edu/~svensson/japan/japan.htm

FIGURE 12.10

THE LIQUIDITY TRAP

Point *F* shows the position of the Japanese economy in recent years. At point *F*, output is below the full-employment level, at the intersection of the curves IS^1 and LM^1. But interest rates are near zero, preventing further stimulus from monetary policy. The figure shows both real and nominal interest rates equal to zero, which is accurate for the case of Japan because inflation and expected inflation were both approximately zero. Note that the *LM* curve is flat at a zero interest rate; this shape reflects the fact that increases in the money supply are powerless to lower the nominal interest rate once it has reached zero. Creating expected inflation may lower the real interest rate and increase output, at point *E*.

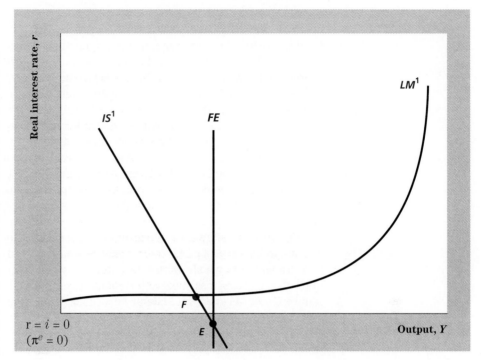

the debates between classicals and Keynesians about whether smoothing the business cycle is sensible, actual macroeconomic stabilization has been much less successful than the simple Keynesian theory suggests.

As discussed earlier in connection with fiscal policy, attempts to stabilize the economy run into some technical problems. First, monetary and fiscal policy must be coordinated, a problem we discussed in the Application, "Fiscal and Monetary Policy in the Great Japanese Slump." Second, because the ability to measure and analyze the economy is imperfect, gauging how far the economy is from full employment at any particular time is difficult. Third, the precise amount that output will increase in response to a monetary or fiscal expansion is not known. These uncertainties make assessing how much of a monetary or fiscal change is needed to restore full employment difficult. Finally, even knowing the size of the policy change needed still would not provide enough information. Because macroeconomic policies take time to implement and more time to affect the economy, their optimal use requires knowledge of where the economy will be six months or a year from now. But such knowledge is, at best, very imprecise.

Because of these problems, aggregate demand management has been likened to trying to hit a moving target in a heavy fog. These problems have not persuaded most Keynesians to abandon stabilization policy; however, many Keynesians agree that policymakers should concentrate on fighting major recessions and not try to "fine-tune" the economy by smoothing every bump and wiggle in output and employment.

Beyond the technical problems associated with trying to find the right policies to stabilize the economy, economists also face the practical problem of convincing policymakers to take their advice.

SUPPLY SHOCKS IN THE KEYNESIAN MODEL

Until the 1970s, the Keynesian business cycle theory focused almost exclusively on aggregate demand shocks as the source of business cycle fluctuations. Because aggregate demand shocks lead to procyclical movements in inflation, however, the Keynesian theory failed to account for the stagflation—high inflation together with a recession—that hit the world economy following the 1973–1975 oil price shock. This experience led to much criticism of the traditional theory by both economists and policymakers, so Keynesians recast the theory to allow for both supply and demand shocks. Although Keynesians would not go so far as to agree with RBC theorists that supply (productivity) shocks are a factor in most recessions, they now concede that there have been occasional episodes—the oil price shocks of the 1970s being the leading examples—in which supply shocks have played a primary role in an economic downturn.

Figure 12.11 shows a Keynesian analysis of the effects of a sharp temporary increase in the price of oil (a similar analysis would apply to other supply shocks, such as a drought). As we showed in Chapter 3, if firms respond to an increase in the price of oil by using less energy, the amount of output that can be produced with the same amount of capital and labour falls. Thus, the increase in the price of oil is an adverse supply shock, which reduces the full-employment level of output and shifts the FE line to the left, from FE^1 to FE^2. After complete wage and price adjustment, which occurs virtually immediately in the basic classical model but only in the long run in the Keynesian model, output falls to its new full-employment level $\bar{Y}_2$. Thus, in the long run (after full wage and price adjustment), the Keynesian analysis and the classical analysis of a supply shock are the same.

However, the Keynesian analysis of the short-run effects of an oil price shock is slightly different from the classical analysis. To understand the short-term effects of

FIGURE 12.11

AN OIL PRICE SHOCK IN THE KEYNESIAN MODEL

An increase in the price of oil is an adverse supply shock that reduces full-employment output from $\bar{Y}_1$ to $\bar{Y}_2$ and, thus, shifts the FE line to the left. In addition, the increase in the price of oil increases prices in sectors that depend heavily on oil, whereas prices in other sectors remain fixed in the short run. Thus, the average price level rises, which reduces the real money supply M/P and shifts the LM curve up and to the left, from LM^1 to LM^2. In the short run, the economy moves to point F, with output falling below the new, lower value of full-employment output and the real interest rate increasing. Because the aggregate quantity of goods demanded at F is less than the full-employment level of output $\bar{Y}_2$, in the long run, the price level falls, partially offsetting the initial increase in prices. The drop in the price level causes the LM curve to shift down and to the right, from LM^2 to LM^3, moving the economy to full-employment equilibrium at point H.

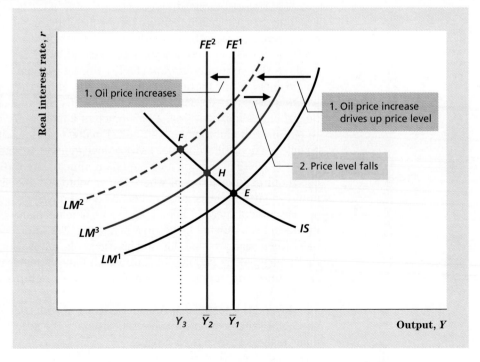

the oil price shock in the Keynesian model, first think about the effects of the increase in the oil price on the general price level. Recall that firms facing menu costs will not change their prices if the "right" prices are only a little different from the preset prices. However, if the right prices are substantially different from the preset prices so that firms would lose considerable profits by maintaining the preset prices, they will change their prices. In the case of a large increase in the price of oil, firms whose costs are strongly affected by the price of oil—including gas stations, suppliers of home heating oil, and airlines, for example—find that the right prices for their products are substantially higher than the preset prices. These oil-dependent firms increase their prices quickly, whereas firms in other sectors maintain their preset prices in the short run. Thus, there is price stickiness in the sense that not all prices adjust to their equilibrium values, and yet the average price level rises in the short run.

Because a sharp increase in the price of oil raises the price level P in the short run, it also reduces the real money supply M/P. A decline in the real money supply shifts the LM curve to left, from LM^1 to LM^2 in Figure 12.11. As drawn, the LM curve shifts farther to the left than the FE line shifts, though this outcome is not logically necessary. The short-run equilibrium is at point F, where LM^2 intersects the IS curve. Because F is to the left of the FE line, the economy is in a recession at F, with output (at Y_3) below the new value of full-employment output, $\overline{Y}_2$. In the short run, the economy experiences stagflation, with both a drop in output and a burst of inflation. Note that according to this analysis, the short-run decline in output has two components: (1) the drop in full-employment output from $\overline{Y}_1$ to $\overline{Y}_2$; and (2) the drop in output below the new full-employment level arising from the shift to the left of the LM curve (the difference between $\overline{Y}_2$ and Y_3).

Supply shocks of the type analyzed in Figure 12.11 pose tremendous difficulties for Keynesian stabilization policies. First, monetary or fiscal policy can do little about the portion of the decline in output resulting from the shift of the FE line; attempts to expand the economy beyond the new full-employment output level $\overline{Y}_2$ will increase output only temporarily and worsen inflation. In contrast, the portion of the output decline arising from the shift to the left of the LM curve (the difference between $\overline{Y}_2$ and Y_3) represents an output level below the full-employment level and could, in principle, be eliminated by expansionary monetary or fiscal policies that raise output to $\overline{Y}_2$. However, by using expansionary policies at point F, rather than doing nothing, the government risks worsening the already-high rate of inflation. Hence in the face of a shock that induces stagflation like the one shown in Figure 12.11, macroeconomic policy can neither avoid a sharp decline in output, nor can it restore output even to its new, lower full-employment level without potentially worsening inflation.

CHAPTER SUMMARY

1. Keynesians are sceptical that a mismatch between workers and jobs can explain all unemployment. They argue that some unemployment is caused by real wages that are rigid and above the level at which the quantities of labour demanded and supplied are equal.

2. One explanation for real-wage rigidity is based on the efficiency wage model, which assumes that workers work harder in response to an increase in the real wage. Firms can attain the highest level of profit by paying the real wage, known as the efficiency wage, that elicits the most worker effort per dollar of wages. If the effort curve relating effort provided by workers to the real wage does not change, the efficiency wage, and hence the real wage actually paid, is rigid.

3. At the efficiency wage, firms demand the level of employment $\bar{N}$ at which the marginal product of labour equals the efficiency wage. If the efficiency wage is above the market-clearing real wage, employment is determined by labour demand. The difference between the quantity of labour supplied and the quantity of labour demanded at the efficiency wage represents unemployment.

4. Full-employment output $\bar{Y}$ is the output that can be produced when employment is at its full-employment level $\bar{N}$ and worker effort is at the level induced by the efficiency wage. The *FE* line in the Keynesian *IS–LM* model is vertical where output equals its full-employment level. In the Keynesian model, full-employment output and the *FE* line are affected by productivity shocks but not by changes in labour supply because changes in labour supply do not affect employment in the efficiency wage model.

5. Keynesians attribute the non-neutrality of money to price stickiness, which means that some firms may not change their prices in the short run, even though the demand for or supply of their product has changed. Price stickiness is contrary to the assumption of the basic classical model that prices and wages are completely flexible.

6. Price stickiness can arise from the profit-maximizing behaviour of monopolistically competitive firms that face menu costs, or costs of changing prices. Such firms are price setters, rather than price takers, and once they set their prices they meet customer demand at that fixed price. These firms readjust prices only occasionally, generally when costs or demand have changed significantly.

7. In the Keynesian model with sticky prices, output is determined in the short run at the intersection of the *IS* and *LM* curves. The economy can be off the *FE* line in the short run because firms are willing to meet demand at predetermined prices. The level of employment in the short run is given by the effective labour demand curve, which shows the amount of labour needed to produce any given amount of output. In the long run, after prices and wages have completely adjusted, the *LM* curve moves to restore general equilibrium with full employment.

8. The short-run and long-run equilibria in the Keynesian model can also be analyzed with the *AD–AS* model. The short-run equilibrium is represented by the intersection of the downward-sloping aggregate demand (*AD*) curve and the horizontal short-run aggregate supply (*AS*) curve. In short-run equilibrium, monopolistically competitive firms produce whatever level of output is demanded at the fixed price level. Eventually, however, the price level adjusts and the economy reaches its long-run equilibrium, represented by the intersection of the *AD* curve and the vertical long-run aggregate supply (*LRAS*) curve. In long-run equilibrium, output equals its full-employment level, $\bar{Y}$.

9. In the Keynesian model, an increase in the money supply shifts the *LM* curve down and to the right, raising output and lowering the real interest rate in the short run. Thus, money is not neutral in the short run. In the long run, however, money is neutral; monetary expansion raises the price level proportionally but has no real effects.

10. In the Keynesian model, an increase in government purchases or a cut in taxes shifts the *IS* curve up and to the right, raising output and the real interest rate in the short run. In the long run, output returns to the full-employment level but the real interest rate increases. Fiscal policy is not neutral in the long run because it affects the composition of output among consumption, investment, and government purchases.

11. Keynesians attribute most business cycles to aggregate demand shocks. These shocks hit the *IS* curve (changes in government purchases, desired consumption, or desired investment) or the *LM* curve (changes in money supply or money demand). Keynesian business cycle theory, which has traditionally emphasized the importance of aggregate demand shocks, can account for the procyclical behaviour of employment, money, inflation, and investment. To explain the procyclical behaviour of average labour productivity, the Keynesian theory must include the additional assumption that firms hoard labour—that is, they employ more workers than necessary during recessions.

12. Macroeconomic stabilization, also called aggregate demand management, is the use of monetary or fiscal policy to try to eliminate recessions and keep the economy at full employment. The Keynesian theory suggests that macroeconomic stabilization is both desirable and possible. However, practical problems include the difficulty of measuring and forecasting the state of the economy and determining how much monetary and fiscal stimulus is needed at any particular time. Keynesian anti-recessionary policies also lead to a higher price level than would occur in the absence of policy changes.

13. Following the oil price shocks of the 1970s, the Keynesian theory was modified to allow for supply shocks as well. Supply shocks lead to stagflation (a combination of inflation and recession) and pose great difficulties for stabilization policy.

KEY TERMS

aggregate demand management, p. 470
aggregate demand shocks, p. 463
effective labour demand curve, p. 455
efficiency wage, p. 446
efficiency wage model, p. 444

effort curve, p. 444
liquidity trap, p. 470
macroeconomic stabilization, p. 470
marginal cost, p. 454
markup, p. 454
menu cost, p. 451
monopolistic competition, p. 451
multiplier, p. 460
pass-through, p. 454
perfect competition, p. 451
price stickiness, p. 449
pricing to market, p. 454
real-wage rigidity, p. 443
turnover costs, p. 444

REVIEW QUESTIONS

1. Define *efficiency wage*. What assumption about worker behaviour underlies the efficiency wage theory? Why does it predict that the real wage will remain rigid even if there is an excess supply of labour?

2. How is full-employment output $\overline{Y}$ determined in the Keynesian model with efficiency wages? In this model, how is full-employment output affected by changes in productivity (supply shocks)? How is it affected by changes in labour supply?

3. What is price stickiness? Why do Keynesians believe that allowing for price stickiness in macroeconomic analysis is important?

4. Define *menu cost*. Why might small menu costs lead to price stickiness in monopolistically competitive markets but not in perfectly competitive markets? Why can a monopolistically competitive firm profitably meet demand at its fixed price when actual demand is greater than the firm anticipated?

5. What does the Keynesian model predict about monetary neutrality (both in the short run and in the long run)? Compare the Keynesian predictions about neutrality with those of the basic classical model and the extended classical model with misperceptions.

6. In the Keynesian model, how do increased government purchases affect output and the real interest rate in the short run? in the long run? How do increased government purchases affect the composition of output in the long run?

7. Describe three alternative responses available to policymakers when the economy is in recession. What are the advantages and disadvantages of each strategy? Be sure to discuss the effects on employment, the price level, and the composition of output. What are some of the practical difficulties in using macroeconomic stabilization policies to fight recessions?

8. Use the Keynesian model to explain the procyclical behaviour of employment, money, inflation, and investment.

9. What does the Keynesian model predict about the cyclical behaviour of average labour productivity? How does the idea of labour hoarding help bring the prediction of the model into conformity with the business cycle facts?

10. According to the Keynesian analysis, in what two ways does an adverse supply shock reduce output? What problems do supply shocks create for Keynesian stabilization policies?

NUMERICAL PROBLEMS

1. A firm identifies the following relationship between the real wage it pays and the effort exerted by its workers.

Real Wage	Effort
8	7
10	10
12	15
14	17
16	19
18	20

The marginal product of labour for this firm is

$$MPN = \frac{E(100 - N)}{15},$$

where E is the effort level and N is the number of workers employed. If the firm can pay only one of the six wage levels shown, which should it choose? How many workers will it employ? There are 200 workers in the town where the firm is located, all willing to work at a real wage of 8. Does this change your answer to the first part of this question? If so, how?

2. An economy is described by the following equations:

Desired consumption	$C^d = 130 + 0.5(Y - T) - 500r.$
Desired investment	$I^d = 100 - 500r.$
Government purchases	$G = 100.$
Taxes	$T = 100.$
Real money demand	$L = 0.5Y - 1000r.$
Money supply	$M = 1,320.$
Full-employment output	$\overline{Y} = 500.$

Assume that expected inflation is zero so that money demand depends directly on the real interest rate.

a. Write the equations for the *IS* and *LM* curves. (These equations express the relationship between r and Y when the goods and asset markets are in equilibrium.)

b. Calculate the full-employment values of output, the real interest rate, the price level, consumption, and investment.

c. Now suppose that because of investor optimism about the future marginal product of capital, the investment function becomes

$$I^d = 200 - 500r.$$

Assuming that the economy was initially at full employment, what are the new values of output, the real interest rate, the price level, consumption, and investment in the short run? in the long run? Show your results graphically.

3. Consider the following economy:

Desired consumption	$C^d = 325 + 0.5(Y - T) - 500r.$
Desired investment	$I^d = 200 - 500r.$
Government purchases	$G = 150.$
Taxes	$T = 150.$
Real money demand	$L = 0.5Y - 1,000r.$
Money supply	$M = 6,000.$
Full-employment output	$\overline{Y} = 1,000.$

a. Calculate the full-employment values of the real interest rate, the price level, consumption, and investment.

b. Now suppose that government purchases are increased to 250, with no change in current taxes. Assuming that the economy was initially at full employment, what are the new values of output, the real interest rate, the price level, consumption, and investment in the short run? in the long run?

c. Repeat part (b) for an increase in the money supply to 7,200. Assume that $G = 150$.

4. An economy is described by the following equations:

Desired consumption	$C^d = 600 + 0.8(Y - T) - 500r.$
Desired investment	$I^d = 400 - 500r.$
Real money demand	$L = 0.5Y - 2,000i$, for $i > 0.$

Government purchases G and taxes T both equal 1000. The initial price level P equals 2.0, and expected inflation π^e is zero. Full-employment output $\overline{Y}$ is 8000. Notice that the real money demand function above is defined only for positive values of the nominal interest rate. We assume that when the nominal interest rate equals zero, people are willing to hold as much money as the central bank wishes to supply; this assumption implies that the *LM* curve becomes horizontal for zero values of the nominal interest rate.

a. Show that in this economy the requirement that the nominal interest rate must be greater than or equal to zero is not consistent with full employment.

That is, the economy is in a "liquidity trap." Can monetary policy alone restore full employment in this economy? Why or why not?

b. Find a combination of the money supply M and government purchases G that restores full employment while keeping the nominal interest rate at zero. Discuss the relevance of this policy to the case of Japan in the 1990s. Assume that the price level and inflation expectations are unchanged.

5. An open economy is described by the following equations:

Desired consumption	$C^d = 120 + 0.5(Y - T) - 200r$.
Desired investment	$I^d = 120 - 200r$.
Net exports	$NX = 60 + 0.05Y_{FOR} - 100r$.
Government purchases	$G = 100$.
Taxes	$T = 100$.
Real money demand	$L = 0.8Y - 200r$.
Money supply	$M = 10{,}800$.
Foreign output	$Y_{FOR} = 1{,}000$.
Full-employment output	$\bar{Y} = 700$.

a. Write the equation for the aggregate demand curve. (*Hint*: Find the equations describing goods market equilibrium and asset market equilibrium. Use these two equations to eliminate the real interest rate. For any given price level, the equation of the aggregate demand curve gives the level of output that satisfies both goods market equilibrium and asset market equilibrium.)

b. Suppose that $P = 18$. What are the short-run values of output, the real interest rate, consumption, net exports, and investment?

c. What are the long-run equilibrium values of output, the real interest rate, consumption, investment, net exports, and the price level?

6. (Appendix 12.A) Consider an economy in which all workers are covered by contracts that specify the nominal wage and give the employer the right to choose the amount of employment. The production function is

$$Y = 20\sqrt{N},$$

and the corresponding marginal product of labour is

$$MPN = \frac{10}{\sqrt{N}}.$$

Suppose that the nominal wage $W = 20$.

a. Derive an equation that relates the real wage to the amount of labour demanded by firms (the labour demand curve).

b. For the nominal wage of 20, what is the relation between the price level and the amount of labour demanded by firms?

c. What is the relation between the price level and the amount of output supplied by firms? Graph this relation.

Now suppose that the IS and LM curves of the economy (the goods market and asset market equilibrium conditions) are described by the following equations:

IS curve	$Y = 120 - 500r$.
LM curve	$M/P = 0.5Y - 500r$.

d. The money supply M is 300. Use the IS and LM equations to derive a relation between output Y and the price level P. This relation is the equation for the aggregate demand curve. Graph this relation on the same axis as the relation between the price level and the amount of output supplied by firms (the aggregate supply curve) from part (c).

e. What are the equilibrium values of the price level, output, employment, the real wage, and the real interest rate?

f. Now suppose that the money supply M is 135. What are the equilibrium values of the price level, output, employment, the real wage, and the real interest rate?

7. (Appendix 12.B) Consider the economy described in Numerical Problem 3.

a. What are the values of α_{IS}, β_{IS}, α_{LM}, β_{LM}, and ℓ_r for this economy? (You will have to refer back to Appendix 9.A for definitions of these coefficients.)

b. Suppose that the price level is fixed at $\bar{P} = 15$. What are the short-run equilibrium values of output and the real interest rate?

c. With the price level still fixed at $\bar{P} = 15$, suppose that government purchases increase from $G = 150$ to $G = 250$. What are the new values of α_{IS} and the short-run equilibrium level of output?

d. Use Eq. (12.B.5) to compute the government purchases multiplier. Use your answer to compute the short-run change in Y resulting from an increase in government purchases from $G = 150$ to $G = 250$. How does your answer here compare with your answer in part (c)?

ANALYTICAL PROBLEMS

1. According to the Keynesian IS–LM model, what is the effect of each of the following on output, the real interest rate, employment, and the price level? Distinguish between the short run and the long run.

a. Increased tax incentives for investment (the tax breaks for investment are offset by lump-sum tax increases that keep total current tax collections unchanged).

b. Increased tax incentives for saving (as in part (a), lump-sum tax increases offset the effect on total current tax collections).

c. A wave of investor pessimism about the future profitability of capital investments.

d. An increase in consumer confidence, as consumers expect that their incomes will be higher in the future.

2. According to the Keynesian *IS–LM* model, what is the effect of each of the following on output, the real interest rate, employment, and the price level? Distinguish between the short run and the long run.

   a. Financial deregulation allows banks to pay a higher interest rate on chequing accounts.

   b. The introduction of debit cards greatly reduces the amount of money that people need for transactions.

   c. A severe water shortage causes sharp declines in agricultural output and increases in food prices.

   d. A temporary beneficial supply shock affects most of the economy, but no individual firm is affected sufficiently to change its prices in the short run.

3. Suppose that the Bank of Canada has a policy of increasing the money supply when it observes that the economy is in recession. However, suppose that about six months are needed for an increase in the money supply to affect aggregate demand, which is about the same amount of time needed for firms to review and reset their prices. What effects will the Bank's policy have on output and price stability? Does your answer change if (a) the Bank has some ability to forecast recessions or (b) price adjustment takes longer than six months?

4. Classical economists argue that using fiscal policy to fight a recession does not make workers better off. Suppose, however, that the Keynesian model is correct. Relative to a policy of doing nothing, does an increase in government purchases that brings the economy to full employment make workers better off? In answering the question, discuss the effects of the fiscal expansion on the real wage, employment, consumption, and current and future taxes. How does your answer depend on (a) the direct benefits of the government spending program, and (b) the speed with which prices adjust in the absence of fiscal stimulus?

5. Some labour economists argue that it is useful to think of the labour market as being divided into two sectors: a primary sector, where "good" (high-paying, long-term) jobs are located, and a secondary sector, which has "bad" (low-paying, short-term) jobs. Suppose that the primary sector has a high marginal product of labour and (because effort is costly for firms to monitor) firms pay an efficiency wage. The secondary sector has a low marginal product of labour and no efficiency wage; instead, the real wage in the secondary sector adjusts so that the quantities of labour demanded and supplied are equal in that sector. Workers are alike, and all would prefer to work in the primary sector. However, workers who cannot find jobs in the primary sector work in the secondary sector.

   What are the effects of each of the following on the real wage, employment, and output in both sectors?

   a. Expansionary monetary policy increases the demand for primary sector output.

   b. Immigration increases the labour force.

   c. The effort curve changes so that a higher real wage is needed to elicit the greatest effort per dollar in the primary sector. Effort exerted at the higher real wage is the same as before the change in the effort curve.

   d. There is a temporary productivity improvement in the primary sector.

   e. There is a temporary productivity improvement in the secondary sector.

APPENDIX 12.A

LABOUR CONTRACTS AND NOMINAL-WAGE RIGIDITY

In the Keynesian theory, the non-neutrality of money is a consequence of nominal rigidity. In this chapter, we emphasized nominal-price rigidity. An alternative nominal rigidity that could account for the non-neutrality of money, which many Keynesians emphasize, is nominal-wage rigidity. Nominal-wage rigidity could reflect long-term labour contracts between firms and unions in which wages are set in nominal terms (the case we study here). In terms of the *AD–AS* framework, the difference between nominal-price rigidity and nominal-wage rigidity is that nominal-price rigidity implies a horizontal short-run aggregate supply curve, whereas nominal-wage rigidity implies a short-run aggregate supply curve that slopes upward. However, this difference does not really affect the results obtained from the Keynesian model. In particular, in the Keynesian model with nominal-wage rigidity, money remains non-neutral in the short run and neutral in the long run.

THE SHORT-RUN AGGREGATE SUPPLY CURVE WITH LABOUR CONTRACTS

In Canada, most labour contracts specify employment conditions and nominal wages for a period of one to three years. Although labour contracts specify the nominal wage rate, they usually do not specify the total amount of employment. Instead, employers unilaterally decide how many hours will be worked and whether workers will be laid off. These factors imply that the short-run aggregate supply curve slopes upward.

We can see why the short-run aggregate supply curve slopes upward when labour contracts prespecify the nominal wage by considering what happens when the price level increases. With the nominal wage W already determined by the contract, an increase in the price level P reduces the real wage w, or W/P. In response to the drop in the real wage, firms demand more labour. Because firms unilaterally choose the level of employment, the increase in the amount of labour demanded leads to an increase in employment and, therefore, an increase in output. Thus, an increase in the price level leads to an increase in the amount of output supplied, as shown by the *SRAS* curves in Figure 12.A.1

NON-NEUTRALITY OF MONEY

Money is non-neutral in the short run in the model with long-term labour contracts, as illustrated in Figure 12.A.1. The initial general equilibrium is at point E, where the initial aggregate demand curve AD^1 intersects the short-run aggregate supply curve $SRAS^1$. A 10% increase in the money supply shifts the *AD* curve up to AD^2. (For any level of output, the price level is 10% higher on AD^2 than on AD^1.) In the short run, the rise in the money supply increases the price level to P_2 and output to Y_2 at point F. Output is higher than its full-employment level at F because the rise in prices lowered the real wage, which leads firms to employ more labour and produce more output.

FIGURE 12.A.1

MONETARY NON-
NEUTRALITY WITH
LONG-TERM CONTRACTS

With long-term labour contracts that fix the nominal wage in the short run, an increase in the price level lowers the real wage and induces firms to employ more labour and produce more output. Thus, the short-run aggregate supply curve $SRAS^1$ slopes upward. When nominal wages are rigid, money is not neutral. From the initial equilibrium point E a 10% increase in the money supply shifts the AD curve up, from AD^1 to AD^2. In the short run, both output and the price level increase, as shown by point F. Over time, contracts are renegotiated and nominal wages rise to match the increase in prices. As wages rise, the short-run aggregate supply curve shifts up, from $SRAS^1$ to $SRAS^2$ so that general equilibrium is restored at H. At H, both the price level P and the nominal wage W have risen by 10% so the real wage is the same as it was initially, and firms supply the full-employment level of output $\overline{Y}$.

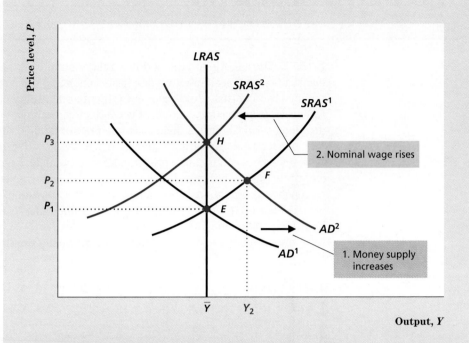

At the short-run equilibrium point, F, however, workers will be dissatisfied because their real wages are lower than they had expected. Over time, as contracts are renewed or renegotiated, nominal wages will rise to offset the increase in prices. At any price level, a rise in the nominal wage also raises the real wage, inducing firms to employ less labour and produce less output. Thus, rising nominal wages cause the short-run aggregate supply curve to shift up, from $SRAS^1$ to $SRAS^2$. Eventually, general equilibrium is restored at point H.

In the long run at point H, the price level rises to P_3, which is 10% higher than its initial value P_1. At H, the nominal wage W has also increased by 10% so that the real wage W/P has returned to its initial value. With the real wage back at its original value, firms employ the same amount of labour and produce the same amount of output ($\overline{Y}$) as they did at the initial equilibrium point, E. Thus, as in the Keynesian model based on efficiency wages and price stickiness, in the Keynesian model with nominal-wage rigidity, money is neutral in the long run but not in the short run.

Although nominal-wage rigidity arising from labour contracts can explain short-run monetary non-neutrality, some economists object to this explanation. One objection is that less than a third of the labour force in Canada is unionized and covered by long-term labour contracts. However, many non-union workers receive wages similar to those set in union contracts. For example, although most non-union workers do not have formal wage contracts, they may have "implicit contracts" with their employers, or informal unwritten arrangements for comparable wages.

A second objection is that many labour contracts contain cost-of-living adjustments (COLAs), which tie the nominal wage to the overall price level, as measured, for example, by the consumer price index. Contracts with *complete* indexation increase the nominal wage by the same percentage as the increase in the price level. If wages are completely indexed to the price level, the short-run aggregate supply curve is vertical and money is neutral. To show why, let us suppose that the price level increases by 6%. If labour contracts are completely indexed, nominal wages also increase by 6% and the real wage W/P remains unchanged. Because the real wage does not change, firms choose the same levels of employment and output independent of the price level.

However, in most Canadian labour contracts wages are not completely indexed to prices. In recent years, fewer than half the workers covered by major private industry bargaining agreements have had any COLA provisions at all. Furthermore, most contracts with COLA provisions have partial rather than complete indexation. For example, under a contract that calls for 50% indexation, the nominal wage will increase by 50% of the overall rate of increase in prices. Thus, if the price level increases by 6%, the nominal wage increases by 3%. As a result, the real wage falls by 3% (a 3% increase in the nominal wage W minus a 6% increase in the price level P). The reduction in the real wage induces firms to increase employment and production. Thus, with partial indexation the short-run aggregate supply curve again slopes upward, and money is not neutral in the short run. On the other hand, COLA provisions were most widespread (and long-term contracts least widespread) in the high-inflation 1970s, which suggests that contracts do eventually adjust to inflation.

A third and final objection is that this theory predicts that real wages will be countercyclical, contrary to the business cycle fact that real wages are procyclical. For example, at point F in Figure 12.A.1 output is higher than the full-employment level, but the real wage is lower than at full employment (indeed, the low real wage induces firms to produce the extra output). Thus, the theory holds that real wages will fall in booms—that is, the real wage is countercyclical—which is inconsistent with the evidence.

However, perhaps both supply shocks and aggregate demand shocks affect real wages. For the real business cycle theory we showed that if productivity shocks cause cyclical fluctuations, the real wage should be procyclical, perhaps strongly so. A combination of supply shocks (which cause the real wage to move procyclically) and aggregate demand shocks (which, as in Figure 12.A.1, cause the real wage to move countercyclically) might average out to a real wage that is at least mildly procyclical.

APPENDIX 12.B

The Multiplier in the Keynesian Model

In this chapter, we defined the multiplier associated with any particular type of spending as the short-run change in total output resulting from a one-unit change in that type of spending. Here, we use the analysis in Appendix 9.A to derive the multiplier associated with government purchases G. We proceed in three steps: First, we calculate the effect on α_{IS} (the intercept of the IS curve in Eq. 9.A.14) of an increase in G. Then, we calculate the effect on the short-run equilibrium value of Y, shown by Eq. (9.A.27), of an increase in α_{IS}. Finally, we combine these two effects to calculate the effect on output, Y, of an increase in G.

To calculate the effect on α_{IS} of an increase in G, we repeat the definition of α_{IS}, Eq. (9.A.15):

$$\alpha_{IS} = \frac{c_0 + i_0 + G - c_y t_0}{c_r + i_r},$$ (12.B.1)

where c_0, i_0, c_Y, c_r, i_r, and t_0 are parameters that determine desired consumption and desired investment (see Appendix 9.A). If G increases by ΔG, then α_{IS} increases by ΔG, then α_{IS} increases by $\Delta G/(c_r + i_r)$, so

$$\Delta\alpha_{IS} = \frac{\Delta G}{c_r + i_r}.$$ (12.B.2)

Next, recall from Eq. (9.A.27) that, in the short run when $P = \bar{P}$, the level of output is

$$Y = \frac{\alpha_{IS} - \alpha_{LM} + (1/\ell_r)(M/\bar{P})}{\beta_{IS} + \beta_{LM}}.$$ (12.B.3)

Observe from Eq. (12.B.3) that, if α_{IS} increases by $\Delta\alpha_{IS}$, output, Y, increases by $\Delta\alpha_{IS}/(\beta_{IS} + \beta_{LM})$, or

$$\Delta Y = \frac{\Delta\alpha_{IS}}{\beta_{IS} + \beta_{LM}}.$$ (12.B.4)

Finally, if we substitute the right-hand side of Eq. (12.B.2) for $\Delta\alpha_{IS}$ on the right-hand side of Eq. (13.B.4) and then divide both sides of the resulting equation by ΔG, we obtain

$$\frac{\Delta Y}{\Delta G} = \frac{1}{(c_r + i_r)(\beta_{IS} + \beta_{LM})}.$$ (12.B.5)

The right-hand side of Eq. (12.B.5) is the increase in short-run equilibrium output, Y, that occurs for each one-unit increase in government purchases, G. In other words, it is the government purchases multiplier. Similar calculations show that changes in desired consumption or desired investment (as reflected in the terms c_0 and i_0) have the same multiplier as government purchases.

Because c_r, i_r, β_{IS}, and β_{LM} are all positive, the multiplier is positive. However, depending on the specific values of those parameters, the multiplier may be greater or less than 1. A case in which the multiplier is likely to be large occurs when the LM curve is horizontal (that is, when the slope of the LM curve β_{LM} is 0). If the LM curve is horizontal, shifts in the IS curve induced by changes in spending have relatively large effects on output. Recall that Eq. (9.A.16) gives the slope of the IS curve, β_{IS}, as $[1 - (1 - t)c_Y]/(c_r + i_r)$. Making this substitution and setting the slope of the LM curve, β_{LM}, at 0 yield a simple form of the multiplier:

$$\frac{\Delta Y}{\Delta G} = \frac{1}{1 - (1 - t)c_Y}. \qquad (12.B.6)$$

For example, suppose that the marginal propensity to consume, c_Y, is 0.8 and that the tax rate, t, is 0.25. Then the multiplier defined in Eq. (12.B.6) is $1/[1 - (0.75)(0.8)] = 1/0.4$, or 2.5.

Chapter 13

UNEMPLOYMENT AND INFLATION

In the last several chapters, we focused on the concepts of the business cycle, macroeconomic stabilization, and classical and Keynesian approaches to business cycle analysis. Although these concepts are central to today's macroeconomics, actual policy discussions rarely involve such abstract terms. Policy debates tend to focus on highly publicized economic statistics, such as inflation and unemployment. To make a stronger connection between business cycle theories and policy debates, we now take a closer look at unemployment and inflation, first together and then separately.

Unemployment and inflation—sometimes referred to as the "twin evils" of macroeconomics—are among the most difficult and politically sensitive economic issues that policymakers face. High rates of unemployment and inflation generate intense public concern because their effects are direct and visible: Almost everyone is affected by rising prices, and few workers can be confident that they will never lose their jobs.

Moreover, there is a longstanding idea in macroeconomics that unemployment and inflation are somehow related. In the first part of this chapter, we discuss in some detail the concept of the Phillips curve—an empirical relationship between inflation and unemployment. According to the Phillips curve, inflation tends to be low when unemployment is high and high when unemployment is low. The Phillips curve relationship raises some important questions about how the economy works and how macroeconomic policies should be used.

We then look at unemployment and inflation separately. We examine the costs that each imposes on society and consider the options that policymakers have for dealing with these problems. This chapter begins Part IV of the book, the purpose of which is to explore macroeconomic policymaking in greater detail. Following the discussion of inflation and unemployment in this chapter, Chapter 14 takes a closer look at institutions and debates related to the making of monetary policy, and Chapter 15 provides a similar overview of fiscal policy.

13.1 UNEMPLOYMENT AND INFLATION: IS THERE A TRADE-OFF?

Newspaper editorials and public discussions about economic policy often refer to the "trade-off" between inflation and unemployment. The idea is that to reduce inflation, the economy must tolerate high unemployment, or that to reduce unemployment, more inflation must be accepted. This section examines the idea of an inflation–unemployment trade-off and its implications for macroeconomic policy.

The origin of the idea of a trade-off between inflation and unemployment was a 1958 article by economist A. W. Phillips, of the London School of Economics.[1] Phillips examined 97 years of British data on unemployment and nominal wage growth data; he found that historically, unemployment tended to be low in years when nominal wages grew rapidly and high in years when nominal wages grew slowly. Economists who built on Phillips's work shifted its focus slightly by looking at the link between unemployment and inflation—that is, the growth rate of prices—rather than the link between unemployment and the growth rate of wages. During the 1960s, many statistical studies examined inflation and unemployment data for numerous countries and time periods, finding, in many cases, a negative relationship between the two variables. This negative empirical relationship between unemployment and inflation is known as the **Phillips curve**.

A striking example of a Phillips curve, shown in Figure 13.1, occurred in Canada during the 1960s. The Canadian economy expanded throughout most of the 1960s, with unemployment falling and inflation rising steadily. In Figure 13.1, the inflation rate is measured on the vertical axis, and the unemployment rate is measured on the horizontal axis. Note that years, such as 1961, that had high unemployment also had low inflation, and that years, such as 1967, that had high inflation also had low unemployment. The data produce a clear downward-sloping relation between inflation and unemployment—that is, a Phillips curve. The experience of several countries in the 1960s, which came after Phillips's article had been published and widely disseminated, was viewed by many as a confirmation of his basic finding.

The policy implications of these findings were much debated. Initially, the Phillips curve seemed to offer policymakers a "menu" of combinations of inflation and unemployment from which they could choose. Indeed, during the 1960s, some economists argued that by accepting a modest amount of inflation, macroeconomic policymakers could keep the unemployment rate low indefinitely. This belief seemed to be borne out during the 1960s, when rising inflation was accompanied by falling unemployment.

In the following decades, however, this relationship between inflation and unemployment failed to hold: Figure 13.2 shows inflation and unemployment for the period 1970–2001. During those years, unlike the 1960s, there seemed to be no reliable relationship between unemployment and inflation. From the perspective of the Phillips curve, the most puzzling period was the mid-1970s, during which the country experienced high inflation and high unemployment simultaneously (stagflation). In 1975, for example, unemployment reached 6.9% of the labour force, and the annual inflation rate was 10.8%. High unemployment, together with high inflation, is inconsistent with the Phillips curve.

---

1. "The "Relation between Unemployment and the Rate of Change of Money Wage Rates in the United Kingdom, 1861–1957," *Economica*, November 1958, pp. 283–299.

FIGURE 13.1

THE PHILLIPS CURVE AND THE CANADIAN ECONOMY DURING THE 1960s

During the 1960s, Canadian rates of inflation seemed to lie along a Phillips curve. Inflation rose and unemployment fell fairly steadily during this decade, and policymakers apparently had decided to live with higher inflation in order to reduce unemployment.

Source: Unemployment rate, 1963–1965: *Historical Statistics of Canada*, Series D233; 1966–1969: *Canadian Economic Observer, Historical Statistical Supplement*, Table 8; CPI inflation rate: *Canadian Economic Observer, Historical Statistical Supplement*, Table 12.

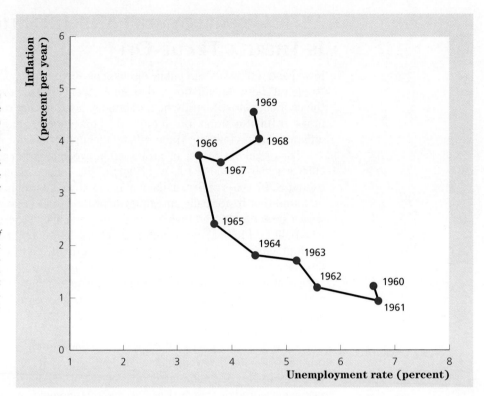

FIGURE 13.2

INFLATION AND UNEMPLOYMENT IN CANADA, 1970–2001

The figure shows the combinations of inflation and unemployment experienced in Canada each year from 1970 to 2001. Unlike the situation during the 1960s (see Figure 13.1), after 1970, a clear negative relationship between inflation and unemployment did not seem to exist.

Source: CPI inflation rate: *Canadian Economic Observer, Historical Statistical Supplement*, Table 12; unemployment rate: Table 8.

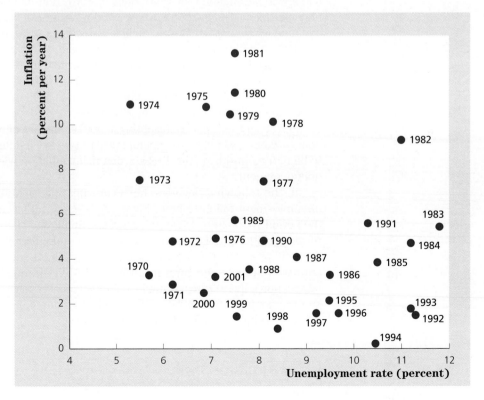

The original empirical results of Phillips and others who extended his work, together with the unexpected experience of the economy after 1970, raises at least three important questions:

- Why was the original Phillips curve relationship between inflation and unemployment frequently observed historically, as in the cases of the United Kingdom in the century before 1958 and Canada in the 1960s?

- Why did the simple negative relationship between inflation and unemployment that seemed to exist during the 1960s in Canada vanish after 1970? In other words, was there, in fact, no systematic relationship between inflation and unemployment in the Canadian economy after 1970?

- Does the Phillips curve actually provide a menu of choices from which policymakers can choose? For example, by electing to maintain a high inflation rate can policymakers guarantee a *permanently* low rate of unemployment?

Economic theory provides reasonable answers to these questions; in particular, it explains the collapse of the Phillips curve after 1970. Interestingly, the key economic analysis of the Phillips curve—which predicted that this relationship would not be stable—was done during the 1960s, before the Phillips curve had actually broken down. Thus, we have at least one example of economic theorists predicting an important development in the economy that policymakers and the public did not anticipate.

The Expectations-Augmented Phillips Curve

Although the Phillips curve seemed to describe adequately the unemployment–inflation relationship in several countries in the 1960s, during the second half of the decade, some economists, notably Milton Friedman,[2] of the University of Chicago, and Edmund Phelps,[3] of Columbia University, questioned the logic of the Phillips curve. Friedman and Phelps argued—purely on the basis of economic theory—that there should not be a stable negative relationship between inflation and unemployment. Instead, a negative relationship should exist between *unanticipated* inflation (the difference between the actual and expected inflation rates) and *cyclical* unemployment (the difference between the actual and natural unemployment rates).[4] Although these distinctions appear to be merely technical, they are crucial in understanding the relationship between the actual rates of inflation and unemployment.

Before discussing the significance of their analyses, we need to explain how Friedman and Phelps arrived at their conclusions. To do so, we use the extended classical model, which includes the misperceptions theory. (Analytical Problem 3 at the end of the chapter asks you to perform a similar analysis using the Keynesian model.) We proceed in two steps, first considering an economy at full employment with steady, fully anticipated inflation. In this economy, both unanticipated inflation and cyclical unemployment are zero. Second, we consider what happens when

---

2. "The Role of Monetary Policy," *American Economic Review*, March 1968, pp. 1–17.
3. "Wage Dynamics and Labor Market Equilibrium," in Edmund Phelps, ed., *Microeconomic Foundations of Employment and Inflation Theory*, New York: W.W. Norton, 1970, pp. 124–166.
4. In Chapter 3, we defined cyclical unemployment. Recall that the natural rate of unemployment is the unemployment rate that exists when output is at its full-employment level. The natural rate exceeds zero because of frictional and structural unemployment, also defined in Chapter 3.

aggregate demand growth increases unexpectedly. In this case, both positive unanticipated inflation (inflation greater than expected) and negative cyclical unemployment (actual unemployment lower than the natural rate) occur. This outcome confirms the Friedman–Phelps point that a negative relationship exists between unanticipated inflation and cyclical unemployment.

We develop the first step of this analysis by using the extended classical model to analyze an economy with steady inflation (Figure 13.3). We assume that this economy is in full-employment equilibrium in which the money supply has been growing at 10% per year for many years and is expected to continue to grow at this rate indefinitely. With the money supply growing by 10% per year, the aggregate demand curve shifts up by 10% each year, from AD^1 in year 1 to AD^2 in year 2, and so on. For simplicity, we assume that full-employment output $\bar{Y}$ is constant, but relaxing that assumption would not affect our basic conclusions.

In Figure 13.3, the short-run aggregate supply (SRAS) curve shifts up by 10% each year. Why? With the growth in money supply fully anticipated, there are no misperceptions. Instead, people expect the price level to rise by 10% per year (a 10% inflation rate), which, in turn, causes the SRAS curve to shift up by 10% per year. With no misperceptions, the economy remains at full employment with output at $\bar{Y}$. For example, when the expected price level is 100 in year 1, the SRAS curve is $SRAS^1$. At point E, the price level is 100 (the same as the expected price level) and output is $\bar{Y}$. In year 2, the expected price level is 110, and the SRAS curve is $SRAS^2$. In year 2, equilibrium occurs at point F, again with output of $\bar{Y}$ and equal expected and actual price levels. Each year, both the AD curve and the SRAS curve shift up by 10%, increasing the actual price level and expected price level by 10% and maintaining output at its full-employment level.

FIGURE 13.3

ONGOING INFLATION IN THE EXTENDED CLASSICAL MODEL

If the money supply grows by 10% every year, the AD curve shifts up by 10% every year, from AD^1 in year 1 to AD^2 in year 2, and so on. If the money supply has been growing by 10% per year for some time and the rate of inflation has been 10% for some time, the expected rate of inflation is also 10%. Thus, the expected price level also grows by 10% each year, from 100 in year 1 to 110 in year 2, and so on. The 10% annual increase in the expected price level shifts the SRAS curve up by 10% each year, for example, from $SRAS^1$ in year 1 to $SRAS^2$ in year 2. The economy remains in full-employment equilibrium at the intersection of the AD curve and the SRAS curve in each year (point E in year 1 and point F in year 2), with output at $\bar{Y}$, unemployment at the natural rate of unemployment $\bar{u}$, and inflation and expected inflation both at 10% per year.

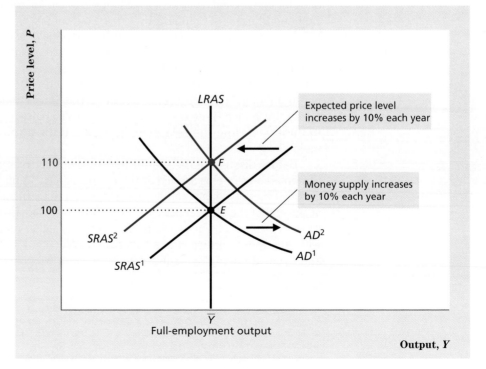

What happens to unemployment in this economy? Because output is continuously at its full-employment level $\overline{Y}$, unemployment remains at the natural rate $\overline{u}$. With unemployment at its natural rate, cyclical unemployment is zero. Hence this economy has zero unanticipated inflation and zero cyclical unemployment.

Against this backdrop of 10% monetary growth and 10% inflation, suppose now that in year 2, the money supply grows by 15%, rather than by the expected 10% (Figure 13.4). In this case, instead of being 10% higher than AD^1 (as shown by $AD^{2,\ old}$), the aggregate demand curve in year 2 will be 15% higher than AD^1 (as shown by $AD^{2,\ new}$). If this increase in the rate of monetary growth is *unanticipated* at the beginning of year 2, the expected price level in year 2 remains at 110, and the short-run aggregate supply curve is $SRAS^2$, as before. The short-run equilibrium in year 2 is at point G, the intersection of the $AD^{2,\ new}$ and $SRAS^2$ curves. At G, the price level is 113, so the actual rate of inflation in year 2 is 13%. Because the expected rate of inflation was 10%, the 13% inflation rate implies unanticipated inflation of 3% in year 2. Further, because output is above its full-employment level $\overline{Y}$ at G, the actual unemployment rate is below the natural rate and cyclical unemployment is negative.

Why is output above its full-employment level in year 2? Note that in year 2, the 13% rate of inflation is less than the 15% rate of money growth but greater than the 10% expected rate of inflation. Because the price level grows by less than does the nominal money supply in year 2, the real money supply M/P increases, lowering the real interest rate and raising the aggregate quantity of goods demanded above $\overline{Y}$. At the same time, because the price level grows by more than expected, the aggregate quantity of goods supplied also is greater than $\overline{Y}$ as producers are fooled into thinking that the relative prices of their products have increased.

Producers cannot be fooled about price behaviour indefinitely, however. In the long run, producers learn the true price level, the economy returns to full employment, and the inflation rate again equals the expected inflation rate, as in Figure 13.3. In the meantime, however, as long as actual output is higher than full-employment output $\overline{Y}$ and actual unemployment is below the natural rate $\overline{u}$, the actual price level must be higher than the expected price level. Indeed, according to the misperceptions theory, output can be higher than $\overline{Y}$ only when prices are higher than expected (and, therefore, when inflation is also higher than expected).

Thus, in this economy, when the public correctly predicts aggregate demand growth and inflation, unanticipated inflation is zero, actual unemployment equals the natural rate, and cyclical unemployment is zero (see Figure 13.3). However, if aggregate demand growth unexpectedly speeds up, the economy faces a period of positive unanticipated inflation and negative cyclical unemployment (see Figure 13.4). Similarly, an unexpected slowdown in aggregate demand growth could occur, causing the AD curve to rise more slowly than expected; for a time unanticipated inflation would be negative (actual inflation less than expected) and cyclical unemployment would be positive (actual unemployment greater than the natural rate).

The relationship between unanticipated inflation and cyclical unemployment implied by this analysis is

$$\pi - \pi^e = -h(u - \overline{u}),$$

where

$\pi - \pi^e =$ unanticipated inflation (the difference between actual inflation π and expected inflation π^e);

$u - \overline{u} =$ cyclical unemployment (the difference between the actual unemployment rate u and the natural unemployment rate $\overline{u}$);

FIGURE 13.4

UNANTICIPATED INFLATION
IN THE EXTENDED
CLASSICAL MODEL

If the money supply has been growing by 10% per year for a long time and is expected to continue growing by 10%, the expected price level increases by 10% each year. The 10% increase in the expected price level shifts the SRAS curve up from $SRAS^1$ in year 1 to $SRAS^2$ in year 2. Then, if the money supply actually increases by 15% in year 2, rather than by the expected 10%, the AD curve is $AD^{2,\ new}$, rather than $AD^{2,\ old}$. As a result of higher-than-expected money growth, output increases above $\overline{Y}$ in year 2, and the price level increases to 113, at point G. Because the price level rises by 13%, rather than the expected 10%, unanticipated inflation is 3% in year 2. This unanticipated inflation is associated with output higher than $\overline{Y}$ and unemployment below the natural rate $\overline{u}$ (negative cyclical unemployment).

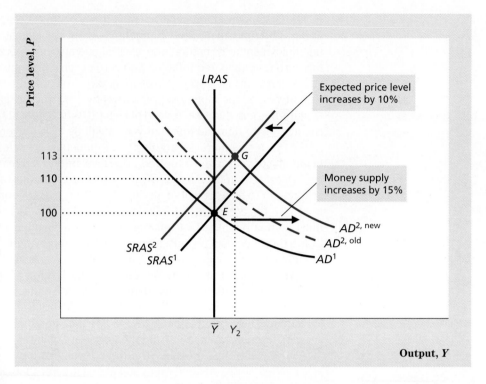

$h = $ a positive number that measures the strength of the relationship between unanticipated inflation and cyclical unemployment.

The preceding equation expresses mathematically the idea that unanticipated inflation will be positive when cyclical unemployment is negative, negative when cyclical unemployment is positive, and zero when cyclical unemployment is zero.[5] If we add π^e to both sides of the equation, it becomes

$$\pi = \pi^e - h(u - \overline{u}). \tag{13.1}$$

Equation (13.1) describes the expectations-augmented Phillips curve. According to the **expectations-augmented Phillips curve**, actual inflation π exceeds expected inflation π^e if the actual unemployment rate u is less than the natural rate $\overline{u}$; and actual inflation is less than expected inflation if the unemployment rate exceeds the natural rate.

THE SHIFTING PHILLIPS CURVE

Let us return to the original Phillips curve, which links the levels of inflation and unemployment in the economy. The insight gained from the Friedman–Phelps analysis is that the relationship illustrated by the Phillips curve depends on the expected rate of inflation and the natural rate of unemployment. If either factor changes, the Phillips curve will shift.

---

5. The equation also implies that the relationship between unanticipated inflation and cyclical unemployment is linear, but this is for convenience only. The relationship of the two variables might as easily be a curve as a line.

CHANGES IN THE EXPECTED RATE OF INFLATION

Figure 13.5 shows how a change in the expected inflation rate affects the relationship between inflation and unemployment, according to the Friedman–Phelps theory. The curve PC^1 is the Phillips curve for an expected rate of inflation of 3%. What identifies the expected rate of inflation as 3% along PC^1? Equation (13.1) indicates that when the actual unemployment rate equals the natural rate (6% in this example), the actual inflation rate equals the expected inflation rate. Thus, to determine the expected inflation rate on a Phillips curve, we find the inflation rate at the point where the actual unemployment rate equals the natural rate. For instance, at point A on curve PC^1, the unemployment rate equals the natural rate, and the actual and expected rates of inflation both equal 3%. As long as the expected inflation rate remains at 3% (and the natural unemployment rate remains at 6%), the Phillips curve PC^1 will describe the relationship between inflation and unemployment.

Now, suppose that the expected rate of inflation increases from 3% to 12%. Figure 13.5 shows that this 9 percentage point increase in the expected rate of inflation shifts the Phillips curve up by 9 percentage points at each level of the unemployment rate, from PC^1 to PC^2. When the actual unemployment rate equals the natural rate on PC^2 (at point B), the inflation rate is 12%, confirming that the expected inflation rate is 12% along PC^2. Comparing PC^2 and PC^1 reveals that an increase in the expected inflation rate shifts the Phillips curve relationship between inflation and unemployment up and to the right.

CHANGES IN THE NATURAL RATE OF UNEMPLOYMENT

The Phillips curve relationship between inflation and unemployment also is shifted by changes in the natural unemployment rate, as illustrated by Figure 13.6. The Phillips curve PC^1 shows a natural unemployment rate at 6% and an expected

FIGURE 13.5

THE SHIFTING PHILLIPS CURVE: AN INCREASE IN EXPECTED INFLATION

The Friedman–Phelps theory implies that there is a different Phillips curve for every expected inflation rate. For example, PC^1 is the Phillips curve when the expected rate of inflation is 3%. To verify this claim, note from Eq. (13.1) that when the actual unemployment rate equals the natural rate $\bar{u}$ (6% here), the actual inflation rate equals the expected inflation rate. At point A, the unemployment rate equals the natural rate and the inflation rate equals 3% on PC^1, so the expected inflation rate is 3% on PC^1. Similarly, at point B on PC^2, where the unemployment rate equals its natural rate, the inflation rate is 12%, so the expected inflation rate is 12% along PC^2. Thus, an increase in the expected inflation rate from 3% to 12% shifts the Phillips curve up and to the right, from PC^1 to PC^2.

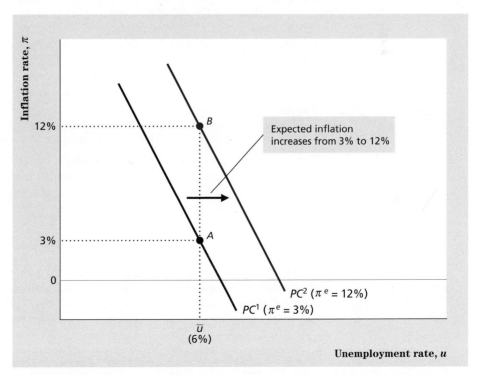

FIGURE 13.6

THE SHIFTING PHILLIPS
CURVE: AN INCREASE IN
THE NATURAL
UNEMPLOYMENT RATE

According to the Friedman–
Phelps theory, an increase in
the natural unemployment rate
shifts the Phillips curve up and
to the right. At point A on PC^1,
the actual inflation rate and the
expected inflation rate are
equal at 3%, so the natural
unemployment rate equals the
actual unemployment rate at
A, or 6%. Thus, PC^1 is the
Phillips curve when the natural
unemployment rate is 6% and
the expected inflation rate is
3%, as in Figure 13.5. If the
natural unemployment rate
increases to 7%, with expected
inflation unchanged, the
Phillips curve shifts to PC^3. At
point C on PC^3, both expected
and actual inflation equal 3%,
so the natural unemployment
rate equals the actual unemployment rate at C, or 7%.

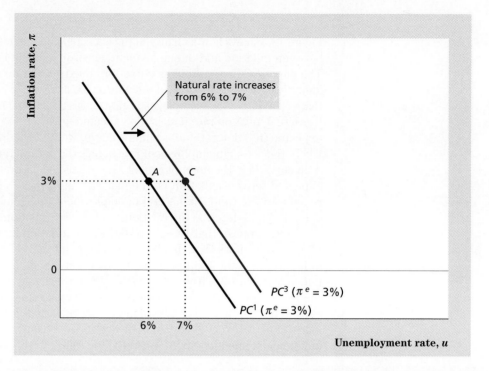

inflation rate at 3% (PC^1 in Figure 13.6 is the same as PC^1 in Figure 13.5). Now,
suppose that the natural unemployment rate increases to 7% but that the expected
inflation rate remains unchanged at 3%. As Figure 13.6 shows, the increase in the
natural unemployment rate causes the Phillips curve to shift, from PC^1 to PC^3.

To confirm that the natural unemployment rate corresponding to Phillips curve
PC^3 in Figure 13.6 is 7%, look at point C on PC^3: At C, where the actual and expected
inflation rates are equal, the unemployment rate is 7%. Thus, the natural
unemployment rate associated with Phillips curve PC^3 is 7%. This example illustrates
that—like an increase in expected inflation—an increase in the natural unemployment
rate causes the Phillips curve relationship between inflation and unemployment to
shift up and to the right.

SUPPLY SHOCKS AND THE PHILLIPS CURVE

The Friedman–Phelps theory holds that changes in either expected inflation or the
natural unemployment rate will shift the Phillips curve. One type of economic
disturbance that is likely to affect both factors is a supply shock. Recall that an
adverse supply shock causes a burst of inflation, which may lead people to expect
higher inflation.[6] An adverse supply shock also tends to increase the natural
unemployment rate, although the reasons for this effect are different for the classical
and Keynesian models.

Recall that from the classical perspective, an adverse supply shock raises the
natural rate of unemployment by increasing the degree of mismatch between workers
and jobs. For example, an oil price shock eliminates jobs in heavy-energy-using
industries but increases employment in energy-providing industries.

6. The inflationary impact of a supply shock will be reinforced if, in an attempt to moderate the rise in
unemployment caused by the shock, the central bank increases the money supply.

In the Keynesian model, recall that much of the unemployment that exists even when the economy is at the full-employment level is blamed on rigid real wages. In particular, if the efficiency wage is above the market-clearing real wage, the amount of labour supplied at the efficiency wage will exceed the amount of labour demanded at that wage (see Figure 12.2), leading to persistent structural unemployment. An adverse supply shock has no effect on the supply of labour,[7] but it does reduce the marginal product of labour and, thus, labour demand. With a rigid efficiency wage, the drop in labour demand increases the excess of labour supplied over labour demanded, raising the amount of unemployment that exists when the economy is at full employment. Thus, as in the classical model, the Keynesian model predicts that an adverse supply shock will raise the natural unemployment rate.

Because adverse supply shocks raise both expected inflation and the natural unemployment rate, according to the Friedman–Phelps analysis, they should cause the Phillips curve to shift up and to the right. Similarly, beneficial supply shocks should shift the Phillips curve down and to the left. Overall, the Phillips curve should be particularly unstable during periods of supply shocks.

THE SHIFTING PHILLIPS CURVE IN PRACTICE

Our analysis of the shifting Phillips curve (see Figures 13.5 and 13.6) helps answer the basic questions about the Phillips curve raised earlier in the chapter. The first question was: Why did the original Phillips curve relationship between inflation and unemployment apply to many historical cases, including Canada during the 1960s? The Friedman–Phelps analysis shows that a negative relationship between the levels of inflation and unemployment holds *as long as expected inflation and the natural unemployment rate are approximately constant*. As shown in Figure 13.9 later in this chapter, the natural unemployment rate changes relatively slowly, and during the 1960s, it was approximately constant. Expected inflation probably was also nearly constant in Canada in the 1960s because at that time, people were used to low and stable inflation and inflation remained low for most of the decade. Thus, not surprisingly, the Canadian inflation and unemployment data for the 1960s seem to lie along a single Phillips curve (see Figure 13.1).

The second question was: Why did the Phillips curve relationship, so apparent in Canada in the 1960s, seem to disappear after 1970 (see Figure 13.2)? The answer suggested by the Friedman–Phelps analysis is that in the period after 1970, the expected inflation rate and the natural unemployment rate varied considerably more than they had in the 1960s, causing the Phillips curve relationship to shift erratically.

Contributing to the shifts of the Phillips curve after 1970 were the two large supply shocks associated with sharp increases in the price of oil that hit the Canadian economy in 1973–1974 and 1979–1980. Recall that adverse supply shocks are likely to increase both expected inflation and the natural rate of unemployment, shifting the Phillips curve up and to the right. Oil prices also varied considerably during the 1980s, declining precipitously in the middle of the decade and then temporarily rising again after the Iraqi invasion of Kuwait in August 1990.

Beyond the direct effects of supply shocks, other forces may have increased the variability of expected inflation and the natural unemployment rate after 1970. As we discuss later in the chapter, the natural unemployment rate rose during this

---

7. This statement is strictly true only for a temporary adverse supply shock. A permanent adverse supply shock, if it reduces expected future wages, would increase labour supply and thus cause an even larger rise in the natural rate of unemployment.

period as a result of labour force composition changes and faster structural changes in the economy.

Expected inflation probably varied more after 1970 because actual inflation varied more (see Figure 2.2 for the Canadian inflation rate for the period 1951–2000). After being relatively low for a long time, inflation, driven by monetary and fiscal policies that had probably been over-expansionary for several years, emerged as a problem at the end of the 1960s. The 1970s were a period of high and erratic inflation, the result of the oil price shocks and macroeconomic policies that again were probably too expansionary, especially in the latter part of the decade. In contrast, following the anti-inflationary policies of the Bank of Canada and other central banks from 1979 through 1982, inflation returned to a relatively low level during the 1980s. To the extent that expected inflation followed the path of actual inflation—high and erratic in the 1970s, low in the 1980s—our analysis suggests that the Phillips curve relationship between inflation and unemployment would not have been stable over the period.

Does the unstable Phillips curve during the period 1970–2001 imply that there was no systematic relationship between inflation and unemployment during that period? The answer is, no. According to the Friedman–Phelps analysis, a negative relationship between *unanticipated* inflation and *cyclical* unemployment should appear in the data, even if expected inflation and the natural unemployment rate are changing. Measures of unanticipated inflation and cyclical unemployment for each year during the period 1963–2001 are shown in Figure 13.7. These measures are approximate because we cannot directly observe either expected inflation (needed to calculate unanticipated inflation) or the natural unemployment rate (needed to find cyclical unemployment). We assumed that expected inflation for each year was the average inflation rate of the previous two years, and we used estimates of the natural unemployment rate presented later in the chapter in Figure 13.9.[8]

Figure 13.7 suggests that despite the instability of the traditional Phillips curve relationship between inflation and unemployment, a negative relationship between unanticipated inflation and cyclical unemployment did exist during the period 1963–2001, as predicted by the Friedman–Phelps analysis (compare Figure 13.7 with Figure 13.2). In particular, note that inflation was much lower than expected and that cyclical unemployment was high during 1982 and 1983, and again during 1992 and 1993, years that followed attempts to reduce inflation through tight monetary policy.

MACROECONOMIC POLICY AND THE PHILLIPS CURVE

We have addressed two of the questions about the Phillips curve raised earlier in the chapter—the questions of why the Phillips curve was observed in historical data and why it seemed to shift after 1970. We still must answer the third question: Can the Phillips curve be thought of as a "menu" of inflation–unemployment combinations from which policymakers can choose? For example, can policymakers reduce the unemployment rate by increasing the rate of inflation (moving up and to the left along the Phillips curve)?

---

8. In Figure 13.7, the point corresponding to the year 1976 lies below the curve defined by the rest of the points. The year 1976 was the first year of wage-and-price controls, and inflation in 1976 fell to 5% from more than 10% in 1974 and 1975. Our estimate of expected inflation for 1976 is based on inflation rates in the previous two years and so does not allow for the effect of the controls. Thus, our estimate of expected inflation may be too high, resulting in an estimate of unanticipated inflation that is too low. The controls may also explain why the point corresponding to the year 1978 lies above the curve. If expected inflation at the time controls were removed was higher than our estimate (based on the previous two years, under controls), then our estimate of unanticipated inflation will be too high.

FIGURE 13.7

THE EXPECTATIONS-AUGMENTED PHILLIPS CURVE IN CANADA, 1963–2001

The expectations-augmented Phillips curve is a negative relationship between unanticipated inflation and cyclical unemployment. The figure shows this relationship for the years 1963 to 2001 in Canada. Unanticipated inflation equals actual inflation minus expected inflation, where expected inflation in any year is measured here as the average inflation rate for the preceding two years. Cyclical unemployment for each year is the actual unemployment rate minus an estimate of the natural unemployment rate for that year (see Figure 13.9). Note that years in which unanticipated inflation is high usually are years in which cyclical unemployment is low.

Source: Unemployment rate, 1963–1965: *Historical Statistics of Canada*, Series D233; 1966–2001: *Canadian Economic Observer, Historical Statistical Supplement*, Table 8; natural rate of unemployment: see Figure 13.9; CPI inflation rate: *Canadian Economic Observer, Historical Statistical Supplement*, Table 12.

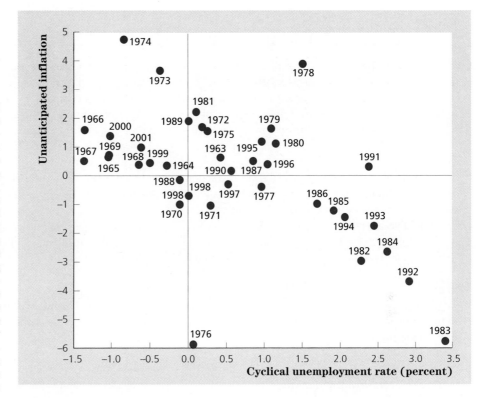

According to the expectations-augmented Phillips curve, unemployment will fall below the natural rate only when inflation is unanticipated. So the question becomes: Can macroeconomic policy be used systematically to create unanticipated inflation?

Classical and Keynesian economists disagree on the answer to this question. Classicals argue that wages and prices adjust quickly in response to new economic information, including information about changes in government policies. Furthermore, classicals believe that people have rational expectations, meaning that they make intelligent forecasts of future policy changes. Because prices and price-level expectations respond quickly to new information, the government cannot keep actual inflation above expected inflation—as would be needed to drive unemployment below the natural rate—except perhaps for a very short time. According to classicals, policies (such as more rapid monetary expansion) that increase the growth rate of aggregate demand act primarily to raise actual and expected inflation and so do not lead to a sustained reduction in unemployment. Because any systematic attempt to affect the unemployment rate will be thwarted by the rapid adjustment of inflation expectations, classicals conclude that the Phillips curve does not represent a usable trade-off for policymakers. (Box 13.1, on the next page, explores a general lesson for policymakers of the shifting Phillips curve.)

In contrast, Keynesians contend that policymakers do have some ability—in the short run, at least—to create unanticipated inflation and, thus, to bring unemployment below the natural rate.[9] Although many Keynesians accept the notion that people have rational expectations, they argue that the expected rate of inflation

---

9. As we discussed in Chapter 12, Keynesian economists also believe that macroeconomic policy can be used to return the unemployment rate to its natural level, if the economy starts out in a recession or a boom.

Box 13.1 THE LUCAS CRITIQUE

Suppose that you observed, in a particular season, that the Winnipeg Blue Bombers of the Canadian Football League punted 100% of the time when faced with third down in their own territory. Could you safely conclude, on the basis of this empirical evidence, that the Bombers would punt on third down in their own territory next season? In most cases, you probably could safely make this prediction, even if you did not know anything about football. But what if, during the off-season, the rules were changed to allow five attempts to make a first down? Would you still expect the Bombers to follow historical precedent and punt on third down? Certainly, no one familiar with football would expect them to follow their old strategy, which would be foolish under the new rules. The simple lesson from this example is that when the rules of the game change, people's behaviour also changes.*

In an influential article,[†] Robert E. Lucas, Jr., of the University of Chicago, applied this lesson to macroeconomic policymaking. Frequently, in attempting to forecast the effects of a new set of policies, economists and policymakers assume that historical relationships between macroeconomic variables will continue to hold after the new policies are in place. Lucas objected to this assumption, asserting what has become known as the *Lucas critique*. According to the Lucas critique, because new policies change the economic "rules" and, thus, affect economic behaviour, no one can safely assume that historical relationships between variables will hold when policies change.

A good example of the Lucas critique in action is the shifting Phillips curve. Historically, there seemed to be a stable relationship between inflation and unemployment, which led some policymakers to believe that they could permanently reduce unemployment by increasing inflation. However, as we have discussed, when policymakers allowed inflation to rise, the public's inflation expectations also rose. As a result, the Phillips curve shifted and the historical relationship between inflation and unemployment broke down.

The main message of the Lucas critique for economists is that in order to predict the effects of policy changes on the economy, they must understand how economic behaviour will change under the new policies. Understanding the impact of policy changes on behaviour—particularly the introduction of policies that have not been tried before—requires the use of economic theory as well as empirical analysis.

---

*The example is from Thomas Sargent, *Rational Expectations and Inflation*, New York: Harper & Row, 1986, pp. 1–2.
[†]"Econometric Policy Evaluation: A Critique," in K. Brunner and A. H. Meltzer, eds., *Carnegie-Rochester Conference Series on Public Policy*, vol. 1, 1976.

---

that should be included in the expectations-augmented Phillips curve is the forecast of inflation made at the time that the oldest sticky prices in the economy were set. Because of price stickiness, when policymakers cause aggregate demand to rise above the expected level, time is needed for prices to fully reflect this new information. In the meantime, some prices reflect older information, and the rate of inflation is higher than the expected inflation rate based on this older information. In response to increased inflation, therefore, unemployment may remain below the natural rate for a while.

THE LONG-RUN PHILLIPS CURVE

Although classicals and Keynesians disagree about whether the Phillips curve relationship can be exploited to reduce unemployment temporarily, they agree that policymakers cannot keep the unemployment rate *permanently* below the natural rate by maintaining a high rate of inflation. Expectations about inflation eventually will adjust so that the expected and actual inflation rates are equal, or $\pi^e = \pi$. The expectations-augmented Phillips curve (Eq. 13.1) implies that, when $\pi^e = \pi$, the actual unemployment rate u equals the natural unemployment rate $\bar{u}$. Thus, the actual unemployment rate equals the natural rate in the long run, regardless of the inflation rate maintained.

The long-run relationship of unemployment and inflation is shown by the **long-run Phillips curve**. In the long run, because unemployment equals the natural rate regardless of the inflation rate, the long-run Phillips curve is a vertical line at $u = \bar{u}$, as shown in Figure 13.8.

The vertical long-run Phillips curve is related to the long-run neutrality of money, discussed in Chapters 11 and 12. Classicals and Keynesians agree that changes in the money supply will have no long-run effects on real variables, including unemployment. The vertical long-run Phillips curve carries the notion of monetary neutrality one step further by indicating that changes in the growth rate of money, which lead to changes in the inflation rate, also have no real effects in the long run.

At best, the Phillips curve can be exploited only temporarily, so why would policymakers attempt to reduce unemployment by creating surprise inflation? One possibility is that stimulating the economy may help the incumbent political party win elections; see the Box, "The Political Environment: Macroeconomic Performance and Opinion Polls," p. 498.

13.2 The Problem of Unemployment

In the rest of the chapter, we look more closely at unemployment and inflation, beginning with unemployment in this section. We start by discussing the costs of unemployment, then consider the factors that determine the long-run unemployment level, and conclude by exploring some ways in which macroeconomic policy can address unemployment.

Figure 13.8

The Long-run Phillips curve

Because people will not permanently overestimate or underestimate the rate of inflation, in the long run, the expected and actual inflation rates are equal and the actual unemployment rate equals the natural unemployment rate. Because in the long run, actual unemployment equals the natural rate regardless of the inflation rate, the long-run Phillips curve is vertical.

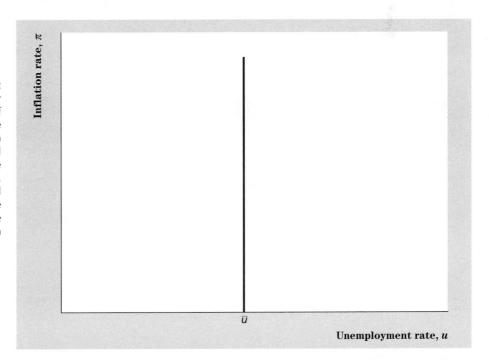

THE POLITICAL ENVIRONMENT

MACROECONOMIC PERFORMANCE AND OPINION POLLS

Among the many issues affecting the popularity of successive federal governments, macroeconomic policy and performance are among the most important. There seems little doubt, for example, that the 1990–1992 recession severely damaged the re-election prospects of the federal Progressive Conservatives.

A study by Daniel Richards,* of Tufts University, tried to measure the effect of macroeconomic performance on the support for the incumbent party (either Liberal or Progressive Conservative) from 1957 to 1990. Richards measured support as the percentage of voters who told Gallup Poll Canada each quarter that they would vote for the party in power if an election were held soon. He controlled for a variety of political influences on this support including separate effects of each prime minister, occurrences of national party conventions, and a "honeymoon" effect according to which the support for an incumbent party should gradually decline during its period of office.

Even with these political effects allowed for, two macroeconomic variables seemed to have significant effects on a government's popularity. First, voter support fell when GDP was volatile around its trend level. One interpretation of this finding is that voters believe there is a role for stabilization policy, as described in Chapter 12. They know that macroeconomic policy cannot permanently alter the level of GDP, but they blame governments that fail to stabilize GDP.

Second, voters withdraw their support (at least in opinion polls) from governments if the inflation rate is too high or too low. Surprisingly, Richards found that voter support was at its highest when the inflation rate was near 7%. This estimate is subject to some sampling error, like all statistical estimates, but even so, it seems clear that it is much greater than zero. One interpretation of this finding is that voters do not prefer high inflation *per se* but that they are concerned about the costs of disinflation (discussed later in this chapter).

Does voting in federal elections reflect these opinion polls and, hence, macroeconomic performance? Here, there are fewer observations, but the indicators of poor macroeconomic performance (differences between output and its trend and between inflation and 7%) were large in 1963, when the Pearson Liberals replaced the Diefenbaker Conservatives, and in 1984, when the Mulroney Conservatives replaced the Trudeau–Turner Liberals. In late 1990, support for the federal Progressive Conservative government was 25 percentage points below the value it would have taken without a recession and disinflation, according to the statistical estimates.

Finally, if voter support depends on macroeconomic performance, why don't governments alter their policies to maximize their support? According to the theory of "political business cycles," we should see governments practising expansionary policies before elections. However, the historical evidence does not provide much support for this type of cycle in macroeconomic policy. Economists at the University of Calgary have found little evidence of a federal political business cycle in Canada, but some evidence that provincial taxes follow such a cycle.[†] One problem with the theory may be the assumption that incumbents are motivated only by the prospects of re-election, which ignores the possibility that politicians have other goals, such as promoting policies that they favour. If different parties have different goals—in addition to re-election—then their macroeconomic policies may differ.

A second problem with the political business cycle theory may be that it does not allow for rational expectations. As we have seen in studying the expectations-augmented Phillips curve, it may be only unexpected changes in policy that affect output and unemployment. If voters expect a government to expand aggregate demand late in its term, then the expansion will have little effect on output. Recently, some theories that combine rational expectations and competing parties have had some success in accounting for observed policies.[‡]

---

* "Do Canadians Want Zero Inflation? Some Evidence from a Model with 'Sophisticated' Voters," *Canadian Public Policy*, December 1992, pp. 413–424.

[†] See Apostolos Serletis and Panos Afxentiou, "Electoral and Partisan Cycle Regularities in Canada," *Canadian Journal of Economics*, February 1998, pp. 28–46; Ronald Kneebone and Kenneth McKenzie, "Electoral and Partisan Cycles in Fiscal Policy: An Examination of Canadian Provinces," *International Tax and Public Finance*, November 2001, pp. 753–774.

[‡] See, for example, Alberto Alesina, "Macroeconomics and Politics," in Stanley Fischer, ed., *NBER Macroeconomics Annual*, Cambridge, Mass.: M.I.T. Press, 1988, pp. 13–52.

THE COSTS OF UNEMPLOYMENT

There are two principal costs of unemployment. The first is the loss of output that occurs because fewer people are productively employed. This cost is borne disproportionately by unemployed workers themselves, in terms of the income they lose because they are out of work. However, because the unemployed may stop paying taxes and instead receive unemployment insurance benefits or other government payments, society (in this case, taxpayers) also bears some of the output cost of unemployment.

How big is the output cost of unemployment? One estimate is provided by **Okun's law**, a rule-of-thumb that states that each percentage point of *cyclical* unemployment is associated with a loss equal to 2% of full-employment output. Thus, if full-employment output is $1,000 billion, Okun's law indicates that each percentage point of unemployment sustained for one year reduces output by $20 billion.

The loss of output predicted by Okun's law reflects not only the direct impact of increased unemployment but also other labour market changes that occur during recessions, such as shorter workweeks, reduced labour force participation, and lower productivity. Thus, the output cost of unemployment estimated by Okun's law is probably too high. Nevertheless, an output loss that was only one-quarter of that predicted by Okun's law would still be a significant cost, particularly if it were borne largely by the relatively poor and disadvantaged members of society.

The other substantial cost of unemployment is the personal or psychological cost faced by unemployed workers and their families. This cost is especially important for workers suffering long spells of unemployment and for the chronically unemployed. Workers without steady employment for long periods lose job skills and self-esteem, and suffer from stress.

The costs of unemployment are real and serious, but two offsetting factors should be noted. First, to the extent that unemployed workers engage in economically productive activities, such as searching for a job or acquiring new skills, the loss of output arising from current unemployment may be compensated for by increased output in the future. In particular, frictional unemployment—the result of workers and firms seeking appropriate matches—raises future productivity and output and, thus, may impose little net economic cost, or even lead to an economic gain.

A second offsetting factor is that unemployed people have more leisure time—to spend with family and friends, work around the house, and so on. However, the benefits of extra leisure time decrease as the amount of leisure increases, and most unemployed workers would not feel that increased leisure was adequate compensation for their lost income.

THE LONG-TERM BEHAVIOUR OF THE UNEMPLOYMENT RATE

Classical and Keynesian economists agree that although the actual unemployment rate may deviate from the natural unemployment rate in the short run, in the long run, the actual rate equals the natural rate. Thus, understanding the behaviour of unemployment in all but the short run requires identifying the determinants of the natural rate of unemployment. In Chapter 3, we discussed the reasons for the natural unemployment rate always being greater than zero; here we focus more narrowly on the reasons for changes in the natural rate in recent years in Canada, the United States, and Europe.

THE CHANGING NATURAL RATE

The natural unemployment rate corresponds to full-employment output. Unfortunately, because we cannot be sure when the economy is at full employment, we cannot directly observe the natural rate and, so, must estimate it. Inevitably, therefore, there is some uncertainty about the value of the natural rate at any particular time. Figure 13.9 shows estimated values of the natural unemployment rate, along with the actual unemployment rate, for the period 1963–2001. Andrew Burns, then of the Economic Council of Canada, estimated levels of the natural rate before 1986, on the basis of his research; we estimated the levels of the natural rate since 1986. Most current estimates, including those in Figure 13.9, suggest a natural unemployment rate of about 7.5% of the labour force. In comparison, most estimates of the natural rate for the 1950s and 1960s were in the range of 4% to 5%. Hence, the natural unemployment rate in Canada apparently has risen by roughly 3 percentage points over the last 40 years.

Giving a fully satisfactory explanation of the rise in the natural rate of unemployment is difficult, but part of the increase seems to have been the result of demographic changes. Figure 13.10(a) shows unemployment levels for workers in different demographic groups (age, gender) in Canada. Note that young workers (aged 15 through 24 years) have higher unemployment rates than adults, and for much of the post–World War II period (but not recently), women have had a higher unemployment rate than men.

A principal reason that youth and (until recently) women have had higher unemployment rates is that these workers are less likely than adult males to hold long-term, stable jobs. Workers younger than 24 years have high unemployment rates both because they move in and out of the labour force frequently while they are in

FIGURE 13.9

ACTUAL AND NATURAL UNEMPLOYMENT RATES IN CANADA

The figure shows the actual unemployment rate and an estimate of the natural rate of unemployment in Canada for the period 1963–2001. The difference between the actual and natural unemployment rates is the cyclical unemployment rate. Note that the natural rate of unemployment rose from the 1960s to the 1980s but has been more stable since.

Source: Unemployment rate, 1963–1965: *Historical Statistics of Canada,* Series D233; 1966–1997: *Canadian Economic Observer, Historical Statistical Supplement,* Table 8; natural rate of unemployment, 1963–1986: based on Andrew Burns, "The Natural Rate of Unemployment: Canada and the Provinces," Chapter 3 in Surendra Gera, ed., *Canadian Unemployment,* Ottawa: Economic Council of Canada, 1991; 1986–2001: estimated by the authors as a weighted average of the actual unemployment rate and the previous natural rate.

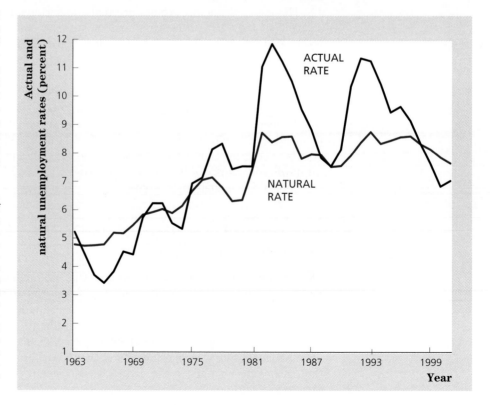

FIGURE 13.10

UNEMPLOYMENT RATES BY DEMOGRAPHIC GROUP AND REGION

(a) The figure shows Canadian unemployment rates since 1966 for men over age 25 years, women over age 25 years, and youth (ages 15 to 24 years) of both genders. Young workers have much higher unemployment rates than older workers, and for much of the period (though not recently) women have had higher unemployment rates than men.

Source: Statistics Canada, CANSIM Series D984970, D984986, D984955.

(b) The figure shows un-employment rates for selected provinces from 1966 to 2000. The average value of the unemployment rate differs systematically across provinces. Although the changes in the provincial unemployment rates from year to year have a common pattern, there also are movements specific to each province. For example, during the 1990–1992 recession, unemployment rates rose much more in Nova Scotia and Ontario than in Saskatchewan.

Source: *Canadian Economic Observer, Historical Statistical Supplement,* Table 42.

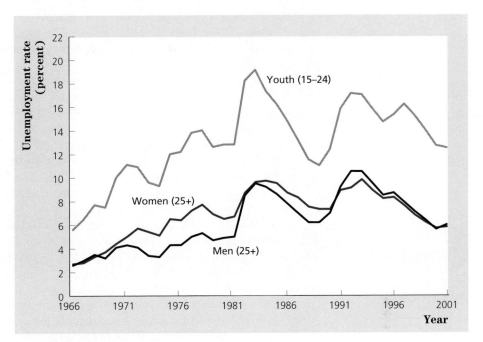

(a) Unemployment by age and sex

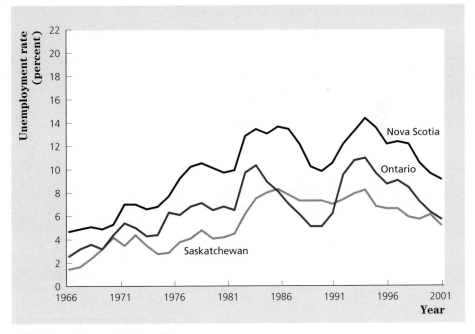

(b) Unemployment by province

school and because many work at low-skill jobs that do not provide long-term employment. However, the incidence of unemployment falls with age, as workers gain skills and experience. A cause of the historically higher unemployment rate for women is that traditionally, women have spent more time than men in taking care of children and, thus, have had more interruptions in their careers. For women, moving in and out of the labour force often involves periods of unemployment.

Since World War II, young workers and women have emerged as a large portion of the Canadian labour force. This shift in the composition of the labour force toward groups that have higher unemployment rates may have raised the overall unemployment rate.

The demographic explanation of the increase in the natural unemployment rate has some merit but is incomplete for two reasons. First, the changes in labour force composition by age and gender account only for a portion—probably less than 1 percentage point—of the increase in the natural rate. Indeed, some demographic changes—such as the relative increase in university- or college-educated workers, who typically have low unemployment rates—work in the direction of reducing the natural rate. Second, the unemployment rate has risen *within* each demographic category. Thus, even if there had been no change in labour force composition, the overall unemployment rate would have risen.

Another factor that may have contributed to the increase in the natural unemployment rate is a faster pace of structural change in the economy, which has taken several forms. Technological changes have increased the skill levels that firms demand from workers, reducing the employment opportunities for low-skilled or poorly educated workers (see the Application, "Technical Change and Wage Inequality," p. 83). Also, some industries and regions have grown significantly while others were suffering long-term declines; notably, the share of jobs in manufacturing has fallen, while that in services has risen. Both changes worsen the problem of mismatch between jobs and workers, raising frictional and structural unemployment and hence the natural rate.[10] An example of structural unemployment is shown in Figure 13.10(b), which graphs unemployment rates for selected provinces. Note that the unemployment rate in Nova Scotia, for example, is persistently higher than the rate in Saskatchewan.

Finally, changes in the system of unemployment insurance (UI) during the past 30 years probably also have raised the natural rate of unemployment. We discuss this effect below.

HYSTERESIS IN UNEMPLOYMENT

One very useful way to collect evidence on the causes of the rise in the natural unemployment rate is to study the unemployment experiences of different countries, which may have been subject to different demographic and institutional changes. For example, dramatic increases in the natural rate of unemployment occurred during the 1980s in several countries in Western Europe.

For 30 years after World War II, many Western European countries maintained low unemployment rates. Then, after the oil price shocks and worldwide recessions of the 1970s, unemployment rates in those countries rose sharply. (Unemployment rates for France, the United States, and Canada are compared in Figure 13.11.) The unemployment rate in the United States also rose to high levels during the 1970s but fell quickly during the recovery that followed the 1981–1982 recession. In contrast, unemployment rates in Western Europe remained high throughout most of the decade, falling temporarily during the late 1980s but rising again in the early 1990s. This long-term increase in the Western European unemployment rate from only 1% to 3% of the labour force in the early 1970s to much higher levels in the 1980s

---

10. See Lucie Samson, "A Study of the Impact of Sectoral Shifts on Aggregate Unemployment in Canada," *Canadian Journal of Economics*, August 1985, pp. 518–530, and Janet Neelin, "Sectoral Shifts and Canadian Unemployment," *Review of Economics and Statistics*, November 1987, pp. 718–722. See also the papers on structural aspects of unemployment in *Canadian Public Policy*, July 2000.

FIGURE 13.11

UNEMPLOYMENT RATES IN THE UNITED STATES AND FRANCE

The figure shows unemployment rates in the United States and France, graphed alongside the Canadian unemployment rate, for 1966–2000. While the US and Canadian unemployment rates declined after the 1981–1982 and 1990–1992 recessions, the unemployment rate in France (and is some other western European countries) rose from less than 3% in the early 1970s to more than 12% in the mid-1990s. The persistence of high unemployment suggests that the natural unemployment rate also increased. The increase in the natural rate, in response to an increase in actual unemployment, is an example of hysteresis.

Source: Canadian unemployment rate: *Canadian Economic Observer, Historical Statistical Supplement,* Table 8; European and US unemployment rates: *OECD Historical Statistics,* Table 2.15, various issues; updates from *IMF World Economic Outlook.*

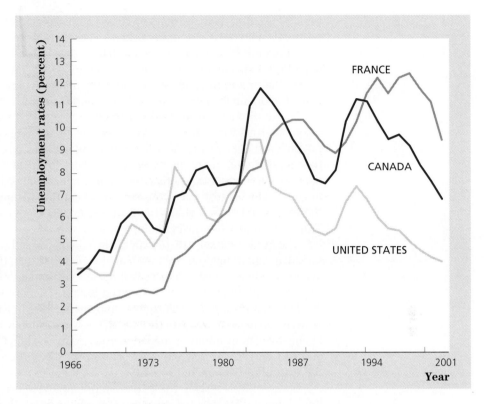

reflects an increase in the natural unemployment rate of 5 percentage points or more, according to some estimates. What accounts for this apparent large increase in the natural unemployment rate in Western Europe?

Some economists use a term taken from physics, hysteresis, to describe the behaviour of European unemployment. Applied to unemployment, **hysteresis** means that the natural unemployment rate changes in response to the actual unemployment rate, rising if the actual rate is above the natural rate and falling if the actual rate is below the natural rate. According to the proponents of hysteresis theory, the rise in unemployment rates in Western Europe (and perhaps Canada) in the mid-1970s, originally because of such factors as rising oil prices and contractionary macroeconomic policies, also increased the natural unemployment rate. This increase, in turn, helps account for the continued high actual unemployment rate in these countries. When these countries return to long-run equilibrium with full employment, the actual rate equals the new higher natural rate.

There are several explanations of hysteresis in European unemployment. First, some economists suggest that when a high unemployment rate idles workers for a long period of time, their skills deteriorate (or the workers fail to get training in the first place). Lower skill levels increase the mismatch between workers and firms and raise the natural unemployment rate.

Second, some economists argue that the bureaucratic aspects of firms and unions, as well as government regulation, interfere with the adjustment of the labour market in Western Europe. For example, in some European countries, the government severely restricts the ability of firms to fire workers. Because firms know that firing workers is difficult, they are reluctant to hire additional workers unless they are confident that they will not have to reduce their workforces for a long time. Thus, after many workers were laid off in the mid-1970s, firms were reluctant to rehire them or to hire new workers. These labour market regulations are more widespread in France and Germany than in the United Kingdom, which provides a test of this explanation for persistence in unemployment rates. The unemployment rate in the United Kingdom has declined by almost 5 percentage points since 1993, while the unemployment rates in France and Germany have remained high.

Third, the **insider–outsider theory** suggests that when a union negotiates a labour contract with a firm, it seeks the highest real wage (including fringe benefits) possible without causing the firm to cut employment. This union behaviour is in the best interests of currently employed workers, or insiders. But think about what happens if a contract is negotiated when unemployment is high. If the union succeeds in getting the highest wage consistent with continued employment of the insiders, the wage will be too high for the firm to increase employment and hire outsiders. Thus, outsiders will remain unemployed.

The insider–outsider theory applies in a unionized setting. Because European and Canadian labour markets are more highly unionized than the US labour market, the insider–outsider theory predicts that hysteresis is quantitatively more important in Europe and Canada than in the United States. This prediction is consistent with the fact that during the 1980s, unemployment rates in Europe and Canada came down much more slowly than they did in the United States. Another difference is that unemployment insurance is more generous in Europe and Canada than in the United States. Box 13.2 discusses the implications of this difference for the behaviour of the natural rate of unemployment.

Is there hysteresis in the Canadian unemployment rate? A study by Stephen R.G. Jones, of McMaster University, has reviewed all the evidence for Canada.[11] Jones's main conclusion was that while the persistence in the unemployment rate cannot be completely explained, there is no evidence of hysteresis. One reason that testing for hysteresis (feedback from the actual unemployment rate to the natural rate) is difficult is that estimates of the natural rate of unemployment are quite imprecise. For example, Daniel Gordon, of the University of Calgary, and Lars Osberg and Mark Setterfield, of Dalhousie University, tried to estimate the natural rate for adult men in Canada for the period from 1956 to 1987.[12] They found that small changes in how they deduced the value of the natural rate led to a wide range of possible values. This uncertainty about the value of the natural rate also makes measuring cyclical unemployment difficult.

POLICIES TO REDUCE THE NATURAL RATE OF UNEMPLOYMENT

Although we call the rate of unemployment toward which the economy gravitates in the long run the "natural" rate of unemployment, we do not mean to imply that it is necessarily desirable or optimal. Many people would argue that for both economic and social reasons, economic policies should be used to try to lower the natural unemployment rate. Although no surefire method for reducing the natural rate exists, several strategies have been suggested:

---

11. *The Persistence of Unemployment: Hysteresis in Canadian Labour Markets*, Kingston: McGill-Queen's University Press, 1995.

12. "Searching for a Will o' the Wisp: An Empirical Study of the NAIRU in Canada," *European Economic Review*, January 1992, pp. 119–136. Also see the symposium on the natural rate of unemployment in the *Journal of Economic Perspectives*, Winter 1997.

Box 13.2 THE EFFECT OF UNEMPLOYMENT INSURANCE ON UNEMPLOYMENT

Unemployment rates in Canada and the United States were very similar in the 1960s and 1970s but have diverged since about 1982, as Figure 13.11 shows. During the past 20 years, Canada's unemployment rate was 2 percentage points higher than the rate in the United States on average.

One explanation for this gap involves differences in the measurement of unemployment across the two countries. In Canada, the unemployed include searchers aged 15 years (who tend to have a high unemployment rate), whereas only those 16 and over are counted in the United States. Canadians on layoff are counted as unemployed for 26 weeks, whereas in the United States, workers on layoff are dropped from the count after 30 days. People who look at job advertisements are counted as unemployed in Canada, but not in the United States, which again adds to measured unemployment. However, these differences in definition also applied during the 1970s, and Canadian unemployment rates now are higher for all groups, so measurement differences probably cannot explain the increase and persistence in the gap.

Although this gap may seem discouraging from the Canadian perspective, David Card, of the University of California at Berkeley, and Craig Riddell, of the University of British Columbia, have shown that during the 1980s, employment rates were actually very similar in the two countries.[*] Thus, the different unemployment rates in the 1980s reflected the fact that in Canada people who were not working were more likely to be classified as unemployed than as not in the labour force (see Table 3.5) than they were in the United States. This observation raises the possibility that participation in the labour force (along with layoffs and lengthy search) was encouraged by Canada's more generous system of unemployment insurance (UI).

The generosity of UI involves several factors:

1. The *replacement ratio*, which measures the size of unemployment benefits relative to lost wages;
2. The benefit *duration*, which measures the amount of time that an unemployed worker may receive benefits;
3. *Eligibility requirements*, which specify who can collect UI benefits.

Card and Riddell examined many features of Canadian and US unemployment insurance and concluded that the differences explain part of the gap between the two countries' unemployment rates.

However, Canadian UI became more generous in 1971–1972, yet the gap with the US unemployment rate did not appear until the 1980s. Moreover, the gap persisted in the 1990s, when Canadian UI became substantially less generous. In the 1990s, Canadian UI (renamed Employment Insurance (EI) in 1996) was reformed several times. The benefit duration fell, the replacement ratio was reduced for repeat users, and eligibility requirements (now based on hours of work in the previous year, rather than weeks) also became more restrictive. For example, workers who quit jobs without cause were no longer eligible for EI. Partly as a result of these changes, only about 40% of unemployed workers were eligible for EI in 1998 (down from a ratio of 80% in 1990). This reduced eligibility partly accounts for the large surpluses in the federal government's EI account.

If unemployment insurance does not explain the gap, then what does? During the 1990s, rates of growth of employment were lower in Canada than in the United States. Riddell and Andrew Sharpe, of the Centre for the Study of Living Standards, surveyed research on the gap and concluded that cyclical factors explain much of it.[†] The recession of the early 1990s was more severe in Canada than in the United States, and the recovery slower. If this explanation is correct, then perhaps the gap, though very persistent, will not be permanent.

---

[*]"A Comparative Analysis of Unemployment in Canada and the United States," Chapter 5 in David Card and Richard B. Freeman, eds., *Small Differences That Matter: Labor Markets and Income Maintenance in Canada and the United States*, Chicago: University of Chicago Press and NBER, 1993.
[†]W. Craig Riddell and Andrew Sharpe, "The Canada–US Unemployment Rate Gap: An Introduction and Overview," *Canadian Public Policy*, February 1998, pp. S1–S37. See also W. Craig Ridell, "Canadian Labour Market Performance in International Perspective," *Canadian Journal of Economics*, November 1999, pp. 1097–1134.

1. *Government support for job training and worker relocation.* Firms have strong incentives to find and train capable workers, and unemployed workers have equally strong incentives to find productive jobs. However, some economists argue that the private incentives to match workers and jobs still are not as strong as they should be. For example, firms may be reluctant to train workers if they fear that once trained, the workers will leave for other firms. Similarly, in deciding whether to retrain for a new job, an unemployed worker will not take into account the gain of his re-employment to taxpayers, who will no longer be responsible for financing his unemployment benefits. Thus, a case can be made for policy measures, such as tax credits or subsidies for training or relocating unemployed workers. If these measures had their desired effect, the mismatch between workers and jobs would be eliminated more quickly and the natural unemployment rate would fall.

2. *Increased labour market flexibility.* Currently, government regulations mandate minimum wages, working conditions, workers' fringe benefits, conditions for firing a worker, and many other terms of employment. Such regulations may be well intentioned but they also increase the cost of hiring additional workers, particularly workers with limited skills and experience. Some other regulations limit labour mobility between provinces. New and existing labour market regulations should be carefully reviewed to ensure that their benefits outweigh the costs they impose in higher unemployment.

3. *Unemployment insurance reform.* Although unemployment insurance provides essential support for the unemployed, it may also increase the natural unemployment rate by increasing the time that the unemployed spend looking for work and by increasing the incentives for firms to lay off workers during slack times. Further reforms to unemployment insurance that preserve its function of supporting the unemployed but reduce incentives for increased unemployment may be needed. For example, payroll taxes on employers might be changed to force employers that use temporary layoffs extensively to bear a greater portion of the unemployed benefits that their workers receive. However, since a majority of unemployed workers in Canada are not eligible for unemployment insurance (see Box 13.2), the most likely remaining reform is a reduction in the premiums paid by workers and employers, which would encourage firms to hire more workers.

4. *A high-pressure economy?* Classical and Keynesian economists generally agree that macroeconomic stabilization policies cannot be used to affect the natural rate of unemployment; in other words, the long-run Phillips curve is vertical. However, some proponents of the hysteresis theory take issue with this view. They argue that if monetary and fiscal policy are used aggressively to keep unemployment as low as possible—a "high-pressure economy"—then, following the principle of hysteresis, the natural rate will eventually fall. So, for example, if current employment is stimulated by monetary expansion, workers may be able to acquire more on-the-job training, which reduces mismatch and lowers the natural unemployment rate in the long run. Opponents of this suggestion point out that there is less evidence of hysteresis in Canada than in Europe. Opponents also express concern that a high-pressure strategy would reignite inflation.

13.3 THE PROBLEM OF INFLATION

In the federal election of June 1974, Prime Minister Trudeau called wage and price controls "a proven disaster looking for a new place to happen." Yet in October 1975, with the inflation rate near 11%, the Liberal government announced a three-year program of wage and price controls, to be administered by the Anti-Inflation Board (AIB). What caused the government to undertake this dramatic U-turn, with the associated political costs? During the late 1980s, the Canadian inflation rate hovered near 5%. The Bank of Canada introduced a set of targets for reducing this rate, with the goal of zero inflation. Why did the Bank undertake this policy? In this section, we look at inflation, beginning with a discussion of inflation costs and then turning to the question of what can be done to control inflation.

THE COSTS OF INFLATION

The costs of inflation depend primarily on whether consumers, investors, workers, and firms are able to predict the inflation before it occurs. To illustrate this point, we discuss two extreme cases: an inflation that everyone is able to predict and an inflation that comes as a complete surprise.

PERFECTLY ANTICIPATED INFLATION

Let us first consider the case of an inflation that is perfectly anticipated by the public. Imagine, for example, that everyone knew that the inflation rate would be 4% per year. To keep things simple, assume also no change in relative prices so that the prices of all individual goods and services also are rising at the rate of 4% per year.

Why then does a fully anticipated inflation impose any costs? The prices you pay for groceries, movie tickets, and other goods would increase by 4% per year but so would your nominal wage or the nominal value of the goods or services you produce. Because your nominal income is rising along with prices, your purchasing power is not hurt by the perfectly anticipated inflation.[13]

What about the money that you hold in your savings account? Although inflation reduces the purchasing power of money, perfectly anticipated inflation would not hurt the value of your savings account. The reason is that the nominal interest rate would adjust to offset the drop in the purchasing power of money. For instance, with a zero inflation rate and a nominal interest rate on savings deposits of 3%, the real interest rate is also 3% per year. If inflation rises to a perfectly anticipated rate of 4% per year, an increase in the nominal interest rate to 7% per year will leave the real interest rate unchanged at 3%. Because both savers and banks care only about the real interest rate, when inflation rises to 4% banks should be willing to offer 7% nominal interest, and savers should be willing to accept that nominal return. Thus, neither banks nor savers are hurt by an anticipated increase in inflation.[14]

The suggestion that perfectly anticipated inflation imposes no economic costs is not quite correct: Inflation erodes the value of currency, which leads people to keep less currency on hand—for example, by going to the bank or the automatic teller machine to make withdrawals every week instead of twice a month. Similarly, inflation may induce firms to reduce their cash holdings by introducing computerized cash management systems or adding staff to the accounting department. The costs in time and effort incurred by people and firms who are trying to minimize their holdings of cash are called **shoe leather costs**. For modest inflation rates, shoe leather

---

13. It may be true that psychologically, people think of increases in their wages arising from ongoing inflation as being earned and, thus, "fair," but that increases in the prices they pay because of inflation are "unfair." This is a confusion, although one that may have real political consequences if it causes the public to demand strong action on inflation.

14. This argument ignores the fact that interest is taxed on a nominal basis. If the after-tax real interest rate is to be kept constant, the nominal interest rate will have to rise by somewhat more than the increase in inflation.

costs are small but not completely trivial. For example, the shoe leather costs of a 10% perfectly anticipated inflation have been estimated to be about 0.3% of GDP, which is about $3 billion per year in Canada.[15]

A second cost of perfectly anticipated inflation arises from menu costs, or the costs of changing nominal prices. When there is inflation and prices are continually rising, sellers of goods and services must use resources to change nominal prices. For instance, mail-order firms have to print and mail catalogues frequently to report the increases in prices. Although some firms face substantial menu costs, for the economy as a whole these costs probably are small. Furthermore, technological progress, such as the introduction of electronic scanners in supermarkets, reduces the cost of changing prices.

UNANTICIPATED INFLATION

Much of the public's aversion to inflation is aversion to unanticipated inflation— inflation that is different from the rate expected. For example, if everyone expects the inflation rate to be 4% per year, but it actually is 6% per year, unanticipated inflation is 2% per year.

What is the effect of 6% inflation if (1) you expected 4% inflation, and (2) your savings account pays 7% interest? When inflation is 6% per year instead of 4% per year, the actual real interest rate on your savings account is only 1% per year (the nominal interest rate of 7% minus the inflation rate of 6%) instead of the 3% per year that you expected. By earning a lower actual real interest rate, you lose as a result of the unanticipated inflation. However, your loss is the bank's gain because the bank pays a lower real interest rate than it expected. Note that the roles would have been reversed if the actual inflation rate had been lower than expected; in that case, the real interest rate that you earn, and that the bank has to pay, would be higher than anticipated.

Similarly, suppose that your nominal salary is set in advance. If inflation is higher than expected, the real value of your salary is less than you expected, and your loss is your employer's gain. If inflation is lower than expected, however, you benefit and your employer loses.

These examples show that a primary effect of unanticipated inflation is to transfer wealth from one person or firm to another. People who lend or save at fixed interest rates (creditors) and those with incomes set in nominal terms are hurt by unanticipated inflation, whereas people who borrow at fixed interest rates (debtors) or who must make fixed nominal payments are helped by unanticipated inflation.

For the economy as a whole, a transfer of wealth from one group to another is not a net loss of resources and, hence, does not represent a true cost. However, from the viewpoints of individual people and firms in the economy, the *risk* of gaining or losing wealth as a result of unanticipated inflation is unwelcome. Because most people do not like risk, the possibility of significant gains or losses arising from unexpected inflation makes people feel worse off and, hence, is a cost of unanticipated inflation. Furthermore, any resources that people use in forecasting inflation and trying to protect themselves against the risks of unanticipated inflation represent an additional cost. However, some of these costs of unanticipated inflation can be eliminated by contracts that are indexed to the price level (see Box 13.3).

---

15. See Stanley Fischer, "Towards an Understanding of the Costs of Inflation: II," in K. Brunner and A. Meltzer, eds., *Carnegie-Rochester Conference Series on Public Policy*, vol. 15, Autumn 1981.

Box 13.3 INDEXED CONTRACTS

In principle, much of the risk of gains and losses associated with unanticipated inflation can be eliminated by using contracts in which payments are indexed to inflation. If a bank wanted to offer a guaranteed 3% real interest rate on savings accounts, for instance, it could index the nominal interest rate to the rate of inflation by offering to pay a nominal interest rate equal to 3% plus whatever the rate of inflation turns out to be. Then, if the actual inflation rate is 6%, the bank would end up paying a nominal interest rate of 9%—giving the depositor the promised 3% real interest rate. Similarly, other financial contracts, such as loans, mortgages, and bonds, can be indexed to protect the real rate of return against unanticipated inflation. Wage payments set by labour contracts can also be indexed to protect workers and employers against unanticipated inflation (we discussed the macroeconomic effects of wage indexation in Appendix 12.A).

How widespread is indexing? Most financial contracts in Canada are not indexed to the rate of inflation, although since 1991, the federal government has offered "real return bonds" that compensate investors for CPI inflation. Payments on some long-term financial contracts (adjustable-rate mortgages, for example) are indexed to nominal interest rates, such as the prime rate charged by banks or the Treasury bill interest rate. Because nominal interest rates move roughly in step with inflation, these long-term financial contracts are to some extent indexed

to inflation. Many labour contracts in Canada are indexed to the rate of inflation through provisions called cost-of-living adjustments, or COLAs. They provide for some increase in nominal wages if inflation is higher than expected, but usually a 1% increase in unanticipated inflation results in somewhat less than a 1% adjustment of wages. Because the public often expresses concern about inflation, economists are puzzled that indexed contracts are not more widely used in Canada.

In contrast, in countries that have experienced high and unpredictable inflation rates, indexed contracts are common. A case in point is Israel, which had a CPI inflation rate of 445% per year in 1984. At that time, over 80% of liquid financial assets in Israel were indexed: For example, long-term government bonds were indexed to the CPI, and banks offered short-term deposits whose purchasing power was tied to that of the US dollar. However, the fraction of financial assets that were indexed decreased after the Israeli hyperinflation ended in the second half of 1985.*

———————————

*See Stanley Fischer, "Israeli Inflation and Indexation," in J. Williamson, ed., *Inflation and Indexation: Argentina, Brazil, Israel,* Institute for International Economics, 1985, reprinted in Stanley Fischer, *Indexing, Inflation, and Economic Policy,* Cambridge, Mass.: M.I.T. Press, 1986; and Zalman F. Shiffer, "Adjusting to High Inflation: The Israeli Experience," *Federal Reserve Bank of St. Louis Review,* May 1986, pp. 18–29.

Another cost of unanticipated inflation relates to the fact that prices serve as signals in a market economy. For example, if wheat becomes more expensive than corn, that is a signal to consumers to switch from wheat to corn and to farmers to produce more wheat and less corn. However, the prices that act as signals in the economy are *relative* prices, such as the price of wheat relative to the price of corn. Knowing that wheat is so many dollars per tonne does not help the consumer and farmer make good economic decisions unless they also know the price of corn. When inflation is unanticipated, particularly if it is erratic, people may confuse changes in prices arising from changes in the general price level with changes in prices arising from shifts in the supply of or demand for individual goods. Because the signals provided by prices may be distorted by unanticipated inflation, the market economy works less efficiently. In addition, when there is a great deal of uncertainty about the true inflation rate, people must spend time and effort learning about different prices, by comparison shopping, for example.

THE COSTS OF HYPERINFLATION

Hyperinflation occurs when the inflation rate is extremely high for a sustained period of time.[16] We mentioned the German hyperinflation of 1922–1923 in Chapter 1, and there are many other examples. During a 12-month period beginning in August 1945, the average rate of inflation in Hungary was 19,800% *per month*.[17] In the more recent hyperinflation in Bolivia, the annual rate of inflation was 1,281% in 1984, and soared to 11,750% in 1985, before dropping to 276% in 1986.[18] The costs of inflation during these hyperinflations were much greater than the costs associated with moderate inflation. For example, when prices are increasing at such mind-boggling rates, the incentives to minimize holdings of currency are powerful and the resulting shoe leather costs are enormous. In severe hyperinflations workers are paid much more frequently—perhaps even more than once a day—and they rush out to spend their money (or to convert their money into some other form, such as a foreign currency) before prices rise even further. The time and energy devoted to getting rid of currency as fast as possible wastes resources and disrupts production.

One early casualty of hyperinflations is the government's ability to collect taxes. In a hyperinflation, taxpayers have an incentive to delay paying their taxes as long as possible. Because tax bills usually are set in nominal terms, the longer the taxpayer delays, the less the real value of that obligation is. The real value of taxes collected by the government falls sharply during hyperinflations, with destructive effects on the government's finances and its ability to provide public services.

Finally, the disruptive effect of inflation on market efficiency that we discussed earlier becomes most severe in the case of a hyperinflation. If prices change so often that they cease to be reliable indicators of the supply of and demand for different goods and services, markets cannot allocate resources efficiently.

FIGHTING INFLATION: THE ROLE OF INFLATIONARY EXPECTATIONS

Basically, inflation occurs when the aggregate quantity of goods demanded at any particular price level is rising more quickly than the aggregate quantity of goods supplied at that price level. (Figure 13.3 illustrates such a situation.) Many factors can cause rapid increases in the aggregate quantity of goods demanded relative to the aggregate quantity supplied. Among these sources of inflation are increases in consumption or investment spending, expansionary fiscal policies, and adverse supply shocks. However, as discussed in Chapter 7, in general, the only factor that can create *sustained* rises in aggregate demand and, thus, ongoing inflation is a high rate of money growth.

If rapid money growth is inflationary, why do central banks permit rapid monetary expansion? As mentioned in Chapter 7 (and discussed in more detail in Chapter 15), in developing or war-torn countries governments may not be able to raise enough revenue by taxing or borrowing, so they print money to finance their spending.

---

16. Philip Cagan, in his classic study of hyperinflation ("The Monetary Dynamics of Hyperinflation," in Milton Friedman, ed., *Studies in the Quantity Theory of Money*, Chicago: University of Chicago Press, 1956), defined a hyperinflation as beginning in the month in which the rate of inflation first exceeds 50% per month.
17. *Ibid.*, Table 1.
18. See Table 7.3, Juan-Antonio Morales, "Inflation Stabilization in Bolivia," in Michael Bruno, Guido De Tella, Rudiger Dornbusch, and Stanley Fischer, eds., *Inflation Stabilization: The Experience of Israel, Argentina, Brazil, Bolivia, and Mexico*, Cambridge, Mass.: M.I.T. Press, 1988.

However, in industrialized countries not engaged in or recovering from a war, governments usually are able either to tax or borrow enough to cover their expenditures. In these countries, rapid money growth usually is the result of past attempts to use expansionary monetary policy to fight recessions, not balanced by tighter monetary policies in periods when output is above the full-employment level.

Because ongoing inflation generally is the result of rapid money growth, the prescription for stopping inflation appears to be simple: Reduce the rate of money growth. Unfortunately, the process of **disinflation**—the reduction of the inflation rate—by slowing money growth may lead to a serious recession. In terms of the expectations-augmented Phillips curve, Eq. (13.1), if macroeconomic policy succeeds in reducing inflation below the expected rate, unemployment will rise above the natural rate. Unemployment will remain above the natural rate until expected inflation falls to the new, lower actual inflation rate.

Is there some way to reduce inflation without incurring serious unemployment costs? The expectations-augmented Phillips curve suggests one possibility: If the public's expected rate of inflation could be lowered as actual inflation was being brought down, unemployment would not have to rise above the natural rate. (You should confirm that in Eq. 13.1, if actual inflation π and expected inflation π^e fall by the same amount, cyclical unemployment $u - \bar{u}$ does not increase.) That is, if expected inflation can be reduced, the original Phillips curve relating inflation and unemployment can be shifted down and to the left, reducing the rate of inflation associated with any level of unemployment.

But how can policymakers reduce the public's inflationary expectations? In the rest of this section, we discuss some suggested approaches for reducing both inflation and inflationary expectations.

RAPID VERSUS GRADUAL DISINFLATION

Some classical economists have proposed that disinflation should be implemented quickly by a rapid and decisive reduction in the growth rate of the money supply—a strategy sometimes referred to as **cold turkey**. Because a cold-turkey disinflation is dramatic and highly visible to the public, proponents of this policy argue that it will quickly and substantially reduce inflationary expectations, particularly if the policy is announced well in advance. If expected inflation falls sufficiently, the expectations-augmented Phillips curve implies that the unemployment costs of the disinflation will be minimal.

However, most Keynesian economists disagree with the idea that rapid disinflation can be achieved without significant costs in terms of increased cyclical unemployment. They argue that because of such factors as menu costs and nominal wage contracts, several years may be required for prices and wages to adjust to a disinflationary policy; during the adjustment period, cyclical unemployment could be high. Further, Keynesians point out that the cold-turkey strategy may not lower inflation expectations because people may expect the government to abandon the policy if the resulting unemployment reaches politically intolerable levels.

Because they fear the possible unemployment consequences of the cold-turkey strategy, many Keynesians recommend a policy of **gradualism**, or reducing the rate of money growth and inflation gradually over a period of years. Keynesians argue that a gradual approach, which gives prices, wages, and expectations more time to adjust to the disinflation, will raise the unemployment rate by less than the cold-turkey strategy—although the period during which unemployment exceeds the natural rate may be longer. They further argue that because the policy will be viewed as sustainable politically, gradualism may be as effective as the cold-turkey approach at reducing inflationary expectations. The results of one study comparing cold turkey and gradualism are discussed in Box 13.4.

Box 13.4 THE SACRIFICE RATIO

To reduce inflation, tight monetary and fiscal policies must be used to slow the growth rate of aggregate demand. However, if these policies are not perfectly anticipated, they will also cause output and employment to fall below their full-employment levels—at least for a time. This loss of output and jobs is an important cost that must be weighed against the benefits of inflation-reducing policies.

Economists sometimes use the sacrifice ratio to measure the cost of lowering the inflation rate. The **sacrifice ratio** is the amount of output lost when the inflation rate is reduced by 1 percentage point. For example, according to a study by Laurence Ball, of Johns Hopkins University,* during the disinflation of the early 1980s, the inflation rate in Canada fell by 7.83 percentage points (from a rate of 11.60% per year to 3.77% per year). For the 16 quarters of this disinflation, Ball estimated the total loss in output caused by inflation-reducing policies to be 18.58% of one year's potential GDP. Dividing the output loss of 18.58% of potential GDP by the 7.83 percentage point reduction in inflation yields a sacrifice ratio of 2.37 for this episode. We can interpret this result as saying that each percentage point by which Canadian inflation was reduced during the early 1980s cost the country 2.37% of a year's potential GDP.

Using quarterly data for nine countries, Ball calculated the sacrifice ratio for 28 disinflations that occurred during the 1960s, 1970s, and 1980s. The accompanying table reports the average sacrifice ratio he found for each country and demonstrates that the output cost of reducing inflation may vary considerably. The average sacrifice ratio ranges from less than 1 in France, the United Kingdom, and Japan to almost 3 in Germany. In other words, reducing inflation in Germany is three times more expensive, in terms of lost output, than it is in those other industrialized countries. What accounts for these differences?

Average Sacrifice Ratios by Country

Australia	1.00
Canada	1.50
France	0.75
Germany	2.92
Italy	1.74
Japan	0.93
Switzerland	1.57
United Kingdom	0.79
United States	2.39

By comparing the characteristics of the different countries in his sample, Ball found that one factor affecting the sacrifice ratio is the flexibility of the labour market. Countries in which wages adjust relatively slowly to changes in labour supply and demand—owing, for example, to heavy government regulation of the labour market—tend to have higher sacrifice ratios. This finding makes sense because countries with inflexible labour markets should take longer to reach long-run equilibrium following an unexpected slowing of the growth of aggregate demand. Ball also found that rapid disinflations tend to have lower sacrifice ratios than do slow disinflations, which is a bit of evidence in favour of the cold turkey approach, rather than gradualism.

Ball's results are interesting but should be interpreted with some caution. One problem is that determining exactly how much output loss can be attributed to a particular set of anti-inflationary policies is not easy. For example, to calculate the output loss owing to disinflation, we have to estimate the amount of output if there had been no disinflation, which is difficult. If the output loss calculation is wrong, the sacrifice ratio calculation will also be wrong. Such factors as supply shocks, which affect both output and inflation, can also distort the calculation of sacrifice ratios. Thus, at best, the sacrifice ratio is a rough measure of the costs of reducing inflation.

---

*"What Determines the Sacrifice Ratio?" in N. Gregory Mankiw, ed., *Monetary Policy*, Chicago: University of Chicago Press, 1994, pp. 155–188.

WAGE AND PRICE CONTROLS

Frustrated by the costs and difficulties of reducing inflation by reducing money growth, policymakers in some countries have taken a more direct approach and imposed wage and price controls—legal limits on the ability of firms to raise wages or prices. These controls have sometimes been used in wartime, and peacetime supporters of wage–price controls (or of *incomes policies*, as wage–price controls are also called) argue that by using the force of law to stop price increases the government can "break the back" of inflationary expectations, allowing a disinflation to proceed without serious unemployment consequences.

Critics of price controls make two points. First, price controls are likely to cause shortages. In a free market the ever-changing forces of supply and demand lead to changes in relative prices, with the prices of some products rising more rapidly than the prices of others. If price controls prevent the price of a product from rising to the level at which quantity supplied equals quantity demanded, there will be excess demand for the product, that is, a shortage. These shortages and the disruptions they cause are a major cost of price controls.[19]

Second, critics dispute that wage–price controls have a major effect on the public's inflation expectations. Although controls stop inflation for the moment, because they cause shortages and disrupt the economy, they eventually have to be removed. Knowing that the controls are temporary, people may expect even greater inflation in the future.

One factor that may affect expectations of inflation during the period of controls is how the government handles monetary and fiscal policy. If macroeconomic policies allow aggregate demand to continue to grow rapidly, people may expect renewed inflation when the controls are lifted (see Analytical Problem 5 at the end of the chapter). In the United States, this failure to reduce aggregate demand growth appears to have been the problem with the Nixon wage–price controls that began in 1971 (see the following Application). But if controls are accompanied by tight monetary and fiscal policy, the idea that inflation will not resume when controls are lifted is more plausible.

APPLICATION

THE NIXON AND TRUDEAU WAGE–PRICE CONTROLS

After increasing gradually during the 1960s, the US inflation rate in 1970 and 1971 hovered at about 5% per year. Attempts to control this inflation by tighter monetary and fiscal policies were not successful. Thus, on August 15, 1971, in a surprise announcement, President Nixon instituted a program of price controls in the United States. The controls began with a 90-day price freeze, known as Phase I, that prevented any prices from increasing. The program evolved haphazardly in response to economic events, reaching Phase IV before the program was finally terminated in April 1974.

As predicted by the basic economics of supply and demand, shortages developed during the period of price controls. To try to prevent shortages, the government exempted some prices, including the prices of raw agricultural products—feed grains, for example—from controls. But prices of final products, such as "broilers" (chickens sold to consumers in grocery stores), remained subject to controls. As feed grain

---

19. Tax-based incomes policies are sometimes suggested as a way of avoiding this problem, but there are few experiences with such schemes.

prices increased, broiler producers could no longer make a profit by paying for feed grain at an uncontrolled price while selling broilers at a controlled price. When this profit squeeze caused broilers to disappear from grocery shelves, the government reclassified broilers as a raw agricultural product so that the price of broilers was no longer controlled. Broilers reappeared on the shelves but at 50% higher prices.[20] Shortages of other goods, including lumber and various steel products, also developed.

To study whether price controls succeeded in reducing inflation after the controls were lifted, Robert J. Gordon[21] conducted a statistical analysis of inflation in the United States during and after the period of price controls. He concluded that price controls reduced the rate of inflation during the period they were in effect (August 1971–April 1974). However, after the price controls were eliminated in April 1974, Gordon found that prices rose rapidly so that by the third quarter of 1975, the price level had reached the same level that it would have attained had there been no controls. In other words, the reduction in the rate of inflation during the period of controls was completely offset by an acceleration of inflation after price controls were removed. A probable reason that inflation accelerated after the removal of controls is that for political reasons the Nixon administration continued to use expansionary monetary and fiscal policy during the period of controls (see the "political business cycle" described in the Political Environment box on p. 498).

Later in the 1970s, the Canadian experience with peacetime controls was somewhat different. In October 1975, the federal government introduced a three-year program of wage and price controls, to be supervised by the Anti-Inflation Board. The Board monitored prices and profits as well as major wage settlements. Estimates by Louis Christofides, of Guelph University, and David Wilton, of the University of Waterloo, suggest that the policy reduced the rate of wage inflation by about 3% per year and had a somewhat smaller effect on CPI inflation.[22] Moreover, there does not seem to be evidence of a "catch-up" or acceleration in inflation when controls were removed in 1978.[23]

For several reasons, the Canadian controls were more successful than their US counterparts. First, they were accompanied by appropriate monetary and fiscal policies, a part of the policy that was announced at the same time as the controls. Second, the AIB enforced gradually declining norms for wage increases (8% in the first year, 6% in the second year, and 4% in the third year), rather than a cold-turkey freeze on wages. Without this gradual decline, workers whose contracts came up for renewal in 1976, say, would have received much lower real wages than those who negotiated contracts in early 1975 before the controls were imposed. By minimizing this potential source of unfairness, the program gained more support from the general public.

However, the prices of up to 40% of the components of the CPI, including food and energy, were not controlled. During this period, the federal government allowed Canadian energy prices to rise toward world levels, which added to inflation. In addition, the nominal effective exchange rate fell by about 10% during the AIB

20. See George P. Shultz and Kenneth W. Dam, "The Life Cycle of Wage and Price Controls," in G. Shultz and K. Dam, eds., *Economic Policy Beyond the Headlines*, Stanford, Calif.: Stanford Alumni Association, 1977.

21. "The Impact of Aggregate Demand on Prices," *Brookings Papers on Economic Activity*, 1975: 3, pp. 613–655.

22. "Wage Controls in Canada (1975:3–1978:2): A Study of Their Impact on Negotiated Base Wage Rates," Ottawa: Anti-Inflation Board, 1979.

23. For a detailed review of the AIB period, see David A. Wilton and David M. Prescott, *Macroeconomics: Theory and Policy in Canada*, Toronto: Addison-Wesley, 1987, pp. 355–364.

period. To the extent this depreciation was passed through into higher import prices, domestic prices rose. For these reasons actual inflation was roughly 10% in 1978 and 1979. Although inflation might have been even higher without wage and price controls, it therefore seems doubtful that the program reduced inflation expectations other than very temporarily.

CREDIBILITY AND REPUTATION

Classicals and Keynesians agree that for disinflation to be achieved without high unemployment costs, reducing the public's expected inflation rate is important. Perhaps the most important factor determining how quickly expected inflation adjusts is the credibility, or believability, of the government's announced disinflationary policy. If the government (in the person of the Minister of Finance or the Governor of the Bank of Canada, for example) announces a policy to reduce the inflation rate—and if workers, consumers, and firms believe that the government means what it says—expected inflation should drop fairly rapidly.

How can a government improve its credibility with the public? One desirable way would be for the government to develop a reputation for carrying through on its promises; then, when it announced a disinflation program, people would likely take this announcement seriously. Unfortunately, time is needed to develop such a reputation, and changes in government may lead to relatively frequent changes in the people who make policy decisions.

Another strategy is to organize policymaking institutions in ways that create credibility with the public. For example, a strong and independent central bank, run by someone with well-known anti-inflation views, may have credibility with the public when it announces a disinflationary policy. However, if the central bank is controlled directly by the government—and is, therefore, exposed to intense political pressure when unemployment rises—an announced disinflationary program is likely to be less credible. We explore the relationship among institutional structure, government credibility, and inflation expectations in greater detail in Chapter 14.

CHAPTER SUMMARY

1. Following the famous 1958 article by A. W. Phillips, empirical studies often showed that inflation is high when unemployment is low and low when unemployment is high. This negative empirical relationship between inflation and unemployment is called the Phillips curve. Inflation and unemployment in Canada conformed to the Phillips curve during the 1960s but not during the 1970s and 1980s.

2. Economic theory suggests that in general, the negative relationship between inflation and unemployment should not be stable. Instead, in an economy in which there are unanticipated changes in the growth rate of aggregate demand, there should be a negative relationship between unanticipated inflation and cyclical unemployment. In particular, when actual and expected inflation are equal (so that unanticipated inflation is zero), the actual unemployment rate will equal the natural unemployment rate (so that cyclical unemployment is zero). This negative relationship between unanticipated inflation and cyclical unemployment is called the expectations-augmented Phillips curve.

3. According to the theory of the expectations-augmented Phillips curve, a stable negative relationship between inflation and unemployment (a Phillips curve) will be observed only if expected inflation and the natural unemployment rate are constant. An increase in expected inflation or an increase in the natural unemployment rate shifts the Phillips curve up and to the right. Adverse supply shocks typically increase both expected inflation and the natural unemployment rate and also shift the Phillips curve up and to the right. Major supply shocks during the 1970s, a rising natural unemployment rate, and highly variable expected inflation rates explain why the Phillips curve shifted erratically in Canada after about 1970.

4. According to the expectations-augmented Phillips curve, macroeconomic policy can reduce unemployment below the natural rate only by surprising the public with higher-than-expected inflation. Classical economists argue that because of rational expectations and rapid price adjustment, policy cannot be used systematically to create inflation higher than expected; thus, policymakers cannot usefully exploit the Phillips curve relationship by trading higher inflation for lower unemployment. Keynesians believe that because not all prices adjust rapidly to reflect new information, policymakers are able to create surprise inflation temporarily and, thus, trade off inflation and unemployment in the short run.

5. Classicals and Keynesians agree that in the long run, expected and actual inflation rates are equal. Thus, in the long run, the actual unemployment rate equals the natural rate, regardless of the inflation rate. Reflecting the fact that there is no long-run trade-off between inflation and unemployment, the long-run Phillips curve is vertical at the natural unemployment rate.

6. The costs of unemployment include output lost when fewer people are working and the personal or psychological costs for unemployed workers and their families.

7. In the long run, the unemployment rate is determined by the natural unemployment rate. According to some estimates, the natural unemployment rate in Canada rose during the 1970s and 1980s but has since stabilized. Explanations for the changes in the natural rate of unemployment include demographic changes in the labour force and changes in the system of unemployment insurance.

8. The actual unemployment rate displays hysteresis if the natural rate increases whenever the actual rate is above the natural rate and decreases whenever the actual unemployment rate is below the natural rate. Hysteresis is thought to be a particularly serious problem in Western Europe and may be important in Canada. Explanations for hysteresis include loss of skills by the unemployed, bureaucratic and legal barriers to labour market adjustment, and wage-setting practices by unions that favour the currently employed (insiders) over those who are currently unemployed (outsiders).

9. Policies to reduce the natural unemployment rate include government support for job training and worker relocation, policies to increase labour market flexibility, and unemployment insurance reform. Some proponents of the hysteresis theory argue that pushing down the actual unemployment rate by means of expansionary policies (a "high-pressure" economy) will ultimately reduce the natural rate as well.

10. The costs of inflation depend on whether the inflation was anticipated or unanticipated. The costs of anticipated inflation, which (except in extreme inflations) are relatively minor, include shoe leather costs (resources used by individuals and firms to reduce their holdings of currency) and menu costs (costs of changing posted prices during an inflation). Unanticipated inflation causes unpredictable transfers of wealth among individuals and firms. The risk of unpredictable gains and losses, and the resources that people expend in trying to reduce this risk, are costs of unanticipated inflation. Unanticipated inflation may also reduce the efficiency of the market system by making it more difficult for people to observe relative prices.

11. Disinflation is a reduction in the rate of inflation. Attempts to disinflate by slowing money growth will cause cyclical unemployment to rise if actual inflation falls below expected inflation. To reduce the unemployment cost of disinflation, the public's expected inflation rate should be brought down along with the actual inflation rate. Strategies for reducing expected inflation include rapid and decisive reduction in the growth rate of the money

supply (the cold-turkey approach), wage and price controls, and taking measures to improve the credibility of government policy announcements.

KEY TERMS

cold turkey, p. 511
disinflation, p. 511
expectations-augmented Phillips curve, p. 490
gradualism, p. 511
hyperinflation, p. 510
hysteresis, p. 503
insider–outsider theory, p. 504
long-run Phillips curve, p. 497
Okun's law, p. 499
Phillips curve, p. 485
sacrifice ratio, p. 512
shoe leather costs, p. 507

KEY EQUATION

$$\pi = \pi^e - h(u - \bar{u}) \qquad (13.1)$$

The expectations-augmented Phillips curve states that unanticipated inflation, $\pi - \pi^e$, is negatively related to cyclical unemployment, $u - \bar{u}$. The expectations-augmented Phillips curve also implies that inflation, π, is negatively related to unemployment, u, only if the expected inflation rate π^e and the natural unemployment rate $\bar{u}$ are constant. Changes in the expected inflation rate or in the natural unemployment rate cause the relationship between inflation and unemployment—the traditional Phillips curve—to shift.

REVIEW QUESTIONS

1. What is the Phillips curve? Does the Phillips curve relationship hold for Canadian data? Explain.

2. How does the expectations-augmented Phillips curve differ from the traditional Phillips curve? According to the theory of the expectations-augmented Phillips curve, under what conditions should the traditional Phillips curve relationship appear in the data?

3. How do changes in the expected inflation rate account for the behaviour of the Phillips curve in the 1970s, 1980s, and 1990s in Canada? What role do supply shocks play in explaining the behaviour of the Phillips curve in Canada?

4. Can policymakers exploit the Phillips curve relationship by trading more inflation for less unemployment in the short run? in the long run? Explain both the classical and Keynesian points of view.

5. Why is the natural unemployment rate an important economic variable? What factors explain the changes in the natural rate over time in Canada, the United States, and Europe? What government policies, if any, might be used to reduce the natural unemployment rate?

6. Give two costs of anticipated inflation and two costs of unanticipated inflation. How is the magnitude of each affected if, instead of a moderate inflation, hyperinflation occurs?

7. What is the greatest potential cost associated with disinflation? How does the responsiveness of the public's inflation expectations affect the size of this potential cost?

8. Discuss at least two strategies for reducing expected inflation rapidly. What are the pros and cons of these strategies?

NUMERICAL PROBLEMS

1. Consider an economy in long-run equilibrium with an inflation rate π of 12% (0.12) per year and a natural unemployment rate $\bar{u}$ of 6% (0.06). The expectations-augmented Phillips curve is

$$\pi = \pi^e - 2(u - \bar{u}).$$

Assume that Okun's law holds so that a 1 percentage point increase in the unemployment rate maintained for one year reduces GDP by 2.0% of full-employment output.

a. Consider a two-year disinflation. In the first year, $\pi = 0.04$ and $\pi^e = 0.08$. In the second year, $\pi = 0.04$ and $\pi^e = 0.04$. In the first year, what is the unemployment rate? By what percentage does output fall short of full-employment output? In the second year, what is the unemployment rate? By what percentage does output fall short of full-employment output?

b. Now consider a four-year disinflation according to the following table:

Year	1	2	3	4
π	0.08	0.04	0.04	0.04
π^e	0.10	0.08	0.06	0.04

What is the unemployment rate in each of the four years? By what percentage does output fall short of full-employment output each year? What is the sacrifice ratio for this disinflation?

2. Consider the following extended classical economy (in which the misperceptions theory holds):

AD	$Y = 300 + 10(M/P)$.
SRAS	$Y = \bar{Y} + P - P^e$.
Okun's law	$(Y - \bar{Y})/\bar{Y} = -2.0(u - \bar{u})$.
Full-employment output	$\bar{Y} = 500$.
Natural unemployment rate	$\bar{u} = 0.06$.

a. Suppose that the money supply $M = 1,000$ and that the expected price level $P^e = 50$. What are the short-run equilibrium values of output Y, the price level P, and the unemployment rate u? What are the long-run equilibrium values of these three variables?

b. Now suppose that an unanticipated increase raises the nominal money supply to $M = 1,260$. What are the new short-run equilibrium values of output Y, the price level P, and the unemployment rate u? What are the new long-run equilibrium values of these three variables? In general, are your results consistent with an expectations-augmented Phillips curve?

3. In a certain economy, the expectations-augmented Phillips curve is

$$\pi = \pi^e - 2(u - \bar{u})$$

and

$$\bar{u} = 0.06.$$

a. Graph the Phillips curve of this economy for an expected inflation rate of 0.10. If the central bank chooses to keep the actual inflation rate at 0.10, what will be the unemployment rate?

b.   An aggregate demand shock (resulting from increased government spending) raises expected inflation to 0.12 (the natural unemployment rate is unaffected). Graph the new Phillips curve and compare it with the curve you drew in part (a). What happens to the unemployment rate if the central bank holds actual inflation at 0.10? What happens to the Phillips curve and the unemployment rate if the central bank announces that it will hold inflation at 0.10 after the aggregate demand shock, and this announcement is fully believed by the public?

c. Suppose that a supply shock (a drought) raises expected inflation to 0.12 and raises the natural unemployment rate to 0.08. Repeat part (b).

4. Consider the following extended classical economy:

AD	$Y = 400 + 5 (M/P)$.
SRAS	$Y = \bar{Y} + 40(P - P^e)$.
Okun's law	$(Y - \bar{Y})/\bar{Y} = -2.0(u - \bar{u})$.
Full-employment output	$\bar{Y} = 800$.
Natural unemployment rate	$\bar{u} = 0.08$.

a. Suppose that the nominal money supply has been constant for many years at $M = 2,000$ and is expected to remain constant forever. What are the equilibrium values of the price level P, the expected price level P^e, output Y, and the unemployment rate u?

b. Suppose that as a complete surprise the nominal money supply increases to $M = 2,912$. What are the short-run equilibrium values of the price level P (Hint: It is a whole number), the expected price level P^e, output Y, and the unemployment rate u? What are the values of cyclical unemployment and unanticipated inflation?

c. What is the slope of the expectations-augmented Phillips curve? (Hint: The slope of the expectations-augmented Phillips curve is $-h$ in Eq. 13.1.)

ANALYTICAL PROBLEMS

1. Suppose that the government institutes a program to help unemployed workers learn new skills, find new jobs, and relocate as necessary to take the new jobs.

a. If this program reduces structural unemployment, what is the effect on the expectations-augmented Phillips curve and the long-run Phillips curve?

b. The government program is expensive, and critics argue that a cheaper way to cut unemployment would be by monetary expansion. Comment.

2. Two extended classical economies (in which the misperceptions theory holds) differ only in one respect: In economy A money growth and inflation have been low and stable for many years, but in economy B, money growth and inflation have fluctuated erratically between very low and very high levels. When producers in economy B observe changes in the prices of the goods they produce, from past experience they usually attribute these changes to fluctuations in the overall price level, rather than to changes in the relative prices of their goods.

Will the slope of the short-run aggregate supply curve for economy B be flatter or steeper than the slope of the curve for economy A? What about the slope of the Phillips curve?

3. In this problem, you are asked to show that the expectations-augmented Phillips curve (derived in the text using the extended classical model) can be derived using the Keynesian model.

Consider a Keynesian economy in which full-employment output is constant and in which the nominal money supply has been growing at 10% per year for some time and is expected to keep growing at that rate in the future. To avoid some technical complications, suppose that instead of growing continuously over time, the money supply is increased by 10% each December 31 and then held constant until the next December 31. Monopolistically competitive firms reset their prices on December 31 of each year at the level that they expect will allow them to sell the full-employment level of output during the coming year. Inflation is measured as the percentage change in prices between January 1 and December 31 of each year.

a. Show how the *AD* curve, *SRAS* curve, output, the price level, and the expected price level evolve over time in this economy. What are the values of unanticipated inflation and cyclical unemployment?

b. Now, suppose that on June 30, 2003, the money supply is unexpectedly raised by an additional 5%. However, the central bank announces—and it is believed by firms—that this extra increase in the money supply is a one-time-only increase and that next December 31 the central bank will return to its policy of increasing the money supply by 10%. (Thus, the total increase in the money supply between January 1, 2003, and December 31, 2003, is 15%.) Firms do not change prices until December 31, as usual, but when they do they respond fully to the new information about money supply growth.

What are the actual and unanticipated inflation rates during 2003? Is cyclical unemployment positive, negative, or zero (on average) during 2003? Relate your results to the expectations-augmented Phillips curve.

4. Some economists have suggested that someday we will live in a "cashless society," in which all businesses (including stores) and banks will be linked to a centralized accounting system. In this system you will be able to pay for purchases directly from your bank account without using cash. What are the costs of anticipated inflation in a cashless society? What are the costs of unanticipated inflation?

5. To fight an ongoing 10% inflation, the government makes raising wages or prices illegal. However, the government continues to increase the money supply (and hence aggregate demand) by 10% per year. The economy starts at full-employment output, which remains constant.

a. Using the Keynesian *AD–AS* framework, show the effects of the government's policies on the economy. Assume that firms meet the demand at the fixed price level.

b. After several years in which the controls have kept prices from rising, the government declares victory over inflation and removes the controls. What happens?

6. How would each of the following changes likely affect the natural unemployment rate?

a. A new law prohibits people from seeking employment before age 18 years.

b. A new internet service, CareerOwl.ca, makes it easy for people to check on the availability of jobs around the country.

c. The length of time that unemployed workers can receive Employment Insurance doubles.

d. A shift in the public's buying habits greatly expands the demand for sophisticated consumer electronics while reducing the demand for traditional consumer goods and services, such as clothing and restaurant meals.

e. Tight monetary policy, introduced to reduce the inflation rate, drives the economy into a recession.

Chapter 14

MONETARY POLICY AND THE BANK OF CANADA

Monetary policy is one of the two principal tools available for affecting macroeconomic behaviour. (The other, fiscal policy, is discussed in Chapter 15.) Monetary policy decisions have widespread implications for the economy. The macroeconomic models that we have presented predict that changes in the money supply will affect nominal variables, such as the price level and the nominal exchange rate. In addition, theories that allow for non-neutrality (including the extended classical theory with misperceptions and the Keynesian theory) imply that in the short run, monetary policy also affects real variables, such as real GDP, the real interest rate, and the unemployment rate. Because monetary policy has such pervasive economic effects, the central bank's announcements and actions are closely monitored by the media, financial market participants, and the general public.

In this chapter, we look more closely at monetary policy, concentrating first on the basic question of how the country's money supply is determined. In previous chapters, we have assumed, for simplicity, that the money supply is determined by the central bank. We now demonstrate that although a country's central bank (such as the Bank of Canada) can exert strong influence over the level of the money supply, the money supply also is affected by the banking system's behaviour and the public's decisions.

In the second part of the chapter, we explore the question: How should the central bank conduct monetary policy? Not surprisingly, because of classical and Keynesian differences over the effects of monetary policy and the desirability of trying to smooth the business cycle (Chapters 11 and 12), the question is controversial. Some Keynesians argue that monetary authorities should have considerable latitude to try to offset cyclical fluctuations. Opposing this view, both classical economists and a group of economists called *monetarists* believe that monetary policy should not be left to the discretion of the central bank but, instead, should be governed by simple rules. Although establishing rules for monetary policy might seem to tie policymakers' hands unnecessarily, monetarists and classicals argue that the use of rules would lead to a more stable and less inflationary economy in the long run. After examining the arguments for and against the use of rules, we discuss the effectiveness of rules-based monetary policies in Canada and other countries. We also discuss how the debate about rules is related to questions of how monetary policymaking institutions should be designed. For example, should the central bank be largely independent from the rest of the government, or should it be more directly controlled by the federal parliament and cabinet?

14.1 PRINCIPLES OF MONEY SUPPLY DETERMINATION

How is the country's money supply determined? So far, we have assumed that the money supply, M, is controlled directly by the central bank. Although this assumption is a useful simplification, it is not literally true. The central bank's control of the money supply is only indirect and depends to some extent on the structure of the economy.

Most generally, three groups affect the money supply: the central bank, depository institutions, and the public.

1. In nearly all countries, the **central bank** is the governmental institution responsible for monetary policy.[1] Examples of central banks are the Bank of Canada, the Federal Reserve System in the United States, the European Central Bank, and the Bank of Japan.

2. **Depository institutions** are privately owned banks, trust companies, credit unions, and caisses populaires that accept deposits from and make loans directly to the public. We refer to depository institutions as banks, for short.

3. The public includes every person or firm (except banks) that holds money, either as currency and coin or as deposits in banks—in other words, virtually the whole private economy outside of the banking system.

Before investigating how these groups interact to set the money supply in a financially complex country, such as Canada, we begin with an example of a primitive agricultural economy, which we call Agricola. Examining the introduction of money and the development of banking in Agricola identifies clearly the factors involved in the determination of the money supply. Additionally, the development of the monetary and banking systems in fictitious Agricola loosely parallels the actual evolution of such systems over the centuries in many countries.

THE MONEY SUPPLY IN AN ALL-CURRENCY ECONOMY

The imaginary country of Agricola is an agricultural nation that produces a variety of fruits, nuts, vegetables, and grains. Initially, Agricola has no money supply, so all trading is done by barter, or the direct trading of goods for goods. Recall, however, that a trading system based on barter is extremely inconvenient (Chapter 7). Under a barter system, a farmer who wants to trade barley for pomegranates must find someone willing to exchange pomegranates for barley, which involves a costly and time-consuming search.

The benevolent leader of Agricola recognizes this inconvenience and decides to create a national money to ease trade among the people. The first step in establishing a national money is to create a government agency called the Agricolan Central Bank. The Central Bank then prints paper certificates[2] and decrees the value of each certificate to be one florin (abbreviated fl), which becomes the national currency of Agricola. The government of Agricola prohibits anyone other than the Agricolan Central Bank from printing these certificates.

To get the florins into general circulation, the Central Bank uses them to buy some real assets from the public. In the agricultural economy of Agricola, real assets

---

1. Most industrialized countries established central banks in the 19th century or early 20th century. Prior to the establishment of central banks, national treasury or finance departments often were responsible for currency issue and other matters pertaining to the money supply.

2. In most countries, the actual printing of paper money is done by a separate agency, not by the central bank itself.

are storable agricultural products, such as coconuts, so the Central Bank uses newly printed florins to buy coconuts from the public. Why do people in Agricola willingly surrender valuable coconuts in exchange for paper certificates? In general, people accept paper money in payment for goods, services, or assets because they expect to be able to use it to buy other goods, services, or assets in the future. In other words, people accept paper money because they believe that other people also will accept it. The belief that money has value becomes self-justifying: If most people believe that money has value, then it has value.[3] The government helps convince the public that paper money has value, usually by decreeing that the money is *legal tender*—that is, creditors are required to accept the money in settlement of debts—and by stating its own willingness to accept money from the public in payment of taxes.

Suppose that the people of Agricola accept the new currency and that the Central Bank trades one million florins to the public for one million coconuts. The balance sheet of the Agricolan Central Bank is

Agricolan Central Bank			
ASSETS		LIABILITIES	
Coconuts	1,000,000 fl	Currency	1,000,000 fl

On the left-hand side of the balance sheet are the Central Bank's assets—what it owns or is owed, in this case, the coconuts. On the right-hand side are the bank's liabilities—what it owes to others. Because the florins are technically debt obligations of the Central Bank, they are entered as liabilities on the balance sheet. The liabilities of the Central Bank that are usable as money are called the **monetary base**, or, equivalently, **high-powered money**. The monetary base of Agricola is, thus, one million florins.

Assume that Agricola initially has no banking system. With no banks and hence no bank deposits, the total money supply is the currency held by the public. That is, the paper certificates distributed by the Agricolan Central Bank are used directly as money. Thus, the money supply in Agricola equals one million florins, which, in turn, equals the monetary base (the liabilities of the Agricolan Central Bank). Hence, *in an all-currency economy (one with no bank deposits) the money supply equals the monetary base*.

THE MONEY SUPPLY UNDER FRACTIONAL RESERVE BANKING

As the people of Agricola become financially more sophisticated, a system of private banks emerges. The banks announce their willingness to accept deposits from the public.

For the time being, let us assume that because currency is easily lost or stolen, Agricolans want to hold all their money in bank deposits, rather than in currency. After the Agricolans deposit all their currency (one million florins) in banks, the combined, or consolidated, balance sheet of all the banks is

---

3. Also possible is that no one believes that money has value, which would again be a self-justifying belief because no one would then accept money in payment. In the next section, we will see an example of this outcome in Canadian history.

Consolidated Balance Sheet of Banks			
ASSETS		LIABILITIES	
Currency	1,000,000 fl	Deposits	1,000,000 fl

The banking system's assets are the one million paper florins in bank vaults. The banking system's liabilities are the deposits, which are the banks' debts or obligations to the public. The balance sheet of the Central Bank remains the same.

Liquid assets held by banks to meet the demands for withdrawals by depositors or to pay the cheques drawn on depositors' accounts are called **bank reserves**. In general, bank reserves comprise currency held by private banks in their vaults and deposits held by private banks at the Central Bank. Here, all bank reserves are held as currency in the banks' vaults. Note that the bank reserves equal total deposits of 1,000,000 fl. This type of banking system is called **100% reserve banking** because bank reserves equal 100% of deposits. Under 100% reserve banking, banks are nothing more than a safekeeping service for the public's currency. Indeed, the only way that banks could cover their expenses and make a profit under 100% reserve banking would be to charge depositors a fee for holding their money for them (that is, to pay negative interest on deposits).

However, one day, an enterprising Agricolan banker notices that the paper florins the bank has accepted from depositors are just sitting idly in neat stacks in the bank's vault. True, a few florins flow out when a depositor writes a cheque to someone who banks elsewhere, or when a depositor switches an account to another bank. However, this outflow is balanced by a roughly equivalent inflow, when the bank's depositors receive cheques drawn on other banks or the bank attracts a depositor away from another bank. The banker calculates that keeping florins in the vault equal to, say, 20% of outstanding deposits would more than cover this random ebb and flow. The remaining 80% of the florins on deposit could be lent to earn interest for the bank!

Under the Agricolan banker's scheme, the reserves held by the bank will equal only a fraction of the bank's outstanding deposits. In this case, the **reserve–deposit ratio**, or reserves divided by deposits, equals 20%. A banking system in which banks hold only a fraction of their deposits in reserve so that the reserve–deposit ratio is less than one, is called **fractional reserve banking**. Fractional reserve banking is profitable for banks because instead of sitting in the vault earning no interest for the bank, a portion of the funds received from depositors can be used to make interest-earning loans.

All the bankers of Agricola quickly grasp the idea of fractional reserve banking and decide to hold reserves of 20% of deposits and lend the other 80% (800,000 fl) to farmers. The farmers use the loans to buy fertilizer for their farms. The sellers of the fertilizer receive 800,000 fl in payment, and because everyone prefers having bank deposits to holding currency, they deposit the 800,000 fl in the banking system. After these deposits are made all the florins are back in the banks, and the consolidated balance sheet of the banking system is

Consolidated Balance Sheet of Banks			
ASSETS		LIABILITIES	
Currency (reserves)	1,000,000 fl	Deposits	1,800,000 fl
Loans to farmers	800,000 fl		
Total	1,800,000 fl	Total	1,800,000 fl

The banks' assets now include the 800,000 fl in loans to farmers (the loans are owed to the banks, so they are assets of the banks). The banks' assets also include one million paper florins: 200,000 fl originally kept in reserve plus the 800,000 fl deposited by the sellers of the fertilizer.

The banks' consolidated liabilities equal 1,800,000 fl in deposits: the 1,000,000 fl in original deposits, and the 800,000 fl in new deposits from the fertilizer sellers.

At this point, as the bankers examine their balance sheets, they note that their reserves (holdings of paper florins) are back up to 1,000,000 fl. Their deposits equal 1,800,000 fl. On the basis of the principle that reserves need be only 20% of deposits, their reserves of 1,000,000 fl are too high. The bankers need to hold only 360,000 fl, or 0.20(1,800,000 fl). The other 640,000 fl, or 1,000,000 fl – 360,000 fl, can be lent again to earn more interest.

So, the banks make additional interest-bearing loans in the amount of 640,000 fl. The banks' borrowers use the funds to make purchases. As before, these florins eventually are re-deposited in the banking system. At this point, the consolidated balance sheet of all the banks is

Consolidated Balance Sheet of Banks

ASSETS		LIABILITIES	
Currency (reserves)	1,000,000 fl	Deposits	2,440,000 fl
Loans to farmers	1,440,000 fl		
Total	2,440,000 fl	Total	2,440,000 fl

The assets of the banks now include one million paper florins (the 360,000 fl kept as reserves and the 640,000 fl re-deposited by the public) and 1,440,000 fl in loans (the 800,000 fl of first-round loans and the 640,000 fl of second-round loans). The liabilities are 2,440,000 fl in deposits (the 1,800,000 fl from earlier deposits and the 640,000 fl in new deposits).

The process does not stop here. Checking their balance sheets after this latest round of loans and re-deposits, the bankers find that their reserves (1,000,000 fl) still exceed 20% of their deposits, or 0.20(2,440,000 fl) = 488,000 fl. So, yet another round of loans and re-deposits of loaned funds will occur.

This process of **multiple expansion of loans and deposits**, in which fractional reserve banking increases an economy's loans and deposits, will stop only when the reserves of the banking system equal 20% of its deposits. The reserves of the banks always equal 1,000,000 fl (the entire supply of paper florins) at the end of each round, so the process will stop when total bank deposits equal 1,000,000 fl/0.20, or 5,000,000 fl. At this final point the consolidated balance sheet of the banks is

Consolidated Balance Sheet of Banks

ASSETS		LIABILITIES	
Currency (reserves)	1,000,000 fl	Deposits	5,000,000 fl
Loans to farmers	4,000,000 fl		
Total	5,000,000 fl	Total	5,000,000 fl

At this final stage, the ratio of reserves to deposits equals the ratio desired by banks (20%). No further expansion of loans and deposits can occur after this point because the ratio of reserves to deposits is at its minimum acceptable level. What is the money supply in Agricola at the end of this process? Recall that the public does not hold any currency but, instead, deposits any currency received in the banking system, where it is held in the form of bank reserves. The reserves in the banks' vaults are not available for transactions and, thus, are not counted as money. However, the public *is* holding deposits. Because they are liquid and can be used for transactions, bank deposits are counted as part of the money supply.[4] Indeed, as there is no public holding of currency in Agricola, bank deposits are the money supply. Therefore, the money supply equals 5,000,000 fl, or the total quantity of deposits.

What is the relationship between the money supply and the monetary base with fractional reserve banking and no holding of currency by the public? We use the following variables to answer this question algebraically:

M = the money supply;
$BASE$ = the monetary base;
DEP = total bank deposits;
RES = total bank reserves;
res = the banks' desired reserve–deposit ratio = RES/DEP.

With no currency being held by the public, the money supply equals the quantity of bank deposits:

$$M = DEP. \tag{14.1}$$

For any level of deposits DEP, the amount of reserves that banks want to hold is $(res)(DEP)$. At the end of the multiple-expansion process, bank reserves must equal the amount of currency distributed by the Central Bank (the monetary base). Therefore,

$$(res)(DEP) = BASE. \tag{14.2}$$

Solving Eq. (14.2) for deposits yields $DEP = BASE/res$. Because the money supply equals deposits in this example,

$$M = DEP = \frac{BASE}{res}. \tag{14.3}$$

Hence, *in an economy with fractional reserve banking and no currency held by the public, the money supply equals the monetary base divided by the reserve–deposit ratio*. In Agricola, the monetary base is 1,000,000 fl, and the reserve–deposit ratio chosen by the banks is 0.20. The money supply is, therefore, 1,000,000 fl/ 0.20, or 5,000,000 fl, as we have already shown.

The multiple expansion of loans and deposits allows the economy to create a money supply that is much larger than the monetary base. Each unit of monetary base allows 1/*res* units of money to be created, leading to a money supply that is a multiple of the monetary base. Because each unit of monetary base permits creation of several units of money supply, the base is also called *high-powered money*.

BANK RUNS

Fractional reserve banking works on the assumption that outflows and inflows of reserves will roughly balance and, in particular, that a large fraction of a bank's

---

4. Recall from Chapter 7 that the most narrowly defined monetary aggregate M1 includes demand deposits and other chequable deposits. Slightly less liquid deposits, such as savings deposits and time deposits, are included in broader monetary aggregates.

depositors will never want to withdraw their funds at the same time. If a large number of depositors attempt to withdraw currency simultaneously (more than 20% of the bank's deposits in Agricola), the bank will run out of reserves and be unable to meet all its depositors' demands for cash.

Historically, in Canada, there were episodes in which rumours circulated that a particular bank had made some bad loans and was at risk of becoming bankrupt. On the principle of "better safe than sorry," the bank's depositors lined up to withdraw their money. From the depositors' perspective, withdrawal avoided the risk that the bank would fail and not be able to pay off depositors in full. A large-scale, panicky withdrawal of deposits from a bank is called a **bank run**. Even if the rumours about the bank's loans proved untrue, a large enough run could exhaust the bank's reserves and force it to close. To stop a run, a bank had to convince customers that it was "sound"—financially solvent—and had plenty of funds available. More recently, the Bank of Canada and federal and provincial regulators (along with deposit insurance) have played roles in preventing bank runs.

THE MONEY SUPPLY WITH BOTH PUBLIC HOLDINGS OF CURRENCY AND FRACTIONAL RESERVE BANKING

In most economies, the public holds some currency (as at first in Agricola), and there is also a fractional reserve banking system (as later in Agricola). Currency in the public's hands and bank deposits both may be used for transactions, so both are forms of money. When the public holds both currency, CU, and bank deposits, DEP, the money supply M is

$$M = CU + DEP. \tag{14.4}$$

In this situation, the monetary base has two uses: Some of the monetary base is held as currency by the public, and the rest is held as reserves by banks. Therefore, the monetary base equals the sum of the two, or

$$BASE = CU + RES. \tag{14.5}$$

The central bank may control the amount of monetary base but does not directly control the money supply. To relate the money supply to the monetary base, we first divide the money supply, Eq. (14.4), by the monetary base, Eq. (14.5), to get

$$\frac{M}{BASE} = \frac{CU + DEP}{CU + RES}. \tag{14.6}$$

Next, we divide both the numerator and the denominator on the right-hand side of Eq. (14.6) by DEP to obtain

$$\frac{M}{BASE} = \frac{(CU/DEP) + 1}{(CU/DEP) + (RES/DEP)}. \tag{14.7}$$

The right-hand side of Eq. (14.7) contains two important ratios. The first is the **currency–deposit ratio** (CU/DEP, or cu), which is the ratio of the currency held by the public to the public's deposits in banks. The currency–deposit ratio is determined by the public and depends on the amount of money the public wants to hold as currency versus the amount it wants to hold as deposits. The public can raise the currency–deposit ratio to any level that it wants by withdrawing currency from banks (which increases currency held and reduces deposits); similarly, by depositing currency in banks, the public can lower the currency–deposit ratio.

The second important ratio on the right-hand side of Eq. (14.7) is the reserve–deposit ratio (*RES/DEP*, or *res*), which we have already discussed. The reserve–deposit ratio is determined by banks' decisions about how much of their deposits to lend.[5]

When the process of multiple expansion of loans and deposits is complete, the currency–deposit ratio equals the ratio desired by the public, *cu*, and the reserve–deposit ratio equals the ratio desired by the banks, *res*. Substituting *cu* for *CU/DEP* and *res* for *RES/DEP* in Eq. (14.7) and multiplying both sides of Eq. (14.7) by *BASE*, we obtain

$$M = \left(\frac{cu+1}{cu+res}\right)BASE. \tag{14.8}$$

Equation (14.8) states that the money supply is a multiple of the monetary base. The relation of the money supply to the monetary base depends on the currency–deposit ratio chosen by the public and the reserve–deposit ratio chosen by banks. The factor $(cu + 1)/(cu + res)$, which is the number of dollars of money supply that can be created from each dollar of monetary base, is called the **money multiplier**. The money multiplier will be greater than 1 as long as *res* is less than 1 (that is, with fractional reserve banking). Note that if the public holds no currency ($cu = 0$), the money multiplier equals $1/res$, or the same value as that in Agricola when all money was held as bank deposits (Eq. 14.3).

Table 14.1 uses Canadian data to illustrate the money multiplier and the relation among currency, reserves, monetary base, and the money supply. With these data, you can verify that the currency–deposit ratio is 0.4127 and that the reserve–deposit ratio is 0.0447. Thus, the money multiplier, $(cu + 1)/(cu + res)$, equals 3.088. You may verify this formula by dividing the money supply ($125,297 million) by the monetary base ($40,571 million) to obtain 3.088.

It can be shown algebraically that the money multiplier decreases when either the currency–deposit ratio *cu* or the reserve–deposit ratio res increases.[6] Recall that the reason that the monetary base gets "multiplied" is that under fractional

TABLE 14.1

The Monetary Base, the Money Multiplier, and the Money Supply in Canada

Currency outside banks, *CU*	$36,606 million
Bank reserves, *RES*	$3,965 million
Monetary base, *BASE* (=*CU* + *RES*)	$40,571 million
Deposits, *DEP*	$89,691 million
Money supply, *M* (=*CU* + *DEP*)	$125,297 million
Reserve–deposit ratio, *res* (=*RES/DEP*)	0.0447
Currency–deposit ratio, *cu* (=*CU/DEP*)	0.4127
Money multiplier, $(cu + 1)/(cu + res)$	3.088
Ratio of money supply to base, *M/BASE*	3.088

Source: *Bank of Canada Banking and Financial Statistics*, January 2002, Tables C1 and E1. Deposits are personal chequing and current accounts and the money supply is M1. Data are for November 2001. Reprinted with permission from the Bank of Canada.

---

5. In some countries, but not Canada, government regulations may set minimum levels for banks' reserve–deposit ratios.

6. That the money multiplier decreases when *cu* increases is not obvious, as *cu* appears in both the numerator and the denominator of the money multiplier. However, as you can confirm by trying numerical examples or by taking a derivative, an increase in *cu* reduces the money multiplier as long as *res* is less than 1, which must always be the case under fractional reserve banking.

reserve banking, banks use some of the currency received as deposits to make loans to the public. The public can either hold the money it borrows from banks as currency or redeposit its borrowings in the banking system, but in either case, the result is a higher total money supply than existed before the loans were made. When the reserve–deposit ratio rises, banks lend a smaller fraction of each dollar of deposits, creating less money for the same amount of monetary base; thus, an increase in the reserve–deposit ratio lowers the money multiplier. When the currency–deposit ratio rises, the public puts a smaller fraction of its money in banks, which means that banks have less money to loan. With banks lending less, less money is created from the same amount of monetary base, again reducing the money multiplier.

OPEN-MARKET OPERATIONS

We have shown how the monetary base and the money multiplier determine the money supply. To change the level of the money supply, a central bank must change the amount of monetary base or change the money multiplier. For now, we focus on the most direct and frequently used way of changing the money supply: raising or lowering the monetary base. For any value of the money multiplier, Eq. (14.8) indicates that a change in the monetary base will cause a proportional change in the money supply.

Suppose that the Agricolan Central Bank decides to increase the monetary base by 10%, from 1,000,000 to 1,100,000 fl. How would it actually do so? First, the Central Bank has to print the extra 100,000 fl. Then, it can use the 100,000 new florins to buy assets (coconuts) from the public. After purchasing the additional coconuts, the Agricolan Central Bank's balance sheet is

Agricolan Central Bank			
ASSETS		LIABILITIES	
Coconuts	1,100,000 fl	Currency	1,100,000 fl

By purchasing 100,000 fl of coconuts, the Central Bank puts 100,000 more paper certificates (florins) into circulation. The monetary base, which is the same as the total liabilities of the Central Bank, rises to 1,100,000 fl. If the money multiplier remains unchanged, the money supply also increases by 10%.

Suppose, instead, that the Agricolan Central Bank wanted to reduce the monetary base by 10%. To do so, it would sell 100,000 fl of coconuts to the public for 100,000 fl in currency. The 100,000 fl collected by the Central Bank are retired from circulation. (The retired florins are not treated as assets of the Central Bank; if you paid off a debt and retrieved your IOU, you would not consider the IOU to be an asset.) The Agricolan Central Bank's balance sheet now is

Agricolan Central Bank			
ASSETS		LIABILITIES	
Coconuts	900,000 fl	Currency	900,000 fl

The Agricolan Central Bank's liabilities outstanding (the monetary base) have been reduced to 900,000. With a constant money multiplier, the money supply will fall proportionately.

Recall (Chapter 7) that a purchase of assets by the central bank is called an **open-market purchase**.[7] It increases the monetary base and, thus, the money supply. A sale of assets to the public by the central bank is called an **open-market sale**. It reduces the monetary base and the money supply. Open-market purchases and sales are collectively called open-market operations. Open-market operations are the most direct way for central banks to change their national money supplies.

However, the Bank of Canada has observed that the money multiplier in Canada is rather unstable, and so, it has not tried to use base control to precisely influence the money supply. Instead, it has affected the monetary base so as to influence short-term interest rates. In Section 14.2 we discuss the Bank of Canada's methods in detail.

14.2 MONETARY CONTROL IN CANADA

The principles of money supply determination developed in the Agricola example can be applied directly to actual economies by adding a few institutional details. In this section, we link these general principles to monetary institutions in Canada.

THE BANK OF CANADA

The Canadian central bank, the Bank of Canada, was created in 1934, on the basis of a recommendation by a Royal Commission chaired by Lord Macmillan, and was modelled on the Bank of England. In part, the Bank was established for political reasons. During the Great Depression, there was widespread dissatisfaction with the operation of the monetary system, and the depth of the Depression was sometimes blamed on the system. This view led the newly founded Co-operative Commonwealth Federation (CCF), the precursor of the New Democratic Party, to call for the public ownership of banks. At the same time, the Social Credit government in Alberta was promoting a monetary expansion. The Alberta government tried to restrict the operation of banks, but its legislation was struck down by the Supreme Court of Canada. It also issued its own money, which turned out to be valueless when no one (not even the government itself) would accept it as payment. These responses show how deep the distrust of the monetary and banking system ran, particularly in the provinces worst hit by the Depression.

The Bank operated as a private corporation until 1938 and is now a Crown Corporation, with headquarters in Ottawa. It is directed by a Board of Directors, which includes the governor, the senior deputy governor, the deputy minister of finance, and 12 part-time directors. The part-time directors are private citizens, appointed for three-year terms. The governor is appointed by the board, with the government's approval, for a renewable seven-year term.

On paper, the Bank seems to be an arm of the government. The governor must make an annual report to the minister of finance, must manage the government's debt, its deposits with chartered banks, and its foreign exchange reserves, and must consult regularly with the minister. If these consultations do not lead to an agreement on monetary policy, then the government may issue a public directive, with which the Bank must comply.

---

7. The term *open market* refers to the fact that the central bank's transactions with the public take place in regular asset markets that are open to and used by the public.

However, a leading commentator on Canadian monetary policy, Peter Howitt, of Brown University, has argued that for several reasons, the Bank has much more independence than the Bank of Canada Act might suggest.[8] For example, since the government has ultimate responsibility for monetary policy, it refrains from public criticism of the Bank's actions. While the government may issue a directive to the Bank, it has not done so since the Act was amended in 1967 to allow this. It is understood that if a directive were issued the governor would resign, which would severely damage the government's credibility in financial markets.

The government cannot readily influence policy through the Board of Directors either. The directors are appointed on a part-time basis, serve overlapping terms, and are not experts on monetary policy (bankers and economists are not allowed to sit on the board). The minutes of board meetings, published in the *Bank of Canada Review* suggest that the board acts as a rubber stamp (see "The Political Environment" box, p. 541, for a discussion of alternative ways of governing the Bank). The government can influence the Bank directly by not renewing the governor's appointment when it expires (as occurred in 1994 when Gordon Thiessen succeeded John Crow), or it could amend the Bank of Canada Act. In either case, though, it cannot directly control short-term monetary policy.

THE BANK OF CANADA'S BALANCE SHEET

The balance sheet of the Bank of Canada at the end of November 2001 is shown in Table 14.2. The Bank's largest asset by far is its holdings of government securities (bonds). Indeed, the Bank owns about 10% of outstanding Treasury bills. It also owns foreign currencies and makes loans (advances) to banks, which count as assets for the Bank.

TABLE 14.2

The Balance Sheet of the Bank of Canada (Millions of Dollars)

Assets		Liabilities	
Treasury bills	$12,251	Notes in circulation	
		In banks	$3,513
Other government securities	$25,986	Outside banks	$36,606
Advances to members of the		Deposits	
Canadian Payments		Government of Canada	$2,321
Association	$394	Members of the Canadian	
		Payments Association	$452
Foreign currency deposits	$335	Foreign central banks	$763
Other assets	$4,689		

Addenda

Reserves = bank deposits at Bank of Canada + currency at banks = $3,965 million

Monetary base = currency outside banks + reserves = $40,571 million

Source: *Bank of Canada Banking and Financial Statistics*, January 2002, Tables B2, C1, and E1. Data are for November 2001. To simplify accounting, we have counted coins as liabilities of the Bank of Canada even though they are issued by the Royal Canadian Mint. Reprinted with permission from the Bank of Canada.

---

8. See Peter Howitt, "Canada," Chapter 14 in Michele Fratianni and Dominick Salvatore, eds., *Monetary Policy in Developed Countries*, Westport, Conn.: Greenwood Press, 1993.

The largest liability of the Bank is currency in circulation. Some of this currency ($3,513 million) is held in private banks. The remainder of currency outstanding, $36,606 million, is held by the public and corresponds to what we label *CU*. The other principal liabilities of the Bank are deposits made by members of the Canadian Payments Association, a cheque-clearing organization of banks. In accepting deposits from banks, the Bank of Canada acts as the "banks' bank." Chartered banks make deposits at the Bank of Canada because it is a convenient way of holding reserves and of settling their accounts with other banks.

These accounts at the Bank of Canada ($452 million), together with currency at banks, sometimes called vault cash, ($3,513 million), equal the total reserves of the banking system ($3,965 million), what we call *RES*. Recall from Eq. (14.5) and Table 14.1 that the monetary base equals bank reserves ($3,965 million) plus currency outside banks ($36,606 million), or $40,571 million. The monetary base can be calculated equivalently as the sum of total currency outstanding ($40,119 million) plus bank deposits at the Bank of Canada ($452 million), which again is $40,571 million.

Other liabilities of the Bank of Canada are the deposits there that are owned by foreign central banks and by the federal government.

TOOLS OF MONETARY POLICY

OVERNIGHT RATES

To understand how the Bank of Canada influences the money supply, first recall that most money in Canada is in the form of demand deposits. Each day, millions of cheques are written on these bank accounts, and so, balances must be transferred between banks. Suppose that a $100 cheque is written on an account at the National Bank and deposited at the Royal Bank. The same day, an $80 cheque is written on an account at the Royal Bank and deposited at the National Bank. Rather than transferring $100 one way and then $80 the other way, the banks make only the net transfer: $20 from the National Bank to the Royal Bank. To make these transfers, the banks hold balances at the Bank of Canada, called clearing or **settlement balances** (shown in Table 14.2 as deposits of members of the Canadian Payments Association). In Canada, banks are not required to hold reserves at the central bank, but 13 large banks and credit union associations called **direct clearers** do so to settle these net transfers. At the end of the day, in this example, $20 is transferred from the National Bank's account at the Bank of Canada to the Royal Bank's account.

The main system for clearing cheques in Canada is the Large Value Transfer System (LVTS). Financial institutions that clear cheques but do not take part in the LVTS hold accounts with larger banks, who, in turn, hold settlement balances at the Bank of Canada on their behalf.

If a bank finds itself with a larger balance than it needs to meet its settlement obligations, then it can lend some of its balances (reserves) to another bank for one day, charging an interest rate called the **overnight rate**. The Bank of Canada implements monetary policy by influencing this very short-term interest rate. The Bank announces a range or operating band of 0.5 percentage points for the overnight rate on eight preset dates each year (or at other times in unusual circumstances). The centre of this band is the **target overnight rate**, which is the key indicator of the stance of monetary policy.

To ensure that the overnight rate remains within the 0.5 percentage point band, the Bank is prepared to lend at the interest rate at the top of the band (called the **Bank rate**). This puts a ceiling on the overnight interest rate, for banks would not

FIGURE 14.1

THE OVERNIGHT RATE AND THE BANK OF CANADA OPERATING BAND, 2001

The heavy lines show the lower and upper edges of the Bank of Canada's operating band for the overnight interest rate. The light line shows the actual overnight rate. The data are daily, so weekends and holidays appear as gaps. The overnight rate deviates very little from the target overnight rate (not shown) which is the centre of the operating band. Note that the Bank of Canada lowered the band on each of the eight, preset dates during 2001 on which policy announcements were made.

Source: *Bank of Canada Banking and Financial Statistics*, Table F1. Reprinted with the permission of the Bank of Canada.

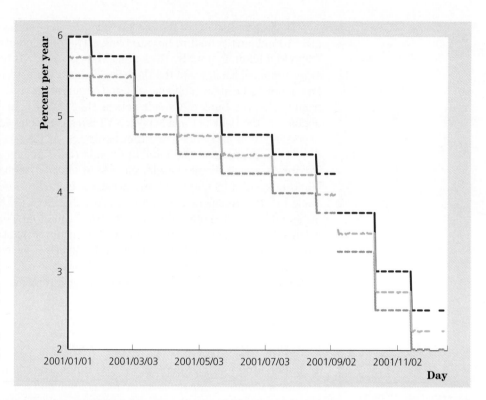

borrow at a higher rate than the one offered by the Bank of Canada. Conversely, the Bank pays interest on deposits at the rate given by the bottom edge of the band, which places a floor under the overnight rate. In practice, most transactions in the overnight market are between banks, at roughly the target overnight rate. Figure 14.1 shows the operating band for the overnight rate during 2001, and the actual overnight rate. During 2001 the Bank lowered the band eight times.

To see how this operating band affects the money supply, let us consider a situation in which the Bank of Canada wishes to loosen monetary policy. Suppose that the Bank announces that it is lowering its target for the overnight interest rate. To bring about this change, the Bank could offer advances to banks at the upper edge of the newly lowered band. Any increase in these advances would show up as an increase in the assets of the Bank, on the left-hand side of its balance sheet (see Table 14.2). A bank accepting an advance would be credited with an increased deposit balance at the Bank of Canada, which would increase the monetary base. Thus, you can think of this as an expansionary monetary policy brought about by a traditional open-market purchase of assets, but one in which the assets are advances to banks. The key feature is that the Bank of Canada announces the target interest rate, then stands ready to offer advances to make that interest rate the market-clearing one.[9]

This increase in the monetary base allows an increase in the money supply. Since reserves are higher, banks expand their own loans and deposits to restore their reserve-deposit ratios. As a result, the money supply rises. Conversely, an increase in the overnight rate leads to a decrease in the money supply. Once again, the money supply and interest rates move in opposite directions, just as we have described from Chapter 9 on, in discussing shifts in the *LM* curve.

---

9. A detailed and clear description of the Bank of Canada's operating procedures is given by Frederic S. Mishkin and Apostolos Serletis, *The Economics of Money, Banking, and Financial Markets.* Toronto: Addison Wesley Longman, 2002, Chapter 17.

In practice, when banks need reserves they most often borrow them from other banks (at the overnight rate), rather than from the Bank of Canada (at the higher Bank rate). However, the Bank of Canada's willingness to lend at the Bank rate serves as a reminder that a central bank exists partly to prevent financial crises (such as bank runs) by serving as a **lender of last resort**. The central bank fulfills this function by standing ready to lend reserves to banks that need cash to meet depositors' demands or settlement needs.

So far, we have described how the Bank of Canada influences the overnight rate and how that rate, in turn, affects the money supply. How does the Bank affect interest rates on bank accounts and mortgages? As we saw in Chapter 4, interest rates on different assets tend to move together. Again, suppose that the Bank of Canada lowers its operating band for the overnight rate. If the overnight rate falls, banks with adequate reserves will choose to invest in some higher-yielding assets, rather than holding reserves. But if many banks react this way, then the returns offered on other assets will tend to fall as lenders compete for those investments. Thus, other interest rates will adjust if the change in the overnight rate persists. For example, the prime rate (the loan rate charged by banks to their best customers) adjusts fairly quickly to changes in the overnight rate. Interest rates on mortgages, savings deposits, and guaranteed investment certificates (GICs) also adjust, though with some delays. Figure 14.2 shows the target overnight rate, the prime rate, and the one-year mortgage rate during the period from 1994 to 2001.

OPEN-MARKET OPERATIONS

Like the Agricola Central Bank, the Bank of Canada can change the money supply through open-market operations. To increase the money supply, for example, the

FIGURE 14.2

SHORT-TERM INTEREST RATES, 1994–2001

The figure shows monthly averages of the target overnight interest rate, the prime rate, and the interest rate on one-year mortgages during the period 1994–2001. Changes in the target overnight rate lead to similar changes in the interest rates administered by banks on loans and mortgages. This is a key way in which monetary policy influences the economy.

Source: *Bank of Canada Banking and Financial Statistics*, Table F1. Reprinted with permission from the Bank of Canada.

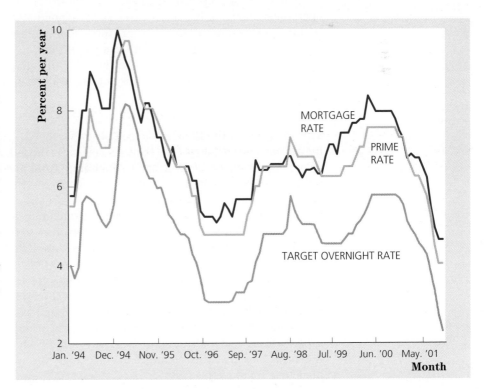

Bank could conduct an open-market purchase, in which it would buy Government of Canada securities (instead of coconuts, as in Agricola) from the public. A purchase of $100 million in securities would increase the Bank's assets by $100 million. To pay for these securities, the Bank would write a cheque on itself, redeemable by a bank either as a deposit at the Bank or as cash. In either case, the monetary base would rise by $100 million. This open-market purchase would lower interest rates and raise the money supply. Because of the money multiplier, an increase in the monetary base translates into a larger increase in the money supply.

Similarly, to reduce the money supply, the Bank may make an open-market sale. The Bank could sell $100 million of government securities to the public, receiving cheques drawn on banks in exchange. The Bank's assets would fall by $100 million (it owns $100 million less in securities). The Bank would use the $100 million in cheques it receives to eliminate $100 million in deposits of banks so that the monetary base would fall by $100 million. This would tend to raise interest rates and lower the money supply.

Although the Bank of Canada most often implements policy by influencing the overnight rate, it sometimes also uses open-market operations to affect interest rates and the money supply. For example, the Bank might wish to target the value of the overnight interest rate within its operating band. It can do this using transactions called **Special Purchase and Resale Agreements** (SPRAs, sometimes called repos) and **Sale and Repurchase Agreements** (SRAs). In an SPRA transaction, the Bank of Canada buys short-term government securities from banks and investment dealers and then sells them back on the next day. When the Bank buys these securities, it pays for them by adding to the seller's settlement balance. As we have seen, this increase in settlement balances will tend to put downward pressure on the overnight interest rate. SRAs have the opposite effect.

The Bank may also use 91-day (three-month) Treasury bills in its open-market operations, though it has not done so since the mid-1990s. In this way, it could try to influence somewhat longer-term (three-month) interest rates directly, rather than through overnight rates. For example, if the Bank wishes to reduce interest rates it could buy Treasury bills and reinforce the effect of a change in the Bank rate. Open-market operations of this kind are widely used internationally.

THE EXCHANGE FUND ACCOUNT

The asset side of the Bank of Canada's balance sheet (see Table 14.2) includes its foreign currency holdings. The Bank also manages the federal government's holdings of various currencies in the separate **exchange fund account**. These reserves can be used to intervene in the foreign exchange market. But as we saw in Chapter 10, monetary policy and exchange rate policy are really the same thing. To see this more concretely, suppose that US interest rates rise so that the Canadian dollar depreciates, as investors demand US dollars in order to buy high-yielding US bonds. The Bank may be concerned that the depreciation will be passed through into domestic inflation, and so, it may try to counteract the depreciation.

One way it can do this is by selling US dollars in exchange for Canadian dollars. This additional demand for Canadian dollars will tend to increase the value of the Canadian dollar. However, the Bank's sale of foreign exchange reserves reduces its assets, just as an open-market sale of government securities does. Thus, the money supply will fall, and interest rates rise. This is exactly what we showed in Chapter 10: A central bank that tries to target the exchange rate will have to devote domestic monetary policy to this task.

INTERMEDIATE TARGETS

In conducting monetary policy, the Bank of Canada has certain goals, or ultimate targets, such as price stability and stable economic growth. In trying to reach these goals, the Bank can use the monetary policy tools, or **instruments**, that we have discussed: its operating band for overnight rates and open-market operations. The problem the Bank faces is how to use the instruments that it controls directly in order to achieve its desired goals. Because there are several steps between the overnight rate and the ultimate behaviour of prices and economic activity—and because these steps often cannot be predicted accurately—the Bank has sometimes used intermediate targets to guide monetary policy. **Intermediate targets**, also sometimes called indicators, are macroeconomic variables that the Bank cannot control directly but can influence fairly predictably and that, in turn, are related to the goals the Bank is trying to achieve.

The most important and frequently used intermediate targets are the exchange rate and monetary aggregates, such as M1 and M2. By influencing short-term interest rates, the Bank can influence other interest rates in the economy. In turn, these rates affect the exchange rate, with increases in domestic rates tending to cause appreciation of the Canadian dollar. From 1962 to 1970, Canada had a fixed exchange rate, which can be thought of as an intermediate target. Peter Howitt has suggested that the Bank also operated with the exchange rate as an informal intermediate target in the mid-1980s.[10]

As we have seen, the Bank also can influence the monetary aggregates. From 1975 to 1982, the Bank followed publicly announced intermediate targets for the growth rate of M1. More recently, the Bank has directly targeted the inflation rate since 1991, rather than use an intermediate target (the Application, "Money-Growth Targeting and Inflation Targeting," on p. 550, discusses the historical experience with both types of targets). Sometimes, the general level of nominal interest rates (or the Treasury bill rate, for example) is suggested as an intermediate target. For example, the Bank might try to smooth variations in interest rates over time. Like the exchange rate and monetary aggregates, short-term nominal interest rates influence the state of the macroeconomy, without directly determining economic welfare. All three variables qualify as intermediate targets because they are affected in a predictable way by the Bank's policies, and because they, in turn, affect the economy.

In Chapter 10, we showed that the Bank cannot simultaneously target the exchange rate and the money supply. The same lesson applies to interest rates. For example, suppose that the Bank were trying to target both the money supply and the Treasury bill rate and that the pre-established targets called for an increase in both variables. How could the Bank meet these targets simultaneously? If it lowered its operating band in order to raise the money supply, it would lower, rather than raise, the overnight rate and, hence, the Treasury bill rate. Alternatively, if the Bank raised its operating band for the overnight rate in order to raise interest rates, the money supply would fall, instead of rising, as required. Thus, in general, the Bank cannot simultaneously meet targets for both interest rates and the money supply, unless those targets are set to be consistent with each other.

Why would the Bank of Canada ever want to target interest rates? Figure 14.3 shows a situation in which this strategy is useful. When the LM curve is LM^1, the economy is at full-employment equilibrium at point E, with output at $\overline{Y}$ and a real

---

10. See Peter Howitt, *Monetary Policy in Transition: A Study of Bank of Canada Policy*, 1982–1985, Toronto: C. D. Howe Institute, 1986.

FIGURE 14.3

INTEREST RATE TARGETING

The figure shows an economy that is buffeted by nominal shocks. Changes in money demand cause the *LM* curve to shift between LM^2 and LM^3 and aggregate demand to move erratically between Y_2 and Y_3. A Bank policy of keeping the real interest rate at r_1, by making open-market purchases whenever the interest rate exceeds r_1 and by making open-market sales whenever the interest rate falls below r_1, will keep the economy at full employment at *E*.

FIGURE 14.3

INTEREST RATE TARGETING

The figure shows an economy that is buffeted by nominal shocks. Changes in money demand cause the *LM* curve to shift between LM^2 and LM^3 and aggregate demand to move erratically between Y_2 and Y_3. A Bank policy of keeping the real interest rate at r_1, by making open-market purchases whenever the interest rate exceeds r_1 and by making open-market sales whenever the interest rate falls below r_1, will keep the economy at full employment at *E*.

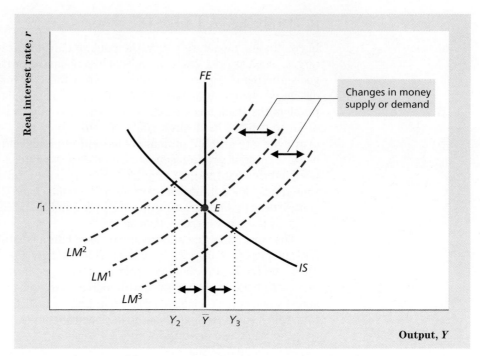

interest rate of r_1. Suppose that most of the shocks hitting the economy are nominal shocks, including shocks to money demand due to financial innovations (as discussed in Chapter 7). Without intervention by the Bank, these nominal shocks cause the *LM* curve to shift between LM^2 and LM^3, leading aggregate demand to shift erratically between Y_2 and Y_3. In either the extended classical model or the Keynesian model, random shifts in aggregate demand cause undesirable cyclical fluctuations in the economy.

The Bank could reduce the instability caused by nominal shocks by using monetary policy to hold the real interest rate at r_1. The Bank actually influences nominal interest rates, but over a short period of time in which expected inflation is constant, targeting nominal interest rates and targeting real interest rates are the same. Whenever the *LM* curve shifted up to LM^2, the Bank could use its tools to increase the money supply to restore the *LM* curve to LM^1; similarly, shifts of the *LM* curve to LM^3 could be offset by reductions in the money supply to return the *LM* curve to LM^1. In this case, stabilizing the intermediate target, the interest rate, also would stabilize output at its full-employment level. For interest rate targeting to be a good strategy, however, nominal shocks must be the main source of instability.[11] As discussed in Analytical Problem 2 at the end of the chapter, if other types of shocks to the economy are more important than nominal shocks, the use of monetary policy to stabilize the interest rate could instead destabilize output.

MAKING MONETARY POLICY IN PRACTICE

The *IS–LM* or *AD–AS* analysis of monetary policy suggests that using monetary policy to affect output and prices is a relatively simple matter. All that the Bank of

---

11. The argument for smoothing interest rates because of shifts in the *LM* curve was made by the Bank in the 1970s. See William White, "Alternative Monetary Targets and Control Instruments in Canada: Criteria for Choice," *Canadian Journal of Economics*, November 1979, pp. 590–604.

Canada needs to do is change the money supply enough to shift the *LM* curve or the *AD* curve to the desired point. In reality, however, making monetary policy is a complex, ongoing process. Two important practical issues that policymakers have to deal with are the lags in the effects of monetary policy on the economy and uncertainty about the channels through which monetary policy works.

LAGS IN THE EFFECTS OF MONETARY POLICY

If changes in the money supply led to immediate changes in output or prices, then using monetary policy to stabilize the economy would be relatively easy. The central bank would simply have to adjust its policy instruments until the economy attained full employment with stable prices. Unfortunately, most empirical evidence suggests that changes in monetary policy take a fairly long time to affect the economy.

Recent research on Canadian monetary policy by David Cushman, of the University of Saskatchewan, and Tao Zha, of the Federal Reserve Bank of Atlanta, suggests the following pattern of lags.[12] First, nominal interest rates and the nominal exchange rate react quickly to a change in monetary policy. Both rise promptly after a tightening of monetary policy, for example. The impact on the exchange rate is greater than on interest rates, though, and the nominal appreciation lasts about twelve months.

In contrast, output and (especially) the price level take much longer to respond to the change in monetary policy. Real GDP barely responds to tighter monetary policy within the first several months, and the full, negative effect is not felt until about six months after the change in policy. Prices respond even more slowly than output, and the negative effect of a monetary contraction on the price level is very gradual.

The long lags in the operation of monetary policy make it very difficult to use this policy instrument with precision.[13] Because of these long lags, the Bank of Canada cannot base its decisions on current levels of output and inflation alone. Instead, it must try to forecast what the economy will be doing six months to two years in the future—and make policy based on those forecasts. Because economic forecasts often are inaccurate, monetary policymaking has sometimes been likened to trying to steer a ship in dense fog.

An illustration of the problems raised by the delayed effects of monetary policy is the recent debate about how aggressive the Bank of Canada should be in its anti-inflationary policies. In 1998, the Bank engaged several times in *pre-emptive strikes* on inflation, raising the Bank rate (that is, tightening monetary policy), even though the current inflation rate was low. Critics of the Bank asked why tightening monetary policy was necessary when inflation was not currently a problem. The response of the Bank of Canada was that it was not responding to current inflation but, rather, to forecasts of inflation a year or more into the future. The Bank was correct in asserting that because of lags in the effects of monetary policy, it is necessary to try to anticipate future inflation, rather than reacting only to current inflation. But because of the difficulties in forecasting inflation, there was plenty of room for debate about how tight monetary policy needed to be in order to prevent future inflation.

---

12. "Identifying Monetary Policy in a Small Open Economy under Flexible Exchange Rates," *Journal of Monetary Economics*, August 1997, pp. 433–448. See also Ben Fung and Rohit Gupta, "Cash Setting, the Call Loan Rate, and the Liquidity Effect in Canada," *Canadian Journal of Economics*, November 1997, pp. 1057–1082.
13. Indeed, as we discuss shortly, a group of economists called monetarists argue that these long lags make monetary policy next to worthless as a tool for stabilizing the economy.

THE CHANNELS OF MONETARY POLICY TRANSMISSION

Another practical difficulty faced by monetary policymakers is determining exactly how monetary policy affects the economy. So far, we have determined two primary ways in which monetary policy affects economic activity and prices. First, according to the Keynesian *IS–LM* analysis (see Chapter 12), a reduction in the money supply raises *real interest rates*, which, in turn, reduces aggregate demand (spending by consumers and firms). Declining aggregate demand leads to falling output and prices, relative to trends. The effects of monetary policy on the economy that work through changes in real interest rates are called the **interest rate channel** of monetary policy.

Second, in open economies, a tightening of monetary policy raises the real exchange rate (see Chapter 10). A higher real exchange rate, by making domestic goods more expensive for foreigners and foreign goods cheaper for domestic residents, reduces the demand for the home country's net exports. All else being equal, this reduced demand for net exports also reduces aggregate demand, depressing output and prices.[14] The effects of monetary policy working through changes in the real exchange rate are called the **exchange rate channel**.

According to some economists, a tightening of monetary policy also works by reducing both the supply and demand for credit, a mechanism referred to as the **credit channel** of monetary policy.[15] On the supply side of the credit market, according to this theory, tight monetary policy leads to reduced lending by banks. The reason is that, as we showed earlier in this chapter, a tightening of monetary policy reduces bank reserves and, thus, the quantity of customer deposits that banks can accept. With fewer deposits on hand, banks have a smaller quantity of funds available to lend, so some consumers and firms are unable to obtain credit. On the demand side of the credit market, tight monetary policy has the effect of making potential borrowers less "creditworthy" or less eligible for loans. The reason is that high interest rates add to a borrowing firm's interest costs and lower its profitability, making it harder for the firm to obtain loans.

Controversy swirls about the relative importance of these different channels of monetary policy. That, in turn, increases the difficulty that policymakers have in judging the stance of monetary policy at any particular time. For example, suppose that the Bank of Canada observes that real interest rates are currently high but that the dollar has been falling. Is monetary policy tight or not? It is hard to say, unless we know the relative strengths of the interest rate channel and the exchange rate channel.

14.3 THE CONDUCT OF MONETARY POLICY: RULES VERSUS DISCRETION

How should monetary policy be used? On some aspects of this question, there is broad agreement. Most classicals and Keynesians agree that money is neutral in the long run so that changes in money growth affect inflation but not real variables in the long run. Therefore, most would accept that the main long-run goal of monetary policy should be to maintain a low and stable inflation rate. However, there is much

---

14. As discussed in Chapter 10, actual net exports need not decline following a tightening of monetary policy because the effect of falling domestic income on import demand may outweigh the real exchange rate effects. However, the higher real exchange rate taken by itself reduces net exports.
15. For a survey of the theory and evidence for the credit channel, see Ben Bernanke and Mark Gertler, "Inside the Black Box: The Credit Channel of Monetary Policy Transmission," *Journal of Economic Perspectives*, Fall 1995, pp. 27–48.

less agreement about the effects of monetary policy and its appropriate use in the short run (Chapters 11 and 12). Most Keynesians believe that monetary policy can and should be used to smooth the business cycle, but most classicals do not. In this section, we revisit the debate about the appropriate use of monetary policy by addressing a long-standing question in macroeconomics: Should monetary policy be conducted according to fixed rules or at the discretion of the central bank?

The use of rules in monetary policy has been advocated primarily by a group of economists called monetarists and by classical macroeconomists. Supporters of **rules** believe that monetary policy should be essentially automatic. In particular, in monetary policy, the central bank should be required to follow a set of simple, prespecified, and publicly announced rules. Many such rules can be imagined. For example, the Bank of Canada might be instructed to increase the monetary base by 1% each quarter. An alternative rule, which has been used historically, is to require the central bank to conduct monetary policy to keep the price of gold at a predetermined level (this rule was the essence of the gold standard). One might also imagine a rule that permits the Bank of Canada to respond to the state of the economy; see Box 14.1 for a discussion of such a rule.

Although the exact form of the rule chosen is not crucial, supporters of the rules-based approach emphasize that the monetary rule should be simple; there cannot be dozens of exceptions and conditions. Furthermore, the rule should be stated in terms of variables that the Bank can control directly or nearly directly. Because a central bank can control the monetary base fairly precisely, a prespecified growth rate for the monetary base is acceptable as a rule. But as the Bank's control over, say, the national unemployment rate is indirect and imperfect, an instruction to the Bank to "keep the unemployment rate at 4%" is not acceptable to advocates of a rules-guided monetary policy.

The opposite of the rules approach, which has been supported by most (though not all) Keynesian economists, is called **discretion**. The idea behind discretion is that the central bank should be free to conduct monetary policy in any way that it believes will advance the ultimate objectives of low and stable inflation, high economic growth, and low unemployment. In particular, the central bank should continuously monitor the economy and, using the advice of economic experts, should change the money supply as needed to best achieve its goals. Because a strategy of discretion involves active responses by the central bank to changes in economic circumstances, such a strategy sometimes is called *activist*.

From this description of rules and discretion, you may have trouble understanding why many economists advocate the use of rules. After all, why should anyone arbitrarily and unnecessarily tie the hands of the central bank? The idea that giving the central bank the option of responding to changing economic conditions is always better than putting monetary policy in a straitjacket dictated by rules is the essence of the Keynesian case for discretion.

This basic argument for discretion is sound, but a strong case also may be made for rules. Next, we discuss the traditional monetarist argument for rules. We then consider a relatively new argument for rules: that the use of rules increases the credibility of the central bank.

THE MONETARIST CASE FOR RULES

Monetarism emphasizes the importance of monetary factors in the macroeconomy. Although monetarists have included numerous outstanding economists, the dominant

Box 14.1 THE TAYLOR RULE

Advocates of the use of rules in monetary policy believe that central banks should be required to follow a set of simple, prespecified, and publicly announced rules when setting monetary policy instruments. Nothing in the concept of rules, however, necessarily prohibits a central bank from responding to the state of the economy, as long as these responses are built into the rule itself. An example of a monetary policy rules that allows a central bank to take economic conditions into account is the so-called **Taylor rule**, introduced by John Taylor,* currently the US Undersecretary of the Treasury for International Affairs.

The Taylor rule is given by:

$$i = \pi + 0.02 + 0.5\,y + 0.5(\pi - 0.02),$$

where

> i = the nominal overnight interest rate (the Bank of Canada's policy instrument)
> π = the rate of inflation over the previous four quarters
> $y = (Y - \overline{Y})/\overline{Y}$ = the percentage deviation of output from full-employment output

The Taylor rule requires that the *real* overnight rate, $i - \pi$, responds to (1) the difference between output and full-employment output, and (2) the difference between inflation and target, here taken to be 2% or 0.02. An inflation rate of 2% is the mid-point of the Bank of Canada's target range for the rate of CPI inflation.

If the economy is "overheating," with output growing more rapidly than full-employment output and inflation rising, the Taylor rule would have the Bank of Canada tighten monetary policy by raising the real overnight interest rate. Conversely, if the economy is weakening, with output and inflation declining, the Taylor rule indicates that the real overnight rate be reduced, thereby easing monetary policy. Both responses are consistent with the standard practices of central banks. For example, Taylor showed that historically, his relatively simple rule describes actual behaviour of the US Federal Reserve quite accurately.

Unlike some advocates of rules, Taylor has not argued that central banks follow his rule slavishly and mechanically. Rather, he would have his rule serve as a guideline for monetary policy. Deviations from the rule would be permitted when, in the judgement of the policymakers, special circumstances prevailed. Nevertheless, for the idea of a policy rule to have meaning, a central bank would have to commit to following the rule (or staying very close to it) the great majority of the time.

*"Discretion versus Policy Rules in Practice," *Carnegie-Rochester Conference Series on Public Policy*, 1993, pp. 195–214.

figure and leader of the group is Milton Friedman. For many years, Friedman has argued that monetary policy should be conducted by rules, and this idea has become an important part of monetarist doctrine.[16]

The monetarist argument for rules may be broken down into a series of propositions.

> Proposition 1. *Monetary policy has powerful short-run effects on the real economy. In the longer run, however, changes in the money supply have their primary effect on the price level.*

Friedman's research on US monetary history (with Anna Schwartz) provided some of the earliest and best evidence that changes in the money supply can be non-neutral in the short run (Chapter 11). Friedman and other monetarists believe that fluctuations in the money supply historically have been one of the most

---

16. Friedman's 1959 book, *A Program for Monetary Stability* (New York: Fordham University Press) presents a clear early statement of his views. For an outline of monetarism, see Douglas D. Purvis, "Monetarism: A Review," *Canadian Journal of Economics*, February 1980, pp. 96–122.

THE POLITICAL ENVIRONMENT

HOW SHALL WE GOVERN THE GOVERNOR?

Peter Howitt has argued that the governors of the Bank of Canada, though influenced by their staff, the financial community, and public opinion, have played key roles in Canadian monetary policy. During its history, the Bank has had seven governors: Graham Towers (1935–1954); James Coyne (1955–1961); Louis Rasminsky (1961–1973); Gerald Bouey (1973–1987); John Crow (1987–1994); Gordon Thiessen (1994–2001); and David Dodge (2001–). If the pattern of monetary policy has noticeably reflected the views of individual governors, then the rules governing the governor are particularly important.

Most of these rules are in the Bank of Canada Act, which dates from the Bank's establishment in the 1930s. However, the Act was revised in the 1960s after a conflict between Governor Coyne and the Diefenbaker government led to Mr. Coyne's resignation.* The revision spelled out how the government could issue a public directive to the Bank to change its policy. By a convention made clear by Governor Rasminsky, the governor would resign if he or she could not carry out such a directive in good conscience. Perhaps partly because of the consequences of a resignation, no directive has ever been issued.

In the early 1980s, the Bank faced harsh criticism when nominal interest rates rose to 20%. In the mid-1980s, some provincial premiers accused the Bank of following a restrictive, high-interest-rate policy when growth was stronger in Ontario and Quebec than in some other provinces. Most recently, the disinflation of the early 1990s brought much debate about the Bank's goals.

David Laidler, of the University of Western Ontario, has argued that the Bank of Canada is working well but that it is perceived to be working badly.[†] He made two suggestions for amendments to the Bank of Canada Act to correct this problem.

First, he proposed that the Bank's mandate focus on price stability as a goal. At present, the Act also mentions exchange rate stability and stabilization of business cycles as goals of the Bank. Laidler argued that these additional goals bring unnecessary criticism on the Bank, when it cannot achieve all of them. As we have seen, scepticism about using monetary policy to limit business cycles is a key element in monetarism, and writing the price-stability goal into the Act might enhance the Bank's credibility. Since the Bank began targetting inflation in 1991, the inflation targets have been jointly announced by the Bank and the Department of Finance, a format which may serve this purpose.

Laidler's second suggestion was to give more power to the Board of Directors of the Bank and to give provincial governments a role in their appointment. He suggested that directors be appointed on a full-time basis, for long terms, from lists submitted by provincial governments. This might add to the political legitimacy of the Bank's actions and remove the focus on a single individual, the governor, in discussions of monetary policy. At the same time, the Bank's independence from day-to-day government control would be maintained. Although Laidler's suggestion has not been acted on, since 1994, the decisions of the Bank have been attributed to a six-member Governing Council comprising the governor and deputy governors. This change may reduce the personal identification of the governor with monetary policy.

Criticism of the Bank during the disinflation of 1990–1991 led to some suggestions for change being included in the federal government's constitutional proposals in September 1991. The suggestions included focusing the Bank's mandate on price stability and making the appointment of a governor subject to the approval of a newly elected federal senate. While nothing came of these proposals, the governance of the Bank may again become controversial if Quebec sovereignty is established. Most economists seem to agree that a sovereign Quebec and the Rest of Canada (ROC) would continue to form a monetary union, with Quebec having representation on the board and a share in the profits of the central bank.[‡] Negotiating the details of these new arrangements would probably be difficult, though.

---

*For a spirited Keynesian critique of the Bank at that time see H. Scott Gordon, *The Economists versus the Bank of Canada*, Toronto: Ryerson Press, 1961.

[†]David E. W. Laidler, *How Shall We Govern the Governor?: A Critique of the Governance of the Bank of Canada*, Toronto: C. D. Howe Institute, 1991.

[‡]See David E. W. Laidler and William B. P. Robson, *Two Nations, One Money? Canada's Monetary System Following a Quebec Secession*, Toronto: C. D. Howe Institute, 1991.

significant—if not the most significant—sources of business cycle fluctuations. On long-run neutrality, Friedman (along with Edmund Phelps) was one of the first to argue that because prices eventually adjust to changes in the money supply, the effect of money on real variables can only be temporary (Chapter 13).

> Proposition 2. *Despite the powerful short-run effect of money on the economy, there is little scope for using monetary policy actively to try to smooth business cycles.*

Monetarists back this proposition with several ideas (several of which we discussed in connection with macroeconomic policy more generally in earlier chapters). First, time is needed for the central bank and other agencies to gather and process information about the current state of the economy. These information lags may make it difficult for the central bank to determine whether the economy actually is in a recession and whether a change in policy is appropriate.

Second, there is considerable uncertainty about how much effect a given change in interest rates or the money supply will have on the economy and how long the effect will take to occur. Monetarists argue that there are *long and variable lags* between monetary policy actions and their economic results. From empirical research monetarists claim that on average, monetary changes take about a year to have a significant impact on the economy (that is, the lag is long). Furthermore, the time required for policy to have an effect is unpredictable and may vary from as little as six months to as much as 18 months (the lag is variable).

Third, wage and price adjustment, although not instantaneous, is so fast that by the time the central bank recognizes that the economy is in a recession and increases the money supply, the economy may already be heading out of the recession. If the expansion in the money supply stimulates the economy with a lag of about a year, the stimulus may take effect when output has already recovered and the economy is in a boom. In this case, the monetary expansion will cause the economy to overshoot full employment and cause prices to rise. Thus, the monetary increase, intended to fight the recession, may actually be destabilizing (causing more variability of output than there would have been otherwise), as well as inflationary.

> Proposition 3. *Even if there is some scope for using monetary policy to smooth business cycles, the central bank cannot be relied on to do so effectively.*

One reason that monetarists do not trust central banks to manage an activist monetary policy effectively is political. For example, the central bank might be pressured to stimulate the economy during an election year. If timed reasonably well, an election-year monetary expansion could expand output and employment just before voters go to the polls, with the inflationary effects of the policy not being felt until after the incumbents were safely re-elected (see the box, "The Political Environment: Macroeconomic Performance and Opinion Polls," Chapter 13, p. 498).

More fundamentally, though, monetarists' scepticism about discretion arises from their interpretation of macroeconomic history. From his work with Anna Schwartz, Friedman concluded that for whatever reason—incompetence, shortsightedness, or bad luck—monetary policy historically has been a greater source of economic instability than stability. The primary example cited by Friedman was the 1929–1933 period in the United States, when the Federal Reserve System (the central bank in the United States, also known as the Fed) was unable or unwilling to stop the money supply from falling by one-third in the wake of widespread runs on US banks. Friedman and Schwartz argued that this monetary contraction was one of the main causes of the Great Depression. Thus, Friedman concluded that eliminating monetary policy as a source of instability would substantially improve macroeconomic performance.

How could the central bank be removed as a source of instability? This question leads to Friedman's policy recommendation, the last proposition:

> Proposition 4. *The central bank should choose a specific monetary aggregate (such as M1 or M2) and commit itself to making that aggregate grow at a fixed percentage rate, year in and year out.*

For monetarists, the crucial step in eliminating the central bank as a source of instability is to get it to give up activist, or discretionary, monetary policy and to commit itself—publicly and in advance—to following some rule. Although the exact choice of a rule is not critical, monetarists believe that a constant-money-growth rule would be a good choice for two reasons. First, the central bank has considerable influence, though not complete control, over the rate of money growth. Thus, if money growth deviated significantly from its target, the central bank could not easily blame the deviation on forces beyond its control. Second, monetarists argue that steady money growth would lead to smaller cyclical fluctuations than the supposedly "countercyclical" monetary policies utilized historically. They conclude that a constant-money-growth rate would provide a "stable monetary background" that would allow economic growth to proceed without concern about monetary instability.

Monetarists do not advocate a sudden shift from discretionary monetary policy to a low, constant rate of money growth. Instead, they envision a transition period in which the Bank of Canada, by gradual preannounced steps, would steadily reduce the growth rate of money. Ultimately, the growth rate of the monetary aggregate selected would be consistent with an inflation rate near zero. Importantly, after the constant growth rate has been attained, the Bank would not respond to modest economic downturns by changing money growth but would continue to follow the policy of maintaining a fixed rate of money growth. However, some monetarists appear to leave open the possibility that the monetary rule could be temporarily suspended in the face of major economic crises, such as a depression.

Canadian monetary policy has been assessed from a monetarist point of view in a series of studies sponsored by the C. D. Howe Institute.[17] These studies have made the case for rules (as in Propositions 2 and 3) and generally argued that the Bank should use M2 as an intermediate target (as in Proposition 4), rather than focusing on a narrower aggregate, interest rates, or the exchange rate.

RULES AND CENTRAL BANK CREDIBILITY

Much of the monetarist argument for rules rests on pessimism about the competence or political reliability of central banks. Economists who are more optimistic about the ability of the government to intervene effectively in the economy (which includes many Keynesians) question the monetarist case for rules. A "policy optimist" could argue as follows:

---

17. The studies include Peter Howitt, *Monetary Policy in Transition: A Study of Bank of Canada Policy, 1982–1985*, Toronto: C. D. Howe Institute, 1986; and David E. W. Laidler and William B. P. Robson, *The Great Canadian Disinflation: The Economics and Politics of Monetary Policy in Canada, 1988–1993*, Toronto: C. D. Howe Institute, 1993.

Monetary policy may have performed badly in the past. However, as time passes, we learn more about the economy and the use of policy gets better. For example, Canadian monetary policy clearly was handled better after World War II than during the Great Depression. Imposing rigid rules just as we are beginning to learn how to use activist policy properly would be foolish. As to the issue of political reliability, that problem affects fiscal policymakers and, indeed, all our branches of government. We just have to trust in the democratic process to ensure that policymakers will take actions that for the most part are in the best interests of the country.

For policy optimists, this reply to the monetarist case for rules seems perfectly satisfactory. During the past two decades, however, a new argument for rules has been developed that applies even if the central bank knows exactly how monetary changes affect the economy and is completely public-spirited. Thus, the new argument for rules is a challenge even to policy optimists. It holds that the use of monetary rules can improve the **credibility** of the central bank, or the degree to which the public believes central bank announcements about future policy, and that the credibility of the central bank influences how well monetary policy works.

DAD, THE KIDS, AND THE GAME: CREDIBLE THREATS AND COMMITMENT

To help explain what credibility is, why it may be enhanced by rules, and why it may be important to monetary policy, let us look at a simple example drawn from family life. Knowing that Mom will be going to a business meeting, Dad has bought tickets to a basketball game for himself and the two kids, Junior and Sis. Dad likes basketball, as do the kids. Unfortunately, the kids also like to fight with each other. Dad has warned the kids: "Don't fight. If you do, we just won't go to the basketball game." Dad cannot go to the basketball game without both kids because Mom will not be home to babysit, and on such short notice, he will not be able to find a sitter. We are interested in the following questions about the behaviour of Dad and the kids: (1) Will the kids fight? (2) Will Dad take the kids to the basketball game?

Before we analyze this situation, let us discuss it informally. The kids know that because Dad wants to go to the game himself, he will be reluctant to impose the punishment he has threatened. That is, Dad's threat is not credible (believable) to the kids. Therefore, the kids will fight anyway, assuming that when push comes to shove, Dad will not be able to bring himself to waste the tickets and they will go to the game.

Figure 14.4, on the next page, illustrates this situation. The two columns of the diagram correspond to the two possible actions that the kids can take: *fight* and *don't fight*. The two rows correspond to the two actions that Dad can take: *go to game* and *don't go to game*. Each of the four squares in the diagram, thus, refers to a possible outcome: Square A corresponds to the outcome *kids fight and Dad takes kids to game*; square B refers *to kids don't fight and Dad takes kids to game*; and so on.

Dad and the kids each have preferences about the four possible outcomes. Let us measure preferences in terms of points: The more points someone assigns to an outcome, the more he or she likes it. Dad likes basketball, so let us assume that he assigns 2 points to going to the game. Also, he assigns 1 point to having the kids not fight. The total number of points Dad assigns to each outcome is shown in each square. Dad's preferred outcome (worth 3 points) is B, in which the kids do not fight and they all go to the game. Dad's worst outcome is C, in which the kids fight and no one goes to the game, an outcome that gets 0 points from Dad.

The kids also like basketball, and they also assign 2 points to going to the game. However, they also like to fight, and they assign 1 point to fighting. The kids' point

FIGURE 14.4

THE GAME BETWEEN DAD AND THE KIDS

Each square represents a combination of an action by the kids and an action by Dad. The points assigned to each combination of actions (shown in each square) measure how much each set of players likes each outcome. The kids "move" first by picking a column; then Dad "moves" by picking a row. The equilibrium is outcome A, in which the kids fight and still get to go to the game.

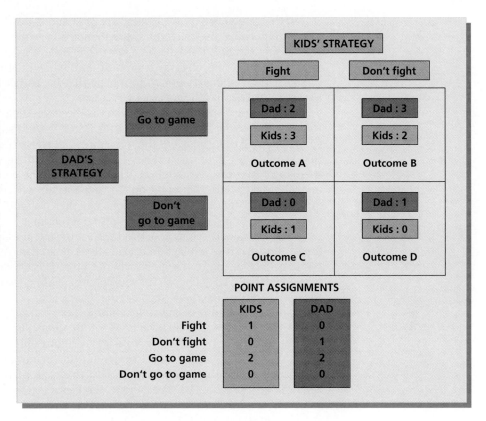

totals for each outcome are also shown in each box. The kids' favourite outcome, worth 3 points, is A (they fight and still get to go to the game). Their least favourite outcome, worth 0 points, is D (no fight and no game).

The sequence of actions is as follows: First, the kids decide whether to fight (after hearing the warning), and then Dad decides whether to take the kids to the game. In Figure 14.4 the kids get to pick the column (*fight* or *don't fight*). After the kids pick the column, Dad gets to pick whether they will be in the top square (*go to game*) or the bottom square (*don't go to game*). We assume that at each stage, both the kids and Dad make the choices that attain their preferred outcome.

The kids reason as follows:

> Suppose we pick *fight* (the left column). That leaves Dad with the choice of A (*go to game*) or C (*don't go to game*). Outcome A is worth 2 points to Dad; C is worth 0 points. So, Dad will pick A over C and, if we fight, we still get to go to the game. If we *pick don't fight* (the right column), Dad will pick B over D, so we also go to the game in that case. But because we like to fight, and we get to go to the game in either case, we might as well fight.

In terms of Figure 14.4, the kids know that once they factor in their Dad's response, they effectively have a choice between A and B. They prefer A to B, so they pick the left column (that is, they fight).

This type of diagram is a standard tool from a branch of mathematics, much used in economics, called game theory. **Game theory** explores situations (games) in which strategy is used by individuals (players) to achieve their goals, possibly at the expense of the other players. An equilibrium of a game is an outcome that occurs if all players do the best they can for themselves.

In the game here, the "players" are Dad and the kids. The equilibrium of the game is outcome A, in which the kids fight and still go to the game. Outcome A is the equilibrium because the kids recognize that Dad's threat is not credible; he has a strong incentive to back away from his threat when the time comes to carry it out. Indeed, if Dad is smart enough to realize that his threat has no force, he will not bother to make it in the first place.

Is there some way for Dad to make his threat credible and thereby get the kids to behave? Yes; the key to credibility for Dad is to find some way by which he can commit himself to carrying out the threat. In other words, Dad must convince the kids that should they fight, he will have *no choice* but to keep everybody home from the game. Suppose, for example, that Dad gives the game tickets to Mom, with instructions to hide them and not to reveal their whereabouts if the kids fight. Suppose that Mom is indifferent about whether Dad and the kids go to the game and can be counted on to carry out these instructions.

How does Mom's hiding the tickets affect the equilibrium of the game? Formally, the effect is to cross out square A (kids fight, go to game) as a possible outcome. If the kids fight, going to the game will not be a possible choice for Dad. Thus, the kids know that if they choose the left column (*fight*), Dad will be forced to choose square C (*don't go to game*), an outcome that yields 1 point for the kids. On the other hand, if the kids choose the right column (*don't fight*), Dad's preferred choice between his options B and D will be B (*go to game*). Because the kids prefer B (2 points) to C (1 point), they will pick the right column and not fight. The key conclusion of this analysis is that by committing in advance to carry out his threat, Dad has made his threat credible. If the kids act in their own best interests, Dad achieves the outcome (B) that he likes the best.

A GAME BETWEEN THE CENTRAL BANK AND FIRMS

We can use game theory to think about the credibility of the central bank. Consider a situation in which the macroeconomy is in general equilibrium so that the *IS* and *LM* curves cross at the *FE* line (point *E* in Figure 14.5(a)). Initially, suppose that both the money supply and the price level are growing steadily at 10% per year. As *M* and *P* are growing at the same rate, the real money supply *M/P* is constant, and the *LM* curve, LM^1, remains fixed and passes through *E*. Thus, the economy is initially at full employment with the unemployment rate at the natural rate, say, 6%, and the inflation equal to 10% per year.

The central bank (the Bank of Canada, let us say) wants to reduce the inflation rate to zero without increasing the unemployment rate. Suppose that the Bank makes the following announcement to all the firms in the economy:

> There is no reason why we should be suffering from this 10% inflation. Let us make a deal. If you businesses hold prices *P* constant this period, rather than raising them by 10%, we will hold the money supply *M* constant. With *M* and *P* both constant, the real money supply *M/P* will not change and the *LM* curve will not shift. Thus, the economy will remain at full employment, with an unemployment rate of 6%, but we will all be better off with no inflation. However, if you insist on raising prices, we will still keep the money supply constant. In this case, the real money supply *M/P* will fall by 10%, the *LM* curve will shift up and to the left to LM^2, and we will all suffer from both high unemployment and continued inflation (point *F*).

How will the firms respond to this statement by the Bank? As we show, the Bank's threat to reduce the real money supply if firms raise prices is not credible because the Bank does not want a recession. As a result, the firms will go ahead and raise prices.

FIGURE 14.5

THE GAME BETWEEN THE
BANK AND THE FIRMS

(a) This part of the figure shows the possible outcomes of the game between the Bank and the firms. Initially, the economy is at point E (full employment) with 10% inflation. The real money supply M/P depends both on the price level P chosen by firms and the money supply M chosen by the Bank. If the real money supply does not change, the economy remains at full employment at E. If the real money supply falls, the LM curve shifts from LM^1 to LM^2, and the economy goes into a recession with 9% unemployment at point F. If the real money supply increases, the LM curve shifts from LM^1 to LM^3, and the economy goes into a boom with 3% unemployment at point H.

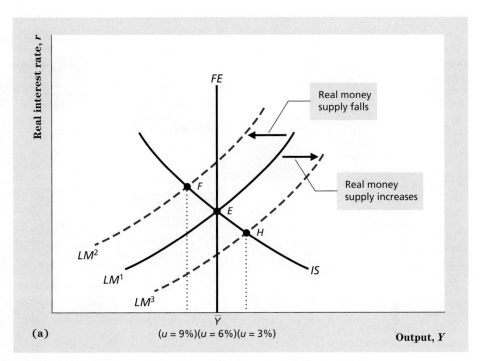

The game between the Bank and the firms is analyzed formally in Figure 14.5(b). The firms' choices, *raise P* (by 10%) and *don't raise P*, correspond to the two columns of the diagram. The Bank's two choices, *raise M* (by 10%) and *don't raise M* correspond to the two rows. Square A represents the outcome *firms raise P and Bank raises M*; square B represents the outcome *firms don't raise P and Bank raises M*; and so on.

What happens to the economy in each case? Determining what happens to inflation is easy: In squares A and C, firms raise prices by 10%, so inflation π is 10%; in squares B and D firms do not raise prices, so $\pi = 0$.

What about unemployment? In square A, both money and prices rise by 10%, so M/P is unchanged and the economy remains at full employment (point E in Figure 14.5(a)). Similarly, in square D, neither M nor P changes, so M/P is unchanged and the economy remains at full employment. Thus, in squares A and D, the unemployment rate u remains at the natural rate of 6%. In square C, P rises, but M does not. Thus, M/P falls, the LM curve shifts up and to the left to LM^2, and the economy goes into recession at point F in Figure 14.5(a), with the unemployment rate increasing to 9%. Finally, in square B, M rises, but P does not, so M/P rises, and the LM curve shifts down and to the right to LM^3. In this case, the economy goes into a boom (point H in Figure 14.5(a)), and the unemployment rate falls to 3%.

The next step is to determine the points that each player assigns to each outcome. Let us start with the Bank, which does not like inflation. It assigns 1 point to zero inflation (B and D) and no points to a positive rate of inflation (A and C). However, the Bank also does not like unemployment. It assigns 0 points to the natural unemployment rate (A and D), 1 point to unemployment below the natural rate (B), and –1 point to unemployment above the natural rate (C). The total point scores for the Bank are shown in each square. The Bank's preferred outcome is B, with no inflation and 3% unemployment; its least favourite outcome is C, with 10% inflation and 9% unemployment.

FIGURE 14.5

(b) This part of the figure shows the possible moves in the game between the Bank and the firms. The firms move first by deciding whether to raise the price level P, choosing the column. Then, the Bank moves by deciding whether to increase the money supply M, choosing the row. If M and P both rise (outcome A) or both stay the same (outcome D), the real money supply is unchanged, and the economy remains at full employment at point E in (a). In outcome B, M increases and P remains the same; thus, the real money supply rises and unemployment falls as at point H in (a). In outcome C, M remains the same and P increases, so the real money supply falls and unemployment increases as at point F in (a). Point assignments show the preferences of the Bank and firms for each outcome. The equilibrium of the game is outcome A, in which the firms raise prices and the Bank increases the money supply.

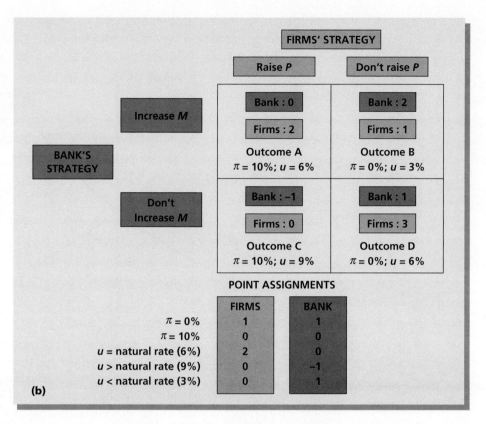

(b)

The firms' profits are maximized on the *FE* line, that is, when the economy is at full employment. Therefore, the firms assign 2 points to the natural unemployment rate (A and D). Firms prefer zero inflation to positive inflation, so they assign 1 point to zero inflation (B and D). Total scores for firms are also shown in each box.

Now, let us find the equilibrium, assuming that firms first decide whether to raise prices and then the Bank decides whether to increase the money supply. The firms reason as follows:

> Suppose that we raise prices. This action leaves the Bank the choice between outcomes A and C. The Bank does not want a recession, so it will choose A; that is, it will increase the money supply. If we do not raise prices, the Bank has a choice of B or D. The Bank prefers B to D because with no inflation, it prefers unemployment below the natural rate to unemployment at the natural rate. In this case, the Bank also will increase the money supply. Therefore, no matter what we do, the Bank will increase the money supply. The Bank's claim that it will maintain a constant money supply if we raise prices just is not credible. If we raise prices we get outcome A, and if we do not raise prices we get outcome B. We prefer A to B (we would rather be at full employment than off the *FE* line and above full employment), so we will raise prices.

The equilibrium of the game is, therefore, outcome A, in which the firms raise prices and the Bank (failing to carry through on its threat) raises the money supply. Because the Bank's threat is not credible, the firms ignore it. Note that *both the Bank and the firms prefer outcome D (full employment and no inflation) to the equilibrium outcome A.* Yet because the Bank's promise to hold the money supply constant is not credible, the economy does not attain outcome D.

In contrast, suppose that the Bank could credibly promise not to increase the money supply under any circumstances and that the firms believed this promise. The firms would reason: "If we raise prices, the Bank will pick outcome C (inflation and a recession). If we do not raise prices, the Bank will pick D (no inflation and no recession). We prefer D to C, so we will not raise prices."

The equilibrium in this case would be outcome D, which is preferred by everyone to the no-credibility outcome A. In outcome D, disinflation is achieved without increasing unemployment because the central bank is credible.

RULES, COMMITMENT, AND CREDIBILITY

The formal analysis shows why central bank credibility is important. If a central bank is credible, it can reduce money growth and inflation without incurring high unemployment. But how can a central bank achieve credibility?

One possibility is for the central bank to develop a reputation for carrying out its promises. Suppose that in the preceding example firms raise their prices, fully expecting the Bank to increase the money supply. However, the Bank holds the money supply constant, causing a recession. The next time, the firms may take the Bank's promises more seriously, and the economy may attain outcome D. Similarly, if Dad crosses up the kids and refuses to take them to the game after they fight, he will improve his reputation for carrying out his threats; the next time, the kids may take him seriously.

The problem with this strategy is that it may involve serious costs while the reputation is being established: The economy suffers a recession while the central bank establishes its reputation; Dad and the kids miss the game while Dad establishes his. Is there some less costly way to achieve credibility?

Advocates of rules suggest that by forcing the central bank to keep its promises, rules may substitute for reputation in establishing credibility. Suppose that there is an ironclad rule—ideally, enforced by some outside agency—that the Bank must gradually reduce the growth of the money supply. Observing the existence of this rule, the firms might well believe that money supply growth is going to decline no matter what, and painless disinflation (outcome D) can be achieved. Similarly, in the case with Dad and the kids, if there is an unbreakable family rule that fighting suspends all privileges—and Mom is there to help enforce it—Dad's threat not to go to the game might be more credible. Note that if it increases credibility, a rule improves central bank performance, even if the central bank is competent and public-spirited. Hence, this reason for monetary policy rules is different from the monetarists' argument presented earlier.

How do advocates of discretion respond to the credibility argument for rules? Keynesians argue that there may be a trade-off between credibility and flexibility. For a rule to establish credibility, it must be virtually impossible to change—otherwise, no one will believe that the Bank will stick to it. In the extreme, the monetary growth rule would be added as an amendment to the constitution, which could then be changed only at great cost and with long delays. But if a rule is completely unbreakable, what happens (ask the Keynesians) if some unexpected crisis arises—for example, a new depression? In that case, the inability of the Bank to take corrective action—that is, its lack of flexibility—could prove disastrous. Therefore, Keynesians argue, establishing a rule ironclad enough to create credibility for the central bank would, by eliminating policy flexibility, also create unacceptable risks.

Application

Money-Growth Targeting and Inflation Targeting

The decade of the 1970s, with its combination of high unemployment and high inflation, led many central banks around the world to wonder whether monetary policy could be handled more effectively. Since then, many have experimented with alternative monetary policy strategies in the hope of improving macroeconomic performance. In response to economists' arguments for the importance of credibility, many of these strategies have involved public announcements by central banks of their goals, accompanied by attempts to convince the public that monetary policymakers were committed to those goals. In this Application, we discuss the experience with two such strategies: money-growth targeting and inflation targeting.[18]

Money-growth targeting is the older of the two strategies. The Bundesbank (the central bank of Germany) introduced money-growth targets in 1975, following a run-up in inflation, and Germany adhered to this strategy until the formation of the European Monetary Union in 1999. Other countries that adopted some sort of money-growth targeting during the 1970s included the United States, Canada, the United Kingdom, and Switzerland.

When using a strategy of *money-growth targeting*, the central bank announces in advance the rate of growth of money that it will try to achieve over the next year (or perhaps longer). In principle, the target growth rate of money is set so as to be consistent with the central bank's desired levels of inflation and real output growth; hitting the targeted rate of growth of money is understood to be the central bank's most important objective. Initially, Germany targeted the growth of a broad money aggregate called central bank money (CBM), a weighted sum of currency, chequing accounts, savings accounts, and time deposits. In most years, the Bundesbank came reasonably close to achieving its stated targets, although there were exceptions, as in 1978 when the Bundesbank overshot its money-growth targets as part of an international effort to strengthen the US dollar.

The United States also began to experiment with money-growth targeting in 1975, when the Fed announced target growth ranges for three different monetary aggregates: M1, M2, and M3. Because the Fed, like any central bank, has only one instrument at its disposal—the control of the monetary base—attempting to control the growth rate of three separate monetary aggregates at the same time was not realistic; indeed, the Fed was not able to accomplish this feat, often badly missing its announced targets. Monetarists have argued that in choosing three different monetary aggregates to target simultaneously, the Fed revealed that it was not very serious about adhering to a money-growth rule.

In Canada, the Bank of Canada announced explicit targets for the growth rate of M1 starting in 1975. The Bank began with a 10% to 15% range for M1 growth, and planned to gradually lower this range. At the same time, wage and price controls were also put in place to control inflation (see the Application, "The Nixon and

---

18. For assessments and historical analyses of these approaches, see Ben Bernanke and Frederic Mishkin, "Central Bank Behavior and the Strategy of Monetary Policy: Observations from Six Industrialized Countries," in Olivier Blanchard and Stanley Fischer, eds., *NBER Macroeconomics Annual*, 1992; and Bernanke and Mishkin, "Inflation Targeting: A New Strategy for Monetary Policy?" *Journal of Economic Perspectives*, Spring 1997.

Trudeau Wage–Price Controls," in Chapter 13). Monetarists disagreed with several aspects of the Bank's policy. For example, no targets for subsequent years were announced at the initial date, subsequent announcements were not made on a regular basis, and growth rates used base periods that were earlier than the announcement dates. Nevertheless, M1 growth rates fell substantially during this period.

According to the arguments advanced by monetarists, maintaining a low and steady growth rate of money should lead to low inflation and stable output and employment growth. Most countries, including Canada, did experience a substantial reduction in inflation during the early 1980s. Often, however, output and employment growth were unstable. For example, Germany, the United States, Canada, and the United Kingdom all suffered sharp increases in unemployment in the early 1980s, during the period of their money-growth targeting experiments. In Canada, the targets were de-emphasized in 1981 and officially dropped in 1982. In the United States, the Fed reduced its reliance on money-growth targets in 1982 and emphasized interest-rate targeting, though it did not drop money-growth targets entirely until 1993. Many other countries also abandoned or weakened their reliance on money-growth targeting during the 1980s, the principal exceptions being Germany and Switzerland, whose central banks continued to announce money-growth targets.

Why was money-growth targeting abandoned? The Bank of Canada's explanation was that because of rapid changes in the Canadian financial system, at times during the 1970s and 1980s, the demand for money was quite unstable and unpredictable (see the Application, "Financial Innovation and 'A Place to Stand'" in Chapter 7). Recall that if money demand is so unstable that the *LM* curve moves randomly back and forth, then varying the money supply to keep interest rates constant leads to a more stable aggregate demand curve than does holding the money stock at a fixed level (see Figure 14.3). In the Bank's view, sharp changes in the demand for money (unstable velocity) made money-growth targeting an ineffective strategy. Instability of money demand also contributed to the abandonment of money-growth targets in the United States and the United Kingdom. Germany's more tightly regulated financial system changed less during the 1980s than those of other countries, reducing the Bundesbank's problems with unstable money demand. But even the Bundesbank was forced to switch from targeting central bank money to targeting M3 in 1987 because the relationship between the former aggregate and the economy appeared to have become too unstable.

The end of money-growth targeting in many countries left central banks groping for a new strategy. Since 1990, a number of countries—including Canada, Sweden, the United Kingdom, Spain, Israel, Brazil and Australia—have adopted an alternative strategy called inflation targeting.[19] In Canada, inflation targets were introduced in a joint statement by the Bank of Canada and the federal government in early 1991, with a target for the end of 1992 of 3% for the 12-month increase in the CPI. At the same time, targets for 1994 and 1995 of 2.5% and 2% were announced, with a band of plus and minus 1 percentage point around them. The 1% to 3% target range was renewed in December 1993 and February 1998 and again in May 2001 to apply until the end of 2006.

---

19. For a review of international experiences with inflation targets, see Ben Bernanke, Thomas Laubach, Frederic Mishkin, and Adam Posen, *Inflation Targeting: Lessons from the International Experience*, Princeton: Princeton University Press, 1998.

The Canadian inflation target is for the CPI, but the Bank of Canada also monitors and reports on an index called CPIX, which excludes the eight most volatile prices from the CPI: fruit,vegetables, gasoline, fuel oil, natural gas, intercity transportation, tobacco, and mortgage-interest costs. The Bank argues that the less volatile CPIX is a reliable measure of the underlying trend in the CPI so that monitoring it may save the Bank from reacting to some temporary price changes that will soon be reversed.

When using a strategy of *inflation targeting*, as the name implies, the central bank targets one of its ultimate goals, the rate of inflation, rather than targeting an intermediate variable (such as money growth). A strategy of inflation targeting does not preclude the use of monetary policy to help stabilize output or other macroeconomic variables in the short run. However, by announcing an inflation target, the central bank signals that hitting that target in the longer run is its first priority.[20]

Relative to money-growth targeting, inflation targeting has advantages and disadvantages. One clear advantage is that inflation targeting sidesteps the problem of money demand instability. Under an inflation-targeting strategy, if money demand changes, there is nothing to prevent the central bank from adjusting the money supply to compensate.[21] Another advantage of inflation targeting is that explaining to the public that the central bank is trying to achieve a certain rate of inflation (which most people understand) is easier than explaining that it is trying to achieve a certain growth rate of M2 (which most people do not understand). Better communication of the central bank's goals should make the public and the financial markets less uncertain about what the central bank is going to do and may increase the accountability of the central bank. For these reasons, the Bank of Canada has published a semi-annual *Monetary Policy Report* since 1995, to try to publicize its goals and describe the prospects for inflation.

A major disadvantage of inflation targeting is that inflation responds to policy actions only with a long lag. As a result, the central bank cannot easily judge which policy actions are needed in order to hit the inflation target, and the public cannot easily determine whether the central bank is living up to its promises. Thus, inflation-targeting central banks may miss their targets, losing credibility as a result. Whether inflation targeting will be the preferred strategy for monetary policy in the future, and perhaps spread to the US Federal Reserve and the new European Central Bank, remains to be seen.

Has inflation targeting added to the credibility of the Bank of Canada? The 1990–1992 recession in Canada was more severe than in the United States, which suggests that either Canada faced different shocks or that Canada had a tighter monetary policy and the Bank's announcement of its low inflation goals did not immediately add to its credibility. However, the Bank met its inflation targets during the 1990s, which may

---

20. Inflation targeting does not qualify as a policy rule in the strict sense, for two reasons. First, it involves targeting a goal variable (inflation), rather than an instrument of policy, such as an interest rate or the monetary base. Second, this approach allows the central bank to exercise some discretion in the short run, as long as it meets the inflation target in the longer run. Advocates of inflation targeting hope that this approach will combine the credibility benefits of a strict rule with the advantage of having some degree of policy discretion.

21. As Figure 14.3 shows, this compensation for money demand shocks occurs automatically when interest rates are used as intermediate targets. Most central banks that set inflation targets for the longer run also use interest rates as their intermediate target in the short run. There is no conflict between short-run interest-rate targeting and long-run inflation targeting, as long as the interest rate is periodically adjusted in a way consistent with the long-run inflation target.

add to its future credibility. David Johnson, of Wilfrid Laurier University, has studied a survey of professional forecasters in Canada, and found that inflation targeting did have some impact on expected inflation in the early 1990s.[22] The question of whether inflation targeting can improve the sacrifice ratio cannot be answered from a single episode, such as the 1990–1992 recession, though, but must await further international experience with inflation targets.

OTHER WAYS TO ACHIEVE CENTRAL BANK CREDIBILITY

Besides announcing targets for money growth or inflation, are there other ways to increase the central bank's credibility and, thus, improve the performance of monetary policy? Three possibilities have been suggested: (1) to appoint a "tough" central banker; (2) to change central bankers' incentives; and (3) to increase the central bank's independence.

1. *Appointing a "tough" central banker.* By definition, a credible central bank is one that will be believed by the public when it states its intention to reduce money growth and inflation. One way to increase credibility is for the government to appoint a central bank governor who strongly dislikes inflation and who people believe is willing to accept increased unemployment, if necessary, to bring inflation down. Thus, when US President Jimmy Carter faced a serious inflation problem in 1979, he appointed Paul Volcker—an imposing individual with a strong anti-inflation reputation—to be chairman of the Fed. In appointing a "tough" central banker, Carter hoped to convince the financial markets and the public that he was serious about reducing inflation. Volcker succeeded in getting rid of inflation, but because unemployment rose significantly in the process, his appointment did not completely solve the credibility problem.[23]

2. *Changing central bankers' incentives.* A second way to enhance the central bank's credibility is to give its leadership strong incentives to be "tough" on inflation (and to ignore any unemployment costs associated with disinflation).[24] If the incentives are strong enough and are publicly known, people may find the central bank's anti-inflation pronouncements to be credible. An interesting recent example of this approach is a law passed in New Zealand that sets explicit inflation targets for the central bank and provides for the replacement of the head of the central bank if those targets are not met. Inflation has come down significantly in New Zealand, but unemployment has risen. Again, credibility problems have not been completely solved.

3. *Increasing central bank independence.* A third strategy is to increase the independence of the central bank from the other parts of the government—for example, by limiting the legal ability of the legislature to interfere in monetary policy decisions. The rationale is that a more independent central bank will be less subject to short-term political pressures to try to expand output and employment (say, before an election) and will be more strongly committed to maintaining a low long-run inflation rate. Because the public will recognize that an independent central bank is less subject to political pressures, announcements made by the central bank should be more credible.

---

22. "Expected Inflation in Canada 1988–1995: An Evaluation of Bank of Canada Credibility and the Effect of Inflation Targets," *Canadian Public Policy* 1997, pp. 233–258.

23. The point that appointing a tough central banker may improve central bank credibility was made by Kenneth Rogoff, "The Optimal Degree of Commitment to an Intermediate Monetary Target," *Quarterly Journal of Economics*, November 1985, pp. 1169–1189. Keynesians might argue that Volcker was credible but that long-lived stickiness in wages and prices led unemployment to increase in 1981–1982 anyway.

24. An analysis of central bankers' incentives is Carl Walsh's, "Optimal Contracts for Central Bankers," *American Economic Review*, March 1995, pp. 150–167.

FIGURE 14.6

CENTRAL BANK
INDEPENDENCE AND
INFLATION

The figure compares average inflation to an index of central bank independence from the rest of the government (higher values of the index imply that the central bank is more independent) for each of 16 countries for the period 1955–1988. It shows that countries with more independent central banks have lower average inflation rates.

Source: Based on Alberto Alesina and Lawrence Summers, "Central Bank Independence and Macroeconomic Performance," *Journal of Money, Credit and Banking*, May 1993, pp. 151–162, Table A1 and Fig. 1a.

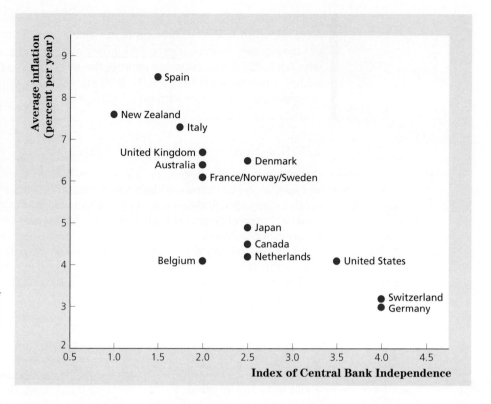

Considerable evidence supports the idea that independent central banks are more credible. Figure 14.6, taken from a study by Alberto Alesina and Lawrence Summers, of Harvard University,[25] shows the relationship between central bank independence and inflation in 16 industrialized countries. The vertical axis measures average inflation for each country for the period 1955–1988. The horizontal axis shows an index of central bank independence (based on such factors as the ease with which the government can dismiss the head of the central bank or reverse central bank decisions). Countries with relatively independent central banks, such as Germany, Switzerland, and the United States, clearly have lower long-run inflation rates than countries without independent central banks, such as the United Kingdom, New Zealand,[26] Italy, and Spain. A similar figure in the Alesina–Summers study shows that countries with independent central banks do not have higher long-run rates of unemployment. This evidence supports the idea that increased central bank independence raises credibility and, thus, lowers the unemployment cost of keeping inflation low.

---

25. "Central Bank Independence and Macroeconomic Performance," *Journal of Money, Credit and Banking*, May 1993, pp. 151–162.

26. The evaluation of the independence of New Zealand's central bank preceded the recent reforms in New Zealand's central banking laws mentioned earlier. Central banks in France, Spain, Japan, and the United Kingdom also were made more independent during the 1990s.

CHAPTER SUMMARY

1. Three groups help determine the money supply: the central bank, private banks, and the general public. The central bank influences the monetary base, which is the quantity of central bank liabilities that can be used as money. The monetary base equals the sum of bank reserves (deposits by banks at the central bank plus currency in the vaults of banks) and currency in circulation. Private banks and the general public interact to determine the money multiplier, which is the ratio of the money supply to the monetary base.

2. In an all-currency economy the monetary base consists entirely of currency in circulation. Therefore, the money supply equals the monetary base, and the money multiplier equals 1.

3. In an economy with fractional reserve banking and no currency held by the public, the money supply is $1/res$ times the monetary base, where res is the ratio of reserves to deposits desired by banks. The money supply is greater than the monetary base in this case because banks lend part of the deposits they receive. When those funds are redeposited in the banking system, bank deposits and, thus, the money supply increase.

4. In an economy with both fractional reserve banking and currency in circulation, the money multiplier equals $(cu + 1)/(cu + res)$, where cu is the public's desired ratio of currency to deposits. The money supply equals deposits plus currency in circulation and also equals the money multiplier times the monetary base. An increase in the desired currency–deposit ratio cu or in the desired reserve–deposit ratio res reduces the money multiplier.

5. The central bank can affect the size of the monetary base and, thus, the money supply through open-market operations. An open-market sale (in which central bank assets are sold for currency or bank reserves) reduces the monetary base. An open-market purchase (in which the central bank uses money to buy assets, such as government securities, from the public) increases the monetary base.

6. The Canadian central bank is called the Bank of Canada. The Bank is headed by a governor who reports to a board of directors. Ultimately, the federal government is responsible for monetary policy, though the Bank has considerable independence. The Bank serves as a lender of last resort, implements monetary policy, and acts as fiscal agent for the federal government.

7. The Bank of Canada affects the Canadian money supply primarily through changes in the overnight interest rate. Changes in monetary policy are signalled with the target overnight rate, the centre of the operating band for the overnight rate. Open-market operations also may be used to influence interest rates.

8. The Bank may focus on intermediate targets, such as monetary aggregates, or short-term interest rates to guide monetary policy. Stabilizing interest rates is a useful strategy when fluctuations in money demand would otherwise cause the LM curve to shift randomly back and forth.

9. The channels through which monetary policy has its effects include the interest rate channel, the exchange rate channel, and the credit channel. These channels work with lags, so policy must be based on forecasts of future macroeconomic variables.

10. Monetary policy may be conducted either by rules or by discretion. Under rules, the central bank is required to follow a simple predetermined rule for monetary policy, such as a requirement for constant money growth, and is not allowed to respond to current economic conditions. Under discretion, the central bank is expected to monitor the economy and use monetary policy actively to maintain full employment and to keep inflation low. Discretion for monetary policy is usually favoured by Keynesians, who argue that it gives central banks maximum flexibility to stabilize the economy.

11. Monetarists, led by Milton Friedman, argue that because of information problems and lags between the implementation of policy changes

and their effects, the scope for using monetary policy to stabilize the economy is small. Furthermore, they argue, central banks cannot be relied on to use active monetary policy wisely and in the public interest. Monetarists advocate a constant-growth-rate rule for the money supply in order to discipline the central bank and keep monetary fluctuations from destabilizing the economy.

12. An additional argument for rules is that they increase central bank credibility. Supporters of rules claim that the use of ironclad rules will cause the public to believe the central bank if it says (for example) that money supply growth will be reduced, with the implication that inflation can be reduced without a large increase in unemployment.

13. Although some countries have experimented with money-growth targets—similar in spirit to the monetarists' constant-growth-rate rule—central banks have not been willing or able to make strong commitments to meet their targets. One reason for their reluctance is that fluctuations in the demand for money have led the relationship between specific monetary aggregates and the macroeconomy to be unstable or unpredictable at times. Since 1991, the Bank of Canada has targeted inflation directly, which requires that monetary policy responds to forecasts of future inflation. Whether inflation targeting reduces the unemployment costs of disinflation remains an open question.

14. Possible alternatives for increasing a central bank's credibility are to appoint a central banker who is "tough" on inflation; to increase central bankers' incentives to reduce inflation; and to increase the central bank's independence from other parts of the government.

KEY TERMS

Bank rate, p. 531
bank reserves, p. 523
bank run, p. 526
central bank, p. 521
credibility, p. 544
credit channel, p. 538
currency–deposit ratio, p. 526
depository institutions, p. 521
direct clearers, p. 531

discretion, p. 539
exchange fund account, p. 534
exchange rate channel, p. 538
fractional reserve banking, p. 523
game theory, p. 545
high-powered money, p. 522
instruments, p. 535
interest rate channel, p. 538
intermediate targets, p. 535
lender of last resort, p. 533
monetarism, p. 539
monetary base, p. 522
money multiplier, p. 527
multiple expansion of loans and deposits, p. 524
100% reserve banking, p. 523
open-market purchase, p. 529
open-market sale, p. 529
overnight rate, p. 531
reserve–deposit ratio, p. 523
rules, p. 539
Sale and Repurchase Agreement, p. 534
settlement balances, p. 531
Special Purchase and Resale Agreement, p. 534
target overnight rate, p. 531
Taylor rule, p. 540

KEY EQUATIONS

$$M = CU + DEP \qquad (14.4)$$

The money supply, M, is the sum of currency in circulation, CU, and deposits held by the public at banks, DEP.

$$BASE = CU + RES \qquad (14.5)$$

The monetary base, or the liabilities of the central bank that are usable as money, equals the sum of currency in circulation, CU, and bank reserves, RES.

$$M = \left(\frac{cu+1}{cu+res} \right) BASE \qquad (14.8)$$

The money supply, M, equals the monetary base times the money multiplier, $(cu + 1)/(cu + res)$, where cu is the currency–deposit ratio chosen by the public and res is the reserve–deposit ratio chosen by banks.

REVIEW QUESTIONS

1. Define *monetary base*. What is the relationship between the monetary base and the money supply in an all-currency economy?

2. Define *money multiplier*. What is the value of the money multiplier in a system of 100% reserve banking? What is the value of the money multiplier in a system of fractional reserve banking, if all money is held in the form of deposits? Why is the money multiplier higher under fractional reserve banking than under 100% reserve banking?

3. Discuss how actions of the public and banks can cause the money multiplier to rise or fall. Does the fact that the public and banks can affect the money multiplier imply that the central bank cannot control the money supply? Why, or why not?

4. How can the Bank of Canada affect bank reserves and overnight interest rates using its operating band for the overnight rate? How do changes in overnight rates affect other interest rates and the money supply?

5. What is the effect on interest rates and the money supply of an open-market purchase of Treasury bills?

6. What are intermediate targets? How do they differ from monetary policy goals? List the two principal types of intermediate targets that the Bank of Canada has used.

7. What are the three channels of monetary policy? Explain each channel briefly.

8. "It is plain to see that discretion is a better way to run monetary policy than following a rule because a policy of discretion gives the central bank the ability to react to news about the economy." What is the monetarist response to the statement? What is the more recent argument for using rules rather than discretion?

9. Has the use of money-growth or inflation targets significantly improved central bank credibility? Besides adopting such targets, what other actions can a country take to increase the credibility of its central bank?

NUMERICAL PROBLEMS

1. The Agricolan monetary base is 1,000,000 florins. The public always holds half its money supply as currency and half as deposits. Banks hold 20% of deposits in the form of reserves. Starting with the initial creation of a monetary base that accompanies the purchase by the central bank of 1,000,000 fl worth of coconuts from the public, show the consolidated balance sheet of the banks after they first receive deposits, after a first round of loans and redeposits, and after a second round of loans and redeposits. (*Hint*: Don't forget that the public keeps only half its money in the form of bank deposits.)

Show the balance sheets of the central bank, the banking system, and the public at the end of the process of multiple expansion of loans and deposits. What is the final value of the money supply?

2. Answer the following:
a. The money supply is $6,000,000, currency held by the public is $2,000,000, and the reserve–deposit ratio is 0.25. Find deposits, bank reserves, the monetary base, and the money multiplier.

b. In a different economy, vault cash is $1,000,000, deposits by depository institutions at the central bank are $4,000,000, the monetary base is $10,000,000, and bank deposits are $20,000,000. Find bank reserves, the money supply, and the money multiplier.

3. When the real interest rate increases, banks have an incentive to lend a greater portion of their deposits, which reduces the reserve–deposit ratio. In particular, suppose that

$$res = 0.4 - 2r,$$

where *res* is the reserve–deposit ratio and r is the real interest rate. The currency–deposit ratio is 0.4, the price level is fixed at 1.0, and the monetary base is 60. The real quantity of money demanded is

$$L(Y, i) = 0.5Y - 10i,$$

where Y is real output and i is the nominal interest rate. Assume that expected inflation is zero so that the nominal interest rate and the real interest rate are equal.
a. If $r = i = 0.10$, what are the reserve–deposit ratio, the money multiplier, and the money supply? For what real output Y does a real interest rate of 0.10 clear the asset market?
b. Repeat part (a) for $r = i = 0.05$.
c. Suppose that the reserve–deposit ratio is fixed at the value you found in part (a) and is not affected by interest rates. If $r = i = 0.05$, for what output Y does the asset market clear in this case?
d. Is the *LM* curve flatter or steeper when the reserve–deposit ratio depends on the real interest rate than when the reserve–deposit ratio is fixed? Explain your answer in economic terms.

4. This question asks you to analyze a game played by two players, player I and player II. Player I can choose one of two actions, A and B. Player II also has two actions to choose from, a and b. Both players are affected by their own action and by the action of the other player. The points that each player assigns to each possible outcome (combination of actions) are shown in the following table.

Outcome	Points for Player I	Points for Player II
(A, a)	2	2
(A, b)	5	0
(B, a)	0	5
(B, b)	3	3

The first row indicates that if player I chooses action A and player II chooses action a, player I gets 2 points and player II gets 2 points. The more points a player gets, the happier she is with the outcome. Players do not care about how many points the other player gets.

a. If player I moves (chooses an action) first and then player II moves, what action will each player take? (Set up a game theory diagram like Figure 14.4.) What is the outcome of the game? Does your answer change if player II moves first?

b. Suppose that player I moves first, but before player I moves, player II announces which action (a or b) she will take when it is her turn. Player II's announcement is legally binding. What is the outcome of the game now?

c. Before player I makes the first move, player II is allowed to make a threat, telling player I what action she will take on her turn if player I chooses A and what action she will take if player I chooses B. Player II's threats are legally binding. What is the outcome of the game now? Is player I made worse off or better off by player II's ability to threaten her?

ANALYTICAL PROBLEMS

1. How would each of the following affect the Canadian money supply? Explain.

a. Banks decide to hold more reserves as a precaution against bank runs.

b. People withdraw cash from their bank accounts for Christmas shopping.

c. The Bank of Canada sells gold to the public.

d. The introduction of automatic teller machines, which allow people to withdraw cash from the bank as needed, makes deposits relatively more convenient.

e. The federal government sells $20 billion of new government bonds to the Bank of Canada. The proceeds of the sale are used to pay government employees.

f. The Bank of Canada sells some of its government securities in Tokyo for yen.

2. Suppose that the central bank strictly followed a rule of keeping the real interest rate at 3% per year. That rate happens to be the real interest rate consistent with the economy's initial general equilibrium.

a. Assume that the economy is hit only by money demand shocks. Under the central bank's rule, how will the money supply respond to money demand shocks? Will the rule make aggregate demand more stable or less stable than it would be if the money supply were constant?

b. Assume that the economy is hit only by *IS* shocks. Under the central bank's interest-rate rule, how will the money supply behave? Will the interest-rate rule make aggregate demand more stable or less stable than it would be if the money supply were constant? Will the central bank be able to follow its rule in the long run?

c. Assume that the economy is hit only by supply shocks (shocks to the *FE* line). Repeat part (b).

3. Suppose that the Bank of Canada were committed to following the Taylor rule, given in Box 14.1, p. 540. For each of the following types of shocks, determine whether the use of the Taylor rule would tend to be stabilizing or destabilizing, or would have an ambiguous effect, relative to a policy of leaving the money supply unchanged. Consider the behaviour of both output and inflation.

a. An increase in money demand.

b. A temporary increase in government purchases.

c. An adverse supply shock.

d. A decline in consumer confidence.

e. An increase in export demand.

4. In the game between the Bank and the firms shown diagrammatically in Figure 14.5(b), what happens if the Bank does not value having the unemployment rate below the natural rate $\bar{u}$? Specifically, assume that the Bank assigns 0 points to a situation in which u equals $\bar{u}$ and assigns −1 points to a situation in which u is either above or below $\bar{u}$. How does this modification affect the outcome of the game? (Assume that if the Bank is indifferent between two actions, it chooses the one that makes the firms better off.)

5. Why do many governments have policies against negotiating with hostage-taking terrorists? Under what conditions, if any, are such policies likely to reduce hostage taking? Discuss the analogy to monetary rules.

Chapter 15

GOVERNMENT SPENDING AND ITS FINANCING

At every level of government, fiscal policy—government decisions about how much to spend, what to spend for, and how to finance its spending—is of central importance. Politicians and the public understand that the government's fiscal choices have a direct impact on the "bread and butter" issues of how much they pay in taxes and what government benefits and services they receive. Equally important are the effects of fiscal policy on the economy. In recent years, people have become more aware of the macroeconomic effects of fiscal policy as the economic implications of government budget deficits, tax reform, and other aspects of fiscal policy have been extensively debated.

This chapter takes a closer look at fiscal policy and its macroeconomic effects. To provide some background, we begin with definitions and facts about the government's budget. We then discuss some basic fiscal policy issues, including the effects of government spending and taxes on economic activity, the burden of government debt, and the link between budget deficits and inflation.

15.1 THE GOVERNMENT BUDGET: SOME FACTS AND FIGURES

Before getting into the analytical issues of fiscal policy, we set the stage by looking at the components of the government budget and their recent trends. We discuss three main aspects of the budget: (1) expenditure; (2) tax revenues, or receipts; and (3) the budget deficit or surplus. Our discussion reviews and builds on Chapter 2, which introduced basic budget concepts.

GOVERNMENT EXPENDITURE

Government expenditure, the total spending by the government during a period of time, is divided into three primary categories: government purchases, transfer payments, and interest payments.

1. *Government purchases* are government spending on currently produced goods and services. Examples are spending on schools, defence, highway repairs, and government workers' salaries.
2. *Transfer payments* are payments made to individuals for which the government does not receive current goods or services in exchange. Examples of transfers include old age security payments, veteran and civil service pensions, foreign aid, unemployment insurance benefits, and welfare payments. We also include

subsidies to businesses in this category. About one-third of federal transfers go to other levels of government, mainly to provincial governments as equalization payments and for spending on health, postsecondary education, and welfare payments. To avoid double-counting, these intergovernmental transfers are netted out in the measurement of transfers, so we count only transfers to households and firms.

3. *Interest payments* are the interest paid to the holders of government bonds, such as Treasury bills or Canada Savings Bonds.

In Canada, total government expenditure (federal, provincial, and local) is about 41% of GDP. Figure 15.1 shows the trends since 1926 in total expenditure and in its three main categories, expressed as a percentage of GDP. The most obvious feature of Figure 15.1 is the enormous increase in government purchases during World War II: In 1944, when the war effort was at its peak, government purchases exceeded 40% of GDP. After falling to 10% of GDP in the late 1940s, the share of GDP devoted to government purchases has risen to about 22%.

Figure 15.1 also shows that transfer payments increased during the Great Depression due to the provision of relief and then again in 1946 due to payments to veterans. Transfers rose steadily as a share of GDP from the early 1950s until the early 1990s, tripling their share of GDP during that 40-year period. Transfers are currently about 12% of GDP. The long-term increase in transfer payments is the result of the creation of new social programs (such as old age security), the expansion of benefits under existing programs (such as unemployment insurance), and the increased number of people covered by the various programs. Conversely, the recent decline in transfer payments reflects the contraction in some of these programs, such as Employment Insurance.

FIGURE 15.1

GOVERNMENT
EXPENDITURE: FEDERAL,
PROVINCIAL, AND LOCAL,
1926–2000

The figure shows the behaviour since 1926 of the three major components of government expenditure, as well as total current expenditure, for all levels of government combined and measured as a percentage of GDP. Government purchases rose most sharply during World War II. Transfer payments have risen steadily as a share of GDP, particularly during recessions. Interest payments have risen more recently as a share of GDP.

Source: Government expenditure, all levels, in millions of dollars, by categories: *Canadian Economic Observer, Historical Statistical Supplement,* Table 3; GDP in millions of dollars: Table 1.

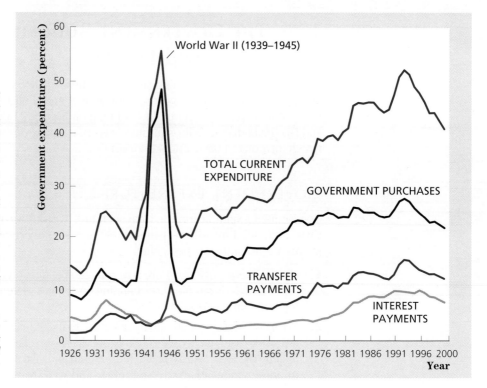

Finally, Figure 15.1 shows how interest payments have evolved. Because interest payments are smaller than the other two categories of expenditure, they appear to fluctuate less. However, interest payments rose sharply as a percentage of GDP in three periods. First, interest payments more than doubled from 3.6% of GDP in 1929 to 7.6% of GDP in 1933, reflecting the large amount of borrowing done to finance the spending during the Depression. Second, interest payments rose from 2.9% of GDP in 1942 to 4.6% of GDP in 1946 because of wartime borrowing. Third, interest payments doubled during the 1980s, rising from about 4.5% in the late 1970s to about 9% of GDP in the 1990s. This increase reflects both higher rates of borrowing by Canadian governments and the generally high level of interest rates during the 1980s. Only in the late 1990s did interest payments begin to decline as a share of GDP.

How does the rate of government expenditure in Canada compare with rates in other countries with similar living standards? Because official accounting rules for measuring the government budget vary widely among countries, the answer is not as straightforward as you might think. Nevertheless, Table 15.1 compares the ratios of government spending to GDP for 19 countries in the Organization for Economic Cooperation and Development (OECD). The table shows ratios for both central government spending (federal, in Canada) and total government spending (including provincial and local, in Canada). Canada's rate of government spending is comparable to those of Western European countries but higher than those in Japan and the United States. Many of these cross-country differences reflect differences in the scale of social welfare programs.

REVENUE

On the revenue side of the government's budget, the main components are tax receipts. There are two principal components of tax receipts: direct taxes, and indirect taxes. The third main source of revenue is investment income. Figure 15.2

TABLE 15.1

Government Spending in Thirteen OECD Countries, Percentage of GDP, 1996

Country	Central Government	All Government
Sweden	41.2	62.3
France	42.2	55.0
Finland	50.4	54.5
Belgium	49.6	52.9
Austria	42.0	51.8
Netherlands	44.3	49.3
Germany	35.3	49.1
Canada	21.7	44.5
United Kingdom	37.7	43.0
Iceland	36.5	38.2
Japan	27.1	35.9
Australia	25.4	34.5
United States	22.7	34.4

Source: *OECD, National Accounts, 1984–1996*, Volume II, Detailed Tables.

FIGURE 15.2

REVENUE: FEDERAL, PROVINCIAL, AND LOCAL, 1926–2000

The figure shows the history of revenues in several categories for all levels of government combined and measured as a percentage of GDP. Total revenue has risen over the past 75 years. Most of the increase is accounted for by increases in direct taxes.

Source: Government revenue, all levels, in millions of dollars, by categories: *Canadian Economic Observer, Historical Statistical Supplement*, Table 3; GDP in millions of dollars: Table 1.

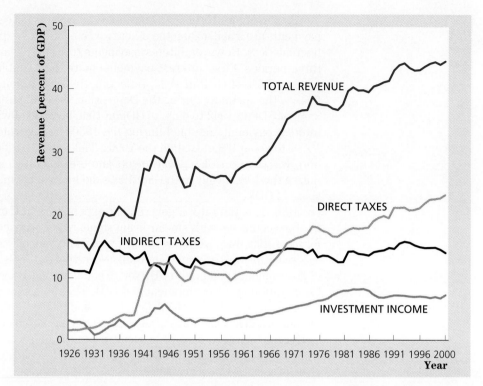

shows the history of revenues from these three main categories in Canada, all expressed as a percentage of GDP. Note that the share of taxes in GDP has risen steadily, from 16% of GDP in 1926 to roughly 44% of GDP in 2000.

The largest category of tax receipts is *direct taxes*, which, in turn, are divided into taxes paid by persons and those paid by enterprises. Direct taxes paid by persons include the personal income tax (both federal and provincial), property taxes, and Employment Insurance contributions. Direct taxes paid by enterprises include the corporate income tax, though revenue from this source has grown much more slowly than personal direct taxes. As Figure 15.2 shows, direct taxes increased dramatically during World War II, and they account for most of the growth in total revenue as a share of GDP since then.

The second category of revenue is *indirect taxes*, which includes the revenue from sales taxes (such as provincial sales taxes and the federal goods and services tax) and from customs duties. This type of revenue has not grown as a share of GDP over the past 75 years.

The final category of revenue is *investment income*, which includes revenue from loans to Crown corporations, to farmers, and to students, for example. In Figure 15.2, this series also includes the revenue from the sale of government assets. This revenue source has been a stable proportion of GDP in recent years.

THE COMPOSITION OF REVENUE AND EXPENDITURE: THE FEDERAL GOVERNMENT VERSUS PROVINCIAL AND LOCAL GOVERNMENTS

The components of government spending shown in Figure 15.1 and the components of revenue shown in Figure 15.2 lump together federal, provincial, and local governments. For most purposes of macroeconomic analysis, combining federal, provincial, and local fiscal policy is the most sensible course. The macroeconomic effect of a new highway-building program, for example, should not depend on whether the new highways are financed from federal, provincial, or local budgets—or from a combination of those budgets. In this respect, the recent tendency of many news stories about fiscal policy to focus on provincial as well as federal government budgets is worthwhile. The Political Environment box, "Federal–Provincial Fiscal Policy Coordination" discusses why the two types of budgets should be studied together.

Nevertheless, it is useful to know that in Canada federal government budgets have a much different composition, on both the expenditure and the revenue sides, from those of provincial and local governments. The box, "In Touch with the Macroeconomy: Provincial Economic Accounts" (on p. 565) describes some of the differences among provinces. A summary of the major components of both the federal and the combined provincial and local government budgets for 2000 is given in Table 15.2, on the next page. Note in particular the following points:

1. *Goods and services.* Two-thirds of provincial and local spending is for goods and services. In contrast, less than a quarter of federal spending is for goods and services. *About four-fifths of government spending on goods and services in Canada is done by provincial and local governments.*

2. *Transfer payments.* The federal government spends a larger share of its budget on transfer payments to individuals than provincial and local governments do. Total transfer payments by the federal government are larger that those of provincial and local governments because about 18% of its spending is a transfer to provincial and local governments, making up 10% of their revenue.

3. *Interest payments.* Because of the large quantity of federal government bonds outstanding, interest payments are an important component of federal spending. The contrast with provincial and local governments is even more striking if we look at net interest payments: interest payments minus investment income. Net interest payments in 2000 were $31.9 billion for the federal government and –$31.8 billion for provincial and local governments. The value for provincial and local governments is negative because they made asset sales, included in investment income.

4. *Composition of revenue.* About 58% of federal government revenue comes from personal taxes (primarily the federal income tax), while only about 15% of federal revenues are from corporate income taxes. Indirect taxes make up 20% of federal revenue. In contrast, indirect taxes account for about 35% of provincial and local revenue. About 28% of provincial and local revenues come from personal taxes (both income taxes and property taxes). As already mentioned, provincial and local governments also count as revenue the transfers they receive from the federal government.

SURPLUSES OR DEFICITS

Government expenditure need not equal revenue in each period. In Chapter 2, we showed that when government revenue exceeds expenditure, there is a government budget surplus (or simply a surplus), and when expenditure exceeds revenue, there is a government budget deficit. For ease of reference, we write the definition of the surplus as

$$\text{surplus} = \text{revenue} - \text{expenditure}$$
$$= \text{tax revenue} - \text{government purchases} - \text{transfers} - \text{net interest}$$
$$= T - G - TR - INT. \tag{15.1}$$

TABLE 15.2

Government Expenditure and Revenue, 2000

	Federal		Provincial and Local	
	Billions of Dollars	**Percentage of Expenditure**	**Billions of Dollars**	**Percentage of Expenditure**
Expenditure				
Goods and services	42.8	23.9	184.6	65.3
Transfers to persons and businesses	59.6	33.3	65.8	23.3
Transfers to provinces and local governments	32.2	18.0	—	—
Interest payments	44.2	24.7	32.4	11.4
Total expenditure	178.8	100.0	282.8	100.0

	Federal		Provincial and Local	
	Billions of Dollars	**Percentage of Revenue**	**Billions of Dollars**	**Percentage of Revenue**
Revenue				
Direct taxes from persons	112.1	57.7	85.8	28.0
Direct taxes from enterprises	30.4	15.6	15.7	5.1
Indirect taxes	39.5	20.3	108.2	35.3
Transfers from federal government	—	—	32.2	10.5
Investment income*	12.3	6.3	64.2	21.1
Total revenue	194.3	100.0	306.1	100.0
Surplus (deficit if negative; revenue minus expenditure)	15.5		23.3	
Primary surplus (deficit if negative; surplus plus net interest payments)	47.4		−8.5	

*Investment income includes sales of assets.

Source: *Canadian Economic Observer, Historical Statistical Supplement*, 2000/01, Table 3.

IN TOUCH WITH THE MACROECONOMY

PROVINCIAL ECONOMIC ACCOUNTS

In Table 15.2, we have grouped all provinces together (as well as grouping provincial and local governments together). This aggregation sometimes obscures striking differences between provinces in expenditure, revenue, and deficits. We also have not looked at the regional allocation of federal government spending and revenue. In general, the federal government may not spend the same amount in a province that it raises there as revenue.

Fortunately, as part of the System of National Accounts, Statistics Canada provides annual data on provincial and territorial economies for each year since 1961 in the *Provincial Economic Accounts*. The accounts contain GDP accounting for each province and they divide public expenditure and revenue within each province into the components accounted for by each level of government.

The accompanying table shows the federal government's expenditure and revenue for each province, along with the corresponding entries for provincial and local governments combined, for 1998. You can see that the federal government ran a deficit in each of the provinces shown, except Ontario, British Columbia, and Alberta, where it ran surpluses.* The pattern of the federal government surplus or deficit across provinces reflects equalization payments, differences in the Canada Health and Social Transfer to different provinces, and sometimes automatic stabilizers. For example, if a recession is more severe in certain provinces, federal spending there will rise.

In 1998, consolidated provincial and local governments ran surpluses, except in Quebec, Ontario, and New Brunswick. The provincial economic accounts also would allow us to calculate spending or revenue per capita or per dollar of provincial GDP.

*These entries do not sum to the federal deficit for 1998 because of data revisions and because of federal expenditure and revenue in the territories and outside Canada.

Expenditure and Revenue by Level of Government in each Province, 1998 (Millions of Dollars)

	Federal			Provincial and Local		
	Expenditure	**Revenue**	**Surplus**	**Expenditure**	**Revenue**	**Surplus**
British Columbia	18,329	20,582	2,253	32,538	32,748	210
Alberta	12,643	18,327	5,684	21,763	24,231	2,468
Saskatchewan	6,167	4,469	–1,698	8,001	8,600	599
Manitoba	7,756	5,152	–2,604	9,566	9,927	361
Ontario	51,665	69,416	17,751	88,660	88,290	–370
Quebec	38,921	33084	–5,837	64,279	61,823	–2,456
New Brunswick	5,699	2,983	–2,716	5,338	5,283	–55
Nova Scotia	7,952	3,850	–4,102	6,588	6,775	187
Prince Edward Island	1,226	572	–654	995	1,017	22
Newfoundland	5,128	1,868	–3,260	4,506	4,718	212

Source: *Provincial Economic Accounts, Annual Estimates*, Statistics Canada, cat. no. 13–213, Tables 6, 7 and 8. Surpluses are defined as government saving, as elsewhere in Section 15.1.

A second surplus concept, called the **primary government budget surplus**, excludes net interest from government expenditure:

$$\text{primary surplus} = \text{tax revenue} - \text{expenditure} + \text{net interest}$$
$$= \text{tax revenue} - \text{government purchases} - \text{transfers}$$
$$= T - G - TR. \tag{15.2}$$

The primary surplus is the amount by which tax revenue exceeds government purchases and transfers; the primary surplus minus net interest payments equals the surplus. Figure 15.3 illustrates the relationship between the two concepts.

Why have two surplus concepts? The reason is that each answers a different question. The standard or total budget surplus answers the question: How much can the government pay down its debt and still pay for its total expenditure? Similarly, the deficit measures how much the government must borrow to pay for its spending.

The primary surplus answers the question: Can the government afford its *current* programs? If the primary surplus is zero, the government is collecting just enough tax revenue to pay for its current purchases of goods and services and its current social programs (as reflected by transfer payments). If there is a primary surplus, then current tax revenue can pay for more than current government purchases and social programs. Net interest payments are ignored in the primary surplus or deficit because they represent not current program costs but costs of past expenditures financed by government borrowing.

Figure 15.4 shows the surplus and primary surplus for all levels of government combined as a percentage of GDP, since 1926. During the Great Depression governments ran deficits, but they also ran primary surpluses as they made net interest payments. During World War II, the government financed only part of the war effort with taxes and, thus, ran large primary and overall deficits. Large deficits (using both concepts) also occurred in the early 1980s and early 1990s. In the late 1990s, overall surpluses reappeared for the first time in 20 years.

FIGURE 15.3

THE RELATIONSHIP BETWEEN THE TOTAL BUDGET SURPLUS AND THE PRIMARY BUDGET SURPLUS

The standard measure of the total government budget surplus is the amount by which revenue exceeds government expenditure. The primary surplus is the amount by which revenue exceeds government purchases plus transfers. The primary budget surplus equals the total budget surplus plus net interest payments.

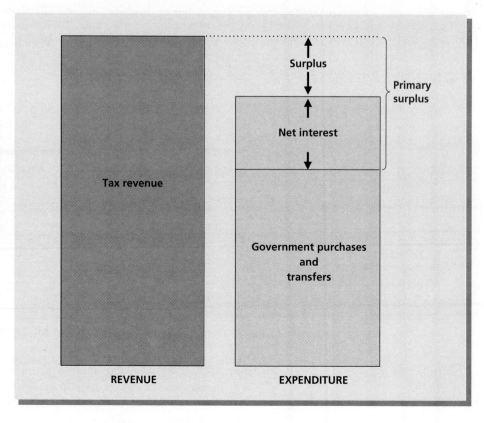

FIGURE 15.4

SURPLUS AND PRIMARY SURPLUS: FEDERAL, PROVINCIAL, AND LOCAL, 1926–2000

The figure shows the total government budget surplus and the primary surplus, both measured as a percentage of GDP, since 1926. The government ran large deficits during World War II. Deficits and primary deficits also were large during the early 1980s and early 1990s. Primary surpluses re-appeared in 1995, and total surpluses followed in 1997.

Source: Same as Figures 15.1 and 15.2.

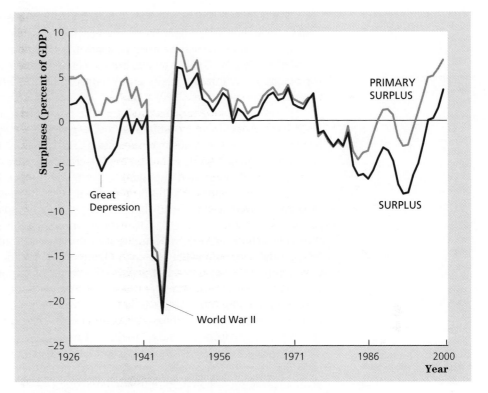

15.2 GOVERNMENT SPENDING, TAXES, AND THE MACROECONOMY

How does fiscal policy affect the performance of the macroeconomy? Economists emphasize three main ways by which government spending and taxing decisions influence macroeconomic variables, such as output, employment, and prices: (1) aggregate demand, (2) government capital formation, and (3) incentives.

FISCAL POLICY AND AGGREGATE DEMAND

Fiscal policy can affect economic activity by influencing the total amount of spending in the economy, or aggregate demand. Recall that aggregate demand is represented by the intersection of the *IS* and *LM* curves. In either the classical or the Keynesian *IS–LM* model, an increase in government purchases reduces desired national saving and shifts the *IS* curve up and to the right, thereby raising aggregate demand.

Classical and Keynesian economists have different beliefs about the effect of tax changes on aggregate demand. Classicals usually accept the Ricardian equivalence proposition, which says that lump-sum tax changes do not affect desired national saving and, thus, have no impact on the *IS* curve or aggregate demand.[1] Keynesians generally disagree with this conclusion; in the Keynesian view, a cut (for example) in taxes is likely to stimulate desired consumption and reduce desired national saving, thereby shifting the *IS* curve up and to the right and raising aggregate demand.

---

1. We introduced the Ricardian equivalence in Chapter 4. We discuss this idea further in Section 15.3.

Classicals and Keynesians also disagree over the question of whether fiscal policy should be used to fight the business cycle. Classicals generally reject attempts to smooth business cycles, by fiscal policy or by other means. In contrast, Keynesians argue that using fiscal policy to stabilize the economy and maintain full employment—for example, by cutting taxes and raising spending when the economy is in a recession—is desirable.

However, even Keynesians admit that the use of fiscal policy as a stabilization tool is difficult. A significant problem is *lack of flexibility*. The government's budget has many purposes besides macroeconomic stabilization, such as providing income support for eligible groups, developing the country's infrastructure (roads, bridges, and public buildings), and supplying government services (education and health). Much of government spending is committed years in advance (as in hydroelectric projects) or even decades in advance (as for pensions). Expanding or contracting total government spending rapidly for macroeconomic stabilization purposes is, thus, difficult without either spending wastefully or compromising other fiscal policy goals. Taxes are somewhat easier to change than spending, but the tax laws also have many different goals and may be the result of a fragile political compromise (between levels of government) that is not easily altered.

Compounding the problem of inflexibility is the problem of *long time lags* that result from the slow-moving political process by which fiscal policy is made (see the Political Environment box, "Federal–Provincial Fiscal Policy Coordination"). This lag makes effective countercyclical use of fiscal policy difficult because (for example), by the time an anti-recession fiscal measure actually had an impact on the economy, the recession might already be over.

AUTOMATIC STABILIZERS AND THE FULL-EMPLOYMENT SURPLUS OR DEFICIT

One way to get around the problems of fiscal policy inflexibility and long lags that impede the use of countercyclical fiscal policies is to build automatic stabilizers into the budget. **Automatic stabilizers** are provisions in the budget that cause government spending to rise or taxes to fall automatically—without legislative action—when GDP falls. Similarly, when GDP rises, automatic stabilizers cause spending to fall or taxes to rise without any need for direct legislative action.

A good example of an automatic stabilizer is Employment Insurance. When the economy goes into a recession and unemployment rises, more people receive employment benefits, which are paid automatically without further action by Parliament. Thus, the Employment Insurance component of transfers rises during recessions, making fiscal policy automatically more expansionary.[2]

Quantitatively, the most important automatic stabilizer is the income tax system. When the economy goes into a recession, people's incomes fall, and they pay less income tax. This "automatic tax cut" helps cushion the drop in disposable income and (according to Keynesians) prevents aggregate demand from falling as far as it might otherwise. Likewise, when people's incomes rise during a boom, the government collects more income tax revenue, which helps restrain the increase in aggregate demand. Keynesians argue that this automatic fiscal policy is a major reason for the increased stability of the economy since World War II.

---

2. This statement assumes that the Keynesian view is right so that an increase in transfers—which is equivalent to a reduction in taxes—raises aggregate demand.

THE POLITICAL ENVIRONMENT

FEDERAL-PROVINCIAL FISCAL POLICY COORDINATION

In studying the macroeconomic effects of federal fiscal policy, we need also to keep track of provincial fiscal policy. For example, suppose that the federal government reduces income tax rates as part of tax reform or as part of an expansionary policy. If provincial governments respond by raising their income tax rates by the same amount, then the behaviour of the private sector will not change. As another example, suppose that the federal government reduces its planned transfers to provincial and local governments, to try to reduce its deficit. Provincial governments may increase taxes, in response to the decline in their revenue, but their deficits may rise, too. If provincial taxes do not increase, then the deficit of the public sector, as a whole, may be unchanged by the change in fiscal policy at one level because the policy is not coordinated. As these examples show, studying the macroeconomic impact of a change in fiscal policy begins with finding the net change in policy by both levels of government.

A reduction in transfers from one level of government to another is sometimes called "off-loading." The federal government transfers funds to provincial governments for spending on health, postsecondary education, and social assistance in the form of the Canada Health and Social Transfer (CHST). The CHST was reduced as part of the federal government's deficit-reduction strategy in the mid-1990s. Also, different recipient governments were treated differently, with Alberta, British Columbia, and Ontario receiving smaller transfers per capita. Several provincial governments also reduced transfers to local governments during this period.

The CHST is distinct from equalization payments, which are made to provincial governments in relatively poor provinces so that they may provide public services comparable with those in other provinces while keeping per capita tax burdens roughly equal across provinces. Both types of transfers are made on a per capita basis. But because provincial populations change, information from the census may show that provinces have been treated differently.

The allocation of spending and revenue between levels of government is known as "fiscal federalism." The example of off-loading suggests that this allocation is largely determined by the federal government, but in fact, all levels are constrained by the constitution. Moreover, the coordination of fiscal policy involves elements of bargaining and strategy. Perhaps the most notable recent example is the bargaining between the federal government and most provincial governments over sales tax harmonization, reform of the Canada Pension Plan, and the scale of payroll taxes.

A side effect of automatic stabilizers is that government budget surpluses tend to fall (or deficits rise) in recessions because government spending automatically rises and taxes automatically fall when GDP declines. Similarly, the surplus tends to rise in booms. In order to distinguish changes in the surplus or deficit caused by recessions or booms from changes caused by other factors, some economists advocate the use of a surplus measure called the full-employment surplus or deficit. The **full-employment surplus** or **full-employment deficit** indicates what the government budget balance *would be*—given the tax and spending policies currently in force—if the economy were operating at its full-employment level.[3] The full-employment surplus is also called the cyclically adjusted or *structural surplus*. Because it eliminates the effects of automatic stabilizers, the full-employment surplus measure is affected primarily by changes in fiscal policy reflected in new legislation. In particular, expansionary fiscal changes—such as increases in government spending programs or (in the Keynesian model) reduced tax rates—lower the full-employment surplus, whereas contractionary fiscal changes raise the full-employment surplus.

---

3. In practice, the calculation of full-employment deficits uses the Keynesian assumption that recessions reflect deviations from full employment, rather than the classical assumption that (in the absence of misperceptions) recessions reflect changes in full-employment output.

Figure 15.5 shows the actual and full-employment surpluses (as percentages of GDP) for all levels of government since 1970. Note that the full-employment surplus substantially exceeded the actual budget surplus during the recessions of 1981–1982 and 1990–1992 when output was below its full-employment level. The difference between the two surplus measures reflects the importance of automatic stabilizers in federal and provincial budgets.

GOVERNMENT CAPITAL FORMATION

The health of the economy depends not only on *how much* the government spends but also on *how* it spends its resources. For example, as we discussed in Chapter 6, the quantity and quality of public infrastructure—roads, schools, hospitals, and so on—are potentially important for the rate of economic growth. Thus, the formation of **government capital**—long-lived physical assets owned by the government—is one way that fiscal policy affects the macroeconomy. The government budget affects not only physical capital formation but also human capital formation. At least part of government expenditures on health and education are an investment, in the sense that they will lead to a more productive workforce in the future.

In Canada, the government budget accounting system distinguishes between expenditures on current items, such as the salaries of police officers or agricultural subsidies, and expenditures on capital items, such as the construction of mass transit systems. When the deficit is measured on a current basis, capital spending is not included as part of government spending. The resulting measure in the national accounts is called "saving" and is defined as follows:

FIGURE 15.5

FULL-EMPLOYMENT AND
ACTUAL BUDGET
SURPLUSES, 1970–2000

The actual and full-employment budget surpluses for all levels of government are shown as a percentage of GDP. The actual budget surplus (the blue line) was less than the full-employment surplus (the black line) by substantial amounts during the 1981–1982 and 1990–1992 recessions, reflecting the importance of automatic stabilizers.

Source: Department of Finance, *Fiscal Reference Tables*, 2001, Table 46. Reproduced with the permission of the Minister of Public Works and Government Services Canada, 2002.

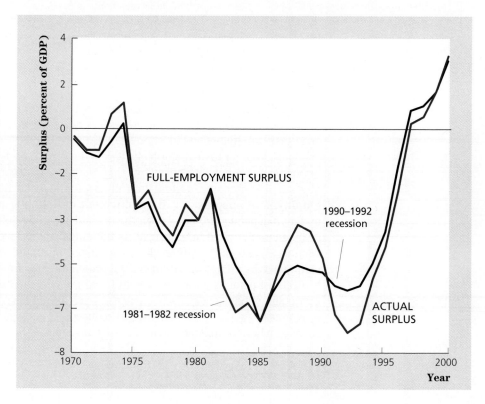

$$
\begin{aligned}
\text{saving} \; &= \; S_{\text{govt}} \\
&= \; T - (G + TR + INT) \\
&= \; \text{surplus}
\end{aligned}
\tag{15.3}
$$

In 2000, saving by all levels of government in Canada was $37.7 billion. When saving is measured in this way, government purchases include only the component of public investment that is needed to maintain the stock of public capital, by offsetting depreciation. This makes sense because depreciation can be thought of as current spending. So, to measure government spending including investment, Statistics Canada subtracts depreciation from G (so as not to count it twice) and then adds all public investment. The result is called "net lending":

$$
\begin{aligned}
\text{net lending} \; &= \; T - (G + TR + INT - dK_{\text{govt}} + I_{\text{govt}}) \\
&= \; \text{saving} + dK_{\text{govt}} - I_{\text{govt}}
\end{aligned}
\tag{15.4}
$$

New investment usually exceeds depreciation, so net lending is less than saving, or the surplus that includes investment spending is less than the surplus based on current spending only. In 2000, net lending was $34 billion.

INCENTIVE EFFECTS OF FISCAL POLICY

The third way in which fiscal policy affects the macroeconomy is by its effects on incentives. Tax policies in particular can affect economic behaviour by changing the financial rewards to various activities. For example, Chapter 4 showed how tax rates influence the incentives of households to save and of firms to make capital investments.

AVERAGE VERSUS MARGINAL TAX RATES

To analyze the effects of taxes on economic incentives, we need to distinguish between average and marginal tax rates. The **average tax rate** is the total amount of taxes paid by a person (or a firm), divided by the person's before-tax income. The **marginal tax rate** is the fraction of an *additional* dollar of income that must be paid in taxes. For example, suppose that in a particular country, no taxes are levied on the first $10,000 of income, and a 25% tax is levied on all income above $10,000 (see Table 15.3). Under this income tax system, a person with an income of $18,000 pays a tax of $2,000. Thus, her average tax rate is 11.1% ($2,000 in taxes divided by $18,000 in before-tax income). However, this taxpayer's marginal tax rate is 25% because a $1 increase in her income will increase her taxes by $0.25. Table 15.3 shows that everyone with an income higher than $10,000 faces the same marginal tax rate of 25% but that the average tax rate increases with income.

TABLE 15.3

Marginal and Average Tax Rates: An Example
(Total Tax = 25% of Income over $10,000)

Income	Income – $10,000	Tax	Average Tax Rate	Marginal Tax Rate
$ 18,000	$ 8,000	$ 2,000	11.1%	25%
50,000	40,000	10,000	20.0%	25%
100,000	90,000	22,500	22.5%	25%

We can show why the distinction between average and marginal tax rates is important by considering the individual's decision about how much labour to supply. The effects of a tax increase on the amount of labour supplied depend strongly on whether average or marginal taxes are being increased. Economic theory predicts that an increase in the average tax rate, with the marginal tax rate held constant, will *increase* the amount of labour supplied at any (before-tax) real wage. In contrast, theory predicts that an increase in the marginal tax rate, with the average tax rate held constant, will *decrease* the amount of labour supplied at any real wage.

To explain these conclusions, let us first consider the effects of a change in the average tax rate. Returning to our example from Table 15.3, imagine that the marginal tax rate stays at 25% but that now all income over $8,000 (rather than all income over $10,000) is subject to a 25% tax. The taxpayer with an income of $18,000 finds that her tax bill has risen from $2,000 to $2,500, or 0.25 ($18,000 –$8000), so her average tax rate has risen from 11.1% to 13.9%, or $2,500/$18,000. As a result, the taxpayer is $500 poorer. Because she is effectively less wealthy, she will increase the amount of labour she supplies at any real wage (see Summary table 4, p. 79). Hence, an increase in the average tax rate, holding the marginal tax rate fixed, shifts the labour supply curve (in a diagram with the before-tax real wage on the vertical axis) to the right.[4]

Now consider the effects of an increase in the marginal tax rate, with the average tax rate constant. Suppose that the marginal tax rate on income is raised from 25% to 40% and is accompanied by other changes in the tax law that keep the average tax rate—and, thus, the total amount of taxes paid by the typical taxpayer—the same. To be specific, suppose that the portion of income not subject to tax is increased from $10,000 to $13,000. Then, for the taxpayer earning $18,000, total taxes are $2,000, or 0.40($18,000 –$13,000), and the average tax rate of 11.1%, or $2,000/$18,000, is the same as it was under the original tax law.

With the average tax rate unchanged, the taxpayer's wealth is unaffected, and so, there is no change in labour supply stemming from a change in wealth. However, the increase in the marginal tax rate implies that the taxpayer's after-tax reward for each extra hour worked declines. For example, if her wage is $20 per hour before taxes, at the original marginal tax rate of 25%, her actual take-home pay for each extra hour of work is $15 ($20 minus 25% of $20, or $5, in taxes). At the new marginal tax rate of 40% the taxpayer's take-home pay for each extra hour of work is only $12 ($20 in before-tax wages minus $8 in taxes). Because extra hours of work no longer carry as much reward in terms of real income earned, at any specific before-tax real wage the taxpayer is likely to work fewer hours and enjoy more leisure, instead. Thus, if the average tax rate is held fixed, an increase in the marginal tax rate causes the labour supply curve to shift to the left.[5]

APPLICATION

THE POVERTY TRAP

According to the analysis of this section, a reduction in marginal tax rates should lead to an increase in labour supply. While the direction of this change is not controversial,

---

4. In terms of the analysis of Chapter 3, the increase in the average tax rate has a pure income effect on labour supply.

5. In terms of the discussion in Chapter 3, a change in the marginal tax rate with no change in the average tax rate has a pure substitution effect on labour supply.

the size of this effect is. In the United States, a group of economists, politicians, and journalists have argued for an approach to economic policy known as **supply-side economics**. Their basic belief is that all aspects of economic behaviour—such as labour supply, saving, and investment—respond to economic incentives and, in particular, to incentives provided by the tax code. "Supply-siders" go further, claiming that the incentive effects of tax policy are much larger than most economists have traditionally believed. In particular, supply-siders argue that the amount of labour supplied would increase substantially as a result of income tax reductions.

While supply-side economics has not been as influential in Canada, there has been considerable debate about Canadian marginal income tax rates. For example, the reductions in income tax rates in British Columbia in 2001 were defended on the grounds that they would increase labour supply. More broadly, some commentators have argued that marginal tax rates, which are higher in Canada than in the United States, discourage the labour supply of highly skilled workers, by encouraging them to emigrate.[6]

You may be surprised to learn that some of the highest marginal tax rates are faced by relatively poor Canadians. These high effective marginal tax rates are possible because transfers under several social programs depend on a household's income. As income rises, the benefits may fall (perhaps suddenly at some cut-off point) in order to limit the transfers to high-income earners. A household that earns an additional dollar in wages may lose almost as much in benefits, as its income rises above a cut-off point. According to our analysis, these high marginal tax rates (combined with low average tax rates) should act to discourage labour supply. This situation is known as the **poverty trap**.

Figure 15.6 shows the effective marginal tax rate (combined federal and provincial) for a one-earner couple with two children, in Ontario in 2000. As income rises along the horizontal axis, eligibility for social assistance, the Canada child tax benefit, the national child benefit (introduced in 1998), and the GST credit declines. As a result, disposable income does not rise as fast as earned income because additional wage earnings are offset by lost benefits and tax credits. The implied marginal tax rates are measured on the vertical axis and, at many income levels, are greater than 70%.

Eliminating the poverty trap is challenging for two reasons. First, defraying the costs that low-income workers face when entering the labour force costs money. Recently, the federal government has enriched the working income supplement to the child tax benefit so that the benefit does not drop as rapidly with income. But avoiding disincentive effects without making a transfer universal, and expensive, remains a challenge. Second, removing the trap requires coordination between the federal government, which is responsible for most refundable income-tax credits, and provincial governments, which administer social assistance. An example of such coordination occurred in 1997, when the federal government enriched the child tax benefit, while provincial governments simultaneously reduced welfare payments for children and re-directed their spending to programs (such as day care or school meals) that benefit poor children, whether their parents receive social assistance or not.

---

6. For annual assessments of Canada's tax system and comparisons with other countries, see each year's issue of *OECD Economic Surveys: Canada.*

FIGURE 15.6

THE POVERTY TRAP

The figure shows the effective marginal tax rate for a one-earner couple with two children, in Ontario in 2000, graphed against family income. As earnings rise, eligibility for benefits declines so that marginal tax rates may be very high even at low levels of income. Labour supply is discouraged because only skilled workers can enter the labour force to the right of the highest marginal tax rates.

Source: Department of Finance. Reproduced with the permission of the Minister of Public Works and Government Services Canada, 2002.

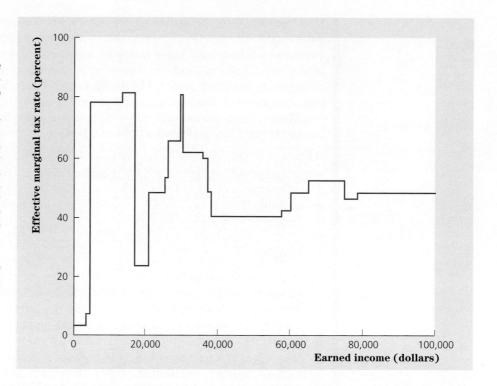

TAX-INDUCED DISTORTIONS AND TAX RATE SMOOTHING

Because taxes affect economic incentives, they change the pattern of economic behaviour. If the invisible hand of free markets is working properly, the pattern of economic activity in the absence of taxes is the most efficient, so changes in behaviour caused by taxes reduce economic welfare. Tax-induced deviations from efficient, free-market outcome are called **distortions**.

To illustrate the idea of a distortion, let us go back to the example of the worker whose before-tax real wage is $20. Because profit-maximizing employers demand labour up to the point that the marginal product of labour equals the real wage, the real output produced by an extra hour of the worker's labour (her marginal product) also is $20. Now, suppose that the worker is willing to sacrifice leisure to work an extra hour if she receives at least $14 in additional real earnings. Because the value of what the worker can produce in an extra hour of labour exceeds the value that she places on an extra hour of leisure, her working the extra hour is economically efficient.

In an economy without taxes, this efficient outcome occurs because the worker is willing to work the extra hour for the extra $20 in real wages. She would also be willing to work the extra hour if the marginal tax rate on earnings were 25% because at a marginal tax rate of 25%, her after-tax real wage is $15, which exceeds the $14 real wage minimum that she is willing to accept. However, if the marginal tax rate rises to 40% so that the worker's after-tax wage falls to only $12, she would decide that it is not worth her while to work the extra hour, even though for her to do so would have been economically efficient. The difference between the number of hours the worker would have worked had there been no tax on wages and the number of hours she actually works when there is a tax reflects the distorting effect of the tax. The higher the tax rate is, the greater the distortion is likely to be.

Because doing entirely without taxes is not possible, the problem for fiscal policymakers is how to raise needed government revenues while keeping distortions relatively small. Because high tax rates are particularly costly in terms of economic efficiency, economists argue that keeping tax rates roughly constant at a moderate level is preferable to alternate periods of very low and very high tax rates. For example, if the government's spending plans require it to levy a tax rate that over a number of years averages 20%, most economists would advise the government *not* to set the tax rate at 30% half the time and 10% the other half. The reason is the large distortions that the 30% tax rate would cause in the years that it was effective. A better strategy is to hold the tax rate constant at 20%. A policy of maintaining stable tax rates so as to minimize distortions is called **tax rate smoothing**.

Has the federal government had a policy of tax rate smoothing? If it were trying to smooth tax rates, the government would prepare for anticipated expenditures (due to recessions, say) by raising some revenue in advance. While this does not seem to happen, the idea of tax smoothing is still useful. For example, what explains the Canadian government's huge deficit during World War II (see Figure 15.4)? The alternative to deficit financing of the war would have been a large wartime increase in tax rates, coupled with a drop in tax rates when the war was over. But high tax rates during the war would have distorted the economy when productive efficiency was especially important. By financing the war through borrowing, the government effectively spread the needed tax increase over a long period of time (as the debt was repaid), rather than raising current taxes by a large amount. This action is consistent with the idea of tax smoothing.

15.3 GOVERNMENT DEFICITS AND DEBT

The single number in the federal government's budget that is the focus of most public debate is the size of the budget deficit or surplus. During the 1980s and early 1990s, a series of unprecedentedly large (for peacetime) deficits led to a barrage of claims and counterclaims about the potential impact of big deficits on the economy. Then the emergence of budget surpluses in the late 1990s brought a debate about paying down public debt. In the rest of this chapter, we discuss the government budget deficit or surplus, the government debt, and their effects on the economy.

THE GROWTH OF THE GOVERNMENT DEBT

There is an important distinction between the government budget surplus or deficit and the government debt (also called the national debt). The government budget surplus or deficit (a flow variable) is the difference between expenditures and tax revenues in any fiscal year. Box 15.1 (on p. 577), "How Large Is the Federal Surplus?" discusses different ways in which the surplus or deficit may be measured. The **government debt** (a stock variable) is the total value of government bonds outstanding at any particular time. Because the excess of government expenditures over revenues equals the amount of new borrowing that the government must do— that is, the amount of new government debt that it must issue—any year's deficit (measured in dollar, or nominal, terms) equals the change in the debt in that year. We can express the relationship between government debt and the budget deficit by

$$\Delta B = \text{nominal government budget deficit}$$
$$= - \text{nominal government budget surplus,} \tag{15.5}$$

where ΔB is the change in the nominal value (or face value) of government bonds outstanding.

In a period of persistently large budget deficits, such as that experienced recently by Canada, the nominal value of the government's debt will grow quickly. For example, between 1979 and 1997, federal government debt outstanding increased tenfold in nominal terms, from $59 billion in 1979 to $588 billion in 1997. Measured in terms of 1992 dollars, the (real) value of federal government debt outstanding in 1997 was more than four times as large as in 1979. However, 1997 marked the end of the sequence of deficits. In that year, the federal government began to run nominal budget surpluses, which led to reductions in debt.

Because countries with a high GDP have relatively more resources available to pay the principal and interest on the government's bonds, a useful measure of government indebtedness is the quantity of government debt outstanding divided by the GDP, or the *debt–GDP ratio*. Figure 15.7 shows the history of the debt–GDP ratio in Canada. The upper curve shows the federal debt–GDP ratio, while the lower curve shows the debt–GDP ratio for provincial governments.

A striking feature of Figure 15.7 is the large increase in the debt–GDP ratio that occurred during World War II when the government sold bonds to finance the war effort. By the end of the war the debt–GDP ratio exceeded 100%, implying that the value of government debt outstanding was greater than a year's GDP. Over the following 30 years, the government steadily reduced its indebtedness relative to GDP. Beginning in about 1976, though, greater budget deficits caused the debt–GDP ratio to rise. By the mid-1990s, the combined federal–provincial debt–GDP ratio was at a postwar high. It peaked in 1996, then began to decline. Currently, Canada's debt–GDP ratio remains higher than the ratios in the United States or the United Kingdom, but it is significantly lower than the ratios in Italy and Japan. Moreover, Japan's debt–GDP ratio, unlike Canada's, is continuing to rise.

FIGURE 15.7

RATIOS OF FEDERAL AND PROVINCIAL DEBT TO GDP

The upper curve shows the ratio of federal government net debt to GDP, for the period 1926–2001. The lower curve shows the ratio of debt to GDP for provincial governments, for the period 1977–2000. The federal debt–GDP ratio was high during the Great Depression, rose dramatically during World War II, then rose again after 1976, peaking in 1996. The provincial ratio rose rapidly during the 1990–1992 recession.

Source: GDP: *Canadian Economic Observer, Historical Statistical Supplement*, Table 1 or CANSIM D14816; net federal debt: CANSIM D469420; net provincial debt: CANSIM D465851.

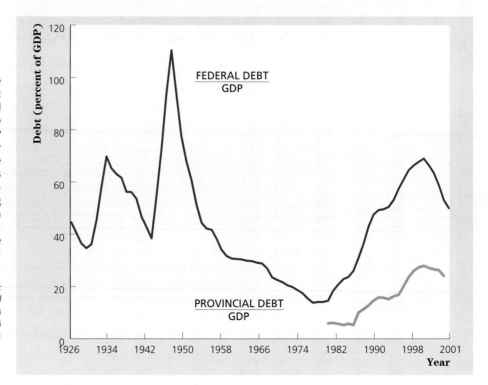

Box 15.1 How Large Is the Federal Surplus?

The measures of the federal surplus or federal deficit we present in this chapter are on a "national accounts" basis. They are consistent with the other data we present from the system of national accounts and are easy to look up. In 2000, the federal surplus on this basis was $15.5 billion. However, two other ways of measuring the federal surplus also are common. These two alternatives are quoted for fiscal years, which run from April 1 to March 31. Thus, neither is comparable with the surplus recorded in the national accounts, which applies to a calendar year. First, when the federal government presents its budget, it quotes the surplus on a "public accounts" or "budgetary" basis. For the 2000–2001 fiscal year, the budgetary surplus was $17.1 billion.

One source of the budgetary surplus in 2000–2001 was the excess of Employment Insurance (EI) premiums over benefits, which amounted to $7.3 billion. Though this amount is not in a separate fund, the size of this gap between revenue from payroll taxes and EI benefits has led some economists, and provincial governments, to argue for a reduction in EI premiums.

The public accounts exclude certain "non-budgetary" items, such as loans and advances by the government, the accounts of the pension plan of government employees, and revenue from the Exchange Fund Account. When these items are added to the public accounts deficit, we have the "financial requirements" surplus, which gives the amount by which debt can be reduced. These other accounts had a deficit in 2000–2001, and so, the financial requirements surplus was $10.2 billion.

The main source of the difference between the budgetary balance and the financial requirements balance was the Exchange Fund Account, which had a deficit of $8.8 billion. The federal government paid down its debt by $10 billion during the 2000–2001 fiscal year, while the remaining $0.2 billion of the financial requirements surplus was used to add to the government's cash balance. The national accounts surplus includes some of these special funds, and so, typically, it falls in between the public accounts and financial requirements surpluses. A good place to read about these measures, components of spending

and revenue, and debt is the *Annual Financial Report of the Government of Canada*, published each autumn by the Department of Finance.

Note that the financial requirements measure of the surplus reflects a broader definition of the government, to include the public service pension fund. When this fund runs a surplus, it might seem that the government's fiscal position is rosier than suggested by the budgetary balance. However, only the part of such a surplus that exceeds the actuarial requirements of the pension funds represents a genuine improvement in the government's financial situation. Counting revenue from the government's pension fund on the federal government's books can be thought of as a form of borrowing. It reduces the amount of additional borrowing the government needs to do, but it adds to the government's liabilities, in this case in the form of future financial obligations to retirees.

The federal government's budget does not include the Canada Pension Plan. During 2000, the CPP ran a surplus of $3.5 billion, while the QPP surplus was $427 million. The CPP must run surpluses today because the proportion of the population eligible for retirement benefits will be much larger in 25 years.

Can we be sure that the CPP will not be a drain on the federal budget in future years? A pay-as-you-go pension scheme can be made more secure by (a) raising the premiums or contributions paid by workers; (b) reducing the benefits or eligibility; or (c) earning a higher rate of return on the fund's investments. In recent years, reforms to the CPP have raised the premiums (from 6% of eligible earnings in 1997 to 9.9% in 2003). At the same time, the management of some CPP funds has been transferred to the CPP Investment Board (CPPIB), with the goal of diversifying the fund's asset holdings, which previously were invested entirely in provincial government bonds. These reforms have made the CPP actuarially sound, in the sense that contributions and investment earnings will be sufficient to pay for pensions and disability payments.

One reason to emphasize that the Canadian federal government's surplus does not include the CPP is that the situation is different in the United States. There,

continued

the federal surplus does include the Social Security system, which accounts for most of the large surpluses run by the US federal government in the late 1990s. Ironically, though, these surpluses probably are not large enough to place the Social Security system on a secure financial footing, unlike the CPP. Some combination of reforms—such as raising contributions or delaying the eligibility age—probably will be necessary in the United States.

These examples show show how difficult it may be to interpret the deficit. For this reason, Laurence Kotlikoff, of Boston University, has argued that the current deficit is not useful as an indicator of fiscal policy.* We examine research on alternate measures in the box "Generational Accounts," on p. 583.

---

*Laurence Kotlikoff, "The Deficit is Not a Well-Defined Measure of Fiscal Policy," *Science*, August 1988, pp. 791–795.

We can describe changes in the debt–GDP ratio over time by the following formula (derived in Appendix 15.A at the end of the chapter):

$$\text{growth rate of debt –GDP ratio } = \frac{\text{primary deficit}}{B} + i - \text{ growth rate of nominal GDP } , \tag{15.6}$$

where B is the nominal quantity of government bonds outstanding and i is the nominal interest rate. Recall that the primary deficit is the total budget deficit less interest payments, measured here in nominal terms. Equation (15.6) emphasizes three factors that cause the debt–GDP ratio to rise quickly:

- A high primary deficit
- A high interest rate, which increases the interest payments the government must make on its outstanding debt and, thus, increases the total budget deficit
- A slow rate of GDP growth

Equation (15.6) helps account for the pattern of the debt–GDP ratio shown in Figure 15.7. The sharp increase during World War II was the result of large primary deficits. In contrast, for the three decades after World War II, the federal government's primary deficit was small or even negative and interest rates were generally lower than GDP growth, so the debt–GDP ratio declined. The debt–GDP ratio increased during the 1980s and 1990s because the federal primary deficit was relatively high and because interest rates exceeded GDP growth rates for much of the period.

The turnaround in the debt–GDP ratio in 1996 can also be explained using Equation (15.6). As the economy slowly recovered from the 1990–1992 recession, nominal interest rates fell, and the growth rate of nominal GDP rose. At the same time, the federal government and most provincial governments began to run primary surpluses. These three factors combined to reduce the debt–GDP ratio.[7]

---

7. For a detailed history of the debt-GDP ratio, see Ron Kneebone and John Leach, "The Accumulation of Public Debt in Canada," *Canadian Public Policy*, September 2001, pp. 297–312.

THE BURDEN OF THE GOVERNMENT DEBT ON FUTURE GENERATIONS

People often express concern that the billions of dollars of federal and provincial government debt accumulated in recent years will impose a crushing financial burden on their children and grandchildren, who will someday be taxed to pay off these debts. In this view, high rates of government borrowing amount to "robbing the future" to pay for government spending that is too high or taxes that are too low in the present.

This conventional argument ignores the fact that most Canadian government bonds are owned by Canadian citizens. Therefore, although our descendants someday may face heavy taxes to pay the interest and principal of the government debt, these future taxpayers also will inherit the outstanding government bonds and, thus, will be the *recipients* of most of those interest and principal payments. To a substantial degree, we owe the government debt to ourselves, so the debt is not a burden in the same sense that it would be if it were owed entirely to outsiders.

Although the popular view of the burden of the government debt is faulty, economists have pointed out several ways in which the government debt can become a burden on future generations. First, if tax rates have to be raised substantially in the future to pay off the debt, the resulting distortions could cause the economy to function less efficiently and impose costs on future generations.

The need to run surpluses also can lead to other distortions. Meeting interest obligations severely limits the scope for countercyclical fiscal policy as a stabilization tool and also may lead to reductions in public investment. Some economists also argue that heavily indebted governments face higher interest rates than they otherwise would, which creates further pressure for tax increases and spending reductions.

Second, most people hold small amounts of government bonds (perhaps through pension funds) or no government bonds at all. In the future, people who hold few or no bonds may have to pay higher taxes to pay off the government debt than they receive in interest and principal payments; they also may receive fewer public services. People holding large quantities of bonds may receive more in interest and principal than they pay in increased taxes. Bondholders are richer on average than non-bondholders, so the need to service the government debt might lead to a transfer of resources from the relatively poor to the relatively rich. However, this transfer could be offset by other tax and transfer policies—for example, by raising taxes on high-income people.

The third argument is probably the most significant: Many economists claim that government deficits reduce national saving; that is, when the government runs a deficit, the economy accumulates less domestic capital and fewer foreign assets than it would have if the deficit had been lower. The second effect on domestic consumption is particularly relevant for Canada, which is a small open economy; government deficits most likely lead to current account deficits, rather than less domestic capital formation. If this argument is correct, deficits will lower the standard of living for our children and grandchildren, both because they may inherit a smaller capital stock and especially because they will have to pay more interest to foreigners than they otherwise would have. This reduction in the future standard of living would constitute a true burden of the government debt.

Crucial to this argument, however, is the idea that government budget deficits reduce national saving. As we have mentioned at several points in this book (notably in Chapter 4), the question of whether budget deficits affect national saving is highly controversial. We devote most of the rest of this section to further discussion of this issue.

BUDGET DEFICITS AND NATIONAL SAVING: RICARDIAN EQUIVALENCE REVISITED

Under what circumstances will an increased government budget deficit cause national saving to fall? Virtually all economists agree that an increase in the deficit caused by a rise in government purchases—say, to fight a war—reduces national saving and imposes a real burden on the economy. However, whether a deficit caused by a cut in current taxes or an increase in current transfers reduces national saving is much less clear. Recall that advocates of Ricardian equivalence argue that tax cuts or increases in transfers will not affect national saving, whereas its opponents disagree.

RICARDIAN EQUIVALENCE: AN EXAMPLE

To illustrate Ricardian equivalence, let us suppose that holding its current and planned future purchases constant, the government cuts this year's taxes by $100 per person. (Assuming that the tax cut is a lump sum allows us to ignore incentive effects.) What impact will this reduction in taxes have on national saving? In answering this question, we first recall the definition of national saving (Eq. 2.8):

$$S = Y - C - G. \tag{15.7}$$

Equation (15.7) states that national saving S equals output Y less consumption C and government purchases G.[8] If we assume that government purchases G are constant and that output Y is fixed at its full-employment level, we know from Eq. (15.7) that the tax cut will reduce national saving S only if it causes consumption C to rise. Advocates of Ricardian equivalence assert that if current and planned future government purchases are unchanged, a tax cut will not affect consumption and, thus, will not affect national saving.

   Why wouldn't a tax cut that raises after-tax incomes cause people to consume more? The answer is that—if current and planned future government purchases do not change—a tax cut today must be accompanied by an offsetting increase in expected future taxes. To see why, note that if current taxes are reduced by $100 per person, without any change in government purchases, the government must borrow an additional $100 per person by selling bonds. Suppose that the bonds are one-year bonds that pay a real interest rate r. In the following year, when the government repays the principal ($100 per person) and interest ($100 \times r$ per person) on the bonds, it will have to collect an additional $100(1 + r)$ per person in taxes. Thus, when the public learns of the current tax cut of $100 per person, they should also expect their taxes to increase by $100(1 + r)$ per person next year.[9]

   Because the current tax cut is balanced by an increase in expected future taxes, it does not make taxpayers any better off in the long run despite raising their current after-tax incomes. Indeed, after the tax cut, *taxpayers' abilities to consume today and in the future are the same as they were originally*. That is, if no one consumes more in response to the tax cut—so that each person saves the entire $100 increase in after-tax income—in the following year, the $100 per person of additional saving will grow to $100(1 + r)$ per person. This additional $100(1 + r)$ per person is precisely the amount needed to pay the extra taxes that will be levied in the future, leaving people able to consume as much in the future as they had originally planned.

---

8.   We assume that net factor payments from abroad, *NFP*, are zero.

9.   The government might put the tax increase off for two, three, or more years. Nevertheless, the general conclusion that the current tax cut must be offset by future tax increases would be unchanged.

Because people are not made better off by the tax cut (which must be coupled with a future tax increase), they have no reason to consume more today. Thus, national saving should be unaffected by the tax cut, as supporters of Ricardian equivalence claim.

RICARDIAN EQUIVALENCE ACROSS GENERATIONS

The argument for Ricardian equivalence rests on the assumption that current government borrowing will be repaid within the lifetimes of people who are living today. In other words, any tax cuts received today are offset by the higher taxes that people must pay later. But what if some of the debt the government is accumulating will be repaid not by the people who receive the tax cut but by their children or grandchildren? In that case, would not people react to a tax cut by consuming more?

Harvard economist Robert Barro[10] has shown that, in theory, Ricardian equivalence may still apply even if the current generation receives the tax cut and future generations bear the burden of repaying the government's debt. To state Barro's argument in its simplest form, let us imagine an economy in which every generation has the same number of people and suppose that the current generation receives a tax cut of $100 per person. With government purchases held constant, this tax cut increases the government's borrowing and outstanding debt by $100 per person. However, people currently living are not taxed to repay this debt; instead, this obligation is deferred until the next generation. To repay the government's increased debt, the next generation's taxes (in real terms) will be raised by $100(1 + R)$ per person, where $1 + R$ is the real value of a dollar borrowed today at the time the debt is repaid.[11]

Seemingly, the current generation of people, who receive the tax cut, should increase their consumption because the reduction in their taxes is not expected to be balanced by an increase in taxes during their lifetimes. However, Barro argued that people in the current generation should not increase their consumption in response to a tax cut if they care about the well-being of the next generation. Of course, people do care about the well-being of their children, as is reflected, in part, in the economic resources devoted to children, including funds spent on children's health and education, gifts, and inheritances.

How does the concern of this generation for the next affect the response of people to a tax cut? A member of the current generation who receives a tax cut—call him Joe—might be inclined to increase his own consumption, all else being equal. But, Barro argues, Joe should realize that for each dollar of tax cut he receives today, his son Joe Junior will have to pay $1 + R$ dollars of extra taxes in the future. Can Joe do anything on his own to help out Joe Junior? The answer is, yes. Suppose that instead of consuming his $100 tax cut, Joe saves the $100 and uses the extra savings to increase Joe Junior's inheritance. By the time the next generation is required to pay the government debt, Joe Junior's extra inheritance plus accumulated interest will be $100 (1 + R)$, or just enough to cover the increase in Joe Junior's taxes. Thus, by saving his tax cut and adding these savings to his planned bequest, Joe can keep both his own consumption and Joe Junior's consumption the same as they would have been if the tax cut had never occurred.

---

10. "Are Government Bonds Net Wealth?" *Journal of Political Economy*, November/December 1974, pp. 1095–1117.

11. For example, if the debt is to be repaid in 30 years and r is the one-year real interest rate, then $(1 + R) = (1 + r)^{30}$.

Furthermore, Barro points out, Joe *should* save all his tax cut for Joe Junior's benefit. Why? If Joe consumes even part of his tax cut, he will not leave enough extra inheritance to allow Joe Junior to pay the expected increase in his taxes, and so, Joe Junior will have to consume less than he could have if there had been no tax cut for Joe. But if Joe wanted to increase his own consumption at Joe Junior's expense, he could have done so without changes in the tax laws—for example, by contributing less to Joe Junior's university tuition payments or by planning to leave a smaller inheritance. That Joe did not take these actions shows that he was satisfied with the division of consumption between himself and Joe Junior that he had planned before the tax cut was enacted; there is no reason that the tax cut should cause this original consumption plan to change. Therefore, if Joe and other members of the current generation do not consume more in response to a tax cut, Ricardian equivalence should hold even when debt repayment is deferred to the next generation.

This analysis can be extended to allow for multiple generations and in other ways. These extensions do not change the main point, which is that if taxpayers understand that they are ultimately responsible for the government's debt, they should not change their consumption in response to changes in taxes or transfers that are unaccompanied by changes in planned government purchases. As a result, deficits created by tax cuts should not reduce national saving and, therefore, should not burden future generations.

DEPARTURES FROM RICARDIAN EQUIVALENCE

The arguments for Ricardian equivalence are logically sound, and this idea has greatly influenced economists' thinking about deficits. Although 25 years ago, most economists would have taken for granted that a tax cut would substantially increase consumption, today, there is much less agreement about this claim. In some countries, such as Canada and Israel, Ricardian equivalence seems to have worked quite well at times. In particular, declines in government saving seem to have been offset by increases in private saving. On the other hand, Ricardian equivalence seemed to fail spectacularly in the 1980s in the United States, when high government budget deficits were accompanied by extremely low rates of national saving. The experience of twin deficits and surpluses in Canada (see Figure 5.9) also may reflect a failure of Ricardian equivalence.[12]

Our judgement is that tax cuts that lead to increased government borrowing probably affect consumption and national saving, although the effect may be small. We base this conclusion on the experiences of Canada during the 1990s and the United States in the 1980s and on the fact that there are some theoretical reasons to expect Ricardian equivalence not to hold exactly. The main arguments against Ricardian equivalence are the possible existence of borrowing constraints, consumers' shortsightedness, the failure of some people to leave bequests, and the non-lump-sum nature of most tax changes.

---

12. For surveys of the evidence by a supporter and an opponent of Ricardian equivalence, respectively, see Robert Barro, "The Ricardian Approach to Budget Deficits," *Journal of Economic Perspectives*, Spring 1989, pp. 37–54; and B. Douglas Bernheim, "Ricardian Equivalence: An Evaluation of Theory and Evidence," in Stanley Fischer, ed., *NBER Macroeconomics Annual*, Cambridge, Mass.: M.I.T. Press, 1987.

Box 15.2 GENERATIONAL ACCOUNTS

How are the costs and benefits of a government program, such as the Canada and Quebec Pension Plans, distributed among the population? We could try to answer this question by noting that in a particular year, say, 2002, Pension Plan benefits were received primarily by older people, while younger people paid most of the taxes used to fund those benefits. However, to conclude that these public pension plans help old people at the expense of young people fails to recognize that the currently retired paid contributions (taxes) when they were young and that the people who are paying taxes today will someday receive benefits. A better way to measure how the costs and benefits of public pension plans are distributed would be to compare taxes paid and benefits received by various individuals over their entire *lifetimes*. For example, by forecasting the lifetime pattern of taxes and benefits of a worker who is currently 30 years old, we could determine whether, overall, a pension plan is a "good deal" for that worker, whereas looking only at one year would not allow us to conclude anything about whether the worker should be satisfied to be participating in the system.

The same lifetime perspective can be applied to all government taxes and transfers combined to see how any group of people—members of a particular generation for example—fares in terms of benefits and burdens.* Philip Oreopoulos, of the University of Toronto, has estimated the taxes that will be paid and the transfers (including education) that will be received for each generation of Canadians, including future generations.** The difference between taxes paid and transfers received is called net tax payments.

Some of his results are summarized in the accompanying table, which shows the present value of net tax payments for Canadians of various ages in 1995. (Appendix 4.A describes how to construct present values.) The payments are in US dollars to allow comparisons with generational accounts in other countries. These net tax payments are negative for those over 60 years, reflecting the fact that income taxes decline and transfers (such as those through health spending or under the CPP/QPP) tend to rise for seniors. (The taxes they paid earlier in their lives are not included.) The present values are largest for those early in their working lives, who have many tax-paying years ahead of them. For those under 20 years of age, the values are positive but lower because they may still receive transfers in the form of education.

Perhaps the most interesting numbers in the table are the last two, which give the net tax payments for those born in 1995 and also for future generations. Oreopoulos estimated that future generations, with net tax payments of $58,000, would face only slightly higher lifetime taxes than newborns, with net tax payments of $56,300. This comparison shows that Canada is approximately in intergenerational fiscal balance, in that future generations are not predicted to be significantly worse or better off than those just born. The fiscal balance partly stems from the gradual increase in CPP/QPP contributions from 1997 to 2002, which reduced the expected tax burden on future generations. It also reflects the decision of the federal government to pay down some of its debt.

Comparing the net tax payments of newborns with those of future generations does not show this same balance in all countries. For the US, future generations face a larger net tax payment than recent ones. For Japan, Italy, and Germany, future generations will face net tax payments more than 75% greater than those faced by current children, unless there are significant changes in fiscal policy (including public pensions) in those countries.

Canadian Generational Accounts

Age in 1995	Present Value of Net Tax Payments (thousands of US dollars)
90	−10.9
80	−79.8
70	−87.9
60	−44.8
50	50.8
40	134.5
30	183.3
20	177.0
10	99.0
0	56.3
Future Generations	58.0

---

*This method has been developed and applied to the United States by Alan Auerbach, Jagadeesh Gokhale, and Laurence Kotlikoff, "Generational Accounting: A Meaningful Way to Evaluate Fiscal Policy," *Journal of Economic Perspectives*, Winter 1994, pp. 73–94. For some applications to Canada, see Miles Corak, ed., *Government Finances and Generational Equity*, Statistics Canada, 1997.
**"Canada: On the Road to Fiscal Balance," Chapter 9 in *Generational Accounting Around the World* (eds. A. Auerbach, L.J. Kotlikoff, and W. Leibfritz) University of Chicago Press, 1999.

1. *Borrowing constraints.* Many people would be willing to consume more if they could find lenders who would extend them credit. However, consumers often face limits, known as *borrowing constraints*,[13] on the amounts that they can borrow. A person who wants to consume more, but who is unable to borrow to do so, will be eager to take advantage of a tax cut to increase consumption. Thus, the existence of borrowing constraints may cause Ricardian equivalence to fail.

2. *Shortsightedness.* In the view of some economists, many people are shortsighted and do not understand that as taxpayers they are ultimately responsible for the government's debt. For example, some people may determine their consumption by simple "rules of thumb," such as the rule that a family should spend fixed percentages of its current after-tax income on food, clothing, housing, and so on, without regard for how its income is likely to change in the future. If people are shortsighted, they may respond to a tax cut by consuming more, contrary to the prediction of Ricardian equivalence. However, Ricardians could reply that ultra-sophisticated analyses of fiscal policy by consumers are not necessary for Ricardian equivalence to be approximately correct. For example, if people know generally that big government deficits mean future problems for the economy (without knowing exactly why), they may be reluctant to spend from a tax cut that causes the deficit to balloon, consistent with the Ricardian prediction.

3. *Failure to leave bequests.* If people do not leave bequests, perhaps because they do not care or think about the long-run economic welfare of their children, they will increase their consumption if their taxes are cut, and Ricardian equivalence will not hold. Some people may not leave bequests because they expect their children to be richer than they are and, thus, not need any bequest. If people continue to hold this belief after they receive a tax cut, they will increase their consumption and again Ricardian equivalence will fail.

4. *Non-lump-sum taxes.* In theory, Ricardian equivalence holds only for lump-sum tax changes, with each person's change in taxes being a fixed amount that does not depend on the person's economic decisions, such as how much to work or save. As we discussed in Section 15.2, when taxes are not lump sum, the level and timing of taxes will affect incentives and, thus, economic behaviour. Thus, non-lump-sum tax cuts will have real effects on the economy, in contrast to the simple Ricardian view.

We emphasize, though, that with non-lump-sum taxes, the incentive effects of a tax cut on consumption and saving behaviour will depend heavily on the tax structure and on which taxes are cut. For example, a temporary cut in sales taxes would likely stimulate consumption, but a reduction in the tax rate on interest earned on savings accounts might increase saving. Thus, we cannot always conclude that just because taxes are not lump sum, a tax cut will increase consumption. That conclusion has to rest primarily on the other three arguments against Ricardian equivalence that we presented.

15.4 DEFICITS AND INFLATION

In this final section of the chapter, we discuss one more concern that has been expressed about government budget deficits: that deficits are inflationary. We show that the principal link between deficits and inflation is that in some circumstances deficits lead to higher rates of growth in the money supply and that high rates of money growth, in turn, cause inflation.

---

13. Appendix 4.A discussed the effect of borrowing constraints on consumption and their implications for Ricardian equivalence.

THE DEFICIT AND THE MONEY SUPPLY

Inflation—a rising price level—results when aggregate demand increases more quickly than aggregate supply. In terms of the *AD–AS* framework, suppose that the long-run aggregate supply curve (which reflects the productive capacity of the economy) is fixed. Then, for the price level to rise, the aggregate demand curve must rise over time.

Both the classical and Keynesian models of the economy imply that deficits can cause aggregate demand to rise more quickly than aggregate supply, leading to an increase in the price level. In both models, a deficit owing to increased government purchases reduces desired national saving, shifting the *IS* curve upward and causing aggregate demand to rise. This increase in aggregate demand causes the price level to rise.[14] If we assume (as Keynesians usually do) that Ricardian equivalence does not hold, a budget deficit resulting from a cut in taxes or an increase in transfers also reduces desired national saving, increases aggregate demand, and raises the price level. Thus, deficits resulting from expansionary fiscal policies (increased spending or reduced taxes) will be associated with inflation.

However, an increase in government purchases or a cut in taxes causes only a one-time increase in aggregate demand. Therefore, although we expect expansionary fiscal policies to lead to a one-time increase in the price level (that is, a temporary burst in inflation), we do not expect an increase in government purchases or a cut in taxes to cause a *sustained* increase in inflation. In general, the only factor that can sustain an increase in aggregate demand, leading to continuing inflation, is sustained growth in the money supply. Indeed, high rates of inflation are almost invariably linked to high rates of national money growth (Chapter 7). The key question therefore is: Can government budget deficits lead to ongoing increases in the money supply?

The answer is, yes. The link is the printing of money to finance government spending when the government cannot (or does not want to) finance all of its spending by taxes or borrowing from the public. In the extreme case, imagine a government that wants to spend $10 billion (say, on submarines) but has no ability to tax or borrow from the public. One option is for this government to print $10 billion worth of currency and use this currency to pay for the submarines. The revenue that a government raises by printing money is called **seignorage**. Any government with the authority to issue money can use seignorage; governments that do not have the authority to issue money, such as provincial governments in Canada, cannot use seignorage.

Actually, governments that want to finance their deficits through seignorage do not simply print new currency but use an indirect procedure. First, the finance department or treasury authorizes government borrowing equal to the amount of the budget deficit ($10 billion in our example), and a corresponding quantity of new government bonds are printed and sold. Thus, the deficit still equals the change in the outstanding government debt (Eq. 15.5). However, the new government bonds are not sold to the public. Instead, the finance department asks (or requires) the central bank to purchase the $10 billion in new bonds. The central bank pays for its purchases of new bonds by printing $10 billion in new currency,[15] which it gives to the finance department in exchange for the bonds. This newly issued currency enters general circulation when the government spends it (on the submarines, say).

---

14. The classical analysis predicts that an increase in government purchases causes aggregate supply to rise also, but we have assumed that the supply effect is smaller than the demand effect.
15. The new money created by the central bank could also be in the form of deposits at the central bank; the ultimate effect is the same.

Note that the purchase of bonds by the central bank increases the monetary base by the amount of the purchase (see Chapter 14), as when the central bank purchases government bonds on the open market.

The precise relationship between the size of the deficit and the increase in the monetary base is

$$\text{deficit} = \Delta B = \Delta B^p + \Delta B^{cb} = \Delta B^p + \Delta BASE \qquad (15.8)$$

Equation (15.8) states that the (nominal) government budget deficit equals the total increase in (nominal) government debt outstanding, ΔB, which can be divided into additional government debt held by the public, ΔB^p, and by the central bank, ΔB^{cb}. The increase in government debt held by the central bank, in turn, equals the increase in the monetary base, $\Delta BASE$. The increase in the monetary base equals the amount of seignorage collected by the government.

The final link between the budget deficit and the money supply has to do with the relationship between the money supply and the monetary base. In general, the increase in the money supply M equals the money multiplier times the increase in the monetary base (Eq. 14.8). In an all-currency economy, the money supply and the monetary base are the same and the money multiplier is 1. Nothing significant in this discussion depends on the value of the money multiplier, so for simplicity, we focus on an all-currency economy, in which the change in the money supply equals the change in the monetary base. On the basis of this assumption, Eq. (15.8) implies that

$$\text{deficit} = \Delta B = \Delta B^p + \Delta B^{cb} = \Delta B^p + \Delta M, \qquad (15.9)$$

where $\Delta BASE = \Delta M$.

Why would governments use seignorage to finance their deficits, knowing that continued money creation ultimately leads to higher inflation? Under normal conditions, developed countries rarely use seignorage. For example, in recent years, the monetary base in Canada has typically increased by about $1 billion per year, which is about 0.6% of federal government expenditure. Heavy reliance on seignorage usually occurs in war-torn or developing countries, in which military or social conditions dictate levels of government spending well above what the country can raise in taxes or borrow from the public.

As we discussed in Chapter 14, in many countries the central bank has some independence from the government. Will they agree on the amount of seignorage? The government may want to sell bonds to the central bank, to finance its deficit, while the central bank may want to limit its purchases of government bonds, to limit money growth and inflation. When the motives of the government and the central bank conflict in this way, economists sometimes describe the situation as a "game of chicken."[16]

In this game, the government can run large deficits, trying to make the central bank "chicken out" and buy government bonds to prevent interest rates from rising. Meanwhile, the central bank can pursue a zero-inflation target, trying to make the government "chicken out" and reduce its budget deficit. In Canada, this strategic game probably is less important than the game between the Bank of Canada and the private sector, though, because seignorage revenue is small and because the Bank of Canada ultimately answers to the minister of finance.

---

16. See Thomas Sargent, "Interpreting the Reagan Deficits," *Federal Reserve Bank of San Francisco, Quarterly Review*, Fall 1986, pp. 5–12.

REAL SEIGNORAGE COLLECTION AND INFLATION

The amount of real revenue that the government collects from seignorage is closely related to the inflation rate. To examine this link, let us consider an all-currency economy in which real output and the real interest rate are fixed and the rates of money growth and inflation are constant. In such an economy, the real quantity of money demanded is constant[17] and hence, in equilibrium, the real money supply must also be constant. Because the real money supply M/P does not change, the growth rate of the nominal money supply $\Delta M/M$ must equal the growth rate of the price level, or the rate of inflation π:

$$\pi = \frac{\Delta M}{M}.$$

(15.10)

Equation (15.10) expresses the close link between an economy's inflation rate and money growth rate.

How much seignorage is the government collecting in this economy? The *nominal* value of seignorage in any period is the increase in the amount of money in circulation ΔM. Multiplying both sides of Eq. (15.10) by M and rearranging gives an equation for the nominal value of seignorage:

$$\Delta M = \pi M.$$

(15.11)

Real seignorage revenue, R, is the real value of the newly created money, which equals nominal seignorage revenue ΔM divided by the price level P. Dividing both sides of Eq. (15.11) by the price level P gives

$$R = \frac{\Delta M}{P} = \pi \frac{M}{P}.$$

(15.12)

Equation (15.12) states that the government's real seignorage revenue R equals the inflation rate π times the real money supply M/P.

Equation (15.12) illustrates why economists sometimes call seignorage the **inflation tax**. In general, for any type of tax, tax revenue equals the tax rate multiplied by the tax base (whatever is being taxed). In the case of the inflation tax, the tax base is the real money supply and the tax rate is the rate of inflation. Multiplying the tax base (the real money supply) by the tax rate (the rate of inflation) gives the total inflation tax revenue.

How does the government collect the inflation tax and who pays this tax? The government collects the inflation tax by printing money (or by having the central bank issue new money) and using the newly created money to purchase goods and services. The inflation tax is paid by any member of the public who holds money because inflation erodes the purchasing power of money. For example, when the inflation rate is 10% per year, a person who holds currency for a year loses 10% of the purchasing power of that money and, thus, effectively pays a 10% tax on the real money holdings.

Suppose that a government finds that the seignorage being collected does not cover its spending and begins to increase the money supply faster. Will this increase in the money growth rate cause the real seignorage collected by the government to rise? Somewhat surprisingly, it may not. As Eq. (15.12) shows, the real seignorage

---

17. Real money demand depends on real output and the nominal interest rate (we assume that the interest rate paid on money is fixed). Output is constant, and because the real interest rate and the inflation rate are constant, the nominal interest rate also is constant. Thus, the real quantity of money demanded is constant.

collected by the government is the product of two terms—the rate of inflation (the tax rate) and the real money supply (the tax base). By raising the money growth rate, the government can increase the inflation rate. However, at a constant real interest rate, a higher rate of inflation will raise the nominal interest rate, causing people to reduce the real quantity of money held. Thus, whether real seignorage revenue increases when the money growth rate increases depends on whether the rise in inflation π outweighs the decline in real money holdings M/P.

This point is illustrated by Figure 15.8, on the next page, which shows the determination of real seignorage revenue at an assumed constant real interest rate of 3%. The real quantity of money is measured along the horizontal axes, and the nominal interest rate is measured along the vertical axes. The downward-sloping MD curves show the real demand for money; they slope downward because an increase in the nominal interest rate reduces the real quantity of money demanded.

In Figure 15.8(a), the actual and expected rate of inflation is 8% so that (for a real interest rate of 3%) the nominal interest rate is 11%. When the nominal interest rate is 11%, the real quantity of money that people are willing to hold is $15 billion (point H). Using Eq. (15.12), we find that the real value of seignorage revenue is 0.08 ($15 billion), or $1.2 billion. Real seignorage revenue is represented graphically by the area of the shaded rectangle. The rectangle's height equals the inflation rate (8%) and the rectangle's width equals the real quantity of money held by the public ($15 billion).

Figure 15.8(b) shows the real amount of seignorage revenue at two different inflation rates. The real interest rate (3%) and the money demand curve in Figure 15.8(b) are identical to those in Figure 15.8(a). When the rate of inflation is 1% per year, the nominal interest rate is 4%, and the real quantity of money that the public holds is $40 billion. Real seignorage revenue is 0.01($40 billion) = $0.4 billion, or the area of rectangle $ABCD$. Alternatively, when the rate of inflation is 15% per year, the nominal interest rate is 18%, and the real value of the public's money holdings is $5 billion. Real seignorage revenue in this case is $0.75 billion, or the area of rectangle $AEFG$.

Comparing Figure 15.8(a) and Figure 15.8(b) reveals that real seignorage revenue is higher when inflation is 8% per year than when inflation is either 1% per year or 15% per year. Figure 15.9 (on p. 590) shows the relationship between the inflation rate and seignorage revenue. At low inflation rates, an increase in the inflation rate increases real seignorage revenue. However, at high inflation rates, an increase in inflation reduces real seignorage revenue. In Figure 15.9, the maximum possible real seignorage revenue is $1.2 billion, which is achieved at the intermediate level of inflation of 8% per year.

What happens if the government tries to raise more seignorage revenue than the maximum possible amount? If it does so, inflation will rise but the real value of the government's seignorage will fall as real money holdings fall. If the government continues to increase the rate of money creation, the economy will experience a high rate of inflation or even hyperinflation. Inflation will continue until the government reduces the rate of money creation either by balancing its budget or by finding some other way to finance its spending.

In some hyperinflations, governments desperate for revenue raise the rate of money creation well above the level that maximizes real seignorage. For example, in the extreme hyperinflation that hit Germany after World War I, rapid money creation drove the rate of inflation to 322% *per month*. In contrast, in his classic study of the

FIGURE 15.8

THE DETERMINATION OF
REAL SEIGNORAGE REVENUE

(a) The downward-sloping curve *MD* is the money demand function for any level of real income. The real interest rate is assumed to be 3%. When the rate of inflation is 8%, the nominal interest rate is 11%, and the real quantity of money held by the public is $15 billion (point *H*). Real seignorage revenue collected by the government, represented by the area of the shaded rectangle, equals the rate of inflation (8%) times the real money stock ($15 billion), or $1.2 billion.

(b) The money demand function *MD* is the same as in (a), and the real interest rate remains at 3%. When the inflation rate is 1%, the nominal interest rate is 4%, and the real quantity of money held by the public is $40 billion. In this case real seignorage revenue equals the area of the rectangle, *ABCD*, or $0.4 billion. When the rate of inflation is 15%, the nominal interest rate is 18%, and the real money stock held by the public is $5 billion. Real seignorage revenue in this case equals the area of the rectangle *AEFG*, or $0.75 billion.

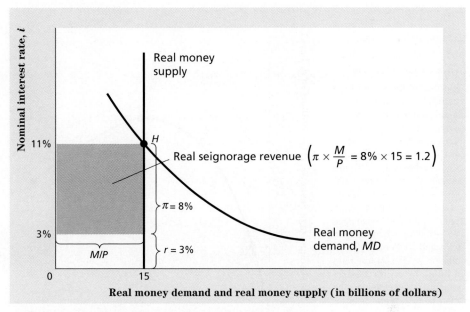

(a) Determination of real seignorage revenue for $\pi = 8\%$

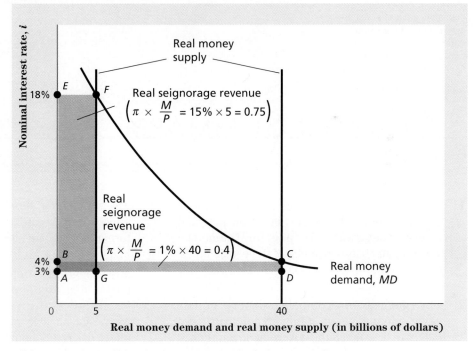

(b) Determination of real seignorage revenue for $\pi = 1\%$ and $\pi = 15\%$

German hyperinflation, Philip Cagan,[18] of Columbia University, calculated that the constant rate of inflation that would have maximized the German government's real seignorage revenue was "only" 20% per month.

---

18. "The Monetary Dynamics of Hyperinflation," in Milton Friedman, ed., *Studies in the Quantity Theory of Money*, Chicago: University of Chicago Press, 1956.

FIGURE 15.9

THE RELATION OF REAL
SEIGNORAGE REVENUE TO
THE RATE OF INFLATION

Continuing the example of
Figure 15.8, this figure shows
the relation of real seignorage
revenue R, measured on the
vertical axis, to the rate of
inflation π, measured on the
horizontal axis. From Figure
15.8(a), when inflation is 8%
per year, real seignorage
revenue is $1.2 billion. From
Figure 15.8(b), real seignorage
is $0.4 billion when inflation
is 1% and $0.75 billion when
inflation is 15%. At low rates
of inflation, an increase in
inflation increases seignorage
revenue. At high rates of
inflation, increased inflation
can cause seignorage revenue
to fall. In this example, the
maximum amount of seignorage revenue the government
can obtain is $1.2 billion,
which occurs when the in-
flation rate is 8%.

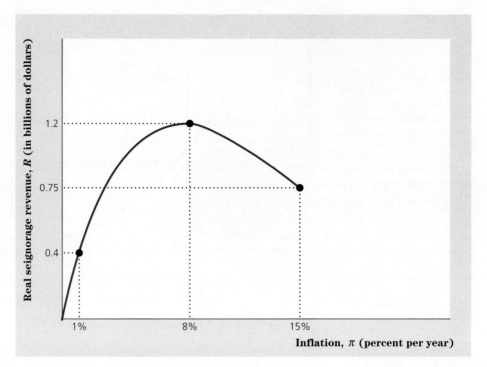

CHAPTER SUMMARY

1. Government expenditures are government purchases of goods and services, transfers, and interest payments. To pay for them, the government collects revenue of three main types: direct taxes, indirect taxes, and investment income.

2. The government budget surplus equals government revenue minus expenditure and indicates how much the government can reduce its debt during the year. A deficit (a negative surplus) indicates how much the government must borrow. The primary government budget surplus is the total surplus plus net interest payments. The primary surplus indicates by how much tax revenue exceeds the cost of current programs (measured by current government purchases and transfers) during the year.

3. Fiscal policy affects the economy through its effects on aggregate demand, government capital formation, and incentives.

4. Increases or decreases in government purchases affect aggregate demand by changing desired national saving and shifting the *IS* curve. If Ricardian equivalence does not hold, as Keynesians usually argue, changes in taxes also affect desired national saving, the *IS* curve, and aggregate demand. Automatic stabilizers in the government's budget allow spending to rise or taxes to fall automatically in a recession, which helps cushion the drop in aggregate demand during a recession. The full-employment surplus is what the surplus would be—given current government spending programs and tax laws—if the economy were at full employment. Because of

automatic stabilizers that increase spending and reduce taxes in recessions, the actual surplus falls below the full-employment surplus in recessions.

5. Government capital formation contributes to the productive capacity of the economy. Government capital formation includes both investment in physical capital (roads, schools) and investment in human capital (education, health care). Official measures of government investment include only investment in physical capital.

6. The average tax rate is the fraction of total income paid in taxes, and the marginal tax rate is the fraction of an additional dollar of income that must be paid in taxes. Changes in average tax rates and changes in marginal tax rates have different effects on economic behaviour. For example, an increase in the average tax rate (with no change in the marginal tax rate) increases labour supply, but an increase in the marginal tax rate (with no change in the average tax rate) decreases labour supply.

7. Policymakers must be concerned about the fact that taxes induce distortions, or deviations in economic behaviour from that which would have occurred in the absence of taxes. One strategy for minimizing distortions is to hold tax rates approximately constant over time (tax rate smoothing), rather than alternating between high and low tax rates.

8. The national debt equals the value of government bonds outstanding. The government budget deficit, expressed in nominal terms, equals the change in the government debt. The behaviour of the debt–GDP ratio over time depends on the ratio of the primary deficit to outstanding government debt and on whether the interest rate is greater or less than the GDP growth rate.

9. Deficits are a burden on future generations if they cause national saving to fall because lower national saving means that the country will have less capital and fewer foreign assets than it would have had otherwise. Ricardian equivalence indicates that a deficit caused by a tax cut will not affect consumption and, therefore, will not affect national saving. In the Ricardian view, a tax cut does not affect consumption because the increase in consumers' current income arising from the tax cut is offset by the prospect of increased taxes in the future, leaving consumers

no better off. In theory, Ricardian equivalence still holds if the government debt is not repaid by the current generation, provided that people care about the well being of their descendants and, thus, choose not to consume more at their descendants' expense.

10. Ricardian equivalence may not hold—and, thus, tax cuts may affect national saving—if (1) borrowing constraints prevent some people from consuming as much as they want to; (2) people are shortsighted and do not take expected future changes in taxes into account in their planning; (3) people fail to leave bequests; or (4) tax cuts are not lump sum. The empirical evidence on Ricardian equivalence is mixed.

11. Deficits are linked to inflation when a government finances its deficits by printing money. The amount of revenue that the government raises by printing money is called seignorage. The real value of seignorage equals the inflation rate times the real money supply. Increasing the inflation rate does not always increase the government's real seignorage because higher inflation causes the public to hold a smaller real quantity of money. Attempts to push the collection of seignorage above its maximum can lead to hyperinflation.

KEY TERMS

automatic stabilizers, p. 568
average tax rate, p. 571
distortions, p. 574
full-employment deficit, p. 569
full-employment surplus, p. 569
government capital, p. 570
government debt, p. 575
inflation tax, p. 587
marginal tax rate, p. 571
poverty trap, p. 573
primary government budget surplus, p. 565
seignorage, p. 585
supply-side economics, p. 573
tax rate smoothing, p. 575

KEY EQUATIONS

$$\Delta B = \text{nominal deficit} \qquad (15.5)$$
$$= -\text{nominal surplus}$$

The change in the nominal value of the government debt equals the nominal government deficit.

growth rate of debt–GDP ratio =

$$\frac{\text{primary deficit}}{B} + i - \text{ growth rate of nominal GDP}$$

$$(15.6)$$

The growth rate of the ratio of government debt outstanding to GDP depends on the ratio of the primary deficit to outstanding government debt, B, and on the difference between the nominal interest rate, i, and the growth rate of nominal GDP.

$$\text{deficit} = \Delta B = \Delta B^p + \Delta B^{cb} = \Delta B^p + \Delta M \quad (15.9)$$

The government budget deficit equals the increase in the stock of government debt outstanding, B, which in turn equals the sum of additional holdings of government debt by the public, B^p, and by the central bank, B^{cb}. The increase in debt held by the central bank equals the increase in the monetary base, which in an all-currency economy is the same as the increase in the money supply, M.

$$R = \frac{\Delta M}{P} = \pi \frac{M}{P}$$

$$(15.12)$$

In an all-currency economy, real seignorage revenue, R, equals the increase in the money supply, M, divided by the price level, P. This ratio, in turn, equals the inflation rate (the tax rate on money) multiplied by the real money supply (the tax base).

REVIEW QUESTIONS

1. What are the major components of government expenditure? What are the major sources of government revenue? How does the composition of the federal government's expenditure and revenue differ from that of provincial and local governments?

2. Explain the difference between the overall government budget surplus and the primary surplus. Why are two surplus concepts needed?

3. How is government debt related to the government deficit? What factors contribute to a high growth rate of the debt–GDP ratio?

4. What are the three main ways that fiscal policy affects the macroeconomy? Explain briefly how each channel of policy works.

5. Define *automatic stabilizer* and give an example. For proponents of anti-recessionary fiscal policies, what advantage do automatic stabilizers have over other types of taxing and spending policies?

6. Give a numerical example that shows the difference between the average tax rate and the marginal tax rate on a person's income. For a constant before-tax real wage, which type of tax rate most directly affects how wealthy a person feels? Which type of tax rate affects the reward for working an extra hour?

7. Why do economists suggest that tax rates be kept roughly constant over time, rather than alternating between high and low levels?

8. In what ways is the government debt a potential burden on future generations? What is the relationship between Ricardian equivalence and the idea that government debt is a burden?

9. Discuss four reasons why the Ricardian equivalence proposition is not likely to hold exactly.

10. Define inflation tax (also called seignorage). How does the government collect this tax, and who pays it? Can the government always increase its real revenues from the inflation tax by increasing money growth and inflation?

NUMERICAL PROBLEMS

1. The following budget data are for a country having both a central government and provincial governments:

Central purchases of goods and services	200
Provincial purchases of goods and services	150
Central transfer payments to persons	100
Provincial transfer payments to persons	50
Central to provincial transfers	100
Central tax receipts	500
Provincial tax receipts	100
Interest received from private sector by central government	10
Interest received from private sector by provincial governments	10
Total central government debt	1,000
Total provincial government debt	0
Central government debt held by provincial governments	200
Nominal interest rate	10%

Calculate the overall and primary deficits for the central government, the provincial governments, and the combined governments.

2. Parliament votes a special one-time $1 billion transfer to bail out the buggy whip industry. Tax collections do not change, and no change is planned for at least several years. By how much will this action increase the overall budget surplus and the primary surplus in the year that the transfer is made? in the next year? in the year after that? Assume that the nominal interest rate is constant at 10%.

3. Because of automatic stabilizers, various components of the government's budget depend on the level of output Y. The following are the main components of that budget:

Tax revenues	$1,000 + 0.1Y$
Transfers	$800 - 0.05Y$
Government purchases	1,800
Interest payments	100

Full-employment output is 10,000. Find the actual budget deficit and the full-employment budget deficit for

a. $Y = 12,000.$ **b.** $Y = 10,000.$ **c.** $Y = 8,000.$

In general, how does the relationship between the actual deficit and the full-employment deficit depend on the state of the economy?

4. Suppose that the income tax law exempts income under $8,000 from the tax, taxes income between $8,000 and $20,000 at a 25% rate, and taxes income greater than $20,000 at a 30% rate.

a. Find the average tax rate and the marginal tax rate for someone earning $16,000 and for someone earning $30,000.

b. The tax law is changed so that income of less than $6,000 is untaxed, income from $6,000 to $20,000 is taxed at 20%, and income of more than $20,000 continues to be taxed at 30%. Repeat part (a).

c. How will the tax law change in part (b) affect the labour supply of the person initially making $16,000? How will it affect the labour supply of the person making $30,000?

5. Suppose that all workers value their leisure at 90 goods per day. The production function relating output per day Y to the number of people working per day N is

$$Y = 250N - 0.5N^2.$$

Corresponding to this production function, the marginal product of labour is

$$MPN = 250 - N.$$

a. Assume that there are no taxes. What are the equilibrium values of the real wage, employment N, and output Y? (*Hint*: In equilibrium, the real wage will equal both the marginal product of labour and the value of a day's leisure to workers.)

b. A 25% tax is levied on wages. What are the equilibrium values of the real wage, employment, and output? In terms of lost output, what is the distortion cost of this tax?

c. Suppose that the tax on wages rises to 50%. What are the equilibrium values of the real wage, employment, and output? In terms of lost output,

what is the distortion cost of this higher tax rate? Compare the distortion caused by a 50% tax rate with that caused by a 25% tax rate. Is the distortion caused by a 50% tax rate twice as large, more than twice as large, or less than twice as large as that caused by a 25% tax rate? How does your answer relate to the idea of tax smoothing?

6. Find the largest nominal primary deficit that the government can run without raising the debt–GDP ratio, under each of the following sets of assumptions:

a. Nominal GDP growth is 10%, the nominal interest rate is 12%, and outstanding nominal debt is 1,000.

b. Nominal interest payments are 800, outstanding nominal debt is 10,000, inflation is 6%, and the economy has zero real growth.

7. In this problem, you are asked to analyze the question: By issuing new bonds and using the proceeds to pay the interest on its old bonds, can government avoid ever repaying its debts?

a. Suppose that nominal GDP is $1 billion and the government has $100 million of bonds outstanding. The bonds are one-year bonds that pay a 7% nominal interest rate. The growth rate of nominal GDP is 5% per year. Beginning now the government runs a zero primary deficit forever and pays interest on its existing debt by issuing new bonds. What is the current debt–GDP ratio? What will this ratio be after one, two, five, and 10 years? Suppose that if the debt–GDP ratio exceeds 10, the public refuses to buy additional government bonds. Will the debt–GDP ratio ever reach that level? Will the government someday have to run a primary surplus in order to repay its debts, or can it avoid repayment forever? Why?

b. Repeat part (a) for nominal GDP growth of 8% per year and a nominal interest rate on government bonds of 7% per year.

8. Real money demand in an economy is

$$L = 0.2Y - 500i,$$

where Y is real income and i is the nominal interest rate. In equilibrium, real money demand L equals real money supply M/P. Suppose that Y is 1,000 and the real interest rate r is 0.04.

a. Draw a graph with real seignorage revenue on the vertical axis and inflation on the horizontal axis. Show the values of seignorage for inflation of 0, 0.02, 0.04, 0.06, . . ., 0.30.

b. What inflation rate maximizes seignorage?

c. What is the maximum amount of seignorage revenue?

d. Repeat parts (a) to (c) for Y = 1,000 and r = 0.08.

9. Consider an economy in which the money supply consists of both currency and deposits. The growth rate of the monetary base, the growth rate of the money supply, inflation, and expected inflation all are constant at 10% per year. Output and the real interest rate are constant. Monetary data for this economy as of January 1, 2000, are as follows:

Currency in circulation	$200
Bank reserves	$ 50
Monetary base	$250
Deposits	$600
Money supply	$800

a. What is the nominal value of seignorage over the year? (*Hint*: How much monetary base is created during the year?)

b. Suppose that deposits and bank reserves pay no interest and that banks lend deposits not held as reserves at the market rate of interest. Who pays the inflation tax (measured in nominal terms), and how much do they pay? (*Hint*: The inflation tax paid by banks in this example is negative.)

c. Suppose that deposits pay a market rate of interest. Who pays the inflation tax, and how much do they pay?

ANALYTICAL PROBLEMS

1. Why is some provincial government spending paid for by transfers from the federal government, instead of having every provincial government pay for its own spending by levying taxes on its residents? What are the advantages and disadvantages of such a system?

2. Using the *Canadian Economic Observer, Historical Statistical Supplement,* compare the federal government's budget in 1995 and 2001. Express the main components of federal spending and receipts in each year as fractions of GDP. Have increased surpluses since 1995 been more the result of decreased spending or increases in revenues?

3. Both transfer programs and taxes affect incentives.

Consider a program designed to help the poor that promises each aid recipient a minimum income of $10,000. That is, if the recipient earns less than $10,000, the program supplements his income by enough to bring him up to $10,000.

Explain why this program would adversely affect incentives for low-wage recipients. (*Hint*: Show that this program is equivalent to giving the recipient $10,000, then taxing his labour income at a high marginal rate.) Describe a transfer program that contains better incentives. Would that program have any disadvantages? If so, what would they be?

4. Answer the following:
a. Show that Eq. (15.6), which describes how the debt–GDP ratio evolves, still holds if the primary budget deficit, the outstanding stock of government bonds, the interest rate, and the growth rate of GDP all are expressed in real, rather than nominal, terms. (*Hint*: Use the growth-rate formulas in the Appendix, Section A.7, to show that the growth rate of nominal GDP equals the growth rate of real GDP plus the inflation rate.)
b. Show that if the primary deficit is zero, the real stock of outstanding government debt grows at a rate equal to the real interest rate. (*Hint*: In this case, the government budget deficit is iB, its nominal interest payments.)

5. A consitutional amendment has been proposed that would force the federal and provincial governments to balance their budgets each year so that current expenditure would be no greater than revenue. (Several provinces already have laws something like this.) Discuss some advantages and disadvantages of such an amendment. How would a balanced-budget amendment affect the following, if in the absence of such an amendment the government would run a large deficit?
a. The use of automatic stabilizers
b. The government's ability to "smooth" taxes over time
c. The government's ability to make capital investments.

APPENDIX 15.A

THE DEBT–GDP RATIO

In this Appendix, we derive Eq. (15.6), which shows how the debt–GDP ratio evolves. If we let Q represent the ratio of government debt to GDP, by definition

$$Q = \frac{B}{PY}, \tag{15.A.1}$$

where B is the nominal value of government bonds outstanding (government debt), P is the price level, and Y is real GDP (so that PY is nominal GDP). A useful rule is that the percentage change in any ratio equals the percentage change in the numerator minus the percentage change in the denominator (Appendix, Section A.7). Applying this rule to Eq. (15.A.1) gives

$$\frac{\Delta Q}{Q} = \frac{\Delta B}{B} - \frac{\Delta(PY)}{PY}. \tag{15.A.2}$$

The increase in the nominal value of government bonds ΔB equals the nominal value of the government budget deficit (Eq. 15.5). The budget deficit equals the nominal value of the primary deficit plus interest payments on the government debt so that

$$\Delta B = PD^P + iB, \tag{15.A.3}$$

where D^P is the real value of the primary deficit, PD^P is the nominal value of the primary deficit, i is the nominal interest rate, and iB is the nominal value of interest payments on the government debt. Using Eq. (15.A.3) to substitute for ΔB on the right-hand side of Eq. (15.A.2), we obtain

$$\frac{\Delta Q}{Q} = \frac{PD^P}{B} + i - \frac{\Delta(PY)}{PY}. \tag{15.A.4}$$

As PD^P/B is the ratio of the primary deficit to the government debt and $\Delta(PY)/PY$ is the growth rate of nominal GDP, Eq. (15.A.4) is equivalent to Eq. (15.6).

Appendix

SOME USEFUL ANALYTICAL TOOLS

This Appendix reviews some basic algebraic and graphical tools that are used in this book.

A.1 FUNCTIONS AND GRAPHS

A function is a relationship among two or more variables. For an economic illustration of a function, suppose that in a certain firm, each worker employed can produce five units of output per day. Let

N = the number of workers employed by the firm;
Y = total daily output of the firm.

In this example, the relationship of output Y to the number of workers N is:

$$Y = 5N. \tag{A.1}$$

Equation (A.1) is an example of a function relating the variable Y to the variable N. Using this function, for any number of workers N, we can calculate the total amount of output Y that the firm can produce each day. For example, if $N = 3$, then $Y = 15$.

Functions can be described graphically as well as algebraically. The graph of the function $Y = 5N$, for values of N between 0 and 16, is shown in Figure A.1. Output Y is shown on the vertical axis, and the number of workers N is shown on the horizontal axis. Points on the line $0AB$ satisfy Eq. (A.1). For example, at point A, $N = 4$ and $Y = 20$, a combination of N and Y that satisfies Eq. (A.1). Similarly, at point B, $N = 12.5$ and $Y = 62.5$, which also satisfies the relationship $Y = 5N$. Note that (at B, for example) the relationship between Y and N allows the variables to have values that are not whole numbers. Allowing fractional values of N and Y is reasonable because workers can work part time or overtime, and a unit of output may be only partially completed during a day.

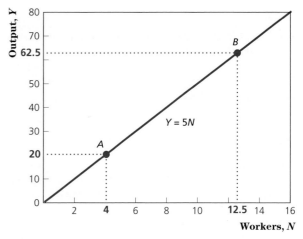

FIGURE A.1
Points on the line $0AB$ satisfy the relationship $Y = 5N$. Because the graph of the function $Y = 5N$ is a straight line, this function is called a linear function.

Functions, such as $Y = 5N$, whose graph is a straight line are called *linear functions*. Functions whose graph is not a line are called *non-linear*. An example of a *non-linear* function is

$$Y = 20\sqrt{N}. \tag{A.2}$$

The graph of the nonlinear function $Y = 20\sqrt{N}$ is shown in Figure A.2, on the next page. All points on the curve satisfy Eq. (A.2). For example, at point C, $N = 4$ and $Y = 20\sqrt{4} = 40$. At point D, $N = 9$ and $Y = 20\sqrt{9} = 60$.

Both examples of functions given so far are exact numerical relationships. We can also write functions in more general terms, using letters or symbols. For example, we might write:

$$Y = G(N). \tag{A.3}$$

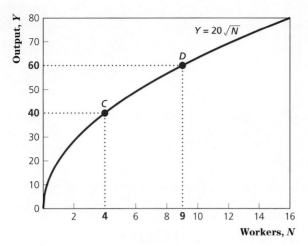

FIGURE A.2

The function $Y = 20\sqrt{N}$, whose graph is shown in this figure, is an example of a nonlinear function.

Equation (A.3) states that there is some general relationship between the number of workers N and the amount of output Y, which is represented by a function G. The numerical functions given in Eqs. (A.1) and (A.2) are specific examples of such a general relationship.

A.2 SLOPES OF FUNCTIONS

Suppose that two variables N and Y are related by a function $Y = G(N)$. Generally speaking, if we start from some given combination of N and Y that satisfies the function G, the *slope* of the function G at that point indicates by how much Y changes when N changes by one unit.

To define the slope more precisely, we suppose that the current value of N is a specific number N_1 so that the current value of Y equals $G(N_1)$. Now, consider what happens if N is increased by an amount ΔN (ΔN is read "the change in N"). Output Y depends on N; therefore, if N changes, Y must also change. The value of N is now $N_1 + \Delta N$, so the value of Y after N increases is $G(N_1 + \Delta N)$. The *change* in Y is

$$\Delta Y = G(N_1 + \Delta N) - G(N_1).$$

The slope of the function G, for an increase in N from N_1 to $N_1 + \Delta N$, is

$$\text{slope} = \frac{\Delta Y}{\Delta N} = \frac{G(N_1 + \Delta N) - G(N_1)}{(N_1 + \Delta N) - N_1}. \quad (A.4)$$

Note that if $\Delta N = 1$, the slope equals ΔY, the change in Y.

Figures A.3 and A.4 show graphically how to determine slopes for the two functions discussed in the preceding section. Figure A.3 shows the graph of the function $Y = 5N$

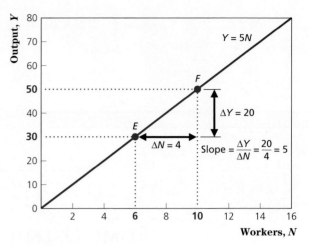

FIGURE A.3

The slope of a function equals the change in the variable on the vertical axis (Y) divided by the change in the variable on the horizontal axis (N). For example, between points E and F, the increase in N, ΔN, equals 4 and the increase in Y, ΔY, equals 20. Therefore, the slope of the function between E and F, $\Delta Y/\Delta N$, equals 5. In general, the slope of a linear function is constant, so the slope of this function between any two points is 5.

(as in Figure A.1). Suppose that we start from point E in Figure A.3, where $N = 6$ and $Y = 30$. If N is increased by 4 (for example), we move to point F on the graph, where $N = 10$ and $Y = 50$. Between E and F, $\Delta N = 10 - 6 = 4$ and $\Delta Y = 50 - 30 = 20$, so the slope $\Delta Y/\Delta N = 20/4 = 5$.

In general, the slope of a linear function is the same at all points. You can prove this result for the linear function $Y = 5N$ by showing that for any change ΔN, $\Delta Y = 5\ \Delta N$. So, for this particular linear function, the slope $\Delta Y/\Delta N$ always equals 5, a constant number.

For a non-linear function, such as $Y = 20\sqrt{N}$, the slope is not constant but depends on both the initial value of N and the size of the change in N. These results are illustrated in Figure A.4, on the next page, which displays the graph of the function $Y = 20\sqrt{N}$ (as in Figure A.2). Suppose that we are initially at point G, where $N = 1$ and $Y = 20$, and we increase N by 8 units. After the increase in N we are at point D, where $N = 9$ and $Y = 20\sqrt{9} = 60$. Between G and D, $\Delta N = 9 - 1 = 8$ and $\Delta Y = 60 - 20 = 40$. Thus, the slope of the function between G and D is $40/8 = 5$. Geometrically, the slope of the function between G and D equals the slope of the straight line between G and D.

Starting once again from point G in Figure A.4, if we instead increase N by 3 units, we come to point C, where $N = 4$ and $Y = 20\sqrt{4} = 40$. In this case $\Delta N = 3$ and $\Delta Y = 40 - 20 = 20$, so the slope between G and C is $20/3 = 6.67$, which is not the same as the slope of 5 that we calculated when earlier we increased N by 8 units. Geometrically, the slope of the line between G and C is greater than the slope

FIGURE A.4

Between points G and D, the change in N (ΔN) is 8 and the change in Y (ΔY) is 40, so the slope of the function between points G and D is $\Delta Y/\Delta N = 40/8 = 5$. This slope is the same as the slope of the line GD. Similarly, the slope of the function between points G and C is $\Delta Y/\Delta N = 20/3 = 6.67$. The slope of the line tangent to point G, which equals 10, approximates the slope of the function for very small changes in N. Generally, when we refer to the slope of a nonlinear function at a specific point, we mean the slope of the line tangent to the function at that point.

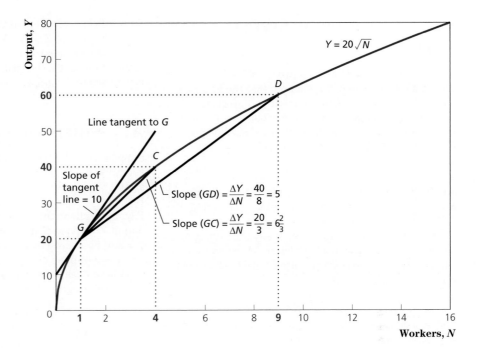

The numerical example illustrated in Figure A.4 shows that the slope of a nonlinear function depends on the size of the increase in N being considered. The slope of a nonlinear function also depends on the point at which the slope is being measured. In Figure A.4, note that the slope of a line drawn tangent to point D, for example, would be less than the slope of a line drawn tangent to point G. Thus, the slope of this particular function (measured with respect to small changes in N) is greater at G than at D.

of the line between G and D; that is, line GC is steeper than line GD.

In Figure A.4, we have also drawn a line that touches but does not cross the graph of the function at point G; this line is *tangent* to the graph of the function at point G. If you start from point G and find the slope of the function for different values of ΔN, you will discover that the smaller the value of ΔN is, the closer the slope will be to the slope of the tangent line. For example, if you compare the slope of line GD (for which $\Delta N = 8$) with the slope of line GC (for which $\Delta N = 3$), you will see that of the two the slope of line GC is closer to the slope of the line tangent to point G. For values of ΔN even smaller than 3, the slope would be still closer to the slope of the tangent line.

These observations lead to an important result: *For small values of ΔN, the slope of a function at any point is closely approximated by the slope of the line tangent to the function at that point.* Unless specified otherwise, in this book, when we refer to the slope of a non-linear function, we mean the slope of the line tangent to the function at the specified point. Thus, in Figure A.4, the slope of the function at point G means the slope of the line tangent to the function at point G, which happens to be 10.[1]

A.3 ELASTICITIES

Like slopes, elasticities indicate how much one variable responds when a second variable changes. Suppose, again, that there is a function relating Y to N, so that when N changes, Y changes as well. The *elasticity* of Y with respect to N is defined to be the percentage change in Y, $\Delta Y/Y$, divided by the percentage change in N, $\Delta N/N$. Writing the formula, we have

$$\text{elasticity of } Y \text{ with respect to } N = \frac{\Delta Y / Y}{\Delta N / N}.$$

Because the slope of a function is $\Delta Y/\Delta N$, we can also write the elasticity of Y with respect to N as the slope times (N/Y).

If the elasticity of Y with respect to N is large, a 1% change in N causes a large percentage change in Y. Thus, a large elasticity of Y with respect to N means that Y is very sensitive to changes in N.

---

1. Showing that the slope of the line tangent to point G equals 10 requires basic calculus. The derivative of the function $Y = 20\sqrt{N}$, which is the same as the slope, is $dY/dN = 10/\sqrt{N}$. Evaluating this derivative at $N = 1$ yields a slope of 10.

A.4 FUNCTIONS OF SEVERAL VARIABLES

A function can relate more than two variables. To continue the example of Section A.1, suppose that the firm's daily output Y depends on both the number of workers N the firm employs and the number of machines (equivalently, the amount of capital) K the firm owns. Specifically, the function relating Y to K and N might be

$$Y = 2\sqrt{K}\sqrt{N}. \tag{A.5}$$

So, if there are 100 machines and 9 workers, by substituting $K = 100$ and $N = 9$ into Eq. (A.5), we get the output $Y = 2\sqrt{100}\sqrt{9} = 2 \times 10 \times 3 = 60$.

We can also write a function of several variables in general terms using symbols or letters. A general way to write the relationship between output Y and the two inputs, capital K and labour N, is

$$Y = F(K, N).$$

This equation is a slight simplification of a relationship called the production function, which we introduce in Chapter 3.

The graph of a function relating three variables requires three dimensions. As a convenient way to graph such a function on a two-dimensional page, we hold one of the right-hand-side variables constant. To graph the function in Eq. (A.5), for example, we might hold the number of machines K constant at a value of 100. If we substitute 100 for K, Eq. (A.5) becomes

$$Y = 2\sqrt{100}\sqrt{N} = 20\sqrt{N}. \tag{A.6}$$

With K held constant at 100, Eq. (A.6) is identical to Eq. (A.2). Like Eq. (A.2), Eq. (A.6) is a relationship between Y and N only and thus can be graphed in two dimensions. The graph of Eq. (A.6), shown as the solid curve in Figure A.5, is identical to the graph of Eq. (A.2) in Figure A.2.

A.5 SHIFTS OF A CURVE

Suppose that the relationship of output Y to machines K and workers N is given by Eq. (A.5) and we hold K constant at 100. As in Section A.4, with K held constant at 100, Eq. (A.5) reduces to Eq. (A.6) and the solid curve in Figure A.5 shows the relationship between workers N and output Y. At point C, in Figure A.5, for example, $N = 4$ and $Y = 20\sqrt{4} = 40$. At point D, where $N = 9, Y = 20\sqrt{9} = 60$.

Now, suppose that the firm purchases additional machines, raising the number of machines K from 100 to 225. If we substitute this new value for K, Eq. (A.5) becomes

$$Y = 2\sqrt{225}\sqrt{N} = 30\sqrt{N}. \tag{A.7}$$

Equation (A.7) is shown graphically as the dashed curve in Figure A.5. Note that the increase in K has shifted the curve up. Because of the increase in the number of machines, the amount of daily output Y that can be produced for any given number of workers N has risen. For example, initially when N equaled 9, output Y equaled 60 (point D in Figure A.5). After the increase in K, if $N = 9$, then $Y = 30\sqrt{9} = 90$ (point J in Figure A.5).

This example illustrates some important general points about the graphs of functions of several variables.

FIGURE A.5

Suppose that output Y depends on capital K and workers N, according to the function in Eq. (A.5). If we hold K fixed at 100, the relationship between Y and N is shown by the solid curve. If K rises to 225 so that more output can be produced with a given number of workers, the curve showing the relationship between Y and N shifts upward, from the solid curve to the dashed curve. In general, a change in any right-hand-side variable that does not appear on an axis of the graph causes the curve to shift.

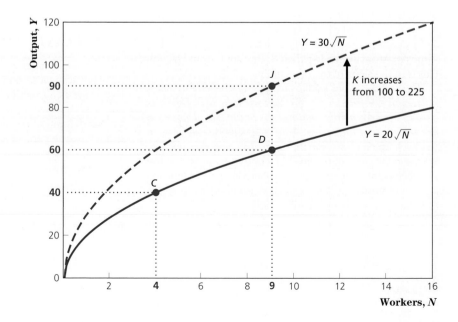

1. To graph a function of several variables in two dimensions, we hold all but one of the right-hand-side variables constant.

2. The one right-hand-side variable that is not held constant (N in this example) appears on the horizontal axis. Changes in this variable do not shift the graph of the function. Instead, changes in the variable on the horizontal axis represent movements along the curve that represents the function.

3. The right-hand-side variables held constant for the purpose of drawing the graph (K in this example) do not appear on either axis of the graph. If the value of one of these variables is changed, the entire curve shifts. In this example, for any number of workers N, the increase in machines K means that more output Y can be produced. Thus, the curve shifts up, from the solid curve to the dashed curve in Figure A.5.

A.6 EXPONENTS

Powers of numbers or variables can be expressed by using superscripts called *exponents*. In the following examples, 2 and 4 are the exponents:

$$5^2 = 5 \times 5, \text{ and } Z^4 = Z \times Z \times Z \times Z.$$

For any numbers Z, a, and b, exponents obey the following rules:

$$Z^a \times Z^b = Z^{a+b}, \text{ and } (Z^a)^b = Z^{ab}.$$

An illustration of the first rule is $5^2 \times 5^3 = (5 \times 5) \times (5 \times 5 \times 5) = 5^5$. An illustration of the second rule is $(5^3)^2 = (5^3) \times (5^3) = (5 \times 5 \times 5) \times (5 \times 5 \times 5) = 5^6$.

Exponents do not have to be whole numbers. For example, $5^{0.5}$ represents the square root of 5. To understand why, note that by the second of the two rules for exponents, $(5^{0.5})^2 = 5^{(0.5)2} = 5^1 = 5$. That is, the square of $5^{0.5}$ is 5. Similarly, for any number Z and any whole number q, $Z^{1/q}$ is the *qth* root of Z. Thus, $5^{0.25}$ means the fourth root of 5, for example. Using exponents, we can rewrite Eq. (A.5) as

$$Y = 2K^{0.5}N^{0.5},$$

where $K^{0.5} = \sqrt{K}$ and $N^{0.5} = \sqrt{N}$.

In general, consider any number that can be expressed as a ratio of two whole numbers p and q. Using the rules of exponents, we have

$$Z^{p/q} = (Z^p)^{1/q} = qth \text{ root of } Z^p.$$

Thus, for example, as 0.7 equals 7/10, $N^{0.7}$ equals the tenth root of N^7. For values of N greater than 1, $N^{0.7}$ is a number larger than the square root of N, $N^{0.5}$, but smaller than N itself.

Exponents also may be zero or negative. In general, the following two relationships hold:

$$Z^0 = 1, \text{ and } Z^{-a} = \frac{1}{Z^a}.$$

Here is a useful way to relate exponents and elasticities: Suppose that two variables Y and N are related by a function of the form

$$Y = kN^a, \tag{A.8}$$

where a is a number and k can be either a number or a function of variables other than N. Then the elasticity of Y with respect to N (see Section A.3) equals a.

A.7 GROWTH RATE FORMULAS

Let X and Z be any two variables, not necessarily related by a function, that are changing over time. Let $\Delta X/X$ and $\Delta Z/Z$ represent the growth rates (percentage changes) of X and Z, respectively. Then, the following rules provide useful approximations (proofs of the various rules are included for reference).

Rule 1. The growth rate of the product of X and Z equals the growth rate of X plus the growth rate of Z.

Proof. Suppose that X increases by ΔX and Z increases by ΔZ. Then the absolute increase in the product of X and Z is $(X + \Delta X)(Z + \Delta Z) - XZ$, and the growth rate of the product of X and Z is

$$\text{growth rate of } (XZ) \tag{A.9}$$

$$= \frac{(X + \Delta X)(Z + \Delta Z) - XZ}{XZ}$$

$$= \frac{(\Delta X)Z + (\Delta Z)X + \Delta X \Delta Z}{XZ}$$

$$= \frac{\Delta X}{X} + \frac{\Delta Z}{Z} + \frac{\Delta X \Delta Z}{XZ}.$$

The last term on the right-hand side of Eq. (A.9), $(\Delta X \Delta Z)/XZ$, equals the growth rate of X, $\Delta X/X$, times the growth rate of Z, $\Delta Z/Z$. This term is generally small; for example, if the growth rates of X and Z are both 5% (0.05), the product of the two growth rates is only 0.25% (0.0025). If we assume that this last term is small enough to ignore, Eq. (A.9) indicates that the growth rate of the product XZ equals the growth rate of X, $\Delta X/X$, plus the growth rate of Z, $\Delta Z/Z$.

Rule 2. The growth rate of the ratio of X to Z is the growth rate of X minus the growth rate of Z.

Proof. Let W be the ratio of X to Z, so $W = X/Z$. Then $X = ZW$. By Rule 1, as X equals the product of Z and W, the growth rate of X equals the growth rate of Z plus the growth rate of W:

$$\frac{\Delta X}{X} = \frac{\Delta Z}{Z} + \frac{\Delta W}{W}.$$

Rearranging this equation to put $\Delta W/W$ on the left-hand side and recalling that $\Delta W/W$ equals the growth rate of (X/Z), we have

$$\text{growth rate of } (X \,/\, Z) = \frac{\Delta X}{X} - \frac{\Delta Z}{Z}. \quad \text{(A.10)}$$

Rule 3. Suppose that Y is a variable that is a function of two other variables X and Z. Then

$$\frac{\Delta Y}{Y} = \eta_{Y,X} \, \frac{\Delta X}{X} + \eta_{Y,Z} \, \frac{\Delta Z}{Z}, \quad \text{(A.11)}$$

where $\eta_{Y,X}$ is the elasticity of Y with respect to X and $\eta_{Y,Z}$ is the elasticity of Y with respect to Z.

Proof (informal). Suppose that only X changes so that $\Delta Z/Z = 0$. Then Eq. (A.11) boils down to the definition of an elasticity, $\eta_{Y,X} = (\Delta Y/Y)/(\Delta X/X)$, as in Section A.3. Similarly, if only Z changes, Eq. (A.11) becomes $\eta_{Y,Z} = (\Delta Y/Y)/(\Delta Z/Z)$, which is the definition of the elasticity of Y with respect to Z. If both X and Z change, Eq. (A.11) indicates that the overall effect on Y is approximately equal to the sum of the individual effects on Y of the change in X and the change in Z.

Rule 4. The growth rate of X raised to the power a, or X^a, is a times the growth rate of X,

$$\text{growth rate of } (X^a) = a \, \frac{\Delta X}{X}. \quad \text{(A.12)}$$

Proof. Let $Y = X^a$. Applying the rule from Eq. (A.8) and setting $k = 1$, we find that the elasticity of Y with respect to X equals a. Therefore, by Eq. (A.11), the growth rate of Y equals a times the growth rate of X. Because $Y = X^a$, the growth rate of Y is the same as the growth rate of X^a, which proves the relationship in Eq. (A.12).

Example: The real interest rate. To apply the growth rate formulas, we derive the equation that relates the real interest rate to the nominal interest rate and the inflation rate, Eq. (2.12).

The real value of any asset, say, a savings account, equals the nominal or dollar value of the asset divided by the price level:

$$\text{real asset value} = \frac{\text{nominal asset value}}{\text{price level}}. \quad \text{(A.13)}$$

The real value of an asset is the ratio of the nominal asset value to the price level, so, according to Rule 2, the growth

rate of the real asset value is approximately equal to the growth rate of the nominal asset value minus the growth rate of the price level. The growth rate of the real value of an interest-bearing asset equals the real interest rate earned by that asset; the growth rate of the nominal value of an interest-bearing asset is the nominal interest rate for that asset; and the growth rate of the price level is the inflation rate. Therefore, Rule 2 implies the relationship

Real interest rate = nominal interest rate − inflation rate,

which is the relationship given in Eq. (2.12).

PROBLEMS

1. Graph the function $Y = 3X + 5$ for $0 \le X \le 5$. What is the slope of this function?
2. Graph the function $Y = X^2 + 2$ for $0 \le X \le 5$. Starting from the point at which $X = 1$, find the slope of the function for $\Delta X = 1$ and $\Delta X = -1$. What is the slope of the line tangent to the function at $X = 1$? (See Problem 3.)
3. For the function $Y = X^2 + 2$, use Eq. (A.4) to write a general expression for the slope. This expression for the slope will depend on the initial value of X, X_1, and on the change in X, ΔX. For values of ΔX sufficiently small that the term $(\Delta X)^2$ can be ignored, show that the slope depends only on the initial value of X, X_1. What is the slope of the function (which is the same as the slope of the tangent line) when $X_1 = 1$?
4. Suppose that the amount of output Y that a firm can produce depends on its amount of capital K and the number of workers employed N, according to the function

$$Y = K^{0.3} N^{0.7}.$$

   a. Suppose that $N = 100$. Give the function that relates Y to K and graph this relationship for $0 \le K \le 50$. (You need calculate only enough values of Y to get a rough idea of the shape of the function.)
   b. What happens to the function relating Y and K and to the graph of the relationship if N rises to 200? If N falls to 50? Give an economic interpretation.
   c. For the function relating Y to K and N, find the elasticity of Y with respect to K and the elasticity of Y with respect to N.
5. Use a calculator to find each of the following:
   a. $5^{0.3}$
   b. $5^{0.3}\, 5^{0.2}$
   c. $(5^{0.25})^2$
   d. $(5^{0.5}\, 5^{0.3})^2\, 5^{0.4}$
   e. $5^{0.2}/5^{0.5}$
   f. $5^{-0.5}$
6. Answer the following:
   a. Nominal GDP equals real GDP times the GDP deflator (see Section 2.4). Suppose that nominal GDP

growth is 12% and real GDP growth is 4%. What is inflation (the rate of growth of the GDP deflator)?

b. The "velocity of money," V, is defined by the equation

$$V = \frac{PY}{M},$$

where P is the price level, Y is real output, and M is the money supply (see Eq. 7.4). In a particular year, velocity is constant, money growth is 10%, and inflation (the rate of growth of the price level) is 7%. What is real output growth?

c. Output Y is related to capital K and the number of workers N by the function

$$Y = 10K^{0.3}N^{0.7}.$$

In a particular year, the capital stock grows by 2% and the number of workers grows by 1%. By how much does output grow?

GLOSSARY

(The number in parentheses after the glossary term is the chapter in which that term first appears or is most extensively discussed.)

absorption: (5) total spending by domestic residents, firms, and governments, equal to $C + I + G$. (p. 169)

activist: (14) describes a policy strategy that involves active responses by the central bank to changes in economic circumstances. See *discretion*. (p. 539)

acyclical: (8) not displaying a regular pattern of behaviour over the business cycle. See *procyclical, countercyclical*. (p. 275)

aggregate demand: (9) the economywide demand for output when the goods market and the asset market are in equilibrium; the level of output corresponding to the intersection of the *IS* and *LM* curves. (p. 320)

aggregate demand (*AD*) curve: (9) in a diagram with output on the horizontal axis and the price level on the vertical axis, the downward-sloping relation between the price level and the economywide demand for output. (p. 320)

aggregate demand for labour: (3) the sum of the labour demands of all employers in an economy. (p. 71)

aggregate demand management: (12) the use of monetary and fiscal policies, which shifts the aggregate demand curve, to try to smooth out the business cycle; also known as macroeconomic stabilization or stabilization policy. (p. 470)

aggregate demand shocks: (12) shocks to the economy that shift the *IS* curve or the *LM* curve and, thus, affect the aggregate demand for output. (p. 463)

aggregate supply: (9) the amount of output supplied by firms in the economy at any given price level; in the long run, when prices and price expectations have adjusted to their equilibrium levels, aggregate supply equals full-employment output. (p. 322)

aggregate supply (*AS*) curve: (9) in a diagram with output on the horizontal axis and the price level on the vertical axis, the relation between the price level and the total amount of output that firms supply. (p. 322)

aggregate supply of labour: (3) the sum of the labour supplied by everyone in the economy. (p. 72)

aggregation: (1) the process of adding individual economic variables to obtain economywide totals. (p. 11)

appreciation: (10) see *nominal appreciation, real appreciation*.

automatic stabilizers: (15) provisions in the government's budget that automatically cause government spending to rise or taxes to fall when GDP falls. (p. 568)

average labour productivity: (1) the amount of output produced per unit of labour input (per worker or per hour of work). (p. 2)

average tax rate: (15) the total amount of taxes paid divided by the taxpayer's income. (p. 571)

balance of payments: (5) the net increase (domestic less foreign) in a country's official reserve assets; also known as the official settlements balance. (p. 164)

balance of payments accounts: (5) the record of a country's international transactions, consisting of the current account and the capital account. (p. 160)

Bank rate: (14) the upper edge of the Bank of Canada's operating band for the overnight interest rate; the interest rate on loans from the Bank to direct clearers. (p. 531)

bank reserves: (14) liquid assets held by banks to meet the demands for withdrawals by depositors or to pay the cheques drawn on depositors' accounts. (p. 523)

bank run: (14) a large-scale withdrawal of deposits from a bank, caused by depositors' fear that the bank may go bankrupt and not pay depositors in full. (p. 526)

boom: (8) in a business cycle, the period of time during which aggregate economic activity grows; also known as an expansion. (p. 265)

borrowing constraint: (4) a restriction imposed by lenders on the amount that someone can borrow. If a borrowing constraint causes an individual to borrow less than he or she would choose to borrow in the absence of the constraint, the borrowing constraint is *binding*; otherwise it is *nonbinding*. (p. 152)

budget constraint: (4) a relation that shows how much current and future consumption a consumer can afford given the consumer's initial wealth, current and future income, and the interest rate. (p. 141)

budget deficit: (1) government expenditure minus government revenue. See *government expenditure, government revenue*. (p. 36)

budget line: (4) the graph of the consumer's budget constraint; the budget line shows graphically the combinations of current and future consumption a consumer can afford given the consumer's initial wealth, current and future income, and the interest rate. (p. 142)

budget surplus: (2) government revenue minus government expenditure. See *government expenditure, government revenue, government saving*. (p. 36)

business cycle: (8) a decline in aggregate economic activity (a contraction or recession) to a low point (a trough), followed by a recovery of activity (an expansion or boom) to a high point (a peak). A complete business cycle can be measured from peak to peak or from trough to trough. (p. 266)

business cycle chronology: (8) a history of the dates of business cycle peaks and troughs. (p. 265)

capital account: (5) the record of a country's international trade in existing assets, either real or financial. (p. 163)

capital account balance: (5) the value of capital inflows (credit items) minus the value of capital outflows (debit items) in a country's capital account. (p. 163)

capital and financial account: (5) the official name for the record of a country's trade in existing assets. (p. 163)

capital good: (2) a good that is produced, is used to produce other goods, and—unlike an intermediate good—is not used up in the same period that it is produced. (p. 28)

capital–labour ratio: (6) the amount of capital per worker, equal to the capital stock divided by the number of workers. (p. 209)

central bank: (14) the governmental institution responsible for monetary policy, such as the Bank of Canada, the Federal Reserve System in the United States, and the Bank of Japan in Japan. (p. 521)

chronically unemployed: (3) workers who are unemployed a large fraction of the time. (p. 91)

classical approach: (1) an approach to macroeconomics based on the assumption that wages and prices adjust quickly to equate quantities supplied and demanded in each market. Classical economists generally argue that free markets are a good way to organize the economy and that the scope for government intervention in the economy—for example, to smooth out the business cycle—should be limited. (p. 16)

closed economy: (1) a national economy that does not have trading or financial relationships with the rest of the world. (p. 7)

coincident variable: (8) a variable with peaks and troughs that occur at about the same time as the corresponding business cycle peaks and troughs. See *lagging variable, leading variable*. (p. 275)

cold turkey: (13) a rapid and decisive reduction in the growth rate of the money supply aimed at reducing the rate of inflation; in contrast with *gradualism*. (p. 511)

co-movement: (8) the tendency of many economic variables to move together in a predictable way over the business cycle. (p. 266)

conditional convergence: (6) the tendency of living standards within groups of countries with similar characteristics to become more equal over time. See *unconditional convergence*. (p. 221)

consumer price index: (2) a price index calculated as the current cost of a fixed basket of consumer goods divided by the cost of the basket in the base period. (p. 43)

consumption: (2) spending by domestic households on final goods and services. (p. 30)

consumption-smoothing motive: (4) the preference of most people for a relatively constant or stable pattern of consumption over time, as opposed to having high consumption at some times and low consumption at others. (p. 103)

contraction: (8) in a business cycle, the period of time during which aggregate economic activity is falling; also known as a recession. (p. 265)

contractionary policy: (12) a monetary or fiscal policy that reduces aggregate demand. (p. 460)

convergence: (6) a tendency of living standards in different countries to become equal over time. See *conditional convergence, unconditional convergence*. (p. 220)

countercyclical: (8) tending to move in the opposite direction of aggregate economic activity over the business cycle (up in contractions, down in expansions). See *procyclical, acyclical*. (p. 275)

credibility: (14) the degree to which the public believes the central bank's announcements about future policy. (p. 544)

credit channel: (14) the effects of monetary policy on credit supply and credit demand, which affect the economy in addition to effects operating through interest rates and exchange rates. (p. 538)

currency: (7) paper money and coin issued by the government; cash. (p. 235)

currency–deposit ratio: (14) the ratio of the currency held by the public to the public's deposits in banks. (p. 526)

currency union: (10) a group of countries that agree to share a common currency. (p. 383)

current account: (5) the record of a country's international trade in currently produced goods and services. (p. 160)

current account balance: (2, 5) payments received from abroad in exchange for currently produced goods and services (including factor services), minus the analogous payments made to foreigners by the domestic economy. (pp. 37, 163)

current transfers: (5) payments made from one country to another that do not correspond to the purchase of any good, service, or asset; examples are foreign aid or gifts by domestic residents to foreigners. (p. 163)

cyclical unemployment: (3) the excess of the actual unemployment rate over the natural rate of unemployment; equivalently, unemployment that occurs when output is below its full-employment level. (p. 92)

debt–GDP ratio: (15) the quantity of government debt outstanding divided by GDP. (p. 576)

deflation: (1) a situation in which the prices of most goods and services are falling over time. (p. 6)

demand for money: (7) the quantity of monetary assets, such as cash and chequing accounts, that people choose to hold in their portfolios. (p. 244)

depository institutions: (14) privately owned banks and other institutions (such as credit unions) that accept deposits from and make loans directly to the public. (p. 521)

depreciation: 1. (2) the amount of capital that wears out during a given period of time. (p. 34) 2. (10) a decline in the exchange rate; see *nominal depreciation, real depreciation*. (p. 345)

depression: (8) a particularly severe and prolonged downturn in economic activity. (p. 265)

desired capital stock: (4) the amount of capital that allows a firm to earn the highest possible expected profit. (p. 117)

devaluation: (10) a reduction in the value of a currency by official government action under a fixed- exchange-rate system. (p. 345)

diminishing marginal productivity: (3) a feature of production functions that implies that the more a particular factor of production is used, the less extra output can be gained by increasing the use of that factor still further (with the usage of other factors of production held constant). For example, for a given capital stock, adding an extra worker increases output more when employment is initially low than when it is initially high. (p. 61)

direct clearers: (14) large banks that hold reserves at the Bank of Canada to settle net transfers. (p. 531)

discouraged workers: (3) people who stop searching for jobs because they have become discouraged by lack of success at finding a job; discouraged workers are not included in the official unemployment rate. (p. 89)

discretion: (14) the freedom of the central bank to conduct monetary policy in any way that it believes will advance the ultimate objectives of low and stable inflation, high economic growth, and low unemployment; in contrast to rules. (p. 539)

disinflation: (13) a fall in the rate of inflation. (p. 511)

distortions: (15) tax-induced deviations in economic behaviour from the efficient, free-market outcome. (p. 574)

duration: (3) the length of time that an unemployment spell lasts. (p. 90)

economic model: (1) a simplified description of some aspect of the economy, usually expressed in mathematical form. (p. 13)

economic theory: (1) a set of ideas about the economy that have been organized in a logical framework. (p. 13)

effective labour demand curve: (12) in a diagram with output on the horizontal axis and the quantity of labour on the vertical axis, an upward-sloping curve that shows how much labour is needed to produce a given amount of output, with productivity, the capital stock, and effort held constant. (p. 455)

effective tax rate: (4) a single measure of the tax burden on capital that summarizes the many provisions of the tax code that affect investment. (p. 122)

efficiency wage: (12) the real wage that maximizes worker effort or efficiency per dollar of real wages received. (p. 446)

efficiency wage model: (12) a model of the labour market in which because workers exert more effort when they receive a higher real wage, profit-maximizing employers choose to pay a real wage that is higher than the real wage that clears the labour market; the efficiency wage model can be used to help explain real-wage rigidity and the existence of unemployment. (p. 444)

effort curve: (12) the relation between the level of effort put forth by workers and the real wage; its positive slope indicates that a higher real wage induces workers to exert greater effort. (p. 444)

empirical analysis: (1) a comparison of the implications of an economic theory or model with real-world data. (p. 13)

employment ratio: (3) the fraction of the adult population that is employed. (p. 89)

endogenous growth theory: (6) a new branch of growth theory that tries to explain productivity growth (hence, the growth rate of output) within a model of economic growth. (p. 222).

equilibrium: (1) a situation in which the quantities demanded and supplied in a market or set of markets are equal. (p. 16)

exchange fund account: (14) the federal government's holdings of foreign exchange, managed by the Bank of Canada; purchases and sales of foreign currencies from this account can influence the exchange rate. (p. 534)

exchange rate: (1, 10) the number of units of foreign currency that can be purchased with one unit of the home currency; also known as the nominal exchange rate. (p. 8, 343)

exchange rate channel: (14) the effects of monetary policy that work through changes in the real exchange rate. (p. 538)

expansion: (8) in a business cycle, the period of time during which aggregate economic activity is rising; also known as a boom. (p. 265)

expansionary policy: (12) a monetary or fiscal policy that increases aggregate demand. (p. 460)

expectations-augmented Phillips curve: (13) an inverse relation between unanticipated inflation and cyclical unemployment. (p. 490)

expected after-tax real interest rate: (4) the nominal after-tax rate of return (equal to the nominal interest rate times 1 minus the tax rate) minus the expected rate of inflation; equals the expected increase in the real value of an asset after payment of taxes on interest income. (p. 111)

expected real interest rate: (2) the nominal interest rate minus the expected rate of inflation; equals the expected increase in the real value of an asset. (p. 49)

expected returns: (7) the rates of return on real or financial assets that financial investors expect to earn. (p. 243)

expenditure approach: (2) a procedure for measuring economic activity by adding the amount spent by all purchasers of final goods and services. (p. 25)

factors of production: (3) inputs to the production process, such as capital goods, labour, raw materials, and energy. (p. 56)

***FE* line**: (9) see *full-employment line*. (p. 295)

final goods and services: (2) goods and services that are the end products of the productive process, in contrast to intermediate goods and services. (p. 28)

financial inflow: (5) a credit (plus) item in a country's financial and capital account that arises when a resident of the country sells an asset to someone in another country. (p. 163)

financial outflow: (5) a debit (minus) item in a country's financial and capital account that arises when a resident of the country buys an asset from abroad. (p. 163)

fiscal policy: (1) policy concerning the level and composition of government spending and taxation. (p. 8)

fixed-exchange-rate system: (10) a system in which exchange rates are set at officially determined levels and are changed only by direct governmental action. (p. 343)

flexible-exchange-rate system: (10) a system in which exchange rates are not officially fixed but are determined by conditions of supply and demand in the foreign exchange market; also known as a floating-exchange-rate system. (p. 343)

floating-exchange-rate system: (10) see *flexible-exchange-rate system*. (p. 343)

flow variable: (2) a variable that is measured per unit of time; an example is GDP, which is measured as output per year or quarter. See *stock variable*. (p. 39)

foreign exchange market: (10) the market in which the currencies of different nations are traded. (p. 343)

fractional reserve banking: (14) a banking system in which banks hold reserves equal to a fraction of their deposits so that the reserve–deposit ratio is less than 1. (p. 523)

frictional unemployment: (3) the unemployment that arises as the result of the matching process in which workers search for suitable jobs and firms search for suitable workers. (p. 91)

full-employment deficit: (15) what the government budget deficit would be, given the tax and spending policies currently in force, if the economy were operating at its full-employment level. (p. 569)

full-employment level of employment: (3) the equilibrium level of employment, achieved after wages and prices fully adjust. (p. 80)

full-employment (*FE*) line: (9) a vertical line representing full-employment output in a diagram with output on the horizontal axis and the real interest rate on the vertical axis. (p. 295)

full-employment output: (3) the level of output that firms supply when wages and prices in the economy have fully adjusted to their equilibrium levels. (p. 80)

full-employment surplus: (15) what the government budget surplus would be, given the tax and spending policies currently in place, if the economy were operating at its full-employment level. (p. 569)

fundamental identity of national income accounting: (2) the accounting identity that states that total production, total income, and total expenditure during a given period are equal. (p. 25)

fundamental value of the exchange rate: (10) the value of the exchange rate that would be determined by the forces of supply and demand in the foreign exchange market, in the absence of government intervention. (p. 374)

game theory: (14) the study of situations (games) in which individuals (players) use strategy in attempting to achieve their goals, possibly at the expense of the other players. (p. 545)

GDP: (2) see *gross domestic product*. (p. 25)

GDP deflator: (2) a measure of the price level, calculated as the ratio of current nominal GDP to current real GDP. (p. 43)

general equilibrium: (9) a situation in which all markets in an economy are simultaneously in equilibrium. (p. 309)

GNP: (2) see *gross national product*. (p. 29)

Golden rule capital-labour ratio: (6) the level of the capital-labour ratio that maximizes consumption per worker in the steady state. (p. 211)

government capital: (15) long-lived physical assets owned by the government, such as roads and public schools. (p. 570)

government debt: (15) the total value of government bonds outstanding at any given time.(p. 575)

government expenditure: (2) the government's purchases of goods and services plus transfers and interest payments. (p. 36)

government purchases: (2) spending by the government on currently produced goods and services. (p. 32)

government revenue: (2) taxes and other revenues collected by the government. (p. 36)

government saving: (2) the government's tax receipts minus its expenditure; equal to the government budget surplus. (p. 36)

gradualism: (13) a prescription for disinflation that involves reducing the rate of monetary growth and the rate of inflation gradually over a period of several years; in contrast to *cold turkey*. (p. 511)

gross domestic product (GDP): (2) the market value of final goods and services newly produced within a nation's borders during a fixed period of time. (p. 25)

gross investment: (4) the total purchase or construction of new capital goods. (p. 124)

gross national product (GNP): (2) the market value of final goods and services newly produced by domestically owned factors of production during a fixed period of time. (p. 29)

growth accounting: (6) a method for dividing total output growth into parts attributable to growth of capital, labour, and productivity. (p. 200)

growth accounting equation: (6) the production function written in growth rate form; it states that the growth rate of output is the sum of (1) the growth rate of productivity, (2) the elasticity of output with respect to capital times the growth rate of capital, and (3) the elasticity of output with respect to labour times the growth rate of labour. (p. 199)

high-powered money: (14) the liabilities of the central bank, consisting of bank reserves and currency in circulation, that are usable as money; also known as the monetary base. (p. 522)

human capital: (6) the productive knowledge, skills, and training of individuals. (p. 223)

hyperinflation: (13) a situation in which the rate of inflation is extremely high for a sustained period of time; one suggested definition is a 50% monthly rate of inflation. (p. 510)

hysteresis: (13) the tendency of the natural rate of unemployment to change in response to the actual unemployment rate, rising if the actual unemployment rate is above the natural rate and falling if the actual unemployment rate is below the natural rate. (p. 503)

income approach: (2) a procedure for measuring economic activity by adding all income received, including taxes and after-tax profits. (p. 24)

income effect: (4) a change in economic behaviour (such as the amount a person saves or works) in response to a change in income or wealth; graphically, a change in behaviour induced by a parallel shift in the budget line. (p. 147)

income effect (of the real interest rate on saving): (4) the tendency of savers to consume more and save less in response to an increase in the real interest rate because they are made wealthier; the tendency of borrowers to consume less and save more in response to an increase in the real interest rate because they are made less wealthy. (p. 110)

income effect (of a higher real wage): (3) the tendency of workers to supply less labour in response to an increase in the real wage; arises because an increase in the real wage makes workers wealthier and leads them to want to consume more leisure. (p. 73)

income elasticity of money demand: (7) the percentage change in money demand resulting from a 1% increase in real income. (p. 249)

income–expenditure identity: (2) the accounting identity that states that total income (product) equals the sum of the four types of expenditure: consumption, investment, government purchases, and net exports. (p. 30)

inconvertible currency: (10) a currency that cannot be traded freely for other currencies, usually because of government-imposed restrictions. (p. 374)

index of leading indicators: (8) a weighted average of 10 economic variables that lead the business cycle, used for forecasting future business activity. (p. 276)

indicators: (14) see *intermediate targets*. (p. 567)

indifference curve: (4) shows graphically the combinations of current and future consumption that yield any given level of utility. (p. 144)

industrial policy: (6) a strategy for economic growth by which the government, using taxes, subsidies, or regulation, attempts to influence the nation's pattern of industrial development. (p. 229)

inflation: (1) a situation in which the prices of most goods and services are rising over time. (p. 6)

inflation tax: (15) the resources raised by the government by issuing money and creating inflation; also known as seignorage. (p. 587)

insider–outsider theory: (13) attributes hysteresis of the natural unemployment rate to the supposed tendency of unions to try to obtain the highest real wage consistent with continued employment of employed members (insiders), without taking account of the interests of unemployed workers (outsiders). See *hysteresis*. (p. 504)

instruments: (14) the policy tools that the Bank of Canada can use to influence the economy; these include the target overnight rate and open-market operations. (p. 535)

interest elasticity of money demand: (7) the percentage change in money demand resulting from a 1% increase (different from a 1 percentage point increase) in the interest rate. (p. 249)

interest rate: (2) the rate of return promised by a borrower to a lender. (p. 45)

interest rate channel: (14) the effects of monetary policy that work through changes in real interest rates. (p. 538)

intermediate goods and services: (2) goods and services that are used up in the production of other goods and services in the same period that they themselves were produced; an example is wheat used up in making bread. (p. 28)

intermediate targets: (14) macroeconomic variables that the Bank of Canada cannot control directly but can influence fairly predictably and that, in turn, are related to the ultimate goals the Bank is trying to achieve; also known as indicators. Examples of intermediate targets are the growth rates of monetary aggregates and short-term interest rates. (p. 535)

intertemporal external balance: (10) the requirement that countries that have positive net exports (lend) today have negative net exports (borrow) in the future, which are offsetting in present-value terms. (p. 392)

inventories: (2) stocks of unsold finished goods, goods in process, and production materials held by firms. (p. 28)

investment: (2) spending for new capital goods, called fixed investment, and increases in firms' inventory holdings, called inventory investment. See *gross investment, net investment*. (p. 30)

invisible hand: (1) the idea (proposed by Adam Smith) that if there are free markets and individuals conduct their economic affairs in their own best interests, the economy as a whole will work well. (p. 16)

IS curve: (9) in a diagram with output on the horizontal axis and the real interest rate on the vertical axis, a downward-sloping curve that shows the value of the real interest rate that clears the goods market for any given value of output. At any point on the *IS* curve, desired national saving equals desired investment (in a closed economy); equivalently, the aggregate quantity of goods demanded equals the aggregate quantity of goods supplied. (p. 297)

Keynesian approach: (1) an approach to macroeconomics based on the assumption that wages and prices may not adjust quickly to equate quantities supplied and demanded in each market. Keynesian economists are more likely than classical economists to argue that government intervention in the economy—for example, to smooth out the business cycle—may be desirable. (p. 17)

labour force: (3) the number of people willing to work, including unemployed people actively searching for work, as well as employed workers. (p. 87)

labour hoarding: (11) a situation that occurs if because of the costs of firing and hiring workers, firms continue to employ some workers in a recession that they otherwise would have laid off. (p. 415)

lagging variable: (8) a variable with peaks and troughs that tend to occur later than the corresponding peaks and troughs in the business cycle. See *coincident variable, leading variable*. (p. 275)

large open economy: (5) an economy that trades with other economies and is large enough to affect the world real interest rate. (p. 181)

leading variable: (8) a variable with peaks and troughs that tend to occur earlier than the corresponding peaks and troughs in the business cycle. See *coincident variable, lagging variable*. (p. 275)

leisure: (3) all off-the-job activities, including eating, recreation, and working in the yard and on the house. (p. 72)

lender of last resort: (14) the role served by a central bank when it stands ready to lend reserves to banks to avoid bank runs or financial crises. (p. 533)

life-cycle model: (4) a multi-period version of the basic two-period model of consumer behaviour that focuses on the patterns of income, consumption, and saving over the various stages of an individual's life. (p. 150)

liquidity: (7) the ease and quickness with which an asset can be exchanged for goods, services, or other assets. (p. 243)

liquidity trap: (12) a situation in which the nominal interest rate is very close to zero, making it impossible for monetary policymakers to expand the economy through further reductions in the interest rate. (p. 470)

LM curve: (9) in a diagram with output on the horizontal axis and the real interest rate on the vertical axis, an upward-sloping curve that shows the value of the real interest rate that clears the asset market for any given value of output. At any point on the *LM* curve, the quantities of money supplied and demanded are equal. (p. 305)

long-run aggregate supply (*LRAS*) curve: (9) in a diagram with output on the horizontal axis and the price level on the vertical axis, a vertical line at full-employment output; indicates that in the long run the supply of output does not depend on the price level. (p. 323)

long-run Phillips curve: (13) in a diagram with unemployment on the horizontal axis and inflation on the vertical axis, a vertical line at the natural rate of unemployment; indicates that in the long run, the unemployment rate equals the natural rate, independent of the rate of inflation. (p. 497)

M1: (7) the most narrowly defined monetary aggregate, made up of currency and travellers' cheques held by the public, demand deposits (personal chequing accounts) at commercial banks, and other chequable deposits. (p. 238)

M2: (7) a monetary aggregate that includes everything in M1 and a number of other assets that are somewhat less moneylike, such as savings deposits and nonpersonal notice deposits. (p. 241)

M2+: (7) a broad monetary aggregate that includes everything in M2 plus accounts at trust and mortgage loan companies, caisses populaires, and credit unions. (p. 241)

M3: (7) a broad monetary aggregate that includes everything in M2 plus further accounts at banks, such as term deposits of businesses and foreign currency accounts. (p. 241)

macroeconomic stabilization: (12) the use of monetary and fiscal policies to moderate cyclical fluctuations and maintain low inflation; also known as aggregate demand management or stabilization policy. (p. 470)

macroeconomics: (1) the study of the structure and performance of national economies and of the policies that governments use to try to affect economic performance. (p. 1)

marginal cost: (12) the cost of producing an additional unit of output. (p. 454)

marginal product of capital (*MPK*): (3) the amount of output produced per unit of additional capital. (p. 60)

marginal product of labour (*MPN*): (3) the amount of output produced per unit of additional labour. (p. 62)

marginal propensity to consume (*MPC*): (4) the amount by which desired consumption rises when current output rises by one unit. (p. 104)

marginal revenue product of labour (*MRPN*): (3) the extra revenue obtained by a firm when it employs an additional unit of labour and sells the resulting increase in output; for competitive firms, equal to the price of output times the marginal product of labour. (p. 65)

marginal tax rate: (15) the fraction of an additional dollar of income that must be paid in taxes. (p. 571)

markup: (12) the difference between the price charged for a good and its marginal cost of production, expressed as a percentage of marginal cost. (p. 454)

medium of exchange: (7) an asset used in making transactions. (p. 236)

menu cost: (12) the cost of changing prices, for example, the cost of printing a new menu or remarking merchandise. (p. 451)

merchandise trade balance: (5) a country's merchandise exports (exports of goods) minus its merchandise imports. (p. 161)

misperceptions theory: (11) predicts that because of producers' inability to observe directly the general price level, the aggregate quantity of output supplied rises above the full-employment level when the aggregate price level is higher than expected; hence the short-run aggregate supply curve is upward-sloping. (p. 425)

monetarism: (14) a school of macroeconomic thought that emphasizes the importance of monetary factors in the macroeconomy, but which opposes the active use of monetary policy to stabilize the economy. (p. 539)

monetary aggregates: (7) the official measures of the money supply, such as M1 and M2. See M1, M2, M2+, M3. (p. 238)

monetary base: (14) the liabilities of the central bank, consisting of bank reserves and currency in circulation, that are usable as money; also known as high-powered money. (p. 522)

monetary neutrality: (9) characterizes an economy in which changes in the nominal money supply change the price level proportionally but have no effect on real variables. The basic classical model predicts neutrality; the classical model with misperceptions and the Keynesian model predict that neutrality holds in the long run but not in the short run. (p. 319)

monetary policy: (1) policies determining the level and rate of growth of the nation's money supply, which are under the control of a government institution known as the central bank (the Bank of Canada in Canada). (p. 9)

money: (7) assets that are widely used and accepted as payment. (p. 235)

money demand function: (7) the function that relates the real demand for money to output and the interest rate paid by non-monetary assets. (p. 247)

money multiplier: (14) the number of dollars of money supply that can be created from each dollar of monetary base, calculated as the ratio of the money supply to the monetary base. (p. 527)

money supply: (7) the total amount of money available in an economy, consisting of currency in circulation and deposits; also known as the money stock. (p. 241)

monopolistic competition: (12) a market situation in which some competition exists but in which a relatively small number of sellers and imperfect standardization of the product allow individual producers to act as price setters, rather than as price takers. (p. 451)

multiple expansion of loans and deposits: (14) in a fractional reserve banking system, the process in which banks lend out some of their deposits, the loaned funds are ultimately redeposited in the banking system, and the new deposits are lent out again; as a result of the multiple-expansion process, the money supply can greatly exceed the monetary base. (p. 524)

multiplier: (12) for any particular type of spending, the short-run change in output resulting from a one-unit change in that type of spending. (p. 460)

national income accounts: (2) an accounting framework used in measuring current economic activity. (p. 22)

national saving: (2) the saving of the economy as a whole, including both private saving (business and household) and government saving. (p. 37)

national wealth: (2) the total wealth of the residents of a country, consisting of the country's domestic physical assets (such as its stock of capital goods and land) and its net foreign assets. (p. 35)

natural rate of unemployment: (3) the rate of unemployment that exists when the economy's output is at its full-employment level; consists of frictional unemployment and structural unemployment. (p. 92)

neoclassical growth model: (6) a model of economic growth based on capital accumulation and population growth, with a constant savings rate (also called the Solow–Swan model). (p. 208)

net exports: (2) exports of goods and services minus imports of goods and services. (p. 32)

net factor payments from abroad (*NFP*): (2) income paid to domestic factors of production by the rest of the world, minus income paid to foreign factors of production by the domestic economy. (p. 29)

net foreign assets: (2) a country's foreign assets (for example, foreign stocks, bonds, and factories owned by domestic residents) minus its foreign liabilities (domestic physical and financial assets owned by foreigners). (p. 40)

net investment: (4) the change in the capital stock over the year, equal to gross investment minus depreciation of existing capital. (p. 124)

no-borrowing, no-lending point: (4) on the budget line, the point at which current consumption equals current income plus initial wealth; if the consumer chooses the consumption combination corresponding to this point, he or she neither borrows nor carries over resources into the future. (p. 154)

nominal appreciation: (10) an increase in the nominal exchange rate in a flexible-exchange-rate system. (p. 345)

nominal depreciation: (10) a decrease in the nominal exchange rate in a flexible-exchange-rate system. (p. 345)

nominal exchange rate: (10) the number of units of foreign currency that can be purchased with one unit of the home currency; also known as the exchange rate. (p. 343)

nominal GDP: (2) the value of an economy's final output measured using current market prices; also known as current-dollar GDP. (p. 41)

nominal interest rate: (2) the rate at which the nominal value of an interest-bearing asset increases over time; equivalent to the market interest rate. (p. 47)

nominal interest rate parity condition: (10) the condition that the difference between the nominal interest rates in two countries equals the rate at which the currency of the country with the higher interest rate is expected to depreciate. (p. 397)

nominal shocks: (11) shocks to money supply or money demand, which cause the *LM* curve to shift. (p. 405)

nominal variables: (2) variables measured in terms of current market prices. (p. 41)

normative analysis: (1) an analysis of policy that tries to determine whether a certain policy should be used; involves both analysis of the consequences of the policy and value judgements about the desirability of those consequences. See *positive analysis*. (p. 15)

official reserve assets: (5) assets held by central banks, other than domestic money or securities, that can be used in making international payments; examples are gold, foreign bank deposits, and special assets created by the International Monetary Fund. (p. 164)

official settlements balance: (5) the net increase (domestic less foreign) in a country's official reserve assets; also known as the balance of payments. (p. 164)

Okun's law: (13) a rule of thumb that says that output falls by 2.0% for each percentage point increase in the cyclical unemployment rate. (p. 499)

100% reserve banking: (14) a banking system in which banks hold reserves equal to 100% of their deposits. (p. 523)

open economy: (1) a national economy that has significant trading and financial relationships with other national economies. (p. 7)

open-economy trilemma: (10) a constraint on monetary policy in which policymakers can adopt only two of fixed exchange rates, mobility of financial capital, and independent monetary policy. (p. 382)

open-market operation: (7) an open-market purchase or sale of assets by the central bank, used to affect the money supply. See *open-market purchase*, *open-market sale*. (p. 242)

open-market purchase: (14) a purchase of assets (such as Treasury bills) from the public by the central bank, used to increase the money supply. (p. 529)

open-market sale: (14) a sale of assets (such as Treasury bills) to the public by the central bank, used to reduce the money supply. (p. 529)

overnight rate: (14) the interest rate charged by one direct clearer to another, for settlement balances lent for one day. (p. 531)

overvalued exchange rate: (10) in a fixed-exchange-rate system, an exchange rate that is higher than its fundamental value. See *fundamental value of the exchange rate*. (p. 374)

participation rate: (3) the fraction of adults who are in the labour force. (p. 89)

pass-through: (12) the extent to which a decrease in the nominal exchange rate leads to an increase in domestic prices. (p. 454)

peak: (8) in a business cycle, the point in time when economic activity stops increasing and begins to decline. (p. 265)

perfect competition: (12) a market situation in which there is a standardized good and many buyers and sellers so that all buyers and sellers are price takers. (p. 451)

permanent income theory: (4) a theory that states that consumption depends on the present value of lifetime resources, with the implication that consumption responds much less to temporary than to permanent changes in income. (p. 149)

persistence: (8) the tendency for declines in economic activity to be followed by further declines and for growth in economic activity to be followed by more growth. (p. 268)

Phillips curve: (13) a downward-sloping relationship between the inflation rate and the unemployment rate; theory suggests that a Phillips curve will be observed in the data only in periods in which expected inflation and the natural rate of unemployment are relatively stable. See *expectations-augmented Phillips curve*, *long-run Phillips curve*. (p. 485)

portfolio allocation decision: (7) a wealth holder's decision about which assets and how much of each asset to hold. (p. 243)

positive analysis: (1) an analysis of the economic consequences of a policy that does not address the question of whether those consequences are desirable. See *normative analysis*. (p. 15)

poverty trap: (15) a situation in which an increase in labour income reduces eligibility for transfers, which implies high marginal tax rates for low-income earners. (p. 573)

present value: (4) the value of a future payment in terms of today's dollars; equal to the amount of money that must be invested today at a given interest rate to be worth the specified payment at the specified date in the future. (p. 143)

present value of lifetime consumption (*PVLC*): (4) the present value of current and future consumption, which equals *PVLR* according to the budget constraint. (p. 143)

present value of lifetime resources (*PVLR*): (4) the present value of current and expected future income plus initial wealth; corresponds to the horizontal intercept of the budget line. (p. 144)

price index: (2) a measure of the average level of prices for some specified set of goods and services, relative to the prices of a specified base period. (p. 43)

price setter: (12) a market participant with some power to set prices; see *monopolistic competition*.

price stickiness: (12) in Keynesian theory, the tendency of prices to adjust only slowly to changes in the economy; also known as price rigidity. (p. 449)

price taker: (12) a market participant who takes the market price as given; see *perfect competition*. (p. 450)

pricing to market: (12) a situation in which firms' prices discriminate across markets, absorbing part of exchange-rate changes in profits and keeping prices stable in each market. (p. 454)

primary government budget deficit: (15) a measure of the deficit that excludes government interest payments from total expenditure; equal to government purchases of goods and services plus transfers minus tax revenues. (p. 565)

primary government budget surplus: (15) a measure of the surplus that excludes government interest payments from total expenditure; equal to the total budget surplus plus net interest payments. (p. 565)

private disposable income: (2) the income of the private sector (households and businesses taken together) after payment of taxes and receipt of transfer payments and interest from the government. (p. 34)

private saving: (2) the saving of the private sector (households and businesses), equal to private disposable income minus consumption. (p. 35)

private sector: (2) the household sector and the business sector taken together. (p. 34)

procyclical: (8) tending to move in the same direction as aggregate economic activity over the business cycle (up in expansions, down in contractions). See *acyclical*, *countercyclical*. (p. 275)

product approach: (2) a procedure for measuring economic activity by adding the market values of goods and services produced, excluding any goods and services used up in intermediate stages of production; equivalently, by summing the values added of all producers. (p. 24)

production function: (3) a function that shows the amount of output that can be produced (by a firm or by an entire economy) by using any given quantities of capital and labour. (p. 56)

productivity: (3) a measure of the overall effectiveness with which the economy uses capital and labour to produce output; also known as total factor productivity. (p. 55)

productivity shock: (11) a change in an economy's production function; equivalently, a change in the amount of output that can be produced using given quantities of capital and labour; also known as a supply shock. (p. 406)

propagation mechanism: (11) an aspect of the economy, such as the behaviour of inventories, that allows short-lived shocks to have longer term effects on the economy. (p. 433)

purchasing power parity: (10) the idea that similar domestic and foreign goods, or baskets of goods, should have the same price in terms of the same currency. (p. 346)

quantity theory of money: (7) a theory that asserts that nominal money demand is proportional to nominal GDP so that velocity is constant. (p. 252)

rational expectations: (11) expectations about the future values of economic variables that are based on reasoned and intelligent examination of available economic data; although they may make forecast errors, people with rational expectations cannot be systematically surprised by changes in macroeconomic policy or in the economy. (p. 431)

real appreciation: (10) an increase in the real exchange rate, which increases the quantity of foreign goods that can be purchased with a given quantity of domestic goods. (p. 346)

real business cycle (RBC) theory: (11) a version of the classical theory that assumes that productivity shocks (supply shocks) are the primary source of cyclical fluctuations. (p. 405)

real depreciation: (10) a fall in the real exchange rate, which decreases the quantity of foreign goods that can be purchased with a given quantity of domestic goods. (p. 346)

real exchange rate: (10) the quantity of foreign goods that can be obtained in exchange for one domestic good. (p. 344)

real GDP: (2) the market value of an economy's final output measured in terms of the prices that prevailed during some fixed base period; also known as constant-dollar GDP. (p. 41)

real interest rate: (2) the rate at which the real value or purchasing power of an interest-bearing asset increases over time; equal to the nominal interest rate minus the rate of inflation. (p. 47)

real interest rate parity condition: (10) the condition that the difference between the real interest rates in two countries equals the rate at which the real exchange rate of the country with the higher real interest rate is expected to fall. (p. 398)

real shocks: (11) disturbances to the "real side" of the economy, such as shocks that affect the production function, the size of the labour force, the real quantity of government purchases, or the spending and saving decisions of consumers; real shocks affect the *IS* curve or the *FE* line. (p. 405)

real variable: (2) a variable measured in terms of the prices of a fixed base year; a measure intended to represent physical quantities produced or used. (p. 41)

real wage: (3) the real value (measured in terms of goods) of what firms must pay per unit of labour input that they employ; equal to the nominal (dollar) wage divided by the price level. (p. 66)

real-wage rigidity: (12) from the Keynesian perspective, the apparent tendency of real wages to move too little over the business cycle to keep the quantity of labour supplied equal to the quantity of labour demanded. (p. 443)

recession: (8) in a business cycle, the period of time during which aggregate economic activity is falling; also known as a contraction. (p. 265)

relative purchasing power parity: (10) the idea that the rate of appreciation of the nominal exchange rate equals the foreign inflation rate minus the domestic inflation rate. (p. 347)

reserve–deposit ratio: (14) the ratio of reserves held by banks to the public's deposits in banks. (p. 523)

reserves: 1. (14) see *bank reserves*. 2. (5) see *official reserve assets*.

revaluation: (10) an increase in the value of a currency by official government action under a fixed-exchange-rate system. (p. 345)

reverse causation: (11) the tendency of expected future changes in output to cause changes in the current money supply in the same direction; used by real business cycle theorists to explain why the money supply leads the cycle. (p. 422)

Ricardian equivalence proposition: (4) the proposition that changes in the government budget deficit caused entirely by changes in (lump-sum) tax collections have no effect on the economy. (p. 115)

risk: (7) the possibility that the actual return received on an asset will be substantially different from the expected return. (p. 243)

rules: (14) a set of simple, prespecified, and publicly announced guidelines for conducting monetary policy; in contrast to discretion. (p. 539)

sacrifice ratio: (13) the amount of output lost when the inflation rate is reduced by one percentage point. (p. 512)

Sale and Repurchase Agreement (SRA): (14) a transaction in which the Bank of Canada sells Treasury bills to banks and investment dealers and then buys them back the next day; it lowers settlement balances and raises the overnight rate. (p. 534)

saving: (2) current income minus spending on current needs. (p. 35)

seignorage: (15) government revenue raised by printing money; also known as the inflation tax. (p. 585)

settlement balances: (14) balances held by direct clearers at the Bank of Canada; also called clearing balances. (p. 531)

shoe leather costs: (13) the costs incurred in the process of economizing on holdings of cash, for example, in more frequent trips to the bank. (p. 507)

short-run aggregate supply (*SRAS*) curve: (9) in a diagram with output on the horizontal axis and the price level on the vertical axis, the relationship between the price level and the amount of output that applies in the short run. In the short run, prices remain fixed, and producers produce the quantity demanded at the fixed price level, so the *SRAS* curve is horizontal. In the extended classical model based on the misperceptions theory, the *SRAS* curve slopes upward, as producers are fooled into supplying more output when the price level is higher than expected; the short run in this model is the period of time during which the expected price level remains unchanged. (p. 322)

small open economy: (5) an economy that trades with other economies but is too small to affect the world real interest rate. (p. 169)

Solow residual: (11) an empirical measure of total factor productivity. (p. 411)

Special Purchase and Resale Agreement (SPRA): (14) a transaction in which the Bank of Canada buys Treasury bills from banks and investment dealers and then sells them back the next day; it raises settlement balances and lowers the overnight rate. (p. 534)

speculative run: (10) a situation in which financial investors, fearing the imminent devaluation of a currency in a fixed-exchange-rate system, rush to sell assets denominated in that currency. (p. 375)

spell of unemployment: (3) see *unemployment spell*. (p. 90)

statistical discrepancy: 1. (2) an amount added to GDP measured by the income approach to so that the total equals GDP measured by the expenditure approach; arises because of errors of measurement and incomplete reporting. (p. 38) 2. (5) an amount added to the sum of the current and capital account balances for this sum to reach its theoretical value of zero. (p. 166)

steady state: (6) a situation in which the economy's output per worker, consumption per worker, and capital stock per worker are constant over time. (p. 209)

stock variable: (2) an economic quantity that is defined at a specific time; examples are wealth or the money supply. See *flow variable*. (p. 39)

store of value: (7) a means of holding wealth over time. (p. 237)

structural unemployment: (3) long-term and chronic unemployment arising from imbalances between the skills and other characteristics of workers in the market and the needs of employers. (p. 91)

substitution effect (of the real interest rate on saving): (4) the tendency of consumers to save more, and thereby substitute future consumption for current consumption, in response to a higher reward for saving. (p. 110)

substitution effect (of a higher real wage): (3) the tendency of workers to substitute work for leisure in response to a higher real wage. (p. 73)

supply shock: (3) a change in an economy's production function, that is, in the amount of output that can be produced by using given quantities of capital and labour; also known as a productivity shock. (p. 62)

supply-side economics: (15) a school of economic thought based on the premise that all aspects of economic behaviour—such as labour supply, saving, and investment—respond strongly to economic incentives, and, in particular, to incentives provided by the tax code. (p. 573)

target overnight rate: (14) the centre of the Bank of Canada's operating band for the overnight interest rate, set through monetary policy. (p. 531)

tax-adjusted user cost of capital: (4) indicates how large the before-tax expected future marginal product of capital must be in order to make a proposed investment profitable; equivalently, the (unadjusted) user cost of capital divided by 1 minus the effective tax rate. (p. 121)

tax rate smoothing: (15) a policy of maintaining stable tax rates over time in order to minimize the distortions created by the tax code. See *distortions*. (p. 575)

Taylor rule: (14) a guideline for monetary policy, it relates the real, target overnight rate to the difference between output and full-employment output and the difference between inflation and its target. (p. 540)

total factor productivity: (3) a measure of the overall efectiveness with which the economy uses capital and labour to produce output; also known as productivity. (p. 57)

trade deficit: (1) a nation's excess of imports over exports. (p. 7)

trade surplus: (1) a nation's excess of exports over imports. (p. 7)

transfers: (2) payments by the government, excluding payments made in exchange for current goods or services; examples of transfers are Old Age Security benefits, unemployment insurance, and welfare payments. (p. 32)

trough: (8) in a business cycle, the time when economic activity stops falling and begins rising. (p. 265)

turning points: (8) peak or troughs in the business cycle. (p. 266)

turnover costs: (12) the costs associated with hiring and training new workers. (p. 444)

unanticipated inflation: (13) the actual rate of inflation minus the rate of inflation that was expected to occur. (p. 508)

unconditional convergence: (6) a tendency for the living standards of different countries to become more equal over time, independently of the particular characteristics of individual countries. See *conditional convergence*. (p. 220)

underground economy: (2) the portion of the economy that includes both legal activities hidden from government record-keepers and illegal activities. (p. 26)

undervalued exchange rate: (10) in a fixed-exchange-rate system, an exchange rate that is lower than its fundamental value. See *fundamental value of the exchange rate*. (p. 376)

unemployment: (1) the number of people who are available for work and actively seeking work but cannot find jobs. (p. 5)

unemployment rate: (3) the fraction of the labour force that is unemployed. (p. 89)

unemployment spell: (3) the period of time that an individual is continuously unemployed. (p. 90)

unit of account: (7) the basic unit for measuring economic value (dollars, for example). (p. 236)

user cost of capital: (4) the expected real cost of using a unit of capital for a specified period of time; equal to the depreciation cost plus the interest cost. (p. 118)

uses-of-saving identity: (2) the accounting identity that states that private saving equals the sum of investment, the government deficit, and the current account balance. (p. 37)

utility: (4) an individual's economic satisfaction or well being. (p. 144)

value added: (2) for any producer, the value of output minus the value of purchased inputs. (p. 24)

velocity: (7) the number of times the money stock "turns over" each period; calculated as nominal GDP divided by the nominal money supply. (p. 251)

wealth: (2) the assets minus the liabilities of an individual, firm, or country; also known as net worth. (p. 35)

world real interest rate: (5) the real interest rate that prevails in the international capital market in which individuals, businesses, and governments borrow and lend across national borders. (p. 170)

Name Index

SUBJECT INDEX